Financial Accounting and Reporting

FOURTEENTH EDITION

Barry Elliott and Jamie Elliott

Financial Times
Prentice Hall
is an imprint of

PEARSON

Harlow, England • London • New York • Boston • San Francisco • Toronto • Sydney • Singapore • Hong Kong
Tokyo • Seoul • Taipei • New Delhi • Cape Town • Madrid • Mexico City • Amsterdam • Munich • Paris • Milan

Pearson Education Limited

Edinburgh Gate
Harlow
Essex CM20 2JE
England

and Associated Companies throughout the world

Visit us on the World Wide Web at:
www.pearsoned.co.uk

First published 1993
Second edition 1996
Third edition 1999
Fourth edition 2000
Fifth edition 2001
Sixth edition 2002
Seventh edition 2003
Eighth edition 2004
Ninth edition 2005
Tenth edition 2006
Eleventh edition 2007
Twelfth edition 2008
Thirteenth edition 2009
Fourteenth edition 2011

Pearson Education is not responsible for the content of third party internet sites.

ISBN: 978-0-273-74444-3

British Library Cataloguing-in-Publication Data
A catalogue record for this book is available from the British Library

Library of Congress Cataloging-in-Publication Data
A catalog record for this book is available from the Library of Congress

10 9 8 7 6 5 4 3 2 1
14 13 12 11 10

Typeset in 10/12 Ehrhardt MT by 35
Printed by Ashford Colour Press Ltd., Gosport

Brief contents

Preface and acknowledgements   xx
Guided tour of MyAccountingLab   xxv

Part 1
INCOME AND ASSET VALUE MEASUREMENT SYSTEMS   1

  1 Accounting and reporting on a cash flow basis   3
  2 Accounting and reporting on an accrual accounting basis   22
  3 Income and asset value measurement: an economist's approach 40
  4 Accounting for price-level changes   59

Part 2
**REGULATORY FRAMEWORK – AN ATTEMPT TO ACHIEVE
UNIFORMITY**   99

  5 Financial reporting – evolution of global standards   101
  6 Concepts – evolution of a global conceptual framework   129
  7 Ethical behaviour and implications for accountants   156
  8 Preparation of statements of comprehensive income and financial position   186
  9 Annual Report: additional financial statements   223

Part 3
**STATEMENT OF FINANCIAL POSITION – EQUITY, LIABILITY
AND ASSET MEASUREMENT AND DISCLOSURE**   255

10 Share capital, distributable profits and reduction of capital   257
11 Off balance sheet finance   283
12 Financial instruments   312
13 Employee benefits   343
14 Taxation in company accounts   375
15 Property, plant and equipment (PPE)   404
16 Leasing   441
17 R&D; goodwill; intangible assets and brands   461
18 Inventories   497
19 Construction contracts   523

Part 4
CONSOLIDATED ACCOUNTS   547

20 Accounting for groups at the date of acquisition   549
21 Preparation of consolidated statements of financial position after the date
    of acquisition   568
22 Preparation of consolidated statements of comprehensive income,
    changes in equity and cash flows   583
23 Accounting for associates and joint ventures   603
24 Accounting for the effects of changes in foreign exchange rates under IAS 21   623

Part 5
INTERPRETATION   639

25 Earnings per share   641
26 Statements of cash flows   668
27 Review of financial ratio analysis   696
28 Analytical analysis – selective use of ratios   736
29 An introduction to financial reporting on the Internet   782

Part 6
ACCOUNTABILITY   799

30 Corporate governance   801
31 Sustainability – environmental and social reporting   838

Index   **884**

Full contents

Preface and acknowledgements   xx
Guided tour of MyAccountingLab   xxv

Part I
INCOME AND ASSET VALUE MEASUREMENT SYSTEMS   1

1 Accounting and reporting on a cash flow basis   3
  1.1   Introduction   3
  1.2   Shareholders   3
  1.3   What skills does an accountant require in respect of external reports?   4
  1.4   Managers   4
  1.5   What skills does an accountant require in respect of internal reports?   5
  1.6   Procedural steps when reporting to internal users   5
  1.7   Agency costs   8
  1.8   Illustration of periodic financial statements prepared under the cash
        flow concept to disclose realised operating cash flows   8
  1.9   Illustration of preparation of statement of financial position   12
  1.10 Treatment of non-current assets in the cash flow model   14
  1.11 What are the characteristics of these data that make them reliable?   15
  1.12 Reports to external users   16
        Summary   16
        Review questions   17
        Exercises   18
        References   21

2 Accounting and reporting on an accrual accounting basis   22
  2.1   Introduction   22
  2.2   Historical cost convention   23
  2.3   Accrual basis of accounting   24
  2.4   Mechanics of accrual accounting – adjusting cash receipts and payments   24
  2.5   Subjective judgements required in accrual accounting – adjusting cash
        receipts in accordance with IAS 18   25
  2.6   Subjective judgements required in accrual accounting – adjusting cash
        payments in accordance with the matching principle   27
  2.7   Mechanics of accrual accounting – the statement of financial position   28
  2.8   Reformatting the statement of financial position   28

2.9	Accounting for the sacrifice of non-current assets	29
2.10	Reconciliation of cash flow and accrual accounting data	32
	Summary	34
	Review questions	34
	Exercises	35
	References	38

3 Income and asset value measurement: an economist's approach — 40

3.1	Introduction	40
3.2	Role and objective of income measurement	40
3.3	Accountant's view of income, capital and value	43
3.4	Critical comment on the accountant's measure	46
3.5	Economist's view of income, capital and value	47
3.6	Critical comment on the economist's measure	53
3.7	Income, capital and changing price levels	53
	Summary	55
	Review questions	55
	Exercises	56
	References	57
	Bibliography	58

4 Accounting for price-level changes — 59

4.1	Introduction	59
4.2	Review of the problems of historical cost accounting (HCA)	59
4.3	Inflation accounting	60
4.4	The concepts in principle	60
4.5	The four models illustrated for a company with cash purchases and sales	61
4.6	Critique of each model	65
4.7	Operating capital maintenance – a comprehensive example	68
4.8	Critique of CCA statements	79
4.9	The ASB approach	81
4.10	The IASC/IASB approach	83
4.11	Future developments	84
	Summary	86
	Review questions	87
	Exercises	88
	References	97
	Bibliography	97

Part 2
REGULATORY FRAMEWORK – AN ATTEMPT TO ACHIEVE UNIFORMITY — 99

5 Financial reporting – evolution of global standards — 101

5.1	Introduction	101
5.2	Why do we need financial reporting standards?	101
5.3	Why do we need standards to be mandatory?	102
5.4	Arguments in support of standards	104

5.5	Arguments against standards	104
5.6	Standard setting and enforcement in the UK under the Financial Reporting Council (FRC)	105
5.7	The Accounting Standards Board (ASB)	106
5.8	The Financial Reporting Review Panel (FRRP)	106
5.9	Standard setting and enforcement in the US	108
5.10	Why have there been differences in financial reporting?	109
5.11	Efforts to standardise financial reports	113
5.12	What is the impact of changing to IFRS?	117
5.13	Progress towards adoption by the USA of international standards	118
5.14	Advantages and disadvantages of global standards for publicly accountable entities	119
5.15	How do reporting requirements differ for non-publicly accountable entities?	119
5.16	Evaluation of effectiveness of mandatory regulations	123
5.17	Move towards a conceptual framework	125
	Summary	125
	Review questions	126
	Exercises	127
	References	127

6 Concepts – evolution of a global conceptual framework — 129

6.1	Introduction	129
6.2	Historical overview of the evolution of financial accounting theory	130
6.3	FASB Concepts Statements	134
6.4	IASC *Framework for the Presentation and Preparation of Financial Statements*	137
6.5	ASB *Statement of Principles 1999*	138
6.6	Conceptual framework developments	149
	Summary	150
	Review questions	152
	Exercises	153
	References	154

7 Ethical behaviour and implications for accountants — 156

7.1	Introduction	156
7.2	The meaning of ethical behaviour	156
7.3	Financial reports – what is the link between law, corporate governance, corporate social responsibility and ethics?	158
7.4	What does the accounting profession mean by ethical behaviour?	159
7.5	Implications of ethical values for the principles versus rules based approaches to accounting standards	161
7.6	The principles based approach and ethics	163
7.7	The accounting standard-setting process and ethics	164
7.8	The IFAC *Code of Ethics for Professional Accountants*	165
7.9	Ethics in the accountants' work environment – a research report	168
7.10	Implications of unethical behaviour for financial reports	169
7.11	Company codes of ethics	172
7.12	The increasing role of whistle-blowing	174
7.13	Why should students learn ethics?	178

	Summary	179
	Review questions	179
	Exercises	182
	References	184

8 Preparation of statements of comprehensive income and financial position — **186**

8.1	Introduction	186
8.2	The prescribed formats – the statement of comprehensive income	187
8.3	The prescribed formats – the statement of financial position	194
8.4	Statement of changes in equity	197
8.5	Has prescribing the formats meant that identical transactions are reported identically?	198
8.6	The fundamental accounting principles underlying statements of comprehensive income and statements of financial position	201
8.7	What is the difference between accounting principles, accounting bases and accounting policies?	201
8.8	What does an investor need in addition to the financial statements to make decisions?	206
	Summary	210
	Review questions	211
	Exercises	212
	References	222

9 Annual Report: additional financial statements — **223**

9.1	Introduction	223
9.2	The value added by segment reports	223
9.3	Detailed review and evaluation of IRFS 8 – *Operating Segments*	224
9.4	IFRS 5 – meaning of 'held for sale'	232
9.5	IFRS 5 – implications of classification as held for sale	232
9.6	Meaning and significance of 'discontinued operations'	233
9.7	IAS 10 – Events after the reporting period	235
9.8	Related party disclosures	237
	Summary	241
	Review questions	241
	Exercises	242
	References	253

Part 3
STATEMENT OF FINANCIAL POSITION – EQUITY, LIABILITY AND ASSET MEASUREMENT AND DISCLOSURE — **255**

10 Share capital, distributable profits and reduction of capital — **257**

10.1	Introduction	257
10.2	Common themes	257
10.3	Total owners' equity: an overview	258
10.4	Total shareholders' funds: more detailed explanation	259
10.5	Accounting entries on issue of shares	262
10.6	Creditor protection: capital maintenance concept	263

10.7 Creditor protection: why capital maintenance rules are necessary 264
10.8 Creditor protection: how to quantify the amounts available to meet creditors' claims 264
10.9 Issued share capital: minimum share capital 265
10.10 Distributable profits: general considerations 265
10.11 Distributable profits: how to arrive at the amount using relevant accounts 267
10.12 When may capital be reduced? 267
10.13 Writing off part of capital which has already been lost and is not represented by assets 268
10.14 Repayment of part of paid-in capital to shareholders or cancellation of unpaid share capital 273
10.15 Purchase of own shares 274
Summary 277
Review questions 277
Exercises 277
References 282

11 Off balance sheet finance **283**
11.1 Introduction 283
11.2 Traditional statements – conceptual changes 283
11.3 Off balance sheet finance – its impact 284
11.4 Illustrations of the application of substance over form 286
11.5 Provisions – their impact on the statement of financial position 289
11.6 ED IAS 37 *Non-financial Liabilities* 297
11.7 ED/2010/1 *Measurement of Liabilities in IAS 37* 303
11.8 Special purpose entities (SPEs) – lack of transparency 304
11.9 Impact of converting to IFRS 305
Summary 306
Review questions 307
Exercises 308
References 311

12 Financial instruments **312**
12.1 Introduction 312
12.2 Financial instruments – the IASB's problem child 312
12.3 IAS 32 *Financial Instruments: Disclosure and Presentation* 315
12.4 IAS 39 *Financial Instruments: Recognition and Measurement* 320
12.5 IFRS 7 *Financial Statement Disclosures* 330
12.6 Financial instruments developments 333
Summary 336
Review questions 337
Exercises 338
References 342

13 Employee benefits **343**
13.1 Introduction 343
13.2 Greater employee interest in pensions 343
13.3 Financial reporting implications 344
13.4 Types of scheme 344

13.5	Defined contribution pension schemes	346
13.6	Defined benefit pension schemes	347
13.7	IAS 19 (revised) *Employee Benefits*	349
13.8	The liability for pension and other post-retirement costs	349
13.9	The statement of comprehensive income	352
13.10	Comprehensive illustration	353
13.11	Plan curtailments and settlements	355
13.12	Multi-employer plans	355
13.13	Disclosures	356
13.14	Other long-service benefits	356
13.15	Short-term benefits	357
13.16	Termination benefits	358
13.17	IFRS 2 *Share-Based Payment*	359
13.18	Scope of IFRS 2	360
13.19	Recognition and measurement	360
13.20	Equity-settled share-based payments	360
13.21	Cash-settled share-based payments	363
13.22	Transactions which may be settled in cash or shares	363
13.23	Transitional provisions	364
13.24	IAS 26 *Accounting and Reporting by Retirement Benefit Plans*	364
	Summary	367
	Review questions	368
	Exercises	370
	References	374
14	**Taxation in company accounts**	**375**
14.1	Introduction	375
14.2	Corporation tax	375
14.3	Corporation tax systems – the theoretical background	376
14.4	Corporation tax systems – avoidance and evasion	377
14.5	Corporation tax – the system from 6 April 1999	380
14.6	IFRS and taxation	381
14.7	IAS 12 – accounting for current taxation	382
14.8	Deferred tax	384
14.9	FRS 19 (the UK standard on deferred taxation)	392
14.10	A critique of deferred taxation	393
14.11	Examples of companies following IAS 12	396
14.12	Value added tax (VAT)	396
	Summary	399
	Review questions	399
	Exercises	400
	References	402
15	**Property, plant and equipment (PPE)**	**404**
15.1	Introduction	404
15.2	PPE – concepts and the relevant IASs and IFRSs	404
15.3	What is PPE?	405
15.4	How is the cost of PPE determined?	406
15.5	What is depreciation?	408
15.6	What are the constituents in the depreciation formula?	411

15.7   How is the useful life of an asset determined?   411
15.8   Residual value   412
15.9   Calculation of depreciation   412
15.10 Measurement subsequent to initial recognition   416
15.11 IAS 36 *Impairment of Assets*   418
15.12 IFRS 5 *Non-Current Assets Held for Sale and Discontinued Operations*   424
15.13 Disclosure requirements   424
15.14 Government grants towards the cost of PPE   425
15.15 Investment properties   427
15.16 Effect of accounting policy for PPE on the interpretation of the
       financial statements   428
       Summary   430
       Review questions   430
       Exercises   431
       References   440

16 Leasing   **441**
16.1   Introduction   441
16.2   Background to leasing   441
16.3   Why was the IAS 17 approach so controversial?   443
16.4   IAS 17 – classification of a lease   444
16.5   Accounting requirements for operating leases   445
16.6   Accounting requirements for finance leases   446
16.7   Example allocating the finance charge using the sum of the
       digits method   447
16.8   Accounting for the lease of land and buildings   451
16.9   Leasing – a form of off balance sheet financing   452
16.10 Accounting for leases – a new approach   453
16.11 Accounting for leases by lessors   455
       Summary   456
       Review questions   456
       Exercises   457
       References   460

17 R&D; goodwill; intangible assets and brands   **461**
17.1   Introduction   461
17.2   Accounting treatment for research and development   461
17.3   Research and development   461
17.4   Why is research expenditure not capitalised?   462
17.5   Capitalising development costs   463
17.6   The judgements to be made when deciding whether to capitalise
       development costs   464
17.7   Disclosure of R&D   465
17.8   Goodwill   466
17.9   The accounting treatment of goodwill   466
17.10 Critical comment on the various methods that have been used to
       account for goodwill   468
17.11 Negative goodwill   470
17.12 Intangible assets   471
17.13 Brand accounting   474

17.14 Justifications for reporting all brands as assets   475
17.15 Accounting for acquired brands   476
17.16 Emissions trading   477
17.17 Intellectual property   479
17.18 Review of implementation of IFRS 3   482
      Summary   484
      Review questions   485
      Exercises   487
      References   495

18 **Inventories**   **497**
18.1 Introduction   497
18.2 Inventory defined   497
18.3 The controversy   498
18.4 IAS 2 *Inventories*   499
18.5 Inventory valuation   500
18.6 Work-in-progress   507
18.7 Inventory control   509
18.8 Creative accounting   510
18.9 Audit of the year-end physical inventory count   512
18.10 Published accounts   513
18.11 Agricultural activity   514
      Summary   517
      Review questions   518
      Exercises   519
      References   522

19 **Construction contracts**   **523**
19.1 Introduction   523
19.2 The accounting issue for construction contracts   523
19.3 Identification of contract revenue   525
19.4 Identification of contract costs   525
19.5 Recognition of contract revenue and expenses   526
19.6 Public–private partnerships (PPPs)   532
      Summary   538
      Review questions   538
      Exercises   539
      References   545

Part 4
CONSOLIDATED ACCOUNTS   **547**

20 **Accounting for groups at the date of acquisition**   **549**
20.1 Introduction   549
20.2 The definition of a group   549
20.3 Consolidated accounts and some reasons for their preparation   549
20.4 The definition of control   551
20.5 Alternative methods of preparing consolidated accounts   552
20.6 The treatment of positive goodwill   554
20.7 The treatment of negative goodwill   554

20.8 The comparison between an acquisition by cash and an exchange
of shares 555
20.9 Non-controlling interests 555
20.10 The treatment of differences between a subsidiary's fair value and
book value 558
20.11 How to calculate fair values 559
Summary 560
Review questions 561
Exercises 562
References 567

**21 Preparation of consolidated statements of financial position
after the date of acquisition 568**
21.1 Introduction 568
21.2 Pre- and post-acquisition profits/losses 568
21.3 Inter-company balances 571
21.4 Unrealised profit on inter-company sales 572
21.5 Provision for unrealised profit affecting a non-controlling interest 577
21.6 Uniform accounting policies and reporting dates 577
21.7 How is the investment in subsidiaries reported in the parent's own
statement of financial position? 578
Summary 578
Review questions 578
Exercises 578
References 582

**22 Preparation of consolidated statements of comprehensive
income, changes in equity and cash flows 583**
22.1 Introduction 583
22.2 Preparation of a consolidated statement of comprehensive income –
the Ante Group 583
22.3 The statement of changes in equity (SOCE) 586
22.4 Other consolidation adjustments 586
22.5 Dividends or interest paid by the subsidiary out of
pre-acquisition profits 587
22.6 A subsidiary acquired part of the way through the year 588
22.7 Published format statement of comprehensive income 590
22.8 Consolidated statements of cash flows 591
Summary 592
Review questions 593
Exercises 593
References 602

23 Accounting for associates and joint ventures 603
23.1 Introduction 603
23.2 Definitions of associates and of significant influence 603
23.3 The treatment of associated companies in consolidated accounts 604
23.4 The Brill Group – the equity method illustrated 604
23.5 The treatment of provisions for unrealised profits 606
23.6 The acquisition of an associate part-way through the year 606
23.7 Joint ventures 608

	Summary	610
	Review questions	610
	Exercises	611
	References	622

24 Accounting for the effects of changes in foreign exchange rates under IAS 21 — **623**

24.1	Introduction	623
24.2	The difference between conversion and translation and the definition of a foreign currency transaction	623
24.3	The functional currency	624
24.4	The presentation currency	624
24.5	Monetary and non-monetary items	624
24.6	The rules on the recording of foreign currency transactions carried out directly by the reporting entity	625
24.7	The treatment of exchange differences on foreign currency transactions	625
24.8	Foreign exchange transactions in the individual accounts of companies illustrated – Boil plc	625
24.9	The translation of the accounts of foreign operations where the functional currency is the same as that of the parent	627
24.10	The use of a presentation currency other than the functional currency	627
24.11	Granby Ltd illustration	628
24.12	Granby Ltd illustration continued	629
24.13	Implications of IAS 21	632
24.14	Critique of use of presentation currency	632
	Summary	633
	Review questions	633
	Exercises	633
	References	637

Part 5
INTERPRETATION — **639**

25 Earnings per share — **641**

25.1	Introduction	641
25.2	Why is the earnings per share figure important?	641
25.3	How is the EPS figure calculated?	642
25.4	The use to shareholders of the EPS	643
25.5	Illustration of the basic EPS calculation	644
25.6	Adjusting the number of shares used in the basic EPS calculation	645
25.7	Rights issues	647
25.8	Adjusting the earnings and number of shares used in the diluted EPS calculation	652
25.9	Procedure where there are several potential dilutions	654
25.10	Exercise of conversion rights during financial year	656
25.11	Disclosure requirements of IAS 33	656
25.12	The Improvement Project	659
25.13	Convergence project	659
	Summary	659
	Review questions	660

	Exercises	661
	References	667

26 Statements of cash flows — 668

26.1	Introduction	668
26.2	Development of statements of cash flows	668
26.3	Applying IAS 7 (revised) Statements of Cash Flows	670
26.4	IAS 7 (revised) format of statements of cash flows	672
26.5	Consolidated statements of cash flows	677
26.6	Analysing statements of cash flows	679
26.7	Critique of cash flow accounting	684
	Summary	685
	Review questions	685
	Exercises	686
	References	695

27 Review of financial ratio analysis — 696

27.1	Introduction	696
27.2	Initial impressions	696
27.3	What are accounting ratios?	697
27.4	Six key ratios	698
27.5	Illustrating the calculation of the six key ratios	703
27.6	Description of subsidiary ratios	706
27.7	Comparative ratios: inter-firm comparisons and industry averages	715
27.8	Limitations of ratio analysis	718
27.9	Earnings before interest, tax, depreciation and amortisation (EBITDA) used for management control purposes	720
	Summary	722
	Review questions	722
	Exercises	723
	References	735

28 Analytical analysis – selective use of ratios — 736

28.1	Introduction	736
28.2	Improvement of information for shareholders	736
28.3	Disclosure of risks and focus on relevant ratios	738
28.4	Shariah compliant companies – why ratios are important	745
28.5	Ratios set by lenders in debt covenants	747
28.6	Predicting corporate failure	749
28.7	Performance related remuneration – shareholder returns	756
28.8	Valuing shares of an unquoted company – quantitative process	760
28.9	Professional risk assessors	764
	Summary	766
	Review questions	767
	Exercises	769
	References	780

29 An introduction to financial reporting on the Internet — 782

29.1	Introduction	782
29.2	The reason for the development of a business reporting language	782

29.3 Reports and the flow of information pre-XBRL 783
29.4 What are HTML, XML and XBRL? 784
29.5 Reports and the flow of information post-XBRL 785
29.6 XBRL and the IASB 786
29.7 Why should companies adopt XBRL? 786
29.8 What is needed to use XBRL for outputting information? 787
29.9 What is needed when receiving XBRL output information? 789
29.10 Progress of XBRL development for internal accounting 794
29.11 Further study 794
Summary 795
Review questions 795
Exercises 796
References 796
Bibliography 797

Part 6
ACCOUNTABILITY 799

30 Corporate governance 801
30.1 Introduction 801
30.2 The concept 801
30.3 Corporate governance effect on corporate behaviour 802
30.4 Pressures on good governance behaviour vary over time 803
30.5 Types of past unethical behaviour 804
30.6 Different jurisdictions have different governance priorities 805
30.7 The effect on capital markets of good corporate governance 806
30.8 The role of accounting in corporate governance 807
30.9 External audits in corporate governance 809
30.10 Corporate governance in relation to the board of directors 814
30.11 Executive remuneration 814
30.12 Market forces and corporate governance 817
30.13 Risk management 818
30.14 Corporate governance, legislation and codes 820
30.15 Corporate governance – the UK experience 822
Summary 832
Review questions 832
Exercises 834
References 836

31 Sustainability – environmental and social reporting 838
31.1 Introduction 838
31.2 How financial reporting has evolved to embrace sustainability reporting 838
31.3 The Triple Bottom Line (TBL) 839
31.4 The Connected Reporting Framework 840
31.5 IFAC Sustainability Framework 842
31.6 The accountant's role in a capitalist industrial society 844
31.7 The accountant's changing role 844
31.8 Sustainability – environmental reporting 845
31.9 Environmental information in the annual accounts 845

31.10 Background to companies' reporting practices   846
31.11 European Commission's recommendations for disclosures in
      annual accounts   847
31.12 Evolution of stand-alone environmental reports   848
31.13 International charters and guidelines   852
31.14 Self-regulation schemes   854
31.15 Economic consequences of environmental reporting   856
31.16 Summary on environmental reporting   857
31.17 Environmental auditing: international initiatives   858
31.18 The activities involved in an environmental audit   859
31.19 Concept of social accounting   861
31.20 Background to social accounting   863
31.21 Corporate social responsibility   866
31.22 Need for comparative data   868
31.23 International initiatives towards triple bottom line reporting   870
      Summary   873
      Review questions   873
      Exercises   875
      References   881
      Bibliography   882

Index   884

Preface and acknowledgements

Our objective is to provide a balanced and comprehensive framework to enable students to acquire the requisite knowledge and skills to appraise current practice critically and to evaluate proposed changes from a theoretical base. To this end, the text contains:

● current IASs and IFRSs;

● illustrations from published accounts;

● a range of review questions;

● exercises of varying difficulty;

● extensive references.

Outline solutions to selected exercises can also be found on the Companion Website (www.pearsoned.co.uk/elliott–elliott).

We have assumed that readers will have an understanding of financial accounting to a foundation or first-year level, although the text and exercises have been designed on the basis that a brief revision is still helpful.

Lecturers are using the text selectively to support a range of teaching programmes for second-year and final-year undergraduate and postgraduate programmes. We have therefore attempted to provide subject coverage of sufficient breadth and depth to assist selective use.

The text has been adopted for financial accounting, reporting and analysis modules on:

● second-year undergraduate courses for Accounting, Business Studies and Combined Studies;

● final-year undergraduate courses for Accounting, Business Studies and Combined Studies;

● MBA courses;

● specialist MSc courses; and

● professional courses preparing students for professional accountancy examinations.

Changes to the fourteenth edition

Accounting standards

UK listed companies, together with those non-listed companies that so choose, have applied international standards from January 2005.

For non-listed companies that choose to continue to apply UK GAAP, the ASB has stated its commitment to progressively bringing UK GAAP into line with international standards.

For companies currently applying FRSSE, this will continue. The IASB issued *IFRS for SMEs* in 2009.

Accounting standards – fourteenth edition updates

Chapters 5 and 6 cover the evolution of global standards and a global Conceptual Framework.

Topics and International Standards are covered as follows:

Chapter 4	Accounting for price-level changes	IAS 29
Chapter 8	Preparation of statements of comprehensive income and financial position	IAS 1, IFRS
Chapter 9	Preparation of published accounts	IAS 8, IAS 10, IAS 24, IFRS 5 and IFRS 8
Chapter 11	Off balance sheet finance	IAS 37
Chapter 12	Financial instruments	IAS 32, IAS 39, IFRS 7 and IFRS 9
Chapter 13	Employee benefits	IAS 19, IAS 26 and IFRS 2
Chapter 14	Taxation in company accounts	IAS 12
Chapter 15	Property, plant and equipment (PPE)	IAS 16, IAS 20, IAS 23, IAS 36, IAS 40 and IFRS 5
Chapter 16	Leasing	IAS 17
Chapter 17	R&D; goodwill and intangible assets; brands	IAS 38 and IFRS 3
Chapter 18	Inventories	IAS 2
Chapter 19	Construction contracts	IAS 11
Chapters 20 to 24 Consolidation		IAS 21, IAS 27, IAS 28, IAS 31 and IFRS 3
Chapter 25	Earnings per share	IAS 33
Chapter 26	Statements of cash flows	IAS 7
Chapter 30	Corporate governance	IFRS 2

Income and asset value measurement systems

Chapters 1 to 4 continue to cover accounting and reporting on a cash flow and accrual basis, the economic income approach and accounting for price-level changes.

The UK regulatory framework and analysis

UK listed companies will continue to be subject to national company law, and mandatory and best practice requirements such as the *Operating and Financial Review* and the *UK Code of Corporate Governance*.

UK regulatory framework and analysis – fourteenth edition changes

The following chapters have been retained and updated as appropriate:

Chapter 7   Ethical behaviour and implications for accountants
Chapter 10 Share capital, distributable profits and reduction of capital

Chapter 11 Off balance sheet finance
Chapter 27 Review of financial ratio analysis
Chapter 28 Analytical analysis – selective use of ratios
Chapter 29 An introduction to financial reporting on the Internet
Chapter 30 Corporate governance
Chapter 31 Sustainability – environmental and social reporting
Chapter 32 Ethics for accountants (now Chapter 7)

Our emphasis has been on keeping the text current and responsive to constructive comments from reviewers.

Recent developments

In addition to the steps being taken towards the development of IFRSs that will receive broad consensus support, regulators have been active in developing further requirements concerning corporate governance. These have been prompted by the accounting scandals in the USA and, more recently, in Europe and by shareholder activism fuelled by the apparent lack of any relationship between increases in directors' remuneration and company performance.

The content of financial reports continues to be subjected to discussion with a tension between preparers, stakeholders, auditors, academics and standard setters; this is mirrored in the tension that exists between theory and practice.

● Preparers favour reporting transactions on a historical cost basis which is reliable but does not provide shareholders with relevant information to appraise past performance or to predict future earnings.

● Shareholders favour forward-looking reports relevant in estimating future dividend and capital growth and in understanding environmental and social impacts.

● Stakeholders favour quantified and narrative disclosure of environmental and social impacts and the steps taken to reduce negative impacts.

● Auditors favour reports that are verifiable so that the figures can be substantiated to avoid them being proved wrong at a later date.

● Academic accountants favour reports that reflect economic reality and are relevant in appraising management performance and in assessing the capacity of the company to adapt.

● Standard setters lean towards the academic view and favour reporting according to the commercial substance of a transaction.

In order to understand the tensions that exist, students need:

● the skill to prepare financial statements in accordance with the historical cost and current cost conventions, both of which appear in annual financial reports;

● an understanding of the main thrust of mandatory and voluntary standards;

● an understanding of the degree of flexibility available to the preparers and the impact of this on reported earnings and the figures in the statement of financial position;

● an understanding of the limitations of financial reports in portraying economic reality; and

● an exposure to source material and other published material in so far as time permits.

Instructor's Manual

A separate Instructors' Manual has been written to accompany this text. It contains fully worked solutions to all the exercises and is of a quality that allows them to be used as over-head transparencies. The Manual is available at no cost to lecturers on application to the publishers.

Website

An electronic version of the Instructors' Manual is also available for download at www.pearsoned.co.uk/elliott-elliott.

Acknowledgements

Financial reporting is a dynamic area and we see it as extremely important that the text should reflect this and be kept current. Assistance has been generously given by colleagues and many others in the preparation and review of the text and assessment material. This fourteenth edition continues to be very much a result of the authors, colleagues, reviewers and Pearson editorial and production staff working as a team and we are grateful to all concerned for their assistance in achieving this.

We owe particular thanks to Ron Altshul, who has updated 'Taxation in company accounts' (Chapter 14); Charles Batchelor formerly of FTC Kaplan for 'Financial instruments' (Chapter 12) and 'Employee benefits' (Chapter 13); Ozer Erman of Kingston University, for 'Share capital, distributable profits and reduction of capital' (Chapter 10); Paul Robins of the Financial Training Company for 'Published accounts' (Chapter 9) and 'Earnings per share' (Chapter 25); Professor Garry Tibbits of the University of Western Sydney 'Ethical behaviour and implications for accountants' (Chapter 7) and 'Corporate governance' (Chapter 30); Hendrika Tibbits of the University of Western Sydney for An introduction to financial reporting on the Internet (Chapter 29); David Towers, formerly of Keele University, for Consolidation chapters; and Martin Howes for inputs to financial analysis.

The authors are grateful for the constructive comments received from the following reviewers who have assisted us in making improvements: Iain Fleming of the University of the West of Scotland; John Morley of the University of Brighton; John Forker of Queen's University, Belfast; Breda Sweeney of NUI Galway; Patricia McCourt Larres of Queen's University, Belfast; and Dave Knight of Leeds Metropolitan University.

Thanks are owed to A.T. Benedict of the South Bank University; Keith Brown formerly of De Montfort University; Kenneth N. Field of the University of Leeds; Sue McDermott of London Metropolitan Business School; David Murphy of Manchester Business School; Bahadur Najak of the University of Durham; Graham Sara of University of Warwick; Laura Spira of Oxford Brookes University.

Thanks are also due to the following organisations: the Accounting Standards Board, the International Accounting Standards Board, the Association of Chartered Certified Accountants, the Association of International Accountants, the Chartered Institute of Management Accountants, the Chartered Institute of Securities and Investment, the Institute of Chartered Accountants of Scotland, Chartered Institute of Public Finance and Accountancy, Chartered Institute of Bankers and the Institute of Investment Management and Research.

We would also like to thank the authors of some of the end-of-chapter exercises. Some of these exercises have been inherited from a variety of institutions with which we have been associated, and we have unfortunately lost the identities of the originators of such material with the passage of time. We are sorry that we cannot acknowledge them by name and hope that they will excuse us for using their material.

We are indebted to Matthew Smith and the editorial team at Pearson Education for active support in keeping us largely to schedule and the attractively produced and presented text.

Finally we thank our wives, Di and Jacklin, for their continued good humoured support during the period of writing and revisions, and Giles Elliott for his critical comment from the commencement of the project. We alone remain responsible for any errors and for the thoughts and views that are expressed.

Barry and Jamie Elliott

Guided tour of MyAccountingLab

MyAccountingLab puts students in control of their own learning through a suite of study and practice tools tied to the online e-book. At the core of **MyAccountingLab** are the following features:

Practice tests

Practice tests for each section of the textbook enable students to test their understanding and identify the areas in which they need to do further work. Lecturers can customise the practice tests or leave students to use the two pre-built tests per chapter.

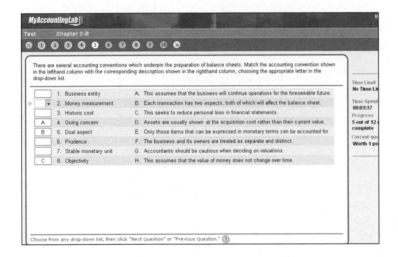

Personalised study plan

The study plan in **MyAccountingLab** helps each student to monitor their own progress, letting them see at a glance exactly which topics they need to practice. **MyAccountingLab** generates a personalised study plan for each student based on his or her results while working through the exercises for each chapter.

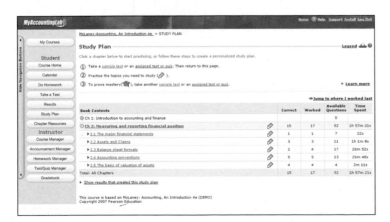

Each student can work through the study plan at their own pace, with instruction provided in the form of detailed, step-by-step solutions to problems. Many of the exercises in **MyAccountingLab** are generated algorithmically, containing different values each time they are used. This means that each student can practice particular concepts as often as they like.

There is also a link to the online textbook from every question in the Study Plan, to assist with learning.

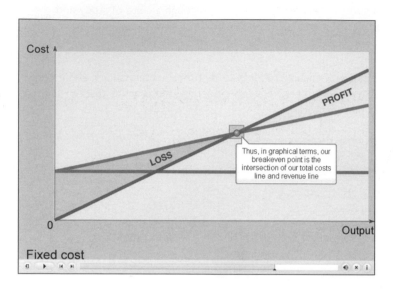

Lecturer training and support

We offer lecturers personalised training and support for **MyAccountingLab**. We have a dedicated team of Technology Specialists whose job it is to support lecturers in their use of our media products, including **MyAccountingLab**. To make contact with your Technology Specialist please email **feedback-cw@pearson.com**.

For a visual walkthrough of how to make the most of **MyAccountingLab**, visit **www.myaccountinglab.com**.

To find details of your local sales representatives go to **www.pearsoned.co.uk/replocator**.

PART I

Income and asset value measurement systems

CHAPTER 1

Accounting and reporting on a cash flow basis

1.1 Introduction

Accountants are communicators. Accountancy is the art of communicating financial information about a business entity to users such as shareholders and managers. The communication is generally in the form of financial statements that show in money terms the economic resources under the control of the management. The art lies in selecting the information that is relevant to the user and is reliable.

Shareholders require periodic information that the managers are accounting properly for the resources under their control. This information helps the shareholders to evaluate the performance of the managers. The performance measured by the accountant shows the extent to which the economic resources of the business have grown or diminished during the year.

The shareholders also require information to **predict future performance**. At present companies are not required to publish forecast financial statements on a regular basis and the shareholders use the report of past performance when making their predictions.

Managers require information in order to control the business and make investment decisions.

Objectives

By the end of this chapter, you should be able to:

- explain the extent to which cash flow accounting satisfies the information needs of shareholders and managers;
- prepare a cash budget and operating statement of cash flows;
- explain the characteristics that makes cash flow data a reliable and fair representation;
- critically discuss the use of cash flow accounting for predicting future dividends.

1.2 Shareholders

Shareholders are external users. As such, they are unable to obtain access to the same amount of detailed historical information as the managers, e.g. total administration costs are disclosed in the published profit and loss account, but not an analysis to show how the figure is made up. Shareholders are also unable to obtain associated information, e.g. budgeted sales and costs. Even though the shareholders own a company, their entitlement to information is restricted.

The information to which shareholders are entitled is restricted to that specified by statute, e.g. the Companies Acts, or by professional regulation, e.g. Financial Reporting Standards, or by market regulations, e.g. Listing requirements. This means that there may be a tension between the **amount** of information that a shareholder would like to receive and the amount that the directors are prepared to provide. For example, shareholders might consider that forecasts of future cash flows would be helpful in predicting future dividends, but the directors might be concerned that such forecasts could help competitors or make directors open to criticism if forecasts are not met. As a result, this information is not disclosed.

There may also be a tension between the **quality** of information that shareholders would like to receive and that which directors are prepared to provide. For example, the shareholders might consider that judgements made by the directors in the valuation of long-term contracts should be fully explained, whereas the directors might prefer not to reveal this information given the high risk of error that often attaches to such estimates. In practice, companies tend to compromise: they do not reveal the judgements to the shareholders, but maintain confidence by relying on the auditor to give a clean audit report.

The financial reports presented to the shareholders are also used by other parties such as lenders and trade creditors, and they have come to be regarded as general-purpose reports. However, it may be difficult or impossible to satisfy the needs of all users. For example, users may have different time-scales – shareholders may be interested in the long-term trend of earnings over three years, whereas creditors may be interested in the likelihood of receiving cash within the next three months.

The information needs of the shareholders are regarded as the primary concern. The government perceives shareholders to be important because they provide companies with their economic resources. It is shareholders' needs that take priority in deciding on the nature and detailed content of the general-purpose reports.[1]

1.3 What skills does an accountant require in respect of external reports?

For external reporting purposes the accountant has a two-fold obligation:

● an obligation to ensure that the financial statements comply with statutory, professional and Listing requirements; this requires the accountant to possess **technical expertise**;

● an obligation to ensure that the financial statements present the substance of the commercial transactions the company has entered into; this requires the accountant to have **commercial awareness**.[2]

1.4 Managers

Managers are internal users. As such, they have access to detailed financial statements showing the current results, the extent to which these vary from the budgeted results and the future budgeted results. Examples of internal users are sole traders, partners and, in a company context, directors and managers.

There is no statutory restriction on the amount of information that an internal user may receive; the only restriction would be that imposed by the company's own policy. Frequently, companies operate a 'need to know' policy and only the directors see all the financial statements; employees, for example, would be most unlikely to receive information that would assist them in claiming a salary increase – unless, of course, it happened to be a time of recession, when information would be more freely provided by management as a means of containing claims for an increase.

1.5 What skills does an accountant require in respect of internal reports?

For the internal user, the accountant is able to tailor his or her reports. The accountant is required to produce financial statements that are specifically relevant to the user requesting them.

The accountant needs to be skilled in identifying the information that is needed and conveying its implication and meaning to the user. The user needs to be confident that the accountant understands the user's information needs and will satisfy them in a language that is understandable. The accountant must be a skilled communicator who is able to instil confidence in the user that the information is:

● relevant to the user's needs;
● measured objectively;
● presented within a time-scale that permits decisions to be made with appropriate information;
● verifiable, in that it can be confirmed that the report represents the transactions that have taken place;
● reliable, in that it is as free from bias as is possible;
● a complete picture of material items;
● a fair representation of the business transactions and events that have occurred or are being planned.

The accountant is a trained reporter of financial information. Just as for external reporting, the accountant needs commercial awareness. It is important, therefore, that he or she should not operate in isolation.

1.5.1 Accountant's reporting role

The accountant's role is to ensure that the information provided is useful for making decisions. For external users, the accountant achieves this by providing a general-purpose financial statement that complies with statute and is reliable. For internal users, this is done by interfacing with the user and establishing exactly what financial information is relevant to the decision that is to be made.

We now consider the steps required to provide relevant information for internal users.

1.6 Procedural steps when reporting to internal users

A number of user steps and accounting action steps can be identified within a financial decision model. These are shown in Figure 1.1.

Note that, although we refer to an accountant/user interface, this is not a single occurrence because the user and accountant interface at each of the user decision steps.

At **step 1**, the accountant attempts to ensure that the decision is based on the appropriate appraisal methodology. However, the accountant is providing a service to a user and,

Figure 1.1 General financial decision model to illustrate the user/accountant interface

USER	USER/ACCOUNTANT INTERFACE	ACCOUNTANT
User step 1 Identify decision and how it is to be made *User step 2* Establish with the accountant the information necessary for decision making *User step 3* Seek relevant data from the accountant		Identify the material information needed by the user Measure the relevant information Prepare report for user to allow user to make decision Provide an understandable report to the user

while the accountant may give guidance, the final decision about methodology rests with the user.

At **step 2**, the accountant needs to establish the information necessary to support the decision that is to be made.

At **step 3**, the accountant needs to ensure that the user **understands** the full impact and financial implications of the accountant's report taking into account the user's level of understanding and prior knowledge. This may be overlooked by the accountant, who feels that the task has been completed when the written report has been typed.

It is important to remember in following the model that the accountant is attempting to satisfy the information needs of the individual user rather than those of a 'user group'. It is tempting to divide users into groups with apparently common information needs, without recognising that a group contains individual users with different information needs. We return to this later in the chapter, but for the moment we continue by studying a situation where the directors of a company are considering a proposed capital investment project.

Let us assume that there are three companies in the retail industry: Retail A Ltd, Retail B Ltd and Retail C Ltd. The directors of each company are considering the purchase of a warehouse. We could assume initially that, because the companies are operating in the same industry and are faced with the same investment decision, they have identical information needs. However, enquiry might establish that the directors of each company have a completely different attitude to, or perception of, the primary business objective.

For example, it might be established that Retail A Ltd is a large company and under the Fisher/Hirshleifer separation theory the directors seek to maximise profits for the benefit of the equity investors; Retail B Ltd is a medium-sized company in which the directors seek to obtain a satisfactory return for the equity shareholders; and Retail C Ltd is a smaller company in which the directors seek to achieve a satisfactory return for a wider range of stakeholders, including, perhaps, the employees as well as the equity shareholders.

The accountant needs to be aware that these differences may have a significant effect on the information required. Let us consider this diagrammatically in the situation where a capital investment decision is to be made, referring particularly to user step 2: 'Establish with the accountant the information necessary for decision making'.

Figure 1.2 Impact of different user attitudes on the information needed in relation to a capital investment proposal

	USER A Directors of Retail A Ltd	USER B Directors of Retail B Ltd	USER C Directors of Retail C Ltd
User attitude	PROFIT MAXIMISER for SHAREHOLDERS	PROFIT SATISFICER for SHAREHOLDERS	PROFIT SATISFICER for SHAREHOLDERS/ STAFF
Relevant data to measure	CASH FLOWS	CASH FLOWS	CASH FLOWS
Appraisal method (decided on by user)	IRR	NPV	NPV
Appraisal criterion (decided on by user)	HIGHEST IRR	NPV but only if positive	NPV possibly even if negative

We can see from Figure 1.2 that the accountant has identified that:

● the relevant financial data are the same for each of the users, i.e. cash flows; but

● the appraisal methods selected, i.e. internal rate of return (IRR) and net present value (NPV), are different; and

● the appraisal criteria employed by each user, i.e. higher IRR and NPV, are different.

In practice, the user is likely to use more than one appraisal method, as each has advantages and disadvantages. However, we can see that, even when dealing with a single group of apparently homogeneous users, the accountant has first to identify the information needs of the particular user. Only then is the accountant able to identify the relevant financial data and the appropriate report. It is the user's needs that are predominant.

If the accountant's view of the appropriate appraisal method or criterion differs from the user's view, the accountant might decide to report from both views. This approach affords the opportunity to improve the user's understanding and encourages good practice.

The diagrams can be combined (Figure 1.3) to illustrate the complete process. The user is assumed to be Retail A Ltd, a company that has directors who are profit maximisers.

The accountant is reactive when reporting to an internal user. We observe this characteristic in the Norman example set out in section 1.8. Because the cash flows are identified as relevant to the user, it is these flows that the accountant will record, measure and appraise.

The accountant can also be proactive, by giving the user advice and guidance in areas where the accountant has specific expertise, such as the appraisal method that is most appropriate to the circumstances.

Figure 1.3 User/accountant interface where the user is a profit maximiser

General model USER	Specific application for Retail A Ltd A PROFIT MAXIMISER		General model ACCOUNTANT	Specific application for Retail A Ltd ACCOUNTANT
Step 1 Decision to be made	Appraise which project warrants capital investment		Identify information needed by the user	User decision criterion is IRR
Step 2 Information needed		**USER/ ACCOUNTANT INTERFACE**	Measure	Measure the project cash flows
	Project with the highest IRR		Prepare report	Prepare report of highest IRR
Step 3 Seek relevant data				
	Report of IRR project		Provide report	Submit report of project with highest IRR per £ invested

1.7 Agency costs[3]

The information in Figure 1.2 assumes that the directors have made their investment decision based on the assumed preferences of the shareholders. However, in real life, the directors might also be influenced by how the decision impinges on their own position. If, for example, their remuneration is a fixed salary, they might select not the investment with the highest IRR, but the one that maintains their security of employment. The result might be suboptimal investment and financing decisions based on risk aversion and over-retention. To the extent that the potential cash flows have been reduced, there will be an agency cost to the shareholders. This agency cost is an opportunity cost – the amount that was forgone because the decision making was suboptimal – and, as such, it will not be recorded in the books of account and will not appear in the financial statements.

1.8 Illustration of periodic financial statements prepared under the cash flow concept to disclose realised operating cash flows

In the above example of Retail A, B and C, the investment decision for the acquisition of a warehouse was based on an appraisal of cash flows. This raises the question: 'Why not continue with the cash flow concept and report the financial changes that occur after the investment has been undertaken using that same concept?'

To do this, the company will record the consequent cash flows through a number of subsequent accounting periods; report the cash flows that occur in each financial period; and produce a balance sheet at the end of each of the financial periods. For illustration we follow this procedure in sections 1.8.1 and 1.8.2 for transactions entered into by Mr S. Norman.

1.8.1 Appraisal of the initial investment decision

Mr Norman is considering whether to start up a retail business by acquiring the lease of a shop for five years at a cost of £80,000.

Our first task has been set out in Figure 1.1 above. It is to establish the information that Mr Norman needs, so that we can decide what data need to be collected and measured. Let us assume that, as a result of a discussion with Mr Norman, it has been ascertained that he is a profit satisficer who is looking to achieve at least a 10% return, which represents the time value of money. This indicates that, as illustrated in Figure 1.2:

● the relevant data to be measured are **cash flows**, represented by the outflow of cash invested in the lease and the inflow of cash represented by the realised operating cash flows;

● the appropriate appraisal method is **NPV**; and

● the appraisal criterion is a **positive NPV** using the discount rate of 10%.

Let us further assume that the cash to be invested in the lease is £80,000 and that the realised operating cash flows over the life of the investment in the shop are as shown in Figure 1.4. This shows that there is a forecast of £30,000 annually for five years and a final receipt of £29,000 in 20X6 when he proposes to cease trading.

We already know that Mr Norman's investment criterion is a positive NPV using a discount factor of 10%. A calculation (Figure 1.5) shows that the investment easily satisfies that criterion.

Figure 1.4 Forecast of realised operating cash flows

	Annually years 20X1–20X5	Cash in year 20X6 after shop closure
	£	£
Receipts from Customers	400,000	55,000
Payments to		
Suppliers	(342,150)	(20,000)
Expense creditors	(21,600)	(3,000)
Rent	(6,250)	(3,000)
Total payments	(370,000)	(26,000)
Realised operating cash flows	30,000	29,000

Figure 1.5 NPV calculation using discount tables

	£	£
Cost of lease		(80,000)
£30,000 annually for 5 years (30,000 × 3.79)	113,700	
£29,000 received in year 6 (29,000 × 0.564)	16,356	
		130,056
Positive net present value		50,056

1.8.2 Preparation of periodic financial statements under the cash flow concept

Having **predicted** the realised operating cash flows for the purpose of making the investment decision, we can assume that the owner of the business will wish to obtain **feedback** to evaluate the correctness of the investment decision. He does this by reviewing the actual results on a regular **timely** basis and **comparing** these with the predicted forecast. Actual results should be reported quarterly, half-yearly or annually in the same format as used when making the decision in Figure 1.4. The actual results provide management with the feedback information required to audit the initial decision; it is a technique for achieving accountability. However, frequently, companies do not provide a report of actual cash flows to compare with the forecast cash flows, and fail to carry out an audit review.

In some cases, the transactions relating to the investment cannot be readily separated from other transactions, and the information necessary for the audit review of the investment cannot be made available. In other cases, the routine accounting procedures fail to collect such cash flow information because the reporting systems have not been designed to provide financial reports on a cash flow basis; rather, they have been designed to produce reports prepared on an accrual basis.

What would financial reports look like if they were prepared on a cash flow basis?

To illustrate cash flow period accounts, we will prepare half-yearly accounts for Mr Norman. To facilitate a comparison with the forecast that underpinned the investment decision, we will redraft the forecast annual statement on a half yearly basis. The data for the first year given in Figure 1.4 have therefore been redrafted to provide a forecast for the half-year to 30 June, as shown in Figure 1.6.

We assume that, having applied the net present value appraisal technique to the cash flows and ascertained that the NPV was positive, Mr Norman proceeded to set up the business on 1 January 20X1. He introduced capital of £50,000, acquired a five-year lease for £80,000 and paid £6,250 in advance as rent to occupy the property to 31 December 20X1. He has decided to prepare financial statements at half-yearly intervals. The information given in Figure 1.7 concerns his trading for the half-year to 30 June 20X1.

Mr Norman was naturally eager to determine whether the business was achieving its forecast cash flows for the first six months of trading, so he produced the statement of

Figure 1.6 Forecast of realised operating cash flows

	Half-year to 30 June 20X1 £
Receipts from	
Customers	165,000
Payments to	
Suppliers	(124,000)
Expense creditors	(18,000)
Rent	(6,250)
Total payments	(148,250)
Realised operating cash flows	16,750

Figure 1.7 Monthly sales, purchases and expenses for six months ended 30 June 20X1

Month	Sales invoiced £	Cash received £	Purchases invoiced £	Cash paid £	Expenses invoiced £	Cash paid £
January	15,000	7,500	16,000		3,400	3,100
February	20,000	17,500	19,000	16,000	3,500	3,400
March	35,000	27,500	29,000	19,000	3,800	3,500
April	40,000	37,500	32,000	29,000	3,900	3,800
May	40,000	40,000	33,000	32,000	3,900	3,900
June	45,000	42,500	37,000	33,000	4,000	3,900
TOTAL	195,000	172,500	166,000	129,000	22,500	21,600

Note: The following items were included under the Expenses invoiced heading:

Expense creditors	– amount
Wages	– £3,100 per month paid in the month
Commission	– 2% of sales invoiced payable one month in arrears

Figure 1.8 Monthly realised operating cash flows

	Jan £	Feb £	Mar £	Apr £	May £	Jun £	Total £
Receipts							
Customers	7,500	17,500	27,500	37,500	40,000	42,500	172,500
Less payments							
Suppliers		16,000	19,000	29,000	32,000	33,000	129,000
Expense creditors	3,100	3,400	3,500	3,800	3,900	3,900	21,600
Rent	6,250						6,250
Realised	(1,850)	(1,900)	5,000	4,700	4,100	5,600	15,650

realised operating cash flows (Figure 1.8) from the information provided in Figure 1.7. From this statement we can see that the business generated positive cash flows after the end of February. These are, of course, only the cash flows relating to the trading transactions.

The information in the 'Total' row of Figure 1.7 can be extracted to provide the financial statement for the six months ended 30 June 20X1, as shown in Figure 1.9.

The figure of £15,650 needs to be compared with the forecast cash flows used in the investment appraisal. This is a form of auditing. It allows the assumptions made on the initial investment decision to be confirmed. The forecast/actual comparison (based on the information in Figures 1.6 and 1.9) is set out in Figure 1.10.

What are the characteristics of these data that make them relevant?

● The data are **objective**. There is no judgement involved in deciding the values to include in the financial statement, as each value or amount represents a verifiable cash transaction with a third party.

Figure 1.9 Realised operating cash flows for the six months ended 30 June 20X1

		£
Receipts from		
Customers		172,500
Payments to		
Suppliers	(129,000)	
Expense creditors	(21,600)	
Rent	(6,250)	
		156,850
Realised operating cash flow		15,650

Figure 1.10 Forecast/actual comparison

		Actual £		Forecast £
Receipts from				
Customers		172,500		165,000
Payment to				
Suppliers	(129,000)			(124,000)
Expense creditors	(21,600)			(18,000)
Rent	(6,250)			(6,250)
Total payments		(156,850)		(148,250)
Realised operating cash flow		15,650		16,750

- The data are **consistent**. The statement incorporates the same cash flows within the periodic financial report of trading as the cash flows that were incorporated within the initial capital investment report. This permits a logical comparison and confirmation that the decision was realistic.
- The results have a **confirmatory** value by helping users confirm or correct their past assessments.
- The results have a **predictive** value, in that they provide a basis for revising the initial forecasts if necessary.[4]
- There is **no requirement for accounting standards** or disclosure of accounting policies that are necessary to regulate accrual accounting practices, e.g. depreciation methods.

1.9 Illustration of preparation of statement of financial position

Although the information set out in Figure 1.10 permits us to compare and evaluate the initial decision, it does not provide a sufficiently sound basis for the following:

- assessing the stewardship over the total cash funds that have been employed within the business;
- signalling to management whether its working capital policies are appropriate.

1.9.1 Stewardship

To assess the stewardship over the total cash funds we need to:

(a) evaluate the effectiveness of the accounting system to make certain that all transactions are recorded;

(b) extend the cash flow statement to take account of the capital cash flows; and

(c) prepare a statement of financial position or balance sheet as at 30 June 20X1.

The additional information for (b) and (c) above is set out in Figures 1.11 and 1.12 respectively.

  The cash flow statement and statement of financial position, taken together, are a means of assessing stewardship. They identify the movement of **all** cash and derive a **net** balance figure. These statements are a normal feature of a sound system of internal control, but they have not been made available to external users.

1.9.2 Working capital policies

By 'working capital' we mean the current assets and current liabilities of the business. In addition to providing a means of making management accountable, cash flows are the raw data required by financial managers when making decisions on the management of working capital. One of the decisions would be to set the appropriate terms for credit policy. For example, Figure 1.11 shows that the business will have a £14,350 overdraft at 30 June 20X1.

Figure 1.11 Cash flow statement to calculate the net cash balance

	Jan £	Feb £	Mar £	Apr £	May £	Jun £	Total £
Operating cash	(1,850)	(1,900)	5,000	4,700	4,100	5,600	15,650
New capital	50,000						50,000
Lease payment	(80,000)						(80,000)
Cash balance	(31,850)	(33,750)	(28,750)	(24,050)	(19,950)	(14,350)	(14,350)

Figure 1.12 Statement of financial position

	Opening 1 Jan 20X1 £	Closing 30 Jun 20X1 £
Capital introduced	50,000	50,000
Net operating cash flow		15,650
	50,000	65,650
Lease		80,000
Net cash balance	50,000	−14,350
	50,000	65,650

If this is not acceptable, management will review its working capital by reconsidering the credit given to customers, the credit taken from suppliers, stock-holding levels and the timing of capital cash inflows and outflows.

If, in the example, it were possible to obtain 45 days' credit from suppliers, then the creditors at 30 June would rise from £37,000 to a new total of £53,500. This increase in trade credit of £16,500 means that half of the May purchases (£33,000/2) would not be paid for until July, which would convert the overdraft of £14,350 into a positive balance of £2,150. As a new business it might not be possible to obtain credit from all of the suppliers. In that case, other steps would be considered, such as phasing the payment for the lease of the warehouse or introducing more capital.

An interesting research report[5] identified that for small firms survival and stability were the main objectives rather than profit maximisation. This, in turn, meant that cash flow indicators and managing cash flow were seen as crucial to survival. In addition, cash flow information was perceived as important to external bodies such as banks in evaluating performance.

1.10 Treatment of non-current assets in the cash flow model

The statement of financial position in Figure 1.12 does not take into account any **unrealised** cash flows. Such flows are deemed to occur as a result of any rise or fall in the realisable value of the lease. This could rise if, for example, the annual rent payable under the lease were to be substantially lower than the rate payable under a new lease entered into on 30 June 20X1. It could also fall with the passing of time, with six months having expired by 30 June 20X1. We need to consider this further and examine the possible treatment of non-current assets in the cash flow model.

Using the cash flow approach, we require an independent verification of the realisable value of the lease at 30 June 20X1. If the lease has fallen in value, the difference between the original outlay and the net realisable figure could be treated as a negative unrealised operating cash flow.

For example, if the independent estimate was that the realisable value was £74,000, then the statement of financial position would be prepared as in Figure 1.13. The fall of £6,000 in realisable value is an unrealised cash flow and, while it does not affect the calculation of the net cash balance, it does affect the statement of financial position.

Figure 1.13 Statement of financial position as at 30 June 20X1 (assuming that there were unrealised operating cash flows)

	£
Capital introduced	50,000
Net operating flow: **realised**	15,650
: **unrealised**	(6,000)
	59,650
Lease: **net realisable value**	74,000
Net cash balance	−14,350
	59,650

The additional benefit of the statement of financial position, as revised, is that the owner is able clearly to identify the following:

- the operating cash inflows of £15,650 that have been realised from the business operations;
- the operating cash outflow of £6,000 that has not been realised, but has arisen as a result of investing in the lease;
- the net cash balance of −£14,350;
- the statement provides a **stewardship-orientated** report: that is, it is a means of making the management accountable for the cash within its control.

1.11 What are the characteristics of these data that make them reliable?

We have already discussed some characteristics of cash flow reporting which indicate that the data in the financial statements are **relevant**, e.g. their predictive and confirmatory roles. We now introduce five more characteristics of cash flow statements which indicate that the information is also **reliable**, i.e. free from bias.[6] These are prudence, neutrality, completeness, faithful representation and substance over form.

1.11.1 Prudence characteristic

Revenue and profits are included in the cash flow statement only when they are realised. Realisation is deemed to occur when cash is received. In our Norman example, the £172,500 cash received from debtors represents the revenue for the half-year ended 30 June 20X1. This policy is described as prudent because it **does not anticipate** cash flows: cash flows are recorded only when they actually occur and not when they are reasonably certain to occur. This is one of the factors that distinguishes cash flow from accrual accounting.

1.11.2 Neutrality characteristic

Financial statements are not neutral if, by their selection or presentation of information, they influence the making of a decision in order to achieve a predetermined result or outcome. With cash flow accounting, the information is not subject to management selection criteria.

Cash flow accounting avoids the tension that can arise between prudence and neutrality because, whilst neutrality involves freedom from deliberate or systematic bias, prudence is a potentially biased concept that seeks to ensure that, under conditions of uncertainty, gains and assets are not overstated and losses and liabilities are not understated.[7]

1.11.3 Completeness characteristic

The cash flows can be verified for completeness provided there are adequate internal control procedures in operation. In small and medium-sized enterprises there can be a weakness if one person, typically the owner, has control over the accounting system and is able to under-record cash receipts.

1.11.4 Faithful representation characteristic

Cash flows can be depended upon by users to represent faithfully what they purport to represent provided, of course, that the completeness characteristic has been satisfied.

1.11.5 Substance over form

Cash flow accounting does not necessarily possess this characteristic which requires that transactions should be accounted for and presented in accordance with their substance and economic reality and not merely their legal form.[8]

1.12 Reports to external users

1.12.1 Stewardship orientation

Cash flow accounting provides objective, consistent and prudent financial information about a business's transactions. It is stewardship-orientated and offers a means of achieving accountability over cash resources and investment decisions.

1.12.2 Prediction orientation

External users are also interested in the ability of a company to pay dividends. It might be thought that the past and current cash flows are the best indicators of future cash flows and dividends. However, the cash flow might be misleading, in that a declining company might sell non-current assets and have a better **net cash position** than a growing company that buys non-current assets for future use. There is also no matching of cash inflows and out-flows, in the sense that a benefit is matched with the sacrifice made to achieve it.

Consequently, it has been accepted accounting practice to view the income statement prepared on the accrual accounting concept as a better predictor of future cash flows to an investor than the cash flow statements that we have illustrated in this chapter.

However, the operating cash flows arising from trading and the cash flows arising from the introduction of capital and the acquisition of non-current assets can become significant to investors, e.g. they may threaten the company's ability to survive or may indicate growth.

In the next chapter, we revise the preparation of the same three statements using the **accrual accounting** model.

1.12.3 Going concern

The Financial Reporting Council suggests in its Consultation Paper *Going Concern and Financial Reporting*[9] that directors in assessing whether a company is a going concern may prepare monthly cash flow forecasts and monthly budgets covering, as a minimum, the period up to the next statement of financial position date. The forecasts would also be supported by a detailed list of assumptions which underlie them.

Summary

To review our understanding of this chapter, we should ask ourselves the following questions.

How useful is cash flow accounting for internal decision making?

Forecast cash flows are relevant for the appraisal of proposals for capital investment.

Actual cash flows are relevant for the confirmation of the decision for capital investment.

Cash flows are relevant for the management of working capital. Financial managers might have a variety of mathematical models for the efficient use of working capital, but cash flows are the raw data upon which they work.

How useful is cash flow accounting for making management accountable?

The cash flow statement is useful for confirming decisions and, together with the statement of financial position, provides a stewardship report. Lee states that 'Cash flow accounting appears to satisfy the need to supply owners and others with stewardship-orientated information as well as with decision-orientated information.'[10]
Lee further states that:

> By reducing judgements in this type of financial report, management can report factually on its stewardship function, whilst at the same time disclosing data of use in the decision-making process. In other words, cash flow reporting eliminates the somewhat artificial segregation of stewardship and decision-making information.[11]

This is exactly what we saw in our Norman example – the same realised operating cash flow information was used for both the investment decision and financial reporting. However, for stewardship purposes it was necessary to extend the cash flow to include **all** cash movements and to extend the statement of financial position to include the **unrealised** cash flows.

How useful is cash flow accounting for reporting to external users?

Cash flow information is relevant:

- as a basis for making internal management decisions in relation to both non-current assets and working capital;
- for stewardship and accountability; and
- for assessing whether a business is a going concern.

Cash flow information is reliable and a fair representation, being:

- objective;
- consistent;
- prudent; and
- neutral.

However, professional accounting practice requires reports to external users to be on an accrual accounting basis. This is because the accrual accounting profit figure is a better predictor for investors of the future cash flows likely to arise from the dividends paid to them by the business, and of any capital gain on disposal of their investment. It could also be argued that cash flows may not be a fair representation of the commercial substance of transactions, e.g. if a business allowed a year's credit to all its customers there would be no income recorded.

REVIEW QUESTIONS

1 Explain why it is the user who should determine the information that the accountant collects, measures and reports, rather than the accountant who is the expert in financial information.

2 'Yuji Ijiri rejects decision usefulness as the main purpose of accounting and puts in its place accountability. Ijiri sees the accounting relationship as a tripartite one, involving the accountor, the

accountee, and the accountant ... the decision useful approach is heavily biased in favour of the accountee ... with little concern for the accountor ... in the central position Ijiri would put fairness.'[12] Discuss Ijiri's view in the context of cash flow accounting.

3 Discuss the extent to which you consider that accounts for a small businessperson who is carrying on business as a sole trader should be prepared on a cash flow basis.

4 Explain why your decision in question 3 might be different if the business entity were a medium-sized limited company.

5 'Realised operating cash flows are only of use for internal management purposes and are irrelevant to investors.' Discuss.

6 'While accountants may be free from bias in the measurement of economic information, they cannot be unbiased in identifying the economic information that they consider to be relevant.' Discuss.

7 Explain the effect on the statement of financial position in Figure 1.13 if the non-current asset consisted of expenditure on industry-specific machine tools rather than a lease.

8 'It is essential that the information in financial statements has a prudent characteristic if the financial statements are to be objective.' Discuss.

EXERCISES

An extract from the solution is provided on the Companion Website (www.pearsoned.co.uk/elliott-elliott) for exercises marked with an asterisk (*).

Question 1

Jane Parker is going to set up a new business on 1 January 20X1. She estimates that her first six months in business will be as follows:

  (i) She will put £150,000 into a bank account for the firm on 1 January 20X1.

 (ii) On 1 January 20X1 she will buy machinery £30,000, motor vehicles £24,000 and premises £75,000, paying for them immediately.

(iii) All purchases will be effected on credit. She will buy £30,000 goods on 1 January and will pay for these in February. Other purchases will be: rest of January £48,000; February, March, April, May and June £60,000 each month. Other than the £30,000 worth bought in January, all other purchases will be paid for two months after purchase.

 (iv) Sales (all on credit) will be £60,000 for January and £75,000 for each month after. Customers will pay for the goods in the fourth month after purchase, i.e. £60,000 is received in May.

  (v) She will make drawings of £1,200 per month.

 (vi) Wages and salaries will be £2,250 per month and will be paid on the last day of each month.

(vii) General expenses will be £750 per month, payable in the month following that in which they are incurred.

(viii) Rates will be paid as follows: for the three months to 31 March 20X1 by cheque on 28 February 20X1; for the 12 months ended 31 March 20X2 by cheque on 31 July 20X1. Rates are £4,800 per annum.

(ix) She will introduce new capital of £82,500 on 1 April 20X1.

(x) Insurance covering the 12 months of 20X1 of £2,100 will be paid for by cheque on 30 June 20X1.

(xi) All receipts and payments will be by cheque.

(xii) Inventory on 30 June 20X1 will be £30,000.

(xiii) The net realisable value of the vehicles is £19,200, machinery £27,000 and premises £75,000.

Required: Cash flow accounting

(i) Draft a cash budget (includes bank) month by month for the period January to June, showing clearly the amount of bank balance or overdraft at the end of each month.

(ii) Draft an operating cash flow statement for the six-month period.

(iii) Assuming that Jane Parker sought your advice as to whether she should actually set up in business, state what further information you would require.

* Question 2

Mr Norman set up a new business on 1 January 20X8. He invested £50,000 in the new business on that date. The following information is available.

1   Gross profit was 20% of sales. Monthly sales were as follows:

Month	Sales £	Month	Sales £
January	15,000	May	40,000
February	20,000	June	45,000
March	35,000	July	50,000
April	40,000		

2   50% of sales were for cash. Credit customers (50% of sales) pay in month following sale.

3   The supplier allowed one month's credit.

4   Monthly payments were made for rent and rates £2,200 and wages £600.

5   On 1 January 20X8 the following payments were made: £80,000 for a five-year lease of business premises and £3,500 for insurances on the premises for the year. The realisable value of the lease was estimated to be £76,000 on 30 June 20X8 and £70,000 on 31 December 20X8.

6   Staff sales commission of 2% of sales was paid in the month following the sale.

Required:

(a) A purchases budget for each of the first six months.

(b) A cash flow statement for the first six months.

(c) A statement of operating cash flows and financial position as at 30 June 20X8.

(d) Write a brief letter to the bank supporting a request for an overdraft.

Question 3

Fred and Sally own a profitable business that deals in windsurfing equipment. They are the only UK agents to import 'Dryline' sails from Germany, and in addition to this they sell a variety of boards and miscellaneous equipment that they buy from other dealers in the UK.

Two years ago they diversified into custom-made boards built to individual customer requirements, each of which was supplied with a 'Dryline' sail. In order to build the boards, they have had to take over larger premises, which consist of a shop front with a workshop at the rear, and employ two members of staff to help.

Demand is seasonal and Fred and Sally find that there is insufficient work during the winter months to pay rent for the increased accommodation and also wages to the extra two members of staff. The four of them could spend October to March in Lanzarote as windsurf instructors and close the UK operation down in this period. If they did, however, they would lose the 'Dryline' agency, as Dryline insists on a retail outlet in the UK for 12 months of the year. Dryline sails constitute 40% of their turnover and carry a 50% mark-up.

Trading has been static and the pattern is expected to continue as follows for 1 April 20X5 to 31 March 20X6:

Sales of boards and equipment (non-custom-built) with Dryline agency: 1 April–30 September £120,000; of this 30% was paid by credit card, which involved one month's delay in receiving cash and 4% deduction at source.

Sixty custom-built boards 1 April–30 September £60,000; of this 15% of the sales price was for the sail (a 'Dryline' 6 m² sail costs Fred and Sally £100; the average price for a sail of the same size and quality is £150 (cost to them)).

Purchasers of custom-built boards take an average of two months to pay and none pays by credit card.

Sales 1 October–31 March of boards and equipment (non-custom-built) £12,000, 30% by credit card as above.

Six custom-built boards were sold for a total of £6,000 and customers took an unexplainable average of three months to pay in the winter.

Purchases were made monthly and paid for two months in arrears.

The average mark-up on goods for resale excluding 'Dryline' sails was 25%. If they lose the agency, they expect that they will continue to sell the same number of sails, but at their average mark-up of 25%. The variable material cost of each custom-made board (excluding the sail) was £500.

Other costs were:
   Wages to employees £6,000 p.a. each (gross including insurance).
   Rent for premises £6,000 p.a. (six-monthly renewable lease) payable on the first day of each month.
   Other miscellaneous costs:
      1 April–30 September   £3,000
      1 October–31 March   £900.

Bank balance on 1 April was £100.

Salary earnable over whole period in Lanzarote:
   Fred and Sally £1,500 each + living accommodation
   Two employees £1,500 each + living accommodation

All costs and income accruing evenly over time.

Required:
(i) Prepare a cash budget for 1 April 20X5 to 31 March 20X6 assuming that:
   (a) Fred and Sally close the business in the winter months.
   (b) They stay open all year.
(ii) What additional information would you require before you advised Fred and Sally of the best course of action to take?

References

1 *Framework for the Preparation and Presentation of Financial Statements*, IASC, 1989, para. 10.
2 *Ibid.*, para. 35.
3 G. Whittred and I. Zimmer, *Financial Accounting: Incentive Effects and Economic Consequences*, Holt, Rinehart & Winston, 1992, p. 27.
4 IASC, *op. cit.*, para. 27.
5 R. Jarvis, J. Kitching, J. Curran and G. Lightfoot, *The Financial Management of Small Firms: An Alternative Perspective*, ACCA Research Report No. 49, 1996.
6 IASC, *op. cit.*, para. 31.
7 *Ibid.*, para. 36.
8 *Ibid.*, para. 35.
9 *Going Concern and Financial Reporting – Proposals V. Revise the Guidance for Directors of Listed Companies.* FRC, 2008, para. 29.
10 T.A. Lee, *Income and Value Measurement: Theory and Practice* (3rd edition), Van Nostrand Reinhold (UK), 1985, p. 173.
11 *Ibid.*
12 D. Solomons, *Making Accounting Policy*, Oxford University Press, 1986, p. 79.

CHAPTER **2**

Accounting and reporting on an accrual accounting basis

2.1 Introduction

The main purpose of this chapter is to extend cash flow accounting by adjusting for the effect of transactions that have not been completed by the end of an accounting period.

Objectives

By the end of this chapter, you should be able to:

- explain the historical cost convention and accrual concept;
- adjust cash receipts and payments in accordance with IAS 18 *Revenue*;
- account for the amount of non-current assets used during the accounting period;
- prepare a statement of income and a statement of financial position;
- reconcile cash flow accounting and accrual accounting data.

2.1.1 Objective of financial statements

The International Accounting Standards Committee (IASC) has stated that the objective of financial statements is to provide information about the financial position, performance and capability of an enterprise that is useful to a wide range of users in making economic decisions.[1]

Common information needs for decision making

The IASC recognises that all the information needs of all users cannot be met by financial statements, but it takes the view that some needs are common to all users: in particular, they have some interest in the financial position, performance and adaptability of the enterprise as a whole. This leaves open the question of which user is the primary target; the IASC states that, as investors are providers of risk capital, financial statements that meet their needs would also meet the needs of other users.[2]

Stewardship role of financial statements

In addition to assisting in making economic decisions, financial statements also show the results of the stewardship of management: that is, the accountability of management for the resources entrusted to it. The IASC view[3] is that users who assess the stewardship do so in order to make economic decisions, e.g. whether to hold or sell shares in a particular company or change the management.

Decision makers need to assess ability to generate cash

The IASC considers that economic decisions also require an evaluation of an enterprise's ability to generate cash, and of the timing and certainty of its generation.[4] It believes that users are better able to make the evaluation if they are provided with information that focuses on the financial position, performance and cash flow of an enterprise.

2.1.2 Financial information to evaluate the ability to generate cash differs from financial information on actual cash flows

The IASC approach differs from the cash flow model used in Chapter 1, in that, in addition to the cash flows and statement of financial position, it includes within its definition of performance a reference to profit. It states that this information is required to assess changes in the economic resources that the enterprise is likely to control in the future. This is useful in predicting the capacity of the enterprise to generate cash flows from its existing resource base.[5]

2.1.3 Statements making up the financial statements published for external users

The IASB stated in 2005[6] that the financial statements published by a company for external users should consist of the following:

● a statement of financial position;
● a statement of comprehensive income;
● a statement of changes in equity;
● a cash flow statement;[7]
● notes comprising a summary of significant accounting policies and other explanatory notes.

In 2007 the IASB stated[8] that a complete set of financial statements should comprise:

● a statement of financial position as at the end of the period;
● a statement of comprehensive income for the period;
● a statement of changes in equity for the period;
● a statement of cash flows for the period;
● notes comprising a summary of significant accounting policies and other explanatory information.

Entities may, however, use other titles in their financial statements. This means that for a period both the pre-2007 and post-2007 titles will be used.

In this chapter we consider two of the conventions under which the statement of comprehensive income and statement of financial position are prepared: the historical cost convention and the accrual accounting concept.

2.2 Historical cost convention

The historical cost convention results in an appropriate measure of the economic resource that has been withdrawn or replaced.

Under it, transactions are reported at the £ amount recorded at the date the transaction occurred. Financial statements produced under this convention provide a basis for determining the outcome of agency agreements with reasonable certainty and predictability because the data are relatively objective.[9]

By this we mean that various parties who deal with the enterprise, such as lenders, will know that the figures produced in any financial statements are objective and not manipulated by subjective judgements made by the directors. A typical example occurs when a lender attaches a covenant to a loan that the enterprise shall not exceed a specified level of gearing.

At an operational level, revenue and expense in the statement of comprehensive income are stated at the £ amount that appears on the invoices. This amount is objective and verifiable. Because of this, the historical cost convention has strengths for stewardship purposes, but inflation-adjusted figures may well be more appropriate for decision usefulness.

2.3 Accrual basis of accounting

The accrual basis dictates when transactions with third parties should be recognised and, in particular, determines the accounting periods in which they should be incorporated into the financial statements. Under this concept the cash receipts from customers and payments to creditors are replaced by revenue and expenses respectively.

Revenue and expenses are derived by adjusting the realised operating cash flows to take account of business trading activity that has occurred during the accounting period, but has not been converted into cash receipts or payments by the end of the period.

2.3.1 Accrual accounting is a better indicator than cash flow accounting of ability to generate cash

The accounting profession generally supports the view expressed by the Financial Accounting Standards Board (FASB) in the USA that accrual accounting provides a better indication of an enterprise's present and continuing ability to generate favourable cash flows than information limited to the financial aspects of cash receipts and payments.[10]

The IASC supported the FASB view in 1989 when it stated that financial statements prepared on an accrual basis inform users not only of past transactions involving the payment and receipt of cash, but also of obligations to pay cash in the future and of resources that represent cash to be received in the future, and that they provide the type of information about past transactions and other events that is most useful in making economic decisions.[11]

Having briefly considered why accrual accounting is more useful than cash flow accounting, we will briefly revise the preparation of financial statements under the accrual accounting convention.

2.4 Mechanics of accrual accounting – adjusting cash receipts and payments

We use the cash flows set out in Figure 1.7. The derivation of the revenue and expenses for this example is set out in Figures 2.1 and 2.2. We assume that the enterprise has incomplete

Figure 2.1 Derivation of revenue

	£
Cash received	172,500
Invoices not paid (= Sales invoiced – Cash received)	22,500
Revenue = Total invoiced	195,000

Figure 2.2 Derivation of expense

	Materials £	Services £
Cash paid	129,000	21,600
Invoices not paid	37,000	900
Expense = Total invoiced	166,000	22,500

records, so that the revenue is arrived at by keeping a record of unpaid invoices and adding these to the cash receipts. Clearly, if the invoices are not adequately controlled, there will be no assurance that the £22,500 figure is correct. This is a relatively straightforward process at a mechanistic level. The uncertainty is not how to adjust the cash flow figures, but when to adjust them. This decision requires managers to make subjective judgements. We now look briefly at the nature of such judgements.

2.5 Subjective judgements required in accrual accounting – adjusting cash receipts in accordance with IAS 18

In Figure 2.1 we assumed that revenue was derived simply by adding unpaid invoices to the cash receipts. In practice, however, this is influenced by the commercial facts underlying the transactions. For example, if the company is a milk producer, the point at which it should report the milk production as revenue will be influenced by the existence of a supply contract. If there is a contract with a buyer, the revenue might be recognised immediately on production.

So that financial statements are comparable, the IASC[12] has set out revenue recognition criteria in IAS 18 *Revenue* in an attempt to identify when performance was sufficient to warrant inclusion in the revenue for the period. It stated that:

In a transaction involving the sale of goods, performance should be regarded as being achieved when the following conditions have been fulfilled:

(a) the seller of the goods has transferred to the buyer the significant risks and rewards of ownership, in that all significant acts have been completed and the seller retains no continuing managerial involvement in, or effective control of, the goods transferred to a degree usually associated with ownership; and

(b) no significant uncertainty exists regarding:

(i) the amount to be received for the goods;

(ii) the costs incurred or to be incurred in producing or purchasing the goods.

The criteria are simple in their intention, but difficult in their application. For instance, at what exact point in the sales cycle is there no significant uncertainty? The enterprise has to decide on the critical event that can support an assumption that revenue may be recognised.

To assist with these decisions, the standard provided an appendix with a number of examples. Figure 2.3 gives examples of critical events.

The amount of detail in the accounting policy for turnover will depend on the range of activities within a business and events occurring during the financial year. For example, the relevant section of the 2008 Annual Report of the Chloride Group,[13] which tests and assembles electronic products, simply reads:

Revenue

Revenue represents the amounts, excluding VAT and similar sales-related taxes, receivable by the Company for goods and services supplied to outside customers in the ordinary course of business. Revenue is recognised when persuasive evidence of an arrangement with a customer exists, products have been delivered or services have been rendered and collectability is reasonably assured.

The revenue recognition policy for Wolseley plc in its 2008 Annual Report[14] is more specific with reference to sales returns as follows:

Revenue

Revenue is the amount receivable for the provision of goods and services falling within the Group's ordinary activities, excluding intra-group sales, estimated and actual sales returns, trade and early settlement discounts, value added tax and similar sales taxes.

Revenue from the provision of goods is recognised when the risks and rewards of ownership of goods have been transferred to the customer. The risks and rewards of ownership of goods are deemed to have been transferred when the goods are shipped to, or are picked up by, the customer.

Revenue from services, other than those that arise from construction service contracts (see below), are recognised when the service provided to the customer has been completed.

Revenue from the provision of goods and all services is only recognised when the amounts to be recognised are fixed or determinable and collectibility is reasonably assured.

Figure 2.3 Extracts from IAS 18 *Revenue* illustrating critical events

Transaction	Critical event
Services Servicing fees included in the price of the product[15]	When the selling price of a product includes an identifiable amount for subsequent servicing for, say, a warranty period, it will normally be appropriate to defer the relevant portion of the selling price and to recognise it as revenue over the appropriate period.
Sales of goods Shipment made giving the buyer right of return[16]	Recognition of revenue in such circumstances will depend on the substance of the agreement. In the case of normal retail sales (e.g. chain store offering money back if not satisfied) it may be appropriate to recognise the sale but to make a suitable provision for returns based on previous experience. In other cases the substance of the agreement may amount to a sale on consignment, in which case the revenue should not be recognised until the goods are sold to a third party.

2.5.1 Inflating revenue

Total revenue can have an impact on the value of a company's shares and a number of companies attempted to raise their market capitalisation by artificially inflating total revenue. In the US the FASB reacted by issuing guidance[17] on the treatment of sales incentives such as slotting fees (these are payments to a retailer to obtain space on shelves or in catalogues) and cooperative advertising programmes. The result of the guidance was that the fees must be deducted from the revenue rather than expensed – the effect is that that revenue is reduced, gross profit is reduced, expenses are reduced but net profit remains unchanged.

The issue of the FASB guidance clarified the position for many companies of what had been a grey area and a number of companies restated their turnover.

For example, the Novartis Group disclosed in its 2002 Annual Report that it had changed its treatment of discounts allowed to customers:

> Sales are recognised when the significant risks and rewards of ownership of the assets have been transferred to a third party and are reported net of sales taxes and rebates. . . . Sales have been restated for all periods presented to treat certain sales incentives and discounts to retailers as sales deductions instead of marketing and distribution expenses.

Note that this does not affect the bottom line but does have an impact on the sales and gross profit figures.

2.6 Subjective judgements required in accrual accounting – adjusting cash payments in accordance with the matching principle

We have seen that the enterprise needs to decide when to recognise the revenue. It then needs to decide when to include an item as an expense in the statement of comprehensive income. This decision is based on an application of the matching principle.

The matching principle means that financial statements must include costs related to the achievement of the reported revenue. These include the internal transfers required to ensure that reductions in the assets held by a business are recorded at the same time as the revenues.

The expense might be more or less than the cash paid. For example, in the Norman example, £37,000 was invoiced but not paid on materials, and £900 on services; £3,125 was prepaid on rent for the six months after June. The cash flow information therefore needs to be adjusted as in Figure 2.4.

Figure 2.4 Statement of comprehensive income for the six months ended 30 June 20X1

	Operating cash flow £	ADJUST cash flow £	Business activity £
Revenue from business activity	172,500	22,500	195,000
Less: Matching expenses			
Transactions for materials	129,000	37,000	166,000
Transactions for services	21,600	900	22,500
Transaction with landlord	6,250	(3,125)	3,125
OPERATING CASH FLOW from business activity	15,650		
Transactions NOT converted to cash or relating to a subsequent period		(12,275)	
PROFIT from business activity			3,375

2.7 Mechanics of accrual accounting – the statement of financial position

The statement of financial position or statement of financial position, as set out in Figure 1.12, needs to be amended following the change from cash flow to accrual accounting. It needs to include the £ amounts that have arisen from trading but have not been converted to cash, and the £ amounts of cash that have been received or paid but relate to a subsequent period. The adjusted statement of financial position is set out in Figure 2.5.

Figure 2.5 Statement of financial position adjusted to an accrual basis

	£
Capital	50,000
Net operating cash flow: **realised**	15,650
Net operating cash flow: **to be realised next period**	(12,275)
	53,375
Lease	80,000
Net cash balance (refer to Figure 1.11)	(14,350)
Net amount of activities not converted to cash or relating to subsequent periods	(12,275)
	53,375

2.8 Reformatting the statement of financial position

The item 'net amount of activities not converted to cash or relating to subsequent periods' is the net debtor/creditor balance. If we wished, the statement of financial position could be reframed into the customary statement of financial position format, where items are classified as assets or liabilities. The IASC defines assets and liabilities in its *Framework*:[18]

- An asset is a resource:
  - controlled by the enterprise;
  - as a result of past events;
  - from which future economic benefits are expected to flow.
- A liability is a present obligation:
  - arising from past events;
  - the settlement of which is expected to result in an outflow of resources.

The reframed statement set out in Figure 2.6 is in accordance with these definitions. Note that the same amount of £3,375 results from calculating the difference in the opening and closing net assets in the statements of financial position as from calculating the residual amount in the statement of comprehensive income. When the amount derived from both approaches is the same, the statement of financial position and statement of comprehensive income are said to **articulate**. The statement of comprehensive income provides the detailed explanation for the difference in the net assets and the amount is the same because the same concepts have been applied to both statements.

Figure 2.6 Reframed statement as at 30 June

	Reframed	
	£	£
CAPITAL	50,000	50,000
Net operating cash flow: **realised**	15,650	
Net operating cash flow: **to be realised**	(12,275)	
NET INCOME		3,375
	53,375	53,375
NON-CURRENT ASSETS	80,000	80,000
NET CURRENT ASSETS		
Net amount of activities not converted to cash	(12,275)	
CURRENT ASSETS		
Trade receivables		22,500
Other receivables: Prepaid rent		3,125
CURRENT LIABILITIES		
Trade payables		(37,000)
Other payables: service suppliers		(900)
Net cash balance	(14,350)	(14,350)
	53,375	53,375

2.9 Accounting for the sacrifice of non-current assets

The statement of comprehensive income and statement of financial position have both been prepared using verifiable data that have arisen from transactions with third parties outside the business. However, in order to determine the full sacrifice of economic resources that a business has made to achieve its revenue, it is necessary also to take account of the use made of the non-current assets during the period in which the revenue arose.

In the Norman example, the non-current asset is the lease. The extent of the sacrifice is a matter of judgement by the management. This is influenced by the prudence principle, which regulates the matching principle. The prudence principle determines the extent to which transactions that have already been included in the accounting system should be recognised in the statement of comprehensive income.

2.9.1 Treatment of non-current assets in accrual accounting

Applying the matching principle, it is necessary to estimate how much of the initial outlay should be assumed to have been revenue expenditure, i.e. used in achieving the revenue of the accounting period. The provisions of IAS 16 on **depreciation** assist by defining depreciation and stating the duty of allocation, as follows:

Depreciation is the systematic allocation of the depreciable amount of an asset over its useful life.[19]

Depreciable amount is the cost of an asset, or other amount substituted for cost in the financial statements, less its residual value.[20]

The depreciation method used should reflect the pattern in which the asset's economic benefits are consumed by the enterprise.[21]

This sounds a rather complex requirement. It is therefore surprising, when one looks at the financial statements of a multinational company such as in the 2005 Annual Report of BP plc, to find that depreciation on tangible assets other than mineral production is simply provided on a straight-line basis of an equal amount each year, calculated so as to write off the cost by equal instalments. In the UK, this treatment is recognised in FRS 15 which states that where the pattern of consumption of an asset's economic benefits is uncertain, a straight-line method of depreciation is usually adopted.[22] The reason is that, in accrual accounting, the depreciation charged to the statement of comprehensive income is a measure of the amount of the economic benefits that have been consumed, rather than a measure of the fall in realisable value. In estimating the amount of service potential expired, a business is following the **going concern assumption**.

2.9.2 Going concern assumption

The going concern assumption is that the business enterprise will continue in operational existence for the foreseeable future. This assumption introduces a constraint on the prudence concept by allowing the account balances to be reported on a depreciated cost basis rather than on a net realisable value basis.

It is more relevant to use the loss of service potential than the change in realisable value because there is no intention to cease trading and to sell the fixed assets at the end of the accounting period.

In our Norman example, the procedure would be to assume that, in the case of the lease, the economic resource that has been consumed can be measured by the amortisation that has occurred due to the effluxion of time. The time covered by the accounts is half a year: this means that one-tenth of the lease has expired during the half-year. As a result, £8,000 is treated as revenue expenditure in the half-year to 30 June.

This additional revenue expenditure reduces the income in the income account and the asset figure in the statement of financial position. The effects are incorporated into the two statements in Figures 2.7 and 2.8. The asset amounts and the income figure in the statement of financial position are also affected by the exhaustion of part of the non-current assets, as set out in Figure 2.8.

It is current accounting practice to apply the same concepts to determining the entries in both the statement of comprehensive income and the statement of financial position. The amortisation charged in the statement of comprehensive income at £8,000 is the same as the amount deducted from the non-current assets in the statement of financial position. As a result, the two statements articulate: the statement of comprehensive income explains the reason for the reduction of £4,625 in the net assets.

How decision-useful to the management is the income figure that has been derived after deducting a depreciation charge?

The loss of £4,625 indicates that the distribution of any amount would further deplete the financial capital of £50,000 which was invested in the company by Mr Norman on setting up the business. This is referred to as **capital maintenance**; the particular capital maintenance concept that has been applied is the **financial capital maintenance concept**.

2.9.3 Financial capital maintenance concept

The financial capital maintenance concept recognises a profit only after the original monetary investment has been maintained. This means that, as long as the cost of the assets

Figure 2.7 Statement of comprehensive income for the six months ending 30 June

	Operating cash flow CURRENT period £	Adjust cash flow £	Business activity CURRENT period £
Revenue from business activity	172,500	22,500	195,000
Less			
Expenditure to support this activity:			
Transactions with suppliers	129,000	37,000	166,000
Transactions with service providers	21,600	900	22,500
Transaction with landlord	6,250	(3,125)	3,125
OPERATING CASH FLOW from activity	15,650		
TRANSACTIONS NOT CONVERTED TO CASH		(12,275)	
INCOME from business activity			3,375
Allocation of non-current asset cost to this period			8,000
INCOME			(4,625)

Figure 2.8 Statement of financial position as at 30 June

	Transaction cash flows £	Notional flows £	Reported £
CAPITAL	50,000		50,000
Net operating cash flow: **realised**	15,650		
Net operating cash flow: **to be realised**	(12,275)		
Net income before depreciation		3,375	
AMORTISATION		(8,000)	
Net income after amortisation			(4,625)
	53,375		45,375
NON-CURRENT ASSETS	80,000	80,000	
Less amortisation		(8,000)	
Net book value			72,000
NET CURRENT ASSETS			
Net amount not converted to cash	(12,275)		
CURRENT ASSETS			
Trade receivables			22,500
Other receivables – prepaid rent			3,125
CURRENT LIABILITIES			
Trade payables			(37,000)
Other payables: service suppliers			(900)
Net cash balance	(14,350)		(14,350)
	53,375		45,375

representing the initial monetary investment is recovered against the profit, by way of a depreciation charge, the initial monetary investment is maintained.

The concept has been described in the IASC *Framework for the Presentation and Preparation of Financial Statements*:

> a profit is earned only if the financial or money amount of the net assets at the end of the period exceeds the financial or money amount of the net assets at the beginning of the period, after excluding any distributions to, and contributions from, owners during the period. Financial capital maintenance can be measured in either nominal monetary units [as we are doing in this chapter] or in units of constant purchasing power [as we will be doing in Chapter 4].[23]

2.9.4 Summary of views on accrual accounting

Standard setters:
The profit (loss) is considered to be a guide when assessing the amount, timing and uncertainty of prospective cash flows as represented by future income amounts. The IASC, FASB in the USA and ASB in the UK clearly state that the accrual accounting concept is more useful in predicting future cash flows than cash flow accounting.

Academic researchers:
Academic research provides conflicting views. In 1986, research carried out in the USA indicated that the FASB view was inconsistent with its findings and that cash flow information was a better predictor of future operating cash flows;[24] research carried out in the UK, however, indicated that accrual accounting using the historical cost convention was 'a more relevant basis for decision making than cash flow measures'.[25]

2.10 Reconciliation of cash flow and accrual accounting data

The accounting profession attempted to provide users of financial statements with the benefits of both types of data, by requiring a cash flow statement to be prepared as well as the statement of comprehensive income and statement of financial position prepared on an accrual basis.

From the statement of comprehensive income prepared on an accrual basis (as in Figure 2.7) an investor is able to obtain an indication of a business's present ability to generate favourable cash flows; from the statement of financial position prepared on an accrual basis (as in Figure 2.8) an investor is able to obtain an indication of a business's continuing ability to generate favourable cash flows; from the cash flow statement (as in Figure 2.9) an investor is able to reconcile the income figure with the change in net cash balance.

Figure 2.9 reconciles the information produced in Chapter 1 under the cash flow basis with the information produced under the accrual basis. It could be expanded to provide information more clearly, as in Figure 2.10. Here we are using the information from Figures 1.9 and 1.12, but within a third statement rather than the statement of comprehensive income and statement of financial position.

2.10.1 Published cash flow statement

IAS 7 *Statement of cash flows*[26] specifies the standard headings under which cash flows should be classified. They are:

Figure 2.9 Reconciliation of income figure with net cash balance

	£
Income per income statement	(4,625)
Add: unrealisable cash outflow	8,000
	3,375
Add: unrealised operating cash flows	12,275
Operating cash flow	15,650
Other sources:	
Capital	50,000
Total cash available	65,650
Applications	
Lease	(80,000)
Net cash balance	(14,350)

Figure 2.10 Statement of cash flows netting amounts that have not been converted to cash

	£	£
Sales	195,000	
Trade receivables	(22,500)	172,500
Purchases	166,000	
Trade payables	(37,000)	(129,000)
Expenses	22,500	
Other payables	(900)	(21,600)
Rent	3,125	
Other receivables: Prepaid rent	3,125	(6,250)
Net cash inflow from operating activities		15,650
Cash flows from investing activities		
Lease		(80,000)
Cash flows from financing activities		
Issue of capital		50,000
Decrease in cash		(14,350)

- cash flows from operating activities;
- cash flows from investing activities;
- cash flows from financing activities;
- net increase in cash and cash equivalents.

To comply with IAS 7, the cash flows from Figure 2.10 would be set out as in Figure 2.11. IAS 7 is mentioned at this stage only to illustrate that cash flows can be reconciled to the accrual accounting data. There is further discussion of IAS 7 in Chapter 26.

Figure 2.11 Cash flow statement in accordance with IAS 7 *Statement of cash flows*

	£
Net cash inflow from operating activities	15,650
Investing activities	
Payment to acquire lease	(80,000)
Net cash outflow before financing	(64,350)
Financing	
Issue of capital	50,000
Decrease in cash	(14,350)
Reconciliation of operating loss to net cash	
inflow from operating activities	£
Operating profit/loss	(4,625)
Amortisation charges	8,000
Increase in trade receivables	(22,500)
Increase in prepayments	(3,125)
Increase in trade payables	37,000
Increase in accruals	900
	15,650

Summary

Accrual accounting replaces cash receipts and payments with revenue and expenses by adjusting the cash figures to take account of trading activity which has not been converted into cash.

Accrual accounting is preferred to cash accounting by the standard setters on the assumption that accrual-based financial statements give investors a better means of predicting future cash flows.

The financial statements are transaction based, applying the historical cost accounting concept which attempts to minimise the need for personal judgements and estimates in arriving at the figures in the statements.

Under accrual-based accounting the expenses incurred are matched with the revenue earned. In the case of non-current assets, a further accounting concept has been adopted, the going concern concept, which allows an entity to allocate the cost of non-current assets over their estimated useful life.

REVIEW QUESTIONS

1 The *Framework for the Preparation and Presentation of Financial Statements* identified seven user groups: investors, employees, lenders, suppliers and other trade creditors, customers, government and the public.

Discuss which of the financial statements illustrated in Chapters 1 and 2 would be most useful to each of these seven groups if they could only receive one statement.

2 'Accrual accounting is preferable to cash flow accounting because the information is more relevant to all users of financial statements.' Discuss.

3 'Cash flow accounting and accrual accounting information are both required by a potential shareholder.' Discuss.

4 'Information contained in a statement of comprehensive income and a statement of financial position prepared under accrual accounting concepts is factual and objective.' Discuss.

5 'The asset measurement basis applied in accrual accounting can lead to financial difficulties when assets are due for replacement.' Discuss.

6 'Accountants preparing financial statements in the UK do not require a standard such as IAS 18 *Revenue*.' Discuss.

7 Explain the revenue recognition principle and discuss the effect of alternative treatments on the reported results of a company.

8 The annual financial statements of companies are used by various parties for a wide variety of purposes. For each of the seven different 'user groups', explain their presumed interest with reference to the performance of the company and its financial position.

EXERCISES

An extract from the solution is provided on the Companion Website (www.pearsoned.co.uk/elliott-elliott) for exercises marked with an asterisk (*).

Question 1

Jane Parker is going to set up a new business in Bruges on 1 January 20X1. She estimates that her first six months in business will be as follows:

(i) She will put €150,000 into the firm on 1 January 20X1.

(ii) On 1 January 20X1 she will buy machinery €30,000, motor vehicles €24,000 and premises €75,000, paying for them immediately.

(iii) All purchases will be effected on credit. She will buy €30,000 goods on 1 January and she will pay for these in February. Other purchases will be: rest of January €48,000; February, March, April, May and June €60,000 each month. Other than the €30,000 worth bought in January, all other purchases will be paid for two months after purchase, i.e. €48,000 in March.

(iv) Sales (all on credit) will be €60,000 for January and €75,000 for each month after that. Customers will pay for goods in the third month after purchase, i.e. €60,000 in April.

(v) Inventory on 30 June 20X1 will be €30,000.

(vi) Wages and salaries will be €2,250 per month and will be paid on the last day of each month.

(vii) General expenses will be €750 per month, payable in the month following that in which they are incurred.

(viii) She will introduce new capital of €75,000 on 1 June 20X1. This will be paid into the business bank account immediately.

(ix) Insurance covering the 12 months of 20X1 of €26,400 will be paid for by cheque on 30 June 20X1.

(x) Local taxes will be paid as follows: for the three months to 31 March 20X1 by cheque on 28 February 20X2, delay due to an oversight by Parker; for the 12 months ended 31 March 20X2 by cheque on 31 July 20X1. Local taxes are €8,000 per annum.

(xi) She will make drawings of €1,500 per month by cheque.

(xii) All receipts and payments are by cheque.

(xiii) Depreciate motor vehicles by 20% per annum and machinery by 10% per annum, using the straight-line depreciation method.

(xiv) She has been informed by her bank manager that he is prepared to offer an overdraft facility of €30,000 for the first year.

Required:

(a) Draft a cash budget (for the firm) month by month for the period January to June, showing clearly the amount of bank balance at the end of each month.

(b) Draft the projected statement of comprehensive income for the first six months' trading, and a statement of financial position as at 30 June 20X1.

(c) Advise Jane on the alternative courses of action that could be taken to cover any cash deficiency that exceeds the agreed overdraft limit.

* Question 2

Mr Norman is going to set up a new business in Singapore on 1 January 20X8. He will invest $150,000 in the business on that date and has made the following estimates and policy decisions:

1   Forecast sales (in units) made at a selling price of $50 per unit are:

Month	Sales units	Month	Sales units
January	1,650	May	4,400
February	2,200	June	4,950
March	3,850	July	5,500
April	4,400		

2   50% of sales are for cash. Credit terms are payment in the month following sale.

3   The units cost $40 each and the supplier is allowed one month's credit.

4   It is intended to hold inventory at the end of each month sufficient to cover 25% of the following month's sales.

5   Administration $8,000 and wages $17,000 are paid monthly as they arise.

6   On 1 January 20X8, the following payments will be made: $80,000 for a five-year lease of the business premises and $350 for insurance for the year.

7   Staff sales commission of 2% of sales will be paid in the month following sale.

Required:

(a) A purchases budget for each of the first six months.

(b) A cash flow forecast for the first six months.

(c) A budgeted statement of comprehensive income for the first six months' trading and a budgeted statement of financial position as at 30 June 20X8.

(d) Advise Mr Norman on the investment of any excess cash.

Question 3

The Piano Warehouse Company Limited was established in the UK on 1 January 20X7 for the purpose of making pianos. Jeremy Holmes, the managing director, had 20 years' experience in the manufacture of pianos and was an acknowledged technical expert in the field. He had invested his life's savings of £15,000 in the company, and his decision to launch the company reflected his desire for complete independence.

Nevertheless, his commitment to the company represented a considerable financial gamble. He paid close attention to the management of its financial affairs and ensured that a careful record of all transactions was kept.

The company's activities during the year ended 31 December 20X7 were as follows:

(i) Four pianos had been built and sold for a total sum of £8,000. Holmes calculated their cost of manufacture as follows:

Materials	£2,000
Labour	£2,800
Overhead costs	£800

(ii) Two pianos were 50% completed at 31 December 20X7. Madrigal Music Limited had agreed to buy them for a total of £4,500 and had made a down-payment amounting to 20% of the agreed sale price. Holmes estimated their costs of manufacture to 31 December 20X7 as follows:

Materials	£900
Labour	£800
Overhead costs	£100

(iii) Two pianos had been rebuilt and sold for a total of £3,000. Holmes paid £1,800 for them at an auction and had spent a further £400 on rebuilding them. The sale of these two pianos was made under a hire purchase agreement under which the Piano Warehouse Company received £1,000 on delivery and two payments over the next two years plus interest of 15% on the outstanding balance.

At the end of the company's first financial year, Jeremy Holmes was anxious that the company's net profit to 31 December 20X7 should be represented in the most accurate manner. There appeared to be several alternative bases on which the transactions for the year could be interpreted. It was clear to him that, in simple terms, the net profit for the year should be calculated by deducting expenses from revenues. As far as cash sales were concerned he saw no difficulty. But how should the pianos that were 50% completed be treated? Should the value of the work done up to 31 December 20X7 be included in the profit of that year, or should it be carried forward to the next year, when the work would be completed and the pianos sold? As regards the pianos sold under the hire purchase agreement, should profit be taken in 20X7 or spread over the years in which a proportion of the revenue is received?

Required:
(a) Prepare a statement of comprehensive income for the year ended 31 December 20X7 on a basis that would reflect conventional accounting principles.
(b) Examine the problems implied in the timing of the recognition of revenues, illustrating your answer by the facts in the case of the Piano Warehouse.
(c) Discuss the significant accounting conventions that would be relevant to profit determination in this case, and discuss their limitations in this context.
(d) Advise the company on alternative accounting treatments that could increase the profit for the year.

Question 4

The following is an extract from the Financial Reporting Review Panel website (www.frrp.org.uk) relating to the Wiggins Group showing the restated financial results.

		Year					
		1995	1996	1997	1998	1999	2000
Turnover	As published	6.4	6.9	19.9	17.8	26.7	49.8
(£m)	Adjustments	(1.5)	(2.6)	(15.6)	(6.7)	(21.6)	(42.5)
	Restated	4.9	4.3	4.3	11.1	5.1	7.3
Profit/(loss)	As published	0.7	1.0	4.9	5.1	12.1	25.1
before tax	Adjustments	(1.3)	(1.9)	(10.2)	(8.5)	(17.2)	(35.0)
(£m)	Restated	(0.6)	(0.9)	(5.3)	(3.4)	(5.1)	(9.9)
Basic EPS	As published	0.14	0.20	0.66	0.64	1.21	2.87
(pence)	Adjustments	(0.26)	(0.38)	(1.67)	(1.14)	(1.91)	(4.06)
	Restated	(0.12)	(0.18)	(1.01)	(0.50)	(0.70)	(1.19)
Net assets	As published	10.2	11.4	17.5	37.5	52.2	45.8
(£m)	Adjustments	(1.3)	(3.2)	(12.0)	(19.8)	(33.8)	(35.4)
	Restated	8.9	8.2	5.5	17.7	18.4	10.4

Revenue recognition

The 1999 accounts contained an accounting policy for turnover in the following terms:

> Commercial property sales are recognised at the date of exchange of contract, providing the Group is reasonably assured of the receipt of the sale proceeds.

The FRRP accepted that this wording was similar to that used by many other companies and was not on the face of it objectionable. In reviewing the company's 1999 accounts the FRRP noted that the turnover and profits recognised under this policy were not reflected in similar inflows of cash; indeed, operating cash flow was negative and the amount receivable within debtors of £46m represented more than the previous two years' turnover of £44m. As a result, the FRRP enquired into the detailed application of the policy.

Required:
Refer to the website and discuss the significance of the revenue recognition criteria on the published results.

References

1 *Framework for the Preparation and Presentation of Financial Statements*, IASC, 1989, para. 12.
2 *Ibid.*, para. 10.
3 *Ibid.*, para. 14.
4 *Ibid.*, para. 15.
5 *Ibid.*, para. 17.
6 IAS 1 *Presentation of Financial Statements*, IASB, revised 2005, para. 8.
7 *Framework for the Preparation and Presentation of Financial Statements*, IASC, 1989, para. 7.
8 IAS 1 *Presentation of Financial Statements*, IASB, revised 2007, para. 10.
9 M. Page, *British Accounting Review*, vol. 24(1), 1992, p. 80.
10 *Statement of Financial Accounting Concepts No. 1, Objectives of Financial Reporting by Business Enterprises*, Financial Accounting Standards Board, 1978.

11 *Framework for the Preparation and Presentation of Financial Statements*, IASC, 1989, para. 20.
12 IAS 18 *Revenue*, IASC, revised 2005, para. 14.
13 http://www.chloridepower.com/en-gb/Chloride-corporate/Investor-relations/Financial-reports/
14 http://annualreport2008.wolseleyplc.com/wol_08/financial_statements/accounting_policies/
15 *Ibid.*, para. 11 of the Appendix.
16 *Ibid.*, para. 2 of the Appendix.
17 EITF 01-9, *Accounting for Consideration Given by a Vendor to a Customer*, FASB, 2001.
18 *Framework for the Preparation and Presentation of Financial Statements*, IASC, 1989, para. 49.
19 IAS 16 *Property, Plant and Equipment*, IASC, revised 2004, para. 6.
20 *Ibid.*, para. 6.
21 *Ibid.*, para. 60.
22 FRS 15 *Tangible Fixed Assets*, ASB, 1999, para. 81.
23 *Framework for the Preparation and Presentation of Financial Statements*, IASC, 1989, para. 102.
24 R.M. Bowen, D. Burgstahller and L.A. Daley, 'Evidence on the relationship between earnings and various measures of cash flow', *Accounting Review*, October 1986, pp. 713–725.
25 J.I.G. Board and J.F.S. Day, 'The information content of cash flow figures', *Accounting and Business Research*, Winter 1989, pp. 3–11.
26 *Statement of cash flows*, IASB, revised 2007.

CHAPTER 3

Income and asset value measurement: an economist's approach

3.1 Introduction

The main purpose of this chapter is to explain the need for income measurement, to compare the methods of measurement adopted by the accountant with those adopted by the economist, and to consider how both are being applied within the international financial reporting framework.

Objectives

By the end of this chapter, you should be able to:

- explain the role and objective of income measurement;
- explain the accountant's view of income, capital and value;
- critically comment on the accountant's measure;
- explain the economist's view of income, capital and value;
- critically comment on the economist's measure;
- define various capital maintenance systems.

3.2 Role and objective of income measurement

Although accountancy has played a part in business reporting for centuries, it is only since the Companies Act 1929 that financial reporting has become income orientated. Prior to that Act, a statement of comprehensive income was of minor importance. It was the statement of financial position that mattered, providing a list of capital, assets and liabilities that revealed the financial soundness and solvency of the business.

According to some commentators,[1] this scenario may be attributed to the sources of capital funding. Until the late 1920s, as in present-day Germany, external capital finance in the UK was mainly in the hands of bankers, other lenders and trade creditors. As the main users of published financial statements, they focused on the company's ability to pay trade creditors and the interest on loans, and to meet the scheduled dates of loan repayment: they were interested in the short-term liquidity and longer-term solvency of the entity.

Thus the statement of financial position was the prime document of interest. Perhaps in recognition of this, the English statement of financial position, until recent times, tended to show liabilities on the left-hand side, thus making them the first part of the statement of financial position read.

The gradual evolution of a sophisticated investment market, embracing a range of financial institutions, together with the growth in the number of individual investors, caused a reorientation of priorities. Investor protection and investor decision-making needs started to dominate the financial reporting scene, and the revenue statement replaced the statement of financial position as the sovereign reporting document.

Consequently, attention became fixed on the statement of comprehensive income and on concepts of accounting for profit. Moreover, investor protection assumed a new meaning. It changed from simply protecting the **capital** that had **been invested** to protecting the **income information** used by investors when making an investment decision.

However, the sight of major companies experiencing severe liquidity problems over the past decade has revived interest in the statement of financial position; while its light is perhaps not of the same intensity as that of the profit and loss account, it cannot be said to be totally subordinate to its accompanying statement of income.

The main objectives of income measurement are to provide:

- a means of control in a micro- and macroeconomic sense;
- a means of prediction;
- a basis for taxation.

We consider each of these below.

3.2.1 Income as a means of control

Assessment of stewardship performance

Managers are the stewards appointed by shareholders. Income, in the sense of net income or net profit, is the crystallisation of their accountability. Maximisation of income is seen as a major aim of the entrepreneurial entity, but the capacity of the business to pursue this aim may be subject to political and social constraints in the case of large public monopolies, and private semi-monopolies such as British Telecommunications plc.

Maximisation of net income is reflected in the earnings per share (EPS) figure, which is shown on the face of the published profit and loss account. The importance of this figure to the shareholders is evidenced by contracts that tie directors' remuneration to growth in EPS. A rising EPS may result in an increased salary or bonus for directors and upward movement in the market price of the underlying security. The effect on the market price is indicated by another extremely important statistic, which is influenced by the statement of comprehensive income: namely, the price/earnings (PE) ratio. The PE ratio reveals the numerical relationship between the share's current market price and the last reported EPS.

Actual performance versus predicted performance

This comparison enables the management and the investing public to use the lessons of the past to improve future performance. The public, as shareholders, may initiate a change in the company directorate if circumstances necessitate it. This may be one reason why management is generally loath to give a clear, quantified estimate of projected results – such an estimate is a potential measure of efficiency. The comparison of actual with projected results identifies apparent underachievement.

The macroeconomic concept

Good government is, of necessity, involved in managing the macroeconomic scene and as such is a user of the income measure. State policies need to be formulated concerning the allocation of economic resources and the regulation of firms and industries, as illustrated by the measures taken by Oftel and Ofwat to regulate the size of earnings by British Telecom and the water companies.

3.2.2 Income as a means of prediction

Dividend and retention policy

The payment of a dividend, its scale and that of any residual income after such dividend has been paid are influenced by the profit generated for the financial year. Other influences are also active, including the availability of cash resources within the entity, the opportunities for further internal investment, the dividend policies of capital-competing entities with comparable shares, the contemporary cost of capital and the current tempo of the capital market.

However, some question the soundness of using the profit generated for the year when making a decision to invest in an enterprise. Their view is that such a practice misunderstands the nature of income data, and that the appropriate information is the prospective cash flows. They regard the use of income figures from past periods as defective because, even if the future accrual accounting income could be forecast accurately, 'it is no more than an imperfect surrogate for future cash flows'.[2]

The counter-argument is that there is considerable resistance by both managers and accountants to the publication of future operating flows and dividend payments.[3] This means that, in the absence of relevant information, an investor needs to rely on a surrogate. The question then arises: which is the best surrogate?

In the short term, the best surrogate is the information that is currently available, i.e. income measured according to the accrual concept. In the longer term, management will be pressed by the shareholders to provide the actual forecast data on operating cash flows and dividend distribution, or to improve the surrogate information.

Suggestions for improving the surrogate information have included the provision of cash earnings per share. More fundamentally, Revsine has suggested that ideal information for investors would indicate the economic value of the business (and its assets) based on expected future cash flows. However, the Revsine suggestion itself requires information on future cash flows that it is not possible to obtain at this time.[4] Instead, he considered the use of replacement cost as a surrogate for the economic value of the business, and we return to this later in the chapter.

Future performance

While history is not a faultless indicator of future events and their financial results, it does have a role to play in assessing the level of future income. In this context, historic income is of assistance to existing investors, prospective investors and management.

Identifying maintainable profit by the analysis of matched costs

Subject to the requirement of enforced disclosure via the Companies Act 2006, as supplemented by various accounting standards, the measurement of income discloses items of income and expenditure necessarily of interest in assessing stewardship success and future prospects. In this respect, exceptional items, extraordinary items and other itemised costs and turnover are essential information.

3.2.3 Basis for taxation

The contemporary taxation philosophy, in spite of criticism from some economists, uses income measurement to measure the taxable capacity of a business entity.

However, the determination of income by the Inland Revenue is necessarily influenced by socioeconomic fiscal factors, among others, and thus accounting profit is subject to adjustment in order to achieve taxable profit. As a tax base, it has been continually eroded as the difference between accounting income and taxable income has grown.[5]

The Inland Revenue in the UK has tended to disallow expenses that are particularly susceptible to management judgement. For example, a uniform capital allowance is substituted for the subjective depreciation charge that is made by management, and certain provisions that appear as a charge in the statement of comprehensive income are not accepted as an expense for tax purposes until the loss crystallises, e.g. a charge to increase the doubtful debts provision may not be allowed until the debt is recognised as bad.

3.3 Accountant's view of income, capital and value

Variations between accountants and economists in measuring income, capital and value are caused by their different views of these measures. In this section, we introduce the accountant's view and, in the next, the economist's, in order to reconcile variations in methods of measurement.

3.3.1 The accountant's view

Income is an important part of accounting theory and practice, although until 1970, when a formal system of propagating standard accounting practice throughout the accountancy profession began, it received little attention in accountancy literature. The characteristics of measurement were basic and few, and tended to be of an intuitive, traditional nature, rather than being spelled out precisely and given mandatory status within the profession.

Accounting tradition of historical cost

The statement of comprehensive income is based on the actual costs of business transactions, i.e. the costs incurred in the currency and at the price levels pertaining at the time of the transactions.

Accounting income is said to be historical income, i.e. it is an *ex post* measure because it takes place after the event. The traditional statement of comprehensive income is historical in two senses: because it concerns a past period, and because it utilises historical cost, being the cost of the transactions on which it is based. It follows that the statement of financial position, being based on the residuals of transactions not yet dealt with in the profit and loss account, is also based on historical cost.

In practice, certain amendments may be made to historical cost in both the statement of comprehensive income and statement of financial position, but historical cost still predominates in both statements. It is justified on a number of counts which, in principle, guard against the manipulation of data.

The main characteristics of historical cost accounting are as follows:

- **Objectivity**. It is a predominantly objective system, although it does exhibit aspects of subjectivity. Its nature is generally understood and it is invariably supported by independent documentary evidence, e.g. an invoice, statement, cheque, cheque counterfoil, receipt or voucher.

- **Factual**. As a basis of fact (with exceptions such as when amended in furtherance of revaluation), it is verifiable and to that extent is beyond dispute.

● **Profit or income concept**. Profit as a concept is generally well understood in a capital market economy, even if its precise measurement may be problematic. It constitutes the difference between revenue and expenditure or, in the economic sense, between opening and closing net assets.

Unfortunately, historical cost is not without its weaknesses. It is not always objective, owing to alternative definitions of revenue and costs and the need for estimates.

We saw in the preceding chapter that revenue could be determined according to a choice of criteria. There is also a choice of criteria for defining costs. For example, although inventories are valued at the lower of cost or net realisable value, the **cost** will differ depending upon the definition adopted, e.g. first-in-first-out, last-in-first-out or standard cost.

Estimation is needed in the case of inventory valuation, assessing possible bad debts, accruing expenses, providing for depreciation and determining the profit attributable to long-term contracts. So, although it is transaction based, there are aspects of historical cost reporting that do not result from an independently verifiable business transaction. This means that profit is not always a unique figure.

Assets are often subjected to revaluation. In an economy of changing price levels, the historical cost system has been compromised by a perceived need to restate the carrying value of those assets that comprise a large proportion of a company's capital employed; e.g. land and buildings. This practice is controversial, not least because it is said to imply that a statement of financial position is a list of assets at market valuation, rather than a statement of unamortised costs not yet charged against revenue.

However, despite conventional accountancy income being partly the result of subjectivity, it is largely the product of the historical cost concept. A typical accounting policy specified in the published accounts of companies now reads as follows:

> The financial statements are prepared under the historical cost conventions as modified by the revaluation of certain fixed assets.

Nature of accounting income

Accounting income is defined in terms of the business entity. It is the excess of revenue from sales over direct and allocated indirect costs incurred in the achievement of such sales. Its measure results in a net figure. It is the numerical result of the matching and accruals concepts discussed in the preceding chapter.

We saw in the preceding chapter that accounting income is transaction based and therefore can be said to be factual, in as much as the revenue and costs have been realised and will be reflected in cash inflow and outflow, although not necessarily within the financial year.

We also saw that, under accrual accounting, the sales for a financial period are offset by the expenses incurred in generating such sales. Objectivity is a prime characteristic of accrual accounting, but the information cannot be entirely objective because of the need to break up the ongoing performance of the business entity into calendar periods or financial years for purposes of accountability reporting. The allocation of expenses between periods requires a prudent estimate of some costs, e.g. the provision for depreciation and bad debts attributable to each period.

Accounting income is presented in the form of the conventional profit and loss account or statement of comprehensive income. This statement of comprehensive income, in being based on actual transactions, is concerned with a past-defined period of time. Thus accounting profit is said to be historic income, i.e. an *ex post* measure because it is after the event.

Nature of accounting capital

The business enterprise requires the use of non-monetary assets, e.g. buildings, plant and machinery, office equipment, motor vehicles, stock of raw materials and work-in-progress.

Such assets are not consumed in any one accounting period, but give service over a number of periods; therefore, the unconsumed portions of each asset are carried forward from period to period and appear in the statement of financial position. This document itemises the unused asset balances at the date of the financial year-end. In addition to listing unexpired costs of non-monetary assets, the statement of financial position also displays monetary assets such as debtor and cash balances, together with monetary liabilities, i.e. moneys owing to trade creditors, other creditors and lenders. Funds supplied by shareholders and retained income following the distribution of dividend are also shown. Retained profits are usually added to shareholders' capital, resulting in what is known as shareholders' funds. These represent the company's equity capital.

The net assets of the firm, i.e. that fund of unconsumed assets which exceeds moneys attributable to creditors and lenders, constitutes the company's net capital, which is the same as its equity capital. Thus the profit and loss account of a financial period can be seen as a linking statement between that period's opening and closing statement of financial positions: in other words, income may be linked with opening and closing capital. This linking may be expressed by formula, as follows:

$$Y_{0-1} = NA_1 - NA_0 + D_{0-1}$$

where Y_{0-1} = income for the period of time t_0 to t_1; NA_0 = net assets of the entity at point of time t_0; NA_1 = net assets of the entity at point of time t_1; D_{0-1} = dividends or distribution during period t_{0-1}.

Less formally: Y = income of financial year; NA_0 = net assets as shown in the statement of financial position at beginning of financial year; NA_1 = net assets as shown in the statement of financial position at end of financial year; D_{0-1} = dividends paid and proposed for the financial year. We can illustrate this as follows:

Income Y_{0-1} for the financial year t_{0-1} as compiled by the accountant was £1,200

Dividend D_{0-1} for the financial year t_{0-1} was £450

Net assets NA_0 at the beginning of the financial year were £6,000

Net assets NA_1 at the end of the financial year were £6,750.

The income account can be linked with opening and closing statements of financial position, namely:

$$\begin{aligned} Y_{0-1} &= NA_1 - NA_0 + D_{0-1} \\ &= £6,750 - £6,000 + £450 \\ &= £1,200 = Y_{0-1} \end{aligned}$$

Thus Y has been computed by using the opening and closing capitals for the period where capital equals net assets.

In practice, however, the accountant would compute income Y by compiling a profit and loss account. So, of what use is this formula? For reasons to be discussed later, the economist finds use for the formula when it is amended to take account of what we call **present values**. Computed after the end of a financial year, it is the *ex post* measure of income.

Nature of traditional accounting value

As the values of assets still in service at the end of a financial period have been based on the unconsumed costs of such assets, they are the by-product of compiling the income financial statement. These values have been fixed not by direct measurement, but simply by an assessment of costs consumed in the process of generating period turnover. We can say, then, that the statement of financial position figure of net assets is a residual valuation after measuring income.

However, it is not a value in the sense of worth or market value as a buying price or selling price; it is merely a **value of unconsumed costs of assets**. This is an important point that will be encountered again later.

3.4 Critical comment on the accountant's measure

3.4.1 Virtues of the accountant's measure

As with the economist's, the accountant's measure is not without its virtues. These are invariably aspects of the historical cost concept, such as objectivity, being transaction based and being generally understood.

3.4.2 Faults of the accountant's measure

Principles of historical cost and profit realisation

The historical cost and profit realisation concepts are firmly entrenched in the transaction basis of accountancy. However, in practice, the two concepts are not free of adjustments. Because of such adjustments, some commentators argue that the system produces a hetero-geneous mix of values and realised income items.[6]

For example, in the case of asset values, certain assets such as land and buildings may have a carrying figure in the statement of financial position based on a revaluation to market value, while other assets such as motor vehicles may still be based on a balance of unallocated cost. The statement of financial position thus pretends on the one hand to be a list of result-ant costs pending allocation over future periods, and on the other hand to be a statement of current values.

Prudence concept

This concept introduces caution into the recognition of assets and income for financial report-ing purposes. The cardinal rule is that income should not be recorded or recognised within the system until it is realised, but unrealised losses should be recognised immediately.

However, not all unrealised profits are excluded. For example, practice is that attribut-able profit on long-term contracts still in progress at the financial year-end may be taken into account. As with fixed assets, rules are not applied uniformly.

Unrealised capital profits

Capital profits are ignored as income until they are realised, when, in the accounting period of sale, they are acknowledged by the reporting system. However, all the profit is recognised in one financial period when, in truth, the surplus was generated over successive periods by gradual growth, albeit unrealised until disposal of the asset. Thus a portion of what are now realised profits applies to prior periods. Not all of this profit should be attributed to the period of sale.

Going concern

The going concern concept is fundamental to accountancy and operates on the assumption that the business entity has an indefinite life. It is used to justify basing the periodic reports of asset values on carrying forward figures that represent unallocated costs, i.e. to justify the non-recognition of the realisable or disposal values of non-monetary assets and, in so doing, the associated unrealised profits/losses. Although the life of an entity is deemed indefinite, there is uncertainty, and accountants are reluctant to predict the future. When they are matching costs with revenue for the current accounting period, they follow the prudence concept of reasonable certainty.

In the long term, economic income and accountancy income are reconciled. The unrealised profits of the economic measure are eventually realised and, at that point, they will be recognised by the accountant's measure. In the short term, however, they give different results for each period.

What if we cannot assume that a business will continue as a going concern?

There may be circumstances, as in the case of Gretag Imaging Holdings AG which in its 2001 Annual Report referred to falling sales and losses, which require a judgement to be made as to the validity of the going concern assumption. The assumption can be supported by showing that active steps are being taken such as restructuring, cost reduction and raising additional share capital which will ensure the survival of the business. If survival is not possible, the business will prepare its accounts using net realisable values, which are discussed in the next chapter.

The key considerations for shareholders are whether there will be sufficient profits to support dividend distributions and whether they will be able to continue to dispose of their shares in the open market. The key consideration for the directors is whether there will be sufficient cash to allow the business to trade profitably. We can see all these considerations being addressed in the following extract from the 2003 Annual Report of Royal Numico N.V.

> #### Going concern
> The negative shareholders' equity . . . results from the impairment of intangible fixed assets . . . Management remains confident that it will be able to sufficiently strengthen shareholders' equity and return to positive shareholders' equity through retained profits . . . and that the negative shareholders' equity will not have an impact on the group's operations, access to funding nor its stock exchange listing.
>
> Based on the cash flow generating capacity of the company and its current financing structure, management is convinced that the company will continue as a going concern. Therefore the valuation principles for assets and liabilities applied are consistent with the prior year and are based on going concern.

3.5 Economist's view of income, capital and value

Let us now consider the economist's tradition of present value and the nature of economic income.

3.5.1 Economist's tradition of present value

Present value is a technique used in valuing a future money flow, or in measuring the money value of an existing capital stock in terms of a predicted cash flow *ad infinitum*.

Present value (PV) constitutes the nature of economic capital and, indirectly, economic income. Given the choice of receiving £100 now or £100 in one year's time, the rational person will opt to receive £100 now. This behaviour exhibits an intuitive appreciation of the fact that £100 today is worth more than £100 one year hence. Thus the mind has **discounted** the value of the future sum: £100 today is worth £100; but compared with today, i.e. **compared with present value**, a similar sum receivable in twelve months' time is worth

less than £100. How much less is a matter of subjective evaluation, but compensation for
the time element may be found by reference to interest: a person forgoing the spending of
£1 today and spending it one year later may earn interest of, say, 10% per annum in compensation for the sacrifice undergone by deferring consumption.

So £1 today invested at 10% p.a. will be worth £1.10 one year later, £1.21 two years
later, £1.331 three years later, and so on. This is the concept of compound interest. It may
be calculated by the formula $(1 + r)^n$, where 1 = the sum invested; r = the rate of interest;
n = the number of periods of investment (in our case years). So for £1 invested at 10% p.a.
for four years:

$$(1 + r)^n = (1 + 0.10)^4$$
$$= (1.1)^4$$
$$= £1.4641$$

and for five years:

$$= (1.1)^5$$
$$= £1.6105, \text{ and so on.}$$

Notice how the **future value** increases because of the compound interest element – it
varies over time – whereas the investment of £1 remains constant. So, conversely, the sum
of £1.10 received at the end of year one has a PV of £1, as does £1.21 received at the end
of year two and £1.331 at the end of year three.

It has been found convenient to construct tables to ease the task of calculating present
values. These show the cash flow, i.e. the future values, at a constant figure of £1 and allow
the investment to vary. So:

$$PV = \frac{CF}{(1 + r)^n}$$

where CF = anticipated cash flow; r = the discount (i.e. interest) rate. So the PV of a cash
flow of £1 receivable at the end of one year at 10% p.a. is:

$$\frac{£1}{(1 + r)^1} = £0.9091$$

and £1 at the end of two years:

$$\frac{£1}{(1 + r)^2} = £0.8264$$

and so on over successive years. The appropriate present values for years three, four and five
would be £0.7513, £0.6830, £0.6209 respectively.

£0.9091 invested today at 10% p.a. will produce £1 at the end of one year. The PV of £1
receivable at the end of two years is £0.8264 and so on.

Tables presenting data in this way are called 'PV tables', while the earlier method compiles
tables usually referred to as 'compound interest tables'. Both types of table are compound
interest tables; only the presentation of the data has changed.

To illustrate the ease of computation using PV tables, we can compute the PV of £6,152
receivable at the end of year five, given a discount rate of 10%, as being £6,152 × £0.6209
= £3,820. Thus £3,820 will total £6,152 in five years given an interest rate of 10% p.a. So
the PV of that cash flow of £6,152 is £3,820, because £3,820 would generate interest of
£2,332 (i.e. 6,152 – 3,820) as compensation for losing use of the principal sum for five years.
Future flows must be discounted to take cognisance of the time element separating cash

flows. Only then are we able to compare like with like by reducing all future flows to the comparable loss of present value.

This concept of PV has a variety of applications in accountancy and will be encountered in many different areas requiring financial measurement, comparison and decision. It originated as an economist's device within the context of economic income and economic capital models, but in accountancy it assists in the making of valid comparisons and decisions. For example, two machines may each generate an income of £10,000 over three years. However, timing of the cash flows may vary between the machines. This is illustrated in Figure 3.1.

Figure 3.1 Dissimilar cash flows

Cash flows		
Machine A	Machine B	Receivable end of year
£	£	
1,000	5,000	1
2,000	4,000	2
7,000	1,000	3
10,000	10,000	

If we simply compare the profit-generating capacity of the machines over the three-year span, each produces a total profit of £10,000. But if we pay regard to the time element of the money flows, the machines are not so equal.

However, the technique has its faults. Future money flows are invariably the subject of **estimation** and thus the actual flow experienced may show variations from forecast. Also, the element of **interest**, which is crucial to the calculation of present values, is **subjective**. It may, for instance, be taken as the average prevailing rate operating within the economy or a rate peculiar to the firm and the element of risk involved in the particular decision. In this chapter we are concerned only with PV as a tool of the economist in evaluating economic income and economic capital.

3.5.2 Nature of economic income

Economics is concerned with the economy in general, raising questions such as: how does it function? how is wealth created? how is income generated? why is income generated? The economy as a whole is activated by income generation. The individual is motivated to generate income because of a need to satisfy personal wants by consuming goods and services. Thus the economist becomes concerned with the individual consumer's psychological state of personal **enjoyment and satisfaction**. This creates a need to treat the economy as a **behavioural entity**.

The behavioural aspect forms a substantial part of micro- and macroeconomic thought, emanating particularly from the microeconomic. We can say that the economist's version of income measurement is microeconomics orientated in contrast to the accountant's business entity orientation.

The origination of the economic measure of income commenced with Irving Fisher in 1930.[7] He saw income in terms of consumption, and consumption in terms of individual perception of personal enjoyment and satisfaction. His difficulty in formulating a standard measure of this personal psychological concept of income was overcome by equating this individual experience with the consumption of goods and services and assuming that the cost of such goods and services formed the measure.

Thus, he reasoned, consumption (C) equals income (Y); so $Y = C$. He excluded savings from income because savings were not consumed. There was no satisfaction derived from savings; enjoyment necessitated consumption, he argued. Money was worthless until spent; so growth of capital was ignored, but reductions in capital became part of income because such reductions had to be spent.

In Fisher's model, capital was a stock of wealth existing at a point in time, and as a stock it generated income. Eventually, he reconciled the value of capital with the value of income by employing the concept of present value. He assessed the PV of a future flow of income by **discounting** future flows using the discounted cash flow (DCF) technique. Fisher's model adopted the prevailing average market rate of interest as the discount factor.

Economists since Fisher have introduced savings as part of income. Sir John Hicks played a major role in this area.[8] He introduced the idea that income was the maximum consumption enjoyed by the individual without reducing the individual's capital stock, i.e. the amount a person could consume during a period of time that still left him or her with the same value of capital stock at the end of the period as at the beginning. Hicks also used the DCF technique in the valuation of capital.

If capital increases, the increase constitutes savings and grants the opportunity of consumption. The formula illustrating this was given in section 3.3, i.e. $Y_{0-1} = NA_1 - NA_0 + D_{0-1}$.

However, in the Hicksian model, $NA_1 - NA_0$, given as £6,750 and £6,000 respectively in the aforementioned example, would have been discounted to achieve present values.

The same formula may be expressed in different forms. The economist is likely to show it as $Y - C + (K_1 - K_0)$ where C = consumption, having been substituted for dividend, and K_1 and K_0 have been substituted for NA_1 and NA_0 respectively.

Hicks's income model is often spoken of as an *ex ante* model because it is usually used for the measurement of **expected** income in advance of the time period concerned. Of course, because it specifically introduces the present value concept, present values replace the statement of financial position values of net assets adopted by the accountant. Measuring income **before the event** enables the individual to estimate the level of consumption that may be achieved without depleting capital stock. Before-the-event computations of income necessitate predictions of future cash flows.

Suppose that an individual proprietor of a business anticipated that his investment in the enterprise would generate earnings over the next four years as specified in Figure 3.2. Furthermore, such earnings would be retained by the business for the financing of new equipment with a view to increasing potential output.

We will assume that the expected rate of interest on capital employed in the business is 8% p.a.

The economic value of the business at K_0 (i.e. at the beginning of year one) will be based on the discounted cash flow of the future four years. Figure 3.3 shows that K_0 is £106,853, calculated as the present value of anticipated earnings of £131,000 spread over a four-year term.

Figure 3.2 Business cash flows for four years

Years	Cash inflows £
1	26,000
2	29,000
3	35,000
4	41,000

Figure 3.3 Economic value at K_0

Year	(a) Cash flow £	(b) $DCF = \dfrac{1}{(1+r)^n}$	(c) $\dfrac{PV}{(a) \times (b)}$ £
K_1	26,000	$\dfrac{1}{(1.08)^1} = 0.9259$	24,073
K_2	29,000	$\dfrac{1}{(1.08)^2} = 0.8573$	24,862
K_3	35,000	$\dfrac{1}{(1.08)^3} = 0.7938$	27,783
K_4	41,000	$\dfrac{1}{(1.08)^4} = 0.7350$	30,135
	$\underline{131,000}$		$\underline{106,853}$

Figure 3.4 Economic value at K_1

Year	(a) Cash flow £	(b) $DCF = \dfrac{-1}{(1+r)^n}$	(c) $\dfrac{PV}{(a) \times (b)}$ £
K_1	26,000	1.0000	26,000
K_2	29,000	$\dfrac{1}{(1+r)^1} = 0.9259$	26,851
K_3	35,000	$\dfrac{1}{(1+r)^2} = 0.8573$	30,006
K_4	41,000	$\dfrac{1}{(1+r)^3} = 0.7938$	32,546
	$\underline{131,000}$		$\underline{115,403}$

The economic value of the business at K_1 (i.e. at the end of year one, which is the same as saying the beginning of year two) is calculated in Figure 3.4. This shows that K_1 is £115,403 calculated as the present value of anticipated earnings of £131,000 spread over a four-year term.

From this information we are able to calculate Y for the period Y_1, as in Figure 3.5. Note that C (consumption) is nil because, in this exercise, dividends representing consumption have not been payable for Y_1. In other words, income Y_1 is entirely in the form of projected capital growth, i.e. savings.

By year-end K_1, earnings of £26,000 will have been received; in projecting the capital at K_2 such earnings will have been reinvested and at the beginning of year K_2 will have a PV of £26,000. These earnings will no longer represent a **predicted** sum because they will have been **realised** and therefore will no longer be subjected to discounting.

Figure 3.5 Calculation of Y for the period Y_1

$$Y = C + (K_1 - K_0)$$
$$Y = 0 + (115,403 - 106,853)$$
$$= 0 + 8,550$$
$$= £8,550$$

The income of £8,550 represents an anticipated return of 8% p.a. on the economic capital at K_0 of £106,853 (8% of £106,853 is £8,548, the difference of £2 between this figure and the figure calculated above being caused by rounding).

As long as the expectations of future cash flows and the chosen interest rate do not change, then Y_1 will equal 8% of £106,853.

What will the anticipated income for the year Y_2 amount to?

Applying the principle explained above, the anticipated income for the year Y_2 will equal 8% of the capital at the end of K_1 amounting to £115,403 = £9,233. This is proved in Figure 3.6, which shows that K_2 is £124,636 calculated as the present value of anticipated earnings of £131,000 spread over a four-year term.

From this information we are able to calculate Y for the period Y_2 as in Figure 3.7. Note that capital value attributable to the end of the year K_2 is being assessed at the beginning of K_2. This means that the £26,000 due at the end of year K_1 will have been received and reinvested, earning interest of 8% p.a. Thus by the end of year K_2 it will be worth £28,080. The sum of £29,000 will be realised at the end of year K_2 so its present value at that time will be £29,000.

If the anticipated future cash flows change, the expected capital value at the successive points in time will also change. Accordingly, the actual value of capital may vary from that forecast by the *ex ante* model.

Figure 3.6 Economic value at K_2

Year	(a) Cash flow	(b) $DCF = \dfrac{1}{(1+r)^n}$	(c) $PV = (a) \times (b)$
	£	£	£
K_1	26,000	1.08	28,080
K_2	29,000	1.0000	29,000
K_3	35,000	0.9259	32,407
K_4	41,000	0.8573	35,149
	131,000		124,636

Figure 3.7 Calculation of Y for the period Y_2

$$Y = C + (K_2 - K_1)$$
$$Y = 0 + (124,636 - 115,403)$$
$$= 0 + 9,233$$
$$= £9,233$$

3.6 Critical comment on the economist's measure

While the income measure enables us to formulate theories regarding the behaviour of the economy, it has inherent shortcomings not only in the economic field, but particularly in the accountancy sphere.

● The calculation of economic capital, hence economic income, is subjective in terms of the present value factor, often referred to as the DCF element. The factor may be based on any one of a number of factors, such as opportunity cost, the current return on the firm's existing capital employed, the contemporary interest payable on a short-term loan such as a bank overdraft, the average going rate of interest payable in the economy at large, or a rate considered justified on the basis of the risk attached to a particular investment.

● Investors are not of one mind or one outlook. For example, they possess different risk and time preferences and will therefore employ different discount factors.

● The model constitutes a compound of unrealised and realised flows, i.e. profits. Because of the unrealised element, it has not been used as a base for computing tax or for declaring a dividend.

● The projected income is dependent upon the success of a planned financial strategy. Investment plans may change, or fail to attain target.

● Windfall gains cannot be foreseen, so they cannot be accommodated in the *ex ante* model. Our prognostic cash flows may therefore vary from the actual flows generated, e.g. an unexpected price movement.

● It is difficult to construct a satisfactory, meaningful statement of financial position detailing the unused stock of net assets by determining the present values of individual assets. Income is invariably the consequence of deploying a group of assets working in unison.

3.7 Income, capital and changing price levels

A primary concern of income measurement to both economist and accountant is the maintenance of the capital stock, i.e. the maintenance of capital values. The assumption is that income can only arise **after** the capital stock has been maintained at the same amount as at the beginning of the accounting period.

However, this raises the question of how we should define the capital that we are attempting to maintain. There are a number of possible definitions:

● **Money capital**. Should we concern ourselves with maintaining the fund of capital resources initially injected by the entrepreneur into the new enterprise? This is indeed one of the aims of traditional, transaction-based accountancy.

● **Potential consumption capital**. Is it this that should be maintained, i.e. the economist's present value philosophy expressed via the discounted cash flow technique?

● **Operating capacity capital**. Should maintenance of productive capacity be the rule, i.e. capital measured in terms of tangible or physical assets? This measure would utilise the current cost accounting system.

Revsine attempted to construct an analytical bridge between replacement cost accounting that maintains the operating capacity, and the economic concepts of **income** and **value**, by demonstrating that the distributable operating flow component of economic income is equal to the current operating component of replacement cost income, and that the unexpected income component of economic income is equal to the unrealisable cost savings of replacement cost income.[9] This will become clearer when the replacement cost model is dealt with in the next chapter.

● **Financial capital**. Should capital be maintained in terms of a fund of general purchasing power (sometimes called 'real' capital)? In essence, this is the consumer purchasing power (or general purchasing power) approach, but not in a strict sense as it can be measured in a variety of ways. The basic method uses a general price index. This concept is likely to satisfy the criteria of the proprietor/shareholders of the entity. The money capital and the financial capital concepts are variations of the same theme, the former being founded on the historic cost principle and the latter applying an adjustment mechanism to take account of changing price levels.

The money capital concept has remained the foundation stone of traditional accountancy reporting, but the operating and financial capital alternatives have played a controversial secondary role over the past twenty-five years.

Potential consumption capital is peculiar to economics in terms of measurement of the business entity's aggregate capital, although, as discussed on pages 49–52, it has a major role to play as a decision-making model in financial management.

3.7.1 Why are these varying methods of concern?

The problem tackled by these devices is that plague of the economy known as 'changing price levels', particularly the upward spiralling referred to as **inflation**. Throughout this chapter we have assumed that there is a stable monetary unit and that income, capital and value changes over time have been in response to operational activity and the interaction of supply and demand or changes in expectations.

Following the historic cost convention, capital maintenance has involved a comparison of opening and closing capital in each accounting period. It has been assumed that the purchasing power of money has remained constant over time.

If we take into account moving price levels, particularly the fall in the purchasing power of the monetary unit due to inflation, then our measure of **income** is affected if we insist upon **maintaining capital in real terms**.

3.7.2 Is it necessary to maintain capital in real terms?

Undoubtedly it is necessary if we wish to prevent an erosion of the operating capacity of the entity and thus its ability to maintain real levels of income. If we do not maintain the capacity of capital to generate the current level of profit, then the income measure, being the difference between opening and closing capitals, will be overstated or overvalued. This is because the capital measure is being understated or undervalued. In other words, there is a danger of dividends being paid out of real capital rather than out of real income. It follows that, if the need to retain profits is overlooked, the physical assets will be depleted.

In accountancy there is no theoretical difficulty in measuring the impact of changing price levels. There are, however, two practical difficulties:

● There are a number of methods, or mixes of methods, available and it has proved impossible to obtain consensus support for one method or compound of methods.

● There is a high element of subjectivity, which detracts from the objectivity of the information.

In the next chapter we deal with inflation and analyse the methods formulated, together with the difficulties that they in turn introduce into the financial reporting system.

Summary

In measuring income, capital and value, the accountant's approach varies from the sister discipline of the economist, yet both are trying to achieve similar objectives.

The accountant uses a traditional transaction-based model of computing income, capital being the residual of this model.

The economist's viewpoint is anchored in a behavioural philosophy that measures capital and deduces income to be the difference between the capital at commencement of a period and that at its end.

The objectives of income measurement are important because of the existence of a highly sophisticated capital market. These objectives involve the assessment of stewardship performance, dividend and retention policies, comparison of actual results with those predicted, assessment of future prospects, payment of taxation and disclosure of matched costs against revenue from sales.

The natures of income, capital and value must be appreciated if we are to understand and achieve measurement. The apparent conflict between the two measures can be seen as a consequence of the accountant's need for periodic reporting to shareholders. In the longer term, both methods tend to agree.

Present value as a concept is the foundation stone of the economist, while historical cost, adjusted for prudence, is that of the accountant. Present value demands a subjective discount rate and estimates that time may prove incorrect; historical cost ignores unrealised profits and in application is not always transaction based.

The economist's measure, of undoubted value in the world of micro- and macro-economics, presents difficulty in the accountancy world of annual reports. The accountant's method, with its long track record of acceptance, ignores any generated profits, which caution and the concept of the going concern deem not to exist.

The economic trauma of changing price levels is a problem that both measures can embrace, but consensus support for a particular model of measurement has proved elusive.

REVIEW QUESTIONS

1 What is the purpose of measuring income?

2 Explain the nature of economic income.

3 The historical cost concept has withstood the test of time. Specify the reasons for this success, together with any aspects of historical cost that you consider are detrimental in the sphere of financial reporting.

4 What is meant by present value? Does it take account of inflation?

5 A company contemplates purchasing a machine that will generate an income of £25,000 per year over each of the next five years. A scrap value of £2,000 is anticipated on disposal. How much would you advise the company to pay for the asset?

6 Discuss the arguments for and against revaluing fixed assets and recognising the gain or loss.

7 To an accountant, net income is essentially a historical record of the past. To an economist, net income is essentially a speculation about the future. Examine the relative merits of these two approaches for financial reporting purposes.

8 Examine and contrast the concepts of profit that you consider to be relevant to:

(a) an economist;

(b) a speculator;

(c) a business executive;

(d) the managing director of a company;

(e) a shareholder in a private company;

(f) a shareholder in a large public company.

EXERCISES

An extract from the solution is provided on the Companion Website (www.pearsoned.co.uk/elliott-elliott) for exercises marked with an asterisk (*).

* Question 1

(a) 'Measurement in financial statements', Chapter 6 of the ASB's *Statement of Principles,* was published in 1999. Amongst the theoretical valuation systems considered is value in use – more commonly known as economic value.

Required:
Describe the Hicksian economic model of income and value, and assess its usefulness for financial reporting.

(b) Jim Bowater purchased a parcel of 30,000 ordinary shares in New Technologies plc for £36,000 on 1 January 20X5. Jim, an Australian on a four-year contract in the UK, has it in mind to sell the shares at the end of 20X7, just before he leaves for Australia. Based on the company's forecast growth and dividend policy, his broker has advised him that his shares are likely to fetch only £35,000 then.

In its annual report for the year ended 31 December 20X4 the company had forecast annual dividend pay-outs as follows:

Year ended: 31 December 20X5, 25p per share
31 December 20X6, 20p per share
31 December 20X7, 20p per share

Required:
Using the economic model of income:
(i) **Compute Jim's economic income for each of the three years ending on the dates indicated above.**
(ii) **Show that Jim's economic capital will be preserved at 1 January 20X5 level. Jim's cost of capital is 20%.**

Question 2

(a) Describe briefly the theory underlying Hicks's economic model of income and capital. What are its practical limitations?

(b) Spock purchased a space invader entertainment machine at the beginning of year one for £1,000. He expects to receive at annual intervals the following receipts: at the end of year one £400; end of year two £500; end of year three £600. At the end of year three he expects to sell the machine for £400.

Spock could receive a return of 10% in the next best investment.

The present value of £1 receivable at the end of a period discounted at 10% is as follows:

End of year one   £0.909
End of year two   £0.826
End of year three £0.751

Required:
Calculate the ideal economic income, ignoring taxation and working to the nearest £.
Your answer should show that Spock's capital is maintained throughout the period and that his income is constant.

Question 3

Jason commenced with £135,000 cash. He acquired an established shop on 1 January 20X1. He agreed to pay £130,000 for the fixed and current assets and the goodwill. The replacement cost of the shop premises was £100,000, stock £10,000 and debtors £4,000; the balance of the purchase price was for the goodwill. He paid legal costs of £5,000. No liabilities were taken over. Jason could have resold the business immediately for £135,000. Legal costs are to be expensed in 20X1.

Jason expected to draw £25,000 per year from the business for three years and to sell the shop at the end of 20X3 for £150,000.

At 31 December 20X1 the books showed the following tangible assets and liabilities:

Cost to the business before any drawings by Jason:	£	He estimated that the net realisable values were:	£
Shop premises	100,000		85,000
Stock	15,500		20,000
Debtors	5,200		5,200
Cash	40,000		40,000
Creditors	5,000		5,000

Based on his experience of the first year's trading, he revised his estimates and expected to draw £35,000 per year for three years and sell the shop for £175,000 on 31 December 20X3.

Jason's opportunity cost of capital was 20%.

Required:
(a) Calculate the following income figures for 20X1:
    (i) accounting income;
    (ii) income based on net realisable values;
    (iii) economic income *ex ante*;
    (iv) economic income *ex post*.
    State any assumptions made.
(b) Evaluate each of the four income figures as indicators of performance in 20X1 and as a guide to decisions about the future.

References

1 T.A. Lee, *Income and Value Measurement: Theory and Practice* (3rd edition), Van Nostrand Reinhold (UK), 1985, p. 20.
2 D. Solomons, *Making Accounting Policy*, Oxford University Press, 1986, p. 132.

3 R.W. Scapens, *Accounting in an Inflationary Environment* (2nd edition), Macmillan, 1981, p. 125.
4 *Ibid.*, p. 127.
5 D. Solomons, *op. cit.*, p. 132.
6 T.A. Lee, *op. cit.*, pp. 52–54.
7 I. Fisher, *The Theory of Interest*, Macmillan, 1930, pp. 171–181.
8 J.R. Hicks, *Value and Capital* (2nd edition), Clarendon Press, 1946.
9 R.W. Scapens, *op. cit.*, p. 127.

Bibliography

American Institute of Certified Public Accountants, *Objectives of Financial Statements*, Report of the Study Group, 1973.
The Corporate Report, ASC, 1975, pp. 28–31.
N. Kaldor, 'The concept of income in economic theory', in R.H. Parker and G.C. Harcourt (eds), *Readings in the Concept and Measurement of Income*, Cambridge University Press, 1969.
T.A. Lee, 'The accounting entity concept, accounting standards and inflation accounting', *Accounting and Business Research*, Spring 1980, pp. 1–11.
J.R. Little, 'Income measurement: an introduction', *Student Newsletter*, June 1988.
D. Solomons, 'Economic and accounting concepts of income', in R.H. Parker and G.C. Harcourt (eds), *Readings in the Concept and Measurement of Income*, Cambridge University Press 1969.
R.R. Sterling, *Theory of the Measurement of Enterprise Income*, University of Kansas Press, 1970.

CHAPTER 4

Accounting for price-level changes

4.1 Introduction

The main purpose of this chapter is to explain the impact of inflation on profit and capital measurement and the concepts that have been proposed to incorporate the effect into financial reports by adjusting the historical cost data. These concepts are periodically discussed but there is no general support for any specific concept among practitioners in the field.

Objectives

By the end of the chapter, you should be able to:

● describe the problems of historical cost accounting (HCA);
● explain the approach taken in each of the inflation adjusting models;
● prepare financial statements applying each model (HCA, CPP, CCA, NRVA);
● critically comment on each model (HCA, CPP, CCA, NRVA);
● describe the approach being taken by standard setters and future developments.

4.2 Review of the problems of historical cost accounting (HCA)

The transaction-based historical cost concept was unchallenged in the UK until price levels started to hedge upwards at an ever-increasing pace during the 1950s and reached an annual rate of increase of 20% in the mid 1970s. The historical cost base for financial reporting witnessed growing criticism. The inherent faults of the system were discussed in Chapter 3, but inflation exacerbates the problem in the following ways:

● Profit is overstated when inflationary changes in the value of assets are ignored.

● Comparability of business entities, which is so necessary in the assessment of performance and growth, becomes distorted.

● The decision-making process, the formulation of plans and the setting of targets may be suboptimal if financial base data are out of date.

● Financial reports become confusing at best, misleading at worst, because revenue is mismatched with differing historical cost levels as the monetary unit becomes unstable.

● Unrealised profits arising in individual accounting periods are increased as a result of inflation.

In order to combat these serious defects, current value accounting became the subject of research and controversy as to the most appropriate method to use for financial reporting.

4.3 Inflation accounting

A number of versions of current value accounting (CVA) were eventually identified, but the current value postulate was said to suffer from the following disadvantages:

- It destroys the factual nature of HCA, which is transaction based: the factual characteristic is to all intents and purposes lost as transaction-based historic values are replaced by judgemental values.
- It is not as objective as HCA because it is less verifiable from auditable documentation.
- It entails recognition of unrealised profit, a practice that is anathema to the traditionalist.
- The claimed improvement in comparability between commercial entities is a myth because of the degree of subjectivity in measuring current value by each.
- The lack of a single accepted method of computing current values compounds the subjectivity aspect. One fault-laden system is being usurped by another that is also faulty.

In spite of these criticisms, the search for a system of financial reporting devoid of the defects of HCA and capable of coping with inflation has produced a number of CVA models.

4.4 The concepts in principle

Several current income and value models have been proposed to replace or operate in tandem with the historical cost convention. However, in terms of basic characteristics, they may be reduced to the following three models:

- current purchasing power (CPP) or general purchasing power (GPP);
- current entry cost or replacement cost (RC);
- current exit cost or net realisable value (NRV).

We discuss each of these models below.

4.4.1 Current purchasing power accounting (CPPA)

The CPP model measures income and value by adopting a price index system. Movements in price levels are gauged by reference to price changes in a group of goods and services in **general** use within the economy. The aggregate price value of this **basket** of commodities-cum-services is determined at a base point in time and indexed as 100. Subsequent changes in price are compared on a regular basis with this base period price and the change recorded. For example, the price level of our chosen range of goods and services may amount to £76 on 31 March 20X1, and show changes as follows:

£76	at 31 March 20X1
£79	at 30 April 20X1
£81	at 31 May 20X1
£84	at 30 June 20X1

and so on.

The change in price may be indexed with 31 March as the base:

20X1	Calculation	Index
31 March	i.e. £76	100
30 April	i.e. $\frac{79}{76} \times 100$	103.9
31 May	i.e. $\frac{81}{76} \times 100$	106.6
30 June	i.e. $\frac{84}{76} \times 100$	110.5

In the UK, an index system similar in construction to this is known as the Retail Price Index (RPI). It is a barometer of fluctuating price levels covering a miscellany of goods and services as used by the average household. Thus it is a **general** price index. It is amended from time to time to take account of new commodities entering the consumer's range of choice and needs. As a model, it is unique owing to the introduction of the concept of gains and losses in **purchasing power**.

4.4.2 Current entry or replacement cost accounting (RCA)

The replacement cost (RC) model assesses income and value by reference to entry costs or current replacement costs of materials and other assets utilised within the business entity. The valuation attempts to replace like with like and thus takes account of the quality and condition of the existing assets. A motor vehicle, for instance, may have been purchased brand new for £25,000 with an expected life of five years, an anticipated residual value of nil and a straight-line depreciation policy. Its HCA carrying value in the statement of financial position at the end of its first year would be £25,000 less £5,000 = £20,000. However, if a similar new replacement vehicle cost £30,000 at the end of year one, then its gross RC would be £30,000; depreciation for one year based on this sum would be £6,000 and the net RC would be £24,000. The increase of £4,000 is a holding gain and the vehicle with a HCA carrying value of £20,000 would be revalued at £24,000.

4.4.3 Current exit cost or net realisable value accounting (NRVA)

The net realisable value (NRV) model is based on the economist's concept of opportunity cost. It is a model that has had strong academic support, most notably in Australia from Professor Ray Chambers who referred to this approach as Continuous Contemporary Accounting (CoCoA). If an asset cost £25,000 at the beginning of year one and at the end of that year it had a NRV of £21,000 after meeting selling expenses, it would be carried in the NRV statement of financial position at £21,000. This amount represents the cash forgone by holding the asset, i.e. the opportunity of possessing cash of £21,000 has been sacrificed in favour of the asset. Depreciation for the year would be £25,000 less £21,000 = £4,000.

4.5 The four models illustrated for a company with cash purchases and sales

We will illustrate the effect on the profit and net assets of Entrepreneur Ltd.

Entrepreneur Ltd commenced business on 1 January 20X1 with a capital of £3,000 to buy and sell second-hand computers. The company purchased six computers on 1 January 20X1 for £500 each and sold three of the computers on 15 January for £900 each.

The following data are available for January 20X1:

	Retail Price Index	Replacement cost per computer £	Net realisable value £
1 January	100		
15 January	112	610	
31 January	130	700	900

The statement of comprehensive incomes and statements of financial position are set out in Figure 4.1 with the detailed workings in Figure 4.2.

4.5.1 Financial capital maintenance concept

HCA and CPP are both transaction-based models that apply the financial capital maintenance concept. This means that profit is the difference between the opening and closing net assets

Figure 4.1 Trading account for the month ended 31 January 20X1

Statements of comprehensive income for the month ended 31 January 20X1

	HCA £		CPP CPP£		RCA £		NRVA £	
Sales	2,700	W1	3,134	W5	2,700	W1	2,700	W1
Opening inventory	—		—		—		—	
Purchases	3,000	W2	3,900	W6	3,000	W2	3,000	W2
Closing inventory	(1,500)	W3	(1,950)	W7	(1,500)	W3	(1,500)	W3
COSA	na		na		330	W10	na	
Cost of sales	1,500		1,950		1,830		1,500	
Holding gain	na		na		na		1,200	W15
Profit	**1,200**		**1,184**		**870**		**2,400**	

Statement of financial position as at 31 January 20X1

	£		CPP£		£		£	
Current assets								
Inventory	1,500	W3	1,950	W7	2,100	W11	2,700	W14
Cash	2,700	W4	2,700		2,700		2,700	
Capital employed	**4,200**		**4,650**		**4,800**		**5,400**	
Capital	3,000		3,900	W8	3,000		3,000	
Holding gains								
On inventory consumed	na		na		330	W12		
On inventory in hand	na		na		600	W13		
Profit	1,200		1,184		870		2,400	
Loss on monetary items	na		(434)	W9	na		na	
	4,200		**4,650**		**4,800**		**5,400**	

na = not applicable

Figure 4.2 Workings (W)

HCA

W1 Sales:	3 × £900 = £2,700	
W2 Purchases:	6 × £500 = £3,000	
W3 Closing inventory:	3 × £500 = £1,500	
W4 Cash:	1 January 20X1 Capital	3,000
	1 January 20X1 Purchases	(3,000)
	1 January 20X1 Balance	nil
	15 January 20X1 Sales	
	3 × £900 =	£2,700
	31 January 20X1 Balance	£2,700

CPP

		CPP£
W5 Sales	£2,700 × 130/112 =	3,134
W6 Purchases	£3,000 × 130/100 =	3,900
W7 Closing inventory	£1,500 × 130/100 =	1,950
W8 Capital	£3,000 × 130/100 =	3,900

W9   Balance of cash was nil until 15 January when sales generated £2,700. This sum was held until 31 January during which period cash, a monetary item, lost purchasing power. The loss of purchasing power is measured by applying the general index to the cash held.

£2,700 × 130/112 − £2,700 = CPP £434.

RCA

W10   Additional replacement cost of inventory consumed as at the date of sale is measured as a cost of sales adjustment (COSA). COSA is calculated as follows:

	3 × £610 =	1,830
Less:	3 × £500 =	1,500
	COSA	£330

W11   Closing inventory: 3 × £700 = £2,100

W12   Holding gains on inventory consumed: as for W10   = £330

W13   Inventory at replacement cost   = 3 × £700 = 2,100
       Less: inventory at cost   = 3 × £500 = 1,500

       Holding gains on closing inventory   £600

NRVA

W14   Closing inventory at net realisable value = 900 × 3 = £2,700

W15   3 × £900 =   2,700
       3 × £500 =   1,500

       Holding gain   £1,200

(expressed in HC £) or the opening and closing net assets (expressed in HC £ indexed for RPI changes) adjusted for any capital introduced or withdrawn during the month.

CPP adjustments

● All historical cost values are adjusted to a common index level for the month. In theory this can be the index applicable to any day of the financial period concerned. However, in practice it has been deemed preferable to use the last day of the period; thus the financial statements show the latest price level appertaining to the period.

● The application of a general price index as an adjusting factor results in the creation of an **alien** currency of **purchasing power**, which is used in place of sterling. Note, particularly, the impact on the entity's sales and capital compared with the other models. **Actual** sales shown on **invoices** will still read £2,700.

● Note the application of the concept of gain or loss on holding monetary items. In this example there is a monetary loss of CPP £434 as shown in Working 9 in Figure 4.2.

4.5.2 Operating capital maintenance concept

Under this concept capital is only maintained if sufficient income is retained to maintain the business entity's physical operating capacity, i.e. its ability to produce the existing level of goods or services. Profit is, therefore, the residual after increasing the cost of sales to the cost applicable at the date of sale.

● Basically, only two adjustments are involved: the additional replacement cost of inventory consumed and holding gains on closing inventories. However, in a comprehensive exercise an adjustment will be necessary regarding fixed assets and you will also encounter a gearing adjustment.

● Notice the concept of holding gains. This model introduces, in effect, unrealised profits in respect of closing inventories. The holding gain concerning inventory consumed at the time of sale has been realised and deducted from what would have been a profit of £1,200. The statement discloses profits of £870.

4.5.3 Capacity to adapt concept

The HCA, CPP and RCA models have assumed that the business will continue as a going concern and only distribute realised profits after retaining sufficient profits to maintain either the financial or operating capital.

The NRVA concept is that a business has the capacity to realise its net assets at the end of each financial period and reinvest the proceeds and that the NRV accounts provide management with this information.

● This produces the same initial profit as HCA, namely £1,200, but a peculiarity of this system is that this realised profit is supplemented by **unrealised** profit generated by holding stocks. Under RCA accounting, such gains are shown in a separate account and are not treated as part of real income.

● This simple exercise has ignored the possibility of investment in fixed assets, thus depreciation is not involved. A reduction in the NRV of fixed assets at the end of a period compared with the beginning would be treated in a similar fashion to depreciation by being charged to the revenue account, and consequently profits would be reduced. An increase in the NRV of such assets would be included as part of the profit.

4.5.4 The four models compared

Dividend distribution

We can see from Figure 4.1 that if the business were to distribute the profit reported under HCA, CPP or NRVA the physical operating capacity of the business would be reduced and it would be paying dividends out of capital:

	HCA	CPP	RCA	NRVA
Realised profit:	1,200	1,184	870	1,200
Unrealised profit	—	—	—	1,200
Profit for month	1,200	1,184	870	2,400

Shareholder orientation

The CPP model is shareholder orientated in that it shows whether shareholders' funds are keeping pace with inflation by maintaining their purchasing power. Only CPP changes the value of the share capital.

Management orientation

The RCA model is management orientated in that it identifies holding gains which represent the amounts required to be retained in order to simply maintain the operating capital.

RCA measures the impact of inflation on the individual firm, in terms of the change in price levels of its **raw materials and assets**, i.e. inflation peculiar to the company, whereas CPP measures general inflation in the economy as a whole. CPP may be meaningless in the case of an individual company. Consider a firm that carries a constant volume of stock valued at £100 in HCA terms. Now suppose that price levels double when measured by a general price index (GPI), so that its inventory is restated to £200 in a CPP system. If, however, the cost of that **particular** inventory has sustained a price change consisting of a five-fold increase, then under the RCA model the value of the stock should be £500.

In the mid 1970s, when the accountancy profession was debating the problem of changing price level measurement, the general price level had climbed by some 23% over a period during which petroleum-based products had risen by 500%.

4.6 Critique of each model

A critique of the various models may be formulated in terms of their characteristics and peculiarities as virtues and defects in application.

4.6.1 HCA

This model's virtues and defects have been discussed in Chapter 3 and earlier in this chapter.

4.6.2 CPP

Virtues

- It is an **objective measure** since it is still transaction based, as with HCA, and the possibility of subjectivity is constrained if a GPI is used that has been constructed by a central agency such as a government department. This applies in the UK, where the Retail Price Index is constructed by the Department for Employment and Learning.

- It is a **measure of shareholders' capital** and that capital's maintenance in terms of purchasing power units. Profit is the residual value after maintaining the money value of capital funds, taking account of changing price levels. Thus it is a measure readily understood by the shareholder/user of the accounts. It can prevent payment of a dividend out of real capital as measured by GPPA.

- It **introduces the concept of monetary items** as distinct from non-monetary items and the attendant concepts of gains and losses in holding net monetary liabilities compared with holding net monetary assets. Such gains and losses are experienced on a disturbing scale in times of inflation. They are **real** gains and losses. The **basic RCA and NRV** models do not recognise such 'surpluses' and 'deficits'.

Defects

- It is **HCA based but adjusted** to reflect general price movements. Thus it possesses the characteristics of HCA, good and bad, but with its values updated in the light of an arithmetic measure of general price changes. The major defect of becoming out of date is mitigated to a degree, but the impact of inflation on the entity's income and capital may be at variance with the rate of inflation affecting the economy in general.

- It may be **wrongly assumed that the CPP statement of financial position is a current value statement**. It is not a current value document because of the defects discussed above; in particular, asset values may be subject to a different rate of inflation than that reflected by the GPI.

- It **creates an alien unit of measurement** still labelled by the £ sign. Thus we have the HCA £ and the CPP £. They are different pounds: one is the bona fide pound, the other is a synthetic unit. This may not be fully appreciated or understood by the user when faced with the financial accounts for the recent accounting period.

- Its **concept of profit is dangerous**. It pretends to cater for changing prices, but at the same time it fails to provide for the additional costs of replacing stocks sold or additional depreciation due to the escalating replacement cost of assets. The inflation encountered by the business entity will not be the same as that encountered by the whole economy. Thus the maintenance of the CPP of shareholders' capital via this concept of profit is not the maintenance of the entity's operating capital in physical terms, i.e. its capacity to produce the same volume of goods and services. The use of CPP profit as a basis for decision making without regard to RCA profit can have disastrous consequences.

4.6.3 RCA

Virtues

- Its **unit of measurement** is the monetary unit and consequently it is understood and accepted by the user of accountancy reports. In contrast, the CPP system employs an artificial unit based on arithmetic relationships, which is different and thus unfamiliar.

- It **identifies and isolates holding gains** from operating income. Thus it can prevent the inadvertent distribution of dividends in excess of operating profit. It satisfies the prudence criterion of the traditional accountant and **maintains the physical operating capacity** of the entity.

- It introduces **realistic current values** of assets in the statement of financial position, thus making the statement of financial position a 'value' statement and consequently more meaningful to the user. This contrasts sharply with the statement of financial position as a list of unallocated carrying costs in the HCA system.

Defects

- It is a **subjective measure**, in that replacement costs are often necessarily based on estimates or assessments. It does not possess the factual characteristics of HCA. It is open to manipulation within constraints. Often it is based on index numbers which themselves may be based on a compound of prices of a mixture of similar commodities used as raw material or operating assets. This subjectivity is exacerbated in circumstances where rapid technological advance and innovation are involved in the potential new replacement asset, e.g. computers, printers.

- It **assumes replacement of assets** by being based on their replacement cost. Difficulties arise if such assets are not to be replaced by similar assets. Presumably, it will then be assumed that a replacement of equivalent value to the original will be deployed, however differently, as capital within the firm.

4.6.4 NRVA

Virtues

- It is a concept readily understood by the user. The value of any item invariably has two measures – a buying price and a selling price – and the twain do not usually meet. However, when considering the value of an **existing** possession, the owner instinctively considers its 'value' to be that in potential sale, i.e. NRV.

- It **avoids the need to estimate depreciation** and, in consequence, the attendant problems of assessing life-span and residual values. Depreciation is treated as the arithmetic difference between the NRV at the end of a financial period and the NRV at its beginning.

- It is **based on opportunity cost** and so can be said to be more meaningful. It is the **sacrificial** cost of possessing an asset, which, it can be argued, is more authentic in terms of being a true or real cost. If the asset were not possessed, its cash equivalent would exist instead and that cash would be deployed in other opportunities. Therefore, NRV = cash = opportunity = cost.

Defects

- It is a **subjective measure** and in this respect it possesses the same major fault as RCA. It can be said to be less prudent than RCA because NRV will tend to be higher in some cases than RCA. For example, when valuing finished inventories, a profit content will be involved.

- It is **not a realistic measure** as most assets, except finished goods, are possessed in order to be utilised, not sold. Therefore, NRV is irrelevant.

- It is **not always determinable**. The assets concerned may be highly specialist and there may be no ready market by which a value can be easily assessed. Consequently, any particular value may be fictitious or erroneous, containing too high a holding gain or, indeed, too low a holding loss.

- It **violates the concept of the going concern**, which demands that the accounts are drafted on the basis that there is no intention to liquidate the entity. Admittedly, this concept was formulated with HCA in view, but the acceptance of NRV implies the possibility of a cessation of trading.

- It is less reliable and verifiable than HC.
- The statement of comprehensive income will report a more volatile profit if changes in NRV are taken to the statement of comprehensive income each year.
- The profit arising from the changes in NRV may not have been realised.

4.7 Operating capital maintenance – a comprehensive example

In Figure 4.1 we considered the effect of inflation on a cash business without fixed assets, credit customers or credit suppliers. In the following example, Economica plc, we now consider the effect where there are non-current assets and credit transactions.

The HCA statements of financial position as at 31 December 20X4 and 20X5 are set out in Figure 4.3 and index numbers required to restate the non-current assets, inventory and monetary items in Figure 4.4.

Figure 4.3 Economica plc HCA statement of financial position

Statements of financial position as at 31 December on the basis of HCA				
		20X5		20X4
	£000	£000	£000	£000
Non-current assets:				
Cost	85,000		85,000	
Depreciation	34,000		25,500	
		51,000		59,500
Current assets:				
Inventory	25,500		17,000	
Trade receivables	34,000		23,375	
Cash and bank	17,000		1,875	
	76,500		42,250	
Current liabilities:				
Trade payables	25,500		17,000	
Income tax	8,500		4,250	
Dividend proposed	5,000		4,000	
	39,000		25,250	
Net current assets	37,500		17,000	
Less: 8% debentures	11,000		11,000	
		26,500		6,000
		77,500		65,500
Share capital and reserves:				
Authorised and issued £1 ordinary shares		50,000		50,000
Share premium		1,500		1,500
Retained earnings		26,000		14,000
		77,500		65,500

Figure 4.4 Index data relating to Economica plc

1　Index numbers as prepared by the Central Statistical Office for non-current assets:

1 January 20X2	100
1 January 20X5	165
1 January 20X6	185
Average for 20X4	147
Average for 20X5	167

2　All non-current assets were acquired on 1 January 20X2. There were no further acquisitions or disposals during the four years ended 31 December 20X5.

3　Indices as prepared by the Central Statistical Office for inventories and monetary working capital adjustments were:

1 October 20X4	115
31 December 20X4	125
15 November 20X4	120
1 October 20X5	140
31 December 20X5	150
15 November 20X5	145
Average for 20X5	137.5

4　Three months' inventory is carried.

5　Depreciation: historical cost based on 10% pa straight-line with residual value of nil:

	£HCA
20X4	8,500,000
20X5	8,500,000

4.7.1 Restating the opening statement of financial position to current cost

The non-current assets and inventory are restated to their current cost as at the date of the opening statement as shown in W1 and W2 below. The increase from HC to CC represents an unrealised holding gain which is debited to the asset account and credited to a reserve account called a current cost reserve, as in W3 below.

The calculations are as follows. First we shall convert the HCA statement of financial position in Figure 4.3, as at 31 December 20X4, to the CCA basis, using the index data in Figure 4.4.

The **non-monetary items**, comprising the non-current assets and inventory, are converted and the converted amounts are taken to the CC statement and the increases taken to the current cost reserve, as follows.

(W1) Property, plant and equipment

	HCA £000	Index			CCA £000	Increase £000
Cost	85,000	$\times \frac{165}{100}$	=		140,250	55,250
Depreciation	25,500	$\times \frac{165}{100}$	=		42,075	16,575
	59,500				98,175	38,675

The CCA valuation at 31 December 20X4 shows a net increase in terms of numbers of pounds sterling of £38,675,000. The £59,500,000 in the HCA statement of financial position will be replaced in the CCA statement by £98,175,000.

(W2) Inventories

	HCA £000		Index		CCA £000		Increase £000
	17,000	×	$\dfrac{125}{120}$	=	17,708	=	708

Note that Figure 4.4 specifies that three months' inventories are held. Thus on average they will have been purchased on 15 November 20X4, on the assumption that they have been acquired and consumed evenly throughout the calendar period. Hence, the index at the time of purchase would have been 120. The £17,000,000 in the HCA statement of financial position will be replaced in the CCA statement of financial position by £17,708,000.

(W3) Current cost reserve

The total increase in CCA carrying values for non-monetary items is £39,383,000, which will be credited to CC reserves in the CC statement. It comprises £38,675,000 on the non-current assets and £708,000 on the inventory.

Note that monetary items do not change by virtue of inflation. Purchasing power will be lost or gained, but the carrying values in the CCA statement will be identical to those in its HCA counterpart. We can now compile the CCA statement as at 31 December 20X4 – this will show net assets of £104,883,000.

4.7.2 Adjustments that affect the profit for the year

The statement of comprehensive income for the year ended 31 December 20X5 set out in Figure 4.5 discloses a profit before interest and tax of £26,350,000. We need to deduct realised holding gains from this profit to avoid the distribution of dividends that would reduce the operating capital. These deductions are a cost of sales adjustment (COSA), a depreciation adjustment (DA) and a monetary working capital adjustment (MWCA). The accounting treatment is to debit the statement of comprehensive income and credit the current cost reserve.

The adjustments are calculated as follows.

(W4) Cost of sales adjustment (COSA) using the average method

We will compute the cost of sales adjustment by using the average method. The average purchase price index for 20X5 is 137.5. If price increases have moved at an even pace throughout the period, this implies that consumption occurred, on average, at 30 June, the mid-point of the financial year.

	HCA £000		Adjustment		CCA £000		Difference £000
Opening inventory	17,000	×	$\dfrac{137.5}{120}$	=	19,479	=	2,479
Purchases	—		—		—		—
	17,000				19,479		
Closing inventory	(25,500)	×	$\dfrac{137.5}{145}$	=	24,181	=	1,319
	(8,500)				(4,702)		3,798

Figure 4.5 Economica plc HCA statement of comprehensive income

Statement of comprehensive income for the year ended
31 December 20X5, on the basis of HCA

		20X5		20X4
		£000		£000
Turnover		42,500		38,250
Less: Cost of sales		(12,070)		(23,025)
Gross profit		30,430		15,225
Less: Distribution costs	2,460		2,210	
Less: Administrative expenses	1,620		1,540	
		(4,080)		(3,750)
Profit before interest and tax		26,350		11,475
Interest		(880)		(880)
Profit before tax		25,470		10,595
Income tax expense		(8,470)		(4,250)
Profit after tax		17,000		6,345
Dividend		(5,000)		(4,000)
Retentions		12,000		2,345
Balance b/f		14,000		11,655
Balance c/f		26,000		14,000
EPS		34p		13p

The impact of price changes on the cost of sales would be an increase of £3,798,000, causing a profit decrease of like amount and a current cost reserve increase of like amount.

(W5) Depreciation adjustment: average method

As assets are consumed throughout the year, the CCA depreciation charge should be based on average current costs.

	HCA	Adjustment	CCA	Difference
	£000		£000	£000
Depreciation	8,500	$\times \dfrac{167}{100}$ =	14,195	= 5,695

(W6) Monetary working capital adjustment (MWCA)

The objective is to transfer from the statement of comprehensive income to CC reserve the amount by which the need for monetary working capital (MWC) has increased due to rising price levels. The change in MWC from one statement of financial position to the next will be the consequence of a combination of changes in volume and escalating price movements. Volume change may be segregated from the price change by using an average index.

	20X5	20X4		Change
	£000	£000		£000
Trade receivables	34,000	23,375		
Trade payables	25,500	17,000		
MWC =	8,500	6,375	Overall change =	2,125

The MWC is now adjusted by the average index for the year.
This adjustment will reveal the change in volume.

$$\left(8,500 \times \frac{137.5}{150}\right) - \left(6,373 \times \frac{137.5}{125}\right)$$

=	7,792	–	7,012	= Volume change	780
So price change =				1,345

The profit before interest and tax will be reduced as follows:

	£000	£000
Profit before interest and tax		26,350
Less:		
COSA	(3,798)	
DA	(5,695)	
MWCA	(1,345)	
Current cost operating adjustments		(10,838)
Current cost operating profit		15,512

The adjustments will be credited to the current cost reserve.

4.7.3 Unrealised holding gains on non-monetary assets as at 31 December 20X5

The holding gains as at 31 December 20X4 were calculated in section 4.7.1 above for non-current assets and inventory. A similar calculation is required to restate these at 20X5 current costs for the closing statement of financial position. The calculations are as in Working 7 below.

(W7) Non-monetary assets

		£000
(i)	Holding gain on non-current assets	
	Revaluation at year-end	
	Non-current assets at 1 January 20X5 (as W1) at CCA revaluation	140,250
	CCA value at 31 December 20X5 = $140,250 \times \dfrac{185}{165} =$	157,250
	Revaluation holding gain for 20X5 to CC reserve in W8	**17,000**

This holding gain of £17,000,000 is transferred to CC reserves.

(ii) Backlog depreciation on non-current assets

CCA aggregate depreciation at 31 December 20X5 for
CC statement of financial position

	£000
$= £HCA\ 34,000,000 \times \dfrac{185}{100}$ in CC statement of financial position	62,900
Less: CCA aggregate depreciation at 1 January 20X5 (as per W1 and statement of financial position at 1 January 20X5)	42,075
Being CCA depreciation as revealed between opening and closing statements of financial position	20,825
But CCA depreciation charged in revenue accounts (i.e. £8,500,000 in £HCA plus additional depreciation of £5,695,000 per W5) =	14,195
So total backlog depreciation to CC reserve in W8	**6,630**

The CCA value of non-current assets at 31 December 20X5:	£000
Gross CCA value (above)	157,250
Depreciation (above)	62,900
Net CCA carrying value in the CC statement of financial position in W8	**94,350**

This £6,630,000 is backlog depreciation for 20X5. Total backlog depreciation is not expensed (i.e. charged to revenue account) as an adjustment of HCA profit, but is charged against CCA reserves. The net effect is that the CC reserve will increase by £10,370,000, i.e. £17,000,000 – £6,630,000.

(iii) Inventory valuation at year-end

CCA valuation at 31 December 20X5

£HCA000		£CCA000	£CCA000
= 25,500	× 150/145 =	26,379 = increase of	879

CCA valuation at 1 January 20X5 (per W2)

= 17,000	× 125/120 =	17,708 = increase of	708
Inventory holding gain occurring during 20X5 to W8			**171**

4.7.4 Current cost statement of financial position as at 31 December 20X5

The current cost statement as at 31 December 20X5 now discloses non-current assets and inventory adjusted by index to their current cost and the retained profits reduced by the current cost operating adjustments. It appears as in Working 8 below.

(W8) Economica plc: CCA statement of financial position as at 31 December 20X5

Non-current assets	£000	20X5 £000	£000	20X4 £000
Cost	157,250 (W7(i))		140,250 (W1)	
Depreciation	62,900 (W7(ii))		42,075 (W1)	
		94,350 (W7(ii))		98,175
Current assets				
Inventory	26,379 (W7(iii))		17,708 (W2)	
Trade receivables	34,000		23,375	
Cash	17,000		1,875	
	77,379		42,958	
Current liabilities				
Trade payables	25,500		17,000	
Income tax	8,500		4,250	
Dividend proposed	5,000		4,000	
	39,000		25,250	
Net current assets	38,379		17,708	
Less: 8% debentures	11,000		11,000	
		27,379		6,708
		121,729		104,883
Financed by				
Share capital: authorised and issued £1 shares		50,000		50,000
Share premium		1,500		1,500
* CC reserve		55,067		39,383
** Retained profit		15,162		14,000
Shareholders' funds		121,729		104,883

* CC reserve	£000	£000
Opening balance		39,383 (W3)
Holding gains		
Non-current assets	17,000 (W7(i))	
Inventory	171 (W7(iii))	
		17,171
COSA	3,798 (W4)	
MWCA	1,345 (W6)	
Less: backlog depreciation	(6,630) (W7(ii))	(1,487)
		55,067

** Retained profit

Opening balance		14,000 (Figure 4.5)
HCA profit for 20X5	12,000	
COSA	(3,798)(W4)	
Extra depreciation	(5,695)(W5)	
MWCA	(1,345)(W6)	
		1,162
CCA profit for 20X5		15,162

4.7.5 How to take the level of borrowings into account

We have assumed that the company will need to retain £10,838,000 from the current year's earnings in order to maintain the physical operating capacity of the company. However, if the business is part financed by borrowings then part of the amount required may be assumed to come from the lenders. One of the methods advocated is to make a gearing adjustment. The gearing adjustment that we illustrate here has the effect of reducing the impact of the adjustments on the profit after interest, i.e. it is based on the realised holding gains only.

The gearing adjustment will change the carrying figures of CC reserves and retained profit, but not the shareholders' funds, as the adjustment is compensating. The gearing adjustment cannot be computed before the determination of the shareholders' interest because that figure is necessary in order to complete the gearing calculation.

Gearing adjustment

The CC operating profit of the business is quantified after making such retentions from the historical profit as are required in order to maintain the physical operating capacity of the entity. However, from a shareholder standpoint, there is no need to maintain in real terms the portion of the entity financed by loans that are fixed in monetary values. Thus, in calculating profit attributable to shareholders, that part of the CC adjustments relating to the proportion of the business financed by loans can be deducted:

(W9) Gearing adjustment =

$$\frac{\text{Average net borrowings for year}}{\left(\begin{array}{c}\text{Average net borrowings}\\ \text{for year}\end{array}\right) + \left(\begin{array}{c}\text{Average shareholders' funds}\\ \text{for year}\end{array}\right)} \times \begin{array}{c}\text{Aggregate}\\ \text{adjustments}\end{array}$$

This formula is usually expressed as $\dfrac{L}{(L+S)} \times A$

where L = loans (i.e. net borrowings); S = shareholders' interest or funds; A = adjustments (i.e. extra depreciation + COSA + MWCA). Note that $L/(L+S)$ is often expressed as a percentage of A (see example below where it is 6.31%).

Net borrowings

This is the sum of all liabilities less current assets, excluding items included in MWC or utilised in computing COSA. In this instance it is as follows:

Note: in some circumstances (e.g. new issue of debentures occurring during the year) a weighted average will be used.

	Closing balance £000	Opening balance £000
Debentures	11,000	11,000
Income tax	8,500	4,250
Cash	(17,000)	(1,875)
Total net borrowings, the average of which equals L	2,500	13,375

$$\text{Average net borrowings} = \frac{2,500,000 + 13,375,000}{2} = £7,937,500$$

Net borrowings plus shareholders' funds

Shareholders' funds in CC £ (inclusive of proposed dividends)	126,729	108,883
Add: net borrowings	2,500	13,375
	129,229	122,258

Or, alternatively:

	£000	£000
Non-current assets	94,350	98,175
Inventory	26,379	17,708
MWC	8,500	6,375
	129,229	122,258

$$\text{Average } L + S = \frac{129,229,000 + 122,258,000}{2}$$

$$= 125,743,500$$

$$\text{So gearing} = \frac{L}{L+S} \times A$$

$$\frac{£7,937,500}{125,743,500} \times \frac{(\text{COSA} + \text{MWCA} + \text{Extra depreciation})}{(3,798,000 + 1,345,000 + 5,695,000)}$$

$$= 6.31\% \text{ of } £10,838,000 = £683,877, \text{ say } \textbf{£684,000}$$

Thus the CC adjustment of £10,838,000 charged against historical profit may be reduced by £684,000 due to a gain being derived from net borrowings during a period of inflation as shown in Figure 4.6. The £684,000 is shown as a deduction from interest payable.

Figure 4.6 Economica plc CCA statement of income

Economica plc CCA statement of comprehensive income for year ended 31 December 20X5
(i.e. under the operating capital maintenance concept)

		£000
Turnover		42,500
Cost of sales		(12,070)
Gross profit		30,430
Distribution costs		(2,460)
Administrative expenses		(1,620)
Historical cost operating profit		26,350
Current cost operating adjustments		**(10,838)**
Current cost operating profit		15,512
Interest payable	(880)	
Gearing adjustment	**684**	(196)
Current profit on ordinary activities before taxation		15,316
Tax on profit on ordinary activities		(8,470)
Current cost profit for the financial year		6,846
Proposed dividends		(5,000)
Current cost profit retained		1,846
EPS		13.7p

4.7.6 The closing current cost statement of financial position

The closing statement with the non-current assets and inventory restated at current cost and the retained profit adjusted for current cost operating adjustments as reduced by the gearing adjustment is set out in Figure 4.7.

4.7.7 Real Terms System

The Real Terms System combines both CPP and current cost concepts. This requires a calculation of total unrealised holding gains and an inflation adjustment as calculated in Workings 10 and 11 below.

(W10) Total unrealised holding gains to be used in Figure 4.8

[Closing statement of financial position at CC – Closing statement of financial position at HC] – [Opening statement of financial position at CC – Opening statement of financial position at HC]
= (£121,729,000 – £77,500,000) – (£104,883,000 – £65,500,000) = £4,846,000
       (W8)   (Figure 4.3)   (Working 8)   (Figure 4.3)

Figure 4.7 Economica plc CCA statement of financial position

		Economica plc CCA statement of financial position as at 31 December 20X5		
20X4			*20X5*	
£000	£000	*Non-current assets*	£000	£000
140,250		Property, Plant and Equipment	157,250	
42,075		Depreciation	62,900	
	98,175			94,350
		Current assets		
17,708		Inventory	26,379	
23,375		Trade receivables	34,000	
1,875		Cash	17,000	
42,958			77,379	
		Current liabilities		
17,000		Trade payables	25,500	
		Other payables		
4,250		— income tax	8,500	
4,000		— proposed dividend	5,000	
25,250			39,000	
	17,708	*Net current assets*		38,379
		Non-current liabilities		
	(11,000)			(11,000)
	6,708			27,379
	104,883			121,729
	£000	*Capital and reserves*		£000
	50,000	Called-up share capital		50,000
	1,500	Share premium account		1,500
	53,383	Total of other reserves		70,229
	104,883			121,729
		Analysis of 'Total of other reserves'		
	£000			£000
	14,000	Statement of income		15,846
	39,383	Current cost reserve		54,383
	53,383			70,229

continued

Figure 4.7 (continued)

Movements on reserves

(a) Statement of income: £000
    Balance at 1 January 20X5   14,000 (from Figure 4.5)
    Current cost retained profit   1,846 (from Figure 4.6)

    Balance at 31 December 20X5   15,846

(b) Current cost reserve:

	Total £000	Non-current assets £000	Inventory £000	MWCA £000	Gearing £000
Balance as at 1 January 20X5	39,383	38,675	708		
Movements during the year:					
Unrealised holding gains in the year	10,541	10,370	171		
Gearing adjustment	(684)				(684)
MWCA	1,345			1,345	
COSA	3,798		3,798		
Balance as at 31 December 20X5	54,383	49,045	4,677	1,345	(684)

(W11) General price index numbers to be used to calculate the inflation adjustment in Figure 4.8

General price index at 1 January 20X5 $= 317.2$
General price index at 31 December 20X5 $= 333.2$
Opening shareholders' funds at CC × Percentage change in GPI during the year =

$$104,883,000 \times \frac{333.2 - 317.2}{317.2} = £5,290,435, \text{ say } £5,290,000$$

The GPP (or CPP) real terms financial capital

The real terms financial capital maintenance concept may be incorporated within the CCA system as in Figure 4.8 by calculating an inflation adjustment.

4.8 Critique of CCA statements

Considerable effort and expense are involved in compiling and publishing CCA statements. Does their usefulness justify the cost? CCA statements have the following uses:

1 The operating capital maintenance statement reveals CCA profit. Such profit has removed inflationary price increases in raw materials and other inventories, and thus is more realistic than the alternative HCA profit.

2 Significant increases in a company's buying and selling prices will give the HCA profit a holding gains content. That is, the reported HCA profit will include gains consequent upon holding inventories during a period when the cost of buying such inventories increases. Conversely, if specific inventory prices fall, HCA profit will be reduced as it takes account of losses sustained by holding inventory while its price drops. Holding gains and losses are quite different from operating gains and losses. HCA profit does not distinguish between the two, whereas CCA profit does.

Figure 4.8 Economica plc real terms statement of comprehensive income

Economica plc CCA statement of income under the real terms system
for the year ended 31 December 20X5

	£000	£000
Historical cost profit after tax for the financial year		17,000
Add: Total unrealised holding gains arising during the year (see W10)	4,846	
Less: Realised holding gains previously recognised as unrealised	none	
	4,846	
Less: Inflation adjustment to CCA shareholders' funds (W11)	(5,290)	
Real holding gains		(444)
Total real gains		16,556
Deduct: proposed dividends		5,000
Amount retained		11,556

Real terms system: analysis of reserves

20X4		20X5
£000		£000
53,383	*Statement of income*	64,939
—	Financial capital maintenance reserve	5,290
53,383		70,229

Movements on reserves

	Income statement	Financial capital maintenance reserve
	£000	£000
Balances at 1 January 20X5	53,383	—
Amount retained	11,556	—
Inflation adjustment for year		5,290
Balances as at 31 December 20X5	64,939	5,290

3 HCA profit might be adjusted to reflect the moving price level syndrome:

(a) by use of the operating capital maintenance approach, which regards only the CCA **operating** profit as the authentic result for the period and which treats any holding gain or loss as a movement on reserves;

(b) by adoption of the real terms **financial** capital maintenance approach, which applies a general inflation measure via the RPI, combined with CCA information regarding holding gains.

Thus the statement can reveal information to satisfy the demands of the management of the entity itself – as distinct from the shareholder/proprietor, whose awareness of inflation may centre on the RPI. In this way the concern of operating management can be accommodated with the different interest of the shareholder. The HCA profit would fail on both these counts.

4   CC profit is important because:

(a) it quantifies cost of sales and depreciation after allowing for changing price levels; hence trading results, free of inflationary elements, grant a clear picture of entity activities and management performance;

(b) resources are maintained, having eliminated the possibility of paying dividend out of real capital;

(c) yardsticks for management performance are more comparable as a time series within the one entity and between entities, the distortion caused by moving prices having been alleviated.

4.9 The ASB approach

The ASB has been wary of this topic. It is only too aware that standard setters in the past have been unsuccessful in obtaining a consensus on the price level adjusting model to be used in financial statements. The chronology in Figure 4.9 illustrates the previous attempts to deal with the topic. Consequently, the ASB has clearly decided to follow a gradualist approach and to require uniformity in the treatment of specific assets and liabilities where it is current practice to move away from historical costs.

The ASB view was set out in a Discussion Paper, *The Role of Valuation in Financial Reporting*, issued in 1993.[1] The ASB had three options when considering the existing system of modified historic costs:

● to remove the right to modify cost in the statement of financial position;

● to introduce a coherent current value system immediately;

● to make *ad hoc* improvements to the present modified historic cost system.

Figure 4.9 Standard setters' unsuccessful attempts to replace HCA

1974   Statement of Accounting Practice SSAP 7 *Accounting for Changes in the Purchasing Power of Money* advocating the CPP model.

1975   *Inflation Accounting*, Report of the Inflation Accounting Committee (The Sandilands Report) advocating current cost accounting (CCA) rather than the CPP, RCA or NRVA model. The CCA system recommended by Sandilands was based on the deprival value of an asset, i.e. the value based on the loss, direct or indirect, sustainable by an entity if it were to be deprived of the asset concerned.

1984   SSAP 16 *Current Cost Accounting* was issued by the ASC requiring listed companies to produce CCA accounts as their primary financial report. There was widespread non-compliance and a new exposure draft ED 35 was issued effectively retaining HCA accounts as the primary financial report with supplementary current cost information.

1985   SSAP 16 was withdrawn and the ASC issued *Accounting for the Effects of Changing Prices: A Handbook*. The Handbook was interesting in that it set out four valuation bases if the financial capital maintenance concept was applied and four valuation bases if the operating capital maintenance concept was applied. Its preferred options were CCA under the financial capital maintenance concept which it referred to as real terms accounting (RTA) and CCA under the operating capital maintenance concept.

4.9.1 Remove the right to modify cost in the statement of financial position

This would mean pruning the system back to one rigorously based on the principles of historical costs, with current values shown by way of note.

This option has strong support from the profession not only in the UK, e.g. 'in our view . . . the most significant advantage of historical cost over current value accounting . . . is that it is based on the actual transactions which the company has undertaken and the cash flows that it has generated . . . this is an advantage not just in terms of reliability, but also in terms of relevance',[2] but also in the USA, e.g. 'a study showed that users were opposed to replacing the current historic cost based accounting model . . . because it provides them with a stable and consistent benchmark that they can rely on to establish historical trends'.[3]

Although this would have brought UK practice into line with that of the USA and some of the EU countries, it has been rejected by the ASB. This is no doubt on the basis that the ASB wishes to see current values established in the UK in the longer term.

4.9.2 Introduce a coherent current value system immediately

This would mean developing the system into one more clearly founded on principles embracing current values. One such system, advocated by the ASB in Chapter 6 of its *Statement of Accounting Principles*, is based on **value to the business**. The value to the business measurement model is eclectic in that it draws on various current value systems. The approach to establishing the value to the business of a specific asset is quite logical:

● If an asset is worth replacing, then use replacement cost (RC).

● If it is **not** worth replacing, then use:

 value in use (economic value) if it is worth keeping; **or**

 net realisable value (NRV) if it is **not** worth keeping.

The reasoning is that the value to the business is represented by the action that would be taken by a business if it were to be deprived of an asset – this is also referred to as the **deprival value**.

For example, assume the following:

	£
Historical cost	200,000
Accumulated depreciation (6 years straight line)	120,000
Net book value	80,000
Replacement cost (gross)	300,000
Aggregate depreciation	180,000
Depreciated replacement cost	120,000
Net realisable value (NRV)	50,000
Value in use (discounted future income)	70,565

If the asset were destroyed then it would be irrational to replace it at its depreciated replacement cost of £120,000 considering that the asset only has a value in use of £70,565.

However, the ASB did not see it as feasible to implement this system at that time because 'there is much work to be done to determine whether or not it is possible to devise a system that would be of economic relevance and acceptable to users and preparers of financial statements in terms of sufficient reliability without prohibitive cost'.[4]

Make *ad hoc* improvements to the present modified historical cost system

The ASB favoured this option for removing anomalies, on the basis that practice should be evolutionary and should follow various ASB pronouncements (e.g. on the revaluation of properties and quoted investments) on an *ad hoc* basis. The *Statement of Accounting Principles* continues to envisage that a mixed measurement system will be used and it focuses on the mix of historical cost and current value to be adopted.[5]

It is influenced in choosing this option by the recognition that there are anxieties about the costs and benefits of moving to a full current value system, and by the belief that a considerable period of experimentation and learning would be needed before such a major change could be successfully introduced.[6]

Given the inability of the standard setters to implement a uniform current value system in the past, it seems a sensible, pragmatic approach for the ASB to recognise that it would fail if it made a similar attempt now.

This approach has been applied in FRS 3 with the requirement for a new primary financial statement, the statement of total recognised gains and losses (see Chapter 8 for further discussion) to report unrealised gains and losses arising from revaluation.

The historical cost based system and the current value based system have far more to commend them than the *ad hoc* option chosen by the ASB. However, as a short-term measure, it leaves the way open for the implementation in the longer term of its preferred value to the business model.

4.10 The IASC/IASB approach

The IASB has struggled in the same way as the ASB in the UK in deciding how to respond to inflation rates that have varied so widely over time. Theoretically there is a case for inflation-adjusting financial statements whatever the rate of inflation but standard setters need to carry the preparers and users of accounts with them – this means that there has to be a consensus that the traditional HCA financial statements are failing to give a true and fair view. Such a consensus is influenced by the current rate of inflation.

When the rates around the world were in double figures, there was pressure for a **mandatory** standard so that financial statements were comparable. This led to the issue in 1983 of IAS 15 *Information Reflecting the Effects of Changing Prices* which required companies to restate the HCA accounts using either a general price index or replacement costs with adjustments for depreciation, cost of sales and monetary items.

As the inflation rates fell below double figures, there was less willingness by companies to prepare inflation-adjusted accounts and so, in 1989, the mandatory requirement was relaxed and the application of IAS 15 became **optional**.

In recent years the inflation rates in developed countries have ranged between 1% and 4% and so in 2003, twenty years after it was first issued, IAS 15 was **withdrawn** as part of the ASB Improvement Project.

These low rates have not been universal outside the developed world and there has remained a need to prepare inflation-adjusted financial statements where there is hyperinflation and the rates are so high that HCA would be misleading.

4.10.1 The IASB position where there is hyperinflation

What do we mean by hyperinflation?

IAS 29 *Financial Reporting in Hyperinflationary Economies* states that hyperinflation occurs when money loses purchasing power at such a rate that comparison of amounts from transactions that have occurred at different times, even within the same accounting period, is misleading.

What rate indicates that hyperinflation exists?

IAS 29 does not specify an absolute rate – this is a matter of qualitative judgement – but it sets out certain pointers, such as people preferring to keep their wealth in non-monetary assets, people preferring prices to be stated in terms of an alternative stable currency rather than the domestic currency, wages and prices being linked to a price index, or the cumulative inflation rate over three years approaching 100%.

Countries where hyperinflation has occurred recently include Angola, Burma and Turkey.

How are financial statements adjusted?

The current year financial statements, whether HCA or CCA, must to be restated using the domestic measuring unit current at the statement of financial position date; if the current year should be the first year that restatement takes place then the opening statement of financial position also has to be restated.

Illustration of disclosures in IAS 29 adjusted accounts

The following is an extract from the 2002 accounts of Turkiye Petrol Rafinerileri.

> IAS 29 requires that financial statements prepared in the currency of a hyperinflationary economy be stated in terms of the measuring unit current at the statement of financial position date and the corresponding figures for previous periods be restated in the same terms. One characteristic that leads to the classification of an economy as hyperinflationary is a cumulative three-year inflation rate approaching 100%. Such cumulative rate in Turkey was 227% for the three years ended 31 December 2002 based on the wholesale price index announced by the Turkish State Institute of Statistics. The restatement has been calculated by means of conversion factors based on the Turkish countrywide wholesale price index (WPI).
>
> The index and corresponding conversion factors for year-ends are as follows (1994 average = 100)

	Index	*Conversion factor*
Year ended 31 December 1999	1,979.5	3.2729
Year ended 31 December 2000	2,626.0	2.4672
Year ended 31 December 2001	4,951.7	1.3083
Year ended 31 December 2002	6,478.8	1.0000

> ● Monetary assets and liabilities are not restated.
>
> ● Non-monetary assets and liabilities are restated by applying to the initial acquisition cost and any accumulated depreciation for fixed assets the relevant conversion factors reflecting the increase in WPI from date of acquisition.
>
> ● All items in the statements of income are restated.

4.11 Future developments

A mixed picture emerges when we try to foresee the future of changing price levels and financial reporting. The accounting profession has been reluctant to abandon the HC concept in favour of a 'valuation accounting' approach. In the UK and Australia many companies have stopped revaluing their non-current assets, with a large proportion opting instead to revert to the historical cost basis with the two main factors influencing management's decision being cost effectiveness and future reporting flexibility.[7]

The pragmatic approach is prevailing with each class of asset and liability being considered on an individual basis. For example, non-current assets are reported at depreciated replacement cost unless this is higher than the economic value we discussed in Chapter 3; financial assets are reported at market value (exit value in the NRV model); current assets reported at lower of HC and NRV. In each case the resulting changes, both realised and unrealised, in value will find their way into the financial performance statement(s).

Fair values

A number of IFRSs now require or allow the use of fair values e.g. IFRS 3 *Business Combinations* in which fair value is defined as 'the amount for which an asset could be exchanged or a liability settled between knowledgeable, willing parties in an arm's length transaction'. This is equivalent to the NRVA model discussed above. It is defined as an exit value rather than a cost value but like NRVA it does not imply a forced sale, i.e. it is the best value that could be obtained.

It is interesting to note that in the US there is a view that financial statements should be primarily decision-useful. This is a move away from the position adopted by the IASB in its conceptual framework in which it states that financial statements have two functions – one to provide investors with the means to assess stewardship and the other the means to make sound economic decisions.

How will financial statements be affected if fair values are adopted?

The financial statements will have the same virtues and defects as the NRVA model (section 4.6.4 above). Some concerns have been raised that reported annual income will become more volatile and the profit that is reported may contain a mix of realised and unrealised profits. Supporters of the use of fair values see the income and statement of financial position as more relevant for decision making whilst accepting that the figures might be less reliable and not as effective as a means of assessing the stewardship by the directors.

Stewardship

Before the growth of capital markets, stewardship was the primary objective of financial reporting. This is reflected in company law, which viewed management as agents of the shareholders who should periodically provide an account of their performance to explain the use they have made of the resources that the owners put under their control, i.e. it is a means of governance by providing *retrospective* accountability.

With the growth of capital markets, the ability to generate cash flows became important when making decisions as to whether to buy, sell or hold shares, i.e. it is concerned with *prospective* performance.

This has given rise to an ongoing debate over the relative importance of stewardship reporting and there is a fundamental difference between the US and Europe. In the US, stewardship is seen as secondary to decision-usefulness, whereas in Europe reporting the past use of resources is seen as just as important as reporting the future wealth-generating potential of those resources.

In their efforts to agree on a common approach, the IASB and FASB issued a Discussion Paper *Preliminary Views on an Improved Conceptual Framework for Financial Reporting* which proposed that the converged framework should specify only one objective of financial reporting, namely the provision of information useful in making future resource allocation decisions. However, there is a strong argument to support the explicit recognition of two equal objectives.

The first is retrospective and stewardship based, and helps investors to assess the management: Have their strategies been effective? Have the assets been protected? Have the resources produced an adequate return? The second is prospective, helping investors to make a judgement as to future performance – a judgement that might well be influenced by their assessment of the past.

It is interesting to note that the IASB Framework[8] currently supports the importance of financial statements as a means of assessing stewardship stating:

> Financial statements also show the results of the stewardship of management, or the accountability of management for the resources entrusted to it. Those users who wish to assess the stewardship or accountability of management do so in order that they make economic decisions; these decisions may include, for example, whether to hold or sell their investment in the enterprise or whether to reappoint or replace the management.

Any revision to the conceptual framework should hold firm to equal weight being given to retrospective and prospective objectives.

The gradualist approach

It is very possible that the number of international standards requiring or allowing fair values will increase over time and reflect the adoption on a piecemeal basis. In the meantime, efforts[9] are in hand for the FASB and IASB to arrive at a common definition of fair value which can be applied to value assets and liabilities where there is no market value available. Agreeing a definition, however, is only a part of the exercise. If analysts are to be able to compare corporate performance across borders, then it is essential that both the FASB and the IASB agree that all companies should adopt fair value accounting – it has been proving difficult to gain acceptance for this in the US.

This means that in the future historical cost and realisation will be regarded as less relevant[10] and investors, analysts and management will need to come to terms with increased volatility in reported annual performance.

Summary

The traditional HCA system reveals disturbing inadequacies in times of changing price levels, calling into question the value of financial reports using this system. Considerable resources and energy have been expended in searching for a substitute model able to counter the distortion and confusion caused by an unstable monetary unit.

Three basic models have been developed: RCA, NRVA and CPP. Each has its merits and defects; each produces a different income value and a different capital value. However, it is important that inflation-adjusted values be computed in order to avoid a possible loss of entity resources and the collapse of the going concern.

The contemporary financial reporting scene is beset by problems such as the emergence of brand accounting, the debate on accounting for goodwill, the need for more informative revenue accounts and a sudden spate of financial scandals involving major industrial conglomerations. These have combined to raise questions regarding the adequacy of the annual accounts and the intrinsic validity of the auditors' report.

In assessing future prospects, it would seem that more useful financial information is needed. This need will be met by changes in the reporting system, which are beginning to include some form of 'value accounting' as distinct from HC accounting. Such value accounting will probably embrace inflationary adjustments to enable comparability to be maintained, as far as possible, in an economic environment of changing prices.

REVIEW QUESTIONS

1 (a) Explain the limitations of HCA when prices are rising.

   (b) Why has the HCA model survived in spite of its shortcomings in times of inflation?

2 Explain the features of the CPP model in contrast with those of the CCA model.

3 What factors should be taken into account when designing a system of accounting for inflation?

4 To what extent are CCA statements useful to an investor?

5 Compare the operating and financial capital maintenance concepts.

6 'Historical cost accounting is the worst possible accounting convention, until one considers the alternatives.' Discuss this statement in relation to CPP, CCA and NRVA.

7 'To be relevant to investors, the profit for the year should include both realised and unrealised gains/losses.' Discuss.

8 Discuss the effect on setting performance bonuses for staff if financial performance for a period contains both realised and unrealised gains/losses.

9 'The relevant financial performance figure for an investor is the amount available for distribution at the statement of financial position date.' Discuss.

10 'Financial statements should reflect realistically the performance and position of an organisation, but most of the accountant's rules conflict directly with the concept of realism.' Discuss.

11 Explain why financial reports prepared under the historical cost convention are subject to the following major limitations:

 • inventory is undervalued;

 • the depreciation charge to the statement of comprehensive income is understated;

 • gains and losses on net monetary assets are undisclosed;

 • statement of financial position values are understated;

 • periodic comparisons are invalidated.

12 Explain how each of the limitations in question 11 could be overcome.

13 In April 2000 the G4 + 1 Group acknowledged that market exit value is generally regarded as the basis for fair value measurement of financial instruments and was discussing the use of the deprival value model for the measurement of non-financial assets or liabilities, especially in cases in which the item is highly specialised and not easily transferable in the market in its current condition. The deprival value model would require that an asset or liability be measured at its replacement cost, net realisable value, or value in use, depending on the particular circumstances.

   (a) Discuss reasons why financial and non-financial assets should be measured using different bases.

   (b) Explain what is meant by 'depending on the particular circumstances'.

14 Explain the criteria for determining whether hyperinflation exists.

15 '...the IASB's failure to decide on a capital maintenance concept is regrettable as users have no idea as to whether total gains represent income or capital and are therefore unable to identify a meaningful "bottom line"'.[11] Discuss.

EXERCISES

An extract from the solution is provided on the Companion Website (www.pearsoned.co.uk/elliott-elliott) for exercises marked with an asterisk (*).

* Question 1

Shower Ltd was incorporated towards the end of 20X2, but it did not start trading until 20X3. Its historical cost statement of financial position at 1 January 20X3 was as follows:

	£
Share capital, £1 shares	2,000
Loan (interest free)	8,000
	£10,000
Non-current assets, at cost	6,000
Inventory, at cost (4,000 units)	4,000
	£10,000

A summary of Shower Limited's bank account for 20X3 is given below:

		£	£
1 Jan 20X3	Opening balance		nil
30 Jun 20X3	Sales (8,000 units)		20,000
Less			
29 Jun 20X3	Purchase (6,000 units)	9,000	
	Sundry expenses	5,000	14,000
31 Dec 20X3	Closing balance		£6,000

All the company's transactions are on a cash basis.

The non-current assets are expected to last for five years and the company intends to depreciate its non-current assets on a straight-line basis. The non-current assets had a resale value of £2,000 at 31 December 20X3.

Notes
1 The closing inventory is 2,000 units and the inventory is sold on a first-in-first-out basis.
2 All prices remained constant from the date of incorporation to 1 January 20X3, but thereafter, various relevant price indices moved as follows:

		Specific indices	
	General price level	Inventory	Non-current assets
1 January 20X3	100	100	100
30 June 20X3	120	150	140
31 December 20X3	240	255	200

Required:
Produce statements of financial position as at December 20X3 and statements of comprehensive incomes for the year ended on that date on the basis of:
  (i)   historical cost;
  (ii) current purchasing power (general price level);
  (iii) replacement cost;
  (iv) continuous contemporary accounting (NRVA).

Question 2

The finance director of Toy plc has been asked by a shareholder to explain items that appear in the current cost statement of comprehensive income for the year ended 31.8.20X9 and the statement of financial position as at that date:

		£	£
Historical cost profit			143,000
Cost of sales adjustment	(1)	10,000	
Additional depreciation	(2)	6,000	
Monetary working capital adjustment	(3)	2,500	18,500
Current cost operating profit before tax			124,500
Gearing adjustment	(4)		2,600
CCA operating profit			127,100
Non-current assets at gross replacement cost		428,250	
Accumulated current cost depreciation	(5)	(95,650)	332,600
Net current assets			121,400
12% debentures			(58,000)
			396,000
Issued share capital			250,000
Current cost reserve	(6)		75,000
Retained earnings			71,000
			396,000

Required:
(a) Explain what each of the items numbered 1–6 represents and the purpose of each.
(b) What do you consider to be the benefits to users of providing current cost information?

Question 3

The statements of financial position of Parkway plc for 20X7 and 20X8 are given below, together with the income statement for the year ended 30 June 20X8.

	Statement of financial position					
	20X8			20X7		
	£000	£000	£000	£000	£000	£000
Non-current assets	Cost	Depn	NBV	Cost	Depn	NBV
Freehold land	60,000	—	60,000	60,000	—	60,000
Buildings	40,000	8,000	32,000	40,000	7,200	32,800
Plant and machinery	30,000	16,000	14,000	30,000	10,000	20,000
Vehicles	40,000	20,000	20,000	40,000	12,000	28,000
	170,000	44,000	126,000	170,000	29,200	140,800
Current assets						
Inventory		80,000			70,000	
Trade receivables		60,000			40,000	
Short-term investments		50,000			—	
Cash at bank and in hand		5,000			5,000	
		195,000			115,000	
Current liabilities						
Trade payables		90,000			60,000	
Bank overdraft		50,000			45,000	
Taxation		28,000			15,000	
Dividends		15,000			10,000	
		183,000			130,000	
Net current assets			12,000			(15,000)
			138,000			125,800
Financed by						
Ordinary share capital			80,000			80,000
Share premium			10,000			10,000
Retained profits			28,000			15,800
			118,000			105,800
Long-term loans			20,000			20,000
			138,000			125,800

Statement of comprehensive income of Parkway plc
for the year ended 30 June 20X8

	£000

Sales	738,000
Cost of sales	620,000
Gross profit	118,000

Notes

1   The freehold land and buildings were purchased on 1 July 20X0. The company policy is to depreciate buildings over 50 years and to provide no depreciation on land.
2   Depreciation on plant and machinery and motor vehicles is provided at the rate of 20% per annum on a straight-line basis.
3   Depreciation on buildings and plant and equipment has been included in administration expenses, while that on motor vehicles is included in distribution expenses.
4   The directors of Parkway plc have provided you with the following information relating to price rises:

	RPI	Inventory	Land	Buildings	Plant	Vehicles
1 July 20X0	100	60	70	50	90	120
1 July 20X7	170	140	290	145	135	180
30 June 20X8	190	180	310	175	165	175
Average for year ending 30 June 20X8	180	160	300	163	145	177

Required:

(a) Making and stating any assumptions that are necessary, and giving reasons for those assumptions, calculate the monetary working capital adjustment for Parkway plc.

(b) Critically evaluate the usefulness of the monetary working capital adjustment.

Question 4

Raiders plc prepares accounts annually to 31 March. The following figures, prepared on a conventional historical cost basis, are included in the company's accounts to 31 March 20X5.

1   In the income statement:

	£000	£000
(i) Cost of goods sold:		
Inventory at 1 April 20X4	9,600	
Purchases	39,200	
	48,800	
Inventory at 31 March 20X5	11,300	37,500
(ii) Depreciation of equipment		8,640

2   In the statement of financial position:

	£000	£000
(iii) Equipment at cost	57,600	
Less: Accumulated depreciation	16,440	41,160
(iv) Inventory		11,300

The inventory held on 31 March 20X4 and 31 March 20X5 was in each case purchased evenly during the last six months of the company's accounting year.

Equipment is depreciated at a rate of 15% per annum, using the straight-line method. Equipment owned on 31 March 20X5 was purchased as follows: on 1 April 20X2 at a cost of £16 million; on 1 April 20X3 at a cost of £20 million; and on 1 April 20X4 at a cost of £21.6 million.

	Current cost of inventory	Current cost of equipment	Retail Price Index
1 April 20X2	109	145	313
1 April 20X3	120	162	328
30 September 20X3	128	170	339
31 December 20X3	133	175	343
31 March/1 April 20X4	138	180	345
30 September 20X4	150	191	355
31 December 20X4	156	196	360
31 March 20X5	162	200	364

Required:

(a) Calculate the following current cost accounting figures:
   (i)   The cost of goods sold of Raiders plc for the year ended 31 March 20X5.
   (ii) The statement of financial position value of inventory at 31 March 20X5.
   (iii) The equipment depreciation charge for the year ended 31 March 20X5.
   (iv) The net statement of financial position value of equipment at 31 March 20X5.

(b) Discuss the extent to which the figures you have calculated in (a) above (together with figures calculated on a similar basis for earlier years) provide information over and above that provided by the conventional historical cost statement of comprehensive income and balance sheet figures.

(c) Outline the main reasons why the standard setters have experienced so much difficulty in their attempts to develop an accounting standard on accounting for changing prices.

Question 5

The historical cost accounts of Smith plc are as follows:

Smith plc Statement of comprehensive income for the year ended 31 December 20X8		
	£000	£000
Sales		2,000
Cost of sales:		
Opening inventory 1 January 20X8	320	
Purchases	1,680	
	2,000	
Closing inventory at 31 December 20X8	280	
		1,720
Gross profit		280
Depreciation	20	
Administration expenses	100	
		120
Net profit		160

Statement of financial position of Smith plc as at 31 December 20X8

	20X7		20X8	
Non-current assets	£000		£000	
Land and buildings at cost	1,360		1,360	
Less aggregate depreciation	(160)		(180)	
	1,200		1,180	
Current assets				
Inventory	320		280	
Trade receivables	80		160	
Cash at bank	40		120	
	440		560	
Trade payables	200		140	
		240		420
		1,440		1,600
Ordinary share capital		800		800
Retained profit		640		800
		1,440		1,600

Notes

1 Land and buildings were acquired in 20X0 with the buildings component costing £800,000 and depreciated over 40 years.
2 Share capital was issued in 20X0.
3 Closing inventories were acquired in the last quarter of the year.
4 RPI numbers were:

Average for 20X0	120
20X7 last quarter	216
At 31 December 20X7	220
20X8 last quarter	232
Average for 20X8	228
At 31 December 20X8	236

Required:

 (i) Explain the basic concept of the CPP accounting system.
(ii) Prepare CPP accounts for Smith plc for the year ended 20X8.
    The following steps will assist in preparing the CPP accounts:
    (a) Restate the statement of comprehensive income for the current year in terms of £CPP at the year-end.
    (b) Restate the closing statement of financial position in £CPP at year-end, but excluding monetary items, i.e. trade receivables, trade payables, cash at bank.
    (c) Restate the opening statement of financial position in £CPP at year-end, but including monetary items, i.e. trade receivables, trade payables and cash at bank, and showing equity as the balancing figure.
    (d) Compare the opening and closing equity figures derived in (b) and (c) above to arrive at the total profit/loss for the year in CPP terms. Compare this figure with the CPP profit calculated in (a) above to determine the monetary gain or monetary loss.
    (e) Reconcile monetary gains/loss in (d) with the increase/decrease in net monetary items during the year expressed in £CPP compared with the increase/decrease expressed in £HC.

* Question 6

Aspirations Ltd commenced trading as wholesale suppliers of office equipment on 1 January 20X1, issuing ordinary shares of £1 each at par in exchange for cash. The shares were fully paid on issue, the number issued being 1,500,000.

The following financial statements, based on the historical cost concept, were compiled for 20X1.

Aspirations Ltd

Statement of comprehensive income for the year ended 31 December 20X1

	£	£
Sales		868,425
Purchases	520,125	
Less: Inventory 31 December 20X1	24,250	
Cost of sales		495,875
Gross profit		372,550
Expenses	95,750	
Depreciation	25,250	
		121,000
Net profit		251,550

Statement of financial position as at 31 December 20X1

	Cost	Depreciation	
Non-current assets	£	£	£
Freehold property	650,000	6,500	643,500
Office equipment	375,000	18,750	356,250
	1,025,000	25,250	999,750
Current assets			
Inventories		24,250	
Trade receivables		253,500	
Cash		1,090,300	
		1,368,050	
Current liabilities		116,250	
	1,251,800		
Non-current liabilities		500,000	751,800
			1,751,550
Issued share capital			
1,500,000 £1 ordinary shares			1,500,000
Retained earnings			251,550
			1,751,550

The year 20X1 witnessed a surge of inflation and in consequence the directors became concerned about the validity of the revenue account and statement of financial position as income and capital statements. Index numbers reflecting price changes were:

Specific index numbers reflecting replacement costs

	1 January 20X1	31 December 20X1	Average for 20X1
Inventory	115	150	130
Freehold property	110	165	127
Office equipment	125	155	145
General price index numbers	135	170	155

Regarding current exit costs

Inventory is anticipated to sell at a profit of 75% of cost.

The value of assets at 31 December 20X1 was

	£
Freehold property	640,000
Office equipment	350,000

Initial purchases of inventory were effected on 1 January 20X1 amounting to £34,375; the balance of purchases was evenly spread over the 12-month period. The non-current assets were acquired on 1 January 20X1 and, together with the initial inventory, were paid for in cash on that day.

Required:
Prepare the accounts adjusted for current values using each of the three proposed models of current value accounting: namely, the accounting methods known as replacement cost, general (or current) purchasing power and net realisable value.

Question 7

Antonio Rossi set up a part-time business on 1 November 2004 buying and selling second-hand sports cars. On 1 November 2004 he commenced business with $66,000 which he immediately used to purchase ten identical sports cars costing $6,600 each, paying in cash. On 1 May 2005 he sold seven of the sports cars for $8,800 each receiving the cash immediately. Antonio estimates that the net realisable value of each sports car remaining unsold was $8,640 as at 31 October 2005.

The replacement cost of similar sports cars was $6,800 as at 1 May 2005 and $7,000 as at 31 October 2005, and the value of a relevant general price index was 150 as at 1 November 2004, 155 as at 1 May 2005 and 159 as at 31 October 2005.

Antonio paid the proceeds from the sales on 1 May 2005 into a special bank account for the business and made no drawings and incurred no expenses over the year ending 31 October 2005.

Antonio's accountant has told him that there are different ways of calculating profit and financial position and has produced the following figures:

Current purchasing power accounting Profit and Loss Account for the year ended 31 October 2005

	$
Sales	63,190
less Cost of sales	48,972
	14,218
Loss on monetary item	(1,590)
CPP net income	12,628

Balance sheet as at 31 October 2005

Assets	$
Inventory	20,988
Cash	61,600
	82,588
Financed by:	
Opening capital	69,960
Profit for the year	12,628
	82,588

Current cost accounting Profit and Loss Account for the year ended 31 October 2005

Historical cost profit	15,400
less Cost of sales adjustment	1,400
Current cost income	14,000

Balance sheet as at 31 October 2005

Asset	$
Inventory	21,000
Cash	61,600
	82,600
Financed by:	
Opening capital	66,000
Current cost reserve	2,600
Profit for the year	14,000
	82,600

Required:
(a) Prepare Antonio's historical cost profit and loss account for the year ended 31 October 2005 and his balance sheet as at 31 October 2005.
(b) (i) Explain how the figures for Sales and Cost of sales were calculated for the current purchasing power profit and loss account. You need not provide detailed calculations.
    (ii) Explain what the 'loss on monetary item' means. In what circumstances would there be a profit on monetary items?
(c) (i) Explain how the 'cost of sales adjustment' was calculated and what it means. You need not provide detailed calculations.
    (ii) Identify and explain the purpose of any three other adjustments which you might expect to see in a current cost profit and loss account prepared in this way.
(d) State, giving your reasons, which of the three bases gives the best measure of Antonio's financial performance and financial position.

(The Association of International Accountants)

References

1 *The Role of Valuation in Financial Reporting*, ASB, 1993.
2 Ernst & Young, *UK GAAP* (4th edition), 1994, p. 91.
3 *The Information Needs of Investors and Creditors*, AICPA Special Committee on Financial Reporting.
4 *The Role of Valuation in Financial Reporting*, ASB, 1993, para. 31(ii).
5 *Statement of Accounting Principles*, ASB, December 1999, para. 6.4.
6 *The Role of Valuation in Financial Reporting*, ASB, 1993, para. 33.
7 Ernst & Young, 'Revaluation of non-current assets', Accounting Standard, Ernst & Young, January 2002, www.ey.com/Global/gcr.nsf/Australia.
8 *Framework for the Preparation and Presentation of Financial Statements*, IASC, 1989, adopted by IASB 2001, para. 14.
9 SFAS 157 *Fair value measurement*, FASB, 2006.
10 A. Wilson, 'IAS: the challenge for measurement', *Accountancy*, December 2001, p. 90.
11 N. Fry and D. Bence, 'Capital or income?', *Accountancy*, April 2007, p. 81.

Bibliography

Accounting for Changes in the Purchasing Power of Money, SSAP 7, ASC, 1974.
Accounting for Stewardship in a Period of Inflation, The Research Foundation of the ICAEW, 1968.
W.T. Baxter, *Accounting Values and Inflation*, McGraw Hill, 1975.
W.T. Baxter, *Depreciation*, Sweet and Maxwell, 1971.
W.T. Baxter, *Inflation Accounting*, Philip Alan, 1984.
W.T. Baxter, *The Case for Deprival Accounting*, ICAS, 2003.
R.J. Chambers, *Accounting Evaluation and Economic Behaviour*, Prentice Hall, 1966.
R.J. Chambers, 'Second thoughts on continuous contemporary accounting', *Abacus*, September 1970.
E.O. Edwards and P.W. Bell, *The Theory and Measurement of Business Income*, University of California Press, 1961.
J.R. Hicks, *Value and Capital* (2nd edition), OUP, 1975.
R.A. Hill, 'Economic income and value: the price level problem', *ACCA Students' Newsletter*, November 1987.
T.A. Lee, *Cash Flow Accounting*, Van Nostrand Reinhold, 1984.
T.A. Lee (ed.), *Developments in Financial Reporting*, Philip Alan, 1981.
T.A. Lee, *Income and Value Measurement: Theory and Practice* (3rd edition), Van Nostrand Reinhold (UK), 1985, Chapter 5.
'A quickfall: the elementary arithmetic of measuring real profit', *Management Accounting*, April 1980.
D.R. Myddleton, *On a Cloth Untrue – Inflation Accounting: The Way Forward*, Woodhead-Faulkner, 1984.
R.H. Parker and G.C. Harcourt (eds), *Readings in the Concept and Measurement of Income*, Cambridge University Press, 1969.
F. Sandilands (Chairman), *Inflation Accounting – Report of the Inflation Accounting Committee*, HMSO Cmnd 6225, 1975, pp. 139–155 and Chapter 9.
D. Tweedie and G. Whittington, *Capital Maintenance Concepts*, ASC, 1985.
D. Tweedie and G. Whittington, *The Debate on Inflation in Accounting*, Cambridge University Press, 1985.
G. Whittington, 'Inflation accounting: all the answers from Deloitte, Haskins and Sells', distinguished lecture series, Cardiff, 5 March 1981, reproduced in *Contemporary Issues in Accounting*, Pitman/Farringdon, 1984.

PART 2

Regulatory framework – an attempt to achieve uniformity

Financial reporting – evolution of global standards

5.1 Introduction

The main purpose of this chapter is to describe the movement towards global standards.

Objectives

By the end of the chapter, you should be able to:

- describe the UK, US and IASB standard setting bodies;
- critically discuss the arguments for and against standards;
- describe the reasons for differences in financial reporting;
- describe the work of international bodies in harmonising and standardising financial reporting;
- explain the impact on financial reporting of changing to IFRS;
- describe the progress being made towards a single set of global international standards;
- describe and comment on the ASB approach to financial reporting by smaller entities;
- describe and comment on the IASB approach to financial reporting by small and medium-sized entities.

5.2 Why do we need financial reporting standards?

Standards are needed because accounting numbers are important when defining contractual entitlements. Contracting parties frequently define the rights between themselves in terms of accounting numbers.[1] For example, the remuneration of directors and managers might be expressed in terms of a salary plus a bonus based on an agreed performance measure, e.g. Johnson Matthey's 2009 Annual Report states:

> Annual Bonus – which is paid as a percentage of basic salary under the terms of the company's Executive Compensation Plan (which also applies to the group's 170 or so most senior executives). The executive directors' bonus award is based on consolidated underlying profit before tax (PBT) compared with the annual budget. The board of directors rigorously reviews the annual budget to ensure that the budgeted PBT is sufficiently stretching.
>
> An annual bonus payment of 50% of basic salary (prevailing at 31st March) is paid if the group meets the annual budget. This bonus may rise on a straight line basis to 75%

of basic salary if the group achieves PBT of 105% of budget and a maximum 100% of basic salary may be paid if 110% of budgeted PBT is achieved. PBT must reach 95% of budget for a minimum bonus of 15% to be payable. The Committee has discretion to vary the awards made.

However, there is a risk of irresponsible behaviour by directors and managers if it appears that earnings will not meet performance targets. They might be tempted to adopt measures that increase the PBT but which are not in the best interest of the shareholders.

This risk is specifically addressed in the Johnson Matthey Annual Report as shown in the following extract:

> The Committee has discretion in awarding annual bonuses and is able to consider corporate performance on environmental, social and governance issues when awards are made to executive directors. The Committee ensures that the incentive structure for senior management does not raise environmental, social and governance risks by inadvertently motivating irresponsible behaviour.

This would not preclude companies from taking typical steps such as **deferring discretionary expenditure,** e.g. research, advertising, training expenditure; **deferring amortisation,** e.g. making optimistic sales projections in order to classify research as development expenditure which can be capitalised; and **reclassifying** deteriorating current assets as non-current assets to avoid the need to recognise a loss under the lower of cost and net realisable value rule applicable to current assets.

The introduction of a mandatory standard that changes management's ability to adopt such measures **affects wealth distribution** within the firm. For example, if managers are unable to delay the amortisation of development expenditure, then bonuses related to profit will be lower and there will effectively have been a transfer of wealth from managers to shareholders.

5.3 Why do we need standards to be mandatory?

Mandatory standards are needed, therefore, to define the way in which accounting numbers are presented in financial statements, so that their measurement and presentation are less subjective. It had been thought that the accountancy profession could obtain uniformity of disclosure by persuasion but, in reality, the profession found it difficult to resist management pressures.

During the 1960s the financial sector of the UK economy lost confidence in the accountancy profession when internationally known UK-based companies were seen to have published financial data that were materially incorrect. Shareholders are normally unaware that this occurs and it tends only to become public knowledge in restricted circumstances, e.g. when a third party has a **vested interest** in revealing adverse facts following a takeover, or when a company falls into the hands of an administrator, inspector or liquidator, **whose duty it is to enquire and report** on shortcomings in the management of a company.

Two scandals which disturbed the public at the time, GEC/AEI and Pergamon Press,[2] were both made public in the restricted circumstances referred to above, when financial reports prepared from the same basic information disclosed a materially different picture.

5.3.1 GEC takeover of AEI in 1967

The first calamity for the profession involved GEC Ltd in its takeover bid for AEI Ltd when the pre-takeover accounts prepared by the old AEI directors differed materially from the post-takeover accounts prepared by the new AEI directors.

AEI profit forecast for 1967 as determined by the old AEI directors

AEI Ltd produced a **profit forecast of £10 million** in November 1967 and recommended its shareholders to reject the GEC bid. The forecast had the blessing of the auditors, in as much as they said that it had been prepared on a fair and reasonable basis and in a manner consistent with the principles followed in preparing the annual accounts. The investing public would normally have been quite satisfied with the forecast figure and the process by which it was produced. Clearly, AEI would not subsequently have produced other information to show that the picture was materially different from that forecast.

However, GEC was successful with its bid and as a result it was GEC's directors who had control over the preparation of the AEI accounts for 1967.

AEI profit for 1967 as determined by the new AEI directors

Under the control of the directors of GEC the accounts of AEI were produced for 1967 showing **a loss of £4.5 million**. Unfortunately, this was from basic information that was largely the same as that used by AEI when producing its profit forecast.

There can be two reasons for the difference between the figures produced. Either the facts have changed or the judgements made by the directors have changed. In this case, it seems there was a change in the facts to the extent of a post-acquisition closure of an AEI factory; this explained £5 million of the £14.5 million difference between the forecast profit and the actual loss. The remaining £9.5 million arose because of differences in judgement. For example, the new directors took a different view of the value of stock and work-in-progress.

5.3.2 Pergamon Press

Audited accounts were produced by Pergamon Press Ltd for 1968 showing a profit of approximately £2 million.

An independent investigation by Price Waterhouse suggested that this profit should be reduced by 75% because of a number of unacceptable valuations, e.g. there had been a failure to reduce certain stock to the lower of cost and net realisable value, and there had been a change in policy on the capitalisation of printing costs of back issues of scientific journals – they were treated as a cost of closing stock in 1968, but not as a cost of opening stock in 1968.

5.3.3 Public view of the accounting profession following these cases

It had long been recognised that accountancy is not an exact science, but it had not been appreciated just how much latitude there was for companies to produce vastly different results based on the same transactions. Given that the auditors were perfectly happy to sign that accounts showing either a £10 million profit or a £4.5 million loss were true and fair, the public felt the need for action if investors were to have any trust in the figures that were being published.

The difficulty was that each firm of accountants tended to rely on precedents within its own firm in deciding what was true and fair. This is fine until the public becomes aware that profits depend on the particular firm or partner who happens to be responsible for the audit. The auditors were also under pressure to agree to practices that the directors wanted because there were no professional mandatory standards.

This was the scenario that galvanised the City press and the investing public. An embarrassed, disturbed profession announced in 1969, via the ICAEW, that there was a majority view supporting the introduction of Statements of Standard Accounting Practice to supplement the legislation.

5.4 Arguments in support of standards

The setting of standards has both supporters and opponents. In this section we discuss credibility, discipline and comparability.

Credibility

The accountancy profession would lose all credibility if it permitted companies experiencing similar events to produce financial reports that disclosed markedly different results simply because they could select different accounting policies. Uniformity was seen as essential if financial reports were to disclose a true and fair view. However, it has been a continuing view in the UK that standards should not be a comprehensive code of rigid rules – they were not to supersede the exercise of informed judgement in determining what constituted a true and fair view in each circumstance.

Discipline

It could be argued that if companies were left to their own devices without the need to observe standards, they would eventually be disciplined by the financial market, for example, an incorrect capitalisation of research expenditure as development would eventually become apparent when sales growth was not as expected by the market. However, this could take a long time. Better to have mandatory standards in place to protect those who rely on the annual accounts when making credit, loan and investment decisions.

Directors are under pressure to maintain and improve the market valuation of their company's securities. There is a temptation, therefore, to influence any financial statistic that has an impact on the market valuation, such as the trend in the earnings per share (EPS) figure, the net asset backing for the shares or the gearing ratios which show the level of borrowing.

This is an ever-present risk and the Financial Reporting Council showed awareness of the need to impose discipline when it stated in its annual review, November 1991, para. 2.4, that the high level of company failures in the then recession, some of which were associated with **obscure financial reporting**, damaged confidence in the high standard of reporting by the majority of companies.

Comparability

In addition to financial statements allowing investors to evaluate the management's perform-ance i.e. their stewardship, they should also allow investors to make predictions of future cash flows and comparisons with other companies.

In order to be able to make valid inter-company comparisons of performance and trends, investors need relevant and reliable data that have been standardised. If companies were to continue to apply different accounting policies to identical commercial activities, innocently or with the deliberate intention of disguising bad news, then investors could be misled in making their investment decisions.

5.5 Arguments against standards

We have so far discussed the arguments in support of standard setting. However, there are also arguments against. These are consensus-seeking and overload.

Consensus-seeking

Consensus-seeking can lead to the issuing of standards that are over-influenced by those with easiest access to the standard setters – particularly as the subject matter becomes more complex, as with e.g. capital instruments.

Overload

Standard overload is not a new charge. However, it takes a number of conflicting forms, e.g.:

- There are too many/too few standards.
- Standards are too detailed/not sufficiently detailed.
- Standards are general-purpose and fail to recognise the differences between large and small entities and interim and final accounts.
- There are too many standard setters with differing requirements, e.g. FASB, IASB, ASB, and national Stock Exchange listing requirements.

5.6 Standard setting and enforcement in the UK under the Financial Reporting Council (FRC)

The FRC was set up in 1990 as an independent regulator to set and enforce accounting standards. It operated through the Accounting Standards Board (ASB) and the Financial Reporting Review Panel (FRRP) to encourage high-quality financial reporting. Due to its success in doing this, the government decided, following corporate disasters such as Enron in the USA, to give it a more proactive role from 2004 onwards in the areas of corporate governance, compliance with statutes and accounting and auditing standards.

The FRC structure has evolved to meet changing needs. This is illustrated by two recent changes. For example, its implementation of the recommendation of the Morris Review[3] in 2005 that the FRC should oversee the regulation of the actuarial profession by creating the Board for Actuarial Standards and then by its restructuring of its own Council and Main Board by merging the two into a single body to make the FRC more effective with regard to strategy.

The FRC's structure in 2009 is shown in Figure 5.1.

Figure 5.1 The Financial Reporting Council organisation chart

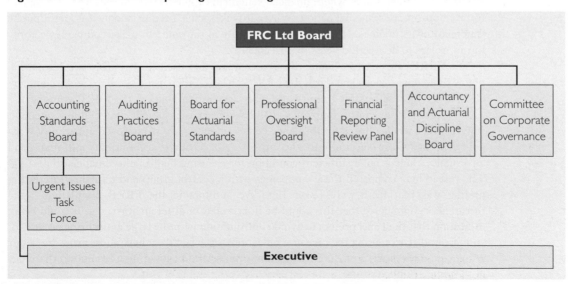

5.7 The Accounting Standards Board (ASB)

The ASB issues mandatory standards (SSAPs and FRSs), confirms that SORPs are not in conflict with its mandatory standards and issues statements of best practice (such as those on OFR and Interim Reports).

5.7.1 SSAPs and FRSs

There are a number of extant standards relating to each of the financial statements. For example, there are standards relating to the measurement and disclosure of assets in the statement of financial position covering goodwill, research and development, tangible non-current assets and inventories and of liabilities covering deferred tax, current tax and pension liabilities.

A full list of current standards is available on the FRC website http://www.frc.org.uk/asb/technical/standards.cfm

5.7.2 Statements of Recommended Practice (SORPs)

SORPs are produced for specialised industries or sectors to supplement accounting standards and are checked by the Financial Sector and Other Special Industries Committee and the Committee on Accounting for Public-benefit Entities to ensure that they are not in conflict with current or future FRSs.

There are SORPs issued by specialised industry bodies such as the Oil Industry Accounting Committee and the Association of British Insurers and by not-for-profit bodies such as the Charity Commission and Universities UK.

5.8 The Financial Reporting Review Panel (FRRP)

The FRRP has a policing role with responsibility for overseeing some 2,500 companies. It is completely independent of the ASB. It has a solicitor as chairman and the other members include accountants, bankers and lawyers. Its role is to review material departures from accounting standards and, where financial statements are defective, to require the company to take appropriate remedial action. Where it makes such a requirement, it issues a public statement of its findings. It has the right to apply to the court to make companies comply but it prefers to deal with defects by agreement.

The FRRP cannot create standards. If a company has used an inappropriate accounting policy that contravenes a standard, the FRRP can act. If there is no standard and a company chooses the most favourable from two or more accounting policies, the FRRP cannot act.

A research study[4] into companies that have been the subject of a public statement suggests that when a firm's performance comes under severe strain, even apparently well-governed firms can succumb to the pressure for creative accounting, and that good governance alone is not a sufficient condition for ensuring high-quality financial reporting. The researchers compared these companies with a control group and a further interesting finding was that there were fewer Big Five auditors in the FRRP population – the researchers commented that this could be interpreted in different ways, e.g. it could be an indication that the Panel prefers to avoid confrontation with the large audit firms because of an increased risk of losing the case or a reflection of the fact that these audit firms are better at managing the politics of the investigation process and negotiating a resolution that does not lead to a public censure.

5.8.1 Criticism of the FRRP for being reactive

The FRRP has, since its establishment in 1988, been a reactive body responding to issues appearing in individual sets of accounts to which it is alerted by public or specific complaint. This led to the criticism that the FRRP was not addressing significant financial reporting issues and was simply dealing with disclosure matters that had readily been detected. The Panel consequently commissioned a pilot study in 2000 which reviewed selected companies for non-compliance. The pilot study revealed no major incidents of non-compliance and in November 2001 the FRRP decided that a proactive approach was unnecessary.

5.8.2 Investor pressure for a more proactive stance

However, regulatory bodies have to be responsive to a material change in investor attitudes and act if there is likely to be a loss of confidence in financial reports which could damage the capital markets. Such a loss of confidence arose following the US accounting scandals such as Enron. Regulators could no longer be simply reactive even though there had been no evidence in the UK of material non-compliance.

Proactive stance – European initiative

The Committee of European Securities Regulators (CESR), at the request of the European Commission, has developed proposals which would require enforcement bodies to take a proactive approach. In its *Proposed Statement of Principles of Enforcement of Accounting Standards in Europe* issued in 2002, it proposed that there should be a selection of companies and documents to be examined using a risk-based approach or a mixed model where a risk-based approach is combined with a rotation and/or a sampling approach – a pure rotation approach or a pure reactive approach would not be acceptable.[5]

Proactive stance – UK initiative

The Coordinating Group on Accounting and Auditing Issues recommended in its Final Report in 2003 that the FRRP should press ahead urgently with developing a proactive element to its work.[6]

The FRRP response to the new requirement for a proactive approach

The Panel proposed that there should be:

● a stepped implementation with a minimum of 300 accounts being reviewed from 2004;

● the development of a risk-based approach to the selection of published accounts taking account of the risk that a particular set of accounts will not give a true and fair view of market stability and investor confidence.

Reviews should comprise an initial desk-check of selected risk areas or whole sets of accounts followed, where appropriate, with correspondence to chairpersons.

Whilst adopting a proactive approach, the FRRP has raised concerns that stakeholders might have a false expectation that the Panel is providing a guarantee that financial statements are true and fair, stressing that no system of enforcement can or should guarantee the integrity of a financial reporting regime.

5.8.3 The Financial Reporting Review Panel Activity Report

The Panel reported in its 2008 Report that it had reviewed 300 sets of accounts, been approached by 138 companies for further information or explanation and 88 companies had undertaken to reflect the Panel's comments in their future reporting. Most of this occurred pre-June 2007, before the dislocation in the markets.

Since June 2007, there have been major uncertainties that affect management's estimates of assets and liabilities in the Statement of Financial Position and the amount of revenue to recognise in the Statement of Comprehensive Income where measurement may be unreliable.

The Panel continues to take a consensual approach but it is important that directors, if they are to reduce the risk of Panel questioning, are transparent about specific risks and uncertainties that their companies are likely to experience.

The FRRP has announced (FRRP PN 123) the sectors on which it will be focusing in 2010/11. These are Commercial property, Advertising, Recruitment, Media and Information technology. These sectors have been selected because, as companies come out of recession and experience possible cash flow difficulties, discretionary spending might be reduced or delayed. The FRRP is planning to pay particular attention to the accounts of those companies which appear to apply aggressive policies compared with their peers.

5.9 Standard setting and enforcement in the US

Reporting standards are set by the Financial Accounting Standards Board (FASB) and enforced by the Securities Exchange Commission.

5.9.1 Standard setting by the FASB and other bodies

The Financial Accounting Standards Board (FASB) is responsible for setting accounting standards in the USA. The FASB is financed by a compulsory levy on public companies, which should ensure its independence. (The previous system of voluntary contributions ran the risk of major donors trying to exert undue influence on the Board.) FASB issues the following documents:

- Statements of Financial Accounting Standards, which deal with specific issues;
- Statements of Concepts, which give general information;
- Interpretations, which clarify existing standards.

There are other mandatory pronouncements from the Emerging Issues Task Force, the Accounting Principles Board (APB) which publishes Opinions and the American Institute of Certified Public Accountants (AICPA) which publishes Accounting Practice Bulletins and Opinions.

5.9.2 Enforcement by the SEC

The Securities and Exchange Commission (SEC) is responsible for requiring the publication of financial information for the benefit of shareholders. It has the power to dictate the form and content of these reports. The largest companies whose shares are listed must register with the SEC and comply with its regulations. The SEC monitors financial reports filed in great detail and makes useful information available to the public via its website (www.sec.gov). However, it is important to note that the majority of companies fall outside of the SEC's jurisdiction.

5.10 Why have there been differences in financial reporting?

Although there have been national standard-setting bodies, this has not resulted in uniform standards. A number of attempts have been made to identify reasons for differences in financial reporting.[7] The issue is far from clear but most writers agree that the following are among the main factors influencing the development of financial reporting:

- the character of the national legal system;
- the way in which industry is financed;
- the relationship of the tax and reporting systems;
- the influence and status of the accounting profession;
- the extent to which accounting theory is developed;
- accidents of history;
- language.

We will consider the effect of each of these.

5.10.1 The character of the national legal system

There are two major legal systems, that based on common law and that based on Roman law. It is important to recognise this because the legal systems influence the way in which behaviour in a country, including accounting and financial reporting, is regulated.

Countries with a legal system based on common law include England and Wales, Ireland, the USA, Australia, Canada and New Zealand. These countries rely on the application of equity to specific cases rather than a set of detailed rules to be applied in all cases. The effect in the UK, as far as financial reporting was concerned, was that there was limited legislation regulating the form and content of financial statements until the government was required to implement the EC Fourth Directive. The directive was implemented in the UK by the passing of the Companies Act 1981 and this can be seen as a watershed because it was the first time that the layout of company accounts had been prescribed by statute in England and Wales.

English common law heritage was accommodated within the legislation by the provision that the detailed regulations of the Act should not be applied if, in the judgement of the directors, strict adherence to the Act would result in financial statements that did not present a true and fair view.

Countries with a legal system based on Roman law include France, Germany and Japan. These countries rely on the codification of detailed rules, which are often included within their companies legislation. The result is that there is less flexibility in the preparation of financial reports in those countries. They are less inclined to look to fine distinctions to justify different reporting treatments, which is inherent in the common law approach.

However, it is not just that common law countries have fewer codified laws than Roman law countries. There is a fundamental difference in the way in which the reporting of commercial transactions is approached. In the common law countries there is an established practice of creative compliance. By this we mean that the spirit of the law is elusive[8] and management is more inclined to act with creative compliance in order to escape effective legal control. By creative compliance we mean that management complies with the form of the regulation but in a way that might be against its spirit, e.g. structuring leasing agreements in the most acceptable way for financial reporting purposes.

5.10.2 The way in which industry is financed

Accountancy is the art of communicating relevant financial information about a business entity to users. One of the considerations to take into account when deciding what is relevant is the way in which the business has been financed, e.g. the information needs of equity investors will be different from those of loan creditors. This is one factor responsible for international financial reporting differences because the predominant provider of capital is different in different countries.[9] Figure 5.2 makes a simple comparison between domestic equity market capitalisation and Gross Domestic Product (GDP).[10] The higher the ratio, the greater the importance of the equity market compared with loan finance.

We see that in the USA companies rely more heavily on individual investors to provide finance than in Europe or Japan. An active stock exchange has developed to allow shareholders to liquidate their investments. A system of financial reporting has evolved to satisfy a stewardship need where prudence and conservatism predominate, and to meet the capital market need for fair information[11] which allows interested parties to deal on an equal footing where the accruals concept and the doctrine of substance over form predominate. It is important to note that whilst equity has gained importance in all areas over the past ten years European statistics are *averages* that do not fully reflect the variation in sources of finance used between, say, the UK (equity investment is very important) and Germany (lending is more important). These could be important factors in the development of accounting.

In France and Germany, as well as equity investment having a lower profile historically, there is also a significant difference in the way in which shares are registered and transferred. In the UK, individual shareholders are entered onto the company's Register of Members. In France and Germany, many shares are bearer shares, which means that they are not registered in the individual investor's name but are deposited with a bank that has the authority to exercise a proxy. It could perhaps appear at first glance that the banks have

Figure 5.2 Domestic equity market capitalisation/gross domestic product

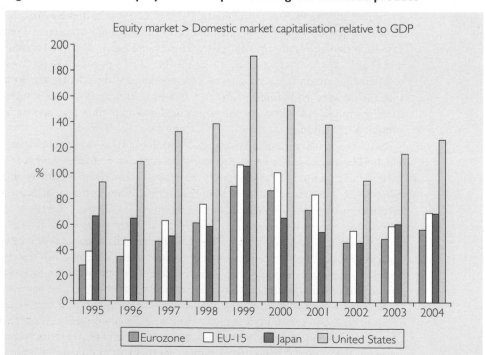

undue influence, but they state that, in the case of proxy votes, shareholders are at liberty to cast their votes as they see fit and not to follow the recommendations of the bank.[12] In addition to their control over proxy votes, the Big Three German banks, the Deutsche Bank, the Dresdner Bank and the Commerzbank, also have significant direct equity holdings, e.g. in 1992 the Deutsche Bank had a direct holding of 28% in Daimler Benz.[13]

There was an investigation carried out in the 1970s by the Gessler Commission into the ties between the Big Three and large West German manufacturing companies. The Commission established that the banks' power lay in the combination of the proxy votes, the tradition of the house bank which kept a company linked to one principal lender, the size of the banks' direct equity holdings and their representation on company supervisory boards.[14]

In practice, therefore, the banks are effectively both principal lenders and shareholders in Germany. As principal lenders they receive internal information such as cash flow forecasts which, as a result, is also available to them in their role as nominee shareholders. We are not concerned here with questions such as conflict of interest and criticisms that the banks are able to exert undue influence. Our interest is purely in the financial reporting implications, which are that the banks have sufficient power to obtain all of the information they require without reliance on the annual accounts. Published disclosures are far less relevant than in, say, the UK.

During the 1990s there was a growth in the UK and the USA of institutional investors, such as pension funds, which form an ever-increasing proportion of registered shareholders. In theory, the information needs of these institutional investors should be the same as those of individual investors. However, in practice, they might be in a position to obtain information by direct access to management and the directors. One effect of this might be that they will become less interested in seeking disclosures in the financial statements – they will have already picked up the significant information at an informal level.

5.10.3 The relationship of the tax and reporting systems

In the UK separate rules have evolved for computing profit for tax and computing profit for financial reporting purposes in a number of areas. The legislation for tax purposes tends to be more prescriptive, e.g. there is a defined rate for capital allowances on fixed assets, which means that the reduction in value of fixed assets for tax purposes is decided by the government. The financial reporting environment is less prescriptive but this is compensated for by requiring greater disclosure. For example, there is no defined rate for depreciating fixed assets but there is a requirement for companies to state their depreciation accounting policy. Similar systems have evolved in the USA and the Netherlands.

However, certain countries give primacy to taxation rules and will only allow expenditure for tax purposes if it is given the same treatment in the financial accounts. In France and Germany, the tax rules effectively become the accounting rules for the accounts of individual companies, although the tax influence might be less apparent in consolidated financial statements.

This can lead to difficulties of interpretation, particularly when capital allowances, i.e. depreciation for tax purposes, are changed to secure public policy objectives such as encouraging investment in fixed assets by permitting accelerated write-off when assessing taxable profits. In fact, the depreciation charge against profit would be said by a UK accountant not to be fair, even though it could certainly be legal or correct.[15]

Depreciation has been discussed to illustrate the possibility of misinterpretation because of the different status and effect of tax rules on annual accounts. Other items that require careful consideration include inventory valuations, bad debt provisions, development expenditure and revaluation of non-current assets. There might also be public policy arrangements that are unique to a single country, e.g. the existence of special reserves to reduce taxable profits was common in Scandinavia. It has recently been suggested that level of connection between tax and financial reporting follows a predictable pattern.[16]

5.10.4 The influence and status of the accounting profession

The development of a capital market for dealing in shares created a need for reliable, relevant and timely financial information. Legislation was introduced in many countries requiring companies to prepare annual accounts and have them audited. This resulted in the growth of an established and respected accounting profession able to produce relevant reports and attest to their reliability by performing an audit.

In turn, the existence of a strong profession had an impact on the development of accounting regulations. It is the profession that has been responsible for the promulgation of accounting standards and recommendations in a number of countries, such as the UK, the USA, Australia, Canada and the Netherlands.

In countries where there has not been the same need to provide market-sensitive information, e.g. in Eastern Europe in the 1980s, accountants have been seen purely as bookkeepers and have been accorded a low status. This explains the lack of expertise among financial accountants. There was also a lack of demand for financial management skills because production targets were set centrally without the emphasis for maximising the use of scarce resources at the business entity level. The attributes that are valued in a market economy such as the exercise of judgement and the determination of relevant information were not required. This position has changed rapidly and there has been a growth in the training, professionalism and contribution for both financial and management accountants as these economies become market economies.

5.10.5 The extent to which accounting theory is developed

Accounting theory can influence accounting practice. Theory can be developed at both an academic and professional level, but for it to take root it must be accepted by the profession. For example, in the UK, theories such as current purchasing power and current cost accounting first surfaced in the academic world and there were many practising accountants who regarded them then and still regard them now, as academic.

In the Netherlands, professional accountants receive academic accountancy training as well as the vocational accountancy training that is typical in the UK. Perhaps as a result of that, there is less reluctance on the part of the profession to view academics as isolated from the real world. This might go some way to explaining why it was in the Netherlands that we saw general acceptance by the profession for the idea that for information to be relevant it needed to be based on current value accounting. Largely as a result of pressure from the Netherlands, the Fourth Directive contained provisions that allowed member states to introduce inflation accounting systems.[17]

Attempts have been made to formulate a conceptual framework for financial reporting in countries such as the UK, the USA, Canada and Australia,[18] and the International Standards Committee has also contributed to this field. One of the results has been the closer collaboration between the regulatory bodies, which might assist in reducing differences in underlying principles in the longer term.

5.10.6 Accidents of history

The development of accounting systems is often allied to the political history of a country. Scandals surrounding company failures, notably in the USA in the 1920s and 1930s and in the UK in the 1960s and 1980s, had a marked impact on financial reporting in those countries. In the USA the Securities and Exchange Commission was established to control listed companies, with responsibility to ensure adequate disclosure in annual accounts. Ever-increasing control over the form and content of financial statements through improvements in the accounting standard-setting process has evolved from the difficulties that arose in the UK.

International boundaries have also been crossed in the evolution of accounting. In some instances it has been a question of pooling of resources to avoid repeating work already carried out elsewhere, e.g. the Norwegians studied the report of the Dearing Committee in the UK before setting up their new accounting standard-setting system in the 1980s.[19] Other changes in nations' accounting practices have been a result of external pressure, e.g. Spain's membership of the European Community led to radical changes in accounting,[20] while the Germans influenced accounting in the countries they occupied during the Second World War.[21] Such accidents of history have changed the course of accounting and reduced the clarity of distinctions between countries.

5.10.7 Language

Language has often played an important role in the development of different methods of accounting for similar items. Certain nationalities are notorious for speaking only their own language, which has prevented them from benefiting from the wisdom of other nations. There is also the difficulty of translating concepts as well as phrases, where one country has influenced another.

5.11 Efforts to standardise financial reports

Both the European Union (EU) and the International Accounting Standards Board have been active in seeking to standardise financial reports.

5.11.1 The European Union[22]

The European Economic Community was established by the Treaty of Rome in 1957 to promote the free movement of goods, services, people and capital. It was renamed in 1993 the European Union (the EU).

A major aim has been to create a single financial market that requires access by investors to financial reports which have been prepared using common financial reporting standards. The initial steps were the issue of accounting directives – these were the Fourth Directive, the Seventh Directive and the Eighth Directive.

The **Fourth Directive** – this prescribed the information to be published by individual companies:

- annual accounts comprising a profit and loss account and statement of financial position with supporting notes to the accounts;
- a choice of formats, e.g. vertical or horizontal presentation;
- the assets and liabilities to be disclosed;
- the valuation rules to be followed, e.g. historical cost accounting;
- the general principles underlying the valuations, e.g. prudence to avoid overstating asset values and understating liabilities, and consistency to allow for inter-period comparisons;
- various additional information such as research and development activity and any material events that have occurred after the end of the financial year.

The directive needs to be routinely updated to reflect changing commercial conditions, e.g. additional provisions relating to the reporting of off-balance sheet commitments.

The **Seventh Directive** requires:

- the consolidation of subsidiary undertakings across national borders, i.e. world-wide;
- uniform accounting policies to be followed by all members of the group;
- the elimination of the effect of inter-group transactions, e.g. eliminating inter-company profit and cancelling inter-company debt;
- the use of the formats prescribed in the Fourth Directive adjusted for the treatment of minority interests.

The **Eighth Directive** issued in 1984 defined the qualifications of persons responsible for carrying out the statutory audits of the accounting documents required by the Fourth and Seventh Directives.

Just as the Fourth and Seventh Directives have been updated to reflect changing commercial practices, so the Eighth Directive has required updating. In the case of the Eighth Directive the need has been to restore investor confidence in the financial reporting system following the financial scandals in the US with Enron and in the EU with Parmalat.

The amended directive requires:

- independent audit committees to have one financial expert as a member;
- audit committees to recommend an auditor for shareholder approval;
- audit partners to be rotated every seven years;
- public oversight to ensure quality audits;
- the group auditor bears full responsibility for the audit report even where other audit firms may have audited subsidiaries around the world.

It clarifies the duties and ethics of statutory auditors but has not prohibited auditors from carrying out consultancy work which some strongly criticise on the grounds that it compromises the independence of auditors.

5.11.2 The International Accounting Standards Board

The International Accounting Standards Committee (IASC) was established in 1973 by the professional accounting bodies of Australia, Canada, France, Germany, Japan, Mexico, the Netherlands, the UK, Ireland and the USA.

The IASC was restructured, following a review between 1998 and 2000, to give an improved balance between geographical representation, technical competence and independence.[23] The nineteen trustees of the IASC represent a range of geographical and professional interests and are responsible for raising the organisation's funds and appointing the members of the Board and the Standing Interpretations Committee (SIC). The International Accounting Standards Board (IASB) has responsibility for all technical matters including the preparation and implementation of standards. The IASB website (www.iasb.org.uk) explains that:

The IASB is committed to developing, in the public interest, a single set of high quality, understandable and enforceable global accounting standards that require transparent and comparable information in general purpose financial statements. In addition, the IASB co-operates with national accounting standard-setters to achieve convergence in accounting standards around the world.

The IASB adopted all current IASs and began issuing its own standards, International Financial Reporting Standards (IFRSs). The body of IASs, IFRSs and associated interpretations are referred to collectively as 'IFRS'.

The process of producing a new IFRS is similar to the processes of some national accounting standard setters. Once a need for a new (or revised) standard has been identified, a steering committee is set up to identify the relevant issues and draft the standard. Drafts are produced at varying stages and are exposed to public scrutiny. Subsequent drafts take account of comments obtained during the exposure period. The final standard is approved by the Board and an effective date agreed. IFRS currently in effect are referred to throughout the rest of this book. The IASC also issued a *Framework for the Preparation and Presentation of Financial Statements*.[24] This continues to assist in the development of accounting standards and improve harmonisation by providing a basis for reducing the number of accounting treatments permitted by IFRS. Translations of IFRS have been prepared and published, making the standards available to a wide audience, and the IASB has a mechanism to issue interpretations of the standards.

It is interesting to see how by 2009 more than 100 jurisdictions have permitted or mandated the use of IFRS and the process is continuing throughout the world.

Position in the EU

The EU recognised that the Accounting Directives which provided accounting rules for limited liability companies were not, in themselves, sufficient to meet the needs of companies raising capital on the international securities markets. There was a need for more detailed standards so that investors could have adequate and transparent disclosures that would allow them to assess risks and opportunities and make inter-company comparisons – standards that would result in annual reports giving a fair view.

The IASB is the body that produces such standards and from 2005 the EU required[25] the consolidated accounts of all listed companies to comply with International Financial Reporting Standards. However, to give the IFRS legal force within the EU, each IFRS has to be endorsed by the EU.

Position in non-EU countries

The role of IFRSs in the following non-EU countries is:

- Australia – issues IFRSs as national equivalents.

- Canada – plans to adopt IFRSs as Canadian Financial Reporting Standards, effective 2011.

- China – all listed companies in China must comply with IFRS from 1 January 2007.

- India – plans to adopt IFRSs as Indian Financial Reporting Standards, effective 2011.

- Japan – in 2005 the Accounting Standards Board of Japan (ASBJ) and the IASB launched a joint project to establish convergence between Japanese GAAP and IFRS with full convergence to be achieved by 2011. It is important to recognise that existing Japanese GAAP financial statements are of a high standard with many issuers listed on international exchanges. The effect of convergence will give an additional advantage of being more comparable to other listed companies using global standards.

- Malaysia – plans to bring Malaysian GAAP into full convergence with IFRSs, effective 1 January 2012.

- New Zealand – issues IFRSs as national equivalents.

- Singapore – the Accounting Standards Council is empowered to prescribe accounting standards and the broad policy intention is to adopt IFRS after considering whether any modifications are required.

It is important to note that if a company wishes to describe its financial statements as complying with IFRS, IAS 1 requires the financial statements to comply with all the requirements of each applicable standard and each applicable interpretation. This clearly outlaws the practice of 'IAS-lite' reporting, observed in the 1990s, where companies claimed compliance with IASs while neglecting some of their more onerous requirements.

Extant IFRS are as follows:

IAS 1   Presentation of financial statements

IAS 2   Inventories

IAS 7   Statement of cash flows

IAS 8   Accounting policies, changes in accounting estimates and errors

IAS 10   Events after the reporting period

IAS 11   Construction contracts

IAS 12   Income taxes

IAS 16   Property, plant and equipment

IAS 17   Leases

IAS 18   Revenue

IAS 19   Employee benefits

IAS 20   Accounting for government grants and disclosure of government assistance

IAS 21   The effects of changes in foreign exchange rates

IAS 23   Borrowing costs

IAS 24   Related party disclosures

IAS 26   Accounting and reporting by retirement benefit plans

IAS 27   Consolidated and separate financial statements

IAS 28   Investments in associates

IAS 29   Financial reporting in hyperinflationary economies

IAS 31   Interests in joint ventures

IAS 32   Financial instruments: Presentation

IAS 33   Earnings per share

IAS 34   Interim financial reporting

IAS 36   Impairment of assets

IAS 37   Provisions, contingent liabilities and contingent assets

IAS 38   Intangible assets

IAS 39   Financial instruments: recognition and measurement

IAS 40   Investment properties

IAS 41   Agriculture

IFRS 1   (Revised) First-time adoption of International Financial Reporting Standards

IFRS 2   Share-based payment

IFRS 3   (Revised) Business combinations

IFRS 4   Insurance contracts

IFRS 5   Non-current assets held for sale and discontinued operations

IFRS 6   Exploration for and evaluation of mineral resources

IFRS 7   Financial instruments disclosures

IFRS 8   Operating segments

IFRS 9   Financial Instruments (Phase 1)

5.12 What is the impact of changing to IFRS?

Making the transition to IFRS is no trivial task for companies, as comparative figures must also be restated. As the date of transition approaches many companies have published restatements reconciling previously published figures with figures computed and presented in accordance with IFRS. These reconciliations have proved a fertile ground for surveys by firms of accountants and academics.

15.12.1 Net income change

In some instances the changes have a dramatic effect on headline figures, e.g. the Dutch company, Wessanen, reported an increase of over 400% in its net income figure when the Dutch GAAP accounts were restated under IFRS. In other cases, there may be some large adjustments to individual balances, but the net effect may be less obvious.

15.12.2 Asset and liability changes

In certain countries there will be major changes in specific components of equity in the year of transition as particular assets or liabilities fall to be recognised (differently) from in the past. For example, the European hotel group, Accor, reported a reduction in total assets of only 1% when its 2004 statement of financial position was restated from French GAAP to IFRS, but within this, 'other receivables and accruals' had fallen by €294 million, a reduction of over 30% of the previously reported balance. In the UK many companies have made increased provisions for deferred tax liabilities on revalued properties and Australian companies have made large adjustments to their statements of financial position through the de-recognition of intangible assets.

In the short term, these changes in reported figures can have important consequences for companies' contractual obligations (e.g. they may not be able to maintain the level of liquidity required by their loan agreements) and their ability to pay dividends. There may be motivational issues to consider where staff bonuses have traditionally been based on reported accounting profit. As a result, companies may find that they need to adjust their management accounting system to align it more closely with IFRS.

15.12.3 Volatility in the accounts

In most countries the use of IFRS will mean that earnings and statement of financial position values will be more volatile than in the past. This could be quite a culture shock for analysts and others used to examining trends that follow a fairly predictable straight line.

While the change to IFRS has been covered in the professional and the more general press, it is not clear whether users of financial statements fully appreciate the effect of the change in accounting regulations, although surveys by KPMG (www.kpmg.co.uk/pubs/215748.pdf) and PricewaterhouseCoopers (www.pwchk.com/home/eng/ifrs_euro_investors_view_feb2006.html) indicated that most analysts and investors were confident that they understood the implications of the change.

5.13 Progress towards adoption by the USA of international standards

Global standards will only be achieved when the US fully adopts IFRSs to replace existing US GAAP. This process started in October 2002 when the IASB and the SEC jointly published details of what is known as the Norwalk Agreement. This included an undertaking to make their financial reporting standards fully compatible as soon as possible and to coordinate future work programmes to maintain that compatibility and to eventually mandate the use of IFRS by US listed companies. The process started with the Norwalk Agreement, followed by the IASB carrying out a Convergence Programme and finally joint standards being issued. The detailed progress was as follows.

5.13.1 The Norwalk Agreement

At their joint meeting in Norwalk in 2002, the Financial Accounting Standards Board (FASB) and the International Accounting Standards Board (IASB) committed to the development of high-quality, compatible accounting standards that could be used for both domestic and cross-border financial reporting aiming to:

● make their existing financial reporting standards fully compatible by undertaking a short-term project aimed at removing a variety of individual differences between US GAAP and International Financial Reporting Standards; and

● remove other differences between IFRSs and US GAAP remaining at 1 January 2005 (when IFRS became compulsory for consolidated accounts in Europe) through coordination of their future work programmes by undertaking discrete, substantial projects on which both Boards would work concurrently.

5.13.2 The Short-term Project

The aim was for the IASB and FASB to remove minor differences by changing their standard. For example, the IASB was to change IAS 11 *Construction Contracts*, IAS 12 *Income Taxes*, IAS 14 *Segment Reporting* and IAS 28 *Joint Ventures*, and the FASB was to change Inventory costs, Earnings per share and Research and Development costs.

By 2008 a number of projects were completed. For example, the FASB issued new or amended standards to bring standards in line with IFRS, e.g. it adopted the IFRS approach to accounting for research and development assets acquired in a business combination (SFAS 141R); in others the IASB converged IFRS with US GAAP, e.g. the new standard on borrowing costs (IAS 23 revised) and segment reporting (IFRS 8), and proposed changes to IAS 12 *Income taxes*.

The SEC was sufficiently persuaded by the progress made by the Boards that in 2007 it removed the reconciliation requirement for non-US companies that are registered in the USA and accepts the use IFRSs as issued by the IASB.

5.13.3 Plans for 2009–16

The intention is for the development of agreed standards to continue with a view to US publicly traded companies being permitted on a phased basis to use IFRS for their financial reports by 2015.

However, there is uncertainty at this time whether the target dates can be achieved because:

- attention might be diverted towards reacting to the credit crunch with an emphasis on going concern considerations and a review of fair value accounting; and

- there might be a political pressure on the SEC by members in Congress to delay mandating the use of IFRS for US companies; they might perhaps consider the lead time to be over-ambitious and also question the quality and universal enforceability of IFRS standards. It has to be recognised that it is a major step for the US to move from its rule based US GAAP to the IASB principle based IFRSs.

The SEC is considering (and perhaps have to be satisfied on?) progress in a number of areas such as improvements in IFRSs, IASB funding and accountability, the interface between XBRL and IFRS and improvements in IFRS education and training. There is a risk in setting out these requirements that the process is delayed or changes/improvements are rushed through. However, it is clear that, in principle, the SEC is fully committed to all US companies being eventually mandated to start using IFRS in their SEC filings.

5.14 Advantages and disadvantages of global standards for publicly accountable entities

Publicly accountable entities are those whose debt or equity is publicly traded. Many are multinational and listed on a stock exchange in more than one country. The main advantages arising from the development of international standards are that it reduces the cost of reporting under different standards, makes it easier to raise cross-border finance, leads to a decrease in firms' costs of capital with a corresponding increase in share prices and means that it is possible for investors to compare performance.

However, one survey[26] carried out in the UK indicated that finance directors and auditors surveyed felt that IFRSs undermined UK reporting integrity. In particular, there was little support for the further use of fair values as a basis for financial reporting which was regarded as making the accounts less reliable with comments such as, 'I think the use of fair values increases the subjective nature of the accounts and confuses unqualified users.'

There was further reference to this problem of understanding with a further comment: 'IFRS/US GAAP have generally gone too far – now nobody other than the Big 4 technical departments and the SEC know what they mean. The analyst community doesn't even bother trying to understand them – so who exactly do the IASB think they are satisfying?'

5.15 How do reporting requirements differ for non-publicly accountable entities?

Governments and standard setters have realised that there are numerous small and medium-sized businesses that do not raise funds on the stock exchange and do not prepare general purpose financial statements for external users.

5.15.1 Role of small firms in the UK economy

Small firms play a major role in the UK economy and are seen to be the main job creators. Interesting statistics on SMEs from a report[27] carried out by Warwick Business School showed:

By size:

2,200,000 businesses have no employees (about 61% of SMEs).

1,450,000 businesses have an annual turnover of less than £50,000 (about 40% of SMEs).

350,000 businesses have less than £10,000 worth of assets.

By legal form:

Almost two in three businesses are sole traders (2,400,000 businesses).

Less than one in four businesses are limited liability companies (870,000 businesses).

About one in ten businesses are partnerships (including limited liability partnerships).

By age:

The majority of businesses (51%) are aged more than fifteen years (1,900,000 businesses).

About 7% of SMEs are start-ups (aged less than two years) (250,000 businesses).

By growth rate:

About 11% of businesses (320,000 businesses) are high growth businesses, having an average turnover growth of 30%, or more, per annum over a period going back up to three years.

Certain companies are relieved of statutory and mandatory requirements on account of their size.

5.15.2 Statutory requirements

Every year the directors are required to submit accounts to the shareholders and file a copy with the Registrar of Companies. In recognition of the cost implications and need for different levels of privacy, there is provision for small and medium-sized companies to file abbreviated accounts.

A small company satisfies two or more of the following conditions:

● Turnover does not exceed £6.5 million.

● Assets do not exceed £3.26 million.

● Average number of employees does not exceed 50.

The company is excused from filing a profit and loss account, and the directors' report and statement of financial position need only be an abbreviated version disclosing major asset and liability headings. Its privacy is protected by excusing disclosure of directors' emoluments.

A medium-sized company satisfies two or more of the following conditions:

● Turnover does not exceed £25.9 million.

● Assets do not exceed £12.9 million.

● Average number of employees does not exceed 250.

It is excused far less than a small company: the major concession is that it need not disclose sales turnover and cost of sales, and the profit and loss account starts with the gross profit figure. This is to protect its competitive position.

5.15.3 National standards

Countries are permitted to adopt IFRS for publicly accountable entities and adopt their own national standards for non-publicly accountable entities. In the UK it is proposed to allow smaller entities to adopt the national standard Financial Reporting Standard for Smaller Entities (FRSSE) or the IFRS for SMEs issued by the IASB in July 2009.

First FRSSE issued[28]

In 1997 the ASB issued the first FRSSE. There was a concern as to the legality of setting different measurement and disclosure requirements, the ASB took legal advice which confirmed that smaller entities can properly be allowed exemptions or differing treatments in standards and UITFs provided such differences were justified **on rational grounds**.

How can rational grounds be established?

The test as to whether a decision is rational is based on obtaining answers to nine questions. If there are more negative responses than positive, there are rational grounds for a different treatment. The nine questions can be classified as follows:

Generic relevance

1 Is the standard essential practice for all entities?

2 Is the standard likely to be widely relevant to small entities?

Proprietary relevance

3 Would the treatment required by the standard be readily recognised by the proprietor or manager as corresponding to their understanding of the transaction?

Relevant measurement requirements

4 Is the treatment compatible with that used by the Inland Revenue in computing tax?

5 Are the measurement methods in a standard reasonably practical for small entities?

6 Is the accounting treatment the least cumbersome?

User relevance

7 Is the standard likely to meet information needs and legitimate expectations of the users?

8 Is the disclosure likely to be meaningful and comprehensible to users?

Expanding statutory provision

9 Do the requirements of the standard significantly augment the treatment required by statute?

How are individual standards dealt with in the FRSSE?

Standards have been dealt with in seven ways as explained in (a) to (g) below:

(a) Adopted without change

FRSSE adopted certain standards and UITFs without change.

(b) Not addressed

Certain standards were not addressed in the FRSSE, e.g. FRS 22 *Earnings per share*.

(c) Statements relating to groups are cross-referenced

If group accounts are to be prepared the FRSSE contains the cross-references required, e.g. to FRS 2 *Accounting for Subsidiary Undertakings*.

(d) Disclosure requirements removed

Certain standards apply but the disclosure requirement is removed, e.g. FRS 10 *Goodwill and Intangible Assets*.

(e) Disclosure requirements reduced

Certain standards apply but there is a reduced disclosure requirement, e.g. SSAP 9 *Stocks and Long-Term Contracts* applies but there is no requirement to sub-classify stock nor to disclose the accounting policy.

(f) Increased requirements

Certain standards are included with certain of the requirements reduced and other requirements increased, e.g. under FRS 8 *Related Party Disclosures* a new paragraph has been added, clarifying that the standard requires the disclosure of directors' personal guarantees for their company's borrowings.

(g) Main requirements included

Certain standards have their main requirements included, e.g. FRS 5 Reporting the substance of transactions, FRS 16 *Current Tax*, FRS 18 *Accounting Policies*, FRS 19 *Deferred Tax*.

The revised FRSSE

A revised FRSSE was issued in 2008 to incorporate changes in company law arising from the Companies Act 2006, which defines small companies as having an annual turnover of up to £6.5 million. No changes were made to the requirements that are based upon Generally Accepted Accounting Practice. Entities adopting the FRSSE continue to be exempt from applying all other accounting standards which reduces the volume of standards that a small entity needs to apply. They may of course still choose not to adopt the FRSSE and to comply with the other UK accounting standards and UITF Abstracts instead or, if they are companies, international accounting standards.

5.15.4 IFRS for SMEs

The IASB issued IFRS for SMEs in July 2009. The approach follows that adopted by the ASB with (a) some topics omitted e.g. earnings per share and segment reports, (b) simpler options allowed e.g. expensing rather than capitalising borrowing costs, (c) simpler recognition e.g. following an amortisation rather than an annual impairment review for goodwill and (d) simpler measurement e.g. using the cost method for associates rather than the equity method. SMEs are not prevented from adopting other options available under full IFRS and may elect to do this if they so decide.

However, in defining an SME it has moved away from the size tests towards a definition based on qualitative factors such as public accountability whereby an SME would be a business that does not have public accountability. Public accountability is implied if outside stakeholders have a high degree of either investment, commercial or social interest and if the majority of stakeholders have no alternative to the external financial report for financial information. The decision whether a business should be permitted to adopt IASB SME standards will be left to national jurisdictions subject to the right of any of the owners to require compliance with the full IFRSs.

Taking account of user needs and cost/benefit can be a complex task[29] and requires judgements to be made. For example:

User needs

Non-publicly accountable companies have a narrower range of users of their financial statements than publicly accountable companies which frequently have a detailed knowledge of the company with the facility to obtain information beyond the financial statements. This means that they may have less need to rely on the published financial statements.

However, whereas with publicly accountable companies there is a clear understanding that the primary user is the equity investor, the question remains for SMEs as to (a) the primary user, e.g. is it the non-managing owner, the long-term lender, the trade creditor or the tax authorities, and (b) what are the primary user's needs, e.g. maximising long-term growth, medium-term viability or short-term liquidity. Questions remain such as whether the financial statements need to be a stewardship report or decision-useful and, then, how are the characteristics such as relevance, reliability and comparability to be ranked and prioritised.

The approach to SME reporting has varied around the world. For example, in the USA there has not been an SME reporting regime in the sense of compliance with FRSs and IFRSs but SMEs have been permitted to prepare financial statements that are tax compliant; the IASB has only recently addressed the topic of SME reporting; in the UK the ASB has produced FRSSE, in drafting which it has taken a pragmatic approach when deciding which FRS provisions need not be applied by SMEs.

There is now a general awareness that the users of non-publicly-accountable companies are extremely diverse and steps are being taken to involve them in the standard-setting process, e.g. in Canada the Accounting Standards Board (AcSB) established a Differential Reporting Advisory Committee (DRAC) in 2000 as a standing committee to provide input to the standard-setting process by acting as a communication conduit for users, preparers and auditors of SMEs. In its response to the IASB Discussion Paper, *Preliminary Views on Accounting Standards for Small and Medium-sized Entities (SMEs)*, the AcSB restated that the approach taken by DRAC was to make a decision based on a cost/benefit approach making the interesting point that, as there were often fewer users of the financial statements, the cost per user could be excessive.

However, it appears that the research necessary to provide a rationale and conceptual approach to user needs is still some way off and the pragmatic approach taken by the ASB will inform financial reporting standards for SMEs for some time to come.

5.16 Evaluation of effectiveness of mandatory regulations

The events in the Sketchley plc takeover in 1990 suggest that mandatory regulations will not be effective.[30]

● In November 1989 Sketchley reported a fall in pre-tax profits for the half-year ended 30 December 1989 from £7.2 million to £5.4 million.

● In February 1990 Godfrey Davis Holdings made a bid to take over Sketchley.

● In March 1990 Sketchley issued a defence document forecasting pre-tax profits for the year ended 31 March 1990 of £6 million. Godfrey Davis Holdings withdrew in the light of these poor results.

● In March 1990, one week later, the Compass Group made a bid. Sketchley appointed a new management team and this second bid was defeated.

The new management team decided that the company had not made a profit of £6 million for the year ended 31 March 1990 after all – it had made a loss of £2 million.

Figure 5.3 Sketchley plc 1990 preliminary results

Sketchley plc 1990 preliminary results

		£000
(a)	Effect of more prudent accounting judgement (exercised by the new management team)	
	Reassessment of bad and doubtful debts	3,358
	Reassessment of stock provisions	2,770
	Write-off of fixed assets	773
		6,901
(b)	Provision for redundancy costs	554
(c)	Other items, including the effect of accounting policy changes	557
		8,012
	Profit before taxation, as forecast	6,000
	Loss before taxation, as reported	2,012

This has a familiar ring. It is very like the AEI situation of 1967, almost twenty-five years before. The adjustments made are shown in Figure 5.3.

Of course, it is not too difficult to visualise the motivation of the old and new management teams. The old team would take as favourable a view as possible of the asset values in order to resist a bid. The new team would take as unfavourable a view as possible, so that their performance would appear that much better in the future. It is clear, however, that the adjustments only arose on the change of management control, and without such a change we would have been basing investment decisions on a set of accounts that showed a £6 million profit rather than a £2 million loss.

There is often mention of the expectation gap, whereby shareholders appear to have lost faith in financial statements. The situation just discussed does little to persuade them that they are wrong. After all, what is the point of a regulatory system that ensures that the accounts present a fair view until the very moment when such a requirement is really necessary?

The area of provisioning and the exercise of judgement have finally been addressed by the regulators with the issue of national and international standards dealing with provisions.

5.16.1 Has the need for standards and effective enforcement fallen since 1990?

We only need to look at the unfortunate events with Enron and Ahold to arrive at an answer.

Enron

This is a company that was formed in the mid 1980s and became by the end of the 1990s the seventh-largest company in revenue terms in the USA. However, this concealed the fact that it had off balance sheet debts and that it had overstated its profits by more than $500 million – falling into bankruptcy (the largest in US corporate history) in 2001.

Ahold

In 2003 Ahold, the world's third-largest grocer, reported that its earnings for the past two years were overstated by more than $500 million as a result of local managers recording promotional allowances provided by suppliers to promote their goods at a figure greater than the cash received. This may reflect on the pressure to inflate profits when there are option schemes for managers.

5.17 Move towards a conceptual framework

The process of formulating standards has encouraged a constructive appraisal of the policies being proposed for individual reporting problems and has stimulated the development of a conceptual framework. For example, the standard on leasing introduced the idea in UK standards of considering the commercial substance of a transaction rather than simply the legal position.

When the ASC was set up in the 1970s there was no clear statement of accounting principles other than that accounts should be prudent, be consistent, follow accrual accounting procedures and be based on the initial assumption that the business would remain a going concern.

The immediate task was to bring some order into accounting practice. The challenge of this task is illustrated by the ASC report *A Conceptual Framework for Financial Accounting and Reporting: The Possibilities for an Agreed Structure* by R. Macve, published in 1981, which considered that the possibility of an agreed body of accounting principles was remote at that time.

However, the process of setting standards has stimulated accounting thought and literature to the point where, by 1989, the IASB had issued the *Framework for the Presentation and Preparation of Financial Statements*, IASC. In 1994, the ASB produced its exposure drafts of *Statement of Accounting Principles*, which appeared in final form in December 1999.

The development of conceptual frameworks is discussed further in Chapter 6.

Summary

It is evident from cases such as AEI/GEC and the Wiggins Group (see Question 4 in Chapter 2) that management cannot be permitted to have total discretion in the way in which it presents financial information in its accounts and rules are needed to ensure uniformity in the reporting of similar commercial transactions. Decisions must then be made as to the nature of the rules and how they are to be enforced.

In the UK the standard-setting bodies have tended to lean towards rules being framed as general principles and accepting the culture of voluntary compliance with explanation for any non-compliance.

Although there is a preference on the part of the standard setters to concentrate on general principles, there is a growing pressure from the preparers of the accounts for more detailed illustrations and explanations as to how the standards are to be applied.

Standard setters have recognised that small and medium-sized businesses are not publicly accountable to external users and are given the opportunity to prepare financial statements under standards specifically designed to be useful and cost effective.

The expansion in the number of multinational enterprises and transnational investments has led to a demand for a greater understanding of financial statements prepared in a range of countries. This has led to pressure for a single set of high quality international accounting standards. IFRS are being used increasingly for reporting to capital markets. At the same time, national standards are evolving to come into line with IFRS.

REVIEW QUESTIONS

1 Why is it necessary for financial reporting to be subject to (a) mandatory control and (b) statutory control?

2 How is it possible to make shareholders aware of the significance of the exercise of judgement by directors which can turn profits of £6 million into losses of £2 million?

3 'The effective working of the financial aspects of a market economy rests on the validity of the underlying premises of integrity in the conduct of business and reliability in the provision of information. Even though in the great majority of cases that presumption is wholly justified, there needs to be strong institutional underpinning.

   'That institutional framework has been shown to be inadequate. The last two to three years have accordingly seen a series of measures by the financial and business community to strengthen it. Amongst these has been the creation of the Financial Reporting Council and the bodies which it in turn established.'[31]

Discuss the above statement with particular reference to one of the following institutions: Accounting Standards Board, Financial Reporting Review Panel, and Urgent Issues Task Force. Illustrate with reference to publications or decisions from the institution you have chosen to discuss.

4 The increasing perception is that IFRS is overly complex and is complicating the search for appropriate forms of financial reporting for entities not covered by the EU Regulation.[32] Discuss whether (a) the current criteria for defining small and medium companies are appropriate; and (b) having a three-tiered approach with FRSSE for small, IFRS SME for medium-sized, and IFRS for large private companies might alleviate the problem.

5 'The most favoured way to reduce information overload was to have the company filter the available information set based on users' specifications of their needs.'[33] Discuss how this can be achieved given that users have differing needs.

6 'Every medium-sized European company should be required to prepare their financial reports in accordance with an IFRSSE which is similar in content to the UK's FRSSE.' Discuss.

7 Research[34] has indicated that narrative reporting in annual reports is not neutral, with good news being highlighted more than is supported by the statutory accounts and more than bad news. Discuss whether mandatory or statutory regulation could enforce objectivity in narrative disclosures and who should be responsible for such enforcement.

8 How does the regulatory framework for financial reporting in the UK differ from that in the USA? Which is better for particular interest groups and why?

9 Is it appropriate that scandal should have a role in the development of accounting regulation. Compare the reaction to the Enron financial statements in the early part of the twenty-first century with the reaction to the financial statements of AEI and Pergamon Press in the 1960s.

10 'The current differences between IASs and US GAAP are extensive and the recent pairing of the US Financial Accounting Standards Board and IASB to align IAS and US GAAP will probably result in IAS moving further from current UK GAAP.'[35]

Discuss the implication of this on any choice that non-listed UK companies might make regarding complying with IFRS rather than UK GAAP after 2005.

EXERCISES

Question 1

Constructive review of the regulators.

Required:
(a) Obtain a copy of the Financial Reporting Council's Annual Review.
(b) Prepare a profile of the members of the ASB.
(c) Comment on the strengths and weaknesses revealed by the profile.
(d) Advise (with reasons) on changes that you consider would strengthen the ASB.

Question 2

Obtain the financial statements of two companies based in different countries. Review the accounting policies notes. Analyse what the policies tell you about the regulatory environment in which the two companies are operating.

Question 3

Consider the interest of the tax authorities in financial reporting regulations. Explain why national tax authorities might be concerned about the transition from domestic accounting standards to IFRS in companies' annual reports.

References

1 G. Whittred and I. Zimmer, *Financial Accounting Incentive Effects and Economic Consequences*, Holt, Rinehart & Winston, 1992, p. 8.
2 E.R. Farmer, *Making Sense of Company Reports*, Van Nostrand Reinhold, 1986, p. 16.
3 www.hm-treasury.gov.uk/press_morris_05.htm
4 K. Peasnell, P. Pope and S. Young, 'Breaking the rules', *Accountancy International*, February 2000, p. 76.
5 CESR, *Proposed Statement of Principles of Enforcement of Accounting Standards in Europe*, CESR02–188b Principle 13, October 2002.
6 Coordinating Group on Accounting and Auditing Issues, *Final Report*, January 2003, para. 4.22.
7 C. Nobes and R. Parker, *Comparative International Accounting* (7th edition), Pearson Education, 2002, pp. 17–33.
8 J. Freedman and M. Power, *Law and Accountancy: Conflict and Cooperation in the 1990s*, Paul Chapman Publishing Ltd, 1992, p. 105.
9 For more detailed discussion see C. Nobes, 'Towards a general model of the reasons for international differences in financial reporting', *Abacus*, vol. 3, no. 2, 1998, pp. 162–187.
10 Source: www.eurocapitalmarkets.org/files/images/equity_capGDP_col.jpg
11 C. Nobes, *Towards 1992*, Butterworths, 1989, p. 15.
12 C. Randlesome, *Business Cultures in Europe* (2nd edition), Heinemann Professional Publishing, 1993, p. 27.
13 J.D. Daniels and L.H. Radebaugh, *International Business* (8th edition), Addison Wesley, 1998, p. 818.
14 Randlesome, *op. cit.*, p. 25.
15 Nobes, *op. cit.*, p. 8.
16 C. Nobes and H.R. Schwencke, 'Modelling the links between tax and financial reporting: a longitudinal examination of Norway over 30 years up to IFRS adoption', *European Accounting Review*, vol. 15, no. 1, 2006, pp. 63–87.

17 Nobes and Parker, *op. cit.*, pp. 73–75.

18 See S.P. Agrawal, P.H. Jensen, A.L. Meader and K. Sellers, 'An international comparison of conceptual frameworks of accounting', *The International Journal of Accounting*, vol. 24, 1989, pp. 237–249.

19 *Accountancy*, June 1989, p. 10.

20 See, e.g., B. Chauveau, 'The Spanish *Plan General de Contabilidad*: Agent of development and innovation?', *European Accounting Review*, vol. 4, no. 1, 1995, pp. 125–138.

21 See, e.g., P.E.M. Standish, 'Origins of the *Plan Comptable Général*: a study in cultural intrusion and reaction', *Accounting and Business Research*, vol. 20, no. 80, 1990, pp. 337–351.

22 http://ec.europa.eu/internal_market/accounting/ias_en.htm#regulation

23 For further details see *Accountancy*, International Edition, December 1999, p. 5.

24 *Framework for the Preparation and Presentation of Financial Statements*, IASC, 1989, adopted by IASB 2001.

25 EU, *Regulation of the European Parliament and of the Council on the Application of International Accounting Standards*, Brussels, 2002.

26 V. Beattie, S. Fearnley and T. Hines, 'Does IFRS undermine UK reporting integrity?', *Accountancy*, December 2008, pp. 56–57.

27 S. Fraser, *Finance for Small and Medium-Sized Enterprises: A Report on the 2004 UK Survey of SME Finances*, Centre for Small and Medium-Sized Enterprises, Warwick Business School, University of Warwick http://www.wbs.ac.uk/downloads/research/wbs-sme-main.pdf

28 *Financial Reporting Standard for Smaller Entities*, ASB, 1997.

29 G. Edwards, 'Performance measures', *CA Magazine*, October 2004.

30 *Student Financial Reporting*, ICAEW, 1991/2, p. 17.

31 *The State of Financial Reporting*, Financial Reporting Council Second Annual Review, November 1992.

32 S. Fearnley and T. Hines, 'How IFRS has Destabilised Financial Reporting for UK Non-Listed Entities', *Journal of Financial Regulation and Compliance*, 2007, 15(4), pp. 394–408.

33 V. Beattie, *Business Reporting: The Inevitable Change?*, ICAS, 1999, p. 53.

34 V. Tauringana and C. Chong, 'Neutrality of narrative discussion in annual reports of UK listed companies', *Journal of Applied Accounting Research*, 2004, 7(1), pp. 74–107.

35 Y. Dinwoodie and P. Holgate, 'Singing from the same songsheet?', *Accountancy*, May 2003, pp. 94–95

CHAPTER 6

Concepts – evolution of a global conceptual framework

6.1 Introduction

The main purpose of this chapter is to discuss the rationale underlying financial reporting standards.

Objectives

By the end of the chapter, you should be able to:

- discuss how financial accounting theory has evolved;
- discuss the accounting principles set out in:
  - the International Framework;
  - the UK Statement of Principles;
  - FASB Statements of Financial Accounting Concepts;
- comment critically on rule-based and principles-based approaches.

6.1.1 Different countries meant different financial statements

In the previous chapter we discussed the evolution of national and international accounting standards. The need for standards arose initially as a means of the accounting profession protecting itself against litigation for negligence by relying on the fact that financial statements complied with the published professional standards. The standards were based on existing best practice and little thought was given to a theoretical basis.

Standards were developed by individual countries and it was a reactive process. For example, in the US the Securities and Exchange Commission (SEC) was set up in 1933 to restore investor confidence in financial reporting following the Great Depression. The SEC is an enforcement agency that enforces compliance with US GAAP, which comprises rule-based standards issued by the FASB.

There has been a similar reactive response in other countries often reacting to major financial crises and fraud, which has undermined investor confidence in financial statements. As a result, there has been a variety of national standards with national enforcement, e.g. in the UK principles-based standards are issued by the ASB and enforced by the Financial Reporting Review Panel.

With the growth of the global economy there has been a corresponding growth in the need for global standards so that investors around the world receive the same fair view of a company's results regardless of the legal jurisdiction in which the company is registered.

National standards varied in their quality and in the level of enforcement. This is illustrated by the following comment[1] by the International Forum on Accountancy Development (IFAD):

> **Lessons from the crisis**
>
> . . . the Asian crisis showed that under the forces of financial globalisation it is essential for countries to improve . . . the supervision, regulation and transparency of financial systems . . . Efficiency of markets requires reliable financial information from issuers. With hindsight, it was clear that local accounting standards used to prepare financial statements did not meet international standards. Investors, both domestic and foreign, did not fully understand the weak financial position of the companies in which they were investing.

We will see in this chapter that, in addition to the realisation that global accounting standards were required, there was also growing interest in basing the standards on a conceptual framework rather than fire-fighting with pragmatic standards often dealing with an immediate problem. However, just as there have been different national standards, so there have been different conceptual frameworks.

Rationale for accounting standards

It is interesting to take a historical overview of the evolution of the financial accounting theory underpinning standards and guiding standard setters to see how it has moved through three phases from the empirical inductive to the deductive and then to a formalised conceptual framework.

6.2 Historical overview of the evolution of financial accounting theory

Financial accounting practices have not evolved in a vacuum. They are dynamic responses to changing macro and micro conditions which may involve political, fiscal, economic and commercial changes, e.g.:

- How to take account of changing prices?
  - Ignore and apply historical cost accounting.
  - Ignore if inflation is low as is the present situation in many European countries.
  - Have a modified historical cost system where tangible non-current assets are revalued which has been the norm in the UK.
  - Have a coherent current cost system as implemented in the 1970s in the Netherlands.
- How to deal with changing commercial practices?
  - Ignore if not a material commercial practice, e.g. leasing in the early 1970s.
  - Apply objective, tightly defined, legalistic-based criteria, e.g. to define finance and operating leases.
  - Apply subjective criteria, e.g. assess the economic substance of a leasing transaction to see if a finance lease because the risks and rewards have substantially been passed to the lessee.
  - Accept that it is not possible to effectively regulate companies to achieve consistent treatment of similar economic transactions unless there is a common standard enforced.

It is clear from considering just these two questions that there could be a variety of accounting treatments for similar transactions and, if annual financial reports are to be useful in making economic decisions,[2] there is a need for uniformity and consistency in reporting.

Attempts to achieve consistency have varied over time.

- An **empirical inductive approach** was followed by the accounting profession prior to 1970.
  This resulted in standards or reporting practices that were based on rationalising what happened in practice, i.e. it established best current practice as the norm. Under this approach there was a general disclosure standard, e.g. IAS 1 *Disclosure of Accounting Policies*, and standards for major specific items, e.g. IAS 2 *Inventories*.

- A **deductive approach** followed in the 1970s.
  This resulted in standards or reporting practices that were based on rationalising what happened in practice, i.e. it established best current practice as the norm but there was also an acceptance of alternatives. Under this approach the accounting theoretical underpinning of the standards was that accounts should be prepared on an accrual basis, with the matching of revenue and related costs and assuming that the business was a going concern. Standards tended to deal with specific major items, for example, a measurement standard for inventories or disclosure of accounting policies, for example, how non-current assets were depreciated. Both types of standard were responding to the fact that there were a number of alternative accounting treatments for the same commercial transaction.

- A **conceptual framework approach** was promoted in the 1980s.
  It was recognised that standards needed to be decision-useful, that they should satisfy cost/benefit criteria and that their implementation could only be achieved by consensus. Consensus was generally only achievable where there was a clearly perceived rationale underprinning a standard and, even so, alternative treatments were required in order to gain support.

- A conceptual framework approach in the twenty-first century – the mandatory model.
  Under this approach standard setters do not permit alternative treatments.

6.2.1 Empirical inductive approach

The empirical inductive approach looked at the practices that existed and attempted to generalise from them.

This tended to be how the technical departments of accounting firms operated. By rationalising what they did, they ensured that the firm avoided accepting different financial reporting practices for similar transactions, e.g. accepting unrealised profit appearing in the statement of comprehensive income of one client and not in another. The technical department's role was to advise partners and staff, i.e. it was a **defensive role** to avoid any potential charge from a user of the accounts that they had been misled.

Initially a technical circular was regarded as a private good and distribution was restricted to the firm's own staff. However, it then became recognised that it could benefit the firm if its practices were accepted as the industry benchmark, so that in the event of litigation it could rely on this fact.

When the technical advice ceased to be a private good, there was a perceived additional benefit to the firm if the nature of the practice could be changed from being a positive statement, i.e. this is how we report profits on uncompleted contracts, to a **normative** statement, i.e. this is how we report *and* this is how all other financial reporters *ought* to report.

Consequently, there has been a growing trend since the 1980s for firms to publish rationalisations for their financial reporting practices. It has been commercially prudent for them to do so. It has also been extremely helpful to academic accountants and their students.

Typical illustrations of the result of such empirical induction are the wide acceptance of the historical cost model and various concepts such as matching and realisation that we discussed in Chapter 2. The early standards were produced under this regime, e.g. the standard on inventory valuation.

This approach has played an important role in the evolution of financial reporting practices and will continue to do so. After all, it is the preparers of the financial statements and their auditors who are first exposed to change, whether economic, political or commercial. They are the ones who have to think their way through each new problem that surfaces, for example, how to measure and report financial instruments. This means that a financial reporting practice already exists by the time the problem comes to the attention of theoreticians.

The major reasons that it has been felt necessary to try other approaches are both pragmatic and theoretical.

Pragmatic reason

The main pragmatic reason is that the past procedure, whereby deduction was dependent upon generalisation from existing practice within each individual accounting practice, has become untenable. The accelerating rate of economic, political and commercial change leaves too little time for effective and uniform practices to evolve.

Theoretical reasons

The theoretical reasons relate to the acceptability of the income determined under the traditional historical cost model. There are three principal reasons:

- **True income**. We have seen that economists had a view that financial reports should report a true income, which differed from the accountants' view.
- **User-defined income – public**. There is a view that there may be a number of relevant incomes depending upon differing user needs which may be regarded as public goods.
- **User-defined income – private**. There is a view that there may be a number of relevant incomes depending upon differing user needs which may be regarded as private rather than public goods.

It was thought that the limitations implicit in the empirical inductive approach could be overcome by the deductive approach.

6.2.2 Deductive approach

The deductive approach is not dependent on existing practice, which is often perceived as having been tainted because it has been determined by finance directors and auditors. However, the problem remains: from whose viewpoint is the deduction to be made?

Possible alternatives to the preparers and auditors of the accounts are economists and users. However, economists are widely perceived as promoting unrealistic models and users as having needs so diverse that they cannot be realistically satisfied in a single set of accounts. Consider the attempts made to define income. Economists have supported the concept of a true income, while users have indicated the need for a range of relevant incomes.

True income

We have already seen in Chapter 3 that there is a significant difference between the accountant's income and the economist's income applying the ideas of Fisher and Hicks.

User needs and multiple incomes

Multiple measures of income, derived from the general price level adjusted accounting model, the replacement cost accounting model and the exit price accounting model, were considered in Chapter 4. Each model provides information that is relevant for different purposes, e.g. replacement cost accounting produces an income figure that indicates how much is available for distribution while still maintaining the operating capacity of the entity.

These income figures were regarded as a public good, i.e. cost-free to the user. Latterly, it has been recognised that there is a cost implication to the production of information, i.e. that it is not a public good; that standards should be capable of being empirically tested; and that consideration should be given to the economic consequences of standards. This has resulted in a concern that standards should deal with economic substance rather than form, e.g. the treatment of leases in IAS 17.[3]

It could be argued that the deductive approach to income, whether an economist's defined income or a theoretician's multiple income, has a basic weakness in that it gives priority to the information needs of only one user group – the investors. In the UK the ASB is quite explicit about this. The *Framework* is less clear about the primary focus, stating that financial statements are prepared to provide information that is useful in making economic decisions. The ASB has been supported by other academics[4] who have stated:

> As we have already noted that the needs of investors, creditors, employees and customers are not fundamentally different, it seems safe to look to the needs of present and potential investors as a guide . . .

There is little independent evidence put forward to support this view.

Where do we stand now?

We have seen that accounting theory was initially founded on generalisations from the accounting practices followed by practitioners. Then came the deductive approach of economists and theoreticians. The latter were not transaction based and were perceived to be too subjective relying on future cash flows.

The practitioners have now staked their claim to create accounting theory or a conceptual framework through the IASB. The advantage of this is that the conceptual framework will be based on consensus.

Conceptual framework

The framework does not seek to be seen as creating standards where none exist nor to override existing standards.

Its objectives are to assist:

- standard setters in the development of future standards so that there is a rational basis for reducing the number of alternatives in existing standards;
- preparers in applying standards and in having a principles basis for the treatment of matters not covered by a standard;
- auditors in satisfying themselves that financial statements being audited are in conformity with the Framework principles; and
- stakeholders when interpreting the financial statements.

We will now consider the evolution of conceptual frameworks from the earliest attempts in the 1970s by the FASB with the issue of Concepts Statements, which were picked up by the IASC with its *Framework for the Presentation and Preparation of Financial Statements* and developed by national standard setters. In this chapter we will review the Statement of Principles produced by the ASB, the UK national standard-setting body.

We will then discuss the collaboration taking place between the FASB, the IASB and a whole range of national standard-setting bodies.

6.3 FASB Concepts Statements

The FASB was the originator of attempts to create a conceptual framework with the issue of a series of Concepts Statements as a basis for financial accounting and reporting standards. It is easy to overlook this fact, particularly as the present preference for principles rather than rules in standard setting has tended to cast the FASB as rule bound. Instead it was in the lead when it came to formulating a conceptual framework. We will consider four of the statements below.

6.3.1 Concepts Statement No. 1: Objectives of Financial Reporting by Business Enterprises[5]

Financial reporting should provide information to present and potential investors and creditors that is understandable by a user who has a reasonable knowledge of business activities and useful in making rational investment and credit decisions. Such decisions are based on an assessment of the amounts, timing and uncertainty of prospective net cash inflows, i.e. ascertaining whether or not there is enough cash to pay creditors on time, cover capital expenditure and pay dividends.

The Concept Statement identified two reasons for providing information about past activities:

- investment and credit decisions are in part based on an evaluation of past performance; and

- owners require information as to the stewardship by the management of their use of resources.

Financial reporting should provide information about resources and claims, and reason for changes, i.e. a statement of financial position and a statement of cash flows, and information about past financial performance, i.e. a statement of financial performance. These statements allow users to check movements in operating capital and financing, see how cash has been spent and assess solvency, liquidity and profitability. Financial reporting is not restricted to financial statements but also includes non-financial and supplementary information.

6.3.2 Concepts Statement No. 2: Qualitative characteristics of Accounting Information[6]

Figure 6.1 illustrates how close the *Statement of Principles* (see section 6.5.3) and Concepts Statement No. 2 are in their approach.

6.3.3 Concepts Statement No. 6: Elements of Financial Statements[7]

This Statement defines ten elements. These include seven elements that appear in the *Statement of Principles* (see section 6.5.4) with slight differences in their definition. These are:

- **Assets** – probable future economic benefits obtained or controlled by a particular entity as a result of past transactions or events.

- **Liabilities** – probable future sacrifices of economic benefits arising from present obligations to transfer assets or provide services to other entities in the future as a result of past transactions or events.

- **Equity** – the residual interest in the assets of an entity that remains after deducting its liabilities. In a business enterprise, the equity is the ownership interest.

Figure 6.1 A hierarchy of accounting qualities

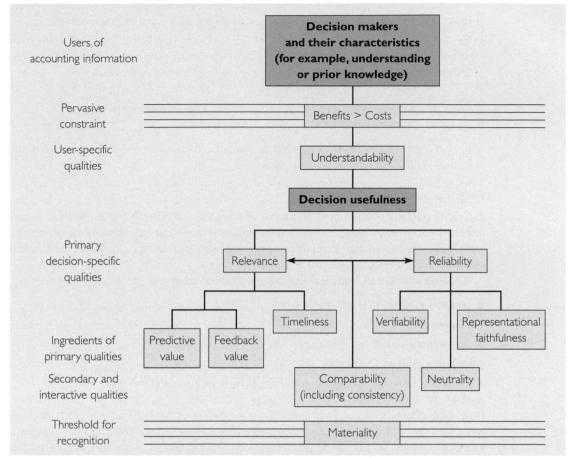

Source: Concept 2, Figure 1 from FASB, 1980, p. 13.

- **Investments by owners** – increases in equity. Assets are most commonly received as investments by owners but it might also include services or taking on liabilities of the enterprise.

- **Distributions to owners** – decreases in equity resulting from transferring assets, rendering services or incurring liabilities by the enterprise to owners. Distributions to owners decrease ownership interest (or equity).

- **Gains** – increases in equity (net assets) from peripheral or incidental transactions of an entity and from all other transactions and other events and circumstances affecting the entity except those that result from revenues or investments by owners.

- **Losses** – decreases in equity (net assets) from peripheral or incidental transactions of an entity and from all other transactions and other events and circumstances affecting the entity except those that result from expenses or distributions to owners.

  The Statement also defines three additional elements:

- **Comprehensive income** – the change in equity during a period from transactions and other events and circumstances from non-owner sources. It includes all changes in equity during a period except those resulting from investments by owners and distributions to owners.

- **Revenues** – inflows or other enhancements of assets of an entity or settlements of its liabilities (or a combination of both) from delivering or producing goods, rendering services, or other activities that constitute the entity's ongoing major or central operations.

- **Expenses** – outflows or other using up of assets or incurring liabilities (or a combination of both) from delivering or producing goods, rendering services or carrying out other activities that constitute the entity's ongoing major or central operations.

6.3.4 Concepts Statement No. 5: Recognition and Measurement in Financial Statements of Business Enterprises[8]

This statement defines financial statements, sets out recognition criteria for inclusion in the statements and comments on measurement.

Financial statements

Financial statements are a central feature of financial reporting being a principal means of communicating financial information to those outside an entity. Financial reporting also includes useful information that is better provided by other means, e.g. notes to the financial statements and supplementary information.

A full set of financial statements for a period should show:

- financial position at the end of the period;
- earnings for the period;
- comprehensive income for the period;
- cash flows during the period;
- investments by and distributions to owners during the period.

Recognition criteria

An item and information about it should meet four fundamental recognition criteria to be recognised and should be recognised when the criteria are met, subject to a cost–benefit constraint and a materiality threshold. Those criteria are:

- **Definitions**.   The item meets the definition of an element of financial statements.
- **Measurability**.   It has a relevant attribute measurable with sufficient reliability.
- **Relevance**.   The information about it is capable of making a difference in user decisions.
- **Reliability**.   The information is representationally faithful, verifiable and neutral.

Measurement

Attributes

Items currently reported in the financial statements are measured by different attributes as described in Chapters 3 and 4 above (e.g. historical cost, current (replacement) cost, current market value, net realisable value and present value of future cash flows), depending on the nature of the item and the relevance and reliability of the attribute measured.

Monetary unit

The monetary unit or measurement scale in current practice in financial statements is nominal units of money, that is, unadjusted for changes in purchasing power of money over time. The Board expects that nominal units of money will continue to be used to measure items recognised in financial statements.

6.4 IASC *Framework for the Presentation and Preparation of Financial Statements*[9]

The Framework differs from the International Financial Reporting Standard (IFRS) in that it does not define standards for the recognition, measurement and disclosure of financial information nor does it override any specific IFRS. However, if there is no IFRS for a particular situation, managers should consider the principles set out in the Framework when developing an accounting policy, which should aim at providing the most useful information to users of the entity's financial statements.

This exposure draft deals with the following:

● The objective of financial statements.
The **objective** of financial statements is that they should provide information about the financial position, performance and changes in financial position of an enterprise that is useful to a wide range of potential users in making economic decisions.

● The qualitative characteristics that determine the usefulness of information in financial statements.
The **qualitative characteristics** that determine the usefulness of information are **relevance** and **reliability**. Comparability is a qualitative characteristic that interacts with both relevance and reliability. Materiality provides a threshold or cut-off point rather than being a primary qualitative characteristic. The balance between cost and benefit is a persuasive constraint rather than a qualitative characteristic.

● The definition, recognition and measurement of elements from which financial statements are constructed.
The **definition** of an element is given in para. 46:

Financial statements portray the financial effects of transactions and other events by grouping the effects into broad classes according to their economic characteristics. These broad classes are termed the **elements** of financial statements. The elements directly related to the measurement of financial position in the statement of financial position are assets, liabilities and equity. The elements directly related to the measurement of performance in the profit and loss account are income and expense.

● The exposure draft defines each of the elements. For example, an asset is defined in para. 53: 'The future economic benefit embodied in an asset is the potential to contribute, directly or indirectly, to the flow of cash and cash equivalents to the enterprise.'

● It defines when an element is to be **recognised**. For example, in para. 87 it states: 'An asset is recognised in the statement of financial position when it is probable that the future economic benefits will flow to the enterprise and the asset has an attribute that can be measured reliably.'
Regarding **measurement**, it comments in para. 99:

The measurement attribute most commonly adopted by enterprises in preparing their financial statements is historical cost. This is usually combined with other measurement attributes, such as realisable value. For example, inventories are usually carried at the lower of cost and net realisable value, and marketable securities may be carried at market value, that is, their realisable value. Furthermore, many enterprises combine historical costs and current costs as a response to the inability of the historical cost model to deal with the effects of changing prices of non-monetary assets.

- The document deals in a similar style with the other elements.
- The concepts of capital, capital maintenance and profit.
- Finally, regarding the concepts of **capital**, **capital maintenance** and **profit**, the IASC comments:

> At the present time, it is not the intention of the Board of the IASC to prescribe a particular measurement model (i.e. historical cost, current cost, realisable value, present value) . . . This intention will, however, be reviewed in the light of world developments.

An appropriate capital maintenance model is not specified but the Framework mentions historical cost accounting, current cost accounting, net realisable value (as discussed in Chapter 4) and present value models (as discussed in Chapter 3).

The Framework has initiated the development of conceptual frameworks by other national standard setters for both private sector and public sector financial statements. Since then and up to the present day other jurisdictions have been influenced when drafting their own national conceptual frameworks, for example, Australia, Canada, New Zealand, South Africa and the UK have similar conceptual frameworks.

One of the earliest conceptual frameworks developed subsequently was that developed by the ASB in the UK as the *Statement of Principles* – this expanded on the ideas underlying the Framework and the ASB deserves praise for this.

6.5 ASB *Statement of Principles* 1999[9]

The *Statement* fleshes out the ideas contained in the Framework.

As Sir David Tweedie, Chairman of the ASB, commented, 'The Board has developed its *Statement of Principles* in parallel with its development of accounting standards . . . It is in effect the Board's compass for when we navigate uncharted waters in the years ahead. This is essential reading for those who want to know where the Board is coming from, and where it is aiming to go.'

The statement contains eight chapters dealing with key issues. Each of the chapters is commented on below.

6.5.1 Chapter 1: 'The objective of financial statements'

The *Statement of Principles* follows the IASC *Framework* in the identification of user groups.

The statement identifies the investor group as the primary group for whom the financial statements are being prepared. It then states the information needs of each group as follows:

- **Investors**. These need information to:
  - assess the stewardship of management, e.g. in safeguarding the entity's resources and using them properly, efficiently and profitably;
  - take decisions about management, e.g. assessing need for new management;
  - take decisions about their investment or potential investment, e.g. deciding whether to hold, buy or sell shares and assessing the ability to pay dividends.
- **Lenders**. These need information to:
  - determine whether their loans and interest will be paid on time;
  - decide whether to lend and on what terms.

- **Suppliers**. These need information to:
  - decide whether to sell to the entity;
  - determine whether they will be paid on time;
  - determine longer-term stability if the company is a major customer.

- **Employees**. These need information to:
  - assess the stability and profitability of the company;
  - assess the ability to provide remuneration, retirement benefits and employment opportunities.

- **Customers**. These need information to:
  - assess the probability of the continued existence of the company taking account of their own degree of dependence on the company, e.g. for future provision of specialised replacement parts and servicing product warranties.

- **Government and other agencies**. These need information to:
  - be aware of the commercial activities of the company;
  - regulate these activities;
  - raise revenue;
  - produce national statistics.

- **Public**. Members of the public need information to:
  - determine the effect on the local economy of the company's activities, e.g. employment opportunities, use of local suppliers;
  - assess recent developments in the company's prosperity and changes in its activities.

The information needs of which group are to be dominant?

Seven groups are identified, but there is only one set of financial statements. Although they are described as general-purpose statements, a decision has to be made about which group's needs take precedence.

The *Statement of Principles* identifies the **investor** group as the defining class of user, i.e. the primary group for whom the financial statements are being prepared.

It takes the view that financial statements 'are able to focus on the common interest of users'. The common interest is described thus: 'all potential users are interested, to a varying degree, in the financial performance and financial position of the entity as a whole'.

This means that it is a prerequisite that the information must be relevant to the investor group. This suggests that any need of the other groups that is not also a need of the investors will not be met by the financial statements.

The 1995 Exposure Draft stated: 'Awarding primacy to investors does not imply that other users are to be ignored. The information prepared for investors is useful as a frame of reference for other users, against which they can evaluate more specific information that they may obtain in their dealings with the enterprise.'

It is important, therefore, for all of the other users to be aware that this is one of the principles. If they require specific disclosures that might be relevant to them, they will need to take their own steps to obtain them, particularly where there is a conflict of interest. For example, if a closure is being planned by the directors, it may be in the investors' interest for the news to be delayed as long as possible to minimise the cost to the company; employees, suppliers, customers and the public must not expect any assistance from the financial statements – their information needs are not the primary concern.

What information should be provided to satisfy the information needs?

The *Statement* proposes that information is required in four areas: financial performance, financial position, generation and use of cash, and financial adaptability.

Financial performance

Financial performance is defined as the return an entity obtains from the resources it controls. This return is available from the profit and loss account and provides a means to assess past management performance, how effectively resources have been utilised and the capacity to generate cash flows.

Financial position

Financial position is available from an examination of the statement of financial position and includes:

● the economic resources controlled by an entity, i.e. assets and liabilities;
● financial structure, i.e. capital gearing indicating how profits will be divided between the different sources of finance and the capacity for raising additional finance in the future;
● liquidity and solvency, i.e. current and liquid ratios;
● capacity to adapt to changes – see below under **Financial adaptability**.

Generation and use of cash

Information is available from the cash flow statement which shows cash flows from operating, investment and financing activities providing a perspective that is largely free from allocation and valuation issues. This information is useful in assessing and reviewing previous assessments of cash flows.

Financial adaptability

This is an entity's ability to alter the amount and timing of its cash flows. It is desirable in order to be able to cope with difficult periods, e.g. when losses are incurred and to take advantage of unexpected investment opportunities. It is dependent on factors such as the ability, at short notice, to:

● raise new capital;
● repay capital or debt;
● obtain cash from disposal of assets without disrupting continuing business, i.e. realise readily marketable securities that might have been built up as a liquid reserve;
● achieve a rapid improvement in net cash flows from operations.

6.5.2 Chapter 2: 'The reporting entity'

This chapter focuses on identifying when an entity should report and which activities to include in the report.

When an entity should report

The principle is that an entity should prepare and publish financial statements if:

● there is a legitimate demand for the information, i.e. it is the case both that it is decision-useful and that benefits exceed the cost of producing the information; and
● it is a cohesive economic unit, i.e. a unit under a central control that can be held accountable for its activities.

Which activities to include

The principle is that those activities should be included that are within the direct control of the entity, e.g. assets and liabilities which are reported in its own statement of financial position, or indirect control, e.g. assets and liabilities of a subsidiary of the entity which are reported in the consolidated statement of financial position.

Control is defined as (a) the ability to deploy the resources and (b) the ability to benefit (or to suffer) from their deployment. Indirect control by an investor can be difficult to determine. The test is not to apply a theoretical level of influence such as holding $x\%$ of shares but to review the relationship that exists between the investor and investee in practice, such as the investor having the power to veto the investee's financial and operating policies and benefit from its net assets.

6.5.3 Chapter 3: 'The qualitative characteristics of financial information'

The *Statement of Principles* is based on the IASC *Framework* and contains the same four principal qualitative characteristics relating to the content of information and how the information is presented. The two primary characteristics relating to content are the need to be relevant and reliable; the two relating to presentation are the need to be understandable and comparable. The characteristics appear diagrammatically in Figure 6.2.

From the diagram we can see that for information content to be **relevant** it must have:

- the ability to influence the economic decisions of users;
- predictive value, i.e. help users to evaluate or assess past, present or future events; or
- confirmatory value, i.e. help users to confirm their past evaluations.

For information to be **reliable** it must be:

- free from material error, i.e. transactions have been accurately recorded and reported;
- a faithful representation, i.e. reflecting the commercial substance of transactions;

Figure 6.2 What makes financial information useful?

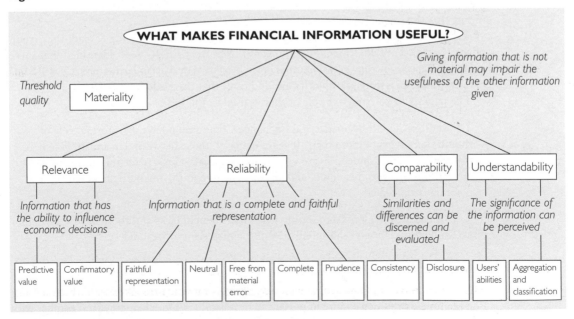

- neutral, i.e. not presented in a way to achieve a predetermined result;
- prudent, i.e. not creating hidden reserves or excessive provisions, deliberately under-stating assets or gains, or deliberately overstating liabilities or losses;
- complete, i.e. the information is complete subject to a materiality test.

To be useful, the financial information also needs to be **comparable** over time and between companies and **understandable**.

It satisfies the criteria for understandability if it is capable of being understood by a user with a reasonable knowledge of business activities and accounting, and a willingness to study the information with reasonable diligence. However, the trade-off between relevance and reliability comes into play with the requirement that complex information that is relevant to economic decision making should not be omitted because some users find it too difficult to understand. There is no absolute answer where there is the possibility of a trade-off and it is recognised by the ASB that the relative importance of the characteristics in different cases is a matter of judgement.

The chapter also introduces the idea of **materiality** as a threshold quality and any item that is not material does not require to be considered further. The statement recognises that no information can be useful if it is not also material by introducing the idea of a threshold quality which it describes as follows: 'An item of information is material to the financial statements if its misstatement or omission might reasonably be expected to influence the economic decisions of users of those financial statements, including their assessment of management's stewardship.'[10]

First, this means that it is justified not to report immaterial items which would impose unnecessary costs on preparers and impede decision makers by obscuring material informa-tion with excessive detail.

Secondly, it means that the important consideration is not user expectation (e.g. users might expect turnover to be accurate to within 1%) but the effect on decision making (e.g. there might only be an effect if turnover were to be more that 10% over- or understated in which case, only errors exceeding 10% are material).

It also states that 'Materiality depends on the size of the item or error judged in the particular circumstances of its omission or misstatement.' The need to exercise judgement means that the preparer needs to have a benchmark.

A discussion paper issued in January 1995 by the Financial Reporting & Auditing Group of the ICAEW entitled *Materiality in Financial Reporting FRAG 1/95* identified that there are few instances where an actual figure is given by statute or by standard setters, e.g. FRS 6,[11] para. 76 refers to a material minority and indicates that this is defined as 10%.

The paper also referred to a rule of thumb used in the USA:

> The staff of the US Securities and Exchange Commission have an informal rule of thumb that errors of more than 10% are material, those between 5% and 10% may be material and those under 5% are usually not material. These percentages are applied to gross profit, net income, equity and any specific line in the financial statements that is potentially misstated.

The ASB has moved away from setting percentage benchmarks and there is now a need for more explicit guidance on the application of the materiality threshold.

Unresolved trade-offs

There are a number of characteristics where there is no guidance given as to the trade-off. For example, is relevance more important than reliability? Does being neutral conflict with prudence? Does relevance require a faithful representation and does a faithful representation require the information to be verifiable?

Unresolved relative importance

The approach taken has to be to regard decision usefulness as paramount. It is not clear where this leaves accountability and stewardship. There are unresolved questions such as, for example, whether comparability is as important as relevance or reliability.

6.5.4 Chapter 4: 'The elements of financial statements'

This chapter gives guidance on the items that *could* appear in financial statements. These are described as **elements** and have the following essential features:

- **Assets**. These are rights to future economic benefits controlled by an entity as a result of past transactions or events.
- **Liabilities**. These are obligations of an entity to transfer future economic benefits as a result of past transactions or events, i.e. ownership is not essential.
- **Ownership interest**. This is the residual amount found by deducting all liabilities from assets which belong to the owners of the entity.
- **Gains**. These are increases in ownership interest not resulting from contributions by the owners.
- **Losses**. These are decreases in ownership interest not resulting from distributions to the owners.
- **Contributions by the owners**. These are increases in ownership interest resulting from transfers from owners in their capacity as owners.
- **Distributions to owners**. These are decreases in ownership interest resulting from transfers to owners in their capacity as owners.

These definitions have been used as the basis for developing standards, e.g. assessing the substance of a transaction means identifying whether the transaction has given rise to new assets or liabilities, defined as above.

6.5.5 Chapter 5: 'Recognition in financial statements'

The objective of financial statements is to disclose in the statement of financial position and the profit and loss account the effect on the assets and liabilities of **transactions**, e.g. purchase of stock on credit and the effect of **events**, e.g. accidental destruction of a vehicle by fire. This implies that transactions are recorded under the double entry principle with an appropriate debit and credit made to the element that has been affected, e.g. the asset element (stock) and the liability element (creditors) are debited and credited to recognise stock bought on credit. Events are also recorded under the double entry principle, e.g. the asset element (vehicle) is derecognised and credited because it is no longer able to provide future economic benefits and the loss element resulting from the fire damage is debited to the profit and loss account. The emphasis is on determining the effect on the assets and liabilities, e.g. the increase in the asset element (stock), the increase in the liability element (creditors) and the reduction in the asset element (vehicle).

This emphasis has a particular significance for application of the matching concept in preparing the profit and loss account. The traditional approach to allocating expenditure across accounting periods has been to identify the costs that should be matched against the revenue in the profit and loss account and carry the balance into the statement of financial position, i.e. the allocation is driven by the need to match costs to revenue. The *Statement of Principles* approach is different in that it identifies the amount of the expenditure to be recognised as an asset and the balance is transferred to the profit and loss account, i.e. the question is 'Should this expenditure be recognised as an asset (capitalised) and, if so, should any part of it be derecognised (written off as a loss element)?'

This means that the allocation process now requires an assessment as to whether an asset exists at the statement of financial position date by applying the following test:

1 If the future economic benefits are eliminated at a single point in time, it is at that point that the loss is recognised and the expenditure derecognised, i.e. the debit balance is transferred to the profit and loss account.

2 If the future economic benefits are eliminated over several accounting periods – typically because they are being consumed over a period of time – the cost of the asset that comprises the future economic benefits will be recognised as a loss in the performance statement over those accounting periods, i.e. written off as a loss element as their future economic benefit reduces.

The result of this approach should not lead to changes in the accounts as currently prepared but it does emphasise that matching cost and revenue is not the main driver of recognition, i.e. the question is not 'How much expenditure should we match with the revenue reported in the profit and loss account?' but rather 'Are there future economic benefits arising from the expenditure to justify inclusion in the statement of financial position?' and, if not, derecognise it, i.e. write it off.

Dealing with uncertainty

There is almost always some uncertainty as to when to recognise an event or transaction, e.g. when is the asset element of raw material inventory to be disclosed as the asset element work-in-progress? Is it when an inventory requisition is issued, when the storekeeper isolates it in the inventory to be issued bay, when it is issued onto the workshop floor, when it begins to be worked on?

The *Statement of Principles* states that the principle to be applied if a transaction has created or added to an existing asset or liability is to recognise it if:

1 sufficient evidence exists that the new asset or liability has been created or that there has been an addition to an existing asset or liability; and

2 the new asset or liability or the addition to the existing asset or liability can be measured at a monetary amount with sufficient reliability.

The use of the word sufficient reflects the uncertainty that surrounds the decision when to recognise and the *Statement* states: 'In the business environment, uncertainty usually exists in a continuum, so the recognition process involves selecting the point on the continuum at which uncertainty becomes acceptable.'[12]

Before that point it may, for example, be appropriate to disclose by way of note to the accounts a contingent liability that is possible (less than 50% chance of crystallising into a liability) but not probable (more than 50% chance of crystallising).

Sufficient reliability

Prudence requires more persuasive evidence of the measurement for the recognition of items that result in an increase in ownership interest than for the recognition of items that do not. However, the exercise of prudence does not allow for the omission of assets or gains where there is sufficient evidence of occurrence and reliability of measurement, or for the inclusion of liabilities or losses where there is not. This would amount to the deliberate understatement of assets or gains, or the deliberate overstatement of liabilities or losses.

Reporting gains and losses

Chapter 5 does not address the disclosure treatment of gains and losses. A change in assets or liabilities might arise from three classes of past event: transactions, contracts for future performance and other events such as a change in market price.

If the change in an asset is offset by a change in liability, there will be no gain or loss. If the change in asset is not offset by a change in liability, there will be a gain or loss. If there is a gain or loss, a decision is required as to whether it should be recognised in the profit and loss account or in the statement of total recognised gains and losses.

Recognition in profit and loss account

For a gain to be recognised in the profit and loss account, it must have been earned and realised. **Earned** means that no material transaction, contract or other event must occur before the change in the assets or liabilities will have occurred; **realised** means that the conversion into cash or cash equivalents must either have occurred or be reasonably assured.

Profit, as stated in the profit and loss account, is used as a prime measure of performance. Consequently, prudence requires particularly good evidence for the recognition of gains.

It is important to note that in this chapter the ASB is following a **statement of financial position orientated** approach to measuring gains and losses. The conventional profit and loss account approach would identify the **transactions** that had been undertaken and allocate these to financial accounting periods.

6.5.6 Chapter 6: 'Measurement in financial statements'

The majority of listed companies in the UK use the mixed measurement system whereby some assets and liabilities are measured using historical cost and some are measured using a current value basis. The *Statement of Principles* envisages that this will continue to be the practice and states that the aim is to select the basis that:

● provides information about financial performance and financial position that is useful in evaluating the reporting entity's cash-generation abilities and in assessing its financial adaptability;

● carries values which are sufficiently reliable: if the historical cost and current value are equally reliable, the better measure is the one that is the most relevant; current values may frequently be no less reliable than historical cost figures given the level of estimation that is required in historical cost figures, e.g. determining provisions for bad debts, stock provisions, product warranties;

● reflects what the asset and liability represents: e.g. the relevance of short-term investments to an entity will be the specific future cash flows and these are best represented by current values.

ASB view on need for a current value basis of measurement

The *Statement* makes the distinction[13] between return *on* capital – i.e. requiring the calculation of accounting profit – and return *of* capital – i.e. requiring the measurement of capital and testing for capital maintenance. The *Statement* makes the point that the financial capital maintenance concept is not satisfactory when *significant* general or specific price changes have occurred.

ASB gradualist approach

The underlying support of the ASB for a gradualist move towards the use of current values is reflected in 'Although the objective of financial statements and the qualitative character-istics of financial information, in particular relevance and reliability may not change . . . as markets develop, measurement bases that were once thought unreliable may become reliable. Similarly, as access to markets develops, so a measurement basis that was once thought insufficiently relevant may become the most relevant measure available.'[14]

Determining current value

Current value systems could be defined as replacement cost (entry value), net realisable value (exit value) or value in use (discounted present value of future cash flows). The approach of the *Statement* is to identify the value to the business by selecting from these three alter-natives the measure that is most relevant in the circumstances. This measure is referred to as deprival value and represents the loss that the entity would suffer if it were deprived of the asset.

The value to the business is determined by considering whether the company would replace the asset. If the answer is *yes*, then use replacement cost; if the answer is *no* but the asset is worth keeping, then use value in use; and if *no* and the asset is not worth keeping, then use net realisable value.

This can be shown diagrammatically as in Figure 6.3.

How will value to the business be implemented?

The ASB is being pragmatic by following an incremental approach to the question of measurement stating that 'practice should develop by evolving in the direction of greater use of current values consistent with the constraints of reliability and cost'. This seems a sensible position for the ASB to take. Its underlying views were clear when it stated that 'a real terms capital maintenance system improves the relevance of information because it shows current operating margins as well as the extent to which holding gains and losses reflect the effect of general inflation, so that users of real terms financial statements are able to select the particular information they require'.[15]

Policing the mixed measurement system

Many companies have adopted the modified historical cost basis and revalued their fixed assets on a selective basis. However, this piecemeal approach allowed companies to cherry-pick the assets they wish to revalue on a selective basis at times when market values have risen. The ASB have adopted the same approach as IAS 16.[16]

Figure 6.3 Value to the business

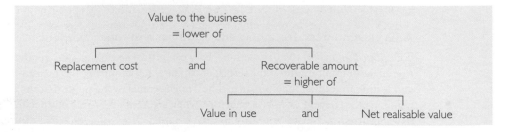

The fair value measurement system

A value to the business approach (often referred to as deprival value) was presented as a logical approach to selecting a value to be recognised in financial statements. Standard setters, e.g. the FASB are currently considering requiring fair values to be the most relevant values for stakeholders.[17]

Does the fair value measurement system make current cost and deprival value redundant?

It is interesting to consider the analysis set out in the Discussion Paper *Measurement Bases for Financial Reporting – Measurement on Initial Recognition*.[18] This is a discussion paper prepared by the staff at the Canadian Accounting Standards Board which was issued (but not adopted) by the IASB in March 2006 for comment. The discussion paper proposes a four-level measurement hierarchy for assets and liabilities when they are initially recognised. The four levels start with two levels where there is a market (fair) value available, i.e. Level 1 – where there are observable market prices and Level 2 – where there are accepted valuation models or techniques. The third and fourth levels deal with transactions where a substitute has to be found for market value – this takes us back to the bases discussed in Chapter 4. For example, when an asset cannot be reliably measured under Level 1 or 2 then the deprival value approach is proposed.

6.5.7 Chapter 7: 'Presentation of financial information'

Chapter 7 states that the objective of the presentation adopted is to communicate clearly and effectively and in as simple and straightforward manner as is possible without loss of relevance or reliability and without significantly increasing the length of the financial statements.

The point about length is well made given the length of current annual reports and accounts. Recent examples include Jenoptik AG extending to eighty-one pages, Sea Containers Ltd seventy-six pages and Hugo Boss over one hundred pages.

The *Statement* analyses the way in which information should be presented in financial statements to meet the objectives set out in Chapter 1. It covers the requirement for items to be aggregated and classified and outlines good presentation practices in the statement of financial performance, statement of financial position, cash flow statement and accompanying information, e.g.:

Statement of financial performance

Good presentation involves:

- Recognising only gains and losses.
- Classifying items by function, e.g. production, selling, administrative and nature, e.g. interest payable.
- Showing separately amounts that are affected in different ways by economic or commercial conditions, e.g. continuing, acquired and discontinued operations, segmental geographical information.
- Showing separately:
  - items unusual in amount or incidence;
  - expenses that are not operating expenses, e.g. financing costs and taxation;
  - expenses that relate primarily to future periods, e.g. research expenditure.

Statement of financial position

Good presentation involves:

- Recognising only assets, liabilities and ownership interest.
- Classifying assets so that users can assess the nature, amounts and liquidity of available resources.
- Classifying assets and liabilities so that users can assess the nature, amounts and timing of obligations that require or may require liquid resources for settlement.
- Classifying assets by function, e.g. show fixed assets and current assets separately.

Accompanying information

Typical information includes chairman's statement, directors' report, operating and financial review, highlights and summary indicators.

The *Statement* states that the more complex an entity and its transactions become, the more users need an objective and comprehensive analysis and explanation of the main features underlying the entity's financial performance and financial position.

Good presentation involves discussion of:

- The main factors underlying financial performance, including the principal risks, uncertainties and trends in main business areas and how the entity is responding.
- The strategies adopted for capital structure and treasury policy.
- The activities and expenditure (other than capital expenditure) that are investment in the future.

It is interesting to note the *Statement* view that highlights and summary indicators, such as amounts and ratios that attempt to distil key information, cannot on their own adequately describe or provide a basis for meaningful analysis or prudent decision making. It does, however, state: 'That having been said, well-presented highlights and summary indicators are useful to users who require only very basic information, such as the amount of sales or dividends.' The ASB will be giving further consideration to this view that there is a need for a really brief report.

6.5.8 Chapter 8: 'Accounting for interests in other entities'

Interests in other entities can have a material effect on the company's own financial performance and financial position and need to be fully reflected in the financial statements. As an example, an extract from the 2006 Annual Report and Accounts of Stagecoach plc shows:

	Company statement of financial position	Consolidated statement of financial position
Tangible assets	£0.1m	£893.4m
Investments	£964.9m	—

In deciding whether to include the assets in the consolidated statement of financial position, a key factor is the degree of influence exerted over the activities and resources of the investee:

- If the degree of influence allows control of the operating and financial policies, the financial statements are aggregated.
- If the investor has joint control or significant influence, the investor's share of the gains and losses are recognised in the consolidated statement of comprehensive income and reflected in the carrying value of the investment.

However, there is no clear agreement on the treatment of interests in other entities, and further developments can be expected.

6.6 Conceptual framework developments

The FASB in America and the IASB have been collaborating on revising the IASB Framework and the FASB Concepts Statements (e.g. Statement 1: Objectives of financial reporting by business enterprise). The intention is to adopt a principles-based approach. This is also supported also by a report[19] from the Institute of Chartered Accountants of Scotland which concludes that the global convergence of accounting standards cannot be achieved by a 'tick-box' rules-driven approach but should rely on judgement-based principles.

A principles-based approach allows companies the flexibility to deal with new situations.

A rules-based approach provides the auditor with protection against litigious claims because it can be shown that other auditors would have adopted the same accounting treatment. However, following the Enron disaster, the rules-based approach was heavily criticised in America and it was felt that a principles-based approach would have been more effective in preventing it.

A rules-based approach means that financial statements are more comparable. Recognising that a principles-based approach could lead to different professional judgements for the same commercial activity, it is important that there should be full disclosure and transparency.

6.6.1 Piecemeal development

The IASB and FASB started a convergence project in 2004 to prepare an agreed Framework over eight phases. These are:

● Phase A: Objective and qualitative characteristics (Final chapter published).
● Phase B: Elements and recognition (DP expected Q4 of 2010).
● Phase C: Measurement (DP Q4 2010).
● Phase D: Reporting entity (ED Q1 2010).
● Phase E: Presentation and disclosure.
● Phase F: Purpose and status of framework.
● Phase G: Applicability to not-for-profit entities.
● Phase H: Other issues, if necessary.

The main points of Phase A Chapter 1 (Objective of Financial Reporting) and Chapter 2 (Qualitative Characteristics and Constraints of Decision-useful Financial Reporting Information) are described below.

The objective of financial reporting

The fundamental objective of general purpose financial reporting is to provide financial information about the reporting entity that is useful to present and potential equity investors when making investment decisions and assessing stewardship. The fundamental objective does not specifically mention stewardship although there is an acceptance that reviewing past performance has an implication for assessing future cash flows. There is also a presumption that such general-purpose financial statements will satisfy the information needs of lenders and others such as customers, suppliers and employees.

Qualitative characteristics and constraints of decision-useful financial reporting information

There are two fundamental qualitative characteristics if information is to be decision-useful and not misleading. These are relevance and faithful representation.

There are other characteristics that may make the information more useful. These are comparability, consistency, verifiability, timeliness and understandability.

Some characteristics were considered but not included on the grounds that they were covered by the above characteristics. For instance, true and fair was not included because it was considered to be equivalent to faithful representation.

As with other frameworks, there are constraints on the information to be disclosed. These are materiality, defined in the usual way as being information whose omission or misstatement could influence decisions, and cost, if this exceeds the benefit of providing the information.

We can see that the project by the IASB to develop an agreed Conceptual Framework is progressing in a piecemeal fashion with only Chapters 1 and 2 finalised and the date for the finalisation of some of the other chapters still to be announced. This might be seen as a strength in that time and thought are being given to the project. However, there is also a downside as seen in the ASB response to the IASB (see www.frc.org.uk/documents/ pagemanager/asb/Conceptual_framework/Conceptual%20Framework%20IASB%20ED_ ASB%20Response_Final.pdf) which expressed concern that:

- The current Framework applies to financial *statements* rather than financial **reporting**. If it is to be extended to financial reporting, this could include other areas such as prospectuses, news releases, management's forecasts but this has not been defined.

- There is a risk that the piecemeal approach could lead to internal inconsistencies and decisions being made in the earlier chapters could have as yet unforeseen adverse consequences.

- The consequences of adopting the entity approach on the remainder of the Framework may be extensive. For example, there is a link between the stewardship objective and the proprietary view and that by dismissing that view from the Framework entirely may lead to difficulties for entities in providing information in the financial reports that fulfils that objective.

The last point concerning the implication for stewardship reporting reflects the US influence on the Framework with less emphasis being given to it.

The piecemeal approach perhaps reflects the differences that need to be resolved between the IASB and FASB from differences in terminology, for example, substituting *faithful representation* for *reliability* to more fundamental differences relating to the scope of the Framework, for example, its very objective and its boundaries as to whether it relates to financial *statements* or financial *reports*.

Summary

Directors and accountants are constrained by a mass of rules and regulations which govern the measurement, presentation and disclosure of financial information. Regulations are derived from three major sources: the legislature in the form of statutes, the accountancy profession in the form of standards, and the Financial Services Authority in the form of Listing Rules.

There have been a number of reports relating to financial reporting. The preparation and presentation of financial statements continue to evolve. Steps are being taken to provide a conceptual framework and there is growing international agreement on the setting of global standards.

User needs have been accepted as paramount; qualitative characteristics of information have been specified; the elements of financial statements have been defined precisely; the presentation of financial information has been prescribed; and comparability between companies is seen as desirable.

However, the intention remains to produce financial statements that present a fair view. This is not achieved by detailed rules and regulations, and the exercise of judgement will continue to be needed. This opens the way for creative accounting practices that bring financial reporting and the accounting profession into disrepute. Strenuous efforts will continue to be needed from the auditors, the ASB, the Review Panel and the Financial Reporting Council to contain the use of unacceptable practices. The regulatory bodies show that they have every intention of accepting the challenge.

The question of the measurement base that should be used has yet to be settled. The measurement question still remains a major area of financial reporting that needs to be addressed.

The Framework sees the objective of financial statements as providing information about the financial position, performance and financial adaptability of an enterprise that is useful to a wide range of users in making economic decisions. It recognises that they are limited because they largely show the financial effects of past events and do not necessarily show non-financial information. On the question of measurement the view has been expressed that:

> historical cost has the merit of familiarity and (to some extent) objectivity; current values have the advantage of greater relevance to users of the accounts who wish to assess the current state or recent performance of the business, but they may sometimes be unreliable or too expensive to provide. It concludes that practice should develop by evolving in the direction of greater use of current values to the extent that this is consistent with the constraints of reliability, cost and acceptability to the financial community.[20]

There are critics[21] who argue that the concern with recording current asset values rather than historical costs means that:

> the essential division between the IASC and its critics is one between those who are more concerned about where they want to be and those who want to be very clear about where they are now. It is a division between those who see the purpose of financial statements as taking economic decisions about the future, and those who see it as a basis for making management accountable and for distributing the rewards among the stakeholders.

Finally, it is interesting to give some thought to extracts from two publications which indicate that there is still a long way to go in the evolution of financial reporting, and that there is little room for complacency.

The first is from *The Future Shape of Financial Reports*:

> As Solomons[22] and *Making Corporate Reports Valuable* discussed in detail, the then system of financial reporting in the UK fails to satisfy the purpose of providing information to shareholders, lenders and others to appraise past performance in order to form expectations about an organisation's future performance in five main respects:

1 ... measures of performance ... are based on original or historical costs ...

2 Much emphasis is placed on a single measure of earnings per share ...

3 ... insufficient attention is paid to changes in an enterprise's cash or liquidity position ...

4 The present system is essentially backward looking ...

5 Emphasis is often placed on the legal form rather than on the economic substance of transactions ...[23]

We have seen that some of these five limitations are being addressed, but not all, e.g. the provision of projected figures.

The second extract is from *Making Corporate Reports Valuable*:

The present statement of financial position almost defies comprehension. Assets are shown at depreciated historical cost, at amounts representing current valuations and at the results of revaluations of earlier periods (probably also depreciated); that is there is no consistency whatsoever in valuation practice. The sum total of the assets, therefore, is meaningless and combining it with the liabilities to show the entity's financial position does not in practice achieve anything worthwhile.[24]

The IASC has taken steps to deal with the frequency of revaluations but the criticism still holds in that there will continue to be financial statements produced incorporating mixed measurement bases.

The point made by some critics remains unresolved:

Accountability and the IASC's decision usefulness are not compatible. Forward-looking decisions require forecasts of future cash flows, which in the economic model are what determines the values of assets. These values are too subjective to form the basis of accountability. The definition of assets and the recognition rules restrict assets to economic benefits the enterprise controls as a result of past events and that are measurable with sufficient reliability. But economic decision making requires examination of all sources of future cash flows, not just a restricted sub-set of them.[25]

In the USA, Australia, Canada, the UK and the IASB, the approach has been the same, i.e. commencing with a consideration of the objectives of financial statements, qualitative characteristics of financial information, definition of the elements, and when these are to be recognised in the financial statements. There is a general agreement on these areas. Agreement on measurement has yet to be reached. A global framework is being developed between the IASB and the FASB and it is interesting to see that the same tensions exist, for example, between accountability and decision-usefulness.

REVIEW QUESTIONS

1 (a) Name the user groups and information needs of the user groups identified by the IASC *Framework for the Presentation and Preparation of Financial Statements*.

   (b) Discuss the effect of the Framework on current financial reporting practice.

2 The workload on the IASB in seeking to converge standards with the FASB has diverted resources from dealing with more fundamental problems such as off-balance sheet issues. Discuss.

3 R. MacVe in *A Conceptual Framework for Financial Accounting and Reporting: The Possibilities for an Agreed Structure* suggested that the search for a conceptual framework was a political process. Discuss the effect that this thinking has had and will have on standard setting.

4 (a) In 1999 in the UK, the ASB published the *Statement of Principles*. Explain what you consider to be the purpose and status of the *Statement*.

(b) Chapter 4 of the *Statement* identifies and defines what the ASB believes to be the elements that make up financial statements. Define any four of the elements and explain how, in your opinion, the identification and definition of the elements of financial statements would enhance financial reporting.

5 'The replacement of accrual accounting with cash flow accounting would avoid the need for a conceptual framework.'[26] Discuss.

6 Financial accounting theory has accumulated a vast literature. A cynic might be inclined to say that the vastness of the literature is in sharp contrast to its impact on practice.

(a) Describe the different approaches that have evolved in the development of accounting theory.

(b) Assess its impact on standard setting.

(c) Discuss the contribution of accounting theory to the understanding of accounting practice, and suggest contributions that it might make in the future.

7 The President of the ICAEW has proposed that regulators from developed and developing countries start talking to agree a set of principles for universal application that could underpin the regulation of accounting and auditing. Discuss the extent to which the IASC Framework provides such a set of principles in dealing with the complexities of global business.

8 Explain the different ways in which future economic benefits may arise in a pharmaceutical company.

9 As fair values may be unreliable and mislead users into thinking that the statement of financial position shows the net worth of an entity, historical costs are preferable for reporting assets and liabilities in the statement of financial position. Discuss.

10 Rules-based accounting adds unnecessary complexity, encourages financial engineering and does not necessarily lead to a 'true and fair view' or a 'fair presentation'. Discuss.

11 The key qualitative characteristics in the Framework are relevance and reliability. Preparers of financial statements may face a dilemma in satisfying both criteria at once. Discuss.

12 An asset is defined in the Framework as a resource which an entity controls as a result of past events and from which future economic benefits are expected to flow to the entity. Discuss whether property, plant and equipment automatically qualify as assets.

EXERCISES

Question 1

The following extract is from *Conceptual Framework for Financial Accounting and Reporting: Elements of Financial Statements and Their Measurement*, FASB 3, December 1976.

The benefits of achieving agreement on a conceptual framework for financial accounting and reporting manifest themselves in several ways. Among other things, a conceptual framework can (1) guide the body responsible for establishing accounting standards, (2) provide a frame of reference for resolving accounting questions in the absence of a specific promulgated standard, (3) determine bounds for judgement in preparing financial statements, (4) increase financial statement users' understanding of and confidence in financial statements, and (5) enhance comparability.

Required:
(a) Define a conceptual framework.
(b) Critically examine why the benefits provided in the above statements are likely to flow from the development of a conceptual framework for accounting.

Question 2

The following extract is from 'Comments of Leonard Spacek', in R.T. Sprouse and M. Moonitz, *A Tentative Set of Broad Accounting Principles for Business Enterprises*, Accounting Research Study No. 3, AICPA, New York, 1962, reproduced in A. Belkaoui, *Accounting Theory*, Harcourt Brace Jovanovich.

A discussion of assets, liabilities, revenue and costs is premature and meaningless until the basic principles that will result in a fair presentation of the facts in the form of financial accounting and financial reporting are determined. This fairness of accounting and reporting must be for and to people, and these people represent the various segments of our society.

Required:
(a) Explain the term 'fair'.
(b) Discuss the extent to which the IASB conceptual framework satisfies the above definition.

Question 3

The following is an extract from *Accountancy Age*, 25 January 2001.

A powerful and 'shadowy' group of senior partners from the seven largest firms has emerged to move closer to edging control of accounting standards from the world's accountancy regulators... they form the Global Steering Committee... The GSC has worked on plans to improve standards for the last two years after scathing criticism from investors that firms produced varying standards of audit in different countries.

Discuss the effect on standard setting if control were to be edged from the world's accountancy regulators.

References

1 For IFAD refer to www.iasplus.com/resource/ifad.htm.
2 *Framework for the Preparation and Presentation of Financial Statements*, IASC, 1989, Preface.
3 IAS 17 revised, *Leases*, IASC, 1994.
4 D. Solomons, *Guidelines for Financial Reporting Standards*, ICAEW, 1989, p. 32.
5 Statement of Financial Accounting No. 1: Objectives of Financial Reporting by Business Enterprises, FASB, November 1978.
6 Statement of Financial Accounting Concepts No. 2: Qualitative characteristics of Accounting Information, FASB, May 1980.
7 Statement of Financial Accounting Concepts No. 6: Elements of Financial Statements, FASB, December 1985.

8 Statement of Financial Accounting Concepts No. 5: Recognition and Measurement in Financial Statements of Business Enterprises, FASB, December 1984.

9 *Statement of Principles for Financial Reporting*, ASB, 1999.

10 *Ibid.*, para. 3.27.

11 FRS 6 *Acquisition and Mergers*, ASB, 1994.

12 *Statement of Principles for Financial Reporting*, ASB, 1999, para. 5.10.

13 *Ibid.*, para. 6.42.

14 *Ibid.*, para. 6.25.

15 *Statement of Principles for Financial Reporting*, ASB, 1995, para. 5.37.

16 IAS 16 *Property, Plant and Equipment*, IASC, revised 1998, para. 34.

17 SFAS No 157 *Fair Value Measurements*, FASB, October 2005.

18 Discussion Paper *Measurement Bases for Financial Reporting – Measurement on Initial Recognition*, ACSB, www.acsbcanada.org/index.cfm/ci_id/185/la_id/1.htm

19 ICAS, *Principles not rules – a question of judgement*, www.icas.org.uk/site/cms/contentView Article.asp?article=4597.

20 A. Lennard, 'The peg on which standards hang', *Accountancy*, January 1996, p. 80.

21 S. Fearnley and M. Page, 'Why the ASB has lost its bearings', *Accountancy*, April 1996, p. 94.

22 D. Solomons, *op. cit.*

23 J. Arnold *et al.*, *The Future Shape of Financial Reports*, ICAEW/ICAS, 1991.

24 *Making Corporate Reports Valuable*, ICAS, 1988, p. 35.

25 S. Fearnley and M. Page, *loc. cit.*

26 R. Skinner, *Accountancy*, January 1990, p. 25.

CHAPTER **7**

Ethical behaviour and implications for accountants

7.1 Introduction

The main purpose of this chapter is for you to have an awareness of the need for ethical behaviour by accountants to complement the various accounting and audit standards issued by the International Accounting Standards Board (IASB), the International Auditing and Assurance Standards Board (IAASB) and professional accounting bodies.

> ### Objectives
>
> By the end of this chapter, you should be able to:
>
> - discuss the meaning of ethical behaviour;
> - understand why accountants need to apply a high level of ethical behaviour to their daily activities;
> - know the sources and intent of the professional guidance in relation to ethical matters;
> - appreciate how approaches to standard setting, laws and cultures influence our ethical standards;
> - describe the various techniques to facilitate whistle-blowing when there are genuine breaches of appropriate legal and moral standards.

7.2 The meaning of ethical behaviour

Individuals in an organisation have their own ethical guidelines which may vary from person to person. These may perhaps be seen as social norms which can vary over time. For example, the relative importance of individual and societal responsibility varies over time.

7.2.1 Individual ethical guidelines

Individual ethical guidelines or personal ethics are the result of a varied set of influences or pressures. As an individual each of us 'enjoys' a series of ethical pressures or influences including the following:

- parents – the first and, according to many authors, the most crucial influence on our ethical guidelines;
- family – the *extended* family which is common in Eastern societies (aunts, uncles, grand-parents and so on) can have a significant impact on personal ethics; the *nuclear* family

which is more common in Western societies (just parent(s) and siblings) can be equally as important but more narrowly focused;

- social group – the ethics of our 'class' (either actual or aspirational) can be a major influence;

- peer group – the ethics of our 'equals' (again either actual or aspirational) can be another major influence;

- religion – ethics based in religion are more important in some cultures, e.g. Islamic societies have some detailed ethics demanded of believers as well as major guidelines for business ethics. However, even in supposedly secular cultures, individuals are influenced by religious ethics;

- culture – this is also a very effective formulator of an individual's ethics;

- professional – when an individual becomes part of a professional body then they are subject to the ethics of the professional body.

Given the variety of inputs, it is natural that there will be a variety of views on what is acceptable ethical behaviour. For example, as an accounting student, how would you handle ethical issues? Would you personally condone cheating? Would you refrain from reporting cheating in exams and assignments by friends? Would you resent other students being selfish, such as hiding library books which are very helpful for an essay? Would you resent cheating in exams by others because you do not cheat and therefore are at a disadvantage? Would that resentment be strong enough to get you to report the fact that there is cheating to the authorities even if you did not name the individuals involved?

7.2.2 Professional ethical guidelines

A managing director of a well known bank described his job as deciding contentious matters for which, after extensive investigation by senior staff, there was no obvious solution. The decision was referred to him because all proposed solutions presented significant downside risks for the bank. Ethical behaviour can be similarly classified. There are matters where there are clearly morally correct answers and there are dilemmas where there are conflicting moral issues.

In this chapter we will endeavour to increase your awareness of the moral issues in the accounting profession. We will also help you identify those problems where there are clear cut solutions, and encourage more searching and sensitive analysis of the complex issues.

Professional codes of conduct tend to provide solutions to common issues which the profession has addressed many times and therefore has had ample opportunity to apply the most experienced and knowledgeable minds to find the best solutions. Thus the professional code of ethics is only the starting point in the sense that it can never cover all the ethical issues an accountant will face and does not absolve accountants from dealing with other ethical dilemmas.

How will decisions be viewed?

Another aspect of ethical behaviour is that others will often be judging the morality of action using hindsight or whilst coming from another perspective. This is the 'how would it appear on the front page of the newspaper?' aspect. So being aware of what could happen is often part of ethical sensitivity. In other words, being able to anticipate possible outcomes or how other parties will view what you have done is a necessary part of identifying that ethical issues have to be addressed.

What if there are competing solutions?

Thus *ethical behaviour involves making decisions which are as morally correct and fair as you can*, recognising that sometimes there will be have to be decisions in relation to two or more competing aspects of what is morally correct which are in unresolvable conflict. One has to be sure that any trade-offs are made for the good of society and that decisions are not blatantly or subtly influenced by self-interest. They must appear fair and reasonable when reviewed subsequently by an uninvolved outsider who is not an accountant. This is because the community places its trust in professionals because they have expertise that others do not, but at the same time it is necessary to retain that trust.

7.3 Financial reports – what is the link between law, corporate governance, corporate social responsibility and ethics?

7.3.1 Law in relation to ethics

The law is the codification into binding rules of those minimum standards of behaviour which parliament sees as essential in a civilised society. These laws reflect societal values and by implication reflect the history and religious beliefs of the community. In other words, they reflect the ethical norms in that society. As minimum standards they do not provide a complete list of ethical guidelines. Compliance with laws which require accountants to follow accounting standards may not give a comprehensive indication of the company's financial position. To give a fairer representation they may have to be supplemented by additional information.

Thus ethical behaviour requires that the annual report be fair to all parties. A famous economist by the name of Baumol[1] provides an interesting concept of superfairness which would help with this type of ethical decision. He says if you didn't know what side of the transaction you were going to be on, what would you consider to be fair? If you didn't know whether you were going to be a company executive, or an auditor, or a buyer of shares, or a seller of shares, what do you think would be a fair representation of the company's performance and financial position? To give a simple example consider a mother who is tired of her two children arguing over who gets the biggest slice of cake. So she gives the whole cake to one child and says cut it into halves and your brother will have first choice of a piece of cake. The child will cut the cake as carefully as possible into two equal halves as the brother will choose whatever appears to be the larger piece of cake, leaving the cutter with the other piece. This is a simple application of superfairness in which neither party is in a position to argue that they were treated unfairly.

The other concern with legal guides is that they can be slow to change and an accountant will be judged by contemporary ethical standards as well as the legal requirements.

7.3.2 Corporate governance in relation to ethics

Corporate governance refers to the systems in place to avoid or resolve potential conflicts of interest. The presence of conflicts of interest means it is possible for one or more parties to make decisions which favour themselves at the expense of others. The possibility of unfair behaviour does not necessarily mean that unethical behaviour will occur. However, the objective of a corporate governance system is to reduce or remove the opportunity for unethical or self-interested behaviour in much the same way as internal controls are there to make it more difficult to commit fraud. They don't guarantee that fraud or unethical behaviour will not occur but they protect the honest from temptation, and they make it much harder for the dishonest to commit unethical behaviour in the areas covered by the system.

Thus corporate governance provides mechanisms in principal–agent situations which reduce the opportunity for unethical behaviour. By principal–agent situations we mean that directors are appointed to look after the interests of shareholders, and have power to act on behalf of shareholders (and thus are agents of shareholders) in situations where shareholders are unable to observe their behaviour. There is therefore a trust relationship and directors have a moral and legal obligation to act in the interests of shareholders. However, there is an element of ambiguity in that different shareholders may have different objectives such as different time horizons. Therefore, since it is sometimes difficult to prove impropriety, the presence of safeguards such as corporate governance mechanism is reassuring. We will be discussing corporate governance in more detail in Chapter 30.

7.3.3 Corporate social responsibility in relation to ethics

Corporate social responsibility (CSR) refers to the process of taking into consideration the financial, social and environmental considerations when making decisions as opposed to an emphasis solely on the financial impacts. Those who take a very narrow view of the corporation believe that the corporation should focus on achieving maximum returns to shareholders. If in the process they pollute the environment or cause social disruption in the community they ignore the cost unless they are likely to be held financially responsible. Ethical behaviour stimulates greater attention to social responsibility and comprehensive accounting. We will be discussing CSR in more detail in Chapter 31.

7.4 What does the accounting profession mean by ethical behaviour?

It is interesting to first consider the legal profession and its view of ethical behaviour and any implication this has for the accounting profession.

7.4.1 The legal profession and ethical behaviour

Kronman[2] wrote a book called *The Lost Lawyer* in which he noted and lamented the change in orientation of the legal profession and of the large legal firms. He said that until recently the lawyers saw themselves as serving the community and that resulted in good incomes. As a consequence, they saw themselves as guardians of the legal system and tried to implement the spirit as well as words of the laws. They saw themselves as professionals with the associated responsibility of safeguarding the interests of the public rather than the narrow interests of their clients.

Kronman made the point that, as law firms grew, there was a shift of emphasis in those firms to seeing themselves as businesses. As businesses, their objective changed to maximising partner incomes, preferably equivalent to those earned by the executives in the large corporations for whom they work. It is not that they don't have ethics; it is just that their frame of reference has shifted. Accordingly they see ethical questions in a different light. Kronman saw the middle-tier law firms as the new upholders of professional values.

7.4.2 The accounting profession and ethical behaviour

It could be argued that the development of the professional accounting firms has mirrored the development of legal practices. Duska and Duska[3] say of accounting:

This tension between the demands of professionalism and the demands of business has created an identity crisis in the industry today.

Duska and Duska[4] proceed to say that the greatest challenge to the accounting profession is to place the interests of clients and the public ahead of their profit-making interests.

This is illustrated by the demise of Arthur Andersen but this firm was not alone at the time. For example, the following extract[5] reads:

> The year [2002] that Arthur Andersen surrendered its licenses to practice Certified Public Accounts, it came under fire for questionable accounting practices in five other cases – overstating cash flow at WorldCom; inflating transaction volumes for clients CMS Energy and Dynergy; improper booking of cost overruns at Halliburton; and inflating revenue at Global Crossing. It should be noted Arthur Andersen was not alone – all 'big five' were involved in improper accounting of one form or other, from conflict of interest, misleading accounting practices to falsifying accounts.

In addition to the pressure to achieve improved profits, accounting firms were under pressure from clients to ignore problems or to structure transactions in a way that concealed the substance of the transaction and the resulting risks. Investors became extremely sceptical of the reliability of financial statements. Confidence that financial reports give a fair view is important for the successful operation of capital markets and led in the USA to the Sarbanes–Oxley Act (SOX) and also to pressure being exerted on the standard setters themselves.

7.4.3 The Sarbanes–Oxley Act (SOX)

It is interesting to note that following the collapse of both Enron and WorldCom in the USA public sentiment was so strong that the Sarbanes–Oxley Act (called SOX) was passed, which placed personal responsibility on the CEO and the CFO for the accounts, with serious penalties for misleading accounts. Also auditors had to confirm that companies had adequate systems and internal controls. Following the collapse of Arthur Andersen and/or the introduction of SOX, a large number of companies had to restate/revise their previous accounts. This raises questions as to the ethics of those who were responsible for the preparation and auditing of those restated accounts. However, there is resistance from business and, in spite of the progress in terms of better accounting, there has recently been a push by industry and commerce to wind-back the SOX provisions particularly in relation to smaller listed entities.

7.4.4 Negative pressures on standard setters

Standard setters have been under pressure which could result in lower quality or expedient accounting as reflected in FASB and SEC rulings. This pressure comes from industry and commerce both directly, and indirectly through threats from the legislators who are beholden to industry. For example, there were proposals to replace the SEC's role in standard setting by transferring the role to a new regulator. The proposal was unsuccessful[6] but illustrates the pressures that can be brought to bear on the standard setters in the US.

The SEC has statutory authority to establish financial accounting and reporting standards for publicly held companies under the Securities Exchange Act of 1934. Historically, however, the SEC has supported FASB's independence and relied on FASB and its predecessors in the private sector to set accounting standards.

The original amendment, which was introduced by Rep. Ed Perlmutter, D-Colo., would have transferred the SEC's accounting standards oversight authority to a proposed new regulator with a mandate to take an active role in accounting standards that it deemed could pose systemic risks.

The amendment that was passed acknowledged that the proposed systemic risk regulator that would be created under the bill would have the ability to comment, like other interested parties, on FASB standards-setting issues.

7.5 Implications of ethical values for the principles versus rules based approaches to accounting standards

It is common in the literature for authors to quote Milton Friedman as indicating that the role of business is to be focused on maximising profits, and also to cite Adam Smith as justification for not interfering in business affairs. In many cases those arguments are misinterpreting the authors.

Milton Friedman recognised that what businessmen should do was maximise profits **within the norms of society**. He knew that without laws to give greater certainty in regard to business activities, and the creation of trust, it was not possible to have a highly efficient economy. Thus he accepted laws which facilitated business transactions and norms in society which also helped to create a cooperative environment. Thus the norms in society set the minimum standards of ethical and social activity which businesses must engage in to be acceptable to those with whom they interact.

Adam Smith (in *The Wealth of Nations*) did not say do not interfere with business, rather, he assumed the existence of the **conditions necessary to facilitate fair and equitable exchanges**. He also suggested that government should interfere to prevent monopolies but should not interfere as a result of lobbying of business groups because their normal behaviour is designed to create monopolies. He also assumed those who did not meet ethical standards might make initial gains but would be found out and shunned. His other major book (*The Theory of Moral Sentiments*) was one on morality so there is no doubt that he thought that ethics were a normal and essential part of society and business.

7.5.1 How does this relate to accounting standards?

The production of accounting standards is only the starting point in the application of accounting standards. We have seen that accountants can apply the standards to the letter of the law and still not achieve reporting that conveys the essence or substance of the performance and financial state of the business. This is because businesses can structure transactions so as to avoid the application of a standard.

The simplest example of this is leasing. In the various jurisdictions, accounting for leases started from the proposition that leases can be divided into two categories, namely, those which involve longer-term commitments and those which are short term in nature or can be cancelled at anytime without substantial penalties. The long-term leases have traditionally been capitalised and appear in the statement of financial position (balance sheet). On the other hand, short-term lease payments are recognised as expenses as they are incurred and the commitments are shown as a note to the accounts. If a company does not want to capitalise a lease, it can approach the financier to change the terms of the lease so that it won't fall into the long-term category.

It is that type of gamesmanship which has worried accounting standard setters. The issue is whether such games are appropriate, and if they aren't, why haven't they been prevented by the ethical standards of the accountants?

7.5.2 How does the accounting profession attempt to ensure that financial reports reflect the substance of a transaction?

We have seen that standards have been set in many national jurisdictions and now internationally by the IASB, in order to make financial statements fair and comparable. The number of standards varies between countries and is described as rules based or principles based according to the number of standardised accounting treatments.

Rules based

Where there are many detailed standards as in the US, the system is described as rules based in that it attempts to specify the uniform treatment for many types of transactions. This is both a strength and also a weakness in that the very use of precise standards as the only criteria leads to the types of games to get around the criteria that were mentioned earlier for lease accounting. When companies have done that, such as in the Enron case, the regulators are influenced to adopt the wider override criteria to support (or replace) the rules.

Principles based

Where there are fewer standards as in the UK, the system is referred to as principles based. In the principles based system there is greater reliance on the application of the true and fair override to (a) report unusual situations and (b) address the issue of whether the accounts prepared in accordance with existing standards provide a fair picture for the decisions to be made by the various users and provide additional information where necessary.

These are positive applications of the override provision. However, the override criteria can also be misused. For example, many companies during the dot com boom around the year 2000 produced statements of **normalised** earnings. The argument was that they were in the set up phase and many of the costs they were incurring were one offs. To get a better understanding of the business readers were said to need to know what an ongoing result was likely to be. So they removed set up costs and produced **normalised** or **sustainable** earnings which suggested the company was inherently profitable. Unfortunately many of these companies failed because those one off costs were not one off and had to be maintained to keep a customer base.

However, the current discussions about IFRS being principles based whereas the USA GAAP is rules based is incorrect in that in neither case do the starting principles justify non-compliance with standards. It is true that the USA has more standards which have been developed for specific applications but that is not a difference in approach but rather a reflection that more effort has been addressed to more different circumstances. Having more choices as sometimes occurs in IFRS is not a principles based approach unless the choices made are not based on personal preferences but rather on reasoning which has to be justified on the basis of first principles. In addition, it could be argued that general purpose accounts (whether rules based or principles based) can never be appropriate for many purposes for which they are routinely used.

The decision has been agreed by the US and IASB that principles based approach should be adopted. This still leaves unanswered the question as to whether this approach can give a true and fair view to every stakeholder. Shareholders are recognised in all jurisdictions but the rights of other parties may vary according to the legal system. When, for example, do the rights of lenders become paramount? Should the accounts be tailored to suit employees when the legal system in some jurisdictions recognises companies are not just there to support owners but have major responsibilities to recognise the preservation of employment wherever possible?

The above discussion is designed to provide a feel for the type of issues which are relevant for the discussion of rules versus principles.

7.6 The principles based approach and ethics

The preceding discussion looked at the principle of true and fair or its equivalent from an accountant's perspective, but ultimately what it means will be determined by the courts. They might take a different perspective again, which is one of the problems of having a criterion which is subjective and liable to be defined more precisely after the event.

If accounting is to be primarily or partially principles based, those principles need to be clearly spelt out in such a manner that those applying them, and those that are reviewing their application, clearly understand what they mean. Furthermore, those who will adjudicate in disputes over whether the criteria have been properly applied, which normally only occurs when substantial sums have been lost or unfairly gained, must at least have basically the same perspective. This is not to suggest law courts have to follow accountants. In application it is probable that the accountants will have to adopt the stance of the courts irrespective of whether they have correctly understood the subtleties of accounting. This means the principles must be expressed in everyday language. True and fair could perhaps be applied but it would have to have an everyday interpretation, such as Rawls[7] expressed when he spoke of justice as fairness or what Baumol called superfairness.

It would, in order to avoid ambiguity, have to spell out 'fair to whom and for what purpose'. This is because at the present time society is in a process of reassessing the role of business relative to the demands by society to achieve high employment rates, to overcome environmental problems and to achieve fair treatment of all countries. Essentially this is suggesting that, given the changing orientation, consideration may have to be given to ethical criteria even if there is only a partial shift from a shareholder orientation to a balancing of competing claims in society. Daniel Friedman[8] says: 'The greatest challenge is to realign morals and markets so that they work together, rather than at cross purposes.' This will need a balancing act specific to the problem faced. In other words, it would have to be principle driven.

7.6.1 Are principles linked to accounting standards?

The next issue is linking principles with accounting standards. The current conceptual framework assumes that we need to produce general purpose financial accounts using understandability, relevance, reliability, and comparability as guiding criteria. However, the individual standards do not demonstrate how those principles lead to the standards which have been produced. Only if that linkage is demonstrated can the standard setters demonstrate to accountants generally how to go from general principles to detailed applications. This is important if the intent is to go from basic principles which must be the underlying starting points. If principles are to dominate when there are no standards which are applicable, such as the case of a unique industry or to a new application, then practitioners could look to the derivation of existing standards to learn how to work out appropriate treatments for their previously unaddressed situation. Also in applying existing accounting standards, their intent should be evident from their derivation. Then accountants would have an obligation to apply the intent rather than being able to justify their avoidance through technical manoeuvring. However, if the intent is to be guided by principles, it should also be possible to justify non-compliance with standards if the assumptions made in formulating the standards do not hold in a specific case.

7.6.2 What are the implications of the above discussion?

Ethics has two major areas where it could impact on the principles based approach. These are that (a) ethics informs the principles and (b) cultural differences may lead to different principles being applied.

(a) Ethics could supply all or part of the criteria used to derive and evaluate potential principles or could be part of the principles themselves. Also the way in which principles are used will not lead to good outcomes unless the accountants preparing and reviewing accounts have high moral standards. An accountant in preparing accounts will always have a potential clash between what his employer and superior wants and what is best from an ethical or community perspective.

(b) If norms, laws and ethics are an integral part of the formulation of accounting principles then there may be grounds for different accounting being applicable to different countries. If the purpose of accounting is not the same in all countries with some countries placing, say, greater emphasis on the impact on employees or the community then the principles must differ. Further, it raises the question of how cultural norms and religion affect ethics both in coverage and how they interpret the individual guidelines. It brings into question the assumption that shareholders in every country have identical information needs and apply identical ethical criteria in assessing a company's operations.

An interesting piece of research compared the attitudes of students in the USA and the UK to cheating and found the US students more likely to cheat.[9] The theoretical basis of the research was that different cultural characteristics, such as uncertainty avoidance or conversely the tolerance for ambiguity, lead to different attitudes to ethics. This means uniform ethical guidelines will not lead to uniform applications in multinational companies unless the corporate culture is much stronger than the country culture. This has implications for multinational businesses that want the accounts prepared in different countries to be uniform in quality. It is significant for audit firms that want their sister firms in other countries to apply the same standards to audit judgements. It is important to investment firms that are making investments throughout the world on the understanding that accounting and ethical standards mean the same things in all major security markets.

Where there are differences in legal and cultural settings then potentially the correct accounting will also differ if a principles based approach is adopted. Currently, Western concepts dominate accounting but if the world power base shifts to either being made up of several world centres of influence, or a new dominant world power, the principles of accounting may have to reflect that.

7.7 The accounting standard-setting process and ethics

Standard setters seem to view the process as similar to physics in the sense of trying to set standards with a view to achieving an objective measure of reality. However, some academics suggest that such an approach is inappropriate because the concepts of profit and value are not physical attributes but 'man made' dimensions. For instance, for profit we measure the progress of the business but the concept of progress is a very subjective attribute which has traditionally omitted public costs such as environmental and social costs. The criteria of fairness has been seen as satisfied by preparing profit statements on principles such as going concern and accrual when measuring profit and neutrality when presenting the profit statement.

What if fairness is defined differently? For example, the idea of basing accounting on the criteria of fairness to all stakeholders (financiers, workers, suppliers, customers and the community) was made by Leonard Spacek[10] before the formation of the FASB. However, this view was not appreciated by the profession at that time. We now see current developments in terms of environmental and social accounting which are moves in that direction but, even so, CSR is not incorporated into the financial statements prepared under IFRSs and constitutes supplementary information that is not integrated into the accounting measures themselves.

The accounting profession sees ethical behaviour in standard setting as ensuring that accounting is neutral. Their opponents think that neutrality is impossible and that accounting has a wide impact on society and thus to be ethical the impact on all parties affected should be taken into consideration.

The accounting profession does not address ethics at the macro level other than pursuing neutrality, but rather focus their attention on actions after the standards and laws are in place. The profession seeks to provide ethical standards which will increase the probability of those standards being applied in an ethical fashion at the micro level where accountants apply their individual skills.

The accounting profession through its body the International Federation of Accountants (IFAC) has developed a *Code of Ethics for Professional Accountants*.[11] That code looks at fundamental principles as well as specific issues which are frequently encountered by accountants in public practice, followed by those commonly faced by accountants in business. The intention is that the professional bodies and accounting firms 'shall not apply less stringent standards than those stated in this code' (p. 4).

7.8 The IFAC *Code of Ethics for Professional Accountants*

The IFAC Fundamental Principles are:

i) 'A distinguishing mark of the accountancy profession is its acceptance of the responsibility to act in the public interest . . .' (100.1)

ii) 'A professional accountant shall comply with the following fundamental principles:

   a) *Integrity* – to be straightforward and honest in all professional and business relationships.

   b) *Objectivity* – to not allow bias, conflict of interest or undue influence of others to override professional or business judgments.

   c) *Professional Competence and Due Care* – to maintain professional knowledge and skill at the level required to ensure that a client or employer receives competent professional services based on current developments in practice, legislation and techniques and act diligently and in accordance with applicable technical and professional standards.

   d) *Confidentiality* – to respect the confidentiality of information acquired as a result of professional and business relationships and, therefore, not disclose any such information to third parties without proper and specific authority, unless there is a legal or professional right or duty to disclose, nor use the information for the personal advantage of the professional accountant or third parties.

   e) *Professional Behaviour* – to comply with relevant laws and regulations and avoid any action that discredits the profession' (100.5).

7.8.1 Acting in the public interest

The first underlying statement that accountants should act in the public interest is probably more difficult to achieve than is imagined. This requires accounting professionals to stand firm against accounting standards which are not in the public interest, even when the politicians and company executives may be pressing for their acceptance. Due to the fact that, in the conduct of an audit, the auditors have dealings mainly with the management, it is easy to lose sight of who the clients actually are. For example, the expression 'audit clients' is commonly used in professional papers and academic books when they are referring to the management of the companies being audited. It immediately suggests a relationship which is biased towards management when, legally, the client may be either the shareholders as a group or specific stakeholders. Whilst it is a small but subtle distinction, it could be the start of a misplaced orientation towards seeing the management as the client.

7.8.2 Fundamental principles

The five fundamental principles are probably uncontentious guides to professional conduct. It is the application of those guides in specific circumstances which provides the greatest challenges. The IFAC paper provides guidance in relation to public accountants covering appointments, conflicts of interest, second opinions, remuneration, marketing, acceptance of gratuities, custody of client assets, objectivity, and independence. In regard to accountants in business they provide guidance in the areas of potential conflicts, preparation and reporting of information, acting with sufficient expertise, financial interests, and inducements.

It is not intended to provide all the guidance which the IFAC code of ethics provides, and if students want that detail they should consult the original document. This chapter will provide a flavour of the coverage relating to accountants in public practice and accountants in business.

7.8.3 Problems arising for accountants in practice

Appointments

Before accepting appointments, public accountants should consider the desirability of accepting the client given the business activities involved, particularly if there are questions of their legality. They also need to consider (a) whether the current accountant of the potential client has advised of any professional reasons for not becoming involved and (b) whether they have the competency required considering the industry and their own expertise. Nor should they become involved if they already provide other services which are incompatible with being the auditor or if the size of the fees would threaten their independence. (Whilst it is not stated in the code, the implication is that it is better to avoid situations which are likely to lead to difficult ethical issues.)

Second opinions

When an accountant is asked to supply a second opinion on an accounting treatment, it is likely that the opinion will be used to undermine an accountant who is trying to do the right thing. It is therefore important to ascertain that all relevant information has been provided before issuing a second opinion, and if in doubt decline the work.

Remuneration

Remuneration must be adequate to allow the work to be done in a professional manner.

Commissions received from other parties must not be such as to make it difficult to be objective when advising your client and in any event must at least be disclosed to clients. Whilst not discussed in the document, the involvement of accountants in personal financial planning has raised ethical issues where the investment vehicle rewards the accountants with commissions. Some accountants have addressed that by passing the commissions on to their client and charging a flat fee for the consulting.

Marketing

Marketing should be professional and should not exaggerate or make negative comments about the work of other professionals.

Independence

Accountants and their close relatives should not accept gifts, other than insubstantial ones, from clients. IFAC para. 280.2 provides that:

> A professional accountant in public practice who provides an assurance service shall be independent of the assurance client. Independence of mind and in appearance is necessary to enable the professional accountant in public practice to express a conclusion.

Professional firms have their own criterion level as to the value of gifts that can be accepted. For example, the following is an extract from the KPMG Code of Conduct:

> Qn: I manage a reproduction center at a large KPMG office. We subcontract a significant amount of work to a local business. The owner is very friendly and recently offered to give me two free movie passes. Can I accept the passes?

> Ans: Probably. Here, the movie passes are considered a gift because the vendor is not attending the movie with you. In circumstances where it would not create the appearance of impropriety, you may accept reasonable gifts from third parties such as our vendors, provided that the value of the gift is not more than $100 and that you do not accept gifts from the same vendor more than twice in the same year.

7.8.4 Problems arising for accountants in business

In relation to accountants in business, the major problem identified by the code seems to be the financial pressures which arise from substantial financial interests in the form of shares, options, pension plans and dependence on employment income to support themselves and their dependants. When these depend on reporting favourable performance, it is difficult to withstand the pressure.

Every company naturally wants to present its results in the most favourable way possible and investors expect this and it is part of an accountant's expertise to do this. However, the ethical standards require compliance with the law and accounting standards subject to the overriding requirement for financial statements to present a fair view. Misreporting and the omission of additional significant material which would change the assessment of the financial position of the company are unacceptable.

Accountants need to avail themselves of any internal steps to report pressure to act unethically, and if that fails to produce results, they need to be willing to resign.

7.8.5 Threats to compliance with the fundamental principles

The IFAC document has identified five types of threats to compliance with their fundamental principles and they will be outlined below. The objective of outlining these potential threats is to make you sensitive to the types of situations where your ethical judgements may be clouded and where you need to take extra steps to ensure you act ethically. The statements are deliberately broad to help you handle situations not covered specifically by the guidelines. IFAC para. 100.12 provides that:

Threats fall into one or more of the following categories:

(a) Self-interest threat – the threat that a financial or other interest will inappropriately influence the accountant's judgment or behaviour;

(b) Self-review threat – the threat that a professional will not appropriately evaluate the results of a previous judgment made or service performed by the professional accountant, or by another individual within the professional accountant's firm or employing organization, or on which the accountant will rely when forming a judgment as part of providing a current service;

(c) Advocacy threat – the threat that a professional will promote a client's or employer's position to the point that the professional accountant's objectivity is compromised;

(d) Familiarity threat – the threat that due to a long or close relationship with a client or employer, a professional accountant will be too sympathetic to their interests or too accepting of their work; and

(e) Intimidation threat – the threat that a professional accountant will be deterred from acting objectively because of actual or perceived pressures, including attempts to exercise undue influence over the professional accountant.

7.9 Ethics in the accountants' work environment – a research report

The Institute of Chartered Accountants in Scotland issued a discussion paper report[12] entitled 'Taking Ethics to Heart', based on research into the application of ethics in practice. This section will discuss some of the findings of that report.

From a student's perspective, one of the interesting findings was that many accountants could not remember the work on ethics which they did as students and therefore had little to draw upon to guide them when problems arose. There was agreement that students need to get more experience in dealing with case studies so as to enhance their ethical decision making skills. This should be reinforced throughout their careers by continuing professional development. The training should sensitise accountants so that they can easily recognise ethical situations and develop skills in resolving the dilemmas.

Exposure to ethical issues is usually low for junior positions, although even then there can be clear and grey issues. For example, padding an expense claim or overstating overtime are clear issues, whereas how to deal with information that has been heard in a private conversation between client staff is less clear. What if a conversation is overheard where one of the factory staff says that products have been despatched at the year end which are known to be defective? Would your response be different if you had been party to the conversation? Would your response be different if it had been suggested that there was a risk of injury due to the defect? Is it ethical to inform your manager or is it unethical not to inform?

Normally exposure to ethical issues increases substantially at the manager level and continues at senior management positions. However the significance of ethical decision making has increased with the expansion of the size of both companies and accounting practices. The impact of decisions can be more widespread and profound. Further, there has been an increase in litigation potentially exposing the accountant to more external review. Greater numbers of accounting and auditing standards can lead to a narrower focus making it harder for individual accountants to envisage the wider ethical dimensions and to get people to consider more than the detailed rules.

Given the likelihood of internal or external review, the emphasis that many participants in the study placed on asking 'how would this decision look to others?' seems a sensible criterion. In light of that emphasis by participants in the research it is interesting to consider the 'Resolving Conflicts' section of BT PLC's document called *The Way We Work*[13] which among other things says:

> How would you explain your decision to your colleagues in different countries?
>
> How would you explain your decision to your family or in public?
>
> Does it conflict with your own or BT's commitment to integrity?

This emphasis on asking how well ethical decisions would stand public scrutiny, including scrutiny in different countries, would be particularly relevant to accountants in businesses operating across national borders.

The role of the organisational setting in improving or worsening ethical decision making was given considerable attention in the ICAS report. A key starting point is having a set of ethical policies which are practical and are reinforced by the behaviour of senior management. Another support is the presence of clearly defined process for referring difficult ethical decisions upward in the organisation.

For those in small organisations, there needs to be an opportunity for those in difficult situations to seek advice about the ethical choice or the way to handle the outcomes of making an ethical stand. Most professional bodies either have senior mentors available or have organised referrals to bodies specialising in ethical issues.

The reality is that some who have taken ethical stands have lost their jobs, but some of those who haven't stood their ground have lost their reputations or their liberty.

7.10 Implications of unethical behaviour for financial reports

One of the essential aspects of providing complete and reliable information which are taken seriously by the financial community is to have a set of rigorous internal controls. However, ultimately those controls are normally dependent on checks and balances within the system and the integrity of those with the greatest power within the system. In other words, the checks and balances, such as requiring two authorisations to issue a cheque or transfer money, presume that at least one of those with authority will act diligently and will be alert to the possibility of dishonest or misguided behaviour by the other. Further, if necessary or desirable, they will take firm action to prevent any behaviour that appears suspicious. The internal control system depends on the integrity and diligence, in other words the ethical behaviour of the majority of the staff in the organisation.

7.10.1 Increased cost of capital

The presence of unethical behaviour in an organisation will raise questions about the reliability of the accounts. If unethical behaviour is suspected by investors, they will probably raise the cost of capital for the individual business. If there are sufficient cases of unethical behaviour across all companies, the integrity of the whole market will be brought into question and the liquidity of the whole market is reduced. That would affect the cost of funds across the board and increase the volatility of share prices.

7.10.2 Hidden liabilities

The other dimension related to the presence of unethical behaviour is associated with hidden liabilities. To illustrate, if a firm cuts corners in terms of quality control, there will be future costs in terms of satisfying warranties and perhaps the undermining of the value of goodwill.

If suppliers are treated unethically and unfairly, they may in the longer term refuse to supply or make the supply more expensive. Alternatively they may consolidate activities by mergers so as to increase their bargaining power. Once again the value of intangibles of the purchaser may be undermined.

A liability, particularly an environmental one, might not crystallise for a number of years as with the James Hardie Group in Australia. The James Hardie Group was a producer of asbestos sheeting whose fibres can in the long-term damage the lungs and lead to death. A number of senior executives of the company themselves died from this. The company was slow in taking the product off the market after the potentially dangerous nature of the product was demonstrated although it has for a number of years now only produced and sold the safe alternative fibre board. The challenge the company faced was the long gestation period between the exposure to the dust from the asbestos and the appearance of the symptoms of the disease. It can be up to 40 years before victims find out that they have a death sentence. The company reorganised so that there was a separate entity which was responsible for the liabilities and that entity was supposed to have sufficient funds to cover future liabilities as they came to light. When it was apparent that the funds set aside were grossly inadequate and that the assessment of adequacy had been based on old data rather than using the more recent data which showed an increasing rate of claims, there was widespread community outrage. As a result, the James Hardie Group felt that irrespective of its legal position, it had to negotiate with the state government and the unions to set aside a share of its cash flows from operations each year to help the victims. Thus the unfair arrangements set in place came back to create the equivalent of liabilities and did considerable damage to the public image of the company. This also made some people reluctant to be associated with the company as customers or employees. The current assessment of liability (as at 2009) is set out in a KPMG Actuarial Report.[14]

7.10.3 Auditor reaction to risk of unethical behaviour

In addition to the above type items, unethical behaviour should make auditors and investors scrutinise accounts more closely. Following the experiences with companies such as Enron, the auditing standards have placed greater emphasis on auditors being sceptical. This means that if they identify instances of unethical behaviour, they should ask more searching questions. Depending on the responses they get, they may need to undertake more testing to satisfy themselves of the reliability of the accounts.

7.10.4 Risk of fraud

There is an increasing need to be wary of unethical behaviour by management leading to fraud.

Jennings[15] points out that while most of the major frauds that make the headlines tend to be attributed to a small number of individuals, there has to be many other participants who allowed it to happen. For every CEO who bleeds the company through companies paying for major personal expenses, or through gross manipulation of accounts, or back dating of options, there has to be a considerable number of people who know what is happening but who choose not to bring it to the attention of the appropriate authorities. The appropriate authority could be the board of directors, or the auditors or regulatory authorities. She attributes this to the culture of the organisation and suggests there are seven signs of ethical collapse in an organisation. They include pressure to maintain the numbers, dissent and bad news are not welcome, iconic CEOs surrounding themselves by young executives whose careers are dependent on them, a weak board of directors, numerous conflicts of interest, innovation abounds, and where goodness in some areas is thought to atone for evil in others.

Others have suggested that companies with high levels of takeover activity and high leverage often are prime candidates for fraud because of the pressures to achieve the numbers. Also if the attitude is that the sole purpose of the firm is to make money subject to compliance with the letter of the law, that is also a warning sign.

The ICSA Report[16] *Taking Ethics to Heart* noted that it appeared that the current business and commercial environment placed an enormous pressure on accountants, wherever they work, which may result in decisions and judgements that compromise ethical standards. It noted also that increased commercial pressures on accountants may be viewed by many within the profession as heralding a disquieting new era.

The accountant working within business has a different set of problems due to the dual position as an employee and a professional accountant. There is a potential clash of issues where the interests of the business could be at odds with professional standards.

7.10.5 Action by professional accounting bodies to assist members

The various professional bodies approach things in different ways. For example, the ICAEW established the Industrial Members Advisory Committee on Ethics (IMACE) in the late 1970s to give specific advice to members with ethical problems in business. This is supported by a strong local support network as well as a national helpline for the guidance of accountants. At the moment IMACE is dealing with 200 to 300 problems per year but this is more a reflection of the numbers of chartered accountants in business than a reflection on the lack of ethical problems.

The type of problem raised is a good indication of the ethical issues raised for accountants in business. They include:

- requests by employers to manipulate tax returns;
- requests to produce figures to mislead shareholders;
- requests to conceal information;
- requests to manipulate overhead absorption rates to extort more income from customers (an occurrence in the defence industries);
- requests to authorise and conceal bribes to buyers and agents, a common request in some exporting businesses;
- requests to produce misleading projected figures to obtain additional finance;
- requests to conceal improper expense claims put in by senior managers;
- requests to over- or undervalue assets;
- requests to misreport figures in respect of government grants;
- requests for information which could lead to charges of 'insider dealing';
- requests to redefine bad debts as 'good' or vice versa.

For accountants in industry, the message is that if your employer has a culture which is not conducive to high ethical values then a good career move would be to look for employment elsewhere. For auditors, the message is that the presence of symptoms suggested above is grounds for employing greater levels of scepticism in the audit.

7.11 Company codes of ethics

Most companies now adopt codes of ethics. They may have alternative titles such as our values, codes of conduct, and codes of ethics. For example, BP has a code of conduct whose coverage, which is listed below, is what one would expect of a company involved in its industry and its activities covering a large number of countries. Its Code of Conduct includes the following major categories:

- Our commitment to integrity.
- Health, safety, security and the environment.
- Employees.
- Business partners.
- Governments and communities.
- Company assets and financial integrity.

Note that or the time of writing (June 2010), BP's code of conduct is under close scrutiny due to the oil drilling disaster in the Gulf of Mexico.

However, the challenge is to make the code an integral part of the day-to-day behaviour of the company and to be perceived as doing such by outsiders. Obviously top management has to act in ways so as to reinforce the values of the code and to eliminate existing activities which are incompatible with the new values.

BP has been criticised for behaviour inconsistent with its values but such behaviour may relate to actions taken before the adoption of the code.[17]

Thus it is important to ensure that the corporate behaviour is consistent with the code of conduct, that staff are rewarded for ethical behaviour and suffer penalties for non-compliance. Breaches, irrespective of whether they are in the past, are difficult to erase from the memories of society.

Stohl et al.[18] suggest that the content of codes of conduct can be divided into three levels.

- Level 1 – there is an attempt to ensure that the company is in compliance with all the laws which impact on it in the various countries in which it operates.

- Level 2 – focuses on ensuring fair and equitable relations with all parties with which the company has direct relations. In this category would be the well publicised adverse publicity which Nike received when it was alleged that their subcontractors were exploiting child labour in countries where such treatment is legal. The adverse publicity and boycotts meant that many companies reviewed their operations and expanded their codes to cover such situations and thus moved into the second level of ethic awareness.

- Level 3 – is where the companies take a global perspective and recognise their responsibility to contribute to the likelihood of peace and favourable global environmental conditions. In most companies the level one concerns are more dominant than level two than the level three. European firms are more likely than US to have a level-three orientation.

7.11.1 Conflict between codes and targets

On the one hand, we see companies developing Codes of Ethical Conduct whilst on the other hand we see some of these same companies developing Management by Objectives which set staff unachievable targets and create pressures that lead to unethical behaviour. Where this occurs there is the risk that an unhealthy corporate climate may develop resulting in the manipulation of accounting figures and unethical behaviour.

There is a view[19] that there is a need to create an ethical climate that transcends a compliance approach to ethics and focuses instead on fostering socially harmonious relationships. An interesting article[20] proceeds to make the argument that the recent accounting scandals may be as much a reflection of a deficient corporate climate, with its concentration on setting unrealistic targets and promoting competition between the staff, as of individual moral failures of managers.

7.11.2 Multinationals face special problems

The modern multinational companies experience special problems in relation to ethics. Firstly, the transactions are often extremely large, so that there are greater pressures to bend the rules so as to get the business. Secondly, the ethical values as reflected in some of the countries may be quite different from those in the head office of the group. One company did business in a developing country where the wages paid to public officials were so low as to be insufficient to support a family even at the very modest living standards of that country. Many public officials had a second job so as to cope. Others saw it as appropriate to demand kick backs in order for them to process any government approvals as for them there was a strong ethical obligation to ensure their family was properly looked after which in their opinion outweighs their obligation to the community.

Is it ethical for other nations to condemn such behaviour in the extreme cases? Should a different standard apply? What is the business to do if that is the norm in a country? Some may decline to do business in those countries, others may employ intermediaries. In the latter case, a company sells the goods to an intermediary company which then resells the goods in the problem country. The intermediary obviously has to pay fees and bribes to make the sale but that is not the concern of the multinational company! They deliberately do not ask the intermediary what they do. However, it could become a concern if a protest group identifies the questionable behaviour of the agent and decides to hold the multinational responsible. A third option is to just pay the fees and bribes. The problem with the second and third positions is that they may be held responsible by one of the countries in which they operate which has laws making it illegal to corrupt public officials in their country or any other country. Also there is the problem that if companies pay bribes that behaviour reinforces the corrupt forces in the target country which, in turn, makes it difficult for the government of that country to eliminate corruption.

The Serious Fraud office in the UK[21] and the Department of Justice in the US are actively investigating corrupt practices. For example, in 2010 BAE Systems had to pay substantial fines for being involved in bribery. In the USA it had to pay $USD400 million to settle allegations of bribery in relation to arms deals with Saudi Arabia. The Serious Fraud Office in the UK made it pay £30 million in relation to over-priced military radar sold to Tanzania whilst taking into account the implementation by BAE Systems of substantial ethical and compliance reforms. Part of the fines is being passed on to the people of Tanzania to compensate for the damage done.

7.11.3 The support given by professional bodies in the designing of ethical codes

There are excellent support facilities available. For example, the Chartered Association of Certified Accountants website (www.accaglobal.com) makes a toolkit available for accountants who might be involved with designing a code of ethics. The site also provides an overview which considers matters such as why ethics are important, links to other related sites, e.g. the Center for Ethics and Business from Loyola Marymount University in Los Angeles[22] with a quiz to establish one's ethical style as an ethic of justice or an ethic of care and a toolkit[23] to assist in the design of a code of ethics.

7.12 The increasing role of whistle-blowing

It is recognised that normally when the law or an ethical code is being broken by a company, a range of people inside and outside the company are aware of the illegal activities or have sufficient information to raise suspicions. To reduce the likelihood of illegal activity or to help identify its occurrence, a number of regulatory organisations have set up mechanisms for whistle-blowing to occur. Also a number of companies have set up their own units, often through a consulting firm, whereby employees can report illegal activities and breaches of a firm's code of ethics or any other activities which are likely to bring a company into disrepute.

Immunity to the first party to report

For example, in many countries the regulatory authority responsible for pursuing price fixing has authority to give immunity or favourable treatment to the first party to report the occurrence of price fixing. It may be possible for the person's lawyer to ascertain whether the item has already been reported without disclosing the identity of the client. This arrangement is in place because of the difficulty of collecting information on such activities of sufficient quality and detail to successfully prosecute. For example, British Airways was fined about £270 million after it admitted collusion in fixing the prices of fuel surcharges. The US Department of Justice fined it $300 million (£148 million) for colluding on how much extra to charge on passenger and cargo flights, to cover fuel costs and UK's Office of Fair Trading fined it £121.5 million, after it held illegal talks with rival Virgin Atlantic. Virgin was given immunity after it reported the collusion and was not fined.

Anonymous whistle-blowing

In the case of large companies, it is difficult for top management to be fully informed as to whether subordinates throughout the organisation are acting responsibly. One solution has been to arrange for an accounting firm to have a contact number where people can anonymously report details of breaches of the law or breaches of ethics or other activities impacting on the good name of the company. It has to be anonymous for several reasons. Firstly people will often be reporting on activities which they have been 'forced' to do or on activities of their superior or colleagues. Given that those colleagues will not take kindly to being reported on, and are capable of making life very difficult for the informant, it is important that reports can be made anonymously. Also even those who are not directly affected will often view whistle-blowing as letting the side down. The whistle-blower, if identified, could well be ostracised. Whilst firms having anonymous hot lines may well support individuals if they ask for it, whistle-blowers need to realise from the beginning that ultimately they may have to seek alternative employment. This is not to suggest they shouldn't blow the whistle. Rather it is to reflect the history of whistle-blowers. However, this should be contrasted with the alternative. If the behaviour you are being required to undertake exposes you to criminal actions, it is better to do the hard work now than suffer the consequences of lost reputation, possibly lost liberty, severe financial penalties, and the stress of drawn out law cases. If you are not involved but are just trying to prevent the company from getting further into negative territory, you may be doing many people a favour. You may prevent the company from getting into a position from which there may be no recovery. You will avoid other people from suffering the same stress which you are under.

Take Enron as an example. The collapse of the company meant many people lost their job and a substantial portion of their superannuation. Others served time in prison. This included executives, and external parties who benefited from or supported the illegal or unethical behaviour. Also the events surrounding the failure contributed to the series of events which destroyed their auditors Arthur Andersen. If someone had blown the whistle much earlier then perhaps a number of those serious consequences would never have occurred. As it was, the staff member who raised the issue of dubious accounting with the CEO, Kenneth Lay, shortly before the collapse, made it harder for him to deny responsibility when he was tried for fraud.

Proportionate response

In spite of the above comments, it is important to keep in mind that the steps taken should reflect the seriousness of the event and that the whistle-blowing should be the final strategy rather than the first. In other words, the normal actions should be to use the internal forums such as debating issues in staff meetings or raising the issue with an immediate superior or their boss when the superior is not approachable for some reason. Nor are disagreements over business issues a reason for reporting. The motivation should be to report breaches which represent legal, moral or public interest concerns and not matters purely relating to differences of opinion on operational issues, personality differences or jealousy.

Government support

There are legal protections against victimisation but it would be more useful if the government provided positive support such as assistance with finding other employment or, perhaps, some form of financial reward to compensate for public spirited actions that actually lead to professional or financial hardship for the whistle-blower.

7.12.1 The role of financial reporting authorities

The financial markets are very dependent on the presence of trust in the integrity of the system and all major players in its operation. It is noticeable that in periods when there have been lower levels of trust participation rates have fallen, prices are lower and prices are more volatile. To maintain trust in the system, financial regulatory authorities monitor inappropriate behaviour and take action against offenders. We comment briefly on the FINRA in the US and the Accounting and Actuarial Disciplinary Board in the UK.

FINRA (Financial Industry Regulatory Authority)

In announcing its creation of the 'Office of the Whistleblower' on 5 March 2009 the FINRA said:[24]

> Some of FINRA's most significant enforcement actions have resulted from investor complaints or anonymous insider tips. They include FINRA's 2007 action against Citigroup Global Markets, ordering the firm to pay a $3 million fine and $12.2 million in restitution to customers to settle charges of misleading Bell South employees in North and South Carolina at early retirement seminars; FINRA's 2006 fine of $5 million against Merrill Lynch to resolve charges related to supervisory violations at its customer Call Center; FINRA's 2005 landmark action against the Kansas firm

Waddell & Reed, Inc., in which the firm was fined $5 million and ordered to pay $11 million in restitution to customers to resolve charges related to variable annuity switching; and, FINRA's 2002 action against Credit Suisse First Boston to resolve charges of siphoning tens of millions of dollars of customers' profits in exchange for 'hot' IPO shares, which resulted in a $50 million fine imposed by FINRA and an additional $50 million fine imposed by the Securities and Exchange Commission.

The Accounting and Actuarial Disciplinary Board

In the UK there is the Accounting and Actuarial Disciplinary Board which investigates and hears complaints. It has on its web pages[25] details of pending cases and reports on completed cases. People with complaints are referred to the relevant accounting professional bodies (ICAEW, ACCA, CIMA, CIFPA) which will try to resolve the issues and if appropriate will refer them to the tribunal.

Whistle-blowing – protection in the UK

In the UK the Public Interest Disclosure Act came into force in 1999 protecting whistle-blowers who raised genuine concerns about malpractice from dismissal and victimisation in order to promote the public interest. The scope of malpractice is wide-ranging, including, e.g. the covering up of a suspected crime, a civil offence such as negligence, a miscarriage of justice, and health and safety or environmental risks.

Whistle-blowing – policies

Companies should have in place a policy which gives clear guidance to employees on the appropriate internal procedures to follow if there is a suspected malpractice. Employees, including accountants and internal auditors, are expected to follow these procedures as well as acting professionally and in accordance with their own professional code.

The following is an extract from the Vodafone 2009 Annual Report:

Ethics

Vodafone's success is underpinned by our commitment to ethical conduct in the way we do business and interact with key stakeholders.

Business principles

Our *Business Principles* define how we intend to conduct our business and our relationships with key stakeholders. They require employees to act with honesty, integrity and fairness.

The principles cover ethical issues including:

- Bribery and corruption
- Conflicts of interest
- Human rights.

The Business Principles set a policy of zero tolerance on bribery and corruption. Our *Anti-corruption Compliance Guidelines* help ensure employees comply with all applicable anti-corruption laws and regulations. We have also introduced an anti-bribery online training course.

Reporting violations

Employees can report any potential violations of the Business Principles to their line manager or local human resources manager in the first instance. Alternatively, they can raise concerns anonymously to our Group Audit Director or our Group Human Resources Director via an online whistle-blowing system.

Our Duty to Report policy applies to *suppliers* and contractors as well as employees. Concerns can be reported either by contacting Vodafone's Group Fraud Risk and Security Department directly, or via a third party confidential telephone hotline service. The line is available 24 hours a day. All calls are taken by an independent organisation with staff trained to handle calls of this nature.

However, although the whistle-blowing policies might have been followed and the accountants protected by the provisions of the Public Interest Disclosure Act, it could result in a breakdown of trust making their position untenable; this means that a whistle-blower might be well advised to have an alternative position in mind.

Breach of confidentiality

Auditors are protected from the risk of liability for breach of confidence provided that:

- disclosure is made in the public interest;
- disclosure is made to a proper authority;
- there is no malice motivating the disclosure.

7.12.2 Legal requirement to report – national and international regulation

It is likely that there will be an increase in formal regulation as the search for greater transparency and ethical business behaviour continues. We comment briefly on national and international regulation relating to money laundering and bribery.

Money laundering – overview

There are various estimates of the scale of money laundering ranging up to over 2% of global gross domestic product. Certain businesses are identified as being more prone to money laundering, e.g. import/export companies and cash businesses such as antiques and art dealers, auction houses, casinos and garages. However, the avenues are becoming more and more sophisticated with methods varying between countries, e.g. in the UK there is the increasing use of smaller non-bank institutions, whereas in Spain it includes cross-border carrying of cash, money-changing at bureaux de change and investment in real estate.

Money laundering – implications for accountants

In 2006 the Auditing Practices Board (APB) in the UK issued a revised Practice Note 12 *Money Laundering* which required auditors to take the possibility of money laundering into account when carrying out their audit and to report to the appropriate authority if they become aware of suspected laundering.

In 1999 there was also guidance from the professional accounting bodies, e.g. *Money Laundering: Guidance Notes for Chartered Accountants* issued by the Institute of Chartered Accountants which deal with the statute law, regulations and professional requirements in relation to the avoidance, recognition and reporting of money laundering.

Money laundering – the Financial Action Task Force (FATF)

The Financial Action Task Force (FATF) is an independent inter-governmental body that develops and promotes policies to protect the global financial system against money laundering and terrorist financing. Recommendations issued by the FATF define criminal justice and regulatory measures that should be implemented to counter this problem. These Recommendations also include international co-operation and preventive measures to be taken by financial institutions and others such as casinos, real estate dealers, lawyers and accountants. The Recommendations are recognised as the global anti-money laundering (AML) and counter-terrorist financing (CFT) standard.

The FATF issued a report[26] in 2009 titled *Money Laundering Through the Football Sector*. This report identified the vulnerabilities of the sector arising from transactions relating to the ownership of football clubs, the transfer market and ownership of players, betting activities and image rights, sponsorship and advertising arrangements. The report is an excellent introduction to the complex web that attracts money launderers.

7.13 Why should students learn ethics?

Survival of the profession

There is debate over whether the attempts to teach ethics are worthwhile. However this chapter is designed to raise awareness of how important ethics are to the survival of the accounting profession. Accounting is part of the system to create trust in the financial information provided. The financial markets will not operate efficiently and effectively if there is not a substantial level of trust in the system. Such trust is a delicate matter and if the accounting profession is no longer trusted then there is no role for them to play in the system. In that event, the accounting profession will vanish. It may be thought that the loss of trust is so unlikely that it need not be contemplated. But who imagined that Arthur Andersen as we knew it would vanish from the scene so quickly? As soon as the public correctly or incorrectly decided that it could no longer trust Arthur Andersen, the business crashed.

A future role for accountants in ethical assurance

The accountant within business could also be seeing a growth in the ethical policing role as internal auditors take on the role of assessing the performance of managers as to their adherence to the ethical code of the organisation. This is already partially happening as conflicts of interest are often highlighted by internal audits and comments raised on managerial practices. This is after all a traditional role for accountants, ensuring that the various codes of practice of the organisation are followed. The level of adherence to an ethical code is but another assessment for the accountant to undertake.

Implications for training

If, as is likely, the accountant has a role in the future as 'ethical guardian', additional training will be necessary. This should be done at a very early stage, as in the USA, where accountants wishing to be Certified Public Accountants (CPAs) are required to pass formal exams on ethical practices and procedures before they are allowed the privilege of working in practice. Failure in these exams prevents the prospective accountant from practising in the business environment.

In the UK, for example, ethics is central to the ACCA Qualification in recognition that values, ethics and governance are themes which organisations are now embedding into company business plans and expertise in these areas is highly sought after in today's employment market. ACCA has adopted a holistic approach to a student's ethical development through the use of 'real-life' case studies and embedding ethical issues within the exam syllabi. For example, the ACCA's Paper P1, *Professional Accountant*, covers personal and professional ethics, ethical frameworks and professional values, as applied in the context of the accountant's duties and as a guide to appropriate professional behaviour and conduct in a variety of situations. In addition, as part of their ethical development, students will be required to complete a two-hour online training module, developed by ACCA. This will give students exposure to a range of real-life ethical case studies and will require them to reflect on their own ethical behaviour and values. Students will be expected to complete the ethics module before commencing their professional-level studies. Similar initiatives are being taken by the other professional accounting bodies.

Summary

At the macro level, the existence of the profession and the careers of all of us are dependent on the community perception of the profession as being ethical. Students need to be very conscious of that as they are the profession of the future.

At a more micro level, all accountants will face ethical issues during their careers whether they recognise them or not. This chapter attempts to make you more aware of the existence of ethical questions. The simplest way to increase awareness is to ask the question:

● Who is directly or indirectly affected by this accounting decision?

Then the follow up question is:

● If I were in their position, how would I feel about the accounting decision in terms of its fairness? (This is Rawls' (1971, revised 1999) and Baumol's (1982) superfairness proposal).

By increasing awareness of the impact of decisions, including accounting decisions, on other parties hopefully the dangers of decisions which are unfair will be recognised. By facing the implications head on, the accountant is less likely to make the wrong decisions. Also keep in mind those accountants who never set out to be unethical but by a series of small incremental decisions found themselves at the point of no return. The personal consequences of being found to be unethical can cover financial disasters, a long period of stress as civil or criminal cases wind their way through the courts, and at the extreme suicide or prison.

Another aspect of this chapter has been the attempt to highlight the vulnerability of companies to accusations of both direct and indirect unethical impacts and hence the need to be aware of trends to increasing levels of accountability.

Finally, you need to be aware of the avenues for getting assistance if you find yourself under pressure to ignore ethics or to turn a blind eye to the inappropriate behaviour of others. You should be aware of built-in avenues for addressing such concerns within your own organisation. Further, you should make yourself familiar with the assistance your professional body can give, such as providing experienced practitioners to discuss your options and the likely advantage and disadvantages of those alternatives.

REVIEW QUESTIONS

1 Explain in your own words the meaning of ethics.

2 Explain the link between corporate governance and ethical decision making.

3 Identify two ethical issues which university students experience and where do they look for guidance. How useful is that guidance? (Whilst the examples do not have to be personal accounts, they do have to be real student issues.)

4 The following is an extract from a *European Accounting Review*[27] article:

> On the teaching front, there is a pressing need to challenge more robustly the tenets of modern day business, and specifically accounting, education which have elevated the principles of property rights and narrow self-interest above broader values of community and ethics.

Discuss how such a challenge might impact on accounting education.

5 The International Association for Accounting Education and Research states that: 'Professional ethics should pervade the teaching of accounting' (www.iaaer.org). Discuss how this can be achieved on an undergraduate accounting degree.

6 As a trainee auditor what ethical issues are you most likely to encounter?

7 Do some research on the failure of Enron and identify and explain at least one instance of unethical behaviour of an accounting or financial executive flowing from a self-interest threat.

8 Explain what you think are four common types of ethical issues associated with (a) auditing, (b) public practice, (c) accounting in a corporate environment.

9 In the ICAS report one accountant suggested that where a company is required to recast its accounts then all the accountants associated with those incorrect accounts, whether they be the preparer or the auditor or a director, should be investigated by the professional bodies for a potential breach of ethics. Discuss why this should or should not occur.

10 An interesting ethical case arose when an employee of a Swiss bank stole records of the accounts of international investors. The records were then offered for sale to the German government on the basis that many of them would represent unreported income and thus provide evidence of tax evasion? Should the government buy the records? Provide arguments for and against.

11 Look up the web page of a major company (other than one mentioned in this chapter) and report on the following aspects of the whistle-blowing arrangements:

(a) Is the whistle-blowing arrangement in-house or with a third party?

(b) If a third party handles the reporting, is that party seen as relatively independent of the company or might a whistle-blower perceive the relationship as too close?

(c) What is the range of activities which the reporting agency suggests are the type of activities that would lead to the use of the reporting arrangements?

12 In relation to the following scenarios explain why it is a breach of ethics and what steps could have been taken to avoid the issue:

(a) The son of the accountant of a company is employed during the university holiday period to undertake work associated with preparation for a visit of the auditors.

(b) A senior executive is given a first class seat to travel to Chicago to attend an industry fair where the company is launching a new product. The executive decides to cash in the ticket and to get two economy class tickets so her boyfriend can go with her. The company picks up the hotel bill and she reimburses the difference between what it would have cost if she went alone and the final bill. The frequent flier points were credited to her personal frequent flier account. Would it make any difference if the company were not launching a new product at the fair?

(c) You pay a sizeable account for freight on the internal shipping of product deliveries in an underdeveloped country. At morning tea the gossip is that the company is paying bribes to a general in the underdeveloped country as protection money.

(d) The credit card statement for the managing director includes payments to a casino. The managing director says it is for the entertainment of important customers.

(e) You are processing a payment for materials which have been approved for repairs and maintenance when you realise the delivery is not to one of the business addresses of the company.

13 In each of the following scenarios outline the ethical problem and suggest ways in which the organisation may solve the problem and prevent its reoccurrence.

(a) A director's wife uses his company car for shopping.

(b) Groceries bought for personal use are included on a director's company credit card.

(c) A director negotiates a contract for management consultancy services but it is later revealed that her husband is a director of the management consultancy company.

(d) The director of a company hires her son for some holiday work within the company but does not mention the fact to her fellow directors.

(e) You are the accountant to a small engineering company and you have been approached by the chairman to authorise the payment of a fee to an overseas government employee in the hope that a large contract will be awarded.

(f) Your company has had some production problems which have resulted in some electrical goods being faulty (possibly dangerous) but all production is being dispatched to customers regardless of condition.

14 In each of the following scenarios outline the ethical or potential ethical problem and suggest ways in which the ethical problem could be resolved or avoided:

(a) Your company is about to sign a contract with a repressive regime in South America for equipment which **could** have a military use. Your own government has given you no advice on this matter.

(b) Your company is in financial difficulties and a large contract has just been gained in partnership with an overseas supplier which employs children as young as seven years old on its production line. The children are the only wage earners for their families and there is no welfare available in the country where they live.

(c) You are the accountant in a large manufacturing company and you have been approached by the manufacturing director to prepare a capital investment proposal for a new production line. After your calculations the project meets **none** of the criteria necessary to allow the project to proceed but the director instructs you to change the financial forecast figures to ensure the proposal is approved.

(d) Review the last week's newspapers and select **three** examples of failures of business ethics and justify your choice of examples.

(e) The company deducts from the monthly payroll employees' compulsory contribution to their superannuation accounts. The payment to the superannuation fund, which also includes the company's matching contribution, is only being made six monthly because the cash flow of the company is tight following rapid expansion.

15 It has sometimes been argued that there is no need to impose more regulations on auditors because the risk of being sued is so significant, and the amount of the potential awards against auditors so large that auditors, out of self-interest, will be conscientious in their tasks. Examine this argument in detail and whether the evidence supports the argument.

16 Should ethics be applicable at the standard-setting level? Express and justify your own views on this as distinct from repeating the material in the chapter.

17 Refer to the Ernst & Young Code of Conduct and discuss the Questions they suggest when putting their Global Code of Conduct into action.[28]

18 Discuss the role of the accounting profession in the issue of ethics.

19 How might a company develop a code of ethics for its own use?

20 Outline the advantages and disadvantages of a written code of ethics.

21 (a) Obtain an ethical statement from:

   (i) a commercial organisation;

   (ii) a charitable organisation.

   (b) Review each statement for content and style.

   (c) Compare each of the two statements and highlight any areas of difference which, in your view, reflect the different nature of the two organisations.

22 Lord Borrie QC has said[29] of the Public Interest Disclosure Bill that came into force in July 1999 that the new law would encourage people to recognise and identify with the wider public interest, not just their own private position and it will reassure them that if they act reasonably to protect the legitimate interest of others, the law will not stand idly by should they be vilified or victimised. Confidentiality should only be breached, however, if there is a statutory obligation to do so. Discuss.

23 The management of a listed company has a fiduciary duty to act in the best interest of the share-holders and it would be unethical for the management to act in the interest of other shareholders if this did not maximise the existing earnings per share. Discuss.

24 The financial director of a listed company makes many decisions which are informed by statute, e.g. the Companies Act and the Public Interest Disclosure Act, and by mandatory pronounce-ments by, e.g. the ASB, the APB and his professional accounting body. What guidance is available when there is a need for an ethical decision which does not contravene statutory or mandatory demands – how can there be confidence that the decision is right?

25 Confidentiality means that an accountant in business has a loyalty to the business which employs him/her which is greater than any commitment to a professional code of ethics. Discuss.

26 It has been said that football clubs are seen by criminals as the perfect vehicles for money laundering. Discuss the reason for this view.

EXERCISES

Question 1

You have recently qualified and set up in public practice under the name Patris Zadan. You have been approached to provide accounting services for Joe Hardiman. Joe explains that he has had a lawyer set up six businesses and he asks you to do the books and to handle tax matters. The first thing you notice is that he is running a number of laundromats which are largely financed by relatives from overseas. As the year progresses, you realise those businesses are extremely profitable given industry averages.

Required:
Discuss – What do you do?

Question 2

Joe Withers is the chief financial officer for Withco plc responsible for negotiating bank loans. It has been the practice to obtain loans from a number of merchant banks. He has recently met Ben Billings who had been on the same undergraduate course some years earlier. They agree to meet for a game of squash and during the course of the evening Joe learns that Ben is the chief loans officer at the Swift Merchant Bank.

During the next five years Joe negotiates all of the company's loan requirements through Swift and Ben arranges for Joe to receive substantial allocations in initial public offerings. Over that period Joe has done quite well out of taking up allocations and selling them within a few days on the market.

Required:
Discuss the ethical issues.

Question 3

Kim Lee is a branch accountant in a multinational company Green Cocoa plc responsible for purchasing supplies from a developing country. Kim Lee is authorised to enter into contracts up to $100,000 for any single transaction. Demand in the home market is growing and head office is pressing for an increase in supplies. A new government official in the developing country says that Kim needs an export permit from his department and that he needs a payment to be made to his brother in law for consulting services if the permit is to be granted. Kim quickly checks alternative sources and finds that the normal price combined with the extra 'facilitation fee' is still much cheaper than the alternative sources of supply. Kim faces two problems, namely, whether to pay the bribe and, if so, how to record it in the accounts so it is not obvious what it is.

Required:
Discuss the ethical issues.

Question 4

Jemma Burrett is a public practitioner. Four years earlier she had set up a family trust for a major client by the name of Simon Trent. The trust is for the benefit of Simon and his wife Marie. Marie is also a client of the practice and the practice prepares her tax returns. Subsequently Marie files for divorce. In her claim for a share of the assets she claims a third share of the business and half the other assets of the family which are listed. The assets of the family trust are not included in the list.

Required:
Discuss the ethical issues raised by the case and what action the accountant should take (if any).

Question 5

George Longfellow is a financial controller with a listed industrial firm which has a long period of sustained growth. This has necessitated substantial use of external borrowing.

During the great financial crisis it has become harder to roll over the loans as they mature. To make matters worse sales revenues have fallen 5% for the financial year, debtors have taken longer to pay, and margins have fallen. The managing director has said that he doesn't want to report a loss for the first time in the company's history as it might scare financiers.

The finance director (FD) has told George to make every effort to get the result to come out positively. He suggests that a number of expenses should be shifted to prepayments, provisions for doubtful debts should be lowered, and that new assets should not be depreciated in the year of purchase but rather should only commence depreciation in the next financial year on the argument that new assets take a while to become fully operational.

In the previous year the company had moved into a new line of business where a small number of customers paid in advance. Because these were exceptional the auditors were persuaded to allow you to avoid the need to make the systems more sophisticated to decrease revenue and to recognise a liability. After all, it was immaterial in the overall group. Fortunately that new line of business has grown substantially in the current financial year and it was suggested that the auditors be told that the revenue in advance should not be taken out of sales because a precedent had been set the year before.

George saw this as a little bit of creative accounting and was reluctant to do what he was instructed. When he tentatively made this comment to the FD, he was assured that this was only temporary to ensure the company could refinance and that next year, when the economy recovered, all the discretionary adjustments would be reversed and everyone would be happy. After all, the employment of the 20,000 people who work for the group depends upon the refinancing and it was not as if the company was not going to be prosperous in the future. The FD emphasised that the few adjustments were, after all, a win–win situation for everyone and George was threatening the livelihood of all of his colleagues – many with children and mortgage payments to meet.

Required:
Discuss who would or could benefit or lose from the finance director's proposals.

References

1 W.J. Baumol, *Superfairness: Applications and Theory*, 1982.
2 A.T. Kronman, *The Lost Lawyer*, Cambridge, MA: The Belknap Press of Harvard University Press, 1993.
3 R.F. Duska and B.S. Duska, *Accounting Ethics*, Oxford: Blackwell Publishing, 2003, p. 174.
4 *Ibid.*, p. 189.
5 http://gaap-standard-accounting-practices.suite101.com/article.cfm/arthur_andersen_agrees_to_pay_16m
6 M.G. Lamoreaux, 'House Panel eases threat to FASB independence', *Journal of Accountancy*, November 2009 (http://www.journalofaccountancy.com/Web/20092357.htm).
7 J. Rawls, *A Theory of Justice*, Oxford: Oxford University Press, 1971, 1999.
8 D. Friedman, *Morals and Markets*, New York: Palgrave Macmillan, 2008.
9 S.B. Salter, D.M. Guffey and J.J. McMillan, 'Truth, consequences and culture: a comparative examination of cheating and attitudes about cheating among U.S. and U.K. students', *Journal of Business Ethics*, Vol. 31, N. 1, May 2001, pp. 37–50(14).
10 L. Spacek, 'The need for an accounting court', *The Accounting Review*, 1958, pp. 368–379.
11 IFAC, *Code of Ethics for Professional Accountants*.
12 C. Helliar and J. Bebbington, *Taking Ethics to Heart*, ICSA, 2004; www.icas.org.uk/site/cms/download/res_helliar_bebbington_Report.pdf
13 www.btplc.com/TheWayWeWork/Businesspractice/twww_english.pdf
14 www.ir.jameshardie.com.au/jh/asbestos_compensation.jsp
15 M.M. Jennings, *Seven Signs of Ethical Collapse: Understanding What Causes Moral Meltdowns in Organizations*, New York, St. Martin's Press, 2006.
16 Helliar and Bebbington, *Taking Ethics to Heart*.
17 S. Beder, *Beyond Petroleum* (www.uow.edu.au/~sharonb/bp.html).

18 C. Stohl, M. Stohl and L. Popova, 'A New Generation of Codes of Ethics', *Journal of Business Ethics*, vol. 90, 2009, pp. 607–622.

19 T. Morris, *If Aristotle Ran General Motors*, New York: Henry Holt, 1997, pp. 118–145.

20 J.F. Castellano, K. Rosenweig and H.P. Roehm, 'How Corporate Culture Impacts Unethical Distortion of Financial Numbers', *Management Accounting Quarterly*, Summer 2004, vol. 5, no. 4.

21 www.sfo.gov.uk/press-room/latest-press-releases/press-releases-2010/bae-systems-plc.aspx

22 www.lmu.edu/Page23070.aspx

23 www.ethics.org

24 FINRA Announces Creation of 'Office of the Whistleblower' (www.finra.org/Newsroom? NewsReleases/2009?P118095, accessed 8.02.2010).

25 www.frc.org.uk/aadb

26 www.oecd.org/dataoecd/7/41/43216572.pdf

27 D. Owen, 'CSR after Enron: a role for the academic accounting profession?', *European Accounting Review*, vol. 14, no. 2, 2005.

28 www.ey.com/Publication/vwLUAssets/Ernst-Young_Global_Code_of_Conduct/$FILE/EY_ Code_of_Conduct.pdf

29 W. Raven, 'Social auditing', *Internal Auditor*, February 2000, p. 8.

CHAPTER **8**

Preparation of statements of comprehensive income and financial position

8.1 Introduction

The published accounts of a listed company are intended to provide a report to enable shareholders to assess current year stewardship and management performance and to predict future cash flows. In order to assess stewardship and management performance, there have been mandatory requirements for standardised presentation, using formats prescribed by International Financial Reporting Standards.

The main standard that will be considered in this chapter is IAS 1 *Presentation of Financial Statements*.

Each company sends an annual report and accounts to its shareholders. It is the means by which the directors are accountable for their stewardship of the assets and their handling of the company's affairs for the **past year**. It consists of financial data which may have been audited and narrative comment which may be reviewed by the auditors to check that it does not present a picture that differs from the financial data (i.e. that the narrative is not misleading).

The financial data consist of four financial statements. These are the statement of comprehensive income, the statement of financial position, the statement of changes in equity and the statement of cash flows – supported by appropriate explanatory notes, e.g. showing the make-up of inventories and the movement in non-current assets.

The narrative report from the directors satisfies two needs: (a) to explain what has been achieved in the current year and (b) to assist existing and potential investors to make their own predictions of cash flows of future years.

Objectives

By the end of this chapter, you should be able to:

- understand the structure and content of published financial statements;
- explain the nature of the items within published financial statements;
- prepare the main primary statements that are required in published financial statements;
- comment critically on the information included in published financial statements.

8.2 The prescribed formats – the statement of comprehensive income

The statement of comprehensive income includes all recognised gains and losses in the period including those that were previously recognised in equity.

IAS 1 allows a company to choose between two formats for detailing income and expenses. The two choices allow for the analysis of costs in different ways and the formats[1] are as follows:

- **Format 1**: Vertical with costs analysed according to function e.g. cost of sales, distribution costs and administration expenses; or
- **Format 2**: Vertical with costs analysed according to nature e.g. raw materials, employee benefits expenses, operating expenses and depreciation.

Many companies use Format 1 (unless there is any national requirement to use Format 2) with the costs analysed according to function. If this format is used the information regarding the nature of expenditure (e.g. raw materials, wages and depreciation) must be disclosed in a note to the accounts.

8.2.1 Classification of operating expenses and other income by function

In order to arrive at its operating profit (a measure of profit often recognised by many companies), a company needs to classify all of the operating expenses of the business into one of four categories:

- cost of sales;
- distribution and selling costs;
- administrative expenses;
- other operating income or expense.

We comment briefly on each to explain how a company might classify its trading transactions.

8.2.2 Cost of sales

Expenditure classified under cost of sales will typically include direct costs, overheads, depreciation and amortisation expense and adjustments. The items that might appear under each heading are:

- Direct costs: direct materials purchased; direct labour; other external charges that comprise production costs from external sources, e.g. hire charges and subcontracting costs.
- Overheads: variable production overheads; fixed production overheads.
- Depreciation and amortisation: depreciation of non-current assets used in production and impairment expense.
- Adjustments: capitalisation of own work as a non-current asset. Any amount of the costs listed above that have been incurred in the construction of non-current assets for retention by the company will not appear as an expense in the statement of comprehensive income: it will be capitalised. Any amount capitalised in this way would be treated for accounting purposes as a non-current asset and depreciated.

8.2.3 Distribution costs

These are costs incurred after the production of the finished article and up to and including transfer of the goods to the customer. Expenditure classified under this heading will typically include the following:

- warehousing costs associated with the operation of the premises, e.g. rent, rates, insurance, utilities, depreciation, repairs and maintenance and wage costs, e.g. gross wages and pension contributions of warehouse staff;

- promotion costs, e.g. advertising, trade shows;

- selling costs, e.g. salaries, commissions and pension contributions of sales staff; costs associated with the premises, e.g. rent, rates; cash discounts on sales; travelling and entertainment;

- transport costs, e.g. gross wages and pension contributions of transport staff, vehicle costs, e.g. running costs, maintenance and depreciation.

8.2.4 Administrative expenses

These are the costs of running the business that have not been classified as either cost of sales or distribution costs. Expenditure classified under this heading will typically include:

- administration, e.g. salaries, commissions, and pension contributions of administration staff;

- costs associated with the premises, e.g. rent, rates;

- amounts written off the receivables that appear in the statement of financial position under current assets;

- professional fees.

8.2.5 Other operating income or expense

Under this heading a company discloses material income or expenses derived from ordinary activities of the business that have not been included elsewhere. If the amounts are not material, they would not be separately disclosed but included within the other captions. Items classified under these headings may typically include the following:

- income derived from intangible assets, e.g. royalties, commissions;

- income derived from third-party use of property, plant and equipment that is surplus to the current productive needs of the company;

- income received from employees, e.g. canteen, recreation fees;

- payments for rights to use intangible assets not directly related to operations, e.g. licences.

8.2.6 Finance costs

In order to arrive at the profit for the period interest received or paid and investment income is disclosed under the Finance cost heading.

8.2.7 Preparation of statements of income from a trial balance

The following illustrates the steps for preparing internal and external statements from the trial balance. These are:

- prepare the trial balance;

- identify year end adjustments;

- prepare an internal Income Statement;

- analyse expenses by function into: Cost of sales, Distribution costs, Administrative expenses, Other income and expenses and Finance costs;

- prepare a Statement of comprehensive income for publication.

8.2.8 The trial balance

The trial balance for Illustrious SpA is shown in Figure 8.1.

Figure 8.1 The trial balance for Illustrious SpA as at 31 December 20X1

	€000	€000
Issued share capital		17,250
Retained earnings		57,500
Long-term loan		63,250
Bank overdraft		8,625
Provision for taxation		5,750
Trade payables		29,900
Depreciation – equipment		3,450
– vehicles		9,200
Freehold land	57,500	
Freehold buildings	57,500	
Equipment	14,950	
Motor vehicles	20,700	
Inventory at 1 January 20X1	43,125	
Trade receivables	28,750	
Cash in hand	4,600	
Purchases	258,750	
Bank interest	1,150	
Directors' remuneration	1,150	
Dividends	1,725	
Fees – audit	1,150	
Interest on debentures	6,325	
Insurance	3,450	
Salaries and wages	18,055	
Motor expenses	9,200	
Taxation	5,750	
Hire charges	300	
Light and power	920	
Miscellaneous expenses	275	
Stationery, courier	1,840	
Repairs and maintenance	2,760	
Sales		345,000
	539,925	539,925

8.2.9 Identify year end adjustments

The following information relating to accruals and prepayments has not yet been taken into account in the amounts shown in the trial balance:

- Inventory at cost at 31 December 20X1 was €25,875,000.
- Depreciation is to be provided as follows:
    - 2% on freehold buildings using the straight-line method;
    - 10% on equipment using the reducing balance method;
    - 25% on motor vehicles using reducing balance.
- €2,300,000 was prepaid for repairs and €5,175,000 has accrued for wages.
- Freehold buildings were revalued at €77,500,000.

8.2.10 Preparation of an internal statement of income after year end adjustments

A statement of income prepared for internal purposes is set out in Figure 8.2. We have arranged the expenses in descending monetary value. The method for doing this is not

Figure 8.2 Statement of income of Illustrious SpA for the year ended 31 December 20X1

		€000	€000
Sales			345,000
Less:			
Opening inventory		43,125	
Purchases		258,750	
		301,875	
Closing inventory		25,875	
Cost of sales			276,600
Gross profit			69,000
Less Expenses:			
Salaries and wages	W1	23,230	
Motor expenses		9,200	
Debenture interest		6,325	
Depreciation	W2	5,175	
Insurance		3,450	
Stationery, courier		1,840	
Fees – audit		1,150	
Bank interest		1,150	
Directors' remuneration		1,150	
Light and power		920	
Repairs and maintenance	W3	460	
Hire charges		300	
Miscellaneous expenses		275	
			54,625
Profit before tax			14,375
Taxation			5,750
Profit after tax			8,625
Dividends (are disclosed in Statement of Changes in Equity)			1,725
Retained earnings			6,900

prescribed and companies are free to organise the items in a number of ways, for example, listing in alphabetical order.

W1 Salaries and wages:

€18,055,000 + accrued €5,175,000 = €23,230,000

W2 Depreciation:

Buildings   2% of €57,500,000 = €1,150,000

Equipment   10% of (€14,950,000 − €3,450,000) = €1,150,000

Vehicles   25% of (€20,700,000 − €9,200,000) = €2,875,000

Total   = €5,175,000

W3 Repairs:

€2,760,000 − prepayment €2,300,000 = €460,000

8.2.11 An analysis of expenses by function

An analysis of expenses would be carried out in practice in order to classify these under their appropriate function heading. In the exercises that are set for classwork and examinations the expenses are often allocated rather than apportioned. For example, the insurance expense might be allocated in total to administration expense.

We have included apportionment in this example to give an understanding of the process that would occur in practice and is also met in some examination questions.

In order to analyse the costs, we need to consider each item in the detailed statement of income. Each item will be allocated to a classification or apportioned if it relates to more than one of the classifications. This requires the company to make a number of assumptions about the basis for allocating and apportioning. The process is illustrated in Figure 8.3.

Companies are required to be consistent in their treatment but we can see from the assumptions that have been made that costs may be apportioned differently by different companies.

8.2.12 Preparation of statement of comprehensive income – other comprehensive income

When IAS 1 was revised in 2008 the profit and loss account or 'income statement' was replaced by the statement of comprehensive income and a new section of 'Other comprehensive income' was added to the previous statement of income.

The recognised gains and losses reported as Other comprehensive income are gains and losses that were previously recognised directly in equity and presented in the statement of changes in equity. Such gains and losses arose, for example, from the revaluation of non-current assets and from other items that are discussed later in chapters on Financial Instruments and Employee Benefits e.g. equity investments held as Available-for-sale and Actuarial gains on defined benefit pension plans.

IAS 1 allows a choice in the way 'Other comprehensive income' is reported. It can be presented as a separate statement or as an extension of the Statement of income. In our example we have presented 'Other comprehensive income' as an extension of the Statement of income.

Figure 8.3 Assumptions made in analysing the costs

N1 An analysis of salaries and wages	Total €000	Cost of sales €000	Distribution costs €000	Administration expenses €000
Factory staff	12,075	12,075		
Warehouse staff and drivers	8,280		8,280	
Accounts department	575			575
Sales staff	2,300		2,300	
	23,230	12,075	10,580	575
N2 An analysis of depreciation				
Freehold buildings	1,150	575	287.5	287.5
Equipment	1,150	575	287.5	287.5
Motor vehicles (allocated)	2,875		2875	
	5,175	1,150	3,450	575
N3 An apportionment of operating expenses on the basis of space occupied				
Motor expenses (allocated)	9,200		9,200	
Insurance	3,450	1,725	862.5	862.5
Stationery, courier	1,840	920	460	460
Light and power	920	460	230	230
Repairs and maintenance	460	230	115	115
Hire charges	300	150	75	75
Miscellaneous expenses	275	137.5	68.75	68.75
	16,445	3,622.5	11,011.25	1,811.25
N4 Directors' remuneration and audit fees				
Audit fees	1,150			1,150
Directors' remuneration	1,150	575		575
	2,300	575		1,725
TOTAL (N1 + N2 + N£ + N4)	47,150	17,422.5	25,041.25	4,686.25
Add materials	276,000	276,000		
TOTALS for Statement of income	323,150	293,422.5	25,041.25	4,686.25

In this example, there is a revaluation surplus and this needs to be added to the profit on ordinary activities for the year in order to arrive at the comprehensive income. This is shown in Figure 8.4.

8.2.13 Presentation using IAS 1 Alternative method (Format 2)

If Format 2 is used, the expenses are classified as change in inventory, raw materials, employee benefits expense, other expenses and depreciation. The Statement of income reports the same operating profit as for Illustrious SpA.

Figure 8.4 Illustrious SpA statement of comprehensive income redrafted into Format 1 style

Statement of comprehensive income of Illustrious SpA for the year ended 31 December 20X1

	€000
Revenue	345,000.00
Cost of sales	293,422.50
Gross profit	51,577.50
Distribution costs	25,041.25
Administrative expenses	4,686.25
Operating profit	21,850.00
Finance costs	7,475.00
Profit on ordinary activities before tax	14,375.00
Taxation	5,750.00
Profit for the year	8,625.00
Other comprehensive income:	
Gains on property revaluation	20,000.00
Comprehensive income	28,625.00

Format 2	€000	€000
Revenue		345,000
Decrease in inventory	(17,250)	
Raw materials	(258,750)	(276,000)
Employee benefits expense		
Salaries	(23,230)	
Directors	(1,150)	(24,380)
Other expenses		
Motor expenses	(9,200)	
Insurance	(3,450)	
Stationery	(1,840)	
Audit fees	(1,150)	
Light and power	(920)	
Repairs	(460)	
Hire charges	(300)	
Miscellaneous	(275)	(17,595)
Depreciation	(5,175)	(5,175)
Operating profit		21,850

8.2.14 What information would be disclosed by way of note to the statement of comprehensive income?

There would be a note giving details of certain items that have been charged in arriving at the Operating Profit. These include items that are:

● sensitive, such as the makeup of the amounts paid to the auditors showing separately the audit fees and the non-audit fees such as for restructuring and for tax advice; and

● subject to judgement, such as the charges for depreciation; and

● exceptional, such as unusually high impairment of trade receivables. These should be disclosed separately either by way of note or on the face of the statement of comprehensive income if that degree of prominence is necessary in order to give a fair view.

For Illustrious SpA the note would read as follows:

Operating profit is stated after charging:

	€000
Depreciation	5,175

8.3 The prescribed formats – the statement of financial position

Let us now consider the prescribed formats for the statement of financial position, the accounting rules that govern the values at which the various assets are included in the statement and the explanatory notes that are required to accompany the statement.

8.3.1 The prescribed format

IAS 1 specifies which items are to be included on the face of the statement of financial position – these are referred to as alpha headings (a) to (r). It does not prescribe the order and presentation that is to be followed. It would be acceptable to present the statement as assets less liabilities equalling equity, or total assets equalling total equity and liabilities. The example given in IAS 1 follows the approach of total assets equalling total equity and liabilities.

The information that must be presented on the face of the statement is:

(a) Property, plant and equipment;

(b) Investment property;

(c) Intangible assets;

(d) Financial assets (excluding amounts shown under (e), (h) and (i));

(e) Investments accounted for using the equity method;

(f) Biological assets;

(g) Inventories;

(h) Trade and other receivables;

(i) Cash and cash equivalents;

(j) The total of assets classified as held for sale and assets included in disposal group classified as held for sale in accordance with IFRS 5 *Non-current Assets Held for Sale and Discontinued Operations*;

(k) Trade and other payables;

(l) Provisions;

(m) Financial liabilities (excluding amounts shown under (j) and (k));

(n) Liabilities and assets for current tax, as defined in IAS 12 *Income Taxes*;

(o) Deferred tax liabilities and deferred tax assets, as defined in IAS 12;

(p) Liabilities included in disposal groups classified as held for sale in accordance with IFRS 5;

(q) Non-controlling interests, presented within equity; and

(r) Issued capital and reserves attributable to equity holders of the parent.

IAS 1 does not absolutely prescribe that enterprises need to split assets and liabilities into current and non-current. However, it does state that this split would need to be done if the nature of the business indicates that it is appropriate. In almost all cases it would be appropriate to split items into current and non-current. If an enterprise decides that it is more relevant and reliable not to split the assets and liabilities into current and non-current on the face of the statement of financial position, they should be presented broadly in order of their liquidity. Not all headings will, of course, be applicable to all companies.

8.3.2 The accounting rules for asset valuation

International standards provide different valuation rules and some choice exists as to which rules to use. Many of the items in the financial statements are held at historical cost but variations to this principle may be required by different accounting standards. Some of the different bases are:

Property, plant and equipment	Can be presented at either historical cost or market value depending upon accounting policy chosen from IAS 16.[2]
Financial assets	Certain classes of financial asset are required to be recognised at fair value per IAS 39.[3]
Inventory	IAS 2 requires that this is included at the lower of cost and net realisable value.[4]
Provisions	IAS 37 requires the discounting to present value of some provisions.[5]

Illustrious SpA statement of financial position

The statement in Figure 8.5 follows the headings set out in para 8.3.1 above.

Figure 8.5 Illustrious SpA statement of financial position as at 31 December 20X1

	€000	€000	€000
Non-current assets			
Property, plant and equipment			152,825
Current assets			
Inventory	25,875		
Receivables	28,750		
Cash at bank and in hand	4,600		
Prepayments	2,300	61,525	
Current liabilities			
Payables	29,900		
Accruals	10,925		
Bank overdraft	8,625	49,450	
Net current assets			
Total assets less current liabilities			12,075
Non-current liabilities			164,900
Debentures			
			63,250
Equity			101,650
Share capital			
Reduction reserve			17,250
Retained earnings			20,000
			64,400
			101,650

8.3.3 What are the explanatory notes that accompany a statement of financial position?

We will consider (a) notes giving greater detail of the makeup of items that appear in the statement of financial position, (b) notes providing additional information to assist predicting future cash flows, and (c) notes giving information of interest to other stakeholders.

(a) Notes giving greater detail of the makeup of statement of financial position figures

Each of the alpha headings may have additional detail disclosed by way of a note to the accounts. For example, inventory of £25.875 million in the statement of financial position may have a note of its detailed makeup as follows:

	£m
Raw materials	11.225
Work-in-progress	1.500
Finished goods	13.150
	25.875

Property, plant and equipment normally has a schedule as shown in Figure 8.6. From this the net book value is read off the total column for inclusion in the statement of financial position.

(b) Notes giving additional information to assist prediction of future cash flows

These are notes intended to assist in predicting future cash flows. They give information on matters such as capital commitments that have been contracted for but not provided in the

Figure 8.6 Disclosure note: Property, plant and equipment movements

	Freehold Property €000	Equipment €000	Motor Vehicles €000	Total €000
Cost/valuation				
As at 1 January 20X1	115,000	14,950	20,700	150,650
Revaluation	20,000			20,000
Additions				
Disposals				
As at 31 December 20X1	135,000	14,950	20,700	170,650
Accumulated depreciation				
As at 1 January 20X1		3,450	9,200	12,650
Charge for the year	1,150	1,150	2,875	5,175
As at 31 December 20X1	1,150	4,600	12,075	17,825
Net book value				
As at 31 December 20X1	**133,850**	**10,350**	**8,625**	**152,825**
As at 31 December 20X0	115,000	11,500	11,500	138,000

accounts and capital commitments that have been authorised but not contracted for; future commitments, e.g. share options that have been granted; and contingent liabilities, e.g. guarantees given by the company in respect of overdraft facilities arranged by subsidiary companies or customers.

(c) Notes giving information that is of interest to other stakeholders

An example is information relating to staff. It is common for enterprises to provide a disclosure of the average number of employees in the period or the number of employees at the end of the period. IAS 1 does not require this information but it is likely that many businesses would provide and categorise the information, possibly following functions such as production, sales, administration. Suggested forms of presentation for Staff costs are shown in Figure 8.7.

Figure 8.7 Staff costs

Operating profit is stated after charging:

Staff costs £xxx

The average number of employees during the period was as follows:

	Number employed
Production	XXX
Distribution	XXX
Sales	XXX
Research and development	XXX
Administration	XXX

This shows categorisation by function. Also acceptable would be categorisation by operating segment or no categorisation at all. However, because there is no standard form of presentation, it is not always sufficient for the prediction of cash flows if the costs are not analysed under function headings.

Employees themselves might be interested when, for example, attempting to assess a company's view that redundancies, short-time working and pay restrictions are actually necessary. The annual report is not the only source of information – there might be stand alone Employee Reports and information obtained during labour negotiations such as the ratio of short-term and long-term assets to employee, the capital–labour ratios and the average sales and net profits per employee in the company compared, if possible, to benchmarks from the same economic sector.

8.4 Statement of changes in equity

A primary statement called 'Statement of changes in equity' should be presented with the same prominence as the other primary statements. The statement is designed to show the comprehensive income for the period and the effects of any prior period adjustments, reconciling the movement in equity from the beginning to the end of the period. An entity must also disclose, either in the statement of changes in equity or in the notes, the amount of distributions to owners and the amount of dividends per share. The statement for Illustrious is shown in Figure 8.8.

Figure 8.8 Statement of Changes in Equity for the year ended 31 December 20X1

	Share capital	Retained earnings	Revaluation Surplus	Total
Balance as at 1 January 20X1	17,250	57,500		74,750
Changes in equity for 20X1				
Dividends		(1,725)		(1,725)
Total comprehensive income for the year		8,625	20,000	28,625
Balance as at 31 December 20X1	17,250	64,400	20,000	101,650

8.5 Has prescribing the formats meant that identical transactions are reported identically?

That is the intention, but there are various reasons why there may still be differences. For example, let us consider the Cost of sales figure. This figure is derived under the accrual accounting concept which means that:

(a) the cash flows have been adjusted by the management in order to match the expense that management considers to be associated with the sales achieved; and

(b) additional adjustments may have been made to increase the cost of sales, for example, if it is estimated that the net realisable value of the closing inventory is less than cost.

Clearly, when management adjust the cash flow figures they are exercising their judgement, and it is impossible to ensure that the management of two companies faced with the same economic activity would arrive at the same adjustment.

We will now consider some of reasons for differences in calculating the cost of sales – these are (a) how inventory is valued, (b) the choice of depreciation policy, (c) management attitudes and (d) the capability of the accounting system.

(a) Differences arising from the choice of the inventory valuation method

Different companies may assume different physical flows when calculating the cost of direct materials used in production. This will affect the inventory valuation. One company may assume a first-in–first-out (FIFO) flow, where the cost of sales is charged for raw materials used in production as if the first items purchased were the first items used in production. Another company may use an average basis.

This is illustrated in Figure 8.9 for a company that started trading on 1 January 20X1 without any opening inventory and sold 40,000 items on 31 March 20X1 for £4 per item.

Inventory valued on a FIFO basis is £60,000 with the 20,000 items in inventory valued at £3 per item, on the assumption that the purchases made on 1 January 20X1 and 1 February 20X1 were sold first. Inventory valued on an average basis is £40,000 with the 20,000 items in inventory valued at £2 per item on the assumption that sales made in March cannot be matched with a specific item.

The effect on the gross profit percentage would be as shown in Figure 8.10. This demonstrates that, even from a single difference in accounting treatment, the gross profit for the same transaction could be materially different in both absolute and percentage terms.

Figure 8.9 Effect on sales of using FIFO and weighted average

Physical flow assumption	Items	£	FIFO £	Average £
Raw materials purchased				
On 1 Jan 20X1 at £1 per item	20,000	20,000		
On 1 Feb 20X1 at £2 item	20,000	40,000		
On 1 Mar 20X1 at £3 per item	20,000	60,000		
On 1 Mar 20X1 in inventory	60,000	120,000	120,000	120,000
On 31 Mar 20X1 in inventory	20,000		60,000	40,000
Cost of sales	40,000		60,000	80,000

Figure 8.10 Effect of physical inventory flow assumptions on the percentage gross profit

	Items	FIFO £	Average £	% difference in gross profit
Sales	40,000	160,000	160,000	
Cost of sales	40,000	60,000	80,000	
		100,000	80,000	
Gross profit %		62.5%	50%	25%

How can the investor determine the effect of different assumptions?

Although companies are required to disclose their inventory valuation policy, the level of detail provided varies and we are not able to quantify the effect of different inventory valuation policies.

For example, a clear description of an accounting policy is provided by AstraZeneca in Figure 8.11. Even so, it does not allow the user to know how net realisable value was determined. Was it, for example, primarily based upon forecasted short-term demand for the product?

Figure 8.11 AstraZeneca inventory policy (2009) annual report

Inventories

Inventories are stated at the lower of cost or net realisable value. The first in, first out or an average method of valuation is used. For finished goods and work in progress, cost includes directly attributable costs and certain overhead expenses (including depreciation). Selling expenses and certain other overhead expenses (principally central administration costs) are excluded. Net realisable value is determined as estimated selling price less all estimated costs of completion and costs to be incurred in selling and distribution.

Write downs of inventory occur in the general course of business and are included in cost of sales in the income statement.

While we can carry out academic exercises as in Figure 8.10 and we are aware of the effect of different inventory valuation policies on the level of profits, it is not possible to carry out such an exercise in real life.

(b) Differences arising from the choice of depreciation method and estimates

Companies may make different choices:

- the accounting base to use e.g. historical cost or revaluation; and
- the method that is used to calculate the charge e.g. straight-line or reducing balance.

Companies make estimates that might differ:

- assumptions as to an asset's productive use, e.g. different estimates made as to the economic life of an asset; and
- assumptions as to the total cost to be expensed, e.g. different estimates of the residual value.

(c) Differences arising from management attitudes

Losses might be anticipated and measured at a different rate. For example, when assessing the likelihood of the net realisable value of inventory falling below the cost figure, the management decision will be influenced by the optimism with which it views the future of the economy, the industry and the company. There could also be other influences. For example, if bonuses are based on net income, there is an incentive to over-estimate the net realisable value; whereas, if management are preparing a company for a management buy-out, there is an incentive to underestimate the net realisable value in order to minimise the net profit for the period.

(d) Differences arising from the capability of the accounting system to provide data

Accounting systems within companies differ. Costs collected by one company may well not be collected by another company. Also the apportionment of costs might be more detailed with different proportions being allocated or apportioned.

8.5.1 Does it really matter under which heading a cost is classified in the statement of comprehensive income provided it is not omitted?

The gross profit figure is a measure of production efficiency and it will be affected if costs are allocated (or not) to cost of sales from one of the other expense headings.

When comparing a company's performance care is needed to see how the profit used by the management in their Financial Highlights is selected. For example, in the 2010 financial statements of the ITOCHU Corporation the Gross trading profit is used:

	1st Half FY 2010	1st Half FY 2009	Increase (Decrease)	%	Outlook for FY 2010	Progress(%)
Net income attributable to ITOCHU	55.3	139.1	(83.8)	(60.2%)	130.0	42.6%
Revenue	1,651.0	1,496.7	154.3	10.3%		
Gross trading profit	440.0	542.1	(102.1)	(18.8%)	950.0	46.3%

The decreases in their Textile and Machinery business was explained as follows:

Textile	Due to market slowdown in textile materials, fabrics, apparels despite increase from an acquisition of SANKEI CO., LTD.
Machinery	Due to reduced transactions in automobile and construction machinery business, and decrease in sales volume by the absence of ship trading transactions in the previous 1st H.

In the 2008 Wolseley Annual Report, however, the profit used is Trading profit defined as Operating profit before exceptional items and the amortisation and impairment of acquired intangibles. The choice might be consistent or it might be to emphasise that exceptional items and amortisation charges have a material impact on the Trading profit, for example, the effect on Wolseley is to reduce its trading profit by more than 50%.

8.6 The fundamental accounting principles underlying statements of comprehensive income and statements of financial position

IAS 1 (paras 15–46) requires compliance with the fundamental accounting principles such as accruals, materiality and aggregation, going concern and consistency of presentation.

A concept not specifically stated in IAS 1 is prudence, which is an important principle in the preparation of financial statements. The *Framework* states that reliable information in the financial statements must be prudent[6] and this implies that a degree of caution should be exercised in making judgements or estimates. Prudence does not allow the making of excessive or unnecessary provisions that would deliberately understate net assets and therefore render the financial statements unreliable.

8.6.1 Disclosure of accounting policies

The accounting policies adopted can make a significant difference to the financial statements. It is important for investors to be aware of the policies and to be confident that management will not change them on an *ad hoc* basis to influence the results. IAS 1 (para. 10) therefore requires a company to state the accounting policies adopted by the company in determining the amounts shown in the Statements of comprehensive income and financial position and to apply them consistently. We have already illustrated above the effect of choosing different inventory valuation policies and the effect if a company were not consistent.

8.7 What is the difference between accounting principles, accounting bases and accounting policies?

Accounting principles

All companies are required to comply with the broad accounting principles of going concern, consistency, accrual accounting, materiality and aggregation. If they fail to comply, they must disclose, quantify and justify the departure from the principle.

Accounting bases

These are the methods that have been developed for applying the accounting principles. They are intended to restrict the subjectivity by identifying a range of acceptable methods. For example, assets may be valued according to the historical cost convention or the alternative accounting rules. Bases have been established for a number of assets, e.g. non-current assets and inventories.

Figure 8.12 Extract from the financial statements of the Nestlé Group

Property, Plant and Equipment

Property, plant and equipment are shown in the statement of financial position at their historical cost. Depreciation is provided on components that have homogeneous useful lives by using the straightline method so as to depreciate the initial cost down to the residual value over the estimated useful lives. The residual values are 30% on head office, 20% on distribution centres for products stored at ambient temperature and nil for all other asset types.

The useful lives are as follows:

Buildings	20–35 years
Machinery and equipment	10–20 years
Tools, furniture, information technology and sundry equipment	3–8 years
Vehicles	5 years
Land is not depreciated	

Useful lives, components and residual amounts are reviewed annually. Such a review takes into consideration the nature of the assets, their intended use and the evolution of technology.

Depreciation of property, plant and equipment is allocated to the appropriate headings of expenses by function in the statement of comprehensive income. Financing costs incurred during the course of construction are expenses. Premiums capitalized for leasehold land and buildings are amortised over the length of the lease.

Accounting policies

Accounting policies are chosen by a company as being the most appropriate to the company's circumstances and **best able to produce a fair view**. They typically disclose the accounting policies followed for the basis of accounting, i.e. historical or alternative accounting rules, and asset valuation, e.g. for inventory, stating whether it uses FIFO or other methods and for property, plant and equipment, stating whether depreciation is straight-line or another method.

As an example, there might be a detailed description as shown by the Nestlé Group in Figure 8.12 or a more general description as shown in the AstraZeneca policy statement in Figure 8.13.

8.7.1 How do users know the effect of changes in accounting policy?

Accounting policies are required by IAS 1 to be applied consistently from one financial period to another. It is only permissible to change an accounting policy if required by a Standard or if the directors consider that a change results in financial statements that are reliable and more relevant. When a change occurs IAS 8 requires:

- the comparative figures of the previous financial period to be amended if possible;
- the disclosure of the reason for the change, the effect of the adjustment in the statement of comprehensive income of the period and the effect on all other periods presented with the current period financial statements.

Figure 8.13 Extract from the financial statements of AstraZeneca

Property, Plant and Equipment

The Group's policy is to write off the difference between the cost of each item of property, plant and equipment and its residual value systematically over its estimated useful life. Assets under construction are not depreciated.

Reviews are made annually of the estimated remaining lives and residual values of individual productive assets, taking account of commercial and technological obsolescence as well as normal wear and tear. Under this policy it becomes impractical to calculate average asset lives exactly. However, the total lives range from approximately thirteen to fifty years for buildings, and three to fifteen years for plant and equipment. All items of property, plant and equipment are tested for impairment when there are indications that the carrying value may not be recoverable. Any impairment losses are recognised immediately in the income statement.

8.7.2 What is meant by a fair view?

This may be referred to as giving a fair presentation or a true and fair view.

8.7.3 IAS I requirements – fair presentation

IAS 1 requires financial statements to give a fair presentation of the financial position, financial performance and cash flows of an enterprise. In para. 17 it states that:

In virtually all circumstances, a fair presentation is achieved by compliance with applicable IFRSs. A fair presentation also requires an entity:

(a) to select and apply accounting policies in accordance with IAS 8 *Accounting Policies, Changes in Accounting Estimates and Errors*. IAS 8 sets out a hierarchy of authoritative guidance that management considers in the absence of a Standard or an Interpretation that specifically applies to an item;

(b) to present information, including accounting policies, in a manner that provides relevant, reliable, comparable and understandable information;

(c) to provide additional disclosures when compliance with the specific requirements in IFRSs is insufficient to enable users to understand the impact of particular transactions, other events and conditions on the entity's financial position and financial performance.

8.7.4 True and fair view

The Companies Act 2006 requires financial statements to give a true and fair view. Auditors are required to give an opinion on true and fair.

8.7.5 Legal opinions – true and fair

True and fair is a legal concept and can be authoritatively decided only by a court. However, the courts have never attempted to define 'true and fair'. In the UK the Accounting Standards Committee (ASC) obtained a legal opinion which included the following statements:

It is however important to observe that the application of the concept involves **judgement in questions of degree**. The information contained in the accounts must be accurate and comprehensive to within acceptable limits. What is acceptable and how is this to be achieved?

Reasonable businessmen and accountants may differ over the degree of accuracy or comprehensiveness which in particular cases the accounts should attain.

Equally, there may sometimes be **room for differences over the method** to adopt in order to give a true and fair view, cases in which there may be more than one true and fair view of the same financial position.

Again, because true and fair involves questions of degree, we think **that cost effectiveness must play a part** in deciding the amount of information which is sufficient to make accounts true and fair.

Accounts will not be true and fair unless the information they contain is **sufficient in** quantity and quality to satisfy the reasonable expectations of the readers to whom they are addressed.[7]

A further counsel's opinion was attained by the Accounting Standards Board (ASB) in 1991 and published[8] in its foreword to Accounting Standards. It advised that accounting standards are an authoritative source of accounting practice and it is now the norm for financial statements to comply with them. In consequence the court may take accounting standards into consideration when forming an opinion on whether the financial statements give a true and fair view.

However, an Opinion obtained by the FRC in May 2008 advised that true and fair still has to be taken into consideration by preparers and auditors of financial statements. Directors have to consider whether the statements are appropriate and auditors have to exercise professional judgement when giving an audit opinion – it is not sufficient for either directors or auditors to reach a conclusion solely because the financial statements were prepared in accordance with applicable accounting standards.

8.7.6 Fair override

IAS 1 recognises that there may be occasions when application of an IAS might be misleading and departure from IAS treatment is permitted. This is referred to as the fair override provision. If a company makes use of the override it is required to explain why compliance with IASs would be misleading and also give sufficient information to enable the user to calculate the adjustments required to comply with the standard.

The true and fair concept is familiar to the UK and Netherlands accounting professions. Many countries, however, view the concept of the true and fair view with suspicion since it runs counter to their legal systems. In Germany the fair override provision has not been directly implemented and laws are interpreted according to their function and objectives. It appears that the role of true and fair in the European context is to act as a protection against over-regulation. Since the wider acceptance of IASs has been occurring in recent years, the financial statements of many more companies and countries are fulfilling the principle of a true and fair view.

Although IAS 1 does not refer to true and fair, the International Accounting Standards Regulation 1606/2002 (para. 9) states that: 'To adopt an international accounting standard for application in the Community, it is necessary . . . that its application results in a true and fair view of the financial position and performance of an enterprise'.

When do companies use the fair override?

It can occur for a number[9] of reasons:

● Accounting standards may prescribe one method, which contradicts company law and thus requires an override, e.g. providing no depreciation on investment properties.

● Accounting standards may offer a choice between accounting procedures, at least one of which contradicts company law. If that particular choice is adopted, the override should be invoked, e.g. grants and contributions not shown as deferred income.

An example of this is shown in the extract from the 2005 Annual Report of Severn Trent:

Grants and contributions

Grants and contributions received in respect of non infrastructure assets are treated as deferred income and are recognised in the profit and loss account over the useful economic life of those assets. In accordance with industry practice, grants and contributions relating to infrastructure assets have been deducted from the cost of fixed assets.

This is not in accordance with Schedule 4 to the Act, which requires assets to be shown at their purchase price or production cost and hence grants and contributions to be presented as deferred income. This departure from the requirements of the Act is, in the opinion of the Directors, necessary to give a true and fair view as, while a provision is made for depreciation of infrastructure assets, finite lives have not been determined for these assets, and therefore no basis exists on which to recognise grants or contributions as deferred income. The effect of this departure is that the cost of fixed assets is £398.5 million lower than it would otherwise have been (2004: £362.6 million).

Those grants and contributions relating to the maintenance of the operating capability of the infrastructure network are taken into account in determining the depreciation charged for infrastructure assets.

● Accounting standards may allow some choice but prefer a particular method which is consistent with company law, but the alternative may not be consistent, e.g. not amortising goodwill (prior to IAS requirement for impairment review).

● There may be a legal requirement but no accounting standard. Failure to comply with the law would require a True and Fair override, e.g. current assets being reported at market value rather than at cost.

● There may be an accounting standards requirement which is overridden, e.g. not providing depreciation on non-current assets.

8.7.7 Fair override can be challenged

Although companies may decide to adopt a policy that is not in accordance with IFRS and rely on the fair override provision, this may be challenged by the Financial Reporting Review Panel and the company's decision overturned, e.g. although Eurovestech had adopted an accounting policy in its 2005 and 2006 accounts not to consolidate two of its subsidiaries because its directors considered that to do so would not give a true and fair view, the FRRP decision was that this was unacceptable because the company was unable to demonstrate special circumstances warranting this treatment.

8.8 What does an investor need in addition to the financial statements to make decisions?

Investors attempt to estimate future cash flows when making an investment decision. As regards future cash flows, these are normally perceived to be influenced by past profits, the asset base as shown by the statement of financial position and any significant changes.

In order to assist shareholders to predict future cash flows with an understanding of the risks involved, more information has been required by the IASB. This has taken two forms:

● more quantitative information in the accounts, including:
  – segmental analysis;
  – the impact of changes on the operation, e.g. a breakdown of turnover, costs and profits for both new and discontinued operations;
  – and the existence of related parties (these are discussed in the next chapter); and
● more qualitative information, including:
  – Mandatory disclosures;
  – Chairman's report;
  – Directors' report;
  – Best practice disclosures: Operating and Financial Review;
  – Business Review in the Directors' report.

We will comment briefly on the qualitative disclosures.

8.8.1 Mandatory disclosures

When making future predictions investors need to be able to identify that part of the net income that is likely to be maintained in the future. IAS 1 provides assistance to users in this by requiring that certain items are separately disclosed. These are items within the ordinary activities of the enterprise which are of such size, nature or incidence that their separate disclosure is required in the financial statements in order for the financial statements to show a fair view.

These items are not extraordinary and must, therefore, be presented above the tax line. It is usual to disclose the nature and amount of these items in a note to the financial statements, with no separate mention on the face of the statement of comprehensive income; however, if sufficiently material, they can be disclosed on the face of the statement.

Examples of the type of items[10] that may give rise to separate disclosures are:

● the write-down of assets to realisable value or recoverable amount;
● the restructuring of activities of the enterprise, and the reversal of provisions for restructuring;
● disposals of items of property, plant and equipment;
● disposals of long-term investments;
● discontinued operations;
● litigation settlements;
● other reversals of provisions.

8.8.2 Additional qualitative information – Chairman's Report

This often tends to be a brief upbeat comment on the current year. For example, the following is a brief extract from Findel plc's 2008 annual report to illustrate the type of information provided.

> Sales from ongoing businesses in our Home Shopping division increased by 22% to £403.5m (2007: £330.7m) with benchmark operating profit increasing to £50.3m (2007: £47.6m). The Home Shopping division now comprises a number of leading brands, each with its own unique appeal and market. Statutory sales for the Home Shopping division were £409.8m (2007: £368.3m) with statutory operating profit of £41.0m (2007: £19.2m).
>
> 2007/08 was the first full trading year for our cash with order division in which it generated £137.5m in sales with net operating margins of 7%. We experienced strong sales growth from Kitbag as it launched three more Premier League football club sites and moved into cricket, rugby, motorsport and tennis. We also benefited from a particularly good profit performance from Kleeneze following its integration into our Accrington site.
>
> The main feature in the year for the cash with order brands was their relocation and integration. This was a huge undertaking and inevitably created some distraction, although we are pleased with the results.

8.8.3 Directors' Report

The paragraph headings from Findel's 2008 annual report illustrate the type of information that is published. The report headings were:

- Activities
- Review of the year and future prospects
- Dividends
- Capital structure
- Suppliers' payment policy
- Directors
- Employees
- Substantial holdings
- Auditors.

There is a brief comment under each heading, for example:

Activities
The principal activities of the Group are home shopping and educational supplies through mail order catalogues and the provision of outsourced healthcare services.

Review of the Year and Future Prospects
The key performance indicators which management consider important are:

- operating margins
- average order value
- retention rates in Home Shopping
- on-time collections and deliveries within Healthcare.

8.8.4 OFR Reporting Standard RS 1

The ASB published RS 1 in 2005. This is not a statutory Standard and is intended to inform best practice. The intention was that directors should focus on the information needs specific to their company and its shareholders rather than follow a rigid list of items to be disclosed. RS 1 assisted directors in this approach by setting down certain principles and providing illustrations of Key Performance Indicators.

The OFR's guiding principles

The seven principles were that the OFR should:

1 reflect the directors' view of the business;

2 focus on matters that are relevant to investors in assessing the strategies adopted and the potential for those strategies to succeed. Whilst maintaining the primacy of meeting investors' needs, directors should take a 'broad view' in deciding what should be included in their OFR, on the grounds that the decisions and agendas of other stakeholders can influence the performance and value of a company;

3 have a forward-looking orientation with an analysis of the main trends and factors which are likely to affect the entity's future development, performance and position;

4 complement as well as supplement the financial statements with additional explanations of amounts included in the financial statements;

5 be comprehensive and understandable but avoid the inclusion of too much information that is not directly relevant;

6 be balanced and neutral – in this way the OFR can produce reliable information;

7 be comparable over time – the ability to compare with other entities in the same industry or sector is encouraged.

Key performance indicators (KPIs)

There has been a concern that OFR would lack quantifiable information. This was addressed with a list of potentially useful KPIs. These covered a wide range of interests including:

- Economic measures of ability to create value (with the terms defined)
  - Return on capital employed

    Capital employed defined for example as Intangible assets + property, plant and equipment + investments + accumulated goodwill amortisation + inventories + trade accounts receivable + other assets including prepaid expenses
  - Economic profit type measures

    Economic profit = Profit after tax and non-controlling interests, excluding goodwill amortisation – cost of capital
- Market positioning
  - Market position
  - Market share

    Market share, being company revenue over estimated market revenue
- Development, performance and position
  - A number of the measures used to monitor the development, performance and position of the company may be traditional financial measures

- Cash conversion rate: rate at which profit is converted into cash
- Asset turnover rates
- Directors often supplement these with other measures common to their industry to monitor their progress towards stated objectives, e.g.
  - Average revenue per user (customer)
  - Number of subscribers
  - Sales per square foot
  - Percentage of revenue from new products
  - Number of products sold per customer
  - Products in the development pipeline
  - Cost per unit produced
- Persons with whom the entity has relations and which could have a significant impact
  - Customers: how do they view the service provided?
    - Measure customer retention
  - Employees: how do they feel about the company?
    - Employee satisfaction surveys
    - Health and safety measures
  - Suppliers: how do they view the company?
  - Regulators: how do they view the company?
- Environmental matters
  - Quantified measures of water and energy usage
- Social and community issues
  - Public health issues, such as obesity, perceived safety issues related to high use of mobile phones
  - Social risks existing in the supply chain such as the use of child labour and payment of fair wages
  - Diversity in either the employee or customer base
  - Impact on the local community, e.g. noise, pollution, transport congestion
  - Indigenous and human rights issues relating to communities local to overseas operations
  - Receipts from and payments to shareholders
  - Other resources
  - Brand strength
  - Intellectual property
  - Intangible assets.

8.8.5 Additional qualitative information – Business Review in the Directors' Report

This is a requirement in the UK. The intention is that the Review should provide a balanced and comprehensive analysis of the business including social and environmental aspects to allow shareholders to assess how directors have performed their statutory duty to promote the company's success. The government is taking the view that matters required by the Reporting Statement such as 'Trends and factors affecting the development, performance and position of the business and KPIs' would be required to be included in the Business Review *where necessary*, i.e. in those circumstances where it were thought to be necessary in order to provide a balanced and comprehensive analysis of the development, performance and position of the business, or describe the principal risks and uncertainties facing the business. It could well be that in practice companies will satisfy the requirements of the Reporting Statement and include within the Business Review a cut-down version of that information.

8.8.6 ASB review of narrative reporting

In 2006 the ASB (www.accountancyfoundation.com/asb/press/pub1228.html) carried out reviews of narrative reporting by FTSE 100 companies. It identified that there was good reporting of descriptions of their business and markets, strategies and objectives and the current development and performance of the business and an increase in companies providing environmental and social information.

However, it also identified the need for improvement in identifying Key financial and non-financial Performance Indicators; describing off-balance sheet positions and the principal risks with an explanation as to how these will be managed.

As far as forward-looking information was concerned, it might well be that the protection offered by the safe harbour provisions in the Companies Act 2006 could encourage companies to avoid choosing to make bland statements that are of little use to shareholders. The safe harbour provisions protect directors from civil liability in respect of omissions or statements made in the narrative reports unless the omissions were to dishonestly conceal material information or the statements were untrue or misleading and made recklessly or in bad faith.

8.8.7 How decision-useful is the statement of comprehensive income?

IAS 1 now requires a statement of comprehensive income as a primary financial statement. There has been ongoing discussion as to the need for such a statement. Some commentators[11] argue that there is no decision-usefulness in providing the comprehensive net income figure for investors whereas others[12] take the opposite view. Intuitively, one might take a view that investors are interested in the total movement in equity regardless of the cause which would lead to support for the comprehensive income figure. However, given that there is this difference of opinion and research findings, this would seem to be an area open to further empirical research to further test the decision-usefulness of each measure to analysts.

Interesting research[13] has since been carried out which supports the view that Net Income and Comprehensive Income are both decision-useful. The findings suggested that comprehensive income was more decision-relevant for assessing share returns and traditional net income more decision-relevant for setting executive bonus incentives.

Summary

In order to assess stewardship and management performance, there have been mandatory requirements for standardised presentation, using formats prescribed by International Financial Reporting Standards. There have also been mandatory requirements for the disclosure of accounting policies, which allow shareholders to make comparisons between years.

There is an increasing pressure for additional disclosures such as KPIs and improved narrative reporting to help users assess the stewardship and assist in making predictions as to future cash flows.

REVIEW QUESTIONS

1 Explain why two companies carrying out identical trading transactions could produce different gross profit figures.

2 A statement of comprehensive income might contain the following profit figures:

> Gross profit
> Profit from operations
> Profit before tax
> Net profit from ordinary activities
> Net profit for the period.

Explain when you would use each profit figure for analysis purposes, e.g. profit from operations may be used in the percentage return on capital employed.

3 Classify the following items into cost of sales, distribution costs, administrative expenses, other operating income or item to be disclosed after trading profit:

(a) Personnel department costs

(b) Computer department costs

(c) Cost accounting department costs

(d) Financial accounting department costs

(e) Bad debts

(f) Provisions for warranty claims

(g) Interest on funds borrowed to finance an increase in working capital

(h) Interest on funds borrowed to finance an increase in property plant and equipment.

4 'We analyze a sample of UK public companies that invoked a TFV override during 1998–2000 to assess whether overrides are used opportunistically. We find overrides increase income and equity significantly, and firms with weaker performance and higher levels of debt employ overrides that are more costly...financial statements are not less informative than control sample.'[14]

Discuss the enquiries and action that you think an auditor should take to ensure that the financial statements give a more true and fair view than from applying standards.

5 When preparing accounts under Format 1, how would a bad debt that was materially larger than normal be disclosed?

6 'Annual accounts have been put into such a straitjacket of overemphasis on uniform disclosure that there will be a growing pressure by national bodies to introduce changes unilaterally which will again lead to diversity in the quality of disclosure. This is both healthy and necessary.' Discuss.

7 Explain the relevance to the user of accounts if expenses are classified as 'administrative expenses' rather than as 'cost of sales'.

8 IAS 1 *Presentation of Financial Statements* requires 'other comprehensive income' items to be included in the statement of comprehensive income and it also requires a statement of changes in equity.

Explain the need for publishing this information, and identify the items you would include in them.

EXERCISES

An extract from the solution is provided on the Companion Website (www.pearsoned.co.uk/elliott-elliott) for exercises marked with an asterisk (*).

Question 1

Basalt plc is a wholesaler. The following is its trial balance as at 31 December 20X0.

	Dr £000	Cr £000
Ordinary share capital: £1 shares		300
Share premium		20
General reserve		16
Retained earnings as at		
1 January 20X0		55
Inventory as at 1 January 20X0	66	
Sales		962
Purchases	500	
Administrative costs	10	
Distribution costs	6	
Plant and machinery – cost	220	
Plant and machinery –		
provision for depreciation		49
Returns outwards		25
Returns inwards	27	
Carriage inwards	9	
Warehouse wages	101	
Salesmen's salaries	64	
Administrative wages and salaries	60	
Hire of motor vehicles	19	
Directors' remuneration	30	
Rent receivable		7
Trade receivables	326	
Cash at bank	62	
Trade payables		66
	1,500	1,500

The following additional information is supplied:

(i) Depreciate plant and machinery 20% on straight-line basis.

(ii) Inventory at 31 December 20X0 is £90,000.

(iii) Accrue auditors' remuneration £2,000.

(iv) Income tax for the year will be £58,000 payable October 20X1.

(v) It is estimated that 7/11 of the plant and machinery is used in connection with distribution, with the remainder for administration. The motor vehicle costs should be allocated to distribution.

Required:
Prepare a statement of income and statement of financial position in a form that complies with IAS 1. No notes to the accounts are required.

* Question 2

The following trial balance was extracted from the books of Old NV on 31 December 20X1.

	€000	€000
Sales		12,050
Returns outwards		313
Provision for depreciation		
Plant		738
Vehicles		375
Rent receivable		100
Trade payables		738
Debentures		250
Issued share capital – ordinary €1 shares		3,125
Issued share capital – preference shares (treated as equity)		625
Share premium		350
Retained earnings		875
Inventory	825	
Purchases	6,263	
Returns inwards	350	
Carriage inwards	13	
Carriage outwards	125	
Salesmen's salaries	800	
Administrative wages and salaries	738	
Land	100	
Plant (includes €362,000 acquired in 20X1)	1,562	
Motor vehicles	1,125	
Goodwill	1,062	
Distribution costs	290	
Administrative expenses	286	
Directors' remuneration	375	
Trade receivables	3,875	
Cash at bank and in hand	1,750	
	19,539	19,539

Note of information not taken into the trial balance data:

(a) Provide for:
   (i) An audit fee of €38,000.
   (ii) Depreciation of plant at 20% straight-line.
   (iii) Depreciation of vehicles at 25% reducing balance.
   (iv) The goodwill suffered an impairment in the year of €177,000.
   (v) Income tax of €562,000.
   (vi) Debenture interest of €25,000.

(b) Closing inventory was valued at €1,125,000 at the lower of cost and net realisable value.

(c) Administrative expenses were prepaid by €12,000.

(d) Land was to be revalued by €50,000.

Required:

(a) Prepare a statement of income for internal use for the year ended 31 December 20X1.

(b) Prepare a statement of comprehensive income for the year ended 31 December 20X1 and a statement of financial position as at that date in Format 1 style of presentation.

Question 3

HK Ltd has prepared its draft trial balance to 30 June 20X1, which is shown below.

Trial balance at 30 June 20X1		
	$000	$000
Freehold land	2,100	
Freehold buildings (cost $4,680)	4,126	
Plant and machinery (cost $3,096)	1,858	
Fixtures and fittings (cost $864)	691	
Goodwill	480	
Trade receivables	7,263	
Trade payables		2,591
Inventory	11,794	
Bank balance	11,561	
Development grant received		85
Profit on sale of freehold land		536
Sales		381,600
Cost of sales	318,979	
Administration expenses	9,000	
Distribution costs	35,100	
Directors' emoluments	562	
Bad debts	157	
Auditors' remuneration	112	
Hire of plant and machinery	2,400	
Loan interest	605	
Dividends paid during the year – preference	162	
Dividends paid during the year – ordinary	426	
9% loan		7,200
Share capital – preference shares (treated as equity)		3,600
Share capital – ordinary shares		5,400
Retained earnings		6,364
	407,376	407,376

The following information is available:

(a) The authorised share capital is 4,000,000 9% preference shares of $1 each and The authorised share capital is 4,000,000 9% preference shares of $1 each and 18,000,000 ordinary shares of 50c each.

(b) Provide for depreciation at the following rates:

   (i) Plant and machinery 20% on cost
   (ii) Fixtures and fittings 10% on cost
   (iii) Buildings 2% on cost

   Charge all depreciation to cost of sales.

(c) Provide $5,348,000 for income tax.

(d) The loan was raised during the year and there is no outstanding interest accrued at the year-end.

(e) Government grants of $85,000 have been received in respect of plant purchased during the year and are shown in the trial balance. One-fifth is to be taken into profit in the current year.

(f) During the year a fire took place at one of the company's depots, involving losses of $200,000. These losses have already been written off to cost of sales shown in the trial balance. Since the end of the financial year a settlement of $150,000 has been agreed with the company's insurers.

(g) $500,000 of the inventory is obsolete. This has a realisable value of $250,000.

(h) Acquisitions of property, plant and equipment during the year were:

Plant $173,000   Fixtures $144,000

(i) During the year freehold land which cost $720,000 was sold for $1,316,000.

(j) A final ordinary dividend of 3c per share is declared and was an obligation before the year-end, together with the balance of the preference dividend. Neither dividend was paid at the year-end.

(k) The goodwill has not been impaired.

(l) The land was revalued at the year end at $2,500,000.

Required:
(a) **Prepare the company's statement of comprehensive income for the year to 30 June 20X1 and a statement of financial position as at that date, complying with the relevant accounting standards in so far as the information given permits.**
    (All calculations to nearest $000.)
(b) **Explain the usefulness of the schedule prepared in (b).**

Question 4

Phoenix plc trial balance at 30 June 20X7 was as follows:

	£000	£000
Freehold premises	2,400	
Plant and machinery	1,800	540
Furniture and fittings	620	360
Inventory at 30 June 20X7	1,468	
Sales		6,465
Administrative expenses	1,126	
Ordinary shares of £1 each		4,500
Trade investments	365	
Revaluation reserve		600
Development cost	415	
Share premium		500
Personal ledger balances	947	566
Cost of goods sold	4,165	
Distribution costs	669	
Overprovision for tax		26
Dividend received		80
Interim dividend paid	200	
Retained earnings		488
Disposal of warehouse		225
Cash and bank balances	175	

The following information is available:

1. Freehold premises acquired for £1.8 million were revalued in 20X4, recognising a gain of £600,000. These include a warehouse, which cost £120,000, was revalued at £150,000 and was sold in June 20X7 for £225,000. Phoenix does not depreciate freehold premises.

2. Phoenix wishes to report Plant and Machinery at open market value which is estimated to be £1,960,000 on 1 July 20X6.

3. Company policy is to depreciate its assets on the straight-line method at annual rates as follows:

Plant and machinery	10%
Furniture and fittings	5%

4. Until this year the company's policy has been to capitalise development costs, to the extent permitted by relevant accounting standards. The company must now write off the development costs, including £124,000 incurred in the year, as the project no longer meets the capitalisation criteria.

5. During the year the company has issued one million shares of £1 at £1.20 each.

6. Included within administrative expenses are the following:

Staff salary (including £125,000 to directors)	£468,000
Directors' fees	£96,000
Audit fees and expenses	£86,000

7. Income tax for the year is estimated at £122,000.

8. Directors propose a final dividend of 4p per share declared and an obligation, but not paid at the year-end.

Required:
In respect of the year ended 30 June 20X7:
(a) The statement of comprehensive income.
(b) The statement of financial position as at 30 June 20X7.
(c) The statement of movement of property, plant and equipment.

Question 5

The following is an extract from the trial balance of Imecet at 31 October 2005:

	$000	$000
Property valuation	8,000	
Factory at cost	2,700	
Administration building at cost	1,200	
Delivery vehicles at cost	500	
Sales		10,300
Inventory at 1 November 2004	1,100	
Purchases	6,350	
Factory wages	575	
Administration expenses	140	
Distribution costs	370	
Interest paid (6 months to 30 April 2005)	100	
Accumulated profit at 1 November 2004		3,701
10% Loan stock		2,000
$1 Ordinary shares (incl. issue on 1 May 2005)		4,000
Share premium (after issue on 1 May 2005)		1,500
Dividends (paid 1 June 2005)	400	
Revaluation reserve		2,500
Deferred tax		650

Other relevant information:

(i) One million $1 Ordinary shares were issued 1 May 2005 at the market price of $1.75 per ordinary share.

(ii) The inventory at 31 October 2005 has been valued at $1,150,000.

(iii) A current tax provision for $350,000 is required for the period ended 31 October 2005 and the deferred tax liability at that date has been calculated to be $725,000.

(iv) The property has been further revalued at 31 October 2005 at the market price of $9,200,000.

(v) No depreciation charges have yet been recognised for the year ended 31 October 2005.

The depreciation rates are:

Factory – 5% straight-line.
Administration building – 3% straight-line.
Delivery vehicles – 25% reducing balance. The accumulated depreciation at 31 October 2004 was $10,000. There were no new vehicles acquired in the year to 31 October 2005.

Required:
(a) Prepare the Income Statement for Imecet for the year ended 31 October 2005.
(b) Prepare the statement of changes in equity for Imecet for the year ended 31 October 2005.

(The Association of International Accountants)

* Question 6

Olive A/S, incorporated with an authorised capital consisting of one million ordinary shares of €1 each, employs 646 persons, of whom 428 work at the factory and the rest at the head office. The trial balance extracted from its books as at 30 September 20X4 is as follows:

	€000	€000
Land and buildings (cost €600,000)	520	—
Plant and machinery (cost €840,000)	680	—
Proceeds on disposal of plant and machinery	—	180
Fixtures and equipment (cost €120,000)	94	—
Sales	—	3,460
Carriage inwards	162	—
Share premium account	—	150
Advertising	112	—
Inventory on 1 Oct 20X3	211	—
Heating and lighting	80	—
Prepayments	115	—
Salaries	820	—
Trade investments at cost	248	—
Dividend received (net) on 9 Sept 20X4	—	45
Directors' emoluments	180	—
Pension cost	100	—
Audit fees and expense	65	—
Retained earnings b/f	—	601
Sales commission	92	—
Stationery	28	—
Development cost	425	—
Formation expenses	120	—
Receivables and payables	584	296
Interim dividend paid on 4 Mar 20X4	60	—
12% debentures issued on 1 Apr 20X4	—	500
Debenture interest paid on 1 Jul 20X4	15	—
Purchases	925	—
Income tax on year to 30 Sept 20X3	—	128
Other administration expenses	128	—
Bad debts	158	—
Cash and bank balance	38	—
Ordinary shares of €1 fully called	—	600
	5,960	5,960

You are informed as follows:

(a) As at 1 October 20X3 land and buildings were revalued at €900,000. A third of the cost as well as all the valuation is regarded as attributable to the land. Directors have decided to report this asset at valuation.

(b) New fixtures were acquired on 1 January 20X4 for €40,000; a machine acquired on 1 October 20X1 for €240,000 was disposed of on 1 July 20X4 for €180,000, being replaced on the same date by another acquired for €320,000.

(c) Depreciation for the year is to be calculated on the straight-line basis as follows:

Buildings: 2% p.a.
Plant and machinery: 10% p.a.
Fixtures and equipment: 10% p.a.

(d) Inventory, including raw materials and work-in-progress on 30 September 20X4, has been valued at cost at €364,000.

(e) Prepayments are made up as follows:

	€000
Amount paid in advance for a machine	60
Amount paid in advance for purchasing raw materials	40
Prepaid rent	15
	€115

(f) In March 20X3 a customer had filed legal action claiming damages at €240,000. When accounts for the year ended 30 September 20X3 were finalised, a provision of €90,000 was made in respect of this claim. This claim was settled out of court in April 20X4 at €150,000 and the amount of the underprovision adjusted against the profit balance brought forward from previous years.

(g) The following allocations have been agreed upon:

	Factory	Administration
Depreciation of buildings	60%	40%
Salaries other than to directors	55%	45%
Heating and lighting	80%	20%

(h) Pension cost of the company is calculated at 10% of the emoluments and salaries.

(i) Income tax on 20X3 profit has been agreed at €140,000 and that for 20X4 estimated at €185,000. Corporate income tax rate is 35% and the basic rate of personal income tax 25%.

(j) Directors wish to write off the formation expenses as far as possible without reducing the amount of profits available for distribution.

Required:
Prepare for publication:
(a) The Statement of Comprehensive Income of the company for the year ended 30 September 20X4, and
(b) the Statement of Financial Position as at that date along with as many notes (other than the one on accounting policy) as can be provided on the basis of the information made available.
(c) the Statement of Changes in Equity.

Question 7

Raffles Ltd trades as a wine wholesaler with a large warehouse in Asia. The trainee accountant at Raffles Ltd has produced the following draft accounts for the year ended 31 December 20X6.

Statement of comprehensive income

	$
Sales	1,628,000
Less: Cost of sales	1,100,000
Gross profit	528,000
Debenture interest paid	9,000
Distribution costs	32,800
Audit fees	7,000
Impairment of goodwill	2,500
Income tax liability on profits	165,000
Interim dividend	18,000
Dividend received from Diat P'or plc	(6,000)
Bank interest	3,000
Over provision of income tax in prior years	(4,250)
Depreciation	
Land and buildings	3,000
Plant and machinery	10,000
Fixtures and fittings	6,750
Administrative expenses	206,300
Net profit	74,900

Draft statement of financial position at 31 December 20X6

	$		$
Bank balance	12,700	Inventory	156,350
10% debentures 20X9	180,000	Receivables	179,830
Ordinary share capital		Land and buildings	238,000
50c nominal value	250,000	Plant and machinery	74,000
Trade payables	32,830	Fixtures and fittings	20,250
Income tax			
Creditor	165,000	Goodwill	40,000
Retained earnings	172,900	Investments at cost	130,000
Revaluation reserve	25,000		
	838,430		838,430

The following information is relevant:

1 The directors maintain that the investments in Diat P'or plc will be held by the company on a continuing basis and that the current market value of the investments at the period end was $135,000. However, since the period end there has been a substantial fall in market prices and these investments are now valued at $90,000.

2 The authorised share capital of Raffles Ltd is 600,000 ordinary shares.

3 During the year the company paid shareholders the proposed 20X5 final dividend of $30,000. This transaction has already been recorded in the accounts.

4 The company incurred $150,000 in restructuring costs during the year. These have been debited to the administrative expenses account. The trainee accountant subsequently informs you that tax relief of $45,000 will be given on these costs and that this relief has not yet been accounted for in the records.

5 The company employs an average of ten staff, 60% of whom work in the wine purchasing and importing department, 30% in the distribution department and the remainder in the accounts department. Staff costs total $75,000.

6 The company has three directors. The managing director earns $18,000 while the purchasing and distribution directors earn $14,000 each. In addition the directors receive bonuses and pensions of $1,800 each. All staff costs have been debited to the statement of comprehensive income.

7 The directors propose to decrease the bad debt provision by $1,500 as a result of the improved credit control in the company in recent months.

8 Depreciation policy is as follows:

Land and buildings:	No depreciation on land. Buildings are depreciated over 25 years on a straight-line basis. This is to be charged to cost of sales.
Plant and machinery:	10% on cost, charge to cost of sales.
Fixtures and fittings:	25% reducing balance, charge to administration.

9 The directors have provided information on a potential lawsuit. A customer is suing them for allegedly tampering with the imported wine by injecting an illegal substance to improve the colour of the wine. The managing director informs you that this lawsuit is just 'sour grapes' by a jealous customer and provides evidence from the company solicitor which indicates that there is only a small possibility that the claim for $8,000 will succeed.

10 Purchased goodwill was acquired in 20X3 for $50,000. The annual impairment test revealed an impairment of $2,500 in the current year.

11 Plant and machinery of $80,000 was purchased during the year to add to the $20,000 plant already owned. Fixtures and fittings acquired two years ago with a net book value of $13,500 were disposed of. Accumulated depreciation of fixtures and fittings at 1 January 20X6 was $37,500.

12 Land was revalued by $25,000 by Messrs Moneybags, Chartered Surveyors, on an open market value basis, to $175,000 during the year. The revaluation surplus was credited to the revaluation reserve. There is no change in the value of the buildings.

13 Gross profit is stated after charging $15,000 relating to obsolete cases of wine that have 'gone off'. Since that time an offer has been received by the company for its obsolete wine stock of $8,000, provided the company does additional vinification on the wine at a cost of $2,000 to bring it up to the buyer's requirements. A cash discount of 5% is allowed for early settlement and it is anticipated that the buyer will take advantage of this discount.

14 Costs of $10,000 relating to special plant and machinery have been included in cost of sales in error. This was not spotted until after the production of the draft accounts.

Required:

(a) Prepare a statement of comprehensive income for the year ended 31 December 20X6 and a statement of financial position at that date for presentation to the members of Raffles Ltd in accordance with relevant accounting standards.

(b) Produce detailed notes to both statements of Raffles Ltd for the year ended 31 December 20X6.

Question 8

Graydon Ross CFO of Diversified Industries PLC is discussing the publication of the annual report with his managing director Phil Davison. Graydon says: 'The law requires us to comply with accounting standards and at the same time to provide a true and fair view of the results and financial position. As half of the business consists of the crockery and brick making business which your great great grand-mother started, and the other half is the insurance company which your father started, I am not sure that the consolidated accounts are very meaningful. It is hard to make sense of any of the ratios as you don't know what industry to compare them with. What say we also give them the comprehensive income statements and balance sheets of the two subsidiary companies as additional information, and then no one can complain that they didn't get a true and fair view?'

Phil says: 'I don't think we should do that. The more information they have the more questions they will ask. Also they might realise we have been smoothing income by changing our level of pessimism in relation to the provisions for outstanding insurance claims. Anyway I don't want them to interfere with my business. Can't we just include a footnote, preferably a vague one, that stresses we are not comparable to either insurance companies or brick makers or crockery manufacturers because of the unique mix of our businesses? Don't raise the matter with the auditors because it will put ideas into their heads. But if it does come up we may have to charge head office costs to the two subsidiaries. You need to think up some reason why most of the charges should be passed on to the crockery operations. We don't want to show everyone how profitable that area is. I trust you will give that some thought so you will have a good answer ready.'

Required:
Discuss the professional, legal and ethical implications for Ross.

References

1 IAS 1, *Presentation of Financial Statements*, December 2008.
2 IAS 16 *Property, Plant and Equipment*, IASC, revised 1998, paras 28–29.
3 IAS 39 *Financial Instruments: Recognition and Measurement*, IASC, 1998, para. 69.
4 IAS 2 *Inventories*, IASC, revised 1993, para. 6.
5 IAS 37 *Provisions, Contingent Liabilities and Contingent Assets*, IASC, 1998, para. 45.
6 *Framework for the Preparation and Presentation of Financial Statements*, IASC, 1989, para. 46.
7 K. Wild and A. Guida, *Touche Ross Financial Reporting Manual* (3rd edition), Butterworth, 1990, p. 433.
8 K. Wild and C. Goodhead, *Touche Ross Financial Reporting Manual* (4th edition), Butterworth, 1994, p. 5.
9 LBS Accounting Subject Area Working Paper No. 031 *An Empirical Investigation of the True and Fair Override*, Gilad Livne and Maureen McNichols (www.bm.ust.hk/acct/acsymp2004/Papers/Livne.pdf).
10 IAS 1, para. 86.
11 D. Dhaliwal, K. Subramnayam and R. Trezevant, 'Is comprehensive income superior to net income as a measure of firm performance?', *Journal of Accounting and Economics*, 26:1, 1999, pp. 43–67.
12 D. Hirst and P. Hopkins, 'Comprehensive income reporting and analysts' valuation judgments', *Journal of Accounting Research*, 36 (Supplement), 1998, pp. 47–74.
13 G.C. Biddles and Jong-Hag Choi, 'Is comprehensive income irrelevant?', 12 June 2002. Available at SSRN: http://ssrn.com/abstract=316703.
14 G. Livne and M.F. McNichols, 'An empirical investigation of the true and fair override', *Journal of Business, Finance and Accounting*, pp. 1–30, January/March 2009.

CHAPTER 9

Annual Report: additional financial statements

9.1 Introduction

The main purpose of this chapter is to explain the additional content in an Annual Report that assists users to make informed estimates of future financial performance.

Objectives

By the end of this chapter, you should be able to:

- discuss the value segmental information adds to published financial statements;
- understand and evaluate the structure and content of Segmental Reports and discuss the major provisions of IFRS 8 *Operating Segments*;
- explain the criteria laid out in IFRS 5 *Non-current assets held for sale and discontinued operations* that need to be satisfied before an asset (or disposal group) is classified as 'held for sale';
- explain the accounting significance of classifying an asset or disposal group as 'held for sale';
- explain the meaning of the term 'discontinued operations' and discuss the impact of such operations on the statement of comprehensive income;
- understand the effect on financial statements of events occurring after the end of the reporting period in accordance with IAS 10;
- identify Related Parties in accordance with IAS 24 (revised November 2009).

9.2 The value added by segment reports

In this section we review the reasons for and importance of segment reporting in the analysis of financial statements. We will also summarise the progress to date in developing an internationally accepted financial reporting standard on this subject.

9.2.1 The benefits of segment reporting

The majority of listed and other large entities derive their revenues and profits from a number of sources (or segments). This has implications for the investment strategy of the entity as different segments require different amounts of investment to support their activities. Conventionally produced statements of financial position and statements of comprehensive income capture financial position and financial performance in a single column of figures.

Segment reports provide a more detailed breakdown of key numbers from the financial statements. Such a breakdown potentially allows a user to:

● appreciate more thoroughly the results and financial position by permitting a better understanding of past performance and thus a better assessment of future prospects;

● be aware of the impact that changes in significant components of a business may have on the business as a whole;

● be more aware of the balance between the different operations and thus able to assess the quality of the entity's reported earnings, the specific risks to which the company is subject, and the areas where long-term growth may be expected.

9.2.2 Constraints on comparison between entities

Segment reporting is intrinsically subjective. This means that there are likely to be major differences in the way segments are determined, and because costs, for instance, may be allocated differently by entities in the same industry it is difficult to make inter-entity comparisons at the segment level and the user still has to take a great deal of responsibility for the interpretation of that information.

9.2.3 Progress in developing an internationally agreed standard on segment reporting

A number of domestic standard setters have developed a standard on this subject. For example, in the UK, SSAP 25 *Segmental Reporting*, was issued in June 1990 with a scope that included listed and very large entities. Its objective was to assist users in evaluating the different business segments and geographical regions of a group and how they would affect its overall results. This particular standard is of questionable benefit as it contained a 'get-out' clause that allowed entities not to give the required disclosures if the directors believed that to do so would be 'seriously prejudicial' to the reporting entity.

In 1997 the predecessor body to the IASB issued IAS 14 – *Segment reporting*. IAS 14 applied to listed entities only and required such entities to identify reportable segments based on geographical and 'type of business' grounds. One or other of the segment types had to be designated the primary reportable segments whilst the other type was to be the secondary reportable segments. The disclosures that had to be given were prescriptive and, at least in theory, consistent across entities.

The issue of segment reporting has been one that was on the agenda of the convergence project between the IASB and the FASB (the primary setter of standards in the United States of America). IFRS 8 *Operating segments* was issued in November 2006 following joint consultation between the two bodies.

9.3 Detailed review and evaluation of IRFS 8 – *Operating Segments*[1]

9.3.1 Overview and scope

The IASB published IFRS 8 *Operating Segments* in November 2006 as part of the IASB convergence project with US GAAP. IFRS 8 replaces IAS 14 and aligns the international rules with the requirements of SFAS 131 *Disclosures about Segments of an Enterprise and Related Information*. Once adopted, IFRS and US GAAP will be the same, except for some very minor differences.

The scope of IFRS 8 remains the same as IAS 14. It applies to separate or individual financial statements of an entity (and to consolidated financial statements of a group with a parent):

● whose debt or equity instruments are traded in a public market; or

● that files, or is in the process of filing, its financial statements with a securities commission or other regulatory organisation for the purpose of issuing any class of instruments in the public market.

If an entity not within the scope of IFRS 8 chooses to prepare information about segments that does not comply with IFRS 8, it should not be described as segment information.

9.3.2 Effective date

IFRS 8 is mandatory for periods beginning on or after 1 January 2009, but earlier adoption is allowed. However, EU companies could not adopt IFRS 8 until it was endorsed by the EU. This endorsement took place in late 2007. When the new standard is adopted, the comparatives need to be restated, unless the cost would be excessive.

9.3.3 Key changes from IAS 14

IFRS 8 adopts the management approach to segment reporting and the disclosure of information used to manage the business rather than the strict rule based IAS 14 disclosures. The three key areas of difference between IFRS 8 and IAS 14 are:

● identification of segments;

● measurement of segment information; and

● disclosures.

9.3.4 Identification of segments

IFRS 8 requires the identification of operating segments on the basis of internal reports that are regularly reviewed by the entity's chief operating decision maker (CODM) in order to allocate resources to the segment and assess its performance. Under IFRS 8 there will be a single set of operating segments rather than the primary and secondary segments of IAS 14.

Also, per IFRS 8 a segment that sells exclusively or mainly to other operating segments of the group meets the definition of an operating segment if the business is managed in that way. IAS 14 limited reportable segments to those that earn a majority of revenue from external customers.

Criteria for identifying a segment

An operating segment is a component of an entity:

(a) that engages in business activities from which it may earn revenues and incur expenses (including revenues and expenses relating to other components of the same entity);

(b) whose operating results are regularly reviewed by the entity's chief operating decision maker, to make decisions about resources to be allocated to the segment and to assess its performance; and

(c) for which discrete financial information is available.

Not every part of the entity will necessarily be an operating segment. For example, a corporate headquarters may not earn revenues.

Criteria for identifying the chief operating decision maker

The 'chief operating decision maker' may be an individual or a group of directors or others. The key identifying factors will be those of performance assessment and resource allocation. Some organisations may have overlapping sets of components for which managers are responsible, e.g. some managers may be responsible for specific geographic areas and others for products worldwide. If the CODM reviews the operating results of both sets of components, the entity shall determine which constitutes the operating segments using the core principles (a)–(c) above.

9.3.5 Identifying *reportable* segments

Once an operating segment has been identified, a decision has to be made as to whether it has to be reported. The segment information is required to be reported for any operating segment that meets any of the following criteria:

(a) its reported revenue, from internal and external customers, is 10% or more of the combined revenue (internal and external) of all operating segments; or

(b) the absolute measure of its reported profit or loss is 10% or more of the greater, in absolute amount of (i) the combined profit of all operating segments that did not report a loss and (ii) the combined reported loss of all operating segments that reported a loss; or

(c) its assets are 10% or more of the combined assets of all operating segments.

Failure to meet any of the criteria does not, however, preclude a company from reporting a segment's results. Operating segments that do not meet any of the criteria may be disclosed, if management think the information would be useful to users of the financial statements.

The 75% test

If the total external revenue of the reportable operating segments is less than 75% of the entity's revenue, additional operating segments should be identified as reportable segments (even if they don't meet the criteria in (a)–(c) above) until 75% of the entity's revenue is included.

Combining segments

Like IAS 14, IFRS 8 includes detailed guidance on which operating segments may be combined to create a reportable segment, e.g. if they have mainly similar products, processes, customers, distribution methods and regulatory environments.

Although IFRS 8 does not specify a maximum number of segments, it suggests that if the reportable segments exceed 10, the entity should consider whether a practical limit had been reached, as the disclosures may become too detailed.

EXAMPLE ● Varia plc is a large training and media entity with an important international component. It operates a state-of-the-art management information system which provides its directors with the information they require to plan and control the various businesses. The directors' reporting requirements are quite detailed and information is collected about the following divisions: Exam-based Training, E-Learning, Corporate Training, Print Media, Online Publishing and Cable Television. The following information is available for the year ended 31 December 2009:

Division	Total Revenue	Profit	Assets
	£m	£m	£m
Exam-based Training	360	21	176
E-Learning	60	3	13
Corporate Training	125	5	84
Print Media	232	27	102
Online Publishing	124	2	31
Cable TV	73	5	39
	974	63	445

Which of Varia plc's divisions are reportable segments in accordance with IFRS 8 Operating Segments?

Solution

- The revenues of **Exam-based Training**, **Corporate Training**, **Print Media** and **Online Publishing** are clearly more than 10% of total revenues and so these segments are reportable.

- All three numbers for **E-Learning and Cable TV** are under 10% of entity totals for revenue, profit and assets and so, unless these segments can validly be combined with others for reporting purposes, they are not reportable separately, although Varia could choose to provide separate information.

As a final check we need to establish that the combined revenues of reportable segments we have identified (£360 million + £125 million + £232 million + £124 million = £841 million) is at least 75% of the total revenues of Varia of £974 million. £841 million is 86% of £974 million so this condition is satisfied. Therefore no other segments need to be added.

9.3.6 Measuring segment information

IFRS 8 specifies that the amount reported for each segment should be the measures reported to the chief operating decision maker for the purposes of allocating resources and assessing performance. IAS 14 required the information to be measured in accordance with the accounting policies adopted for presenting and preparing information in the consolidated accounts.

IAS 14 defined segment revenue, segment expense, segment result, segment assets, and segments liabilities. IFRS 8 does not define these terms, but requires an explanation of how segment profit or loss and segment assets and segment liabilities are measured for each reportable segment.

Allocations and adjustments to revenues and profit should only be included in segment disclosures if they are reviewed by the CODM.

9.3.7 Disclosure requirements for reportable segments

The principle in IFRS 8 is that an entity should disclose 'information to enable users to evaluate the nature and financial effect of the business activities in which it engages and the economic environment in which it operates'.

IFRS 8 requires disclosure of the following segment information:

(i) Factors used to identify the entity's operating segments, including the basis of organisation (for example, whether management organises the entity around products and services, geographical areas, regulatory environments, or a combination of factors and whether segments have been aggregated).

(ii) Types of products and services from which each reportable segment derives its revenues.

(iii) A measure of profit or loss and total assets for each reportable segment.

(iv) A measure of liabilities for each reportable segment if it is regularly provided to the chief operating decision maker.

(v) The following items **if** they are disclosed in the performance statement reviewed by the chief operating decision maker:

- revenues from external customers;
- revenues from transactions with other operating segments;
- interest revenue;
- interest expense;
- depreciation and amortisation;
- 'exceptional' items;
- interests in profits and losses of associates and JVs (under equity method);
- income tax income or expense;
- other material non-cash items.

(vi) The following items **if** they are regularly provided to the chief operating decision maker:

- the amount of investment in associates and JVs accounted for by the equity method;
- total amounts for additions to non-current assets other than financial instruments, deferred tax assets, post-employment benefit assets, and rights arising under insurance contracts.

(vii) Reconciliations of profit or loss and assets to the group totals for the entity.

9.3.8 Entity wide disclosures

IFRS 8 requires the following entity wide disclosures, even for those with a single reportable segment:

(i) Revenue from external customers for each product or service, or groups of similar products or services.

(ii) Revenues from external customers (a) attributed to the entity's country of domicile and (b) attributed to all foreign countries in total. If revenues from external customers from an individual country are material, they should be disclosed separately.

(iii) Non-current assets (other than financial instruments, deferred tax assets, post-employment benefits assets and rights under insurance contracts) located in (a) the entity's country of domicile and (b) all other foreign countries. If assets in individual foreign countries are material, they should be disclosed separately.

(iv) The information in (i)–(iii) above should be based on the financial information that is used to produce the entity's financial statements.

(v) Reliance on major customers. If revenues from a single external customer are 10% or more of the entity's total revenue, it must disclose that fact and the segment reporting the revenue. It need not disclose the identity of the major customer or the amount of the revenue.

A 'single customer' is deemed to be entities under common control and a government (national, state, local) and entities known to be under the control of that government shall be considered to be a single customer.

These disclosures are not required if the information is not available and if the costs to develop it would be excessive, in which case this fact should be disclosed. These entity wide disclosures are also not needed if they have already been given under the reportable segment information described in 9.3.7 above.

9.3.9 Evaluation of the impact of IFRS 8

IFRS 8 was developed in part to converge with US practice but also because there was a boilerplate feel to IAS 14 which meant that it was presented by management to accommodate IAS 14 requirements whilst not being seen as important information for management. Some commentators have suggested that the disclosures under IFRS 8 may be more meaningful, as it will be information which the management believe to be important in running the business.

Companies will produce a single set of segmental information for internal and external purposes, which may reduce costs. This does not necessarily mean less information will be disclosed – in fact it may be more, depending on the information that is reviewed by the chief operating decision maker.

Although there may be little impact on the way some entities report segment information, for others it will involve very significant changes to the way they identify reportable segments and disclose segment information. There may be greater diversity in reporting, for example, some companies may report a combination of business and geographic segments, others may identify a single set of segments, say the different business segments.

IFRS 8 requires a much greater disclosure of information than IAS 14. In particular, separate disclosure of both segment assets and segment liabilities are required and the basis of inter-segment pricing. In addition, the information disclosed, for some entities, may be very different from under IAS 14 and the reconciliations to the financial statements may be difficult to understand. How this is to be presented to external users of the accounts should be considered. It is important that investors and analysts know what to expect and what the new disclosures mean.

Continuing concerns following the issue of IAS 8

Despite the existence of IFRS 8, there are many concerns about the extent of segmental disclosure and its limitations must be recognised. A great deal of discretion is imparted to the directors concerning the **definition of each segment**. However, 'the factors which provide guidance in determining an industry segment are often the factors which lead a company's management to organise its enterprise into divisions, branches or subsidiaries'. There is discretion concerning the **allocation of common costs** to segments on a reasonable basis. There is flexibility in the **definition of some of the items** to be disclosed (particularly net assets).

These concerns have been recognised at government level and will be held under review as, for example, by the European Parliament.

European Parliament reservations

In November 2007 the European Parliament accepted the Commission's proposal to endorse IFRS 8, incorporating US Statement of Financial Accounting Standard No. 131

into EU law, which will require EU companies listed in the European Union to disclose segmental information in accordance with the 'through-the-eyes-of-management' approach.

However, it regretted[2] that the impact assessment carried out by the Commission did not sufficiently take into account the interests of users as well as the needs of small and medium-sized companies located in more than one Member State and companies operating only locally. Its view was that such impact assessments must incorporate quantitative information and reflect a balancing of interests among stakeholders. It did not accept that the convergence of accounting rules was a one-sided process where one party (the IASB) simply copies the financial reporting standards of the other party (the FASB). In particular it expressed reservations that disclosure of geographical information on the basis of IFRS 8 would be comparable to that disclosed under IAS 14. It took a strong line by requiring the Commission to follow closely the application of IFRS 8 and to report back to Parliament no later than 2011, *inter alia*, regarding reporting of geographical segments, segment profit or loss, and the use of non-IFRS measures. This underlines that if the Commission discovers deficiencies in the application of IFRS 8 it has a duty to rectify such deficiencies.

Given the global nature of multinationals' activities, the pressure for country-by-country disclosures seems well based and of interest to investors.

UK reservations

The FRRP reviewed a sample of 2009 interim accounts and 2008 annual accounts. On the basis of this review, the FRRP has highlighted situations where companies were asked to provide additional information:

- Only one operating segment is reported, but the group appears to be diverse with different businesses or with significant operations in different countries.
- The operating analysis set out in the narrative report differs from the operating segments in the financial report.
- The titles and responsibilities of the directors or executive management team imply an organisational structure which is not reflected in the operating segments.
- The commentary in the narrative report focuses on non-IFRS measures whereas the segmental disclosures are based on IFRS amounts.

It also suggested a number of questions that directors should ask themselves when preparing segmental reports such as:

- What are the key operating decisions made in running the business?
- Who makes the key operating decisions?
- Who are the segment managers and who do they report to?
- How are the group's activities reported in the information used by management?
- Have the reported segment amounts been reconciled to the IFRS aggregate amounts?
- Do the reported segments appear consistent with their internal reporting?

9.3.10 Sample disclosures under IFRS 8

1 Format for disclosure of segment profits or loss, assets and liabilities

	Hotels £m	Software £m	Finance £m	Other £m	Totals £m
Revenue from external customers	800	2,150	500	100(a)	3,550
Intersegment revenue	—	450	—	—	450
Interest revenue	125	250	—	—	375
Interest expense	95	180	—	—	275
Net interest revenue (b)	—	—	100	—	100
Depreciation & amortisation	30	155	110	—	295
Reportable segment profit	27	320	50	10	407
Other material non-cash items – impairment of assets	20	—	—	—	20
Reportable segment assets	700	1,500	5,700	200	8,100
Expenditure for reportable segment non-current assets	100	130	60	—	290
Reportable segment liabilities	405	980	3,000	—	4,385

(a) Revenue from segments below the quantitative thresholds are attributed to four operating divisions. Those segments include a small electronics company, a warehouse leasing company, a retailer and an undertakers. None of these segments has ever met any of the quantitative thresholds for determining reportable segments.

(b) The finance segment derives most of its revenue from interest. Management primarily relies on net interest revenue, not the gross revenue and expense amounts, in managing that segment. Therefore, as permitted by paragraph 23, only net interest is disclosed.

2 Reconciliations of reportable segment revenues and assets

Reconciliations are required for every material item disclosed, the following are just sample reconciliations.

Revenues	£m
Total revenues for reportable segments	3,900
Other revenues	100
Elimination of intersegment revenues	(450)
Entity's revenue	3,550

Profit or loss	£m
Total profit or loss for reportable segments	397
Other profit or loss	10
Elimination of inter-segment profits	(50)
Unallocated amounts:	
Litigation settlement received	50
Other corporate expenses	(75)
Adjustment to pension expense in consolidation	(25)
Income before tax expense	307

Assets	£m
Total assets for reportable segments	7,900
Other assets	200
Elimination of receivables from corporate headquarters	(100)
Other unallocated amounts	150
Entity's assets	8,150

3 Information about major customers

Sample disclosure might be:

> Revenues from one customer of the software and hotels segments represent approximately £400 million of the entity's total revenue.

(NB: disclosure is not required of the customer's name or of the revenue for each operating segment.)

9.4 IFRS 5 – meaning of 'held for sale'

IFRS 5 *Non-current assets held for sale and discontinued operations*[3] deals, as its name suggests, with two separate but related issues. The first is the appropriate reporting of an asset (or group of assets – referred to in IFRS 5 as a 'disposal group') that management has decided to dispose of.

IFRS 5 states that an asset (or disposal group) is classified as 'held for sale' if its carrying amount will be recovered principally through a sale transaction rather than through continuing use. It further provides that the asset or disposal group must be available for immediate sale in its present condition and its sale must be **highly probable**. For the sale to be highly probable IFRS 5 requires that:

- The appropriate level of management must be committed to a plan to sell the asset or disposal group.
- An active programme to locate a buyer and complete the plan must have been initiated.
- The asset or disposal group must be actively marketed for sale at a price that is reasonable in relation to its current fair value.
- The sale should be expected to qualify for recognition as a completed sale within one year from the date of classification.
- Actions required to complete the plan should indicate that it is unlikely that significant changes to the plan will be made or that the plan will be withdrawn.

There is a pragmatic recognition that there may be events outside the control of the enterprise which prevent completion within one year. In such a case the held for sale classification is retained, provided there is sufficient evidence that the entity remains committed to its plan to sell the asset or disposal group and has taken all reasonable steps to resolve the delay.

It is important to note that IFRS 5 specifies that this classification is appropriate for assets (or disposal groups) that are to be **sold**. The classification does not apply to assets or disposal groups that are to be **abandoned**.

9.5 IFRS 5 – implications of classification as held for sale

Assets, or disposal groups, that are classified as held for sale should be removed from their previous position in the statement of financial position and shown under a single 'held for sale' caption – usually as part of **current** assets. Any liabilities directly associated with disposal groups that are classified as held for sale should be separately presented within liabilities.

As far as disposal groups are concerned, it is acceptable to present totals on the face of the statement of financial position, with a more detailed breakdown in the notes. The following is a note disclosure from the published financial statements of Unilever for the year ended 31 December 2009:

Assets classified as held for sale

	2009 £m	2008 £m
Disposal groups held for sale		
Property, plant and equipment	7	7
Inventories	1	15
	8	22
Non-current assets held for sale		
Property, plant and equipment	9	14
	17	36

Depreciable assets that are classified as 'held for sale' should not be depreciated from classification date, as the classification implies that the intention of management is primarily to recover value from such assets through sale, rather than through continued use.

When assets (or disposal groups) are classified as held for sale their carrying value(s) at the date of classification should be compared with the 'fair value less costs to sell' of the asset (or disposal group). If the carrying value exceeds fair value less costs to sell then the excess should be treated as an impairment loss. In the case of a disposal group, the impairment loss should be allocated to the specific assets in the order specified in IAS 36 – *Impairment*.

9.6 Meaning and significance of 'discontinued operations'

9.6.1 Meaning

IFRS 5 defines a discontinued operation as a component of an entity that, during the reporting period, either:

- has been disposed of (whether by sale or abandonment); or
- has been classified as held for sale, and ALSO
  - represents a separate major line of business or geographical area of operations; or
  - is part of a single coordinated plan to dispose of a separate major line of business or geographical area of operations; or
  - is a subsidiary acquired exclusively with a view to resale (probably as part of the acquisition of an existing group with a subsidiary that does not fit into the long term plans of the acquirer).

The IFRS defines a component as one which comprises operations and cash flows that can be clearly distinguished, operationally and for financial reporting purposes, from the rest of the entity. This definition is somewhat subjective and the IASB is considering amending this definition to align it with that of an operating segment in IFRS 8 (see section 9.3.4 above).

9.6.2 Significance

The basic significance is that the results of discontinued operations should be separately disclosed from those of other, continuing, operations in the statement of comprehensive income. As a minimum, on the face of the statement, entities should show, as a single amount, the total of:

- the post-tax profit or loss of discontinued operations; and
- the post-tax gain or loss recognised on the measurement to fair value less cost to sell or on the disposal of the assets or disposal group(s) constituting the discontinued operation.

Further analysis of this amount is required, either on the face of the statement of comprehensive income or in the notes into:

- the revenue, expenses and pre-tax profit or loss of discontinued operations;
- the related income tax expense as required by IAS 12;
- the gain or loss recognised on the measurement to fair value less costs to sell or on the disposal of the assets or disposal group(s) constituting the discontinued operation; and
- the related income tax expense as required by IAS 12.

The net cash flows attributable to the operating, investing and financing activities of discontinued operations also need to be disclosed separately. As for the disclosures mentioned above for the statement of comprehensive income, these can also either be made on the face of the statement of cash flows or in the notes.

Where an operation meets the criteria for classification as discontinued in the current period, then the comparatives should be amended to show the results of the operation as discontinued even though, in the previous period, the operation did not meet the relevant criteria.

An example of the required disclosures is given below – these relate to Vodafone.

Disposals and discontinued operations

India – Bharti Airtel Limited

On 9 May 2007 and in conjunction with the acquisition of Vodafone Essar, the Group entered into a share sale and purchase agreement in which a Bharti group company irrevocably agreed to purchase the Group's 5.60% direct shareholding in Bharti Airtel Limited. During the year ended 31 March 2008, the Group received £654 million in cash consideration for 4.99% of such shareholding and recognised a net gain on disposal of £250 million, reported in non-operating income and expense. The Group's remaining 0.61% direct shareholding was transferred in April 2008 for cash consideration of £87 million.

Japan – Vodafone K.K.

On 17 March 2006, the Group announced an agreement to sell its 97.7% holding in Vodafone K.K. to SoftBank. The transaction completed on 27 April 2006, with the Group receiving cash of approximately ¥1.42 trillion (£6.9 billion), including the repayment of intercompany debt of ¥0.16 trillion (£0.8 billion). In addition, the Group received non-cash consideration with a fair value of approximately ¥0.23 trillion (£1.1 billion), comprised of preferred equity and a subordinated loan. SoftBank also assumed debt of approximately ¥0.13 trillion (£0.6 billion). Vodafone K.K. represented a separate geographical area of operation and, on this basis, Vodafone K.K. was treated as a discontinued operation in Vodafone Group Plc's annual report for the year ended 31 March 2006.

Income statement and segment analysis of discontinued operations

	2007 £m	2006 £m
Segment revenue	**520**	**7,268**
Inter-segment revenue	—	(2)
Net revenue	**520**	**7,266**
Operating expenses	(402)	(5,667)
Depreciation and amortisation[1]	—	(1,144)
Impairment loss	—	(4,900)
Operating profit/(loss)	**118**	**(4,445)**
Net financing costs	8	(3)

	2007 £m	2006 £m
Profit/(loss) before taxation	**126**	**(4,448)**
Taxation relating to performance of discontinued operations	(15)	7
Loss on disposal[2]	(747)	—
Taxation relating to the classification of the discontinued operations	145	(147)
Loss for the financial year from discontinued operations[3]	**(491)**	**(4,588)**

(NB: The single amounts shown above were the numbers that were presented in the consolidated income statement.)

Notes:

(1) Including gains and losses on disposal of fixed assets.

(2) Includes £794 million of foreign exchange differences transferred to the income statement on disposal.

(3) Amount attributable to equity shareholders for the year to 31 March 2008 was nil (2007: £(494) million; 2006: £(4,598) million).

Loss per share from discontinued operations

	2007 Pence per share	2006 Pence per share
Basic loss per share	(0.90)	(7.35)
Diluted loss per share	(0.90)	(7.35)

Cash flows from discontinued operations

	2007 £m	2006 £m
Net cash flows from operating activities	135	1,651
Net cash flows from investing activities	(266)	(939)
Net cash flows from financing activities	(29)	(536)
Net cash flows	**(160)**	**176**
Cash and cash equivalents at the beginning of the financial year	161	4
Exchange loss on cash and cash equivalents	(1)	(19)
Cash and cash equivalents at the end of the financial year	**—**	**161**

9.7 IAS 10 – events after the reporting period[4]

IAS 10 requires preparers of financial statements to evaluate events that occur after the reporting date but before the financial statements are authorised for issue by the directors.

Events in this period are referred to as 'Events after the Reporting Period'. In certain circumstances the financial statements should be adjusted to reflect the occurrence of such events.

9.7.1 Adjusting events

These are events after the reporting period that provide additional evidence of conditions that exist at the year end date. Examples of such events include, but are not limited to:

- After date sales of inventory that provide additional evidence of the net realisable value of the inventory at the reporting date.
- Evidence received after the year end that provides additional evidence of the appropriate measurement of a liability that existed at the reporting date.
- The revaluation of an asset such as a property that indicates the likelihood of impairment **at the reporting date**.

As you might expect, IAS 10 requires that the occurrence of adjusting events should lead to the financial statements themselves being adjusted.

9.7.2 Non-adjusting events

These are events occurring after the reporting period that concern conditions that did not exist at the statement of financial position date. Examples would include:

- an issue shares after the reporting date;
- acquisition of new businesses after the reporting date;
- the loss or other decline in value of assets due to events occurring after the end of the reporting period.

IAS 10 states that the financial statements should not be adjusted upon the occurrence of non-adjusting events. However where non-adjusting events are material, IAS 10 requires disclosure of:

- the nature of the event; and
- an estimate of the financial effect, or a statement that such an estimate cannot be made.

The following is an extract from the 2003 Annual Report of Manchester United:

> **Events after the reporting period**
> After the reporting date, the playing registrations of two footballers have been acquired for a total consideration including associated costs of £18,063,000 of which £7,393,000 is due for payment after more than one year.

9.7.3 Dividends

IAS 10 states that dividends declared after the reporting period are not to be treated as liabilities in the financial statements. A dividend is 'declared' when its payment is no longer at the discretion of the reporting entity. For interim dividends, this does not usually occur until the dividend is actually paid. For final dividends this usually occurs when the shareholders approve the dividend at a general meeting to approve the financial statements, which cannot take place until the financial statements have been prepared! Therefore, the concept of a 'dividend liability' for equity shares has effectively disappeared.

9.7.4 Going concern issues

Deterioration in the operating results or other major losses that occur after the period end are basically non-adjusting events. However, if they are of such significance as to affect the going concern basis of preparation of the financial statements then this impacts on the numbers in the financial statements because the going concern assumption would no longer be appropriate. In this limited set of circumstances an event that would normally be non-adjusting is effectively treated as adjusting.

9.8 Related party disclosures

The users of financial statements would normally assume that the transactions of an entity have been carried out at arms length and under terms which are in the best interests of the entity. The existence of related party relationships **may** mean that this assumption is not appropriate. The purpose of IAS 24 is to define the meaning of the term 'related party' and prescribe the disclosures that are appropriate for transactions with related parties (and in some cases for their mere existence). From the outset it is worth remembering that the term 'party' could refer to an individual **or** to another entity.

9.8.1 Definition of 'related party' – a person

IAS 24 *Related party disclosures*[5] breaks the definition down into two main sections: A person, or a close member of that person's family (P) is a related party to the reporting entity (E) if:

- P has control or joint control over E.
- P has significant influence over E.
- P is a member of the key management personnel of E.

Close members of the family of P are those family members who may be expected to influence, or be influenced by, P in their dealings with E and include:

- P's children and spouse or domestic partner; and
- children of the spouse or domestic partner; and
- dependants of P or P's spouse or domestic partner.

Key management personnel of E are those persons having authority and responsibility for planning, directing and controlling the activities of E, directly or indirectly including any director (whether executive or otherwise) of E.

9.8.2 Definition of related party – another entity

Another entity (AE) is related to E if:

- E and AE are members of the same group (which means that each parent, subsidiary and fellow subsidiary is related to the others).
- AE is an associate or joint venture of E (or of a group of which E is a member), or vice versa.
- E and AE are both joint ventures of the same third party.

- E is the joint venture of a third entity and AE is an associate of the third entity, or vice versa.
- AE is a post-employment benefit plan for the benefit of either E or an entity related to E. If E is such a plan, then the sponsoring employees are also related to E.
- AE is controlled or jointly controlled by any person that is a related party of E (see 9.8.1 above).

9.8.3 Parties deemed not to be related parties

IAS 24 emphasises that it is necessary to carefully consider the substance of each relationship to see whether or not a related party relationship exists. However, the standard highlights a number of relationships that would not normally lead to related party status:

- two entities simply because they have a director or other member of the key management personnel in common or because a member of the key management personnel of one entity has significant influence over the other entity;
- two venturers simply because they share control over a joint venture;
- providers of finance, trade unions, public utilities or government departments in the course of their normal dealings with the entity;
- a single customer, supplier, franchisor, distributor or general agent with whom an entity transacts a significant volume of business merely by virtue of the resulting economic dependence.

9.8.4 Disclosure of controlling relationships

IAS 24 requires that relationships between a parent and its subsidiaries be disclosed irrespective of whether there have been transactions between them. Where the entity is controlled, it should disclose:

- the name of its parent;
- the name of its ultimate controlling party (which could be an individual or another entity);
- if neither the parent nor the ultimate controlling party produces consolidated financial statements available for public use, the name of the next most senior parent that does produce such statements.

9.8.5 Disclosure of compensation of key management personnel

'Compensation' in this context includes employee benefits as defined in IAS 19 – *Employee benefits* – including those 'share based' employee benefits to which IFRS 2 – *Share-based payment* – applies. These disclosures are required under the following headings:

- short-term employee benefits;
- post-employment benefits;
- other long-term benefits (e.g. accrued sabbatical leave);
- termination benefits;
- share-based payment.

9.8.6 Disclosure of related party transactions

A related party transaction is a transfer of resources or obligations between a reporting entity and a related party, regardless of whether a price is charged. Where such transactions have occurred, the entity should disclose the nature of the related party relationship as well as information about those transactions and outstanding balances to enable a user to understand the potential effect of the relationship on the financial statements. As a minimum, the disclosures should include:

- the amount of the transactions;
- the amount of the outstanding balances and:
  - their terms and conditions, including whether they are secured, and the nature of the consideration to be provided in settlement; and
  - details of any guarantees given or received;
- provisions for doubtful debts related to the amount of outstanding balances; and
- the expense recognised during the period in respect of bad or doubtful debts due from related parties.

These disclosures should be given separately for each of the following categories:

- the parent;
- entities with joint control or significant influence over the reporting entity;
- subsidiaries;
- associates;
- joint ventures in which the entity is a venturer;
- key management personnel of the entity or its parent;
- other related parties.

The following are examples of transactions that are disclosed if they are with a related party:

- purchases or sale of goods, property or other assets;
- rendering or receiving of services;
- leases;
- transfers of research and development;
- transfers under licence agreements;
- transfers under finance agreements;
- provision of guarantees;
- future commitments;
- settlement of liabilities on behalf of the entity or by the entity on behalf of the related party.

The following extract from the Unilever 2009 Annual Report is an example of the required disclosures:

30 Related party transactions

The following related party balances existed with associate or joint venture businesses at 31 December:

Related party balances	*€ million* 2009	*€ million* 2008
Trading and other balances due from joint ventures	231	240
Trading and other balances due from/(to) associates	5	(33)

Joint ventures

Unilever completed the restructuring of its Portuguese business as at 1 January 2007. Sales by Unilever group companies to Unilever Jeronimo Martins and Pepsi Lipton International were €91 million and €14 million in 2009 (2008: €84 million and €12 million) respectively. Sales from Jeronimo Martins to Unilever group companies were €46 million in 2009 (2008: €48 million). Balances owed by/(to) Unilever Jerónimo Martins and Pepsi Lipton International at 31 December 2009 were €230 million and €1 million (2008: €238 million and €2 million) respectively.

Associates

At 31 December 2009 the outstanding balance receivable from Johnson Diversey Holdings Inc. was €5 million (2008: balance payable was €33 million). Agency fees payable to Johnson Diversey in connection with the sale of Unilever branded products through their channels amounted to approximately €20 million in 2009 (2008: €24 million).

Langholm Capital Partners invests in private European companies with above-average longer-term growth prospects. Since the Langholm fund was launched in 2002, Unilever has invested €76 million in Langholm, with an outstanding commitment at the end of 2009 of €21 million. Unilever has received back a total of €123 million in cash from its investment in Langholm.

Physic Ventures is an early stage venture capital fund based in San Francisco, focusing on consumer-driven health, wellness and sustainable living. Unilever has invested €20 million in Physic Ventures since the launch of the fund in 2007. At 31 December 2009 the outstanding commitment with Physic Ventures was €43 million.

9.8.7 Exemption from disclosures re: government-related entities

A reporting entity is exempt from the detailed disclosures referred to in 9.7 above in relation to related party transactions and outstanding balances with:

● a government that has control, joint control or significant influence over the reporting entity; and

● another entity that is a related party because the same government has control, joint control or significant influence over both parties.

If this exemption is applied, the reporting entity is nevertheless required to make the following disclosures about transactions with government-related entities:

● the name of the government and the nature of its relationship with the reporting entity;

● the following information in sufficient detail to enable users of the financial statements to understand the effect of related party transactions:
  – the nature and amount of each individually significant transaction; and
  – for other transactions that are collectively, but not individually, significant, a qualitative or quantitative indication of their extent.

The reason for the exemption is essentially pragmatic. In some jurisdictions where government control is pervasive it can be difficult to identify other government related entities. In some circumstances the directors of the reporting entity may be genuinely unaware of the related party relationship. Therefore, the basis of conclusions to IAS 24 (BC 43) states that, in the context of the disclosures that **are** needed in these circumstances:

> The objective of IAS 24 is to provide disclosures necessary to draw attention to the possibility that the financial position and profit or loss may have been affected by the existence of related parties and by transactions and outstanding balances, including commitments, with such parties. To meet that objective, IAS 24 requires some disclosure when the exemption applies. Those disclosures are intended to put users on notice that related party transactions have occurred and to give an indication of their extent. The Board did not intend to require the reporting entity to identify **every** government-related entity, or to quantify in detail **every** transaction with such entities, because such a requirement would negate the exemption.

Summary

The published accounts of a listed company are intended to provide a report to enable shareholders to assess current year stewardship and management performance and to predict future cash flows.

In order to assist shareholders to predict future cash flows with an understanding of the risks involved, more information has been required by the IASB. This has taken two forms:

1 more quantitative information in the accounts, e.g. segmental analysis, and the impact of changes on the operation, e.g. a breakdown of turnover, costs and profits for both new and discontinued operations; and

2 more qualitative information, e.g. related party disclosures and events occurring after the reporting period.

REVIEW QUESTIONS

1 Explain the criteria that have to be satisfied when identifying an operating segment.

2 Explain the criteria that have to be satisfied to identify a reportable segment.

3 Explain why it is necessary to identify a chief operating decision maker and describe the key identifying factors.

4 Explain the conditions set out in IFRS 5 for determining whether operations have been discontinued and the problems that might arise in applying them.

5 Explain the conditions that must be satisfied if a non-current asset is to be reported in the statement of financial position as held for sale.

6 'Annual accounts have been put into such a straitjacket of overemphasis on uniform disclosure that there will be a growing pressure by national bodies to introduce changes unilaterally which will again lead to diversity in the quality of disclosure. This is both healthy and necessary.' Discuss.

7 Explain the circumstances in which an event that is normally non-adjusting is required to be adjusted.

8 Explain how to identify key personnel for the purposes of IAS 24 and why this is considered to be important.

EXERCISES

An extract from the solution is provided on the Companion Website (www.pearsoned.co.uk/elliott-elliott) for exercises marked with an asterisk (*).

* Question 1

Filios Products plc owns a chain of hotels through which it provides three basic services; restaurant facilities, accommodation, and leisure facilities. The latest financial statements contain the following information:

Statement of financial position of Filios Products

	£m
ASSETS	
Non-current assets at book value	1,663
Current assets	
Inventories and receivables	381
Bank balance	128
	509
Total Assets	**2,172**
EQUITY AND LIABILITIES	
Equity	
Share capital	800
Retained earnings	1,039
	1,839
Non-current liabilities:	
Long-term borrowings	140
Current liabilities	193
Total Equity and liabilities	**2,172**

Statement of comprehensive income of Filios Products

	£m	£m
Revenue		1,028
Less: Cost of sales	684	
Administration expenses	110	
Distribution costs	101	
Interest charged	14	(909)
Net profit		119

The following breakdown is provided of the company's results into three divisions and head office:

	Restaurants £m	Hotels £m	Leisure £m	Head office £m
Revenue	508	152	368	—
Cost of sales	316	81	287	—
Administration expenses	43	14	38	15
Distribution costs	64	12	25	—
Interest charged	10	—	—	4
Non-current assets at book value	890	332	364	77
Inventories and receivables	230	84	67	—
Bank balance	73	15	28	12
Payables	66	40	56	31
Long-term borrowings	100	—	—	40

Required:

(a) Outline the nature of segmental reports and explain the reason for presenting such information in the published accounts.

(b) Prepare a segmental statement for Filios Products plc for complying, so far as the information permits, with the provisions of IFRS 8 – *Operating Segments* – so as to show for each segment and the business as a whole:
  (i) Revenue;
  (ii) Profit;
  (iii) Net assets.

(c) Examine the relative performance of the operating divisions of Filios Products. The examination should be based on the following accounting ratios:
  (i) Operating profit percentage;
  (ii) Net asset turnover;
  (iii) Return on net assets.

Question 2

IAS 10 deals with events after the reporting period.

Required:

(a) Define the period covered by IAS 10.

(b) Explain when should the financial statements be adjusted?

(c) Why should non-adjusting events be disclosed?

(d) A customer made a claim for £50,000 for losses suffered by the late delivery of goods. The main part (£40,000) of the claim referred to goods due to be delivered before the year end. Explain how this would be dealt with under IAS 10.

(e) After the year end a substantial quantity of inventory was destroyed in a fire. The loss was not adequately covered by insurance. This event is likely to threaten the ability of the business to continue as a going concern. Discuss the matters you would consider in making a decision under IAS 10.

(f) The business entered into a favourable contract after the year end that would see its profits increase by 15% over the next three years. Explain how this would be dealt with under IAS 10.

* Question 3

Epsilon is a listed entity. You are the financial controller of the entity and its consolidated financial statements for the year ended 31 March 2009 are being prepared. The board of directors is responsible for all key financial and operating decisions, including the allocation of resources.

Your assistant is preparing the first draft of the statements. He has a reasonable general accounting knowledge but is not familiar with the detailed requirements of all relevant financial reporting standards. There are two issues on which he requires your advice and he has sent you a note as shown below:

Issue 1

We intend to apply IFRS 8 – *Operating Segments* – in this year's financial statements. I am aware that this standard has attracted a reasonable amount of critical comment since it was issued in November 2006.

The board of directors receives a monthly report on the activities of the five significant operational areas of our business. Relevant financial information relating to the five operations for the year to 31 March 2009, and in respect of our Head office, is as follows:

Operational area	Revenue for year to 31 March 2009 $000	Profit/(loss) for year to 31 March 2009 $000	Assets at 31 March 2009 $000
A	23,000	3,000	8,000
B	18,000	2,000	6,000
C	4,000	(3,000)	5,000
D	1,000	150	500
E	3,000	450	400
Sub-total	49,000	2,600	19,900
Head office	Nil	Nil	6,000
Entity total	49,000	2,600	25,900

I am unsure of the following matters regarding the reporting of operating segments:

● How do we decide on what our operating segments should be?

● Should we report segment information relating to head office?

● Which of our operational areas should report separate information? Operational areas A, B and C exhibit very distinct economic characteristics but the economic characteristics of operational areas D and E are very similar.

● Why has IFRS8 attracted such critical comment?

Issue 2

I note that on 31 January 2009 the board of directors decided to discontinue the activities of a number of our subsidiaries. This decision was made, I believe, because these subsidiaries did not fit into the long-term plans of the group and the board did not consider it likely that the subsidiaries could be sold. This decision was communicated to the employees on 28 February 2009 and the activities of the subsidiaries affected were gradually curtailed starting on 1 May 2009, with an expected completion date of 30 September 2009. I have the following information regarding the closure programme:

(a) All the employees in affected subsidiaries were offered redundancy packages and some of the employees were offered employment in other parts of the group. These offers had to be accepted or rejected by 30 April 2009. On 31 March 2009 the directors estimated that the cost of redundancies would be $20 million and the cost of relocation of employees who accepted alternative employment would be $10 million. Following 30 April 2009 these estimates were revised to $22 million and $9 million respectively.

(b) Latest estimates are that the operating losses of the affected subsidiaries for the six months to 30 September 2009 will total $15 million.

(c) A number of the subsidiaries are leasing properties under non-cancellable operating leases. I believe that at 31 March 2009 the present value of the future lease payments relating to these properties totalled $6 million. The cost of immediate termination of these lease obligations would be $5 million.

(d) The carrying values of the freehold properties owned by the affected subsidiaries at 31 March 2008 totalled $25 million. The estimated net disposal proceeds of the properties are $29 million and all properties should realise a profit.

(e) The carrying value of the plant and equipment owned by the affected subsidiaries at 31 March 2008 was $18 million. The estimated current disposal proceeds of this plant and equipment is $2 million and its estimated value in use (including the proceeds from ultimate disposal) is $8 million.

I am unsure regarding a number of aspects of accounting for this decision by the board. Please tell me how the decision to curtail the activities of the three subsidiaries affects the financial statements.

Required:
Draft a reply to the questions raised by your assistant.

Question 4

Epsilon is a listed entity. You are the financial controller of the entity and its consolidated financial statements for the year ended 30 September 2008 are being prepared. Your assistant, who has prepared the first draft of the statements, is unsure about the correct treatment of a transaction and has asked for your advice. Details of the transaction are given below.

On 31 August 2008 the directors decided to close down a business segment which did not fit into its future strategy. The closure commenced on 5 October 2008 and was due to be completed on 31 December 2008. On 6 September 2008 letters were sent to relevant employees offering voluntary redundancy or redeployment in other sectors of the business. On 13 September 2008 negotiations commenced with relevant parties with a view to terminating existing contracts of the business segment and arranging sales of its assets. Latest estimates of the financial implications of the closure are as follows:

(i) Redundancy costs will total $30 million, excluding the payment referred to in (ii) below.

(ii) The pension plan (a defined benefit plan) will make a lump sum payment totalling $8 million to the employees who accept voluntary redundancy in termination of their rights under the plan. Epsilon will pay this amount into the plan on 31 January 2009. The actuaries have advised that the accumulated pension rights that this payment will extinguish have a present value of $7 million and this sum is unlikely to alter significantly before 31 January 2009.

(iii) The cost of redeploying and retraining staff who do not accept redundancy will total $6 million.

(iv) The business segment operates out of a leasehold property that has an unexpired lease term of ten years from 30 September 2008. The annual lease rentals on this property are $1 million, payable on 30 September in arrears. Negotiations with the owner of the freehold indicate that the owner would accept a single payment of $5.5 million in return for early termination of the lease. There are no realistic opportunities for Epsilon to sub-let this property. An appropriate rate to use in any discounting calculations is 10% per annum. The present value of an annuity of $1 receivable annually at the end of years 1 to 10 inclusive using a discount rate of 10% is $6.14.

(v) Plant having a net book value of $11 million at 30 September 2008 will be sold for $2 million.

(vi) The operating losses of the business segment for October, November and December 2008 are estimated at $10 million.

Your assistant is unsure of the extent to which the above transactions create liabilities that should be recognised as a closure provision in the financial statements. He is also unsure as to whether or not the results of the business segment that is being closed need to be shown separately.

Required:
Explain how the decision to close down the business segment should be reported in the financial statements of Epsilon for the year ended 30 September 2008.

Question 5

Omega prepares financial statements under International Financial Reporting Standards. In the year ended 31 March 2007 the following transactions occurred:

Transaction 1
On 1 April 2006 Omega began the construction of a new production line. Costs relating to the line are as follows:

Details	Amount
	$000
Costs of the basic materials (list price $12.5 million less a 20% trade discount)	10,000
Recoverable sales taxes incurred, not included in the purchase cost.	1,000
Employment costs of the construction staff for the three months to 30 June 2006 (Note 1)	1,200
Other overheads directly related to the construction (Note 2)	900
Payments to external advisors relating to the construction	500
Expected dismantling and restoration costs (Note 3)	2,000

Note 1
The production line took two months to make ready for use and was brought into use on 30 June 2006.

Note 2
The other overheads were incurred in the two months ended 31 May 2006. They included an abnormal cost of $300,000 caused by a major electrical fault.

Note 3
The production line is expected to have a useful economic life of eight years. At the end of that time Omega is legally required to dismantle the plant in a specified manner and restore its location to an acceptable standard. The figure of $2 million included in the cost estimates is the amount that is expected to be incurred at the end of the useful life of the production plant. The appropriate rate to use in any discounting calculations is 5%. The present value of $1 payable in eight years at a discount rate of 5% is approximately $0.68.

Note 4
Four years after being brought into use, the production line will require a major overhaul to ensure that it generates economic benefits for the second half of its useful life. The estimated cost of the overhaul, at current prices, is $3 million.

Note 5
Omega computes its depreciation charge on a monthly basis.

Note 6
No impairment of the plant had occurred by 31 March 2007.

Transaction 2
On 31 December 2006 the directors decided to dispose of a property that was surplus to requirements. They instructed selling agents to procure a suitable purchaser and advertised the property at
a commercially realistic price.

The property was being measured under the revaluation model and had been revalued at $15 million
on 31 March 2006. The depreciable element of the property was estimated as $8 million at 31 March
2006 and the useful economic life of the depreciable element was estimated as 25 years from that
date. Omega depreciates its non-current assets on a monthly basis.

On 31 December 2006 the directors estimated that the market value of the property was $16 million,
and that the costs incurred in selling the property would be $500,000. The property was sold on
30 April 2007 for $15.55 million, being the agreed selling price of $16.1 million less selling costs
of $550,000. The actual selling price and costs to sell were consistent with estimated amounts as at
31 March 2007.

The financial statements for the year ended 31 March 2007 were authorised for issue on 15 May 2007.

Required:
Show the impact of the construction of the production line and the decision to sell the property
on the income statement of Omega for the year ended 31 March 2007, and on its balance sheet as
at 31 March 2007. You should state where in the income statement and the balance sheet relevant
balances will be shown. You should make appropriate references to international financial reporting
standards.

(IFRS)

Question 6

Omega prepares financial statements under International Financial Reporting Standards. In the year
ended 31 March 2007 the following transaction occurred:

Omega follows the revaluation model when measuring its property, plant and equipment. One of its
properties was carried in the balance sheet at 31 March 2006 at its market value at that date of
$5 million. The depreciable amount of this property was estimated at $3.2 million at 31 March 2006
and the estimated future economic life of the property at 31 March 2006 was 20 years.

On 1 January 2007 Omega decided to dispose of the property as it was surplus to requirements
and began to actively seek a buyer. On 1 January 2007 Omega estimated that the market value of
the property was $5.1 million and that the costs of selling the property would be $80,000. These
estimates remained appropriate at 31 March 2007.

The property was sold on 10 June 2007 for net proceeds of $5.15 million.

Required:
Explain, with relevant calculations, how the property would be treated in the financial statements
of Omega for the year ended 31 March 2007 and the year ending 31 March 2008.

Question 7

(a) In 20X3 Arthur is a large loan creditor of X Ltd and receives interest at 20% p.a. on this loan. He also has a 24% shareholding in X Ltd. Until 20X1 he was a director of the company and left after a disagreement. The remaining 76% of the shares are held by the remaining directors.

(b) Brenda joined Y Ltd, an insurance broking company, on 1 January 20X0 on a low salary but high commission basis. She brought clients with her that generated 30% of the company's 20X0 revenue.

(c) Carrie is a director and major shareholder of Z Ltd. Her husband, Donald, is employed in the company on administrative duties for which he is paid a salary of £25,000 p.a. Her daughter, Emma, is a business consultant running her own business. In 20X0 Emma carried out various consultancy exercises for the company for which she was paid £85,000.

(d) Fred is a director of V Ltd. V Ltd is a major customer of W Ltd. In 20X0 Fred also became a director of W Ltd.

Required:
Discuss whether parties are related in the above situations.

Question 8

Maxpool plc, a listed company, owned 60% of the shares in Ching Ltd. Bay plc, a listed company, owned the remaining 40% of the £1 ordinary shares in Ching Ltd. The holdings of shares were acquired on 1 January 20X0.

On 30 November 20X0 Ching Ltd sold a factory outlet site to Bay plc at a price determined by an independent surveyor.

On 1 March 20X1 Maxpool plc purchased a further 30% of the £1 ordinary shares of Ching Ltd from Bay plc and purchased 25% of the ordinary shares of Bay plc.

On 30 June 20X1 Ching Ltd sold the whole of its fleet of vehicles to Bay plc at a price determined by a vehicle auctioneer.

Required:
Explain the implications of the above transactions for the determination of related party relationships and disclosure of such transactions in the financial statements of (a) Maxpool Group plc, (b) Ching Ltd and (c) Bay plc for the years ending 31 December 20X0 and 31 December 20X1.

(ACCA)

Question 9

The following trial balance has been extracted from the books of Hoodurz as at 31 March 2006:

	$000	$000
Administration expenses	210	
Ordinary share capital, $1 per share		600
Trade receivables	470	
Bank overdraft		80
Provision for warranty claims		205
Distribution costs	420	
Non-current asset investments	560	
Investment income		75
Interest paid	10	
Property, at cost	200	
Plant and equipment, at cost	550	
Plant and equipment, accumulated depreciation (at 31.3.2006)		220
Accumulated profits (at 31.3.2005)		80
Loans (repayable 31.12.2010)		100
Purchases	960	
Inventories (at 31.3.2005)	150	
Trade payables		260
Sales		2,010
2004/2005 final dividend paid	65	
2005/2006 interim dividend paid	35	
	3,630	3,630

The following information is relevant:

(i) The trial balance figures include the following amounts for a disposal group that has been classified as 'held for sale' under IFRS 5 *Non-Current Assets Held for Sale and Discontinued Operations*:

	$000
Plant and equipment, at cost	150
Plant and equipment, accumulated depreciation	15
Trade receivables	70
Bank overdraft	10
Trade payables	60
Sales	370
Inventories (at 31.12.2005)	25
Purchases	200
Administration expenses	55
Distribution costs	60

The disposal group had no inventories at the date classified as 'held for sale'.

(ii) Inventories (excluding the disposal group) at 31.3.2006 were valued at $160,000.

(iii) The depreciation charges for the year have already been accrued.

(iv) The income tax for the year ended 31.3.2006 is estimated to be $74,000. This includes $14,000 in relation to the disposal group.

(v) The provision for warranty claims is to be increased by $16,000. This is classified as administration expense.

(vi) Staff bonuses totalling $20,000 for administration and $20,000 for distribution are to be accrued.

(vii) The property was acquired during February 2006, therefore, depreciation for the year ended 31.3.2006 is immaterial. The directors have chosen to use the fair value model for such an asset. The fair value of the property at 31.3.2006 is $280,000.

Required:

Prepare for Hoodruz:

(a) an income statement for the year ended 31 March 2006; and

(b) a balance sheet as at 31 March 2006.

Both statements should comply as far as possible with relevant International Financial Reporting Standards. No notes to the financial statements are required nor is a statement of changes in equity, but all workings should be clearly shown.

(The Association of International Accountants)

Question 10

The following is the draft trading and income statement of Parnell Ltd for the year ending 31 December 2003:

	$m	$m
Revenue		563
Cost of sales		310
		253
Distribution costs	45	
Administrative expenses	78	
		123
Profit on ordinary activities before tax		130
Tax on profit on ordinary activities		45
Profit on ordinary activities after taxation – all retained		85
Profit brought forward at 1 January 2003		101
Profit carried forward at 31 December 2003		186

You are given the following additional information, which is reflected in the above statement of comprehensive income only to the extent stated:

1 Distribution costs include a bad debt of $15 million which arose on the insolvency of a major customer. There is no prospect of recovering any of this debt. Bad debts have never been material in the past.

2 The company has traditionally consisted of a manufacturing division and a distribution division. On 31 December 2003, the entire distribution division was sold for $50 million; its book value at the time of sale was $40 million. The profit on disposal was credited to administrative expenses. (Ignore any related income tax.)

3 During 2003, the distribution division made sales of $100 million and had a cost of sales of $30 million. There will be no reduction in stated distribution costs or administration expenses as a result of this disposal.

4 The company owns offices which it purchased on 1 January 2001 for $500 million, comprising $200 million for land and $300 million for buildings. No depreciation was charged in 2001 or 2002, but the company now considers that such a charge should be introduced. The buildings were

expected to have a life of 50 years at the date of purchase, and the company uses the straight-line basis for calculating depreciation, assuming a zero residual value. No taxation consequences result from this change.

5   During 2003, part of the manufacturing division was restructured at a cost of $20 million to take advantage of modern production techniques. The restructuring was not fundamental and will **not** have a material effect on the nature and focus of the company's operations. This cost is included under administration expenses in the statement of comprehensive income.

Required:

(a) State how each of the items 1–5 above must be accounted for in order to comply with the requirements of international accounting standards.

(b) Redraft the income statement of Parnell Ltd for 2003, taking into account the additional information so as to comply, as far as possible, with relevant standard accounting practice. Show clearly any adjustments you make. Notes to the accounts are not required. Where an IAS recommends information to be on the face of the income statement it could be recorded on the face of the statement.

(The Chartered Institute of Bankers)

* Question 11

Springtime Ltd is a UK trading company buying and selling as wholesalers fashionable summer clothes. The following balances have been extracted from the books as at 31 March 20X4:

	£000
Auditor's remuneration	30
Income tax based on the accounting profit:	
For the year to 31 March 20X4	3,200
Overprovision for the year to 31 March 20X3	200
Delivery expenses (including £300,000 overseas)	1,200
Dividends: final (proposed – to be paid 1 August 20X4)	200
interim (paid on 1 October 20X3)	100
Non-current assets at cost:	
Delivery vans	200
Office cars	40
Stores equipment	5,000
Dividend income (amount received from listed companies)	1,200
Office expenses	800
Overseas operations: closure costs of entire operations	350
Purchases	24,000
Sales (net of sales tax)	35,000
Inventory at cost:	
At 1 April 20X3	5,000
At 31 March 20X4	6,000
Storeroom costs	1,000
Wages and salaries:	
Delivery staff	700
Directors' emoluments	400
Office staff	100
Storeroom staff	400

Notes:

1 Depreciation is provided at the following annual rates on a straight-line basis: delivery vans 20%; office cars 25%; stores 1%.

2 The following taxation rates may be assumed: corporate income tax 35%; personal income tax 25%.

3 The dividend income arises from investments held in non-current investments.

4 It has been decided to transfer an amount of £150,000 to the deferred taxation account.

5 The overseas operations consisted of exports. In 20X3/X4 these amounted to £5,000,000 (sales) with purchases of £4,000,000. Related costs included £100,000 in storeroom staff and £15,000 for office staff.

6 Directors' emoluments include:

Chairperson	100,000	
Managing director	125,000	
Finance director	75,000	
Sales director	75,000	
Export director	25,000	(resigned 31 December 20X3)
	£400,000	

Required:

(a) **Produce a statement of comprehensive income suitable for publication and complying as far as possible with generally accepted accounting practice.**

(b) **Comment on how IFRS 5 has improved the quality of information available to users of accounts.**

Question 12

As the financial controller of SEAS Ltd, you are responsible for preparing the company's financial statements and are at present finalising these for the year ended 31 March 20X8 for presentation to the board of directors. The following items are material:

(i) Costs of £250,000 arose from the closure of the company's factory in Garratt, which manufactured coffins. Owing to a declining market, the company has withdrawn from this type of business prior to the year-end.

(ii) You discover that during February 20X8, whilst you were away skiing, the cashier took advantage of the weakness in internal control to defraud the company of £30,000.

(iii) During the year ended 31 March 20X8, inventories of obsolete electrical components had to be written down by £250,000 owing to foreign competitors producing them more cheaply.

(iv) At a board meeting held on 30 April 20X8, the directors signed an agreement to purchase the business of Mr Hacker (a small computer manufacturer) for the sum of £100,000.

(v) £300,000 of development expenditure, which had been capitalised in previous years, was written off during the year ended 31 March 20X8. This became necessary due to foreign competitors' price cutting, which cast doubt on the recovery of costs from future revenue.

(vi) Dynatron Ltd, a customer, owed the company £50,000 on 31 March 20X8. However, on 15 May 20X8 it went into creditors' voluntary liquidation. Of the £50,000, £40,000 is still outstanding and the liquidator of Dynatron is expected to pay approximately 25p in the pound to unsecured creditors.

(vii) On 30 April 20X8, the company made a 1 for 4 rights issue to the ordinary shareholders, which involved the issue of 50,000 £1 ordinary shares for a sum of £62,500.

Required:

Explain how you will treat the above financial statements, and give a brief explanation of why you are adopting your proposed treatment.

References

1 IFRS 8 *Operating Segments*, IASB, 2006.
2 www.europarl.europa.eu/sides/getDoc.do?Type=TA&Reference=P6-TA-2007-0526&language=EN
3 IFRS 5 *Non-current assets held for sale and discontinued operations*, IASB (revised 2009).
4 IAS 10 *Events after the Reporting Period*, IASB (revised 2003).
5 IAS 24 *Related party disclosures*, IASB (revised 2009).

PART **3**

Statement of financial position – equity, liability and asset measurement and disclosure

Share capital, distributable profits and reduction of capital

10.1 Introduction

The main purpose of this chapter is to explain the issue and reduction of capital and distributions to shareholders in the context of creditor protection.

Objectives

After completing this chapter, you should be able to:

- describe the reasons for the issue of shares;
- describe the rights of different classes of shares;
- prepare accounting entries for issue of shares;
- explain the rules relating to distributable profits;
- explain when capital may be reduced;
- prepare accounting entries for reduction of capital;
- discuss the rights of different parties on a capital reduction.

10.2 Common themes

Companies may be financed by equity investors, loan creditors and trade creditors. Governments have recognised that for an efficient capital market to exist the rights of each of these stakeholders need to be protected. This means that equity investors require a clear statement of their powers to appoint and remunerate directors and of their entitlement to share in residual income and net assets; loan creditors and trade creditors require assurance that the directors will not distribute funds to the equity investors before settling outstanding debts in full.

Statutory rules have, therefore, evolved which attempt a balancing act by protecting the creditors on the one hand, e.g. by restricting dividend distributions to realised profits, whilst, on the other hand, not unduly restricting the ability of companies to organise their financial affairs, e.g. by reviewing a company's right to purchase and hold Treasury shares. Such rules may not be totally consistent between countries but there appear to be some common themes in much of the legislation. These are:

- Share capital can be broadly of two types, equity or preference.
- Equity shares are entitled to the residual income in the statement of comprehensive income after paying expenses, loan interest and tax.

- Equity itself is a residual figure in that the standard setters have taken the approach of defining assets and liabilities and leaving equity capital as the residual difference in the statement of financial position.

- Equity may consist of ordinary shares or equity elements of **participating** preference shares and compound instruments which include debt and equity, i.e. where there are conversion rights when there must be a split into their debt and equity elements, with each element being accounted for separately.

- Preference shares are not entitled (unless participating) to share in the residual income but may be entitled to a fixed or floating rate of interest on their investment.

- Distributable reserves equate to retained earnings when these have arisen from realised gains.

- Trade payables require protection to prevent an entity distributing assets to shareholders if creditors are not paid in full.

- Capital restructuring may be necessary when there are sound commercial reasons.

However, the rules are not static and there are periodic reviews in most jurisdictions, e.g. the proposal that an entity should make dividend decisions based on its ability to pay rather than on the fact that profits have been realised.

- The distributable reserves of entities are those that have arisen due to realised gains and losses (retained profits), as opposed to unrealised gains (such as revaluation reserves).

- There must be protection for trade payables to prevent an entity distributing assets to shareholders to the extent that the trade payables are not paid in full. An entity must retain net assets at least equal to its share capital and non-distributable reserves (a capital maintenance concept).

- The capital maintenance concept also applies with regard to reducing share capital, with most countries generally requiring a replacement of share capital with a non-distributable reserve if it is redeemed.

Because all countries have company legislation and these themes are common, the authors felt that, as the UK has relatively well developed company legislation, it would be helpful to consider such legislation as illustrating a typical range of statutory provisions. We therefore now consider the constituents of total shareholders' funds (also known as total owners' equity) and the nature of distributable and non-distributable reserves. We then analyse the role of the capital maintenance concept in the protection of creditors, before discussing the effectiveness of the protection offered by the Companies Act 2006 in respect of both private and public companies.

10.3 Total owners' equity: an overview

Total owners' equity consists of the issued share capital stated at nominal (or par) value, non-distributable and distributable reserves. Here we comment briefly on the main constituents of total shareholders' funds. We go on to deal with them in greater detail in subsequent sections.

10.3.1 Right to issue shares

Companies incorporated[1] under the Companies Act 2006 are able to raise capital by the issue of shares and debentures. There are two main categories of company: private limited companies and public limited companies. Public limited companies are designated by the letters plc and have the right to issue shares and debentures to the public. Private limited companies are often family companies; they are not allowed to seek share capital by invitations to the public. The shareholders of both categories have the benefit of limited personal indemnity, i.e. their liability to creditors is limited to the amount they agreed to pay the company for the shares they bought.

10.3.2 Types of share

Broadly, there are two types of share: ordinary and preference.

Ordinary shares

Ordinary shares, often referred to as equity shares, carry the main risk and their bearers are entitled to the residual profit after the payment of any fixed interest or fixed dividend to investors who have invested on the basis of a fixed return. Distributions from the residual profit are made in the form of dividends, which are normally expressed as pence per share.

Preference shares

Preference shares usually have a fixed rate of dividend, which is expressed as a percentage of the nominal value of the share. The dividend is paid before any distribution to the ordinary shareholders. The specific rights attaching to a preference share can vary widely.

10.3.3 Non-distributable reserves

There are a number of types of **statutory** non-distributable reserve, e.g. when the paid-in capital exceeds the par value as a share premium. In addition to the statutory non-distributable reserves, a company might have restrictions on distribution within its memorandum and articles, stipulating that capital profits are non-distributable as dividends.

10.3.4 Distributable reserves

Distributable reserves are normally represented by the retained earnings that appear in the statement of financial position and belong to the ordinary shareholders. However, as we shall see, there may be circumstances where credits that have been made to the statement of comprehensive income are not actually distributable, usually because they do not satisfy the **realisation** concept.

Although the retained earnings in the statement of financial position contain the cumulative residual distributable profits, it is the earnings per share (EPS), based on the post-tax earnings for the year as disclosed in the profit and loss account, that influences the market valuation of the shares, applying the price/earnings ratio.

When deciding whether to issue or buy back shares, the directors will therefore probably consider the impact on the EPS figure. If the EPS increases, the share price can normally be expected also to increase.

10.4 Total shareholders' funds: more detailed explanation

10.4.1 Ordinary shares – risks and rewards

Ordinary shares (often referred to as equity shares) confer the right to:

- share proportionately in the rewards, i.e.:
  - the residual profit remaining after paying any loan interest or fixed dividends to investors who have invested on the basis of a fixed return;
  - any dividends distributed from these residual profits;
  - any net assets remaining after settling all creditors' claims in the event of the company ceasing to trade;
- share proportionately in the risks, i.e.:
  - lose a proportionate share of invested share capital if the company ceases to trade and there are insufficient funds to pay all the creditors and the shareholders in full.

10.4.2 Ordinary shares – powers

The owners of ordinary shares generally have one vote per share which can be exercised on a routine basis, e.g. at the Annual General Meeting to vote on the appointment of directors, and on an *ad hoc* basis, e.g. at an Extraordinary General Meeting to vote on a proposed capital reduction scheme.

However, there are some companies that have issued non-voting ordinary shares which may confer the right to a proportional share of the residual profits but not to vote.

Non-voting shareholders can attend and speak at the Annual General Meeting but, as they have no vote, are unable to have an influence on management if there are problems or poor performance – apart from selling their shares.

The practice varies around the world and is more common in continental Europe. In the UK, institutional investors have made it clear since the early 1990s that they regard it as poor corporate governance and companies have taken steps to enfranchise the non-voting shareholders. The following is an extract from a letter from John Laing plc to shareholders setting out its enfranchisement proposals:

LAING SETS OUT ENFRANCHISEMENT PROPOSALS 23 March 2000
John Laing plc today issues enfranchisement proposals to change the Group voting structure.

The key points are as follows:

- Convert the Ordinary A (non-voting) Shares into Ordinary Shares
- All redesignated shares to have full voting rights ranking pari passu in all respects with the existing Ordinary Shares
- Compensatory Scrip Issue for holders of existing Ordinary Shares of one New Ordinary Share for every 20 Ordinary Shares held [authors' note: this is in recognition of the fact that the proportion of votes of the existing ordinary shareholders has been reduced – an alternative approach would be to ask the non-voting shareholders to pay a premium in exchange for being given voting rights]
- EGM to be held on 18th May 2000

Reasons for enfranchisement

- To increase the range of potential investors in the Company which the Directors believe should enhance the marketability and liquidity of the Company's Shares.
- To enable all classes of equity shareholders, who share the same risks and rewards, to share the same voting rights.
- To ensure the Company has maximum flexibility to manage its capital structure in order to reduce its cost of capital and to enhance shareholder value.

In other countries, however, there may be sound commercial reasons why non-voting shares are issued. In Japan, for example, the Japanese Commercial Code was amended in 2002 to allow companies to issue shares with special rights, e.g. power to veto certain company decisions, and to increase the proportion of non-voting shares in issue. The intention was to promote successful restructuring of ailing companies and stimulate demand for Japanese equity investments.

10.4.3 Methods and reasons for issuing shares

Methods of issuing shares

Some of the common methods of issuing shares are: *offer for subscription*, where the shares are offered directly to the public; *placings*, where the shares are arranged (placed) to be bought by financial institutions; and *rights issues*, whereby the new shares are offered to the existing shareholders at a price below the market price of those shares. The rights issue might be priced significantly below the current market price but this may not mean that the shareholder is benefiting from cheap shares as the price of existing shares will be reduced, e.g. the British Telecommunications plc £5.9 billion rights issue announced in 2001 made UK corporate history in that no British company had attempted to raise so much cash from its shareholders. The offer was three BT shares for every ten held and, to encourage take-up, the new shares were offered at a deeply discounted rate of £3 which was at a 47% discount to the share price on the day prior to the launch.

Reasons for issuing shares

- **For future investment**, e.g. Watford Leisure plc (Watford Football Club) offered and placed 540,000,000 ordinary shares and expected to raise cash proceeds of about £4.7 million. The company has since been floated on the AIM.

- **As consideration on an acquisition**, e.g. Microsoft Corp. acquired Great Plains Software Incorporated, a leading supplier of mid-market business applications. The acquisition was structured as a stock purchase and was valued at approximately $1.1 billion. Each share of Great Plains common stock was exchanged for 1.1 shares of Microsoft common stock.

- **To shareholders to avoid paying out cash from the company's funds**, e.g. the Prudential plc Annual Report 2009 has a scrip dividend scheme which enables shareholders to receive new ordinary shares instead of the cash dividends they would normally receive. This means they can build up their shareholding in Prudential without going to the market to buy new shares and so will not incur any dealing costs or stamp duty.

- **To directors and employees to avoid paying out cash in the form of salary from company's funds**, e.g. in the Psion 2000 Annual Report the note on directors' remuneration stated:

Name	As at 1/1/00	Exercised	As at 31.12.00	Option price	Market price
M.M. Wyatt	150,000	150,000	—	£0.73	£12.09

- **To shareholders to encourage re-investment**, e.g. some companies operate a Dividend Reinvestment Plan whereby the dividends of shareholders wishing to reinvest are pooled and reinvested on the Stock Exchange. A typical Plan is operated by GKN where the Plan is operated through a special dealing arrangement.

- **To shareholders by way of a rights issue** to shore up statement of financial positions weakened in the credit crisis by reducing debt and to avoid breaching debt covenants, e.g. in February 2009 the Cookson Group plc announced a 12 for 1 Rights Issue to raise net proceeds of approximately £240 million in order to provide a more suitable capital structure for the current environment and enhance covenant and longer-term liquidity headroom under current debt facilities.

- **To loan creditors in exchange for debt**, e.g. Sirius XM, a satellite radio station, with about $1 billion debt due to mature in February 2009, in January 2009 exchanged shares for $2\frac{1}{2}\%$ convertible debt.
- **To obtain funds for future acquisitions**, e.g. SSL International, a successful company that had outperformed the FTSE All-Share index 2008, raised £87 million to fund its medium-term growth plans. Other companies were raising funds to acquire assets that were being sold by companies needing to obtain cash to reduce their debt burden.
- **To reduce levels of debt** to avoid credit rating agencies downgrading the company which would make it difficult or more expensive to borrow.
- **To overcome liquidity problems**, e.g. Brio experienced liquidity problems and refinanced with the isue of SK300 million shares to raise over £25 million.

10.4.4 Types of preference shares

The following illustrate some of the ways in which specific rights can vary.

Cumulative preference shares
Dividends not paid in respect of any one year because of a lack of profits are accumulated for payment in some future year when distributable profits are sufficient.

Non-cumulative preference shares
Dividends not paid in any one year because of a lack of distributable profits are permanently forgone.

Participating preference shares
These shares carry the right to participate in a distribution of additional profits over and above the fixed rate of dividend after the ordinary shareholders have received an agreed percentage. The participation rights are based on a precise formula.

Redeemable preference shares
These shares may be redeemed by the company at an agreed future date and at an agreed price.

Convertible preference shares
These shares may be converted into ordinary shares at a future date on agreed terms. The conversion is usually at the preference shareholder's discretion.

There can be a mix of rights, e.g. Getronics entered into an agreement in 2005 with its cumulative preference shareholders whereby Getronics had the right in 2009 to repurchase (redeem) the shares and, if it did not redeem the shares, the cumulative preference shareholders had the right to convert into ordinary shares.

10.5 Accounting entries on issue of shares

10.5.1 Shares issued at nominal (par) value

If shares are issued at nominal value, the company simply debits the cash account with the amount received and credits the ordinary share capital or preference share capital, as appropriate, with the **nominal value** of the shares.

10.5.2 Shares issued at a premium

The market price of the shares of a company, which is based on the prospects of that company, is usually different from the par (nominal) value of those shares.

On receipt of consideration for the shares, the company again debits the cash account with the amount received and credits the ordinary share capital or preference share capital, as appropriate, with the **nominal value** of the shares.

Assuming that the market price exceeds the nominal value, a premium element will be credited to a share premium account. The share premium is classified as a **non-distributable reserve** to indicate that it is not repayable to the shareholders who have subscribed for their shares: it remains a part of the company's permanent capital.

The accounting treatment for recording the issue of shares is straightforward. For example, the journal entries to record the issue of 1,000 £1 ordinary shares at a market price of £2.50 per share payable in instalments of:

on application	on 1 January 20X1	25p
on issue	on 31 January 20X1	£1.75 including the premium
on first call	on 31 January 20X2	25p
on final call	on 31 January 20X4	25p

would be as follows:

1 Jan 20X1	Dr	Cr
	£	£
Cash account	250	
Application account		250
31 Jan 20X1	**Dr**	**Cr**
	£	£
Cash account	1,750	
Issue account		1,750
31 Jan 20X1	**Dr**	**Cr**
	£	£
Application account	250	
Issue account	1,750	
Share capital account		500
Share premium in excess of par value		1,500

The first and final call would be debited to the cash account and credited to the share capital account on receipt of the date of the calls.

10.6 Creditor protection: capital maintenance concept

To protect creditors, there are often rules relating to the use of the total shareholders' funds which determine how much is distributable.

As a general rule, the paid-in share capital is not repayable to the shareholders and the reserves are classified into two categories: distributable and non-distributable. The directors have discretion as to the amount of the distributable profits that they recommend for distribution as a dividend to shareholders. However, they have no discretion as to the treatment of the non-distributable funds. There may be a statutory requirement for the company to retain within the company net assets equal to the non-distributable reserves. This requirement is to safeguard the interests of creditors and is known as **capital maintenance**.

10.7 Creditor protection: why capital maintenance rules are necessary

It is helpful at this point to review the position of unincorporated businesses in relation to capital maintenance.

10.7.1 Unincorporated businesses

An unincorporated business such as a sole trader or partnership is not required to maintain any specified amount of capital within the business to safeguard the interests of its creditors. The owners are free to decide whether to introduce or withdraw capital. However, they remain personally liable for the liabilities incurred by the business, and the creditors can have recourse to the personal assets of the owners if the business assets are inadequate to meet their claims in full.

When granting credit to an unincorporated business, the creditors may well be influenced by the personal wealth and apparent standing of the owners and not merely by the assets of the business as disclosed in its financial statements. This is why in an unincorporated business there is no external reason for the capital and the profits to be kept separate.

In partnerships, there are frequently internal agreements that require each partner to maintain his or her capital at an agreed level. Such agreements are strictly a matter of contract between the owners and do not prejudice the rights of the business creditors.

Sometimes owners attempt to influence creditors unfairly, by maintaining a lifestyle in excess of what they can afford, or try to frustrate the legal rights of creditors by putting their private assets beyond their reach, e.g. by transferring their property to relatives or trusts. These subterfuges become apparent only when the creditors seek to enforce their claim against the private assets. Banks are able to protect themselves by seeking adequate security, e.g. a charge on the owners' property.

10.7.2 Incorporated limited liability company

Because of limited liability, the rights of creditors against the private assets of the owners, i.e. the shareholders of the company, are restricted to any amount unpaid on their shares. Once the shareholders have paid the company for their shares, they are not personally liable for the company's debts. Creditors are restricted to making claims against the assets of the company.

Hence, the legislature considered it necessary to ensure that the shareholders did not make distributions to themselves such that the assets needed to meet creditors' claims were put beyond creditors' reach. This may be achieved by setting out statutory rules.

10.8 Creditor protection: how to quantify the amounts available to meet creditors' claims

Creditors are exposed to two types of risk: the business risk that a company will operate unsuccessfully and will be unable to pay them; and the risk that a company will operate successfully, but will pay its shareholders rather than its creditors.

The legislature has never intended trade creditors to be protected against ordinary business risks, e.g. the risk of the debtor company incurring either trading losses or losses that might arise from a fall in the value of the assets following changes in market conditions.

In the UK, the Companies Act 2006 requires the amount available to meet creditors' claims to be calculated by reference to the company's annual financial statements. There are two possible approaches:

- The **direct** approach which requires the **asset** side of the statement of financial position to contain assets with a realisable value sufficient to cover all outstanding liabilities.

- The **indirect** approach which requires the **liability** side of the statement of financial position to classify reserves into distributable and non-distributable reserves (i.e. respectively, available and not available to the shareholders by way of dividend distributions).

The Act follows the indirect approach by specifying capital maintenance in terms of the total shareholders' funds. However, this has not stopped certain creditors taking steps to protect themselves by following the direct approach, e.g. it is bank practice to obtain a mortgage debenture over the assets of the company. The effect of this is to disadvantage the trade creditors. The statutory restrictions preventing shareholders from reducing capital accounts on the liability side are weakened when management grants certain parties priority rights against some or all of the company's assets.

We will now consider total shareholders' funds and capital maintenance in more detail, starting with share capital. Two aspects of share capital are relevant to creditor protection: minimum capital requirements and reduction of capital.

10.9 Issued share capital: minimum share capital

The creditors of public companies may be protected by the requirements that there should be a minimum share capital and that capital should be reduced only under controlled conditions.

In the UK, the minimum share capital requirement for a public company is currently set at £50,000 or its euro equivalent although this can be increased by the Secretary of State for the Department for Business, Innovation and Skills.[2] A company is not permitted to commence trading unless it has issued this amount. However, given the size of many public companies, it is questionable whether this figure is adequate.

The minimum share capital requirement refers to the nominal value of the share capital. In the UK, the law requires each class of share to have a stated nominal value. This value is used for identification and also for capital maintenance. The law ensures that a company receives an amount that is at least equal to the nominal value of the shares issued, less a controlled level of commission, by prohibiting the issue of shares at a discount and by limiting any underwriting commissions on an issue. This is intended to avoid a material discount being granted in the guise of commission. However, the requirement is concerned more with safeguarding the relative rights of existing shareholders than with protecting creditors.

There is effectively no minimum capital requirement for private companies. We can see many instances of such companies having an issued and paid-up capital of only a few £1 shares, which cannot conceivably be regarded as adequate creditor protection. The lack of adequate protection for the creditors of private companies is considered again later in the chapter.

10.10 Distributable profits: general considerations

We have considered capital maintenance and non-distributable reserves. However, it is not sufficient to attempt to maintain the permanent capital accounts of companies unless there are clear rules on the amount that they can distribute to their shareholders as profit. Without such rules, they may make distributions to their shareholders out of capital. The question of what can legitimately be distributed as profit is an integral part of the concept of capital maintenance in company accounts. In the UK, there are currently statutory definitions of the amount that can be distributed by private, public and investment companies.

10.10.1 Distributable profits: general rule for private companies

The definition of distributable profits under the Companies Act 2006 is:

> Accumulated, realised profits, so far as not previously utilised by distribution or capitalisation, less its accumulated, realised losses, as far as not previously written off in a reduction or reorganisation of capital.

This means the following:

- Unrealised profits cannot be distributed.
- There is no difference between realised revenue and realised capital profits.
- All accumulated net realised profits (i.e. realised profits less realised losses) on the statement of financial position date must be considered.

On the key question of whether a profit is realised or not, the Companies Act (para. 853) simply says that realised profits or realised losses are

> such profits or losses of the company as fall to be treated as realised in accordance with principles generally accepted, at the time when the accounts are prepared, with respect to the determination for accounting purposes of realised profits or losses.

Hence, the Act does not lay down detailed rules on what is and what is not a realised profit; indeed, it does not even refer specifically to 'accounting principles'. Nevertheless, it would seem reasonable for decisions on realisation to be based on generally **accepted accounting principles** at the time, subject to the court's decision in cases of dispute.

10.10.2 Distributable profits: general rule for public companies

According to the Companies Act, the undistributable reserves of a public company are its share capital, share premium, capital redemption reserve and also 'the excess of accumulated unrealised profits over accumulated unrealised losses at the time of the intended distribution and ... any reserves not allowed to be distributed under the Act or by the company's own Memorandum or Articles of Association'.

This means that, when dealing with a public company, the distributable profits have to be reduced by any net unrealised loss.

10.10.3 Investment companies

The Companies Act 2006 allows for the special nature of some businesses in the calculation of distributable profits. There are additional rules for investment companies in calculating their distributable profits. For a company to be classified as an investment company, it must invest its funds mainly in securities with the aim of spreading investment risk and giving its members the benefit of the results of managing its funds.

Such a company has the option of applying one of two rules in calculating its distributable profits. These are either:

- the rules that apply to public companies in general, but excluding any realised capital profits, e.g. from the disposal of investments; or
- the company's accumulated realised revenue less its accumulated realised and unrealised revenue losses, provided that its assets are at least one and a half times its liabilities both before and after such a distribution.

The reasoning behind these special rules seems to be to allow investment companies to pass the dividends they receive to their shareholders, irrespective of any changes in the values of their investments, which are subject to market fluctuations. However, the asset cover ratio of liabilities can easily be manipulated by the company simply paying creditors, whereby the ratio is improved, or borrowing, whereby it is reduced.

10.11 Distributable profits: how to arrive at the amount using relevant accounts

In the UK, the Companies Act 2006 stipulates that the distributable profits of a company must be based on **relevant accounts**. Relevant accounts may be prepared under either UK GAAP or EU adopted IFRS. On occasions a new IFRS might have the effect of making a previously realised item reclassified as unrealised, which would then become undistributable. For a more detailed description on the determination of realised profits for distribution refer to the ICAEW Technical Release 7/08 (www.icaew.co.uk). These would normally be the audited annual accounts, which have been prepared according to the requirements of the Act to give a true and fair view of the company's financial affairs. In the case of a qualified audit report, the auditor is required to prepare a written statement stating whether such a qualification is material in determining a company's distributable profit. Interim dividends are allowed to be paid provided they can be justified on the basis of the latest annual accounts, otherwise interim accounts will have to be prepared that would justify such a distribution.

10.11.1 Effect of fair value accounting on decision to distribute

In the context of fair value accounting, volatility is an aspect where directors will need to consider their fiduciary duties. The fair value of financial instruments may be volatile even though such fair value is properly determined in accordance with IAS 39 *Financial Instruments: Recognition and Measurement*. Directors should consider, as a result of their fiduciary duties, whether it is prudent to distribute profits arising from changes in the fair values of financial instruments considered to be volatile, even though they may otherwise be realised profits in accordance with the technical guidance.

10.12 When may capital be reduced?

Once the shares have been issued and paid up, the contributed capital together with any payments in excess of par value are normally regarded as permanent. However, there might be commercially sound reasons for a company to reduce its capital and we will consider three such reasons. These are:

● writing off part of capital which has already been lost and is not represented by assets;

● repayment of part of paid-up capital to shareholders or cancellation of unpaid share capital;

● purchase of own shares.

In the UK it has been necessary for both private and public companies to obtain a court order approving a reduction of capital. In line with the wish to reduce the regulatory burden on private companies the government legislated[3] in 2008 for private companies to be able to reduce their capital by special resolution subject to the directors signing a solvency statement to the effect that the company would remain able to meet all of its liabilities for at least a year. At the same time a reserve arising from the reduction is treated as realised and may be distributed, although it need not be and could be used for other purposes, e.g. writing off accumulated trading losses.

10.13 Writing off part of capital which has already been lost and is not represented by assets

This situation normally occurs when a company has accumulated trading losses which prevent it from making dividend payments under the rules relating to distributable profits. The general approach is to eliminate the debit balance on retained earnings by setting it off against the share capital and non-distributable reserves.

10.13.1 Accounting treatment for a capital reduction to eliminate accumulated trading losses

The accounting treatment is straightforward. A capital reduction account is opened. It is debited with the accumulated losses and credited with the amount written off the share capital and reserves.

For example, assume that the capital and reserves of Hopeful Ltd were as follows at 31 December 20X1:

	£
200,000 ordinary shares of £1 each	200,000
Statement of comprehensive income	(180,000)

The directors estimate that the company will return to profitability in 20X2, achieving profits of £4,000 per annum thereafter. Without a capital reduction, the profits from 20X2 must be used to reduce the accumulated losses. This means that the company would be unable to pay a dividend for forty-five years if it continued at that level of profitability and ignoring tax. Perhaps even more importantly, it would not be attractive for shareholders to put additional capital into the company because they would not be able to obtain any dividend for some years.

There might be statutory procedures such as the requirement for the directors to obtain a special resolution and court approval to reduce the £1 ordinary shares to ordinary shares of 10p each. Subject to satisfying such requirements, the accounting entries would be:

	Dr £	Cr £
Capital reduction account	180,000	
Statement of income:		180,000
Transfer of debit balance		
Share capital	180,000	
Capital reduction account:		180,000
Reduction of share capital		

Accounting treatment for a capital reduction to eliminate accumulated trading losses and loss of value on non-current assets – losses borne by equity shareholders

Companies often take the opportunity to revalue all of their assets at the same time as they eliminate the accumulated trading losses. Any loss on revaluation is then treated in the same way as the accumulated losses and transferred to the capital reduction account.

For example, assume that the capital and reserves and assets of Hopeful Ltd were as follows at 31 December 20X1:

	£	£
200,000 ordinary shares of £1 each		200,000
Statement of income		(180,000)
		20,000
Non-current assets		
Plant and equipment		15,000
Current assets		
Cash	17,000	
Current liabilities		
Trade payables	12,000	
Net current assets		5,000
		20,000

The plant and equipment is revalued at £5,000 and it is resolved to reduce the share capital to ordinary shares of 5p each. The accounting entries would be:

	Dr	Cr
	£	£
Capital reduction account	190,000	
Statement of income		180,000
Plant and machinery:		10,000
Transfer of accumulated losses and loss on revaluation		
Share capital	190,000	
Capital reduction account:		190,000
Reduction of share capital to 200,000 shares of 5p each		

The statement of financial position after the capital reduction shows that the share capital fairly reflects the underlying asset values:

	£	£
200,000 ordinary shares of 5p each		10,000
		10,000
Non-current assets		
Plant and equipment		5,000
Current assets		
Cash	17,000	
Current liabilities		
Trade payables	12,000	5,000
		10,000

The pro forma statement of financial position shown in Figure 10.1 is from the Pilkington's Tiles Group plc's 2002 Annual Report. It shows the position when the company proposed the creation of distributable reserves after a substantial deficit in the reserves had been caused by the writing down of an investment – this was to be achieved by transferring to the profit and loss account the sums currently standing to the credit of the capital redemption reserve and share premium account.

The proposal was the subject of a special resolution to be confirmed by the High Court – the court would consider the proposal taking creditor protection into account. The company recognised this with the following statement:

the Company will need to demonstrate to the satisfaction of the High Court that no creditor of the Company who has consented to the cancellations will be prejudiced by them. At present, it is anticipated that the creditor protection will take the form of an undertaking ... not to treat as distributable any sum realised ... which represents the realisation of hidden value in the statement of financial position.

Figure 10.1 Pilkington's Tiles Group pro forma balance sheet assuming the competition of the restructuring plan

	31 March 2002 £000	Adjustment £000	Adjusted balance £000
Capital and reserves			
Share capital	9,247		9,247
Share premium	25,429	(25,429)	—
Capital redemption reserve	645	(645)	—
Merger reserve	(1,001)	1,001	—
Revaluation reserve	1,581	—	1,581
Profit and loss account	(21,738)	25,073	3,335
Equity shareholders' funds	14,163	—	14,163

10.13.2 Accounting treatment for a capital reduction to eliminate accumulated trading losses and loss of value on non-current assets – losses borne by equity and other stakeholders

In the Hopeful Ltd example above, the ordinary shareholders alone bore the losses. It might well be, however, that a reconstruction involves a compromise between shareholders and creditors, with an amendment of the rights of the latter. Such a reconstruction would be subject to any statutory requirements within the jurisdiction, e.g. the support, say, of 75% of each class of creditor whose rights are being compromised, 75% of each class of shareholder and the permission of the court. For such a reconstruction to succeed there needs to be reasonable evidence of commercial viability and that anticipated profits are sufficient to service the proposed new capital structure.

Assuming in the Hopeful Ltd example that the creditors agree to bear £5,000 of the losses, the accounting entries would be as follows:

	£	£
Share capital	185,000	
Creditors	5,000	
Capital reduction account:		190,000
Reduction of share capital to 200,000 shares of 7.5p each		

Reconstruction schemes can be complex, but the underlying evaluation by each party will be the same. Each will assess the scheme to see how it affects their individual position.

Trade payables

In their decision to accept £5,000 less than the book value of their debt, the trade payables of Hopeful Ltd would be influenced by their prospects of receiving payment if Hopeful were to cease trading immediately, the effect on their results without Hopeful as a continuing customer and the likelihood that they would continue to receive orders from Hopeful following reconstruction.

Loan creditors

Loan creditors would take into account the expected value of any security they possess and a comparison of the opportunities for investing any loan capital returned in the event of liquidation with the value of their capital and interest entitlement in the reconstructed company.

Preference shareholders

Preference shareholders would likewise compare prospects for capital and income following a liquidation of the company with prospects for income and capital from the company as a going concern following a reconstruction.

Relative effects of the scheme

In practice, the formulation of a scheme will involve more than just the accountant, except in the case of very small companies. A merchant bank, major shareholders and major debenture holders will undoubtedly be concerned. Each vested interest will be asked for its opinion on specific proposals: unfavourable reactions will necessitate a rethink by the accountant. The process will continue until a consensus begins to emerge.

Each stakeholder's position needs to be considered separately. For example, any attempt to reduce the nominal value of all classes of shares and debentures on a proportionate basis would be unfair and unacceptable. This is because a reduction in the nominal values of pre-ference shares or debentures has a different effect from a reduction in the nominal value of ordinary shares. In the former cases, the dividends and interest receivable will be reduced; in the latter case, the reduction in nominal value of the ordinary shares will have no effect on dividends as holders of ordinary shares are entitled to the residue of profit, whatever the nominal value of their shares.

Total support may well be unachievable. The objective is to maintain the company as a going concern. In attempting to achieve this, each party will continually be comparing its advantages under the scheme with its prospects in a liquidation.

Illustration of a capital reconstruction

XYZ plc has been making trading losses, which have resulted in a substantial debit balance on the profit and loss account. The statement of financial position of XYZ plc as at 31 December 20X3 was as follows:

		£000
Ordinary share capital (£1 shares)		1,000
Less: Accumulated losses	Note 1	(800)
		200
10% debentures (£1)		600
Net assets at book value	Note 2	800

Notes:
1 The company is changing its product and markets and expects to make £150,000 profit before interest and tax every year from 1 January 20X4.
2 (a) The estimated break-up or liquidation value of the assets at 31 December 20X3 was £650,000.
  (b) The going concern value of assets at 31 December 20X3 was £700,000.

The directors are faced with a decision to liquidate or reconstruct. Having satisfied themselves that the company is returning to profitability, they propose the following reconstruction scheme:

- Write off losses and reduce asset values to £700,000.
- Cancel all existing ordinary shares and debentures.
- Issue 1,200,000 new ordinary shares of 25p each and 400,000 12.5% debentures of £1 each as follows:
  - the existing shareholders are to be issued with 800,000 ordinary 25p shares;
  - the existing debenture holders are to be issued with 400,000 ordinary 25p shares and the new debentures.

The stakeholders, i.e. the ordinary shareholders and debenture holders, have first to decide whether the company has a reasonable chance of achieving the estimated profit for 20X4. The company might carry out a sensitivity analysis to show the effect on dividends and interest over a range of profit levels.

Next, stakeholders must consider whether allowing the company to continue provides a better return than that available from the liquidation of the company. Assuming that it does, they assess the effect of allowing the company to continue without any reconstruction of capital and with a reconstruction of capital.

The accountant writes up the reconstruction accounts and produces a statement of financial position after the reconstruction has been effected.

The accountant will produce the following information:

Effect of liquidating

	£	Debenture holders £	Ordinary shareholders £
Assets realised	650,000		
Less: Prior claim	(600,000)	600,000	
Less: Ordinary shareholders	(50,000)		50,000
	—	600,000	50,000

This shows that the ordinary shareholders would lose almost all of their capital, whereas the debenture holders would be in a much stronger position. This is important because it might influence the amount of inducement that the debenture holders require to accept any variation of their rights.

Company continues without reconstruction

	£	Debenture holders £	Ordinary shareholders £
Expected annual income:			
Expected operating profit	150,000		
Debenture interest	(60,000)	60,000	
Less: Ordinary dividend	(90,000)		90,000
Annual income	—	60,000	90,000

However, as far as the ordinary shareholders are concerned, no dividend will be allowed to be paid until the debit balance of £800,000 has been eliminated, i.e. there will be no dividend for more than nine years (for simplicity the illustration ignores tax effects).

Company continues with a reconstruction

	£	Debenture holders £	Ordinary shareholders £
Expected annual income:			
Expected operating profit	150,000		
Less: Debenture interest	(50,000)	50,000	
(12.5% on £400,000)			
Less: Dividend on shares	(33,000)	33,000	
Less: Ordinary dividend	(67,000)		67,000
Annual income	—	83,000	67,000

How will debenture holders react to the scheme?

At first glance, debenture holders appear to be doing reasonably well: the £83,000 provides a return of almost 14% on the amount that they would have received in a liquidation (83,000/600,000 × 100), which exceeds the 10% currently available, and it is £23,000 more than the £60,000 currently received. However, their exposure to risk has increased because £33,000 is dependent upon the level of profits. They will consider their position in relation to the ordinary shareholders.

For the ordinary shareholders the return should be calculated on the amount that they would have received on liquidation, i.e. 134% (67,000/50,000 × 100). In addition to receiving a return of 134%, they would hold two-thirds of the share capital, which would give them control of the company.

A final consideration for the debenture holders would be their position if the company were to fail after a reconstruction. In such a case, the old debenture holders would be materially disadvantaged as their prior claim will have been reduced from £600,000 to £400,000.

Accounting for the reconstruction

The reconstruction account will record the changes in the book values as follows:

Reconstruction account

	£000		£000
Statement of comprehensive income	800	Share capital	1,000
Assets (losses written off)	100	Debentures (old debentures cancelled)	600
Ordinary share capital (25p)	300		
12.5% debentures (new issue)	400		
	1,600		1,600

The post-reconstruction statement of financial position will be as follows:

Ordinary share capital (25p)	300,000
12.5% debentures of £1	400,000
	700,000

10.14 Repayment of part of paid-in capital to shareholders or cancellation of unpaid share capital

This can occur when a company wishes to reduce its unwanted liquid resources. It takes the form of a pro rata payment to each shareholder and may require the consent of the creditors.

At the same time, the Directors need to retain sufficient to satisfy the company's capital investment requirements. The following is an extract from the AstraZeneca 2005 Annual Report:

Dividend and share re-purchases

In line with the policy stated last year, the Board intends to continue its practice of growing dividends in line with earnings (maintaining dividend cover in the two to three times range) whilst substantially distributing the balance of cash flow via share re-purchases. During 2005, we returned $4,718 million out of free cash of $6,052 million to shareholders through a mix of share buy-backs and dividends. The Board firmly believes that the first call on free cash flow is business need and, having fulfilled that, will return surplus cash flow to shareholders.

The primary business need is to build the product pipeline by supporting internal and external opportunities. Accordingly, in 2006, the Board intends to re-purchase shares at around the same level as 2005, with any balance of free cash flow available firstly for investment in the product pipeline or subsequent return to shareholders.

10.15 Purchase of own shares

This might take the form of the redemption of redeemable preference shares, the purchase of ordinary shares which are then cancelled and the purchase of ordinary shares which are not cancelled but held in treasury.

10.15.1 Redemption of preference shares

In the UK, when redeemable preference shares are redeemed, the company is required either to replace them with other shares or to make a transfer from distributable reserves to non-distributable reserves in order to maintain permanent capital. The accounting entries on redemption are to credit cash and debit the redeemable preference share account.

10.15.2 Buyback of own shares – intention to cancel

There are a number of reasons for companies buying back shares. These provide a benefit when taken as:

● a strategic measure, e.g. recognising that there is a lack of viable investment projects, i.e. expected returns being less than the company's weighted average cost of capital and so returning excess cash to shareholders to allow them to search out better growth investments;

● a defensive measure, e.g. an attempt to frustrate a hostile takeover or to reduce the power of dissident shareholders;

● a reactive measure, e.g. taking advantage of the fact that the share price is at a discount to its underlying intrinsic value or stabilising a falling share price;

● a proactive measure, e.g. creating shareholder value by reducing the number of shares in issue which increases the earnings per share, or making a distribution more tax efficient than the payment of a cash dividend;

● a tax efficient measure, e.g. Rolls Royce made a final payment to shareholders in 2004 of 5.00p, making a total of 8.18p per ordinary share (2003 8.18p), stating that: 'The Company will continue to issue B Shares in place of dividends in order to accelerate the recovery of its advance corporation tax.'

There is also a potential risk if the company has to borrow funds in order to make the buyback, leaving itself liable to service the debt. Where it uses free cash rather than loans it is attractive to analysts and shareholders. For example, in the BP share buyback scheme (one of the UK's largest), the chief executive, Lord Browne, said that any free cash generated from BP's assets when the oil price was above $20 a barrel would be returned to investors over the following three years.

10.15.3 Buyback of own shares – treasury shares

The benefits to a company holding treasury shares are that it has greater flexibility to respond to investors' attitude to gearing, e.g. reissuing the shares if the gearing is perceived to be too high. It also has the capacity to satisfy loan conversions and employee share options without the need to issue new shares which would dilute the existing shareholdings.

National regimes where buyback is already permitted

In Europe and the USA it has been permissible to buy back shares, known as treasury shares, and hold them for reissue. In the UK this has been permissible since 2003. There are two common accounting treatments – the cost method and the par value method. The most common method is the cost method, which provides the following:

On purchase

● The treasury shares are debited at gross cost to a Treasury Stock account – this is deducted as a one-line entry from equity, e.g. a statement of financial position might appear as follows:

Owners' equity section of statement of financial position

	£
Common stock, £1 par, 100,000 shares authorised, 30,000 shares issued	30,000
Paid-in capital in excess of par	60,000
Retained earnings	165,000
Treasury Stock (15,000 shares at cost)	(15,000)
Total owners' equity	240,000

In some countries, e.g. Switzerland, the treasury shares have been reported in the statement of financial position as a financial asset. When a company moves to IAS this is not permitted and it is required that the shares are disclosed as negative equity.

On resale

● If on resale the sale price is higher than the cost price, the Treasury Stock account is credited at cost price and the excess is credited to Paid-in Capital (Treasury Stock).

● If on resale the sale price is lower than the cost price, the Treasury Stock account is credited with the proceeds and the balance is debited to Paid-in Capital (Treasury Stock). If the debit is greater than the credit balance on Paid-in Capital (Treasury Stock), the difference is deducted from retained earnings.

The UK experience

Treasury shares have been permitted in the UK since 2003. The regulations relating to Treasury shares are now contained in the Companies Act 2006.[4] These regulations permit companies with listed shares that purchase their own shares out of distributable profits to hold them 'in treasury' for sale at a later date or for transfer to an employees' share scheme.

There are certain restrictions whilst shares are held in treasury, namely:

- Their aggregate nominal value must not exceed 10% of the nominal value of issued share capital (if it exceeds 10% then the excess must be disposed of or cancelled).
- Rights attaching to the class of share – e.g. receiving dividends, and the right to vote – cannot be exercised by the company.

Treasury shares – cancellation

- Where shares are held as treasury shares, the company may at any time cancel some or all of the shares.
- If shares held as treasury shares cease to be qualifying shares, then the company must cancel the shares.
- On cancellation the amount of the company's share capital is reduced by the nominal amount of the shares cancelled.

The Singapore experience

It is interesting to note that until 1998 companies in Singapore were not permitted to purchase their own shares and had to rely on obtaining a court order to reduce capital. It was realised, however, that regimes such as those in the UK allowed a quicker and less expensive way to return capital to shareholders. UK experience meant that public companies were able to return capital if there were insufficient investment opportunities, and private companies were able to repurchase shares to resolve disputes between family members or minority and majority shareholders.

The following criteria apply:

- the company should have authority under its Articles of Association;
- the repayment should be from distributable profits that are realised;
- the creditors should be protected by requiring the company to be solvent before and after the repayment (assets and liabilities to be restated to current values for this exercise);
- on-market acquisitions require an ordinary resolution;
- selective off market acquisitions require a special resolution because of the risk that directors may manipulate the transaction.

The amount paid by the company will be set against the carrying amount of the contributed capital, i.e. the nominal value plus share premium attaching to the shares acquired and the retained earnings. In order to maintain capital, there will be a transfer from retained earnings to a capital redemption reserve. For example, a payment of $100,000 to acquire shares with a nominal value of $20,000 would be recorded as:

	Dr	Cr
Share capital	$20,000	
Retained earnings	$80,000	
Cash		$100,000

Being purchase of 20,000 $1 shares for $100,000 and their cancellation

Retained earnings	$20,000	
Capital redemption reserve		$20,000

Being the creation of capital redemption reserve to maintain capital.

Summary

Creditors of companies are not expected to be protected against ordinary business risks as these are taken care of by financial markets, e.g. through the rates of interest charged on different capital instruments of different companies. However, the creditors are entitled to depend on the non-erosion of the permanent capital unless their interests are considered and protected.

The chapter also discusses the question of capital reconstructions and the need to consider the effect of any proposed reconstruction on the rights of different parties.

REVIEW QUESTIONS

1 What is the relevance of dividend cover if dividends are paid out of distributable profits?

2 How can distributable profits become non-distributable?

3 Why do companies reorganise their capital structure when they have accumulated losses?

4 What factors would a loan creditor take into account if asked to bear some of the accumulated loss?

5 Explain a debt/equity swap and the reasons for debt/equity swaps, and discuss the effect on existing shareholders and loan creditors.

EXERCISES

An extract from the solution is provided on the Companion Website (www.pearsoned.co.uk/elliott-elliott) for exercises marked with an asterisk (*).

Question I

The draft statement of financial position of Telin plc at 30 September 20X5 was as follows:

	£000		£000
Ordinary shares of £1 each, fully paid	12,000	Product development costs	1,400
12% preference shares of £1 each, fully paid	8,000	Sundry assets	32,170
Share premium	4,000	Cash and bank	5,450
Retained (distributable) profits	4,600		
Payables	10,420		
	39,020		39,020

Preference shares of the company were originally issued at a premium of 2p per share. The directors of the company decided to redeem these shares at the end of October 20X5 at a premium of 5p per share. They also decided to write off the balances on development costs and discount on debentures (see below).

All write-offs and other transactions are to be entered into the accounts according to the provisions of the Companies Acts and in a manner financially advantageous to the company and to its shareholders.

The following transactions took place during October 20X5:

(a) On 4 October the company issued for cash 2,400,000 10% debentures of £1 each at a discount of 2½%.

(b) On 6 October the balances on development costs and discount of debentures were written off.

(c) On 12 October the company issued for cash 6,000,000 ordinary shares at a premium of 10p per share. This was a specific issue to help redeem preference shares.

(d) On 29 October the company redeemed the 12% preference shares at a premium of 5p per share and included in the payments to shareholders one month's dividend for October.

(e) On 30 October the company made a bonus issue, to all ordinary shareholders, of one fully paid ordinary share for every 20 shares held.

(f) During October the company made a net profit of £275,000 from its normal trading operations. This was reflected in the cash balance at the end of the month.

Required:
(a) **Write up the ledger accounts of Telin plc to record the transactions for October 20X5.**
(b) **Prepare the company's statement of financial position as at 31 October 20X5.**
(c) **Briefly explain accounting entries which arise as a result of redemption of preference shares.**

* Question 2

The following is the statement of financial position of Alpha Ltd as on 30 June 20X8:

	£000 Cost	£000 Accumulated depreciation	£000
Non-current assets			
Freehold property	46	5	41
Plant	85	6	79
	131	11	120
Investments			
Shares in subsidiary company		90	
Loans		40	130
Current assets			
Inventory		132	
Trade receivables		106	
		238	
Current liabilities			
Trade payables		282	
Bank overdraft		58	
		340	
Net current liabilities			(102)
Total assets less liabilities			148
Capital and reserves			
250,000 8½% cumulative redeemable preference shares of £1 each fully paid			250
100,000 ordinary shares of £1 each 75p paid			75
			325
Retained earnings			(177)
			148

The following information is relevant:

1   There are contingent liabilities in respect of (i) a guarantee given to bankers to cover a loan of £30,000 made to the subsidiary and (ii) uncalled capital of 10p per share on the holding of 100,000 shares of £1 each in the subsidiary.

2   The arrears of preference dividend amount to £106,250.

3   The following capital reconstruction scheme, to take effect as from 1 July 20X8, has been duly approved and authorised:

   (i) the unpaid capital on the ordinary shares to be called up;

   (ii) the ordinary shares thereupon to be reduced to shares of 25p each fully paid up by cancelling 75p per share and then each fully paid share of 25p to be subdivided into five shares of 5p each fully paid;

   (iii) the holders to surrender three of such 5p shares out of every five held for reissue as set out below;

   (iv) the $8^1/2$% cumulative preference shares together with all arrears of dividend to be surrendered and cancelled on the basis that the holder of every 50 preference shares will pay to Alpha a sum of £30 in cash, and will be issued with;

      (a) one £40 convertible $7^3/4$% note of £40 each, and

      (b) 60 fully paid ordinary shares of 5p each (being a redistribution of shares surrendered by the ordinary shareholders and referred to in (iii) above);

   (v) the unpaid capital on the shares in the subsidiary to be called up and paid by the parent company whose guarantee to the bank should be cancelled;

   (vi) the freehold property to be revalued at £55,000;

   (vii) the adverse balance on retained earnings to be written off, £55,000 to be written off the shares in the subsidiary and the sums made available by the scheme to be used to write down the plant

Required:
(a) **Prepare a capital reduction and reorganisation account.**
(b) **Prepare the statement of financial position of the company as it would appear immediately after completion of the scheme.**

Question 3

A summary of the statement of financial position of Doxin plc, as at 31 December 20X0, is given below;

	£		£
800,000 ordinary shares of		Assets other than bank	
£1 each	800,000	(at book values)	1,500,000
300,000 6% preference			
shares of £1 each	300,000	Bank	200,000
General reserves	200,000		
Payables	400,000		
	1,700,000		1,700,000

During 20X1, the company:

(i) Issued 200,000 ordinary shares of £1 each at a premium of 10p per share (a specific issue to redeem preference shares).

(ii) Redeemed all preference shares at a premium of 5%. These were originally issued at 25% premium.

(iii) Issued 4,000 7% debentures of £100 each at £90.

(iv) Used share premium, if any, to issue fully paid bonus shares to members.

(v) Made a net loss of £500,000 by end of year which affected the bank account.

Required:

(a) Show the effect of each of the above items in the form of a moving statement of financial position (i.e. additions/deductions from original figures) and draft the statement of financial position of 31 December 20XI.

(b) Consider to what extent the interests of the creditors of the company are being protected.

Question 4

Discuss the advantages to a company of:

(a) purchasing and cancelling its own shares;

(b) purchasing and holding its own shares in treasury.

* Question 5

Speedster Ltd commenced trading in 1986 as a wholesaler of lightweight travel accessories. The company was efficient and traded successfully until 2000 when new competitors entered the market selling at lower prices which Speedster could not match. The company has gradually slipped into losses and the bank is no longer prepared to offer overdraft facilities. The directors are considering liquidating the company and have prepared the following statement of financial position and supporting information:

Statement of financial position (000s)		
Non-current assets		
Freehold land at cost		1,500
Plant and equipment (NBV)		1,800
Current assets		
Inventories	600	
Trade receivables	1,200	
	1,800	
Current liabilities		
Payables	1,140	
Bank overdraft (secured on the plant and equipment)	1,320	
	2,460	
Net current assets		(660)
Non-current liabilities		
Secured loan (secured on the land)		(1,200)
		1,440
Financed by		
Ordinary shares of £1 each		3,000
Statement of comprehensive income		(1,560)
		1,440

Supporting information

(i) The freehold land has a market value of £960,000 if it is continued in use as a warehouse. There is a possibility that planning permission could be obtained for a change of use allowing the warehouse to be converted into apartments. If planning permission were to be obtained, the company has been advised that the land would have a market value of £2,500,000.

(ii) The net realisable values on liquidation of the other assets are:

Plant and equipment	£1,200,000
Inventory	£450,000
Trade receivables	£1,050,000

(iii) An analysis of the payables indicated that there would be £300,000 owing to preferential creditors for wages, salaries and taxes.

(iv) Liquidation costs were estimated at £200,000

Required:
Prepare a statement showing the distribution on the basis that:
(a) planning permission was not obtained; and
(b) planning permission was obtained.

Question 6

Delta Ltd has been developing a lightweight automated wheelchair. The research costs written off have been far greater than originally estimated and the equity and preference capital has been eroded as seen on the statement of financial position.

The following is the statement of financial position of Delta Ltd as at 31.12.20X9:

	£000	£000
Intangible assets		
Development costs		300
Non-current assets		
Freehold property	800	
Plant, vehicles and equipment	650	1,450
		1,750
Current assets		
Inventory	480	
Trade receivables	590	
Investments	200	
	1,270	
Current liabilities		
Trade payables	(1,330)	
Bank overdraft	(490)	(550)
		1,200
10% debentures (secured on freehold premises)		(1,000)
Total assets less liabilities		200
Capital and reserves		
Ordinary shares of 50p each		800
7% cumulative preference shares of £1 each		500
Retained earnings (debit)		(1,100)
		200

The finance director has prepared the following information for consideration by the board:

1 Estimated current and liquidation values were estimated as follows:

	Current values £000	Liquidation values £000
Capitalised development costs	300	–
Freehold property	1,200	1,200
Plant and equipment	600	100
Inventory	480	300
Trade receivables	590	590
Investments	200	200
		2,390

2 If the company were to be liquidated there would be disposal costs of £100,000.

3 The preference dividend had not been paid for five years.

4 It is estimated that the company would make profits before interest over the next five years of £150,000 rising to £400,000 by the fifth year.

5 The directors have indicated that they would consider introducing further equity capital.

6 It was the finance director's opinion that for any scheme to succeed , it should satisfy the following conditions:

(a) The shareholders and creditors should have a better benefit in capital and income terms by reconstructing rather than liquidating the company.

(b) The scheme should have a reasonable possibility of ensuring the long-term survival of the company.

(c) There should be a reasonable assurance that there will be adequate working capital.

(d) Gearing should not be permitted to become excessive.

(e) If possible, the ordinary shareholders should retain control.

Required:

(a) **Advise the unsecured creditors of the minimum that they should accept if they were to agree to a reconstruction rather than proceed to press for the company to be liquidated.**

(b) **Propose a possible scheme for reconstruction.**

(c) **Prepare the statement of financial position of the company as it would appear immediately after completion of the scheme.**

References

1 Companies Act 2006.
2 *Ibid.*, section 764.
3 Companies (Reduction of Share Capital) Order 2008.
4 The Companies Act 2006, paras 724–732.

CHAPTER 11

Off balance sheet finance

11.1 Introduction

The main purpose of this chapter is to introduce the concept of 'off-balance sheet finance' which arises when accounting treatments allow companies not to recognise assets and liabilities that they control or on which they suffer the risks and enjoy the rewards. Various accounting standards have been issued to try to ensure that the statement of financial position properly reflects assets and liabilities such as IAS 37 *Provisions, Contingent Liabilities and Contingent Assets* and IAS 10 *Events after the Reporting Period*. Also the conceptual framework of accounting is important in how it requires the substance of transactions to be reflected when giving reliable information in financial statements.

Objectives

By the end of this chapter, you should be able to:

- understand and explain why it is important that companies reflect as accurately as possible their assets and liabilities, and the implications if assets and liabilities are not reflected on the statement of financial position;
- understand and explain the concept of substance over form and why it is important in accounting;
- account for provisions, contingent liabilities and contingent assets under IAS 37 and explain the potential changes the IASB is considering in relation to provisions.

11.2 Traditional statements – conceptual changes

Accountants have traditionally followed an objective, transaction-based, book-keeping system for recording financial data and a conservative, accrual-based system for classifying into income and capital and reporting to users and financial analysts. Capital gearing was able to be calculated from the balance sheet on the assumption that it reported all of the liabilities used in the debt/equity ratio; and income gearing was able to be calculated from the income statement on the assumption that it reported all interest expense.

However, since the 1950s there has been a growth in the use of off balance sheet finance and complex capital instruments. The financial analyst can no longer assume that all liabilities are disclosed in the residual balances that appear in the traditional balance sheet and all interest expense is disclosed as such in the income statement when assessing risks and returns. Off balance sheet finance has made it impossible to use ratios to make valid inter-period or inter-firm comparisons based on the published financial statements.

11.3 Off balance sheet finance – its impact

Off balance sheet finance is the descriptive phrase for all financing arrangements where strict recognition of the legal aspects of the individual contract results in the exclusion of liabilities and associated assets from the statement of financial position. The impact of such transactions is to understate resources (assets) and obligations (liabilities) to the detriment of the true and fair view.[1] The analyst cannot determine the amount of capital employed or the real gearing ratio when attempting to assess risk and it could be said that the financial statements do not provide a fair view of the financial position, particularly if there are contracts for extended periods with heavy penalties for early termination.

This can happen as an innocent side-effect of the transaction-based book-keeping system. For example, when a company undertakes the long-term hire of a machine by payment of annual rentals, the rental is recorded in the income statement, but the machine, because it is not owned by the hirer, will not be shown in the hirer's statement of financial position.

If the facility to hire did not exist, the asset could still be used and a similar cash outflow pattern incurred by purchasing it with the aid of a loan. A hiring agreement, if perceived in terms of its **accounting substance** rather than its **legal form**, has the same effect as entering into a loan agreement to acquire the machine.

The true and fair view can also be compromised by deliberate design when the substance of transactions is camouflaged by relying on a strictly legal distinction. For example, loan capital arrangements were concealed from shareholders and other creditors by a legal subterfuge to which management and lenders were party.

One of the earliest measures to bring liabities into the balance sheet taken by standard setters was that relating to accounting for leases.

11.3.1 Substance over form

IAS 17 *Leases*[2] was the first formal imposition of the principle of accounting for substance over legal form, aiming to ensure that the legal characteristics of a financial agreement did not obscure its commercial impact. In particular, it was intended to prevent the commercial level of gearing from being concealed.

The standard's aim of getting the liability onto the statement of financial position is gradually being achieved but it has proved difficult with some companies structuring lease contracts to have leases, which are in substance finance leases, classified as operating leases. The effect has been that the asset and liability did not appear on the statement of financial position and so the debt/equity ratio was artificially lower and the return on capital employed artificially higher.

The explosive growth of additional and complex forms of financial arrangements during the 1980s focused attention on the need to increase the disclosure and awareness of such arrangements and led to substance over form being included as one of the qualities of reliable information in the *Framework for the Preparation and Presentation of Financial Statements*.

11.3.2 *Framework for the Preparation and Presentation of Financial Statements*

The *Framework* makes the following observations relating to the reliability characteristic:

Reliability

To be useful, information must also be reliable. Information has the quality of reliability when it is free from material error and bias and can be depended upon by users to **represent faithfully** that which it either purports to represent or could reasonably be expected to represent.

Faithful representation

To be reliable, information must represent faithfully the transactions and other events it either purports to represent or could reasonably be expected to represent. Thus, for example, a balance sheet should represent faithfully the transactions and other events that result in **assets, liabilities and equity** of the entity at the reporting date which meet the recognition criteria.

Substance over form

If information is to represent faithfully the transactions and other events that it purports to represent, it is necessary that they be accounted for and presented in accordance with their **substance and economic reality and not merely their legal form**.

The key points are that faithful representation requires that assets, liabilities and equity be reported in the statement of financial position in accordance with their substance. In fact, it is difficult to see how a faithful representation could be achieved if the economic reality of transactions were not reported in accordance with their commercial substance.

11.3.3 Accounting for substance over form

The IASB has not issued a standard on accounting for substance over form and therefore guidance must be sought from the *Framework for the Preparation and Presentation of Financial Statements* which we see from above provides that:

> a balance sheet should represent faithfully the transactions and other events that result in **assets, liabilities and equity**.

This means that to account for substance we need to consider the definitions of assets and liabilities as these will dictate the substance of a transaction. If a transaction or item meets the definition of an asset or liability and certain recognition criteria, it should be recognised on the statement of financial position regardless of the legal nature of the transaction or item.

The definitions of assets and liabilities[3] are as follows:

- An **asset** is a resource controlled by an entity as a result of past events and from which future economic benefits are expected to flow to the entity.

- A **liability** is a present obligation of the entity arising from past events, the settlement of which is expected to result in an outflow from the entity of resources embodying economic benefits.

The definitions emphasise **economic benefits controlled** (assets) and **economic benefits transferable** (liabilities) – not legal ownership of, or title to, assets and possession of legal responsibilities for liabilities.

11.3.4 How to apply the definitions

This involves the consideration of key factors in analysing the commercial implications of an individual transaction. The key factors are:

1 **Substance** must first be identified by determining whether the transaction has given rise to new assets or liabilities for the reporting entity and whether it has changed the entity's existing assets and liabilities.

2 **Rights** or other access to benefits (i.e. possession of an asset) must be evidenced by the entity's exposure to risks inherent in the benefits, taking into account the likelihood of those risks having a commercial effect in practice.

3 **Obligations** to transfer benefits (i.e. acceptance of a liability) must be evidenced by the existence of some circumstance by which the entity is unable to avoid, legally or commercially, an outflow of benefits.

4 **Options, guarantees or conditional provisions** incorporated in a transaction should have their commercial effect assessed within the context of all the aspects and implications of the transaction in order to determine what assets and liabilities exist.

11.3.5 When is recognition required in the statement of financial position?

Having applied the definition to determine the existence of an asset or liability, it is then necessary to decide whether to include the asset or liability in the statement of financial position. This decision necessitates:

● sufficient evidence that a transfer of economic benefits is probable; and

● that monetary evaluation of the item is measurable with sufficient reliability.[4]

11.4 Illustrations of the application of substance over form

The following examples relating to consignment stocks, sale and repurchase agreements and debt factoring show how to identify the substance of a transaction. In each case it is essential in order to obtain accurate figures for the current assets – this in turn has an effect on the Current and Acid test ratios.

11.4.1 Inventory on consignment

Risks and rewards remain with the consignor

Inventory on consignment normally remains the property of the consignor until the risks and rewards have been transferred to the consignee, usually when a sale has been made by the consignee or the consignee takes legal ownership of the goods. This is illustrated by the following extract from the 2008 Annual Report of Imperial Tobacco:

Revenue is recognized on products on consignment when these are sold by the consignee.

The 2008 Annual Report of Deere and Company refers specifically to the risks and rewards of ownership as follows:

Revenue Recognition
Sales of equipment and service parts are recorded when the sales price is determinable and the risks and rewards of ownership are transferred to independent parties based on the sales agreements in effect. In the US and most international locations, this transfer occurs primarily when goods are shipped. In Canada and some other international locations, certain goods are shipped to dealers on a consignment basis under which the risks and rewards of ownership are not transferred to the dealer. Accordingly, in these locations, sales are not recorded until a retail customer has purchased the goods.

Risks and rewards transferred to the consignee

However, there are circumstances where, although the legal ownership is retained by the consignor, the economic risks and rewards are transferred to the consignee. It is necessary for these transactions to determine the commercial impact of the transaction.

How is the commercial impact determined?

By consignment, we normally understand that the consignee has the right to return the goods. However, a contract might vary this right and so we need to consider rights of each party to have the inventory returned to the consignor.

Effect of penalty provisions

The agreement may contain an absolute right of return of the inventory to the consignor, but in practice penalty provisions may effectively neutralise the right so that inventory is never returned.

EXAMPLE ● Producer P plc supplies leisure caravans to caravan dealer C Ltd on the following terms:

1 Each party has the option to have the caravans returned to the producer.

2 C Ltd pays a rental charge of 1% per month of the cost price of the caravan as consideration for exhibiting the caravan in its showrooms.

3 The eventual sale of a caravan necessitates C Ltd remitting to P plc the lower of:

   (a) the ex-factory price of the caravan when first delivered to C Ltd; or

   (b) the current ex-factory price of the caravan, less all rentals paid to date.

4 If the caravans remain unsold for six months, C Ltd must pay for each unsold caravan on the terms specified above.

To some extent, the risks and rewards of ownership are shared between both parties and the substance is not always easy to identify. However, in practice we must decide in favour of one party because it is not acceptable to show the caravans partly on each party's statement of financial position.

The factors in favour of treating the consigned goods as inventory of P plc are:

● P plc's right to demand the return of the vans;

● C Ltd's ability to return the vans to P plc;

● P plc is deriving a rental income per caravan for six months or until the time of sale, whichever occurs first.

The factors in favour of treating the goods as the inventory of C Ltd are:

● C Ltd's obligation to pay for unsold vans at the end of six months;

● the payment of a monthly rental charge: this may be considered as interest on the amount outstanding;

● C Ltd's payment need not exceed the ex-works price existing at the time of supply.

However, if C Ltd has an **unrestricted** right to return the caravans before the six months have elapsed it can, in theory, avoid the promise to pay for the caravans. Indeed, providing the ex-works cost has not increased beyond the rental (i.e. 1% per month), the company can recover the sum of the rental. However, the right might not be unrestricted, for example, disputes may develop if the exhibited caravans suffer wear and tear considered excessive by

P plc and the return is not accepted. Because the substance is not always easy to identify, a decision may be delayed in practice to observe how the terms actually operated, on the basis that what actually transpired constitutes the substance.

11.4.2 Sale and repurchase agreements

Sale and repurchase agreements appear in a variety of guises. The essential ingredient is that the original holder or purported vendor of the asset does not relinquish physical control: it retains access to the economic benefits and carries exposure to the commercial risks. In short, the characteristics of a normal sale are absent. Substance would deem that such a transaction should be treated as non-sale, the asset in question remaining in the statement of financial position of the purported vendor.

In deciding whether it is a sale or a finance agreement, consider which party enjoys the benefits and suffers the risk between sale and repurchase. In the simplest version of this kind of contract, this will usually be indicated by the prices at which the two transactions are arranged. If the prices are market prices current at the date of each transaction, risks and rewards of ownership rest with the buyer for the period between the two transactions. But if the later price displays any arithmetic linking with the former, this suggests a relationship of principal and interest between the two dates. Thus benefits and risk reside with the original entity-seller, who is in effect a borrower; the original entity-buyer is in effect a lender as in the following example.

EXAMPLE ● A company specialising in building domestic houses sells a proportion of its landholding to a merchant bank for £750,000 on 25 March 20X5, agreeing to repurchase the land for £940,800 on 24 March 20X7. The land remains under the control and supervision of the vendor.

Substance deems this contract to be a financing arrangement. The risks and rewards of ownership have not been transferred to the bank. Money has been borrowed on the security of the land. The bank is to receive a fixed sum of the capital of £750,000 and an additional £190,800 at the end of a two-year term. This equates in effect to compound interest at 12% per annum. The statement of financial position should retain the land as an asset, the cash inflow of £750,000 being displayed as a loan, redeemed two years later by its repayment at £750,000 plus the accrued interest of £190,800. Accounting for the substance of the transaction will result in a higher debt/equity ratio and a lower Return on Total Assets.

11.4.3 Debt factoring

Factoring is a means of accelerating the cash inflow by selling trade receivables to a third party, with the sales ledger administration being retained by the entity or handed over to the third party – this is purely a practical consideration, for example, the entity might have the better collection facilities.

How to determine whether the factoring is a sale of trade receivables or a borrowing arrangement

We need to consider whether the transaction really is a sale in substance, or merely a borrowing arrangement with collateral in the form of accounts receivable. In practice, this means identifying who bears the risk of ownership.

The main risk of ownership of trade receivables is the bad debt risk and the risk of slow payment. If these risks have been transferred to a third party the substance of the factoring arrangement is a genuine sale of accounts receivable, but if these risks are retained by the enterprise the factoring arrangement is in substance a loan arrangement. To decide on the transference of risks, the details of the agreement with the third party must be established.

If the agreement transfers the debts **without recourse** then the third party accepts the risks and will have no recourse to the enterprise in the event of non-payment by the debtor. The receipt of cash by the enterprise from the third party in this situation would be recorded to reduce the balance of receivables in the statement of financial position.

If the agreement transfers the debts **with recourse** then the third party has not accepted the risks and in the event of default by the debtor the third party will seek redress from the enterprise. The substance of this arrangement is a financing transaction and therefore any cash received by the enterprise from the third party will be recorded as a liability until the debtor pays. Only at that point do the risk and the obligation to repay the third party disappear.

The above examples of substance over form concentrate on the fair representation of assets and liabilities on the statement of financial position, i.e. if a transaction creates something that meets the definition of an asset or liability, it should be recognised. If, on the other hand, the risks and rewards of an asset are passed to another party, it should be derecognised from the statement of financial position regardless of the legal nature of the transaction.

11.5 Provisions – their impact on the statement of financial position

The IASC approved IAS 37 *Provisions, Contingent Liabilities and Contingent Assets*[5] in July 1998. The key objective of IAS 37 is to ensure that appropriate recognition criteria and measurement bases are applied and that sufficient information is disclosed in the notes to enable users to understand their nature, timing and amount.

The IAS sets out a useful **decision tree**, shown in Figure 11.1, for determining whether an event requires the creation of a provision, the disclosure of a contingent liability or no action.

In June 2005 the IASB issued an exposure draft, IAS 37 *Non-Financial Liabilities*, to revise IAS 37.

We will now consider IAS 37 treatment of provisions, contingent liabilities and contingent assets.

11.5.1 Provisions

IAS 37 is mainly concerned with provisions and the distorting effect they can have on profit trends, income and capital gearing. It defines a provision as 'a liability of uncertain timing or amount'.

In particular it targets 'big bath' provisions that companies historically have been able to make. This is a type of creative accounting that it has been tempting for directors to make in order to smooth profits without any reasonable certainty that the provision would actually be required in subsequent periods. Sir David Tweedie, the chairman of the IASB, has said:

> A main focus of [IAS 37] is 'big-bath' provisions. Those who use them sometimes pray in aid of the concept of prudence. All too often however the provision is wildly excessive and conveniently finds its way back to the statement of comprehensive income in a later period. The misleading practice needs to be stopped and [IAS 37] proposes that in future provisions should only be allowed when the company has an unavoidable obligation – an **intention** which may or may not be fulfilled will **not be enough**. Users of accounts can't be expected to be mind readers.

Figure 11.1 Decision tree

Figure 11.1 Decision tree

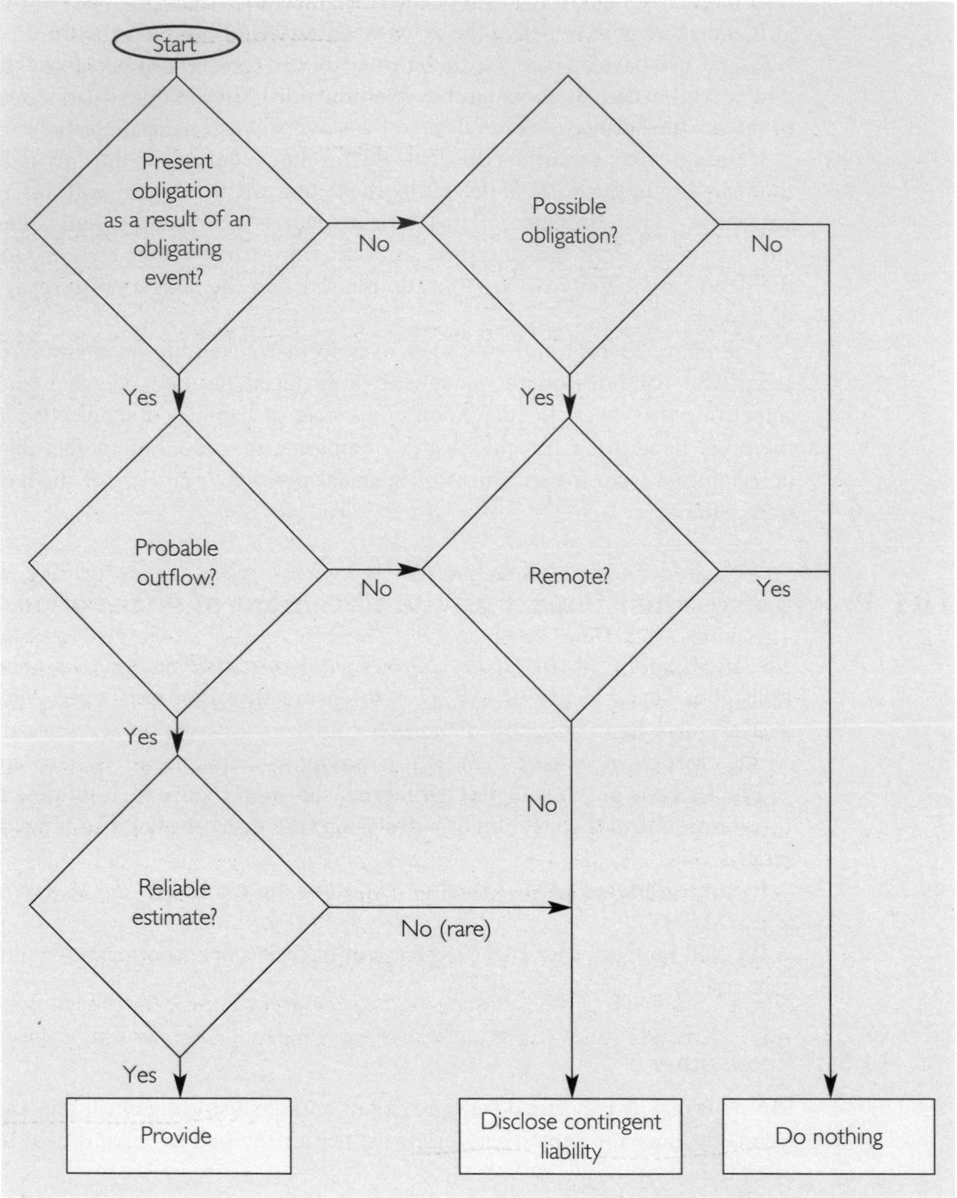

11.5.2 What are the general principles that IAS 37 applies to the recognition of a provision?

The general principles are that a provision should be recognised when:[6]

(a) an entity has a **present obligation** (legal or constructive) **as a result of past events**;

(b) it is **probable** that a transfer of **economic benefits will be required to settle the obligation**;

(c) **a reliable estimate** can be made of the amount of the obligation.

Provisions by their nature relate to the future. This means that there is a need for estimation and IAS 37 comments[7] that **the use of estimates is an essential part of the preparation of financial statements and does not undermine their reliability**.

The IAS addresses the uncertainties arising in respect of present obligation, past event, probable transfer of economic benefits and reliable estimates when deciding whether to recognise a provision.

Present obligation

The test to be applied is whether it is more likely than not, i.e. more than 50% chance of occurring. For example, if involved in a disputed lawsuit, the company is required to take account of all available evidence including that of experts and of events after the reporting period to decide if there is a greater than 50% chance that the lawsuit will be decided against the company.

Where it is more likely that no present obligation exists at the period end date, the company discloses a contingent liability, unless the possibility of a transfer of economic resources is remote.

Past event[8]

A past event that leads to a present obligation is called an **obligating event**. This is a new term with which to become familiar. This means that the company has no realistic alternative to settling the obligation. The IAS defines no alternative as being only where the settlement of the obligation can be enforced by law or, in the case of a constructive obligation, where the event creates valid expectations in other parties that the company will discharge the obligation.

The IAS stresses that it is only those obligations arising from past events existing independently of a company's future actions that are recognised as provisions, e.g. clean-up costs for unlawful environmental damage that has occurred require a provision; environmental damage that is not unlawful but is likely to become so and involve clean-up costs will not be provided for until legislation is virtually certain to be enacted as drafted.

Probable transfer of economic benefits[9]

The IAS defines probable as meaning that the event is more likely than not to occur. Where it is not probable, the company discloses a contingent liability unless the possibility is remote.

11.5.3 What are the general principles that IAS 37 applies to the measurement of a provision?

IAS 37 states[10] that the amount recognised as a provision should be the *best estimate* of the expenditure required to settle the present obligation at the period end date.

Best estimate is defined as the amount that a company would rationally pay to settle the obligation or to transfer it to a third party. The estimates of outcome and financial effect are determined by the judgement of management supplemented by experience of similar transactions and reports from independent experts. Management deal with the uncertainties as to the amount to be provided in a number of ways:

- A class obligation exists
  - where the provision involves a large population of items such as a warranty provision, statistical analysis of expected values should be used to determine the amount of the provision.

- A single obligation exists
  - where a single obligation is being measured, the individual most likely outcome may be the best estimate;
  - however, there may be other outcomes that are significantly higher or lower indicating that expected values should be determined.

For example, a company had been using unlicensed parts in the manufacture of its products and, at the year end, no decision had been reached by the court. The plaintiff was seeking damages of $10 million.

In the draft accounts a provision had been made of $5.85 million. This had been based on the entity's lawyers estimate that there was a 20% chance that the plaintiff would be unsuccessful and a 25% chance that the entity would be required to pay $10 million and a 55% chance of $7 million becoming payable to the plaintiff. The provision had been calculated as 25% of $0 + 55% of $7 million + 20% of $10 million.

The finance director disagreed with this on the grounds that it was more likely than not that there would be an outflow of funds of $7 million and required an additional $1.15 million to be provided.

Management must avoid creation of excessive provisions based on a prudent view:

- Uncertainty does not justify the creation of excessive provisions[11]
  - if the projected costs of a particular adverse outcome are estimated on a prudent basis, that outcome should not then be deliberately treated as more probable than is realistically the case.

The IAS states[12] that 'where the effect of the time value of money is material, the amount of a provision should be the present value of the expenditures expected to be required to settle the obligation'.

Present value is arrived at[13] by discounting the future obligation at 'a pre-tax rate (or rates) that reflect(s) current market assessments of the time value of money and the risks specific to the liability. The discount rate(s) should not reflect risks for which future cash flow estimates have been adjusted.'

If provisions are recognised at present value, a company will have to account for the unwinding of the discounting. As a simple example, assume a company is making a provision at 31 December 2008 for an expected cash outflow of €1 million on 31 December 2010. The relevant discount factor is estimated at 10%. Assume the estimated cash flows do not change and the provision is still required at 31 December 2009.

	€000
Provision recognised at 31 December 2008 (€1m × 1/1.121)	826
Provision recognised at 31 December 2009 (€1m × 1/1.1)	909
Increase in the provision	83

This increase in the provision is purely due to discounting for one year in 2009 as opposed to two years in 2008. This increase in the provision must be recognised as an expense in profit or loss, usually as a finance cost, although IAS 37 does not make this mandatory.

The extract from the 2005/2006 Annual Report of Scottish Power highlights the unwinding of the discounting policy:

Mine reclamation and Closure costs

Provision was made for mine reclamation and closure costs when an obligation arose out of events prior to the statement of financial position date. The amount recognized was the present value of the estimated future expenditure determined in accordance with local conditions and requirements. A corresponding asset was also created of an amount equal to the provision. This asset, together with the cost of the mine, was subsequently depreciated on a unit of production basis. The unwinding of the discount was included within finance costs.

11.5.4 Application of criteria illustrated

Scenario 1

An offshore oil exploration company is required by its licence to remove the rig and restore the seabed. Management have estimated that 85% of the eventual cost will be incurred in removing the rig and 15% through the extraction of oil. The company's practice on similar projects has been to account for the decommissioning costs using the 'unit of production' method whereby the amount required for decommissioning was built up year by year, in line with production levels, to reach the amount of the expected costs by the time production ceased.

Decision process

1 **Is there a present obligation as a result of a past event?**
   The construction of the rig has created a legal obligation under the licence to remove the rig and restore the seabed.

2 **Is there a probable transfer of economic benefits?**
   This is probable.

3 **Can the amount of the outflow be reasonably estimated?**
   A best estimate can be made by management based on past experience and expert advice.

4 **Conclusion**
   A provision should be created of 85% of the eventual future costs of removal and restoration.
      This provision should be discounted if the effect of the time value of money is material.
      A provision for the 15% relating to restoration should be created when oil production commences.

The unit of production method is not acceptable in that the decommissioning costs relate to damage already done.

Scenario 2

A company has a private jet costing £24 million. Air regulations required it to be overhauled every four years. An overhaul costs £1.6 million. The company policy has been to create a provision for depreciation of £2 million on a straight-line basis over twelve years and an annual provision of £400,000 to meet the cost of the required overhaul every four years.

Decision process

1 **Is there a present obligation as a result of a past obligating event?**
   There is no present obligation. The company could avoid the cost of the overhaul by, for example, selling the aircraft.

2 **Conclusion**
   No provision for cost of overhaul can be recognised. Instead of a provision being recognised, the depreciation of the aircraft takes account of the future incidence of maintenance costs, i.e. an amount equivalent to the expected maintenance costs is depreciated over four years.

11.5.5 Disclosures

Specific disclosures,[14] for each material class of provision, should be given as to the amount recognised at the year-end and about any movements in the year, e.g.:

- **Increases in provisions** – any new provisions; any increases to existing provisions; and, where provisions are carried at present value, any change in value arising from the passage of time or from any movement in the discount rate.

- **Reductions in provisions** – any amounts utilised during the period; management are required to review provisions at each reporting date and
  - adjust to reflect the current best estimates; and
  - if it is no longer probable that a transfer of economic benefits will be required to settle the obligation, the provision should be reversed.

Disclosures need not be given in cases where to do so would be seriously prejudicial to the company's interests. For example, an extract from the Technotrans 2002 Annual Report states:

> A competitor filed patent proceedings in 2000, . . . the court found in favour of the plaintiff . . . paves the way for a claim for compensation which may have to be determined in further legal proceedings . . . the particulars pursuant to IAS 37.85 are not disclosed, in accordance with IAS 37.92, in order not to undermine the company's situation substantially in the ongoing legal dispute.

- **A provision for future operating losses** should not be recognised (unless under a contractual obligation) **because there is no obligation at the reporting date**. However, where a contract becomes onerous (see next point) and cannot be avoided, then a provision should be made.

  This can be contrasted to cases where a company supplies a product as a loss leader to gain a foothold in the market. In the latter case, the company may cease production at any time. Accordingly, no provision should be recognised as no obligation exists.

A provision should be recognised if there is an onerous contract. An onerous contract is one entered into with another party under which the unavoidable costs of fulfilling the contract exceed the revenues to be received and where the entity would have to pay compensation to the other party if the contract was not fulfilled. A typical example in times of recession is the requirement to make a payment to secure the early termination of a lease where it has been imossible to sub-let the premises. This situtaion could arise where there has been a down-turn in business and an entity seeks to reduce its annual lease payments on premises that are no longer required.

The nature of an onerous contract will vary with the type of business activity. For example, the following is an extract from the Kuoni Travel Holding AG 2001 Annual Report when it created a provision of over CHF80m:

> The provision for onerous contracts covers the loss anticipated in connection with excess flight capacity at Scandinavian charter airline Novair for the period up to the commencement of the 2005 summer season and resulting from the leasing agreement for an Airbus A-330. Until this time, the aircraft will be leased, for certain periods only to other airlines at the current low rates prevailing in the market. The leasing agreement will expire in autumn 2007.

- **A provision for restructuring** should only be recognised when there is a commitment supported by:

(a) a detailed formal plan for the restructuring identifying at least:

   (i) the business or part of the business concerned;

   (ii) the principal locations affected;

   (iii) details of the approximate number of employees who will receive compensation payments;

   (iv) the expenditure that will be undertaken; and

   (v) when the plan will be implemented; and

(b) has raised a valid expectation in those affected that it will carry out the restructuring by implementing its restructuring plans or announcing its main features to those affected by it.

- **A provision for restructuring should not be created merely on the intention to restructure**. For example, a management or board decision to restructure taken before the reporting date does not give rise to a constructive obligation at the reporting date unless the company has, before the reporting date:

  – started to implement the restructuring plan, e.g. dismantling plant or selling assets;

  – announced the main features of the plan with sufficient detail to raise the valid expectation of those affected that the restructuring will actually take place.

- **A provision for restructuring** should only include the direct expenditures arising from the restructuring which are necessarily entailed and not associated with the ongoing activities of the company. For example, the following costs which relate to the future conduct of the business are not included:

  – retraining costs; relocation costs; marketing costs; investment in new systems and distribution networks.

- **A provision for environmental liabilities** should be recognised at the time and to the extent that the entity becomes obliged, legally or constructively, to rectify environmental damage or to perform restorative work on the environment. This means that a provision should be set up only for the entity's costs to meet its *legal* obligations. It could be argued that any provision for any additional expenditure on environmental issues is a public relations decision and should be written off.

- **A provision for decommissioning costs** should be recognised to the extent that decommissioning costs relate to damage already done or goods and services already received.

11.5.6 The use of provisions

Only expenditures that relate to the original provision are to be set against it because to set expenditures against a provision that was originally recognised for another purpose would conceal the impact of two different events.

Illustration of accounting policy from Scottish Power 2005/06 Annual Report

Mine reclamation and closure costs

Provision was made for mine reclamation and closure costs when an obligation arose out of events prior to the statement of financial position date. The amount recognised was the present value of the estimated future expenditure determined in accordance with local conditions and requirements. A corresponding asset was also created of an amount equal to the provision. This asset, together with the cost of the mine, was subsequently depreciated on a unit of production basis. The unwinding of the discount was included within finance costs.

11.5.7 Contingent liabilities

IAS 37 deals with provisions and contingent liabilities within the same IAS because the IASB regarded all provisions as contingent as they are uncertain in timing and amount. For the purposes of the accounts, it distinguishes between provisions and contingent liabilities in that:

● Provisions are a present obligation requiring a probable transfer of economic benefits that can be reliably estimated – a provision can therefore be recognised as a liability.

● Contingent liabilities fail to satisfy these criteria, e.g. lack of a reliable estimate of the amount; not probable that there will be a transfer of economic benefits; yet to be confirmed that there is actually an obligation – a contingent liability cannot therefore be recognised in the accounts but may be disclosed by way of note to the accounts or not disclosed if an outflow of economic benefits is remote.

Where the occurrence of a contingent liability becomes sufficiently probable, it falls within the criteria for recognition as a provision as detailed above and should be accounted for accordingly and recognised as a liability in the accounts.

Where the likelihood of a contingent liability is possible, but not probable and not remote, disclosure should be made, for each class of contingent liability, where practicable, of:

(a) an estimate of its financial effect, taking into account the inherent risks and uncertainties and, where material, the time value of money;

(b) an indication of the uncertainties relating to the amount or timing of any outflow; and

(c) the possibility of any reimbursement.

For example, an extract from the 2003 Annual Report of Manchester United plc informs as follows:

Contingent liabilities
Transfer fees payable
Under the terms of certain contracts with other football clubs in respect of player transfers, certain additional amounts would be payable by the Group if conditions as to future team selection are met. The maximum that could be payable is £12,005,000 (2002 £12,548,000).
Guarantee on behalf of associate
Manchester United PLC has undertaken to guarantee the property lease of its associate, Timecreate Limited. The lease term is 35 years with annual rentals of £400,000.

11.5.8 Contingent assets

A contingent asset is a possible asset that arises from past events whose existence will be confirmed only by the occurrence of one or more uncertain future events not wholly within the entity's control.

Recognition as an asset is only allowed if the asset is *virtually certain*, i.e. and therefore by definition no longer contingent.

Disclosure by way of note is required if an inflow of economic benefits is *probable*. The disclosure would include a brief description of the nature of the contingent asset at the reporting date and, where practicable, an estimate of their financial effect taking into account the inherent risks and uncertainties and, where material, the time value of money.

No disclosure is required where the chance of occurrence is anything less than probable. For the purposes of IAS 37, probable is defined as more likely than not, i.e. more than a 50% chance.

11.6 ED IAS 37 *Non-financial Liabilities*

In June 2005, the International Accounting Standards Board (IASB) proposed amendments to IAS 37 *Provisions, Contingent Liabilities and Contingent Assets*. The new title strips IAS 37 of the words 'Provisions', 'Contingent' and 'Assets' and adds the term 'Non-financial' to create the new title IAS 37 *Non-financial Liabilities*. It is interesting to see that the new Standard has been developed around the *Framework*'s definitions of an asset and a liability.

It appears that the word 'non-financial' has been added to distinguish the subject from 'financial liabilities' which are covered by IAS 32 and IAS 39.

11.6.1 The 'old' IAS 37 Provisions, Contingent Liabilities and Contingent Assets

To understand the 'new' approach in ED IAS 37 (Non-financial liabilities), it is necessary first to look at the 'old' IAS 37. The old treatment can be represented by the following table:

Probability	Contingent liabilities	Contingent assets
Virtually certain	Liability	Asset
Probable ($p > 50\%$)	Provide	Disclose
Possible ($p < 50\%$)	Disclose	No disclosure
Remote	No disclosure	No disclosure

Note that contingent liabilities are those items where the probability is less than 50% ($p < 50\%$). Where, however, the liability is probable, i.e. the probability is $p > 50\%$, the item is classified as a provision and not a contingent liability. Normally, such a provision will be reported as the product of the value of the potential liability and its probability.

Note that the approach to contingent assets is different in that the 'prudence' concept is used which means that only virtually certain assets are reported as an asset. If the probability is probable, i.e. $p > 50\%$ then contingent assets are disclosed by way of a note to the accounts and if the probability is $p < 50\%$ then there is no disclosure.

Criticisms of the 'old' IAS 37

The criticisms included the following:

- The 'old' IAS 37 was not even-handed in its treatment of contingent assets and liabilities. In ED IAS 37 the treatment of contingent assets is similar to contingent liabilities, and provisions are merged into the treatment of contingent liabilities.

- The division between 'probable' and 'possible' was too strict/crude (at the $p = 50\%$ level) rather than being proportional. For instance, if a television manufacturer was considering the need to provide for guarantee claims (e.g. on televisions sold with a three-year warranty), then it is probable that each television sold would have a less than 50% chance of being subject to a warranty claim and so no provision would need to be made. However, if the company sold 10,000 televisions, it is almost certain that there would be some claims which would indicate that a provison should be made. A company could validly take either treatment, but the effect on the financial statements would be different.

- If there was a single possible legal claim, then the company could decide it was 'possible' and just disclose it in the financial statements. However, a more reasonable treatment would be to assess the claim as the product of the amount likely to be paid and its probability. This latter treatment is used in the new ED IAS 37.

11.6.2 Approach taken by ED IAS 37 *Non-financial Liabilities*

The new proposed standard uses the term 'non-financial liabilities' which it defines as 'a liability other than a financial liability as defined in IAS32 *Financial Instruments: Presentation*'. In considering ED IAS 37, we will look at the proposed treatment of contingent liabilities/provisions and contingent assets, starting from the *Framework's* definitions of a liability and an asset.

The *Framework*'s definition

The *Framework*, para. 91, requires a liability to be recognised as follows:

> A liability is recognised in the statement of financial position when it is probable that an outflow of resources embodying economic benefits will result from the settlement of a present obligation and the amount at which the settlement will take place can be measured reliably.

ED IAS 37 approach to provisions

Considering a provision first, old IAS 37 (para. 10) defines it as follows:

> A provision is distinguished from other liabilities because there is uncertainty about the timing or amount of the future expenditure required in settlement.

ED IAS 37 argues that a provision should be reported as a liability, as it satisfies the *Framework*'s definition of a liability. It makes the point that there is no reference in the *Framework* to 'uncertainty about the timing or amount of the future expenditure required in settlement'. It considers a provision to be just one form of liability which should be treated as a liability in the financial statements.

Will the item 'provision' no longer appear in financial statements?

One would expect that to be the result of the ED classification. However, the proposed standard does not take the step of prohibiting the use of the term as seen in the following extract (para. 9):

> In some jurisdictions, some classes of liabilities are described as provisions, for example those liabilities that can be measured only by using a substantial degree of estimation. Although this [draft] Standard does not use the term 'provision', it does not prescribe how entities should describe their non-financial liabilities. Therefore, entities may describe some classes of non-financial liabilities as provisions in their financial statements.

ED IAS 37 approach to contingent liabilities

Now considering contingent liabilities, old IAS 37 (para. 10) defines these as:

(a) a possible obligation that arises from past events and whose existence will be confirmed only by the occurrence or non-occurrence of one or more uncertain future events not wholly within the control of the entity; or

(b) a present obligation that arises from past events, but is not recognised because:
   (i) it is not probable that an outflow of resources embodying economic benefits will be required to settle the obligation; or
   (ii) the amount of the obligation cannot be measured with sufficient reliability.

This definition means that the old IAS 37 has taken the strict approach of using the term 'possible' ($p < 50\%$) when it required no liability to be recognised.

ED IAS 37 is different in that it takes a two-stage approach in considering whether 'contingent liabilities' are 'liabilities'. To illustrate this, we will take the example of a restaurant where some customers have suffered food poisoning.

First determine whether there is a present obligation

The restaurant's year end is 30 June 20X6. If the food poisoning took place after 30 June 20X6, then this is not a 'present obligation' at the year end, so it is not a liability. If the food poisoning occurred up to 30 June, then it is a 'present obligation' at the year end, as there are possible future costs arising from the food poisoning. This is the first stage in considering whether the liability exists.

Then determine whether a liability exists

The second stage is to consider whether a 'liability' exists. The *Framework*'s definition of a liability says it is a liability if 'it is probable that an outflow of resources will result from the settlement of the present obligation'. So, there is a need to consider whether any payments (or other expenses) will be incurred as a result of the food poisoning. This may involve settling legal claims, other compensation or giving 'free' meals. The estimated cost of these items will be the liability (and expense) included in the financial statements.

The rationale

ED IAS 37 explains this process as:

- the unconditional obligation (stage 1) establishes the liability; and
- the conditional obligation (stage 2) affects the amount that will be required to settle the liability.

The liability being the amount that the entity would rationally pay to settle the present obligation or to transfer it to a third party on the statement of financial position date. Often, the liability will be estimated as the product of the maximum liability and the probability of it occurring, or a decision tree will be used with a number of possible outcomes (costs) and their probability.

In many cases, the new ED IAS 37 will cover the 'possible' category for contingent liabilities and include the item as a liability (rather than as a note to the financial statements). This gives a more 'proportional' result than the previously strict line between 'probable' ($p > 50\%$) (when a liability is included in the financial statements) and 'possible' ($p < 50\%$) (when only a note is included in the financial statements and no charge is included for the liability).

What if they cannot be measured reliably?

For other 'possible' contingent liabilities, which have not been recognised because they cannot be measured reliably, the following disclosure should be made:

- a description of the nature of the obligation;
- an explanation of why it cannot be measured reliably;
- an indication of the uncertainties relating to the amount or timing of any outflow of economic benefits; and
- the existence of any rights to reimbursement.

What disclosure is required for maximum potential liability?

ED IAS 37 does not require disclosure of the maximum potential liability, e.g. the maximum damages if the entity loses the legal case.

11.6.3 Measured reliably

The *Framework* definition of a liability includes the condition 'and the amount at which the settlement will take place can be measured reliably'. This posed a problem when drafting ED IAS 37 because of the concern that an entity could argue that the amount of a contingent liability could not be measured reliably and that there was therefore no need to include it as a liability in the financial statements – i.e. to use this as a 'cop out' to give a 'rosier' picture in the financial statements. Whilst acknowledging that in many cases a non-financial liability cannot be measured exactly, it considered that it could (and should) be estimated. It then says that cases where the liability cannot be measured reliably are 'extremely rare'. We can see from this that the ED approach is that 'measured reliably' does not mean 'measured exactly' and that cases where the liability 'cannot be measured reliably' will be 'extremely rare'.

11.6.4 Contingent asset

The *Framework*, para. 89, requires recognition of an asset as follows:

> An Asset is recognised in the statement of financial position when it is probable that the future economic benefits will flow to the entity and the asset has a cost or value that can be measured reliably.

Note that under the old IAS 37, contingent assets included items where they were 'probable' (unlike liabilities, when this was called a 'provision'). However, probable contingent assets are not included as an asset, but only included in the notes to the financial statements.

The ED IAS 37 approach

ED IAS 37 takes a similar approach to 'contingent assets' as it does to 'provisions/contingent liabilities'. It abolishes the term 'contingent asset' and replaces it with the term 'contingency'. The term contingency refers to uncertainty about the amount of the future economic benefits embodied in an asset, rather than uncertainty about whether an asset exists.

Essentially, the treatment of contingent assets is the same as contingent liabilities. The first stage is to consider whether an asset exists and the second stage is concerned with valuing the asset (i.e. the product of the value of the asset and its probability). A major change is to move contingent assets to IAS 38 *Intangible Assets* (and not include them in IAS 37).

The treatment of 'contingent assets' under IAS 38 is now similar to that for 'contingent liabilities/provisions'. This seems more appropriate than the former 'prudent approach' used by the 'old' IAS 37.

11.6.5 Reimbursements

Under the 'old' IAS 37 an asset could be damaged or destroyed, when the expense would be included in profit or loss (and any future costs included as a provision). If the insurance claim relating to this loss was made after the year-end, it is likely that no asset could be included in the financial statements as compensation for the loss, as the insurance claim was 'not certain'. In reality, this did not reflect the true situation when the insurance claim would compensate for the loss, and there would be little or no net cost.

With the new rules under ED IAS 37, the treatment of contingent assets and contingent liabilities is the same, so an asset would be included in the statement of financial position as the insurance claim, which would offset the loss on damage or destruction of the asset. But, ED IAS 37 says the liability relating to the loss (e.g. the costs of repair) must be stated separately from the asset for the reimbursement (i.e. the insurance claim) – they cannot be netted off (although they will be in profit or loss).

11.6.6 Constructive and legal obligations

The term 'constructive obligation' is important in determining whether a liability exists. ED IAS 37 (para. 10) defines it as:

> A constructive obligation is a present obligation that arises from an entity's past actions when:
>
> **(a)** by an established pattern of past practice, published policies or a sufficiently specific current statement, the entity has indicated to other parties that it will accept particular responsibilities, and
>
> **(b)** as a result, the entity has created a valid expectation in those parties, that they can reasonably rely on it to discharge those responsibilities.

It also defines a legal obligation as follows:

> A legal obligation is a present obligation that arises from the following:
>
> **(a)** a contract (through its explicit or implicit terms)
>
> **(b)** legislation, or
>
> **(c)** other operating law.

A contingent liability/provision is a liability only if it is either a constructive and/or a legal obligation. Thus, an entity would not normally make a provision (recognise a liability) for the potential costs of rectifying faulty products outside their guarantee period.

11.6.7 Present value

ED IAS 37 says that future cash flows relating to the liability should be discounted at the pre-tax discount rate. Unwinding of the discount would still need to be recognised as an interest cost.

11.6.8 Subsequent measurement and de-recognition

On subsequent measurement, ED IAS 37 says the carrying value of the non-financial liability should be reviewed at each reporting date. The non-financial liability should be derecognised when the obligation is settled, cancelled or expires.

11.6.9 Onerous contracts

If a contract becomes onerous, the entity is required to recognise a liability as the present obligation under the contract. However, if the contract becomes onerous as a result of the entity's own actions, the liability should not be recognised until it has taken the action.

11.6.10 Restructurings

ED IAS 37 says:

> An entity shall recognise a non-financial liability for a cost associated with a restructuring only when the definition of a liability has been satisfied.

There are situations where management has made a decision to restructure and the ED provides that in these cases 'a decision by the management of an entity to undertake a restructuring is not the requisite past event for recognition of a liability. A cost associated with a restructuring is recognised as a liability on the same basis as if that cost arose independently of the restructuring.

11.6.11 Other items

These include the treatment of termination costs and future operating losses where the approach is still to assess whether a liability exists. The changes to termination costs will require an amendment to IAS 19 *Employee Benefits*. In the case of termination costs, these are only recognised when a liability is incurred: e.g. the costs of closure of a factory become a liability only when the expense is incurred and redundancy costs become a liability only when employees are informed of their redundancy. In the case of future operating losses, these are not recognised as they do not relate to a past event.

Under the new ED IAS 37, the liability arises no earlier than under the 'old' IAS 37 and sometimes later.

11.6.12 Disclosure

ED IAS 37 requires the following disclosure of non-financial liabilities:

For each class of non-financial liability, the carrying amount of the liability at the period-end together with a description of the nature of the obligation.

For any class of non-financial liability with uncertainty about its estimation:

(a) a reconciliation of the carrying amounts at the beginning and end of the period showing:
   (i) liabilities incurred;
   (ii) liabilities derecognised;
   (iii) changes in the discounted amount resulting from the passage of time and the effect of any change in the discount rate; and
   (iv) other adjustments to the amount of the liability (e.g. revisions in the estimated cash flows that will be required to settle it);

(b) the expected timing of any resulting outflows of economic benefits;

(c) an indication of the uncertainties about the amount or timing of those outflows. If necessary, to provide adequate information on the major assumptions made about future events;

(d) the amount of any right to reimbursement, stating the amount of any asset that has been recognised

If a non-financial liability is not recognised because it cannot be measured reliably, that fact should be disclosed together with:

(a) a description of the nature of the obligation;

(b) an explanation of why it cannot be measured reliably;

(c) an indication of the uncertainties relating to the amount or timing of any outflow of economic benefits; and

(d) the existence of any right to reimbursement.

11.6.13 Conclusion on ED IAS 37 Non-financial Liabilities

This proposed standard makes significant changes to the subject of 'Provisions, Contingent Liabilities and Contingent Assets', which are derived from the general principles of accounting. Its good features include:

(a) It is conceptually sound by basing changes on the *Framework*'s definitions of an asset and a liability.

(b) It is more appropriate that the treatment of provisions/contingent liabilities and contingent assets should be more 'even handed'.

(c) It avoids the 'strict' breaks at 50% probability between 'probable' and 'possible'. It uses probability in estimating the liability down (effectively) to 0%.

(d) The definition of a constructive obligation has been more clearly defined.

(e) It overcomes the previous anomaly of not allowing reimbursements after the year-end (e.g. where there is an unsettled insurance claim at the year-end).

However, in some ways it could be argued that the proposed standard goes too far, particularly in its new terminology:

(a) The abolition of the term 'contingent liability' and not defining 'provision'. The new term 'non-financial liability' does not seem as meaningful as 'contingent liability'. It would seem better (more meaningful) to continue to use the term 'contingent liability' and make this encompass provisions (as it does for contingent assets).

(b) It would seem more appropriate to continue to include 'contingent assets' in this Standard, rather than move them to 'intangible assets', as the treatment of these items is similar to 'contingent liabilities'.

ED IAS 37 has proved to be a controversial exposure draft where there have been significant discussions surrounding the potential changes. This project is proceeding in parallel with other projects that the IASB has in development, such as leasing and revenue recognition, and the outcomes of those projects may influence the direction the IASB takes.

11.7 ED/2010/1 *Measurement of Liabilities in IAS 37*

This ED is a limited re-exposure of a proposed amendment to IAS 37. It deals with only one of the measurement requirements for liabilities. The ED proposes that the non-financial liability should be measured at the amount that the entity would rationally pay to be relieved of the liability.

If the liability cannot be cancelled or transferred, the liability is measured as the present value of the resources required to fulfil the obligation. It may be that the resources required are uncertain. If so, the expected value is estimated based on the probability weighted average of the outflows. The expected value is then increased to take into account the risk that the actual outcome might be higher, estimating the amount a third party would require to take over this risk.

If the liability can be cancelled or transferred, there is a choice available – to fulfil the obligation, to cancel the obligation or to transfer the liability. The logical choice is to choose the lower of the present value of fulfilling the obligation and the amount that would have to be paid to either cancel or transfer.

Potential impact on ratios and transparency

A new standard that applies this measurement approach will not have an identical impact on all entities – some will have to include higher non-liabilities on their statement of financial position, others will have to reduce the non-liabilities. This means that there will be different impacts on returns on equity, gearing and debt covenants.

Given the process of establishing expected values and risk adjustments, it might be that additional narrative explanation will be required in the annual report – particularly if the non-liabilities are material.

11.8 Special purpose entities (SPEs) – lack of transparency

Investors rely on the financial statements presenting a true and fair view of material items. Whilst an SPE might be set up for a commercially acceptable purpose such as to finance the purchase of non-current assets it can also be designed to conceal from investors the existence of material liabilities or losses or the payment of fees to directors of the sponsor company. In the case of Enron it is reported that there was concealment of all three such material items.

11.8.1 How does an SPE operate?

Typically there are four parties involved, namely,

- the sponsor (a company such as Enron that wishes to acquire a non-current asset but wants to keep the asset and liability off the balance sheet);
- the SPE (this is the entity that will borrow the funds to acquire the non-current asset);
- the lender (a bank or institution prepared to advance funds to the SPE to acquire the asset); and
- the independent investor (who puts in at least 3% of the cost of the asset and who technically controls the SPE).

As far as the sponsor is concerned, both the asset and the liability are off the balance sheet and the sponsor enters into a lease arrangement with the SPE to make lease payments to cover the loan repayments. If required by the lender, the sponsor might also arrange for a guarantee to be provided using its own share price strength or through another party. As we recognised in the UK prior to the introduction of FRS 5, by keeping debt off the balance sheet a company's creditworthiness is improved.

The second problem was that investors were unable to rely on advice from analysts. It is reported that analysts failed to follow sound financial analysis principles, being under pressure to hype the shares, e.g. to keep the share price up particularly where their employers, such as investment banks, were making significant advisory fees.[15]

The third problem was that investors were not alerted by the auditors to the fact that such liabilities, losses and the payment of fees existed. It could be that the auditors were convinced that the financial statements complied with the requirements of US GAAP and that the SPEs did not therefore need to be consolidated. If that were the case, it could be argued that the auditor was acting professionally in reporting that the financial statements complied with US GAAP.

11.9 Impact of converting to IFRS

Owing to the importance of the statement of financial position, the impact of converging to IFRS on the statement must be considered. Changes to the statement of financial position can arise from (a) corrections that result in a change in the total assets and liabilities and (b) reclassification that do not result in any increase or decrease in total assets and liabilities.

(a) IFRS corrections

The general changes to assets and liabilities, together with an example, are shown below.
As regards liabilities, this may arise from:

● the recognition of new liabilities onto the statement of financial position, e.g. provisions for environmental and decommissioning costs; and

● the derecognition of existing liabilities, e.g. provisions for future restructuring costs that are no longer permitted to be created.

As regards assets, this may arise from:

● the recognition of new assets, e.g. derivative financial assets; and

● the derecognition of existing assets, e.g. start-up costs and research that had been currently capitalised.

(b) IFRS reclassifications

For some companies the main impact might, however, arise from the reclassification of existing assets and liabilities. This is illustrated with the following extract from the Annual Report of Arinso International – in Figure 11.2 – which converted to IFRS in 2003 and restated its 2002 statement of financial position.

Changes might affect the perceptions of risk by different investors and can therefore potentially affect the ability of companies to raise capital and provide adequate returns to investors. It is important therefore that users have an understanding of any economic impact arising from any changes.

Investors may be interested in the effect on retained earnings and distributable profits, e.g. retained earnings have increased by €1,567,936; loan creditors may be interested in the effect on non-current liabilities where there has been a decrease to €378,724 from €1,111,803 with an impact on gearing and the possibility in some companies of improved compliance with debt covenants; and creditors may be interested in the effect on liquidity with the current ratio falling from 3.6:1 to 1.5:1.

There might be difficulties in differentiating real changes in performance from the impact of the new IFRS requirements. It will be important for companies to highlight the economic impact of any changes on their business strategy, treasury management, financing, profitability and dividends, e.g. Barclays have indicated that there will be little impact on profit after tax and earnings per share but that there will be an impact on the statement of financial position as off balance sheet items are brought on to the statement of financial position.

Figure 11.2 Extract from Arinso 2002 restated balance sheet

	Belgian GAAP	IFRS
Non-current assets	16,389,061	15,420,553
Current assets		
Trade receivables	34,787,200	35,125,168
Other current assets	48,490,267	50,343,150
	99,666,528	100,888,871
Equity	61,704,696	61,704,696
Retained earnings	9,484,114	11,052,050
Non-current liabilities	1,111,803	378,724
Current liabilities		
Trade payables	9,675,272	23,056,366
Other current liabilities	17,690,643	4,697,035
	99,666,528	100,888,871

Summary

Traditional book-keeping resulted in the production of a statement of financial position that was simply a list of unused and unpaid balances on account at the close of the financial year. It was intrinsically a document confirming the double entry system but it was used by investors and analysts to assess the risk inherent in the capital structure.

Unfortunately the transaction-based nature of book-keeping created a statement of financial position incapable of keeping pace with a developing financial market of highly sophisticated transactions. By operating within the legal niceties, management was able to keep future benefits and obligations off the statement of financial position. It was also possible for capital instruments of one kind to masquerade as those of another – sometimes by accident, but often by design. This dilution in the effectiveness of the statement of financial position had to be remedied.

The IASB has addressed the problem from first principles by requiring consideration to be given to the definitions of assets and liabilities; to the accounting substance of a transaction over its legal form; to the elimination of off balance sheet finance; and to the standardisation of accounting treatment in respect of items such as leases and capital instruments.

As a consequence, the statement of financial position is rapidly becoming the primary reporting vehicle. In so doing it is tending to be seen as a efinitive statement of assets used and liabilities incurred by the reporting entity.

The process of change is unlikely to be painless, and considerable controversy will doubtless arise about whether a transaction falls within the IASB definition of an asset or liability; whether it should be recognised; and how it should be disclosed. This will remain an important developing area of regulation and the IASB is to be congratulated on its approach, which requires accountants to exercise their professional judgement.

REVIEW QUESTIONS

1 Some members of the board of directors of a company deliberating over a possible source of new capital believe that irredeemable debentures carrying a fixed annual coupon rate would suffice. They also believe that the going concern concept of the financial statements would obviate the need to include the debt thereon: the entity is a going concern and there is no intention to repay the debt; therefore disclosure is unwarranted. Discuss.

2 The Notes in the BG Group 2007 Annual Report included the following extract:

Provisions for liabilities and charges
Decommissioning

	2007	2006
	£m	£m
As at 1 January	311	260
Unwinding of discount	16	13

Decommissioning costs
The estimated cost of decommissioning at the end of the producing lives of fields is reviewed at least annually and engineering estimates and reports are updated periodically. Provision is made for the estimated cost of decommissioning at the statement of financial position date, to the extent that current circumstances indicate BG Group will ultimately bear this cost.

Explain why the provision has been increased in 2006 and 2007 by the unwinding of discount and why these increases are for different amounts.

3 As a sales incentive, a computer manufacturer, Burgot SA, offers to buy back its computers after three years at 25% of the original selling price, so providing the customer with a guaranteed residual value which would be exercised if he or she were unable to achieve a higher price in the second-hand market.

Discuss the substance of this transaction and conclude on how the transaction should be presented in the financial statements of the customer.

4 A boat manufacturer, Swann SpA, supplies its dealers on a consignment basis, which allows either Swann SpA or a dealer to require a boat to be returned. Each dealer has to arrange insurance for the boats held on consignment.

When a boat is sold to a customer, the dealer pays Swann SpA the lower of:

● the delivery price of the boat as at the date it was first supplied; or

● the current delivery price less the insurance premiums paid to date of sale.

If a boat is unsold after three months, the dealer has to pay on the same terms.

Discuss, with reasons, whether boats held by the dealers on consignment should appear as inventory in the statement of financial position of Swann SpA or the dealer.

5 Discuss the problems of interpreting financial reports when there are events after the reporting date, and the extent to which you consider IAS 10 should be amended. Illustrate your decisions with practical examples as appropriate.

6 D Ltd has a balance on its receivable's account of £100,000. Previous experience would anticipate bad debts to a maximum of 3%. The company adopts a policy of factoring its receivables. Explain how the transaction would be dealt with in the books of D Ltd under each of the following independent sets of circumstances:

(i) The factoring agreement involves a sole payment of £95,000 to complete the transaction. No further payments are to be made or received by either party to the agreement.

(ii) The receivables are transferred to the factoring entity on receipt of £93,000. The agreement provides for further payments, which will vary on the basis of timing and receipts from debtors. Interest is chargeable by the factor on a daily basis, based on the outstanding amount at the close of the day's transactions. The factor also has recourse to D Ltd for the first £10,000 of any loss.

7   Mining, nuclear and oil companies have normally provided an amount each year over the life of an enterprise to provide for decommissioning costs. Explain why the IASB considered this to be an inappropriate treatment and how these companies would be affected by IAS 37 *Provisions, Contingent Liabilities and Contingent Assets* and ED IAS 37 *Non-financial Liabilities*.

8   The following note appeared in the Jarvis plc 2004 Annual Report:

Provision against onerous lease liabilities

The provision reflects the anticipated costs arising from the Group's decision not to occupy new premises on which it has entered into a long-term lease…

Discuss the criteria for assessing whether a contract is onerous.

9   The following note appeared in the Eesti Telekom 2003 Annual Report:

Factoring of receivables

The factoring of receivables is the sale of receivables. Depending on the type of factoring contract, the buyer acquires the right to sell the receivables back to the seller (factoring with recourse) or there is no right to resell and all the risks and rewards are transferred from the seller to the buyer (factoring without recourse).

Explain how the accounting treatment would differ between a non-recourse and a recourse factoring agreement.

EXERCISES

An extract from the solution is provided on the Companion Website (www.pearsoned.co.uk/elliott-elliott) for exercises marked with an asterisk (*).

Question 1

(a) Provisions are particular kinds of liabilities. It therefore follows that provisions should be recognised when the definition of a liability has been met. The key requirement of a liability is a present obligation and thus this requirement is critical also in the context of the recognition of a provision. IAS 37 *Provisions, Contingent Liabilities and Contingent Assets* deals with this area.

Required:
(i) Explain why there was a need for detailed guidance on accounting for provisions.
(ii) Explain the circumstances under which a provision should be recognised in the financial statements according to IAS 37 *Provisions, Contingent Liabilities and Contingent Assets*.

(b) World Wide Nuclear Fuels, a public limited company, disclosed the following information in its financial statements for the year ending 30 November 20X9:

The company purchased an oil company during the year. As part of the sale agreement, oil has to be supplied to the company's former holding company at an uneconomic rate for a period of five years. As a result, a provision for future operating losses has been set up of $135m, which relates solely to the uneconomic supply of oil. Additionally the oil company is exposed to environmental liabilities arising out of its past obligations, principally in respect of soil and ground water restoration costs, although currently there is no legal obligation to carry out the work. Liabilities for environmental costs are provided for when the group determines a formal plan of action on the closure of an inactive site. It has been decided to provide for $120m in respect of the environmental liability on the acquisition of the oil company. World Wide Nuclear Fuels has a reputation for ensuring the preservation of the environment in its business activities. The company is also facing a legal claim for $200 million from a competitor who claims they have breached a patent in one of their processes. World Wide Nuclear Fuels has obtained legal advice that the claim has little chance of success and the insurance advisers have indicated that to insure against losing the case would cost $20 million as a premium.

Required:
Discuss whether the provision has been accounted for correctly under IAS 37 *Provisions, Contingent Liabilities and Contingent Assets*, and whether any changes are likely to be needed under ED IAS 37.

Question 2

The directors of Apple Pie plc at the September 20X5 board meeting were expressing concern about falling sales and the lack of cash to meet a dividend for the current year ending 31 December at the same rate as the previous year. They suggested to the finance director that:

● equipment with a book value of £40 million as at the beginning of the year and an estimated useful economic life of three years should be sold for £62.5 million;

● the £62.5 million and £40 million should be included in the sales and cost of sales for the period resulting in an improvement of £22.5 million in profit which would cover the proposed dividend;

● the equipment should then be leased back at 1 October 20X5 for the remainder of its economic life. The commercial rate of interest for a similar lease agreement had been 10%.

Required:
Draft the finance director's response to their suggestion and indicate the effect on the financial statements as at 31 December 20X5 if the lease agreement is entered into on 1 October 20X5.

* Question 3

On 20 December 20X6 one of Incident plc's lorries was involved in an accident with a car. The lorry driver was responsible for the accident and the company agreed to pay for the repair to the car. The company put in a claim to its insurers on 17 January 20X7 for the cost of the claim. The company expected the claim to be settled by the insurance company except for a £250 excess on the insurance policy. The insurance company may dispute the claim and not pay out, however, the company believes that the chance of this occurring is low. The cost of repairing the car was estimated as £5,000, all of which was incurred after the year end.

Required:
Explain how this item should be treated in the financial statements for the year ended 31 December 20X6 according to both IAS 37 and ED IAS 37 *Non-financial Liabilities*.

Question 4

Plasma Ltd, a manufacturer of electrical goods, guarantees them for 12 months from the date of purchase by the customer. If a fault occurs after the guarantee period, but is due to faulty manufacture or design of the product, the company repairs or replaces the product. However, the company does not make this practice widely known.

Required:
Explain how repairs after the guarantee period should be treated in the financial statements.

Question 5

In 20X6 Alpha AS made the decision to close a loss-making department in 20X7. The company proposed to make a provision for the future costs of termination in the 20X6 profit or loss. Its argument was that a liability existed in 20X6 which should be recognised in 20X6. The auditor objected to recognising a liability, but agreed to recognition if it could be shown that the management decision was irrevocable.

Required:
Discuss whether a liability exists and should be recognised in the 20X6 statement of financial position.

Question 6

Easy View Ltd had started business publishing training resource material in ring binder format for use in primary schools. Later it diversified into the hiring out of videos and had opened a chain of video hire shops. With the growing popularity of a mail order video/dvd supplier the video hire shops had become loss-making.

The company's year end was 31 March and in February the financial director (FD) was asked to prepare a report for the board on the implications of closing this segment of the business.

The position at the board meeting on 10 March was as follows:

1   It was agreed that the closure should take place from 1 April 2010 to be completed by 31 May 2010.

2   The premises were freehold except for one that was on a lease with six years to run. It was in an inner city shopping complex where many properties were empty and there was little chance of sub-letting. The annual rent was £20,000 per annum. Early termination of the lease could be negotiated for a figure of £100,000. An appropriate discount rate is 8%.

3   The office equipment and vans had a book value of £125,000 and it was expected to realise £90,000, a figure tentatively suggested by a dealer who indicated that he might be able to complete by the end of April.

4   The staff had been mainly part-time and casual employees. There were 45 managers, however, who had been with the company for a number of years. These were happy to retrain to work with the training resources operation. The cost of retraining to use publishing software was estimated at £225,000

5   Losses of £300,000 were estimated for the current year and £75,000 for the period until the closure was complete.

A week before the meeting the managing director made it clear to the FD that he wanted the segment to be treated as a discontinued operation so that the Continuing operations could reflect the profitable training segment's performance.

Required:
Draft the finance director's report to present to the MD before the meeting to clarify the financial reporting implications.

References

1 K.V. Peasnell and R.A.Yaansah, *Off-Balance Sheet Financing*, ACCA, 1988.
2 IAS 17 *Leases*, IASC, revised 1997.
3 *Framework for the Preparation and Presentation of Financial Statements*, IASC, 1989, para. 49.
4 *Ibid.*, para. 86.
5 IAS 37 *Provisions, Contingent Liabilities and Contingent Assets*, IASC, 1998.
6 *Ibid.*, para. 2.
7 *Ibid.*, para. 25.
8 *Ibid.*, para. 17.
9 *Ibid.*, para. 23.
10 *Ibid.*, para. 36.
11 *Ibid.*, para. 43.
12 *Ibid.*, para. 45.
13 *Ibid.*, para. 47.
14 *Ibid.*, para. 84.
15 B. Singleton-Green, 'Enron – how the fraud worked', *Accountancy*, May 2002, pp. 20–21.

CHAPTER 12

Financial instruments

12.1 Introduction

Accounting for financial instruments has proven to be one of the most difficult areas for the IASB to provide guidance on, and the current standards are far from perfect. In 2009 the IASB began a process to amend the existing financial instrument accounting with the issue of revised guidance on the recognition and measurement of financial instruments. It is expected over 2010 that new guidance on impairment, hedging and derecognition of assets and liabilities will also be issued. The new guidance is unlikely to be mandatory until 2013. In this chapter we will consider the main requirements of IAS 32 *Financial Instruments: Presentation*, IAS 39 *Financial Instruments: Recognition and Measurement* and IFRS 7 *Financial Instruments: Disclosure* as well as the main changes introduced by the revised standard, IFRS 9 *Financial Instruments* and the likely changes in accounting for impairment of financial assets.

Objectives

By the end of this chapter, you should be able to:

- define what financial instruments are and be able to outline the main accounting requirements under IFRS;
- comment critically on the international accounting requirements for financial instruments and understand why they continue to prove both difficult and controversial topics in accounting;
- account for different types of common financial instrument that companies may use.

12.2 Financial instruments – the IASB's problem child

International accounting has had standards on financial instruments since the late 1990s and, ever since they were introduced, they have proved the most controversial requirements of IFRS. In the late 1990s, in order to make international accounting standards generally acceptable to stock exchanges, the International Accounting Standards Committee (forerunner of the International Accounting Standards Board) introduced IAS 32 and 39. These standards drew heavily on US GAAP as that was the only comprehensive regime that had guidance in this area. Even now some national accounting standards, such as the UK regime, do not have compulsory comprehensive accounting standards on financial instruments for all companies.

Ever since their issue the guidance on financial instruments has been criticised by users, preparers, auditors and others and has also been the only area of accounting that has caused real political problems. As this text is being written in early 2010 the IASB is being put under pressure from the G20 nations and the European Union to look at its guidance and it has committed to revise the standards by the end of 2010.

12.2.1 Rules versus principles

IAS 32 and 39 are sourced from US GAAP (although not fully consistent with US GAAP) and this has led to one of the first major criticisms of the guidance, that it is too 'rules' based. The international accounting standards aim to be a principles based accounting regime where the accounting standards establish good principles that underpin the accounting treatments but not every possible situation or transaction is covered in guidance. Generally US GAAP, whilst still having underpinning principles, tends to have a significantly greater number of 'rules' and as a result IAS 32 and 39 have significant and detailed rules within them.

The difficulty with the rules based approach is that some companies claim that they cannot produce financial statements that reflect the intent behind their transactions. For example, an area we will be considering in this chapter is hedge accounting. Some companies have claimed that the very strict hedge accounting requirements in IAS 39 are so difficult to comply with that they cannot reflect what they consider are genuine hedge transactions appropriately in their financial statements. The extract below is from the 2007 Annual Report of Rolls Royce and shows that there can be a significant difference between reported earnings under IFRS and the 'underlying' performance of the business:

> On the basis described below, underlying profit before tax was £800 million (2006 £705 million). The adjustments are detailed in note 2 on page 77.
>
> The published profit before tax reduced to £733 million from £1,391 million in 2006. This is primarily due to reduced benefits from the unrealised fair value derivative contracts, lower benefit from foreign exchange hedge reserve release and finally the recognition of past service costs for UK pension schemes, all of which are excluded from the calculation of underlying performance.
>
> The Group is exposed to fluctuations in foreign currency exchange rates and commodity price movements. These exposures are mitigated through the use of currency and commodity derivatives for which the Group does not apply hedge accounting.
>
> As a result, reported earnings do not reflect the economic substance of derivatives that have been closed out in the financial year, but do include unrealised gains and losses on derivatives which will only affect cash flows when they are closed out at some point in the future.
>
> Underlying earnings are presented on a basis that shows the economic substance of the Group's hedging strategies in respect of transactional exchange rate and commodity price movements. Further information is included within key performance indicators on page 20 of this report.

12.2.2 The 2008 financial crisis

The financial crisis that began in 2008 highlighted problems with IAS 39 and caused more political intervention in accounting standard setting than had previously been seen. Also the IASB were forced into a position where it had to change an accounting standard without any due process, an action which the IASB felt was necessary but that has drawn widespread criticism.

As you read the chapter you will appreciate that IAS 39 requires different measurement bases for different types of financial assets and liabilities. How a company determines which measurement to use, broadly the choice being fair value or amortised cost, depends on how instruments are classified, there being four different asset classifications allowed by IAS 39. Many banks in the financial crisis were caught in a position where they had loan assets measured at fair value, and the fair value of those loans was reducing significantly, with the potential for major losses.

Banks will keep their loan assets generally in two books, a 'trading' book where the loans are measured at fair value through profit or loss, and a 'banking' book where the loans are measured at amortised cost. Up to October 2008 under IAS 39 if a company chose to measure its financial assets or liabilities at fair value through profit or loss it was not allowed to subsequently reclassify those loans and start measuring them at amortised cost. Many banks had included loans in the 'trading' book which, because of illiquidity in financial markets they could not sell, and for which the market values significantly reduced. The losses on revaluation were all going to be charged against their profit and this was causing some concern.

The issue came to a head when the European Union, through work carried out by the French, identified that under US GAAP reclassification was allowed and therefore European banks were potentially in a worse position than their American counterparts. The European Union concluded that this was unacceptable and that if IAS 39 was not altered they would 'carve out' the section of IAS 39 restricting the transfer and not make that part of the standards relevant to EU businesses. This was perceived as a major threat by the IASB, in particular to its convergence work with US GAAP, and therefore the IASB amended IAS 39 to allow reclassification. For the first time ever an amendment was made that had not been issued as a discussion paper or exposure draft, it was simply a change to the standard. This has led to significant criticism of the IASB and calls for its due process to be revisited to ensure this does not happen again.

The political interest in accounting has continued with global politicians putting pressure on the IASB to speed up its work on certain areas. In addition it has led to calls for the IASB to examine the way it operates and its governance: a number of governments are concerned that a board, on which they have no representation, can set accounting standards which have to be followed by companies in their country. To highlight how high these issues have been on the agenda of politicians the following are extracts from the G20 communiqué issued after the meeting on 15 November 2008:

Strengthening Transparency and Accountability
Immediate Actions by March 31, 2009.
The key global accounting standards bodies should work to enhance guidance for valuation of securities, also taking into account the valuation of complex, illiquid products, especially during times of stress.

Accounting standard setters should significantly advance their work to address weaknesses in accounting and disclosure standards for off balance sheet vehicles.

Regulators and accounting standard setters should enhance the required disclosure of complex financial instruments by firms to market participants.

With a view toward promoting financial stability, the governance of the international accounting standard setting body should be further enhanced, including by undertaking a review of its membership, in particular in order to ensure transparency, accountability, and an appropriate relationship between this independent body and the relevant authorities.

Promoting Integrity in Financial Markets Immediate Actions by March 31, 2009.
Medium-term actions
The key global accounting standards bodies should work intensively toward the objective of creating a single high-quality global standard.

Regulators, supervisors, and accounting standard setters, as appropriate, should work with each other and the private sector on an ongoing basis to ensure consistent application and enforcement of high-quality accounting standards.

It is likely that 2010 will see further changes in the accounting standards in response to the financial crisis, not only for measurement of financial instruments that was addressed by IFRS 9 but also in areas such as consolidation, derecognition of financial assets, impairment and structured entities and securitisation.

12.3 IAS 32 *Financial Instruments: Disclosure and Presentation*[1]

The dynamic nature of the international financial markets has resulted in a great variety of financial instruments from traditional equity and debt instruments to derivative instruments such as futures or swaps. These instruments are a mixture of on and off balance sheet instruments, and they can significantly contribute to the risks that an enterprise faces. IAS 32 was introduced to highlight to users of financial statements the range of financial instruments used by an enterprise and how they affect the financial position, performance and cash flows of the enterprise.

IAS 32 only considers the areas of presentation of financial instruments; recognition and measurement are considered in a subsequent standard, IAS 39.

12.3.1 Scope of the standard

IAS 32 should be applied by all enterprises and should consider all financial instruments with the exceptions of:

(a) share-based payments as defined in IFRS 2;

(b) interests in subsidiaries as defined in IAS 27;

(c) interests in associates as defined in IAS 28;

(d) interests in joint ventures as defined in IAS 31;

(e) employers' rights and ligations under employee benefit plans;

(f) rights and obligations arising under insurance contracts (except embedded derivatives requiring separate accounting under IAS 39).

12.3.2 Definition of terms[2]

The following definitions are used in IAS 32 and also in IAS 39, which is to be considered later.

A **financial instrument** is any contract that gives rise to both a financial asset of one enterprise and a financial liability or equity instrument of another enterprise.

A **financial asset** is any asset that is:

(a) cash;

(b) a contractual right to receive cash or another financial asset from another entity;

(c) a contractual right to exchange financial instruments with another entity under conditions that are potentially favourable; or

(d) an equity instrument of another entity.

A **financial liability** is any liability that is a contractual obligation:

(a) to deliver cash or another financial asset to another entity; or

(b) to exchange financial instruments with another entity under conditions that are potentially unfavourable.

An **equity instrument** is any contract that evidences a residual interest in the assets of an entity after deducting all of its liabilities.

Following the introduction of IAS 39 extra clarification was introduced into IAS 32 in the application of the definitions. First, a commodity-based contract (such as a commodity future) is a financial instrument if either party can settle in cash or some other financial instrument. Commodity contracts would not be financial instruments if they were expected to be settled by delivery, and this was always intended.

The second clarification is for the situation where an enterprise has a financial liability that can be settled either with financial assets or the enterprise's own equity shares. If the number of equity shares to be issued is variable, typically so that the enterprise always has an obligation to give shares equal to the fair value of the obligation, they are treated as a financial liability.

12.3.3 Presentation of instruments in the financial statements

Two main issues are addressed in the standard regarding the presentation of financial instruments. These issues are whether instruments should be classified as liabilities or equity instruments, and how compound instruments should be presented.

Liabilities v equity

IAS 32 follows a substance approach[3] to the classification of instruments as liabilities or equity. If an instrument has terms such that there is an obligation on the enterprise to transfer financial assets to redeem the obligation then it is a liability instrument regardless of its legal nature. Preference shares are the main instrument where in substance they could be liabilities but legally are equity. The common conditions on the preference share that would indicate it is to be treated as a liability instrument are as follows:

- annual dividends are compulsory and not at the discretion of directors; or
- the share provides for mandatory redemption by the issuer at a fixed or determinable amount at a future fixed or determinable date; or
- the share gives the holder the option to redeem upon the occurrence of a future event that is highly likely to occur (e.g. after the passing of a future date).

If a preference share is treated as a liability instrument, it is presented as such in the statement of financial position and also any dividends paid or payable on that share are calculated in the same way as interest and presented as a finance cost in the statement of comprehensive income. The presentation on the statement of comprehensive income could be as a separate item from other interest costs but this is not mandatory. Any gains or losses on the redemption of financial instruments classified as liabilities are also presented in profit or loss.

Impact on companies

The presentation of preference shares as liabilities does not alter the cash flows or risks that the instruments give, but there is a danger that the perception of a company may change. This presentational change has the impact of reducing net assets and increasing gearing. This could be very important, for example, if a company had debt covenants on other borrowings that required the maintenance of certain ratios such as gearing or interest cover. Moving preference shares to debt and dividends to interest costs could mean the covenants are breached and other loans become repayable.

In addition, the higher gearing and reduced net assets could mean the company is perceived as more risky, and therefore a higher credit risk. This in turn might lead to a reduction in the company's credit rating, making obtaining future credit more difficult and expensive.

These very practical issues need to be managed by companies converting to IFRS from a local accounting regime that treats preference shares as equity or non-equity funds. Good communication with users is key to smoothing the transition.

Compound instruments[4]

Compound instruments are financial instruments that have the characteristics of both debt and equity. A convertible loan, which gives the holder the option to convert into equity shares at some future date, is the most common example of a compound instrument. The view of the IASB is that the proceeds received by a company for these instruments are made up of two parts, a debt obligation and an equity option, and following the substance of the instruments IAS 32 requires that the two parts be presented separately, a 'split accounting' approach.

The split is made by measuring the debt part and making the equity the residual of the proceeds. This approach is in line with the definitions of liabilities and equity, where equity is treated as a residual. The debt is calculated by discounting the cash flows on the debt at a market rate of interest for similar debt without the conversion option.

The following is an extract from the 2007 Balfour Beatty Annual Return relating to convertible preference shares:

> The Company's cumulative convertible redeemable preference shares are regarded as a compound instrument, consisting of a liability component and an equity component. The fair value of the liability component at the date of issue was estimated using the prevailing market interest rate for a similar non-convertible instrument. The difference between the proceeds of issue of the preference shares and the fair value assigned to the liability component, representing the embedded option to convert the liability into the Company's ordinary shares, is included in equity.
>
> The interest expense on the liability component is calculated by applying the market interest rate for similar non-convertible debt prevailing at the date of issue to the liability component of the instrument. The difference between this amount and the dividend paid is added to the carrying amount of the liability component and is included in finance charges, together with the dividend payable, in the statement of comprehensive income.

Illustration for compound instruments

Rohan plc issues 1,000 £100 5% convertible debentures at par on 1 January 2000. The debentures can either be converted into 50 ordinary shares per £100 of debentures, or redeemed at par at any date from 1 January 2005. Interest is paid annually in arrears on 31 December. The interest rate on similar debentures without the conversion option is 6%.

To split the proceeds the debt value must be calculated by discounting the future cash flows on the debt instrument.

The value of debt is therefore:

Present value of redemption payment (discounted @ 6%)	£74,726
Present value of interest (5 years) (discounted @ 6%)	£21,062
Value of debt	£95,788
Value of the equity proceeds: (£100,000 − £95,788)	
(presented as part of equity)	£4,212

The extract below from Balfour Beatty shows the impact of compound instruments when spilt accounting was adopted in 2004:

Extract from Balfour Beatty IFRS restatement of 2004 results
Preference shares:
The Group's £136m outstanding convertible redeemable preference shares included within 'Shareholders' funds' at 31 December 2004 under UK GAAP are, under IAS 32, regarded as a compound instrument consisting of a liability (£112m, including £10m deferred tax) and an equity component (£19m). The preference dividend is shown in the statement of comprehensive income as an interest expense.

	UK GAAP	IAS 32 Adjusted
Capital and reserves		
Called-up share capital	213	212
Share premium account	150	15
Equity component of preference shares	—	19
Non-current liabilities		
Liability component of preference shares	—	(102)

Perpetual debt

Following a substance approach, perpetual or irredeemable debt could be argued to be an equity instrument as opposed to a debt instrument. IAS 32, however, takes the view that it is a debt instrument because the interest must be paid (as compared to dividends which are only paid if profits are available for distribution and if directors declare a dividend approved by the shareholders), and the present value of all the future obligations to pay interest will equal the proceeds of the debt if discounted at a market rate. The proceeds on issue of a perpetual debt instrument are therefore a liability obligation.

12.3.4 Calculation of finance costs on liability instruments

The finance costs will be changed to profit or loss. The finance cost of debt is the total payments to be incurred over the life-span of that debt less the initial carrying value. Such costs should be allocated to profit or loss over the life-time of the debt at a constant rate of interest based on the outstanding carrying value per period. If a debt is settled before maturity, any profit or loss should be reflected immediately in profit or loss – unless the substance of the settlement transaction fails to generate any change in liabilities and assets.

Illustration of the allocation of finance costs and the determination of carrying value

On 1 January 20X6 a company issued a debt instrument of £1,000,000 spanning a four-year term. It received from the lender £890,000, being the face value of the debt less a discount of £110,000. Interest was payable yearly in arrears at 8% per annum on the principal sum of £1,000,000. The principal sum was to be repaid on 31 December 20X9.

To determine the yearly finance costs and year-end carrying value it is necessary to compute:

● the aggregate finance cost;

● the implicit rate of interest carried by the instrument (also referred to as the effective yield);

● the finance charge per annum; and

● the carrying value at successive year-ends.

Aggregate finance cost
This is the difference between the total future payments of interest plus principal, less the net proceeds received less costs of the issue, i.e. £430,000 in column (i) of Figure 12.1.

Figure 12.1 Allocation of finance costs and determination of carrying value

	(i) Cash flows £000		(ii) Finance charge to Statement of comprehensive income £000		(iii) Carrying value in balance sheet £000
At 1 Jan 20X6	(890)	(1,000 – 110)	—		890
At 31 Dec 20X6	80	(8% × 1,000)	103.2	(11.59% × 890)	913.2
At 31 Dec 20X7	80	(8% × 1,000)	105.8	(11.59% × 913.2)	939.2
At 31 Dec 20X8	80	(8% × 1,000)	108.8	(11.59% × 939)	967.8
At 31 Dec 20X9	1,080	(1,000 + (8% × 1,000))	112.2	(11.59% × 967.8)	—
Net cash flow	430	= Cost	430		

Implicit rate of interest carried by the instrument
This can be computed by using the net present value (NPV) formula:

$$\sum_{t=1}^{t=n} \frac{At}{1+r} - I = 0$$

where A is forecast net cash flow in year Λ, t time (in years), n the life-span of the debt in years, r the company's annual rate of discount and I the initial net proceeds. Note that the application of this formula can be quite time-consuming. A reasonable method of assessment is by interpolation of the interest rate.

The aggregate formula given above may be disaggregated for calculation purposes:

$$\sum_{t=1}^{t=n} \frac{A1}{(1+r)} + \frac{A2}{(1+r)^2} + \frac{A3}{(1+r)^3} + \frac{A4}{(1+r)^4} - I = 0$$

Using the data concerning the debt and assuming (allowing for discount and costs) an implicit constant rate of, say, 11%:

$$\Sigma = \frac{80,000}{(1.11)^1} + \frac{80,000}{(1.11)^2} + \frac{80,000}{(1.11)^3} + \frac{1,080,000}{(1.11)^4} - 890,000 = 0$$

$$= 72,072 + 64,930 + 58,495 + 711,429 - 890,000 = +16,926$$

The chosen implicit rate of 11% is too low. We now choose a higher rate, say 12%:

$$\Sigma = \frac{80,000}{(1.12)^1} + \frac{80,000}{(1.12)^2} + \frac{80,000}{(1.12)^3} + \frac{1,080,000}{(1.12)^4} - 890,000 = 0$$

$$= 71,429 + 63,776 + 56,942 + 686,360 - 890,000 = -11,493$$

This rate is too high, resulting in a negative net present value. Interpolation will enable us to arrive at an implicit rate:

$$11\% + \left[\frac{16,926}{16,926 + 11,493} \times (12\% - 11\%) \right]$$

$$= 11\% + 0.59\% = 11.59\%$$

This is a trial and error method of determining the implicit interest rate. In this example the choice of rates, 11% and 12%, constituted a change of only 1%. It would be possible to choose, say, 11% and then 14%, generating a 3% gap within which to interpolate. This wider margin would result in a less accurate implicit rate and an aggregate interest charge at variance with the desired £430,000 of column (ii). The aim is to choose interest rates as close as possible to either side of the monetary zero, so that the exact implicit rate may be computed.

The object is to determine an NPV of zero monetary units, i.e. to identify the discount rate that will enable the aggregate future discounted net flows to equate to the initial net proceeds from the debt instrument. In the above illustration, a discount (interest) rate of 11.59% enables £430,000 to be charged to profit or loss after allowing for payment of all interest, costs and repayment of the face value of the instrument.

The finance charge per annum and the successive year-end carrying amounts
The charge to the statement of comprehensive income and the carrying values in the statement of financial position are shown in Figure 12.1.

12.3.5 Offsetting financial instruments[5]

Financial assets and liabilities can only be offset and presented net if the following conditions are met:

(a) the enterprise has a legally enforceable right to set off the recognised amounts; and

(b) the enterprise intends either to settle on a net basis, or to realise the asset and settle the liability simultaneously.

IAS 32 emphasises the importance of the intention to settle on a net basis as well as the legal right to do so. Offsetting should only occur when the cash flows and therefore the risks associated with the financial asset and liability are offset and therefore to present them net in the statement of financial position shows a true and fair view.

Situations where offsetting would not normally be appropriate are:

- several different financial instruments are used to emulate the features of a single financial instrument;

- financial assets and financial liabilities arise from financial instruments having the same primary risk exposure but involve different counterparties;

- financial or other assets are pledged as collateral for non-recourse financial liabilities;

- financial assets are set aside in trust by a debtor for the purpose of discharging an obligation without those assets having been accepted by the creditor in settlement of the obligation;

- obligations incurred as a result of events giving rise to losses are expected to be recovered from a third party by virtue of a claim made under an insurance policy.

12.4 IAS 39 *Financial Instruments: Recognition and Measurement*

IAS 39 is the first comprehensive standard on the recognition and measurement of financial instruments and completes the guidance that was started with the introduction of IAS 32.

12.4.1 Scope of the standard

IAS 39 should be applied by all enterprises to all financial instruments except those excluded from the scope of IAS 32 (see above) and the following additional instruments:

● rights and obligations under leases to which IAS 17 applies (except for embedded derivatives);

● equity instruments of the reporting entity including options, warrants and other financial instruments that are classified as shareholders' equity;

● contracts between an acquirer and a vendor in a business combination to buy or sell or acquire at a futue date;

● rights to payments to reimburse the entity for expenditure it is required to make to settle a liability under IAS 37.

12.4.2 Definitions of four categories of financial instruments

The four categories are (a) financial assets or liabilities at fair values through profit or loss, (b) held-to-maturity investments, (c) loans and receivables, and (d) available-for-sale financial assets. The definition of each is as stated below.

(a) Financial assets or liabilities at fair values through profit or loss

Assets and liabilities under this category are reported in the financial statements at fair value. Changes in the fair value from period to period are reported as a component of net income. There are two types of investments that are accounted for under this heading, namely, *held-for trading investments* and *designated on initial recognition*.

Held-for-trading investments
These are financial instruments where (i) the investor's principal intention is to sell or repurchase a security in the near future and where there is normally active trading for profit-taking in the securities, or (ii) they are part of a portfolio of identified financial instruments that are managed together and for which there is evidence of a recent pattern of short-term profit-taking, or (iii) they are derivatives. This category includes commercial papers, certain government bonds and treasury bills.
   A **derivative** is a financial instrument:

● whose value changes in response to the change in a specified interest rate, security price, commodity price, foreign exchange rate, index of prices or rates, a credit rating or credit index or similar variable (sometimes called the 'underlying');

● that requires no initial net investment or an initial net investment that is smaller than would be required for other types of contract that would be expected to have a similar response to changes in market factors; and

● that is settled at a future date.

Designated on initial recognition
A company has the choice of designating as fair value through profit or loss on the initial recognition of an investment in the following situations:

● it eliminates or significantly reduces a measurement or recognition inconsistency (sometimes referred to as 'an accounting mismatch') that would otherwise arise from measuring assets or liabilities or recognising the gains and losses on them on different bases; or

- a group of financial assets, financial liabilities or both is managed and performance is evaluated on a fair value basis, in accordance with a documented risk management or investment strategy; or
- the financial asset or liability contains an embedded derivative that would otherwise require separation from the host.

The following is an extract from the Fortis Consolidated Financial Statements 2007 Annual Report:

Financial assets at fair value through profit or loss include:

(i) financial assets held for trading, including derivative instruments that do not qualify for hedge accounting

(ii) financial assets that Fortis has irrevocably designated at initial recognition or first-time adoption of IFRS as held at fair value through profit or loss, because:

- the host contract includes an embedded derivative that would otherwise require separation

- it eliminates or significantly reduces a measurement or recognition inconsistency ('accounting mismatch')

- it relates to a portfolio of financial assets and/or liabilities that are managed and evaluated on a fair value basis.

Prior to October 2008 it was prohibited to transfer instruments either into or out of the fair value through profit or loss category after initial recognition of the instrument. Following significant pressure that the international standards were more restrictive than US GAAP in this area, the IASB amended the standard to allow reclassification of financial instruments in rare circumstances. The financial crisis of 2008 was deemed to be a rare situation that would justify reclassification.

The reclassification requirements allow instruments to be transferred from fair value through profit and loss to the loans and receivables category. They also allow reclassifications from the available for sale category (discussed later) to the loans and receivables category. The IASB allowed a short-term exemption from the general requirement that the transfer is at fair value, and permitted the transfers to be undertaken at the fair values of instruments on 1 July 2008, a date before significant reductions in fair value on debt instruments arose.

(b) Held-to-maturity investments

Held-to-maturity investments consist of instruments with fixed or determinable payments and fixed maturity for which the entity positively intends and has the ability to hold to maturity. For items to be classified as held-to-maturity an entity must justify that it will hold them to maturity. The tests that a company must pass to justify this classification are summarised in Figure 12.2.

The investments are initially measured at fair value (including transaction costs) and subsequently measured at amortised cost using the effective interest method, with the periodic amortisation recorded in the statement of comprehensive income. As they are reported at amortised cost, temporary fluctuations in fair value are not reflected in the entity's financial statements.

Such investments include corporate and government bonds and redeemable preference shares which can be held to maturity. It does not include investments that are those designated as at fair value through profit or loss on initial recognition, those designated as available for sale and those defined as loans and receivables. It also does not include ordinary shares in other entities because these do not have a maturity date.

Figure 12.2 Tests for classification as held-to-maturity investment

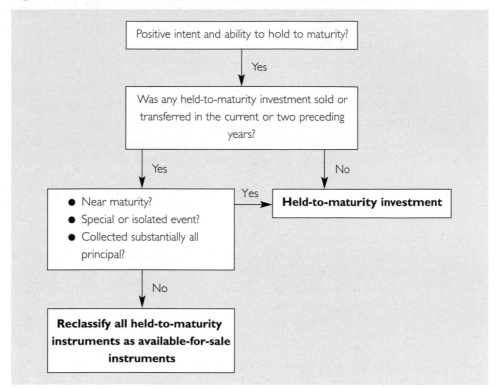

(c) Loans and receivables

Loans and receivables include financial assets with fixed or determinable payments that are not quoted in an active market. They are initially measured at fair value (including transaction costs) and subsequently measured at amortised cost using the effective interest method, with the periodic amortisation in the statement of comprehensive income.

Amortised cost is normally the amount at which a financial asset or liability is measured at initial recognition minus principal repayments, minus the cumulative amortisation of any premium and minus any write-down for impairment.

This category includes trade receivables, accrued revenues for services and goods, loan receivables, bank deposits and cash at hand. It does not include financial assets held for trading, those designated on initial recognition as at fair value through profit or loss, those available-for-sale and those for which the holder may not recover substantially all of its initial investment, other than because of credit deterioration.

(d) Available-for-sale financial assets

A common financial asset that would be classified as available-for-sale would be equity investments in another entity.

On initial recognition an asset is reported at cost and at period-ends it is restated to fair value with changes in fair value reported under *Other comprehensive income*. If the fair value falls below amortised cost and the fall is not estimated to be temporary, it is reported in the investor's statement of comprehensive income.

The fair value of publicly traded securities is normally based on quoted market prices at the year-end date. The fair value of securities that are not publicly traded is assessed using a variety of methods and assumptions based on market conditions existing at each year-end date referring to quoted market prices for similar or identical securities if available or employing other techniques such as option pricing models and estimated discounted values of future cash flows.

Available-for-sale does not include debt and equity securities classified as held for trading or held-to-maturity.

Example of accounting for an available-for-sale financial asset: the acquisition by Brighton plc of shares in Hove plc

On 1 September 20X9 Brighton purchased 15 million of the 100 million shares in Hove for £1.50 per share. This purchase was made with a view to further purchases in future. The Brighton directors are not able to exercise any influence over the operating and financial policies of Hove. The shares are currently in the Statement of Financial Position as at 31 December 20X9 at cost and the fair value of a share was £1.70.

Accounting treatment at the year end

Brighton owns 15% of the Hove issued shares. As the directors are not able to exercise any influence, the investment is dealt with under IAS 39 *Financial Instruments: Measurement Recognition* and under its provisions the investment is an available for sale financial asset. This means that it is to be valued at fair value, with gains or losses taken to equity.

In this case the investment is valued at £25.5 million (15 million × £1.70) and the gain of £3 million (15 million × (£1.70 – £1.50)) is taken to equity through other comprehensive income.

Headings under which reported

Assets are reported as appropriate in the Statement of position under Other non-current assets, Trade and Other Receivables, Interest-bearing Receivables, Cash and Cash Equivalents. Financial liabilities measured at amortised cost comprises financial liabilities, such as borrowings, trade payables, accrued expenses for services and goods, and certain provisions settled in cash and are reported in the position statement under Long-term and Short-term Borrowings, Other Provisions, Other Long-term Liabilities, Trade Payables and Other Current Liabilities.

Impact of classification on the financial statements

The impact of the classification of financial instruments on the financial statements is important as it affects the value of assets and liabilities and also the income recognised. For example, assume that Henry plc had the following financial assets and liabilities at its year-end. All the instruments had been taken out at the start of the current year:

1 A forward exchange contract. At the period-end date the contract was an asset with a fair value of £100,000.

2 An investment of £1,000,000 in a 6% corporate bond. At the period-end date the market rate of interest increased and the bond fair value fell to £960,000.

3 An equity investment of £500,000. This investment was worth £550,000 at the period-end.

The classification of these instruments is important and choices are available as to how they are accounted for. For example, the investment in the corporate bond above could be accounted for as a held-to-maturity investment if Henry plc had the intent and ability to hold it to maturity, or it could be an available-for-sale investment if so chosen by Henry. The bond and the equity investment could even be recognised as fair value through profit or loss if they met the criteria to be designated as such on initial recognition.

To highlight the impact on the financial statements, the tables below show the accounting positions for the investments on different assumptions. Not all possible classifications are shown in the tables:

Option 1

Instrument	Classification	Statement of financial position	Profit or loss	Other comprehensive income
Forward contract	FV–P&L	£100,000	£100,000	—
Corporate bond	Held-to-maturity	£1,000,000	*(£60,000)	—
Equity investment	Available-for-sale	£550,000	—	£50,000

* *Interest on the bond of £1,000,000 × 6%*

The bond is not revalued because held-to-maturity investments are recognised at amortised cost.

Option 2

Instrument	Classification	Statement of financial position	Profit or loss	Other comprehensive income
Forward contract	FV–P&L	£100,000	£100,000	—
Corporate bond	Available-for-sale	£960,000	(£60,000)	(£40,000)
Equity investment	Available-for-sale	£550,000	—	£50,000

Interest is still recognised on the bond but at the year-end it is revalued through equity to its fair value of £960,000.

Option 3

Instrument	Classification	Statement of financial position	Profit or loss	Other comprehensive income
Forward contract	FV–P&L	£100,000	£100,000	—
Corporate bond	Held-to-maturity	£1,000,000	(£60,000)	—
Equity investment	FV–P&L	£550,000	£50,000	—

The equity investment is revalued through profit and loss as opposed to through other comprehensive income as it would be if classified as available-for-sale.

12.4.3 Recognition of financial instruments

Initial recognition

A financial asset or liability should be recognised when an entity becomes party to the contractual provisions of the instrument. This means that derivative instruments must be recognised if a contractual right or obligation exists.

Derecognition

Financial assets should only be derecognised when the entity transfers the risks and rewards that comprise the asset. This could be because the benefits are realised, the rights expire or the enterprise surrenders the benefits.

If it is not clear whether the risks and reward have been transferred, the entity considers whether control has passed. If control has passed, the entity should derecognise the asset; whereas if control is retained, the asset is recognised to the extent of the entity's continuing involvement in the asset.

On derecognition any gain or loss should be recorded in profit or loss. Also any gains or losses previously recognised in reserves relating to the asset should be transferred to the profit or loss on sale.

Financial liabilities should only be derecognised when the obligation specified in the contract is discharged, cancelled or expires.

The rule on the derecognition of liabilities does mean that it is not acceptable to write off liabilities. In some industries this will lead to a change in business practice. For example, UK banks are not allowed to remove dormant accounts from their statements of financial position as the liability has not been legally extinguished.

12.4.4 Embedded derivatives

Sometimes an entity will enter into a contract that includes both a derivative and a host contract – with the effect that some of the cash flows of the combined instrument vary in a similar way to a stand-alone derivative. Examples of such embedded derivatives could be a put option on an equity instrument held by an enterprise, or an equity conversion feature embedded in a debt instrument.

An embedded instrument should be separated from the host contract and accounted for as a derivative under IAS 39 if all of the following conditions are met:

(a) the economic characteristics and risks of the embedded derivative are not closely related to the economic characteristics and risks of the host contract;

(b) a separate instrument with the same terms as the embedded derivative would meet the definition of a derivative; and

(c) the hybrid instrument is not measured at fair value with changes in fair value reported in profit or loss.

If an entity is required to separate the embedded derivative from its host contract but is unable to separately measure the embedded derivative, the entire hybrid instrument should be treated as a financial instrument held at fair value through profit or loss and as a result changes in fair value should be reported through profit or loss.

12.4.5 Measurement of financial instruments

Initial measurement

Financial assets and liabilities (other than those at fair value through profit or loss) should be initially measured at fair value plus transaction costs. In almost all cases this would be at cost. For instruments at fair value through profit and loss, transaction costs are not included.

Subsequent measurement

Figure 12.3 summarises the way that financial assets and liabilities are to be subsequently measured after initial recognition.

The measurement after initial recognition is at either fair value or amortised cost. The only financial instruments that can be recognised at cost (not amortised) are equity investments for which there is no measurable fair value. These should be very rare.

The fair value is the amount for which an asset could be exchanged, or a liability settled, between knowledgeable, willing parties in an arm's-length transaction.

The methods for fair value measurement allow a number of different bases to be used for the assessment of fair value. These include:

Figure 12.3 Subsequent measurement

Category	Measurement
Financial assets at fair value through profit or loss*	Fair value without any deduction for transaction costs on sale or disposal.
Held-to-maturity investments	Amortised cost using the effective interest method
Loans and receivables	Amortised cost using the effective interest method
Available-for-sale financial assets*	Fair value without any deduction for transaction costs on sale or disposal
Financial liabilities at fair value through profit or loss	Fair value
Other financial liabilities	Amortised cost using the effective interest method

* If these categories include unquoted equity instruments (or derivative liabilities that are settled in unquoted equity instruments) where fair value cannot be measured reliably then they are measured at cost. This however should be very rare.

- published market prices;
- transactions in similar instruments;
- discounted future cash flows;
- valuation models.

The method used will be the one which is most reliable for the particular instrument.

In the 2008 financial crisis there were calls on the IASB to either abolish or suspend the fair value measurement basis in IAS 39 as it has been perceived as requiring companies to recognise losses greater than their true value. The reason for this is that some claim the market value is being distorted by a lack of liquidity in the markets and that markets are not functioning efficiently with willing buyers and sellers. The IASB has resisted the calls but has issued guidance on valuation in illiquid markets that emphasises the different ways that fair value can be determined. For instruments that operate in illiquid markets there is sometimes a need to value the instruments based on valuation models and discounted cash flows, however these models take into account factors that a market participant would consider in the current circumstances.

Amortised cost is calculated using the effective interest method on assets and liabilities. For the definition of effective interest it is necessary to look at IAS 39, para. 9. The effective rate is defined as:

'the rate that exactly discounts estimated future cash receipts or payments through the expected life of the financial instrument'.

The definition then goes on to require that the entity shall:

- estimate cash flows considering all contractual terms of the financial instrument (for example, prepayment, call and similar options), but not future credit losses;

● include all necessary fees and points paid or received that are an integral part of the effective yield calculation (IAS 18);

● make a presumption that the cash flows and expected life of a group of similar financial instruments can be estimated reliably.

Illustration of the effective yield method

George plc lends £10,000 to a customer for fixed interest based on the customer paying 5% interest per annum (annually in arrears) for 2 years, and then 6% fixed for the remaining 3 years with the full £10,000 repayable at the end of the 5-year term.

The tables below show the interest income over the loan period assuming:

(a) it is not expected that the customer will repay early (effective rate is 5.55% per annum derived from an internal rate of return calculation); and

(b) it is expected the customer will repay at the end of year 3 but there are no repayment penalties (effective rate is 5.3% per annum derived from an internal rate of return calculation).

The loan balance will alter as follows:

No early repayment

Period	B/F	Interest income (5.55%)	Cash received	C/F
Year 1	10,000	555	(500)	10,055
Year 2	10,055	558	(500)	10,113
Year 3	10,113	561	(600)	10,074
Year 4	10,074	559	(600)	10,033
Year 5	10,033	557	(10,600)	(10)*

* Difference due to rounding

Early repayment

Period	B/F	Interest income (5.3%)	Cash received	C/F
Year 1	10,000	530	(500)	10,030
Year 2	10,030	532	(500)	10,062
Year 3	10,062	533	(10,600)	(5)*

* Difference due to rounding

Gains or losses on subsequent measurement

When financial instruments are remeasured to fair value the rules for the treatment of the subsequent gain or loss are as shown in Figure 12.4. Gains or losses arising on financial

Figure 12.4 Gains or losses on subsequent measurements

Instrument	Gain or loss
Instruments at fair value through profit or loss	Profit or loss
Available-for-sale	Equity (except for impairments and foreign exchange gains and losses) until derecognition, at which time the cumulative gain/loss in equity is recognised in profit or loss. Dividend income is recognised in profit or loss when the right to receive payment is established.

instruments that have not been remeasured to fair value will arise either when the assets are impaired or the instruments are derecognised. These gains and losses are recognised in profit or loss for the period.

12.4.6 Hedging

If a financial instrument has been taken out to act as a hedge, and this position is clearly identified and expected to be effective, hedge accounting rules should be followed.

There are three types of hedging relationship:

1 Fair value hedge

A hedge of the exposure to changes in fair value of a recognised asset or liability or an unrecognised firm commitment that will affect reported net income. Any gain or loss arising on remeasuring the hedging instrument and the hedged item should be recognised in profit or loss in the period.

2 Cash flow hedge

A hedge of the exposure to variability in cash flows that is attributable to a particular risk associated with the recognised asset or liability and that will affect reported net income. A hedge of foreign exchange risk on a firm commitment may be a cash flow or a fair value hedge. The gain or loss on the hedging instrument should be recognised directly in other comprehensive income. Any gains or losses recognised in other comprehensive income should be included in profit or loss in the period that the hedged item affects profit or loss. If the instrument being hedged results in the recognition of a non-financial asset or liability, the gain or loss on the hedging instrument can be recognised as part of the cost of the hedged item.

Cash flow hedge illustrated

Harvey plc directors agreed at their July 2006 meeting to acquire additional specialist computer equipment in September 2007 at an estimated cost of $500,000.

The company entered into a forward contract in July 2006 to purchase $500,000 in September 2007 and pay GBP260,000. At the year-end in December 2006 the $ has appreciated and has a sterling value of GBP276,000.

At the year-end the increase of GBP16,000 will be debited to Forward Contract and credited to a hedge reserve.

In September 2007 when the equipment is purchased the 16,000 will be deducted in its entirety from the Equipment carrying amount or transferred as a reduction of the annual depreciation charge.

3 Net investment hedge

A hedge of an investment in a foreign entity. The gain or loss on the hedging instrument should be recognised directly in other comprehensive income to match against the gain or loss on the hedged investment.

Conditions for hedge accounting

In order to be able to apply the hedge accounting techniques detailed above, an entity must meet a number of conditions. These conditions are designed to ensure that only genuine hedging instruments can be hedge accounted, and that the hedged positions are clearly identified and documented.

The conditions are:

- at the inception of the hedge there is formal documentation of the hedge relationship and the enterprise's risk management objective and strategy for undertaking the hedge;
- the hedge is expected to be highly effective at inception and on an ongoing basis in achieving offsetting changes in fair values or cash flows;
- the effectiveness of the hedge can be reliably measured, that is the fair value of the hedged item and the hedging instrument can be measured reliably;
- for cash flow hedges, a forecasted transaction that is the subject of the hedge must be highly probable; and
- the hedge was assessed on an ongoing basis and determined actually to have been effective throughout the accounting period (effective between 80% and 125%).

12.5 IFRS 7 *Financial Statement Disclosures*[6]

12.5.1 Introduction

This standard came out of the ongoing project of improvements to the accounting and disclosure requirements relating to financial instruments.

For periods before those starting on or after 1 January 2007 disclosures in respect of financial instruments were governed by two standards:

1 IAS 30 *Disclosures in the financial statements of banks and similar financial institutions*; and

2 IAS 32 *Financial instruments: disclosure and presentation*.

In drafting IFRS 7, the IASB:

- reviewed existing disclosures in the two standards, and removed duplicative disclosures;
- simplified the disclosure about concentrations of risk, credit risk, liquidity risk and market risk under IAS 32; and
- transferred disclosure requirements from IAS 32.

12.5.2 Main requirements

The standard applies to all entities, regardless of the quantity of financial instruments held. However, the extent of the disclosures required will depend on the extent of the entity's use of financial instruments and of its exposure to risk.

The standard requires disclosure of:

- the significance of financial instruments for the entity's financial position and performance (many of these disclosures were previously in IAS 32); and
- qualitative and quantitative information about exposure to risks arising from financial instruments, including specified minimum disclosures about credit risk, liquidity risk, and market risk.

The qualitative disclosures describe management's objectives, policies and processes for managing those risks.

The quantitative disclosures provide information about the extent to which the entity is exposed to risk, based on the information provided internally to the entity's key management personnel.

For the disclosure of the significance of financial instruments for the entity's financial position and performance a key aspect will be to clearly link the statement of financial position and the statement of comprehensive income to the classifications in IAS 39. The requirements from IFRS in this respect are as follows:

8 The carrying amounts of each of the following categories, as defined in IAS 39, shall be disclosed either on the face of the statement of financial position or in the notes:
  (a) financial assets at fair value through profit or loss, showing separately (i) those designated as such upon initial recognition and (ii) those classified as held for trading in accordance with IAS 39;
  (b) held-to-maturity investments;
  (c) loans and receivables;
  (d) available-for-sale financial assets;
  (e) financial liabilities measured at amortised cost.

9 An entity shall disclose the following items of income, expense, gains or losses either on the face of the financial statements or in the notes:
  (a) net gains or net losses on:
      (i) financial assets or financial liabilities at fair value through profit or loss, showing separately those on financial assets or financial liabilities designated as such upon initial recognition, and those on financial assets or financial liabilities that are classified as held for trading in accordance with IAS 39;
      (ii) available-for-sale financial assets, showing separately the amount of gain or loss recognised directly in equity during the period and the amount removed from equity and recognised in profit or loss for the period;
      (iii) held-to-maturity investments;
      (iv) loans and receivables; and
      (v) financial liabilities measured at amortised cost;
  (b) total interest income and total interest expense (calculated using the effective interest method) for financial assets or financial liabilities that are not at fair value through profit or loss;
  (c) fee income and expense (other than amounts included in determining the effective interest rate) arising from:
      (i) financial assets or financial liabilities that are not at fair value through profit or loss; and
      (ii) trust and other fiduciary activities that result in the holding or investing of assets on behalf of individuals, trusts, retirement benefit plans, and other institutions;
  (d) interest income on impaired financial assets accrued in accordance with paragraph AG93 of IAS 39; and
  (e) the amount of any impairment loss for each class of financial asset.

EXAMPLE ● Extract from the disclosures given by Findel plc in 2008 compliant with IFRS 7:

FINANCIAL INSTRUMENTS

Capital risk management
The group manages its capital to ensure that entities in the group will be able to continue as going concerns while maximising the return to stakeholders through the optimisation of the debt and equity balance. The capital structure of the group consists

of debt (£399,492,000), which includes the borrowings disclosed in note 25, cash and cash equivalents (£12,767,000) and equity attributable to equity holders of the parent, comprising issued capital (£4,255,000), reserves (£52,233,000) and retained earnings (£73,803,000) as disclosed in notes 30 to 33.

Externally imposed capital requirement
The group is not subject to externally imposed capital requirements.

Significant accounting policies
Details of the significant accounting policies and methods adopted, including the criteria for recognition, the basis of measurement and the basis on which income and expenses are recognised, in respect of each class of financial asset, financial liability and equity instrument are disclosed in note 1 to the financial statements.

Categories of financial instruments

	Carrying value	
	2008	2007
	£000	£000
Financial assets		
Held for trading	457	274
Loans and receivables (including cash and cash equivalents)	325,108	255,017
Financial liabilities		
Held for trading	315	127
Amortised cost	501,274	420,856

Financial risk management objectives
The group's financial risks include market risk (including currency risk and interest risk), credit risk, liquidity risk and cash flow interest rate risk. The group seeks to minimise the effects of these risks by using derivative financial instruments to manage its exposure. The use of financial derivatives is governed by the group's policies approved by the board of directors. The group does not enter into or trade financial instruments, including derivative financial instruments, for speculative purposes.

Market risk
The group's activities expose it primarily to the financial risks of changes in foreign currency exchange rates and interest rates. The group enters into a variety of derivative financial instruments to manage its exposure to interest rate and foreign currency risk, including:

● forward foreign exchange contracts to hedge the exchange rate risk arising on the purchase of inventory in US dollars; and

● interest rate swaps to mitigate the risk of rising interest rates.

Foreign currency risk management
The group undertakes certain transactions denominated in foreign currencies. Hence, exposures to exchange rate fluctuations arise. Exchange rate exposures are managed utilising forward foreign exchange contracts. The carrying amounts of the group's foreign currency denominated monetary assets and monetary liabilities at the reporting date are as follows:

	Assets		Liabilities	
	2008	2007	2008	2007
	£000	£000	£000	£000
Euro	3,286	1,436	(14)	(572)
Hong Kong dollar	—	396	(213)	(290)
US dollar	3,132	3,328	(3,419)	(2,730)

Foreign currency sensitivity analysis

A significant proportion of products sold through the group's Home Shopping and Educational Supplies divisions are procured through the group's Far East buying office. The currency of purchase for these goods is principally the US dollar, with a proportion being in Hong Kong dollars.

The following table details the group's sensitivity to a 10% increase and decrease in the Sterling against the relevant foreign currencies. 10% represents management's assessment of the reasonably possible change in foreign exchange rates. The sensitivity analysis includes only outstanding foreign currency denominated monetary items and adjusts their translation at the period end for a 10% change in foreign currency rates. The sensitivity analysis includes external loans as well as loans to foreign operations within the group where the denomination of the loan is in a currency other than the currency of the lender or the borrower. A positive number below indicates an increase in profit and other equity where the Sterling strengthens 10% against the relevant currency. For a 10% weakening of the Sterling against the relevant currency, there would be an equal and opposite impact on the profit and other equity, and the balances below would be negative.

	Euro Currency impact		Hong Kong dollar Currency impact		US dollar Currency impact	
	2008	2007	2008	2007	2008	2007
	£000	£000	£000	£000	£000	£000
Profit or loss and equity	(297)	(79)	19	(10)	(1,291)	(984)

[These are an extract from the disclosures; full disclosures can be seen in Findel plc 2008 Annual Report.]

12.5.3 Effective date

The standard must be applied for annual accounting periods commencing on or after 1 January 2007, although early adoption is encouraged.

IAS 32 was renamed[7] in 2005 as *Financial Instruments: Presentation*, following the transfer of the disclosure requirements to IFRS 7.

12.6 Financial instruments developments

As a result of the 2008 financial crisis and the subsequent criticism of the accounting standards on financial instruments, the IASB committed to revising IAS 39 and replacing it with a simpler standard that was easier to apply. In order to be able to progress this project quickly, the IASB split the project into a number of areas and IFRS 9 *Financial Instruments* is the outcome of the first part of the project. The areas to be considered are:

(i) recognition and measurement (IFRS 9);

(ii) impairment and the effective yield model;

(iii) hedge accounting;

(iv) derecognition of financial assets and liabilities;

(v) financial liability measurement.

By early 2010 the IASB had issued IFRS 9 and had also issued an exposure draft on the impairment model and derecognition, hedge accounting guidance is expected in 2010. IFRS 9 is mandatory from accounting periods beginning on or after 1 January 2013, but earlier adoption is permitted.

12.6.1 IFRS 9 – Recognition and measurement

As discussed earlier in this chapter, the existing IAS 39 is complex involving four different potential classifications of financial assets (held to maturity, loans and receivables, available for sale and fair value through profit or loss), each with its own measurement requirements. These classifications can be difficult to apply and also can give inconsistencies between entities and between the accounting and the commercial intentions of some instruments (highlighted in the changes made to IAS 39 to allow reclassification in 2008). The primary focus of the IASB was to simplify these categories and also to be clearer in how to determine which instruments are recognised in each category.

Classification

IFRS 9 only has two measurement bases for financial assets, fair value or amortised cost, and only allows gains and losses on equity instruments to be presented in other comprehensive income, fair value gains and losses on other instruments are recognised in profit or loss. The diagram in Figure 12.5 summarises the classification approach.

Figure 12.5 The classification approach of IFRS 9

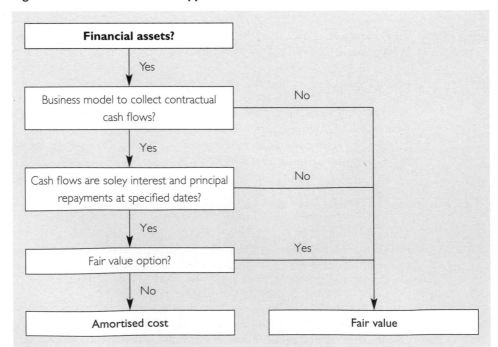

The two key factors in determining the accounting treatment are the business model adopted by an entity for the instrument and the nature of the cash flows. The alternative business models could be to collect principal and interest or to trade the instruments by selling them on for example, and the contractual cash flows requirement ensures that an instrument held at amortised cost only exhibits basic loan features of repayment of interest and capital. IFRS 9 does however retain the fair value option in IAS 39 although it is not expected to be as significant a choice as the first two criteria will generally determine the treatment. Reclassification between the categories is only acceptable if an entity changes its business model, and only applies retrospectively.

Presentation of gains and losses

Once the measurement at fair value or amortised cost is determined, the standard gives a choice of the presentation of fair value gains and losses only for equity instruments. Any debt instruments or derivatives are measured at fair value with gains and losses in profit or loss. However, for equity instruments which are not trading instruments there is a choice for entities to present the gains and losses from movements in fair value in other comprehensive income. This choice is irrevocable and therefore subsequent reclassification is not appropriate.

12.6.2 Impairment of financial assets

The issues surrounding impairment have proved difficult for the IASB and they have faced significant pressure to change the current impairment models in IAS 39, in particular for instruments measured at amortised cost. To the date of writing this text the IASB has issued an exposure draft on amortised cost and impairment but final guidance has not been issued. Below we discuss the major concern that the IASB has been asked to address and its initial proposals in the exposure draft, ED/2009/12 *Financial Instruments: Amortised Cost and Impairment*.

Incurred v expected losses

The debate on impairment largely revolves around whether financial asset impairment should be calculated following an incurred or expected loss model. IAS 39 uses an incurred loss model, however, in the 2008 financial crisis many commentators have suggested that this model delayed the recognition of losses on loans resulting in misleading results for financial institutions. The key difference between the two approaches is that an incurred loss model only provides for impairments when an event has occurred that causes that impairment. An expected loss model, however, provides for impairment if there is reason to expect that it will arise at some point over the life of the loan even if it has not arisen at the balance sheet date. For example, if a bank makes a loan to a customer and the customer becomes unemployed and therefore defaults on the loan, under the incurred loss model an impairment would only be recognised when the customer loses his job. Under the expected loss model, the bank would have made an estimate of the likelihood of the customer losing his job from the inception of the loan and provide based on that probability. The provision on the expected loss model is therefore recognised earlier but it does depend much more on the estimation and judgement of management of a company.

ED/2009/12 has been issued to address impairment and the way that the amortised cost method of accounting is applied. The ED proposes an expected loss model but does this by proposing changes in the way that the amortised cost model is applied. The amortised cost model determines an effective interest rate by determining the rate at which the initial loan and the cash flows over its life are discounted to zero, effectively the internal rate of return on the loan. The current IAS 39 requires the rate to be determined on cash flows before future credit losses, whereas the exposure draft requires the calculation on cash flows including expected future credit losses. Every period the expected cash flows need to be adjusted and discounted back at the original effective rate, and difference in the loan value is adjusted against profit or loss. The impact of this new approach is that losses would tend to be recognised earlier and no separate impairment model is required; if impairment is expected, the cash flow estimates will automatically adjust for that. It is still to be seen how straightforward the approach will be in practice and whether financial institutions can adapt their systems and processes easily to the revised approach.

12.6.3 Derecognition of financial assets

The IASB is looking at derecognition of financial assets as a separate project to the replacement of IAS 39. By early 2010 an exposure draft had been issued but it was not clear in its approach and consequently any new standard may differ from the approach in the exposure draft. As with impairment, there are two distinct views on the basis on which derecognition decisions should be made and the members of the IASB continue to debate which approach is preferable. The two approaches differ in that one considers prior ownership of an asset should influence continuing recognition, whereas the other approach does not consider prior ownership in the decision to recognise an asset. To illustrate this consider the example below.

Illustration of derecognition approaches

A company owns a portfolio of receivables worth €1 million. It sells the receivables to a finance company for €1 million and gives the finance company a guarantee over default in any of the receivable balances provided that the finance company continues to hold them.

Approach 1 – The company has not transferred the significant risks and rewards of ownership or control of the receivables (restriction on finance company selling) and therefore they should not be derecognised. The €1 million received on sale should be treated as a liability.

Approach 2 – The company has sold the receivables and only has left a credit default guarantee which should be recognised as a derivative at fair value with gains and losses in profit or loss.

Currently IAS 39 uses a version of approach 1, however, if a company had simply given a guarantee on €1 million of another entity's debts, approach 2 would be used. Supporters of approach 2 say that the obligation is no different regardless of whether the receivables had been previously owned and therefore it is inconsistent to have different accounting treatments. We need to await the outcome of the IASB deliberations to get a final position on this issue.

Summary

This chapter has given some insight into the difficulties and complexities of accounting for financial instruments and the ongoing debate on this topic, highlighted by the financial crisis that began in 2008. The approach of the IASB is to adhere to the principles contained in the *Framework* but to also issue guidance that is robust enough to prevent manipulation and abuse. Whether the IASB has achieved this is open to debate. Some might view the detailed requirements of the standards, particularly IAS 39, to be so onerous that companies will not be able to show their real intentions in the financial statements. This would be particularly true, for instance, with the detailed criteria on hedging. These criteria have led to many businesses not hedge accounting even though they are hedging commercially to manage their risks. The hedge accounting criteria do not fit with the way they run or manage their risk profiles.

The standards are still developing and problems have already been identified. Since December 2003 there have already been many amendments to the standards.

As can be seen there is much to criticise these standards about, but it should be borne in mind that the IASB has grasped this issue better than many other standard setters. Financial instruments may be complex and subject to debate but guidance is required in this area, and the IASB has given guidance where many others have not.

In addition to giving an insight into the development of standards, our aim has been that you should be able to calculate the debt/equity split on compound instruments and the finance cost on liability instruments and classify and account for the four categories of financial instrument.

REVIEW QUESTIONS

1 Explain what is meant by the term split accounting when applied to convertible debt or convertible preference shares and the rationale for splitting.

2 Discuss the implications for a business if a substance approach is used for the reporting of convertible loans.

3 Explain how a gain or loss on a forward contract is dealt with in the accounts if the contract is not completed until after the period end.

4 Explain how redeemable preference shares, perpetual debt, loans and equity investments are reported in the financial statements.

5 The authors[8] contend that the use of current valuations can present an inaccurate view of a firm's true financial status. When assets are illiquid, current value represents only a guess. When assets participate in an economic 'bubble', current value is invariably unsustainable. Accounting standards, the authors conclude, should be flexible enough to fairly assess value in these circumstances. Discuss the alternatives that standard setters could permit in order to fairly assess values in an illiquid market.

6 Disclosure of the estimated fair values of financial instruments is better than adjusting the values in the financial statements with the resulting volatility that affects earnings and gearing ratios. Discuss.

7 Companies were permitted in 2009 to reclassify financial instruments that were initially designated as at fair value through profit. Critically discuss the reasons for the standard setters changing the existing standard.

8 Explain the difference between the incurred loss model and the expected loss model in determining impairment and suggest limitations of both approaches.

9 The only true way to simplify IAS 39 would be for all financial assets and liabilities to be measured at fair value with gains and losses recognised in profit or loss. Discuss.

EXERCISES

An extract from the solution is provided on the Companion Website (www.pearsoned.co.uk/elliott-elliott) for exercises marked with an asterisk (*).

* Question 1

On 1 April year 1, a deep discount bond was issued by DDB AG. It had a face value of £2.5 million covering a five-year term. The lenders were granted a discount of 5%. The coupon rate was 10% on the principal sum of £2.5 million, payable annually in arrears. The principal sum was repayable in cash on 31 March year 5. Issuing costs amounted to £150,000.

Required:
Compute the finance charge per annum and the carrying value of the loan to be reported in each year's profit or loss and statement of financial position respectively.

Question 2

On 1 October year 1, RPS plc issued one million £1 5% redeemable preference shares. The shares were issued at a discount of £50,000 and are due to be redeemed on 30 September Year 5. Dividends are paid on 30 September each year.

Required:
Show the accounting treatment of the preference shares throughout the life-span of the instrument calculating the finance cost to be charged to profit or loss in each period.

Question 3

October 20X1, Little Raven plc issued 50,000 debentures, with a par value of £100 each, to investors at £80 each. The debentures are redeemable at par on 30 September 20X6 and have a coupon rate of 6%, which was significantly below the market rate of interest for such debentures issued at par. In accounting for these debentures to date, Little Raven plc has simply accounted for the cash flows involved, namely:

● On issue: Debenture 'liability' included in the statement of financial position at £4,000,000.

● Statements of comprehensive income: Interest charged in years ended 30 September 20X2, 20X3 and 20X4 (published accounts) and 30 September 20X5 (draft accounts) – £300,000 each year (being 6% on £5,000,000).

The new finance director, who sees the likelihood that further similar debenture issues will be made, considers that the accounting policy adopted to date is not appropriate. He has asked you to suggest a more appropriate treatment.

Little Raven plc intends to acquire subsidiaries in 20X6.

Statements of comprehensive income for the years ended 30 September 20X4 and 20X5 are as follows:

	Y/e 30 Sept 20X5 (Draft) £000	Y/e 30 Sept 20X4 (Actual) £000
Turnover	6,700	6,300
Cost of sales	(3,025)	(2,900)
Gross profit	3,675	3,400
Overheads	(600)	(550)
Interest payable – debenture	(300)	(300)
– others	(75)	(50)
Profit for the financial year	2,700	2,500
Retained earnings brought forward	4,300	1,800
Retained earnings carried forward	7,000	4,300

Extracts from the statement of financial position are:

	At 30 Sept 20X5 (Draft) £000	At 30 Sept 20X4 (Actual) £000
Share capital	2,250	2,250
Share premium	550	550
Retained earnings	7,000	4,300
	9,800	7,100
6% debentures	4,000	4,000
	13,800	11,100

Required:
(a) Outline the considerations involved in deciding how to account for the issue, the interest cost and the carrying value in respect of debenture issues such as that made by Little Raven plc. Consider the alternative treatments in respect of the statement of comprehensive income and refer briefly to the appropriate statement of financial position disclosures for the debentures. Conclude in terms of the requirements of IAS 32 (on accounting for financial instruments) in this regard.
(b) Detail an alternative set of entries in the books of Little Raven plc for the issue of the debentures and subsequently; under this alternative the discount on the issue should be dealt with under the requirements of IAS 32. The constant rate of interest for the allocation of interest cost is given to you as 11.476%. Draw up a revised statement of comprehensive income for the year ended 30 September 20X5 – together with comparatives – taking account of the alternative accounting treatment.

Question 4

On 1 January 2009 Henry Ltd issued a convertible debenture for €200 million carrying a coupon interest rate of 5%. The debenture is convertible at the option of the holders into 10 ordinary shares for each €100 of debenture stock on 31 December 2013. Henry Ltd considered borrowing the €200 million through a conventional debenture that repaid in cash, however, the interest rate that could be obtained was estimated at 7%, therefore Henry Ltd decided on the issue of the convertible.

Required:
Show how the convertible bond issue will be recognised on 1 January 2009 and determine the interest charges that are expected in the statement of comprehensive income over the life of the convertible bond.

* **Question 5**

George plc adopted IFRS for the first time on 1 January 2008 and has three different instruments whose accounting George is concerned will change as a result of the adoption of the standard. The three instruments are:

1 An investment in 15% of the ordinary shares of Joshua Ltd, a private company. This investment cost €50,000, but had a fair value of €60,000 on 1 January 2008, €70,000 on 31 December 2008 and €65,000 on 31 December 2009.

2 An investment of €40,000 in 6% debentures. The debentures were acquired at their face value of €40,000 on 1 July 2007 and pay interest half yearly in arrears on 31 December and 30 June each year. The bonds have a fair value of €41,000 at 1 January 2008, €43,000 at 31 December 2008 and €38,000 at 31 December 2009.

3 An interest rate swap taken out to swap floating rate interest on an outstanding loan to fixed rate interest. Since taking out the swap the loan has been repaid, however, George plc decided to retain the swap as it was 'in the money' at 1 January 2008. The fair value of the swap was a €10,000 asset on 1 January 2008, however, it became a liability of €5,000 by 31 December 2008 and the liability increased to €20,000 by 31 December 2009. In 2008 George paid €1,000 to the counterparty to the swap and in 2009 paid €5,000 to the counterparty.

Required:
Show the amount that would be recognised for all three instruments in the statement of financial position, in profit and loss and in other comprehensive income on the following assumptions:
(i) Equity and debt investments are available for sale.
(ii) Where possible, investments are treated as held to maturity.
(iii) Where equity investments are treated as fair value through profit and loss and debt investments are treated as loans and receivables.

Question 6

Isabelle Limited borrows £100,000 from a bank on the following terms:

(i) Arrangement fees of £2,000 are charged by the bank and deducted from the initial proceeds on the loan;

(ii) Interest is payable at 5% for the first 3 years of the loan and then increases to 7% for the remaining 2 years of the loan;

(iii) The full balance of £100,000 is repaid at the end of year 5.

Required:
(a) What interest should be recognised in the statement of comprehensive income for each year of the loan?
(b) If Isabelle Limited repaid the loan after 3 years for £100,000 what gain or loss would be recognised in the statement of comprehensive income?

Question 7

A company borrows on a floating rate loan, but wishes to hedge against interest variations so swaps the interest for fixed rate. The swap should be perfectly effective and has zero fair value at inception. Interest rate increase and therefore the swap becomes a financial asset to the company at fair value of £5 million.

Required:

Describe the impact on the financial statements for the following situations:

(a) The swap is accounted for under IAS 39, but is not designated as a hedge.

(b) The swap is accounted for under IAS 39, and is designated as a hedge.

Question 8

Charles plc is applying IAS 32 and IAS 39 for the first time this year and is uncertain about the application of the standard. Charles plc balance sheet is as follows:

	£000	Financial asset/liability	IAS 32/39?	Category	Measurement
Non-current assets					
Goodwill	2,000				
Intangible	3,000				
Tangible	6,000				
Investments					
Corporate bond	1,500				
Equity trade					
investments	900				
	13,400				
Current assets					
Inventory	800				
Receivables	700				
Prepayments	300				
Forward contracts					
(note 1)	250				
Equity investments					
held for future sale	1,200				
	3,250				
Current liabilities					
Trade creditors	(3,500)				
Lease creditor	(800)				
Income tax	(1,000)				
Forward contracts					
(note 1)	(500)				
	(5,800)				
Non-current liabilities					
Bank loan	(5,000)				
Convertible debt	(1,800)				
Deferred tax	(500)				
Pension liability	(900)				
	(8,200)				
Net assets	**2,650**				

Note

1   The forward contracts have been revalued to fair value in the balance sheet. They do not qualify as hedging instruments.

Required:

For the above balance sheet consider whether, under the IAS 39:

(i) Which items on the balance sheet are financial assets/liabilities?

(ii) Are the balances within the scope of IAS 39?

(iii) How they should be classified under IAS 39:

HTM	Held to maturity
LR	Loans and receivables
FVPL	Fair value through profit and loss
AFS	Available for sale
FL	Financial liabilities

(iv) How they should be measured under IAS 39:

FV	Fair value
C	Amortised cost

Assume that the company only includes items in 'fair value through profit and loss' when required to do so, and also chooses where possible to include items in 'loans and receivables'.

References

1 IAS 32 *Financial Instruments: Disclosure and Presentation*, IASC, revised 1998.

2 *Ibid.*, para. 5.

3 *Ibid.*, para. 18.

4 *Ibid.*, para. 23.

5 *Ibid.*, para. 33.

6 IFRS 7 *Financial Instruments: Disclosures*, IASB, 2005.

7 IAS 32 *Financial Instruments: Presentation*, IASB, revised 2005.

8 S. Fearnley and S. Sunder 'Bring Back Prudent', *Accountancy*, 2007, 140(1370), pp. 76–77.

CHAPTER 13

Employee benefits

13.1 Introduction

In this chapter we consider the application of IAS 19 *Employee Benefits*.[1] IAS 19 is concerned with the determination of the cost of retirement benefits in the financial statements of **employers** having retirement benefit plans (sometimes referred to as 'pension schemes', 'superannuation schemes' or 'retirement benefit schemes'). The requirements of IFRS 2 *Share-Based Payment* will also be considered here. Even though IFRS 2 covers share-based payments for almost any good or service a company can receive, in practice it is employee service that is most commonly rewarded with share-based payments. We also consider the disclosure requirements of IAS 26 *Accounting and Reporting by Retirement Benefit Plans*.[2]

Objectives

By the end of this chapter, you should be able to:

- critically comment on the approaches to pension accounting that have been used under International Accounting Standards;
- understand the nature of different types of pension plan and account for the different types of pension plan that companies may have;
- explain the accounting treatment for other long-term and short-term employee benefit costs;
- understand and account for share-based payments that are made by companies to their employees;
- outline the required approach of pension schemes to presenting their financial position and performance.

13.2 Greater employee interest in pensions

The percentages of pensioners and public pension expenditure are increasing.

	% of population over 60		*Public pensions as % of GDP*
	2000	*2040*	*2040*
	%	*% (projected)*	*% (projected)*
Germany	24	33	18
Italy	24	37	21
Japan	23	34	15
UK	21	30	5
US	17	29	7

This has led to gloomy projections that countries could even be bankrupted by the increasing demand for state pensions. In an attempt to avert what governments see as a national disaster, there have been increasing efforts to encourage private funding of pensions.

As people become more and more aware of the possible failure of governments to provide adequate basic state pensions, they recognise the advisability of making their own provision for their old age. This has raised their expectation that their employers should offer a pension scheme and other post-retirement benefits. These have increased, particularly in Ireland, the UK and the USA, and what used to be a 'fringe benefit' for only certain categories of staff has been broadened across the workforce. This has been encouraged by various governments with favourable tax treatment of both employers' and employees' contributions to pension schemes.

13.3 Financial reporting implications

The provision of pensions for employees as part of an overall remuneration package has led to the related costs being a material part of the accounts. The very nature of such arrangements means that the commitment is a long-term one that may well involve estimates. The way the related costs are allocated between accounting periods and are reported in the financial statements needs careful consideration to ensure that a fair view of the position is shown.

In recent years there has been a shift of view on the way that pension costs should be accounted for. The older view was that pension costs (as recommended by IAS 19 prior to its revision in 1998) should be matched against the period of the employee's service so as to create an even charge for pensions in the statement of comprehensive income, although the statement of financial position amount could have been misleading. The more recent approach is to make the statement of financial position more sensible, but perhaps accept greater variation in the pension cost in the statement of comprehensive income. The new view is the one endorsed by IAS 19 (revised) and is the one now in use by companies preparing accounts to international accounting standards.

Before examining the detail of how IAS 19 (revised) requires pensions and other long-term benefits to be accounted for, we need to consider the types of pension scheme that are commonly used.

13.4 Types of scheme

13.4.1 *Ex gratia* arrangements

These are not schemes at all but are circumstances where an employer agrees to grant a pension to be paid for out of the resources of the firm. Consequently these are arrangements where pensions have not been funded but decisions are made on an *ad hoc* or case-by-case basis, sometimes arising out of custom or practice. No contractual obligation to grant or pay a pension exists, although a constructive obligation may exist which would need to be provided for in accordance with IAS 37 *Provisions, Contingent Liabilities and Contingent Assets*.

13.4.2 Defined contribution schemes

These are schemes in which the employer undertakes to make certain contributions each year, usually a stated percentage of salary. These contributions are usually supplemented by contributions from the employee. The money is then invested and, on retirement, the employee gains the pension benefits that can be purchased from the resulting funds.

Such schemes have uncertain future benefits but fixed, predetermined costs. Schemes of this sort were very common among smaller employers but fell out of fashion for a time. In recent years, due to the fixed cost to the company and the resulting low risk to the employer for providing a pension, these schemes have become increasingly popular. They are also popular with employees who regularly change employers, since the funds accrued within the schemes are relatively easy to transfer.

The contributions may be paid into a wide variety of plans, e.g. government plans to ensure state pensions are supplemented (these may be optional or compulsory), or schemes operated by insurance companies.

The following is an extract from the 2007 Annual Report of Nokia:

Pensions

The Group's contributions to defined contribution plans and to multi-employer and insured plans are charged to the profit and loss account in the period to which the contributions relate.

Know how much to receive

13.4.3 Defined benefit schemes

Under these schemes the employees will, on retirement, receive a pension based on the length of service and salary, usually final salary or an average of the last few (usually three) years' salary.

These schemes form the majority of company pension schemes. They are, however, becoming less popular when new schemes are formed because the cost to employers is uncertain and there are greater regulatory requirements being introduced.

Whilst the benefits to the employee are not certain, they are more predictable than under a defined contribution scheme. The cost to the employer, however, is uncertain as the employer will need to vary the contributions to the scheme to ensure it is adequately funded to meet the pension liabilities when employees eventually retire.

The following is an extract from the accounting policies in the 2007 Annual Report of the Nestlé Group:

Employee benefits

The liabilities of the Group arising from defined benefit obligations, and the related current service cost, are determined using the projected unit credit method. Valuations are carried out annually for the largest plans and on a regular basis for other plans. Actuarial advice is provided both by external consultants and by actuaries employed by the Group. The actuarial assumptions used to calculate the benefit obligations vary according to the economic conditions of the country in which the plan is located.

Such plans are either externally funded, with the assets of the schemes held separately from those of the Group in independently administered funds, or unfunded with the related liabilities carried in the statement of financial position.

For the funded defined benefit plans, the deficit or excess of the fair value of plan assets over the present value of the defined benefit obligation is recognised as a liability or an asset in the statement of financial position, taking into account any unrecognised past service cost. However, an excess of assets is recognised only to the extent that it represents a future economic benefit which is actually available to the Group, for example in the form of refunds from the plan or reductions in future contributions to the plan. When such excess is not available or does not represent a future economic benefit, it is not recognised but is disclosed in the notes.

Actuarial gains and losses arise mainly from changes in actuarial assumptions and differences between actuarial assumptions and what has actually occurred. They are recognised in the period in which they occur outside the statement of comprehensive income directly in equity under the statement of recognised income and expense. The Group performs full pensions and retirement benefits reporting once a year, in December, at which point actuarial gains and losses for the period are determined.

For defined benefit plans the actuarial cost charged to the statement of comprehensive income consists of current service cost, interest cost, expected return on plan assets and past service cost. Recycling to the statement of comprehensive income of accumulated actuarial gains and losses recognised against equity is not permitted by IAS 19. The past service cost for the enhancement of pension benefits is accounted for when such benefits vest or become a constructive obligation.

The accounting policy is quite complex to apply and we will illustrate the detailed calculations involved below.

13.4.4 Equity compensation plans

IAS 19 does not specify recognition or measurement requirements for equity compensation plans such as shares or share options issued to employees at less than fair value. The valuation of share options has proved an extremely contentious topic and we will consider the issues that have arisen. IFRS 2 *Share-Based Payment* covers these plans.[3]

The following is an extract from the accounting policies in the 2007 Annual Report of the Nestlé Group:

> The Group has equity-settled and cash-settled share-based payment transactions.
>
> Equity-settled share-based payment transactions are recognised in the statement of comprehensive income with a corresponding increase in equity over the vesting period. They are fair valued at grant date and measured using the Black and Scholes model. The cost of equity-settled share-based payment transactions is adjusted annually by the expectations of vesting, for the forfeitures of the participants' rights that no longer satisfy the plan conditions, as well as for early vesting.
>
> Liabilities arising from cash-settled share-based payment transactions are recognised in the statement of comprehensive income over the vesting period. They are fair valued at each reporting date and measured using the Black and Scholes model. The cost of cash-settled share-based payment transactions is adjusted for the forfeitures of the participants' rights that no longer satisfy the plan conditions, as well as for early vesting.

13.5 Defined contribution pension schemes

Defined contribution schemes (otherwise known as money purchase schemes) have not presented any major accounting problems. The cost of providing the pension, usually a percentage of salary, is recorded as a remuneration expense in the statement of comprehensive income in the period in which it is due. Assets or liabilities may exist for the pension contributions if the company has not paid the amount due for the period. If a contribution was payable more than twelve months after the reporting date for services rendered in the current period, the liability should be recorded at its discounted amount (using a discount rate based on the market rate for high-quality corporate bonds).

Disclosure is required of the pension contribution charged to the statement of comprehensive income for the period.

Illustration of Andrew plc defined contribution pension scheme costs

Andrew plc has payroll costs of £2.7 million for the year ended 30 June 2009. Andrew plc pays pension contributions of 5% of salary, but for convenience paid £10,000 per month standard contribution with any shortfall to be made up in the July 2009 contribution.

Statement of comprehensive income charge

The pension cost is £2,700,000 × 5%   £135,000

Statement of financial position

The amount paid over the period is £120,000 and therefore an accrual of £15,000 will be made in the statement of financial position at 30 June 2009.

13.6 Defined benefit pension schemes

13.6.1 Position before 1998

To consider the accounting requirements for defined benefit pension schemes it is useful to look at the differences between the original IAS 19 and IAS 19 as revised in 1998. By looking at the original IAS 19 it is possible to see why a revision was necessary and what the revision to the standard was trying to achieve.

Statement of comprehensive income

Under the original pre-1998 standard both the costs and the fund value were computed on an actuarial basis. The valuation was needed to give an estimate of the costs of providing the benefits over the remaining service lives of the relevant employees. This was normally done in such a way as to produce a pension cost that was a level percentage of both the current and future pensionable payroll. Both the accounting standard and the actuarial professional bodies gave guidance on the assumptions and methods to be employed in the valuation and required that those guidelines were followed.

Treatment of variations from regular costs

If a valuation gave rise to a variation in the regular costs, it would normally be allocated over the remaining service lives of the employees. If, however, a variation arose out of a surplus or deficit arising from a significant reduction in pensionable employees, it was recognised when it arose unless such treatment was not prudent and involved the anticipating of income.

Statement of financial position

This was a much simpler approach and was based purely on the accruals principle for defined benefit pension schemes. The difference between cumulative pension costs charged in the statement of comprehensive income and the money paid either as pensions or contributions to a scheme or fund was shown as either a prepayment or an accrual. In effect the statement of financial position value was a balancing figure representing the difference between the amounts charged against the statement of comprehensive income and the amounts paid into the fund.

Illustration of Hart plc defined benefit pension scheme under the pre-1998 approach

Hart plc operates a defined benefit pension scheme on behalf of its employees. At an actuarial valuation in early 2008 the following details were calculated:

Regular service costs (per annum)	£10,000
Estimated remaining average service lives of staff	10 years
Surplus on scheme at 31 December 2007	£30,000

Hart plc has been advised to eliminate the surplus on the scheme by taking a three-year contribution holiday, and then returning to regular service cost contributions.

The financial statements over the remaining service lives of the employees would show the following amounts:

Year	Contribution	Statement of comprehensive income charge	Statement of financial position liability
	£	£	£
2008	Nil	7,000	7,000
2009	Nil	7,000	14,000
2010	Nil	7,000	21,000
2011	10,000	7,000	18,000
2012	10,000	7,000	15,000
2013	10,000	7,000	12,000
2014	10,000	7,000	9,000
2015	10,000	7,000	6,000
2016	10,000	7,000	3,000
2017	10,000	7,000	—
	70,000		

The statement of comprehensive income charge is the total contributions paid over the period (£70,000) divided by the average remaining service lives of ten years. The effect of this is to spread the surplus over the remaining service lives in the statement of comprehensive income.

13.6.2 Problems of the old standard

The old IAS 19 had a number of problems in its approach which needed to be addressed by the revised standard.

A misleading statement of financial position

Making the statement of financial position accrual or prepayment a balancing figure based on the comparison of the amount paid and charged to date could be very misleading. In the above illustration it can be seen that the statement of financial position shows a liability even though there is a surplus on the fund. A user of the financial statements who was unaware of the method used to account for the pension scheme could be misled into believing that contributions were owed to the pension fund.

Current emphasis is on getting the statement of financial position to report assets and liabilities more accurately

There is an issue regarding the consistency of the presentation of the pension asset or liability with that of other assets and liabilities. Accounting is moving towards ensuring that the statement of financial position shows a sensible position with the statement of comprehensive income recording the change in the statement of financial position. Accounting for pension schemes under the old IAS 19 does not do this.

The old IAS 19 was also inconsistent with the way that US GAAP would require pensions to be accounted for, although in its defence it was consistent with the approach adopted by UK GAAP.

Valuation basis

The old IAS 19 required the use of an actuarial valuation basis for both assets and liabilities of the fund in deciding what level of contribution was required and whether any surplus or deficit had arisen. In addition the liabilities of the fund (i.e. the obligation to pay future pensions) were discounted at the expected rate of return on the assets. These approaches to valuation are difficult to justify and could give rise to unrealistic pension provision being made.

13.7 IAS 19 (revised) *Employee Benefits*

After a relatively long discussion and exposure period IAS 19 (revised) was issued in 1998 and it redefined how all employee benefits were to be accounted for.

IAS 19 has chosen to follow an 'asset or liability' approach to accounting for the pension scheme contributions by the employer and, therefore, it defines how the statement of financial position asset or liability should be built up. The statement of comprehensive income charge is effectively the movement in the asset or liability. The pension fund must be valued sufficiently regularly so that the statement of financial position asset or liability is kept up to date. The valuation would normally be done by a qualified actuary and is based on actuarial assumptions.

13.8 The liability for pension and other post-retirement costs

The liability for pension costs is made up from the following amounts:

(a) the present value of the defined benefit obligation at the period end date;

(b) plus any actuarial gains (less actuarial losses) not yet recognised;

(c) minus any past service cost not yet recognised;

(d) minus the fair value at the period end date of plan assets (if any) out of which the obligations are to be settled directly.

If this calculation comes out with a negative amount, the company should recognise a pension asset in the statement of financial position. There is a limit on the amount of the asset, if the asset calculated above is greater than the total of:

(i) any unrecognised actuarial losses and past service cost; plus

(ii) the present value of any future refunds from the scheme or reductions in future contributions.

Within IAS 19 there are rules regarding the maximum pension asset that can be created. Effective from 1 January 2009, IFRIC 14 *Limit on a Defined Benefit Asset, Minimum Funding Requirements and their Interaction* was issued that provides further guidance in respect of the maximum pension asset than can be recognised. It gives guidance that where a pension has minimum funding obligations to cover future pension service these reduce the amount of the asset that can be recognised.

Each of the elements making up the asset or liability position (a) to (d) above can now be considered.

13.8.1 Obligations of the fund

The pension fund obligation must be calculated using the 'projected unit credit method'. This method of allocating pension costs builds up the pension liability each year for an extra year of service and a reversal of discounting. Discounting of the liability is done using the market yields on high-quality corporate bonds with similar currency and duration.

The Grado illustration below shows how the obligation to pay pension accumulates over the working life of an employee.

Grado illustration

A lump sum benefit is payable on termination of service and equal to 1% of final salary for each year of service. The salary in year 1 is £10,000 and is assumed to increase at 7% (compound) each year. The discount rate used is 10%. The following table shows how an obligation (in £) builds up for an employee who is expected to leave at the end of year 5. For simplicity, this example ignores the additional adjustment needed to reflect the probability that the employee may leave service at an earlier or later date.

Year	1	2	3	4	5
Benefit attributed to prior years	0	131	262	393	524
Benefit attributed to current year (1% of final salary)*	131	131	131	131	131
Benefit attributed to current and prior years	131	262	393	524	655
Opening obligation (present value of benefit attributed to prior years)	—	89	196	324	476
Interest at 10%	—	9	20	33	48
Current service cost (present value of benefit attributed to current year)	89	98	108	119	131
Closing obligation (present value of benefit attributed to current and prior years)**	89	196	324	476	655

* Final salary is £10,000 × (1.07)^4 = £13,100.
** Discounting the benefit attributable to current and prior years at 10%.

13.8.2 Actuarial gains and losses

Actuarial gains or losses result from changes either in the present value of the defined benefit obligation or changes in the market value of the plan assets. They arise from experience adjustments – that is, differences between actuarial assumptions and actual experience. Typical reasons for the gains or losses would be:

● unexpectedly low or high rates of employee turnover;
● the effect of changes in the discount rate;
● differences between the **actual** return on plan assets and the **expected** return on plan assets.

Accounting treatment

Since a revision of IAS 19 in 2004 there has been a choice of accounting treatment for actuarial gains and losses. One approach follows a '10% corridor' and requires recognition of gains and losses in the profit or loss whereas an alternative makes no use of the corridor and requires gains and losses to be recognised in other comprehensive income.

10% corridor approach

- If actual gains and losses are greater than the higher of 10% of the present value of the defined benefit obligation or 10% of the market value of the plan assets, the excess gains and losses should be charged or credited to the profit or loss over the average remaining service lives of current employees. Any shorter period of recognition of gains or losses is acceptable, provided it is systematic.

- If beneath the 10% thresholds, they can be part of the defined benefit liability for the year, however, the standard also allows them to be recognised in the profit or loss.

Any actuarial gains and losses that are recognised in the profit or loss are recognised in the periods following the one in which they arise. For example, if an actuarial loss arose in the year ended 31 December 2007 that exceeded the 10% corridor and therefore required recognition in the statement of comprehensive income, that recognition would begin in the 2008 year. This means that to calculate the income statement charge or credit for the current year the cumulative unrecognised gains or losses at the end of the previous year are compared to the corridor at the end of the previous year (or the beginning of the current year).

The comprehensive illustration in section 13.10 below illustrates this treatment.

Equity recognition approach

It is acceptable to recognise actuarial gains and losses immediately in other comprehensive income.

This approach has the benefit over the corridor approach in that it does not require any actuarial gains and losses to be recognised in profit or loss; however, its drawback comes in volatility on the statement of financial position. Under this approach all actuarial gains and losses are recognised and therefore no unrecognised ones are available for offset against the statement of financial position asset or liability. As the actuarial valuations are based on fair values the volatility could be significant.

13.8.3 Past service costs

Past service costs are costs that arise for a pension scheme as a result of improving the scheme or when a business introduces a plan. They are the extra liability in respect of previous years' service by employees. Do note, however, that past service costs can only arise if actuarial assumptions did not take into account the reason why they occurred. Typically they would include:

- estimates of benefit improvements as a result of actuarial gains (if the company proposes to give the gains to the employees);
- the effect of plan amendments that increase or reduce benefits for past service.

Accounting treatment

The past service cost should be recognised on a straight-line basis over the period to which the benefits vest. If already vested, the cost should be recognised immediately in profit or loss in the statement of comprehensive income. A benefit vests when an employee satisfies preconditions. For example, if a company offered a scheme where employees would only be entitled to a pension if they worked for at least five years, the benefits would vest as soon as they started their sixth year of employment. The company will still have to make provision for pensions for the first five years of employment (and past service costs could arise in this period), as these will be pensionable service years provided the employees work for more than five years.

13.8.4 Fair value of plan assets

This is usually the market value of the assets of the plan (or the estimated value if no immediate market value exists). The plan assets exclude unpaid contributions due from the reporting enterprise to the fund.

13.8.5 Impact on net assets

For many businesses the implication on net assets on moving to the asset or liability approach to pensions required by IAS 19 has been significant. The extract below shows the impact on the net assets of Balfour Beatty for 2004, when they adopted IFRS.

Extract from Balfour Beatty financial statements

Net assets

Reconciliation of net assets	£m
Net assets – UK GAAP at 31 December 2004	413
IFRS 3 – Goodwill amortisation not charged	17
IAS 19 – Retirement benefit obligations (net of tax)	(174)
IFRS 2/IAS 12 – Share-based payments – tax effects	5
IAS 10 – Elimination of provision for proposed dividend	16
IAS 12 – Deferred taxation	(4)
Net assets – IFRS restated at 31 December 2004	273

13.9 The statement of comprehensive income

The statement of comprehensive income charge for a period should be made up of the following parts:

(a) current service cost;

(b) interest cost;

(c) the expected return on any plan assets;

(d) actuarial gains and losses to the extent that they are recognised under the 10% corridor;

(e) past service cost to the extent that it is recognised;

(f) the effect of any curtailments or settlements.

If a company takes the option of recognising all actuarial gains and losses outside profit or loss then they are recognised in full in the 'other comprehensive income' section of the statement of comprehensive income.

The items above are all the things that cause the statement of financial position liability for pensions to alter and the statement of comprehensive income is consequently based on the movement in the liability. Because of the potential inclusion of actuarial gains and losses and past service costs in comprehensive income the total comprehensive income is liable to fluctuate much more than the charge made under the original IAS 19.

13.10 Comprehensive illustration

The following comprehensive illustration is based on an example in IAS 19 (revised)[4] and demonstrates how a pension liability and profit or loss charge is calculated. The example does not include the effect of curtailments or settlements. This illustration demonstrates the 10% corridor approach for actuarial gains and losses.

Illustration

The following information is given about a funded defined benefit plan. To keep the computations simple, all transactions are assumed to occur at the year-end. The present value of the obligation and the market value of the plan assets were both 1,000 at 1 January 20X1. The average remaining service lives of the current employees is ten years.

	20X1	20X2	20X3
Discount rate at start of year	10%	9%	8%
Expected rate of return on plan assets			
at start of year	12%	11%	10%
Current service cost	160	140	150
Benefits paid	150	180	190
Contributions paid	90	100	110
Present value of obligations at 31 December	1,100	1,380	1,455
Market value of plan assets at 31 December	1,190	1,372	1,188

1000 + 100 interest

In 20X2 the plan was amended to provide additional benefits with effect from 1 January 20X2. The present value as at 1 January 20X2 of additional benefits for employee service before 1 January 20X2 was 50, all for vested benefits.

Required:
Show how the pension scheme would be shown in the accounts for 20X1, 20X2 and 20X3.

Solution to the comprehensive illustration

Step 1 Change in the obligation
The changes in the present value of the obligation must be calculated and used to determine what, if any, actuarial gains and losses have arisen. This calculation can be done by comparing the expected obligations at the end of each period with the actual obligations as follows:

Change in the obligation:

	20X1	20X2	20X3
Present value of obligation, 1 January	1,000	1,100	1,380
Interest cost	100	99	110
Current service cost	160	140	150
Past service cost – vested benefits	—	50	—
Benefits paid	(150)	(180)	(190)
Actuarial (gain) loss on obligation			
(balancing figure)	*(10)*	*171*	*5*
Present value of obligation, 31 December	1,100	1,380	1,455

Step 2 Change in the assets

The changes in the fair value of the assets of the fund must be calculated and used to determine what, if any, actuarial gains and losses have arisen. This calculation can be done by comparing the asset values at the end of each period with the actual asset values.

Change in the assets:

	20X1	20X2	20X3
Fair value of plan assets, 1 January	1,000	1,190	1,372
Expected return on plan assets	120	131	137
Contributions	90	100	110
Benefits paid	(150)	(180)	(190)
Actuarial gain (loss) on plan assets			
(balancing figure)	130	131	(241)
Fair value of plan assets, 31 December	1,190	1,372	1,188

Step 3 The 10% corridor calculation

The limits of the '10% corridor' need to be calculated in order to establish whether actuarial gains or losses exceed the corridor limit and therefore need recognising in profit or loss. Actuarial gains and losses are recognised in profit or loss if they exceed the 10% corridor, and they are recognised by being amortised over the remaining service lives of employees.

The limits of the 10% corridor (at 1 January) are set at the greater of:

(a) 10% of the present value of the obligation before deducting plan assets (100, 110 and 138); and

(b) 10% of the fair value of plan assets (100, 119 and 137).

	20X1	20X2	20X3
Limit of '10% corridor' at 1 January	100	119	138
Cumulative unrecognised gains (losses) –			
1 January	—	140	98
Gains (losses) on the obligation	10	(171)	(5)
Gains (losses) on the assets	130	131	(241)
Cumulative gains (losses) before amortisation	140	100	(148)
Amortisation of excess over ten years			
(see working)	—	(2)	—
Cumulative unrecognised gains (losses) –			
31 December	140	98	(148)

Working: $\dfrac{(140 - 119)}{10 \text{ yrs}} = 2$ – amortisation charge in 20X2.

Step 4 Calculate the profit or loss entry

	20X1	20X2	20X3
Current service cost	160	140	150
Interest cost	100	99	110
Expected return on plan assets	(120)	(131)	(137)
Recognised actuarial (gains) losses		(2)	
Recognised past service cost			50
Profit or loss charge	*140*	*156*	*123*

Step 5 Calculate the statement of financial position entry

	20X1	20X2	20X3
Present value of obligation, 31 December	1,100	1,380	1,455
Fair value of assets, 31 December	(1,190)	(1,372)	(1,188)
Unrecognised actuarial gains (losses) –			
from Step 3	140	98	(148)
Liability in statement of financial position	*50*	*106*	*119*

13.11 Plan curtailments and settlements

A curtailment of a pension scheme occurs when a company is committed to make a material reduction in the number of employees of a scheme or when the employees will receive no benefit for a substantial part of their future service. A settlement occurs when an enterprise enters into a transaction that eliminates any further liability from arising under the fund.

The accounting for a settlement or curtailment is that a gain or loss is recognised in profit or loss when the settlement or curtailment occurs. The gain or loss on a curtailment or settlement should comprise:

(a) any resulting change in the present value of the defined benefit obligation;

(b) any resulting change in the fair value of the plan assets;

(c) any related actuarial gain/loss and past service cost that had not previously been recognised.

Before determining the effect of the curtailment the enterprise must remeasure the obligations and the liability to get it to the up-to-date value.

13.12 Multi-employer plans

The definition of a multi-employer plan per IAS 19[5] is that it is a defined contribution or defined benefit plan that:

(a) pools the assets contributed by various enterprises that are not under common control; and

(b) uses those assets to provide benefits to employees of more than one enterprise, on the basis that contribution and benefit levels are determined without regard to the identity of the enterprise that employs the employees concerned.

An enterprise should account for a multi-employer defined benefit plan as follows:

- account for its share of the defined benefit obligation, plan assets and costs associated with the plan in the same way as for any defined benefit plan; or
- if insufficient information is available to use defined benefit accounting it should:
  - account for the plan as if it were a defined contribution plan; and
  - give extra disclosures.

In 2004 the IASB revised IAS 19 and changed the position for group pension plans in the financial statements of the individual companies in the group. Prior to the revision a group pension scheme could not be treated as a multi-employer plan and therefore any group schemes would have had to be split across all the individual contributing companies. The amendment to IAS 19, however, made it acceptable to treat group schemes as multi-employer schemes. This means that the defined benefit accounting is only necessary in the consolidated accounts and not in the individual company accounts of all companies in the group. The requirements for full defined benefit accounting are required in the individual sponsor company financial statements.

This amendment to IAS 19 was not effective until accounting periods commencing in 2006; however, earlier adoption was allowed.

13.13 Disclosures

The major disclosure requirements[6] of the standard are:

- the enterprise's accounting policy for recognising actuarial gains and losses;
- a general description of the type of plan;
- a reconciliation of the assets and liabilities including the present value of the obligations, the market value of the assets, the actuarial gains/losses and the past service cost;
- a reconciliation of the movement during the period in the net liability;
- the total expense in the statement of comprehensive income broken down into different parts;
- the actual return on plan assets;
- the principal actuarial assumptions used as at the period end date.

13.14 Other long-service benefits

So far in this chapter we have considered the accounting for post-retirement costs for both defined contribution and defined benefit pension schemes. As well as pensions, IAS 19 (revised) considers other forms of long-service benefit paid to employees.[7] These other forms of long-service benefit include:

(a) long-term compensated absences such as long-service or sabbatical leave;
(b) jubilee or other long-service benefits;
(c) long-term disability benefits;
(d) profit-sharing and bonuses payable twelve months or more after the end of the period in which the employees render the related service;
(e) deferred compensation paid twelve months or more after the end of the period in which it is earned.

The measurement of these other long-service benefits is not usually as complex or uncertain as it is for post-retirement benefits and therefore a more simplified method of accounting is used for them. For other long-service benefits any actuarial gains and losses and past service costs (if they arise) are recognised immediately in profit or loss and no '10% corridor' is applied.

This means that the statement of financial position liability for other long-service benefits is just the present value of the future benefit obligation less the fair value of any assets that the benefit will be settled from directly.

The profit or loss charge for these benefits is therefore the total of:

(a) current service cost;

(b) interest cost;

(c) expected return on plan assets (if any);

(d) actuarial gains and losses;

(e) past service cost;

(f) the effect of curtailments or settlements.

13.15 Short-term benefits

In addition to pension and other long-term benefits considered earlier, IAS 19 gives accounting rules for short-term employee benefits.

Short-term employee benefits include items such as:

1 wages, salaries and social security contributions;

2 short-term compensated absences (such as paid annual leave and paid sick leave) where the absences are expected to occur within twelve months after the end of the period in which the employees render the related employee service;

3 profit-sharing and bonuses payable within twelve months after the end of the period in which the employees render the related service; and

4 non-monetary benefits (such as medical care, housing or cars) for current employees.

All short-term employee benefits should be recognised at an undiscounted amount:

• as a liability (after deducting any payments already made); and

• as an expense (unless another international standard allows capitalisation as an asset).

If the payments already made exceed the undiscounted amount of the benefits, an asset should be recognised only if it will lead to a future reduction in payments or a cash refund.

Compensated absences

The expected cost of short-term compensated absences should be recognised:

(a) in the case of accumulating absences, when the employees render service that increases their entitlement to future compensated absences; and

(b) in the case of non-accumulating compensated absences, when the absences occur.

Accumulating absences occur when the employees can carry forward unused absence from one period to the next. They are recognised when the employee renders services regardless of whether the benefit is vesting (the employee would get a cash alternative if they left employment) or non-vesting. The measurement of the obligation reflects the likelihood of employees leaving in a non-vesting scheme.

It is common practice for leave entitlement to be an accumulating absence (perhaps restricted to a certain number of days) but for sick pay entitlement to be non-accumulating.

Profit-sharing and bonus plans

The expected cost of a profit-sharing or bonus plan should only be recognised when:

(a) the enterprise has a present legal or constructive obligation to make such payments as a result of past events; and

(b) a reliable estimate of the obligation can be made.

13.16 Termination benefits[8]

These benefits are treated separately from other employee benefits in IAS 19 (revised) because the event that gives rise to the obligation to pay is the termination of employment as opposed to the service of the employee.

The accounting treatment for termination benefits is consistent with the requirements of IAS 37 and the rules concern when the obligation should be provided for and the measurement of the obligation.

Recognition

Termination benefits can only be recognised as a liability when the enterprise is demonstrably committed to either:

(a) terminate the employment of an employee or group of employees before the normal retirement date; or

(b) provide termination benefits as a result of an offer made in order to encourage voluntary redundancy.

The enterprise would only be considered to be demonstrably committed to a termination when a detailed plan for the termination is made and there is no realistic possibility of withdrawal from that plan. The plan should include as a minimum:

● the location, function and approximate number of employees whose services are to be terminated;

● the termination benefits for each job classification or function;

● the time at which the plan will be implemented.

In June 2005 the IASB issued an exposure draft of IAS 37 *Provisions, Contingent Liabilities and Contingent Assets*. When they issued this exposure draft they also proposed an amendment to IAS 19 regarding provisions for termination benefits. The proposal is that for voluntary redundancy payments provision can only be made once the employees have accepted the offer as opposed to when the detailed plan has been announced. The IASB view is that this is the date the payment becomes an obligation.

Measurement

If the termination benefits are to be paid more than twelve months after the period end date, they should be discounted, at a discount rate using the market yield on good quality corporate bonds. Prudence should also be exercised in the case of an offer made to encourage voluntary redundancy, as provision should only be based on the number of employees expected to accept the offer.

13.17 IFRS 2 *Share-Based Payment*

Share awards either directly through shares or through options are very common ways of rewarding employee performance. These awards align the interests of the directors with those of the shareholders and, as such, are aimed at motivating the directors to perform in the way that benefits the shareholders. In particular, there is a belief that they will motivate the directors towards looking at the long-term success of the business as opposed to focusing solely on short-term profits. They have additional benefits also to the company and employees, for example in relation to cash and tax. If employees are rewarded in shares or options, the company will not need to pay out cash to reward the employees, and in a start-up situation where cash flow is very limited this can be very beneficial. Many dotcom companies initially rewarded their staff in shares for this reason. There are also tax benefits to employees with shares in some tax regimes which give an incentive to employees to accept share awards.

Whilst commercially share-based payments have many benefits, the accounting world has struggled in finding a suitable way to account for them. IAS 19 only covered disclosure requirements for share-based payments and had no requirements for the recognition and measurement of the payments when it was issued. The result of this was that many companies who gave very valuable rewards to their employees in the form of shares or options did not recognise any charge associated with this. The IASB addressed this by issuing, in February 2004, IFRS 2 *Share-Based Payment* which is designed to cover all aspects of accounting for share-based payments.

13.17.1 Should an expense be recognised?

Historically there has been some debate about whether a charge should be recognised in the statement of comprehensive income for share-based payments. One view is that the reward is given to employees in their capacity as shareholders and, as a result, it is not an employee benefit cost. Also supporters of the 'no-charge' view claimed that to make a charge would be a double hit to earnings per share in that it would reduce profits and increase the number of shares, which they felt was unreasonable.

Supporters of a charge pointed to opposite arguments that claimed having no charge underestimated the reward given to employees and therefore overstated profit. The impact of this was to give a misleading view of the profitability of the company. Also, making a charge gave comparability between companies who rewarded their staff in different ways. Comparability is one of the key principles of financial reporting.

For many years these arguments were not resolved and no standard was in issue but the IASB has now decided that a charge is appropriate and they have issued IFRS 2. In drawing up IFRS 2 a number of obstacles had to be overcome and decisions had to be made, for example:

(i) What should the value of the charge be – fair value or intrinsic value?

(ii) At what point should the charge be measured – grant date, vesting date or exercise date?

(iii) How should the charge be spread over a number of periods?

(iv) If the charge is made to the statement of comprehensive income, where is the opposite entry to be made?

(v) What exemptions should be given from the standard?

IFRS 2 has answered these questions, and when introduced it made substantial changes to the profit recognised by many companies. In the UK, for example, the share-based payments charge for many businesses was one of their largest changes to profit on adopting IFRS.

13.18 Scope of IFRS 2

IFRS 2 proposes a comprehensive standard that would cover all aspects of share-based payments. Specifically IFRS 2 covers:

- equity-settled share-based payment transactions, in which the entity receives goods or services as consideration for equity instruments issued;
- cash-settled share-based payment transactions, in which the entity receives goods or services by incurring liabilities to the supplier of those goods or services for amounts that are based on the price of the entity's shares or other equity instruments; and
- transactions in which the entity receives goods or services and either the entity or the supplier of those goods or services may choose whether the transaction is settled in cash (based on the price of the entity's shares or other equity instruments) or by issuing equity instruments.

There are no exemptions from the provisions of the IFRS except for:

(a) acquisitions of goods or other non-financial assets as part of a business combination; and

(b) acquisitions of goods or services under derivative contracts where the contract is expected to be settled by delivery as opposed to being settled net in cash.

13.19 Recognition and measurement

The general principles of recognition and measurement of share-based payment charges are as follows:

- Entities should recognise the goods or services acquired in a share-based payment transaction over the period the goods or services are received.
- The entity should recognise an increase in equity if the share-based payment is equity-settled and a liability if the payment is a cash-settled payment transaction.
- The share-based payment should be measured at fair value.

13.20 Equity-settled share-based payments

For equity-settled share-based payment transactions, the entity shall measure the goods and services received, and the corresponding increase in equity:

- **directly** at the fair value of the goods and services received, unless that fair value cannot be estimated reliably;
- **indirectly**, by reference to the fair value of the equity instruments granted, if the entity cannot estimate reliably the fair value of the goods and services received.

For transactions with employees, the entity shall measure the fair value of services received by reference to the fair value of the equity instruments granted, because typically it is not possible to estimate reliably the fair value of the services received.

In transactions with the employees the IASB has decided that it is appropriate to value the benefit at the fair value of the instruments granted at their *grant date*. The IASB could have picked a number of different dates at which the options could have been valued:

- grant date – the date on which the options are given to the employees;
- vesting date – the date on which the options become unconditional to the employees;
- exercise date – the date on which the employees exercise their options.

The IASB went for the grant date as it felt that the grant of options was the reward to the employees and not the exercise of the options. This means that after the grant date any movements in the share price, whether upwards or downwards, do not influence the charge to the financial statements.

Employee options

In order to establish the fair value of an option at grant date the market price could be used (if the option is traded on a market), but it is much more likely that an option pricing model will need to be used. Examples of option pricing models that are possible include:

- *Black–Scholes.* An option pricing model used for options with a fixed exercise date that does not require adjustment for the inability of employees to exercise options during the vesting period; or
- *Binomial model.* An option pricing model used for options with a variable exercise date that will need adjustment for the inability of employees to exercise options during the vesting period.

Disclosures are required of the principle assumptions used in applying the option pricing model.

IFRS 2 does not recommend any one pricing model but insists that whichever model is chosen a number of factors affecting the fair value of the option such as exercise price, market price, time to maturity and volatility of the share price must be taken into account. In practice the Black–Scholes model is probably most commonly used, however, many companies vary the model to some extent to ensure it fits with the precise terms of their options.

Once the fair value of the option has been established at the grant date it is charged to profit or loss over the vesting period. The vesting period is the period in which the employees are required to satisfy conditions, for example service conditions, that allow them to exercise their options. The vesting period might be within the current financial accounting period and all options exercised.

EXAMPLE ● Employees were granted options to acquire 100,000 shares at $20 per share if still in employment at the end of the financial year. The market value of an option was $1.50 per share. All employees exercised their option at the year end and the company received $2,000,000. There will be a charge in the income statement of $150,000. Although the company has not transferred cash, it has transferred value to the employees. IFRS 2 requires the charge to be measured as the market value of the option i.e. £1.50 per share.

However, it is more usual for options to be exercised over longer periods. In which case, the charge is spread over the vesting period by calculating a revised cumulative charge each year, and then apportioning that over the vesting period with catch-up adjustments made to amend previous under- or over-charges to profit or loss. The illustration below shows how this approach works.

When calculating the charge in profit or loss the likelihood of options being forfeited due to non-market price conditions (e.g., because the employees leave in the conditional period) should be adjusted for. For non-market conditions the charge is amended each year to reflect any changes in estimates of the numbers expected to vest.

The charge cannot be adjusted, however, for market price conditions. If, for example, the share price falls and therefore the options will not be exercised due to the exercise price being higher than market price, no adjustment can be made. This means that if options are 'under water' the statement of comprehensive income will still be recognising a charge for those options.

The charge is made to the statement of comprehensive income but there was some debate about how the credit entry should be made. The credit entry must be made either as a liability or as an entry to equity, and the IASB has decided that it should be an entry to equity. The logic for not including a liability is that the future issue of shares is not an 'obligation to transfer economic benefits' and therefore does not meet the definition of a liability. When the shares are issued it will increase the equity of the company and be effectively a contribution from an owner.

Even though the standard specifies that the credit entry is to equity, it does not specify which item in equity is to be used. In practice it seems acceptable either to use a separate reserve or to make the entry to retained earnings. If a separate reserve is used and the options are not ultimately exercised, this reserve can be transferred to retained earnings.

Illustration of option accounting

A Ltd issued share options to staff on 1 January 20X0, details of which are as follows:

Number of staff	1,000
Number of options to each staff member	500
Vesting period	3 years
Fair value at grant date (per option)	£3
Expected employee turnover (per annum)	5%

In the 31 December 20X1 financial statements, the company revised its estimate of employee turnover to 8% per annum for the three-year vesting period.

In the 31 December 20X2 financial statements, the actual employee turnover had averaged 6% per annum for the three-year vesting period.

Options vest as long as the staff remain with the company for the three-year period.

The charge for share-based payments under IFRS 2 would be as follows:

Year-ended 31 December 20X0
In this period the charge would be based on the original terms of the share option issue.

The total value of the option award at fair value at the grant date is:

	£000
1000 staff × 500 options × £3 × $(0.95 \times 0.95 \times 0.95)$	1,286

The charge to the statement of comprehensive income for the period is therefore:

£1,286 ÷ 3	427

Year ended 31 December 20X1
In this year the expected employee turnover has risen to 8% per annum. The estimate of the effect of the increase is taken into account.

Amended total expected share option award at grant date:

	£000	£000
1000 staff × 500 options × £3 × $(0.92 \times 0.92 \times 0.92)$		1,168

The charge to the statement of comprehensive income is therefore

£1,168 × $^2/_3$	779	
Less: recognised to date	(427)	
		352

Year ended 31 December 20X2

The actual number of options that vest is now known.

The actual value of the option award that vests at the grant date is:

	£000	£000
1000 staff × 500 options × £3 × (0.94 × 0.94 × 0.94)		1,246

The charge to the statement of comprehensive income is therefore:

Total value over the vesting period	1,246	
Less: recognised to date	(779)	
		467

Re-priced options

If an entity re-prices its options, for instance in the event of a falling share price, the incremental fair value should be spread over the remaining vesting period. The incremental fair value per option is the difference between the fair value of the option immediately before re-pricing and the fair value of the re-priced option.

13.21 Cash-settled share-based payments

Cash-settled share-based payments result in the recognition of a liability. The entity shall measure the goods or services acquired and the liability incurred at fair value. Until the liability is settled, the entity shall remeasure the fair value of the liability at each reporting date, with any changes in fair value recognised in profit or loss.

For example, an entity might grant share appreciation rights to employees as part of their pay package, whereby the employees will become entitled to a future cash payment (rather than an equity instrument), based on the increase in the entity's share price from a specified level over a specified period.

The entity shall recognise the services received, and a liability to pay for those services, as the employees render service. For example, some share appreciation rights vest immediately, and the employees are therefore not required to complete a specified period of service to become entitled to the cash payment. In the absence of evidence to the contrary, the entity shall presume that the services rendered by the employees in exchange for the share appreciation rights have been received. Thus, the entity shall recognise immediately the services received and a liability to pay for them. If the share appreciation rights do not vest until the employees have completed a specified period of service, the entity shall recognise the services received, and a liability to pay for them, as the employees render service during that period.

The liability shall be measured, initially and at each reporting date until settled, at the fair value of the share appreciation rights, by applying an option pricing model, taking into account the terms and conditions on which the share appreciation rights were granted, and the extent to which the employees have rendered service to date. The entity shall remeasure the fair value of the liability at each reporting date until settled.

Disclosure is required of the difference between the amount that would be charged to the statement of comprehensive income if the share appreciation rights are paid out in cash as opposed to being paid out with shares.

13.22 Transactions which may be settled in cash or shares

Some share-based payment transactions can be settled in either cash or shares with the settlement option being either with the supplier of the goods or services and/or with the entity.

The accounting treatment is dependent upon which counterparty has the choice of settlement.

Supplier choice

If the supplier of the goods or services has the choice over settlement method, the entity has issued a compound instrument. The entity has an obligation to pay out cash (as the supplier can take this choice), but also has issued an equity option, as the supplier may decide to take equity to settle the transaction. The entity therefore recognises both a liability and an equity component.

The fair value of the equity option is the difference between the fair value of the offer of the cash alternative and the fair value of the offer of the equity payment. In many cases these are the same value, in which case the equity option has no value.

Once the split has been determined, each part is accounted for in the same way as other cash-settled or equity-settled transactions.

If cash is paid in settlement, any equity option recognised may be transferred to a different category in equity. If equity is issued, the liability is transferred to equity as the consideration for the equity instruments issued.

Entity choice

For a share-based payment transaction in which an entity may choose whether to settle in cash or by issuing equity instruments, the entity shall determine whether it has a present obligation to settle in cash and account for the share-based payment transaction accordingly. The entity has a present obligation to settle in cash if the choice of settlement in equity instruments is not substantive, or if the entity has a past practice or a stated policy of settling in cash.

If such an obligation exists, the entity shall account for the transaction in accordance with the requirements applying to cash-settled share-based payment transactions.

If no such obligation exists, the entity shall account for the transaction in accordance with the requirements applying to equity-settled transactions.

13.23 Transitional provisions

For equity-settled share-based payment transactions, the entity shall apply the requirements of IFRS 2 to grants of shares, options or other equity instruments that were granted after 7 November 2002 that had not yet vested at the effective date of this IFRS (1 January 2005). For first-time adopters of the standard the same retrospective date applies, options granted after 7 November 2002.

For liabilities arising from share-based payment transactions existing at the effective date of this IFRS, the entity shall apply retrospectively the requirements of this IFRS, except that the entity is not required to measure vested share appreciation rights (and similar liabilities in which the counterparty holds vested rights to cash or other assets of the entity) at fair value. Such liabilities shall be measured at their settlement amount (i.e. the amount that would be paid on settlement of the liability had the counterparty demanded settlement at the date the liability is measured).

13.24 IAS 26 *Accounting and Reporting by Retirement Benefit Plans*

This standard provides complementary guidance in addition to IAS 19 regarding the way that the pension fund should account and report on the contributions it receives and the obligations it has to pay pensions. The standard mainly contains the presentation and disclosure requirements of the schemes as opposed to the accounting methods that they should adopt.

13.24.1 Defined contribution plans

The report prepared by a defined contribution plan should contain a statement of net assets available for benefits and a description of the funding policy.

With a defined contribution plan it is not normally necessary to involve an actuary, since the pension paid at the end is purely dependent on the amount of fund built up for the employee. The obligation of the employer is usually discharged by the employer paying the agreed contributions into the plan. The main purpose of the report of the plan is to provide information on the performance of the investments, and this is normally achieved by including the following statements:

(a) a description of the significant activities for the period and the effect of any changes relating to the plan, its membership and its terms and conditions;

(b) statements reporting on the transactions and investment performance for the period and the financial position of the plan at the end of the period; and

(c) a description of the investment policies.

13.24.2 Defined benefit plans

Under a defined benefit plan (as opposed to a defined contribution plan) there is a need to provide more information, as the plan must be sufficiently funded to provide the agreed pension benefits at the retirement of the employees. The objective of reporting by the defined benefit plan is to periodically present information about the accumulation of resources and plan benefits over time that will highlight an excess or shortfall in assets.

The report that is required should contain[9] either:

(a) a statement that shows:
   (i) the net assets available for benefits;
   (ii) the actuarial present value of promised retirement benefits, distinguishing between vested benefits and non-vested benefits; and
   (iii) the resulting excess or deficit; or

(b) a statement of net assets available for benefits including either:
   (i) a note disclosing the actuarial present value of promised retirement benefits, distinguishing between vested benefits and non-vested benefits; or
   (ii) a reference to this information in an accompanying report.

The most recent actuarial valuation report should be used as a basis for the above disclosures and the date of the valuation should be disclosed. IAS 26 does not specify how often actuarial valuations should be done but suggests that most countries require a triennial valuation.

When the fund is preparing the report and using the actuarial present value of the future obligations, the present value could be based on either projected salary levels or current salary levels. Whichever has been used should be disclosed. The effect of any significant changes in actuarial assumptions should also be disclosed.

Report format

IAS 26 proposes three different report formats that will fulfil the content requirements detailed above. These formats are:

(a) A report that includes a statement that shows the net assets available for benefits, the actuarial present value of promised retirement benefits, and the resulting excess or deficit. The report of the plan also contains statements of changes in net assets available for benefits and changes in the actuarial present value of promised retirement benefits. The report may include a separate actuary's report supporting the actuarial present value of promised retirement benefits.

(b) A report that includes a statement of net assets available for benefits and a statement of changes in net assets available for benefits. The actuarial present value of the promised retirement benefits is disclosed in a note to the statements. The report may also include a report from an actuary supporting the actuarial value of the promised retirement benefits.

(c) A report that includes a statement of net assets available for benefits and a statement of changes in net assets available for benefits with the actuarial present value of promised retirement benefits contained in a separate actuarial report.

In each format a trustees' report in the nature of a management or directors' report and an investment report may also accompany the statements.

13.24.3 All plans – disclosure requirements[10]

For all plans, whether defined contribution or defined benefit, some common valuation and disclosure requirements exist.

Valuation

The investments held by retirement benefit plans should be carried at fair value. In most cases the investments will be marketable securities and the fair value is the market value. If it is impossible to determine the fair value of an investment, disclosure should be made of the reason why fair value is not used.

Market values are used for the investments because this is felt to be the most appropriate value at the report date and the best indication of the performance of the investments over the period.

Disclosure

In addition to the specific reports detailed above for defined contribution and defined benefit plans, the report should also contain:

(a) a statement of net assets available for benefits disclosing:
- assets at the end of the period suitably classified;
- the basis of valuation of assets;
- details of any single investment exceeding either 5% of the net assets available for benefits or 5% of any class or type of security;
- details of any investment in the employer;
- liabilities other than the actuarial present value of promised retirement benefits;

(b) a statement of changes in net assets for benefits showing the following:

- employer contributions;
- employee contributions;
- investment income such as interest or dividends;
- other income;
- benefits paid or payable;
- administrative expenses;
- other expenses;
- taxes on income;
- profits or losses on disposal of investment and changes in value of investments;
- transfers from and to other plans;

(c) a summary of significant accounting policies;

(d) a description of the plan and the effect of any changes in the plan during the period.

Summary

Accounting for employee benefits has always been a difficult problem with different views as to the appropriate methods.

The different types of pension scheme and the associated risks add to the difficulties in terms of accounting. The accounting treatment for these benefits has recently changed with the current view that the asset or liability position takes priority over the profit or loss charge. However, one consequence of giving the statement of financial position priority is that this change to the statement of comprehensive income can be much more volatile and this is considered by some to be undesirable.

Within the international community agreement does not exist on how these benefits should be accounted for. An interesting recent development is the option to use 'other comprehensive income' to record variations from the normal pension costs, i.e. for actuarial gains and losses, rather than taking them to profit or loss. The latest revisions do give significant choice to the companies in how they account for their pension schemes, which could be a criticism of the standard. Pension accounting is a very difficult area to gain global agreement on, and therefore IAS 19 (revised) could be construed as an early step towards more global convergence.

IFRS 2 is the first serious attempt of the IASB to deal with the accounting for share-based payments. It requires companies to recognise that a charge should be made for share-based payments and, in line with other recent standards such as financial instruments, it requires that charge to be recognised at fair value. There has been criticism of the standard in that it brings significant estimation into assessing the amount of charges to profit; however, overall the standard has been relatively well received with companies coping well with its requirements so far. What is unclear at present is whether the requirements will change the way that companies reward their staff; for this we will have to wait and see.

REVIEW QUESTIONS

1 Outline the differences between a defined benefit and a defined contribution pension scheme.

2 If a defined contribution pension scheme provided a pension that was 6% of salary each year, the company had a payroll cost of €5 million, and the company paid €200,000 in the year, what would be the statement of comprehensive income charge and the statement of financial position liability at the year-end?

3 'The approach taken in IAS 19 before its 1998 revision was to match an even pension cost against the period the employees provided service. This follows the accruals principle and is therefore fundamentally correct.' Discuss.

4 Under the revised IAS 19 (post 1998) what amount of actuarial gains and losses should be recognised in profit or loss?

5 Past service costs are recognised under IAS 19 (revised) immediately if the benefit is 'vested'. In what circumstances would the benefits not be vested?

6 What is the required accounting treatment for a curtailment of a defined benefit pension scheme?

7 What distinguishes a termination benefit from the other benefits considered in IAS 19 (revised)?

8 The issue of shares by companies, even to employees, should not result in a charge against profits. The contribution in terms of service that employees give to earn their rewards are contributions as owners and not as employees and when owners buy shares for cash there is no charge to profit. Discuss.

9 The use of option pricing models to determine the charges to profit or loss brings undesired estimation and subjectivity into the financial statements. Discuss.

10 Briefly summarise the required accounting if a company gives their staff a cash bonus directly linked to the share price.

11 Explain what distinguishes the different types of share-based payment, equity-settled, cash-settled and equity with a cash alternative.

12 A plc issues 50,000 share options to its employees on 1 January 2006, which the employees can only exercise if they remain with the company until 31 December 2008. The options have a fair value of £5 each on 1 January 2006.

It is expected that the holders of options over 8,000 shares will leave A plc before 31 December 2008.

In March 2006 adverse press comments regarding A plc's environmental policies and a downturn in the stock market cause the share price to fall significantly to below the exercise price on the options. The share price is not expected to recover in the foreseeable future.

Required
What charge should A plc recognise for share options in the financial statements for the year-ended 31 December 2006?

13 The following are extracts from the financial statements of Heidelberger Druckmaschinen AG showing the accounting policy and detailed notes regarding the provision of pensions according to IAS 19. As can be seen the disclosures are quite complex but they attempt to give a sensible statement of financial position and statements of comprehensive income position.

Accounting policy disclosure

Provisions for pensions and similar obligations comprise both the provision obligations of the Group under defined benefit plans and defined contribution plans. Pension obligations are determined according to the projected unit credit method (IAS 19) for defined benefit plans. Actuarial expert opinions are obtained annually in this connection. Calculations are based on an assumed trend of 3.5% (previous year: 2.5%) for the growth in pensions, and a discount rate of 6.0% (previous year: 6.0%). The probability of death is determined according to Heubec's current mortality tables as well as comparable foreign mortality tables.

In the case of defined contribution plans (for example, direct insurance policies), compulsory contributions are offset directly as an expense. No provisions for pension obligations are formed, as in these cases our Company does not have any liability over and above its liability to make premium payments.

Provisions for pensions and similar obligations (Note 15 in the financial statements)

We maintain benefit programs for the majority of employees for the period following their retirement – either a direct program or one financed by payments of premiums to private institutions. The level of benefits payments depends on the conditions in particular countries. The amounts are generally based on the term of employment and the salary of the employees. The liabilities include both those arising from current pensions as well as vested pension rights for pensions payable in the future. The pension payments expected following the beginning of benefit payment are accrued over the entire service time of the employee.

The provisions for pensions and similar obligations are broken down as follows:

	31 Mar 98	31 Mar 99
Net present value of the pension claims	408,208	445,054
Adjustment amount based on (not offset) actuarial profits/losses	−12,843	−18,225
Provisions for pensions and similar obligations	395,365	426,829

The amount of €18,225 thousand (previous year: €12,843 thousand), which is not yet adjusted arises largely from profits/losses in connection with deviations of the actual income trends from the assumptions that were the basis of the calculation. As soon as it exceeds 10% of total liabilities, this amount is carried as an expense over the average remaining period of service of the staff (IAS 19).

The expense for the pension plan is broken down as follows:

	31 Mar 98	31 Mar 99
Expense for pension claims added during the financial year*	16,902	17,084
Interest expense for claims already acquired	21,583	22,855
Net additions to pension provision	38,485	39,939
Expenses for other pension plans*	14,848	19,407
	53,333	59,346

* The expense for the pension plan included under personnel expenses totals 36,491 thousand (previous year: 31,750 thousand).

We include interest expenses for already acquired pension claims under interest and similar expenses.

Required:
(a) Explain the projected unit credit method for determining pension obligations for defined benefit plans.
(b) Why does the company need to use a discount rate?
(c) Explain the reference to the 10% corridor.

370 • Statement of financial position – equity, liability and asset measurement and disclosure

EXERCISES

An extract from the solution is provided on the Companion Website (www.pearsoned.co.uk/elliott-elliott) for exercises marked with an asterisk (*).

Question 1

Kathryn

Kathryn plc, a listed company, provides a defined benefit pension for its staff, the details of which are given below.

Pension scheme

As at the 30 April 2004, actuaries valued the company's pension scheme and estimated that the scheme had assets of £10.5 million and obligations of £10.2 million (using the valuation methods prescribed in IAS 19).

The actuaries made assumptions in their valuation that the assets would grow by 11% over the coming year to 30 April 2005, and that the obligations were discounted using an appropriate corporate bond rate of 10%. The actuaries estimated the current service cost at £600,000. The actuaries informed the company that pensions to retired directors would be £800,000 during the year, and the company should contribute £700,000 to the scheme.

At 30 April 2005 the actuaries again valued the pension fund and estimated the assets to be worth £10.7 million, and the obligations of the fund to be £10.9 million.

Assume that contributions and benefits are paid on the last day of each year.

Required:
(a) Explain the reasons why IAS 19 was revised in 1998, moving from an actuarial income driven approach to a market-based asset and liability driven approach. Support your answer by referring to the *Framework Document* principles.
(b) Show the extracts from the statement of comprehensive income and statement of financial position of Kathryn plc in respect of the information above for the year ended 30 April 2005. You do not need to show notes to the accounts.

[The accounting policy adopted by Kathryn plc is to recognise actuarial gains and losses immediately in other comprehensive income as allowed by IAS 19 in its 2004 amendment.]

* Question 2

Donna Inc

Donna Inc operates a defined benefit pension scheme for staff. The pension scheme has been operating for a number of years but not following IAS 19. The finance director is unsure of which accounting policy to adopt under IAS 19 because he has heard very conflicting stories. He went to one presentation in 2003 that referred to a '10% corridor' approach to actuarial gains and losses, recognising them in profit or loss, but went to another presentation in 2004 that said actuarial gains and losses could be recognised in other comprehensive income.

The pension scheme had market value of assets of £3.2 million and a present value of obligations of £3.5 million on 1 January 2002. There were no actuarial gains and losses brought forward into 2002.

The details relevant to the pension are as follows (in 000s) are:

	2002	2003	2004
Discount rate at start of year	6%	5%	4%
Expected rate of return on plan assets at start of year	10%	9%	8%
Current service cost	150	160	170
Benefits paid	140	150	130
Contributions paid	120	120	130
Present value of obligations at 31 December	3,600	3,500	3,200
Market value of plan assets at 31 December	3,400	3,600	3,600

In all years the average remaining service lives of the employees was ten years. Under the 10% corridor approach any gains or losses above the corridor would be recognised over the average remaining service lives of the employees.

Required:
Advise the finance director of the differences in the approach to actuarial gains and losses following the '10% corridor' and the recognition in equity. Illustrate your answer by showing the impact on the pension for 2002 to 2004 under both bases.

Question 3

The following information (in £m) relates to the defined benefit scheme of Basil plc for the year ended 31 December 20X7:

Fair value of plan assets at 1 January 20X7 £3,150 and at 31 December 20X7 £2,384; contributions £26; current service cost £80; benefits paid £85; past service cost £150; present value of the obligation at 1 January 20X7 £3,750 and at 31 December 20X7 £4,192.

The discount rate was 7% at 31 December 20X6 and 8% at 31 December 20X7. The expected rate of return on plan assets was 9% at 31 December 20X6 and 10% at 31 December 20X7.

Required:
Show the amounts that will be recognised in the statement of comprehensive income and statement of financial position for Basil plc for the year ended 31 December 20X7 under IAS 19 *Employee Benefits* and the movement in the net liability.

* Question 4

C plc wants to reward its directors for their service to the company and has designed a bonus package with two different elements as follows. The directors are informed of the scheme and granted any options on 1 January 20X7.

1   Share options over 300,000 shares that can be exercised on 31 December 20Y0. These options are granted at an exercise price of €4 each, the share price of C plc on 1 January 20X7. Conditions of the options are that the directors remain with the company, and the company must achieve an average increase in profit of at least 10% per year, for the years ending 31 December 20X7 to 31 December 20X9. C plc obtained a valuation on 1 January 20X7 of the options which gave them a fair value of €3.

No directors were expected to leave the company but, surprisingly, on 30 November 20X9 a director with 30,000 options did leave the company and therefore forfeited his options. At the

31 December 20X7 and 20X8 year-ends C plc estimated that they would achieve the profit targets (they said 80% sure) and by 31 December 20X9 the profit target had been achieved.

By 31 December 20Y0 the share price had risen to €12 giving the directors who exercised their options an €8 profit per share on exercise.

2   The directors were offered a cash bonus payable on 31 December 20X8 based on the share price of the company. Each of the five directors was granted a €5,000 bonus for each €1 rise in the share price or proportion thereof by 31 December 20X8.

On 1 January 20X7 the estimated fair value of the bonus was €75,000; this had increased to €85,000 by 31 December 20X7, and the share price on 31 December 20X8 was €8 per share.

Required
Show the accounting entries required in the years ending 31 December 20X7, 20X8 and 20X9 for the directors' options and bonus above.

Question 5

The following information is available for the year ended 31 March 20X6 (values in $m):

Present value of scheme liabilities at 1 April 20X5 $1,007; Fair value of plan assets at 1 April 20X5 $844; Benefits paid $44; Expected return on plan assets $67; Contributions paid by employers $16; Current service costs $28; Past service costs $1; Actuarial gains on assets $31; Actuarial losses on liabilities $10; Interest costs $58.

Required:
(a) Calculate the net liability to be recognised in the statement of financial position.
(b) Show the amounts recognised in the statement of comprehensive income.

Question 6

(a) IAS 19 *Employee Benefits* was amended in December 2004 to allow a choice of methods for the recognition of actuarial gains and losses.

Required:
Explain the treatments of actuarial gains and losses currently permitted by IAS 19.

(b) The following information relates to the defined benefit employees compensation scheme of an entity:

Present value of obligation at start of 2008 ($000)		20,000
Market value of plan assets at start of 2008 ($000)		20,000
Expected annual return on plan assets		10%
Discount rate per year		8%
	2008	2009
	$000	$000
Current service cost	1,250	1,430
Benefits paid out	987	1,100
Contributions paid by entity	1,000	1,100
Present value of obligation at end of the year	23,000	25,500
Market value of plan assets at end of the year	21,500	22,300

Actuarial gains and losses outside the 10% corridor are to be recognised in full in the income statement. Assume that all transactions occur at the end of the year.

Required:
(a) Calculate the present value of the defined benefit plan obligation as at the start and end of 2008 and 2009 showing clearly any actuarial gain or loss on the plan obligation for each year.
(b) Calculate the market value of the defined benefit plan assets as at the start and end of 2008 and 2009 showing clearly any actuarial gain or loss on the plan assets for each year.
(c) Applying the 10% corridor show the total charge in respect of this plan in the income statement for 2008 and the statement of comprehensive income for 2009.

(The Association of International Accountants)

Question 7

On 1 October 2005 Omega granted 50 employees options to purchase 500 shares in the entity. The options vest on 1 October 2007 for those employees who remain employed by the entity until that date. The options allow the employees to purchase the shares for $10 per share. The market price of the shares was $10 on 1 October 2005 and $10.50 on 1 October 2006. The market value of the options was $2 on 1 October 2005 and $2.60 on 1 October 2006. On 1 October 2005 the directors estimated that 5% of the relevant employees would leave in each of the years ended 30 September 2006 and 2007 respectively. It turned out that 4% of the relevant employees left in the year ended 30 September 2006 and the directors now believe that a further 4% will leave in the year ended 30 September 2007.

Required:
Show the amounts that will appear in the balance sheet of Omega as at 30 September 2006 in respect of the share options and the amounts that will appear in the income statement for the year ended 30 September 2006.

You should state where in the balance sheet and where in the income statement the relevant amounts will be presented. Where necessary you should justify your treatment with reference to appropriate international financial reporting standards.

(Dip IFR December 2006)

* Question 8

On 1 January 20X1 the company obtained a contract in order to keep the factory in work but had obtained it on a very tight profit margin. Liquidity was a problem and there was no prospect of offering staff a cash bonus. Instead, the company granted its 80 production employees share options for 1,000 shares each at £10 per share. There was a condition that they would only vest if they still remained in employment at 31 December 20X2. The options were then exercisable during the year ended 31 December 20X3. Each option had an estimated fair value of £6.5 at the grant date.

At 31 December 20X1:

The fair value of each option at 31 December 20X1 was £7.5.

4 employees had left.

It was estimated that 16 of the staff would have left by 31 December 20X2.

The share price had increased from £9 on 1 January 20X1 to £9.90.

Required:
Calculate the charge to the income statement for the year ended 31 December 20X1.

References

1 IAS 19 *Employee Benefits*, IASB, amended 2002.
2 IAS 26 *Accounting and Reporting by Retirement Benefit Plans*, IASC, reformatted 1994.
3 IFRS 2 *Share-Based Payment*, IASB, 2004.
4 IAS 19, Appendix 1.
5 *Ibid.*, para. 7.
6 *Ibid.*, para. 120.
7 *Ibid.*, para. 126.
8 *Ibid.*, para. 132.
9 IAS 26, para. 28.
10 *Ibid.*, para. 32.

CHAPTER 14

Taxation in company accounts

14.1 Introduction

The main purpose of this chapter is to explain the corporation tax system and the accounting treatment of deferred tax.

> ### Objectives
>
> By the end of the chapter, you should be able to:
>
> - discuss the theoretical background to corporation tax systems;
> - critically discuss tax avoidance and tax evasion;
> - prepare deferred tax calculations;
> - critically discuss deferred tax provisions.

14.2 Corporation tax

Limited companies, and indeed all corporate bodies, are treated for tax purposes as being legally separate from their proprietors. Thus, a limited company is itself liable to pay tax on its profits. This tax is known as **corporation tax**. The shareholders are only accountable for tax on the income they receive by way of any dividends distributed by the company. If the shareholder is an individual, then **income tax** becomes due on their dividend income received.

This is in contrast to the position in a partnership, where each partner is individually liable for the tax on that share of the pre-tax profit that has been allocated. A partner is taxed on the profit and not simply on drawings. Note that it is different from the treatment of an employee who is charged tax on the amount of salary that is paid.

In this chapter we consider the different types of company taxation and their accounting treatment. The International Accounting Standard that applies specifically to taxation is IAS 12 *Income Taxes*. The standard was last modified radically in 1996, further modified in part by IAS 10 in 1999 and revised by the IASB in 2000. Those UK unquoted companies that choose not to follow international standards will follow FRS 16 *Current Tax* and FRS 19 *Deferred Tax*.

Corporation tax is calculated under rules set by Parliament each year in the Finance Act. The Finance Act may alter the existing rules; it also sets the rate of tax payable. Because of this annual review of the rules, circumstances may change year by year, which makes comparability difficult and forecasting uncertain.

The reason for the need to adjust accounting profits for tax purposes is that although the tax payable is based on the accounting profits as disclosed in the profit and loss account, the tax rules may differ from the accounting rules which apply prudence to income recognition. For example, the tax rules may not accept that all the expenses which are recognised by the accountant under the IASB's *Framework for the Preparation and Presentation of Financial Statements* and the IAS 1 *Presentation of Financial Statements* accrual concept are deductible when arriving at the taxable profit. An example of this might be a bonus, payable to an employee (based on profits), which is payable in arrear but which is deducted from accounting profit as an accrual under IAS 1. This expense is only allowed in calculating taxable profit on a cash basis when it is paid in order to ensure that one taxpayer does not reduce his potential tax liability before another becomes liable to tax on the income received.

The accounting profit may therefore be lower or higher than the taxable profit. For example, the Companies Acts require that the formation expenses of a company, which are the costs of establishing it on incorporation, must be written off in its first accounting period; the rules of corporation tax, however, state that these are a capital expense and cannot be deducted from the profit for tax purposes. This means that more tax will be assessed as payable than one would assume from an inspection of the published profit and loss account.

Similarly, although most businesses would consider that entertaining customers and other business associates was a normal commercial trading expense, it is not allowed as a deduction for tax purposes.

A more complicated situation arises in the case of depreciation. Because the directors have the choice of method of depreciation to use, the legislators have decided to require all companies to use the same method when calculating taxable profits. If one thinks about this, then it would seem to be the equitable practice. Each company is allowed to deduct a uniform percentage from its profits in respect of the depreciation that has arisen from the wear and tear and diminution in value of fixed assets.

The substituted depreciation that the tax rules allow is known as a **capital allowance**. The capital allowance is calculated in the same way as depreciation; the only difference is that the rates are those set out in the Finance Acts. At the time of writing, some commercial fixed assets (excluding land and buildings) qualify for a capital allowance far in excess of depreciation in the accounts. There are restricted allowances, called industrial buildings allowances, for certain categories of buildings used in manufacturing. Just as the depreciation that is charged by the company under accrual accounting is substituted by a capital allowance, profits or losses arising on the sale of fixed assets are not used for tax purposes.

14.3 Corporation tax systems – the theoretical background

It might be useful to explain that there are three possible systems of company taxation (classical, imputation and partial imputation).[1] These systems differ solely in their tax treatment of the relationship between the limited company and those shareholders who have invested in it.

14.3.1 The classical system

In the classical system, a company pays tax on its profits, and then the shareholders suffer a second and separate tax liability when their share of the profits is distributed to them. In effect, the dividend income of the shareholder is regarded as a second and separate source of income from that of the profits of the company. The payment of a dividend creates an additional tax liability which falls directly on the shareholders. It could be argued that this double taxation is inequitable when compared to the taxation system on unincorporated bodies where the rate of taxation suffered overall remains the same whether or not profits are withdrawn from the business. It is suggested that this classical system discourages the distribution of profits to shareholders since the second tranche of taxation (the tax on dividend income of the shareholders) only becomes payable on payment of the dividend, although some argue that the effect of the burden of double taxation on the economy is less serious than it might seem.[2] Austria, Belgium, Denmark, the Netherlands and Sweden have classical systems.

14.3.2 The imputation system

In an imputation system, the dividend is regarded merely as a flow of the profits on each sale to the individual shareholders, as there is considered to be merely one source of income which could either be retained in the company or distributed to the shareholders. It is certainly correct that the payment of a dividend results from the flow of monies into the company from trading profits, and that the choice between retaining profits to fund future growth and the payment of a dividend to investing shareholders is merely a strategic choice unrelated to a view as to the nature of taxable profits. In an imputation system the total of the tax paid by the company and by the shareholder is unaffected by the payment of dividends and the tax paid by the company is treated as if it were also a payment of the individual shareholders' liabilities on dividends received. It is this principle of the flow of net profits from particular sales to individual shareholders that has justified the repayment of tax to shareholders with low incomes or to non-taxable shareholders of tax paid by the limited company, even though that tax credit has represented a reduction in the overall tax revenue of the state because the tax credit repaid also represented a payment of the company's own corporation tax liability. If the dividend had not been distributed to such a low-income or non-taxable shareholder who was entitled to repayment, the tax revenue collected would have been higher overall. France and Germany have such an imputation system. The UK modified its imputation system in 1999, so that a low-income or non-taxable shareholder (such as a charity) could no longer recover any tax credit.

14.3.3 The partial imputation system

In a partial imputation system only part of the underlying corporation tax paid is treated as a tax credit.

14.3.4 Common basis

All three systems are based on the taxation of profits earned as shown under the same basic principles used in the preparation of financial statements.

14.4 Corporation tax systems – avoidance and evasion

Governments have to follow the same basic principles of management as individuals. To spend money, there has to be a source of funds. The sources of funds are borrowing and income. With governments, the source of income is taxation. As with individuals, there is a practical limit as to how much they can borrow; to spend for the benefit of the populace, taxation has to be collected. In a democracy, the tax system is set up to ensure that the more prosperous tend to pay a greater proportion of their income in order to fund the needs of the poorer; this is called a progressive system. As Franklin Roosevelt, the American politician, stated, 'taxes, after all, are the dues that we pay for the privileges of membership in an organised society'.[3] Corporation tax on company profits represents 10% of the taxation collected by HM Revenue & Customs in the UK from taxes on income and wages.

It appears to be a general rule that taxpayers do not enjoy paying taxation (despite the fact that they may well understand the theory underpinning the collection of taxation). This fact of human nature applies just as much to company directors handling company resources as it does to individuals. Every extra pound paid in taxation by a company reduces the resources available for retention for funding future growth.

14.4.1 Tax evasion

Politicians often complain about tax evasion. Evasion is the illegal (and immoral) manipulation of business affairs to escape taxation. An example could be the directors of a family-owned company taking cash sales for their own expenditure. Another example might be the payment of a low salary (below the threshold of income tax) to a family member not working in the company, thus reducing profits in an attempt to reduce corporation tax. It is easy to understand the illegality and immorality of such practices. Increasingly the distinction between tax avoidance and tax evasion has been blurred.[4] When politicians complain of tax evasion, they tend not to distinguish between evasion and avoidance.

14.4.2 Tax avoidance

Tax avoidance could initially be defined as a manipulation of one's affairs, within the law, so as to reduce liability; indeed, as it is legal, it can be argued that it is not immoral. There is a well established tradition within the UK that 'every man is entitled if he can to order his affairs so that the tax attaching under the appropriate Acts is less than it otherwise would be'.[5]

Indeed the government deliberately sets up special provisions to reduce taxes in order to encourage certain behaviours. The more that employers and employees save for employee retirement, the less social security benefits will be paid out in the future. Thus both companies and individuals obtain full relief against taxation for pension contributions. Another example might be increased tax depreciation (capital allowances) on capital investment, in order to increase industrial investment and improve productivity within the UK economy.

The use of such provisions, as intended by the legislators, is not criticised by anyone, and might better be termed 'tax planning'. The problem area lies between the proper use of such tax planning, and illegal activities. This 'grey area' could best be called 'tax avoidance'.

The Institute for Fiscal Studies has stated:

> We think it is impossible to define the expression 'tax avoidance' in any truly satisfactory manner. People routinely alter their behaviour to reduce or defer their taxation liabilities. In doing so, commentators regard some actions as legitimate tax planning and others as tax avoidance. We have regarded tax avoidance (in contra-indication to legitimate . . . tax planning) as action taken to reduce or defer tax liabilities in a way Parliament plainly did not intend. . . .[6]

The law tends to define tax avoidance as an artificial element in the manipulation of one's affairs, within the law, so as to reduce liability.[7]

14.4.3 The problem of distinguishing between avoidance and evasion

The problem lies in distinguishing clearly between legal avoidance and illegal evasion. It can be difficult for accountants to walk the careful line between helping clients (in tax avoidance) and colluding with them against HM Revenue and Customs.[8]

When clients seek advice, accountants have to be careful to ensure that they have integrity in all professional and business relationships. Integrity implies not merely honesty but fair dealing and truthfulness. 'In all dealings relating to the tax authorities, a member must act honestly and do nothing that might mislead the authorities.'[9]

As an example to illustrate the problems that could arise, a client company has carried out a transaction to avoid taxation, but failed to minute the details as discussed at a directors' meeting. If the accountant were to correct this act of omission in arrear, this would be a move from tax avoidance towards tax evasion. Another example of such a move from tax avoidance to tax evasion might be where an accountant in informing the Inland Revenue of a tax-avoiding transaction fails to detail aspects of the transaction which might show it in a disadvantageous light.

Companies can move profit centres from high-taxation countries to low-taxation countries by setting up subsidiaries therein. These areas, known in extreme cases as tax havens, are disliked by governments.

Tax havens are countries with very low or nil tax rates on some or all forms of income. They could be classified into two groups:

1 the zero rate and low tax havens,
2 the tax haven that imposes tax at normal rates but grants preferential treatment to certain activities.

Group 1 countries tend to be small economies that make up for the absence of taxation on profits and earnings by the use of taxes on sales. This group of tax havens is disliked by governments of larger economies. Gibraltar[10] took the European Commission to court over its ruling that it should not run a tax regime more favourable than that in the UK, and succeeded in its claim in the Court of the First Instance. Both Spain and the European Commission are appealing against this decision on numerous points of law, and it is clear that the policies of Gibraltar remain under attack. In February 2009 the European Union proposed an attack on the secrecy of banking in such tax havens.

Ireland is an example of the second group, with its manufacturing incentives under which a special low rate of tax applies to manufacturing operations located there.

The use of zero rate and low-tax havens could be considered a form of tax avoidance, although sometimes they are used by tax evaders for their lack of regulation.

Companies can make use of government approved investment schemes to reduce (or 'shelter') their tax liability, although there have recently been examples of improper (or abusive) schemes where short-term transactions were taken solely for taxation purposes. On 26 August 2005 the US Justice Department obtained an admission by and penalties of $456 million from the USA KPMG accounting firm over such a scheme.[11] The agreement reached with the Justice Department requires permanent restrictions on KPMG tax practice in the USA.[12] A few partners in the firm had set up a scheme for clients and misled the US Internal Revenue Service. Whilst the schemes may or may not have been legal, the misleading information certainly resulted in tax evasion. The dangers of starting to act improperly were illustrated in an in an e-mail obtained by the Senate Committee in which a senior KPMG tax adviser told his colleagues that even if regulators took action against their sales strategies for a tax shelter known as OPIS the potential profits from these deals would still greatly exceed the possible court penalties.[13]

14.5 Corporation tax – the system from 6 April 1999

A company pays corporation tax on its income. When that company pays a dividend to its shareholders it is distributing some of its taxed income among the proprietors. In an imputation system the tax paid by the company is 'imputed' to the shareholders who therefore receive a dividend which has already been taxed.

This means that, from the paying company's point of view, the concept of gross dividends does not exist. From the paying company's point of view, the amount of dividend paid shown in the profit and loss account will equal the cash that the company will have paid.

However, from the shareholder's point of view, the cash received from the company is treated as a net payment after deduction of tax. The shareholders will have received, with the cash dividend, a note of a tax credit, which is regarded as equal to basic rate income tax on the total of the dividend plus the tax credit. For example:

	£
Dividend being the cash paid by the company and disclosed in the company's profit and loss account	400.00
Imputed tax credit of 1/9 of dividend paid (being the rate from 6 April 1999)	44.44
Gross dividend	444.44

The imputed tax credit calculation (as shown above) has been based on a basic tax rate of 10% for dividends paid, being the basic rate of income tax on dividend income from 6 April 1999. This means that an individual shareholder who only pays basic rate income tax has no further liability in that the assumption is that the basic rate tax has been paid by the company. A non-taxpayer cannot obtain a repayment of tax.

Although a company pays corporation tax on its income, when that company pays a dividend to its shareholders it is still considered to be distributing some of its taxed income among the proprietors. In this system the tax payable by the company is 'imputed' to the shareholders who therefore receive a dividend which has already been taxed. This means that, from the paying company's point of view, the concept of 'gross' dividends does not exist. From the paying company's point of view, the amount of dividends paid shown in the profit and loss account will equal the cash that the company will have paid to the shareholders.

The essential point is that the dividend paying company makes absolutely no deduction from the dividend **nor is any payment made by the company to the HM Revenue and Customs**. The addition of 1/9 of the dividend paid as an imputed tax credit is purely nominal. A tax credit of 1/9 of the dividend will be deemed to be attached to that dividend (in effect an income tax rate of 10%). That credit is notional in that no payment of the 10% will be made to the HM Revenue and Customs.[14] The payment of taxation is not associated with dividends.

Large companies (those with taxable profits of over £1,500,000) pay their corporation tax liability in quarterly instalments starting within the year of account, rather than paying their corporation tax liability nine months thereafter. The payment of taxation is not associated with the payment of dividends. Smaller companies pay their corporation tax nine months after the year-end.

It has been argued that the imputation system has encouraged the payment of dividends, and consequently discourages firms from reinvesting earnings. Since 1985, both investment and the ratio of dividend payments to GDP had soared in Britain relative to the USA, but it is not obvious that such trends are largely attributable to tax policy.[15] It has been suggested that the corporation tax system (from 5 April 1999) would tend to discourage companies from paying 'excessive' dividends because the major pressure for dividends has come in the past from pension fund investors who previously could reclaim the tax paid, and that the decrease in cash flow to the company caused by payment of quarterly corporation tax payments might tend to assist company directors in resisting dividend increases to compensate for this loss.

14.5.1 Advance corporation tax – the system until 5 April 1999

A company pays corporation tax on its income. Statute previously required that when a company paid a dividend it was required to make a payment to the Inland Revenue equal to the total tax credit associated with that dividend. This payment was called 'advance corporation tax' (ACT) because it was a payment on account of the corporation's tax liability that would be paid on the profits of the accounting period. When the company eventually made its payment of the corporation tax liability, it was allowed to reduce the amount paid by the amount already paid as ACT. The net amount of corporation tax that was paid after offsetting the ACT was known as **mainstream corporation tax**. The total amount of corporation tax was no greater than that assessed on the taxable profits of the company; there was merely a change in the timing of the amount of tax paid by paying it in two parts – the ACT element and the mainstream corporation tax element.

What would have been the position if the company had declared a dividend but had not paid it out to the shareholders by the date of the statement of financial position? In such a case the ACT could only have been offset against the corporation tax in the accounting period during which the tax was actually paid. The offset of ACT against corporation tax was effectively restricted to the ACT rate multiplied by the company's profits chargeable to corporation tax. A further refinement was that for offset purposes the ACT rate was multiplied by the UK profit – this does not include profits generated overseas. Should a distribution have exceeded the chargeable profits for that period, then the ACT could not be recovered immediately. Under tax law, such unrelieved ACT could be carried back against corporation tax payments in the preceding six years or forward against future liabilities indefinitely.

Unrecovered ACT would have appeared in the statement of financial position as an asset. At this point the accountant must have considered the prudence concept. In order for it to have remained as such on the statement of financial position it must have been (a) reasonably certain and (b) foreseeable that it would be recoverable at a future date. If the ACT could be reasonably seen as recoverable then it should have been shown on the statement of financial position as a deferred asset. If, for any reason, it seemed improbable that there would be sufficient future tax liabilities to 'cover' the ACT, then it had to be written off as irrecoverable. This payment of ACT stopped on 5 April 1999 with a change in the imputation system. Companies which had paid tax for which they had not yet had relief against mainstream corporation tax at 5 April 1999 are permitted to carry it forward against future corporation tax liabilities – this carry-forward is called **shadow ACT**.

14.6 IFRS and taxation

European Union law requires listed companies to draw up their consolidated accounts according to IFRS for accounting periods beginning after 1 January 2005 (with adjusted comparative figures for the previous year). United Kingdom law has been amended to allow the Inland Revenue to accept accounts drawn up in accordance with GAAP ('generally accepted accounting practice'), which is defined as IFRS or UK GAAP (UK Generally Accepted Accounting Practice).[16]

Although the Accounting Standards Board (ASB) intends to bring its standards into accordance with IFRS (but not necessarily identical with them), it will take several years to do this. Consequently two different standards will be acceptable for some years. The move towards IFRS is leading to a detailed study of accounting theory and principles, so that the accounting treatment may eventually become the benchmark standard for taxation purposes, although this will take several years to reach fruition (if it proves to be attainable).

The Inland Revenue and the professional bodies have anticipated the potential impact of the move to IFRS. For some years at least, the legislation will have to provide for different treatment of specific items under UK GAAP and IFRS.

The Finance Act 2004 included legislation which ensured that companies that adopted IFRS to draw up their accounts would receive broadly equivalent tax treatment to companies that continue to use UK GAAP.[17] The intention of these provisions is to defer the major tax effects of most transitional adjustments until the tax impact becomes clearer.

The Pre-Budget Report of 2 December 2004 proposed further tax changes to ensure this policy of deferring tax effects of these accounting changes, for which the Chancellor of the Exchequer further confirmed his support in his Budget of 16 March 2005.

The clearest intimation of the intention to defer major tax effects is shown by the proposals for special purpose securitisation companies. These are certain companies where borrowing is located in a separate company in order to protect from insolvency. Under the proposed provisions, these companies would continue to use the previous accounting practice for taxation purposes for a further year, thus avoiding a significant tax charge on items that would not have been treated as income under UK GAAP. Another example is that there will be difficulties under IAS 39 where hedging profits are taken into account before they are realised, and tax law will ignore these volatile items.

A deliberate decision had already been made during the discussion of the Finance Act 2003 not to follow the changes in the treatment of share-based payments to employees that would not only follow from IFRS 2 but also from FRS 20 (under UK GAAP).[18]

IAS 8 includes adjustments for fundamental errors in the statement of changes in equity, but the legislation specifically excludes the tax effects of these.

Further provisions have been introduced to mitigate the tax liabilities that could arise from the adoption of IFRS. It remains to be seen whether the taxation effects of any significant changes in profit resulting from the change from UK GAAP to IFRS will be deferred until UK GAAP becomes truly aligned with IFRS.

IFRS will not remain static. The IASB Project on the 'Financial Reporting of all Profit-Oriented Entities' (for under consideration is the development of a standard 'performance statement') will lead to further significant changes from UK GAAP. Such a move from the present Profit and Loss Account would lead to the need for a decision whether it could be used for tax purposes and what further adjustments would be needed for tax assessment purposes.

At least for the time being, any significant effects of the change to IFRS will be deferred for tax purposes.

14.7 IAS 12 – accounting for current taxation

The essence of IAS 12 is that it requires an enterprise to account for the tax consequences of transactions and other events in the same way that it accounts for the transactions and other events themselves. Thus, for transactions and other events recognised in the statement of comprehensive income, any related tax effects are also recognised in the statement of comprehensive income.

The details of how IAS 12 requires an enterprise to account for the tax consequences of transactions and other events follow below.

Statement of comprehensive income disclosure

The standard (para. 77) states that the tax expense related to profit or loss from ordinary activities should be presented on the face of the statement of comprehensive income. It also provides that the major components of the tax expense should be disclosed separately. These separate components of the tax expense may include (para. 80):

(a) current tax expense for the period of account;

(b) any adjustments recognised in the current period of account for prior periods (such as where the charge in a past year was underprovided);

(c) the amount of any benefit arising from a previously unrecognised tax loss, tax credit or temporary difference of a prior period that is used to reduce the current tax expense; and

(d) the amount of tax expense (income) relating to those changes in accounting policies and fundamental errors which are included in the determination of net profit or loss for the period in accordance with the allowed alternative treatment in IAS 8 *Net Profit or Loss for the Period, Fundamental Errors and Changes in Accounting Policies*.

Statement of financial position disclosure

The standard states that current tax for current and prior periods should, to the extent unpaid, be recognised as a liability. If the amount already paid in respect of current and prior periods exceeds the amount due for those periods, the excess should be recognised as an asset.

The treatment of tax losses

As regards losses for tax purposes, the standard states that the benefit relating to a tax loss that can be carried back to recover current tax of a previous period should be recognised as an asset. Tax assets and tax liabilities should be presented separately from other assets and liabilities in the statement of financial position. An enterprise should offset (para. 71) current tax assets and current tax liabilities if, and only if, the enterprise:

(a) has a legally enforceable right to set off the recognised amounts; and

(b) intends either to settle on a net basis, or to realise the asset and settle the liability simultaneously.

The standard provides (para. 81) that the following should also be disclosed separately:

(a) tax expense (income) relating to extraordinary items recognised during the period,

(b) an explanation of the relationship between tax expense (income) and accounting profit in either or both of the following forms:

　(i) a numerical reconciliation between tax expense (income) and the product of accounting profit multiplied by the applicable tax rate(s), disclosing also the basis on which the applicable tax rate(s) is (are) computed; or

　(ii) a numerical reconciliation between the average effective tax rate and the applicable tax rate, disclosing also the basis on which the applicable tax rate is computed,

(c) an explanation of changes in the applicable tax rate(s) compared to the previous accounting period.

The relationship between tax expense and accounting profit

The standard sets out the following example in Appendix B of an explanation of the relationship between tax expense (income) and accounting profit:

Current Tax Expense

	X5	X6
Accounting profit	8,775	8,740
Add		
Depreciation for accounting purposes	4,800	8,250
Charitable donations	500	350
Fine for environmental pollution	700	—
Product development costs	250	250
Health care benefits	2,000	1,000
	17,025	18,590
Deduct		
Depreciation for tax purposes	(8,100)	(11,850)
Taxable profit	8,925	6,740
Current tax expense at 40%	3,570	
Current tax expense at 35%		2,359

IAS 12 and FRS 16

IAS 12 is similar to FRS 16 *Current Tax*, which UK non-quoted companies that choose not to follow international standards can choose to adopt.

There are very few rules for calculating current tax in UK GAAP, although in practice the calculation will be largely similar to that under IAS 12. FRS 16 does not go into the detail of calculating current tax, but it does, however, clarify the treatment of withholding taxes and the effect they have on the statement of comprehensive income.

14.8 Deferred tax

14.8.1 IAS 12 – background to deferred taxation

The profit on which tax is paid may differ from that shown in the published profit and loss account. This is caused by two separate factors.

Permanent differences

One factor that we looked at above is that certain items of expenditure may not be legitimate deductions from profit for tax purposes under the tax legislation. These differences are referred to as **permanent** differences because they will not be allowed at a different time and will be permanently disallowed, even in future accounting periods.

Timing differences

Another factor is that there are some other expenses that are legitimate deductions in arriving at the taxable profit which are allowed as a deduction for tax purposes at a later date. These might be simply **timing** differences in that tax relief and charges to the profit and loss account occur in different accounting periods. The accounting profit is prepared on an accruals basis but the taxable profit might require certain of the items to be dealt with on a cash basis. Examples of this might include bonuses payable to senior management, properly included in the financial statements under the accruals concept but not eligible for tax relief until actually paid some considerable time later, thus giving tax relief in a later period.

Temporary differences

The original IAS 12 allowed an enterprise to account for deferred tax using the statement of comprehensive income liability method which focused on timing differences. IAS 12 (revised) requires the statement of financial position liability method, which focuses on temporary differences, to be used. Timing differences are differences between taxable profit and accounting profit that originate in one period and reverse in one or more subsequent periods. Temporary differences are differences between the tax base of an asset or liability and its carrying amount in the statement of financial position. The tax base of an asset or liability is the amount attributed to that asset or liability for tax purposes. All timing differences are temporary differences.

The most significant temporary difference is depreciation. The depreciation charge made in the financial statements must be added back in the tax calculations and replaced by the official tax allowance for such an expense. The substituted expense calculated in accordance with the tax rules is rarely the same amount as the depreciation charge computed in accordance with IAS 16 *Property, Plant and Equipment*.

Capital investment incentive effect

It is common for legislation to provide for higher rates of tax depreciation than are used for accounting purposes, for it is believed that the consequent deferral of taxation liabilities serves as an incentive to capital investment (this incentive is not forbidden by European Union law or the OECD rules). The classic effect of this is for tax to be payable on a lower figure than the accounting profit in the earlier years of an asset's life because the tax allowances usually exceed depreciation in the earlier years of an asset's life. In later accounting periods, the tax allowances will be lower than the depreciation charges and the taxable profit will then be higher than the accounting profit that appears in the published profit and loss account.

Deferred tax provisions

The process whereby the company pays tax on a profit that is lower than the reported profit in the early years and on a profit that is higher than reported profit in later years is known as **reversal**. Given the knowledge that, ultimately, these timing differences will reverse, the accruals concept requires that consideration be given to making provision for the future liability in those early years in which the tax payable is calculated on a lower figure. The provision that is made is known as a **deferred tax provision**.

Alternative methods for calculating deferred tax provisions

As you might expect, there has been a history of disagreement within the accounting profession over the method to use to calculate the provision. There have been, historically, two methods of calculating the provision for this future liability – the **deferral** method and the **liability** method.

The deferral method

The deferral method, which used to be favoured in the USA, involves the calculation each year of the tax effects of the timing differences that have arisen in that year. The tax effect is then debited or credited to the profit and loss account as part of the tax charge; the double entry is effected by making an entry to the deferred tax account. This deferral method of

Figure 14.1 Deferred tax provision using deferral method

		ACCOUNTS (depreciation)	TAX (allowances)	DIFFERENCE (temporary)	TAX (rate)
		£	£	£	
01.0.1.1996	Cost of asset	10,000	10,000		
31.12.1996	Depreciation/tax	1,000	2,500	1,500	25%
	Allowance	9,000	7,500	1,500	
31.12.1997	Depreciation/tax	1,000	1,875	875	25%
	Allowance	8,000	5,625	2,375	
31.12.1998	Depreciation/tax	1,000	1,406	406	25%
	Allowance	7,000	4,219	2,781	
31.12.1999	Depreciation/tax	1,000	1,055	55	24%
	Allowance	6,000	3,164	2,836	
31.12.2000	Depreciation/tax	1,000	791	(209)	24%
	Allowance	5,000	2,373	2,627	

calculating the tax effect ignores the effect of changing tax rates on the timing differences that arose in earlier periods. This means that the total provision may consist of differences calculated at the rate of tax in force in the year when the entry was made to the provision.

The liability method

The liability method requires the calculation of the total amount of potential liability each year at current rates of tax, increasing or reducing the provision accordingly. This means that the company keeps a record of the timing differences and then recalculates at the end of each new accounting period using the rate of corporation tax in force as at the date of the current statement of financial position.

To illustrate the two methods we will take the example of a single asset, costing £10,000, depreciated at 10% using the straight-line method, but subject to a tax allowance of 25% on the reducing balance method. The workings are shown in Figure 14.1. This shows, that, if there were no other adjustments, for the first four years the profits subject to tax would be lower than those shown in the accounts, but afterwards the situation would reverse.

Charge to statement of comprehensive income under the deferral method

The deferral method would charge to the profit and loss account each year the variation multiplied by the current tax rate, e.g. 1996 at 25% on £1,500 giving £375.00, and 1999 at 24% on £55 giving £13.20. This is in accordance with the accruals concept which matches the tax expense against the income that gave rise to it. Under this method the deferred tax provision will be credited with £375 in 1997 and this amount will not be altered in 1999 when the tax rate changes to 24%. In the example, the calculation for the five years would be as in Figure 14.2.

Charge to statement of comprehensive income under the liability method

The liability method would make a charge so that the total balance on deferred tax equalled the cumulative variation multiplied by the current tax rate. The intention is that the statement of financial position liability should be stated at a figure which represents the tax effect as at

Figure 14.2 Summary of deferred tax provision using the deferral method

Year ended	Timing difference £	Basic rate %	Deferred tax charge in year £	Deferred tax provision (deferral method) £
31.12.1996	1,500	25%	375.00	375.00
31.12.1997	875	25%	218.75	593.75
31.12.1998	406	25%	101.50	695.25
31.12.1999	55	24%	13.20	708.45
31.12.2000	(209)	24%	(50.16)	658.29

the end of each new accounting period. This means that there would be an adjustment made in 1999 to recalculate the tax effect of the timing difference that was provided for in earlier years. For example, the provision for 1997 would be recalculated at 24%, giving a figure of £360 instead of the £375 that was calculated and charged in 1997. The decrease in the expected liability will be reflected in the amount charged against the profit and loss account in 1997. The £15 will in effect be credited to the 1997 profit statement.

The effect on the charge to the 2000 profit statement (Figures 14.2 and 14.3) is that there will be a charge of £13.20 using the deferral method and a **credit** of £14.61 using the liability method. The £14.61 is the reduction in the amount provided from £695.25 at the end of 1999 to the £680.64 that is required at the end of 2000.

World trend towards the liability method

There has been a move in national standards away from the deferral method towards the liability method, which is a change of emphasis from the statement of comprehensive income to the statement of financial position because the deferred tax liability is shown at current rates of tax in the liability method. This is in accordance with the IASB's conceptual framework which requires that all items in the statement of financial position, other than shareholders' equity, must be either assets or liabilities as defined in the framework. Deferred tax as it is calculated under the traditional deferral method is not in fact a calculation of a liability, but is better characterised as deferred income or expenditure. This is illustrated by the fact that the sum calculated under the deferral method is not recalculated to take account of changes in the rate of tax charged, whereas it is recalculated under the liability method.

Figure 14.3 Deferral tax provision using the liability method

Year ended	Temporary difference £	Basic rate	Deferred tax charge in year £	Deferred tax provision (deferral method) £	Rate in 2000	Deferred tax provision (liability method) £
31.12.1997	1,500	25%	375.00	375.00	24%	360.00
31.12.1998	875	25%	218.75	593.75	24%	210.00
31.12.1999	406	25%	101.50	695.25	24%	97.44
31.12.2000	55	24%	13.20	708.45	24%	13.20
				708.45		680.64

The world trend towards using the liability method also results in a change from accounting only for timing differences to accounting for temporary differences.

Temporary versus timing: conceptual difference

These temporary differences are defined in the IASB standard as 'differences between the carrying amount of an asset or liability in the statement of financial position and its tax base'.[19] The conceptual difference between these two views is that under the liability method provision is made for only the future reversal of these timing differences whereas the temporary difference approach provides for the tax that would be payable if the company were to be liquidated at statement of financial position values (i.e. if the company were to sell all assets at statement of financial position values).

The US standard SFAS 109 argues the theoretical basis for these temporary differences to be accounted for on the following grounds:

> A government levies taxes on net taxable income. Temporary differences will become taxable amounts in future years, thereby increasing taxable income and taxes payable, upon recovery or settlement of the recognised and reported amounts of an enterprise's assets or liabilities . . . A contention that those temporary differences will never result in taxable amounts . . . would contradict the accounting assumption inherent in the statement of financial position that the reported amounts of assets and liabilities will be recovered and settled, respectively; thereby making that statement internally inconsistent.[20]

A consequence of accepting this conceptual argument in IAS 12 is that provision must also be made for the potential taxation effects of asset revaluations.

14.8.2 IAS 12 – deferred taxation

The standard requires that the financial statements are prepared using the liability method described above (which is sometimes known as the statement of financial position liability method).

An example of how deferred taxation operates follows.

EXAMPLE ● An asset which cost £150 has a carrying amount of £100. Cumulative depreciation for tax purposes is £90 and the tax rate is 25% as shown in Figure 14.4.

The tax base of the asset is £60 (cost of £150 less cumulative tax depreciation of £90). To recover the carrying amount of £100, the enterprise must earn taxable income of £100, but will only be able to deduct tax depreciation of £60. Consequently, the enterprise will pay taxes of £10 (£40 at 25%) when it recovers the carrying amount of the asset. The difference between the carrying amount of £100 and the tax base of £60 is a taxable temporary difference of £40. Therefore, the enterprise recognises a deferred tax liability of £10 (£40 at 25%)

Figure 14.4 Cumulative depreciation

	In accounts	For tax
Cost	150	150
Depreciation	50	90
Carrying amount	100	60

Figure 14.5 Deferred tax liability

Income to recover	
Carrying amount	£100
Carrying amount for tax	£60
Temporary difference	£40
Tax rate	25%
Deferred tax	£10

representing the income taxes that it will pay when it recovers the carrying amount of the asset as shown in Figure 14.5.

The accounting treatment over the life of an asset

The following example, taken from IAS 12,[21] illustrates the accounting treatment over the life of an asset.

EXAMPLE ● An enterprise buys equipment for £10,000 and depreciates it on a straight-line basis over its expected useful life of five years. For tax purposes, the equipment is depreciated at 25% per annum on a straight-line basis. Tax losses may be carried back against taxable profit of the previous five years. In year 0, the enterprise's taxable profit was £5,000. The tax rate is 40%. The enterprise will recover the carrying amount of the equipment by using it to manufacture goods for resale. Therefore, the enterprise's current tax computation is as follows:

Year	1	2	3	4	5
Taxable income (£)	2,000	2,000	2,000	2,000	2,000
Depreciation for tax purposes	2,500	2,500	2,500	2,500	0
Tax profit (loss)	(500)	(500)	(500)	(500)	2,000
Current tax expense (income) at 40%	(200)	(200)	(200)	(200)	800

The enterprise recognises a current tax asset at the end of years 1 to 4 because it recovers the benefit of the tax loss against the taxable profit of year 0.

The temporary differences associated with the equipment and the resulting deferred tax asset and liability and deferred tax expense and income are as follows:

Year	1	2	3	4	5
Carrying amount (£)	8,000	6,000	4,000	2,000	0
Tax base	7,500	5,000	2,500	0	0
Taxable temporary difference	500	1,000	1,500	2,000	0
Opening deferred tax liability	0	200	400	600	800
Deferred tax expense (income)	200	200	200	200	(800)
Closing deferred tax liability	200	400	600	800	0

The enterprise recognises the deferred tax liability in years 1 to 4 because the reversal of the taxable temporary difference will create taxable income in subsequent years. The enterprise's statement of comprehensive income is as follows:

Year	1	2	3	4	5
Income (£)	2,000	2,000	2,000	2,000	2,000
Depreciation	2,000	2,000	2,000	2,000	2,000
Profit before tax	0	0	0	0	0
Current tax expense (income)	(200)	(200)	(200)	(200)	800
Deferred tax expense (income)	200	200	200	200	(800)
Total tax expense (income)	0	0	0	0	0
Net profit for the period	0	0	0	0	0

Further examples of items that could give rise to temporary differences are:

- Retirement benefit costs may be deducted in determining accounting profit as service is provided by the employee, but deducted in determining taxable profit either when contributions are paid to a fund by the enterprise or when retirement benefits are paid by the enterprise. A temporary difference exists between the carrying amount of the liability (in the financial statements) and its tax base (the carrying amount of the liability for tax purposes); the tax base of the liability is usually nil.

- Research costs are recognised as an expense in determining accounting profit in the period in which they are incurred but may not be permitted as a deduction in determining taxable profit (tax loss) until a later period. The difference between the tax base (the carrying amount of the liability for tax purposes) of the research costs, being the amount the taxation authorities will permit as a deduction in future periods, and the carrying amount of nil is a deductible temporary difference that results in a deferred tax asset.

Treatment of asset revaluations

The original IAS 12 permitted, but did not require, an enterprise to recognise a deferred tax liability in respect of asset revaluations. If such assets were sold at the revalued sum then a profit would arise that could be subject to tax. IAS 12 as currently written requires an enterprise to recognise a deferred tax liability in respect of asset revaluations.

Such a deferred tax liability on a revalued asset might not arise for many years, for there might be no intention to sell the asset. Many would argue that IAS 12 should allow for such timing differences by discounting the deferred liability (for a sum due many years in advance is certainly recognised in the business community as a lesser liability than the sum due immediately, for the sum could be invested and produce income until the liability would become due; this is termed the time value of money). The standard does not allow such discounting.[22] Indeed, it could be argued that in reality most businesses tend to have a policy of continuous asset replacement, with the effect that any deferred liability will be further deferred by these future acquisitions, so that the deferred tax liability would only become payable on a future cessation of trade. Not only does the standard preclude discounting, it also does not permit any account being made for future acquisitions by making a partial provision for the deferred tax.

Accounting treatment of deferred tax following a business combination

In a business combination that is an acquisition, the cost of the acquisition is allocated to the identifiable assets and liabilities acquired by reference to their fair values at the date of the exchange transaction. Temporary differences arise when the tax bases of the identifiable assets and liabilities acquired are not affected by the business combination or are affected differently. For example, when the carrying amount of an asset is increased to fair value but the tax base of the asset remains at cost to the previous owner, a taxable temporary difference arises which results in a deferred tax liability. Paragraph B16(i) of IFRS 3 *Business Combinations* prohibits discounting of deferred tax assets acquired and deferred tax liabilities assumed in a business combination as does IAS 12 (revised). IAS 12 states that deferred tax should not be provided on goodwill if amortisation of it is not allowable for tax purposes (as is the case in many states). Deferred tax arising on a business combination that is an acquisition is an exception to the rule that changes in deferred tax should be recognised in the statement of comprehensive income (rather than as an adjustment by way of a note to the financial statements).

Another exception to this rule relates to items charged (or credited) directly to equity. Examples of such items are:

● a change in the carrying amount arising from the revaluation of property, plant and equipment (IAS 16 *Property, Plant and Equipment*);

● an adjustment to the opening balance of retained earnings resulting from either a change in accounting policy that is applied retrospectively or the correction of an error (IAS 8 *Accounting Policies, Changes in Accounting Estimates and Errors*);

● exchange differences arising on the translation of the financial statements of a foreign entity (IAS 21 *The Effects of Changes in Foreign Exchange Rates*);

● amounts arising on initial recognition of the equity component of a compound financial instrument.

Deferred tax asset

A deferred tax asset should be recognised for the carry-forward of unused tax losses and unused tax credits to the extent that it is probable that future taxable profit will be available against which the unused tax losses and unused tax credits can be utilised.

At each statement of financial position date, an enterprise should reassess unrecognised deferred tax assets. The enterprise recognises a previously unrecognised deferred tax asset to the extent that it has become probable that future taxable profit will allow the deferred tax asset to be recovered. For example, an improvement in trading conditions may make it more probable that the enterprise will be able to generate sufficient taxable profit in the future for the deferred tax asset.

The International Accounting Standards Board (IASB), as part of the convergence project with the United States Financial Accounting Standards Board (FASB), proposed to amend IAS 12 with a new IFRS.

The published Exposure Draft (ED/2009/2) was similar to IAS 12, although it would seem that deferred tax liabilities net of deferred tax assets under the changes would be altered. This led to considerable discussion. It would be instructive to look at the points raised.

Two particular issues arose from the papers. Firstly it was proposed that the tax base of an asset used to calculate any deferred tax would be the tax base on disposal and not that on its final use. Many assets held in the United Kingdom, particularly buildings, have no tax base whilst in use because they do not have any form of tax deduction, whereas on disposal there will be one because of a calculations of tax liability on capital profits. Many deferred tax calculations would have to be reworked. It could be argued that the revised deferred tax charge would represent tax on future profits arising on sale rather than a reversal of past differences between book and tax depreciation.

Secondly the new IFRS would consider the recognition and measurement of differences in interpretation of the law between tax authorities and companies (termed 'uncertain tax positions'), where both current and deferred tax liabilities will be adjusted for the weighted average of possible outcomes of tax in dispute. Apart from the difficulty in assessing such probabilities, company directors may well prove averse to accounting for their opinions proving to be incorrect.

The proposals proved contentious. At one extreme was the argument that at a time when there are many other issues to deal with relating to the financial crisis, it was not the right time to pursue this project. Amongst the proponents of this point was the CIMA (the Chartered Institute of Management Accountants). Although it might seem improper to take such a pragmatic (and indeed 'political') approach, it must be remembered that in order for changes in policy to be accepted generally the view of company management must accept the logic and mechanism of proposed changes.

A more fundamental view was that the theoretical background to the proposals had not been fully considered, and the proposals represented minor changes to a 'weak standard' rather than seeking a fundamental review of tax accounting. Amongst those putting forward this view was the ICAEW – the Institute of Chartered Accountants in England and Wales.

At the October 2009 joint meeting of the IASB and the FASB, both boards indicated that they would consider undertaking a fundamental review of accounting for income taxes at some time in the future. In the meantime, the IASB is considering which issues it should address in a limited-scope project to amend IAS 12.

14.9 FRS 19 (the UK standard on deferred taxation)

Those UK unquoted companies that choose not to follow international standards will follow FRS 19 *Deferred Tax*.

Accounting for deferred tax in the UK pre-dates the issue of accounting standards.

Prior to the issue of standards, companies applied an accounting practice known as 'tax equalisation accounting', whereby they recognised that accounting periods should each be allocated an amount of income tax expense that bears a 'normal relationship to the income shown in the statement of comprehensive income', and to let reported income taxes follow reported income has been the objective of accounting for income taxes ever since.[23] There is also an economic consequence that flows from the practice of tax equalisation in that the trend of reported after-tax income is smoothed, and there is less likelihood of pressure for a cash dividend distribution based on the crediting of the tax benefit of capital investment expenditure to the early years of the fixed assets.

There followed a period of very high rates of capital allowances and, with a naive belief that this situation would continue and allow permanent deferral, companies complained that to provide full provision was unrealistic and so in 1977 the concept of **partial provision** was introduced in which deferred tax was only provided in respect of timing differences that were likely to be reversed. The argument was that if the company continued with the replacement of fixed assets, and if the capital allowances were reasonably certain to exceed the depreciation in the foreseeable future, it was unrealistic to make charges against the profit and create provisions that would not crystallise. This would merely lead to the appearance of an ever-increasing provision on the statement of financial position.

The *Foreword to Accounting Standards* published in June 1993 by the Accounting Standards Board (ASB) states that 'FRSs are formulated with due regard to international developments . . . the Board supports the IASC in its aim to harmonise' and that 'where the requirements of an accounting standard and an IAS differ, the accounting standard should be followed'.

Professor Andrew Lennard, then Assistant Technical Director of the ASB, confirmed during a lecture on 17 March 1999 that this was a matter where there was a divergence of view between the ASB and international regulators, where the ASB was unhappy to account in full for deferred tax where there was no discounting for long delays until the anticipated payment; indeed he expressed his exasperation with the topic in stating that 'he wished deferred tax accounting would go away'.[24] Applying the full provision method is more consistent with both international practice and the ASB's draft *Statement of Principles* (as modified in March 1999). However, a criticism of the full provision method in the past was that it could, if the company had a continuous capital expenditure programme, lead to a build-up of large liabilities that may fall due only far into the future, if at all.

The significant differences between FRS 19 and IAS 12 are:

1 Under FRS 19 there is a general requirement that a deferred tax charge **should not be recognised on revaluation gains** on non-monetary assets which are revalued to fair values on the acquisition of a business. IAS 12 requires tax on revaluations.

2 Under FRS 19 **discounting of deferred taxation liabilities is made optional**. The ASB had stated its belief that, in principle, deferred tax should be discounted, but has taken the view that discounting should be optional so as to give a choice to the preparer of the accounts. However, although discounting appears to be an attractive method for allowing for the delay in payment of the liability, it has been pointed out that in some cases where capital expenditure is uneven, then an unexpected effect of discounting both the initial and final cash flow effects could be to turn an eventual liability into an initial asset.[25] IAS 12 does not allow such discounting.[26]

The ASB is aware that the break with international standards is undesirable. Indeed it has been suggested that the ASB developed and implemented FRS 19 with a view that it would 'encourage the International Accounting Standards Committee to think again' about IAS 12.[27]

The ASB is considering the diverging views as to whether UK GAAP should be aligned with IFRS.

14.10 A critique of deferred taxation

It could be argued that deferred tax is not a legal liability until it accrues. The consequence of this argument would be that deferred tax should not appear in the financial statements, and financial statements should:

● present the tax expense for the year equal to the amount of income taxes that has been levied based on the income tax return for the year;

● accrue as a receivable any income refunds that are due from taxing authorities or as a payable any unpaid current or past income taxes;

● disclose in the notes to the financial statements differences between the income tax bases of assets and liabilities and the amounts at which they appear in the statement of financial position.

The argument is that the process of accounting for deferred tax is confusing what **did** happen to a company, i.e. the agreed tax payable for the year, and what **did not** happen to the company, which is the tax that would have been payable if the adjustments required by the tax law for timing differences had not occurred. It is felt that the investor should be provided with details of the tax charge levied on the profits for the year and an explanation of factors that might lead to a different rate of tax charge appearing in future financial statements. The argument against adjusting the tax charge for deferred tax and the creation of a deferred tax provision holds that shareholders are accustomed to giving consideration to many other imponderables concerning the amount, timing and uncertainty of future cash receipts and payments, and the treatment of tax should be considered in the same way. This view has received support from others,[28] who have held that tax attaches to taxable income and not to the reported accounting income and that there is no legal requirement for the tax to bear any relationship to the reported accounting income. Indeed it has been argued that 'deferred tax means income smoothing'.[29]

Before discussing the arguments it is appropriate to consider the economic reality of deferred taxation.

Those industries which are capital-intensive tend to have benefited from tax deferral by way of accelerated tax depreciation on plant investment, and it could be suggested that their accounts do not truly reflect the economic reality without provision for deferred taxation. Studies in the UK certainly support this view.

In the UK it has not been the practice to make full provision for deferred taxation. 'Full provision' refers to the fact that **the potential liability to deferred taxation has not been reduced** to allow for the view of management that the entire liability will not be paid in the future as a result of timing differences because the taxation benefits of future capital investments will result in a further deferral of taxation liability. In the UK, the deferred taxation liability has been reduced to allow for the effects of these anticipated future investments.

Terry Smith points out in Table 17.2 of his *Accounting for Growth*[30] that according to the companies' own figures their estimated EPS would fall as follows if full provision for deferred tax were made:

British Airways	36.4%
Severn Trent	25.3%
British Gas	20.5% (based on CCA earnings of 15.1p per share adjusted to exclude restructuring costs)
TI Group	13.8%

In his Table 17.3 he lists companies which expected an EPS fall of over 10% and with more than 10% of shareholders' funds in unprovided deferred tax:

	Estimated impact on historic gearing of full provision	
	From	*To*
	%	%
British Airways	148	214
BP	67	78
British Gas	56	68

He points out in his Table 17.4 that five of the companies he lists without any exposure to an increase in deferred tax charge are some of the UK's most successful and conservatively financed large companies.

	Tax rate (%)
General Electric	32
Marks & Spencer	32
Reuters	32
GUS	33
Wolseley	33

In the light of such economic facts, it is possible to understand why business managers might oppose deferred tax accounting, for it would lower their company stock valuation, whereas investment advisers might support deferred tax accounting as enabling them to form a better view of future prospects. Academic research has shown the extent of corporate lobbying against the full provision of deferred taxation liabilities.[31] IAS 12 is believed to be deeply unpopular with company directors. Whilst IASB believes the standard makes tax more transparent, the ICAEW suggests that the deferred tax charge will act as a disincentive to the adoption of IFRS (particularly because the adoption of IFRS will force companies to create a deferred tax liability on the revaluation of assets or subsidiaries).[32] In the change from the use of UK GAAP to IFRS, UK companies have started[33] to provide for deferred taxation on valuation gains. The following companies showed a deferred tax charge on these gains and a decrease in Shareholder's Equity as follows:

	£ million
Slough Estates plc	30.5
Brixton plc	68.1
Great Portland Estates plc	34.8

It has been argued[34] that IAS 12 uses definitions of assets and liabilities that are different to those otherwise used in IFRS and consequently require an entry to record taxes on future income. This argument, whilst initially attractive, ignores the fact that additional asset value has been created on the statement of financial position.

It is suggested that the arguments for and against deferred taxation accounting must be based solely on the theory underpinning accounting, and unaffected by commercial considerations.

It is also suggested that the above arguments against the use of deferred tax accounting are unconvincing if one considers the IASB's underlying assumption about accrual accounting, as stated in the *Framework*:

> In order to meet their objectives, financial statements are prepared on the accrual basis of accounting ... Financial statements prepared on the accrual basis inform users not only of past transactions involving the payment and receipt of cash but also of obligations to pay cash in the future and of resources that represent cash to be received in the future.[35]

This underlying assumption confirms that deferred tax accounting makes the fullest possible use of accrual accounting.

Pursuing this argument further the *Framework* states:

> The future economic benefit embodied in an asset is the potential to contribute, directly or indirectly, to the flow of cash and cash equivalents to the enterprise. The potential may be a productive one that is part of the operating activities of the enterprise.[36]

If a statement of financial position includes current market valuations based on this view of an asset, it is difficult to argue logically that the implicit taxation arising on this future economic benefit should not be provided for at the same time. The previous argument for excluding the deferred tax liability cannot therefore be considered persuasive on this basis.

On the other hand, it is stated in the *Framework* that 'An essential characteristic of a liability is that the enterprise has a present obligation.'[37] One could argue solely from these words that deferred tax is not a liability, but this conflicts with the argument based on the definition of an asset; consequently when considered in context this does not provide a sustainable argument against a deferred tax provision. The fact is that accounting practice has moved definitively towards making such a provision for deferred taxation.

The legal argument that deferred tax is not a legal liability until it accrues runs counter to the criterion of substance over form which gives weight to the economic aspects of the event rather than the strict legal aspects. The *Framework* states:

> **Substance Over Form**
> If information is to represent faithfully the transactions and other events that it purports to represent, it is necessary that they are accounted for and presented in accordance with their substance and economic reality and not merely their legal form. The substance of transactions or other events is not always consistent with that which is apparent from their legal or contrived form.[38]

It is an interesting fact that substance over form has achieved a growing importance since the 1980s and the legal arguments are receiving less recognition. Investments are made on economic criteria, investors make their choices on the basis of anticipated cash flows, and such flows would be subject to the effects of deferred taxation.

14.11 Examples of companies following IAS 12

Figure 14.6 is from the Roche Group 2009 Annual Report. Figure 14.7 is from the Bayer Group 2008 Annual Report. It should be noted that these published examples do not always comply in full with all aspects of IAS 12 (revised).

14.12 Value added tax (VAT)

VAT is one other tax that affects most companies and for which there is an accounting standard (SSAP 5 *Accounting for Value Added Tax*), which was established on its introduction. This standard was issued in 1974 when the introduction of value added tax was imminent and

Figure 14.6 Extract from Roche Group 2009 Annual Accounts

6. Income taxes

Income tax expenses | in millions of CHF

	2009	2008
Current income taxes	(3,701)	(3,617)
Adjustments recognised for current tax of prior periods	160	35
Deferred income taxes	671	277
Total income (expense)	**(2,870)**	**(3,305)**

Since the Group operates internationally, it is subject to income taxes in many different tax jurisdictions. The Group calculates its average expected tax rate as a weighted average of the tax rates in the tax jurisdictions in which the Group operates. This rate changes from year to year due to changes in the mix of the Group's taxable income and changes in local tax rates. The Group's effective tax rate can be reconciled to the Group's average expected tax rate as follows:

continued

Figure 14.6 *(continued)*

Reconciliation of the Group's effective tax rate

	2009	2008
Average expected tax rate	22.1%	23.0%
Tax effect of		
— Utilisation of previously unrecognised tax losses	–0.1%	–0.2%
— Non-taxable income/non-deductible expenses	+0.7%	+1.2%
— Genentech equity compensation plans	+0.1%	+0.5%
— Other differences	–1.3%	–1.1%
Group's effective tax rate before exceptional items	**21.5%**	**23.4%**

Income tax assets (liabilities) | in millions of CHF

	2009	2008	2007
Current income taxes			
— Assets	244	268	263
— Liabilities	(2,478)	(2,193)	(2,215)
Net current income tax assets (liabilities)	**(2,234)**	**(1,925)**	**(1,952)**
Deferred income taxes			
— Assets	2,573	1,829	1,317
— Liabilities	(1,099)	(1,409)	(1,527)
Net deferred income tax assets (liabilities)	**1,474**	**420**	**(210)**

Deferred income tax assets are recognised for tax loss carry forwards only to the extent that realisation of the related tax benefit is probable. The Group has unrecognised tax losses, including valuation allowances, as follows:

Unrecognised tax losses: expiry

	2009 Amount (mCHF)	2009 Applicable tax rate	2008 Amount (mCHF)	2008 Applicable tax rate
Within one year	—	—	—	—
Between one and five years	90	24%	68	22%
More than five years	480	19%	223	31%
Total unrecognised tax losses	**570**	**20%**	**291**	**29%**

Deferred income tax liabilities have not been established for the withholding tax and other taxes that would be payable on the unremitted earnings of certain foreign subsidiaries, as such amounts are currently regarded as permanently reinvested. These unremitted earnings totalled 26.5 billion Swiss francs at 31 December 2009 (2008: 41.7 billion Swiss francs).

there was considerable worry within the business community on its accounting treatment. We can now look back, having lived with VAT for well over two decades, and wonder, perhaps, why an SSAP was needed. VAT is essentially a tax on consumers collected by traders and is accounted for in a similar way to PAYE income tax, which is a tax on employees collected by employers.

Figure 14.7 Extract from Bayer Group 2009 Annual Accounts

14. Income taxes

The breakdown of income taxes by origin is as follows:

Income Tax Expense by Origin

	2008	2009
	€ million	€ million
Income taxes paid or accrued		
Germany	(161)	(186)
other countries	(651)	(476)
	(812)	**(662)**
Deferred taxes		
from temporary differences	323	430
from interest carryforwards	11	(11)
from tax loss carryforwards	(168)	(291)
from tax credits	10	23
	176	**151**
Total	**(636)**	**(511)**

Expiration of Unusable Tax Credits and Tax Loss Carryforwards

	Tax credits		Tax loss carryforwards	
	Dec. 31, 2008	Dec. 31, 2009	Dec. 31, 2008	Dec. 31, 2009
	€ million	€ million	€ million	€ million
One year	—	—	2	—
Two years	—	—	9	23
Three years	—	—	58	28
Four years	—	—	51	39
Five years	—	—	111	123
Thereafter	—	32	170	255
Total	**—**	**32**	**401**	**468**

IAS 18 (para. 8) makes clear that the same principles are followed:

Revenue includes only the gross inflows of economic benefits received and receivable by the enterprise on its own account. Amounts collected on behalf of third parties such as sales taxes, goods and services taxes and value added taxes are not economic benefits which flow to the enterprise and do not result in increases in equity. Therefore, they are excluded from revenue.[39]

14.12.1 The effects of the standard

The effects of the standard vary depending on the status of the accounting entity under the VAT legislation. The term 'trader' appears in the legislation and is the terminology for a business entity. The 'traders' or companies, as we would normally refer to them, are classified under the following headings:

(a) Registered trader

For a registered trader, accounts should only include figures net of VAT. This means that the VAT on the sales will be deducted from the invoice amount. The VAT will be payable to the government and the net amount of the sales invoice will appear in the profit and loss account in arriving at the sales turnover figure. The VAT on purchases will be deducted from the purchase invoice. The VAT will then be reclaimed from the government and the net amount of the purchases invoice will appear in the profit and loss account in arriving at the purchases figure.

The only exception to the use of amounts net of VAT is when the input tax is not recoverable, e.g. on entertaining and on 'private' motor cars.

(b) Non-registered or exempt trader

For a company that is classified as non-registered or exempt, the VAT that it has to pay on its purchases and expenses is not reclaimable from the government. Because the company cannot recover the VAT, it means that the expense that appears in the profit and loss account must be inclusive of VAT. It is treated as part of each item of expenditure and the costs treated accordingly. It will be included, where relevant, with each item of expense (including capital expenditure) rather than being shown as a separate item.

(c) Partially exempt trader

An entity which is partially exempt can only recover a proportion of input VAT, and the proportion of non-recoverable VAT should be treated as part of the costs on the same lines as with an exempt trader. The VAT rules are complex but, for the purpose of understanding the figures that appear in published accounts of public companies, treatment as a registered trader would normally apply.

Summary

The major impact on reported post-tax profits will be the adoption of IAS 12 which will remove the possibility for the discounting of deferred tax on the adoption of the full provisioning method.

There may be significant increase in the deferred tax charge, with the earnings per share correspondingly reduced.

REVIEW QUESTIONS

1 Why does the charge to taxation in a company's accounts not equal the profit multiplied by the current rate of corporation tax?

2 Explain clearly how advance corporation tax arose and its effect on the profit and loss account and the year-end statement of financial position figures. (Use a simple example to illustrate.)

3 Explain how the corporation tax system changed as from April 1999.

4 Deferred tax accounting may be seen as an income-smoothing device which distorts the true and fair view. Explain the impact of deferred tax on reported income and justify its continued use.

5 Explain how dividends received and paid are shown in the accounts.

6 Distinguish between (a) the deferral and (b) the liability methods of company deferred tax.

7 Explain the criteria that a deferred tax provision needs to satisfy under IAS 12 in order to be accepted as a liability in the statement of financial position.

8 Explain the effect of SSAP 5 *Accounting for Value Added Tax*.

EXERCISES

An extract from the solution is provided on the Companion Website (www.pearsoned.co.uk/elliott-elliott) for exercises marked with an asterisk (*).

Question 1

In your capacity as chief assistant to the financial controller, your managing director has asked you to explain to him the differences between tax planning, tax avoidance and tax evasion.

He has also asked you to explain to him your feelings as a professional accountant about these topics.

Write some notes to assist you in answering these questions.

* Question 2

A fixed asset (a machine) was purchased by Adjourn plc on 1 July 20X2 at a cost of £25,000.

The company prepares its annual accounts to 31 March in each year. The policy of the company is to depreciate such assets at the rate of 15% straight line (with depreciation being charged pro rata on a time apportionment basis in the year of purchase). The company was granted capital allowances at 25% per annum on the reducing balance method (such capital allowances are apportioned *pro rata* on a time apportionment basis in the year of purchase).

The rate of corporation tax has been as follows:

Year ended   31 Mar 20X3 20%
              31 Mar 20X4 30%
              31 Mar 20X5 20%
              31 Mar 20X6 19%
              31 Mar 20X7 19%

Required:
(a) Calculate the deferred tax provision using both the deferred method and the liability method.
(b) Explain why the liability method is considered by commentators to place the emphasis on the statement of financial position, whereas the deferred method is considered to place the emphasis on the profit and loss account.

Question 3

The move from the preparation of accounts under UK GAAP to the users of IFRS by United Kingdom quoted companies for years beginning 1 January 2005 had an effect on the level of profits reported. How will those profits arising from the change in accounting standards be treated for taxation purposes?

Question 4

Discuss the arguments for and against discounting the deferred tax charge.

Question 5

Austin Mitchell MP proposed an Early Day Motion in the House of Commons on 17 May 2005 as follows:

> That this House urges the Government to clamp down on artificial tax avoidance schemes and end the … tax avoidance loop-holes that enable millionaires and numerous companies trading in the UK to avoid UK taxes; and further urges the Government to … so that transactions lacking normal commercial substance and solely entered into for the purpose of tax avoidance are ignored for tax purposes, thereby providing certainty, fairness and clarity, which the UK's taxation system requires to prevent abusive tax avoidance, to protect the interests of ordinary citizens who are committed to making their contribution to society, to avoid an unnecessary burden of tax of individual tax-payers and to ensure that companies pay fair taxes on profits generated in this country.

Required:
(a) The Motion refers to tax avoidance. In your opinion, does the Early Day Motion tend to confuse the boundaries between tax avoidance and tax evasion?
(b) The Motion refers to nullifying the effects of tax avoidance to protect the interests of ordinary citizens who are making their contribution to society, to avoid an unnecessary burden of tax on individual taxpayers. If ordinary citizens require such protection, would it be possible to argue that even if tax avoidance were legal, it might well be immoral?

Question 6

Dee For has recently qualified as a pilot and is now intending to set up a private company in the near future to run small charter passenger flights from her home town. Most of her business plan has been written but she has recently learned that the company's forecast statement of comprehensive income and statement of financial position may be incorrect as she has not taken into account the likely impact of deferred tax on those financial statements. She has therefore asked you for help and, following a meeting, the following facts come to light:

(i) The aircraft would cost $1m. It would have a life of five years after which, it would have no residual value and will then be scrapped. Depreciation will be on a straight-line basis.
(ii) The government of the country in which she lives has recently introduced a scheme for new entrepreneurs which provides a tax allowance on capital expenditure of this type of 25% per annum using the reducing balance method. In this country, depreciation is not a deductible expense for tax purposes. Also in this country, a balancing adjustment is allowed whenever the asset is sold or scrapped.
(iii) Corporate income tax is currently set at 30%. It has remained unchanged for many years now and the government has indicated there are no plans to change it.
(iv) The company's forecast annual accounting profit before tax is $2m per annum over the next five years.

Required:
(a) Demonstrate the impact of the above on the company's forecast profit and loss accounts and balance sheets for each of the next five years by comparing the 'nil provision' method with the 'full provision method'.
(b) Explain the 'partial provision' method and whether it could apply to Dee For's company.
(c) Explain how your answer to (a) would be affected by a government announcement that it intends to increase the corporate income tax rate in the near future.

(The Association of International Accountants)

Question 7

The following information is given in respect of Unambitious plc:

(a) Non-current assets consist entirely of plant and machinery. The net book value of these assets as at 30 June 2010 is £100,000 in excess of their tax written-down value.

(b) The provision for deferred tax (all of which relates to fixed asset timing differences) as at 30 June 2010 was £21,000.

(c) The company's capital expenditure forecasts indicate that capital allowances and depreciation in future years will be:

Year ended 30 June	Depreciation charge for year	Capital allowances for year
£	£	£
2011	12,000	53,000
2012	14,000	49,000
2013	20,000	36,000
2014	40,000	32,000
2015	44,000	32,000
2016	46,000	36,000

For the following years, capital allowances are likely to continue to be in excess of depreciation for the foreseeable future.

(d) Corporation tax is to be taken at 21%.

Required:
Calculate the deferred tax charges or credits for the next six years, commencing with the year ended 30 June 2011, in accordance with the provisions of IAS 12.

References

1 OECD, *Theoretical and Empirical Aspects of Corporate Taxation*, Paris, 1974; van den Temple, *Corporation Tax and Individual Income Tax in the EEC*, EEC Commission, Brussels, 1974.
2 G.H. Partington and R.H. Chenhall, *Dividends, distortion and double taxation*, Abacus, June 1983.
3 Franklin D. Roosevelt, 1936 Speech at Worcester, Mass., 1936. Roosevelt Museum.
4 *Countering tax avoidance in the UK: which way forward*, A Report of the Tax Law Review Committee, The Institute of Fiscal Studies, 2009, para. 4.2.
5 Tomlin, L.J. in. *Duke of Westminster v CIR*, HL 1935, 19 TC 490.
6 *Tax Avoidance: A Report by the Tax Law Review Committee*, The Institute For Fiscal Studies 1997, para. 7.
7 *WT Ramsay Ltd v CIR*, HL 1981, 54 TC 101; [1981] STC 174; [1981] 2 WLR 449; [1981] 1 All ER 865.
8 Robert Maas, *Beware tax avoidance drifting into evasion*, Taxline, Tax Planning 2003–2004, Institute of Chartered Accountants in England & Wales.
9 *Professional Conduct in Relation to Taxation*, Ethical Statement 1.308, Institute of Chartered Accountants in England & Wales, para. 2.13 (this is similar to the statements issued by the other accounting bodies).
10 *The Telegraph*, 4 July 2005.
11 *Business Week*, 1 September 2005.
12 The International Tax Planning Association Library, September 2005.
13 'Power Without Responsibility: Tax Avoidance and Corporate Integrity', John Christensen, e-mail of January 2005.

14 R. Altshul, 'Act now', *Accountancy Age*, 5 February 1998, p. 19.

15 William Gale, 'What can America Learn from the British Tax System?', *Fiscal Studies*, vol. 18, no. 4, November 1997.

16 Section 836A *Income and Corporation Taxes Act 1988* (as modified by Finance Act 2004).

17 Sections 50 to 54, under the heading of Accounting Practice, and Schedule 10 (Amendment of enactments that operate by reference to accounting practice), Finance Act 2004.

18 Schedule 23 to Finance Act 2003.

19 IAS 12 *Income Taxes*, IASB revised 2000, para. 5.

20 SFAS 109, *Accounting for Income Taxes*, FASB, 1992, extracts therefrom.

21 IAS 12 *Income Taxes*, IASB revised 2000, Example 1 to Appendix B.

22 IAS 12 *Income Taxes*, IASB revised 2000, para. 54.

23 P. Rosenfield and W.C. Dent, 'Deferred income taxes' in R. Bloom and P.T. Elgers (eds), *Accounting Theory and Practice*, Harcourt Brace Jovanovich, 1987, p. 545.

24 Andrew C. Lennard during a guest lecture at Sunderland Business School.

25 Mike Metcalf, 'Alchemical Accounting', *Accountancy*, November 1999, p. 100.

26 IAS 12 *Income Taxes*, IASB, revised 2000, para. 54.

27 Joan Brown, 'A step closer to harmony', *Accountancy*, January 2001, p. 90.

28 R.J. Chambers, *Tax Allocation and Financial Reporting*, Abacus, 1968.

29 Prof. D.R. Middleton, letters to the Editor, *The Financial Times*, 29 September 1994.

30 Terry Smith, *Accounting for Growth: stripping the camouflage from Company Accounts* (2nd edition), Random House, 1996.

31 'Corporate Lobbying in the UK: analysis of attitudes towards the ASB's 1995 deferred taxation proposals'. G. Geordgiou and C. Roberts, *British Accounting Review*, Dec. 2004, vol. 36, issue 4.

32 'IFRS Update October 2005 – Tax', *Accountancy Age*, 5 October 2005.

33 'International Financial Reporting Standards. Communicating the changes', BDO Stoy Hayward, December 2006.

34 David Cairns, *Accountancy*, October 2006, vol. 138, p. 14.

35 *Framework for the Preparation and Presentation of Financial Statements*, IASB 2001, para. 22.

36 *Ibid.*, para. 53.

37 *Ibid.*, para. 60.

38 *Ibid.*, para. 35.

39 IAS 18 *Revenue*, IASB 2001, para. 8.

CHAPTER 15

Property, plant and equipment (PPE)

15.1 Introduction

The main purpose of this chapter is to explain how to determine the initial carrying value of PPE and to explain and account for the normal movements in PPE that occur during an accounting period.

Objectives

By the end of this chapter, you should be able to:

- explain the meaning of PPE and determine its initial carrying value;
- account for subsequent expenditure on PPE that has already been recognised;
- explain the meaning of depreciation and compute the depreciation charge for a period;
- account for PPE measured under the revaluation model;
- explain the meaning of impairment;
- compute and account for an impairment loss;
- explain the criteria that must be satisfied before an asset is classified as held for sale and account for such assets;
- explain the accounting treatment of government grants for the purchase of PPE;
- identify an investment property and explain the alternative accounting treatment of such properties;
- explain the impact of alternative methods of accounting for PPE on key accounting ratios.

15.2 PPE – concepts and the relevant IASs and IFRSs

For PPE the accounting treatment is based on the accruals or matching concepts, under which expenditure is capitalised until it is charged as depreciation against revenue in the periods in which benefit is gained from its use. Thus, if an item is purchased that has an economic life of two years, so that it will be used over two accounting periods to help earn profit for the entity, then the cost of that asset should be apportioned in some way between the two accounting periods.

However, this does not take into account the problems surrounding PPE accounting and depreciation, which have so far given rise to six relevant international accounting standards. We will consider these problems in this chapter and cover the following:

IAS 16 and IAS 23:

- What is PPE (IAS 16)?
- How is the cost of PPE determined (IAS 16 and IAS 23)?
- How is depreciation of PPE computed (IAS 16)?
- What are the regulations regarding carrying PPE at revalued amounts (IAS 16)?

Other relevant international accounting standards and pronouncements:

- How should grants receivable towards the purchase of PPE be dealt with (IAS 20)?
- Are there ever circumstances in which PPE should not be depreciated (IAS 40)?
- What is impairment and how does this affect the carrying value of PPE (IAS 36)?
- What are the key changes made by the IASB concerning the disposal of non-current assets (IFRS 5)?

15.3 What is PPE?

IAS 16 *Property, Plant and Equipment*[1] defines PPE as tangible assets that are:

(a) held by an entity for use in the production or supply of goods and services, for rental to others, or for administrative purposes; and

(b) expected to be used during more than one period.

It is clear from the definition that PPE will normally be included in the non-current assets section of the statement of financial position.

15.3.1 Problems that may arise

Problems may arise in relation to the interpretation of the definition and in relation to the application of the materiality concept.

The definitions give rise to some areas of practical difficulty. For example, an asset that has previously been held for use in the production or supply of goods or services but is now going to be sold should, under the provisions of IFRS 5, be classified separately on the statement of financial position as an asset 'held for sale'.

Differing accounting treatments arise if there are different assessments of materiality. This may result in the same expenditure being reported as an asset in the statement of financial position of one company and as an expense in the statement of comprehensive income of another company. In the accounts of a self-employed carpenter, a kit of hand tools that, with careful maintenance, will last many years will, quite rightly, be shown as PPE. Similar assets used by the maintenance department in a large factory will, in all probability, be treated as 'loose tools' and written off as acquired.

Many entities have *de minimis* policies, whereby only items exceeding a certain value are treated as PPE; items below the cut-off amount will be expensed through the statement of comprehensive income.

For example, the MAN 2003 Annual Report stated in its accounting policies:

Tangible assets are depreciated according to the straight-line method over their estimated useful lives. Low-value items (defined as assets at cost of €410 or less) are fully written off in the year of purchase.

15.4 How is the cost of PPE determined?

15.4.1 Components of cost[2]

According to IAS 16, the cost of an item of PPE comprises its purchase price, including import duties and non-refundable purchase taxes, plus any directly attributable costs of bringing the asset to working condition for its intended use. Examples of such directly attributable costs include:

(a) the costs of site preparation;

(b) initial delivery and handling costs;

(c) installation costs;

(d) professional fees such as for architects and engineers;

(e) the estimated cost of dismantling and removing the asset and restoring the site, to the extent that it is recognised as a provision under IAS 37 *Provisions, Contingent Liabilities and Contingent Assets*.

Administration and other general overhead costs are not a component of the cost of PPE unless they can be directly attributed to the acquisition of the asset or bringing it to its working condition. Similarly, start up and similar pre-production costs do not form part of the cost of an asset unless they are necessary to bring the asset to its working condition.

15.4.2 Self-constructed assets[3]

The cost of a self-constructed asset is determined using the same principles as for an acquired asset. If the asset is made available for sale by the entity in the normal course of business then the cost of the asset is usually the same as the cost of producing the asset for sale. This cost would usually be determined under the principles set out in IAS 2 *Inventories*.

The normal profit that an enterprise would make if selling the self-constructed asset would not be recognised in 'cost' if the asset were retained within the entity. Following similar principles, where one group company constructs an asset that is used as PPE by another group company, any profit on sale is eliminated in determining the initial carrying value of the asset in the consolidated accounts (this will also clearly affect the calculation of depreciation).

If an item of PPE is exchanged in whole or in part for a dissimilar item of PPE then the cost of such an item is the fair value of the asset received. This is equivalent to the fair value of the asset given up, adjusted for any cash or cash equivalents transferred or received.

15.4.3 Capitalisation of borrowing costs

Where an asset takes a substantial period of time to get ready for its intended use or sale then the entity may incur significant borrowing costs in the preparation period. Under the accruals basis of accounting there is an argument that such costs should be included as a directly attributable cost of construction. IAS 23 *Borrowing Costs* was issued to deal with this issue.

IAS 23 states that borrowing costs that are directly attributable to the acquisition, construction or production of a 'qualifying asset' should be included in the cost of that asset.[4] A 'qualifying asset' is one that necessarily takes a substantial period of time to get ready for its intended use or sale.

Borrowing costs that would have been avoided if the expenditure on the qualifying asset had not been undertaken are eligible for capitalisation under IAS 23. Where the funds are borrowed specifically for the purpose of obtaining a qualifying asset then the borrowing costs that are eligible for capitalisation are those incurred on the borrowing during the period less any investment income on the temporary investment of those borrowings. Where the funds are borrowed generally and used for the purpose of obtaining a qualifying asset then the entity should use a capitalisation rate to determine the borrowing costs that may be capitalised. This rate should be the weighted average of the borrowing costs applicable to the entity, other than borrowings made specifically for the purpose of obtaining a qualifying asset. Capitalisation should commence when:

● expenditures for the asset are being incurred;

● borrowing costs are being incurred;

● activities that are necessary to prepare the asset for its intended use or sale are in progress.

When substantially all the activities necessary to prepare the qualifying asset for its intended use or sale are complete then capitalisation should cease.

One of the key future priorities of the IASB is to converge IFRFS with GAAP in the USA. The equivalent US statement, SFAS 34, also requires capitalisation in relevant cases.

Borrowing costs treatment in the UK

The UK standard that deals with this issue is FRS 15 *Tangible Fixed Assets*. FRS 15 makes the capitalisation of borrowing costs optional, rather than compulsory. FRS 15 requires that the policy be applied consistently however. This used to be the treatment under IAS 23 before that standard was revised in 2007.

15.4.4 Subsequent expenditure

Subsequent expenditure relating to an item of PPE that has already been recognised should normally be recognised as an expense in the period in which it is incurred. The exception to this general rule is where it is probable that future economic benefits in excess of the originally assessed standard of performance of the existing asset will, as a result of the expenditure, flow to the entity. In these circumstances, the expenditure should be added to the carrying value of the existing asset. Examples of expenditure that might fall to be treated in this way include:

● modification of an item of plant to extend its useful life, including an increase in its capacity;

● upgrading machine parts to achieve a substantial improvement in the quality of output;

● adoption of new production processes enabling a substantial reduction in previously assessed operating costs.

Conversely, expenditure that restores, rather than increases, the originally assessed standard of performance of an asset is written off as an expense in the period incurred.

Some assets have components that require replacement at regular intervals. Two examples of such components would be the lining of a furnace and the roof of a building. IAS 16 states[5] that, provided such components have readily ascertainable costs, they should be accounted for as separate assets because they have useful lives different from the items of PPE to which they relate. This means that when such components are replaced they are accounted for as an asset disposal and acquisition of a new asset.

15.5 What is depreciation?

IAS 16 defines depreciation[6] as the systematic allocation of the depreciable amount of an asset over its life. The depreciable amount is the cost of an asset or other amount substituted for cost in the financial statements, less its residual value.

Note that this definition places an emphasis on the consumption in a particular accounting period rather than an average over the asset's life. We will consider two aspects of the definition: the measure of wearing out; and the useful economic life.

15.5.1 Allocation of depreciable amount

Depreciation is a measure of wearing out that is calculated annually and charged as an expense against profits. Under the 'matching concept', the depreciable amount of the asset is allocated over its productive life.

It is important to make clear what depreciation is *not*:

● It is not 'saving up for a new one'; it is not setting funds aside for the replacement of the existing asset at the end of its life; it is the matching of cost to revenue. The effect is to reduce the profit available for distribution, but this is not accompanied by the setting aside of cash of an equal amount to ensure that liquid funds are available at the end of the asset's life.

● It is not 'a way of showing the real value of assets on the statement of financial position' by reducing the cost figure to a realisable value.

We emphasise what depreciation is *not* because both of these ideas are commonly held by non-accountant users of accounts; it is as well to realise these possible misconceptions when interpreting accounts for non-accountants.

Depreciation is currently conceived as a charge for funds **already expended**, and thus it cannot be considered as the setting aside of funds to meet future expenditure. If we consider it in terms of capital maintenance, then we can see that it results in the maintenance of the initial invested monetary capital of the company. It is concerned with the allocation of that expenditure over a period of time, without having regard for the **value** of the asset at any intermediate period of its life.

Where an asset has been revalued the depreciation is based on the revalued amount. This is because the revalued amount has replaced cost (less residual value) as the depreciable amount.

15.5.2 Useful life

IAS 16 defines this as:

(a) the period of time over which an asset is expected to be used by an entity; or

(b) the number of production or similar units expected to be obtained from the asset by an entity.[7]

The IAS 16 definition is based on the premise that almost all assets have a finite useful economic life. This may be true in principle, but it is incredibly difficult in real life to arrive at an average economic life that can be applied to even a single class of assets, e.g. plant. This is evidenced by the accounting policy in the ICI 2005 Annual Report which states:

> **Depreciation and amortization**
> The Group's policy is to write-off the book value of property, plant and equipment, excluding land, and intangible assets and goodwill to their residual value evenly over

their estimated remaining lives. Residual values are reviewed on an annual basis. Reviews are made annually of the estimated remaining lives of individual productive assets, taking account of commercial and technological obsolescence as well as normal wear and tear. Under this policy, the total lives approximate to 32 years for buildings and 14 years for land and equipment and 3 to 5 years for computer software.

In addition to the practical difficulty of estimating economic lives, there are also exceptions where nil depreciation is charged. Two common exceptions found in the accounts of UK companies relate to freehold land and certain types of property.

15.5.3 Freehold land

Freehold land (but not the buildings thereon) is considered to have an infinite life unless it is held simply for the extraction of minerals, etc. Thus land held for the purpose of, say, mining coal or quarrying gravel will be dealt with for accounting purposes as a coal or gravel deposit. Consequently, although the land may have an infinite life, the deposits will have an economic life only as long as they can be profitably extracted. If the cost of extraction exceeds the potential profit from extraction and sale, the economic life of the quarry has ended. When assessing depreciation for a commercial company, we are concerned only with these private costs and benefits, and not with public costs and benefits which might lead to the quarry being kept open.

The following extract from the Goldfields 2006 Annual Report illustrates accounting policies for land and mining assets.

Land
Land is shown at cost and is not depreciated.

Amortisation and depreciation of mining assets
Amortisation is determined to give a fair and systematic charge in the statement of comprehensive income taking into account the nature of a particular ore body and the method of mining that ore body. To achieve this the following calculation methods are used:

● Mining assets, including mine development and infrastructure costs, mine plant facilities and evaluation costs, are amortised over the lives of the mines using the units-of-production method, based on estimated proved and probable ore reserves above infrastructure.

● Where it is anticipated that the mine life will significantly exceed the proved and probable reserves, the mine life is estimated using a methodology that takes account of current exploration information to assess the likely recoverable gold from a particular area. Such estimates are used only for the level of confidence in the assessment and the probability of conversion to reserves.

● At certain of the group's operations, the calculation of amortisation takes into account future costs which will be incurred to develop all the proved and probable ore reserves.

● Proved and probable ore reserves reflect estimated quantities of economically recoverable reserves, which can be recovered in future from known mineral deposits. Certain mining plant and equipment included in mine development and infrastructure are depreciated on a straight-line basis over their estimated useful lives.

Mineral and surface rights
Mineral and surface rights are recorded at cost of acquisition. When there is little likelihood of a mineral right being exploited, or the value of mineral rights have diminished below cost, a write-down is effected against income in the period that such determination is made.

Few jurisdictions have comprehensive accounting standards for extractive activities. IFRS 6 – *Exploration for and Evaluation of Mineral Resources* – is an interim measure pending a more comprehensive view by the ASB in future. IFRS 6 allows an entity to develop an accounting policy for exploration and evaluation assets without considering the consistency of the policy with the IASB framework. This may mean that for an interim period accounting policies might permit the recognition of both current and non-current assets that do not meet the criteria laid down in the IASB Framework. This is considered by some commentators to be unduly permissive. Indeed, about the only firm requirement IFRS 6 can be said to contain is the requirement to test exploration and evaluation assets for impairment whenever a change in facts and circumstances suggests that impairment exists.

15.5.4 Certain types of property

In some jurisdictions certain types of property, e.g. hotels, have not been subject to annual depreciation charges. The rationale for this treatment is that in certain cases regular refurbishment expenditure on such properties is necessary because of their key function within the business. This regular refurbishment expenditure, it is alleged, makes the useful economic lives of such properties infinite, thus removing the need for depreciation.

An example is provided by this extract from the Accounting Policies in the 2003 Annual Report of Punch Taverns plc.

Depreciation – Leased estate
It is the Group's policy to maintain the properties comprising the licensed estate in such a condition that the residual values of the properties, based on prices prevailing at the time of acquisition or subsequent revaluation, are at least equal to their book values. The primary responsibility for the maintenance of such properties, ensuring that they remain in sound operational condition, is normally that of the lessee as required by their lease contracts with the Group. Having regard to this, it is the opinion of the Directors that depreciation of any such property as required by the Companies Act 1985 and generally accepted accounting practice would not be material ... An annual impairment review is carried out on all properties in accordance with FRS 11 and FRS 15.

IAS 16 does not appear to support non-depreciation of PPE other than freehold land in any circumstances. Paragraph 58 of IAS 16 states:

Land and buildings are separable assets and are accounted for separately, even when they are acquired together. With some exceptions, such as quarries and sites used for landfill, land has an unlimited useful life and is therefore not depreciated. Buildings have a limited useful life and are therefore depreciable assets. An increase in the value of the land on which the building stands does not affect the determination of the depreciable amount of the building.

The accounting policy of Punch Taverns plc has since been changed and the following appears in the 2006 Annual Report:

Licensed properties, unlicensed properties and owner-occupied properties 50 years or the life of the lease if shorter.

15.6 What are the constituents in the depreciation formula?

In order to calculate depreciation it is necessary to determine three factors:

1 cost (or revalued amount if the company is following a revaluation policy);
2 economic life;
3 residual value.

A simple example is the calculation of the depreciation charge for a company that has acquired an asset on 1 January 20X1 for £1,000 with an estimated economic life of four years and an estimated residual value of £200. Applying a straight-line depreciation policy, the charge would be £200 per year using the formula of:

$$\frac{\text{Cost} - \text{Estimated residual value}}{\text{Estimated economic life}} = \frac{£1,000 - £200}{4} = £200 \text{ per annum}$$

We can see that the charge of £200 is influenced in all cases by the definition of cost; the estimate of the residual value; the estimate of the economic life; and the management decision on depreciation policy.

In addition, if the asset were to be revalued at the end of the second year to £900, then the depreciation for 20X3 and 20X4 would be recalculated using the revised valuation figure. Assuming that the residual value remained unchanged, the depreciation for 20X3 would be:

$$\frac{\text{Revalued asset} - \text{Estimated residual value}}{\text{Estimated economic life}} = \frac{£900 - £200}{2} = £350 \text{ per annum}$$

15.7 How is the useful life of an asset determined?

The IAS 16 definition of useful life is given in section 15.5.2 above. This is not necessarily the total life expectancy of the asset. Most assets become less economically and technologically efficient as they grow older. For this reason, assets may well cease to have an economic life long before their working life is over. It is the responsibility of the preparers of accounts to estimate the economic life of all assets.

It is conventional for entities to consider the economic lives of assets by class or category, e.g. buildings, plant, office equipment, or motor vehicles. However, this is not necessarily appropriate, since the level of activity demanded by different users may differ. For example, compare two motor cars owned by a business: one is used by the national sales manager, covering 100,000 miles per annum visiting clients; the other is used by the accountant to drive from home to work and occasionally the bank, covering perhaps one-tenth of the mileage.

In practice, the useful economic life would be determined by reference to factors such as repair costs, the cost and availability of replacements, and the comparative cash flows of existing and alternative assets. The problem of optimal replacement lives is a normal financial management problem; its significance in financial reporting is that the assumptions used within the financial management decision may provide evidence of the expected economic life.

15.7.1 Other factors affecting the useful life figure

We can see that there are technical factors affecting the estimated economic life figure. In addition, other factors have prompted companies to set estimated lives that have no relationship to the active productive life of the asset. One such factor is the wish of management to take into account the effect of inflation. This led some companies to reduce the estimated economic life, so that a higher charge was made against profits during the early period of the asset's life to compensate for the inflationary effect on the cost of replacement. The total charge will be the same, but the timing is advanced. This does not result in the retention of funds necessary to replace; but it does reflect the fact that there is at present no coherent policy for dealing with inflation in the published accounts – consequently, companies resort to *ad hoc* measures that frustrate efforts to make accounts uniform and comparable. *Ad hoc* measures such as these have prompted changes in the standards.

15.8 Residual value

IAS 16 defines residual value as the net amount which an entity expects to obtain for an asset at the end of its useful life after deducting the expected costs of disposal. Where PPE is carried at cost, the residual value is initially estimated at the date of acquisition. In subsequent periods the estimate of residual value is revised, the revision being based on conditions prevailing at each statement of financial position date. Such revisions have an effect on future depreciation charges.

Besides inflation, residual values can be affected by changes in technology and market conditions. For example, during the period 1980–90 the cost of small business computers fell dramatically in both real and monetary terms, with a considerable impact on the residual (or second-hand) value of existing equipment.

15.9 Calculation of depreciation

Having determined the key factors in the computation, we are left with the problem of how to allocate that cost between accounting periods. For example, with an asset having an economic life of five years:

	£
Asset cost	11,000
Estimated residual value	
(no significant change anticipated over useful economic life)	1,000
Depreciable amount	10,000

How should the depreciable amount be charged to the statement of comprehensive income over the five years? IAS 16 tells us that it should be allocated on a systematic basis and the depreciation method used should reflect as fairly as possible the pattern in which the asset's economic benefits are consumed. The two most popular methods are **straight-line**, in which the depreciation is charged evenly over the useful life, and **diminishing balance**, where depreciation is calculated annually on the net written-down amount. In the case above, the calculations would be as in Figure 15.1.

Note that, although the diminishing balance is generally expressed in terms of a percentage, this percentage is arrived at by inserting the economic life into the formula as n; the 38% reflects the expected economic life of five years. As we change the life, so we change the percentage that is applied. The normal rate applied to vehicles is 25% diminishing balance; if we apply that to the cost and residual value in our example, we can see that we would be assuming an economic life of eight years. It is a useful test when using reducing balance percentages to refer back to the underlying assumptions.

We can see that the end result is the same. Thus, £10,000 has been charged against income, but with a dramatically different pattern of statement of comprehensive income charges. The charge for straight-line depreciation in the first year is less than half that for reducing balance.

15.9.1 Arguments in favour of the straight-line method

The method is simple to calculate. However, in these days of calculators and computers this seems a particularly facile argument, particularly when one considers the materiality of the figures.

15.9.2 Arguments in favour of the diminishing balance method

First, the charge reflects the efficiency and maintenance costs of the asset. When new, an asset is operating at its maximum efficiency, which falls as it nears the end of its life. This may be countered by the comment that in year 1 there may be 'teething troubles' with new equipment, which, while probably covered by a supplier's guarantee, will hamper efficiency.

Secondly, the pattern of diminishing balance depreciation gives a net book amount that approximates to second-hand values. For example, with motor cars the initial fall in value is very high.

15.9.3 Other methods of depreciating

Besides straight-line and diminishing balance, there are a number of other methods of depreciating, such as the sum of the units method, the machine-hour method and the annuity method. We will consider these briefly.

Sum of the units method

A compromise between straight-line and reducing balance that is popular in the USA is the sum of the units method. The calculation based on the information in Figure 15.1 is now shown in Figure 15.2. This has the advantage that, unlike diminishing balance, it is simple to obtain the exact residual amount (zero if appropriate), while giving the pattern of high initial charge shown by the diminishing balance approach.

Machine-hour method

The machine-hour system is based on an estimate of the asset's service potential. The economic life is measured not in accounting periods but in working hours, and the depreciation is allocated in the proportion of the actual hours worked to the potential total hours available. This method is commonly employed in aviation, where aircraft are depreciated on the basis of flying hours.

Annuity method

With the annuity method, the asset, or rather the amount of capital representing the asset, is regarded as being capable of earning a fixed rate of interest. The sacrifice incurred in using the asset within the business is therefore two-fold: the loss arising from the exhaustion of the service potential of the asset; and the interest forgone by using the funds invested in the business to purchase the fixed asset. With the help of annuity tables, a calculation shows what equal amounts of depreciation, written off over the estimated life of the asset, will reduce the book value to nil, after debiting interest to the asset account on the diminishing

Figure 15.1 Effect of different depreciation methods

	Straight-line (£2,000)	Diminishing balance (38%)	Difference
	£	£	£
Cost	11,000	11,000	
Depreciation for year 1	2,000	4,180	2,180
Net book value (NBV)	9,000	6,820	
Depreciation for year 2	2,000	2,592	592
NBV	7,000	4,228	
Depreciation for year 3	2,000	1,606	(394)
NBV	5,000	2,622	
Depreciation for year 4	2,000	996	(1,004)
NBV	3,000	1,626	
Depreciation for year 5	2,000	618	(1,382)
Residual value	1,000	1,008	

The diminishing balance formula was $1 - \sqrt[n]{(\text{Residual value/Cost})}$

Figure 15.2 Sum of the units method

		£
Cost		11,000
Depreciation for year 1	£10,000 × 5/15	3,333
Net book value (NBV)		7,667
Depreciation for year 2	£10,000 × 4/15	2,667
NBV		5,000
Depreciation for year 3	£10,000 × 3/15	2,000
NBV		3,000
Depreciation for year 4	£10,000 × 2/15	1,333
NBV		1,667
Depreciation for year 5	£10,000 × 1/15	667
Residual value		1,000

amount of funds that are assumed to be invested in the business at that time, as represented by the value of the asset.

Figure 15.3 contains an illustration based on the treatment of a five-year lease which cost the company a premium of £10,000 on 1 January year 1. It shows how the total depreciation charge is computed. Each year the charge for depreciation in the statement of comprehensive income is the equivalent annual amount that is required to repay the investment over the five-year period at a rate of interest of 10% less the notional interest available on the remainder of the invested funds.

An extract from the annuity tables to obtain the annual equivalent factor for year 5 and assuming a rate of interest of 10% would show:

Figure 15.3 Annuity method

Year	Opening written-down value £	Notional interest (10%) £	Annual payment £	Net movement £	Closing written-down value £
1	10,000	1,000	(2,638)	(1,638)	8,362
2	8,362	836	(2,638)	(1,802)	6,560
3	6,560	656	(2,638)	(1,982)	4,578
4	4,578	458	(2,638)	(2,180)	2,398
5	2,398	240	(2,638)	(2,398)	Nil

Year	Annuity $A_{\overline{n}|}^{-1}$
1	1.1000
2	0.5762
3	0.4021
4	0.3155
5	0.2638

Therefore, at a rate of interest of 10% five annual payments to repay an investor of £10,000 would each be £2,638.

A variation of this system involves the investment of a sum equal to the net charge in fixed interest securities or an endowment policy, so as to build up a fund that will generate cash to replace the asset at the end of its life.

This last system has significant weaknesses. It is based on the misconception that depreciation is 'saving up for a new one', whereas in reality depreciation is charging against profits funds already expended. It is also dangerous in a time of inflation, since it may lead management not to maintain the capital of the entity adequately, in which case they may not be able to replace the assets at their new (inflated) prices.

The annuity method, with its increasing net charge to income, does tend to take inflationary factors into account, but it must be noted that the *total* net profit and loss charge only adds up to the cost of the asset.

15.9.4 Which method should be used?

The answer to this seemingly simple question is 'it depends'. On the matter of depreciation IAS 16 is designed primarily to force a fair charge for the use of assets into the statement of comprehensive income each year, so that the earnings reflect a true and fair view.

Straight-line is most suitable for assets such as leases which have a definite fixed life. It is also considered most appropriate for assets with a short working life, although with motor cars the diminishing balance method is sometimes employed to match second-hand values. Extraction industries (mining, oil wells, quarries, etc.) sometimes employ a variation on the machine-hour system, where depreciation is based on the amount extracted as a proportion of the estimated reserves.

Despite the theoretical attractiveness of other methods the straight-line method is, by a long way, the one in most common use by entities that prepare financial statements in accordance with IFRSs. Reasons for this are essentially pragmatic:

- It is the most straightforward to compute.

- In the light of the three additional subjective factors [cost (or revalued amount); residual value; useful life] that need to be estimated, any imperfections in the charge for depreciation caused by the choice of the straight-line method are not likely to be significant.

- It conforms to the accounting treatment adopted by peers. For example, one group reported that it currently used the reducing balance method but, as peer companies used the straight-line method, it decided to change and adopt that policy.

The following accounting policy note comes from the financial statements of BorsodChem Nyct, a Hungarian entity preparing financial statements in accordance with international accounting standards:

> Freehold land is not depreciated. Depreciation is provided using the straight-line methods at rates calculated to write off the cost of the asset over its expected economic useful life. The rates used are as follows:

Buildings	2%
Machinery and other equipment	5–15%
Vehicles	15–20%
Computer equipment	33%

15.9.5 Impairment of assets

IAS 36 *Impairment of Assets*[8] deals with the problems of the measurement, recognition and presentation of material reductions in value of non-current assets both tangible and intangible.

Unless a review is specifically required by another IFRS non-current assets will be required to be reviewed for impairment only if there is some indication that impairment has occurred, e.g. slump in property market or expected future losses.

The IASB's aim is to ensure that relevant assets are recorded **at no more than recoverable amount**. This is defined as being the higher of net selling price and value in use. Value in use is defined as the **present value** of future cash flows obtainable from the asset's continued use using a **discount rate** that is equivalent to the rate of return that the market would expect on an equally risky investment.

We will consider impairment of assets in more detail in section 15.11. However, this issue is also relevant to the computation of the depreciation charge. Paragraph 17 of IAS 36 states:

> If there is an indication that an asset may be impaired this may indicate that the remaining useful life, the depreciation method, or the residual value for the asset need to be reviewed and adjusted under the IAS applicable to the asset, even if no impairment loss is recognised for the asset.

In the case of PPE the relevant IAS is IAS 16 and this indicates that an impairment review may well affect future depreciation charges in the statement of comprehensive income, even if no impairment loss is recognised.

15.10 Measurement subsequent to initial recognition

15.10.1 Choice of models

An entity needs to choose either the cost or the revaluation model as its accounting policy for an entire class of PPE. The cost model (definitely the most common) results in an asset being carried at cost less accumulated depreciation and any accumulated impairment losses.

15.10.2 The revaluation model

Under the revaluation model the asset is carried at revalued amount, being its fair value at the date of the revaluation less any subsequent accumulated depreciation and subsequent accumulated impairment losses. The fair value of an asset is defined in IAS 16 as 'the amount for which an asset could be exchanged between knowledgeable and willing parties in an arm's length transaction'. Thus fair value is basically market value. If a market value is not available, perhaps in the case of partly used specialised plant and equipment that is rarely bought and sold other than as new, then IAS 16 requires that revaluation be based on depreciated replacement cost.

EXAMPLE ● An entity purchased an item of plant for £12,000 on 1 January 20X1. The plant was depreciated on a straight-line basis over its useful economic life, which was estimated at six years. On 1 January 20X3 the entity decided to revalue its plant. No fair value was available for the item of plant that had been purchased for £12,000 on 1 January 20X1 but the replacement cost of the plant at 1 January 20X3 was £21,000.

The carrying value of the plant immediately before the revaluation would have been:

● Cost £12,000

● Accumulated depreciation £4,000 [(£12,000/6) × 2]

● Written-down value £8,000.

Under the principles of IAS 16 the revalued amount would be £14,000 [£21,000 × 4/6]. This amount would be reflected in the financial statements either by:

● showing a revised gross figure of £14,000 and reversing out all the accumulated depreciation charged to date so as to give a carrying value of £14,000; or

● restating both the gross figure and the accumulated depreciation by the proportionate change in replacement cost. This would give a gross figure of £21,000, with accumulated depreciation restated at £7,000 to once again give a net carrying value of £14,000.

15.10.3 Detailed requirements regarding revaluations

The frequency of revaluations depends upon the movements in the fair values of those items of PPE being revalued. In jurisdictions where the rate of price changes is very significant revaluations may be necessary on an annual basis. In other jurisdictions revaluations every three or five years may well be sufficient.

Where an item of PPE is revalued then the entire class of PPE to which that asset belongs should be revalued.[9] A class of PPE is a grouping of assets of a similar nature and use in an entities operations. Examples would include:

● land;

● land and buildings;

● machinery.

This is an important provision because without it entities would be able to select which assets they revalued on the basis of best advantage to the financial statements. Revaluations will usually increase the carrying values of assets and equity and leave borrowings unchanged. Therefore gearing (or leverage) ratios will be reduced. It is important that, if the revaluation route is chosen, assets are revalued on a rational basis.

The following is a further extract from the financial statements of Coil SA, a company incorporated in Belgium that prepares financial statements in euros in accordance with international accounting standards: 'Items of PPE are stated at historical cost modified by revaluation and are depreciated using the straight-line method over their estimated useful lives.'

15.10.4 Accounting for revaluations

When the carrying amount of an asset is increased as a result of a revaluation, the increase should be credited directly to other comprehensive income, being shown in equity under the heading of revaluation surplus. The only exception is where the gain reverses a revaluation decrease previously recognised as an expense **relating to the same asset**.

This means that, in the example we considered under section 15.10.2 above, the revaluation would lead to a credit of £6,000 (£14,000 – £8,000) to other comprehensive income.

If however the carrying amount of an asset is decreased as a result of a revaluation then the decrease should be recognised as an expense. The only exception is where that asset had previously been revalued. In those circumstances the loss on revaluation is charged against the revaluation surplus to the extent that the revaluation surplus contains an amount **relating to the same asset**.

EXAMPLE ● An entity buys freehold land for £100,000 in year 1. The land is revalued to £150,000 in year 3 and £90,000 in year 5. The land is not depreciated.

In year 3 a surplus of £50,000 [£150,000 – £100,000] is credited to equity under the heading 'revaluation surplus'. In year 5 a deficit of £60,000 [£90,000 – £150,000] arises on the second revaluation. £50,000 of this deficit is deducted from the revaluation surplus and £10,000 is charged as an expense. It is worth noting that £10,000 is the amount by which the year 5 carrying amount is lower than the original cost of the land.

Where an asset that has been revalued is sold then the revaluation surplus becomes realised.[10] It may be transferred to retained earnings when this happens but this transfer is not made through the statement of comprehensive income.

Turning again to our example in section 15.10.2, let us assume that the plant was sold on 1 January 20X5 for £5,000. The carrying amount of the asset in the financial statements immediately before the sale would be £7,000 [£14,000 – 2 × £3,500]. This means that a loss on sale of £2,000 would be taken to the statement of comprehensive income. The revaluation surplus of £6,000 would be transferred to retained earnings.

IAS 16 allows for the possibility that the revaluation surplus is transferred to retained earnings as the asset is depreciated. To turn once again to our example, we see that the revaluation on 1 January 20X3 increased the annual depreciation charge from £2,000 [£12,000/6] to £3,500 [£21,000/6]. Following revaluation an amount equivalent to the 'excess depreciation' may be transferred from the revaluation surplus to retained earnings as the asset is depreciated. This would lead in our example to a transfer of £1,500 each year. Clearly if this occurs then the revaluation surplus that is transferred to retained earnings on sale is £3,000 [£6,000 – (2 × £1,500)].

15.11 IAS 36 Impairment of Assets

15.11.1 IAS 36 approach

IAS 36 sets out the principles and methodology for accounting for impairments of non-current assets and goodwill. Where possible, individual non-current assets should be individually tested for impairment. However, where cash flows do not arise from the use of a single non-current asset, impairment is measured for the smallest group of assets which generates income that is largely independent of the company's other income streams. This smallest group is referred to as a cash generating unit (CGU).

Impairment of an asset, or CGU (if assets are grouped), occurs when:

● the carrying amount of an asset or CGU is greater than its recoverable amount; where

   ● carrying amount is the depreciated historical cost (or depreciated revalued amount);

   ● recoverable amount is the higher of net selling price and value in use; where

      – net selling price is the amount at which an asset could be disposed of, less any direct selling costs; and

      – value in use is the present value of the future cash flows obtainable as a result of an asset's continued use, including those resulting from its ultimate disposal.

When impairment occurs, a **revised carrying amount** is calculated for the statement of financial position as follows:

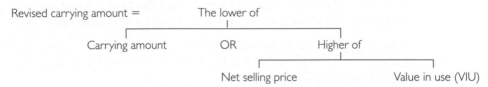

It is not always necessary to go through the potentially time-consuming process of computing the value in use of an asset. If the net selling price can be shown to be higher than the existing carrying value then the asset cannot possibly be impaired and no further action is necessary. However this is not always the case for non-current assets and a number of assets (e.g. goodwill) cannot be sold so several value in use computations are inevitable.

The revised carrying amount is then depreciated over the remaining useful economic life.

15.11.2 Dividing activities into CGUs

In order to carry out an impairment review it is necessary to decide how to divide activities into CGUs. There is no single answer to this – it is extremely judgemental, e.g. if the company has multi-retail sites, the cost of preparing detailed cash flow forecasts for each site could favour grouping.

The risk of grouping is that poorly performing operations might be concealed within a CGU and it would be necessary to consider whether there were any commercial reasons for breaking a CGU into smaller constituents, e.g. if a location was experiencing its own unique difficulties such as local competition or inability to obtain planning permission to expand to a more profitable size.

15.11.3 Indications of impairment

A review for impairment is required when there is an indication that an impairment has actually occurred. The following are indicators of impairment:

● External indicators:

   – a fall in the market value of the asset;

   – material adverse changes in regulatory environment;

   – material adverse changes in markets;

   – material long-term increases in market rates of return used for discounting.

- Internal indicators:
  - material changes in operations;
  - major reorganisation;
  - loss of key personnel;
  - loss or net cash outflow from operating activities if this is expected to continue or is a continuation of a loss-making situation.

If there is such an indication, it is necessary to determine the depreciated historical cost of a single asset, or the net assets employed if a CGU, and compare this with the net realisable value and value in use.

ICI stated in its 2005 Annual Report:

> No depreciation has been provided on land. Impairment reviews are performed where there is an indication of potential impairment. If the carrying value of an asset exceeds the higher of the discounted estimated cash flows from the asset and net realizable value of the asset the resulting impairment is charged to the statement of comprehensive income.

15.11.4 Value in use calculation

Value in use is arrived at by estimating and discounting the income stream. The **income streams**:

- are likely to follow the way in which management monitors and makes decisions about continuing or closing the different lines of business;
- may often be identified by reference to major products or services;
- should be based on reasonable and supportable assumptions;
- should be consistent with the most up-to-date budgets and plans that have been formally approved by management:
  - if for a period beyond that covered by formal budgets and plans should, unless there are exceptional circumstances, assume a steady or declining growth rate;[11]
- should be projected cash flows unadjusted for risk, discounted at a rate of return expected from a similarly risky investment or should be projected risk-adjusted pre-tax cash flows discounted at a risk-free rate.

The **discount rate** should be:

- calculated on a pre-tax basis;
- an estimate of the rate that the market would expect on an equally risky investment excluding the effects of any risk for which the cash flows have been adjusted:[12]
  - increased to reflect the way the market would assess the specific risks associated with the projected cash flows;
  - reduced to a risk-free rate if the cash flows have been adjusted for risk.

The following illustration is from the Roche Holdings Ltd 2003 Annual Report:

> When the recoverable amount of an asset, being the higher of its net selling price and its value in use, is less than the carrying amount, then the carrying amount is reduced to its recoverable amount. This reduction is reported in the statement of comprehensive income as an impairment loss. Value in use is calculated using estimated cash flows,

generally over a five-year period, with extrapolating projections for subsequent years. These are discounted using an appropriate long-term pre-tax interest rate. When an impairment arises the useful life of the asset in question is reviewed and, if necessary, the future depreciation/amortisation charge is amended.

15.11.5 Treatment of impairment losses

If the carrying value exceeds the higher of net selling price and value in use, then an impairment loss has occurred. The accounting treatment of such a loss is as follows:

Asset not previously revalued

An impairment loss should be recognised in the statement of comprehensive income in the year in which the impairment arises.

Asset previously revalued

An impairment loss on a revalued asset is effectively treated as a revaluation deficit. As we have already seen, this means that the decrease should be recognised as an expense. The only exception is where that asset had previously been revalued. In those circumstances the loss on revaluation is charged against the revaluation surplus to the extent that the revaluation surplus contains an amount **relating to the same asset**.

Allocation of impairment losses

Where an impairment loss arises, the loss should ideally be set against the specific asset to which it relates. Where the loss cannot be identified as relating to a specific asset, it should be apportioned within the CGU to reduce the most subjective values first, as follows:

- first, to reduce any goodwill within the CGU;
- then to the unit's other assets, allocated on a pro rata basis;
- however, no individual asset should be reduced below the higher of:
  - its net selling price (if determinable);
  - its value in use (if determinable);
  - zero.

The following is an example showing the allocation of an impairment loss.

EXAMPLE ● A cash generating unit contains the following assets:

	£
Goodwill	70,000
Intangible assets	10,000
PPE	100,000
Inventory	40,000
Receivables	30,000
	250,000

The unit is reviewed for impairment due to the existence of indicators and the recoverable amount is estimated at £150,000. The PPE includes a property with a carrying amount of £60,000 and a market value of £75,000. The net realisable value of the inventory is greater than its carrying values and none of the receivables is considered doubtful.

The table below shows the allocation of the impairment loss

	Pre-impairment £	Impairment £	Post-impairment £
Goodwill	70,000	(70,000)	Nil
Intangible assets	10,000	(6,000)	4,000
PPE	100,000	(24,000)	76,000
Inventory	40,000	Nil	40,000
Receivables	30,000	Nil	30,000
	250,000	(100,000)	150,000

Notes to table:

1 The impairment loss is first allocated against goodwill. After this has been done £30,000 (£100,000 – £70,000) remains to be allocated.

2 No impairment loss can be allocated to the property, inventory or receivables because these assets have a recoverable amount that is higher than their carrying value.

3 The remaining impairment loss is allocated pro-rata to the intangible assets (carrying amount £10,000) and the plant (carrying amount £40,000 (£100,000 – £60,000)).

Restoration of past impairment losses

Past impairment losses in respect of an asset other than goodwill may be restored where the recoverable amount increases due to an improvement in economic conditions or a change in use of the asset. Such a restoration should be reflected in the statement of comprehensive income to the extent of the original impairment previously charged to the statement of comprehensive income, adjusting for depreciation which would have been charged otherwise in the intervening period.

15.11.6 Illustration of data required for an impairment review

Pronto SA has a product line producing wooden models of athletes for export. The carrying amount of the net assets employed on the line as at 31 December 20X3 was £114,500. The scrap value of the net assets at 31 December 20X6 is estimated to be £5,000.

There is an indication that the export market will be adversely affected in 20X6 by competition from plastic toy manufacturers. This means that the net assets employed to produce this product might have been impaired.

The finance director estimated the net realisable value of the net assets at 31 December 20X3 to be £70,000. The value in use is now calculated to check if it is higher or lower than £70,000. If it is higher it will be compared with the carrying amount to see if impairment has occurred; if it is lower the net realisable value will be compared with the carrying amount.

Pronto SA has prepared budgets for the years ended 31 December 20X4, 20X5 and 20X6. The assumptions underlying the budgets are as follows:

Unit costs and revenue:

	£
Selling price	10.00
Buying in cost	(4.00)
Production cost: material, labour, overhead	(0.75)
Head office overheads apportioned	(0.25)
Cash inflow per model	5.00

Estimated sales volumes:

	20X3	20X4	20X5	20X6
Estimated at 31 December 20X2	6,000	8,000	11,000	14,000
Revised estimate at 31 December 20X3	—	8,000	11,000	4,000

Determining the discount rate to be used:

	20X4	20X5	20X6
The rate obtainable elsewhere at the same level of risk is	10%	10%	10%

The discount factors to be applied to each year are then calculated using cost of capital discount rates as follows:

20X4	$1/1.1$	$= 0.909$
20X5	$1/(1.1)^2$	$= 0.826$
20X6	$1/(1.1)^3$	$= 0.751$

15.11.7 Illustrating calculation of value in use

Before calculating value in use, it is necessary to ensure that the assumptions underlying the budgets are reasonable, e.g. is the selling price likely to be affected by competition in 20X6 in addition to loss of market? Is the selling price in 20X5 likely to be affected? Is the estimate of scrap value reasonably accurate? How sensitive is value in use to the scrap value? Is it valid to assume that the cash flows will occur at year-ends? How accurate is the cost of capital? Will components making up the income stream, e.g. sales, materials, labour be subject to different rates of inflation?

Assuming that no adjustment is required to the budgeted figures provided above, the estimated income streams are discounted using the normal DCF approach as follows:

	20X4	20X5	20X6
Sales (models)	8,000	11,000	4,000
Income per model	£5	£5	£5
Income stream (£)	40,000	55,000	20,000
Estimated scrap proceeds			5,000
Cash flows to be discounted	40,000	55,000	25,000
Discounted (using cost of capital factors)	0.909	0.826	0.751
Present value	36,360	45,430	18,775

Value in use = £100,565

15.11.8 Illustration determining the *revised* carrying amount

If the carrying amount at the statement of financial position date exceeds net realisable value and value in use, it is revised to an amount which is the higher of net realisable value and value in use. For Pronto SA:

	£
Carrying amount as at 31 December 20X3	114,500
Net realisable value	70,000
Value in use	100,565
Revised carrying amount	**100,565**

15.12 IFRS 5 *Non-Current Assets Held for Sale and Discontinued Operations*

IFRS 5 sets out requirements for the classification, measurement and presentation of non-current assets held for sale. The requirements which replaced IAS 35 *Discontinuing Operations* were discussed in Chapter 8. The IFRS is the result of the joint short-term project to resolve differences between IFRSs and US GAAP.

Classification as 'held for sale'

The IFRS (para. 6) classifies a non-current asset as 'held for sale' if its carrying amount will be recovered principally through a sale transaction rather than through continuing use. The criteria for classification as 'held for sale' are:

● the asset must be available for immediate sale in its present condition; and

● its sale must be *highly probable*.

The criteria for a sale to be highly probable are:

● the appropriate level of management must be committed to a plan to sell the asset;

● an active programme to locate a buyer and complete the plan must have been initiated;

● the asset must be actively marketed for sale at a price that is reasonable in relation to its current fair value;

● the sale should be expected to qualify for recognition as a completed sale within one year from the date of classification unless the delay is caused by events or circumstances beyond the entity's control and there is sufficient evidence that the entity remains committed to its plan to sell the asset; and

● actions required to complete the plan should indicate that it is unlikely that significant changes to the plan will be made or that the plan will be withdrawn.

Measurement and presentation of assets held for sale

The IFRS requires that assets 'held for sale' should:

● be measured at the lower of carrying amount and *fair value* less costs to sell;

● not continue to be depreciated; and

● be presented separately on the face of the statement of financial position.

The following additional disclosures are required in the notes in the period in which a non-current asset has been either classified as held for sale or sold:

● a description of the non-current asset;

● a description of the facts and circumstances of the sale;

● the expected manner and timing of that disposal;

● the gain or loss if not separately presented on the face of the statement of comprehensive income; and

● the caption in the statement of comprehensive income that includes that gain or loss.

15.13 Disclosure requirements

For each class of PPE the financial statements need to disclose:

- the measurement bases used for determining the gross carrying amount;
- the depreciation methods used;
- the useful lives or the depreciation rates used;
- the gross carrying amount and the accumulated depreciation (aggregated with accumulated impairment losses) at the beginning and end of the period;
- a reconciliation of the carrying amount at the beginning and end of the period.

The style employed by British Sky Broadcasting Group Plc in its 2003 accounts is almost universally employed for this:

Tangible fixed assets (or PPE)

The movements in the year were as follows:

	Freehold land and buildings £m	Short leasehold improvements £m	Equipment, fixtures and fittings £m	Assets in course of construction	Total £m
Group					
Cost					
Beginning of year	37.9	83.3	554.4	29.9	705.5
Additions	0.4	3.2	73.0	24.8	101.4
Disposals	—	—	(10.9)	—	(10.9)
Transfers	—	—	25.8	(25.8)	—
End of year	38.3	86.5	642.3	28.9	796.0

	Freehold land and buildings £m	Short leasehold improvements £m	Equipment, fixtures and fittings £m	Assets in course of construction	Total £m
Depreciation					
Beginning of year	6.0	43.3	313.2	—	362.5
Charge	2.3	4.0	91.6	—	97.9
Disposals	—	—	(10.6)	—	(10.6)
End of year	8.3	47.3	394.2	—	449.8
Net book value					
Beginning of year	31.9	40.0	241.2	29.9	343.0
End of year	30.0	39.2	248.1	28.9	346.2

Additionally the financial statements should disclose:

- the existence and amounts of restrictions on title, and PPE pledged as security for liabilities;
- the accounting policy for the estimated costs of restoring the site of items of PPE;
- the amount of expenditures on account of PPE in the course of construction;
- the amount of commitments for the acquisition of PPE.

15.14 Government grants towards the cost of PPE

The accounting treatment of government grants is covered by IAS 20. The basis of the standard is the accruals concept, which requires the matching of cost and revenue so as to recognise both in the statements of comprehensive income of the periods to which they relate. This should, of course, be tempered with the prudence concept, which requires that revenue is not anticipated. Therefore, in the light of the complex conditions usually attached to grants, credit should not be taken until receipt is assured.

Similarly, there may be a right to recover the grant wholly or partially in the event of a breach of conditions, and on that basis these conditions should be regularly reviewed and, if necessary, provision made.

Should the tax treatment of a grant differ from the accounting treatment, then the effect of this would be accounted for in accordance with IAS 12 *Income Taxes*.

IAS 20

Government grants should be recognised in the statement of comprehensive income so as to match the expenditure towards which they are intended to contribute. If this is retrospective, they should be recognised in the period in which they became receivable.

Grants in respect of PPE should be recognised over the useful economic lives of those assets, thus matching the depreciation or amortisation.

IAS 20 outlines two acceptable methods of presenting grants relating to assets in the statement of financial position:

(a) The first method sets up the grant as deferred income, which is recognised as income on a systematic and rational basis over the useful life of the asset.

EXAMPLE ● An entity purchased a machine for £60,000 and received a grant of £20,000 towards its purchase. The machine is depreciated over four years.

The 'deferred income method' would result in an initial carrying amount for the machine of £60,000 and a deferred income credit of £20,000. In the first year of use of the plant the depreciation charge would be £15,000. £5,000 of the deferred income would be recognised as a credit in the statement of comprehensive income, making the net charge £10,000. At the end of the first year the carrying amount of the plant would be £45,000 and the deferred income included in the statement of financial position would be £15,000.

The following is an extract from the 2006 Go-Ahead Annual Report:

Government grants
Government grants are recognised at their fair value where there is reasonable assurance that the grant will be received and all attaching conditions will be complied with. When the grant relates to an expense item, it is recognised in the statement of comprehensive income over the period necessary to match on a systematic basis to the costs that it is intended to compensate. *Where the grant relates to a non-current asset, value is credited to a deferred income account and is released to the statement of comprehensive income over the expected useful life of the relevant asset.*

(b) The second method deducts the grant in arriving at the carrying amount of the relevant asset. If we were to apply this method to the above example then the initial carrying amount of the asset would be £40,000. The depreciation charged in the first year would be £10,000. This is the same as the net charge to income under the 'deferred credit' method. The closing carrying amount of the plant would be £30,000. This is of course the carrying amount under the 'deferred income method' (£45,000) less the closing deferred income under the 'deferred income method' (£15,000).

The following extract is from the 2006 Annual Report of A & J Muklow plc:

Capital grants
Capital grants received relating to the building or refurbishing of investment properties are deducted from the cost of the relevant property. Revenue grants are deducted from the related expenditure.

The IASB is currently considering drafting an amended standard on government grants. Among the reasons for the Board amending IAS 20 were the following:

- The recognition requirements of IAS 20 often result in accounting that is inconsistent with the *Framework*, in particular the recognition of a deferred credit when the entity has no liability, e.g. the following is an extract from the SSL International plc Annual Report:

  Grant income
  Capital grants are shown in other creditors within the statement of financial position and released to match the depreciation charge on associated assets.

- IAS 20 contains numerous options. Apart from reducing the comparability of financial statements, the options in IAS 20 can result in understatement of the assets controlled by the entity and do not provide the most relevant information to users of financial statements.

In the near future there is the prospect of the IASB issuing a revised standard which requires entities to recognise grants as income as soon as their receipt becomes unconditional. This is consistent with the specific requirements for the recognition of grants relating to agricultural activity laid down in IAS 41 *Agriculture*. This matter is discussed in more detail in Chapter 18.

15.15 Investment properties

While IAS 16 requires all PPEs to be subjected to a systematic depreciation charge, this may be considered inappropriate for properties held as assets but not employed in the normal activities of the entity, rather being held as investments. For such properties a more relevant treatment is to take account of the current market value of the property. The accounting treatment is set out in IAS 40 *Investment Property*.

Such properties may be held either as a main activity (e.g. by a property investment company) or by a company whose main activity is not the holding of such properties. In each case the accounting treatment is similar.

Definition of an investment property[13]

For the purposes of the statement, an investment property is property held (by the owner or by the lessee under a finance lease) to earn rentals or capital appreciation or both.
Investment property does **not** include:

(a) property held for use in the production or supply of goods or services or for administrative purposes (dealt with in IAS 16);

(b) property held for sale in the ordinary course of business (dealt with in IAS 2);

(c) an interest held by a lessee under an operating lease, even if the interest was a long-term interest acquired in exchange for a large up-front payment (dealt with in IAS 17);

(d) forests and similar regenerative natural resources (dealt with in IAS 41 *Agriculture*); and

(e) mineral rights, the exploration for and development of minerals, oil, natural gas and similar non-regenerative natural resources (dealt with in project on Extractive Industries).

Accounting models

Under IAS 40, an entity must choose either:

- a fair value model: investment property should be measured at fair value and changes in fair value should be recognised in the statement of comprehensive income; or

- a cost model (the same as the benchmark treatment in IAS 16 *Property, Plant and Equipment*): investment property should be measured at depreciated cost (less any accumulated impairment losses). An entity that chooses the cost model should disclose the fair value of its investment property.

An entity should apply the model chosen to all its investment property. A change from one model to the other model should be made only if the change will result in a more appropriate presentation. The standard states that this is highly unlikely to be the case for a change from the fair value model to the cost model.

In exceptional cases, there is clear evidence when an entity that has chosen the fair value model first acquires an investment property (or when an existing property first becomes investment property following the completion of construction or development, or after a change in use) that the entity will not be able to determine the fair value of the investment property reliably on a continuing basis. In such cases, the entity measures that investment property using the benchmark treatment in IAS 16 until the disposal of the investment property. The residual value of the investment property should be assumed to be zero. The entity measures all its other investment property at fair value.

15.16 Effect of accounting policy for PPE on the interpretation of the financial statements

A number of difficulties exist when attempting to carry out inter-firm comparisons using the external information that is available to a shareholder.

15.16.1 Effect of inflation on the carrying value of the asset

The most serious difficulty is the effect of inflation, which makes the charges based on historical cost inadequate. Companies have followed various practices to take account of inflation. None of these is as effective as an acceptable surrogate for index adjustment using specific asset indices on a systematic annual basis: this is the only way to ensure uniformity and comparability of the cost/valuation figure upon which the depreciation charge is based.

The method that is currently allowable under IAS 16 is to revalue the assets. This is a partial answer, but it results in lack of comparability of ratios such as gearing, or leverage.

15.16.2 Effect of revaluation on ratios

The rules of double entry require that when an asset is revalued the 'profit' (or, exceptionally, 'loss') must be credited somewhere. As it is not a 'realised' profit, it would not be appropriate to credit the statement of comprehensive income, so a 'revaluation reserve' must be created. As the asset is depreciated, this reserve may be realised to income; similarly, when an asset is ultimately disposed of, any residue relevant to that asset may be taken into income.

One significant by-product of revaluing assets is the effect on gearing. The revaluation reserve, while not distributable, forms part of the shareholders' funds and thus improves the debt/equity ratio. Care must therefore be taken in looking at the revaluation policies and reserves when comparing the gearing or leverage of companies.

The problem is compounded because the carrying value may be amended at random periods and on a selective category of asset.

15.16.3 Choice of depreciation method

There are a number of acceptable depreciation methods that may give rise to very different patterns of debits against the profits of individual years.

15.16.4 Inherent imprecision in estimating economic life

One of the greatest difficulties with depreciation is that it is inherently imprecise. The amount of depreciation depends on the estimate of the economic life of assets, which is affected not only by the durability and workload of the asset, but also by external factors beyond the control of management. Such factors may be technological, commercial or economic. Here are some examples:

● the production by a competitor of a new product rendering yours obsolete, e.g. watches with battery-powered movements replacing those with mechanical movements;

● the production by a competitor of a product at a price lower than your production costs, e.g. imported goods from countries where costs are lower;

● changes in the economic climate which reduce demand for your product.

This means that the interpreter of accounts must pay particular attention to depreciation policies, looking closely at the market where the entity's business operates. However, this understanding is not helped by the lack of requirement to disclose specific rates of depreciation and the basis of computation of residual values. Without such information, the potential effects of differences between policies adopted by competing entities cannot be accurately assessed.

15.16.5 Mixed values in the statement of financial position

The effect of depreciation on the statement of financial position is also some cause for concern. The net book amount shown for non-current assets is the result of deducting accumulated depreciation from cost (or valuation); it is not intended to be (although many non-accountants assume it is) an estimate of the value of the underlying assets. The valuation of a business based on the statement of financial position is extremely difficult.

15.16.6 Different policies may be applied within the same sector

Inter-company comparisons are even more difficult. Two entities following the historical cost convention may own identical assets, which, as they were purchased at different times, may well appear as dramatically different figures in the accounts. This is particularly true of interests in land and buildings.

15.16.7 Effect on the return on capital employed

There is an effect not only on the net asset value, but also on the return on capital employed. To make a fair assessment of return on capital it is necessary to know the current replacement cost of the underlying assets, but, under present conventions, up-to-date valuations are required only for investment properties.

15.16.8 Effect on EPS

IAS 16 is concerned to ensure that the earnings of an entity reflect a fair charge for the use of the assets by the enterprise. This should ensure an accurate calculation of earnings per share. But there is a weakness here. If assets have increased in value without revaluations, then depreciation will be based on the historical cost.

Summary

Before IAS 16 there were significant problems in relation to the accounting treatment of PPE such as the determination of a cost figure and the adjustment for inflation; companies providing nil depreciation on certain types of asset; revaluations being made selectively and not kept current.

With IAS 16 the IASB has made the accounts more consistent and comparable. This standard has resolved some of these problems, principally requiring companies to provide for depreciation and if they have a policy of revaluation to keep such valuations reasonably current and applied to all assets within a class, i.e. removing the ability to cherry-pick which assets to revalue.

However, certain difficulties remain for the user of the accounts in that there are different management policies on the method of depreciation, which can have a major impact on the profit for the year; subjective assessments of economic life that may be reviewed each year with an impact on profits; and inconsistencies such as the presence of modified historical costs and historical costs in the same statement of financial position. In addition, with pure historical cost accounting, where non-current asset carrying values are based on original cost, no pretence is made that non-current asset net book amounts have any relevance to current values. The investor is expected to know that the depreciation charge is arithmetical in character and will not wholly provide the finance for tomorrow's assets or ensure maintenance of the business's operational base. To give recognition to these factors requires the investor to grapple with the effects of lost purchasing power through inflation; the effect of changes in supply and demand on replacement prices; technological change and its implication for the company's competitiveness; and external factors such as exchange rates. To calculate the effect of these variables necessitates not only considerable mental agility, but also far more information than is contained in a set of accounts. This is an area that needs to be revisited by the standard setters.

REVIEW QUESTIONS

1 Define PPE and explain how materiality affects the concept of PPE.

2 Define depreciation. Explain what assets need not be depreciated and list the main methods of calculating depreciation.

3 What is meant by the phrases 'useful life' and 'residual value'?

4 Define 'cost' in connection with PPE.

5 What effect does revaluing assets have on gearing (or leverage)?

6 How should grants received towards expenditure on PPE be treated?

7 Define an investment property and explain its treatment in financial statements.

8 'Depreciation should mean that a company has sufficient resources to replace assets at the end of their economic lives.' Discuss.

EXERCISES

An extract from the solution is provided on the Companion Website (www.pearsoned.co.uk/elliott-elliott) for exercises marked with an asterisk (*).

Question 1

(a) Discuss why IAS 40 *Investment Property* was produced.

(b) Universal Entrepreneurs plc has the following items on its PPE list:

(i) £1,000,000 – the right to extract sandstone from a particular quarry. Geologists predict that extraction at the present rate may be continued for ten years.

(ii) £5,000,000 – a freehold property, let to a subsidiary on a full repairing lease negotiated on arm's-length terms for 15 years. The building is a new one, erected on a greenfield site at a cost of £4,000,000.

(iii) A fleet of motor cars used by company employees. These have been purchased under a contract which provides a guaranteed part exchange value of 60% of cost after two years' use.

(iv) A company helicopter with an estimated life of 150,000 flying hours.

(v) A 19-year lease on a property let out at arm's-length rent to another company.

Required:
Advise the company on the depreciation policy it ought to adopt for each of the above assets.

(c) The company is considering revaluing its interests in land and buildings, which comprise freehold and leasehold properties, all used by the company or its subsidiaries.

Required:
Discuss the consequences of this on the depreciation policy of the company and any special instructions that need to be given to the valuer.

Question 2

Mercury

You have been given the task, by one of the partners of the firm of accountants for which you work, of assisting in the preparation of a trend statement for a client.

Mercury has been in existence for four years. Figures for the three preceding years are known but those for the fourth year need to be calculated. Unfortunately, the supporting workings for the preceding years' figures cannot be found and the client's own ledger accounts and workings are not available.

One item in particular, plant, is causing difficulty and the following figures have been given to you:

12 months ended 31 March	20X6	20X7	20X8	20X9
	£	£	£	£
(A) Plant at cost	80,000	80,000	90,000	?
(B) Accumulated depreciation	(16,000)	(28,800)	(28,080)	?
(C) Net (written down) value	64,000	51,200	61,920	?

The only other information available is that disposals have taken place at the beginning of the financial years concerned:

	Date of		Original	Sales
	Disposal	Original acquisition	cost	proceeds
		12 months ended 31 March	£	£
First disposal	20X8	20X6	15,000	8,000
Second disposal	20X8	20X6	30,000	21,000

Plant sold was replaced on the same day by new plant. The cost of the plant which replaced the first disposal is not known but the replacement for the second disposal is known to have cost £50,000.

Required:
(a) Identify the method of providing for depreciation on plant employed by the client, stating how you have arrived at your conclusion.
(b) Show how the figures shown at line (B) for each of the years ended 31 March 20X6, 20X7 and 20X8 were calculated. Extend your workings to cover the year ended 31 March 20X9.
(c) Produce the figures that should be included in the blank spaces on the trend statement at lines (A), (B) and (C) for the year ended 31 March 20X9.
(d) Calculate the profit or loss arising on each of the two disposals.

Question 3

In the year to 31 December 20X9, Amy bought a new machine and made the following payments in relation to it:

	£	£
Cost as per supplier's list	12,000	
Less: Agreed discount	1,000	11,000
Delivery charge		100
Erection charge		200
Maintenance charge		300
Additional component to increase capacity		400
Replacement parts		250

Required:
(a) State and justify the cost figure which should be used as the basis for depreciation.
(b) What does depreciation do, and why is it necessary?
(c) Briefly explain, without numerical illustration, how the straight-line and diminishing balance methods of depreciation work. What different assumptions does each method make?

(d) Explain the term 'objectivity' as used by accountants. To what extent is depreciation objective?

(e) It is common practice in published accounts in Germany to use the diminishing balance method for PPE in the early years of an asset's life, and then to change to the straight-line method as soon as this would give a higher annual charge. What do you think of this practice? Refer to relevant accounting conventions in your answer.

(ACCA)

* Question 4

The finance director of the Small Machine Parts Ltd company is considering the acquisition of a lease of a small workshop in a warehouse complex that is being redeveloped by City Redevelopers Ltd at a steady rate over a number of years. City Redevelopers are granting such leases for five years on payment of a premium of £20,000.

The accountant has obtained estimates of the likely maintenance costs and disposal value of the lease during its five-year life. He has produced the following table and suggested to the finance director that the annual average cost should be used in the financial accounts to represent the depreciation charge in the profit and loss account.

Table prepared to calculate the annual average cost

Years of life	1	2	3	4	5
	£	£	£	£	£
Purchase price	20,000	20,000	20,000	20,000	20,000
Maintenance/repairs					
Year 2		1,000	1,000	1,000	1,000
3			1,500	1,500	1,500
4				1,850	1,850
5					2,000
	20,000	21,000	22,500	24,350	26,350
Resale value	11,500	10,000	8,010	5,350	350
Net cost	8,500	11,000	14,490	19,000	26,000
Annual average cost	8,500	5,500	4,830	4,750	5,200

The finance director, however, was considering whether to calculate the depreciation chargeable using the annuity method with interest at 15%.

Required:

(a) Calculate the entries that would appear in the statement of comprehensive income of Small Machine Parts Ltd for each of the five years of the life of the lease for the amortisation charge, the interest element in the depreciation charge and the income from secondary assets using the ANNUITY METHOD. Calculate the net profit for each of the five years assuming that the operating cash flow is estimated to be £25,000 per year.

(b) Discuss briefly which of the two methods you would recommend.

The present value at 15% of £1 per annum for five years is £3.35214.

The present value at 15% of £1 received at the end of year 5 is £0.49717.

Ignore taxation.

(ACCA)

Question 5

Simple SA has just purchased a roasting/salting machine to produce roasted walnuts. The finance director asks for your advice on how the company should calculate the depreciation on this machine. Details are as follows:

Cost of machine	SF800,000
Residual value	SF104,000
Estimated life	4 years
Annual profits	SF2,000,000
Annual turnover from machine	SF850,000

Required:

(a) Calculate the annual depreciation charge using the straight-line method and the reducing balance method. Assume that an annual rate of 40% is applicable for the reducing balance method.

(b) Comment upon the validity of each method, taking into account the type of business and the effect each method has on annual profits. Are there any other methods which would be more applicable?

Question 6

(a) IAS 16 *Property, Plant and Equipment* requires that where there has been a permanent diminution in the value of property, plant and equipment, the carrying amount should be written down to the recoverable amount. The phrase 'recoverable amount' is defined in IAS 16 as 'the amount which the entity expects to recover from the future use of an asset, including its residual value on disposal'. The issues of how one identifies an impaired asset, the measurement of an asset when impairment has occurred and the recognition of impairment losses were not adequately dealt with by the standard. As a result the International Accounting Standards Committee issued IAS 36 *Impairment of Assets* in order to address the above issues.

Required:

(i) Describe the circumstances which indicate that an impairment loss relating to an asset may have occurred.

(ii) Explain how IAS 36 deals with the recognition and measurement of the *impairment of assets*.

(b) AB, a public limited company, has decided to comply with IAS 36 *Impairment of Assets*. The following information is relevant to the impairment review:

(i) Certain items of machinery appeared to have suffered a permanent diminution in value. The inventory produced by the machines was being sold below its cost and this occurrence had affected the value of the productive machinery. The carrying value at historical cost of these machines is $290,000 and their net selling price is estimated at $120,000. The anticipated net cash inflows from the machines is now $100,000 per annum for the next three years. A market discount rate of 10% per annum is to be used in any present value computations.

(ii) AB acquired a car taxi business on 1 January 20X1 for $230,000. The values of the assets of the business at that date based on net selling prices were as follows:

	$000
Vehicles (12 vehicles)	120
Intangible assets (taxi licence)	30
Trade receivables	10
Cash	50
Trade payables	(20)
	190

On 1 February 20X1, the taxi company had three of its vehicles stolen. The net selling value of these vehicles was $30,000 and because of non-disclosure of certain risks to the insurance company, the vehicles were uninsured. As a result of this event, AB wishes to recognise an impairment loss of $45,000 (inclusive of the loss of the stolen vehicles) due to the decline in the value in use of the cash generating unit, that is the taxi business. On 1 March 20X1 a rival taxi company commenced business in the same area. It is anticipated that the business revenue of AB will be reduced by 25% leading to a decline in the present value in use of the business, which is calculated at $150,000. The net selling value of the taxi licence has fallen to $25,000 as a result of the rival taxi operator. The net selling values of the other assets have remained the same as at 1 January 20X1 throughout the period.

Required:
Describe how AB should treat the above impairments of assets in its financial statements.

(In part (b) (ii) you should show the treatment of the impairment loss at 1 February 20X1 and 1 March 20X1.)

(ACCA)

* Question 7

Infinite Leisure Group owns and operates a number of pubs and clubs across Europe and South East Asia. Since inception the group has made exclusive use of the cost model for the purpose of its annual financial reporting. This has led to a number of shareholders expressing concern about what they see as a consequent lack of clarity and quality in the group's financial statements.

The CEO does not support use of the alternative to the cost model (the revaluation model), believing it produces volatile information. However, she is open to persuasion and so, as an example of the impact of a revaluation policy, has asked you to carry out an analysis (using data concerning 'Soo²' – one of the group's nightclubs sold during the year to 31 October 2006) to show the impact the revaluation model would have had on the group's financial statements had the model been adopted from the day the club was acquired.

The following extract has been taken from the company's asset register:

Outlet: 'Soo$^{z'}$'

Acquisition data

Date acquired	1 November 2001
Total cost	€10.24m

Cost components:

Plant and equipment

Cost	€0.24m
Economic life	six years
Residual value	nil

Property

Buildings

Cost	€7.0m
Economic life	50 years

Land

Cost	€3.0m

Updates

1 November 2003   Replacement cost of plant & equipment €0.42m. No fair value available (mainly specialised audio visual equipment). No change to economic life. Property revaluation €13m (land €4m, buildings €9m). Future economic life as at 1 November 2003 50 years

Disposal

Date committed to a plan to sell	January 2006
Date sold	June 2006
Net sale price	€9.1m

Sale price components

Plant and equipment	€0.1m
Property	€9.0m

Note: the Group accounts for property and plant and equipment as separate non-current assets in its statement of financial position using straightline depreciation.

Required

Prepare an analysis to show the impact on Infinite Leisure's financial statements for each year the 'Soo$^{z'}$' nightclub was owned had the revaluation model been in place from the day the nightclub was acquired.

(*The Association of International Accountants*)

Question 8

The Blissopia Leisure Group consists of three divisions: Blissopia 1, which operates mainstream bars; Blissopia 2, which operates large restaurants; and Blissopia 3, which operates one hotel – the Eden.

Divisions 1 and 2 have been trading very successfully and there are no indications of any potential impairment. It is a different matter with the Eden however. The Eden is a 'boutique' hotel and was acquired on 1 November 2006 for $6.90m. The fair value (using net selling price) of the hotel's net assets at that date and their carrying value at the year-end were as follows:

	$m	$m
	1.11.06	31.10.07
	Fair value	*Carrying value*
Land and buildings	3.61	3.18
Plant and equipment	0.90	0.81
Cash	1.40	1.12
Vehicles	0.10	0.09
Trade receivables	0.34	0.37
Trade payables	(0.60)	(0.74)
	5.75	4.83

The following facts were discovered following an impairment review as at 31 October 2007:

(i) During August 2007, a rival hotel commenced trading in the same location as the Eden. The Blissopia Leisure Group expects hotel revenues to be significantly affected and has calculated the value-in-use of the Eden to be $3.52m.

(ii) The company owning the rival hotel has offered to buy the Eden (including all of the above net assets) for $4m Selling costs would be approximately $50,000.

(iii) One of the hotel vehicles was severely damaged in an accident whilst being used by an employee to carry shopping home from a supermarket. The vehicle's carrying value at 31 October 2007 was $30,000 and insurers have indicated that as it was being used for an uninsured purpose the loss is not covered by insurance. The vehicle was subsequently scrapped.

(iv) A corporate client, owing $40,000, has recently gone into liquidation. Lawyers have estimated that the company will only receive 25% of the amount outstanding.

Required

Prepare a memo for the directors of the Blissopia Leisure Group explaining how the group should account for the impairment to the Eden Hotel's assets as at 31 October 2007.

(The Association of International Accountants)

Question 9

Cryptic plc extracted its trial balance on 30 June 20X5 as follows:

	£000	£000
Land and buildings at cost	750	—
Plant and machinery at cost	480	—
Accumulated depreciation on plant and machinery at 30 Jun 20X5	—	400
Depreciation on plant and machinery	80	—
Furniture, tools and equipment at cost	380	—
Accumulated depreciation on furniture, etc. at 30 Jun 20X4	—	95
Receivables and payables	475	360
Inventory of raw materials at 30 Jun 20X4	112	—
Work-in-progress at factory cost at 30 Jun 20X4	76	—
Finished goods at cost at 30 Jun 20X4	264	—
Sales including selling taxes	—	2,875
Purchases of raw materials including selling taxes	1,380	—
Share premium account	—	150
Advertising	65	—
Deferred taxation	—	185
Salaries	360	—
Rent	120	—
Retained earnings at 30 Jun 20X4	—	226
Factory power	48	—
Trade investments at cost	240	—
Overprovision for tax for the year ended 30 Jun 20X4	—	21
Electricity	36	—
Stationery	12	—
Dividend received (net)	—	24
Dividend paid on 15 April 20X5	60	—
Other administration expenses	468	—
Disposal of furniture	—	64
Selling tax control account	165	—
Ordinary shares of 50p each	—	1,000
12% Preference shares of £1 each (IAS 32 liability)	—	200
Cash and bank balance	29	—
	5,600	5,600

The following information is relevant:

(i) The company discontinued a major activity during the year and replaced it with another. All non-current assets involved in the discontinued activity were redeployed for the new one. The following expenses incurred in this respect, however, are included in 'Other administration expenses':

	£000
Cancellation of contracts re terminated activity	165
Fundamental reorganisation arising as a result	145

Cryptic has decided to present its results from discontinued operations as a single line on the face of the statement of comprehensive income with analysis in the notes to the accounts as allowed by IFRS 5.

(ii) On 1 January 20X5 the company acquired new land and buildings for £150,000. The remainder of land and buildings, acquired nine years earlier, have NOT been depreciated until this year. The company has decided to depreciate the buildings, on the straight-line method, assuming that one-third of the cost relates to land and that the buildings have an estimated economic life of 50 years. The company policy is to charge a full year of depreciation in the year of purchase and none in the year of sale.

(iii) Plant and machinery was all acquired on 1 July 20X0 and has been depreciated at 10% per annum on the straight-line method. The estimate of useful economic life had to be revised this year when it was realised that if the market share is to be maintained at current levels, the company has to replace all its machinery by 1 July 20X6. The balance in the 'Accumulated provision for depreciation' account on 1 July 20X4 was amended to reflect the revised estimate of useful economic life and the impact of the revision adjusted against the retained earnings brought forward from prior years.

(iv) Furniture acquired for £80,000 on 1 January 20X3 was disposed of for £64,000 on 1 April 20X5. Furniture, tools and equipment are depreciated at 5% p.a. on cost. Depreciation for the current year has not been provided.

(v) Results of the inventory counting at year-end are as follows:

Inventory of raw materials at cost including selling tax	£197,800
Work-in-progress at factory cost	£54,000
Finished goods at cost	£364,000

(vi) The company allocates its expenditure as follows:

	Production cost	Factory overhead	Distribution cost	Administrative expenses
Salaries and wages	65%	15%	5%	15%
Rent	—	60%	15%	25%
Electricity	—	10%	20%	70%
Depreciation of building	—	40%	10%	50%

(vii) The directors wish to make an accrual for audit fees of £18,000 and estimate the income tax for the year at £65,000. £11,000 should be transferred from the deferred tax account. The directors have to pay the preference dividend.

(viii) The following analysis has been made:

	New activity	Discontinued activity
Sales excluding selling taxes	£165,000	£215,000
Cost of sales	£98,000	£155,000
Distribution cost	£16,500	£48,500
Administrative expenses	£22,500	£38,500

(ix) Assume that selling taxes applicable to all purchases and sales is 15%, the basic rate of personal income tax is 25% and the corporate income tax rate is 35%.

Required:
(a) Advise the company on the accounting treatment in respect of information stated in (ii) above.
(b) In respect of the information stated in (iii) above, state whether a company is permitted to revise its estimate of the useful economic life of a non-current asset and comment on the appropriateness of the accounting treatment adopted.
(c) Set out a statement of movement of property, plant and equipment in the year to 30 June 20X5.
(d) Set out for publication the statement of comprehensive income for the year ended 30 June 20X5, the statement of financial position as at that date and any notes other than that on accounting policy, in accordance with relevant standards.

References

1 IAS 16 *Property, Plant and Equipment*, IASB, revised 2004, para. 6.
2 *Ibid.*, para. 16.
3 *Ibid.*, para. 22.
4 IAS 23 *Borrowing Costs*, IASB, revised 2007, para. 8.
5 IAS 16 *Property, Plant and Equipment*, IASB, revised 2004, para. 18.
6 *Ibid.*, para. 6.
7 *Ibid.*, para. 6.
8 IAS 36 *Impairment of Assets*, IASB, 2004.
9 IAS 16 *Property, Plant and Equipment*, IASB, revised 2004, para. 29.
10 *Ibid.*, para. 41.
11 IAS 36 *Impairment of Assets*, IASB, 2004, para. 33.
12 *Ibid.*, paras 55–56.
13 IAS 40 *Investment Property*, IASB, 2004.

CHAPTER **16**

Leasing

16.1 Introduction

The main purpose of this chapter is to introduce the accounting principles and policies that apply to lease agreements.

Objectives

By the end of this chapter, you should be able to:

- critically discuss the reasons for IAS 17;
- account for leases by the lessee;
- account for leases by the lessor;
- critically discuss the reasons for the proposed revision of IAS 17.

16.2 Background to leasing

In this section we consider the nature of a lease; why leasing has become popular; and why it was necessary to introduce IAS 17.

16.2.1 What is a lease?

IAS 17 *Leases* provides the following definition:

A *lease* is an agreement whereby the lessor conveys to the lessee in return for a payment or series of payments the right to use an asset for an agreed period of time.

In practice, there might well be more than two parties involved in a lease. For example, on leasing a car the parties involved are the motor dealer, the finance company and the company using the car.

16.2.2 Why has leasing become popular?

Prior to the issue of IAS 17, three of the main reasons for the popularity of leasing were the tax advantage to the lessor able to make use of depreciation allowances, the commercial advantages to the lessee and the potential for off balance sheet financing.

Commercial advantages for the lessee

There are a number of advantages associated with leases. These are attributable in part to the ability to spread cash payments over the lease period instead of making a one-off lump sum payment. They include the following:

- **Cash flow management.** If cash is used to purchase non-current assets, it is not available for the normal operating activities of a company.
- **Conservation of capital.** Lines of credit may be kept open and may be used for purposes where finance might not be available easily (e.g. financing working capital).
- **Continuity.** The lease agreement is itself a line of credit that cannot easily be withdrawn or terminated due to external factors, in contrast to an overdraft that can be called in by the lender.
- **Flexibility of the asset base.** The asset base can be more easily expanded and contracted. In addition, the lease payments can be structured to match the income pattern of the lessee.

16.2.3 Off balance sheet financing

Leasing provides the lessee with the possibility of off balance sheet financing,[1] whereby a company has the use of an economic resource that does not appear in the statement of financial position, with the corresponding omission of the liability.

An attraction of off balance sheet financing is that the gearing ratio is not increased by the inclusion of the liability.

16.2.4 Why was IAS 17 necessary?

As with many of the standards, action was required because there was no uniformity in the treatment and disclosure of leasing transactions. The need became urgent following the massive growth in the leasing industry and the growth in off balance sheet financing which by 2007 had grown to US$760 billion worldwide.

Leasing has become a material economic resource but the accounting treatment of the lease transaction was seen to distort the financial reports of a company so that they did not represent a true and fair view of its commercial activities.

IAS 17, therefore, required lease agreements that transferred substantially all the risks and rewards to the lessee to be reported in the financial statements. The asset and liability were both brought onto the statement of financial position.

There was some concern that this might have undesirable economic consequences,[2] by reducing the volume of leasing and that the inclusion of the lease obligation might affect the lessee company's gearing adversely, possibly causing it to exceed its legal borrowing powers. However, in the event, the commercial reasons for leasing and the capacity of the leasing industry to structure lease agreements to circumvent the standard prevented a reduction in lease activity. Evidence of lessors varying the term of the lease agreements to ensure that they remained off balance sheet is supported by Cranfield[3] and by Abdel-Khalik *et al.*[4]

A standard was necessary to ensure uniform reporting and to prevent the accounting message being manipulated.

16.2.5 The approach taken by IAS 17

The approach taken by the standard was to distinguish between two types of lease – finance and operating – and recommends different accounting treatment for each. In brief, the definitions were as follows:

- **Finance lease**: a lease that transfers substantially all the risks and rewards of ownership of an asset. Title may or may not eventually be transferred.
- **Operating lease**: a lease other than a finance lease.

Finance leases were required to be capitalised in the lessee's accounts. This means that the leased item should be recorded as an asset in the statement of financial position, and the obligation for future payments should be recorded as a liability in that statement. It was not permissible for the leased asset and lease obligation to be left out of the statement.

In the case of operating leases, the lessee is required only to expense the annual payments as a rental through the statement of comprehensive income.

16.3 Why was the IAS 17 approach so controversial?

The proposal to classify leases into finance and operating leases, and to capitalise those which are classified as finance leases, appears to be a feasible solution to the accounting problems that surround leasing agreements. So, why did the standard setters encounter so much controversy in their attempt to stop the practice of charging all lease payments to the statement of comprehensive income?

The whole debate centres on one accounting policy: **substance over form**. Although this is not cited as an accounting concept in the IASC *Framework*, para. 35 states:

> If information is to represent faithfully the transactions and other events that it purports to represent, it is necessary that they are accounted for and presented in accordance with their substance and economic reality and not merely their legal form.

The real sticking point was that IAS 17 invoked a substance over form approach to accounting treatment that was completely different to the traditional approach, which has strict regard to legal ownership. The IASC argued that in reality there were two separate transactions taking place. In one transaction, the company was borrowing funds to be repaid over a period. In the other, it was making a payment to the supplier for the use of an asset.

The correct accounting treatment for the borrowing transaction, based on its substance, was to include in the lessee's statement of financial position a liability representing the obligation to meet the lease payments, and the correct accounting treatment for the asset acquisition transaction, based on its substance, was to include an asset representing the asset supplied under the lease.

IAS 17, para. 10, states categorically that 'whether a lease is a finance lease or an operating lease depends on the substance of the transaction rather than the form of the contract'.

16.3.1 How do the accounting and legal professions differ in their approach to the reporting of lease transactions?

The accounting profession sees itself as a service industry that prepares financial reports in a dynamic environment, in which the user is looking for reports that reflect commercial reality. Consequently, the profession needs to be sensitive and responsive to changes in commercial practice.

There was still some opposition within the accounting profession to the inclusion of a finance lease in the statement of financial position as an 'asset'. The opposition rested on the fact that the item that was the subject of the lease agreement did not satisfy the existing criterion for classification as an asset because it was not 'owned' by the lessee. To accommodate this, the definition of an asset has been modified from 'ownership' to 'control' and 'the ability to contribute to the cash flows of the enterprise'.

The legal profession, on the other hand, concentrates on the strict legal interpretation of a transaction. The whole concept of substance over form is contrary to its normal practice.

It is interesting to reflect that, whereas an equity investor might prefer the economic resources to be included in the statement of financial position under the substance over form principle, this is not necessarily true for a loan creditor. The equity shareholder is interested in resources available for creating earnings; the lender is interested in the assets available as security.

Another way to view the asset is to think of it as an asset consisting of the ownership of the right to use the facility as opposed to the ownership of the physical item itself. In a way this is similar to owning accounts receivable or a patent or intellectual property. You do not have a physical object but rather a valuable intangible right.

16.4 IAS 17 – classification of a lease

As discussed earlier in the chapter, IAS 17 provides definitions for classifying leases as finance or operating leases, then prescribes the accounting and disclosure requirements applicable to the lessor and the lessee for each type of lease.

The crucial decision in accounting for leases is whether a transaction represents a finance or an operating lease. We have already defined each type of lease, but we must now consider the risks and rewards of ownership.

IAS 17 provides in paragraph 10 a list of the factors that need to be considered in the decision whether risks and rewards of ownership have passed to the lessee. These factors are considered individually and in combination when making the decision, and if met would normally indicate a finance lease:

(a) the lease transfers ownership of the asset to the lessee by the end of the lease term;

(b) the lessee has the option to purchase the asset at a price that is expected to be sufficiently lower than the fair value at the date the option becomes exercisable for it to be reasonably certain, at the inception of the lease, that the option will be exercised;

(c) the lease term is for the major part of the economic life of the asset even if title is not transferred;

(d) at the inception of the lease the present value of the minimum lease payments amounts to at least substantially all of the fair value of the leased asset; and

(e) the leased assets are of such a specialised nature that only the lessee can use them without major modifications.

Leases of land

If land is leased and legal title is not expected to pass at the end of the lease, the lease will be an operating lease. The reason is that the lease can never be for the substantial part of the economic life of the asset (criterion (c) above). This means that if a land and buildings lease is entered into it should be classified as two leases, a land lease which is usually an operating lease and a buildings lease which could be an operating or a finance lease. The lease payments should be allocated between the land and buildings elements in proportion to the relative fair values of the land element and the buildings element of the lease at its inception.

This split is not required by lessees if the land and buildings are an investment property accounted for under IAS 40, and where the fair value model has been adopted.

IAS 17 (revised 1997) included a helpful flow chart, prepared by the IAS secretariat, which represents examples of some possible positions that would normally be classified as finance leases (Figure 16.1).

Figure 16.1 IAS 17 aid to categorising operating and finance leases

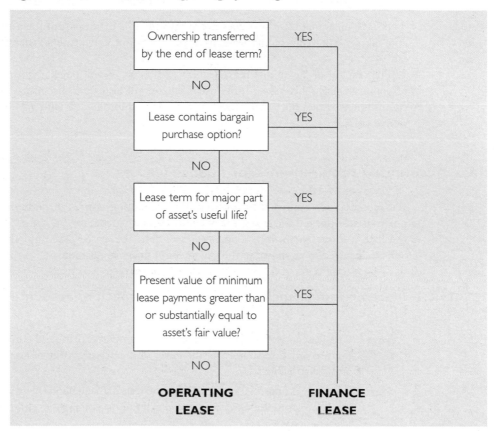

16.5 Accounting requirements for operating leases

The treatment of operating leases conforms to the legal interpretation and corresponds to the lease accounting practice that existed before IAS 17. No asset or obligation is shown in the statement of financial position; the operating lease rentals payable are charged to the statement of comprehensive income on a straight-line basis unless another systematic basis is more representative of the time pattern of the user's benefit.

16.5.1 Disclosure requirements for operating leases

IAS 17 requires that the total of operating lease rentals charged as an expense in the statement of comprehensive income should be disclosed, and these rentals should be broken down for minimum lease payments, contingent costs, and sublease payments. Disclosure is required of the payments that a lessee is committed to make during the next year, in the second to fifth years inclusive, and over five years.

EXAMPLE ● OPERATING LEASE Clifford plc is a manufacturing company. It negotiates a lease to begin on 1 January 20X1 with the following terms:

Term of lease	4 years
Estimated useful life of machine	9 years
Purchase price of new machine	£75,000
Annual payments	£8,000

This is an operating lease as it does not apply only to a major part of the asset's useful life, and the present value of the lease payments does not constitute substantially all of the fair value.

The amount of the annual rental paid – £8,000 p.a. – will be charged to the statement of comprehensive income and disclosed. There will also be a disclosure of the ongoing commitment with a note that £8,000 is payable within one year and £24,000 within two to five years.

16.6 Accounting requirements for finance leases

We follow a step approach to illustrate the accounting entries in both the statement of financial position and the statement of comprehensive income.

When a lessee enters into a finance lease, both the leased asset and the related lease obligations need to be shown in the statement of financial position.

16.6.1 Statement of financial position step approach to accounting for a finance lease

Step 1 The leased asset should be capitalised in property, plant and equipment (and recorded separately) at the lower of the present value of lease payments and its fair value.

Step 2 The annual depreciation charge for the leased asset should be calculated by depreciating the asset over the shorter of its estimated useful life or the lease period.

Step 3 The net book value of the leased asset should be reduced by the annual depreciation charge.

Step 4 The finance lease obligation is a liability which should be recorded. At the inception of a lease **agreement**, the value of the leased asset and the leased liability will be the same.

Step 5 (a) The finance charge for the finance lease should be calculated as the difference between the total of the minimum lease payments and the fair value of the asset (or the present value of the minimum lease payments if lower), i.e. it represents the charge made by the lessor for the credit that is being extended to the lessee.

(b) The finance charge should be allocated to the accounting periods over the term of the lease. Three methods for allocating finance charges are used in practice:

● **Actuarial method.** This applies a constant periodic rate of charge to the balance of the leasing obligation. The rate of return applicable can be calculated by applying present value tables to annual lease payments.

- **Sum of digits method**. This method ('Rule of 78') is much easier to apply than the actuarial method. The finance charge is apportioned to accounting periods on a reducing scale.

- **Straight-line method**. This spreads the finance charge equally over the period of the lease (it is only acceptable for immaterial leases).

Step 6 The finance lease obligation should be reduced by the difference between the lease payment and the finance charge. This means that first the lease payment is used to repay the finance charge, and then the balance of the lease payment is used to reduce the book value of the obligation.

16.6.2 Statement of comprehensive income steps for a finance lease

Step 1 The annual depreciation charge should be recorded.

Step 2 The finance charge allocated to the current period should be recorded.

16.7 Example allocating the finance charge using the sum of the digits method

EXAMPLE ● FINANCE LEASE Clifford plc negotiates another lease to commence on 1 January 20X1 with the following terms:

Term of lease	3 years
Purchase price of new machine	£16,500
Annual payments (payable in advance)	£6,000
Clifford plc's borrowing rate	10%

Finance charges are allocated using the sum of digits method.

16.7.1 Categorise the transaction

First we need to decide whether the lease is an operating or a finance lease. We do this by applying the present value criterion.

- Calculate the fair value:
  Fair value of asset = £16,500

- Calculate the present value of minimum lease payments:

$$£6,000 + \frac{£6,000}{1.1} + \frac{£6,000}{(1.1)^2} = £16,413$$

- Compare the fair value and the present value. It is a finance lease because PV of the lease payments is substantially all of the fair value of the asset.

16.7.2 Statement of financial position steps for a finance lease

Step 1 Capitalise lease at fair value (present value is immaterially different):
  Asset value = £16,500

Step 2 Calculate depreciation (using straight-line method):
  £16,500/3 = £5,500

Step 3 Reduce the asset in the statement of financial position:

Extract as at		31 Dec 20X1	31 Dec 20X2	31 Dec 20X3
ASSET	Opening value	16,500	11,000	5,500
(Right to	Depreciation	5,500	5,500	5,500
use asset)	Closing value	11,000	5,500	—

Or if we keep the asset at cost as in published accounts:

ASSET	Cost	16,500	16,500	16,500
(Right to	Depreciation	5,000	11,000	16,500
use asset)	Net book value	11,000	5,500	—

Step 4 Obligation on inception of finance lease:
Liability = £16,500

Step 5 Finance charge:

Total payments	$3 \times £6,000$	= £18,000
Asset value		= £16,500
		£1,500

Finance charge
Allocated using sum of digits:

Year 1 = 2/(1 + 2) × £1,500 = (£1,000)
Year 2 = 1/(1 + 2) × £1,500 = (£500)

Note that the allocation is only over two periods because the instalments are being made in advance. If the instalments were being made in arrears, the liability would continue over three years and the allocation would be over three years.

Step 6 Reduce the obligation in the statement of financial position:

Statement of financial position (extract) as at		31 Dec 20X1	31 Dec 20X2	31 Dec 20X3
Liability	Opening value	16,500	11,500	6,000
(Obligation	Lease payment	6,000	6,000	6,000
under finance		10,500	5,500	—
lease)	Finance charge	1,000	500	—
	Closing value	11,500	6,000	—

Note that the closing balance on the asset represents unexpired service potential and the closing balance on the liability represents the capital amount outstanding at the period end date.

16.7.3 Statement of comprehensive income step approach to accounting for a finance lease

Step 1 A depreciation charge is made on the basis of use. The charge would be calculated in accordance with existing company policy relating to the depreciation of that type of asset.

Step 2 A finance charge is levied on the basis of the amount of financing outstanding.

Both then appear in the statement of comprehensive income as expenses of the period:

	Extract for year ending		
	31 Dec 20X1	*31 Dec 20X2*	*31 Dec 20X3*
Depreciation	5,500	5,500	5,500
Finance charge	1,000	500	—
Total	6,500	6,000	5,500

16.7.4 Example allocating the finance charge using the actuarial method

In the Clifford example, we used the sum of the digits method to allocate the finance charge over the period of the repayment. In the following example, we will illustrate the actuarial method of allocating the finance charge.

EXAMPLE ● FINANCE LEASE Witts plc negotiates a four-year lease for an item of plant with a cost price of £35,000. The annual lease payments are £10,000 payable in advance. The cost of borrowing for Witts plc is 15%.

First we need to determine whether this is a finance lease. Then we need to calculate the implicit interest rate and allocate the total finance charge over the period of the repayments using the actuarial method.

● Categorise the transaction to determine whether it is a finance lease.

Fair value of asset	$= £35,000$
PV of future lease payments:	
$£10,000 + (10,000 \times a_{\overline{3}|15})$	
$£10,000 + (10,000 \times 2.283)$	$= £32,830$

The PV of the minimum lease payments is substantially the fair value of the asset. The lease is therefore categorised as a finance lease.

● Calculate the 'interest rate implicit in the lease'.

Fair value = Lease payments discounted at the implicit interest rate
$£35,000 \quad = £10,000 + (10,000 \times a_{\overline{3}|i})$
$a_{\overline{3}|i} \quad = £25,000/10,000 = 2.5$
$i \quad = 9.7\%$

● Allocate the finance charge using the actuarial method.

Figure 16.2 shows that the finance charge is levied on the obligation during the period at 9.7%, which is the implicit rate calculated above.

16.7.5 Disclosure requirements for finance leases

IAS 17 requires that assets subject to finance leases should be identified separately and the net carrying amount disclosed. This can be achieved either by separate entries in the property, plant and equipment schedule or by integrating owned and leased assets in this schedule and disclosing the breakdown in the notes to the accounts.

The obligations relating to finance leases can also be treated in two different ways. The leasing obligation should either be shown separately from other liabilities in the statement

Figure 16.2 Finance charge allocation using actuarial method

Period	Obligation (start) £	Rentals paid £	Obligation (during) £	Finance 9.7% £	Obligation (end) £
Year 1	35,000	10,000	25,000	2,425	27,425
Year 2	27,425	10,000	17,425	1,690	19,115
Year 3	19,115	10,000	9,115	885	10,000
Year 4	10,000	10,000	—	—	—

of financial position or integrated into 'current liabilities' and 'non-current liabilities' and disclosed separately in the notes to the accounts.

The notes to the accounts should also analyse the leasing obligations in terms of the timing of the payments. The analysis of the amounts payable should be broken down into those obligations falling due within one year, two to five years, and more than five years.

Note that Figure 16.2 also provides the information required for the period end date. For example, at the end of year 1 the table shows, in the final column, a total obligation of £27,425. This can be further subdivided into its non-current and current components by using the next item in the final column, which represents the amount outstanding at the end of year 2. This amount of £19,115 represents the non-current element, and the difference of £8,310 represents the current liability element at the end of year 1.

This method of calculating the current liability from the table produces a different current figure each year. For example, the current liability at the end of year 2 is £9,115, being £19,115 – £10,000. This has been discussed in *External Financial Reporting*, where the point was made that the current liability should be the present value of the payment that is to be made at the end of the next period, i.e. £10,000 discounted at 9.7%, which gives a present value for the current liability of £9,115 for inclusion at each period end until the liability is discharged.[5] We use the conventional approach in working illustrations and exercises, but you should bear this point in mind.

EXAMPLE ● DISCLOSURE REQUIREMENTS IN THE LESSEE'S ACCOUNTS It is interesting to refer to the disclosures found in published accounts as illustrated by the Nestlé Group accounts.

Extract from the Nestlé Group – Annual Report and Accounts 2008

Accounting policies

Leased assets
Assets acquired under finance leases are capitalised and depreciated in accordance with the Group's policy on property, plant and equipment unless the lease term is shorter. Land and building leases are recognised separately provided an allocation of the lease payments between these categories is reliable. The associated obligations are included under financial liabilities.

Rentals payable under operating leases are expensed.

The costs of the agreements that do not take the legal form of a lease but convey the right to use an asset are separated into lease payments and other payments if the entity has the control of the use or of the access to the asset or takes essentially all the output of the asset. Then the entity determines whether the lease component of the agreement is a finance or an operating lease.

Other notes

Lease commitments
The following charges arise from these commitments:

Operating leases

Lease commitments refer mainly to buildings, industrial equipment, vehicles and IT equipment.

In millions of CHF	2008	2007
	Minimum lease payments future value	
Within one year	609	559
In the second year	487	425
In the third to fifth year inclusive	918	859
After the fifth year	524	571
	2,538	2,414

Finance leases

In millions of CHF	2008		2007	
	Minimum future payments			
	Present value	Future value	Present value	Future value
Within one year	65	67	78	88
In the second year	54	64	100	120
In the third to fifth year inclusive	101	139	146	208
After the fifth year	74	181	122	264
	294	451	446	680

The difference between the future value of the minimum lease payments and their present value represents the discount on the lease obligations.

16.8 Accounting for the lease of land and buildings

Land and buildings are dealt with separately. Each has to be reviewed to determine whether to classify as an operating or finance lease. This is illustrated in the Warehouse Company example.

Let us assume that:

- The Warehouse Company Ltd, whose borrowing rate was 10% per annum, entered into a ten-year lease under which it made payments of $106,886 annually in advance.
- The present value of the land was $500,000 and of the buildings was $500,000.
- The value of the land at the end of ten years was $670,000 and the value of the buildings was $50,000.

Classifying the land segment of the lease

We first need to classify the land lease. As there is no contract to pass title at the end of the contract and the land is expected to increase in value, it is clear that the land segment of the contract does not involve the lessor transferring the risk and benefits to the lessee. This means that the lessee has to account for the lease of the land as an operating lease.

Classifying the building segment of the lease

The building segment of the lease is different. The residual value has fallen to $50,000 which has a present value of $19,275 (50,000 × 0.3855). This means that 96% of the benefit has been transferred (500,000 − 19,275) and the building segment is, therefore, a finance lease.

How to apportion the lease payment in the statement of comprehensive income

The payment should be split at the commencement of the lease according to the fair value of the components covered by the lease. In the case of the land, the present value of the land is $500,000 of which $258,285 (670,000 × 0.3855) represents the present value of the land at the end of the contract so the balance of $241,715 represents the present value of the operating lease. Similarly the amount covered by the finance lease is $480,725. Splitting the lease payment of $106,886 in those proportions (241,715:480,725) gives $35,763 for the land component and $71,123 for the finance lease representing the buildings leased.

How to report in the statement of financial position

For the finance lease covering the building the lessee will have to show a $480,725 asset initially which will be depreciated over the ten years of the lease according to the normal policy of depreciating buildings which are going to last ten years. At the same time a liability representing an obligation to the legal owner of the buildings (the lessor) for the same amount will be created. As lease payments are made the interest component will be treated as an expense and the balance will be used to reduce the liability.

In this example the risk and rewards relating to the building segment were clearly transferred to the lessee. If the residual value had been say, $350,000 rather than $50,000 then the present value at the end of the lease would have been $134,925 which represents 27% of the value. This does not indicate that substantially all the benefits of ownership have been transferred and hence it would be classified as an operating lease. The lessee would not, therefore, capitalise the lease but would charge each period with the same leasing expense.

16.9 Leasing – a form of off balance sheet financing

Prior to IAS 17, one of the major attractions of leasing agreements for the lessee was the off balance sheet nature of the transaction. However, the introduction of IAS 17 required the capitalisation of finance leases and removed part of the benefit of off balance sheet financing.

The capitalisation of finance leases effectively means that all such transactions will affect the lessee's gearing, return on assets and return on investment. Consequently, IAS 17 substantially alters some of the key accounting ratios which are used to analyse a set of financial statements.

Operating leases, on the other hand, are not required to be capitalised. This means that operating leases still act as a form of off statement of financial position financing.[6] Hence, they are extremely attractive to many lessees. Indeed, leasing agreements are increasingly being structured specifically to be classified as operating leases, even though they appear to be more financial in nature.[7]

An important conclusion is that some of the key ratios used in financial analysis become distorted and unreliable in instances where operating leases form a major part of a company's financing.[8]

To illustrate the effect of leasing on the financial structure of a company, we present a buy versus leasing example.

EXAMPLE ● RATIO ANALYSIS OF BUY VERSUS LEASE DECISION Kallend Tiepins plc requires one extra machine for the production of tiepins. The MD of Kallend Tiepins plc is aware that the gearing ratio and the return on capital employed ratio will change depending on whether the company buys or leases (on an operating lease) this machinery. The relevant information is as follows.

The machinery costs £100,000, but it will improve the operating profit by 10% p.a. The current position, the position if the machinery is bought and the position if the machinery is leased are as follows, assuming that lease costs match depreciation charges:

	Current £	Buy £	Lease £
Operating profit	40,000	44,000	44,000
Equity capital	200,000	200,000	200,000
Long-term debt	100,000	200,000	100,000
Total capital employed	300,000	400,000	300,000
Gearing ratio	0.5:1	1:1	0.5:1
ROCE	13.33%	11%	14.66%

It is clear that the impact of a leasing decision on the financial ratios of a company can be substantial.[9] Although this is a very simple illustration, it does show that the buy versus lease decision has far-reaching consequences in the financial analysis of a company.

16.10 Accounting for leases – a new approach

The total annual leasing volume was reported in 2007 as being US$760 billion. Whilst finance leases are reported on the statement of financial position, many of the lease contracts have been classified as operating leases and do not appear on the statement.

There has been criticism on theoretical grounds that this effectively ignores assets and liabilities that fall within the definition of assets and liabilities in the Conceptual Framework and on practical grounds that the difference in the accounting treatment of finance leases and operating leases provides opportunities to structure transactions so as to achieve a particular lease classification. This means that the same transaction could be reported differently by companies and comparability reduced.

Some users have attempted to overcome this by adjusting the statement of financial position to capitalise the operating leases. For example, credit rating agencies capitalise operating lease obligations on the basis that all leasing is a form of financing that creates a claim on future cash flows and the distinction between finance and operating leases is artificial. The approach taken by the credit agency, Standard & Poor, is to capitalise operating leases by discounting the minimum lease commitments using the entity's borrowing rate to calculate the present value of the commitments.

The data in the financial statements is then adjusted, for example, EBITDA is re-calculated with the interest element of the lease payments deducted from the rental figure that had been deducted in arriving at the EBITDA. Other adjustments are made as discussed below in considering the impact on financial statements.

The standard setters (the IASB and FASB) have, therefore, proposed that operating leases give rise to an asset which is the right-of-use and a liability and both should be reported on the statement of financial position.

16.10.1 Impact on financial statements

Where an industry uses operating leases extensively, there could be significant impact on key performance indicators. For example, there is an impact on the Statement of comprehensive income resulting from the rental charge being separated into a depreciation and interest charge, so that the EBITDA figure increases; and an impact on the Statement of cash flows in which the operating cash flow and free cash flow increase; and an impact on the Statement of financial position in which the gearing increases. This is illustrated in an article[10] relating to the retail industry.

Discount rate

The Boards (FASB and IASB) decided that a lessee should initially measure both its right-of-use asset and its lease obligation at the present value of the expected lease payments and that a lessee should discount the lease payments using the lessee's incremental borrowing rate for secured borrowings. It follows from this that a lease with the same terms and conditions would be reported at different amounts by different entities.

This differs from IAS 17 which requires the discount rate to be at the interest rate implicit in the lease and, only if this cannot be determined, at the lessee's incremental borrowing rate.

Contingent rentals

The Boards decided to develop a new approach for contingent lease payments by requiring a lessee to measure contingent rentals based on the lessee's best estimate of the expected lease payments over the term of the lease. However, there is no requirement to probability-weight possible outcomes. For example, if lease rentals are contingent on changes in an index or rate, such as the consumer price index or the prime interest rate, the lessee would measure the contingent rentals using the index or rate existing at the inception of the lease in its initial determination of the best estimate of expected lease payments.

IAS 17 *Leases* is unclear on the issue and contingent rentals have generally not been included in the amount to be recognised. This will presumably be clarified when a revised standard is issued.

Residual value guarantees

The proposal is that these should be based on the lessee's best estimate of the expected lease payments over the term of the lease. IAS 17 *Leases* requires a lease to be classified as a finance lease if the lessee assumes the residual value risk of the asset and the lease liability would be recognised in full.

There are other matters under consideration such as how to treat lease extension options – whether to discount the cash flows for (a) the the initial period where there is no legal or constructive obligation to take up the option, or (b) the total period including the option extension, or (c) the initial period plus a probability adjusted extension period, or (d) the best estimate of the likely total period. Conceptually one would have thought that unless there is a legal or constructive obligation to take up the option then no liability exists which implies that only (a) is conceptually sound, however the preliminary views of the Boards support option (d) above.

16.11 Accounting for leases by lessors

There are essentially two different types of situation.

The first is where a manufacturer enters into a lease to enable a potential purchaser to 'buy' their product. In this situation it is necessary to separate the sale transaction from the leasing transaction. All costs relating to making the sale must be included in calculating the profit or loss on the sale and must not be included in the lease accounting.

The second scenario is where an asset is purchased by the finance company at the request of a client and is then leased to the client. The lease is then classified as a financial lease or as an operating lease, as seen below.

16.11.1 Finance lease

The lessor will recognise a finance lease receivable in its assets. The amount initially shown will be the cost of the asset plus any direct costs necessarily incurred in setting up the lease. Suppose the XYZ plc finance company purchases a machine for $157,000 at the request of Flexible Manufacturing plc which then leases it for $58,000 per annum for three years, payments being made at the commencement of each year. XYZ plc incurs costs of $1,661 to establish the lease.

XYZ plc, the lessor, will record an asset of $158,661 being the amount which is to be recovered from Flexible Manufacturing plc. In addition, it is entitled to interest on the transaction. To ascertain the rate of interest, we ascertain by trial and error the rate of interest which equates the present value of the lease payments ($58,000 in years 0, 1 and 2) to the amount to be recovered, in this case $158,661. The interest rate is 10%.

So at the start of the first year XYZ plc will receive $58,000. Of that $10,066 will be recorded as interest and $47,934 as recovery of the initial investment. (Initial investment $158,661 less immediate recovery of $58,000 leaving a balance of $100,661 outstanding for a year at 10% or $10,066 interest. This means of the $58,000 paid, $10,066 represents interest and the remaining $47,934 is a repayment of capital.) At the end of the first year the lease asset would show as $110,727 ($158,661 − $47,934). Interest recognised in the next year would be $5,273 (10% of (110,727 − 58,000)).

In tabular format:

Year	Recoverable b/f	Rental	Interest @ 10%	Recoverable c/f
1	158,661	58,000	10,066	110,727
2	110,727	58,000	5,273	58,000
3	58,000	58,000	—	
		174,000	15,339	

There are also disclosure requirements relating to the timing of cash flows, unearned finance income, allowances for uncollectible amounts, unguaranteed residuals expected under the contracts, and contingent rents.

16.11.2 Operating leases

The asset will be capitalised at its cost plus the direct cost of arranging the lease. The asset will then be depreciated like any other non-current asset.

The revenue will be matched against periods according to the pattern of benefits received, which in most cases will be on a straight-line basis.

Summary

The initial upturn in leasing activity in the 1970s was attributable to the economy and tax requirements rather than the popularity of lease transactions *per se*. High interest rates, a high inflation rate, 100% first year tax allowances and a sequence of annual losses in the manufacturing industry made leasing transactions extremely attractive to both the lessors and the lessees.

Off balance sheet financing was considered a particular advantage of lease financing. IAS 17 recognised this and attempted to introduce stricter accounting policies and requirements. However, although IAS 17 introduced the concept of 'substance over form', the hazy distinction between finance and operating leases still allows companies to structure lease agreements to achieve either type of lease. This is important because, while stricter accounting requirements apply to finance leases, operating leases can still be used as a form of off statement of financial position accounting.

We do not know the real extent to which IAS 17 is either observed or ignored. However, it is true to say that creative accountants and finance companies are able to circumvent IAS 17 by using 'structured' leases. Future development will change this position considerably.

REVIEW QUESTIONS

1 Can the legal position on leases be ignored now that substance over form is used for financial reporting? Discuss.

2 (a) Consider the importance of the categorisation of lease transactions into operating lease or finance lease decisions when carrying out financial ratio analysis. What ratios might be affected if a finance lease is structured to fit the operating lease classification?

(b) Discuss the effects of renegotiating/reclassifying all operating leases into finance leases. For which industries might this classification have a significant impact on the financial ratios?

3 State the factors that indicate that a lease is a finance lease under IAS 17.

4 The favourite off-balance sheet financing trick used to be leasing. Use any illustrative numerical examples you may wish to:

(a) Define the term 'off-balance sheet on financing' and state why it is popular with companies.

(b) Illustrate what is meant by the above quotation in the context of leases and discuss the accounting treatments and disclosures required by IAS 17 which have limited the usefulness of leasing as an off-balance sheet financing technique.

(c) Suggest two other off-balance sheet financing techniques and discuss the effect that each technique has on statement of financial position assets and liabilities, and on the income statement.

5 The Body Shop International PLC 2004 Annual Report included the following accounting policy:

Leased assets
Assets held under finance leases are capitalised at amounts approximating to the present value of the *minimum lease payments* payable over the term of the lease. The corresponding leasing commitments are shown as amounts payable to the lessor. Depreciation on assets held under finance leases is charged to the income statement.

Leasing payments are analysed between capital and interest components so that the interest element is charged to the income statement over the period of the lease and *approximates to a constant proportion of the balances of capital payments outstanding.*

All other leases are treated as operating leases with annual rentals charged to the income statement on a straight-line basis over the term of the lease.

(a) Explain the meaning of 'minimum lease payments' and 'approximates to a constant proportion of the balances of capital repayments outstanding'.

(b) Explain why it is necessary to use present values and approximate to a constant proportion.

6 Peter Mullen says in an article sent in to the UK Accounting Standards Board (ASB), the following:

the ASB advocates that all leasing type deals should essentially be accounted for in relation to the extent of asset and liability transfer that they involve...

On the first point, the ASB seems to have a point – 90% [for recognition of a finance lease] is unquestionably an arbitrary figure. But 'arbitrariness' is not in itself wrong: indeed often it is necessary. The speeding limit on a motorway is set at 70 mph, a driver driving at 71 mph is therefore breaking the law, where one driving at a 'substantially similar' speed is not. One could easily think of many similar examples where the demands of pragmatism means that a 'bright line' being drawn somewhere is preferable to no line at all. There is only a convincing case for dispensing with arbitrariness in these situations if the replacement does not give rise to something which is equally arbitrary, and this is where the ASB starts to run into problems.

...If assets and liabilities mean what the ASB wants them to mean they have to do so in all circumstances. The range of contracts that give rise to similar liabilities and assets, however is vast.

At a very simple level, Leaseguard has retainer agreements with its clients which are typically between two and four years' duration. Under any sensible extension of ASB's logic these should be capitalised rather than treated as revenue items. Imagine a world, however, where just about every contract for the provision of future services or assets that an organisation enters into is scrutinised for its asset and liability content.

Discuss whether this is a valid argument for not treating all leases in the same manner.

EXERCISES

An extract from the solution is provided on the Companion Website (www.pearsoned.co.uk/elliott-elliott) for exercises marked with an asterisk (*).

* Question 1

On 1 January 20X8, Grabbit plc entered into an agreement to lease a widgeting machine for general use in the business. The agreement, which may not be terminated by either party to it, runs for six years and provides for Grabbit to make an annual rental payment of £92,500 on 31 December each year. The cost of the machine to the lessor was £350,000, and it has no residual value. The machine has a useful economic life of eight years and Grabbit depreciates its property, plant and equipment using the straight-line method.

Required:

(a) Show how Grabbit plc will account for the above transaction in its statement of financial position at 31 December 20X8, and in its statement of comprehensive income for the year then ended, if it capitalises the leased asset in accordance with the principles laid down in IAS 17.

(b) Explain why the standard setters considered accounting for leases to be an area in need of standardisation and discuss the rationale behind the approach adopted in the standard.

(c) The lessor has suggested that the lease could be drawn up with a minimum payment period of one year and an option to renew. Discuss why this might be attractive to the lessee.

* Question 2

(a) When accounting for finance leases, accountants prefer to overlook legal form in favour of commercial substance.

Required:
Discuss the above statement in the light of the requirements of IAS 17 *Leases*.

(b) State briefly how you would distinguish between a finance lease and an operating lease.

(c) Smarty plc finalises its accounts annually on 31 March. It depreciates its machinery at 20% per annum on cost and adopts the 'Rule of 78' for allocating finance charges among different accounting periods. On 1 August 20X7 it acquired machinery on a finance lease on the following agreement:

   (i) a lease rent of £500 per month is payable for 36 months commencing from the date of acquisition;

   (ii) cost of repairs and insurance are to be met by the lessee;

   (iii) on completion of the primary period the lease may be extended for a further period of three years, at the lessee's option, for a peppercorn rent.

   The cash price of the machine is £15,000.

Required:
(1) Set out how all ledger accounts reflecting these transactions will appear in each of the four accounting periods 20X7/8, 20X8/9, 20X9/Y0 and 20Y0/Y1.
(2) Show the statement of comprehensive income entries for the year ended 31 March 20X8 and statement of financial position extracts as at that date.

Question 3

The Mission Company Ltd, whose year-end is 31 December, has acquired two items of machinery on leases, the conditions of which are as follows:

Item Y: Ten annual instalments of £20,000 each, the first payable on 1 January 20X0. The machine was completely installed and first operated on 1 January 20X0 and its purchase price on that date was £160,000. The machine has an estimated useful life of ten years, at the end of which it will be of no value.

Item Z: Ten annual instalments of £30,000 each, the first payable on 1 January 20X2. The machine was completely installed and first operated on 1 January 20X2 and its purchase price on that date was £234,000. The machine has an estimated useful life and is used for 12 years, at the end of which it will be of no value.

The Mission Company Ltd accounts for finance charges on finance leases by allocating them over the period of the lease on the sum of the digits method.

Depreciation is charged on a straight-line basis. Ignore taxation.

Required:

(a) Calculate and state the charges to the statement of comprehensive income for 20X6 and 20X7 if the leases were treated as operating leases.

(b) Calculate and state the charges to the statement of comprehensive income for 20X6 and 20X7 if the leases were treated as finance lease and capitalised using the sum of the digits method for the finance charges.

(c) Show how items Y and Z should be incorporated in the statement of financial position, and notes thereto, at 31 December 20X7, if capitalised.

Question 4

X Ltd entered into a lease agreement on the following terms:

Cost of leased asset	£100,000
Lease term	5 years
Rentals six-monthly in advance	£12,000
Anticipated residual on disposal of the assets at end of lease term	£10,000
Lessee's interest in residual value	97%
Economic life	8 years
Inception date	1 January 20X4
Lessee's financial year-end	31 December
Implicit rate of interest is applied half-yearly	4.3535%

Required:

Show the statement of comprehensive income entries for the years ended 31 December 20X4 and 20X7 and statement of financial position extracts at those dates.

Question 5

At 1 January 20X5 Bridge Finance plc agreed to finance the lease of machinery costing $37,200 to Rapid Growth plc at a lease cost of $10,000 per annum payable at the end of the year, namely 31 December. The period of the lease is five years. Bridge Finance plc incurred direct costs of $708 in setting up the contract.

Required:

Show for Bridge Finance plc the amount that would be charged to the statement of comprehensive income for the year ending 31 December 20X7 and the amount of the leased asset that would appear in the statement of financial position at that date.

Question 6

Alpha entered into an operating lease under which it was committed to five annual payments of £50,000 per year. It was subsequently decided to treat the lease as a Right-of-use asset reported on the Statement of financial position. Alpha's borrowing rate was 10%.

Required:

Calculate the amount to be reported in the Statement of financial position and Statement of comprehensive income.

Question 7

Construction First provides finance and financial solutions to companies in the construction industry. On 1 January 2007 the company agreed to finance the lease of equipment costing $145,080 to Bodge Brothers over its useful life of five years at an annual rental of $39,000 payable annually in arrears. The interest rate associated with this transaction is 10% and Construction First incurred direct costs of $2,761 in setting up the lease.

Construction First agreed with the manufacturer of the equipment to pay the amount owing in 3 equal six-monthly instalments beginning on 31 January 2007.

Required:

Show the entries that would appear in Construction First's statement of income and statement of financial position (balance sheet) for the year ended 31 December 2008 together with comparative figures and an appropriate disclosure note.

(Association of International Accountants)

References

1   G. Allum *et al.*, 'Fleet focus: to lease or not to lease', *Australian Accountant*, September 1989, pp. 31–58; R.L. Benke and C.P. Baril, 'The lease vs. purchase decision', *Management Accounting*, March 1990, pp. 42–46.
2   B. Underdown and P. Taylor, *Accounting Theory and Policy Making*, Heinemann, 1985, p. 273.
3   Cranfield School of Management, *Financial Leasing Report*, Bedford, 1979.
4   Abdel-Khalik *et al.*, 'The economic effects on lessees of FASB Statement No. 13', *Accounting for Leases*, FASB, 1981.
5   R. Main, in *External Financial Reporting*, ed. B. Carsberg and S. Dev, Prentice Hall, 1984.
6   R.H. Gamble, 'Off-balance-sheet diet: greens on the side', *Corporate Cashflow*, August 1990, pp. 28–32.
7   R.L. Benke and C.P. Baril, 'The lease vs. purchase decision', *Management Accounting*, March 1990, pp. 42–46; N. Woodhams and P. Fletcher, 'Operating leases to take bigger market share with changing standards', *Rydge's (Australia)*, September 1985, pp. 100–110.
8   C.H. Volk, 'The risks of operating leases', *Journal of Commercial Bank Lending*, May 1988, pp. 47–52.
9   Chee-Seong Tah, 'Lease or buy?', *Accountancy*, December 1992, pp. 58–59.
10 C.W. Mulford and M. Gram, 'The effects of lease capitalisation on various financial measures: an analysis of the retail industry', *Journal of Applied Research in Accounting and Finance*, 2007, vol. 2, no. 2, pp. 3–13.

CHAPTER 17

R&D; goodwill; intangible assets and brands

17.1 Introduction

The main purpose of this chapter is consider the accounting treatments of:

- research and development;
- goodwill and other intangible assets;
- brands; and
- emissions trading certificates.

Objectives

By the end of this chapter, you should be able to:

- define and explain how to account for research and development (R&D), goodwill and other intangible assets;
- comment critically on the IASB requirements in IAS 38 and IFRS 3;
- account for development costs;
- account for impairment;
- prepare extracts of the entries and disclosure of these items in the statement of comprehensive income and statement of financial position.

17.2 Accounting treatment for research and development

Under IAS 38 *Intangible Assets*,[1] the accounting treatment for research and development (R&D) differs depending on whether the expenditure relates to research expenditure or development expenditure. Broadly speaking, research expenditure must always be charged to the statement of comprehensive income and development expenditure must be capitalised provided a strict set of criteria is met. In this section we will consider how R&D is defined, why research expenditure is written off and the tests for capitalising development expenditure.

17.3 Research and development

IAS 38 *Intangible Assets* defines both research and development expenditure.

17.3.1 Research defined

IAS 38 states[2] 'expenditure on research shall be recognised as an expense when it is incurred'. This means that it cannot be included as an intangible asset in the statement of financial position. The standard gives examples of research activities[3] as:

1 activities aimed at obtaining new knowledge;

2 the search for, evaluation and final selection of, applications of research findings or other knowledge;

3 the search for alternatives for materials, devices, products, processes, systems and services;

4 the formulation, design, evaluation and final selection of possible alternatives for new or improved materials, devices, products, processes, systems or services.

Normally, research expenditure is not related directly to any of the company's products or processes. For instance, development of a high temperature material, which can be used in any aero engine, would be 'research', but development of a honeycomb for a particular engine would be 'development'. Whilst it is in the research phase, the IAS position[4] is that an entity cannot demonstrate that an intangible asset exists that will generate probable future economic benefits. It is this inability that justifies the IAS requirement for research expenditure not to be capitalised but to be charged as an expense when it is incurred.

17.3.2 Development defined

Expenditure is recognised[5] as development if the entity can identify an intangible asset and demonstrate that the asset will generate probable future economic benefits. The standard gives examples of development activities:[6]

(a) the design, construction and testing of pre-production and pre-use prototypes and models;

(b) the design of tools, jigs, moulds and dies involving new technology;

(c) the design, construction and operation of a pilot plant that is not of a scale economically feasible for commercial production;

(d) the design, construction and testing of a chosen alternative for new or improved materials, devices, products, processes, systems or services.

17.4 Why is research expenditure not capitalised?

Many readers will think of research not as a cost but as a strategic investment which is essential to remain competitive in world markets. Indeed, this was the view[7] taken by the House of Lords Select Committee on Science and Technology, stating that 'R&D has to be regarded as an investment which leads to growth, not a cost'. Globally, such expenditure is in excess of 3% of sales, taking place particularly in the advanced technical industries such as pharmaceuticals, where a sustained high level of R&D investment is required – almost 80% occurring in five countries: the USA, Japan, Germany, France and the UK. The regulators, however, do not consider that the expenditure can be classified as an asset for financial reporting purposes.

Why do the regulators not regard research expenditure as an asset?

The IASC in its *Framework for the Preparation and Presentation of Financial Statements* (para. 49) defines an asset as a resource that is controlled by the enterprise, as a result of past events and from which future economic benefits are expected to flow.

Research is controlled by the enterprise and is as a result of past events but there is no reasonable certainty that the intended economic benefits will be achieved. Because of this uncertainty, the accounting profession has traditionally considered it more prudent to write off the investment in research as a cost rather than report it as an asset in the statement of financial position.

It might be thought that this is concealing an asset from investors but in research on both analysts'[8] and accountants'[9] reactions to R&D expenditure Nixon[10] found that: 'Two important dimensions of the corporate reporting accountants' perspective emerge: first, disclosure is seen as more important than the accounting treatment of R&D expenditure and, second, the financial statements are not viewed as the primary channel of communication for information on R&D.'

This highlights the importance of reading carefully the narrative in financial reports. An interesting study in Singapore[11] examined the impact of annual report disclosures on analysts' forecasts for a sample of firms listed on the Stock Exchange of Singapore (SES) and showed that the level of disclosure affected the accuracy of earnings forecasts among analysts and also led to greater analyst interest in the firm.

Management might prefer in general to be able to capitalise research expenditure but there could be circumstances where writing off might be preferred. For example, directors might be pleased to take the expense in a year when they know its impact rather than carry it forward. They are aware of profit levels in the year in which the expenditure arises and could, perhaps, find it embarrassing to take the charge in a subsequent year when profits were lower or the company even reported a trading loss.

Development expenditure, on the other hand, has more probability of achieving future economic benefits and that allows it to be classified as an asset. The regulators, therefore, require such expenditure to be capitalised.

17.5 Capitalising development costs

IAS 38 now requires development costs to be capitalised. However, that has not always been the situation. The development of an accounting standard in this area has been subject to the conflicting demands of the accruals concept (which would favour capitalisation if future benefits could be foreseen) and the prudence concept (which would favour immediate write-off). This led to a compromise whereby companies were allowed a choice of either capitalising or expensing. This element of choice impaired inter-company comparisons and was seen by many analysts as a significant weakness. The IASC responded to this concern and in its *Statement of Intent: Comparability of Financial Statements*,[12] proposed that the choice should be removed and that, if development costs met the conditions for capitalisation, they must be capitalised and depreciated. This is the approach that has since been adopted by IAS 38.[13]

17.5.1 The conditions set out in IAS 38

The relevant paragraph of IAS 38 (para. 57) says an intangible asset for development expenditure must be recognised if and only if an entity can demonstrate **all** of the following:

(a) the technical feasibility of completing the intangible asset so that it will be available for use or sale;

(b) the intention to complete the intangible asset and use or sell it;

(c) its ability to use or sell the intangible asset;

(d) how the intangible asset will generate probable future economic benefits;

(e) the availability of adequate technical, financial and other resources to complete the development and to use or sell the intangible asset;

(f) its ability to measure reliably the expenditure attributable to the intangible asset during its development.

It is important to note that if the answers to all the conditions (a) to (f) above are 'Yes' then the entity *must* capitalise the development expenditure subject to reviewing for impairment. For example, if costs incurred exceed future economic benefits, the lower figure is taken and the difference written off. There is a large element of judgement and if a company does not want to capitalise its development expenditure, it could argue that there is sufficient uncertainty about future development costs, being able to develop the product and/or making profits from future sales, and thus answer 'No' to one of the questions above. This would result in development expenditure not being capitalised.

17.5.2 What costs can be included?

The costs that can be included in development expenditure are similar to those used in determining the cost of inventory (IAS 2 *Inventories*). It is important to note that only expenditure incurred after the project satisfies the IAS 38 criteria can be capitalised – all expenditure incurred prior to this date must be written off as an expense in the statement of comprehensive income.

How is the amortisation charge calculated?

The intangible asset of development costs is usually amortised over the sales of the product (i.e. the charge in 20X5 would be: 20X5 sales/total estimated sales × capitalised development expenditure).

17.6 The judgements to be made when deciding whether to capitalise development costs

The IASB's *Framework for the Preparation and Presentation of Financial Statements* says 'an asset is recognised in the statement of financial position when it is probable that the future economic benefits will flow to the entity and the asset has a cost or value that can be measured reliably'. Let us consider these conditions further.

17.6.1 Cost incurred to date

Costs such as wages and materials can generally be measured reliably although there might be arguments as to the amount of overheads that can be allocated or apportioned to the development activities. This would be a matter for the auditors to satisfy themselves as to the justification for the overhead rates applied.

In determining whether 'it is probable that future economic benefits will flow to the entity' there could still be uncertainties as to both costs and revenues.

17.6.2 Profit measurement – estimating future costs

Current production wages will be known and might be initially high because of 'learning'. It might be assumed in estimating future costs that they are likely to reduce when production quantities increase – but by how much? If the economy unexpectedly grows, there could be higher costs. For example, skilled workers might become more expensive to retain, raw materials such as copper might become more expensive. These factors show how uncertain it is that a product will be profitable, and the potential inaccuracies in estimating this figure.

17.6.3 Profit measurement – estimating future sales

Sales value is the product of the selling price and quantity sold and there may be uncertainties about both of these figures. For some high technology products the selling price might initially be high, but subsequently decline. For instance, high speed microprocessors command a high price when they are released but decline quite quickly as competitors develop faster microprocessors. Also, there is a relationship between quantity sold and the selling price – lowering the selling price will increase sales. This discussion highlights the problems of estimating future sales value.

At what point in time can an asset be recognised?

In the early stages of a development project, usually there are uncertainties over:

(a) whether the project can be completed successfully; and

(b) the costs of developing the product.

Experience tends to indicate that people who develop products are notoriously optimistic. In practice, they encounter many more problems than they imagined and the cost is much greater than estimates. This means that the development project may well be approaching completion before future development costs can be estimated reliably. It may, therefore, be very difficult to satisfy the Framework's statement of an asset as being 'recognised in the statement of financial position when it is probable that the future economic benefits will flow to the entity'. If this statement cannot be satisfied, then the development expenditure cannot be included as an asset in the statement of financial position.

17.7 Disclosure of R&D

R&D is important to many manufacturing companies, such as pharmaceutical companies who develop drugs, car and defence manufacturers. Disclosure is required of the aggregate amount of research and development expenditure recognised as an expense during the period.[14] Normally, this total expenditure will be:

(a) research expenditure;

(b) development expenditure amortised;

(c) development expenditure not capitalised; and

(d) impairment of capitalised development expenditure.

Under IAS 38 more companies may capitalise development expenditure, although many will avoid capitalisation by saying they cannot be certain to make future profits from the sale of the product. The following is the R&D policy extract from the Rolls-Royce Annual Report for the year ended 31 December 2008:

> **Research and development**
> In accordance with IAS 38 'Intangible Assets', expenditure incurred on research and development, excluding known recoverable amounts on contracts, and contributions to shared engineering programmes, is distinguished as relating either to a research phase or to a development phase.
> All research phase expenditure is charged to the statement of comprehensive income. For development expenditure, this is capitalised as an internally generated intangible

asset, only if it meets strict criteria, relating in particular to technical feasibility and generation of future economic benefits.

Expenditure that cannot be classified into these two categories is treated as being incurred in the research phase. The Group considers that, due to the complex nature of new equipemnt programmes, it is not possible to distinguish reliably between research and development activities until relatively late in the programme.

Expenditure capitalised is amortised over its useful economic life, up to an maximum of 15 years from the entry-into-service of the product.

The financial statements (of Rolls-Royce for the year ended 31 December 2008) show capitalised development expenditure of £213 million at the year end, £97 million additions and £46 million amortisation in the year.

17.8 Goodwill

IFRS 3 defines goodwill[15] as: 'future economic benefits arising from assets that are not capable of being individually identified and separately recognised'. The definition effectively affirms that the value of a business as a whole is more than the sum of the accountable and identifiable net assets. Goodwill can be internally generated through the normal operations of an existing business or purchased as a result of a business combination.

17.8.1 Internally generated goodwill

Internally generated goodwill falls within the scope of IAS 38 Intangible assets which states that 'Internally Generated Goodwill (or "self generated goodwill") shall not be recognised as an asset'. If companies were allowed to include internally generated goodwill as an asset in the statement of financial position, it would boost total assets and produce a more favourable view of the statement of financial position, for example, by reducing the gearing ratio.

17.8.2 Purchased goodwill

The key distinction between internally generated goodwill and purchased goodwill is that purchased goodwill has an identifiable 'cost', being the difference between the fair value of the total consideration that was paid to acquire a business and the fair value of the identifiable net assets acquired. This is the initial cost reported in the statement of financial position.

17.9 The accounting treatment of goodwill

Now that we have a definition of goodwill, we need to consider how to account for it in subsequent years. One might have reasonably thought that a simple requirement to amortise the cost over its estimated useful life would have been sufficient. This has been far from the case. Over the past forty years, there have been a number of approaches to accounting for purchased goodwill, including:

(a) writing off the cost of the goodwill directly to reserves in the year of acquisition;

(b) reporting goodwill at cost in the statement of financial position;

(c) reporting goodwill at cost, amortising over its expected life; and

(d) reporting goodwill at cost, but checking it annually for impairment.

The first UK accounting standard SSAP 22 *Accounting for Goodwill* was issued in 1984. This allowed entities two alternative treatments:

1 write off the goodwill directly to reserves in the year of acquisition (option b); or

2 amortise the goodwill to the statement of comprehensive income over its expected life (option c).

Almost all UK companies used treatment 1 above, as it had no effect on reported profit in the current or future years (treatment 2 reduced reported profit because of the amortisation charge). The problem with using treatment 1, however, was that it reduced shareholders' funds, which could become negative. In fact, some advertising agencies reached the situation of having negative shareholders' funds (i.e. the statement of financial position showed the company had negative net worth). As treatment 1 reduces shareholders' funds, it increases the capital gearing of the company (i.e. loans/shareholders' funds) which could lead to a breach of loan covenants making banks and other investors unwilling to provide loans.

17.9.1 The initial IAS 22 treatment

Unlike the UK's SSAP 22, IAS 22 *Business Combinations* (revised 1998) did not allow goodwill to be written off against reserves in the year of acquisition. All companies were required to amortise goodwill over its useful life (option c), thus reducing profits.

17.9.2 The current IFRS 3 treatment

IFRS 3 *Business Combinations* prohibits the amortisation of goodwill. It treats goodwill as if it has an indefinite life with the amount reviewed annually for impairment. If the carrying value is greater than the recoverable value of the goodwill, the difference is written off.

Whereas goodwill amortisation gave rise to an annual charge, impairment losses will arise at irregular intervals. This means that the profit for the year will become more volatile. This is why companies and analysts rely more on the EBITDA (earnings before tax, depreciation and amortisation) when assessing a company's performance, assuming that this is a better indication of maintainable profits.

This is illustrated by the following is an extract from the 2005 Molins plc annual report which shows the volatile effect of impairment charges on maintainable profits:

Consolidated statement of comprehensive income for the year ended 31 December 2005

	Before goodwill impairment and reorganization costs	Goodwill impairment	Reorganisation costs	Total
	M	m	m	M
Revenue	121.4	—	—	121.4
Cost of sales	(85.8)	—	(1.2)	(87.0)
Gross profit	35.6	—	(1.2)	34.4
Other operating income	0.3	—	—	0.3
Distribution expenses	(9.8)	—	(0.2)	(10.0)
Administrative expenses	(18.7)	—	(0.3)	(19.0)
Other operating expenses	(1.2)	(6.7)	(0.5)	(8.4)
Operating profit/(loss)	6.2	(6.7)	(2.2)	(2.7)

17.10 Critical comment on the various methods that have been used to account for goodwill

Let us consider briefly the alternative accounting treatments.

(a) Reporting goodwill unchanged at cost

It is (probably) wrong to keep goodwill unchanged in the statement of financial position, as its value will decline with time. Its value may be *maintained* by further expenditure e.g. continued advertising, but this expenditure is essentially creating 'internally generated goodwill' which is not allowed to be capitalised. Sales of most manufactured products often decline during their life and their selling price falls. Eventually, the products are replaced by a technically superior product. An example is computer microprocessors, which initially command a high price, and high sales. The selling price and sales quantities decline as faster microprocessors are produced. Much of the goodwill of businesses is represented by the products they sell. Hence, it is wrong to not amortise the goodwill.

(b) Writing off the cost of the goodwill directly to reserves in the year of acquisition

A buyer pays for goodwill on the basis that future profits will be improved. It is wrong therefore to write it off in the year of acquisition against previous years in the reserves. The loss in value of the goodwill does not occur at the time of acquisition but occurs over a longer period. The goodwill is losing value over its life, and this loss in value should be charged to the statement of comprehensive income each year. Making the charge direct to reserves stops this charge from appearing in the future income statements.

(c) Amortising the goodwill over its expected useful life

Amortising goodwill over its life could achieve a matching under the accrual concept with a charge in the statement of comprehensive income. However, there are problems (i) in determining the life of the goodwill and (ii) in choosing an appropriate method for amortising.

(i) What is the life of the goodwill?

Companies wishing to minimise the amortisation charge could make a high estimate of the economic life of the goodwill and auditors had to be vigilant in checking the company's justification. The range of lives can vary widely. For example, goodwill paid to acquire a business in the fashion industry could be quite short compared to that paid to acquire an established business with a loyal customer base.

(ii) The method for amortising

Straight-line amortisation is the simplest method. However, as the benefits are likely to be greater in earlier years than later ones, amortisation could use 'actual sales'/'expected total sales' or the reducing balance method.

It could be argued that amortising goodwill is equivalent to depreciating tangible fixed assets as prescribed by IAS 16 *Property, Plant and Equipment* and that the amortisation approach appears to be the best way of treating goodwill in the statement of financial position and statement of comprehensive income. This is effectively following a 'statement of comprehensive income' approach to 'expense' (e.g. depreciation) with the expense charged over the life of the asset or in relation to the profits obtained from the acquisition.

There are difficulties but these should not prevent us from using this method. After all, accountants have to make many judgements when valuing items in the statement of financial position, such as assessing the life of Property, Plant and Equipment, the value of inventory and bad debt provisions.

(d) An annual impairment check

IFRS 3 *Business Combinations* has introduced a new treatment for purchased goodwill when it arises from a business combination (i.e. the purchase of a company which becomes a subsidiary). It assumes that goodwill has an indefinite economic life which means that it is not possible to make a realistic estimate of its economic life and a charge should only be made to the statement of comprehensive income when it becomes impaired.

This is called a 'statement of financial position approach' to accounting, as the charge is only made when the value (in the statement of financial position) falls below its original cost.

The IFRS 3 treatment is consistent with the Framework,[16] which says: 'Expenses are recognised in the statement of comprehensive income when a decrease in future economic benefits related to a decrease in an asset or an increase of a liability has arisen that can be measured reliably.'

Criticism of the statement of financial position approach
However, there has been much criticism of the 'statement of financial position approach' of the Framework.

For example, if a company purchased specialised plant which had a resale value of 5% of its cost, then it could be argued that the depreciation charge should be 95% of its cost immediately after it comes into use. This is not sensible, as the purpose of buying the plant is to produce a product, so the depreciation charge should be over the life of the product.

Alternatively, if the 'future economic benefit' approach was used to value the plant, there would be no depreciation until the future economic benefit was less than its original cost. So, initial sales would incur no depreciation charge, but later sales would have an increased charge.

This example shows the weakness of using 'impairment' and the 'statement of financial position approach' for charging goodwill to the statement of comprehensive income – the charge occurs at the 'wrong time'. The charge should be made earlier when sales, selling prices and profits are high, not when the product becomes 'out of date' and sales and profits are falling.

Why the Impairment charge occurs at the wrong time
Although the IFRS 3 treatment of 'impairment' appears to be correct according to the *Framework*, it could be argued that the impairment approach is not correct, as the charge occurs at the wrong time (i.e. when there is a loss in value, rather than when profits are being made), it is very difficult to estimate the 'future economic benefit' of the goodwill and those estimates are likely to be over-optimistic.

In addition, it means that the treatment of goodwill for IFRS 3 transactions is different from the treatment in IAS 38 *Intangible Assets*. This shows the inconsistency of the standards – they should use a single treatment, either IAS 38 amortisation or IFRS 3 impairment.

17.10.1 Why does the IFRS 3 treatment of goodwill differ from the treatment of intangible assets in IAS 38?

The answer is probably related to the convergence of International Accounting Standards to US accounting standards, and pressure from listed companies.

Convergence pressure

In issuing recent International Standards, the IASB has not only aimed to produce 'world-wide' standards but also standards which are acceptable to US standard setters. The IASB wanted their standards to be acceptable for listing on the New York Stock Exchange (NYSE), so there was strong pressure on the IASB to make their standards similar to US Standards. The equivalent US standard to IFRS 3 uses impairment of goodwill as the charge against profits (rather than amortisation). Thus, IFRS 3 uses the same method and it prohibits amortisation.

Commercial pressure

A further pressure for impairment rather than amortisation comes from listed companies. Essentially, listed companies want to maximise their reported profit, and amortisation reduces profit. For most of the time, companies can argue that the 'future economic benefit' of the goodwill is greater than its original cost (or carrying value if it has been previously impaired), and thus avoid a charge to the statement of comprehensive income. Also, companies could argue that the 'impairment charge' is an unexpected event and charge it as an exceptional item.

In the UK, most companies publicise their 'profit before exceptional items' by separating out the impairment charge as seen in the Molins extract above.

17.11 Negative goodwill

Negative goodwill arises when the amount paid is less than the fair value of the net assets acquired. IFRS 3 says the acquirer should:

(a) reassess the identification and measurement of the acquiree's identifiable assets, liabilities and contingent liabilities and the measurement of the cost of the combination in case the assets have been undervalued or the liabilities overstated; and

(b) recognise immediately in the statement of comprehensive income any excess remaining after that reassessment.

The immediate crediting of negative goodwill to the statement of comprehensive income seems difficult to justify when, as in many situations, the reason why the consideration is less than the value of the net identifiable assets is that there are expected to be future losses or redundancy payments. Whilst the redundancy payments could be included in the 'contingent liabilities' at the date of acquisition, standard setters are very reluctant to allow a provision to be made for future losses (this has been prohibited in recent accounting standards). This means that the only option is to say the negative goodwill should be credited to the statement of comprehensive income at the date of acquisition. This results in the group profit being inflated when a subsidiary with negative goodwill is acquired.

In some ways, it would be better to credit the negative goodwill to the statement of comprehensive income over the years the losses are expected. However, the 'provision for future losses' (i.e. the negative goodwill) does not fit in very well with the Framework's definition of a liability as being recognised 'when it is probable that an outflow of resources embodying economic benefits will result from the settlement of a present obligation and the amount at which the settlement will take place can be measured reliably'. It is questionable whether future losses are a 'present obligation' and whether they can be 'measured reliably', so it is very unlikely that future losses can be included as a liability in the statement of financial position.

17.12 Intangible assets

Standard setters wanted companies to identify any intangible assets that were acquired and not to include them within a global figure of goodwill. This is important because each intangible can then be amortised under IAS 38 over its economic life i.e. there is no assumption that the asset has an indefinite life. Examples of intangible assets that should be recognised and reported in the Statement of financial position are set out in IAS 38.

IAS 38 gives the following examples of classes of intangible assets:[17]

- brand names;
- mastheads and publishing titles;
- computer software;
- licences and franchises;
- copyrights, patents and other industrial property rights, services and operating rights;
- recipes, formulae, models, designs and prototypes;
- intangible assets under development;
- goodwill acquired in a business combination (as we have already seen, IFRS 3 applies here);
- non-current intangible assets classified as held for sale.

17.12.1 Recognition criteria

IAS 38 states that an asset is recognised in respect of an intangible item if the asset is:

Identifiable

One of the difficulties that are faced when considering intangible items is their existence. This is what IAS 38 is examining here. The standard states that for an intangible asset to exist (or be identifiable) it must either be separable or arise from contractual or other legal rights, whether or not the asset can be separately disposed of. This means that in theory a large number of intangible items could create assets.

Controlled by the entity

Control is one of the central features of the Framework definition of an asset. If the entity cannot exercise control over the potential future economic benefits inherent in an item then no asset should be recognised. Therefore, IAS 38 does not normally allow an entity to recognise the potential 'asset' that could be said to exist because of the inherent skills in an assembled workforce. There is generally insufficient control over the workforce to allow asset recognition.

Future economic benefits

Again, it is inherent in the Framework definition of an asset that the potential future economic benefits can be identified with reasonable certainty. If the identifiability and control tests are satisfied then IAS 38 allows recognition of an intangible asset if:

- it is probable that the expected future economic benefits that are attributable to the asset will flow to the entity; and
- the cost of the asset can be measured reliably.

17.12.2 Meaning of 'cost'

IAS 38 states that this depends on the way in which the asset arose.

Separate acquisition

In such circumstances 'cost' has its normal meaning – as long as the other tests are satisfied recognition of an asset is perfectly possible. An example of such an asset would be a payment for a production licence.

Acquired as part of a business combination

In such a case a single payment has been made for the whole business and in order to complete the accounting it is necessary to allocate the cost as far as possible to the identifiable net assets, with the balance being goodwill accounted for under IFRS 3 (see earlier in the chapter). It is here that the concept of 'identifiability' can be applied to intangible items such as:

- customer lists;
- order or production backlogs;
- customer relationships (whether contractual or non-contractual);
- domain names.

If items such as the above have a reliable fair value at the date of acquisition then they can be recognised as separate assets in the statement of financial position of the acquiring company or group.

Internally developed

Based on the reliability criterion, IAS 38 states that only development projects (see earlier in the chapter) that satisfy the stringent criteria laid out in paragraph 57 of the standard can be recognised as internally developed intangibles.

17.12.3 Accounting treatment subsequent to initial recognition

IAS 38 states that recognised intangible non-current assets should be recognised at cost less accumulated amortisation. Revaluation is only permitted if there is an active market in the intangible item. This is relatively unusual for intangible items so revaluations are quite rare.

The asset should be amortised over its estimated useful economic life, in a manner that is very similar to the treatment of property, plant and equipment under IAS 16. Where the estimated useful economic life is indefinite, then no amortisation is required but IAS 38 requires that the asset be subject to annual impairment reviews.

17.12.4 Disclosure of intangible assets under IAS 38

IAS 38 requires the disclosure of the following for each type of intangible asset:[18]

- Whether useful lives are indefinite or finite. For finite useful lives, the useful lives or amortisation rates are used.
- The amortisation methods used for intangible assets with finite useful lives.
- The gross carrying amount and accumulated amortisation at the beginning and end of the period.
- Increases or decreases resulting from revaluations and from impairment losses recognised or reversed directly in equity (IAS 36 *Impairment of Assets*).

Where an intangible asset is assessed as having an indefinite useful life, the carrying value of the asset must be stated[19] along with the reasons for supporting the assessment of an indefinite life. For example:

As stated in the section on R&D, the financial statements must disclose the charge for research and development in the period.[20]

Approaches to valuation of intangible assets

Approaches vary with the nature of the intangible. For example, the purchase of trade names and trademarks means that an entity is relieved from the need to pay royalties which can be estimated and discounted to arrive at a present value for the intangible.

Customer lists and supplier relationships mean that there is an expected greater volume of business than could be achieved using the current assets. These intangibles could be valued by identifying their impact on future cash flows. Under this approach, first the business unit that benefits from the intangible is identified, then the cash flows of the unit are established. The next stage is to deduct from the unit cash flows an estimate of the cash flows arising from the other unit assets (both tangible and intangible) assuming a reasonable rate of return on those assets. The difference represents the cash flows estimated to arise from the acquired intangible which can be discounted to arrive at a present value for financial reporting purposes.

Illustration of disclosures from SABMiller 2009 Annual Report and the KCOM Group 2009 Annual Report

The SABMiller Accounting policy explains the amortisation and impairment policy for intangibles with finite lives as follows:

Intangible assets
Intangible assets are stated at cost less accumulated amortisation on a straight-line basis (if applicable) and impairment losses . . . Amortisation is included within net operating expenses in the statement of comprehensive income . . . Intangible assets with finite lives are amortised over their estimated useful economic lives, and only tested for impairment where there is a triggering event.

SABMiller also report an adjusted Earnings per share figure which excludes amortisation of intangible assets:

The group presents the measure of adjusted basic earnings per share, which excludes the impact of amortisation of intangible assets (other than software) and other non-recurring items including post-tax exceptional items, in order to present a more useful comparison of underlying performance for the years shown in the consolidated financial statements.

The KCOM Accounting policy on recognising internally generated intangible assets and notes as to economic lives are as follows:

(i) The accounting policies state:

Development costs
An internally-generated intangible asset arising from the Group's internal development activities is recognised only if all of the following conditions are met:

- an asset is created that can be identified (such as software and new processes);
- it is probable that the asset created will generate future economic benefits;
- the development cost of the asset can be measured reliably.

Internally-generated intangible assets are amortised on a straight-line basis over their useful lives. Where no internally-generated intangible asset can be recognised, development expenditure is recognised as an expense in the period in which it is incurred. Research costs are expensed to the statement of comprehensive income as and when they are incurred.

(ii) The notes disclose the estimated useful lives for amortisation:

Customer relationships	up to 8 years
Technology and brand	up to 10 years
Software	period of contract up to 5 years
Development	1 year

(iii) Disclosure in the statement of comprehensive income:

	2008	*2007*
Group operating profit	17,673	23,577
Analysed as:		
Group EBITDA	65,312	63,146
Depreciation of property, plant and equipment	(24,023)	(24,192)
Amortisation of intangible assets	(23,616)	(15,377)

17.13 Brand accounting

We have discussed goodwill and intangible assets above but brands deserve a separate consideration because of their major significance in some companies. For example, the following information appears in the 2009 Diageo annual report:

	£m	£m
Total equity (i.e. net assets)		3,936
Intangible assets:		
Brands	4,621	
Goodwill	363	
Other intangible assets	1,122	
Computer software	109	
Total intangible assets		6,215

We can see that brands alone are more than 1.17 times greater than total equity. It is interesting to take a look at the global importance of brands within sectors.

17.13.1 The importance of brands to particular sectors

It is interesting to note that certain sectors have high global brand valuations. For example, the Best Global Brands Report 2008[21] showed beverages (Coca-Cola), computer software (Microsoft), computer services (IBM), computer hardware (Intel), telecoms (Nokia), automotive (Ford), entertainment (Disney), restaurants (McDonald's) and financial services (Citi) as leading global brands.

The Report ranked the top 100 by brand valuation and showed how valuable brands can be, with the top three exceeding $45,000 million (Coca-Cola $66,667 million, IBM $59,031 million and Microsoft $59,007 million) and even the hundredth exceeding $3,000 million (Visa $3,338 million).

This indicates the importance of investors having as much information as possible to assess management's stewardship of brands. If this cannot be reported on the face of the statement of financial position then there is an argument for having an additional statement to assist shareholders including the information that the directors consider when managing brands.

17.14 Justifications for reporting all brands as assets

We now consider some other justifications that have been put forward for the inclusion of brands as a separate asset in the statement of financial position.

17.14.1 Reduce equity depletion

For acquisitive companies it could be attributed to the accounting treatment required for measuring and reporting goodwill. The London Business School carried out research into the 'brands phenomenon' and found that 'a major aim of brand valuation has been to repair or pre-empt equity depletion caused by UK goodwill accounting rules'.[22]

17.14.2 Strengthen the statement of financial position

Non-acquisitive companies do not incur costs for acquiring goodwill, so their reserves are not eroded by writing off purchased goodwill. However, these companies may have incurred promotional costs in creating home-grown brands and it would strengthen the statement of financial position if they were permitted to include a valuation of these brands.[23]

17.14.3 Effect on equity shareholders' funds

Immediate goodwill write-off resulted in a fall in net tangible assets as disclosed by the statement of financial position, even though the market capitalisation of a company increased. One way to maintain the asset base and avoid such a depletion of companies' reserves is to divide the purchased goodwill into two parts: the amount attributable to brands and the remaining amount attributable to pure goodwill.[24] For instance, WPP capitalised two corporate brand names in 1988 and without that capitalisation, the share owners' funds of £187.7 million in the 1998 accounts would have been reduced by £350 million to a negative figure of (£162.3 million). The 2008 Annual Report shows that total equity now exceeds the brand value but would be reduced to a negative figure if goodwill were not included.

17.14.4 Effect on borrowing powers

The borrowing powers of public companies may be expressed in terms of multiples of net assets. In Articles of Association there may be strict rules regarding the multiple that a company must not exceed. In addition, borrowing agreements and Stock Exchange listing agreements are generally dependent on net assets.

17.14.5 Effect on ratios

Immediate goodwill write-off distorted the gearing ratios, but the inclusion of brands as intangible assets minimised this distortion by providing a more realistic value for shareholders' funds.

17.14.6 Effect on management decisions

It is claimed that including brands on the statement of financial position leads to more informed and improved management decision making. The quality of internal decisions is related to the quality of information available to management.[25] As brands represent one of the most important assets of a company, management should be aware of the success or failure of each individual brand. Knowledge about the performance of brands ensures that management reacts accordingly to maintain or improve competitive advantage.

Effect on management decisions – where brands are not capitalised

Whether or not a brand is capitalised, management does take its existence into account when making decisions affecting a company's gearing ratios. For example, in 2007 the Hugo Boss management in explaining its thinking about the advisability of making a Special Dividend payment[26] recognised that one effect was to reduce the book value of equity and increase the gearing ratio but commented:

> The book value of the equity capital of the HUGO BOSS Group will be reduced by the special dividend. However this perception does not take into consideration that the originally created market value 'HUGO BOSS' is not reflected in the book value of the equity capital. This does not therefore mirror the strong economic position of HUGO BOSS fully.

The implication is that the existence of brand value is recognised by the market and leads to a more sustainable market valuation.

There is also evidence[27] that companies with valuable brand names are not including these in their statements of financial position and are not, therefore, taking account of the assets for insurance purposes.

The above are the justifications for recognising internally generated brands as assets. However, IAS 38 prohibits[28] this by saying: 'Internally generated brands, mastheads, publishing titles, customer lists and items similar in substance shall not be recognised as intangible assets.'

17.15 Accounting for acquired brands

Acquired brands require to be valued. In 2009, the International Valuation Standards Council issued an Exposure Draft, *Valuation of Intangible Assets for IFRS Reporting Purposes* (see www.ivsc.org) which considers the need to define more clearly terms used within IFRSs such as 'active' and 'inactive' markets.

A decision is then made in respect of each brand as to whether it should be treated in the financial statements as having a definite or indefinite life. The following is an extract from the accounting policies of WPP in their 2007 Annual Report:

> Corporate brand names and customer related intangibles acquired as part of acquisitions of business are capitalised separately from goodwill as intangible assets if their value can be measured reliably on initial recognition and it is probable that the expected economic benefits that are attributable to the asset will flow to the Group.
>
> Certain corporate brands of the Group are considered to have an indefinite economic life because of the institutional nature of the corporate brand names, their proven ability to maintain market leadership and profitable operations over long periods of time and the Group's commitment to develop and enhance their value. The carrying value of

these intangible assets is reviewed at least annually for impairment and adjusted to the recoverable amount if required.

Amortisation is provided at rates calculated to write off the cost less residual value of each asset on a straight-line basis over its estimated life as follows:

Brand names – 10–20 years
Customer related intangibles – 3–10 years

17.15.1 How effective have IFRS 3 and IAS 38 been?

There is still a temptation for companies to treat the excess paid on acquiring a subsidiary as goodwill. If it is treated as goodwill, then there is no requirement to make an annual amortisation charge. If any part of the excess is attributed to an intangible, then this has to be amortised. For example, in the UK the FRRP required Brewin Dolphin Holdings (PLC) to implement a change of accounting policy in the forthcoming financial statements of the company for the period ended 27 September 2009. The company agreed that intangible assets representing client relationships would now be recognised separately from goodwill.

The Panel's principal concern related to the company's practice of not separately recognising customer related intangible assets in the purchase of investment management businesses. IFRS 3 (2004) *Business Combinations* requires an acquirer to recognise intangible assets separately if they meet the definition of an intangible asset in IAS 38 *Intangible Assets* and their fair value can be measured reliably.

This is a clear indication that the FRRP will be policing the allocation of any excess on acquisitions to ensure that there is appropriate effort to attribute to intangible asset categories if that is the economic reality.

However, even so, the information is limited in that only acquired brands can be reported on the statement of financial position, which gives an incomplete picture of an entity's value. Even with acquired brands, their value can only remain the same or be revised downward following an impairment review. This means that there is no record of any added value that might have been achieved by the new owners to allow shareholders to assess the current stewardship.

17.16 Emissions trading

The European Union Emissions Trading Scheme (EU ETS) was created under the Kyoto Protocol. The programme, started in 2005, caps the amount of carbon dioxide (CO_2) emitted by large installations such as power plants and carbon intensive factories and covers about half of the EU's CO_2 emissions. The aim is to progressively reduce these emissions to 5.2% below their 1990 level by 2012.

The government issues companies with free certificates allowing them to emit a stated amount of CO_2. If a company is not going to emit that quantity of CO_2, it can sell the excess in the market, which companies exceeding the limit can buy. So, these certificates have a value. The 'selling company' (Company A) will sell the entitlement if it either has an excess (in certificates) or the value of the certificate is more than the company's cost of reducing its CO_2 emissions. Similarly, the 'buying company' (Company B) will buy the certificates if it is exceeding its CO_2 emissions limit, or the net revenue resulting from the extra CO_2 emissions is more than the cost of buying the certificates.

The questions are:

● How should these certificates be valued in companies' financial statements? and

● Where should they be included in the statement of financial position?

The three possible situations are:

1 If the company receives the certificates free from the government, their value in the financial statements should be zero. It would be unreasonable to put a value on them in the company's financial statement (e.g. number of tonnes of $CO_2 \times CO_2$ emissions value per tonne). This would be 'boosting the statement of financial position'.

2 If the company is trading in the certificates, they are financial instruments under IAS 39 *Financial Instruments: Recognition and Measurement*. They can be valued at cost, with impairment if their value becomes less than cost. However, it is probably more appropriate to treat them as 'fair value through the profit or loss', value them at market value, and include profits or losses in the statement of comprehensive income.

3 If a company buys the certificates to use in its business, they could be accounted for like inventory and valued at the lower of original cost and net realisable value. When the CO_2 emission takes place, their cost will be included in cost of sales.

Answering the question of 'Where should they be included in the statement of financial position?', they could be included:

● as an intangible asset subject to the conditions studied in this chapter;
● as a financial instrument;
● as a prepayment;
● as inventory.

Considering items (1) to (3) above in turn:

1 if the certificates have no value, they do not appear in the statement of financial position;
2 if they are classified as a financial instrument they will be included in current assets if their life is less than one year;
3 this is a problem which will be considered below.

CO_2 emissions certificates have many characteristics of inventory, and the most appropriate accounting treatment is to treat them like inventory. Normally, they will be valued at cost, and they will be charged as cost of sales when the CO_2 emissions take place. Net realisable value (NRV) will apply when the process which produces the CO_2 makes a loss. NRV will be the value which gives a zero profit from the process, but NRV will not be less than zero (negative). The problem with including them as inventory is that inventory is a physical asset, and these emission certificates are not a physical asset (they are an intangible asset).

The certificates could be a financial instrument and valued either at cost, market value or net realisable value. As they are held for use in a production process (which produces CO_2), market value does not seem appropriate. As the CO_2 is emitted, their value will be reduced and the amount charged to cost of sales. It will be like selling part of a holding of shares, but the 'sale' will be a consumption in a production process. Overall, it does not seem appropriate to include the certificates as a financial instrument, as there are more negative factors than including them as inventory.

The certificates could be included as an intangible asset, like the items considered in this chapter. However, most intangible assets last a number of years, and these certificates will probably be used within a year. The accounting standards prohibit amortisation of certain types of goodwill. This should not apply to emission certificates, as they are being consumed in the production process (i.e. as the CO_2 is being emitted, the units of the emission certificates left diminishes).

It is apparent that emission certificates are a current asset, as their life is probably less than a year, and they are consumed in the production process. They come into the category of 'receivables', although they are not an amount owed by a customer. They are more like a prepayment. The company buys the certificates (like buying insurance for the future) and consumes them in the future. Most prepayments relate to payments in advance for a future period (e.g. a year for insurance). Emission certificates are different, as they are consumed in proportion to the amount of CO_2 emitted in the future. However, they are probably more like a prepayment than the other items considered.

This discussion is 'a view' based on various arguments. It is not a definitive answer. You could consider these and other arguments and come to a different conclusion. It will be interesting to see proposals and a standard approach from the IASB in the future.

Although the scheme has been in operation for over three years, there is no standard treatment. An example of one company's accounting policy is seen in the following extract from the 2008 annual report of British Energy (now part of EDF):

Accounting policy

Under the EU Emissions Trading Scheme (EU ETS), granted carbon allowances received in a period are initially recognised at nil value within intangible assets. Purchased carbon allowances are initially recognised at cost within intangible assets. Allowances granted are apportioned over the year in line with actual and forecast emissions for the relevant emissions year.

A liability is recognised when actual emissions are greater than the granted allowances apportioned for the year. The liability is measured at the cost of purchased allowances up to the level of purchased allowances held, and then at the market price of allowances ruling at the statement of financial position date, with movements in the liability recognised in operating profit.

Forward contracts for the purchase or sale of carbon allowances are measured at fair value with gains and losses arising from changes in fair value recognised in the consolidated statement of comprehensive income in the unrealised net gains or losses on derivative financial instruments and commodity contracts line. On delivery of forward contracts, carbon allowances are capitalised in intangible assets at cost, with any permanent reduction to bring the carrying value in line with market prices being presented within fuel costs. Carbon allowances have a sustainable value and can be used in settlement of the Group's EU ETS obligation at any time within the corresponding EU ETS Phase. As a result, carbon allowances are not amortised.

17.17 Intellectual property

According to the World Intellectual Property Organisation (WIPO), intellectual property refers to creations of the mind: inventions, literary and artistic works and symbols, names, images and designs used in commerce. Intellectual property is divided into two categories, namely:

- **industrial property** which includes inventions (patents), trademarks, industrial designs and geographic indications of source; and
- **copyright** which includes literary and artistic works such as novels, poems, plays, films, musical works, artistic works such as drawings, paintings, photographs and sculptures, and architectural designs. Rights related to copyright include those of performing artistes in their performances, producers of phonograms in their recordings, and those of broadcasters in their radio and television programmes.

WIPO[29] is an international organisation dedicated to promoting the use and protection of works of the human spirit. These works – intellectual property – are expanding the bounds of science and technology and enriching the world of arts. Through its work, WIPO plays an important part in enhancing the quality and enjoyment of life as well as creating real wealth for nations. With headquarters in Geneva, Switzerland, WIPO is one of the sixteen specialised agencies of the United Nations system of organisations. It administers twenty-one international treaties dealing with different aspects of intellectual property protection. The organisation counts 175 nations as member states. Its importance is recognised in the following comment by Peter Drucker (www.wired.com/wired/archive/1.03/druker.html):

> Knowledge has become the 'key resource' of the world economy. The traditional factors of production – land, labour, capital – are becoming restraints rather than driving forces.

And in the UK, a 1998 White Paper[30] placed 'know-how' at the heart of competitiveness.

> Our competitiveness depends on making the most of our distinctive and valuable assets which competitors find hard to imitate. In a modern economy those distinctive assets are increasingly knowledge, skills and creativity rather than traditional factors.

In looking at the relative importance of asset values in businesses, in the 1980s 70% was attributed to tangible assets and 30% to intangible assets. In the mid-1990s, the situation reversed and 30% was tangible assets and 70% intangible assets. More recently 95% has been attributed to intangible assets and 5% to physical and financial assets.

17.17.1 The legal view

As Gallafent, Eastaway and Dauppe[31] suggest the principal characteristic of all forms of intellectual property is the so-called 'incorporeal' nature of that property. It is an abstraction, intangible and as such difficult to protect. To be eligible for legal protection, the author's or inventor's work must have been rendered into some tangible form. The term 'intellectual property' denotes the rights over a tangible object of the person whose mental efforts created it. The rapid development in communications initially created a problem for the practical application of copyright law as in the recent example of the *Napster* case.[32]

17.17.2 Knowledge management

Another term that is currently in use is knowledge management (KM). It has been described as developing business practices and processes that ensure that a business creates, accesses and embeds the knowledge that it needs. Binney[33] sees different elements of the knowledge management spectrum, including, for example, the management of transactional, analytical, process, innovation/creation-based, developmental and asset knowledge.

The first three of these feature as a routine part of a financial and management accountant's work. They are primarily directed towards efficiency savings and cost control and have an impact on the potential revenues and expenses in the statement of comprehensive income:

- transactional KM – the knowledge is embedded in the system, e.g. how to enter a routine order;
- analytical KM – large amounts of data are turned into information, e.g. inter-firm comparison reports;
- process KM – the focus is on codification and improvement of processes, e.g. total quality management;
- developmental KM – the focus is on the transfer of explicit knowledge via training or education and experiential assignments aimed at increasing companies' human capital;

● innovation/creation-based KM – the focus is on providing an environment in which knowledge workers, often from different disciplines, can collaborate to create new knowledge resulting in new products. This can encourage staff retention and reduce the cost of staff turnover and has a strategic value if it results in competitive advantage and increased revenues.

The final element is the one that impacts on the statement of financial position:

● asset KM – the focus is on processes to identify and exploit intellectual property.

As far as financial reporting is concerned, the key requirement is that the intellectual capital should be capable of meeting the criteria established in the *Statement of Principles* for classification as an asset if it is to be reported in the statement of financial position. Satisfying the asset criteria has been the major problem for reporting.

17.17.3 The rise of the new economy

This has been principally driven by information and knowledge. It has been identified by the Organisation for Economic Co-operation and Development (OECD) as explaining the increased prominence of intellectual capital as a business and research topic.[34]

Through a brief examination of the period since the industrial revolution, the following chain of events is observable.[35]

(a) Capital and labour were brought together and the factors of production became localised and accessible.

(b) Firms pushed to increase volumes of production to meet the demands of growing markets.

(c) Firms began to build intangibles like brand equity and reputation (goodwill) in order to create a competitive advantage in markets where new entrants limited the profit-making potential of a strategy of mass production.

(d) Firms invested heavily in information technology to increase the quality of products and improve the speed with which those products could be brought to market.

(e) Firms realised the value of information and worked at managing information and transforming it into the intellectual capital needed to drive the organisation.

At each state of this corporate evolution fixed assets became less important, in relative terms, compared with intangible assets in determining a company's success. Accounting and financial reporting practices, however, have remained largely unchanged.

17.17.4 The OECD definition

The OECD describes intellectual capital[36] as the economic value of two categories of intangible assets of a company:

(a) organisational ('structural') capital; and

(b) human capital.

Structural capital refers to things like proprietary software systems, distribution networks and supply chains. Human capital includes human resources within the organisation (i.e. staff resources) and resources external to the organisation (namely, customers and suppliers). The term intellectual capital has often been treated as being synonymous with intangible assets. The definition by the OECD makes a distinction by identifying intellectual capital as a subset of, rather than the same as, the intangible assets base of a business.

Traditionally, accounting reports have been prepared on the basis of historical cost. This does not provide for the identification and measurement of intangibles in organisations – especially knowledge-based organisations. The limitations of the existing financial reporting systems have resulted in a move towards finding new ways to measure and report on a company's intellectual capital.

Guthrie, while arguing[37] that accountants must find a way to incorporate accurate measures and values of intellectual capital in formal company reports or they will become irrelevant, suggests that the importance of intellectual capital is specifically emphasised in:

● the revolution in information technology and the information society;

● the rising importance of knowledge and the knowledge-based economy;

● the changing patterns of interpersonal activities and the network society;

● the emergence of innovation and creativity as the principal determinant of competitiveness.

In a world of dotcom companies, virtual corporations and a flourishing service industry, book values correlate poorly with market capitalisation.

Intellectual capital is important because a company's intangible assets are a key contributor to its capacity to secure a sustainable competitive advantage. Interest at an academic and professional level is high with an increasing list of articles (see the *Journal of Intellectual Capital*) and research reports.

17.17.5 Intellectual capital disclosures (ICDs) in the annual report

The problem of valuing for financial reporting purposes has meant that investors need to look outside the annual report for information which tends to be predominately narrative. This is highlighted in an ICAEW Research Report[38] which comments:

> A wide range of media were used to report ICDs, with the annual report accounting for less than a third of total ICDs across all reporting media. Furthermore, the pattern of ICDs in the annual report did not reflect the pattern of ICDs in other reports, so examination of ICDs in annual reports was not a good proxy for overall ICD practices in the sample studied . . . disclosures are overwhelmingly narrative. Previous studies have tended to indicate that monetary expression of IC elements in corporate reports is a relatively rare practice (see, for example, Beattie *et al.*, 2004). This current study of UK ICR practices reinforces this observation.

The report also referred to the fact that preparers of reports did not see that the annual report was the appropriate place to be providing stakeholders with new information on intellectual capital – the annual report being seen as having a confirmatory role in relation to information that was already in the public domain.

It would seem that companies do not consider that their market value is undervalued by the omission of an asset 'intellectual property' provided they keep investors and analysts up to date with developments. A contrary approach could be taken by companies that see an economic value in valuing and reporting in acquisition situations, e.g. payment to acquire customer lists.

17.18 Review of implementation of IFRS 3

IFRS 3, *Business Combinations*, was designed to give greater transparency to how companies accounted for acquisitions. However, recent research appears to indicate that IFRS 3 is not always being correctly applied by the UK's leading companies.

In the year following the introduction of IFRS 3, around £40 billion were spent by FTSE 100 companies on acquisitions, and over half of this (53%) was allocated to goodwill. This is directly opposed to the spirit of IFRS 3. Intangible assets accounted for only 30% of all acquisitions, with the remaining 17% attributed to tangible assets less liabilities.

A certain amount of goodwill is, of course, inevitable. A premium will generally have to be paid to convince shareholders to sell their investment. While this premium by definition is more than the sum of the company's assets, it can still be identified. And you would hope that it already had been identified prior to the takeover approach or else how would the acquiring company know that it can make a return on its investment, thereby justifying the acquisition?

Prior to an acquisition, companies would generally identify likely benefits. This would generate a range within which the acquiring company must remain for the deal to make commercial sense. This could include a premium for value the buyer can bring. The premium could be justified by economies of sale, or synergies that are possible such as reducing overheads like head office costs.

17.18.1 Reasons for inadequate reporting

Unfortunately, it appears that this is not being done when reporting under IFRS 3 – goodwill is not being broken out and intangibles are not being identified. There are several reasons for this, including:

1 **To increase profits through reduced amortisation charges**. As goodwill cannot be amortised and intangible assets with finite lives can be, and amortisation is charged to profits, companies are motivated to bolster goodwill and reduce the intangibles.

2 **To minimise impairment charges**. Acquired intangible assets must be tested for impairment annually. Any increase may not be recognised but a fall in value must be reported – implicating management for poor performance. Goodwill also has to be tested for impairment, but the criteria are not so stringent.

3 **Lack of specialist skills**. As this is the first time that companies have been required to report the value of acquired intangibles, they may lack the specialist skills and knowledge required. They may also lack the confidence to value them accurately.

4 **Failure to see the big picture**. As there are so many regulations to comply with and the rules are so complex, there is a danger that companies get so bogged down in the detail that they fail to reassess overall what the business acquisition was about. They fail to see the wood for the trees.

17.18.2 Examples of inadequate reporting

There are many examples of this inadequate reporting, including:

1 **Standard Chartered**: In April 2005, Standard Chartered acquired Korea First Bank for $3.4 billion. Korea First Bank was clearly a substantial business, with 407 branches, 2100 ATMs and 7 km of signage. And although Standard Chartered admits to the significance of Korea First Bank's brand and customers, they only accounted for 7% of the deal value. Goodwill accounted for over half of the acquisition value and is largely unexplained.

2 **WPP**: In March 2005, WPP, one of the world's largest marketing services companies purchased Grey Global Group, for £928 million and allocated no value to its brand. What value was allocated to intangible assets was not broken out – as IFRS 3 stipulates and as WPP has done in the past for acquisitions of similar brands such as JWT, Hill & Knowlton, Ogilvy & Mather and Young and Rubicam Group.

3 **Aviva:** In March 2005, Aviva bought the RAC for £1.1 billion. The RAC has 7 million customers and is one of the most trusted brands in the UK. The brand and customer relationships should most likely have accounted for the majority of the acquisition price whereas they were reported as being worth only £260 million and £132 million respectively, 35% of the total cost. Goodwill dominates and is unexplained.

4 **Kingfisher:** In June 2005 Kingfisher bought OBI, a chain of 13 DIY superstores in China, for its B&Q brand for £144 million, placing no value whatsoever on its brand or customer relationships.

17.18.3 Elements within goodwill but still difficult to value separately

Some of the reasons for this inadequate reporting have already been discussed. But how can goodwill be broken out and valued? Assuming the most common intangible assets, such as brands and customer relationships (which the brand often subsumes anyway), have been valued to reflect reality, the remaining intangibles which are dumped into goodwill can still be valued. In fact, the recognition criteria under IFRS 3 are so broad that it is unlikely that much could actually be included in goodwill. And even if there are such assets, IFRS 3 requires full disclosure and reasons why they have not been valued. This was usually not seen.

There are a number of ways in which goodwill can be identified and valued, some of which are:

1 **Workforce in place:** A business's workforce may not be valued under IFRS 3. Its value, therefore, must be recognised within goodwill. Although difficulties exist in valuing people, it is still possible under certain circumstances.

2 **Synergies:** Synergies are one of the main motivations for acquisitions – being able to strip out certain costs which will increase the efficiency of the acquired company and the acquiring company as well. Such as:

(a) **Cost synergies:** Cost synergies can be rigorously analysed, such as the duplication of head offices or a sales force.

(b) **Sales synergies:** Combining two portfolios of products can achieve synergies through cross-selling, or leveraging the combined portfolio. This can be quantified.

Summary

As business has become more complex and industrial processes more sophisticated, the amount paid to develop or acquire an intangible asset has become significant in comparison to the fixed asset base of some companies. IAS 38 allows intangible assets to be recognised if they are identifiable, if the source of future economic benefits can be identified and controlled, and if they have a measurable 'cost'. This means that separately purchased intangibles are recognised at cost, intangibles acquired as part of a business combination are recognised at fair value, and internally developed intangibles are only recognised if they arise out of a development project that satisfies strict criteria.

Any difference between the cost of an acquired business and the fair value of the identifiable net assets is purchased goodwill, which is accounted for according to IFRS 3. Purchased goodwill is not amortised but reviewed annually for impairment.

REVIEW QUESTIONS

1 Why do standard setters consider it necessary to distinguish between research and development expenditure, and how does this distinction affect the accounting treatment?

2 Discuss the suggestion that the requirement for companies to write off research investment rather than showing it as an asset exposes companies to short-term pressure from acquisitive companies that are damaging to the country's interest.

3 Discuss why the market value of a business may increase to reflect the analysts' assessment of future growth but there is no asset in the statement of financial position.

4 Here is an extract from the Reckitt Benckiser 2007 Annual Report:

	2007 £m	2006 £m
Non-current assets		
Intangible assets		
Brands	2,917	2,936
Goodwill and other intangible assets	894	1,485
PPE	479	425
	4,290	4,846
Total equity	2,385	1,866

The accounting policy states:

> An acquired brand is only recognised on the balance sheet as an intangible asset where it is supported by a registered trademark, is established in the market place, brand earnings are separately identifiable, the brand could be sold separately from the rest of the business and where the brand achieves earnings in excess of those achieved by unbranded products. The value of an acquired brand is determined by allocating the purchase consideration of an acquired business between the underlying fair values of the tangible assets, goodwill and brands acquired.
>
> Brands are not generally amortised, as it is considered that their useful economic lives are not limited.... Their carrying values are reviewed annually by the directors to determine whether there has been any permanent impairment in value and any such reductions in their values are taken to the profit and loss account.

Discuss the suggestion that nothing has been achieved by separating the excess of the payment between goodwill and brands if both are treated in the same way, i.e. reported at cost and reviewed for possible impairment.

5 The following is an extract from the 2008 Cadbury Report: and Accounts:

i) Brands and other intangibles

> Brands and other intangibles that are acquired through acquisition are capitalised on the balance sheet. These brands and other intangibles are valued on acquisition using a discounted cash flow methodology and we make assumptions and estimates regarding future revenue growth, prices, marketing costs and economic factors in valuing a brand. These assumptions reflect management's best estimates but these estimates involve inherent uncertainties, which may not be controlled by management.
>
> Upon acquisition we assess the useful economic life of the brands and intangibles. We do not amortise over 99% of our brands by value. In arriving at the conclusion that a brand has an indefinite life, management considers the fact that we are a brands business and expects to acquire, hold and support brands for an indefinite period. We support our brands through

spending on consumer marketing and through significant investment in promotional support, which is deducted in arriving at Revenue. Many of our brands were established over 50 years ago and continue to provide considerable economic benefits today. We also consider factors such as our ability to continue to protect the legal rights that arise from these brand names indefinitely or the absence of any regulatory, economic or competitive factors that could truncate the life of the brand name. Where we do not consider these criteria to have been met, as was the case with certain brands acquired with Adams, a definite life is assigned and the value is amortised over the life.

Discuss the implication for ratios of maintaining brands at historical cost with the growing emphasis on the use of fair values in financial reporting.

6 Discuss the advantages and disadvantages of the proposal that there should be a separate category of asset in the statement of financial position clearly identified as 'research investment – outcome uncertain'.

7 The Chloride 2005 Annual Report included the following accounting policy for goodwill:

Goodwill is subject to review at the end of the year of acquisition and at any other time when the directors believe that impairment may have occurred. Any impairment would be charged to the profit and loss account in the period in which the loss occurs.

(a) Explain the indications that a review for impairment is required.

(b) Once there are indications of impairment, how is impairment measured?

8 How is 'value in use' calculated for an impairment review? What are the areas of subjectivity?

9 Critically evaluate the basis of the following assertion: 'I am sceptical that it [the impairment test] will work reliably in practice, given the complexity and subjectivity that lie within the calculation.'[39]

10 IFRS 3 has introduced a new concept into accounting for purchased goodwill – annual impairment testing, rather than amortisation. Consider the effect of a change from amortisation of goodwill (in IAS 22) to impairment testing and no amortisation in IFRS 3, and in particular:

● the effect on the financial statements;

● the effect on financial performance ratios;

● the effect on the annual impairment or amortisation charge and its timing;

● which method gives the fairest charge over time for the value of the goodwill when a business is acquired;

● whether impairment testing with no amortisation complies with the IASC's *Framework for the Preparation and Presentation of Financial Statements*;

● why there has been a change from amortisation to impairment testing – is this pandering to pressure from the US FASB and/or listed companies?

11 A research report into the use of IFRS 3 (www.intangiblebusiness.com/Content/2441) concluded:

However IFRS 3 has not been followed, through undervaluing intangible assets acquired with a corresponding exaggeration of goodwill. Throughout there is a lack of disclosure. So the rationale justifying acquisitions is inadequate and £21 billion has been lost in an accounting black hole called goodwill.

Discuss reasons for the undervaluing of intangibles and exaggeration of goodwill.

12 One goodwill impairment indicator is the loss of key personnel.

Discuss two further possible indicators.

EXERCISES

An extract from the solution is provided on the Companion Website (www.pearsoned.co.uk/elliott-elliott) for exercises marked with an asterisk (*).

Question 1

Environmental Engineering plc is engaged in the development of an environmentally friendly personal transport vehicle. This will run on an electric motor powered by solar cells, supplemented by passenger effort in the form of pedal assistance.

At the end of the current accounting period, the following costs have been attributed to the project:

(a) A grant of £500,000 to the Polytechnic of the South Coast Faculty of Solar Engineering to encourage research.

(b) Costs of £1,200,000 expended on the development of the necessary solar cells prior to the decision to incorporate them in a vehicle.

(c) Costs of £5,000,000 expended on designing the vehicle and its motors, and the planned promotional and advertising campaign for its launch on the market in twelve months' time.

Required:
(i) Explain, with reasons, which of the above items could be considered for treatment as deferred development expenditure, quoting any relevant International Accounting Standard.
(ii) Set out the criteria under which any items can be so treated.
(iii) Advise on the accounting treatment that will be afforded to any such items after the product has been launched.

Question 2

As chief accountant at Italin NV, you have been given the following information by the director of research:

Project Luca

	€000
Costs to date (pure research 25%, applied research 75%)	200
Costs to develop product (to be incurred in the year to 30 September 20X1)	300
Expected future sales per annum for 20X2–20X7	1,000

Fixed assets purchased in 20X1 for the project:

Cost	2,500
Estimated useful life	7 years
Residual value	400

(These assets will be disposed of at their residual value at the end of their estimated useful lives.)

The board of directors considers that this project is similar to the other projects that the company undertakes, and is confident of a successful outcome. The company has enough finances to complete the development and enough capacity to produce the new product.

Required:
Prepare a report for the board outlining the principles involved in accounting for research and development and showing what accounting entries will be made in the company's accounts for each of the years ending 30 September 20X1–20X7 inclusive.

Indicate what factors need to be taken into account when assessing each research and development project for accounting purposes, and what disclosure is needed for research and development in the company's published accounts.

* Question 3

Oxlag plc, a manufacturer of pharmaceutical products, has the following research and development projects on hand at 31 January 20X2:

(A) A general survey into the long-term effects of its sleeping pill Chalcedon upon human resistance to infections. At the year-end the research is still at a basic stage and no worthwhile results with any particular applications have been obtained.

(B) A development for Meebach NV in which the company will produce market research data relating to Meebach's range of drugs.

(C) An enhancement of an existing drug, Euboia, which will enable additional uses to be made of the drug and which will consequently boost sales. This project was completed successfully on 30 April 20X2, with the expectation that all future sales of the enhanced drug would greatly exceed the costs of the new development.

(D) A scientific enquiry with the aim of identifying new strains of antibiotics for future use. Several possible substances have been identified, but research is not sufficiently advanced to permit patents and copyrights to be obtained at the present time.

The following costs have been brought forward at 1 February 20X1:

Project	A	B	C	D
			£000	
Specialised laboratory				
Cost	—	—	500	—
Depreciation	—	—	25	—
Specialised equipment				
Cost	—	—	75	50
Depreciation	—	—	15	10
Capitalised development costs	—	—	200	—
Market research costs	—	250	—	—

The following costs were incurred during the year:

Project	A	B	C	D
			£000	
Research costs	25	—	265	78
Market research costs	—	75	—	—
Specialised equipment cost	50	—	—	50

Depreciation on specialised laboratories and special equipment is provided by the straight-line method and the assets have an estimated useful life of 25 and five years respectively. A full year's depreciation is provided on assets purchased during the year.

Required:

(i) Write up the research and development, fixed asset and market research accounts to reflect the above transactions in the year ended 31 January 20X2.

(ii) Calculate the amount to be charged as research costs in the statement of comprehensive income of Oxlag plc for the year ended 31 January 20X2.

(iii) State on what basis the company should amortise any capitalised development costs and what disclosures the company should make in respect of amounts written off in the year to 31 January 20X3.

(iv) Calculate the amounts to be disclosed in the statement of financial position in respect of fixed assets, deferred development costs and work-in-progress.

(v) State what disclosures you would make in the accounts for the year ended 31 January 20X2 in respect of the new improved drug developed under project C, assuming sales begin on 1 May 20X2, and show strong growth to the date of signing the accounts, 14 July 20X2, with the expectation that the new drug will provide 25% of the company's pre-tax profits in the year to 31 January 20X3.

Question 4

International Accounting Standards IFRS 3 and IAS 38 address the accounting for goodwill and intangible assets.

Required:

(a) Describe the requirements of IFRS 3 regarding the initial recognition and measurement of goodwill and intangible assets.

(b) Explain the proposed approach set out by IFRS 3 for the treatment of positive goodwill in subsequent years.

(c) Territory plc acquired 80% of the ordinary share capital of Yukon Ltd on 31 May 20X6. The statement of financial position of Yukon Ltd at 31 May 20X6 was:

Yukon Ltd – Statement of financial position at 31 May 20X6

	£000
Non-current assets	
Intangible assets	6,020
Tangible assets	38,300
	44,320
Current assets	
Inventory	21,600
Receivables	23,200
Cash	8,800
	53,600
Current liabilities	24,000
Net current assets	29,600
Total assets less current liabilities	73,920
Non-current liabilities	12,100
Provision for liabilities and charges	3,586
	58,234
Capital reserves	
Called-up share capital (ordinary shares of £1)	10,000
Share premium account	5,570
Retained earnings	42,664
	58,234

Additional information relating to the above statement of financial position

(i) The intangible assets of Yukon Ltd were brand names currently utilised by the company. The directors felt that they were worth £7 million but there was no readily ascertainable market value at the statement of financial position date, nor any information to verify the directors' estimated value.

(ii) The provisional market value of the land and buildings was £20 million at 31 May 20X6. This valuation had again been determined by the directors. A valuers' report received on 30 November 20X6 stated the market value of land and buildings to be £23 million as at 31 May 20X6. The depreciated replacement cost of the remainder of the tangible fixed assets was £18 million at 31 May 20X6.

(iii) The replacement cost of inventories was estimated at £25 million and its net realisable value was deemed to be £20 million. Trade receivables and trade payables due within one year are stated at the amounts expected to be received and paid.

(iv) The non-current liability was a long-term loan with a bank. The initial loan on 1 June 20X5 was £11 million at a fixed interest rate of 10% per annum. The total amount of the interest is to be paid at the end of the loan period on 31 May 20X9. The current bank lending rate is 7% per annum.

(v) The provision for liabilities and charges relates to costs of reorganisation of Yukon Ltd. This provision had been set up by the directors of Yukon Ltd prior to the offer by Territory plc and the reorganisation would have taken place even if Territory plc had not purchased the shares of Yukon Ltd. Additionally Territory plc wishes to set up a provision for future losses of £10 million which it feels will be incurred by rationalising the group.

(vi) The offer made to all of the shareholders of Yukon Ltd was 2.5 £1 ordinary shares of Territory plc at the market price of £2.25 per share plus £1 cash, per Yukon Ltd ordinary share.

(vii) The directors of Yukon Ltd informed Territory plc that as at 31 May 20X7, the brand names were worthless as the products to which they related had recently been withdrawn from sale because they were deemed to be a health hazard.

(viii) In view of the adverse events since acquisition, the directors of Territory plc have impairment-tested the goodwill relating to Yukon SA, and they estimate its current value is £1 million.

Required:
Calculate the charge for impairment of goodwill in the Group Statement of Comprehensive Income of Territory plc for the accounting period ending on 31 May 20X7.

Question 5

The brands debate

Under IAS 22, the depletion of equity reserves caused by the accounting treatment for purchased goodwill resulted in some companies capitalising brands on their statements of financial position. This practice was started by Rank Hovis McDougall (RHM) – a company which has since been taken over. Martin Moorhouse, the group chief accountant at RHM, claimed that putting brands on the statement of financial position forced a company to look to their value as well as to profits. It served as a reminder to management of the value of the assets for which they were responsible and that at the end of the day those companies which were prepared to recognise brands on the statement of financial position could be better and stronger for it.[40]

There were many opponents to the capitalisation of brands. A London Business School research study found that brand accounting involves too many risks and uncertainties and too much subjective judgement.

In short, the conclusion was that 'the present flexible position, far from being neutral, is potentially corrosive to the whole basis of financial reporting and that to allow brands – whether acquired or home-grown – to continue to be included in the statement of financial position would be highly unwise'.[41]

Required:
Consider the arguments for and against brand accounting. In particular, consider the issues of brand valuation; the separability of brands; purchased vs home-grown brands; and the maintenance/substitution argument.

* Question 6

Brands plc is preparing its accounts for the year ended 31 October 20X8 and the following information is available relating to various intangible assets acquired on the acquisition of Countrywide plc.

(a) A milk quota of 2,000,000 litres at 30p per litre. There is an active market trading in milk and other quotas.

(b) A government licence to experiment with the use of hormones to increase the cream content of milk had been granted to Countrywide shortly before the acquisition by Brands plc. No fee had been required. This is the first licence to be granted by the government and was one of the reasons that Brands acquired Countrywide. The licence is not transferable but the directors estimate that it has a value to the company based on discounted cash flows for a five-year period of £1 million.

(c) A full cream yoghurt sold under the brand name 'Naughty but Nice' was valued by the directors at £2 million. Further enquiry established that a similar brand name had been recently sold for £1.5 million.

Required:
Explain how each of the above items would be treated in the consolidated financial statements using IAS 38.

Question 7

IAS 38 – *Intangible Assets* – was primarily issued in order to identify the criteria that need to be present before expenditure on intangible items can be recognised as an asset. The standard also pre-scribes the subsequent accounting treatment of intangible assets that satisfy the recognition criteria and are recognised in the statement of financial position.

Required:
(a) Explain the criteria that need to be satisfied before expenditure on intangible items can be recognised in the statement of financial position as intangible assets.
(b) Explain how the criteria outlined in (a) are applied to the recognition of separately purchased intangible assets, intangible assets acquired in a business combination, and internally generated intangible assets. You should give an example of each category discussed.
(c) Explain the subsequent accounting treatment of intangible assets that satisfy the recognition criteria of IAS 38.

Iota prepares financial statements to 30 September each year. During the year ended 30 September 20X6 Iota (which has a number of subsidiaries) engaged in the following transactions:

1 On 1 April 20X6 Iota purchased all the equity capital of Kappa and Kappa became a subsidiary from that date. Kappa sells a branded product that has a well-known name and the directors of Iota have obtained evidence that the fair value of this name is $20 million and that it has a useful economic life that is expected to be indefinite. The value of the brand name is not included in

the statement of financial position of Kappa as the directors of Kappa do not consider that it satisfies the recognition criteria of IAS 38 for internally developed intangible assets. However, the directors of Kappa have taken legal steps to ensure that no other entities can use the brand name.

2   On 1 October 20X4 Iota began a project that sought to develop a more efficient method of organising its production. Costs of $10 million were incurred in the year to 30 September 20X5 and debited to the statement of comprehensive income in that year. In the current year the results of the project were extremely encouraging and on 1 April 20X6 the directors of Iota were able to demonstrate that the project would generate substantial economic benefits for the group from 31 March 20X7 onwards as its technical feasibility and commercial viability were clearly evident. Throughout the year to 30 September 20X6 Iota spent $500,000 per month on the project.

Required:

(d) **Explain how both of the above transactions should be recognised in the financial statements of Iota for the year ending 30 September 20X6. You should quantify the amounts recognised and make reference to relevant provisions of IAS 38 wherever possible.**

Question 8

(a) Explain what is meant by 'component depreciation' and its status under international accounting standards.

(b) Trin, a limited liability company, owns its business premises. It has just installed extensive special-ised machinery and fittings in the premises. The estimated remaining useful life is 10 years for the building and 6 years for the machinery and fittings. Trin knows that decommissioning the machinery and fittings in 6 years' time will cost around $910,000 at current prices.

Required:

Explain, with reasons, how Trin should account for the costs of decommissioning its machinery and fittings.

(c) Cozz, a limited liability company, has an asset, purchased on 1 November 2002, which was reported in its balance sheet as at 1 November 2006 as follows:

	$
Cost	240,000
Accumulated depreciation	118,000
	122,000

The accumulated depreciation figure is made up as follows:

	$
Four years' depreciation based on the asset's estimated life of 12 years	80,000
Impairment recognised during the year ended 31 October 2005	20,000
Impairment recognised during the year ended 31 October 2006	18,000
	118,000

As at 31 October 2007 there was no change to the estimate of this asset's economic life or residual value. The asset's recoverable amount was estimated to be $125,000 as at 31 October 2007. Cozz reports this class of assets at historical cost.

Required:

What charge will Cozz make in its income statement for the year ended 31 October 2007 for this asset and how will the asset be reported in the balance sheet as at 31 October 2007?

(d) The following is the summarised balance sheet of Grimsel, a limited liability company, as at 31 October 2007.

		$000
ASSETS		
Non-current assets:		
Property, plant and equipment		7,540
Current assets:		
Inventory	2,230	
Receivables	4,120	
Cash	430	
		6,780
		14,320
LIABILITIES AND EQUITY		
Current liabilities		3,775
Non-current liabilities		12,500
Equity:		
Issued share capital	5,000	
Accumulated losses	6,955	
		(1,955)
		14,320

Grimsel has been a very successful company in its time. However, a series of losses due to a declining share in the market and demands from its bankers for repayment of significant bank debt included in current and non-current liabilities have left its shareholders keen to sell.

Brenner, another limited liability company, operates in the same line of business as Grimsel. Brenner has been very successful and sees an opportunity to acquire Grimsel at a bargain price.

Brenner has successfully concluded negotiations with Grimsel and has agreed a price of $2,000,000 for all the issued share capital of Grimsel.

The following additional information is available:

(i) The value of all the assets and liabilities identified in Grimsel's balance sheet were agreed as fair values for the purposes of the purchase with the exception of the following assets:

Fair values	$000
Property, plant and equipment	8,000
Inventory	2,000
Receivables	3,710

(ii) Grimsel has a deferred income tax asset of $2,200,000. This is not shown in Grimsel's balance sheet because it was unlikely that Grimsel would be able to recover this amount because of its continuing losses. Brenner is trading profitably in the same type of business and will be able to realise this benefit.

(iii) Grimsel has significant patents which were internally developed. These patents are still useful and an independent valuer has given them a fair value of $1,000,000.

(iv) Brenner will also take over Grimsel's customer list. This is a sensitive area. While the customer list was not of much value to Grimsel, the directors of Brenner feel that it could be of significant value but wish to continue keeping it off the balance sheet. An independent valuer has estimated the fair value of the customer list to Brenner as $1,500,000.

Required:
Applying the rules in IFRS 3 calculate the amount of goodwill arising on the acquisition of Grimsel by Brenner.

(e) Summarise the guidance in IFRS 3 when goodwill turns out to be a negative.

(The Association of International Accountants)

Question 9

Ross Neale is the divisional accountant for the Research and Development division of Critical Pharmaceuticals PLC. He is discussing the third-quarter results with Tina Snedden who is the manager of the division. The conversation focuses on the fact that whilst they have already fully committed the development capital expenditure budget for the year, the annual expense budget for research is well under spent because of the staff shortages which occurred in the last quarter. Tina mentions that she is under pressure to meet or exceed her expense budgets this year as the industry is renegotiating prescription costs this year and don't want to be seen to be too profitable.

Ross suggests that there are several strategies they could employ namely:

(a) Several of the subcontractors have us as their largest customer and so we could ask them to describe the services in the fourth quarter, which are essentially development cost, as research costs.

(b) We could ask them to charge us in advance for research work that will be required in quarter one next year without mentioning that it is an advance in documentation. That would be good for them as it would improve their cash flow and it would guarantee that they would get the work next year.

(c) We could ask some of the subcontractors on development projects to charge us in first quarter next year and we could hold out to them that we would give them some better priced projects in next year to compensate them for the interest incurred as a result of the delayed payment.

Required:
Discuss the advantages and disadvantages of adopting these strategies.

Question 10

James Bright has just taken up the position of managing director following the unsatisfactory achievements of the previous incumbent. James arrives as the accounts for the previous year are being finalised. James wants the previous performance to look poor so that whatever he achieves will look good in comparison. He knows that if he can write off more expenses in the previous year, he will have lower expenses in his first year and possibly a lower asset base. He gives directions to the accountants to write off as many bad debts as possible and to make sure accruals can be as high as they can get past the auditors. Further, he wants all brand name assets reviewed using assumptions that the sales levels achieved during the economic downturn are only going to improve slightly over the foreseeable future. Also he mentions that the cost of capital has risen over the period of the financial crisis so the projected benefits are to be discounted at a higher rate. Preferably at a much higher rate than that used in the previous reviews!

Required:
Discuss the accountant's professional responsibility and any ethical questions arising in this case.

References

1 IAS 38 *Intangible Assets*, IASC, revised March 2004.

2 *Ibid.*, para. 54.

3 *Ibid.*, para. 56.

4 *Ibid.*, para. 55.

5 *Ibid.*, para. 58.

6 *Ibid.*, para. 59.

7 B. Nixon and A. Lonie, 'Accounting for R&D: the need for change', *Accountancy*, February 1990, p. 91; B. Nixon, 'R&D disclosure: SSAP 13 and after', *Accountancy*, February 1991, pp. 72–73.

8 A. Goodacre and J. McGrath, 'An experimental study of analysts' reactions to corporate R&D expenditure', *British Accounting Review*, 1997, 29, pp. 155–179.

9 B. Nixon, 'The accounting treatment of research and development expenditure: views of UK company accountants', *European Accounting Review*, 1997, vol. 6, no. 2, pp. 265–277.

10 *Ibid.*

11 Li Li Eng, Hong Kiat Teo, 'The relation between annual report disclosures, analysts' earnings forecast and analysts following: evidence from Singapore', *Pacific Accounting Review*, 1999, vol. 121, no, 1/2, pp. 21–239.

12 *Statement of Intent: Comparability of Financial Statements*, IASC, 1990.

13 IAS 38 *Intangible Assets*, IASC, revised March 2004.

14 IRS 38 *Intangible Assets*, IASC, revised March 2004, para. 126.

15 IFRS 3 *Business Combinations*, IASB, 2004, para. 51.

16 *The Framework for the Preparation and Presentation of Financial Statements*, IASB, April 2001, para. 94.

17 *Ibid.*, para. 119.

18 *Ibid.*, para. 118.

19 *Ibid.*, para. 122.

20 *Ibid.*, para. 126.

21 www.interbrand.com/best_global_brands.aspx

22 P. Barwise, C. Higson, A. Likierman and P. Marsh, *Accounting for Brands*, ICAEW, June 1989; M. Cooper and A. Carey, 'Brand valuation in the balance', *Accountancy*, June 1989.

23 A. Pizzey, 'Healing the rift', *Certified Accountant*, October 1990.

24 'Finance directors say yes to brand valuation', *Accountancy*, January 1990, p. 12.

25 M. Moorhouse, 'Brands debate: wake up to the real world', *Accountancy*, July 1990, p. 30.

26 http://group.hugoboss.com/en/faq_special_dividend.htm

27 M. Gerry, 'Companies ignore value of brands', *Accountancy Age*, March 2000, p. 4.

28 IAS 38 *Intangible Assets*, IASC, revised March 2004, para. 63.

29 www.wipo.org

30 Great Britain, White Paper, *Our Competitive Future: Building the Knowledge Driven Economy*, London, HMSO, 1998.

31 R.J. Gallafent, N.A. Eastaway and V.A. Dauppe, *Intellectual Property Law and Taxation*, Longman, London, 1992.

32 www.riaa.com-news-filings-pdf-napster-PlaintiffsSJM.pdf.url

33 Derek Binney, 'The knowledge management spectrum – a technique for optimising knowledge management strategies', *Journal of Knowledge Management*, vol. 5, no. 1, 2001, pp. 33–42.

34 OECD, *Final Report: Measuring and Reporting Intellectual Capital: Experience, Issues and Prospects*, Paris: OECD, 2000.

35 J. Guthrie and R. Petty, 'Knowledge management: the information revolution has created the need for a codified system of gathering and controlling knowledge', *Company Secretary*, January 1999, vol. 9, no. 1, pp. 38–41; R. Tissen *et al.*, *Value-Based Knowledge Management*, Longman Nederland BV, 1998, pp. 25–44.

36 OECD, 'Guidelines and instructions for OECD Symposium', International Symposium Measuring and Reporting Intellectual Capital: Experiences, Issues and Prospects, June 1999, Amsterdam, OECD, Paris.

37 J. Guthrie, 'Measuring up to change', *Financial Management*, December 2000, CIMA, London, p. 11.

38 J. Unerman, J. Guthrie and M. Striukova, *UK Reporting of Intellectual Capital*, ICAEW, 2007, www.icaew.co.uk

39 R. Paterson, 'Will FRS 10 hit the target?', *Accountancy*, February 1998, pp. 74–75.

40 M. Moorhouse, 'Brands debate: wake up to the real world', *Accountancy*, July 1990, p. 30.

41 P. Barwise, C. Higson, A. Likierman and P. Marsh, *Accounting for Brands*, ICAEW, June 1989; M. Cooper and A. Carey, 'Brand valuation in the balance', *Accountancy*, June 1989.

CHAPTER 18

Inventories

18.1 Introduction

The main purpose of this chapter is to explain the accounting principles involved in the valuation of inventory and biological assets.

Objectives

After finishing this chapter, you should be able to:

- define inventory in accordance with IAS 2;
- explain why valuation has been controversial;
- describe acceptable valuation methods;
- describe procedure for ascertaining cost;
- calculate inventory value;
- explain how inventory could be used for creative accounting;
- explain IAS 41 provisions relating to agricultural activity;
- calculate biological value.

18.2 Inventory defined

IAS 2 *Inventories* defines inventories as assets:

(a) held for sale in the ordinary course of business;

(b) in the process of production for such sale;

(c) in the form of materials or supplies to be consumed in the production process or in the rendering of services.[1]

The valuation of inventory involves:

(a) the establishment of physical existence and ownership;

(b) the determination of unit costs;

(c) the calculation of provisions to reduce cost to net realisable value, if necessary.[2]

The resulting evaluation is then disclosed in the financial statements.

These definitions appear to be very precise. We shall see, however, that although IAS 2 was introduced to bring some uniformity into financial statements, there are many areas where professional judgement must be exercised. Sometimes this may distort the financial statements to such an extent that we must question whether they do represent a 'true and fair' view.

18.3 The controversy

The valuation of inventory has been a controversial issue in accounting for many years. The inventory value is a crucial element not only in the computation of profit, but also in the valuation of assets for statement of financial position purposes.

Figure 18.1 presents information relating to Coats Viyella plc. It shows that the inventory is material in relation to total assets and pre-tax profits. In relation to the profits we can see that an error of 4% in the 2001 interim report inventory value would potentially cause the profits for the group to change from a pre-tax profit to a pre-tax loss. As inventory is usually a multiple rather than a fraction of profit, inventory errors may have a disproportionate effect on the accounts. Valuation of inventory is therefore crucial in determining earnings per share, net asset backing for shares and the current ratio. Consequently, the basis of valuation should be consistent, so as to avoid manipulation of profits between accounting periods, and comply with generally accepted accounting principles, so that profits are comparable between different companies.

Unfortunately, there are many examples of manipulation of inventory values in order to create a more favourable impression. By increasing the value of inventory at the year-end, profit and current assets are automatically increased (and vice versa). Of course, closing inventory of one year becomes opening inventory of the next, so profit is thereby reduced. But such manipulation provides opportunities for profit-smoothing and may be advantageous in certain circumstances, e.g. if the company is under threat of takeover.

Figure 18.2 illustrates the point. Simply by increasing the value of inventory in year 1 by £10,000, profit (and current assets) is increased by a similar amount. Even if the two values are identical in year 2, such manipulation allows profit to be 'smoothed' and £10,000 profit switched from year 2 to year 1.

According to normal accrual accounting principles, profit is determined by matching costs with related revenues. If it is unlikely that the revenue will in fact be received, prudence dictates that the irrecoverable amount should be written off immediately against current revenue.

It follows that inventory should be valued at cost less any irrecoverable amount. But what is cost? Entities have used a variety of methods of determining costs, and these are explored later in the chapter. There have been a number of disputes relating to the valuation of inventory which affected profits (e.g. the AEI/GEC merger of 1967).[3] Naturally, such circumstances tend to come to light with a change of management, but it was considered important that a definitive statement of accounting practice be issued in an attempt to standardise treatment.

Figure 18.1 Coats Viyella plc

	2000	2001 (Half year)
Pre-tax profits (losses) (£m)	(29.9)	9.9
Inventory(£m)	304.2	320.2
Total assets (£m)	1,321.8	1,310.4

Figure 18.2 Inventory values manipulated to smooth income

		Year 1		Year 1 With inventory inflated
Sales		100,000		100,000
Opening inventory	—		—	
Purchases	65,000		65,000	
Less: Closing inventory	5,000		15,000	
COST OF SALES		60,000		50,000
PROFIT		40,000		50,000

		Year 2		Year 2 With inventory inflated
Sales		150,000		150,000
Opening inventory	5,000		15,000	
Purchases	100,000		100,000	
	105,000		115,000	
Less: Closing inventory	15,000		15,000	
COST OF SALES		90,000		100,000
PROFIT		60,000		50,000

18.4 IAS 2 *Inventories*

No area of accounting has produced wider differences in practice than the computation of the amount at which inventory is stated in financial accounts. An accounting standard on the subject needs to define the practices, to narrow the differences and variations in those practices and to ensure adequate disclosure in the accounts.

IAS 2 requires that the amount at which inventory is stated in periodic financial statements should be the total of the lower of cost and net realisable value of the separate items of inventory or of groups of similar items. The standard also emphasises the need to match costs against revenue, and it aims, like other standards, to achieve greater uniformity in the measurement of income as well as improving the disclosure of inventory valuation methods. To an extent, IAS 2 relies on management to choose the most appropriate method of inventory valuation for the production processes used and the company's environment. Various methods of valuation are theoretically available, including FIFO, LIFO and weighted average or any similar method (see below). In selecting the most suitable method, management must exercise judgement to ensure that the methods chosen provide the fairest practical approximation to cost. IAS 2 does not allow the use of LIFO because it often results in inventory being stated in the statement of financial position at amounts that bear little relation to recent cost levels.

At the end of the day, even though there is an International Accounting Standard in existence, the valuation of inventory can provide areas of subjectivity and choice to management. We will return to this theme many times in the following sections of this chapter.

18.5 Inventory valuation

The valuation rule outlined in IAS 2 is difficult to apply because of uncertainties about what is meant by cost (with some methods approved by IAS 2 and others not) and what is meant by net realisable value.

18.5.1 Methods acceptable under IAS 2

The acceptable methods of inventory valuation include FIFO, AVCO and standard cost.

First-in-first-out (FIFO)

Inventory is valued at the most recent 'cost', since the cost of oldest inventory is charged out first, whether or not this accords with the actual physical flow. FIFO is illustrated in Figure 18.3.

Average cost (AVCO)

Inventory is valued at a 'weighted average cost', i.e. the unit cost is weighted by the number of items carried at each 'cost', as shown in Figure 18.4. This is popular in organisations holding a large volume of inventory at fluctuating 'costs'. The practical problem of actually recording and calculating the weighted average cost has been overcome by the use of sophisticated computer software.

Figure 18.3 First-in-first-out method (FIFO)

	Receipts			Issues			Balance		
Date	Quantity	Rate	£	Quantity	Rate	£	Quantity	Rate	£
January	10	15	150				10		150
February				8	15	120	2		30
March	10	17	170				12		200
April	20	20	400				32		600
May				2	15	30			
				10	17	170			
				12	20	240			
				Cost of goods sold		560			
				Inventory			8	20	160

Figure 18.4 Average cost method (AVCO)

	Receipts			Issues			Balance		
Date	Quantity	Rate	£	Quantity	Rate	£	Quantity	Rate	£
January	10	15	150				10		150
February				8	15	120	2		30
March	10	17	170				12		200
April	20	20	400				32		600
May				24	18.75	450			600
				Cost of goods sold		570			
				Inventory			8	18.75	150

The following is an extract from the J Sainsbury plc 2008 Annual Report:

Inventories
Inventories are valued at the lower of cost and net realizable value. Inventories at warehouses are valued on a first-in, first-out basis. Those at retail outlets are valued at calculated average cost prices. Cost includes all direct expenditure and other appropriate attributable costs incurred in bringing inventories to their present location and condition.

Standard cost
In many cases this is the only way to value manufactured goods in a high-volume/high-turnover environment. However, the standard is acceptable only if it approximates to actual cost. This means that variances need to be reviewed to see if they affect the standard cost and for inventory evaluation.

Retail method
IAS 2 recognises that an acceptable method of arriving at cost is the use of selling price, less an estimated profit margin. This method is only acceptable if it can be demonstrated that the method gives a reasonable approximation of the actual cost.

IAS 2 does not recommend any specific method. This is a decision for each organisation based upon sound professional advice and the organisation's unique operating conditions.

18.5.2 Methods rejected by IAS 2

Methods rejected by IAS 2 include LIFO and (by implication) replacement cost.

Last-in-first-out (LIFO)

The cost of the inventory most recently received is charged out first at the most recent 'cost'. The practical upshot is that the inventory value is based upon an 'old cost', which may bear little relationship to the current 'cost'. LIFO is illustrated in Figure 18.5.

Figure 18.5 Last-in-first-out method (LIFO)

Date	Receipts Quantity	Rate	£	Issues Quantity	Rate	£	Balance Quantity	Rate	£
January	10	15	150				10		150
February				8	15	120	2		30
March	10	17	170				12		200
April	20	20	400				32		600
May				20	20	400			
				4	17	68			
				Cost of goods sold		588			
				Inventory			8		132

May closing balance = [(2 × 15) + (6 × 17)]

US companies commonly use the LIFO method as illustrated by this extract from the Wal-Mart Stores Inc 2008 Annual Report:

Inventories

The Company values inventories at the lower of cost or market as determined primarily by the retail method of accounting, using the last-in, first-out ('LIFO') method for substantially all of the Wal-Mart Stores segment's merchandise inventories. Sam's Club merchandise and merchandise in our distribution warehouses are valued based on the weighted average cost using the LIFO method. Inventories of foreign operations are primarily valued by the retail method of accounting, using the first-in, first-out ('FIFO') method. At January 31, 2008 and 2007, our inventories valued at LIFO approximate those inventories as if they were valued at FIFO.

If the LIFO method were to give a result significantly different from that reported using FIFO, then the effect would have to be quantified as in the Wal-Mart 2001 Annual Report:

	2001	2000
	$m	$m
Inventories at replacement cost	21,644	20,171
Less LIFO reserve	202	378
Inventories at LIFO cost	21,442	19,793

The company's summary of significant accounting policies stated that the company used the retail LIFO method. The LIFO reserve shows the cumulative, pre-tax effect on income between the results obtained using LIFO and the results obtained using a more current cost inventory valuation method (e.g. FIFO) – this gave an indication of how much higher profits would have been if FIFO were used.

Replacement cost

The inventory is valued at the current cost of the individual item (i.e. the cost to the organisation of replacing the item) rather than the actual cost at the time of manufacture or purchase. This is an attractive idea since the 'value' of inventory could be seen as the cost at which a similar item could be currently acquired. The problem again is in arriving at a 'reliable' profit figure for the purposes of performance evaluation. Wild fluctuation of profit could occur simply because of such factors as the time of the year, the vagaries of the world weather system or the manipulation of market forces. Let us take three examples, involving coffee, oil and silver.

Coffee. Wholesale prices collapsed over three years (1999–2002) from nearly $2.40 per pound to just under 50 cents. This was the lowest level in thirty years and, allowing for the effects of inflation, coffee became uneconomic to sell and farmers resorted to burning their crop for fuel. The implication for financial reporting was that the objective was to increase the inventory unit cost by 100% by forcing the price back above $1 per pound. What value should be attached to the coffee inventory? 50 cents or the replacement cost of $1 which would create a profit equal to the existing inventory value?

Oil. When the Gulf Crisis of 1990 began, the cost of oil moved from around $13 per barrel to a high of around $29 per barrel in a short time. If oil companies had used replacement cost, this would have created huge fictitious profits. This might have resulted in higher tax payments and shareholders demanding dividends from a profit that existed only on paper. When the Gulf Crisis settled down to a quiet period (before the 1991 military action), the market price of oil dropped almost as dramatically as it had risen. This might have led to fictitious losses for companies in the following financial year with an ensuing loss of business confidence.

This scenario was not unique to the Gulf Crisis and we see the same situation arising with fluctuations in the price of Arab Light which moved from $8.74 per barrel on 31 December 1998 to $24.55 per barrel on 31 December 1999 and down to $17.10 on 31 December 2001 (www.eia.doe.gov). A similar surge occurred in 2008 with prices varying from $40 to $140.

Silver. In the early 1980s a Texan millionaire named Bunker Hunt attempted to make a 'killing' on the silver market by buying silver to force up the price and then selling at the high price to make a substantial profit. This led to remarkable scenes in the UK, with long lines of people outside jewellers wanting to sell items at much higher prices than their 'real' cost. Companies using silver as a raw material (e.g. jewellers, mirror manufacturers, and electronics companies, which use silver as a conductive element) would have been badly affected had they used replacement cost in a similar way to the preceding two cases. The 'price' of silver in effect doubled in a short time, but the Federal Authorities in the USA stepped in and the plan was defeated.

The use of replacement cost is not specifically prohibited by IAS 2 but is out of line with the basic principle underpinning the standard, which is to value inventory at the actual costs incurred in its purchase or production. The IASC *Framework for the Preparation and Presentation of Financial Statements* describes historical cost and current cost as two distinct measurement bases and where a historical cost measurement base is used for assets and liabilities the use of replacement cost is inconsistent.

Although LIFO does not have IAS 2 approval, it is still used in practice. For example, LIFO is commonly used by UK companies with US subsidiaries, since LIFO is the main method of inventory valuation in the USA.

18.5.3 Procedure to ascertain cost

Having decided upon the accounting policy of the company, there remains the problem of ascertaining the cost. In a retail environment, the 'cost' is the price the organisation had to pay to acquire the goods, and it is readily established by reference to the purchase invoice from the supplier. However, in a manufacturing organisation the concept of cost is not as simple. Should we use prime cost, or production cost, or total cost? IAS 2 attempts to help by defining cost as 'all costs of purchase, costs of conversion and other costs incurred in bringing the inventories to their present location and condition'.

In a manufacturing organisation each expenditure is taken to include three constituents: direct materials, direct labour and appropriate overhead.

Direct materials

These include not only the costs of raw materials and component parts, but also the costs of insurance, handling (special packaging) and any import duties. An additional problem is waste and scrap. For instance, if a process inputs 100 tonnes at £45 per tonne, yet outputs only 90 tonnes, the output's inventory value **must** be £4,500 (£45 × 100) and not £4,050 (90 × £45). (This assumes the 10 tonnes loss is a normal, regular part of the process.) An adjustment may be made for the residual value of the scrap/waste material, if any. The treatment of component parts will be the same, provided they form part of the finished product.

Direct labour

This is the cost of the actual production in the form of gross pay and those incidental costs of employing the direct workers (employer's national insurance contributions, additional pension contributions, etc.). The labour costs will be spread over the goods' production.

Appropriate overhead

It is here that the major difficulties arise in calculating the true cost of the product for inventory valuation purposes. Normal practice is to classify overheads into five types and decide whether to include them in inventory. The five types are as follows:

- Direct overheads – subcontract work, royalties.
- Indirect overheads – the cost of running the factory and supporting the direct workers, and the depreciation of capital items used in production.
- Administration overheads – the office costs and salaries of senior management.
- Selling and distribution overheads – advertising, delivery costs, packaging, salaries of sales personnel, and depreciation of capital items used in the sales function.
- Finance overheads – the cost of borrowing and servicing debt.

We will look at each of these in turn, to demonstrate the difficulties that the accountant experiences.

Direct overheads. These should normally be included as part of 'cost'. But imagine a situation where some subcontract work has been carried out on *some* of a company's products because of a capacity problem (i.e. the factory could normally do the work, but due to a short-term problem some of the work has been subcontracted at a higher price/cost). In theory, those items subject to the subcontract work should have a higher inventory value than 'normal' items. However, in practice, the difficulty of identifying such 'subcontracted' items is so great that many companies do not include such non-routine subcontract work in the inventory value as a direct overhead. For example, if a factory produces 1,000,000 drills per month and 1,000 of them have to be sent out because of a machine breakdown, since all the drills are identical it would be very costly and time-consuming to treat the 1,000 drills differently from the other 999,000. Hence the subcontract work would *not* form part of the overhead for inventory valuation purposes (in such an organisation, the standard cost approach would be used when valuing inventory). On the other hand, in a customised car firm producing twenty vehicles per month, special subcontract work would form part of the inventory value because it is readily identifiable to individual units of inventory.

To summarise, any regular, routine direct overhead will be included in the inventory valuation, but a non-routine cost could present difficulties, especially in a high-volume/high-turnover organisation.

Indirect overheads. These always form part of the inventory valuation, as such expenses are incurred in support of production. They include factory rent and rates, factory power and depreciation of plant and machinery; in fact, any indirect factory-related cost, including the warehouse costs of storing completed goods, will be included in the value of inventory.

Administration overheads. This overhead is in respect of the whole business, so only that portion easily identifiable to production should form part of the inventory valuation. For instance, the costs of the personnel or wages department could be apportioned to production on a head-count basis and that element would be included in the inventory valuation. Any production-specific administration costs (welfare costs, canteen costs, etc.) would also be included in the inventory valuation. If the expense cannot be identified as forming part of the production function, it will not form part of the inventory valuation.

Selling and distribution overheads. These costs will not normally be included in the inventory valuation as they are incurred after production has taken place. However, if the goods are on a 'sale or return' basis and are on the premises of the customer but remain the supplier's property, the delivery and packing costs will be included in the inventory value of goods held on a customer's premises.

An additional difficulty concerns the modern inventory technique of 'just-in-time' (JIT). Here, the customer does not keep large inventories, but simply 'calls off' inventory from the supplier and is invoiced for the items delivered. There is an argument for the inventory still in the hands of the supplier to bear more of this overhead within its valuation, since the only selling and distribution overhead to be charged/incurred is delivery. The goods have in fact been sold, but ownership has not yet changed hands. As JIT becomes more popular, this problem may give accountants and auditors much scope for debate.

Finance overheads. Normally these overheads would never be included within the inventory valuation because they are not normally identifiable with production. In a job-costing context, however, it might be possible to use some of this overhead in inventory valuation. Let us take the case of an engineering firm being requested to produce a turbine engine, which requires parts/components to be imported. It is logical for the financial charges for these imports (e.g. exchange fees or fees for letters of credit) to be included in the inventory valuation.

Thus it can be seen that the identification of the overheads to be included in inventory valuation is far from straightforward. In many cases it depends upon the judgement of the accountant and the unique operating conditions of the organisation.

In addition to the problem of deciding **whether** the five types of overhead should be included, there is the problem of deciding **how much** of the total overhead to include in the inventory valuation at the year-end. IAS 2 stipulates the use of 'normal activity' when making this decision on overheads. The vast majority of overheads are 'fixed', i.e. do not vary with activity, and it is customary to share these out over a normal or expected output.

The following is an extract from the Agrana Group 2007/8 Annual Report:

Inventories

Inventories are measured at the lower of cost of purchase and/or conversion and net selling price. The weighted average formula is used. In accordance with IAS 2, the conversion costs of unfinished and finished products include – in addition to directly attributable unit costs – reasonable proportions of the necessary material costs and production overheads inclusive of depreciation of manufacturing plant (based on the assumption of normal capacity utilisation) as well as production-related administrative costs. Financing costs are not taken into account. To the extent that inventories are at risk because of prolonged storage or reduced saleability, a write-down is recognised.

If this expected output is not reached, it is not acceptable to allow the actual production to bear the full overhead for inventory purposes. A numerical example will illustrate this:

Overhead for the year	£200,000	
Planned activity	10,000	units
Closing inventory	3,000	units
Direct costs	£2	per unit
Actual activity	6,000	units

Inventory value based on actual activity

Direct costs	3,000 × £2	£6,000
Overhead	$\dfrac{3,000 \times £200,000}{6,000}$	£100,000
Closing inventory value		£106,000

Inventory value based on planned or normal activity

Direct cost	$3,000 \times £2$	£6,000
Overhead	$\dfrac{3,000 \times £200,000}{10,000}$	£60,000
Closing inventory value		£66,000

Comparing the value of inventory based upon actual activity with the value based upon planned or normal activity, we have a £40,000 difference. This could be regarded as increasing the current year's profit by carrying forward expenditure of £40,000 to set against the following year's profit.

The problem occurs because of the organisation's failure to meet expected output level (6,000 actual versus 10,000 planned). By adopting the **actual activity basis**, the organisation makes a profit out of failure. This cannot be an acceptable position when evaluating performance. Therefore, IAS 2 stipulates **the planned or normal activity model** for inventory valuation. The failure to meet planned output could be due to a variety of sources (e.g. strikes, poor weather, industrial conditions); the cause, however, is classed as abnormal or non-routine, and all such costs should be excluded from the valuation of inventory.

18.5.4 What is meant by net realisable value?

We have attempted to identify the problems of arriving at the true meaning of cost for the purpose of inventory valuation. Net realisable value is an alternative method of inventory valuation if 'cost' does not reflect the true value of the inventory. Prudence dictates that net realisable value will be used if it is lower than the 'cost' of the inventory (however that may be calculated). These occasions will vary among organisations, but can be summarised as follows:

- There is a permanent fall in the market price of inventory. Short-term fluctuations should not cause net realisable value to be implemented.

- The organisation is attempting to dispose of high inventory levels or excessively priced inventory to improve its liquidity position (quick ratio/acid test ratio) or reduce its inventory holding costs. Such high inventory volumes or values are primarily a result of poor management decision making.

- The inventory is physically deteriorating or is of an age where the market is reluctant to accept it. This is a common feature of the food industry, especially with the use of 'sell by' dates in the retail environment.

- Inventory suffers obsolescence through some unplanned development. (Good management should never be surprised by obsolescence.) This development could be technical in nature, or due to the development of different marketing concepts within the organisation or a change in market needs.

- The management could decide to sell the goods at 'below cost' for sound marketing reasons. The concept of a 'loss leader' is well known in supermarkets, but organisations also sell below cost when trying to penetrate a new market or as a defence mechanism when attacked.

Such decisions are important and the change to net realisable value should not be undertaken without considerable forethought and planning. Obsolescence should be a decision based upon sound market intelligence and not a managerial 'whim'. The auditors of companies always examine such decisions to ensure they were made for sound business reasons. The opportunities for fraud in such 'price-cutting' operations validate this level of external control.

Realisable value is, of course, the price the organisation receives for its inventory from the market. However, getting this inventory to market may involve additional expense and effort in repackaging, advertising, delivery and even repairing of damaged inventory. This additional cost must be deducted from the realisable value to arrive at the net realisable value.

A numerical example will demonstrate this concept:

Item	Cost (£)	Net realisable value (£)	Inventory value (£)
1 No. 876	7,000	9,000	7,000
2 No. 997	12,000	12,500	12,000
3 No. 1822	8,000	4,000	4,000
4 No. 2076	14,000	8,000	8,000
5 No. 4732	27,000	33,000	27,000
	(a) 68,000	(b) 66,500	(c) 58,000

The inventory value chosen for the accounts is (c) £58,000, although each item is assessed individually.

18.6 Work-in-progress

Inventory classified as work-in-progress (WIP) is mainly found in manufacturing organisations and is simply the production that has not been completed by the end of the accounting period.

The valuation of WIP must follow the same IAS 2 rules and be the lower of cost or net realisable value. We again face the difficulty of deciding what to include in cost. The three basic classes of cost – direct materials, direct labour and appropriate overhead – will still form the basis of ascertaining cost.

18.6.1 Direct materials

It is necessary to decide what proportion of the total materials have been used in WIP. The proportion will vary with different types of organisation, as the following two examples illustrate:

- If the item is complex or materially significant (e.g. a custom-made car or a piece of specialised machinery), the WIP calculation will be based on actual recorded materials and components used to date.

- If, however, we are dealing with mass production, it may not be possible to identify each individual item within WIP. In such cases, the accountant will make a judgement and define the WIP as being x% complete in regard to raw materials and components. For example, a drill manufacturer with 1 million tools per week in WIP may decide that in respect of raw materials they are 100% complete; WIP then gets the full materials cost of one million tools.

In both cases **consistency** is vital so that, however WIP is valued, the same method will always be used.

18.6.2 Direct labour

Again, it is necessary to decide how much direct labour the items in WIP have actually used. As with direct materials, there are two broad approaches:

- Where the item of WIP is complex or materially significant, the actual time 'booked' or recorded will form part of the WIP valuation.

- In a mass production situation, such precision may not be possible and an accounting judgement may have to be made as to the average percentage completion in respect of direct labour. In the example of the drill manufacturer, it could be that, on average, WIP is 80% complete in respect of direct labour.

18.6.3 Appropriate overhead

The same two approaches as for direct labour can be adopted:

- With a complex or materially significant item, it should be possible to allocate the overhead actually incurred. This could be an actual charge (e.g. subcontract work) or an application of the appropriate overhead recovery rate (ORR). For example, if we use a direct labour hour recovery rate and we have an ORR of £10 per direct labour hour and the recorded labour time on the WIP item is twelve hours, then the overhead charge for WIP purposes is £120.

EXAMPLE ● A custom-car company making sports cars has the following costs in respect of No. 821/C, an unfinished car, at the end of the month:

Materials charged to job 821/C	£2,100
Labour 120 hours @ £4	£480
Overhead £22/DLH × 120 hours	£2,640
WIP value of 821/C	£5,220

This is an accurate WIP value provided *all* the costs have been accurately recorded and charged. The amount of accounting work involved is not great as the information is required by a normal job cost system. An added advantage is that the figure can be formally audited and proven.

- With mass production items, the accountant must either use a budgeted overhead recovery rate approach or simply decide that, in respect of overheads, WIP is $y\%$ complete.

For example, the following is an extract from the Palfinger AG 2006 Annual Report:

Inventories
Materials and production supplies are valued at floating average cost, or at a standard cost in the case of materials supplied by Group companies. Besides direct materials and production costs, goods from in-house production also contain appropriate shares of materials and production overheads. Valuation is at budgeted production costs.

EXAMPLE ● A company produces drills. The costs of a completed drill are:

	£	
Direct materials	2.00	
Direct labour	6.00	
Appropriate overhead	10.00	
Total cost	18.00	(for finished goods inventory value purposes)

The company accountant takes the view that for WIP purposes the following applies:

Direct material	100% complete
Direct labour	80% complete
Appropriate overhead	30% complete

Therefore, for one WIP drill:

Direct material	£2.00 × 100% = £2.00
Direct labour	£6.00 × 80% = £4.80
Appropriate overhead	£10.00 × 30% = £3.00
WIP value	£9.80

If the company has 100,000 drills in WIP, the value is:

100,000 × £9.80 = £980,000

This is a very simplistic view, but the principle can be adapted to cover more complex issues. For instance, there could be 200 different types of drill, but the same calculation can be done on each. Of course, sophisticated software makes the accountant's job mechanically easier.

This technique is particularly useful in processing industries, such as petroleum, brewing, dairy products or paint manufacture, where it might be impossible to identify WIP items precisely. The approach must be consistent and the role of the auditor in validating such practices is paramount.

18.7 Inventory control

The way in which inventory is physically controlled should not be overlooked. Discrepancies are generally of two types: disappearance through theft and improper accounting.[4] Management will, of course, be responsible for adequate systems of internal control, but losses may still occur through theft or lack of proper controls and recording. Inadequate systems of accounting may also cause discrepancies between the physical and book inventories, with consequent correcting adjustments at the year-end.

Many companies are developing in-house computer systems or using bought-in packages to account for their inventories. Such systems are generally adequate for normal recording purposes, but they are still vulnerable to year-end discrepancies arising from errors in establishing the physical inventory on hand at the year-end, and problems connected with the paperwork and the physical movement of inventories.

A major cause of discrepancy between physical and book inventory is the 'cut-off' date. In matching sales with cost of sales, it may be difficult to identify exactly into which period of account certain inventory movements should be placed, especially when the annual inventory count lasts many days or occurs at a date other than the last day of the financial year. It is customary to make an adjustment to the inventory figure, as shown in Figure 18.6. This depends on an accurate record of movements between the inventory count date and the financial year-end.

Auditors have a special responsibility in relation to inventory control. They should look carefully at the inventory counting procedures and satisfy themselves that the accounting

Figure 18.6 Adjusted inventory figure

	£
Inventory on 7 January 20X1	XXX
Less: Purchases	(XXX)
Add: Sales	XXX
Inventory at 31 December 20X0	XXX

arrangements are satisfactory. For example, in September 1987 Harris Queensway announced an inventory reduction of some £15 million in projected profit caused by write-downs in its furniture division. It blamed this on the inadequacy of control systems to 'identify ranges that were selling and ensure their replacement'. Interestingly, at the preceding AGM, no hint of the overvaluation was given and the auditors insisted that 'the company had no problem from the accounting point of view'.[5]

In many cases the auditor will be present at the inventory count. Even with this apparent safeguard, however, it is widely accepted that sometimes an accurate physical inventory take is almost impossible. The value of inventory should nevertheless be based on the best information available; and the resulting disclosed figure should be acceptable and provide a true and fair view on a going concern basis.

In practice, errors may continue unidentified for a number of years,[6] particularly if there is a paper-based system in operation. This was evident when T.J. Hughes reduced its profit for the year ended January 2001 by £2.5–3 million from a forecast £8 million.

18.8 Creative accounting

No area of accounting provides more opportunities for subjectivity and creative accounting than the valuation of inventory. This is illustrated by the report *Fraudulent Financial Reporting: 1987–1997 – An Analysis of U.S. Public Companies* prepared by the Committee of Sponsoring Organizations of the Treadway Commission.[7] This report, which was based on the detailed analysis of approximately 200 cases of fraudulent financial reporting, identified that the fraud often involved the overstatement of revenues and assets with inventory fraud featuring frequently – assets were overstated by understating allowances for receivables, overstating the value of inventory and other tangible assets, and recording assets that did not exist.

This section summarises some of the major methods employed.

18.8.1 Year-end manipulations

There are a number of stratagems companies have followed to reduce the cost of goods sold by inflating the inventory figure. These include:

Manipulating cut-off procedures

Goods are taken into inventory but the purchase invoices are not recorded.

The authors of *Fraudulent Financial Reporting: 1987–1997 – An Analysis of U.S. Public Companies* found that over half the frauds involved overstating revenues by recording revenues prematurely or fictitiously and that such overstatement tended to occur right at the end of the year – hence the need for adequate cut-off procedures. This was illustrated by Ahold's experience in the USA where subsidiary companies took credit for bulk discounts allowed by suppliers before inventory was actually received.

Fictitious transfers

Year-end inventory is inflated by recording fictitious transfers of non-existent inventory, e.g. it was alleged by the SEC that certain officers of the Miniscribe Corporation had increased the company's inventory by recording fictitious transfers of nonexistent inventory from a Colorado location to overseas locations where physical inventory counting would be more difficult for the auditors to verify or the goods are described as being 'in transit'.[8]

Inaccurate inventory records

Where inventory records are poorly maintained it has been possible for senior management to fail to record material shrinkage due to loss and theft as in the matter of Rite Aid Corporation.[9]

Journal adjustments

In addition to suppressing purchase invoices, making fictitious transfers, failing to write off obsolete inventory or recognise inventory losses, the senior management may simply reduce the cost of goods sold by adjusting journal entries, e.g. when preparing quarterly reports by crediting cost of goods and debiting accounts payable.

18.8.2 Net realisable value (NRV)

Although the determination of net realisable value is dealt with extensively in the appendix to IAS 2, the extent to which provisions can be made to reduce cost to NRV is highly subjective and open to manipulation. A provision is an effective smoothing device and allows overcautious write-downs to be made in profitable years and consequent write-backs in unprofitable ones.

18.8.3 Overheads

The treatment of overheads has been dealt with extensively above and is probably the area that gives the greatest scope for manipulation. Including overhead in the inventory valuation has the effect of deferring the overhead's impact and so boosting profits. IAS 2 allows expenses incidental to the acquisition or production cost of an asset to be included in its cost. We have seen that this includes not only directly attributable production overheads, but also those which are indirectly attributable to production and interest on borrowed capital. IAS 2 provides guidelines on the classification of overheads to achieve an appropriate allocation, but in practice it is difficult to make these distinctions and auditors will find it difficult to challenge management on such matters.

The statement suggests that the allocation of overheads included in the valuation needs to be based on the company's normal level of activity. The cost of unused capacity should be written off in the current year. The auditor will insist that allocation should be based on normal activity levels, but if the company underproduces, the overhead per unit increases and can therefore lead to higher year-end values. The creative accountant will be looking for ways to manipulate these year-end values, so that in bad times costs are carried forward to more profitable accounting periods.

18.8.4 Other methods of creative accounting

Over- or understate quantities

A simple manipulation is to show more or less inventory than actually exists. If the commodity is messy and indistinguishable, the auditor may not have either the expertise or the will to verify measurements taken by the client's own employees. This lack of auditor measuring knowledge and involvement allowed one of the biggest frauds ever to take place, which became known as 'the great salad oil swindle'.[10]

Understate obsolete inventory

Another obvious ploy is to include, in the inventory valuation, obsolete or 'dead' inventory. Of course, such inventory should be written off. However, management may be 'optimistic' that it can be sold, particularly in times of economic recession. In high-tech industries, unrealistic values may be placed on inventory that in times of rapid development becomes obsolete quickly.

This can be highly significant, as in the case of Cal Micro.[11] On 6 February 1995, Cal Micro restated its financial results for fiscal year 1994. The bulk of the adjustments to Cal Micro's financial statements – all highly material – occurred in the areas of accounts inventory, accounts receivable and property and, from an originally reported net income of approximately $5.1 million for the year ended 30 June 1994, the restated allowance for additional inventory obsolescence decreased net income by approximately $9.3 million.

Lack of marketability

This is a problem that investors need to be constantly aware of, particularly when a company experiences a downturn in demand but a pressure to maintain the semblance of growth. An example is provided by Lexmark[12] which was alleged to have made highly positive statements regarding strong sales and growth for its printers although there was intense competition in the industry – the company reporting quarter after quarter of strong financial growth whereas the actual position appeared to be very different with unmarketable inventory in excess of $25 million to be written down in the fourth quarter of fiscal year 2001. The share price of a company that conceals this type of information is maintained and allows insiders to offload their shareholding on an unsuspecting investing public.

18.9 Audit of the year-end physical inventory count

The problems of accounting for inventory are highlighted at the company's year-end. This is when the closing inventory figure to be shown in both the statement of comprehensive income and statement of financial position is calculated. In practice, the company will assess the final inventory figure by physically counting all inventory held by the company for trade. The year-end inventory count is therefore an important accounting procedure, one in which the auditors are especially interested.

The auditor generally attends the inventory count to verify both the physical quantities and the procedure of collating those quantities. At the inventory count, values are rarely assigned to inventory items, so the problems facing the auditor relate to the identification of inventory items; their ownership; and their physical condition.

18.9.1 Identification of inventory items

The auditor will visit many companies in the course of a year and will spend a considerable time looking at accounting records. However, it is important for the auditor also to become familiar with each company's products by visiting the shop floor or production facilities during the audit. This makes identification of individual inventory items easier at the year-end. Distinguishing between two similar items can be crucial where there are large differences in value. For example, steel-coated brass rods look identical to steel rods, but their value to the company will be very different. It is important that they are not confused at inventory count because, once recorded on the inventory sheets, values are assigned, production carries on, and the error cannot be traced.

18.9.2 Ownership of inventory items

The year-end cut-off point is important to the final inventory figure, but the business activities continue regardless of the year-end, and some account has to be taken of this. Hence, the

Figure 18.7 Treatment of inventory items

Sales	In inventory	Loading bay
If invoiced to customer	Delete from inventory	Inventory not counted
If credited (i.e. returned)	Include	Include
If not invoiced/credited	Include unless accounting entry falls into this year	Include
Purchases		
If invoiced to company	Include in inventory	Include in inventory
If credited (i.e. to be returned)	Delete from inventory	Delete from inventory
If invoiced/credited	Include unless accounting entry falls into next year	Include

auditor must be aware that the recording of accounting transactions may not coincide with the physical flow of inventory. Inventory may be in one of two locations: included as part of inventory; or in the loading bay area awaiting dispatch or receipt. Its treatment will depend on several factors (see Figure 18.7). The auditor must be aware of all these possibilities and must be able to trace a sample of each inventory entry through to the accounting records, so that:

- if purchase is recorded, but not sale, the item must be in inventory;
- if sale is recorded, purchase must also be recorded and the item should not be in inventory.

18.9.3 Physical condition of inventory items

Inventory in premium condition has a higher value than damaged inventory. The auditor must ensure that the condition of inventory is recorded at inventory count, so that the correct value is assigned to it. Items that are damaged or have been in inventory for a long period will be written down to their net realisable value (which may be nil) as long as adequate details are given by the inventory counter. Once again, this is a problem of identification, so the auditor must be able to distinguish between, for instance, rolls of first quality and faulty fabric. Similarly, items that have been in inventory for several inventory counts may have little value, and further enquiries about their status should be made at the time of inventory count.

18.10 Published accounts

Disclosure requirements in IAS 2 have already been indicated. The standard requires the accounting policies that have been applied to be stated and applied consistently from year to year. Inventory should be sub-classified in the statement of financial position or in the notes to the financial statements so as to indicate the amounts held in each of the main categories in the standard statement of financial position formats. But will the ultimate user of those financial statements be confident that the information disclosed is reliable, relevant and useful? We have already indicated many areas of subjectivity and creative accounting, but are such possibilities material?

In 1982 Westwick and Shaw examined the accounts of 125 companies with respect to inventory valuation and its likely impact on reported profit.[13] The results showed that the effect on profit before tax of a 1% error in closing inventory valuation ranged from a low

Figure 18.8 Impact of a 5% change in closing inventory

Company:	1	2	3	4	5	6	7	8
	£m	£m	£m	£m	£m	£m	£m	£m
Actual inventory	390.0	428.0	1,154.0	509.0	509.0	280.0	360.0	232.0
Actual pre-tax profit	80.1	105.6	479.0	252.5	358.4	186.3	518.2	436.2
Change in pre-tax profit	19.5	21.4	57.7	25.2	25.5	14.0	18.0	11.6
Impact of a 5% change in closing inventory (%)								
(i) Pre-tax profit	24.3	20.0	12.0	10.0	7.1	7.5	3.5	2.7
(ii) Earnings per share	27.0	25.0	12.0	9.3	8.4	6.9	3.4	3.4

Key to companies:
1 Electrical retailer
2 Textile, etc., manufacturer
3 Brewing, public houses, etc.
4 Retailer – diversified
5 Pharmaceutical and retail chemist
6 Industrial paints and fibres
7 Food retailer
8 Food retailer

of 0.18% to a high of 25.9% (in one case) with a median of 2.26%. The industries most vulnerable to such errors were household goods, textiles, mechanical engineering, contracting and construction.

Clearly, the existence of such variations has repercussions for such measures as ROCE, EPS and the current ratio. The research also showed that, in a sample of audit managers, 85% were of the opinion that the difference between a pessimistic and an optimistic valuation of the same inventory could be more than 6%.

IAS 2 has since been strengthened and these results may not be so indicative of the present situation. However, using the same principle, let us take a random selection of eight companies' recent annual accounts, apply a 5% increase in the closing inventory valuation and calculate the effect on EPS (taxation is simply taken at 35% on the change in inventory).

Figure 18.8 shows that, in absolute terms, the difference in pre-tax profits could be as much as £57.7 million and the percentage change ranges from 2.7% to 24%. Of particular note is the change in EPS, which tends to be the major market indicator of performance. In the case of the electrical retailer (company 1), a 5% error in inventory valuation could affect EPS by as much as 27%. The inventory of such a company could well be vulnerable to such factors as changes in fashion, technology and economic recession.

18.11 Agricultural activity

18.11.1 The overall problem

Agricultural activity is subject to special considerations and so is governed by a separate IFRS, namely IAS 41. IAS 41 defines agricultural activity as 'the management by an entity of the biological transformation of biological assets for sale, into agricultural produce or into additional biological assets'. A biological asset is a living animal or plant.

The basic problem is that biological assets, and the produce derived from them (referred to in IAS 41 as 'agricultural produce'), cannot be measured using the cost-based concepts that form the bedrock of IAS 2 and IAS 16. This is because biological assets, such as cattle for example, are not usually purchased, they are born and develop into their current state. Therefore different accounting methods are necessary.

18.11.2 The recognition and measurement of biological assets and agricultural produce

IAS 41 states that an entity should recognise a biological asset or agricultural produce when:

● the entity controls the asset as a result of a past event;

● it is probable that future economic benefits associated with the asset will flow to the entity;

● the fair value or cost of the asset can be measured reliably.

Rather than the usual cost-based concepts of measurement that are used for assets, IAS 41 states that assets of this type should be measured at their fair value less estimated costs of sale. The only (fairly rare) exception to this general measurement principle is if the asset's fair value cannot be estimated reliably. In such circumstances a biological asset is measured at cost (if available). However market values would usually be available for biological assets and agricultural produce.

The following is an extract from the 2005 Holmen AB annual report:

Past practice was for Holmen's forest assets to be stated at acquisition cost adjusted for revaluations. According to IFRS, forest assets are to be divided into growing forest, which is stated in accordance with IAS 41, and land, which is stated in accordance with IAS 16. The application of IAS 41 means that growing forest is to be valued and stated at its fair value on each occasion the accounts are finalized. Changes in fair value are taken into the statement of comprehensive income. In the absence of market prices or other comparable values, biological assets are to be valued at the present value of the future cash flow from the assets. The land on which the trees are growing is valued at acquisition cost in accordance with IAS 16.

The change in financial reporting restatement can have a significant impact on the carrying value in the statement of financial position as shown in the Holmen 2004 restated statement of financial position:

Statement of financial position (MSEK)	31.12.2004	IFRS 3	IAS 41	Total
Assets				
Intangible fixed assets				
Goodwill	491	32		523
Other	36			36
Tangible fixed assets	12,153			12,153
Biological assets	6,201		2,421	8,622

An implication of the measurement principle that is used is that gains or losses on re-measurement will regularly arise. IAS 41 requires that these be taken to the statement of comprehensive income in the relevant period. Statement of comprehensive income amounts can arise from:

● the initial recognition of a biological asset or agricultural produce;

● the change in fair value of previously recognised amounts;

● the costs associated with the agricultural activity.

The following extracts are from the Precious Woods Group's 2005 Annual Report:

General Valuation Principles according to IAS 41
According to IAS 41, biological assets – in the case of Precious Woods, tree plantations – are to be valued annually at fair value. The gain or loss in fair value of these biological assets is reported in net profit. The measurement of biological growth in the field is an important element of this valuation. Initially, at the start of the plantation cycle, the fair value is equal to the standard costs of preparing and maintaining a plantation including the appropriate cost of capital, assuming efficient operations. Toward the end of the plantation cycle the fair value depends solely on the discounted vale of the expected harvest less estimated point-of-sale costs.

The statement of financial position values of the biological assets have developed as follows:

	$
Carrying amount at beginning of year	32,919,820
Net change in fair value of biological assets before harvest	3,743,660
Fair value biological assets harvested 2005	(133,623)
Personnel costs incurred during the year	1,186,661
Depreciation expense	120,267
Other general costs incurred during the year	387,416
Carrying amount end of year	**38,224,201**

18.11.3 An illustrative example

A farmer owned a dairy herd. At the start of the period the herd contained 100 animals that were two years old and fifty newly born calves. At the end of the period a further thirty calves were born. None of the herd died during the period. Relevant fair value details were as follows:

	Start of period	*End of period*
	$	$
Newly born calves	50	55
One-year-old animals	60	65
Two-year-old animals	70	75
Three-year-old animals	75	80

The change in the fair value of the herd is $3,400, made up as follows:

Fair value at end of the year = $100 \times \$80 + 50 \times \$65 + 30 \times \$55 = \$12,900$
Fair value at start of the year = $100 \times \$70 + 50 \times \$50 \qquad = \$9,500$

IAS 41 requires that the change in the fair value of the herd be reconciled as follows:

	$
Price change – opening newly born calves: $50(\$55 - \$50)$	250
Physical change of opening newly born calves: $50(\$65 - \$55)$	500
Price change of opening two-year-old animals: $100(\$75 - \$70)$	500
Physical change of opening two-year-old animals: $100(\$80 - \$75)$	500
Due to birth of new calves: $30 \times \$55$	1,650
Total change	**3,400**

The costs incurred in maintaining the herd would all be charged in the statement of comprehensive income in the relevant period.

18.11.4 Agricultural produce

Examples of agricultural produce would be milk from a dairy herd or crops from a cornfield. Such produce is sold by a farmer in the ordinary course of business and is inventory. The initial carrying value of the inventory at the point of 'harvest' is its fair value less costs to sell at that date. Agricultural entities then apply IAS 2 to the inventory using the initial carrying value as 'cost'.

18.11.5 Land

Despite its importance in agricultural activity, IAS 41 does not apply to agricultural land, which is accounted for in accordance with IAS 16. Where biological assets are physically attached to land (e.g. crops in a field) then it is often possible to compute the fair value of the biological assets by computing the fair value of the combined asset and deducting the fair value of the land alone.

18.11.6 Government grants relating to biological assets

As mentioned in Chapter 15 such grants are not subject to IAS 20 – the general standard on this subject. Under IAS 41 the IASB view is more consistent with the principles of the *Framework* than the provisions of IAS 20. Under IAS 41 grants are recognised as income when the entity becomes entitled to receive it. This removes the fairly dubious credit balance 'Deferred income' that arises under the IAS 20 approach and does not appear to satisfy the *Framework* definition of a liability.

Summary

Examples of differences in inventory valuation are not uncommon.[14] For example, in 1984, Fidelity, the electronic equipment manufacturer, was purchased for £13.4 million.[15] This price was largely based on the 1983/84 profit figure of £400,000. Subsequently, it was maintained that this 'profit' should actually be a loss of £1.3 million – a difference of £1.7 million. Much of this difference was attributable to inventory discrepancies. The claim was contested, but it does illustrate that a disparity can occur when important figures are left to 'professional judgement'.

Another case involved the selling of British Wheelset by British Steel, just before privatisation in 1988, at a price of £16.9 million.[16] It was claimed that the accounts 'were not drawn up on a consistent basis in accordance with generally accepted accounting practice'. If certain inventory provisions had been made, these would have resulted in a £5 million (30%) difference in the purchase price.

Other areas that cause difficulties to the user of published information are the capitalisation of interest and the reporting of write-downs on acquisition. Post-acquisition profits can be influenced by excessive write-downs of inventory on acquisition, which has the effect of increasing goodwill. The written-down inventory can eventually be sold at higher prices, thus improving post-acquisition profits.

Although legal requirements and IAS 2 have improved the reporting requirements, many areas of subjective judgement can have substantial effects on the reporting of financial information.

REVIEW QUESTIONS

1 Discuss why some form of theoretical pricing model is required for inventory valuation purposes.

2 Discuss the acceptability of the following methods of inventory valuation: LIFO; replacement cost.

3 Discuss the application of individual judgement in inventory valuation, e.g. changing the basis of overhead absorption.

4 Explain the criteria to be applied when selecting the method to be used for allocating costs.

5 Discuss the effect on work-in-progress and finished goods valuation if the net realisable value of the raw material is lower than cost at the statement of financial position date.

6 Discuss why the accurate valuation of inventory is so crucial if the financial statements are to show a true and fair view.

7 The following is an extract from the Interbrew 2007 Annual Report:

Inventories

Inventories are valued at the lower of cost and net realizable value. Cost includes expenditure incurred in acquiring the inventories and bringing them to their existing location and condition. The weighted average method is used in assigning the cost of inventories.

The cost of finished products and work in progress comprises raw materials, other production materials, direct labor, other direct cost and an allocation of fixed and variable overhead based on normal operating capacity. Net realizable value is the estimated selling price in the ordinary course of business, less the estimated completion and selling costs.

Discuss the possible effects on profits if the company did not use normal operating activity. Explain an alternative definition for net realisable value and discuss the criterion to be applied when making a policy choice.

8 The following is an extract from the 2007 Annual Report of SIPEF SA:

Auditor's Report

The statutory auditor has confirmed that his audit procedures, which have been substantially completed, have revealed no material adjustments that would have to be made to the accounting information included in this press release.

With regard to the valuation of the biological assets, the statutory auditor draws the reader's attention to the fact that, because of the inherent uncertainty associated with the valuation of the biological assets due to the volatility of the prices of the agricultural produce and the absence of a liquid market, their carrying value may differ from their realisable value.

Given the inherent uncertainty applying IAS 41, discuss (a) whether the pre-IAS 41 practice of value at historical cost would be preferable for the statement of financial position and (b) whether the new requirement to pass unrealised gains and losses through the statement of comprehensive income is more relevant to an investor.

EXERCISES

An extract from the solution is provided on the Companion Website (www.pearsoned.co.uk/elliott-elliott) for exercises marked with an asterisk (*).

Question 1

Sunhats Ltd manufactures patent hats. It carries inventory of these and sells to wholesalers and retailers via a number of salespeople. The following expenses are charged in the profit and loss account:

Wages of: Storemen and factory foremen

Salaries of: Production manager, personnel officer, buyer, salespeople, sales manager, accountant, company secretary

Other: Directors' fees, rent and rates, electric power, repairs, depreciation, carriage outwards, advertising, bad debts, interest on bank overdraft, development expenditure for new type of hat.

Required:

Which of these expenses can reasonably be included in the valuation of inventory?

* Question 2

Purchases of a certain product during July were:

July   1   100 units @ £10.00
     12   100 units @ £9.80
     15   50 units @ £9.60
     20   100 units @ £9.40

Units sold during the month were:

July   10   80 units
     14   100 units
     30   90 units

Required:

Assuming no opening inventories:
(i) Determine the cost of goods sold for July under three different valuation methods.
(ii) Discuss the advantages and/or disadvantages of each of these methods.
(iii) A physical inventory count revealed a shortage of five units. Show how you would bring this into account.

* Question 3

Alpha Ltd makes one standard article. You have been given the following information:

1   The inventory sheets at the year-end show the following items:

Raw materials:
100 tons of steel:
Cost £140 per ton
Present price £130 per ton

Finished goods:
100 finished units:
Cost of materials £50 per unit
Labour cost £150 per unit
Selling price £500 per unit

40 semi-finished units
Cost of materials £50 per unit
Labour cost to date £100 per unit
Selling price £500 per unit (completed)

10 damaged finished units:
Cost to rectify the damage £200 per unit
Selling price £500 per unit (when rectified)

2   Manufacturing overheads are 100% of labour cost.
Selling and distribution expenses are £60 per unit (mainly salespeople's commission and freight charges).

Required:
From the information in notes 1 and 2, state the amounts to be included in the statement of financial position of Alpha Ltd in respect of inventory. State also the principles you have applied.

Question 4

Beta Ltd commenced business on 1 January and is making up its first year's accounts. The company uses standard costs. The company owns a variety of raw materials and components for use in its manufacturing business. The accounting records show the following:

	Standard cost of purchases	Adverse (favourable) variances Price variance	Usage variance
	£	£	£
July	10,000	800	(400)
August	12,000	1,100	100
September	9,000	700	(300)
October	8,000	900	200
November	12,000	1,000	300
December	10,000	800	(200)
Cumulative figures for whole year	110,000	8,700	(600)

Raw materials control account balance at year-end is £30,000 (at standard cost).

Required:
The company's draft statement of financial position includes 'Inventories, at the lower of cost and net realisable value £80,000'. This includes raw materials £30,000: do you consider this to be acceptable? If so, why? If not, state what you consider to be an acceptable figure.

   (*Note:* for the purpose of this exercise, you may assume that the raw materials will realise more than cost.)

Question 5

The statement of comprehensive income of Bottom, a manufacturing company, for the year ending 31 January 20X2 is as follows:

	Bottom
	$000
Revenue	75,000
Cost of sales	(38,000)
Gross profit	37,000
Other operating expenses	(9,000)
Profit from operations	28,000
Investment income	
Finance cost	(4,000)
Profit before tax	24,000
Income tax expense	(7,000)
Net profit for the period	17,000

Note – accounting policies

Bottom has used the LIFO method of inventory valuation but the directors wish to assess the implications of using the FIFO method. Relevant details of the inventories of Bottom are as follows:

Date	Inventory valuation under:	
	FIFO	LIFO
	$000	$000
1 February 20X1	9,500	9,000
31 January 20X2	10,200	9,300

Requirement:

Re-draft the statement of comprehensive income of Bottom using the FIFO method of inventory valuation and explain how the change would need to be recognised in the published financial statements, if implemented.

Question 6

Agriculture is a key business activity in many parts of the world, particularly in developing countries. Following extensive discussions with, and funding from, the World Bank, the International Accounting Standards Committee (IASC) developed an accounting standard relating to agricultural activity. IAS 41 *Agriculture* was published in 2001 to apply to accounting periods beginning on or after 1 January 2003.

Sigma prepares financial statements to 30 September each year. On 1 October 2003 Sigma carried out the following transactions:

● Purchased a large piece of land for $20 million.

● Purchased 10,000 dairy cows (average age at 1 October 2003, two years) for $1 million.

● Received a grant of $400,000 towards the acquisition of the cows. This grant was non-returnable.

During the year ending 30 September 2004 Sigma incurred the following costs:

● $500,000 to maintain the condition of the animals (food and protection).

● $300,000 in breeding fees to a local farmer.

On 1 April 2004, 5,000 calves were born. There were no other changes in the number of animals during the year ended 30 September 2004. At 30 September 2004, Sigma had 10,000 litres of unsold milk in inventory. The milk was sold shortly after the year end at market prices.

Information regarding fair values is as follows:

Item	Fair value less point of sale costs		
	1 October 2003	1 April 2004	30 September 2004
	$	$	$
Land	20 m	22 m	24 m
New born calves (per calf)	20	21	22
Six-month-old calves (per calf)	23	24	25
Two-year-old cows (per cow)	90	92	94
Three-year-old cows (per cow)	93	95	97
Milk (per litre)	0.6	0.55	0.55

Required:

(a) Discuss how the IAS 41 requirements regarding the recognition and measurement of biological assets and agricultural produce are consistent with the IASC Framework for the Preparation and Presentation of Financial Statements.

(b) Prepare extracts from the statement of comprehensive income and the statement of financial position that show how the transactions entered into by Sigma in respect of the purchase and maintenance of the dairy herd would be reflected in the financial statements of the entity for the year ended 30 September 2004. You do not need to prepare a reconciliation of changes in the carrying amount of biological assets.

(ACCA DipIFR 2004)

References

1 IAS 2 *Inventories*, IASB, revised 2004.
2 'A guide to accounting standards – valuation of inventory and work-in-progress', *Accountants Digest*, Summer 1984.
3 M. Jones, 'Cooking the accounts', *Certified Accountant*, July 1988, p. 39.
4 T.S. Dudick, 'How to avoid the common pitfalls in accounting for inventory', *The Practical Accountant*, January/February 1975, p. 65.
5 *Certified Accountant*, October 1987, p. 7.
6 M. Perry, 'Valuation problems force FD to quit', *Accountancy Age*, 15 March 2001, p. 2.
7 The report appears on www.coso.org/index.htm.
8 See www.sec.gov/litigation/admin/34-41729.htm.
9 See www.sec.gov/litigation/admin/34-46099.htm.
10 E. Woolf, 'Auditing the stocks – part II', *Accountancy*, May 1976, pp. 108–110.
11 See www.sec.gov/litigation/admin/34-41720.htm.
12 See http://securities.stanford.edu/1022/LXK01-01/.
13 C. Westwick and D. Shaw, 'Subjectivity and reported profit', *Accountancy*, June 1982, pp. 129–131.
14 E. Woolf, 'Auditing the stocks – part I', *Accountancy*, April 1976, p. 106; 'Auditing the stocks – part II', *Accountancy*, May 1976, pp. 108–110.
15 K. Bhattacharya, 'More or less true, quite fair', *Accountancy*, December 1988, p. 126.
16 R. Northedge, 'Steel attacked over Wheelset valuation', *Daily Telegraph*, 2 January 1991, p. 19.

CHAPTER 19

Construction contracts

19.1 Introduction

The purpose of this chapter is to explain how IAS 11 *Construction Contracts* defines a construction contract and requires it to be recognised and measured in the financial statements. The chapter also considers the structure of public private partnerships that companies may enter into with government bodies, and considers the accounting issues and guidance that exists for contracts of this type.

Objectives

By the end of this chapter, you should be able to:

- identify when IAS 11 *Construction Contracts* is relevant;
- prepare the financial statements to reflect construction contracts appropriately;
- understand what public–private partnerships are and be able to understand how this type of arrangement is reflected in the financial statements.

19.2 The accounting issue for construction contracts

19.2.1 The future of revenue recognition

Accounting for construction and service contracts is a contentious area for the IASB and an area which is likely to see changes in the future as the IASB debates and revises its proposals on revenue recognition. Currently, IFRS has two approaches for recognising revenue: (i) an approach for goods which focuses on the point at which risks and rewards and control pass to the customer as being the basis for recognition, and (ii) an approach for service and construction contracts that recognises revenue over the period work is performed on a percentage completion basis. This percentage of completion approach is defined and explained in both IAS 11 and IAS 18 *Revenue* in its requirements for service contracts. In a discussion paper issued in December 2008 as a joint project with the FASB, the IASB has proposed a method of revenue recognition that attempts to define a principle that can be applied to all revenue for both goods and services and which therefore removes this dual approach. The basis proposed is that revenue basically should be recognised when the contract obligations to the customer have been fulfilled and control of the good or service has been passed to the customer.

The revised approach proposed gives particular problems in its application to service and construction contracts. In the sale of goods it is generally clear when the obligation to the customer has been fulfilled, usually when the good has been delivered and accepted by the customer. However, for service and construction contracts the position is much less clear. For example, it might be argued that the obligations to the customer have only been fulfilled on completion of a contract, or alternatively it might be argued that they are fulfilled as the services are performed. In its discussion paper the IASB highlights that the fulfilment of an obligation to a customer only occurs if the customer has control of the asset that they are receiving. For example, the paper distinguishes between construction work undertaken on the developer's land and construction work undertaken on the customer's land. In the case of construction work undertaken on the developer's land until the development is passed to the customer it is more likely to be viewed as an asset of the developer and therefore the construction work is enhancing the developer's asset and not giving rise to revenue for the developer during the construction phase.

The uncertainty over how to apply the proposed revenue approach to service and construction contracts has caused concern. In its summary of the responses provided to the discussion paper, the IASB highlights that 'many respondents express concern with construction contracts because legal title to, or physical possession of, the *completed* asset might not be transferred until the end of the contract'. Hence, revenue would not be recognised until that point. It thinks that this is inappropriate because it considers many of their contracts to be contracts for construction services that are provided over the contract term. It is unclear as yet how these concerns will be addressed within any revised standard, however, it does appear clear that the IASB believes that an approach based on performance of obligations is appropriate and will be introduced.

19.2.2 IAS 11 *Construction Contracts*

IAS 11 *Construction Contracts* defines a construction contract as:

> A contract specifically negotiated for the construction of an asset or a combination of assets that are closely inter-related or inter-dependent in terms of their design, technology and function or their ultimate purpose or use.

Some construction contracts are **fixed-price contracts**, where the contractor agrees to a fixed contract price, which in some cases is subject to cost escalation clauses. Other contracts are **cost-plus contracts**, where the contractor is reimbursed for allowable costs, plus a percentage of these costs or a fixed fee.

Construction contracts are normally assessed and accounted for individually. However, in certain circumstances construction contracts may be combined or segmented. Combination or segmentation is appropriate when:

● A group of contracts is negotiated as a single package and the contracts are performed together or in a continuous sequence (combination).

● Separate proposals have been submitted for each asset and the costs and revenues of each asset can be identified (segmentation).

A key accounting issue is when the revenues and costs (and therefore net income) under a construction contract should be recognised. There are two possible approaches:

- Only recognise net income when the contract is complete – the *completed contracts method*.
- Recognise a proportion of net income over the period of the contract – the *percentage of completion method*.

IAS 11 requires the latter approach, provided the overall contract result can be predicted with reasonable certainty.

19.3 Identification of contract revenue

Contract revenue should comprise:

(a) The initial amount of revenue agreed in the contract; and

(b) Variations in contract work, claims and incentive payments, to the extent that

   (i) it is probable that they will result in revenue;

   (ii) they are capable of being reliably measured.

Variations to the initially agreed contract price occur due to events such as:

- cost escalation clauses;
- claims for additional revenue by the contractor due to customer-caused delays or errors in specification or design;
- incentive payments where specified performance standards are met or exceeded.

However they occur, the basic criteria of probable receipt and measurability need to be satisfied before variations can be included as revenue.

19.4 Identification of contract costs

IAS 11 classifies costs that can be identified with contracts under three headings:

Costs that directly relate to the specific contract, such as:

- site labour;
- costs of materials;
- depreciation of plant and equipment used on the contract;
- costs of moving plant and materials to and from the contract site;
- costs of hiring plant and equipment;
- costs of design and technical assistance that are directly related to the contract;
- the estimated costs of rectification and guarantee work;
- claims from third parties.

Costs that are attributable to contract activity in general and can be allocated to specific contracts, such as:

- insurance;
- costs of design and technical assistance that are not directly related to a specific contract;
- construction overheads.

Costs of this nature need to be allocated on a systematic and rational basis, based on the normal level of construction activity.

Such other costs as are specifically chargeable to the customer under the terms of the contract. Examples of these would be general administration and development costs for which reimbursement is specified in the terms of the contract.

Contract costs normally include relevant costs from the date the contract is secured to the date the contract is finally completed. If they can be separately identified and reliably measured then costs that are incurred in securing the contract can also be included as part of contract costs if it is probable the contract will be awarded. However, where such costs were previously recognised as an expense in the period in which they were incurred then they are not included in contract costs when the contract is obtained in the subsequent period.

Care needs to be taken to ensure that non-contract costs are not attributed to a contract causing the profit for the year to be inflated. For example, the following is an extract from the Cray Inc 2005 Annual Report:

> Cray has determined that certain costs were incorrectly charged to the product development contract in 2004; this contract is accounted for under the percentage of completion method. This restatement will decrease 2004 revenue by $3.3 million, decrease cost of product revenue by $3.1 million, increase research and development expense by $3.1 million and increase net loss by $3.3 million. There was no impact on cash or short-term investment position.

19.5 Recognition of contract revenue and expenses

IAS 11 states that the revenue and costs associated with a construction contract should be recognised in the statement of comprehensive income as soon as the outcome of the contract can be estimated reliably. This is likely to be possible when:

● the total contract revenue can be measured reliably and it is probable that the related economic benefits will flow to the enterprise;

● the total contract costs (both those incurred to date and those expected to be incurred in the future) can be measured reliably;

● the stage of completion of the contract can be accurately identified.

As stated in section 19.2 above, the method of accounting for construction contracts that is laid down in IAS 11 is the percentage of completion method, which, as we have seen, involves, *inter alia*, identifying the stage of completion of the contract. IAS 11 does not identify a single method that may be used to identify the stage of completion. For many contracts this may involve an external expert (e.g. an architect) confirming that the contract has reached a particular stage of completion. However, alternative methods that might be appropriate include:

● the proportion that contract costs incurred for work performed to date bear to total contract costs;

  – this is the method used, for example, by Johnson Matthey in its 2006 annual report:

Construction contracts

Where the outcome of a construction contract can be estimated reliably, revenue and costs are recognized by reference to the stage of completion. This is normally measured by the proportion that contract costs incurred to date bear to the estimated total contract costs.

● completion of a physical proportion of the contract work.

The appropriate method for recognising net income on a construction contract is to recognise the relevant proportion of total contract income as revenue and the relevant proportion of total contract costs as expenses. Clearly under this process the proportion of net income that is attributable to the work performed to date will be credited in the statement of comprehensive income.

If, exceptionally, the contract is expected to show a loss then the total expected loss is recognised immediately on the grounds of prudence. Where the contract is at too early a stage for an accurate prediction of the overall result then IAS 11 forbids enterprises from recognising any profit. In such circumstances, provided there is no reason to expect that the contract will make an overall loss, then the revenue that is recognised should be restricted to the costs incurred during the year that relate to the contract, which should in turn be recognised as an expense. Clearly in such circumstances the net income recognised is nil.

This is the policy stated in the 2006 Johnson Matthey annual report:

Where the outcome of a construction contract cannot be estimated reliably, contract revenue is recognised to the extent of contract costs incurred that it is probable will be recoverable. Contract costs are recognized as expenses in the period in which they are incurred.

The statement of financial position presentation for construction contracts should show as an asset – *Gross amounts due from customers* – the following net amount:

● total costs incurred to date;
● plus attributable profits (or less foreseeable losses);
● less any progress billings to the customer.

Where for any contract the above amount is negative, it should be shown as a liability – *Gross amounts due to customers*.

Advances – amounts received by the contractor before the related work is performed – should be shown as a liability – effectively a payment on account by the customer.

The financial statements of Eni, an Italian company that prepares financial statements in accordance with US GAAP, show an accounting policy note for inventories that is fairly close to the requirements of IAS 11:

Contract work-in-progress, representing 14% and 12% of inventories at December 31, 1998 and 1999 respectively, is recorded using the percentage-of-completion method. Payments received in advance of construction are subtracted from inventories and any excess of such advances over the value of work performed is recorded as a liability. Contract work-in-progress not invoiced, whose payment is agreed in a foreign currency, is recorded at current exchange rates at year-end. Future losses that exceed the revenues earned are accrued for when the company becomes aware such losses will occur.

This policy is IAS 11 compliant in all respects other than the treatment of advances. IAS 11 requires that these be shown as liabilities until the related work is performed.

19.5.1 IAS 11 Illustrated – Profitable Contract using – Step approach first year of contract

ABC has two construction contracts outstanding at the end of its financial year, 30 June 20X0 Details for Contract A are as follows:

	Contract A £000
Total contract price	25,000
Costs incurred to date	5,500
Anticipated future costs	14,500
Progress billings	—
Advance payments	
% complete 30.6.X0	28%

Step 1 Overall anticipated result

The first step is to predict the overall contract result using the information available at the period end date:

	Contract A £000
Total contract price	25,000
Total expected contract costs:	
Costs to date	(5,500)
Expected future costs	(14,500)
Overall anticipated result	5,000

Step 2 Statement of comprehensive income: revenue entry

The next step is to compute the revenue that will be included in the statement of comprehensive income for the year ended 30 June 20X0:

	Contract A £000
Cumulative revenue (28% of total)	7,000
So revenue for the year	7,000

Step 3 Statement of comprehensive income: expense entry

We now move on to compute the expense that will be recognised:

	Contract A £000
28% of total anticipated costs (use actual)	5,500
Allowance for future losses	Nil
So expense for the year	5,500

Before we move on to the presentation of the contracts, let us summarise the statement of comprehensive income position for the current year:

	Contract A £000
Revenue	7,000
Expense	(5,500)
Net income (expense)	1,500

Step 4 Statement of financial position entries

As far as this statement is concerned, the figures presented will be based on the cumulative amounts. The gross amounts due from customers will be as follows:

	Contract A £000
Costs incurred to date	5,500
Add: recognised profits less recognised losses	1,500
Less: progress billings	—
Gross amounts due from customers	7,000

Note: As no problems had been experienced or were anticipated the company decided that it was appropriate to treat on a percentage completion basis.

19.5.2 Example: Profitable contract – step approach for year 2

ABC has two construction contracts outstanding at the end of its financial year, 30 June 20X1. Details for Contract A are as follows:

	Contract A £000
Total contract price	25,000
Costs incurred to date	14,000
Anticipated future costs	6,000
Progress billings	12,000
Advance payments	4,000
% complete 30.6.X1	60%

Step 1 Overall anticipated result

The first step is to predict the overall contract result using the information available at the period end date (this is unchanged from the year 1 estimate):

	Contract A £000
Total contract price	25,000
Total expected contract costs:	
Costs to date	(14,000)
Expected future costs	(6,000)
Overall anticipated result	5,000

Step 2 Statement of comprehensive income: revenue entry

The next step is to compute the revenue that will be included in the statement of comprehensive income for the year ended 30 June 20X1:

	Contract A £000
Cumulative revenue (60% of total)	15,000
Less: recognised in previous years:	(7,000)
So revenue for the year	8,000

Step 3 Statement of comprehensive income: expense entry

We now move on to compute the expense that will be recognised:

	Contract A
	£000
60% of total anticipated costs	12,000
Allowance for future losses	Nil
Less: recognised in previous years	(5,500)
So expense for the year	6,500

Before we move on to the presentation of the contracts, let us summarise the statement of comprehensive income position, both for the current year and cumulatively:

	Year 1	This year	Contract A Cumulative
	£000	£000	£000
Revenue	7,000	8,000	15,000
Expense	(5,500)	(6,500)	(12,000)
Net income (expense)	1,500	1,500	3,000

Step 4 Statement of financial position entries

As far as this statement is concerned, the figures presented will be based on the cumulative amounts. The gross amounts due from customers will be as follows:

	Contract A
	£000
Costs incurred to date	14,000
Add: recognised profits less recognised losses	3,000
Less: progress billings	(12,000)
Gross amounts due from customers	5,000

19.5.3 Example: Loss making contract – step approach

ABC has two construction contracts outstanding at the end of its financial year, 30 June 20X1. Details for the second, Contract B, are as follows:

	Contract B
	£000
Total contract price	20,000
Costs incurred to date	15,000
Anticipated future costs	9,000
Progress billings	10,000
Advance payments	Nil
% complete 30.6.X1	50%
% complete 30.6.X0	Not possible to determine

Contract B was at an early stage of completion at 30 June 20X0 but there was no indication at that date that it was likely to make a loss. Costs incurred on Contract B to 30 June 20X0 totalled £2,000,000.

Step 1 Overall anticipated result

The first step is to predict the overall contract result using the information available at the period end date:

	Contract B £000
Total contract price	20,000
Total expected contract costs:	
Costs to date	(15,000)
Expected future costs	(9,000)
Overall anticipated result	(4,000)

Step 2 Statement of comprehensive income: revenue entry

The next step is to compute the revenue that will be included in the statement of comprehensive income for the year ended 30 June 20X1:

	Contract B £000
Cumulative revenue (50% of total)	10,000
Less: recognised in previous years	(2,000)
So revenue for the year	8,000

Notice that the revenue that is recognised in the year to 30 June 20X0 for contract B is equal to the costs incurred in that year. This is because, in previous years, the contract was at too early a stage to recognise any profit. Therefore, under IAS 11, the revenue and expense that is recognised is equal to the costs actually incurred on that contract.

Step 3 Statement of comprehensive income: expense entry

We now move on to compute the expense that will be recognised:

	Contract B £000
50% of total anticipated costs	12,000
Allowance for future losses	2,000
Less: recognised in previous years	(2,000)
So expense for the year	12,000

As far as contract B is concerned, recognising 50% of the total contract price and revenue and 50% of the total expected contract costs as expense results in a net expense of £2,000,000 [£10,000,000 – £12,000,000]. The contract is expected to make an overall loss of £4,000,000. Since the contract is expected to be loss-making then the whole of the expected loss must be recognised. This means making an additional charge to expense of £2,000,000 [£4,000,000 – £2,000,000].

Before we move on to the presentation of the contracts, let us summarise the statement of comprehensive income position, both for the current year and cumulatively:

	Year 1 £000	This year £000	Contract B Cumulative £000
Revenue	2,000	8,000	10,000
Expense	2,000	(12,000)	(14,000)
Net income (expense)	—	(4,000)	(4,000)

Step 4 Statement of financial position entries

As far as this statement is concerned, the figures presented will be based on the cumulative amounts. The gross amounts due from customers will be as follows:

	Contract B £000
Costs incurred to date	15,000
Add: recognised profits less recognised losses	(4,000)
Less: progress billings	(10,000)
Gross amounts due from customers	1,000

19.6 Public–private partnerships (PPPs)

PPPs have become a common government policy for public bodies to enter into contracts with private companies which have included contracts for the building and management of transport infrastructure, prisons, schools and hospitals. There are inherent risks in any project and the intention is that the government, through a PPP arrangement, should transfer some or all of such risks to private contractors. For this to work equitably there needs to be an incentive for the private contractors to be able to make a reasonable profit provided they are efficient whilst ensuring that the providers, users of the service, tax payers and employees also receive a fair share of the benefits of the PPP.

Improved public services

It has been recognised that where such contracts satisfy a value for money test it makes economic sense to transfer some or all of the risks to a private contractor. In this way it has been possible to deliver significantly improved public services with:

- increases in the quality and quantity of investment, e.g. by the private contractor raising equity and loan capital in the market rather than relying simply on government funding;

- tighter control of contracts during the construction stage to avoid cost and time overruns, e.g. completing construction contracts within budget and within agreed time – this is evidenced in a report from the National Audit Office[1] which indicates that the majority are completed on time and within budget; and

- more efficient management of the facilities after construction, e.g. maintaining the buildings, security, catering and cleaning of an approved standard for a specified number of years.

PPP defined

There is no clear definition of a PPP. It can take a number of forms, e.g. in the form of the improved use of existing public assets under the Wider Markets Initiative (WMI) or contracts for the construction of new infrastructure projects and services provided under a Private Finance Initiative (PFI).

The Wider Markets Initiative (WMI)[2]

The WMI encourages public sector bodies to become more entrepreneurial and to undertake commercial services based on the physical assets and knowledge assets (e.g. patents, databases) they own in order to make the most effective use of public assets. WMI does not relate to the use of surplus assets – the intention would be to dispose of these. However, becoming more entrepreneurial leads to the need for collaboration with private enterprise with appropriate expertise.

Private Finance Initiative (PFI)

The PFI has been described[3] as a form of public private partnership (PPP) that 'differs from privatisation in that the public sector retains a substantial role in PFI projects, either as the main purchaser of services or as an essential enabler of the project . . . differs from contracting out in that the private sector provides the capital asset as well as the services . . . differs from other PPPs in that the private sector contractor also arranges finance for the project'.

In its 2004 Government Review the HM Treasury stated[4] that:

The Private Finance Initiative is a small but important part of the Government's strategy for delivering high quality public services. In assessing where PFI is appropriate, the Government's approach is based on its commitment to efficiency, equity and accountability and on the Prime Minister's principles of public sector reform. PFI is only used where it can meet these requirements and deliver clear value for money without sacrificing the terms and conditions of staff. Where these conditions are met, PFI delivers a number of important benefits. By requiring the private sector to put its own capital at risk and to deliver clear levels of service to the public over the long term, PFI helps to deliver high quality public services and ensure that public assets are delivered on time and to budget.

The following is an extract showing the capital value of PFI contracts and a breakdown by major departments.

	Breakdown by department	
Department	*Number of signed projects*	*Capital value ($£$m)*
Transport	45	21,432.1
Education and Skills	121	2,922.8
Health	136	4,901.2
Work & Pensions	11	1,341.0
Home Office	37	1,095.8
Defence	52	4,254.8
Scotland	84	2,249.3
Other departments	191	4,502.4
Total	**677**	**42,699.4**

The PFI has meant that more capital projects have been undertaken for a given level of public expenditure and public service capital projects have been brought on stream earlier. However, it has to be recognised that this increased level of activity must be paid for by higher public expenditure in the future, as the stream of payments to the private sector grows – PFI projects have committed the government (and future governments) to a stream of revenue payments to private sector contractors between 2000/01 and 2025/26 of more than £100 billion.

Briefly, then, PFI allows the public sector to enter into a contract (known as a concession) with the private sector to provide quality services on a long-term basis, typically twenty-five to thirty years, so as to take advantage of private sector management skills working under contracts where private finance is at risk.

19.6.1 How does PFI operate?

In principle, private sector companies accept the responsibility for the design; raise the finance; undertake the construction, maintenance and possibly operation of assets for the delivery of public services. In return for this the public sector pays for the project by making annual payments that cover all the costs plus a return on the investment through performance payments.

In practice the construction company and other parties such as the maintenance companies become shareholders in a project company set up specifically to tender for a concession. The project company:

- enters into the contract (the 'concession') with the public sector; then
- enters into two principal subcontracts with
  - a construction company to build the project assets; and
  - a facilities management company to maintain the asset – this is normally for a period of 5 or so years after which time it is re-negotiated.

  NOTE: the project company will pass down to the constructor and maintenance subcontractors any penalties or income deductions that arise as a result of their mismanagement.

- raises a mixture of
  - equity and subordinated debt from the principal private promoters i.e. the construction company and the maintenance company; and
  - long-term debt.

  NOTE: The long-term debt may be up to 90% of the finance required on the basis that it is cheaper to use debt rather than equity. The loan would typically be obtained from banks and would be without recourse to the shareholders of the project company. As there is no recourse to the shareholders, lenders need to be satisfied that there is a reliable income stream coming to the project company from the public sector, i.e. the lender needs to be confident that the project company can satisfy the contractual terms agreed with the public sector.

  The subordinated debt made available to the project company by the promoters will be subordinated to the claims of the long-term lenders in that they will only be repaid after the long-term lenders.

- receives regular payments, usually over a twenty-five to thirty-year period, from the public sector once the construction has been completed to cover the interest, construction, operating and maintenance costs.

  NOTE: Such payments may be conditional on a specified level of performance and the private sector partners need to have carried out detailed investigation of past practice for accommodation type projects and or detailed economic forecasting for throughput projects.

  If, for example, it is an accommodation type project (e.g. prisons, hospitals and schools) then payment is subject to the buildings being available in an appropriate clean and decorated condition – if not, income deductions can result.

  If it is a throughput project (e.g. roads, water) with payment made on basis of throughput such as number of vehicles and litres of water, then payment would be at a fixed rate per unit of throughput and the accuracy of the forecast usage has a significant impact on future income.

- makes interest and dividend payments to the principal promoters.
- returns the infrastructure assets in agreed condition to the public sector at the end of the twenty-five to thirty-year contractual period.

This can be shown graphically as in Figure 19.1.

Figure 19.1 The operation of PFI

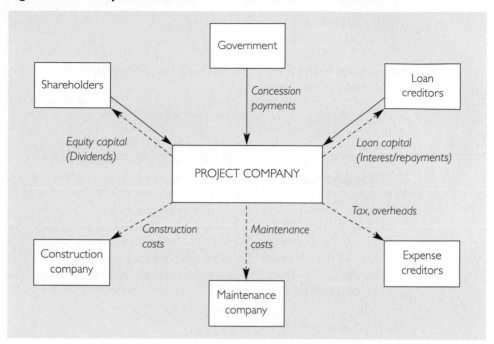

19.6.2 Profit and cash flow profile for the shareholders

Over a typical thirty-year contract the profit and cash flow profiles would follow different growth patterns.

Profit profile

No profits received as dividends during construction. Before completion the depreciation and loan interest charges can result in losses in the early years. As the loans are reduced the interest charge falls and profits then grow steadily to the end of the concession.

Cash flow

As far as the shareholders are concerned, cash flow is negative in the early years with the introduction of equity finance and subordinated loans. Cash begins to flow in when receipts commence from the public sector and interest payments commence to be made on the subordinated loans, say from year 5, and dividend payments start to be made to the equity shareholders, say from year 15.

19.6.3 How is a concession dealt with in the annual accounts of a construction company?

Statement of comprehensive income entries

The accounting treatment will depend on the nature of the construction company's shareholding in the project company. If it has control, then it would consolidate. Frequently, however, it has significant influence without control and therefore accounts for its investment in concessions by taking to the statement of comprehensive income its share of the net income or expense of each concession, in line with IAS 28 Investments in Associates.

19.6.4 How is a concession dealt with in the annual accounts of a concession or project company?

The accounting for service concessions has been a difficult problem for accounting standard setters around the world and different models exist. The main difficulties are in determining the nature of the asset that should be recognised, whether that is a tangible fixed asset, a financial asset or an intangible asset, or even some combination of these different options.

Accounting for concessions in the UK is governed by Financial Reporting Standard 5, Reporting the Substance of Transactions, Application Note F, which is primarily concerned with how to account for the costs of constructing new assets.

Assets constructed by the concession may be either considered as a fixed asset of the concession, or as a long-term financial asset ('contract receivable'), depending on the specific allocation of risks between the concession company and the public sector authority. In practice the main risk is normally the demand risk associated with the usage of the asset, e.g. number of vehicles using a road where the risk remains with the concession company.

Treated as a non-current asset

Where the concession company takes the greater share of the risks associated with the asset, the cost of constructing the asset is considered to be a fixed asset of the concession. The cost of construction is capitalised and depreciation is charged to the statement of comprehensive income over the life of the concession. Income is recognised as turnover in the statement of comprehensive income as it is earned.

Treated as a financial instrument

Where the public sector takes the greater share of the risks associated with the asset, the concession company accounts for the cost of constructing the asset as a long-term contract receivable, being a receivable from the public sector. Finance income on this contract receivable is recorded using a notional rate of return which is specific to the underlying asset, and included as part of non-operating financial income in the statement of comprehensive income.

Under the contract receivable treatment, the revenue received from the public sector is split. The element relating to the provision of services that are considered a separate transaction from the provision of the asset is recognised as turnover in the statement of comprehensive income. The element relating to the contract debtor is split between finance income and repayment of the outstanding principal.

The following is an extract from the Balfour Beatty 2003 Annual Report to illustrate a usage based concession:

Roads

Balfour Beatty's road concessions typically comprise a mixture of new build roads and taking responsibility for the long-term maintenance of roads that the concession has not constructed ('assumed roads').

The income on roads concessions is directly related to the volume of traffic. The new roads are therefore considered to be fixed assets of the concession and are depreciated over the life of the concession, once construction is complete.

The revenue is split into two streams: that relating to the constructed road and that relating to the assumed road. Revenue on the constructed road is recognised as turnover as it is received. Revenue on the assumed road is recognised as turnover as the underlying maintenance obligations are performed. Where revenue is received in advance of performing these obligations, its recognition as turnover is deferred until they are performed.

The total profit earned from a concession will be the same whether it is treated as a fixed asset or a finance asset. There will, however, be a difference in the timing of the profit recognition, and a difference in the presentation of income and expenses in the statement of comprehensive income. When treated as a fixed asset, profits increase over time largely due to the reducing financing costs of the transaction as the outstanding loans are repaid; when treated as a finance asset, the finance income is calculated on the full value of the contract debtor and this finance income falls in line with the principal repayments over the life of the project.

IFRIC 12 *Service Concession Agreements*

For enterprises preparing financial statements in accordance with IFRS, IFRIC 12 was issued in November 2006 and became effective for periods beginning on or after 31 January 2008. As we will see, this interpretation will result in accounting that has some similarities to that laid down for PFI contracts in UK FRS 5, however the presentation of the assets recognised might differ.

Service concession agreements are arrangements where a government or other body grants contracts for the supply of public services to private operators. IFRIC 12 draws a distinction between two types of service concession arrangement.

In one case the operator receives a **financial asset**, specifically an unconditional contractual right to receive cash or another financial asset in return for constructing or upgrading the public sector asset. In the other, an **intangible asset** – a right to charge for use of the public sector asset that it constructs or upgrades. IFRIC 12 allows for the possibility that both types of arrangement may exist within a single contract. Therefore, IFRIC 12 recognises two accounting models:

Under the **financial asset model** the operator receives a financial asset. This arises where the operator has an unconditional contractual right to receive cash or another financial asset from the public sector body for relevant services. This is where the public sector body contractually guarantees to pay the operator:

● specified or determinable amounts; or

● the shortfall, if any, between amounts received from users of the public service and specified or determinable amounts.

The operator measures the intangible asset initially at fair value. Subsequent to initial measurement the financial assets will be accounted for under IAS 39 and will be classified according to that standard. As a result the financial asset could be measured as follows:

● if classified as a 'loan and receivable' it will be measured at amortised cost;

● if classified as 'available for sale' it will be measured at fair value with gains and losses recognised in the other gains and losses section of the statement of comprehensive income; or

● if classified as 'fair value through profit or loss' it will be measured at fair value with gains and losses reflected with net profit or loss in the statement of comprehensive income.

Under the **intangible asset model** the operator recognises an intangible asset to the extent to which it receives a right to charge users of the public service. A right to charge users is not an unconditional right to receive cash because it depends on the extent to which the public uses the service.

The operator measures the financial asset initially at fair value. Subsequent to initial recognition the intangible asset will be recognised in accordance with IAS 38 *Intangible Assets*. Subsequent to initial recognition the assets amortisation or impairment charges will need to be recognised as required by IAS 38.

Revenue is recognised by the operator in accordance with the general recognition principles of IAS 11 and IAS 18.

Summary

Long-term contracts are those that cannot be completed within the current financial year. This means that a decision has to be made as to whether or not to include any profit before the contract is actually completed. The view taken by the standard setters is that contract revenue and costs should be recognised under IAS 11 using the percentage of completion method. There is a proviso that revenue and costs can only be recognised when the amounts are capable of independent verification and the contract has reached a reasonable stage of completion. Although profits are attributed to the financial periods in which the work is carried out, there is a requirement that any foreseeable losses should be recognised immediately in the statement of comprehensive income of the current financial period and not apportioned over the life of the contract.

REVIEW QUESTIONS

1 Discuss the point in a contract's life when it becomes appropriate to recognise profit and the feasibility of specifying a common point, e.g. when contract is 25% complete.

2 'Profit on a contract is not realised until completion of the contract.' Discuss.

3 'Profit on a contract that is not completed is an unrealised holding gain.' Discuss.

4 'There should be one specified method for calculating attributable profit.' Discuss.

5 The Treasury state that 'Talk of PFI liabilities with a present value of £110 million is wrong. Adding up PFI unitary payments and pretending they present a threat to the public finances is like adding up electricity, gas, cleaning and food bills for the next 30 years.' Discuss.

EXERCISES

An extract from the solution is provided on the Companion Website (www.pearsoned.co.uk/elliott-elliott) for exercises marked with an asterisk (*).

Question 1

MACTAR have a series of contracts to resurface sections of motorways. The scale of the contract means several years' work and each motorway section is regarded as a separate contract.

Required:

From the following information, calculate for each contract the amount of profit (or loss) you would show for the year and show how these contracts would appear in the statement of financial position with all appropriate notes.

M1	£m
Contract	3.0
Costs to date	2.1
Estimated cost to complete	0.3
Certified value of work completed to date	1.8
Progress billings applied for to date	1.75
Payment received to date	1.5

M6	£m
Contract sum	2.0
Costs to date	0.3
Estimated cost to complete	1.1
Certified value of work completed to date	0.1
Progress billings applied for to date	0.1
Payments received to date	—

M62	£m
Contract sum	2.5
Costs to date	2.3
Estimated costs to complete	0.8
Certified value of work completed to date	1.3
Progress billings applied for to date	1.0
Payments received to date	0.75

The M62 contract has had **major** difficulties due to difficult terrain, and the contract only allows for a 10% increase in contract sum for such events.

Question 2

At 31 October 20X0, Lytax Ltd was engaged in various contracts including five long-term contracts, details of which are given below:

	1 £000	2 £000	3 £000	4 £000	5 £000
Contract price	1,100	950	1,400	1,300	1,200
At 31 October					
Cumulative costs incurred	664	535	810	640	1,070
Estimated further costs to completion	106	75	680	800	165
Estimated cost of post-completion guarantee rectification work	30	10	45	20	5
Cumulative costs incurred transferred to cost of sales	580	470	646	525	900
Progress billings:					
Cumulative receipts	615	680	615	385	722
Invoiced					
– awaiting receipt	60	40	25	200	34
– retained by customer	75	80	60	65	84

It is not expected that any customers will default on their payments.

Up to 31 October 20X9, the following amounts have been included in the revenue and cost of sales figures:

	1 £000	2 £000	3 £000	4 £000	5 £000
Cumulative revenue	560	340	517	400	610
Cumulative costs incurred transferred to cost of sales	460	245	517	400	610
Foreseeable loss transferred to cost of sales	—	—	—	70	—

It is the accounting policy of Lytax Ltd to arrive at contract revenue by adjusting contract cost of sales (including foreseeable losses) by the amount of contract profit or loss to be regarded as recognised, separately for each contract.

Required:
Show how these items will appear in the statement of financial position of Lytax Ltd with all appropriate notes. Show all workings in tabular form.

* Question 3

During its financial year ended 30 June 20X7 Beavers, an engineering company, has worked on several contracts. Information relating to one of them is given below:

Contract X201

Date commenced	1 July 20X6
Original estimate of completion date	30 September 20X7
Contract price	£240,000
Proportion of work certified as satisfactorily completed (and invoiced) up to 30 June 20X7	£180,000
Progress payments from Dam Ltd	£150,000

Costs up to 30 June 20X7

Wages	£91,000
Materials sent to site	£36,000
Other contract costs	£18,000
Proportion of Head Office costs	£6,000
Plant and equipment transferred to the site (at book value on 1 July 20X6)	£9,000

The plant and equipment is expected to have a book value of about £1,000 when the contract is completed.

Inventory of materials at site 30 June 20X7	£3,000
Expected additional costs to complete the contract:	
Wages	£10,000
Materials (including stock at 30 June 20X7)	£12,000
Other (including Head Office costs)	£8,000

At 30 June 20X7 it is estimated that work to a cost value of £19,000 has been completed, but not included in the certifications.

If the contract is completed one month earlier than originally scheduled, an extra £10,000 will be paid to the contractors. At the end of June 20X7 there seemed to be a 'good chance' that this would happen.

Required:

(a) Show the account for the contract in the books of Beavers up to 30 June 20X7 (including any transfer to the statement of comprehensive income which you think is appropriate).

(b) Show the statement of financial position entries.

(c) Calculate the profit (or loss) to be recognised in the 20X6–X7 accounts.

Question 4

Newbild SA commenced work on the construction of a block of flats on 1 July 20X0.

During the period ended 31 March 20X1 contract expenditure was as follows:

	€
Materials issued from stores	13,407
Materials delivered direct to site	73,078
Wages	39,498
Administration expenses	3,742
Site expenses	4,693

On 31 March 20X1 there were outstanding amounts for wages 396 and site expenses 122, and the stock of materials on site amounted to 5,467.

The following information is also relevant:

1   On 1 July 20X0 plant was purchased for exclusive use on site at a cost of 15,320. It was estimated that it would be used for two years after which it would have a residual value of 5,000.

2   By 31 March 20X1 Newbild SA had received 114,580, being the amount of work certified by the architects up to 31 March 20X1 less a 15% retention.

3   The total contract price is 780,000. The company estimates that additional costs to complete the project will be 490,000. From costing records it is estimated that the costs of rectification and guarantee work will be 2.5% of the contract price.

Required:
(a) **Prepare the contract account for the period, together with a statement showing your calculation of the net income to be taken to the company's statement of comprehensive income on 31 March 20X1. Assume for the purpose of the question that the contract is sufficiently advanced to allow for the taking of profit.**
(b) **Give the values which you think should be included in the figures of revenue and cost of sales, in the statement of comprehensive income, and those to be included in net amounts due to or from the customer in the statement of financial position in respect of this contract.**

* Question 5

Good Progress SpA entered into a contract on 1.1.20X0 at a contract price of 1,000,000 and an estimated total profit of 250,000. The contract was due for completion on 31.12.20X4.

The following information was available.

As at 31.12.20X0:

The contract was 25% complete and an architect's certificate was issued for 250,000.

As at 31.12.20X1:

The contract was 40% complete and an architect's certificate was issued for 400,000.

Required:
Prepare the statement of comprehensive income entries for the years ended 31 December 20X0 and 20X1 and the statement of financial position entries as at those dates.

Question 6

(a) A concession company, WaterAway, has completed the construction of a wastewater plant. The plant will be transferred to the public sector unconditionally after 25 years. The public sector (the grantor) makes payments related to the volume of wastewater processed.

Discuss how this will be dealt with in the statement of comprehensive income and statement of financial position of the concession company.

(b) A concession company, LearnAhead, has built a school and receives income from the public sector (the grantor) based on the availability of the school for teaching.

Discuss how this will be dealt with in the statement of comprehensive income and statement of financial position of the concession company, under IFRIC 12.

Question 7

Quickbuild Ltd entered into a two-year contract on 1 January 20X7 at a contract price of 250,000. The estimated cost of the contract was 150,000. At the end of the first year the following information was available:

- contract costs incurred totalled 70,000;
- inventories still unused at the contract site totalled 10,000;
- progress payments received totalled 60,000;
- other non-contract inventories totalled 185,000.

Required:
(a) Calculate the statement of comprehensive income entries for the contract revenue and the contract costs.
(b) Calculate entries in the statement of financial position for the amounts due from construction contracts and inventories.

Question 8

(a) During 2006, Jack Matelot set up a company, JTM, to construct and refurbish marinas in various ports around Europe. The company's first accounting period ended on 31 October 2006 and during that period JTM won a contract to refurbish a small marina in St Malo, France. During the year ended 31 October 2007, the company won a further two contracts in Barcelona, Spain and Faro, Portugal. The following extract has been taken from the company's contract notes as at 31 October 2007:

Contract:	Barcelona	Faro	St Malo
	€m	€m	€m
Contract value	12.24	10.00	15.00
Work certified:			
To 31 October 2006	—	—	6.00
Year to 31 October 2007	6.50	0.50	3.00
To date	6.50	0.50	9.00
Payments received:			
To 31 October 2006	—	—	5.75
Year to 31 October 2007	3.76	—	1.75
To date	3.76	—	7.50
Invoices sent to client:			
To 31 October 2006	—	—	6.00
Year to 31 October 2007	5.00	0.50	2.76
To date	5.00	0.50	8.76
Costs incurred:			
To 31 October 2006	—	—	6.56
Year to 31 October 2007	11.50	1.50	3.94
To date	11.50	1.50	10.50
Estimated costs to complete:			
As at 31 October 2006			5.44
As at 31 October 2007	4.00	5.50	1.50

Notes

Barcelona:
Experiencing difficulties. Although JTM does not anticipate any cost increases, the client has offered to increase contract value by €0.76m as compensation.

Faro:
No problems.

St Malo:
Work has slowed down during 2007. However, company feels it can continue profitably.

The company uses the value of work certified to estimate the percentage completion of each contract.

Required

For each contract, calculate the profit or loss attributable to the year ended 31 October 2007 and show how it would be recognised in the company's balance sheet at that date. (Show your workings clearly.)

(b) As JTM's 2007 accounts were being prepared, it became evident that the St Malo contract had slowed down due to a dispute with a neighbouring marina which claimed that the JTM refurbishment had damaged part of its quayside. The company has been told that the cost of repairing the damage would be €150,000. Jack Matelot believes it is a fair estimate and, in the interests of completing the contract on time, has decided to settle the claim. He is not unduly concerned about the amount involved as such eventualities are adequately covered by insurance.

Required

How should this event be dealt with in the 2007 accounts?

(c) During 2007, Jack Matelot had two major worries: (i) the operating performance of JTM had not been as good as expected; and (ii) the planned disposal of surplus property (to finance the agreed acquisition of a competitor, MoriceMarinas, and the payment of a dividend) had not been successful. As a result of these circumstances, Jack had been warning shareholders not to expect a dividend for 2007. However, during November 2007, the property was unexpectedly disposed of for €5m; which enabled the payment of a 2007 dividend of €1m and the acquisition of MoriceMarinas for €4m.

Required
How should the above events be dealt with in the 2007 accounts?

(The Association of International Accountants)

References

1 National Audit Office, PFI: Construction Performance Feb. 2003
   www.nao.org.uk/publications/nao_reports/02-03/0203371.pdf
2 *Selling government services into wider markets, Policy and Guidance Notes*, Enterprise and Growth Unit, HM Treasury July 1998
   www.hm-treasury.gov.uk/mediastore/otherfiles/sgswm.pdf
3 Research Paper 01/0117 *Private Finance Initiative*, G. Allen, Economic Policy and Statistics Section, House of Commons, December 2001.
4 www.hm-treasury.gov.uk/documents/public_private_partnerships/ppp_index.cfm?ptr=29

PART **4**

Consolidated accounts

Accounting for groups at the date of acquisition

20.1 Introduction

The main purpose of this chapter is to explain the reasons for and how to prepare consolidated financial statements at the date of acquisition.

> ### Objectives
>
> By the end of this chapter, you should be able to:
>
> - explain the need for consolidated financial statements;
> - define the meaning of the term 'subsidiary';
> - prepare consolidated accounts at the date of acquisition and calculate goodwill for a wholly-owned subsidiary;
> - explain the treatment of goodwill;
> - account for non-controlling interests under the two options available in IFRS 3;
> - understand the need for fair value adjustments and prepare consolidated financial statements reflecting such adjustments.

20.2 The definition of a group

Under IAS 27 *Consolidated and Separate Financial Statements*, a group exists where one enterprise (the parent) **controls**, either directly or **indirectly**, another enterprise (the subsidiary). A group consists of a parent and its subsidiaries.[1] This book will deal only with situations where both the parent and subsidiary enterprises are companies.

20.3 Consolidated accounts and some reasons for their preparation

In most cases a parent company is required by IAS 27 to prepare consolidated financial statements. These show the accounts of a group as though that group were one enterprise. The net assets of the companies in a group will therefore be combined and any inter-company profits and balances eliminated.

Why are groups required to prepare consolidated accounts?

(i) To prevent the preparation of misleading accounts by such means as inflating the sales through selling to another member of a group.

(ii) To provide a more meaningful EPS figure. Consolidated accounts show the full earnings on a parent company's investment while parent's individual accounts only show the dividend received from the subsidiaries.

(iii) To provide a better measurement of the performance of a parent company's directors. In consolidated accounts the total earnings of a group can be compared with its total assets in arriving at a group's return on capital employed (ROCE).

ROCE is regarded as important strategic information. For example, the Danish group FLS Industries A/S stated in its 1999 Financial Results Statement:

Return on capital employed (ROCE)

The FLS Group has decided to introduce value-based management with the overall objective of strengthening the framework for monitoring and controlling the Group's long-term capability for generating earnings. For this purpose a version of EVA^{TM} – Economic Value Added – is used. This entails relating the financial result to the capital it requires and the risk it entails . . .

Although the return on capital employed is not satisfactory, over the past five years the FLS Group has achieved an increasing return on its capital employed. In 1995, ROCE amounted to 6.6%, compared with 10.2% in 1998 and 21.1% in 1999. Adjusted for non-recurring items, ROCE for 1999 amounts to 5.9%.

In 2000 the Group will intensify the focus on optimising capital employed.

Note that in 2004 there was an operational integration of the parent company, FLS Industries A/S, and F.L.Smidth A/S now trading as FLSmidth A/S and that the ROCE for 2005 was 19%.

When may a parent company not be required to prepare consolidated accounts?

It may not be necessary for a parent company to prepare consolidated accounts if the parent is itself a wholly-owned subsidiary and the ultimate parent produces consolidated financial statements available for public use that comply with International Financial Reporting Standards (IFRSs).[2] This situation arises when the ultimate parent exercises control over a company through a subsidiary company's investment as illustrated by the extract from the 2008 Accounts of Eybl International:

Consolidation principles

The consolidation constituency has been disclosed in accordance with IAS 27.12 . . . The Consolidated Annual Report comprises the Annual Report of Eybl International Aktiengesellschaft as parent company as well as the annual financial accounts of 16 subsidiaries that are subject to uniform control by Eybl International Aktiengesellschaft and in which the latter or one of its subsidiaries holds the majority of voting rights.

If the parent company is a partially-owned subsidiary of another entity, then, if its other owners have been informed and do not object, the parent company need not present consolidated financial statements.

When may a parent company exclude a subsidiary from a consolidation?

IAS 27 does not allow subsidiaries to be excluded from consolidation on the grounds of severe long-term restrictions on control, or on the grounds of dissimilar activities. A subsidiary would be accounted for under IFRS 5 *Non-current Assets Held for Sale and Discontinued Operations* if it was acquired exclusively with a view to sale and it meets the criteria in IFRS 5. This is illustrated by an extract from the 2008 GKN annual report:

Basis of consolidation

The statements incorporate the financial statements of the Company and its subsidiaries
. . . Subsidiaries are entities over which, either directly or indirectly, the Company
has control through the power to govern financial operating policies so as to obtain
benefit from their activities. Except as noted below, this power is accompanied by a
shareholding of more than 50% of the voting rights. . . .

In a single case the Company indirectly owns 100% of the voting share capital of an
entity but is precluded from exercising either control or joint control by a contractual
agreement with the United States Department of Defense. In accordance with IAS 27
this entity has been excluded from the consolidation and treated as an investment.

Exclusion is permissible on grounds of non-materiality[3] as the International Accounting
Standards are not intended to apply to immaterial items. For example, the Nissan group
state in its 2009 Annual Report:

Unconsolidated subsidiaries 167

● Domestic companies 106

Nissan Marine Co., Ltd., Shinwa Kogyo Co., Ltd. and others

● Foreign companies 61

Nissan Industrial Equipment Co. and others
These unconsolidated subsidiaries are small in terms of their total assets, sales, net
income or loss, retained earnings and others, and do not have a significant effect
on the consolidated financial statements. As a result, they have been excluded from
consolidation.

Exclusion might also be appropriate where there are substantial minority rights as seen in
the following extract from the 2008 Linde AG annual report:

Scope of consolidation

The Group financial statements comprise Linde AG and all the companies over which
Linde AG exercises direct or indirect control by virtue of its power to govern their
financial and operating policies. . . .

Companies in which Linde AG holds the majority of the voting rights, either directly
or indirectly, but where it is unable to control the company due to substantial minority
rights, are also accounted for using the equity method.

Exclusion on the grounds that a subsidiary's activities are dissimilar from those of the
others within a group cannot be justified.[4] This is because information is required under
IFRS 8 *Operating Segments* on the different activities of subsidiaries, and users of accounts
can, therefore, make appropriate adjustments for their own purposes if required.

20.4 The definition of control

Under IFRS 3 *Business Combinations*, control is defined[5] as 'the power to govern the financial
and operating policies of an entity or business so as to obtain benefits from its activities'.
Control is **assumed** when one party to the combination owns more than half of the voting
rights of the other either directly or through a subsidiary. This is illustrated with the following extract from the 2008 accounts of the Wartsila Corporation:

Principles of consolidation

The consolidated financial statements include the parent company Wartsila Corporation and all subsidiaries in which the parent directly or indirectly holds more than 50 per cent of the voting rights or in which Wartsila is otherwise in control . . .

What if the voting rights acquired are less than half?

Even in this situation, it may still be possible[6] to identify an acquirer when one of the combining enterprises, as a result of the business combination, acquires:

(a) power over more than one-half of the voting rights of the other enterprise by virtue of an agreement with other investors;

(b) power to govern the financial and operating policies of the other enterprise under a statute or an agreement;

(c) power to appoint or remove the majority of the members of the board of directors or equivalent governing body of the other enterprise; or

(d) power to cast the majority of votes at a meeting of the board of directors or equivalent governing body of the other enterprise.

An extract from the 2008 Informa plc Annual Report states:

Basis of consolidation

The consolidated financial statements incorporate the accounts of the Company and all of its subsidiaries . . . Control is achieved where the Company has the power to govern the financial and operating policies of an investee entity so as to obtain benefits from its activities.

20.5 Alternative methods of preparing consolidated accounts

Before IFRS 3 there were two main methods of preparing consolidated statements, the purchase method and the pooling of interests method. The former method was the more common and was used in all cases where one company was seen as acquiring another. IFRS 3 now allows only the purchase method. This should ensure greater comparability of financial statements and remove the incentive to structure combinations in such a way as to produce the desired accounting result.

The purchase method

The **fair value** of the parent company's investment in a subsidiary is set against of the **fair value** of the identifiable net assets in the subsidiary at the date of acquisition. If the investment is greater than the share of net assets then the difference is regarded as the purchase of goodwill – see the Rose Group example below.

EXAMPLE ● THE ROSE GROUP CONSOLIDATED USING THE PURCHASE METHOD

On 1 January 20X0 Rose plc acquired 100% of the 10,000 £1 common shares in Tulip plc for £1.50 per share in cash and gained control. The fair value of the net assets of Tulip plc at that date was the same as the book value. The individual statements of financial position immediately after the acquisition and the group accounts at that date were as follows:

	Rose plc £	Tulip plc £	Group £	
ASSETS				
Non–current assets	20,000	11,000	31,000	Note 2
Goodwill	—	—	1,000	Note 1
Investment in Tulip	15,000	—	—	
Net current assets	8,000	3,000	11,000	Note 2
Net assets	43,000	14,000	43,000	
Share capital	16,000	10,000	16,000	Note 3
Retained earnings	27,000	4,000	27,000	Note 3
	43,000	14,000	43,000	

Note 1. Calculate the goodwill for inclusion in the group accounts:

		£	£
The parent company's investment			15,000
Less: The parent's share of			
a i the subsidiary's share capital	(100% × 10,000)	10,000	
a ii the subsidiary's retained earnings	(100% × 4,000)	4,000	14,000
The difference is goodwill for inclusion in the consolidated statement of financial position.			1,000*

* This is equivalent to the 100% share of net assets, i.e. Non-current assets 11,000 + Net current assets 3,000.

Note 2. Add together the assets and liabilities of the two companies for the group accounts:

		£
Non-current assets other than goodwill (20,000 + 11,000)		31,000
Goodwill	(as calculated in Note 1)	1,000
Net current assets	(8,000 + 3,000)	11,000
		43,000

Note 3. Calculate the consolidated share capital and reserves for the group accounts:

		£
Share capital	(The parent company only)	16,000
Retained earnings	(The parent company only)	27,000
		43,000

Note that:

● In Note 1 the investment in the subsidiary (£15,000) has been set off against the parent company's share of the subsidiary's share capital and reserves (£14,000) and these cancelled inter-company balances do not, therefore, appear in the consolidated accounts.

- In Note 2 the total of the net assets in the group account is the same as the net assets in the individual statement of financial position but the Tulip plc investment in Rose plc's accounts has been replaced by the net assets of Tulip plc of £14,000 **plus** the previously unrecorded £1,000 goodwill.

- In Note 3 the consolidated statement of financial position only includes the share capital and retained earnings of the parent company, because the subsidiary's share capital and retained earnings have been used in the calculation of goodwill.

The adjustments are often set out in a schedule format as follows:

	Rose plc £	Tulip plc £	Adjustments	Group £
ASSETS				
Non-current assets	20,000	11,000		31,000
Goodwill	—	—	1,000 c	1,000
Investment in Tulip	15,000	—	(10,000) a	—
			(4,000) b	
			(1,000) c	
Net current assets	8,000	3,000		11,000
Net assets	43,000	14,000		43,000
Share capital	16,000	10,000	(10,000) a	16,000
Retained earnings	27,000	4,000	(4,000) b	27,000
	43,000	14,000		43,000

Supported by the same notes (Notes 1–3) shown above.

An extract from the 2008 annual report of EnBW Energie Baden-Württemberg AG (EnBW) states:

> Capital consolidation is performed according to the purchase method by offsetting the cost of acquisition against the proportionate revalued equity of the subsidiaries at the date of acquisition.

20.6 The treatment of positive goodwill

Positive purchased goodwill, where the investment exceeds the total of the net assets acquired, should be recognised as an asset with no amortisation. Goodwill must be subject to impairment tests in accordance with IAS 36 *Impairment of Assets*. These tests will be annual, or more frequently if circumstances indicate that the goodwill might be impaired.[7] Once recognised, an impairment loss for goodwill may not be reversed in a subsequent period,[8] which helps in preventing the manipulation of period profits.

20.7 The treatment of negative goodwill

The acquiring company does not always pay more than the fair value of the identifiable net assets. If it pays less then negative goodwill is said to arise.

Negative goodwill, where the fair value of the net assets exceeds the amount of the investment, can arise[9] because –

(a) there have been errors measuring the fair value of either the cost of the combination or the acquiree's identifiable assets, liabilities or contingent liabilities;

(b) future costs such as losses have been taken into account;

(c) there has been a bargain purchase.

Where negative goodwill apparently arises, IFRS 3 requires parent companies to review the fair value exercise to ensure that no assets are overstated or liabilities understated. Assuming this review reveals no errors, then the resulting negative goodwill is recognised immediately in the statement of comprehensive income.

The following is an extract from the 2008 EnBW Annual Report:

Basis of consolidation
Capital consolidation is performed according to the purchase method by offsetting the cost of acquisition against the proportionate revalued equity of the subsidiaries at the date of acquisition.

Assets, liabilities and contingent liabilities are carried at fair value. Any remaining positive differences are recognised as goodwill.

Negative differences are immediately recognised in profit or loss following a review of their calculation.

20.8 The comparison between an acquisition by cash and an exchange of shares

Shares in another company can be purchased with cash or through an exchange of shares. In the former case, the cash will be reduced and exchanged for another asset called 'Investment in the subsidiary company'. If there is an exchange of share, there will be an increase in the share capital and, probably, the share premium of the acquiring company rather than a decrease in cash. There is no effect in either case on the accounts of the acquired company. The purchase price may contain a mixture of cash and shares and possibly other assets as well.

20.9 Non-controlling interests

A parent company does not need to purchase all the shares of another company to gain control. The holders of the remaining shares are collectively referred to as the **non-controlling interest**. They are part owners of the subsidiary. In such a case, therefore, the parent does not **own** all the net assets of the acquired company but does **control** them.

One of the purposes of preparing group accounts is to show the effectiveness of that control and of the directors of the parent company who are responsible for it. Therefore, all of the net assets of the subsidiary will be included in the group statement of financial position and the non-controlling interest will be shown as partly financing those net assets.

IFRS 3 allows for two different methods of measuring the non-controlling interest in the statement of financial position:

● **Method 1** requires that the non-controlling interest be measured at the *proportionate share of the net assets* of the subsidiary at the date of acquisition plus the relevant share of changes in the post-acquisition net assets of the acquired subsidiary. The practical effect of this method is that at each reporting date the non-controlling interest is measured as the share of the net assets of the subsidiary.

- **Method 2** requires that the non-controlling interest be measured at *fair value* at the date of acquisition, plus the relevant share of changes in the post-acquisition net assets of the acquired subsidiary. The practical effect of this method is that at each reporting date the non-controlling interest is measured as the share of the net assets of the subsidiary, plus the goodwill that has been apportioned to the non-controlling interest.

In the group statement of comprehensive income the full profit of the subsidiary is included and the non-controlling interest in it then separately identified. The statement of comprehensive income will be dealt with in more detail in Chapter 22. The effect on the statement of financial position is illustrated in the Bird Group example below.

EXAMPLE ● THE BIRD GROUP

On 1 January 20X0 Bird plc acquired 80% of the 10,000 £1 Ordinary shares in Flower plc for £1.50 per share in cash and gained control. The fair value of the net assets of Flower at that date was the same as the book value. We will first use method 1 to compute the non-controlling interest. The individual statements of financial position immediately after the acquisition and the group accounts at that date were as follows:

	Bird £	Flower £	Group £	
ASSETS				
Non-current assets	20,000	11,000	31,000	Note 3
Goodwill	—	—	800	Note 1
Investment in Flower	12,000	—	—	
Net current assets	11,000	3,000	14,000	Note 3
Net assets	43,000	14,000	45,800	
Share capital	16,000	10,000	16,000	Note 4
Retained earnings	27,000	4,000	27,000	Note 4
	43,000	14,000	43,000	
Non-controlling interest		—	2,800	Note 2
	43,000	14,000	45,800	

Note 1. Calculate goodwill

	£	£
The parent company's investment in Flower		12,000
Less: The parent's share of the subsidiary's share capital (80% × 10,000)	8,000	
The parent's share of the retained earnings (80% × 4,000)	3,200	
(Equivalent to the share of net assets, i.e. 80% × (11,000 + 3,000))		11,200
The difference is goodwill		**800**

Note 2. Calculate the non-controlling interest

The non-controlling interest in the share capital of Flower	(20% × 10,000)	=	2,000
The non-controlling interest in the retained earnings of Flower	(20% × 4,000)	=	800
Represents the non-controlling interest in the net assets of Flower			**2,800**

In published group accounts the non-controlling interest will be shown as a separate item in the equity of the group as follows:

Share capital	16,000
Retained earnings	27,000
Bird shareholders' share of equity	43,000
Non-controlling interest	2,800
Total equity	45,800

Non-controlling interest is, therefore, now shown as part of the ownership of the group rather than as a liability.

Note 3. Add together the assets and liabilities of the two companies for the group accounts

	£
Non-current assets other than goodwill (20,000 + 11,000)	31,000
Goodwill (as calculated in Note 1)	800
Net current assets (11,000 + 3,000)	14,000
	45,800

Note 4. Calculate the consolidated share capital and reserves for the group accounts

		£
Share capital	*(parent company only)*	16,000
Retained earnings	*(parent company only)*	27,000
		43,000

The schedule format would be as follows:

	Bird £	Flower £	Adjustment	Group £
ASSETS				
Non-current assets	20,000	11,000		31,000
Goodwill	—	—	800 a iii	800
Investment in Flower	12,000	—	(8,000) a i	—
			(3,200) a ii	
			(800) a iii	—
Net current assets	11,000	3,000		14,000
Net assets	43,000	14,000		45,800
Share capital	16,000	10,000	(8,000) a i	16,000
			(2,000) b i	
Retained earnings	27,000	4,000	(3,200) a ii	
			(800) b ii	27,000
	43,000	14,000		43,000
Non-controlling interest			2,000 b i	
			800 b ii	2,800
	43,000	14,000		45,800

Let us now consider the impact on the previous example of using method 2 to measure the non-controlling interest. In order to use this method, we need to know the fair value of the non-controlling interest in the subsidiary at the date of acquisition. Let us assume in this case that this fair value is £2,900.

The use of method 2 affects two figures – goodwill and the non-controlling interest. The impact is the goodwill that is attributed to the non-controlling interest and it is computed as follows:

	£
Fair value of non-controlling interest at date of acquisition	2,900
20% (the share attributable to the non-controlling interest) of the net assets at the date of acquisition (£14,000)	(2,800)
Attributable goodwill	100

The consolidated statement of financial position would now be as follows:

	£
Non-current assets other than goodwill	31,000
Goodwill (£800 + £100)	900
Net current assets	14,000
	45,900
Share capital	16,000
Retained earnings	27,000
Non-controlling interest (£2,800 + £100)	2,900
	45,900

Note that we assumed that the fair value of the non-controlling interest at the date of acquisition was £2,900. This figure may well be given in a question. However, if it were necessary to calculate it, one approach would be to calculate the value of the subsidiary at the date of acquisition and take 20% of that figure. The non-controlling interest would be:

20% of the fair value of the subsidiary at the date of acquisition (using share price if available)	£x
Less: 20% of the net assets at the date of acquisition	£y
= Goodwill attributable to the non-controlling interest	£x – £y

We would, however, expect the 20% attributable to the non-controlling interest to be less than the 20% attributable to the parent company which would be normally have paid an additional amount to obtain control.

20.10 The treatment of differences between a subsidiary's fair value and book value

In our examples so far we have assumed that the book value of the net assets in the subsidiary are equal to their fair value. In practice, book value in the parent company and in the subsidiary rarely equals fair value and it is necessary to revalue the group's share of the assets and liabilities of the subsidiary prior to consolidation. Note that, when consolidating, the parent company's assets and liabilities remain unchanged at book value – it is only the subsidiary's that are adjusted for the purpose of the consolidated accounts. If, for example, the non-current assets of Flower in the example above had a fair value of £11,600, the non-current assets would be increased by £600 and a pre-acquisition revaluation reserve created of £600. We will assume the non-controlling interest is measured using method 1.

	Bird £	Flower £	Group £	
ASSETS				
Non-current assets	20,000	11,000	31,600	
Goodwill	—	—	320	Note 1
Investment in Flower	12,000	—	—	
Net current assets	11,000	3,000	14,000	
Net assets	43,000	14,000	45,920	
Share capital	16,000	10,000	16,000	
Retained earnings	27,000	4,000	27,000	
	43,000	14,000	43,000	
Non-controlling interest	—	—	2,920	Note 2
	43,000	14,000	45,920	

Note 1. Goodwill

		£
The parent company's investment in Flower		12,000
Less: The parent's share of the subsidiary's share capital (80% × 10,000)	8,000	
The parent's share of retained earnings (80% × 4,000)	3,200	
The parent's share of the revaluation (80% × 600)	480	
(Equivalent to the share of net assets) 80% × (11,000 + 3,000 + 600)		11,680
The difference is goodwill		320

Note 2. Non-controlling interest

			£
The non-controlling interest in the share capital of Flower	(20% × 10,000)	=	2,000
The non-controlling interest in the retained earnings of Flower	(20% × 4,000)	=	800
The non-controlling interest in the revaluation of the subsidiary's assets	(20% × 600)		120
			2,920

Note 3. Non-current assets (20,000 + 11,000 + 600) = £31,600

It must be stressed that the revaluation of the subsidiary's assets is only necessary for the consolidated accounts. No entries need be made in the individual accounts of the subsidiary or its books of account. The preparation of consolidated accounts is a separate exercise that in no way affects the records of the individual companies.

20.11 How to calculate fair values

IFRS 3 *Business Combinations* gives a definition of fair value as 'The amount for which an asset could be exchanged or a liability settled between knowledgeable, willing parties in an arm's-length transaction.'[10] The detailed guidance for determining fair value is also set out in IFRS 3. The main provisions are as follows:

As from the date of acquisition, an acquirer should:

(a) incorporate into the statement of comprehensive income the results of operations of the acquiree; and

(b) recognise in the statement of financial position the identifiable assets, liabilities and contingent liabilities of the acquiree and any goodwill or negative goodwill arising on the acquisition.

The identifiable assets, liabilities and contingent liabilities acquired that are recognised should be those of the acquiree that existed at the date of acquisition. Liabilities should not be recognised at the date of acquisition if they result from the acquirer's intentions or actions. Therefore liabilities for terminating or reducing the activities of the acquiree should only be recognised where the acquiree has, at the acquisition date, an existing liability for restructuring recognised in accordance with IAS 37 *Provisions, Contingent Liabilities and Contingent Assets*.

Liabilities should also not be recognised for future losses[11] or other costs expected to be incurred as a result of the acquisition, whether they relate to the acquirer or acquiree.

The IFRS sets out the rules for specific assets and liabilities in Appendix B. These are not produced in detail here.

The reason why the net assets of the subsidiary must be revalued at the date of acquisition is to ensure that all profits, both realised and unrealised, are reflected in the value of the net assets at the date of acquisition and to prevent distortion of EPS in periods following the acquisition.

There is a requirement to identify both tangible and intangible assets that are acquired. For example, fair values would be attached to intangibles such as brands and customer lists if these can be measured reliably. If it is not possible to measure reliably, then the goodwill would be reported at a higher figure as in the following extract from the 2008 AstraZeneca Annual Report:

BUSINESS COMBINATIONS AND GOODWILL
On the acquisition of a business, fair values are attributed to the identifiable assets and liabilities and contingent liabilities unless the fair value cannot be measured reliably in which case the value is subsumed into goodwill. Where fair values of acquired contingent liabilities cannot be measured reliably, the assumed contingent liability is not recognised but is disclosed in the same manner as other contingent liabilities. Goodwill is the difference between consideration paid and the fair value of net assets acquired.

Summary

When one company acquires a controlling interest in another and the combination is treated as an acquisition, the investment in the subsidiary is recorded in the acquirer's consolidated statement of financial position at the fair value of the investment.

On consolidation, if the acquirer has acquired less than 100% of the common shares, any differences between the fair values of the assets or liabilities and their face value are recognised in full and the parent and non-controlling interests credited or debited with their respective percentage interests.

Also, on consolidation, any differences between the fair values of the net assets and the consideration paid to acquire them is treated as positive or negative goodwill and dealt with in accordance with IFRS 3 *Business Combinations*.

REVIEW QUESTIONS

1 Explain how negative goodwill may arise and its accounting treatment.

2 Explain how the fair value is calculated for:
   ● tangible non-current assets
   ● inventories
   ● monetary assets.

3 Explain why only the net assets of the subsidiary and not those of the parent are adjusted to fair value at the date of acquisition for the purpose of consolidated accounts.

4 Coil SA/NV is a company incorporated under the laws of Belgium. Its accounts are IAS compliant. It states in its 2003 accounts (in accordance with IAS 27, para. 13):

   Principles of consolidation
   The consolidated Financial statements include all subsidiaries which are controlled by the Parent Company, unless such control is assumed to be temporary or due to long-term restrictions significantly impairing a subsidiary's ability to transfer funds to the Parent Company.

   Required: Discuss whether these are acceptable reasons for excluding a subsidiary from the consolidated financial statements under the revised IAS 27.

5 The 2008 Annual Report of Bayer AG:

   Subsidiaries that do not have a material impact on the Group's net worth, financial position or earnings, either individually or in aggregate, are not consolidated.

   Discuss what criteria might have applied in determining that a subsidiary does not have a material impact.

6 Parent plc acquired Son plc at the beginning of the year. At the end of the year there were intangible assets reported in the consolidated accounts for the value of a domain name and customer lists. These assets did not appear in either the Parent or Son's Statements of Financial Position.

   Required: Discuss why assets only appear in the consolidated accounts.

7 In each of the following cases you are required to give your opinion, with reasons, on whether or not there is a parent/subsidiary under IFRS 3. Suggest any other information, if any, that might be helpful in making a decision.

   (a) Tin acquired 15% of the equity voting shares and 90% of the non-voting preferred shares of Copper. Copper has no other category of shares. The directors of Tin are also the directors of Copper, there is a common head office with shared administration departments and the functions of Copper are mainly the provision of marketing and transport facilities for Tin. Another company, Iron, holds 55% of the equity voting shares of Copper but has never used its voting power to interfere with the decisions of the directors.

   (b) Hat plc owns 60% of the voting equity shares in Glove plc and 25% of the voting equity shares in Shoe plc. Glove owns 30% of the voting equity shares in Shoe plc and has the right to appoint a majority of the directors.

   (c) Morton plc has 30% of the voting equity shares of Berry plc and also has a verbal agreement with other shareholders, who own 40% of the shares, that those shareholders will vote according to the wishes of Morton.

(d) Bean plc acquired 30% of the shares of Pea plc several years ago with the intention of acquiring influence over the operating and financial policies of that company. Pea sells 80% of its output to Bean. While Bean has a veto over the operating and financial decisions of Pea's board of directors it has only used this veto on one occasion, four years ago, to prevent that company from supplying one of Bean's competitors.

EXERCISES

An extract from the solution is provided on the Companion Website (www.pearsoned.co.uk/elliott-elliott) for exercises marked with an asterisk (*).

Questions 1–5

Required:

Prepare the statements of financial position of Parent Ltd and the consolidated statement of financial position as at 1 January 20X7 after each transaction, using for each question the statements of financial position of Parent Ltd and Daughter Ltd as at 1 January 20X7 which were as follows:

	Parent Ltd	Daughter Ltd
	£	£
Ordinary shares of £1 each	40,500	9,000
Retained earnings	4,500	1,800
	45,000	10,800
Cash	20,000	2,000
Other net assets	25,000	8,800
	45,000	10,800

Question 1

(a) Assume that on 1 January 20X7 Parent Ltd acquired all the ordinary shares in Daughter Ltd for £10,800 cash. The fair value of the net assets in Daughter Ltd was their book value.

(b) The purchase consideration was satisfied by the issue of 5,400 new ordinary shares in Parent Ltd. The fair value of a £1 ordinary share in Parent Ltd was £2. The fair value of the net assets in Daughter Ltd was their book value.

Question 2

(a) On 1 January 20X7 Parent Ltd acquired all the ordinary shares in Daughter Ltd for £16,200 cash. The fair value of the net assets in Daughter Ltd was their book value.

(b) The purchase consideration was satisfied by the issue of 5,400 new ordinary shares in Parent Ltd. The fair value of a £1 ordinary share in Parent Ltd was £3. The fair value of the net assets in Daughter Ltd was their book value.

Question 3

(a) On 1 January 20X7 Parent Ltd acquired all the ordinary shares in Daughter Ltd for £16,200 cash. The fair value of the net assets in Daughter Ltd was £12,000.

(b) The purchase consideration was satisfied by the issue of 5,400 new ordinary shares in Parent Ltd. The fair value of a £1 ordinary share in Parent Ltd was £3. The fair value of the net assets in Daughter Ltd was £12,000.

Question 4

On 1 January 20X7 Parent Ltd acquired all the ordinary shares in Daughter Ltd for £6,000 cash. The fair value of the net assets in Daughter Ltd was their book value.

Question 5

On 1 January 20X7 Parent Ltd acquired 75% of the ordinary shares in Daughter Ltd for £9,000 cash. The fair value of the net assets in Daughter Ltd was their book value. Assume in each case that the non-controlling interest is measured using method 1.

Question 6

The following accounts are the consolidated statement of financial position and parent company statement of financial position for Alpha Ltd as at 30 June 20X2.

	Consolidated statement of financial position		Parent company statement of financial position	
	£	£	£	£
Ordinary shares		140,000		140,000
Capital reserve		92,400		92,400
Retained earnings		79,884		35,280
Non-controlling interest		12,329		—
		324,613		267,680
Non-current assets				
Property		127,400		84,000
Plant and equipment		62,720		50,400
Goodwill		85,680		
Investment in subsidiary (50,400 shares)				151,200
Current assets				
Inventory	121,604		71,120	
Trade receivables	70,429		51,800	
Cash at bank	24,360		—	
	216,393		122,920	
Current liabilities				
Trade payables	140,420		80,920	
Income tax	27,160		20,720	
Bank overdraft	—		39,200	
	167,580		140,840	
Working capital		48,813		(17,920)
		324,613		267,680

Notes:

(i) There was only one subsidiary called Beta Ltd.

(ii) There were no capital reserves in the subsidiary.

(iii) Alpha produced inventory for sale to the subsidiary at a cost of £3,360 in May 20X2. The inventory was invoiced to the subsidiary at £4,200 and was still on hand at the subsidiary's warehouse on 30 June 20X2. The invoice had not been settled at 30 June 20X2.

(iv) The retained earnings of the subsidiary had a credit balance of £16,800 at the date of acquisition. No fair value adjustments were necessary.

(v) There was a right of set-off between overdrafts and bank balances.

(vi) The parent owns 90% of the subsidary.

Required:

(a) **Prepare the statement of financial position as at 30 June 20X2 of the subsidiary company from the information given above. The non-controlling interest is measured using method 1.**

(b) **Discuss briefly the main reasons for the publication of consolidated accounts.**

Question 7

Rouge plc acquired 100% of the common shares of Noir plc on 1 January 20X0 and gained control. At that date the statements of financial position of the two companies were as follows:

	Rouge £ million	Noir £ million
ASSETS		
Non-current assets		
Property, plant and equipment	100	60
Investment in Noir	132	
Current assets	80	70
Total assets	312	130
EQUITY AND LIABILITIES		
Ordinary £1 shares	200	60
Retained earnings	52	40
	252	100
Current liabilities	60	30
Total equity and liabilities	312	130

Note: The fair values are the same as the book values.

Required: Prepare a consolidated statement of financial position for Rouge plc as at 1 January 20X0.

* Question 8

Ham plc acquired 100% of the common shares of Burg plc on 1 January 20X0 and gained control. At that date the statements of financial position of the two companies were as follows:

	Ham £000	Burg £000
ASSETS		
Non-current assets		
Property, plant and equipment	250	100
Investment in Burg	90	
Current assets	100	70
Total assets	440	170
EQUITY AND LIABILITIES		
Capital and reserves		
£1 shares	200	100
Retained earnings	160	10
	360	110
Current liabilities	80	60
Total equity and liabilities	440	170

Notes:

1 The fair value is the same as the book value.
2 £15,000 of the negative goodwill arises because the net assets have been acquired at below their fair value and the remainder covers expected losses of £3,000 in the year ended 31/12/20X0 and £2,000 in the following year.

Required:
(a) Prepare a consolidated statement of financial position for Ham plc as at 1 January 20X0.
(b) Explain how the negative goodwill will be treated.

* Question 9

Set out below is the summarised statement of financial position of Berlin plc at 1 January 20X0.

	£000
ASSETS	
Non-current assets	
Property, plant and equipment	250
Current assets	150
Total assets	400
EQUITY AND LIABILITIES	
Capital and reserves	
Share capital (£5 shares)	200
Retained earnings	80
	280
Current liabilities	120
Total equity and liabilities	400

On 1/1/20X0 Berlin acquired 100% of the shares of Hanover for £100,000 and gained control.

Required: Prepare the statement of financial position of Berlin immediately after the acquisition if:
(a) Berlin acquired the shares for cash.
(b) Berlin issued 10,000 common shares of £5 (market value £10.).

Question 10

Bleu plc acquired 80% of the common shares of Verte plc on 1 January 20X0 and gained control. At that date the statements of financial position of the two companies were as follows:

	Bleu £m	Verte £m
ASSETS		
Non-current assets		
Property, plant and equipment	150	120
Investment in Verte	210	
Current assets	108	105
Total assets	468	225

	Bleu £m	Verte £m
EQUITY AND LIABILITIES		
Capital and reserves		
Share capital	300	120
Retained earnings	78	60
	378	180
Current liabilities	90	45
Total equity and liabilities	468	225

Note: The fair values are the same as the book values.

Required: Prepare a consolidated statement of financial position for Bleu plc as at 1 January 20X0. Non-controlling interests are measured using method 1.

Question 11

Base plc acquired 60% of the common shares of Ball plc on 1 January 20X0 and gained control. At that date the statements of financial position of the two companies were as follows:

	Base £000	Ball £000
ASSETS		
Non-current assets		
Property, plant and equipment	250	100
Investment in Ball	90	
Current assets	100	70
Total assets	440	170
EQUITY AND LIABILITIES		
Capital and reserves		
Share capital	200	80
Share premium		20
Retained earnings	160	10
	360	110
Current liabilities	80	60
Total equity and liabilities	440	170

Note:

The fair value of the property, plant and equipment in Ball at 1/1/20X0 was £120,000. The fair value of the non-controlling interest in Ball at 1/1/20X0 was £55,000. The 'fair value method' should be used to measure the non-controlling interest.

Required: Prepare a consolidated statement of financial position for Base as at 1 January 20X0.

Question 12

On 1 January 20X0 Hill plc purchased 70% of the ordinary shares of Valley plc for £1.3 million. The fair value of the non-controlling interest at that date was £0.5 million. At the date of acquisition, Valley's retained earnings were £0.6 million.

The statements of financial position of Hill and Valley at 31 December 20X0 were:

Capital and reserves	Hill (£000)	Valley (£000)
Share capital	5,000	1,000
Retained earnings	3,500	200
	8,500	1,200
Net assets	8,500	1,200

Because of Valley's loss in 20X0, the directors of Hill decided to write down the value of goodwill by £0.3 million. The directors of Hill propose to use Method 2 to calculate goodwill in the consolidated statement of financial position. The goodwill is to be written down in proportion to the respective holdings of Valley's shares by Hill and the non-controlling interest.

Required:

(a) **Calculate the goodwill of Valley relating to Hill plc and the non-controlling interest.**
(b) **Show how the goodwill will be written down at 31 December 20X0, for both Hill plc and the non-controlling interest.**
(c) **Comment on your answer to part (b).**

References

1 IAS 27 *Consolidated and Separate Financial Statements*, IASB, 2008, para. 4.
2 *Ibid.*, para. 10.
3 IAS 1 *Presentation of Financial Statements*, IASB, 2007, para. 31.
4 IAS 27 *Consolidated and Separate Financial Statements*, IASB, 2008, para. 17.
5 IFRS 3 *Business Combinations*, 2008.
6 IAS 27 *Consolidated and Separate Financial Statements*, para. 13.
7 IAS 36 *Impairment of Assets*, 2004, BC 131A.
8 IAS 36 *Impairment of Assets*, IASB, revised 2004, para. 34.
9 IFRS 3 *Business Combinations*, 2008, para. 57.
10 *Ibid.*, Appendix A.
11 *Ibid.*, para. 41.

CHAPTER 21

Preparation of consolidated statements of financial position after the date of acquisition

21.1 Introduction

The main purpose of this chapter is to prepare consolidated financial statements after a period of trading.

Objectives

By the end of this chapter, you should be able to:

- account for the post-acquisition profits of a subsidiary;
- eliminate inter-company balances and deal with reconciling items;
- account for unrealised profits on inter-company transactions.

21.2 Pre- and post-acquisition profits/losses

Pre-acquisition profits

Any profits or losses of a subsidiary made **before** the date of acquisition are referred to as **pre-acquisition profits/losses** in the consolidated financial statements. These are represented by net assets that exist in the subsidiary as at the date of acquisition and, as we have seen in Chapter 20, the fair values of these net assets will be dealt with in the goodwill calculation.

Post-acquisition profits

Any profits or losses made **after** the date of acquisition are referred to as **post-acquisition profits**. Because these will have arisen whilst the subsidiary was under the control of the parent company, they will be included in the group consolidated statement of comprehensive income and so will appear in the retained earnings figure in the statement of financial position. The following example for the Bend Group illustrates the approach to dealing with the pre- and post-acquisition profits.

EXAMPLE ● THE BEND GROUP illustrating the treatment of pre- and post-acquisition profits

1 January 20X1
Bend plc acquired 80% of the 10,000 £1 common shares in Stretch plc for £1.50 per share in cash and so gained control.

- Investment in the subsidiary cost £12,000.
- The retained earnings of Stretch plc were £4,000.
- The fair value of the non-controlling interest at the date of acquisition way £2,950.

Note that the retained earnings are required for the goodwill calculation. We will use method 2 to compute the non-controlling interest.

- The fair value of the non-current assets in Stretch plc was £600 above book value. The fair value of the subsidiary's assets are required for the consolidated statement of financial position. In the subsidiary's own accounts the assets may be left at book values or restated at their fair values. If revalued, they will then become subject to the requirements of IAS 16 *Property, Plant and Equipment*[1] which states that revaluations should be made with sufficient regularity that the statement of financial position figure is not materially different from the fair value at that date. This is one reason why the fair value adjustment is usually treated simply as a consolidation adjustment each year.

At 31 December 20X1

The closing statements of financial position of Bend plc and Stretch plc together with the group accounts were as follows:

	Bend £	Stretch £	Group £	
ASSETS				
Non-current assets	26,000	12,000	38,600	Note 3
Goodwill	—	—	350	Note 1
Investment in Stretch	12,000	—	—	
Net current assets	13,000	4,000	17,000	Note 3
Net assets	51,000	16,000	55,950	
EQUITY				
Share capital	16,000	10,000	16,000	Note 4
Retained earnings	35,000	6,000	36,600	Note 4
	51,000	16,000	52,600	
Non-controlling interest	—	—	3,350	Note 2
	51,000	16,000	55,950	

Note 1. Goodwill calculated as at 1 January 20X1

	£	£
The cost of the parent company's investment in Stretch		12,000

Less:

(a) Share capital
the parent's share of the subsidiary's share capital:
80% × share capital of Stretch .... (80% × 10,000) = 8,000

(b) Pre-acquisition profit
the parent's share of the subsidiary's retained earnings:
80% × retained earnings at 1 January 20X1 .... (80% × 4,000) = 3,200

(c) Fair value adjustment
the parent's share of any change in the book values:
80% × revaluation of fixed assets at 1 January 20X1   (80% × 600)   =   480

	11,680
Goodwill attributable to the parent company shareholders	320

	£
Fair value of non-controlling interest at date of acquisition	2,950
20% of net assets at date of acquisition (10,000 + 4,000 + 600)	(2,920)
Goodwill attributable to the non-controlling interest	30
Total goodwill (£320 + £30)	350

Note 2. Non-controlling interest in the net assets of subsidiary calculated as at 31 December 20X1

		£
(a) Subsidiary share capital		
Non-controlling interest in the share capital of Stretch	(20% × 10,000) =	2,000
(b) Total retained earnings as at 31 December 20X1		
Non-controlling interest in the retained earnings of Stretch (20% × 6,000) =		1,200
(c) Fair value adjustment of subsidiary's fixed assets		
Non-controlling interest in any revaluation reserve	(20% × 600) =	120
Statement of financial position figure for non-controlling interest in the net assets of Stretch as at 31.12.20X1		3,320
Non-controlling interest in goodwill		30
		3,350

Note 3. Add together the assets and liabilities of the parent and subsidiary for the group accounts

	Parent	Subsidiary	Group
	£	£	£
Non-current other than goodwill	26,000 +	(12,000 + Revaluation 600)	38,600
Goodwill	as calculated in Note 1		350
Net current assets	13,000 +	4,000	17,000
Total			**55,950**

Note 4. Calculate the consolidated share capital and reserves for the group accounts

		£	£
Share capital	(parent company only)		16,000
Reserves:			
Retained earnings	(parent company)	35,000	
Parent's share of the **post-acquisition retained profit** of the subsidiary			
80% of (accumulated profit at 31.12.20X1 less accumulated profit at 1.1.20X1)		1,600	
			36,600
Total shareholders' interest			**52,600**

Notes:
1 The £4,000 pre-acquisition retained profit of the subsidiary is needed to calculate the goodwill.
2 The non-controlling shareholders are entitled to their percentage share of the closing net assets. The pre-acquisition and post-acquisition division is irrelevant to the minority – they are entitled to their percentage share of the **total** retained earnings at the date the consolidated statement of financial position is prepared.

21.3 Inter-company balances

We have seen above that we set off the parent's investment in a subsidiary against the parent's share of the subsidiary's share capital and reserves (retained earnings plus/minus revaluation changes) as at the date of acquisition.

However, there are likely to be other balances in the statements of financial position of both the parent and the subsidiary company arising from inter-company (also referred to as intra-group) transactions. These will require adjustment in order that the group accounts do not double count assets and/or liabilities. These are normally referred to as consolidation adjustments and would be authorised as consolidation journal entries by a responsible officer such as the finance director. The following are examples of intra-group or inter-company transactions which we will now consider:

- preferred shares held by a parent in its subsidiary;
- bonds held by a parent in its subsidiary;
- inter-company balances arising from inter-company sales or other transactions such as inter-company loans;
- inter-company dividends payable/receivable.

These are discussed below in relation to preparation of the consolidated statement of financial position and are included in the comprehensive example, the Prose Group, below. Their significance as far as the group income is concerned will be explained when we refer to the preparation of the annual statement of comprehensive income in the next chapter.

21.3.1 Preferred shares

A parent company, in addition to the common shares by which it gained control, may have acquired preferred shares in the subsidiary. If so, any amount paid by the parent company will be included within the investment in subsidiary figure that appears in the parent company's statement of financial position. Just as the common shares represent part of the net assets acquired, so the parent's share of the preferred shares in the subsidiary's statement of financial position will represent part of the net assets acquired and will be included in the calculation of goodwill.

Any preferred shares not held by the parent are part of the non-controlling interest – this applies even though the parent might itself hold less than 50% of the preferred shares – it is not necessary for the parent to hold a majority of the preferred shares.

Where preferred shares are recognised as liabilities of the subsidiary under IAS 32 *Financial Instruments: Presentation and Disclosure,* they are accounted for in the same way as bonds. On consolidation, the preferred shares purchased by the parent and included in the cost of investment will be cancelled out against the liability of the subsidiary.

21.3.2 Bonds

As with the preferred shares, any bonds in the subsidiary's statement of financial position that have been acquired by the parent will represent part of the net assets acquired and will be included in the calculation of goodwill.

However, the amount of bonds not held by the parent will not be part of the non-controlling interest as they do not bestow any rights of ownership on shareholders. They are, effectively, a form of long-term loan, and will be shown as such in the consolidated statement of financial position.

21.3.3 Inter-company balances arising from sales or other transactions

IAS 27 requires inter-company balances to be eliminated in full.[2]

Eliminating inter-company balances

If entries in the parent's records and the subsidiary's records are up to date, the same figure will appear as a balance in the current assets of one company and in the current liabilities of the other. For example, if the parent company has supplied goods invoiced at £1,500 to its subsidiary, there will be a receivable for £1,500 in the parent statement of financial position and a payable for £1,500 in the subsidiary's statement of financial position. These need to be cancelled, i.e. eliminated, before preparing the consolidated accounts. In accounting terminology, this would be described as offsetting.

Reconciling inter-company balances

In practice, temporary differences may arise for such items as inventory or cash in transit that are recorded in one company's books but of which the other company is not yet aware, e.g. goods or cash in transit. In such a case the records will require reconciling and updating before proceeding. In a multinational company, this can be an extremely time-consuming exercise.

The following is an extract from the Sanitec International S.A. 2004 financial statements:

All significant inter-company balances and transactions have been eliminated in consolidation.

21.3.4 Inter-company dividends payable/receivable

If the subsidiary company has declared a dividend before the year-end, this will appear in the current liabilities of the subsidiary company and in the current assets of the parent company and must be cancelled before preparing the consolidated statement of financial position. If the subsidiary is wholly owned by the parent the whole amount will be cancelled. If, however, there is a non-controlling interest in the subsidiary, the non-cancelled amount of the dividend payable in the subsidiary's statement of financial position will be the amount payable to the non-controlling interest and will be reported as part of the non-controlling interest in the consolidated statement of financial position. Where a dividend has not been declared by the year-end date there is no liability under IAS 10 *Events After the Balance Sheet Date* and there should, therefore, be no liability reported under International Accounting Standards.

21.4 Unrealised profit on inter-company sales

Where sales have been made between two companies within the group, there may be an element of profit that has not been realised by the group if the goods have not then been sold on to a third party before the year-end. We will illustrate with the Many Group which consists of a parent, Many plc, and a subsidiary, Few plc.

Intra-group sales realised by sale to a third party (not a group member)

Assume, for example, that Many plc buys £1,000 worth of goods for resale and sells them to Few plc for £1,500, making a profit of £500. At the date of the statement of financial position, if Few plc still has these goods in inventory, the group has not yet made any profit on these goods and the £500 is therefore said to be 'unrealised'. It must be removed from the consolidated statement of financial position by:

- reducing the retained earnings of Many by £500;
- reducing the inventories of Few by £500.

The £500 is called a provision for unrealised profit.

If these goods are eventually sold by Few to customers outside the group for £1,800, the profit made by the group will be £800, the difference between the original cost of the goods to Many, £1,000, and the eventual sales price of £1,800. It follows from this that it is only necessary to provide for an unrealised profit from intra-group sales to the extent that the goods are still in the inventories of the group at the statement of financial position date.

The following extract from the 1999 accounts of Bayer Schering Pharma AG is an example of consolidation policy:

> Inter-company profits and losses, sales, income and expenses, receivables and liabilities between companies included in the consolidation have been eliminated.

The comprehensive example below for the Prose Group incorporates the main points dealt with so far on the preparation of a consolidated statement of financial position.

EXAMPLE ● THE PROSE GROUP

On 1 January 20X1 Prose plc acquired 80% of the equity shares in Verse plc for £21,100, 20% of the preferred shares for £2,000 and 10% of the bonds for £900, and gained control. The retained earnings as at 1 January 20X1 were £4,000. The fair value of the land in Verse was £1,000 above book value. During the year Prose sold some of its inventory to Verse for £3,000, which represented cost plus a mark-up of 25%. Half of these goods are still in the inventory of Verse at 31/12/20X1. Prepare a consolidated statement of financial position as at 31 December 20X1. Note that depreciation is not charged on land. Method 1 is used to compute the non-controlling interest.

Note: Just as in the Bend plc example above, it is helpful to structure the information before preparing your consolidation, as follows:

I January 20X1 – the date of acquisition

- Prose acquired 80% of the equity shares for £21,100 for cash and so gained control.
- Prose acquired 20% of the preferred shares in Verse for £2,000.
- Prose acquired 10% of the bonds in Verse for £900.
- The total cost of the investment is therefore £24,000.
- The retained earnings in Verse were £4,000, i.e. this is the pre-acquisition profit of which 80% will be included in the goodwill calculation.
- The fair value of the non-current assets in Verse was £1,000 above book value, i.e. the non-current assets of the subsidiary will be increased in the consolidated statement of financial position.

During 20X1

- Prose sold some of its inventory to Verse for £3,000, which represented cost plus a mark-up of 25%.

At 31 December 20X1

- Half of the goods sold by Prose were still in the inventory of Verse, i.e. there is unrealised profit, and both the consolidated gross profit and inventories in the consolidated statement of financial position will need to be reduced by the amount unrealised.
- The closing statements of financial position of Prose and Verse at 31 December 20X1 together with the group accounts were as follows:

	Prose £	Verse £	Group £	
ASSETS				
Non-current assets				
(including land)	25,920	43,400	70,320	Note 4
Goodwill	—	—	8,900	Note 1
Investment in Verse	24,000	—	—	Note 1
Current assets				
Inventories	9,600	4,000	13,300	Note 4
Verse current account	8,000			Note 2(bi)
Bond interest receivable	35			Note 2(bii)
Other current assets	1,965	3,350	5,315	Note 4
Total assets	69,520	50,750	97,835	
EQUITY and LIABILITIES				
Equity share capital	24,000	11,000	24,000	Note 5
Preferred shares	4,000	8,000	4,000	Note 5
Retained earnings	30,000	8,500	33,300	Note 5
	58,000	27,500	61,300	
Non-controlling interest	—	—	10,500	Note 3
Non-current liabilities				
Bonds	5,000	7,000	11,300	Note 6
Current liabilities				
Prose current account		8,000		
Bond interest payable		350	315	Note 2(bii)
Other current liabilities	6,520	7,900	14,420	Note 4
	69,520	50,750	97,835	

Note 1. Calculation of goodwill (note that this calculation will be the same as when calculated at the date of acquisition)

	£	£
The cost of the parent company's investment for common shares, additional paid in capital, preferred shares and bonds		24,000

Less:

(a i) parent's share of the **subsidiary's equity share capital**:
80% × common shares of Verse (80% × 11,000) = 8,800

(a ii) parent's share of the subsidiary's retained earnings:
80% × retained earnings balance at
1 January 20X1 (80% × 4,000) = 3,200

(a iii) parent's share of any change in **subsidiary's book values**:
80% × revaluation of land at **1 January 20X1** (80% × 1,000)   =   800

(a iv) parent's share of preferred shares:
20% × **preferred shares** of Verse   (20% × 8,000)   =   1,600

(a v) parent's share of **bonds**:
10% × bonds of Verse   (10% × 7,000)   =   <u>700</u>
                                                         15,100

(a vi) Goodwill in statement of financial position   <u>8,900</u>

Note 2. Inter-company adjustments

(b i) The **current accounts** of £8,000 between the two companies are cancelled. Note that the accounts are equal which indicates that there are no items such as goods in transit or cash in transit which would have required a reconciliation.

(b ii) The **bond interest receivable** by Prose is cancelled with £35 (10% of £350) of the bond interest payable by Verse leaving £315 (90% of £350) payable to outsiders. This is not part of the non-controlling interest as bond holders have no ownership rights in the company.

(b iii) Provision for unrealised profit on the inventory of Verse

The mark-up on the inter-company sales was $£3,000 \times \dfrac{25}{125}$ =   £600

Half the goods are still in inventories at the statement of financial position date so provide
$^{1}/_{2} \times £600$ for the unrealised profit   =   **£300**

Note 3. Calculation of non-controlling interest as at 31/12/20X1

Note that:
● the non-controlling interest is calculated as at the year-end while goodwill is calculated at the date of acquisition.

                                                               £

(c i) Subsidiary share capital
Non-controlling interest in the **equity shares** of Verse   (20% × 11,000) = 2,200

(c ii) Total retained earnings as at 31 December 20X1
Non-controlling interest in the retained earnings of Verse   (20% × 8,500)   1,700

(c iii) Fair value adjustment of subsidiary's non-current assets
Non-controlling interest in the **revaluation** of land   (20% × 1,000)   =   200

(c iv) Subsidiary preferred shares
Non-controlling interest in the **preferred shares** of Verse (80% × 8,000)   = <u>6,400</u>

Statement of financial position figure   <u>10,500</u>

Note 4. Add together the following assets and liabilities of the parent and subsidiary for the group accounts

	Parent	Subsidiary	£
Non-current assets other than goodwill	25,920 +	(43,400 + revaluation 1,000)	= 70,320
Inventories	9,600 +	(4,000 − provision for unrealised profit 300)	= 13,300
Other current assets	1,965 +	3,350	= 5,315
Other current liabilities	6,520 +	7,900	= 14,420

Note 5. Calculate the consolidated share capital and reserves for the group accounts

		£	£
Share capital:			
Equity share capital	(parent company's only)		**24,000**
Preferred shares	(parent company's only)		**4,000**
Retained earnings	(parent company's)	= 30,000	
Less: Provision for unrealised profit		(300)	
			29,700
Parent's share of the **post-acquisition profit** of the subsidiary			
80% × 8,500		6,800	
Less: 80% of pre-acquisition profits	(80% × 4,000)	(3,200)	
			3,600
Retained earnings in the consolidated statement of financial position			**33,300**

Note 6. Bonds

	Parent		Subsidiary		£
Bonds	5,000	+	(7,000 – inter-company 700)	=	**11,300**

The following is presented in schedule format:

	Prose £	Verse £	Adjustments DR	Adjustments CR	Group £
ASSETS					
Non-current assets					
(including land)	25,920	43,400	800 aiii		70,320
			200 ciii		
Goodwill	—	—	8,900 avi		8,900
Investment in Verse	24,000	—		(8,800) ai	
				(3,200) aii	
				(800) aiii	
				(1,600) aiv	
				(700) av	
				(8,900) avi	
Current assets					
Inventories	9,600	4,000		(300) biii	13,300
Verse current account	8,000			(8,000) bi	
Bond interest receivable	35			(35) bii	
Other current assets	1,965	3,350			5,315
Total assets	69,520	50,750			97,835

EQUITY and LIABILITIES

Equity share capital	24,000	11,000	(8,800) ai		24,000
			(2,200) ci		
Preferred shares	4,000	8,000	(1,600) aiv		4,000
			(6,400) civ		
Retained earnings	30,000	8,500	(3,200) aii		
			(1,700) cii		
			(300) biii		33,300
	58,000	27,500			61,300
Non-controlling interest	—	—		2,200 ci	10,500
				1,700 cii	
				200 ciii	
				6,400 civ	
Non-current liabilities					
Bonds	5,000	7,000	(700) av		11,300
Current liabilities					
Prose current account		8,000	(8,000)	2,200	
Bond interest payable		350			315
Other current liabilities	6,520	7,900	(35)	6,400	14,420
	69,520	50,750	42,835	42,835	97,835

21.5 Provision for unrealised profit affecting a non-controlling interest

Where a subsidiary with a non-controlling interest sells goods to a parent company at a mark-up, the non-controlling interest must be charged with their share of any provision for unrealised profit. For example, if Verse had sold goods to Prose for £3,000, including a mark-up of 25%, the non-controlling interest would have been charged with 20% of the provision for unrealised profit (20% × £300) = £60. The group would have been charged with the remaining £240.

21.6 Uniform accounting policies and reporting dates

Consolidated financial statements should be prepared using uniform accounting policies. If it is not practicable then disclosure must be made of that together with details of the items involved.[3]

The financial statements of the parent and subsidiaries used in the consolidated accounts are usually drawn up to the same date but IAS 27 allows up to three months' difference providing that appropriate adjustments are made for significant transactions outside the common period.[4]

Extract from the 2009 Annual Report of the National Grid plc
Where necessary, adjustments are made to bring the accounting policies applied under UK generally accepted accounting principles (UK GAAP), US generally accepted accounting principles (US GAAP) or other frameworks used in the individual financial statements of the Company, subsidiaries and joint ventures into line with those used by the Company in its consolidated financial statements under IFRS. Inter-company transactions are eliminated.

21.7 How is the investment in subsidiaries reported in the parent's own statement of financial position?

IAS 27 gives the parent a choice as to how to report the investment.[5] It can either report the investment at cost, or report it in accordance with the provisions of IAS 39 *Financial Instruments: Recognition and Measurement*. Cost in this context means the fair value of the consideration at the date of acquisition.

Summary

When consolidated accounts are prepared after the subsidiary has traded whilst under the control of the parent, the goodwill calculation remains as at the date of the acquisition but all inter-company transactions have to be eliminated.

REVIEW QUESTIONS

1 The 2006 accounts of Eybl International state:

   Elimination of intra-group balances
   Advances . . . arising in the course of business between the companies included in the consolidation . . . are eliminated.

   (a) Discuss three examples of inter-company (also referred to as intra-group) accounts.

   (b) Explain what is meant by 'have been eliminated'.

   (c) Explain what effect there could be on the reported group profit if inter-company transactions were not eliminated.

2 Explain why the non-controlling interest is calculated as at the year-end whilst goodwill is calculated at the date of acquisition.

3 Explain why pre-acquisition profits of a subsidiary are treated differently from post-acquisition profits.

4 Explain the effect of a provision for unrealised profit on a non-controlling interest:

   (a) where the sale was made by the parent to the subsidiary; and

   (b) where the sale was made by the subsidiary to the parent.

EXERCISES

An extract from the solution is provided on the Companion Website (www.pearsoned.co.uk/elliott-elliott) for exercises marked with an asterisk (*).

Question I

Sweden acquired 100% of the equity shares of Oslo on 1 March 20X1 and gained control. At that date the balances on the reserves of Oslo were as follows:

The Revaluation reserve – Kr10 million
Retained earnings – Kr70 million

The statements of financial position of the two companies at 31/12/20X1 were as follows:

	Sweden Krm	Oslo Krm
ASSETS		
Non-current assets		
Property, plant and equipment	264	120
Investment in Oslo	200	
Current assets	160	140
Total assets	624	260
EQUITY AND LIABILITIES		
Kr10 shares	400	110
Retained earnings	104	80
Revaluation reserve	20	10
	524	200
Current liabilities	100	60
Total equity and liabilities	624	260

Notes:

1 The fair values were the same as the book values on 1/3/20X1.
2 There have been no movements on share capital since 1/3/20X1.
3 20% of the goodwill is to be written off as an impairment loss.
4 Method 1 is to be used to compute the non-controlling interest.

Required:
Prepare a consolidated statement of financial position for Sweden as at 31 December 20X1.

* Question 2

Summer plc acquired 60% of the common shares of Winter Ltd on 30 September 20X1 and gained control. At the date of acquisition, the balance of retained earnings of Winter was £35,000.

At 31 December 20X1 the statements of financial position of the two companies were as follows:

	Summer £000	Winter £000
ASSETS		
Non-current assets		
Property, plant and equipment	200	200
Investment in Winter	141	
Current assets	100	140
Total assets	441	340
EQUITY AND LIABILITIES		
Equity shares	200	180
Retained earnings	161	40
	361	220
Current liabilities	80	120
Total equity and liabilities	441	340

Notes:

1 The fair value of the non-controlling interest at the date of acquisition was £92,000. The non-controlling interest is to be measured using method 2. The fair values of the identifiable net assets of Winter at the date of acquisition were the same as their book values..

2 There have been no movements on share capital since 30/9/20X1.

3 16.67% of the goodwill is to be written off as an impairment loss.

Required:
Prepare a consolidated statement of financial position for Summer plc as at 31 December 20X1.

Question 3

On 30 September 20X0 Gold plc acquired 75% of the equity shares, 30% of the preferred shares and 20% of the bonds in Silver plc and gained control. The balance of retained earnings on 30 September 20X0 was £16,000. The fair value of the land owned by Silver was £3,000 above book value. No adjustment has so far been made for this revaluation.

The statements of financial position of Gold and Silver at 31 December 20X1 were as follows:

	Gold £	Silver £
ASSETS		
Property, plant and equipment (including land)	82,300	108,550
Investment in Silver	46,000	—
Current assets:		
Inventory	23,200	10,000
Silver current account	20,000	
Bond interest receivable	175	
Other current assets	5,000	7,500
Total assets	176,675	126,050
EQUITY AND LIABILITIES		
Equity share capital	60,000	27,600
Preferred shares	10,000	20,000
Retained earnings	75,000	21,200
	145,000	68,800
Non-current liabilities – bonds	12,500	17,500
Current liabilities		
Gold current account		20,000
Bond interest payable	625	875
Other current liabilities	18,550	18,875
Total equity and liabilities	176,675	126,050

Notes:

1 20% of the goodwill is to be written off as an impairment loss.

2 During the year Gold sold some of its inventory to Silver for £3,000, which represented cost plus a mark-up of 25%. Half of these goods are still in the inventory of Silver at 31/12/20X1.

3 There is no depreciation of land.

4 There has been no movement on share capital since the acquisition.

5 Method 1 is to be used to compute the non-controlling interest.

Required:
Prepare a consolidated statement of financial position as at 31 December 20X1.

Question 4

Prop and Flap have produced the following statements of financial position as at 31 October 2008:

| | Prop | | Flap | |
	$m	$m	$m	$m
ASSETS				
Non-current assets				
Plant and equipment		2,100		480
Investments		800		
Current assets				
Inventories	800		280	
Receivables	580		280	
Cash and cash equivalents	400		8	
		1,860		708
Total assets		4,760		1,188
EQUITY and LIABILITIES				
Equity share capital		2,400		680
Retained earnings		860		200
		3,260		880
Non-current liabilities				
Long-term borrowing		400		
Current liabilities				
Payables	1,100		228	
Bank overdraft	—		80	
		1,100		308
Total equity and liabilities		4,760		1,188

The following information is relevant to the preparation of the financial statements of the Prop Group:

(i) Prop acquired 80% of the issued ordinary share capital of Flap many years ago when the retained earnings of Flap were $72 million. Consideration transferred was $800 million. Flap has performed well since acqusition and so far there has been no impairment to goodwill.

(ii) At the date of acquisition the plant and equipment of Flap was revalued upwards by $40 million, although this revaluation was not recorded in the acconts of Flap. Depreciation would have been $32 million greater had it been based on the revalued figure.

(iii) Flap buys goods from Prop upon which Prop earns a margin of 20%. At 31 October 2008 Flap's inventories include $180 million goods purchased from Prop.

(iv) At 31 October 2008 Prop has receivables of $140 million owed by Flap and payables of $60 million owed to Flap.

(v) The market price of the non-controlling interest shares just before Flap's acquisition by Prop was $1.30. It is the group's policy to value the non-controlling interest at fair value.

Required:
Prepare the Prop Group consolidated statement of financial position as at 31 October 2008.

(Association of International Accountants)

References

1 IAS 16 *Property, Plant and Equipment*, IASB, revised 2003, para. 31.
2 IAS 27 *Consolidated and Separate Financial Statements*, IASB, revised 2008, para. 20.
3 *Ibid.*, para. 24.
4 *Ibid.*, paras 22 and 23.
5 *Ibid.*, para. 38.

CHAPTER **22**

Preparation of consolidated statements of comprehensive income, changes in equity and cash flows

22.1 Introduction

The main purpose of this chapter is to explain how to prepare a consolidated statement of comprehensive income.

> **Objectives**
>
> By the end of this chapter, you should be able to:
>
> - prepare a consolidated statement of comprehensive income;
> - eliminate inter-company transactions from a consolidated statement of comprehensive income;
> - attribute comprehensive income to the non-controlling shareholders;
> - prepare a consolidated statement of changes in equity.

22.2 Preparation of a consolidated statement of comprehensive income – the Ante Group

The following information is available:

At the date of acquisition on 1 January 20X1
Ante plc acquired 75% of the common shares and 20% of the preferred shares in Post plc.
  (Shows that Ante had control)
At that date the retained earnings of Post were £30,000.
  (These are pre-acquisition profits and should not be included in the Group profit for the year)
Ante had paid £10,000 more than the fair value of the net assets acquired. Method 1 has been used to measure the non-controlling interest.
  (This represents positive goodwill)

During the year ended 31 December 20X2
Ante had sold Post goods at their cost price of £9,000 plus a mark up of one-third. These were the only inter-company sales.
  (Indicates that the group sales and cost of sales require adjusting)

At the end of the financial year on 31 December 20X2
Half of these goods were still in the inventory at the end of the year.
  (There is unrealised profit to be removed from the Group gross profit)

584 • Consolidated accounts

20% is to be written-off goodwill as an impairment loss.

Dividends paid in the year by group companies were as follows:

	Ante	*Post*
On ordinary shares	40,000	5,000
On preferred shares	—	3,000

Set out below are the individual statements of comprehensive income and statement of changes in equity of Ante and Post together with the consolidated statement of comprehensive income for the year ended 31 December 20X2 with explanatory notes.

Statements of comprehensive income for the year ended 31 December 20X2

	Ante £	*Post* £	*Consolidated* £	
Sales	200,000	120,000	308,000	Notes 1/3
Cost of sales	60,000	60,000	109,500	Notes 1/2/3
Gross profit	140,000	60,000	198,500	
Expenses	59,082	40,000	99,082	Note 4
Impairment of goodwill	—		2,000	Note 5
Profit from operations	80,918	20,000	97,418	
Dividends received – common shares	3,750	—	—	Note 6
Dividends received – preferred shares	600	—	—	Note 6
Profit before tax	85,268	20,000	97,418	
Income tax expense	14,004	6,000	20,004	Note 7
Profit for the period	71,264	14,000	77,414	
Attributable to:				
Ordinary shareholders of Ante (balance)			72,264	
Non-controlling shareholders in Post (Note 8)			5,150	
			77,414	

Profit realised from operations – £97,418 – see Notes 1–5

Adjustments are required to establish the profit **realised** from operations. This entails eliminating the effects of inter-company sales and inventory transferred within the group with a profit loading but not sold at the statement of financial position date and charging any goodwill impairment.

Notes:

1 **Eliminate inter-company sales on consolidation.**

   Cancel the inter-company sales of £12,000 (9,000 + $^1/_3$) by.

   (i) reducing the sales of Ante from £200,000 to £188,000; and

   (ii) reducing the cost of sales of Post by the same amount from £60,000 to £48,000.

2 **Eliminate unrealised profit on inter-company goods still in closing inventory.**

   (i) Ante had sold the goods to Post at a mark up £3,000.

   (ii) Half of the goods remain in the inventory of Post at the year-end.

   (iii) From the group's view there is an unrealised profit of half of the mark-up, i.e. £1,500. Therefore:

   • deduct £1,500 from the gross profit of Ante by adding this amount to the cost of sales;

   • add this amount to a provision for unrealised profit;

- reduce the inventories in the consolidated statement of financial position by the amount of the provision (as explained in the previous chapter).

3 Aggregate the adjusted sales and cost of sales figures for items in Notes 1 and 2.

(i) Add the adjusted sales figures

((200,000 − 12,000 inter-company sales) + 120,000) = £308,000

(ii) Add the adjusted cost of sales figures;

60,000 + (60,000 − 12,000) + 1,500 provision = £109,500

4 Aggregate expenses

No adjustment is required to the parent or subsidiary total figures.

5 Deduct the impairment loss.

The goodwill was given as £10,000, and it has been estimated that there has been a £2,000 impairment loss.

Profit after tax – £97,418

Adjustments are required[1] to establish the profit after tax earned by the group as a whole. This entails eliminating dividends and interest that have been paid to the parent by the subsidiaries. If this were not done, there would be a double counting as these would appear in the profit from operations of the subsidiary, which has been included in the consolidated profit from operations, and again as dividends and interests received by the group.

6 Accounting for inter-company dividends

(i) **The ordinary dividend** £3,750 received by Ante is 75% of the £5,000 dividend paid by Post.

(ii) Cancel the inter-company dividend received by Ante with £3,750 dividend paid by Post, leaving the £1,250 dividend paid by Post to the non-controlling interest.

(iii) **The preferred dividend** of £600 received by Ante is 20% of the £3,000 paid by Post.

(iv) Cancel the £600 preferred dividend received by Ante with £600 of the preferred dividend paid by Post.

(v) the balance of £2,400 remaining was paid to the non-controlling interest.

7 Aggregate the taxation figures.

No adjustment is required to the parent or subsidiary total figures.

Allocation of profit to equity holders and non-controlling interest

Adjustment is required[2] to establish how much of the profit after tax is attributable to equity holders of the parent. This entails allocating the non-controlling interest in the subsidiary company as a percentage of the subsidiary's after-tax figure, as adjusted for any preference dividend (see note 8).

8 Calculate the share of post-taxation profits belonging to the non-controlling interest.

£

Preferred shares – dividend on these shares:

Non-controlling shareholders hold 80% of preferred shares

(80% × 3,000) = 2,400

Common shares – % of profit after tax of the subsidiary *less* preferred share dividend

Non-controlling shareholders hold 25% of the ordinary shares

25% × (14,000 − 3,000) = 2,750

Total non-controlling interest in the profit after tax of the subsidiary **5,150**

22.3 The statement of changes in equity (SOCE)[3]

We will prepare extracts from the consolidated statement of changes in equity for the Ante group (retained earnings columns only). In order to do this, we need the balances on retained earnings at the start of the year. These are as follows:

Ante – £69,336.
Post – £54,000.

The statement will be as follows:

	Ante group	Non-controlling interest	Total
	£	£	£
Opening balance (Notes 1 & 2)	87,336	13,500	100,836
Comprehensive income for the period (from the consolidated statement of comprehensive income)	72,264	5,150	77,414
Dividends paid (Note 3)	(40,000)	(3,650)	(43,650)
Closing balance	119,600	15,000	134,600

Note 1 – Opening balance for the Ante group

	£
Ante's retained earnings at the start of the year	69,336
The group share of Post's retained earnings since acquisition (75% × (54,000 – 30,000))	18,000
	87,336

Note 2 – Opening balance for the non-controlling shareholders

54,000 × 25% = £13,500. The relevant percentage to use is 25% because only **ordinary** shareholders will have any interest in the **retained** profits.

Note 3 – Dividends paid

In the Ante group column the dividends paid are those of the parent only. The parent company's share of Post's dividend cancels out with the parent company's investment income. The non-controlling share is dealt with in their column. The dividends paid to non-controlling shareholders are 25% × £5,000 + 80% × £3,000.

22.4 Other consolidation adjustments

In the above example we dealt with adjustments for intra-group sale of goods, unrealised profit on inventories and dividends received from a subsidiary. There are other adjustments that often appear in examination papers relating to depreciation.

Depreciation adjustment based on fair values

In the example, we assumed that the fair value of the non-current assets acquired was their book value. If the fair value was higher than the book value, we would need to adjust the Cost of sales figure. For example, assume that non-current assets with a book value of

£100,000 were acquired at a fair value of £150,000 and an estimated economic life of five years. The depreciation charge in the subsidairy would have been £20,000 (£100,000/5). The charge in the consolidation should be based on the £150,000 i.e. £30,000 (£150,000/5). A consolidation adjustment is required to charge the £10,000 difference. If there is no information as to the type of non-current asset, then this would be added to the Cost of sales figure. If the type of asset is identified, for example, as delivery lorries, then the adjustment would be made to the approppriate expense e.g. distribution costs.

Adjustment where non-current asset is acquired from a subsidiary

Digdeep plc is a civil engineering company that has a subsidairy, Heavylift plc, that manufactures digging equipment. Assume that at the beginning of the financial year Heavylift sold equipment costing £80,000 to Digdeep for £100,000, It is Digdeep's depreciation policy to depreciate at 5% using the straight line method.

On consolidation, the following adjustments are required:

(i) Revenue is reduced by £20,000 and the asset is reduced by £20,000 to bring the asset back to its cost of £80,000.
   DR: Revenue   £20,000
   CR: Asset   £20,000

(ii) Revenue is then reduced by £80,000 and Cost of sales reduced by £80,000 to eliminate the intra-group sale.
   DR: Revenue   £80,000
   CR: Cost of sales   £80,000

(iii) Depreciation needs to be based on the cost of £80,000 by crediting depreciation and debiting the accumulated depreciation. The depreciation charge was £5,000 (5% of £100,000); it should be £4,000 (5% of £80,000) so the adjustment is:
   DR: Accumulated depreciation   £1,000
   CR: Depreciation in the statement of income   £1,000

Revaluation of non-current assets

The revaluation of non-current assets to fair value on acquisition has an impact on the calculation of goodwill. The only impact on the consolidated statement of income is for the depreciation adjustment discussed above.

Any increase on a revaluation of the parent company's non-current assets will be reported under Other comprehensive income.

22.5 Dividends or interest paid by the subsidiary out of pre-acquisition profits

In the Ante Group example above, we illustrated the accounting treatment where a dividend was paid by a subsidiary out of post-acquisition profits. This showed that, when dividends and interest are received by a parent company from a company it has acquired, they will normally be credited as income in the parent company's statement of comprehensive income.

However, this treatment will not be appropriate where the dividend or interest has been paid out of profits earned by the subsidiary before acquisition. The reason is that the dividend or interest is paid out of the net assets acquired at the date of acquisition and these were paid for in the price paid for the investment. The dividend or interest received by the parent, therefore, is not income but a return of part of the purchase price, which must be reported as such in the parent's statement of financial position. This is illustrated in the Bow plc example below:

Illustration of a dividend paid out of pre-acquisition profits

Bow plc acquired 75% of the shares in Tie plc on 1 January 20X1 for £80,000 when the balance of the retained earnings of Tie was £40,000. There was no goodwill. On 10 January 20X1 Bow received a dividend of £3,000 from Tie out of the profits for the year ended 31/12/20X0. There were no inter-company transactions, other than the dividend. The summarised statements of comprehensive income for the year ended 31/12/20X1 were as follows:

	Bow £	Tie £	Consolidated £
Gross profit	130,000	70,000	200,000
Expenses	50,000	40,000	90,000
Profit from operations	80,000	30,000	110,000
Dividends received from Tie (see note)	3,000	—	—
Profit before tax	83,000	30,000	110,000
Income tax expense	24,000	6,000	30,000
Profit for the period	59,000	24,000	80,000

Note:

The £3,000 dividend received from Tie is not income and must not therefore appear in Bow statement of comprehensive income. The correct treatment is to deduct it from the investment in Tie, which will then become £77,000 (80,000 − 3,000). The consolidation would then proceed as usual.

22.6 A subsidiary acquired part of the way through the year

It would be attractive for a company whose results had not been as good as expected to acquire a profitable subsidiary at the end of the year and take its annual profit into the group accounts. However, this type of window dressing is not permitted and the group can only bring in a subsidiary's profits from the date of the acquisition. The Tight plc example below illustrates the approach.

22.6.1 Illustration of a subsidiary acquired part of the way through the year – Tight plc

The following information is available:

At date of acquisition – 30 September 20X1
Tight acquired 75% of the shares and 20% of the 5% bonds in Loose.
The purchase consideration (amount paid) was £10,000 more than book value.
The book value and fair value were the same amount.
The retained earnings of the Tight Group were £69,336.

During the year
All income and expenses are deemed to accrue evenly through the year and the dividend receivable may be apportioned to pre- and post-acquisition on a time basis.
On 30 June 20X1 Tight sold Loose goods for £4,000 plus a mark-up of one-third.

At end of financial year

The Tight Group prepares its accounts as at 31 December each year.

Half of the intra-group goods were still in inventory at the end of the year.

Set out below are the individual statements of comprehensive income of Tight and Loose together with the consolidated statement of comprehensive income for the year ended 31 December 20X1.

	Tight £	Loose £	Consolidated £	
Revenue	200,000	120,000	**230,000**	Notes 1/2
Cost of sales	60,000	60,000	**75,000**	Note 2
Gross profit	140,000	60,000	155,000	
Expenses	59,082	30,000	**66,582**	Note 3
Interest paid on 5% bonds		10,000	**2,000**	Note 4
Interest received on Loose bonds	2,000		—	
	82,918	20,000	86,418	
Dividends received	3,600	NIL	NIL	Note 5
Profit before tax	86,518	20,000	86,418	
Income tax expense	14,004	6,000	**15,504**	Note 6
Profit for the period after tax	72,514	14,000	70,914	
Attributable to:				
Ordinary shareholders of Tight (balance)			70,039	
Non-controlling shareholders in Loose (Note 7)			875	
			70,914	

Notes:

1 Inter-company sales

These can be ignored as they took place before the date of acquisition.

2 Time-apportion and aggregate the revenue and cost of sales figures.

Group revenue includes a full year for the parent company and three months for the subsidiary (1 October to 31 December),

i.e. £200,000 + (120,000 × $^3/_{12}$) = **£230,000**

Group cost of sales include a full year for the parent company and three months for the subsidiary (1 October – 31 December),

i.e. £60,000 + (60,000 × $^3/_{12}$) = **£75,000**

3 Aggregate the expense.

This includes the whole of the parent and the time-apportioned subsidiary's expenses, i.e. £59,082 + (30,000 × $^3/_{12}$) = **£66,582**

4 Accounting for inter-company interest

The interest received by Tight is apportioned on a time basis: $^9/_{12}$ £2,000 = £1,500 is treated as being pre-acquisition and deducted from the cost of the investment in Loose.

The remainder (£500) is cancelled with £500 of the post-acquisition element of the interest payable by Loose. The interest payable figure in the consolidated financial statements will be the post-acquisition interest less the inter-company elimination, which represents the amount payable to the holders of 80% of the bonds.

Total interest paid 10,000 – pre-acquisition 7,500 – inter-company 500 = **£2,000**

Profit before tax

Inter-company expense items need to be eliminated. These include items such as management charges, consulting fees and interest payments. In this example we illustrate the treatment of interest. Interest is an expense which is normally deemed to accrue evenly over the year and to be apportioned on a time basis.

5 **Accounting for inter-company dividends**

Amount received by Tight	=	£3,600
The dividend received by Tight is apportioned on a time basis, and the pre-acquisition element is credited to the cost of investment in Tight's statement of financial position, i.e. $^9/_{12} \times £3,600$	=	(£2,700)
The post-acquisition element is cancelled with part of the dividend paid in Loose statement of comprehensive income prior to consolidation.	=	(£900)
Amount credited to consolidated statement of comprehensive income		NIL

6 **Aggregate the tax figures.**

This includes the whole of the parent's tax and the time-apportioned part of the subsidiary's tax, i.e. £14,004 + (6,000 × $^3/_{12}$) = £15,504
The group taxation is that of Tight plus $^3/_{12}$ of Loose.

7 **Calculate the share of post-acquisition consolidated profits belonging to the non-controlling interest.**

As only the post-acquisition proportion of the subsidiary's profit after tax has been included in the consolidated statement of comprehensive income, the amount deducted as the non-controlling interest in the profit after tax is also time-apportioned, i.e.
25% × (14,000 × $^3/_{12}$) = £875

22.7 Published format statement of comprehensive income

The statement of comprehensive income follows the classification of expenses by function as illustrated in IAS 1:

	£
Revenue	230,000
Cost of sales	75,000
Gross profit	155,000
Distribution costs	xxxxxx
Administrative expense	xxxxxx
	66,582
	88,418
Finance cost	2,000
	86,418
Income tax expense	15,504
Profit for the period	70,914
Attributable to:	
Equity holders of the parent	70,039
Non-controlling interest	875

22.8 Consolidated statements of cash flows

Statements of cash flow are explained in Chapter 26 for a single company. A consolidated statement of cash flows differs from that for a single company in two respects: there are additional items such as dividends paid to non-controlling interests; and adjustments may be required to the actual amounts to reflect the assets and liabilities brought in by the subsidiary.

22.8.1 Additional items when subsidiary acquired during the year

Adjustments are required if the closing statement of financial position items have been increased or reduced as a result of **non-cash movements**. Such movements occur if there has been a purchase of a subsidiary to reflect the fact that the asset and liabilities from the new subsidiary have not necessarily resulted from cash flows. The following illustrates such adjustments in relation to a subsidiary acquired at the end of the financial year where the net assets of the subsidiary were:

Net assets acquired	*£000*	*In consolidated statement of cash flows the effect will be:*
Working capital:		
Inventory	10	Reduce inventory increase
Trade payables	(12)	Reduce trade payables increase
Non-current assets:		
Vehicles	20	Reduce capital expenditure
Cash/bank:		
Cash	5	Reduce amount paid to acquire subsidiary in investing section
Net assets acquired	23	

Let us assume that the consideration for the acquisition were as follows:

Consideration:		
Shares	10	Reduce share cash inflow
Share premium	10	Reduce share cash inflow
Cash	3	Payment to acquire subsidiary in investing section
	23	

The consolidated statement of cash flows can then be prepared using the indirect method.

Statement of cash flows using the indirect method

	£000	£000
Cash flows from operating activities		
Net profit before tax	500	
Adjustments for:		
Depreciation	102	
Operating profit before working capital changes	602	
Increase in trade and other receivables	(260)	
Increase in inventories (400)		
Less: **inventory brought in on acquisition** 10	(390)	
Decrease in trade payables (40)		
Add: **trade payables brought in on acquisition** (12)	(52)	
Cash generated from operations	160	
Income taxes paid (200 + 190 − 170)	(220)	
Net cash from operating activities		(60)
Cash flows from investing activities		
Purchase of property, plant and equipment (563)		
Less: **vehicles brought in on acquisition** 20	(543)	
Payment to acquire subsidiary	(3)	
Cash acquired with subsidiary	5	
Net cash used in investing activities		(541)
Cash flows from financing activities		
Proceeds from issuance of share capital 300		
Less: **shares issued on acquisition not for cash** (20)	280	
Dividends paid (*from statement of comprehensive income*)	(120)	
Net cash from financing activities		160
Net decrease in cash and cash equivalents		(441)
Cash and cash equivalents at the beginning of the period		72
Cash and cash equivalents at the end of the period		(369)

Supplemental disclosure of acquisition

	£
Total purchase consideration	23,000
Portion of purchase consideration discharged by means of cash or cash equivalents	3,000
Amount of cash and cash equivalents in the subsidiary acquired	5,000

Summary

The retained earnings of the subsidiary brought forward is divided into pre-acquisition profits and post-acquisition profits – the group share of the former are used in the goodwill calculation, and the share of the latter are brought into the consolidated shareholders' equity.

Revenue and cost of sales are adjusted in order to eliminate intra-group sales and unrealised profits.

Finance expenses and income are adjusted to eliminate intra-group payments of interest and dividends.

The non-controlling interest in the profit after tax of the subsidiary is deducted to arrive at the profit for the year attributable to the equity holders of the parent.

The amounts paid as dividends to the parent company's shareholders are shown as deductions in the consolidated statement of changes in equity.

If a subsidiary is acquired during a financial year, the items in its statement of comprehensive income require apportioning. In the illustration in the text we assumed that trading was evenly spread throughout the year – in practice you would need to consider any seasonal patterns that would make this assumption unrealistic, remembering that the important consideration is that the group accounts should only be credited with profits arising whilst the subsidiary was under the parent's control.

REVIEW QUESTIONS

1 Explain why the dividends deducted from the group in the statement of changes in equity are only those of the parent company.

2 Explain how unrealised profits arise from transactions between companies in a group and why it is important to remove them.

3 Explain why it is necessary to apportion a subsidiary's profit or loss if acquired part-way through a financial year.

4 Explain why dividends paid by a subsidiary to a parent company are eliminated on consolidation.

5 Give five examples of inter-company income and expense transactions that will need to be eliminated on consolidation and explain why each is necessary.

6 A shareholder was concerned that following an acquisition the profit from operations of the parent and subsidiary were less than the aggregate of the individual profit from operations figures. She was concerned that the acquisition, which the directors had supported as improving earnings per share, appeared to have reduced the combined profits. She wanted to know where the profits had gone.

Give an explanation to the shareholder.

EXERCISES

An extract from the solution is provided on the Companion website (www.pearsoned.co.uk/elliott-elliott) for exercises marked with an asterisk (*).

* Question 1

Bill plc acquired 80% of the common shares and 10% of the preferred shares in Ben plc on 31 December three years ago when Ben's accumulated retained profits were £45,000. During the year Bill sold Ben goods for £8,000 plus a mark-up of 50%. Half of these goods were still in stock at the end of the year. There was goodwill impairment loss of £3,000. Non-controlling interests are measured using method 1.

The statements of comprehensive income of the two companies for the year ended 31 December 20X1 were as follows:

	Bill	Ben
	£	£
Revenue	300,000	180,000
Cost of sales	90,000	90,000
Gross profit	210,000	90,000
Expenses	88,623	60,000
	121,377	30,000
Dividends received – common shares	6,000	—
Dividends received – preferred shares	450	—
Profit before tax	127,827	30,000
Income tax expense	21,006	9,000
Profit for the period	106,821	21,000

Required:
Prepare a consolidated statement of comprehensive income for the year ended 31 December 20X1.

Question 2

Morn Ltd acquired 90% of the shares in Eve Ltd on 1 January 20X1 for £90,000 when Eve Ltd's accumulated profits were £50,000. On 10 January 20X1 Morn Ltd received a dividend of £10,800 from Eve Ltd out of the profits for the year ended 31/12/20X0. On 31/12/20X1 Morn increased its non-current assets by £30,000 on revaluation. The summarised statements of comprehensive income for the year ended 31/12/20X1 were as follows:

	Morn	Eve
	£	£
Gross profit	360,000	180,000
Expenses	120,000	110,000
	240,000	70,000
Dividends received from Eve Ltd	10,800	—
Profit before tax	250,800	70,000
Income tax expense	69,000	18,000
Profit for the period	181,800	52,000

There were no inter-company transactions, other than the dividend. There was no goodwill.

Required:
Prepare a consolidated statement of comprehensive income for the year ended 31 December 20X1.

Question 3

River plc acquired 90% of the common shares and 10% of the 5% bonds in Pool Ltd on 31 March 20X1. All income and expenses are deemed to accrue evenly through the year. On 31 January 20X1 River sold Pool goods for £6,000 plus a mark up of one-third. 75% of these goods were still in stock at the end of the year. There was a goodwill impairment loss of £4,000. On 31/12/20X1 River increased its non-current assets by £15,000 on revaluation. Non-controlling interests are measured using method 1. Set out below are the individual statements of comprehensive income of River and Pool:

Statements of comprehensive income for the year ended 31 December 20X1

	River £	Pool £
Net turnover	100,000	60,000
Cost of sales	30,000	30,000
Gross profit	70,000	30,000
Expenses	20,541	15,000
Interest payable on 5% bonds		5,000
Interest receivable on Pool Ltd bonds	500	
	49,959	10,000
Dividends received	2,160	NIL
Profit before tax	52,119	10,000
Income tax expense	7,002	3,000
Profit for the period	45,117	7,000

Required:

Prepare a consolidated statement of comprehensive income for the year ended 31 December 20X1.

Question 4

The statements of financial position of Mars plc and Jupiter plc at 31 December 20X2 are as follows:

	Mars £	Jupiter £
ASSETS		
Non-current assets at cost	550,000	225,000
Depreciation	220,000	67,500
	330,000	157,500
Investment in Jupiter	187,500	
Current assets		
Inventories	225,000	67,500
Trade receivables	180,000	90,000
Current account – Jupiter	22,500	
Bank	36,000	18,000
	463,500	175,500
Total assets	**981,000**	**333,000**
EQUITY AND LIABILITIES		
Capital and reserves		
£1 common shares	196,000	90,000
General reserve	245,000	31,500
Retained earnings	225,000	135,000
	666,000	256,500
Current liabilities		
Trade payables	283,500	40,500
Taxation	31,500	13,500
Current account – Mars		22,500
	315,000	76,500
Total equity and liabilities	**981,000**	**333,000**

Statements of comprehensive income for the year ended 31 December 20X2

	£	£
Sales	1,440,000	270,000
Cost of sales	1,045,000	135,000
Gross profit	395,000	135,000
Expenses	123,500	90,000
Dividends received from Jupiter	9,000	NIL
Profit before tax	280,500	45,000
Income tax expense	31,500	13,500
Profit for the period	249,000	31,500
Dividends paid	180,000	11,250
	69,000	20,250
Retained earnings brought forward from previous years	156,000	114,750
	225,000	135,000

Mars acquired 80% of the shares in Jupiter on 1 January 20X0 when Jupiter's retained earnings were £80,000 and the balance on Jupiter's general reserve was £18,000. Non-controlling interests are measured using method 1. During the year Mars sold Jupiter goods for £18,000 which represented cost plus 50%. Half of these goods were still in stock at the end of the year.

During the year Mars and Jupiter paid dividends of £180,000 and £11,250 respectively. The opening balances of retained earnings for the two companies were £156,000 and £114,750 respectively.

Required:
Prepare a consolidated statement of comprehensive income for the year ended 31/12/20X2, a statement of financial position as at that date, and a consolidated statement of changes in equity. Also prepare the retained earnings columns of the consolidated statement of changes in equity for the year.

* Question 5

The statements of financial position of Red Ltd and Pink Ltd at 31 December 20X2 are as follows:

	Red $	Pink $
ASSETS		
Non-current assets	225,000	100,000
Depreciation	80,000	30,000
	145,000	70,000
Investment in Pink Ltd	110,000	
Current assets		
Inventories	100,000	30,000
Trade receivables	80,000	40,000
Current account – Pink Ltd	10,000	
Bank	16,000	8,000
	206,000	78,000
Total assets	**461,000**	**148,000**

EQUITY AND LIABILITIES

Capital and reserves

$1 common shares	176,000	40,000
General reserve	20,000	14,000
Revaluation reserve	25,000	
Retained earnings	100,000	60,000
	321,000	114,000
Current liabilities		
Trade payables	125,996	18,000
Taxation payable	14,004	6,000
Current account – Red Ltd		10,000
	140,000	34,000
Total equity and liabilities	**461,000**	**148,000**

Statements of comprehensive income for the year ended 31 December 20X2

	$	$
Sales	200,000	120,000
Cost of sales	60,000	60,000
Gross profit	140,000	60,000
Expenses	59,082	40,000
Dividends received	3,750	NIL
Profit before tax	84,668	20,000
Income tax expense	14,004	6,000
	70,664	14,000
Surplus on revaluation	25,000	—
Total comprehensive income	**95,664**	**14,000**

Red Ltd acquired 75% of the shares in Pink Ltd on 1 January 20X0 when Pink Ltd's retained earnings were $30,000 and the balance on Pink's general reserve was $8,000. The fair value of the non-controlling interest at the date was £32,000. Non-controlling interests are to be measured using method 2.

On 31 December 20X2 Red revalued its non-current assets. The revaluation surplus of £25,000 was credited to the revaluation reserve.

During the year Pink sold Red goods for $9,000 plus a mark-up of one-third. Half of these goods were still in inventory at the end of the year. Goodwill suffered an impairment loss of 20%.

Required:
Prepare a consolidated statement of comprehensive income for the year ended 31/12/20X2 and a statement of financial position as at that date.

Question 6

Alpha has owned 80% of the equity shares of Beta since the incorporation of Beta. On 1 July 20X6 Alpha purchased 60% of the equity shares of Gamma. The statements of comprehensive income and summarised statements of changes in equity of the three entities for the year ended 31 March 20X7 are given below:

Statement of comprehensive income

	Alpha $'000	Beta $'000	Gamma $'000
Revenue (Note 1)	180,000	120,000	106,000
Cost of sales	(90,000)	(60,000)	(54,000)
Gross profit	90,000	60,000	52,000
Distribution costs	(9,000)	(8,000)	(8,000)
Administrative expenses	(10,000)	(9,000)	(8,000)
Investment income (Note 2)	26,450	Nil	Nil
Finance cost	(10,000)	(8,000)	(5,000)
Profit before tax	87,450	35,000	31,000
Income tax expense	(21,800)	(8,800)	(7,800)
Net profit for the period	65,650	26,200	23,200

Summarised statements of changes in equity

Balance at 1 April 20X6	152,000	111,000	102,000
Net profit for the period	65,650	26,200	23,200
Dividends paid on 31 January 20X7	(30,000)	(13,000)	(15,000)
Revaluation of non-current assets – 20,000 –			
Balance at 31 March 20X7	187,650	144,200	110,200

Notes to the financial statements

Note 1 – Inter-company sales

Alpha sells products to Beta and Gamma, making a profit of 30% on the cost of the products sold. All the sales to Gamma took place in the post-acquisition period. Details of the purchases of the products by Beta and Gamma, together with the amounts included in opening and closing inventories in respect of the products, are given below:

	Purchased in year $'000	Included in opening inventory $'000	Included in closing inventory $'000
Beta	20,000	2,600	3,640
Gamma	10,000	Nil	1,950

Note 2 – Investment income

Alpha's investment income includes dividends received from Beta and Gamma and interest receivable from Beta. The dividend received from Gamma has been credited to the statement of comprehensive income of Alpha without time apportionment. The interest receivable is in respect of a loan of $60 million to Beta at a fixed rate of interest of 6% per annum. The loan has been outstanding for the whole of the year ended 31 March 20X7.

Note 3 – Details of acquisition of shares in Gamma

On 1 July 20X6 Alpha purchased 15 million of Gamma's issued equity shares by a share exchange. Alpha issued 4 new equity shares for every 3 shares acquired in Gamma. The market value of the shares in Alpha and Gamma at 1 July 20X6 was $5 and $5.50 respectively. The non-controlling interest in Gamma is measured using method 1.

The fair values of the net assets of Gamma closely approximated to their carrying values in Gamma's financial statements with the exception of the following items:

(i) A property that had a carrying value of $20 million at the date of acquisition had a market value of $30 million. $16 million of this amount was attributable to the building, which had an estimated useful future economic life of 40 years at 1 July 20X6. In the year ended 31 March 20X7 Gamma had charged depreciation of $200,000 in its own financial statements in respect of this property.

(ii) Plant and equipment that had a carrying value of $6 million at the date of acquisition and a market value of $8 million. The estimated useful future economic life of the plant at 1 July 20X6 was 4 years. None of this plant and equipment had been sold or scrapped prior to 31 March 20X7.

(iii) Inventory that had a carrying value of $3 million at the date of acquisition had a fair value of $3.5 million. This entire inventory had been sold by Gamma prior to 31 March 20X7.

Note 4 – Other information

(i) Gamma charges depreciation and impairment of assets to cost of sales.

(ii) On 31 March 20X7 the directors of Alpha computed the recoverable amount of Gamma as a single cash-generating unit. They concluded that the recoverable amount was $150 million.

(iii) When the directors of Beta and Gamma prepared the individual financial statements of these companies no impairment of any assets of either company was found to be necessary.

(iv) On 31 March 20X7 Beta revalued its non-current assets. This resulted in a surplus of £20,000 which was credited to Beta's revaluation reserve.

Required:
Prepare the consolidated statement of comprehensive income and consolidated statement of changes in equity of Alpha for the year ended 31 March 20X7. Notes to the consolidated statement of comprehensive income are not required. Ignore deferred tax.

Question 7

H Ltd has one subsidiary, S Ltd. The company has held a controlling interest for several years. The latest financial statements for the two companies and the consolidated financial statements for the H Group are as shown below:

Statements of comprehensive income for the year ended 30 September 20X4

	H Ltd £000	S Ltd £000	H Group £000
Turnover	4,000	2,200	5,700
Cost of sales	(1,100)	(960)	(1,605)
	2,900	1,240	4,095
Administration	(420)	(130)	(550)
Distribution	(170)	(95)	(265)
Dividends received	180	—	—
Profit before tax	2,490	1,015	3,280
Income tax	(620)	(335)	(955)
Profit after tax	1,870	680	2,325
Attributable to:			
Equity shareholders of H Ltd			2,155
Non-controlling shareholders in S Ltd			170
			2,325

Statements of financial position at 30 September 20X4

	H Ltd £000	£000	S Ltd £000	£000	H Group £000	£000
Non-current assets:						
Tangible	7,053		2,196		9,249	
Investment in S Ltd	1,700	8,753	—	2,196	—	9,249
Current assets:						
Inventory	410		420		785	
Receivables	535		220		595	
Bank	27	972	19	659	46	1,426
Current liabilities:						
Payables	(300)		(260)		(355)	
Dividend to non-controlling interest	—		—		(45)	
Taxation	(605)	(905)	(375)	(635)	(980)	(1,380)
		8,820		2,220		9,295

	H Ltd £000	S Ltd £000	H Group £000
Share capital	4,500	760	4,500
Retained earnings	4,320	1,460	4,240
	8,820	2,220	8,740
Non-controlling interest	—	—	555
	8,820	2,220	9,295

Goodwill of £410,000 was written off at the date of acquisition following an impairment review.

Required:
(a) Calculate the percentage of S Ltd which is owned by H Ltd.
(b) Calculate the value of sales made between the two companies during the year.
(c) Calculate the amount of unrealised profit which had been included in the inventory figure as a result of inter-company trading and which had to be cancelled on consolidation.
(d) Calculate the value of inter-company receivables and payables cancelled on consolidation.
(e) Calculate the balance on S Ltd's retained earnings when H Ltd acquired its stake in the company. Non-controlling interests are measured using Method 1.

(CIMA)

Question 8

The following are the financial statements of White and its subsidiary Brown as at 30 September 20X9

Statement of income for the year ended 30 September 20X9	White	Brown
	£000	£000
Sales revenue	245,000	95,000
Cost of sales	(140,000)	(52,000)
Gross profit	105,000	43,000
Distribution costs	(12,000)	(10,000)
Admin expenses	(55,000)	(13,000)
Profit from operations	38,000	20,000
Dividend from Brown	7,000	—
Profit before tax	45,000	20,000
Tax	(13,250)	(5,000)
Net profit for the year	31,750	15,000

Statements of financial position as at 30 September 20X9	White	Brown
	£000	£000
Non-current assets:		
Property, plant & equipment	110,000	40,000
Investments – 21 million		
shares in Brown	24,000	—
Current assets:		
Inventory	13,360	3,890
Trade receivables & dividend		
receivable	14,640	6,280
Bank	3,500	2,570
	165,500	52,740

Equity & reserves:	White	Brown
Ordinary shares of £1 each	100,000	30,000
Reserves	9,200	1,000
Retained earnings	27,300	9,280
	136,500	40,280
Current liabilities:		
Trade Payables	9,000	2,460
Dividend declared	20,000	10,000
	165,500	52,740

The following information is also available:

(i) White purchased its ordinary shares in Brown on 1 September 20X4 when Brown had credit balances on reserves of £0.5 million and on retained earnings of £1.5 million.

(ii) At 1 September 20X8 goodwill on the acquisition of Brown was £960,000. The impairment review at 30 September 20X9 reduced this to £800,000.

(iii) During the year ended 30 September 20X9 White sold goods which originally cost £12 million to Brown and were invoiced to Brown at cost plus 40%. Brown still had 30% of these goods in inventory as at 30 September 20X9.

(iv) Brown owed White £1.5 million at 30 September 20X9 for goods supplied during the year.

Required:
(a) Calculate the goodwill arising at the date of acquisition.
(b) Prepare the Consolidated Statement of Income for the year ended 30 September 20X9.

Question 9

Hyson plc acquired 75% of the shares in Green plc on 1 January 20X0 for £6 million when Green plc's accumulated profits were £4.5 million. At acquisition, the fair value of Green's non-current assets were £1.2 million in excess of their carrying value. The remaining life of these non-current assets is six years.

The summarised statements of comprehensive income for the year ended 31.12.X0 were as follows:

	Hyson	Green
	£000	£000
Revenue	23,500	6,400
Cost of sales	16,400	4,700
Gross profit	7,100	1,700
Expenses	4,650	1,240
Profit before tax	2,450	460
Income tax expense	740	140
Profit for the period	1,710	320

There were no inter-company transactions. Depreciation of non-current assets is charged to cost of sales.

Required:
Prepare a consolidated statement of comprehensive income for the year ended 31 December 20X0.

Question 10

Forest plc acquired 80% of the ordinary shares of Bulwell plc some years ago. At acquisition, the fair values of the assets of Bulwell plc were the same as their carrying value. Bulwell plc manufacture plant and equipment.

On 1 January 20X3, Bulwell sold an item of plant & equipment to Forest plc for $2 million. Forest plc depreciate plant and equipment at 10% per annum on cost, and charge this expense to cost of sales. Bulwell plc made a gross profit of 30% on the sale of the plant and equipment to Forest plc.

The income statements of Forest and Bulwell for the year ended 31 December 20X3 are:

	Forest	Bulwell
	$000	$000
Revenue	21,300	8,600
Cost of sales	14,900	6,020
Gross profit	6,400	2,580
Other operating expenses	3,700	1,750
Profit before tax	2,700	830
Taxation	820	250
Profit after tax	1,880	580

Required:
Prepare an income statement for the Forest plc group for the year ended 31 December 20X3.

References

1 IAS 27 *Consolidated and Separate Financial Statements*, IASB, revised 2008, para. 20.
2 *Ibid.*, para. 28.
3 IAS 1 *Presentation of Financial Statements*, IASB, revised 2007, Implementation Guidance.

CHAPTER 23

Accounting for associates and joint ventures

23.1 Introduction

The previous three chapters have focused on the need for consolidated financial statements where an investor has control over an entity. In these circumstances line by line consolidation is appropriate. Where the size of an investment is not sufficient to give sole control, but where the investment gives the investor significant influence or joint control, then a modified form of accounting is appropriate. We will consider this issue further in this chapter.

Objectives

By the end of this chapter, you should be able to:

- define an associate;
- incorporate an associate into the consolidated financial statements using the equity method;
- account for transactions between a group and its associate;
- define a joint venture and describe the three types of joint venture into which a company might enter;
- prepare financial statements incorporating interests in joint ventures.

23.2 Definitions of associates and of significant influence

An associate is an entity over which the investor has significant influence and which is neither a subsidiary nor a joint venture of the investor.[1]

Significant influence is the power to participate in the financial and operating policy decisions of the investee but is not control over these policies.[2]

Significant influence will be assumed in situations where one company has 20% or more of the voting power in another company, unless it can be shown that there is no such influence. Unless it can be shown to the contrary, a holding of less than 20% will be assumed insufficient for associate status. The circumstances of each case must be considered.[3]

IAS 28 suggests that one or more of the following might be evidence of an associate:

(a) representation on the board of directors or equivalent governing body of the investee;

(b) participation in policy-making processes;

(c) material transactions between the investor and the investee;

(d) interchange of managerial personnel; or

(e) provision of essential technical information.[4]

23.3 The treatment of associated companies in consolidated accounts

Associated companies will be shown in consolidated accounts under the equity method, unless the investment meets the criteria of a disposal group held for sale under IFRS 5 *Non-current Assets Held for Sale and Discontinued Operations*. If this is the case it will be accounted for under IFRS 5 at the lower of carrying value and fair value less costs to sell.

The equity method is a method of accounting whereby:

● The investment is reported in the consolidated statement of financial position in the non-current asset section.[5] It is reported initially at cost adjusted, at the end of each financial year, for the post-acquisition change in the investor's share of the net assets of the investee.[6]

● In the consolidated statement of comprehensive income, income from associates is reported after profit from operations together with finance costs and finance expenses.[7] The income reflects the investor's share of the post-tax results of operations of the investee.[8]

23.4 The Brill Group – the equity method illustrated

Brill plc had acquired 80% of Bream plc's ordinary shares in 20X0.

At date of acquisition of shares in associate on 1 January 20X0:

● Brill acquired 20% of the ordinary shares in Cod for £20,000, i.e. Brill was assumed to have significant influence.

● The retained earnings of Cod were £22,500 and the general reserve was £6,000.

Set out below are the consolidated accounts of Brill and its subsidiary Bream and the individual accounts of the associated company, Cod, together with the consolidated group accounts.

23.4.1 Consolidated statement of financial position

Statements of financial position of the Brill Group (parent plus subsidiaries already consolidated) and Cod (an associate company) as at 31 December 20X2:

	Brill and Subsids £	Cod £	Group £	
Non-current assets				
Property, plant and equipment	172,500	59,250	172,500	
Goodwill on consolidation	13,400		13,400	
Investment in Cod	20,000		23,600	Note 1
Current assets				
Inventories	132,440	27,000	132,440	
Trade receivables	151,050	27,000	151,050	
Current account – Cod	2,250		2,250	Note 2
Bank	36,200	4,500	36,200	
	527,840	117,750	531,440	

	Brill and Subsids £	Cod £	Group £
Current liabilities			
Trade payables	110,250	25,500	110,250
Taxation	27,750	6,000	27,750
Current account – Brill		2,250	
	138,000	33,750	138,000
Total net assets	389,840	84,000	393,440
EQUITY			
£1 ordinary shares	187,500	37,500	187,500
General reserve	24,900	9,000	25,500 Note 3
Retained earnings	145,940	37,500	148,940 Note 4
	358,340	84,000	361,940
Non-controlling interest	31,500	—	31,500 Note 5
	389,840	84,000	393,440

Notes:

1 Investment in associate

	£	£
Initial cost of the 20% holding		20,000
Share of post-acquisition reserves of Cod:		
20% (37,500 – 22,500) (retained earnings) =	3,000	
20% (9,000 – 6,000) (general reserves) =	600	3,600
		23,600

Note that unlike subsidiaries the assets and liabilities are not joined line by line with those of the companies in the group.

Where necessary the investment in the associate is tested for impairment under IAS 28.[9]

2 The Cod current account is received from outside the group and must therefore continue to be shown as receivable by the group. **It is not cancelled.**

3 General reserve consists of:

	£
Parent's general reserve	24,900
General reserve of Cod:	
The group share of the post-acquisition retained profits i.e. 20% (9,000 – 6,000) =	600
Consolidated general reserve	25,500

4 Retained earnings consists of:

	£
Parent's retained earnings	145,940
Retained earnings of Cod:	
The group share of the post-acquisition retained profits, i.e. 20% (37,500 – 22,500) =	3,000
Consolidated retained earnings	**148,940**

5 Non-controlling interest

Note that there is no non-controlling interest in Cod. Only the group share of Cod's net assets has been brought into the total net assets above (see note 1).

23.4.2 Consolidated statement of comprehensive income

Statements of comprehensive income for the year ended 31 December 20X2

	Brill and Subsids £	Cod £	Group £	
Sales	329,000	75,000	329,000	
Cost of sales	114,060	30,000	114,060	
Gross profit	214,940	45,000	214,940	
Expenses	107,700	22,500	107,700	
Profit from operations	107,240	22,500	107,240	
Dividends received	1,200	—	NIL	Note 1
Share of associate's profit	—	—	**3,300**	Note 2
Profit before tax	108,440	22,500	110,540	
Income tax expense	27,750	6,000	**27,750**	
Profit for the period	80,690	16,500	82,790	

Notes:
Profit before tax

1 **Dividend received from Cod** is not shown because the share of Cod's profits (before dividend) has been included in the group account (see note 2). To include the dividend as well would be double counting.

2 **Share of Cod's profit after tax** = 20% × £16,500 = **£3,300**

3 As in the statement of financial position, there is no need to account for a non-controlling interest in Cod. This is because the consolidated statement of comprehensive income only ever included the group share of Cod's profits.

4 There are no additional complications in the statement of changes in equity. The group retained earnings column will include the group share of Cod's post-acquisition retained earnings. There will be no additional column for a non-controlling interest in Cod.

23.5 The treatment of provisions for unrealised profits

It is never appropriate in the case of associated companies to remove 100% of any unrealised profit on inter-company transactions because only the group's share of the associate's profit and net assets are shown in the group accounts. This is illustrated in the Zenith example:

EXAMPLE ● Zenith Group made sales to an associate, Nadir plc, at a mark-up of £10,000. All the goods are in the inventory of Nadir at the year-end. Zenith's holding in Nadir was 20%. The Zenith Group will provide for 20% of £10,000 (i.e. £2,000) against the group share of the associate's profit in the statement of comprehensive income and against the group share of the associate's net assets in the statement of financial position.

23.6 The acquisition of an associate part-way through the year

In order to match the cost (the investment) with the benefit (share of the associate's net assets), the associate's profit will only be taken into account from the date of acquiring the holding in the associate. The associate's profit at the date of acquisition represents part of the net assets that are being acquired at that date. The Puff example below is an illustration of the accounting treatment.

In this chapter the adjustment for unrealised profit is made against the group's share of the associate's profit and net assets irrespective of whether the associate is receiving goods from the group (i.e. downstream transactions) or providing goods to the group (i.e. upstream transactions).[10]

23.6.1 The Puff Group

At date of acquisition on 31 March 20X0 of shares in associate:

- Puff plc acquired 30% of the shares in Blow plc.
- At that date the accumulated retained earnings of Blow was £61,500.

During the year:

- On 1/10/20X0 Blow sold Puff goods for £15,000 which was cost plus 25%.
- All income and expenditure for the year in Blow's statement of comprehensive income accrued evenly throughout the year.

At end of financial year on 31 December 20X0:

- 75% of the goods sold to Puff by Blow were still in inventory.

Set out below are the consolidated statement of comprehensive income of Puff and its subsidiaries and the individual statement of comprehensive income of an associated company, Blow, together with the consolidated group statement of comprehensive income.

	Puff and Subsids £	Blow £	Group accounts £	
Revenue	225,000	112,500	225,000	Note 1
Cost of sales	75,000	56,250	75,000	Note 2
Gross profit	150,000	56,250	150,000	
Expenses	89,850	30,000	89,850	
	60,150	26,250	60,150	
Dividends received from associate	1,350	NIL	NIL	Note 3
Share of associate's profit	—	—	3,713	Note 4
Profit before taxation	61,500	26,250	63,863	
Income tax period	15,000	6,750	15,000	
Profit for the period	46,500	19,500	48,863	

Notes:

1. The revenue, cost of sales and all other income and expenses of the associated company are not added on a line by line basis with the those of the parent company and its subsidiaries. The group's share of the profit before taxation of the associate is shown as one figure (see note 4) and added to the remainder of the group's profit before taxation.

2. The group accounts 'cost of sales' figure does not include the provision for unrealised profit, as this has been deducted from the share of the associate's profit.

3. The dividend received of £1,350 is eliminated, being replaced by the group share of its underlying profits.

4 Share of profits after tax of the associate

	£
Profit after tax	19,500
Apportion for 9 months ($^9/_{12} \times 19,500$)	14,625
Less: unrealised profit ($^{25}/_{125} \times 15,000$) $\times 75\%$	2,250
	12,375
Group share (30% $\times$ 12,375)	3,713

5 There is no share of the associated company's retained earnings brought forward because the shares in the associate were purchased during the year.

23.7 Joint ventures

IAS 31 *Interests in Joint Ventures* defines a joint venture as one in which there is a contractual arrangement whereby two or more parties undertake an economic activity that is subject to joint control so that no single venturer is in a position to control the activity unilaterally.[11]

There are a number of ways[12] in which a contractual arrangement may be evidenced, e.g. by a formal contract between the venturers or minutes of discussions between the venturers setting out in writing matters such as:

(a) scope – identifying the activity and its duration;

(b) management – the appointment of managers/directors;

(c) finance – capital contributions and sharing of profits and losses;

(d) stewardship – reporting obligations.

The standard identifies three broad types, namely, **jointly controlled operations, jointly controlled assets** and **jointly controlled entities**.

23.7.1 Jointly controlled operations

The collaborative approach to the manufacture of an aircraft is a good example of this type of joint venture where the wings, body and engine are built by different companies. Each company bears its own costs and takes an agreed contractual share of the revenue from the sale of the aircraft. Each company is responsible for raising its own capital, using its own production capacity and working capital and incurring its own expenses.

Financial reports

The following are reported in the financial statements of each venturer:

(a) the assets that it controls and the liabilities that it incurs; and

(b) the expenses that it incurs and its share of the income that it earns from the sale of goods or services by the joint venture.

23.7.2 Jointly controlled assets

This type of joint venture is one in which the venturers have joint control over the assets contributed to or acquired for the purposes of the joint venture. They do not involve the establishment of a corporation, partnership or other entity. This includes situations where the participants derive benefit from the joint activity through a share of production, rather than by receiving a share of the results of trading.

The common use of an oil pipeline by companies which control and finance it and pay according to the amount of throughput is an example[13] from IAS 31.

Financial reports

The following are reported in the financial statements of each venturer:

(a) its share of the jointly controlled assets, classified according to the nature of the assets;

(b) any liabilities that it has incurred;

(c) its share of any liabilities incurred jointly with the other venturers in relation to the joint venture;

(d) any income from the sale or use of its share of the output of the joint venture, together with its share of any expenses incurred by the joint venture; and

(e) any expenses that it has incurred in respect of its interest in the joint venture.

The following is an extract from the 2005 Rio Tinto annual report:

The Group's proportionate interest in the assets, liabilities, revenues, expenses and cash flows of jointly controlled asset ventures are incorporated into the Group's financial statements under the appropriate headings. In some situations, joint control exists even though the Group has an ownership interest of more than 50 per cent because of the veto rights held by joint venture partners.

23.7.3 Jointly controlled entities

These joint ventures are operated through a corporation or partnership which controls the assets of the joint venture, incurs liabilities and expenses and earns income and enters into contracts in its own name.

Jointly controlled entities are accounted for in group accounts using either the equity accounting method or proportionate consolidation.

Financial reports

A jointly controlled entity maintains its own accounting records[14] and prepares and presents financial statements in the same way as other entities in conformity with International Financial Reporting Standards.

23.7.4 Proportionate consolidation[15]

Proportionate consolidation is a method of accounting whereby a venturer's share of each of the assets, liabilities, income and expenses of a jointly controlled entity is combined line by line with similar items in the venturer's financial statements or reported as separate line items in the venturer's financial statements.

There is a criticism of proportionate consolidation that there is a conceptual problem with the investor reporting in its statement of financial position assets that it does not control. The alternative is to apply equity accounting but this would mean that equity accounting would be applied to two different types of investments, namely, associates in which the investor only has a significant influence and joint ventures in which it has joint control.

The IASB has issued an exposure draft of a proposed amendment to IAS 31 that suggests the withdrawal of proportionate consolidation for joint ventures. This would indeed mean that jointly controlled entities would be accounted for using the equity method in the same way as associates.

23.7.5 Equity accounting method

In the UK joint ventures are generally required to be accounted for using the equity method. IAS 31 takes a different approach in that it permits equity accounting but actively argues against it,[16] saying:

> Some venturers report their interests in jointly controlled entities using the equity method, as described in IAS 28. The use of the equity method is supported by those who argue that it is inappropriate to combine controlled items with jointly controlled items and by those who believe that venturers have significant influence, rather than joint control, in a jointly controlled entity. This Standard does not recommend the use of the equity method because proportional consolidation better reflects the substance and economic reality of a venturer's interest in a jointly controlled entity, that is control over the venturer's share of the future economic benefits. Nevertheless, this Standard permits the use of the equity method, as an allowed alternative treatment, when reporting interests in jointly controlled entities.

Summary

Associates are accounted for using the equity method whereby there is a single-line entry in the statement of financial position for the Investment in Associate, which is carried initially at cost and the balance adjusted annually for the investor's share of the associate's current year's profit or loss.

Joint ventures take a number of forms and, in each case, users need to be able to identify the assets and liabilities committed to the venture and the results in so far as they relate to the venturer. For joint venture entities, IAS 31 permits alternative treatments with investors able to adopt the equity accounting method or proportionate consolidation. The IASB no longer supports the proportionate consolidation method.

REVIEW QUESTIONS

1 The following is an extract from the notes to the 1999 consolidated financial statements of the Chugoku Electric Power Company, Incorporated.

Equity method
Investments in four (three in 1998) affiliated companies (20% to 50% owned) are accounted for by the equity method and, accordingly, are stated at cost adjusted for equity in undistributed earnings and losses from the date of acquisition.

(a) What is another name for most companies which are 20% to 50% owned?

(b) What is meant by the word 'equity' in the above statement?

(c) What are the entries in the statement of comprehensive income under the equity method of accounting?

(d) What are the differences between the equity method and consolidation?

2 Why are associated companies accounted for under the equity method rather than consolidated?

3 How does the treatment of inter-company unrealised profit differ between subsidiaries and associated companies?

4 IAS 28, para. 17, states:

The recognition of income on the basis of distributions received may not be an adequate measure of the income earned by an investor on an investment in an associate.

Explain why this may be so.

5 Where an associate has made losses, IAS 28, para. 30, states:

After the investor's interest is reduced to zero, additional losses are provided for, and a liability is recognised, only to the extent that the investor has incurred legal or constructive obligations or made payments on behalf of the associate. If the associate subsequently reports profits, the investor resumes recognising its share of those profits only after its share of the profits equals the share of losses not recognised.

Explain why profits are recognised only after its share of the profits equals the share of losses not recognised.

6 The result of including goodwill by valuing the non-controlling shares at their market price using Method 2 is to value the non-controlling shares on a different basis to valuing an equity investment in an associate. Discuss whether there should be a uniform approach to both.

EXERCISES

An extract from the solution is provided on the Companion Website (www.pearsoned.co.uk/elliott-elliott) for exercises marked with an asterisk (*).

* Question 1

The following are the financial statements of the parent company Swish plc, a subsidiary company Broom and an associate company Handle.

Statements of financial position as at 31 December 20X3

	Swish £	Broom £	Handle £
ASSETS			
Non-current assets			
Property, plant and equipment at cost	320,000	180,000	100,000
Depreciation	200,000	70,000	21,000
	120,000	110,000	79,000
Investment in Broom	140,000		
Investment in Handle	40,000		
Current assets			
Inventories	120,000	60,000	36,000
Trade receivables	130,000	70,000	36,000
Current account – Broom	15,000		
Current account – Handle	3,000		
Bank	24,000	7,000	6,000
Total current assets	292,000	137,000	78,000
Total assets	592,000	247,000	157,000
EQUITY AND LIABILITIES			
£1 ordinary shares	250,000	60,000	50,000
General reserve	30,000	20,000	12,000
Retained earnings	150,000	120,000	50,000
	430,000	200,000	112,000
Current liabilities			
Trade payables	132,000	25,000	34,000
Taxation payable	30,000	7,000	8,000
Current account – Swish		15,000	3,000
Total equity and liabilities	592,000	247,000	157,000

Statement of comprehensive income for the year ended 31 December 20X3

	£	£	£
Sales	300,000	160,000	100,000
Cost of sales	90,000	80,000	40,000
Gross profit	210,000	80,000	60,000
Expenses	95,000	50,000	40,000
Dividends paid (shown in equity)	40,000	10,000	8,000
Dividends received from Broom and Handle	11,000	NIL	10,000
Profit before tax	126,000	30,000	30,000
Income tax expense	30,000	7,000	8,000
Profit for the period	96,000	23,000	22,000
Dividend paid (shown in equity)	40,000	10,000	8,000

Swish acquired 90% of the shares in Broom on 1 January 20X1 when the balance on the retained earnings of Broom was £60,000 and the balance on the general reserve of Broom was £16,000. Swish also acquired 25% of the shares in Handle on 1 January 20X2 when the balance on Handle's accumulated retained profits was £30,000 and the general reserve £8,000.

During the year Swish sold Broom goods for £16,000, which included a mark-up of one-third. 80% of these goods were still in inventory at the end of the year.

Non-controlling interests are measured using method 1.

Required:
(a) Prepare a consolidated statement of comprehensive income, including the associated company Handle's results, for the year ended 31 December 20X3.
(b) Prepare a consolidated statement of financial position as at 31 December 20X3. The group policy is to measure non-controlling interests using method 1.

Question 2

Set out below are the financial statements of Ant Co., its subsidiary Bug Co. and an associated company Nit Co. for the accounting year-end 31 December 20X9.

Statements of financial position as at 31 December 20X9

	Ant $	Bug $	Nit $
ASSETS			
Non-current assets			
Property, plant and equipment at cost	240,000	135,000	75,000
Depreciation	150,000	52,500	15,750
	90,000	82,500	59,250
Investment in Bug	90,000		
Investment in Nit	30,000		
Current assets			
Inventories	105,000	45,000	27,000
Trade receivables	98,250	52,500	27,000
Current account – Bug	11,250		
Current account – Nit	2,250		
Bank	17,250	5,250	4,500
Total current assets	234,000	102,750	58,500
Total assets	444,000	185,250	117,750
EQUITY AND LIABILITIES			
$1 ordinary shares	187,500	45,000	37,500
General reserve	22,500	15,000	9,000
Retained earnings	112,500	90,000	37,500
	322,500	150,000	84,000
Current liabilities			
Trade payables	99,000	18,750	25,500
Taxation payable	22,500	5,250	6,000
Current account – Ant		11,250	2,250
Total equity and liabilities	444,000	185,250	117,750

Statements of comprehensive income for the year ended 31 December 20X9

	$	$	$
Sales	225,000	120,000	75,000
Cost of sales	67,500	60,000	30,000
Gross profit	157,500	60,000	45,000
Expenses	70,500	37,500	30,000
Dividends received	7,500	NIL	7,500
Profit before tax	94,500	22,500	22,500
Taxation	22,500	5,250	6,000
Profit for the year	72,000	17,250	16,500
Dividends paid in year	30,000	7,500	6,000

Ant Co. acquired 80% of the shares in Bug Co. on 1 January 20X7 when the balance on the retained earnings of Bug Co. was $45,000 and the balance on the general reserve of Bug Co. was $12,000. The fair value of the non-controlling interest in Bug on 1 January 20X7 was £21,000. Group policy is to measure non-controlling interests using method 2. Ant Co. also acquired 25% of the shares in Nit Co. on 1 January 20X8 when the balance on Nit's retained earnings was $22,500 and the general reserve $6,000.

During the year Ant Co. sold Bug Co. goods for $12,000, which included a mark-up of one-third. 90% of these goods were still in inventory at the end of the year.

Required:
(a) Prepare a consolidated statement of comprehensive income for the year ending 31/12/20X9, including the associated company Nit's results.
(b) Prepare a consolidated statement of financial position at 31/12/20X9, including the associated company.

Question 3

Alpha has owned 75% of the equity shares of Beta since the incorporation of Beta. Therefore, Alpha has prepared consolidated financial statements for some years. On 1 July 20X6 Alpha purchased 40% of the equity shares of Gamma. The statements of comprehensive income and summarised statements of changes in equity of the three entities for the year ended 30 September 20X6 are given below:

Statements of comprehensive income

	Alpha $'000	Beta $'000	Gamma $'000
Revenue (Note 1)	150,000	100,000)	96,000
Cost of sales	(110,000)	(78,000)	(66,000)
Gross profit	40,000	22,000	30,000
Distribution costs	(7,000)	(6,000)	(6,000)
Administrative expenses	(8,000)	(7,000)	(7,200)
Profit from operations	25,000	9,000	16,800
Investment income (Note 2)	6,450	Nil	Nil
Finance cost	(5,000)	(3,000)	(4,200)
Profit before tax	26,450	6,000	12,600
Income tax expense	(7,000)	(1,800)	(3,600)
Net profit for the period	19,450	4,200	9,000
Summarised statements of changes in equity			
Balance at 1 October 20X5	122,000	91,000	82,000
Net profit for the period	19,450	4,200	9,000
Dividends paid on 31 July 20X6	(6,500)	(3,000)	(5,000)
Balance at 30 September 20X6	134,950	92,200	86,000

Notes to the financial statements

Note 1 – Inter-company sales

Alpha sells products to Beta and Gamma, making a profit of 25% on the cost of the products sold. All the sales to Gamma took place in the post-acquisition period. Details of the purchases of the products by Beta and Gamma, together with the amounts included in opening and closing inventories in respect of the products, are given below:

	Purchased in year $'000	Included in opening inventory $'000	Included in closing inventory $'000
Beta	20,000	2,000	3,000
Gamma	10,000	Nil	1,500

There were no other inter-company sales between Alpha, Beta or Gamma during the period.

Note 2 – Investment income

Alpha's investment income includes dividends received from Beta and Gamma and interest receivable from Beta. The dividend received from Gamma has been credited to the statement of comprehensive income of Alpha without time apportionment. The interest receivable is in respect of a loan of $20 million to Beta at a fixed rate of interest of 6% per annum. The loan has been outstanding for the whole of the year ended 30 September 20X6.

Note 3 – Details of acquisitions by Alpha

Entity	Date of acquisition	Fair value adjustment at date of acquisition $'000
Beta	1 July 20X5	Nil
Gamma	1 June 20X6	6,400

There has been no impairment of the goodwill arising on the acquisition of Beta or of the investment in Gamma since the dates of acquisition of either entity.

The fair value adjustment has the effect of increasing the fair value of property, plant and equipment above the carrying value in the individual financial statements of Gamma. Group policy is to depreciate property, plant and equipment on a monthly basis over its estimated useful economic life. The estimated life of the property, plant and equipment of Gamma that was subject to the fair value adjustment is five years, with depreciation charged against cost of sales.

Note 4 – other information

- The purchase of shares in Gamma entitled Alpha to appoint a representative to the board of directors of Gamma. This meant that Alpha was potentially able to participate in, and significantly influence, the policy decisions of Gamma.
- No other investor is able to control the operating and financial policies of Gamma, but on one occasion since 1 July 20X6 Gamma made a policy decision with which Alpha did not fully agree.
- Alpha has not entered into a contractual relationship with any other investor to exercise joint control over the operating and financial policies of Gamma.
- All equity shares in Beta carry one vote at general meetings.
- The policy of Alpha regarding the treatment of equity investments in its consolidated financial statements is as follows:
  - Subsidiaries are fully consolidated.
  - Joint ventures are proportionally consolidated.
  - Associates are equity accounted.
  - Other investments are treated as available for sale financial assets.

Your assistant has been reading the working papers for the consolidated financial statements of Alpha for previous years. He has noticed that Beta has been consolidated as a subsidiary and has expressed the view that this must be because Alpha owns more than 50% of its shares. He has further stated that Gamma should be treated as an available-for-sale financial asset since Alpha is unable to control its operating and financial policies.

Required:
(a) Prepare the consolidated statement of comprehensive income and consolidated statement of changes in equity of Alpha for the year ended 30 September 20X6. Notes to the consolidated statement of comprehensive income are not required. Ignore deferred tax.
(b) Assess the observations of your assistant regarding the appropriate method of consolidating Beta and Gamma. Your assessment need NOT include an explanation of the detailed mechanics of consolidation. You should refer to the provisions of international financial reporting standards where you consider they will assist your explanation.

* Question 4

The following are the statements of comprehensive income of four companies for the year ended 31 October 2006, the end of their most recent financial year.

Income statements for the year ended 31 October 2006

	Afjar	Jikki	Hupin	Sofrin
	$000	$000	$000	$000
Revenue	8,890	4,580	4,470	2,760
Cost of sales	(3,000)	(2,200)	(1,800)	(1,700)
Gross profit	5,890	2,380	2,670	1,060
Distribution costs	(900)	(540)	(1,010)	(230)
Administrative expenses	(1,060)	(990)	(1,100)	(250)
Operating profit	3,930	850	560	580
Dividends receivable	410	130		
Interest receivable	230	321	150	
Interest payable	(1,188)	(455)	(380)	
Net profit before taxation	3,382	846	330	580
Income tax expense	(1,000)	(200)	(80)	(100)
Net profit after taxation	2,382	646	250	480
Earnings per share (in cents)	11.9	4.0	2.5	2.4

The following additional information is available:

(a) All shares issued by the companies have a face value of $1.

(b) The companies made the following dividend payments to shareholders during the year ended 31 October 2006:

	Afjar	Jikki	Hupin	Sofrin
	$000	$000	$000	$000
Preference dividend				
– final for 2005, paid March 2006	400	120		
– interim for 2006, paid September 2006	400	120		
Ordinary dividend				
– final for 2005, paid March 2006	800	180	54	76
– interim for 2006, paid September 2006	800	180	54	76

Under IAS 32 *Financial Instruments: Disclosure and Presentation* dividends on preference shares have been included in interest payable.

(c) Afjar owns 60% of the ordinary shares in Jikki, 40% of the shares in Hupin and 25% of the shares in Sofrin. Jikki is a subsidiary of Afjar, Hupin is an associate of Afjar, and Sofrin is a joint venture.

(d) During the year ended 31 October 2006 Afjar sold inventory which had cost $640,000 to Jikki at a mark up of 25%. Jikki had resold 65% of these items by 31 October 2006.

(e) On 1 July 2006 Jikki made a long term loan of $500,000 to Afjar. The loan bears interest at 12% a year payable every six months in arrears.

Required:

Prepare, in so far as the information given permits, the consolidated statement of comprehensive income of Afjar for the year ended 31 October 2006. Your statement of comprehensive income should include a figure for earnings per share with a supportive disclosure note.

(The Association of International Accountants)

Question 5

The statements of comprehensive income for Continent plc, Island Ltd and River Ltd for the year ended 31 December 20X9 were as follows:

	Continent plc	Island Ltd	River Ltd
	€	€	€
Revenue	825,000	220,000	82,500
Cost of sales	(616,000)	(55,000)	(8,250)
Gross profit	209,000	165,000	74,250
Administration costs	(33,495)	(18,700)	(3,850)
Distribution costs	(11,000)	(14,300)	(2,750)
Dividends receivable from Island and River	4,620		
Profit before tax	169,125	132,000	67,650
Income tax	(55,000)	(33,000)	(11,000)
Profit after tax	114,125	99,000	56,650

Continent plc acquired 80% of Island Ltd for €27,500 on 1 January 20X3, when Island Lid's retained earnings were €22,000 and share capital was €5,500. During the year, Island Ltd sold goods costing €2,750 to Continent plc for €3,850. At the year end, 10% of these goods were still in Continent plc's inventory.

Continent plc acquired 40% of River Ltd for €100,000 on 1 January 20X5, when River Ltd's share capital and reserves totalled €41,250 (share capital consisted of 11,000 50c shares). During the year River Ltd sold goods costing €1,650 to Continent plc for €2,200. At the year end, 50% of these goods were still in Continent plc's inventory.

Goodwill in Island Ltd had suffered impairment charges in previous years totalling €2,200 and Goodwill in River Ltd impairment charges totalling €7,700. Impairment has continued during 2009 reducing the Goodwill in Island by €550 and the Goodwill in River by €3,850.

Continent plc includes in its revenue management fees of €5,500 charged to Island Ltd and €2,750 charged to River Ltd. Both companies treat the charge as an administration cost.

Non-controlling interests are measured using method 1.

Required:

Prepare Continent plc's consolidated statement of comprehensive income for the year ended 31 December 20X9.

Question 6

The statements of comprehensive income for Highway plc, Road Ltd and Lane Ltd for the year ended 31 December 20X9 were as follows:

	Highway plc $	Road Ltd $	Lane Ltd $
Revenue	184,000	152,000	80,000
Cost of sales	(48,000)	(24,000)	(16,000)
Gross profit	136,000	128,000	64,000
Administration costs	(13,680)	(11,200)	(20,800)
Distribution costs	(11,200)	(17,600)	(8,000)
Dividends receivable from Road	2,480		
Profit before tax	113,600	99,200	35,200
Income tax	(32,000)	(8,000)	(4,800)
Profit for the period	81,600	91,200	30,400

Highway plc acquired 80% of Road Ltd for $160,000 on 1.1.20X6 when Road Ltd's share capital was $64,000 and reserves were $16,000.

Highway plc acquired 30% of Lane Ltd for $40,000 on 1.1.20X7 when Lane Ltd's share capital was $8,000 and reserves were $8,000.

Goodwill of Road Ltd had suffered impairment charges of $14,400 in previous years and $4,800 was to be charged in the current year. Goodwill of Lane Ltd had suffered impairment charges of $3,520 in previous years and $1,760 was to be charged in the current year.

During the year Road Ltd sold goods to Highway plc for $8,000. These goods had cost Road Ltd $1,600. 50% were still in Highway's inventory at the year end.

During the year Lane Ltd sold goods to Highway plc for $6,400. These goods had cost Lane Ltd $3,200. 50% were still in Highway's inventory at the year end.

Highway's revenue included management fees of 5% of Road and Lane's turnover. Both of those companies have treated the charge as an administration cost.

Non-controlling interests are measured using method 1.

Required:
Prepare Highway's consolidated statement of comprehensive income for the year ended 31.12.20X9.

Question 7

The following are the financial statements of the parent company Alpha plc, a subsidiary company Beta and an associate company Gamma.

Statements of financial position as at 31 December 20X9

	Alpha £	Beta £	Gamma £
ASSETS			
Non-current assets			
Land at cost	540,000	256,500	202,500
Investment in Beta	216,000		
Investment in Gamma	156,600		
Current assets			
Inventories	162,000	54,000	135,000
Trade receivables	108,000	72,900	91,800
Dividend receivable from Beta	12,420		
Current account – Beta	10,800		
Current account – Gamma	13,500		
Cash	237,600	62,100	67,500
Total current assets	544,320	189,000	294,300
Total assets	1,456,920	445,500	496,800
EQUITY AND LIABILITIES			
£1 shares	540,000	67,500	27,000
Retained earnings	769,500	329,400	391,500
	1,309,500	396,900	418,500
Current liabilities			
Trade payables	93,420	24,300	59,400
Dividends payable	54,000	13,500	5,400
Current account – Alpha	—	10,800	13,500
Total equity and liabilities	1,456,920	445,500	496,800

On 1 January 20X5 Alpha plc acquired 80% of Beta plc for £216,000 when Beta plc's share capital and reserves were £81,000, and 30% of Gamma Ltd for £156,600 when Gamma Ltd's share capital and reserves were £40,500. The fair value of the land at the date of acquisition was £337,500 in Beta plc and £270,000 in Gamma Ltd. Both companies have kept land at cost in their statement of financial position. All other assets are recorded at fair value. There have been no further share issues or purchases of land since the date of acquisition.

At the year end, Alpha plc has inventory acquired from Beta plc and Gamma Ltd. Beta plc had invoiced the inventory to Alpha plc for £54,000 – the cost to Beta plc had been £40,500 and Gamma Ltd had invoiced Alpha plc for £13,500 – the cost to Gamma Ltd had been £8,100. Goodwill has been impaired by £52,650. The whole of the impairment relates to Beta.

Non-controlling interests are measured using method 1.

Required:
Prepare Alpha plc's consolidated statement of financial position as at 31.12.20X9.

Question 8

The following are the statements of financial position of Garden plc, its subsidiary Rose Ltd and its associate Petal Ltd:

Statements of financial position as at 31 December 20X9

	Garden £	Rose £	Petal £
ASSETS			
Non-current assets			
Land at cost	240,000		84,000
Land at valuation		180,000	
Investment in Rose	300,000		
Investment in Petal	72,000		
Investments	18,000		
Current assets			
Inventories	15,000	99,000	5,400
Trade receivables	33,000	98,400	1,200
Current account – Rose	18,000		
Current account – Petal	2,400		
Cash	6,600	67,200	300
Total current assets	75,000	264,600	6,900
Total assets	705,000	444,600	90,900
EQUITY AND LIABILITIES			
£1 shares	300,000	120,000	30,000
Revaluation reserve		90,000	
Retained earnings	270,000	216,000	57,600
	570,000	426,000	87,600
Current liabilities			
Trade payables	135,000	3,600	900
Current account – Garden	—	15,000	2,400
Total equity and liabilities	705,000	444,600	90,900

On 1 January 20X3 Garden plc acquired 75% of Rose Ltd for £300,000 when Rose's share capital and reserves were £252,000. At the date of acquisition, the net book value of Rose's non-current assets were £90,000. Rose immediately included the revaluation in its statement of financial position.

On 1 January 20X5 Garden acquired 20% of Petal Ltd for £72,000 when the fair value of Petal's net assets were £42,000.

Goodwill has been impaired in Rose by £77,700 and in Petal by £31,800.

At the year end, Garden plc has inventory acquired from Rose and Petal. Rose had invoiced the inventory to Garden for £6,000 – the cost to Rose had been £1,200 – and Petal had invoiced Garden for £3,000 – the cost to Petal had been £1,800.

Non-controlling interests are measured using method 1.

Required:
Prepare Garden plc's consolidated statement of financial position as at 31.12.20X9.

References

1 IAS 28 *Investments in Associates*, IASB, revised 2003, para. 2.
2 *Ibid.*, para. 2.
3 *Ibid.*, para. 6.
4 *Ibid.*, para. 7.
5 *Ibid.*, para. 38.
6 *Ibid.*, para. 2.
7 IAS 1 *Presentation of Financial Statements*, IASB, revised 2003, Implementation Guidance.
8 IAS 28, para. 2.
9 *Ibid.*, para. 31.
10 *Ibid.*, para. 22.
11 IAS 31 *Interests in Joint Ventures*, IASB, revised 2003, para. 3.
12 *Ibid.*, para. 10.
13 *Ibid.*, para. 20.
14 *Ibid.*, para. 28.
15 *Ibid.*, para. 3.
16 *Ibid.*, paras 38–41.

CHAPTER 24

Accounting for the effects of changes in foreign exchange rates under IAS 21

24.1 Introduction

The increasing globalisation of business means that it is becoming more and more common for entities to enter into transactions that are denominated in a foreign currency. This causes accounting issues because the entity needs to record these transactions in its own currency in order to prepare its financial statements. A further complication is that entities can either enter into such transactions directly or via an overseas operation (a branch or subsidiary that it has established for the purposes of carrying out business in a particular location).

Objectives

By the end of this chapter, you should be able to:

- explain the meaning of the term 'functional currency';
- distinguish between functional currency and presentational currency;
- reflect foreign currency transactions carried out directly by the reporting entity in the financial statements;
- prepare consolidated financial statements to include subsidiaries with a functional currency that differs from the functional currency of the group;
- explain the particular accounting issues involved when a parent has a subsidiary that is located in a hyper-inflationary environment.

24.2 The difference between conversion and translation and the definition of a foreign currency transaction

Conversion is the exchange of one currency for another while **translation** is the expression of another currency in the terms of the currency of the reporting operation. Only in the case of conversion is there a **foreign currency transaction**, which IAS 21 *The Effects of Changes in Foreign Exchange Rates* defines as follows:[1]

A foreign transaction is a transaction, which is denominated in or requires settlement in a foreign currency, including transactions arising when an entity:

(a) buys or sells goods or services whose price is denominated in a foreign currency;

(b) borrows or lends funds when the amounts payable or receivable are denominated in a foreign currency;

(c) otherwise acquires or disposes of assets, or incurs or settles liabilities, denominated in a foreign currency.

24.3 The functional currency

The **functional currency** is the currency of the primary economic environment in which the entity operates.

IAS 21 sets out the factors which a reporting entity (a company preparing financial statements) will consider in determining its functional currency.[2] These are:

(a) the currency:
  (i) that mainly influences sales prices for goods and services; and
  (ii) of the country whose competitive forces and regulations mainly determine the sales prices of its goods and services;

(b) the currency that mainly influences labour, material, and other costs of providing goods and services.

The following factors may also provide evidence of an entity's functional currency:[3]

(a) the currency in which funds from financing activities are generated;

(b) the currency in which the receipts from operating activities are usually retained.

If the functional currency is not obvious from the above, then managers have to make a judgement as to which currency most represents the economic effects of its transactions.

A company must also decide whether or not any of its foreign operations, such as a branch or subsidiary, has the same functional currency. In doing so the following factors will be considered:[4]

(a) Whether the activities of the foreign operation are carried out as an extension of the reporting entity, rather than being carried out with a significant degree of autonomy. An example of the former is when the foreign operation only sells goods imported from the reporting entity and remits the proceeds to it. An example of the latter is when the operation accumulates cash and other monetary items, incurs expenses, generates income and arranges borrowings, all substantially in its local currency.

(b) Whether transactions with the reporting entity are a high or low proportion of the foreign operation's activities.

(c) Whether cash flows from the activities of the foreign operation directly affect the cash flows of the reporting entity and are readily available for remittance to it.

(d) Whether cash flows from the activities of the foreign operation are sufficient to service existing and normally expected debt obligations without funds being made available by the reporting entity.

24.4 The presentation currency[5]

The **presentation currency** is the currency a reporting entity uses for its financial statements. The reporting entity is entitled to present its financial statement in any currency, so that in some cases the presentation currency may differ from the functional currency.

24.5 Monetary and non-monetary items

Monetary items are balances owed by or to an entity that will be settled in cash. Examples will be payables for goods supplied, loans, cash and debtors for goods supplied. Non-monetary assets will include property, plant and equipment, inventory and amounts prepaid for goods.

24.6 The rules on the recording of foreign currency transactions carried out directly by the reporting entity

Initial recognition[6]

All transactions are entered in the books at the spot currency exchange rate between the foreign currency and the functional currency on the transaction date. An average rate may be used for a period where it is appropriate. It will be inappropriate where exchange rates fluctuate significantly. Therefore in practice the spot rate is almost always used.

At subsequent dates

Amounts paid or received in settlement of foreign currency monetary items during an accounting period are translated at the date of settlement.

At the statement of financial position date monetary balances are retranslated at closing rate.

Non-monetary items at historical cost remain at their original rate. Non-monetary items at fair value are translated at the rate on the date the fair value was determined.[7]

24.7 The treatment of exchange differences on foreign currency transactions

Exchange differences arising on the settlement of monetary items or on translating monetary items at rates different from those at which they were translated on initial recognition during the period, or in previous financial statements, must be recognised in the statement of comprehensive income during the period in which they arise,[8] unless the company has entered into a hedging transaction under IAS 39 *Financial Instruments: Recognition and Measurement*. If the parent has taken a foreign loan to act as a hedge against the foreign investment the exchange differences on the loan can be recognised directly in equity to offset the exchange differences on the foreign subsidiary. Hedge accounting is only available if the group meets strict criteria which can prove difficult to meet in practice.

Note that the profits or losses on foreign currency transactions affect the cash flow and are therefore realised.

The following extract is from the Nemetschek AC 1999 group accounts:

In the individual annual accounts of Nemetschek AC and its subsidiaries, business transactions in a foreign currency are valued at the exchange rate at the time of their original posting. Any exchange losses from the valuation of receivables and payables are taken into account up to the statement of financial position cutoff date. Profits and losses from fluctuations in the exchange rate are taken into account as affecting net income.

24.8 Foreign exchange transactions in the individual accounts of companies illustrated – Boil plc

Boil plc is a UK company that buys and sells catering equipment. The following information is available for foreign currency transactions entered into by Boil plc during the year ended 31 December 20X0:

1/11   Buys goods for $30,000 on credit from Nevada Inc
15/11   Sells goods for $40,000 on credit to Union Inc
15/11   Pays Nevada Inc $20,000 for on account for the goods purchased
10/12   Receives $25,000 on account from Union Inc in payment for the goods sold
10/12   Buys machinery for $80,000 from Florida Inc on credit
10/12   Borrowed $60,000 from an American bank; this is held in a dollar bank account
22/12   Pays Florida Inc $80,000 for the machinery

The exchange rates at the relevant dates were:

1/11   £1 = $2.00
15/11   £1 = $2.20
10/12   £1 = $2.40
22/12   £1 = $2.50
31/12   £1 = $2.60

Required:

Calculate the profit or loss on foreign currency to be reported in the financial statements of Boil plc at 31/12/20X0.

(Assume that Boil plc buys foreign currency to pay for goods and non-current assets on the day of settlement and immediately converts into sterling any currency received from sales.)

Solution

We need to calculate any exchange differences on monetary accounts, non-monetary accounts, and sales and purchases as follows:

Monetary accounts

Profits or losses on foreign transactions will arise on monetary accounts from the difference between the exchange rate on the date of the initial transaction and the rate on the date of its settlement or the statement of financial position date, whichever is earlier. Profits or losses on exchange differences will arise on the following monetary accounts:

Nevada Inc   –   Trade payables
Union Inc   –   Trade receivable
Florida Inc   –   Payable for machinery
American bank   –   Payable for a loan

The profit or loss on foreign exchange in these cases will be as follows:

Name of account	Nevada Inc payable	Union Inc receivable	Florida Inc payable	American bank loan payable
Foreign currency at exchange rate on date of initial transaction	$30,000/2.00	$40,000/2.20	$80,000/2.40	$60,000/2.40
	= £15,000	= £18,182	= £33,333	= £25,000
Foreign currency at exchange rate on date of settlement	$20,000/2.20	$25,000/2.40	$80,000/2.50	
	= £9,091	= £10,417	= £32,000	
Foreign currency at exchange rate on date of statement of financial position	$10,000/2.60	$15,000/2.60		$60,000/2.60
	= £3,846	= £5,769		= £23,077
Profit/(loss) on foreign exchange (£)	£2,063	(£1,996)	£1,333	£1,923

Other balances

All other balances, i.e. purchases and sales in the statement of comprehensive income and machinery (non-monetary) will be translated on the day of the initial transaction and no profit or loss on foreign exchange will arise. These balances will therefore appear in the financial statements as follows:

Purchases	$30,000/2.00	= £15,000
Sales	$40,000/2.20	= £18,182
Machinery	$80,000/2.40	= £33,333

The profit or loss on exchange differences is realised as they have either already affected the cash flows of Boil plc or will do so in the foreseeable future. This profit or loss must therefore be taken to the statement of comprehensive income.

24.9 The translation of the accounts of foreign operations where the functional currency is the same as that of the parent

If the functional currency of the foreign operation is the same as that of the parent then this means the foreign operation is primarily influenced by the parent's currency and will be evaluating its financial performance in the parent's currency. Therefore, the financial statements that will be the starting point for the consolidation will be prepared in the 'home' currency and the consolidation will be just as for any other subsidiary.

24.10 The use of a presentation currency other than the functional currency

Whenever the presentation currency is different from the functional currency, it is necessary to translate the financial statements into the presentation currency. In this situation there is no realisation of the exchange gain/loss in the cash flows and therefore any gain/loss will go to reserves.

The translation rules used in this situation are set out in para. 39 of IAS 21 as follows:

(a) assets and liabilities . . . shall be translated at the closing rate at the date of the statement of financial position;

(b) income and expenses . . . shall be translated at exchange rates at the dates of the transactions [or average rate if this is a reasonable approximation]; and

(c) all resulting exchange differences shall be recognised as a separate component of equity.

The following is an extract from the Uniq Group's 2005 Interim Accounts:

Foreign currency translation
Functional and presentation currency
Items included in the financial statements of each of the Group's entities are measured using the currency of the primary economic environment in which the entity operates ('the functional currency'). The consolidated financial statements are presented in pound sterling, rounded to the nearest hundred thousand, which is the Group and Company's functional and presentation currency.

Transactions and balances
Foreign currency transactions are translated into the functional currency using the exchange rates prevailing at the dates of the transactions. Foreign exchange gains and

losses resulting from the settlement of such transactions and from the translation at year-end exchange rates of monetary assets and liabilities denominated in foreign currencies are recognised in the statement of comprehensive income.

Group companies

The results and financial position of all the group entities (none of which has the functional currency of a hyperinflationary economy) that have a functional currency different from the presentation currency are translated into the presentation currency as follows:

(a) assets and liabilities for each statement of financial position presented are translated at the closing rate at the date of that statement of financial position;

(b) income and expenses for each statement of comprehensive income are translated at average exchange rates (unless this average is not a reasonable approximation of the cumulative effect of the rates prevailing on the transaction dates, in which case income and expenses are translated at the dates of the transactions); and

(c) all resulting exchange differences are recognised as a separate component of equity.

On consolidation, exchange differences arising from the translation of the net investment in foreign entities, and of borrowings and other currency instruments designated as hedges of such investments, are taken to shareholders' equity. When a foreign operation is sold, such exchange differences are recognised in the statement of comprehensive income as part of the gain or loss on sale. Goodwill and fair value adjustments arising on the acquisition of a foreign entity are treated as assets and liabilities of the foreign entity and translated at the closing rate.

24.11 Granby Ltd illustration

On 30 June 20X0 Granby Ltd acquired 60% of the common shares of a German subsidiary Berlin Gmbh. At that date the balance on the retained earnings of Berlin was €20,000,000. The summarised statements of comprehensive income and statement of financial position of Granby Ltd and Berlin Gmbh at 30 June 20X3 were as follows:

Statements of comprehensive income for the year ended 30 June 20X3

	Granby Ltd £000	Berlin Gmbh €000
Sales	430,000	140,000
Opening inventories	70,000	21,200
Purchases	250,000	80,000
Closing inventories	25,000	17,200
Cost of sales	295,000	84,000
Gross profit	135,000	56,000
Dividend received	2,400	NIL
Depreciation	40,000	12,000
Other expenses	10,600	4,000
Interest paid	7,000	2,000
Total expenses	57,600	18,000
Profit before taxation	79,800	38,000
Taxation	20,000	12,000
Profit after taxation	59,800	26,000
Dividend paid 30.6.20X3	25,000	8,000

Statements of financial position as at 30 June 20X3

	£000	€000
Non-current assets	140,000	90,000
Investment in Berlin Gmbh	4,500	
Current assets:		
Inventories	25,000	17,200
Trade receivables	60,500	20,000
Berlin Gmbh	4,000	
Cash	11,000	800
	100,500	38,000
Current liabilities:		
Trade payables	60,000	18,000
Granby Ltd		8,000
Taxation	20,000	12,000
	80,000	38,000
Bonds	50,000	16,000
Total assets *less* liabilities	115,000	74,000
Share capital	52,000	6,000
Retained earnings	63,000	68,000
	115,000	74,000

The following information is also available:

1 Exchange rates were as follows:

At 30 June 20X0 £1 = €5
Average for the year ending 30 June 20X3, an approximation of the rate
on the date of trading transactions and expenses £1 = €4
At 30 June/1 July 20X2 £1 = €3.5
At 30 June 20X3 £1 = €2

2 It is assumed that the functional currency of Berlin is the euro.

3 An amount of €1,380,000 was written off goodwill as an impairment charge in the current year, and €2,760,000 in previous years.

4 Non-controlling interests are measured using method 1.

Required:
Prepare consolidated accounts.

24.12 Granby Ltd illustration continued

24.12.1 Solution – note all numbers expressed in '000s.

Stage 1 – Translate the net assets of Berlin into £

This is all done at the closing rate as shown below:

	€'000	£'000
Non-current assets	90,000	45,000
Inventories	17,200	8,600
Trade receivables	20,000	10,000
Cash	800	400
Trade payables	(18,000)	(9,000)
Owing to Granby	(8,000)	(4,000)
Taxation	(12,000)	(6,000)
Bonds	(16,000)	(8,000)
Net assets	74,000	37,000

Stage 2 – compute goodwill on acquisition

Goodwill is treated as a foreign currency asset so this is initially done in euros:

$(£4,500 \times 5) - 60\% (€6,000 + €20,000) = 6,900$ in euros.
€4,140 (€1,380 + €2,760) has been written off as impairment so €2,760 remains.
This is translated at the year end rate to give a figure in the statement of financial position of **£1,380** (€2,760 × ½).

Stage 3 – prepare the consolidated statement of financial position

		£'000
Goodwill (see stage 2 above)		1,380
Non-current assets	(140,000 + 45,000)	185,000
Inventories	(25,000 + 8,600)	33,600
Trade receivables	(60,500 + 10,000)	70,500
Cash	(11,000 + 400)	11,400
Trade payables	(60,000 + 9,000)	(69,000)
Taxation	(20,000 + 6,000)	(26,000)
Bonds	(50,000 + 8,000)	(58,000)
		148,880
Share capital		52,000
Retained earnings	(see below)	82,080
Non-controlling interest	(40% × 37,000)	14,800
		148,880

Working – reconciliation of retained earnings

	£'000
Granby	63,000
Berlin [60% (68,000 – 20,000) × ½]	14,400
Impairment of goodwill (4,140 × ½)	(2,070)
Notional exchange difference on investment in Berlin	6,750
(See note below)	82,080

Note:
The notional exchange difference on the investment in Berlin of €22,500 that would have arisen had the investment been retranslated at the closing rate of 2 is necessary because of the way in which goodwill on consolidation is computed and translated. All other components

of the calculation bar this are already treated at the closing rate so this needs to be too in order to reconcile retained earnings.

This number includes all the exchange differences that have arisen on the consolidation of Granby since the date of acquisition. Some companies would show these exchange differences in a separate foreign exchange reserve but we do not have enough information to separately compute them.

Stage 4 – prepare the consolidated statement of comprehensive income

Note that where foreign subsidiaries are involved it is usually easier to take a 'two statement' approach to the preparation of the statement of comprehensive income. This is because the exchange differences are not shown in profit and loss but are included as 'other comprehensive income'. The statement of comprehensive income itself translates every item relating to Berlin at the average rate for the period, which is €4 to £1.

		£'000
Sales	$(430,000 + (140,000 \times \frac{1}{4}))$	465,000
Cost of sales	$(295,000 + (84,000 \times \frac{1}{4}))$	(316,000)
Gross profit		149,000
Impairment of goodwill	$(1,380 \times \frac{1}{2})$	(690)
Depreciation	$(40,000 + (12,000 \times \frac{1}{4}))$	(43,000)
Other expenses	$(10,600 + (4,000 \times \frac{1}{4}))$	(11,600)
Interest	$(7,000 + (2,000 \times \frac{1}{4}))$	(7,500)
Profit before taxation		86,210
Taxation	$(20,000 + (12,000 \times \frac{1}{4}))$	(23,000)
Profit for the period		63,210
Attributed to:		
Shareholders of Granby 60,610		
Non-controlling interest $(40\% \times 26,000 \times \frac{1}{4})$		2,600
		63,210

Stage 5 – compute the exchange differences

These arise in two ways:

On net assets of Berlin

		Euros	Rate	£'000
At start of period	(balancing figure in euros)	56,000	3.5	16,000
Profit for the period		26,000	4	6,500
Dividend		(8,000)	2	(4,000)
Exchange translation difference (balancing figure in £)		Nil		18,500
At end of period		74,000	2	37,000

On goodwill on consolidation

		Euros	Rate	£'000
At start of period	$(6,900 - 2,760)$	4,140	3.5	1,183
Impairment at the **end** of the period		(1,380)	2	(690)
Exchange translation difference	(balancing figure in £)	Nil		887
At end of period		2,760	2	1,380

Step 6 – prepare the statement of total comprehensive income

		£'000
Consolidated profit for the period		63,210
Other comprehensive income	(18,500 + 887)	19,387
Total comprehensive income		82,597
Attributed to:		
Shareholders of Granby		72,597
Non-controlling interest	(2,600 + (40% × 18,500))	10,000
		82,597

Note that none of the exchange difference on goodwill is allocated to the non-controlling interest because method 1 is used to measure it.

24.13 Implications of IAS 21

IAS 21 was revised in December 2003, and it was at this revision that the concept of the functional and presentation currencies was introduced. Whilst the implications for the standard are not significant for all businesses, they can have an effect. For example, a company may, in the past, have viewed foreign operations as separate to their existing parent business, but under IAS 21 as revised, if the foreign operations have a functional currency the same as the parent business, this is no longer permitted.

Also, the revision to IAS 21 changed the translation rules for statement of comprehensive incomes of businesses with a different functional and presentation currency, and gave new rules for the restatement of goodwill and fair value adjustments. These changes affected profits, net asset values and exchange differences that companies declared.

The following extract from Shell highlights some potential impacts:

> The Group has a range of inter-company funding arrangements in place in order to optimise the sourcing of financing for the Group and optimise the funding of its subsidiaries. IAS 21 is more prescriptive on the treatment of gains and losses taken to reserves [equity], for example, gains/losses where the currency of the loan is neither in the functional currency of the borrower nor of the lender are to be recognised in the statement of comprehensive income. IAS 21 is thus expected to increase volatility in the statement of comprehensive income. However, the Group is currently investigating whether to change its treasury policies to reduce this volatility.

24.14 Critique of use of presentation currency

Multinational companies may have subsidiaries in many different countries, each of which may report by choice or legal requirement internally in their local currency. With globalisation, reporting the group in a presentation currency assists the efficiency of international capital markets, particularly where a group raises funds in more than one market. Although each subsidiary might be controlled through financial statements prepared in the local currency, realism requires the use of a single presentation currency.

Summary

The conversion and translation of foreign currency for presentation in the financial statements has always been a difficult area of accounting with different views on approach. The approach taken in IAS 21 attempts to translate transactions and operations in a way that reflects the economic circumstances of the transaction. This gives no significant problems for individual foreign transactions but has led to two methods being adopted for foreign operations.

A foreign operation which has the same functional currency as its parent is treated as in integral part of the parent operations and therefore is translated in the same way as individual company transactions. A foreign operation with a functional currency different to the parent's (or a company with different functional and presentation currencies) follows different rules.

REVIEW QUESTIONS

1 Discuss the desirability or otherwise of isolating profits or losses caused by exchange differences from other profit or losses in financial statements.

2 How can different relationships between a parent operation and its controlled foreign operation affect the treatment of exchange profits or losses in the consolidated financial statements? Why should the treatment be different?

3 How does the treatment of changes in foreign exchange rates relate to the prudence and accruals concepts?

4 Explain the term functional currency and describe the factors an entity should take into account when determining which is the functional currency.

EXERCISES

An extract from the solution is provided on the Companion Website (www.pearsoned.co.uk/elliott-elliott) for exercises marked with an asterisk (*).

Question 1

Fry Ltd has the following foreign currency transactions in the year to 31/12/20X0:

15/11 Buys goods for $40,000 on credit from Texas Inc

15/11 Sells goods for $60,000 on credit to Alamos Inc

20/11 Pays Texas Inc $40,000 for the goods purchased

20/11 Receives $30,000 on account from Alamos Inc in payment for the goods sold

20/11 Buys machinery for $100,000 from Chicago Inc on credit

20/11 Borrows $90,000 from an American bank

21/12 Pays Chicago Inc $80,000 for the machinery

The exchange rates at the relevant dates were:

15/11 £1 = $2.60

20/11 £1 = $2.40

21/12 £1 = $2.30

31/12 £1 = $2.10

Required:

Calculate the profit or loss to be reported in the financial statements of Fry Ltd at 31/12/20X0.

* Question 2

On 1 January 20X0 Walpole Ltd acquired 90% of the ordinary shares of a French subsidiary Paris SA. At that date the balance on the retained earnings of Paris SA was €10,000. The non-controlling interest in Paris was measured using method 1. No shares have been issued by Paris since acquisition. The summarised statements of comprehensive income and statements of financial position of Walpole Ltd and Paris SA at 31 December 20X2 were as follows:

Statements of comprehensive income for the year ended 31 December 20X2

	Walpole Ltd £000	Paris SA €000
Sales	317,200	200,000
Opening inventories	50,000	22,000
Purchases	180,000	90,000
Closing inventories	60,000	12,000
Cost of sales	170,000	100,000
Gross profit	147,200	100,000
Dividend received from Paris SA	1,800	NIL
Depreciation	30,000	30,000
Other expenses	15,000	7,000
Interest paid	6,000	3,000
Total expenses	51,000	40,000
Profit before taxation	98,000	60,000
Taxation	21,000	15,000
Profit after taxation	77,000	45,000
Dividend paid	20,000	10,000

Statement of financial position as at 31 December 20X2

	£000	€000
Non-current assets	94,950	150,000
Investment in Paris SA	41,050	
Current assets:		
Inventories	60,000	12,000
Trade receivables	59,600	40,000
Paris SA	2,400	
Cash	11,000	11,000
Total current assets	133,000	63,000
Current liabilities:		
Trade payables	45,000	18,000
Walpole Ltd		12,000
Taxation	21,000	15,000
Total current liabilities	66,000	45,000
Debentures	40,000	10,000
Total assets less liabilities	163,000	158,000
Share capital	80,000	60,000
Share premium	6,000	20,000
Revaluation reserve	10,000	12,000
Retained earnings	67,000	66,000
	163,000	158,000

The following information is also available:

(i) The revaluation reserve in Paris SA arose from the revaluation of non-current assets on 1/1/20X2.

(ii) No impairment of goodwill has occurred since acquisition.

(iii) Exchange rates were as follows:

At 1 January 20X0   £1 = €2
Average for the year ending 31 December 20X2   £1 = €4
At 31 December 20X1/1 January 20X2   £1 = €3
At 31 December 20X2   £1 = €5

Required:
Assuming that the functional currency of Paris SA is the euro, prepare the consolidated accounts for the Walpole group at 31 December 20X2.

Question 3

(a) According to IAS 21 *The Effects of Changes in Foreign Exchange Rates*, how should a company decide what its functional currency is?

(b) Until recently Eufonion, a UK limited liability company, reported using the euro (€) as its functional currency. However, on 1 November 2007 the company decided that its functional currency should now be the dollar ($).

The summarised balance sheet of Eufonion as at 31 October 2008 in € million was as follows:

ASSETS		€m
Non-current assets		420
Current assets		
Inventories	26	
Trade and other receivables	42	
Cash and cash equivalents	8	
		76
Total assets		496
EQUITY AND LIABILIITES		
Equity		
Share capital		200
Retained earnings		107
		307
Non-current liabilities	85	
Current liabilities		
Trade and other payables	63	
Current taxation	41	
	104	
Total liabilities		189
Total equity and liabilities		496

Non-current liabilities includes a loan of $70 million which was raised in dollars ($) and translated at the closing rate of $1 = €0.72425.

Trade receivables include an amount of $20 million invoiced in dollars ($) to an American customer which has been translated at the closing rate of $1 = €0.72425.

All items of property, plant and equipment were purchased in euros (€) except for plant which was purchased in British pounds (£) in 2007 and which cost £150 million. This was translated at the exchange rate of £1 = €1.46015 as at the date of purchase. The carrying value of the equipment was £90 million as at 31 October 2008.

Required:
Translate the balance sheet of Eufonion as at 31 October 2008 into dollars ($m), the company's new functional currency.

(c) The directors of Eufonion (as in (b) above) are now considering using the British pound (£) as the company's presentation currency for the financial statements for the year ended 31 October 2009.

Required:
Advise the directors how they should translate the company's income statement for the year ended 31 October 2009 and its balance sheet as at 31 October 2009 into the new presentation currency.

(d) Discuss whether or not a reporting entity should be allowed to present its financial statements in a currency which is different from its functional currency.

(The Association of International Accountants)

References

1 IAS 21 *The Effects of Changes in Foreign Exchange Rates*, IASB, revised 2003, para. 20.
2 *Ibid.*, para. 20.
3 *Ibid.*, para. 10.
4 *Ibid.*, para. 11.
5 *Ibid.*, para. 38.
6 *Ibid.*, para. 21.
7 *Ibid.*, para. 23.
8 *Ibid.*, para. 28.

PART **5**

Interpretation

CHAPTER 25

Earnings per share

25.1 Introduction

The main purpose of this chapter is to undertand the importance of earnings per share (EPS) and the PE ratio as a measure of the financial performance of a company (or 'an enterprise'). This chapter will enable you to calculate the EPS according to IAS 33 both for the current year and prior years, when there is an issue of shares in the year. Also, it will enable you to understand and calculate the diluted earnings per share, for future changes in share capital arising from exercising of share options and conversion of other financial instruments into shares.

Objectives

By the end of the chapter, you should be able to:

- define earnings per share and the PE ratio;
- comment critically on the PE ratio of an enterprise in comparison with the industry average;
- calculate the basic and diluted earnings per share.

25.2 Why is the earnings per share figure important?

One of the most widely publicised ratios for a public company is the price/earnings or PE ratio. The PE ratio is significant because, by combining it with a forecast of company earnings, analysts can decide whether the shares are currently over- or undervalued.[1]

The ratio is published daily in the financial press and is widely employed by those making investment decisions. The following is a typical extract from the *Risk Measurement Service*:[2]

Breweries, Pubs and Restaurants

Company	Price 31/3/98	PE ratio
Company A	453	12.6
Company B	340	39.3
Company C	1,125	19.6

The PE ratio is calculated by dividing the market price of a share by the earnings that the company generated for that share. Alternatively, the PE figure may be seen as a multiple of the earnings per share, where the multiple represents the number of years' earnings required to recoup the price paid for the share. For example, it would take a shareholder in Company B just under forty years to recoup her outlay if all earnings were to be distributed, whereas it would take a shareholder in Company A just over twelve years to recoup his outlay, and one in Company C just under twenty years.

25.2.1 What factors affect the PE ratio?

The PE ratio for a company will reflect investors' confidence and hopes about the international scene, the national economy and the industry sector, as well as about the current year's performance of the company as disclosed in its financial report. It is difficult to interpret a PE ratio in isolation without a certain amount of information about the company, its competitors and the industry within which it operates.

For example, a **high PE ratio** might reflect investor confidence in the existing management team: people are willing to pay a high multiple for expected earnings because of the underlying strength of the company. Conversely, it might also reflect lack of investor confidence in the existing management, but an anticipation of a takeover bid which will result in transfer of the company assets to another company with better prospects of achieving growth in earnings than has the existing team.

A **low PE ratio** might indicate a lack of confidence in the current management or a feeling that even a new management might find problems that are not easily surmounted. For example, there might be extremely high gearing, with little prospect of organic growth in earnings or new capital inputs from rights issues to reduce it.

These reasons for a difference in the PE ratios of companies, even though they are in the same industry, are market-based and not simply a function of earnings. However, the current earnings per share figure and the individual shareholder's expectation of future growth relative to that of other companies also have an impact on the share price.

25.3 How is the EPS figure calculated?

Because of the importance attached to the PE ratio, it is essential that there be a consistent approach to the calculation of the EPS figure. IAS 33 *Earnings per Share*[3] was issued in 1998 for this purpose. A revised version of the standard was issued in 2003.

The EPS figure is of major interest to shareholders not only because of its use in the PE ratio calculation, but also because it is used in the earnings yield percentage calculation. It is a more acceptable basis for comparing performance than figures such as dividend yield percentage because it is not affected by the distribution policy of the directors. The formula is:

$$\text{EPS} = \frac{\text{Earnings}}{\text{Weighted number of ordinary shares}}$$

The standard defines two EPS figures for disclosure, namely,

- **basic** EPS based on ordinary shares currently in issue; and
- **diluted** EPS based on ordinary shares currently in issue *plus* potential ordinary shares.

25.3.1 Basic EPS

Basic EPS is defined in IAS 33 as follows:[4]

- Basic earnings per share is calculated by dividing the net profit or loss for the period attributable to ordinary shareholders by the weighted average number of ordinary shares outstanding during the period.

For the purpose of the BEPS definition:

- **Net profit** is the profit for the period attributable to the parent entity after deduction of preference dividends (assuming preference shares are equity instruments).[5]

- The **weighted average number of ordinary shares** should be adjusted for events, other than the conversion of potential ordinary shares, that have changed the number of ordinary shares outstanding, without a corresponding change in resources.[6]

- An **ordinary share** is an equity instrument that is subordinate to all other classes of equity instruments.[7]

Earnings per share is calculated on the overall profit attributable to ordinary shareholders but also on the profit from continuing operations if this is different to the overall profit for the period.

25.3.2 Diluted EPS

Diluted EPS is defined as follows:

- For the purpose of calculating diluted earnings per share, the net profit attributable to ordinary shareholders and the weighted average number of shares outstanding should be *adjusted for the effects of all dilutive potential ordinary shares.*[8]

  This means that *both* the earnings *and* the number of shares used *may* need to be adjusted from the amounts that appear in the profit and loss account and statement of financial position.

- **Dilutive** means that earnings in the future may be spread over a larger number of ordinary shares.

- **Potential ordinary shares** are financial instruments that may entitle the holders to ordinary shares.

25.4 The use to shareholders of the EPS

Shareholders use the reported EPS to estimate future growth which will affect the future share price. It is an important measure of growth over time. There are, however, limitations in its use as a performance measure and for inter-company comparison.

25.4.1 How does a shareholder estimate future growth in the EPS?

The current EPS figure allows a shareholder to assess the wealth-creating abilities of a company. It recognises that the effect of earnings is to add to the individual wealth of shareholders in two ways: first, by the payment of a dividend which transfers cash from the company's control to the shareholder; and, secondly, by retaining earnings in the company for reinvestment, so that there may be increased earnings in the future.

The important thing when attempting to arrive at an estimate is to review the statement of comprehensive income of the current period and identify the earnings that can reasonably be expected to continue. In accounting terminology, you should identify the **maintainable post-tax earnings** that arise in the **ordinary course of business.**

Companies are required to make this easy for the shareholder by disclosing separately, by way of note, any unusual items and by analysing the profit and loss on trading between discontinuing and continuing activities.

Shareholders can use this information to estimate for themselves the maintainable post-tax earnings, assuming that there is no change in the company's trading activities. Clearly, in a dynamic business environment it is extremely unlikely that there will be no change in the current business activities. The shareholder needs to refer to any information on capital commitments which appear as a note to the accounts and also to the chairman's statement and any coverage in the financial press. This additional information is used to adjust the existing maintainable earnings figure.

25.4.2 Limitations of EPS as a performance measure

EPS is thought to have a significant impact on the market share price. However, there are limitations to its use as a performance measure.

The limitations affecting the use of EPS as an inter-period performance measure include the following:

- It is based on historical earnings. Management might have made decisions in the past to encourage current earnings growth at the expense of future growth, e.g. by reducing the amount spent on capital investment and research and development. Growth in the EPS cannot be relied on as a predictor of the rate of growth in the future.

- EPS does not take inflation into account. Real growth might be materially different from the apparent growth.

The limitations affecting inter-company comparisons include the following:

- The earnings are affected by management's choice of accounting policies, e.g. whether non-current assets have been revalued or interest has been capitalised.

- EPS is affected by the capital structure, e.g. changes in number of shares by making bonus issues.

However, the **rate of growth** of EPS is important and this may be compared between different companies and over time within the same company.

25.5 Illustration of the basic EPS calculation

Assume that Watts plc had post-tax profits for 20X1 of £1,250,000 and an issued share capital of £1,500,000 comprising 1,000,000 ordinary shares of 50p each and 1,000,000 £1 10% preference shares that are classified as equity. The basic EPS (BEPS) for 20X1 is calculated at £1.15 as follows:

	£000
Profit on ordinary activities after tax	1,250
Less preference dividend	(100)
Profit for the period attributable to ordinary shareholders	1,150

$$\text{BEPS} = £1,150,000/1,000,000 \text{ shares} = £1.15$$

Note that it is the *number* of issued shares that is used in the calculation and *not the nominal value* of the shares. The market value of a share is not required for the BEPS calculation.

25.6 Adjusting the number of shares used in the basic EPS calculation

The earnings per share is frequently used by shareholders and directors to demonstrate the growth in a company's performance over time. Care is required to ensure that the number of shares is stated consistently to avoid distortions arising from changes in the capital structure that have changed the number of shares outstanding without a corresponding change in resources during the whole or part of a year. Such changes occur with (a) bonus issues and share splits; (b) new issues and buybacks at full market price during the year; and (c) the bonus element of a rights issue.

We will consider the appropriate treatment for each of these capital structure changes in order to ensure that EPS is comparable between accounting periods.

25.6.1 Bonus issues

A bonus issue, or capitalisation issue as it is also called, arises when a company capitalises reserves to give existing shareholders more shares. In effect, a simple transfer is made from reserves to issued share capital. In real terms, neither the shareholder nor the company is giving or receiving any immediate financial benefit. The process indicates that the reserves will not be available for distribution, but will remain invested in the physical assets of the company. There are, however, more shares.

Treatment in current year

In the Watts plc example, assume that the company increased its shares in issue in 20X1 by the issue of another 1 million shares and achieved identical earnings in 20X1 as in 20X0. The EPS reported for 20X1 would be immediately halved from £1.15 to £0.575. Clearly, this does not provide a useful comparison of performance between the two years.

Restatement of previous year's BEPS

The solution is to restate the EPS for 20X0 that appears in the 20X1 accounts, using the number of shares in issue at 31.12.20X1, i.e. £1,150,000/2,000,000 shares = BEPS of £0.575.

25.6.2 Share splits

When the market value of a share becomes high some companies decide to increase the number of shares held by each shareholder by changing the nominal value of each share. The effect is to reduce the market price per share but for each shareholder to hold the same total value. A share split would be treated in the same way as a bonus issue.

For example, if Watts plc split the 1,000,000 shares of 50p each into 2,000,000 shares of 25p each, the 20X1 BEPS would be calculated using 2,000,000 shares. It would seem that the BEPS had halved in 20X1. This is misleading and the 20X0 BEPS is therefore restated using 2,000,000 shares. The total market capitalisation of Watts plc would remain unchanged. For example, if, prior to the split, each share had a market value of £4 and the company had a total market capitalisation of £4,000,000, after the split each share would have a market price of £2 and the company market capitalisation would remain unchanged at £4,000,000.

25.6.3 New issue at full market value

Selling more shares to raise additional capital should generate additional earnings. In this situation we have a real change in the company's capital and there is no need to adjust any comparative figures. However, a problem arises in the year in which the issue took place. Unless the issue occurred on the first day of the financial year, the new funds would have been *available to generate profits* for only a part of the year. It would therefore be misleading to calculate the EPS figure by dividing the earnings generated during the year by the number of shares in issue at the end of the year. The method adopted to counter this is to use a time-weighted average for the number of shares.

For example, let us assume in the Watts example that the following information is available:

	No. of shares
Shares (nominal value 50p) in issue at 1 January 20X1	1,000,000
Shares issued for cash at market price on 30 September 20X1	500,000

The time-weighted number of shares for EPS calculation at 31 December 20X1 will be:

	No. of shares
Shares in issue for 9 months to date of issue	
$(1,000,000) \times (9/12 \text{ months})$	750,000
Shares in issue for 3 months from date of issue	
$(1,500,000) \times (3/12 \text{ months})$	375,000
Time-weighted shares for use in BEPS calculation	1,125,000

BEPS for 20X1 will be £1,150,000/1,125,000 shares = **£1.02**

25.6.4 Buybacks at market value

Companies are prompted to buy back their own shares when there is a fall in the stock market. The main arguments that companies advance for purchasing their own shares are:

- To reduce the cost of capital when equity costs more than debt.
- The shares are undervalued.
- To return surplus cash to shareholders.
- To increase the apparent rate of growth in BEPS.

The following is an extract from the 2000 Annual Report of EVN AG in respect of both a buyback and a share split, both of which will impact on the EPS figure:

Share buyback programme prolonged
At the 71st Annual General Meeting on January 14, 2000, the EVN Executive Board was given authorisation to purchase company shares up to a maximum of 10% of share capital over 18 months. This authorisation also extends to the resale of the shares via the stock markets. The main aim was the stabilisation of the shareholder structure and the stock market share price. On this basis, the Executive Board decided to repurchase shares initially to the value of 3% of share capital in the period up to September 30, 2000.

Share split
In line with a resolution passed by the 71st Annual General Meeting, EVN AG share capital was reallocated through a 1:3 share split. Shareholders have received three shares for every one in their possession. Share capital, which remains unchanged at Eur 82,878,000 is now divided into 34,200,000 ordinary shares. The measure was aimed at easing the price of the EVN share, thereby stimulating trading and share price development.

The impact on the weighted number of shares is explained by the EVN in Note 52 as follows:

Earnings per share
Due to the 1:3 ratio share split, the number of ordinary shares outstanding totalled 34,200,000. Following the deduction of own shares, the weighted number of shares outstanding is 33,974,310 . . .

In the UK, examples are found amongst the FTSE 100 companies: e.g. in 1998 NatWest Bank purchased 175,000; Rio Tinto 2.965m; BTR 700,020 ordinary shares.[9]

The shares bought back by the company are included in the basic EPS calculation time apportioned from the beginning of the year to the date of buyback.

For example, let us assume in the Watts example that the following information is available:

	No. of shares
Shares (50p nominal value) in issue at 1 January 20X1	1,000,000
Shares bought back on 31 May 20X1	240,000
Profit attributable to ordinary shares	£1,150,000

The time-weighted number of shares for EPS calculation at 31 December 20X1 will be:

1.1.20X1	Shares in issue for 5 months to date of buyback	$1,000,000 \times 5/12$	416,667
31.5.20X1	Number of shares bought back by company	(240,000)	
31.12.20X1	Opening capital less shares bought back	$760,000 \times 7/12$	443,333
	Time-weighted shares for use in BEPS calculation		860,000

BEPS for 20X1 will be £1,150,000/860,000 shares = **£1.34**

Note that the effect of this buyback has been to increase the BEPS for 20X1 from £1.15 as calculated in section 25.5 above. This is a mechanism for management to lift the BEPS and achieve EPS growth.

25.7 Rights issues

A rights issue involves giving existing shareholders 'the right' to buy a set number of additional shares at a price below the fair value which is normally the current market price. A rights issue has two characteristics being both an issue for cash and, because the price is below fair value, a bonus issue. Consequently the rules for *both* a cash issue *and* a bonus issue need to be applied in calculating the weighted average number of shares for the basic EPS calculation.

This is an area where students frequently find difficulty with Step 1 and we will illustrate the rationale without accounting terminology.

The following four steps are required:

Step 1: Calculate the average price of shares before and after a rights issue to identify the amount of the bonus the company has granted.

Step 2: The weighted average number of shares is calculated for current year.

Step 3: The BEPS for current year is calculated.

Step 4: The previous year BEPS is adjusted for the bonus element of the rights issue.

Step 1: Calculate the average price of shares before and after a rights issue to identify the amount of the bonus the company has granted

Assume that Mr Radmand purchased two 50p shares at a market price of £4 each in Watts plc on 1 January 20X1 and that on 2 January 20X1 the company offered a 1:2 rights issue (i.e. one new share for every two shares held) at £3.25 per share.

If Mr Radmand had bought at the market price, the position would simply have been:

		£
2 shares at market price of £4 each on 1 January 20X1	=	8.00
1 share at market price of £4.00 per share on 2 January	=	4.00
Total cost of 3 shares as at 2 January		12.00
Average cost per share unchanged at		4.00

However, this did not happen. Mr Radmand only paid £3.25 for the new share. This meant that the total cost of 3 shares to him was:

		£
2 shares at market price of £4 each on 1 January 20X1	=	8.00
1 share at discounted price of £3.25 on 2 January 20X1	=	3.25
Total cost of 3 shares	=	11.25
Average cost per share (£11.25/3 shares)	=	3.75

The rights issue has had the effect of reducing the cost per share of each of the three shares held by Mr Radmand on 2 January 20X1 by (£4.00 − £3.75) **£0.25 per share**.

The accounting terms applied are:

- Average cost per share after the rights issue (£3.75) is *the theoretical ex-rights value*.
- Amount by which the average cost of each share is reduced (£0.25) is *the bonus element*.

In accounting terminology, Step 1 is described as follows:

Step 1: The bonus element is ascertained by calculating the theoretical ex-rights value, i.e. the £0.25 is ascertained by calculating the £3.75 and deducting it from £4 pre-rights market price

Step 1: Theoretical ex-rights calculation

In accounting terminology, this means that existing shareholders get an element of bonus per share (£0.25) at the same time as the company receives additional capital (£3.25 per new share). The bonus element may be quantified by the calculation of a **theoretical ex-rights price (£3.75)**, which is compared with the last market price (£4.00) prior to the issue; the difference is a bonus. The theoretical ex-rights price is calculated as follows:

		£
2 shares at fair value of £4 each prior to rights issue	=	8.00
1 share at discounted rights issue price of £3.25 each	=	3.25
3 shares at fair value after issue (i.e. ex-rights)	=	11.25
The theoretical ex-rights price is £11.25/3 shares	=	3.75
The bonus element is fair value £4 less £3.75	=	0.25

Note that for the calculation of the number of shares and time-weighted number of shares for a bonus issue, share split and issue at full market price per share the market price per share is not relevant. The position for a rights issue is different and the market price becomes a relevant factor in calculating the number of bonus shares.

Step 2: The weighted average number of shares is calculated for current year

Assume that Watts plc made a rights issue of one share for every two shares held on 1 January 20X1.

There would be no need to calculate a weighted average number of shares. The total used in the BEPS calculation would be as follows:

		No. of shares
Shares to date of rights issue:		
1,000,000 shares held for a full year	=	1,000,000
Shares from date of issue:		
500,000 shares held for full year	=	500,000
Total shares for BEPS calculation		1,500,000

However, if a rights issue is made part way through the year, a time-apportionment is required. For example, if we assume that a rights issue is made on 30 September 20X1, the time-weighted number of shares is calculated as follows:

		No. of shares
Shares to date of rights issue:		
1,000,000 shares held for a full year	=	1,000,000
Shares from date of issue:		
500,000 shares held for 3 months (500,000 × 3/12)	=	125,000
Weighted average number of shares		1,125,000

Note, however, that the 1,125,000 has not taken account of the fact that the new shares had been issued at less than market price and that the company had effectively granted the existing shareholders a bonus. We saw above that when there has been a bonus issue the number of shares used in the BEPS is increased. We need, therefore, to calculate the number of bonus shares that would have been issued to achieve the reduction in market price from £4.00 to £3.75 per share. This is calculated as follows:

Total market capitalisation was 1,000,000 shares @ £4.00 per share	=	£4,000,000
Number of shares that would reduce the market price to £3.75	=	£4,000,000/£3.75
	=	1,066,667 shares
Number of shares prior to issue	=	1,000,000
Bonus shares deemed to be issued to existing shareholders	=	66,667
Bonus share for period of 9 months to date of issue (66,667/12 × 9)	=	**50,000**

The bonus shares for the nine months are added to the existing shares and the time apportioned new shares as follows:

		No. of shares
Shares to date of rights issue:		
1,000,000 shares held for a full year	=	1,000,000
Shares from date of issue:		
500,000 shares held for 3 months (500,000 × 3/12)	=	125,000
Weighted average number of shares		1,125,000
Bonus share:		
66,667 shares held for 9 months (66,667/12 × 9)	=	50,000
		1,175,000

Figure 25.1 Formula approach to calculating weighted average number of shares

					No. of shares
Shares to date of rights issue:					
No. of shares	× Increase by bonus fraction		× Time adjustment		
1,000,000			× 9/12	=	750,000
Bonus:	((1,000,000 × 4/3.75) − 1,000,000)	× 9/12		=	50,000
Shares from date of issue:					
1,500,000	×		× 3/12	=	375,000
Weighted average number of shares					1,175,000

The same figure of 1,175,000 can be derived from the following approach using the relationship between the market price of £4.00 and the theoretical ex-rights price of £3.75 to calculate the number of bonus shares.

The relationship between the actual cum–rights price and theoretical ex-rights price is shown by the bonus fraction:

$$\frac{\text{Actual cum–rights share price}}{\text{Theoretical ex-rights share price}}$$

This fraction is applied to the number of shares before the rights issue to adjust them for the impact of the bonus element of the rights issue. This is shown in Figure 25.1.

Step 3: Calculate BEPS for current year

BEPS for 20X1 is then calculated as £1,150,000 / 1,175,000 shares   =   **£0.979**

Step 4: Adjusting the previous year's BEPS for the bonus element of a rights issue

The 20X0 BEPS of £1.15 needs to be restated, i.e. reduced to ensure comparability with 20X1.

In Step 2 above we calculated that the company had made a bonus issue of 66,667 shares to existing shareholders. In re-calculating the BEPS for 20X0 the shares should be increased by 66,667 to 1,066,667. The restated BEPS for 20X0 is as follows:

Earnings	/	restated number of shares		
£1,150,000	/	1,066,667	=	£1.078125

Assuming that the earnings for 20X0 and 20X1 were £1,150,000 in each year the 20X0 BEPS figures will be reported as follows:

As reported in the 20X0 accounts as at 31.12.20X0 =
£1,150,000/1,000,000   =   **£1.15**
As restated in the 20X1 accounts as at 31.12.20X1 =
£1,150,000/1,066,667   =   **£1.08**

The same result is obtained using the bonus element approach by reducing the 20X0 BEPS as follows by multiplying it by the reciprocal of the bonus fraction:

$$\frac{\text{Theoretical ex-rights fair value per share}}{\text{Fair value per share immediately before the exercise of rights}} = \frac{£3.75}{£4.00}$$

As restated in the 20X1 accounts as at 31.12.20X1 = £1.15 × (3.75/4.00)   =   **£1.08**

25.7.1 Would BEPS for current and previous year be the same if the company had made a separate full market price issue and a separate bonus issue?

This section is included to demonstrate that the BEPS is the same, i.e. £1.08 if we approach the calculation on the assumption that there was a full price issue followed by a bonus issue. This will demonstrate that the BEPS is the same as that calculated using theoretical ex-rights. There are five steps, as follows:

Step 1: Calculate the number of full value and bonus shares in the company's share capital

	No. of shares
Shares in issue *before* bonus	1,000,000
Rights issue at full market price	
(500,000 shares × £3.25 issue price/full market price of £4)	406,250
	1,406,250
Total number of bonus shares	93,750
Total shares	1,500,000

Step 2: Allocate the total bonus shares to the 1,000,000 original shares

(Note that the previous year will be restated using the proportion of original shares: original shares + bonus shares allocated to these original 1,000,000 shares.)

Shares in issue before bonus		1,000,000
Bonus issue applicable to pre-rights:		
93,750 bonus shares × (1,000,000/1,406,250) =		
66,667 shares × 9/12 months	= 50,000	
Bonus issue applicable to post-rights		
93,750 bonus shares × (1,000,000/1,406,250) =		
66,667 shares × 3/12 months	= 16,667	
Total bonus shares allocated to existing 1,000,000 shares		66,667
Total original holding plus bonus shares allocated to that holding		1,066,667

Step 3: Time-weight the rights issue and allocate bonus shares to rights shares

Rights issue at full market price	
500,000 shares × (£3.25 issue price/full market price of £4)	
= 406,250 × 3/12 months	101,563
Bonus issue applicable to rights issue:	
93,750 bonus shares × (406,250/1,406,250) = 27,083 shares × 3/12 months	6,770
Weighted average ordinary shares (includes shares from Steps 2 and 3)	1,175,000

Step 4: BEPS calculation for 20X1

Calculate the BEPS using the post-tax profit and weighted average ordinary shares, as follows:

$$20X1 \ BEPS = \frac{£1,150,000}{£1,175,000} = £0.979$$

Step 5: BEPS restated for 20X0

There were 93,750 bonus shares issued in 20X1. The 20X0 BEPS needs to be reduced, therefore, by the same proportion as applied to the 1,000,000 ordinary shares in 20X1, i.e. 1,000,000:1,066,667

$$20\text{X0 BEPS} \quad \times \text{bonus adjustment} = \text{restated 20X0 BEPS}$$
$$\text{i.e. } 20\text{X0} = £1.15 \times (1,000,000/1,066,667) = £1.08$$

This approach illustrates the rationale for the time-weighted average and the restatement of the previous year's BEPS. The adjustment using the theoretical ex-rights approach produces the same result and is simpler to apply but the rationale is not obvious.

25.8 Adjusting the earnings and number of shares used in the diluted EPS calculation

We will consider briefly what dilution means and the circumstances which require the weighted average number of shares and the net profit attributable to ordinary shareholders used to calculate BEPS to be adjusted.

25.8.1 What is dilution?

In a modern corporate structure, a number of classes of person such as the holders of convertible bonds, the holders of convertible preference shares, members of share option schemes and share warrant holders may be entitled as at the date of the statement of financial position to become equity shareholders at a future date.

If these people exercise their entitlements at a future date, the EPS would be reduced. In accounting terminology, the EPS will have been diluted. The effect on future share price could be significant. Assuming that the share price is a multiple of the EPS figure, any reduction in the figure could have serious implications for the existing shareholders; they need to be aware of the potential effect on the EPS figure of any changes in the way the capital of the company is or will be constituted. This is shown by calculating and disclosing both the basic and 'diluted EPS' figures.

IAS 33 therefore requires a diluted EPS figure to be reported using as the denominator potential ordinary shares that are dilutive, i.e. would decrease net profit per share or increase net loss from continuing operations.[10]

25.8.2 Circumstances in which the number of shares used for BEPS is increased

The holders of convertible bonds, the holders of convertible preference shares, members of share option schemes and the holders of share warrants will each be entitled to receive ordinary shares from the company at some future date. Such additional shares, referred to as potential ordinary shares, *may* need to be added to the basic weighted average number *if they are dilutive*. It is important to note that if a company has potential ordinary shares they are not automatically included in the fully diluted EPS calculation. There is a test to apply to see if such shares actually are dilutive – this is discussed further in section 25.9 below.

25.8.3 Circumstances in which the earnings used for BEPS are increased

The earnings are increased to take account of the post-tax effects of amounts recognised in the period relating to dilutive potential ordinary shares that will no longer be incurred on their conversion to ordinary shares, e.g. the loan interest payable on convertible loans will no longer be a charge after conversion and earnings will be increased by the post-tax amount of such interest.

25.8.4 Procedure where there are share warrants and options

Where options, warrants or other arrangements exist which involve the issue of shares below their fair value (i.e. at a price lower than the average for the period) then the impact is calculated by notionally splitting the potential issue into shares issued at fair value and shares issued at no value for no consideration.[11] Since shares issued at fair value are not dilutive that number is ignored but the number of shares at no value is employed to calculate the dilution. The calculation is illustrated for Watts plc:

Assume that Watts plc had at 31 December 20X1:

- an issued capital of 1,000,000 ordinary shares of 50p each nominal value;

- post-tax earnings for the year of £1,150,000;

- an average market price per share of £4; and

- share options in existence 500,000 shares issuable in 20X2 at £3.25 per share.

The computation of basic and diluted EPS is as follows:

	Per share	Earnings	Shares
Net profit for 20X1		£1,150,000	
Weighted average shares during 20X1			1,000,000
Basic EPS (£1,150,000/1,000,000)	*1.15*		
Number of shares under option			500,000
Number that would have been issued			
At fair value (500,000 × £3.25)/£4			(406,250)
Diluted EPS	1.05	£1,150,000	1,093,750

25.8.5 Procedure where there are convertible bonds or convertible preference shares

The post-tax profit should be adjusted[12] for:

- any dividends on dilutive potential ordinary shares that have been deducted in arriving at the net profit attributable to ordinary shareholders;

- interest recognised in the period for the dilutive potential ordinary shares; and

- any other changes in income or expense that would result from the conversion of the dilutive potential ordinary shares, e.g. the reduction of interest expense related to convertible bonds results in a higher post-tax profit but this could lead to a consequential increase in expense if there were a non-discretionary employee profit-sharing plan.

25.8.6 Convertible preference shares calculation illustrated for Watts plc

Assume that Watts plc had at 31 December 20X1:

- an issued capital of 1,000,000 ordinary shares of 50p each nominal value;
- post-tax earnings for the year of £1,150,000;
- convertible 8% preference shares of £1 each totalling £1,000,000, convertible at one ordinary share for every five convertible preference shares.

The computation of basic and diluted EPS for convertible bonds is as follows:

	Per share	Earnings	Shares
Post-tax net profit for 20X1 (after interest)		£1,150,000	
Weighted average shares during 20X1			1,000,000
Basic EPS (£1,150,000/1,000,000)	£1.15		
Number of shares resulting from conversion			200,000
Add back the preference dividend paid in 20X1		80,000	
Adjusted earnings and number of shares		1,230,000	1,200,000
Diluted EPS (£1,230,000/1,200,000)	£1.025		

25.8.7 Convertible bonds calculation illustrated for Watts plc

Assume that Watts plc had at 31 December 20X1:

- an issued capital of 1,000,000 ordinary shares of 50p each nominal value;
- post-tax earnings after interest for the year of £1,150,000;
- convertible 10% loan of £1,000,000;
- an average market price per share of £4;

and the convertible loan is convertible into 250,000 ordinary shares of 50p each.
The computation of basic and diluted EPS for convertible bonds is as follows:

	Per share	Earnings	Shares
Post-tax net profit for 20X1 (after interest)		£1,150,000	
Weighted average shares during 20X1			1,000,000
Basic EPS (£1,150,000/1,000,000)	£1.15		
Number of shares resulting from conversion			250,000
Interest expense on convertible loan		100,000	
Tax liability relating to interest expense – Assuming the firm's marginal tax rate is 40%		(40,000)	
Adjusted earnings and number of shares		1,210,000	1,250,000
Diluted EPS (£1,210,000/1,250,000)	£0.97		

25.9 Procedure where there are several potential dilutions

Where there are several potential dilutions the calculation must be done in progressive stages starting with the most dilutive and ending with the least.[13] Any potential 'antidilutive' (i.e. potential issues that would increase earnings per share) are ignored.

Assume that Watts plc had at 31 December 20X1:

- an issued capital of 1,000,000 Ordinary shares of 50p each nominal value;
- post-tax earnings after interest for the year of £1,150,000;
- an average market price per share of £4; and
- share options in existence 500,000 shares
  – exercisable in year 20X2 at £3.25 per share;
- convertible 10% loan of £1,000,000
  – convertible in year 20X2 into 250,000 ordinary shares of 50p each;
- convertible 8% preference shares of £1 each totalling £1,000,000
  – convertible in year 20X4 at 1 ordinary share for every **40** preference shares.

There are two steps in arriving at the diluted EPS, namely:

Step 1: Determine the increase in earnings attributable to ordinary shareholders on conversion of potential ordinary shares;

Step 2: Determine the potential ordinary shares to include in the diluted earnings per share.

Step 1: Determine the increase in earnings attributable to ordinary shareholders on conversion of potential ordinary shares

	Increase in earnings	*Increase in number of ordinary shares*	*Earnings per incremental share*
Options			
Increase in earnings			
Incremental shares issued			
for no consideration			
500,000 × (£4 − 3.25)/£4	nil	93,750	nil
Convertible preference shares			
Increase in net profit			
8% of £1,000,000	80,000		
Incremental shares 1,000,000/40		25,000	3.20
10% convertible bond			
Increase in net profit			
£1,000,000 × 0.10 × (60%)	60,000		
(assumes a marginal tax rate of 40%)			
Incremental shares 1,000,000/4		250,000	0.24

Step 2: Determine the potential ordinary shares to include in the computation of diluted earnings per share

	Net profit attributable to continuing operations	*Ordinary shares*	*Per share*
As reported for BEPS	1,150,000	1,000,000	1.15
Options	—	93,750	
	1,150,000	1,093,750	1.05 dilutive
10% convertible bonds	60,000	250,000	
	1,210,000	1,343,750	0.90 dilutive
Convertible preference shares	80,000	25,000	
	1,290,000	1,368,750	0.94 antidilutive

Since the diluted earnings per share is increased when taking the convertible preference shares into account (from 90p to 94p), the convertible preference shares are antidilutive and are ignored in the calculation of diluted earnings per share. The lowest figure is selected and the diluted EPS will, therefore, be disclosed as 90p.

25.10 Exercise of conversion rights during financial year

Shares actually issued will be in accordance with the terms of conversion and will be included in the BEPS calculation on a time-apportioned basis from the date of conversion to the end of the financial year.

25.10.1 Calculation of BEPS assuming that convertible loan has been converted and options exercised during the financial year

This is illustrated for the calculation for the year 20X2 accounts of Watts plc as follows. Assume that Watts plc had at 31 December 20X2:

● an issued capital of 1,000,000 ordinary shares of 50p each as at 1 January 20X2;

● convertible 10% loan of £1,000,000 **converted** on 1 April 20X2 into 250,000 ordinary shares of 50p each;

● share options for 500,000 ordinary shares of 50p each **exercised** on 1 August 20X2.

The weighted average number of shares for BEPS is calculated as follows:

	Net profit attributable to continuing operations	Ordinary shares	Per share
As reported for BEPS	1,150,000	1,000,000	1.15
Options	—	93,750	
	1,150,000	1,093,750	1.05 dilutive
10% convertible bonds	60,000	250,000	
	1,210,000	1,343,750	0.90 dilutive
Convertible preference shares	80,000	25,000	
	1,290,000	1,368,750	0.94 antidilutive

25.11 Disclosure requirements of IAS 33

The standard[14] requires the following disclosures:

For the current year:

● Companies should disclose the basic and diluted EPS figures for profit or loss from continuing operations and for profit or loss with equal prominence, whether positive or negative, on the face of the statement of comprehensive income for each class of ordinary share that has a different right to share in the profit for the period.

● The amounts used as the numerators in calculating basic and diluted earnings per share, and a reconciliation of those amounts to the net profit or loss for the period.

● The weighted average number of shares used as the denominator in calculating the basic and diluted earnings per share and a reconciliation of these denominators to each other.

For the previous year (if there has been a bonus issue, rights issue or share split):

● BEPS and diluted EPS should be adjusted retrospectively.

25.11.1 Alternative EPS figures

In the UK the Institute of Investment Management and Research (IIMR) published Statement of Investment Practice No. 1, entitled *The Definition of Headline Earnings*,[15] in which it identified two purposes for producing an EPS figure:

● as a measure of the company's **maintainable earnings** capacity, suitable in particular for forecasts and for inter-year comparisons, and for use on a per share basis in the calculation of the price/earnings ratio;

● as a factual headline figure for historical earnings, which can be a benchmark figure for the **trading outcome for the year**.

The Institute recognised that the maintainable earnings figure required exceptional or non-continuing items to be eliminated, which meant that, in view of the judgement involved in adjusting the historical figures, the calculation of maintainable earnings figures could not be put on a standardised basis. It took the view that there was a need for an earnings figure, calculated on a standard basis, which could be used as an unambiguous reference point among users. The Institute accordingly defined a **headline earnings** figure for that purpose.

25.11.2 Definition of IIMR headline figure

The Institute criteria for the headline figure are that it should be:

1 **A measure of the trading performance**, which means that it will:
   (a) *exclude* capital items such as profits/losses arising on the sale or revaluation of fixed assets; profits/losses arising on the sale or termination of a discontinued operation and amortisation charges for goodwill, because these are likely to have a different volatility from trading outcomes;
   (b) *exclude* provisions created for capital items such as profits/losses arising on the sale of fixed assets or on the sale or termination of a discontinued operation; and
   (c) *include* abnormal items with a clear note and profits/losses arising on operations discontinued during the year.

2 **Robust**, in that the result could be arrived at by anyone using the financial report produced in accordance with IAS 1 and IFRS 5.

3 **Factual**, in that it will not have been adjusted on the basis of subjective opinions as to whether a cost is likely to continue in the future.

The strength of the Institute's approach is that, by defining a headline figure, it is producing a core definition. Additional earnings, earnings per share and price/earnings ratio figures can be produced by individual analysts, refining the headline figure in the light of their own evaluation of the quality of earnings.

25.11.3 IAS 33 Disclosure requirements

If an enterprise discloses an additional EPS figure using a reported component of net profit other than net profit for the period attributable to ordinary shareholders, IAS 33 requires that:

Figure 25.2 Reconciliation of earnings per share

	2003 Pence per share	2002 Pence per share
As calculated from FRS 14	(4.3)	40.7
Profit on the disposal of discontinued operations	—	(0.7)
Profit on sale of investments	—	(12.0)
Loss on impairment of investment	0.7	
Loss/(profit) on disposal of fixed assets held for resale	0.2	(0.1)
Amortisation of goodwill	10.4	1.5
Headline earnings per share as defined by IIMR	**7.0**	**29.4**
Reorganisation costs	11.9	5.0
Headline earnings per share before items shown above	**18.9**	**34.4**

- It must still use the weighted average number of shares determined in accordance with IAS 33.
- If the net profit figure used is not a line item in the statement of comprehensive income, then a reconciliation should be provided between the figure and a line item which is reported in the statement of comprehensive income.
- The additional EPS figures cannot be disclosed on the face of the statement of comprehensive income.

The extract in Figure 25.2 from the De La Rue 2003 Annual Report is an example of an IIMR-based reconciliation (FRS 14 is the UK equivalent of IAS 33).

25.11.4 Will companies include an alternative EPS figure?

In 1994 Coopers & Lybrand surveyed 100 top UK companies.[16] The survey found that fifty-four companies reported additional EPS figures, which varied from 62% lower to 278% higher than the reported figure. The basis of the most frequently used additional EPS figures was as follows:

Basis of additional EPS	No. of companies
IIMR headline EPS	16
Adjusted for exceptional items reported below operating profit	16
Adjusted for all exceptional items above and below operating profit	13

A number of other bases were used. Commenting on the choice of basis, the authors stated:

> This may result in stability for an individual company, but they certainly do not give rise to comparability across companies. To our surprise, only sixteen of the fifty-four companies used the IIMR headline figures as their EPS. The remainder evidently preferred to tell their own story despite the analysts' announcement of the basis on which they will perform their analysis.

The survey, therefore, also tested the hypothesis that companies would produce an alternative EPS figure where the alternative exceeded the standard figure. The outcome suggested that companies show additional EPS figures primarily to stabilise their earnings figures and not merely to enhance their reported performance.

An interesting recent research study (Young-soo Choi, M. Walker and S. Young, 'Bridging the earnings GAAP', *Accountancy*, February 2005, pp. 77–78) supports the finding that the additional EPS figures provide a better indication of future operating earnings one year ahead.

25.12 The Improvement Project

IAS 33 was one of the IASs revised by the IASB as part of its Improvement Project. The objective of the revised standard was to continue to prescribe the principles for the determination and presentation of earnings per share so as to improve comparisons between different entities and different reporting periods. The Board's main objective when revising was to provide additional guidance on selected complex issues such as the effects of contingently issuable shares and purchased put and call options. However, the Board did not reconsider the fundamental approach to the determination and presentation of earnings per share contained in the original IAS 33.

25.13 Convergence project

The earnings used as the numerator and the number of shares used as the denominator are both calculated differently under IAS 33 and the US SFAS 128 *Earnings per Share* and so produce different EPS figures.

In 2008, as part of the convergence project, the IASB and FASB issued an Exposure Draft which aimed to achieve some convergence in the calculation of the denominator of earnings per share. They are, in the meanwhile, conducting a joint project on financial statement presentation and when they have completed that project and their joint project on liabilities and equity, they may consider whether to conduct a more fundamental review of the method for determining EPS which would look at an agreed approach to determining earnings and number of shares to be used in both the basic and diluted EPS calculation.

Summary

The increased globalisation of stock market transactions places an increasing level of importance on international comparisons. The EPS figure is regarded as a key figure with a widely held belief that management performance could be assessed by the comparative growth rate in this figure. This has meant that the earnings available for distribution, which was the base for calculating EPS, became significant. Management action has been directed towards increasing this figure: sometimes by healthy organic growth; sometimes by buying-in earnings by acquisition; sometimes by cosmetic manipulation, e.g. structuring transactions so that all or part of the cost bypassed the statement of comprehensive income; and at other times by the selective exercise of judgement, e.g. underestimating provisions. Regulation by the IASB has been necessary.

IAS 33 permits the inclusion of an EPS figure calculated in a different way, provided that there is a reconciliation of the two figures. Analysts have expressed the view that EPS should be calculated to show the future maintainable earnings and in the UK have arrived at a formula designed to exclude the effects of unusual events and of activities discontinued during the period.

REVIEW QUESTIONS

1 Explain: (i) basic earnings per share; (ii) diluted earnings per share; (iii) potential ordinary shares; and (iv) limitation of EPS as a performance measure.

2 Why are issues at full market value treated differently from rights issues?

3 In the 1999 Annual Report and Accounts of Associated British Ports Holdings plc, the directors report earnings per share – basic, and earnings per share – underlying, as follows:

Underlying	Goodwill £m	Exceptional amortisation £m	Total items £m	1999 £m	1998 £m
Profit on ordinary activities after tax attributable to shareholders	86.3	(3.8)	(76.9)	5.6	84.1
Dividends	(39.4)	—	—	(39.4)	(37.2)
Retained profit/(loss)	46.9	(3.8)	(76.9)	(33.8)	46.9
Earnings per share – basic	24.6	(1.1)	(21.9)	**1.6p**	22.4p
Earnings per share – underlying				**24.6p**	22.4p

Note 11 Reconciliation of profit used for calculating the basic and underlying earnings per share:

	1999 £m	1998 £m
Profit for year attributable to shareholders for calculating basic earnings per share	**5.6**	84.1
Amortisation of goodwill	3.8	2.0
Impairment of goodwill	60.6	—
Impairment of fixed assets	19.6	—
Profit on sale of fixed assets	(3.3)	(1.2)
Withdrawal from a discontinued business	—	(1.2)
Attributable tax	—	0.3
Profit for year attributable to shareholders for calculating the underlying earnings per share	**86.3**	84.0

The directors state that the underlying basis is a more appropriate basis for comparing performance between periods.

Discuss the relevance of the basic figure of 1.6p reported for 1999.

4 The following note appeared in the 2002 Annual Report of Mercer International Inc.

	2002	2001	2000
Net income (loss) available to shareholders of beneficial interest	€(6,322)	€(2,823)	€32,013
BEPS weighted average number of shares outstanding – basic	16,774,515	16,874,899	16,778,962
Effect of dilutive securities:			
Options	—	—	365,528
Weighted average number of shares outstanding – diluted	16,774,515	16,874,899	17,144,490

For 2002 and 2001 options and warrants were not included in the computation of diluted earnings per share because they were antidilutive. Warrants were not dilutive in 2000.

Explain:

(a) why the BEPS shares were weighted; and

(b) what is meant by antidilutive.

5 Would the following items justify the calculation of a separate EPS figure under IAS 33?

(a) A charge of £1,500 million that appeared in the accounts, described as additional provisions relating to exposure to countries experiencing payment difficulties.

(b) Costs of £14 million that appeared in the accounts, described as redundancy and other non-recurring costs.

(c) Costs of £62.1 million that appeared in the accounts, described as cost of rationalisation and withdrawal from business activities.

(d) The following items that appeared in the accounts:

(i)	Profit on sale of property	£80m
(ii)	Reorganisation costs	£35m
(iii)	Disposal and discontinuance of hotels	£659m

6 Income smoothing describes the management practice of maintaining a steady profit figure.

(a) Explain why managers might wish to smooth the earnings figure. Give three examples of how they might achieve this.

(b) It has been suggested that debt creditors are most at risk from income smoothing by the managers. Discuss why this should be so.

7 In connection with IAS 33 *Earnings per Share*:

(a) Define the profit used to calculate basic and diluted EPS.

(b) Explain the relationship between EPS and the price/earnings (P/E) ratio. Why may the P/E ratio be considered important as a stock market indicator?

8 The following is an extract from the FirstGroup 2004 Annual Report:

Profit for adjusted basic EPS calculation	£112.0m	EPS: £27.3p
Depreciation	£103.0m	EPS: £25.1p
Profit for adjusted cash EPS calculation	£215.0m	EPS: £52.4p

Discuss the relevance of an adjusted cash EPS.

EXERCISES

An extract from the outline solution is provided on the Companion Website (www.pearsoned.co.uk/elliott-elliott) for exercises marked with an asterisk (*).

Question 1

Alpha plc had an issued share capital of 2,000,000 ordinary shares at 1 January 20X1. The nominal value was 25p and the market value £1 per share. On 30 September 20X1 the company made a rights issue of 1 for 4 at a price of 80p per share. The post-tax earnings were £4.5m and £5m for 20X0 and 20X1 respectively.

Required: (i) Calculate the basic earnings per share for 20X1.

(ii) Restate the basic earnings per share for 20X0.

Question 2

Beta Ltd had the following changes during 20X1:

1 January	1,000,000 shares of 50c each
31 March	500,000 shares of 50c each issued at full market price of $5 per share
30 April	Bonus issue made of 1 for 2
31 August	1,000,000 shares of 50c each issued at full market price of $5.50 per share
31 October	Rights issue of 1 for 3. Rights price was $2.40 and market value was $5.60 per share.

Required:

Calculate the time-weighted average number of shares for the basic earnings per share denominator. Note that adjustments will be required for time, the bonus issue and the bonus element of the rights issue.

* Question 3

The computation and publication of earnings per share (EPS) figures by listed companies are governed by IAS 33 *Earnings per Share*.

Nottingham Industries plc
Statement of comprehensive income for the year ended 31 March 20X6
(extract from draft unaudited accounts)

		£000
Profit on ordinary activities before taxation	(Note 2)	(1,000)
Tax on profit on ordinary activities	(Note 3)	(420)
Profit on ordinary activities after taxation		580

Notes:

1 Called-up share capital of Nottingham Industries plc:

   In issue at 1 April 20X5:

   16,000,000 ordinary shares of 25p each
   1,000,000 10% cumulative preference shares of £1 each

   1 July 20X5: Bonus issue of ordinary shares, 1 for 5.
   1 October 20X5: Market purchase of 500,000 of own ordinary shares at a price of £1.00 per share.

2 In the draft accounts for the year ended 31 March 20X6, 'profit on ordinary activities before taxation' is arrived at after charging or crediting the following items:

   (i) accelerated depreciation on fixed assets, £80,000;

   (ii) book gain on disposal of a major operation, £120,000.

3 Profit after tax included a write-back of deferred taxation (accounted for by the liability method) in consequence of a reduction in the rate of corporation tax from 45% in the financial year 20X4 to 40% in the financial year 20X5.

4 The following were charged:

   (i) Provision for bad debts arising on the failure of a major customer, £150,000. Other bad debts have been written off or provided for in the ordinary way.

   (ii) Provision for loss through expropriation of the business of an overseas subsidiary by a foreign government, £400,000.

5 In the published accounts for the year ended 31 March 20X5, basic EPS was shown as 2.2p; fully diluted EPS was the same figure.

6 Dividends paid totalled £479,000.

Required:

(a) On the basis of the facts given, compute the basic EPS figures for 20X6 and restate the basic EPS figure for 20X5, stating your reasons for your treatment of items that may affect the amount of EPS in the current year.

(b) Compute the diluted earnings per share for 20X6 assuming that on 1 January 20X6 executives of Nottingham plc were granted options to take up a total of 200,000 unissued ordinary shares at a price of £1.00 per share: no options had been exercised at 31 March 20X6. The average fair value of the shares during the year was £1.10.

(c) Give your opinion as to the usefulness (to the user of financial statements) of the EPS figures that you have computed.

* Question 4

The following information relates to Simrin plc for the year ended 31 December 20X0:

	£
Turnover	700,000
Operating costs	476,000
Trading profit	224,000
Net interest payable	2,000
	222,000
Exceptional charges	77,000
	145,000
Tax on ordinary activities	66,000
Profit after tax	79,000

Simrin plc had 100,000 ordinary shares of £1 each in issue throughout the year. Simrin plc has in issue warrants entitling the holders to subscribe for a total of 50,000 shares in the company. The warrants may be exercised after 31 December 20X5 at a price of £1.10 per share. The average fair value of shares was £1.28. The company had paid an ordinary dividend of £15,000 and a preference dividend of £9,000.

Required:

(a) Calculate the basic EPS for Simrin plc for the year ended 31 December 20X0, in accordance with best accounting practice.

(b) Calculate the diluted EPS figure, to be disclosed in the statutory accounts of Simrin plc in respect of the year ended 31 December 20X0.

(c) Briefly comment on the need to disclose a diluted EPS figure and on the relevance of this figure to the shareholders.

(d) In the past, the single most important indicator of financial performance has been earnings per share. In what way has the profession attempted to destroy any reliance on a single figure to measure and predict a company's earnings, and how successful has this attempt been?

* Question 5

Gamma plc had an issued share capital at 1 April 20X0 of:

- £200,000 made up of 20p shares.
- 50,000 £1 convertible preference shares receiving a dividend of £2.50 per share:
  - these shares were convertible in 20X6 on the basis of 1 ordinary share for 1 preference share.

There was also loan capital of:

- £250,000 10% convertible loans:
  - the loan was convertible in 20X9 on the basis of 500 shares for each £1,000 of loan;
  - the tax rate was 40%.

Earnings for the year ended 31 March 20X1 were £5,000,000 after tax.

Required:
(a) Calculate the diluted EPS for 20X1.
(b) Calculate the diluted EPS assuming that the convertible preference shares were receiving a dividend of £6 per share instead of £2.50.

Question 6

Delta NV has share capital of €1m in shares of €0.25 each. At 31 May 20X9 shares had a market value of €1.1 each. On 1 June 20X9 the company makes a rights issue of 1 share for every 4 held at €0.6 per share. Its profits were €500,000 in 20X9 and €440,000 in 20X8. The year-end is 30 November.

Required:
Calculate
(a) the theoretical ex-rights price;
(b) the bonus issue factor;
(c) the basic earnings per share for 20X8;
(d) the basic earnings per share for 20X9.

Question 7

The following information is available for X Ltd for the year ended 31 May 20X1:

Net profit after tax and minority interest	£18,160,000
Ordinary shares of £1 (fully paid)	£40,000,000
Average fair value for year of ordinary shares	£1.50

1 Share options have been granted to directors giving them the right to subscribe for ordinary shares between 20X1 and 20X3 at £1.20 per share. The options outstanding at 31 May 20X1 were 2,000,000 in number.

2 The company has £20 million of 6% convertible loan stock in issue. The terms of conversion of the loan stock per £200 nominal value of loan stock at the date of issue were:

Conversion date	No. of shares
31 May 20X0	24
31 May 20X1	23
31 May 20X2	22

No loan stock has as yet been converted. The loan stock had been issued at a discount of 1%.

3 There are 1,600,000 convertible preference shares in issue. The cumulative dividend is 10p per share and each preference share can convert into two ordinary shares. The preference shares can be converted in 20X2.

4 Assume a corporation tax rate of 33% when calculating the effect on income of converting the convertible loan stock.

Required:
(a) Calculate the diluted EPS according to IAS 33.
(b) Discuss why there is a need to disclose diluted earnings per share.

Question 8

(a) The issued share capital of Manfred, a quoted company, on 1 November 2004 consisted of 36,000,000 ordinary shares of 75 cents each. On 1 May 2005 the company made a rights issue of 1 for 6 at $1.46 per share. The market value of Manfred's ordinary shares was $1.66 before announcing the rights issue. Tax is charged at 30% of profits.

Manfred reported a profit after taxation of $4.2 million for the year ended 31 October 2005 and $3.6 million for the year ended 31 October 2004. The published figure for earnings per share for the year ended 31 October 2004 was 10 cents per share.

Required:
Calculate Manfred's earnings per share for the year ended 31 October 2005 and the comparative figure for the year ended 31 October 2004.

(b) Brachly, a publicly quoted company, has 15,000,000 ordinary shares of 40 cents each in issue throughout its financial year ended 31 October 2005. There are also:

- 1,000,000 8.5% convertible preference shares of $1 each in issue. Each preference share is convertible into 1.5 ordinary shares.

- $2,000,000 12.5% convertible loan notes. Each $1 loan note is convertible into 2 ordinary shares.

- Options granted to the company's senior management giving them the right to subscribe for 600,000 ordinary shares at a cost of 75 cents each.

The statement of comprehensive income of Brachly for the year ended 31 October 2005 reports a net profit after tax of $9,285,000 and preference dividends paid of $85,000. Tax on profits is 30%. The average market price of Brachly's ordinary shares was 84 cents for the year ended 31 October 2005.

Required:
Calculate Brachly's basic and diluted earnings per share figures for the year ended 31 October 2005.

(The Association of International Accountants)

Question 9

The capital structure of Chavboro, a quoted company, during the years ended 31 October 2005 and 2006 was as follows:

	$
6,000,000 ordinary shares of 50 cents	3,000,000
10% preferred shares of $1	200,000
300,000 deferred ordinary shares of $1	300,000
12% convertible loan stock	250,000

The company has an executive share option scheme which gives the company's directors the option to purchase a total of 100,000 ordinary shares for $2.10 each. During the year ended 31 October 2006 no shares were issued in accordance with the share incentive scheme and the company's obligations under the scheme remained unchanged.

On 31 August 2006 Chavboro plc made a 1 for 6 rights issue at $2.50 per share. The cum-rights price on the last day of quotation cum rights was $2.85 per share. The shares issued in the rights issue are not included in the figure for ordinary shares given above.

The deferred ordinary shares will not rank for dividends until 1 November 2010 when they will each be divided into two 50 cents ordinary shares ranking *pari passu* with the other ordinary shares then in issue.

The 12% loan stock is convertible into 50 cents ordinary shares on the following terms:

(i)   if the option is exercised on 1 November 2007 each $100 of loan stock can be converted into 40 ordinary shares;

(ii) if the option is exercised on 1 November 2008 each $100 of loan stock can be converted into 35 ordinary shares.

The following information comes from the statement of comprehensive income of the company for the year ended 31 October 2006:

	$
Profit before interest and tax	1,253,000
less Interest	30,000
	1,223,000
less Income tax, at 30%	366,900
Profit attributable to shareholders	856,100

You may assume that the yield on 2.5% government consolidated stock was 7.5% on 1 November 2005 and 6% on 1 November 2006, and that the rate of income tax is 30% throughout. Chavboro plc's reported earnings per share for the year ended 31 October 2005 were 10 cents.

Required:

(a) Calculate Chavboro plc's basic earnings per share in cents for the year ended 31 October 2006.

(b) Calculate Chavboro plc's restated earnings per share in cents for the year ended 31 October 2005.

(c) Calculate Chavboro plc's fully diluted earnings per share in cents for the year ended 31 October 2006.

(d) Calculate Chavboro plc's fully diluted earnings per share in cents for the year ended 31 October 2005.

(e) How can an investor evaluate the quality of the earnings per share figure published in a company's financial statements?

(The Association of International Accountants)

References

1 J. Day, 'The use of annual reports by UK investment analysts', *Accounting Business Research*, Autumn 1986, pp. 295–307.

2 London Business School, *Risk Measurement Service*, April–June 1998, ISBN 0361-3344.

3 IAS 33 *Earnings per Share*, IASB, 2003.

4 *Ibid.*, para. 10.

5 *Ibid.*, para. 12.

6 *Ibid.*, para. 26.

7 *Ibid.*, para. 5.

8 *Ibid.*, para. 31.

9 *Accountancy*, November 1998, p. 73.

10 IAS 33, para. 31.

11 *Ibid.*, para. 45.

12 *Ibid.*, para. 33.

13 *Ibid.*, para. 44.

14 *Ibid.*, paras 66 and 70.

15 Statement of Investment Practice No. 1, *The Definition of Headline Earnings*, IIMR, 1993.

16 Coopers and Lybrand, *EPS and Exceptional Items*, 1994.

CHAPTER **26**

Statements of cash flows

26.1 Introduction

The main purpose of this chapter is to explain the reasons for preparing a statement of cash flows and how to prepare a statement applying IAS 7.

Objectives

By the end of this chapter, you should be able to:

- prepare a statement of cash flows in accordance with IAS 7;
- analyse a statement of cash flows;
- critically discuss their strengths and weaknesses.

26.2 Development of statements of cash flows

At the end of an accounting period, an income statement is prepared which explains the change in the retained earnings at the beginning and end of an accounting period and a further statement prepared to explain the change that has occurred in the assets and liabilities.

There have been three approaches to the format of this further statement. The first, called a Source and Application statement or Funds Flow Statement, was followed by two different formats for Statements of Cash Flows.

26.2.1 Source and application statement

This statement explained the changes between the opening and closing statement of financial position by classifying the changes in non-current assets and long-term capital under two headings:

- **source of funds**, comprising funds from operating and other sources such as sale of fixed assets and issue of shares and loans; and
- **application of funds**, comprising tax paid, dividends paid, fixed asset acquisitions and long-term capital repayments. The difference represented the net change in working capital.

In 1977 IAS 7 *Statement of Changes in Financial Position* was issued, requiring companies to publish a funds flow statement with the annual accounts.[1] This would appear as follows:

Source and Application Statement for the year ended 31.12.20X9

Sources of funds:

Funds from operations	1,000	
Sale of non-current assets	500	
Issue of shares	200	
Issue of debentures	600	
		2,300

Application of funds:

Tax paid	250	
Dividends paid	100	
Purchase of non-current assets	950	
Repayment of capital	120	
Repayment of loans	80	
		1,500
Difference = Change in working capital		800

26.2.2 Statement of cash flows

In 1987 SFAS 95 *Statement of Cash Flows* was published in the USA.[2] It concluded that a cash flow statement should replace the funds flow statement, concentrating on **changes in cash** rather than **changes in working capital**. The statement of cash flows should represent all of a company's cash receipts and cash payments during a period. There was also widespread support for the belief that statements of cash flow **were more decision-useful** and that they should replace the funds flow statement.

In 1992 the IASC issued IAS 7 (revised), which appeared to be based on SFAS 95.[3] It proposed that cash flow statements should replace funds flow statements in financial reporting. Guidelines were given about reporting cash flows, appropriate formats and minimum disclosure. The effect was that the changes in inventories, trade receivables and trade payables were disclosed as separate movements.

A report by the ICAEW Research Board and the ICAS Research Advisory Committee, entitled *The Future Shape of Financial Reports*, recommended a number of reporting reforms.[4] One of the main areas for improvement was reporting a company's cash position. Professor Arnold wrote:

> little attention is paid to the reporting entity's cash or liquidity position. Cash is the lifeblood of every business entity. The report . . . advocates that companies should provide a cash flow statement . . . preferably using the direct method.[5]

An important issue is the relationship of cash flows to the existing financial statements. As the following quotation illustrates, statements of cash flows are not a substitute for the statement of comprehensive income:

> The emphasis on cash flows, and the emergence of the statement of cash flows as an important financial report, does not mean that operating cash flows are a substitute for, or are more important than, net income. In order to analyse financial statements correctly we need to consider **both** operating cash flows and net income.[6]

The overwhelming reason for replacing a funds flow statement with a statement of cash flows was that the latter provides more relevant and useful information to users of financial statements. When used in conjunction with the accrual-adjusted data included in the statement of comprehensive income and the statement of financial position, cash flow information helps to assess liquidity, viability and financial flexibility. This view is held by Henderson and Maness, who stress the need to integrate different types of analysis to achieve an overall assessment of an organisation's financial health: 'cash flow analysis should be used in conjunction with traditional ratio analysis to get a clear picture of the financial position of a firm'.[7]

The financial viability and survival prospects of any organisation rest on the ability to generate net positive cash flows. Cash flows help to reduce an organisation's dependency on external funding, service existing debts and obligations, finance investments, and reward the investors with an acceptable dividend policy. The end-result is that, independent of reported profits, if an organisation is unable to generate sufficient cash, it will eventually fail.

Statements of cash flows can also be used to evaluate any economic decisions related to the financial performance of an organisation. Decisions made on the basis of expected cash flows can be monitored and reviewed whenever additional cash flow information becomes available.

Finally, the quality of information contained in statements of cash flows should be better than that contained in funds flow statements because it is more consistent and neutral. Cash flows can be reliably traced to when a transaction occurred, while funds flows are distorted by the accounting judgements inherent in accrual-adjusted data.[8]

The following extract from Heath and Rosenfield's article on solvency is a useful conclusion to our analysis of the benefits of cash flow statements:

> Solvency is a money or cash phenomenon. A solvent company is one with adequate cash to pay its debts; an insolvent company is one with inadequate cash ... Any information that provides insight into the amounts, timings and certainty of a company's future cash receipts and payments is useful in evaluating solvency. Statements of past cash receipts and payments are useful for the same basic reason that statements of comprehensive income are useful in evaluating profitability: both provide a basis for predicting future performance.[9]

26.3 Applying IAS 7 (revised) *Statements of Cash Flows*

26.3.1 IAS 7 issued

IAS 7 was revised and renamed again in 2008 by the IASB to require companies to issue a statement of cash flows. Its objective was to require companies to provide standardised reports on their cash generation and cash absorption for a period. Its principal feature was the analysis of cash flows under **three** standard headings of 'operating activities', 'investing activities' and 'financing activities'. Accounting commentators said that information on cash is an essential part of a company's financial statements.

26.3.2 Methods of presenting cash flows from operating activities

IAS 7 permitted either the direct or indirect method of presentation to be used.

- The **direct** method reports cash inflows and outflows directly, starting with the major categories of gross cash receipts and payments. This means that cash flows such as receipts from customers and payments to suppliers are stated separately within the operating activities.

- The **indirect** method starts with the profit before tax and then adjusts this figure for non-cash items such as depreciation and changes in working capital.

We will comment briefly on each method.

26.3.3 The direct method

The direct method demonstrates more of the qualities of a true cash flow statement because it provides more information about the sources and uses of cash. This information is not available elsewhere and helps in the estimation of future cash flows.

The principal advantage of the direct method is that it shows operating cash receipts and payments. Knowledge of the specific sources of cash receipts and the purposes for which cash payments were made in past periods may be useful in assessing future cash flows. Disclosure of *cash from customers* could provide additional information about an entity's ability to convert revenues to cash.

When is the direct method beneficial?

One such time is when the user is attempting to predict bankruptcy or future liquidation of the company. A research study looking at the cash flow differences between failed and non-failed companies[10] established that seven cash flow variables and suggested ratios captured statistically significant differences between failed and non-failed firms as much as five years prior to failure. The study further showed that the research findings supported the use of a direct cash flow statement and the authors commented:

> An indirect cash flow statement will not provide a number of the cash flow variables for which we found significant differences between bankrupt and non-bankrupt companies. Thus, using an indirect cash flow statement could lead to ignoring important information about creditworthiness.

The direct method is the method preferred by the standard but preparers have a choice. In the UK the indirect method is often used; in other regions (e.g. Australia) the direct method is more common. It has been proposed in a review of IAS 7 that the direct method should be mandated and the alternative removed and this is the likely requirement in a new standard to eventually replace IAS 7.

26.3.4 The indirect method

The two methods provide different types of information to the users. The indirect method applies changes in working capital to net income.

The principal advantage of the indirect method is that it highlights the differences between operating profit and net cash flow from operating activities to provide a measure of the quality of income. Many users of financial statements believe that such reconciliation is essential to give an indication of the quality of the reporting entity's earnings. Some investors and creditors assess future cash flows by estimating future income and then allowing for accruals adjustments; thus information about past accruals adjustments may be useful to help estimate future adjustments.

A criticism of the indirect method is that the changes calculated from the statements of financial position are adjusted before entering in the statement of cash flows. For example, if there has been a foreign exchange difference or an acquisition the change is adjusted as seen in section 26.5.2 below so that it is not possible for a user to reconcile the two statements. This could be overcome by the inclusion of supplementary information.

Preparer and user response

The IASB indicates that the responses to the discussion paper were mixed with the preparers tending to prefer the indirect method and the users having a mixed response. There was a view that the direct method would be improved if the movements on working capital were disclosed as supplementary information and the indirect method would be improved if the cash from customers and payments to suppliers was disclosed as supplementary information, i.e. both are found useful.

Cash equivalents

IAS 7 recognised that companies' cash management practices vary in the range of short- to medium-term deposits and instruments in their cash and near-cash portfolio. The standard standardised the treatment of near-cash items by applying the following definition when determining whether items should be aggregated with cash in the cash flow statement:

> Cash equivalents are short-term, highly liquid investments which are readily convertible into known amounts of cash and which are subject to an insignificant risk of changes in value.

Near-cash items falling outside this definition were reported under the heading of 'investing activities'.

There has been criticism over the definition of cash equivalents. IAS 7 does give some guidance that a cash equivalent should normally be within three months of maturity at the date of acquisition, but this guidance can create problems. For example, it is not always commercially appropriate to deal with deposits over three months as investing activities as opposed to cash equivalents. The effect of the definition of cash equivalents is to split the activities of corporate treasury departments between investing cash flows and increases or decreases in cash. If cash is put on deposit for more than three months, it is treated as a cash outflow under investing, whereas if deposited for less than three months, it is not shown as actually being a cash flow. This makes analysis of the movements in cash and cash equivalents potentially misleading.

In the UK the cash flow statement reconciles opening and closing cash rather than cash equivalents. A replacement standard will probably follow the UK practice.

26.4 IAS 7 (revised) format of statements of cash flows

The IAS 7 format is set out below and its application to Tyro Bruce illustrated.

26.4.I The IAS 7 format is as follows

Cash flows from operating activities		
Profit before tax	x	
Adjustments for:		
Depreciation	x	
Foreign exchange loss	x	
Investment income	(x)	
Interest expense	x	
Operating profit before working capital changes	x	
Increase in trade and other receivables	(x)	
Decrease in inventories	x	
Decrease in trade payables	(x)	
Cash generated from operations	x	
Interest paid*	(x)	
Income taxes paid	(x)	
Cash flow before extraordinary item	x	
Proceeds from earthquake disaster settlement	x	
Net cash from operating activities		x
Cash flows from investing activities		
Acquisition of subsidiary net of cash acquired	(x)	
Purchase of property, plant and equipment	(x)	
Proceeds from sale of equipment	x	
Interest received*	x	
Dividends received*	x	
Net cash used in investing activities		(x)
Cash flows from financing activities		
Proceeds from issue of share capital	x	
Proceeds from long-term borrowings	x	
Payment of finance lease liabilities	(x)	
Dividends paid*	(x)	
Net cash used in financing activities		(x)
Net increase in cash and cash equivalents		x
Cash and cash equivalents at the beginning of the period		x
Cash and cash equivalents at the end of the period		x

* The position in the statement of cash flows for these items is not precisely defined in IAS 7, and choice exists in the presentation. Interest paid, and interest and dividends received, could either be classified as operating cash flows or as financing (for interest paid) and investing cash flows (for the receipts). Dividends paid could either be presented as financing cash flows or as operating cash flows. However, it is a requirement that whichever presentation is adopted by an enterprise should be consistently applied from year to year.

26.4.2 Step approach to preparation of a statement of cash flows – indirect method

Company X: A step approach to illustrate preparing a statement of cash flows with workings on face of the statements of financial position, statement of comprehensive income and notes.

Step 1: Calculate differences in the Statements of Financial Position and note whether to treat under Operating activities, Investing, Financing or as a cash equivalent.

Statements of Financial Position as at 31.3.20X8 and 31.3.20X9

	Cost	Depn	20X8 NBV	Cost	Depn	20X9 NBV	Difference	Cash Flow section
Non-current assets	2,520	452	2,068	2,760	462	2,298	See PPE note	Investing if there are any acquisitions or disposals
Current assets								
Inventory		800			1,200		400	PBT adjustment/decrease
Trade receivables		640			900		260	PBT adjustment/decrease
Government securities		—			20		20	Cash equivalent
Cash		80			10		70	Cash equivalent
		1,520			2,130			
Current liabilities								
Trade payables		540			500		40	PBT adjustment/decrease
Taxation		190			170		20	Cash flow from operations
Dividends		—			—		—	
Overdraft		8			478		470	Cash equivalent
		738			1,148			
Net current assets			782			982		
			2,850			3,280		
Share capital			1,300			1,400	100	Financing/increase
Share premium a/c			200			400	200	Financing/increase
Retained earnings			1,150			1,150		
Profit for year			—			180		
10% loan 20 × 4			200			150	50	Financing/decrease
			2,850			3,280		

Step 2: Identify any items in the Income statement for the year ended 31.3.20X9 after Profit before Interest and tax (PBIT) to be entered under operating activities, investing or financing.

	£000	£000	
Sales		3,000	
Cost of sales		2,000	
Gross profit		1,000	
Distribution costs	300		
Administrative expenses	180	480	
PBIT		520	
Interest expense		(20)	Add back interest expense to PBT
Profit before tax		500	PBT as the first Operating activities entry
Income tax expense		(200)	Operating activities/decrease
Profit after tax		300	
Dividend paid		120	Financing/decrease
Retained earnings for year		180	

The Cash Flow items can then be entered into the Statement of Cash Flows in accordance with IAS 7.

Cash flows from operating activities		£000
Profit before tax		500
Adjustments for non-cash items:		
Depreciation	From Step 3 (ii)	102
Profit on sale of plant	From Step 3 (iv)	(13)
Interest expense		20
Increase in trade receivables		(260)
Increase in inventories		(400)
Decrease in trade payables		(40)
Cash generated from operations		**(91)**
Interest paid	No accrual or prepayment	(20)
Income taxes paid (Expense +		
(closing accrual − opening accrual))	200 + (190 − 170)	(220)
Net cash used in operating activities		(331)
Cash flows from investing activities		
Purchase of property, plant and equipment	From Step 3 (i)	(560)
Proceeds from sale of equipment	From Step 3 (iii)	241
Net cash used in investing activities		(319)
Cash flows from financing activities		
Proceeds from issue of shares at a premium		300
Redemption of loan		(50)
Dividends paid		(120)
Net cash from financing activities		130
Net increase in cash and cash equivalents		**(520)**
Cash and cash equivalents at beginning of period	80 − 8	72
Cash and cash equivalents at end of the period	(478) − (10 + 20)	**(448)**

Step 3: Refer to the PPE Schedule to identify any acquisitions, disposals and depreciation charges that affect the Cash flows. The Tyro Bruce Schedule showed:

		Cost £000		Depn £000
At 31.3.20X8	Cost	2,520	Accum. depreciation	452
	Additions	**560**	**Charge for year**	**102**
		3,080		554
	Disposal*	320	Disposal	92
At 31.3.20X9		2,760		462

The approach to calculating the effect on a statement of cash flows arising from a disposal of non-current assets depends on whether the information available is the cash proceeds or the profit/loss on disposal. Let us assume a profit of £13,000.

If the question gives the profit/loss figure, then the cash proceeds have to be calculated as: Net book value + profit on disposal = (£320,000 − £92,000) + £13,000 = £241,000.

If the question gives the cash proceeds, then the profit/loss has to be calculated to be used as an adjustment for non-cash items. This would be Cash proceeds − Net book value = £241,000 − £228,000 = £13,000.

From this we can see that there are four impacts:

(i) Additions: The cash of £560,000 paid out on additions will appear under Investing.

(ii) The depreciation charge: This is a non-cash item and the £102,000 will be added back as a non-cash item to the Profit before tax in the Operating activities section.

(iii) Disposal proceeds: The cash received from the disposal will appear under Investing. It is calculated as NBV of £228,000 (320,000 − 92,000) + the profit figure of £13,000 = £241,000.

(iv) Profit on disposal: As the full proceeds of £241,000 are included under Investing, there would be double counting to leave the profit of £13,000 within the Profit before tax figure. It is therefore deducted as a non-cash item from PBT in the Operating activities section.

26.4.3 Statement of cash flows – direct method

One of the criticisms of IAS 7 was that it did not standardise on the use of the direct method. Under the direct method the 'operating activities' of the statement are presented differently to show the actual cash flows from customers and to suppliers and employees. In our example the (91) is calculated and disclosed as below:

Cash flows from operating activities	*£000*
Cash received from customers (a)	2,740
Cash paid to suppliers and employees (b)	(2,831)
Cash generated from operations	(91)

(a) Cash received from customers

	£000
Sales	3,000
Receivables increase	260
	2,740

(b) Cash paid to suppliers and employees

	£000
Cost of sales	2,000
Payables decreased	40
Inventory increase	400
Depreciation	(102)
Profit on sale	13
Distribution costs	300
Administration expenses	180
	2,831

26.4.4 Additional notes required by IAS 7

As well as the presentation on the face of the cash flow statement, IAS 7 requires notes to the cash flow statement to help the user understand the information. The notes that are required are as follows:

Major non-cash transactions

If the entity has entered into major non-cash transactions that are therefore not represented on the face of the cash flow statement sufficient further information to understand the transactions should be provided in a note to the financial statements. Examples of major non-cash transactions might be:

● the acquisition of assets by way of finance leases;

● the conversion of debt to equity.

Components of cash and cash equivalents

An enterprise must disclose the components of cash and cash equivalents and reconcile these into the totals in the statement of financial position. An example of a suitable disclosure in the case of Tyro Bruce is:

	20X9	*20X8*
Cash	10	80
Government securities	20	
Overdraft	(478)	(8)
Cash and cash equivalents	(448)	(72)

Disclosure must also be given on restrictions on the use by the group of any cash and cash equivalents held by the enterprise. These restrictions might apply if, for example, cash was held in foreign countries and could not be remitted back to the parent company.

Segmental information

IAS 7 encourages enterprises to disclose information about operating, investing and financing cash flows for each business and geographical segment. This disclosure is optional. IFRS 8 does not require a cash flow by segment.

26.5 Consolidated statements of cash flows

A consolidated statement of cash flows differs from that for a single company in two respects: there are additional items; and adjustments may be required to the actual amounts.

26.5.1 Additional items

Additional items appear under the operating, investing and financing activities of the cash flow statement as follows:

1 **Operating activities**
   ● Adjust for non-cash income:
      – Share of profit of associate.

2 **Investing activities**
   ● Dividends received:
      – Dividends received from associates.

- Purchase of a subsidiary, interest in an associated/joint venture undertaking or of a business.
- Receipt from the disposal of a subsidiary, interest in an associated/joint venture undertaking or of a business.

3 Financing activities

- Dividends paid to non-controlling interests (this is calculated as non-controlling interests in the opening consolidated statement of financial position plus non-controlling interests in the statement of comprehensive income less non-controlling interests in the closing statement of financial position).

26.5.2 Adjustments to amounts

Adjustments are required if the closing statement of financial position items have been increased or reduced as a result of **non-cash movements**. Such movements occur if there has been a purchase of a subsidiary to reflect the fact that the asset and liabilities from the new subsidiary have not necessarily resulted from cash flows.

Subsidiary acquired during year

For example, if Tyro Bruce had acquired a subsidiary on 31 March 20X9 on the following terms:

Net assets acquired	*£000*	*In the Statement of cash flows the effect will be:*
Working capital:		
Inventory	10	Reduce inventory increase
Trade payables	(12)	Reduce trade payables increase
Non-current assets:		
Vehicles	20	Reduce purchase of PPE
Cash/bank:		
Cash	5	Show as cash acquired in the investing section
Net assets acquired	23	
Consideration from Tyro Bruce:		
Shares	10	Reduce proceeds from issue of shares
Premium	10	Reduce proceeds from issue at a premium
Cash	3	Show as payment to acquire subsidiary in the investing section
	23	

The Tyro Bruce consolidated statement of cash flows prepared using the indirect method would appear as follows on stripping out the non-cash movements.

Statement of cash flows for Tyro Bruce using the indirect method

Cash flows from operating activities		£000	£000
Net profit before tax		500	
Adjustments for:			
Depreciation		102	
Profit on sale of equipment		(13)	
Interest expense		20	
Operating profit before working capital changes		609	
Increase in trade and other receivables		(260)	
Increase in inventories	(400)		
Less: **inventory brought in on acquisition**	10	(390)	
Decrease in trade payables	(40)		
Add: **trade payables brought in on acquisition**	(12)	(52)	
Cash generated from operations		(93)	
Interest paid (*from statement of comprehensive income*)		(20)	
Income taxes paid (200 + 190 − 170)		(220)	
Net cash from operating activities			(333)
Cash flows from investing activities			
Purchase of property, plant and equipment	(560)		
Less: **vehicles brought in on acquisition**	20	(540)	
Proceeds from sale of equipment		241	
Payment to acquire subsidiary		(3)	
Cash acquired with subsidiary		5	
Net cash used in investing activities			(297)
Cash flows from financing activities			
Proceeds from issuance of share capital	300		
Less: **shares issued on acquisition not for cash**	(20)	280	
Repayment of debentures		(50)	
Dividends paid (*from statement of comprehensive income*)		(120)	
Net cash from financing activities			110
Net decrease in cash and cash equivalents			(520)
Cash and cash equivalents at the beginning of the period			72
Cash and cash equivalents at the end of the period			(448)

If there had been a disposal of a subsidiary, the same adjustments would have been required except that they would have been in the opposite direction, e.g. capital expenditure on vehicles would have been increased from £1,120,000 to £1,140,000.

Supplemental disclosure of acquisition

	£
Total purchase consideration	23,000
Portion of purchase consideration discharged by means of cash or cash equivalents	3,000
Amount of cash and cash equivalents in the subsidiary acquired	5,000

26.6 Analysing statements of cash flows

Arranging cash flows into specific classes provides users with relevant and decision-useful information by classifying cash flows as Cash generated from operations, Net cash from operating activities, Net cash flows from investing activities and Net cash flows from financing activities.

Lack of a clear definition

However, this does not mean that companies will necessarily report the same transaction in the same way. Although IAS 7 requires cash flows to be reported under these headings, it does not define operating activities except to say that it includes all transactions and other events that are not defined as investing or financing activities.

Alternative treatments

Alternative treatments for interest and dividends paid could be presented as either operating or financing cash flows. In the UK the problem is solved by adding a fourth category of cash flows titled *Returns on investment and servicing of finance*. Whilst most companies choose to report the dividends as Financing cash flows, when making inter-firm comparisons we need to see which alternative has been chosen. The choice can have a significant impact. If, for example, in the Tyro Bruce illustration the dividends of £120,000 were reported as an operating cash flow, then the Net cash outflow from operating activities would increase from (£333,000) to (£453,000). It does not affect inter-period comparisons.

The classifications assist users in making informed predictions about future cash flows or raising questions for further enquiry which would be difficult to make using traditional accrual-based techniques.[11]

We will briefly comment on the implication of each classification.

26.6.1 Cash generated from operations

In the Tyro Bruce example on page 675 we can see that there has been a significant increase in working capital of £700,000 (£260,000 + £400,000 + £40,000) resulting in a negative cash flow from operations. Lenders look to the cash generated from operations to pay interest and taxation, both of which are unavoidable – it is an indication of the safety margin, i.e. how long a business could continue to pay unavoidable costs.

Lenders in Tyro Bruce concerned with interest cover could see that the cash available to meet interest charges and taxation in the current year has been adversely affected by the significant impact of working capital changes.

Interest cover

Interest cover is normally defined as the number of times the profit before interest and tax covers the interest charge: in the Tyro Bruce example this is 26 times (520/20). The position as disclosed in the statement of cash flows is weaker. There is a negative net cash flow of £91,000 from operating activities which does not cover the interest payment.

Cash debt coverage

In addition to interest cover, lenders want to be satisfied that their loan will be repaid. Failure to do so could lead to a going concern problem for the company. One measure used is to calculate the ratio of cash flow from operations less dividend payments to total debt and, of more immediate interest, to loans that are about to mature. The ratio can be adjusted to reflect the company's current position. For example, if there is a significant cash balance, it might be appropriate to add this to the retained cash flow from operations on the basis that it would be available to meet the loan repayment.

Cash dividend coverage

The ratio of cash flow from operating activities less interest paid to dividends paid indicates the ability to meet the current dividend. If the dividend rate shows a rising trend, dividends declared might be used rather than the cash flow figure. This would give a better indication of the coverage ratio for future dividends.

Future cash flows

There are two aspects to consider when attempting to predict future cash flows from operations. The first is the level of operating cash flow before the investment in working capital; the second is the level of investment in working capital.

26.6.2 Future cash flows from operations

We need to look at previous periods to identify the trend. Trends are important with investors naturally hoping to invest in a company with a rising trend. If there is a loss or a downward trend, this is a cause for concern and investors should make further enquiries to identify any proposed steps to improve the position. This is where narrative may be helpful – the operating and financial review and chairman's statement may give some indication as to how the company will be addressing the situation. For example, is the company planning a cost reduction programme or disposing of loss-making activities? If it is not possible to improve the trend or reverse the negative cash flow, then there could be future liquidity difficulties.

The implication for future cash flow is that such difficulties could have an impact on future discretionary costs, e.g. the curtailment of research, marketing or advertising expenditure; on investment decisions, e.g. postponing capital expenditure; and on financing decisions, e.g. the need to raise additional equity or loan capital.

There are signs that there has been an increase in activity with acquisition of a subsidiary and investment in additional non-current assets. A review of the narrative should answer questions as to the reason for the increase and the likelihood of it being sustained, such as whether there are new markets, new products, change in sales mix, more competitive pricing with use of more efficient plant.

We can see the cash implication, but would need to make further enquiries to establish the reasons for the change and the likelihood of similar cash outflow movements recurring in future years. If, for example, the increased investment in inventory resulted from an increase in turnover, then a similar increase could recur if the forecast turnover continued to increase. If, on the other hand, the increase was due to poor inventory control, then it is less likely that the increase will recur: in fact, quite the opposite as management addresses the problem.

The cash flow statement indicates the cash extent of the change: additional ratios and enquiries are required to allow us to evaluate the change.

26.6.3 Evaluating the investing activities cash flows

These arise from the acquisition and disposal of non-current assets and investments.

It is useful to consider how much of the expenditure is to replace existing non-current assets and how much is to increase capacity. One way is to relate the cash expenditure to the depreciation charge; this indicates that the cash expenditure is more than five times greater than the depreciation charge calculated as follows: [(£540,000/£102,000) × 100].

This seems to indicate a possible increase in productive capacity. However, the cash flow statement does not itemise the expenditure and the non-current asset schedule does not reveal how much was spent on plant.

How much relates to replacing existing non-current assets?

There has been a criticism that it is not possible to assess how much of the investing activities cash outflow related to simply maintaining operations by replacing non-current assets that were worn out rather than to increasing existing capacity with a potential for an increase in turnover and profits. The solution proposed was that investment that merely maintained should be shown as an operating cash flow and that the investing cash flow should be restricted to increasing capacity. The IASB doubted the reliability of such a distinction but there is a view that such an analysis provides additional information, provided the breakdown between the two types of expenditure can be reliably ascertained.

26.6.4 Evaluating the financing cash flows

Additional capital of £300,000 has been raised. After repaying a loan of £50,000 and payment of a dividend of £120,000, it left only £130,000 towards a net outflow of £600,000 (£331,000 + £319,000). The business is heavily reliant on overdraft.

This does not allow us to assess the financing policy of the company, e.g. whether the capital was raised the optimum way. Nor does it allow us to assess whether the company would have done better to provide finance by improved control over its assets, e.g. working capital reduction.[12]

However, it does flag up the need to seek information as to how the business will manage the overdraft. There could be a liquidity problem with a possible requirement to raise additional share capital, possibly by a rights issue.

26.6.5 Free cash flow (FCF)

Free cash flow defined

There is no common definition of FCF. It has been variously defined as:

(a) Net cash flow used in operating activities.

(b) Net cash flow used in operating activities less purchase of non-current assets to maintain the operating capital of the company. However, for an external user of the accounts, it is not possible to split the capital expenditure between assets to maintain as opposed to assets to increase production capacity unless a company makes a voluntary disclosure of this information.

(c) Net cash flow used in operating activities less all capital expenditure (assuming that this is to maintain operating capacity) but excluding acquisitions (on the basis that these do not reflect organic growth).

(d) As for (c) but including acquisitions.

Under the definition in (d), a negative or depressed FCF may not be a disadvantage if it results from investment in high return investments as shown in the following extract from the 2001 Pearson Annual Report:

Free cash flow

Free cash flow per share is a measure of the cash which is freely available, after the payment of interest and tax, for distribution in the form of dividends and for reinvestment in the business. The proceeds of disposals and the cost of acquisitions, together with any substantial integration costs associated with them, are excluded from the calculation. Pearson's total free cash flow has been depressed over the past several years by a high level of investment demands, on our print businesses as well as on the internet. We believe that these investments will help us to sustain a higher rate of sales growth in the future but we also need to ensure that dividends to shareholders are paid from the cash generated by the business.

In the Pearson example the investment has been based on the expected higher sales growth. It should be recognised, however, that there is a risk if a company has significant free cash flow that its managers may be too optimistic about future performance. When they are not reliant on satisfying external funders there could be less constraint on their investment decisions. If there is negative free cash flow then the opposite applies and the business would require external sources of finance to maintain its operating capital.

Use of free cash flow ratios to track trends

Free cash flow as a percentage of revenue indicates what proportion of the revenue is available for discretionary expenditure.

The following is based on the BBA Aviation plc Annual Reports:

Free cash flow margin

	2007	2006	2005	2004
Revenue (millions)	979	950	1,511	1,374
(i) Free cash flow margin %	8.0%	12.5%	11.5%	9.6%
Net cash flow used in operating activities				
(ii) Free cash flow margin %	4.3%	2.9%	6.7%	5.5%
As in (i) less non-current assets purchased				
(iii) Underlying profit before interest and tax	10.7%	10.6%	5.5%	9.2%

Like all ratios they are only flags. It is interesting to hypothesise from the above: the ratios indicate that in each of the years there was a positive operating cash margin with almost 4% being used to purchase non-current assets except in 2006 when there was a 37% decrease in sales but almost 10% used to purchase non-current assets. The effect on the underlying profit ratio was to increase it by over 90% which was maintained in 2007. However, the free cash flow margin had fallen to 8% which might be due to increases in working capital as the net profit ratio was constant.

26.6.6 Voluntary disclosures

IAS 7 (paras 50–52) lists additional information, supported by a management commentary that may be relevant to understanding:

- liquidity, e.g. the amount of undrawn borrowing facilities;
- future profitability, e.g. cash flow representing increases in operating capacity separate from cash flow maintaining operating capacity; and
- risk, e.g. cash flows for each reportable segment to better understand the relationship between the entity's cash flows and each segment's cash flows.

26.6.7 Reconciliation of net cash flows to net debt

In the UK FRS 1 requires companies to reconcile the movement in cash flows to the movement in net debt by way of note in order to **provide information that assists in the assessment of liquidity and solvency**, e.g. investors review net debt levels for signs of financial distress. IAS 7, however, does not require such a disclosure.

By way of illustration, the notes prepared under FRS 1 for Tyro Bruce (see section 26.4.2 above) would appear as follows:

	20X9		20X8	
1 Borrowings	(150)		(200)	
Overdraft	(478)		(8)	
Government securities	20			
Cash	10		80	
		(448)		72
		(598)		(128)

2 Reconcile net cash flow to movement in net debt	
Decrease in cash	(520)
Change in net debt resulting from cash	50
Movement in net debt	(470)
Net debt at beginning	(128)
Net debt at end of period	(598)

3 Analysis of net debt

	20X8	Cash flow	20X9
Cash at bank	80	(520)	10
Government securities			20
Overdraft	(8)		(478)
Debt outstanding	(200)	50	(150)
Net debt	(128)	(470)	(598)

26.7 Critique of cash flow accounting

IAS 7 (revised) applies stricter requirements to the format and presentation of cash flow statements. It still, however, allows companies to choose between the direct and the indirect methods, and the presentation of interest and dividend cash flows. It can be argued, therefore, that it has failed to rectify the problem of a lack of comparability between statements.

An important point is that, in its search for improved comparability, IAS 7 (revised) reduced the scope for innovation. It might be argued that standard setters should not be reducing innovation, but that there should be concerted effort to increase innovation and improve the information available to user groups. The acceptability of innovation is a fundamental issue in a climate that is becoming increasingly prescriptive.

Our final consideration is the option of direct or indirect methods allowed in IAS 7 (revised). The direct method appears to be a genuine format for a cash flow statement, whereas the indirect method is a cross between a cash flow statement and a funds flow statement. Is it appropriate to continue to offer this hybrid format in IAS 7 (revised) as a replacement for a funds flow statement?

Summary

The funds flow statements produced until 1992 were criticised for not highlighting potential financial problems and for allowing too much choice to companies in how items were disclosed. IAS 7 (revised) defines more tightly the format and treatment of individual items within the cash flow statement. This leads to uniformity and greater comparability between companies. However, there is still some criticism of the current IAS 7:

- There are options within IAS 7 for presentation, since either the direct or the indirect method can be used; and there are choices about the presentation of dividends and interest.

- The cash flow statement does not distinguish between discretionary and non-discretionary cash flows, which would be valuable information to users.

- There is no separate disclosure of cash flows for expansion from cash flows to maintain current capital levels. This distinction would be useful when assessing the position and performance of companies, and is not always easy to identify in the current presentation.

- The definition of cash and cash equivalents can cause problems in that companies may interpret which investments are cash equivalents differently, leading to a lack of comparability. Cash flow statements could be improved by removing cash equivalents and concentrating solely on the movement in cash, which is the current UK practice.

REVIEW QUESTIONS

1 The management of any enterprise may put considerable emphasis on the cash flow effects of its decisions and actions, monitoring these with the internal reporting system. Cash flow information is also relevant to those with external interests in the enterprise. Discuss the importance of cash flow information for both internal and external decisions. What internal and external user needs does cash flow reporting satisfy? Is the current cash flow information adequate for these purposes?

2 Many people preferred the direct method for cash flow preparation, but IAS 7 did not require it. Discuss possible reasons for allowing choice and the effectiveness of the IASC's encouragement to companies to use the direct method.

3 Explain the information that a user can obtain from a cash flow statement that cannot be obtained from the current or comparative statements of financial position.

4 Company X has both a large cash balance and high borrowings. Explain why cash might not have been used to reduce debt.

5 Explain how a payment under a finance lease would be treated.

6 Discuss the limitations of a cash flow statement when evaluating a company's control over its working capital.

7 Explain why the non-current assets acquired on the acquisition of a subsidiary during the year have the same effect on the consolidated cash flow statement as an exchange gain of equal amount resulting from the translation at closing rate.

8 There is a view that if a company shows a healthy operating profit but has low or negative operating cash flows, there is a suspicion that earnings manipulation or creative accounting has occurred. Discuss why there should be suspicion.

9 Describe the voluntary disclosures suggested by IAS 7 and discuss whether these shold be made mandatory.

10 Explain how reconciliation of cash flow to movements in net debt could assist in the analysis of the financial statements and discuss whether this should be made mandatory.

EXERCISES

An extract from the solution is provided on the Companion Website (www.pearsoned.co.uk/elliott-elliott) for exercises marked with an asterisk (*).

Question 1

Direct plc provided the following information from its records for the year ended 30 September 20X9:

	€000
Sales	316,000
Cost of goods sold	110,400
Other expenses	72,000
Rent expense	14,400
Dividends	10,000
Amortisation expense –	
PPE	8,000
Advertising expense	4,800
Gain on sale of equipment	2,520
Interest expense	320

	20X9	20X8
Accounts receivable	13,200	15,200
Unearned revenue	8,000	9,600
Inventory	18,400	19,200
Prepaid advertising	0	400
Accounts payable	11,200	8,800
Rent payable	0	1,200
Interest payable	40	0

Required:
Using the direct method of presentation, prepare the cash flows from the operating activities section of the Statement of cash flows for the year ended 30 September 20X9.

Question 2

Almost Ready Ltd had extracted the following information from the statement of comprehensive income and statement of financial position (000s) for the year ended 30 September 20X9:

Proceeds from issue of ordinary shares 405, Dividends paid 1,923, Cash and cash equivalents at beginning of the period 6,539, Dividends from joint ventures 228, Purchase of investments 29, Interest received 43, Tax paid 1,389, Purchase of property 115, Cash and cash equivalents at end of period 9,214, Proceeds from sale of other long term assets 24, Purchase of a business (net of cash acquired) 274, Interest paid 16, Payment of principal under a finance lease 11, Cash generated from operations 5,732.

Required:
Prepare statement of cash flows for the year ended 30 September 20X9.

Question 3*

The following are the financial statements of Riddle plc for the last two years:

The statements of financial position as at 31 March

	20X8		20X9	
	$000	$000	$000	$000
Non-current assets:				
Property, plant and equipment, at cost	540		720	
Less accumulated depreciation	(145)		(190)	
		395		530
Investments		115		140
Current assets:				
Inventory	315		418	
Trade receivables	412		438	
Bank	48	775	51	907
Total assets		1,285		1,577
Capital and reserves:				
Ordinary shares	600		800	
Share premium	40		55	
Retained earnings	217	857	311	1,166
Non-current liabilities:				
12% debentures		250		200
Current liabilities:				
Trade payables	139		166	
Taxation	39	178	45	211
Total equity and liabilities		1,285		1,577

Statement of comprehensive income for the year ended 31 March 20X9

	$000	$000
Revenue		2,460
Cost of sales		1,780
Gross profit		680
Distribution costs	(124)	
Administration expenses	(300)	(424)
Operating profit		256
Interest on debentures		(24)
Profit before tax		232
Tax		(48)
Profit after tax		184

Note: The statement of changes in equity disclosed a dividend of $90,000.

Required:
(a) Prepare the statement of cash flows for Riddle plc for the year ended 31 March 20X9 and show the operating cash flows using the 'indirect method'.
(b) Calculate the cash generated from operations using the 'direct method'.

Question 4

The statements of financial position of Flow Ltd for the years ended 31 December 20X5 and 20X6 were as follows:

	20X5		20X6	
	€	€	€	€
Non-current assets				
Tangible assets				
PPE at cost	1,743,750		1,983,750	
Accumulated depreciation	551,250	1,192,500	619,125	1,364,625
Current assets				
Inventory		101,250		85,500
Trade receivables		252,000		274,500
		1,545,750		1,724,625
Capital and reserves				
Common shares of €1 each		900,000		1,350,000
Share premium				30,000
Retained earnings		387,000		176,625
Current liabilities				
Trade payables		183,750		159,750
Bank overdraft		75,000		8,250
		1,545,750		1,724,625

Note that during the year ended 31 December 20X6:

1 Equipment that had cost 25,500 and with a net book value of 9,375 was sold for 6,225.

2 The company paid a dividend of 45,000.

3 A bonus issue was made at the beginning of the year of 1 bonus share for every 3 shares.

4 A new issue of 150,000 shares was made on 1 July 20X6 at a price of 1.20 for each 1 share.

5 A dividend of 60,000 was declared but no entries had been made in the books of the company.

Required:
Prepare a statement of cash flows for the year ended 31 December 20X6 that complies with IAS 7.

* Question 5

The statements of financial position of Radar plc at 30 September were as follows:

	20X8		20X9	
	$000	$000	$000	$000
Non-current assets:				
Property, plant and equipment, at cost	760		920	
Less accumulated depreciation	(288)		(318)	
		472		602
Investments		186		214
Current assets:				
Inventory	596		397	
Trade receivables	332		392	
Bank	5	933	—	789
Total assets		1,591		1,605
Capital and reserves:				
Ordinary shares	350		500	
Share premium	75		125	
Retained earnings	137	562	294	919
Non-current liabilities:				
12% debentures		400		100
Current liabilities:				
Trade payables	478		396	
Accrued expenses	64		72	
Taxation	87		96	
Overdraft	—		22	
		629		586
Total equity and liabilities		1,591		1,605

The following information is available:

(i) An impairment review of the investments disclosed that there had been an impairment of £20,000.

(ii) The depreciation charge made in the statement of comprehensive income was £64,000.

(iii) Equipment costing £72,000 was sold for £54,000 which gave a profit of £16,000.

(iv) The debentures redeemed in the year were redeemed at a premium of 25%.

(v) The premium paid on the debentures was written off to the share premium account.

(vi) The income tax expense was £92,000.

(vii) A dividend of £25,000 had been paid and dividends of £17,000 had been received.

Required:
Prepare a statement of cash flows for the year ended 30 September using the indirect method.

Question 6

Shown below are the summarised final accounts of Martel plc for the last two financial years:

Statements of financial position as at 31 December

	20X1 £000	20X1 £000	20X0 £000	20X0 £000
Non-current assets				
Tangible				
Land and buildings	1,464		1,098	
Plant and machinery	520		194	
Motor vehicles	140		62	
		2,124		1,354
Current assets				
Inventory	504		330	
Trade receivables	264		132	
Government securities	40		—	
Bank	—		22	
	808		484	
Current liabilities				
Trade payables	266		220	
Taxation	120		50	
Proposed dividend	72		40	
Bank overdraft	184		—	
	642		310	
Net current assets		166		174
Total assets less current liabilities		2,290		1,528
Non-current liabilities				
9% debentures		(432)		(350)
		1,858		1,178

	20X1 £000	20X1 £000	20X0 £000	20X0 £000
Capital and reserves				
Ordinary shares of 50p each fully paid		900		800
Share premium account	120		70	
Revaluation reserve	360		—	
General reserve	100		50	
Retained earnings	378		258	
		958		378
		1,858		1,178

Summarised statement of comprehensive income for the year ending 31 December

	20X1	20X0
	£000	£000
Operating profit	479	215
Interest paid	52	30
Profit before taxation	427	185
Tax	149	65
Profit after taxation	278	120

Additional information:

1 The movement in non-current assets during the year ended 31 December 20X1 was as follows:

	Land and buildings	Plant, etc.	Motor vehicles
	£000	£000	£000
Cost at 1 January 20X1	3,309	470	231
Revaluation	360	—	—
Additions	81	470	163
Disposals	—	(60)	—
Cost at 31 December 20X1	3,750	880	394
Depreciation at 1 January 20X1	2,211	276	169
Disposals	—	(48)	—
Added for year	75	132	85
Depreciation at 31 December 20X1	2,286	360	254

The plant and machinery disposed of during the year was sold for £20,000.

2 During 20X1, a rights issue was made of one new ordinary share for every eight held at a price of £1.50.

3 A dividend of £36,000 (20X0 £30,000) was paid in 20X1. A dividend of £72,000 (20X0 £40,000) was proposed for 20X1. A transfer of £50,000 was made to the general reserve.

Required:

(a) **Prepare a statement of cash flows for the year ended 31 December 20X1, in accordance with IAS 7.**

(b) **Prepare a report on the liquidity position of Martel plc for a shareholder who is concerned about the lack of liquid resources in the company.**

Question 7

The statements of financial position of Maytix as at 31 October 2005 and 31 October 2004 are as follows:

	2005		2004	
	$000	$000	$000	$000
Non-current assets:				
Property, at cost	4,000		3,000	
Plant and equipment, at cost	7,390		4,182	
Less accumulated depreciation	(1,450)		(1,452)	
		9,940		5,730
Current assets:				
Inventory	5,901		4,520	
Trade receivables	2,639		2,233	
Bank	—	8,540	1,007	7,760
		18,480		13,490
Capital and reserves:				
Ordinary shares	5,000		3,500	
Share premium	2,500		1,000	
Retained earnings	2,110	9,610	3,090	7,590
Non-current liabilities:				
10% loan stock		4,750		3,750
Current liabilities:				
Trade payables	1,237		1,700	
Taxation	550		450	
Bank overdraft	2,333	4,120	—	2,150
		18,480		13,490

The statement of comprehensive income of Maytix for the year ended 31 October 2005 is as follows:

	$000	$000
Credit sales		9,500
Cash sales		1,047
Cost of sales		(8,080)
Gross profit		2,467
Distribution costs	(501)	
Administration expenses	(369)	(870)
Operating profit		1,597
Interest on loan stock		(425)
Loss on disposal of non-current assets		(102)
Profit before tax		1,070
Tax		(550)
Profit after tax		520

Notes:
(i) The 'Statement of changes in equity' disclosed a dividend paid figure of $1,500,000 during the year to 31 October 2005.
(ii) The non-current asset schedule revealed the following details:

Property: Additions cost $1,000,000.

Plant and equipment	Cost	Depreciation	NBV
	$000	$000	$000
Balance at 31.10.2004	4,182	(1,452)	2,730
Additions	6,278	—	6,278
Annual charge	—	(540)	(540)
	10,460	(1,992)	8,468
Disposal	(3,070)	542	(2,528)
Balance at 31.10.2005	7,390	(1,450)	5,940

Required:
(a) Prepare the Cash Flow Statement of Maytix for the year ended 31 October 2005. Use the format required by IAS 7 'Cash Flow Statements' and show operating cash flows using the 'indirect method'.
(b) Describe the additional information that would be included in a cash flow statement showing operating cash flows using the direct method and discuss the proposition that such disclosures be made compulsory under IAS 7.

(The Association of International Accountants)

Question 8

Helvatia GmbH is a Swiss company which is a wholly owned subsidiary of Corolli, a UK company. Helvatia GmbH was formed on 1 November 2005 to purchase and manage a property in Zürich in Switzerland. The reporting and functional currency of Helvatia GmbH is the Swiss franc (CHF).

As a financial accountant in Corolli you are converting the financial statements of Helvatia GmbH into £ sterling in order to be consolidated with the results of Corolli which reports in £s.

The following are the summarised income statements and balance sheet (in thousands of Swiss francs) of Helvatia GmbH:

Helvatia GmbH income statement and Retained Earnings for the year ended 31 October 2007

	CHF (000)
Revenue	8,800
Depreciation	(1,370)
Other operating expenses	(1,900)
Net income	5,530
Retained earnings at 1 November 2006	3,760
	9,290
Dividends paid	(1,000)
Retained earnings at 31 October 2007	8,290

Helvatia GmbH balance sheet as at 31 October

Assets		2007 CHF (000)		2006 CHF (000)
Non-current assets				
Land		6,300		3,300
Buildings		12,330		13,700
		18,630		17,000
Current assets				
Receivables	550		1,550	
Cash	5,610		610	
		6,160		2,160
		24,790		19,160
Liabilities and equity				
Non-current liabilities				
Mortgage loan		10,800		10,000
Current liabilities				
Payables		700		400
Equity				
Issued share capital	5,000		5,000	
Retained earnings	8,290	13,290	3,760	8,760
		24,790		19,160

The following exchange rates are available:

	1 Swiss franc = £
At 1 November 2005	0.40
At 1 November 2006	0.55
At 30 November 2006	0.53
At 31 January 2007	0.53
At 31 October 2007	0.45
Weighted average for the year ended 31 October 2007	0.50

The non-current assets and mortgage loan of Helvatia GmbH as at 31 October 2006 all date from 1 November 2005. Helvatia GmbH purchased additional land and increased the mortgage loan on 31 January 2007. There were no other purchases of non-current assets. Land is not depreciated but the building is depreciated at 10% a year using the reducing balance method. Helvatia GmbH's dividends were paid on 31 January 2007.

The sterling equivalent of Helvatia GmbH's retained earnings as at 31 October 2006 was £1,222,000.

Required:
Prepare the following statements for Helvatia GmbH in £000 sterling:

(a) A summarised income statement for the year ended 31 October 2007.
(b) A summarised balance sheet as at 31 October 2007.
(c) A statement of cash flows for the year ended 31 October 2007 using the indirect method. Additional notes are not required.

(The Association of International Accountants)

References

1 IAS 7 *Statement of Changes in Financial Position*, IASC, 1977.
2 SFAS 95 *Statement of Cash Flows*, FASB, November 1987.
3 IAS 7 *Cash Flow Statements*, IASB revised 2005.
4 J. Arnold *et al.*, *The Future Shape of Financial Reports*, ICAEW and ICAS, 1991.
5 J. Arnold, 'The future shape of financial reports', *Accountancy*, May 1991, p. 26.
6 G.H. Sorter, M.J. Ingberman and H.M. Maximon, *Financial Accounting: An Events and Cash Flow Approach*, McGraw-Hill, 1990.
7 J.W. Henderson and T.S. Maness, *The Financial Analyst's Deskbook*, Van Nostrand Reinhold, 1989, p. 12.
8 J. Crichton, 'Cash flow statements – what are the choices?' *Accountancy*, October 1990, p. 30.
9 L.J. Heath and P. Rosenfield, 'Solvency: the forgotten half of financial reporting', in R. Bloom and P.T. Elgers (eds.), *Accounting Theory and Practice*, Harcourt Brace Jovanovich, 1987, p. 586.
10 J.M. Gahlon and R.L. Vigeland, 'Early warning signs of bankruptcy using cash flow analysis', *Journal of Commercial Lending*, December 1988, pp. 4–15.
11 J.W. Henderson and T.S. Maness, *op. cit.*, p. 72.
12 G. Holmes and A. Sugden, *Interpreting Company Reports and Accounts* (5th edition), Woodhead Faulkner, 1995, p. 134.

CHAPTER 27

Review of financial ratio analysis

27.1 Introduction

The main purpose of this chapter is to provide an overview of the use of ratios in the analysis of the statements of comprehensive income and financial position.

Objectives

By the end of the chapter, you should be able to:

- calculate operating, liquidity and activity ratios from an annual report;
- discuss the implication of the ratios;
- describe and draft a report using inter-firm and industry comparative ratios;
- critically discuss the strengths and weaknesses of ratio analysis;
- calculate EBITDA and EBITDA margins for management control purposes.

27.2 Initial impressions

27.2.1 Impressions formed before referring to the annual report

Often, even before looking at the annual report and accounts, analysts have some preconceived ideas and expectations based on global economic conditions and the specific economic conditions affecting the sector. For example, we have seen in the time of the credit crisis that the professional accounting bodies and enforcement agencies have issued warnings to auditors to be aware of the risk that a company's going concern status might be in jeopardy.

Before even opening the annual report there would be questions already forming in the auditor's and analyst's minds, such as:

(a) What is the likely impact of the overall economic conditions on the entity? For example:
- o liquidity might be under pressure;
- o debt covenants might be broken;
- o segments might be sold to obtain funds to reduce debt with profit/loss arising from forced sales.

(b) What is the likely impact of specific economic conditions affecting the sector? For example, the possibility of:
- o a significant fall in revenue, for example, in the building sector;
- o plant closures in the car making sector;
- o exceptional costs arising from cost reduction and redundancy programmes.

(c) What is the possibility of misrepresentation? For example, by:

○ understating liabilities by omitting to record purchase invoices; or

○ overstating inventories by not making appropriate allowances for inventory losses through fall in demand, obsolescence and deterioration; or

○ overstating trade receivables by recording fictitious sales or not making appropriate allowances for doubtful debts; or

○ understating impairment losses on non-current assets to give a better debt to equity ratio.

There has always been a risk of misrepresentation by management tempted to overstate revenues to satisfy performance targets to obtain a bonus. The following is an interesting, although perhaps rather exaggerated, view given by Ian Griffiths who has written a book on creative accounting which questions the reliability of financial statements:

> Every company in the country is fiddling its profits. Every set of published accounts is based on books which have been gently cooked or completely roasted . . . it is the biggest con trick since the Trojan Horse.[1]

27.2.2 Before referring to the financial data in the annual report

It is helpful to take a critical look at the narrative in the report. For example, the following is an extract from the Chief Executive' Review in the 2008 Annual Report of Wienerberger, a major brick making company:

> 2008 marked a clear turning point in the pattern of economic development across the world . . . High write-offs to bank portfolios triggered a loss of confidence in the financial sector and subsequently led to more restrictive lending . . . Companies were forced to cut back on capital expenditure, which in turn led to a loss of jobs and a general decline in consumer confidence . . . We reacted quickly and adjusted our strategy in summer 2008 . . . liquidity has top priority. . . . Our primary task is to reduce fixed costs as quickly as possible.

This indicates that at this time the particular concern was to achieve an adequate, safe cash flow more than expanding revenues.

We should, however, take heed of the warnings from the professional accounting bodies and be open-minded and investigative when confronted by a set of financial statements or, in accounting terms, approach the analysis with a certain degree of scepticism. To quote Griffiths again,

> Whether the differences in accounting treatment and presentation are real or imagined, it is clear that there is scope for tremendous variation in reported figures . . . perhaps the best safeguard is to look upon the annual accounts with a more cynical and jaundiced eye. The myth that the financial statements are an irrefutable and accurate reflection of the company's trading performance for the year must be exploded once and for all. The accounts are little more than an indication of the broad trend.[2]

27.3 What are accounting ratios?

Ratios describe the relationship between different items in the financial statements. Obviously, we could calculate hundreds of ratios from a set of financial statements; the expertise lies in knowing which ratios provide relevant information. For example, an investor would be interested the statement of comprehensive income and the availability of profits to pay dividends, whereas a credit controller of a supplier would be more interested in a customer's ability to pay and would be concentrating on the statement of financial position and liquidity ratios. The relative usefulness of each ratio depends on what aspects of a company's business affairs are being investigated.

In order to evaluate a ratio, it is customary to make a comparison with the previous year's or industry ratios. It is helpful to bear in mind that:

- A comparison is only valid if the same accounting policies have been applied, for example, both periods or companies using historical cost accounting in reporting their non-current assets.
- The ratios are defined in the same way as the definitions of ratios may vary from source to source as concepts and terminology are not universally defined.[3]
- As a ratio compares two values, changes in either of these underlying values over time may be obscured in the final ratio figure. Let us take the example of Radmand plc:

	Net profit	*Capital employed*	*Return on Capital employed*
	£	£	
20X7	100,000	1,000,000	10%
20X8	150,000	1,500,000	10%
20X9	225,000	2,250,000	10%

Although the return on capital employed (ROCE) remains a constant 10% over the years 20X7–20X9, no assumptions can be made about the underlying figures. As we can see, the net profit increased by 50% in both 20X8 and 20X9, and this trend is not ascertainable in the ROCE ratio. The user should be aware that a ratio is not saying anything about the trends of its individual components – only about the combined effect of both components.

In the following paragraph we will illustrate the pyramid approach used by management to produce ratios that can indicate how effectively an entity is operating and managing its resources.

27.4 Six key ratios

In our analysis we identify six key ratios and a number of subsidiary ratios. The key ratios are presented as a pyramid in Figure 27.1. The pyramid illustrates how the constituent parts of each ratio relate to a set of financial statements. It is an approach used by inter-firm comparison organisations to systematically order the ratios that are prepared for members of the scheme.

The key ratios are:

1 Operating return on equity
2 Financial leverage multiplier
3 Return on capital employed (ROCE)
4 Asset turnover
5 Operating margin (operating profit as % of revenue)
6 Current ratio.

Figure 27.1 Pyramid of key ratios

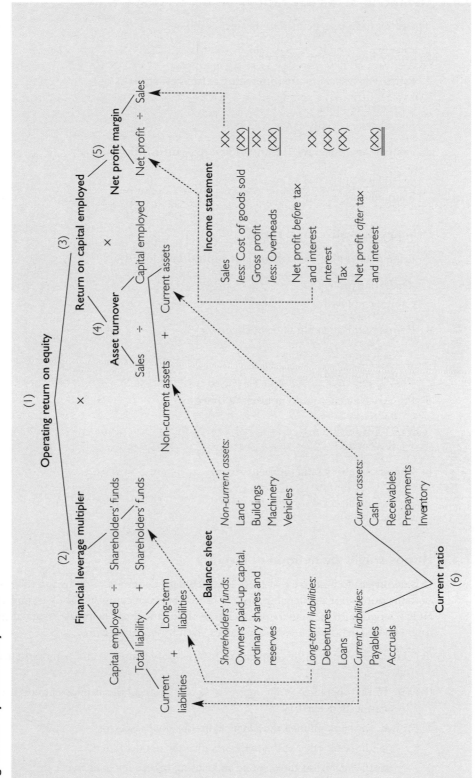

27.4.1 Definition of the key ratios

The ratios have been defined in this text as follows:

Primary investment level ratios

1 Primary investment ratio (**operating return on equity**)

$$\frac{\text{Operating profit}}{\text{Shareholders' equity}}$$

2 Primary financing ratio (**financial leverage multiplier**)

$$\frac{\text{Capital employed}}{\text{Shareholders' equity}}$$

Primary operative level ratios

3 Primary operating ratio (**return on capital employed**)

$$\frac{\text{Operating profit}}{\text{Capital employed}}$$

4 Primary utilisation ratio (**asset turnover**)

$$\frac{\text{Revenue}}{\text{Capital employed}}$$

5 Primary efficiency ratio (**operating margin**)

$$\frac{\text{Operating profit}}{\text{Revenue}}$$

6 Primary liquidity ratio (**current ratio**)

$$\frac{\text{Current assets}}{\text{Current liabilities}}$$

27.4.2 Ratios might be defined differently

It is important to be aware that there is no standard definition of ratios and the make-up of both the numerator and denominator might vary between companies. For example, consider ROCE where both the numerator (operating profit) and the denominator (capital employed) might be defined differently by companies, even in the same sector:

(a) The operating profit used might be before or after interest and before or after income tax.

(b) (i) If the operating profit figure is *before* interest, the capital employed might be variously defined as:

- the book value of the *closing* figure for total assets; or
- the book value of the net assets plus the net debt; or
- the *average* of the opening and closing figures for total assets; or
- the current value of the assets as at the date of the statement of financial position.

This is a method required by some inter-firm comparison schemes in order to make a valid comparison when comparing the ROCE of scheme members.

(ii) If the operating profit figure is *after* interest, the capital employed might be variously taken as:

- the book value of the closing figure for *net* assets; or
- the *average* of the opening and closing figures for net assets; or
- the current value of the net assets as at the date of the statement of financial position.

27.4.3 Discussing the use of the key ratios

1 Primary investment ratio (operating return on equity)

The operating return on equity represents the operating profit before tax as a percentage of the book value of the shareholders' equity. This ratio is at the apex of the ratio pyramid. It is the product of the financial leverage multiplier and the ROCE.

2 Primary financing ratio (financial leverage multiplier)

The financial leverage multiplier expresses how many times bigger the capital employed is than the shareholders' equity. This multiplier demonstrates that assets funded by sources other than the owners will increase the profit or loss of the company relative to shareholders' equity.

3 Primary operating ratio (return on capital employed)

ROCE is a popular indicator of management efficiency and for strategic planning.

Management efficiency

A comparison of the operating profit generated by a company with the total book value of the non-current and current assets indicates how many dollars of profit are obtained from every dollar of resource under management's control. It is useful when making inter-period comparisons for a company.

Strategic planning

ROCE is also used for strategic planning. For example, the following is an extract from the Government Shareholder Executive reporting on the performance of the Royal Mint:[4]

Commentary
The Royal Mint's financial performance improved for the second consecutive year in 2007–08, with a pre-exceptional operating profit of £9.6m. This compared to £8.7m and £1.1m in the two previous years . . . The return on capital employed of 11.5% was substantially above the financial ministerial target of 7.2%.

We have used total (rather than net) assets on the basis that the management are responsible for the use they make of all the assets under their control and operating profit *before* tax. However, as mentioned above there are other definitions. For example, the following is an extract from the 2009 Annual Report of Tesco plc:

Return on capital employed (ROCE)
ROCE is calculated as profit before interest less tax divided by the average of net assets plus net debt plus dividend creditor less net assets held for sale. ROCE is a relative profit measurement that not only incorporates the funds shareholders have invested, but also funds invested by banks and other lenders, and therefore shows the productivity of the assets of the Group.

Note that Tesco has defined capital employed as including net assets plus net debt and for profit as profit less tax but before interest. It is before interest in order that the numerator reflects the resources included in the denominator which includes net debt.

4 Primary utilisation ratio (asset turnover)

The asset turnover ratio measures the number of times that one dollar of assets results in a dollar of revenue. An initial view might be that the more frequently a dollar of revenue is produced the better. Although this ratio can act as a good guide to company performance, it needs to be looked at carefully to establish the reason for any change. If asset turnover increases, then either the total value of revenue is increasing or the capital asset base is decreasing, or both.

If it is because sales are increasing, this is positive if there has been no change in either the sales mix or selling prices. However, the increase might have been achieved at the expense of the profit margin with discounting.

If it is because the capital asset base is reduced, this needs further investigation. For example, it could be caused by a failure to maintain non-current assets with the risk that operating efficiency is affected. This risk is addressed in the following extract from the 2008 Wienerberger Annual Report:

> Maintenance capex was also reduced . . . less than 40% of depreciation. However, these measures in no way endanger the operating performance of our plants.

5 Primary efficiency ratio (operating profit margin)

Operating profit before tax as a percentage of revenue is another widely used ratio in the assessment of company performance and in comparisons with other companies.

The percentage achieved depends on the type of industry a company is operating within (e.g. high-volume/low-margin), the company pricing policies, the sales volumes and cost structure. Any change in the percentage would be investigated to establish the reason. For example, has there been a change in the sales mix, the selling prices, the cost of materials or labour?

6 Primary liquidity ratio (current ratio)

The current ratio is a short-term measure of a company's liquidity position comparing current assets with current liabilities. There is no rule of thumb measure, such as 2:1, that can be applied. The appropriate ratio depends on the industry sector and each individual company's experience. This can be assessed by referring to the times series summaries, as shown in this extract from the 2008 Annual Report of Barloworld, a South African conglomerate:

	2008	2007	2006	2005
Current ratio	1.4	1.5	1.6	1.7

The company has set its own target of >1. The actual ratios indicate that the company's current ratio for 20X8 is within its own normal range and exceeds the company's own target. Whether a current ratio is appropriate depends on the company's financial structure, e.g. is it able to finance the current assets without causing liquidity problems? It is customary to prepare projected cash flows to assess the ability to obtain or convert the assets into cash at a rate that is appropriate to meeting its liabilities on time.

What if the current ratio increases beyond the normal range?

This may arise for a number of reasons, some beneficial, others unwelcome.

Beneficial reasons

- A build-up of inventory in order to support increased sales following an advertising campaign or increasing popular demand as for, say, a PlayStation. Management action will be to establish from a cash budget that the company will not experience liquidity problems from holding such inventory, e.g. there may be sufficient cash in hand or from operations, a short-term loan, extended credit or bank overdraft.

- A permanent expansion of the business which will require continuing higher levels of inventory. Management action will be to consider existing cash resources, future cash flows from operations or arrange additional finance, e.g. equity or long-term borrowings to finance the increased working capital.

Unwelcome reasons

- Operating losses may have eroded the working capital base. Management action will vary according to the underlying problem, e.g. implementing a cost reduction programme, disposing of underperforming segments, arranging a sale of assets or inviting a takeover.

- Inefficient control over working capital, e.g. poor inventory or accounts receivable control allowing a build up of slow moving inventories or doubtful trade receivables.

- Adverse trading conditions, e.g. inventory becoming obsolete or introduction of new models by competitors.

We will see when we discuss subsidiary ratios below that the current ratio is further analysed in terms of its constituent parts i.e. inventory, receivables, payables and cash.

27.5 Illustrating the calculation of the six key ratios

To illustrate we are using the accounts of JD Wetherspoon plc. The company's principal activities are the development and management of public houses.[5] JD Wetherspoon's profit and loss account and statement of financial position for 2002 and 2003 are reproduced in Figure 27.2.

27.5.1 Calculating the six key ratios for JD Wetherspoon

Calculation of the six key ratios

1 **Operating return on equity**

$$2003 \quad \frac{74,983}{318,628} = 23.5\% \qquad\qquad 2002 \quad \frac{70,085}{310,133} = 22.6\%$$

2 **Financial leverage multiplier**

$$2003 \quad \frac{816,250}{318,628} = 2.56 \text{ times} \qquad\qquad 2002 \quad \frac{783,366}{310,133} = 2.53 \text{ times}$$

3 **Return on capital employed**

$$2003 \quad \frac{74,983}{318,628} = 9.19\% \qquad\qquad 2002 \quad \frac{70,085}{783,366} = 8.95\%$$

4 **Asset turnover**

$$2003 \quad \frac{730,913}{816,350} = 0.9 \text{ times} \qquad\qquad 2002 \quad \frac{601,295}{783,366} = 0.77 \text{ times}$$

Figure 27.2 JD Wetherspoon consolidated profit and loss account for year ended 31 July 2003

	2003 £000	2002 £000
Turnover from continuing operations	730,913	601,295
Cost of sales	(621,894)	(503,699)
Gross profit	109,019	97,596
Administrative expenses	(34,036)	(27,511)
Operating profit	74,983	70,085
Net interest payable	(18,844)	(16,517)
Profit on ordinary activities before tax	56,139	53,568
Tax on profit on ordinary activities	(19,744)	(18,152)
Profit on ordinary activities after tax	36,395	35,416
Dividends	(7,434)	(6,902)
Retained profit for the year	28,961	28,514

JD Wetherspoon
Group statement of financial position at 31 July 2003

	2003 £000	2002 £000
Fixed assets		
Tangible assets	773,823	745,041
	773,823	745,041
Current assets		
Stocks	9,601	8,594
Debtors due after more than one year	8,448	7,682
Debtors due after less than one year	9,017	8,237
Investments	301	203
Cash	15,160	13,609
	42,527	38,325
Creditors due within one year	(135,361)	(122,919)
Net current liabilities	(92,834)	(84,594)
Total assets less current liabilities	680,989	660,447
Creditors due after one year	(299,942)	(292,915)
Provisions for liabilities and charges	(62,419)	(57,399)
	318,628	310,133
Capital and reserves		
Called-up share capital	4,149	4,292
Share premium account	126,739	124,819
Capital redemption reserve	165	
Revaluation reserve	22,439	23,386
Profit and loss account	165,136	157,636
Equity shareholders' funds	318,628	310,133

Figure 27.3 Pyramid of ratios

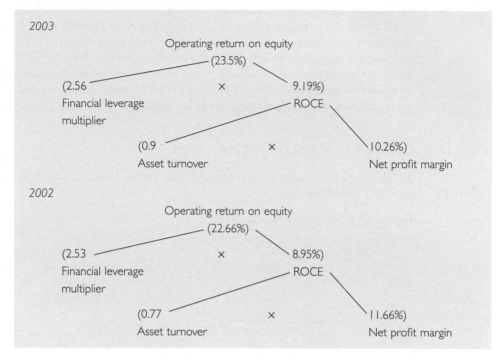

5 **Net profit margin**

$$2003 \quad \frac{74,983}{730,913} = 10.26\% \qquad\qquad 2002 \quad \frac{70,085}{601,295} = 11.66\%$$

6 **Current ratio**

$$2003 \quad \frac{42,527}{135,361} = 0.31{:}1 \qquad\qquad 2002 \quad \frac{38,325}{122,919} = 0.31{:}1$$

Five of these key ratios are shown in the pyramid structure in Figure 27.3.

27.5.2 Interpreting the six key ratios – JD Wetherspoon

There are a number of areas of the business in which further investigations should be carried out. To begin with, the operating return on equity has improved from 22.6% to 23.5%. Disaggregating this ratio we can see that the improvement is due to both an increase in the financial leverage multiplier (2.53 to 2.56) and an increase in the ROCE (8.95% to 9.19%).

The increase in the financial leverage multiplier means that there has been an increased proportion of total liabilities within the capital employed figure. Looking at the statement of financial position, it is evident that long-term loans have risen by nearly £7 million (from £292,915,000 to £299,942,000).

The increase in the ROCE is driven by an improved asset turnover (from 0.77 to 0.9), despite a drop in the net margin (11.66% to 10.26%). The improved asset turnover means that each £ of capital employed (or total assets) produces a higher level of sales. If the decline in net margin is investigated further it is evident that the main cause has been a decline in the gross margin (gross profit/sales) from 16.2% to 14.9%. The declining gross margin might be due to a decline in sales prices or higher cost of sales (which, according to the Wetherspoon annual report, is the main reason).

However, the ratios are calculated on results before exceptional items and the accounts showed an exceptional loss of £2,251,000 arising principally from the sale of 18 pubs. The current ratio is constant at 0.31:1 with the current liabilities much higher than the current assets. Although this appears low, one would need to compare this with the industry average which for brewers is below 0.5:1. The notes to the accounts (not reproduced here) show that trade creditors (accounts payable) have fallen from £54.4 million to £53 million.

27.6 Description of subsidiary ratios

Subsidiary ratios are prepared to support the key ratios. These are set out in Figure 27.4 and provide further ratios for:

Figure 27.4 Subsidiary ratios

Gearing ratios

$$\text{Gearing ratio} = \frac{\text{Total liability} - \text{Current liability}}{\text{Capital employed}}$$

$$\text{Shareholders' ratio} = \frac{\text{Shareholders' funds}}{\text{Capital employed}}$$

$$\text{Interest cover} = \frac{\text{Net profit before interest and tax}}{\text{Interest}}$$

Liquidity ratios

$$(6)\ \text{Current ratio} = \frac{\text{Current assets}}{\text{Current liabilities}}$$

$$\text{Acid test ratio} = \frac{\text{Current assets} - \text{Inventory}}{\text{Current liabilities}}$$

Investment ratios

Earnings per share =

$$\frac{\text{Net profit after tax} - \text{Preference dividends}}{\text{Number of ordinary shares}}$$

$$\text{Price/earnings ratio} = \frac{\text{Share price}}{\text{Earnings per share}}$$

Dividend cover (ordinary shares) =

$$\frac{\text{Net profit after tax} - \text{Preference dividends}}{\text{Dividends on ordinary shares}}$$

$$\text{Dividend yield} = \frac{\text{Dividend on ordinary shares}}{\text{Market value of ordinary shares}}$$

Asset utilisation ratios (turnover ratios)

$$\frac{\text{Sales}}{\text{Non-current assets}}$$

$$\frac{\text{Sales}}{\text{Current assets}}$$

$$\frac{\text{Sales}}{\text{Working capital}}$$

$$\frac{\text{Cost of sales}}{\text{Inventory}}$$

$$\frac{\text{Sales}}{\text{Accounts receivable}}$$

$$\frac{\text{Cost of sales}^a}{\text{Trade payables}}$$

[a]Ideally cost of materials used should be used.

Profitability ratios

$$\frac{\text{Gross profit}}{\text{Sales}}$$

$$\frac{\text{Cost of sales}}{\text{Sales}}$$

$$\frac{\text{Total overheads}}{\text{Sales}}$$

$$\frac{\text{Cost of materials}}{\text{Cost of sales}}$$

$$\frac{\text{Cost of labour}}{\text{Cost of sales}}$$

- capital and income gearing;
- liquidity;
- asset utilisation;
- investment ratios; and
- profitability.

27.6.1 Statement of financial position ratios – capital gearing ratios

Gearing is the relationship between the amounts provided by shareholders and other creditors. The relationship can be expressed using a number of different formulae. For the capital gearing there are two approaches: (a) relate liabilities to total assets or equity and (b) relate equity to total assets:

(a) Relating liabilities to total assets may be variously defined as:
  - long-term debt to total assets;
  - the debt ratio (total debt/total assets);
  - total liabilities to total assets;
  - (total liabilities – provisions) to total assets;
  - the debt-to-equity ratio (net debt/total equity);
  - the debt equity ratio (total debt/total equity).

(b) the equity ratio;
  - equity/asscts.

For the purposes of illustration in this chapter, we are defining gearing as long-term debt to capital employed. A number of companies report the debt/equity ratio as their preferred choice and include total debt rather than long-term debt if a company relies heavily on over-draft facilities.

27.6.2 Statement of income ratios – income gearing

Most companies have borrowings and are committed to paying interest. The security of their interest payment is normally measured by the income gearing ratio which is calculated as the number of times the interest could be paid out of the operating profit. The ratio may be expressed in different ways. For example:

- Earnings before interest, tax, depreciation and amortisation (EBITDA) which emphasises the cash generated from normal operations.
- Operating profit (EBIT) excluding exceptional items.
- Profit before interest – including exceptional items.

The leverage effect

We saw that if capital employed is funded by sources other than equity, then there is a financial leverage impact on the ROCE (refer to section 27.5.1 for an illustration of this by the analysis of JD Wetherspoon's Annual Report with the ROCE of 9.19% being lifted by financial leverage to produce an operating return on equity of 23.5%).

In reviewing the 23.5% we would need to consider whether the assets in the statement of financial position are a fair indication of current values. If the current value of the assets were, say, 10% higher (£897,875) then the operating return on equity would fall by more than 20% from 23.5% to 18.73% (£74,983/£400,235 × 100).

As far as the equity shareholders are concerned, it might appear that the higher the financial leverage the better. However:

- If borrowings are high, it might be difficult to obtain additional loans to take advantage of new opportunities. For example, HSBC raised £12.5 billion by a rights issue on the basis that this would give the bank a competitive advantage over its rivals by restoring its position as having the strongest statement of financial position, i.e. high borrowings limit a company's flexibility.

- Interest has to be paid even in bad years with the risk that loan creditors could put the company into administration if interest is not paid.

How should a potential investor decide on an acceptable level of gearing?

This is initially influenced by the political and economic climate of the time. We have seen that prior to the credit crisis arising in 2007 high gearing was not seen by many as risky and there was a general feeling that borrowing was good, leverage was respectable, and capital gains were inevitable. This might have reduced the importance of questions that would normally have been asked. The questions were:

- If gearing has increased, what were the funds used for? Was it to:
  - restructure debt following inability to meet current repayment terms;
  - finance new maintenance/expansion capex;
  - improve liquid ratios.
- Are the values in the statement of financial position reasonably current? If too low the gearing ratio is overstated.
- How does the gearing compare to other companies in the same sector?
- Is the gearing ratio constant or has it increased over time with heavier borrowing? If higher:
  - further borrowing might be difficult;
  - it might indicate that there has been investment that will lead to higher profits so details are needed as to how the funds borrowed have been used.
- How variable is the rate of interest that is being charged on the borrowings? If rates are falling then equity shareholders benefit but if rates rise then expenses are higher.
- How many times does the earnings before tax cover the interest? A highly geared company is more at risk if the business cycle moves into recession because the company has to continue to service the debts even if sales fall substantially.
- How many times does the cash flow from operations currently cover the interest? This is a useful ratio if profits are not converted into cash, e.g. they might be reinvested in non-current assets.
- How variable is the company's cash flow from operations? A company with a stable cash flow is less at risk so the trend is important.
- What covenants are in place and what is the risk that they might be breached? A breach could lead to a company going into administration or liquidation.
- What is the likely effect of contingent liabilities if they crystallise on the debt ratio? Could it have a significant adverse impact?

A company's attitude to leverage may vary over time

The following is an interesting article in *Management Today*:[6]

The statement of financial position of British business has passed through a truly remarkable transformation over the past two years . . . in every sector and at every level, from giant household names down to modest seven-figure enterprises, all confirm the pattern: gearing levels radically reduced, businesses managing their cash-flow more intelligently than ever before, and deep-seated reluctance to borrow afresh . . . Bank of England statistics show that industrial and commercial companies have been repaying debt steadily since the beginning of 1993 . . . New financing was provided instead by a combination of capital issues (£16 billion) and retained earnings . . . A survey by accountants KPMG of 133 quoted companies in the West Midlands shows the average debt/equity ratio falling between 1992/93 and 1993/94 from 32% to 23% . . . According to Kevin Jennings, director of commercial marketing at National Westminster Bank, there has been a 'major shift in business literacy', in which managers have learned to run higher levels of turnover on lower levels of short-term finance by much more rigorous attention to stocks, debtors and creditors . . . There is, of course, another side to the story. Demand for borrowing may be under control, but what of supply? In the last boom it was undeniably true that banks poured fuel onto the flames by their very aggressive lending policies, driven by the need to fill their own statements of financial position in order to show an adequate return on capital. More recently, the talk has been of a 'flight to quality' . . . a willingness to shrink the lending business in order to stay within acceptable parameters of risk.

We now see the same scenario having been played out ten years later – aggressive lending policies followed by a flight to quality resulting in it being more difficult for companies to obtain loans and a resulting requirement for more new equity funding.

27.6.3 Liquidity ratios

$$\text{Acid test ratio} = \frac{\text{Current assets} - \text{Inventory}}{\text{Current liabilities}}$$

The acid test or quick ratio indicates the company's ability to repay immediate commitments using cash or near-cash. It excludes inventory in order to show the immediate solvency of the company.

The following is an extract from the 2008 Annual Report of Barloworld:

	2008	2007	2006	2005
Quick ratio	0.9	1.0	1.2	1.1

This indicates that the company's quick (or acid test) ratio is within its own normal range and exceeds its own target of >0.5.

27.6.4 Asset utilisation ratios: non-current assets

In order to identify the rate at which revenue is generated from the assets under management's control, we calculate ratios that are referred to as activity ratios. The first of these, which looks at the use of capital employed (defined here as total assets), is the asset turnover ratio where we divide the turnover from the statement of comprehensive income by the capital employed from the statement of financial position. However, before we draw any conclusions from the ratio, we need to review (a) the make-up of the non-current assets when assessing consolidated accounts to see the division between intangible and tangible (b) how the tangible assets have been valued and (c) the age of the assets.

(a) The make-up of non-current assets

This is important because some groups rely on organic growth and have little goodwill, whilst others have achieved growth through material acquisitions. For example, The Kier Group, a building and civil engineering company, relies on organic growth. The following is an extract from its 2008 annual report:

Non-current assets	£176.1m
Goodwill	£5.2m
Revenue	£2,374.2
Asset turnover (including goodwill)	13.5 times
Asset turnover (excluding goodwill)	13.9 times

Compare this with Syskoplan, a software integrator and consultancy company, where goodwill is a significant part of its non-current assets, as shown in the following extract from its 2007 annual report:

Non-current assets	€19.8m
Goodwill	€12.4m
Revenue	€57.5m
Asset turnover (including goodwill)	2.9 times
Asset turnover (excluding goodwill)	7.8 times

Which assets to include in the ratio?

There is an argument that the operational management is only responsible for the effective use of the tangible assets. It could be argued that it is the board that is responsible for the total of the intangible and tangible assets on the basis that it was responsible for the acquisitions which gave rise to the goodwill. This is the reason for the separate calculation for tangible and intangible asset turnover shown in Figure 27.5. If intangible assets are not included, look at any change in ratio of R&D to sales separately.

Figure 27.5 Asset turnover ratio

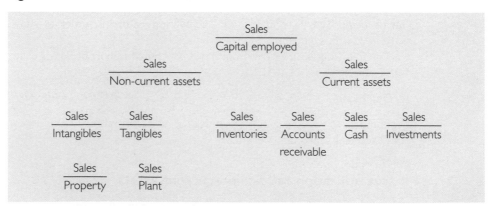

(b) How the tangible assets have been valued

If using the asset turnover ratio to make comparisons with other companies, consider whether valuation is on the same basis, i.e. historical cost or revaluation, the age of the assets if at cost which can be estimated by the amount of accumulated depreciation in relation to the cost figure, and the depreciation policies that have been adopted.

(c) The age of the assets

If assets are heavily depreciated, the ratio will be higher. It is important to read the narrative to check if there are plans for future capital investment and to confirm that the capital base is being maintained. Delaying the replacement of capacity may be chosen or forced on the business in times of recession so it is useful to check if there is a high or low capital expenditure/depreciation ratio.

27.6.5 Asset utilisation ratios: current assets

The activity ratios relating to current assets are broken down into (a) inventory turnover, (b) trade receivables turnover, and (c) trade payables turnover. We will now consider each of these.

(a) Inventory turnover ratio

Inventory control is concerned with minimising the cost of holding inventory. The cost would have been determined by a management accountant taking into account the cost of placing an order, the cost of holding inventory based on the interest rate and the cost of being out of inventory. This is a balancing act with the company trying to avoid tying up too much capital in inventory, yet maintaining sufficient to meet customer demand and maintain continuous production.

In calculating and interpreting the inventory turnover ratio, attention is directed towards, first, assessing whether the level is appropriate by comparing with competitors in the same sector and, secondly, by comparing with previous periods to identify whether there has been any change.

The ratio can be expressed as the number of times inventory turns over:

$$\text{Inventory turnover} = \frac{\text{Sales}}{\text{Inventory}} \text{ or } \frac{\text{Cost of sales}}{\text{Average inventory}} \text{ or more usually } \frac{\text{Cost of sales}}{\text{Closing inventory}}$$

Or as the number of days inventory has been held:

$$\frac{\text{Closing inventory}}{\text{Cost of sales}} \times 365$$

Any change in this ratio must be investigated to determine exactly why the change has occurred. It could be as a result of a proactive business decision, a reaction to economic circumstances or misrepresentation.

(a) Proactive business decision

An example of a planned increase is seen in the following extract from the 1999 Annual Report of Schering AG:

> **Good balance-sheet ratios maintained**
> The balance-sheet ratios demonstrate the healthy financial state of the Schering Group. Inventories and receivable rose to 41% of the balance-sheet total. Among other things, this was due to a build-up of stocks to keep the market supplied during implementation of our European Production Concept and to cater for any problems that might have arisen in connection with Y2K.

(b) Reaction to change in economic circumstances

An example is seen where there has been a decline in demand in the following extract from the 2007 Annual Report of ThyssenKrupp Steel:

> The European steel industry expects business to stabilize at a high level in the coming year. In the short term, however, the inventory overhangs in the market are expected to dampen demand, initially, with possible effects on production.

This has two implications. One is that ThyssenKrupp customers are holding higher inventories which could, in turn, have an effect on ThyssenKrupp's own inventory. This is supported by the figures reported in the ThyssenKrupp 2007 Annual Report:

	2006 €m	2007 €m	% change
Sales	47,125	51,723	9.8%
Inventories	8,069	9,480	17.5%
Inventory turnover ratio (times)	5.8	5.5	

(c) Possibility of misrepresentation

One must be aware of the risk of fraud if the economic climate in which the company is operating has falling profits. For example, what is the temptation to overvalue inventory? A possible sign could be an increase in inventory with a corresponding increase in the gross profit percentage. One reason could be a fraud that has often occurred in the past where a simple accounting entry is made to debit inventory and credit the cost of sales – this should, of course, be detected by normal audit procedures.

Importance of referring to narrative

The ratios are based on the figures in the financial statements. It helps, however, to look beyond the figures to the narrative in the business review for further clues, as in the Cisco Annual Report 2001 *Financial Review – Management's Discussion and Analysis:*

> Inventory purchases and commitments are based upon future demand forecasts. To mitigate the component supply constraints that have existed in the past, we built inventory levels for certain components with long lead times and entered into commitments for certain components. Due to a sudden and significant decrease in demand for our products, inventory levels exceeded our estimated requirements based on demand forecasts.

(b) Trade receivables turnover – collection period

When preparing a cash budget we need to know when, after a credit sale has been made, cash will be received. We would expect it be received within the normal agreed credit period of, say, 30 days. At the period end the number of days that trade receivables have been outstanding is calculated and normally expressed as the number of days of collection period. The turnover ratio is calculated as:

$$\frac{\text{Accounts receivable}}{\text{Sales}} \times 365$$

Before drawing conclusions from the ratio, we need to consider the business climate. In times of recession, access to bank finance becomes more difficult and businesses seeks more trade credit whilst at the same time delaying settling their accounts. The implication is that there could be an increase in the suppliers' accounts of trade receivables and a corresponding increase in trade payables in the purchasers' accounts. This means that there could be both an increase in the volume of trade receivables and an extension of the collection period. Research by Creditsafe (www1.creditsafeuk.com/?id=975&cid=1426&Year=2008) has shown that late payment is a problem in the UK:

> In Britain late payments is a problem which is endemic in businesses of all sizes. 53% of sole traders complain that they suffer from late payments, a figure which rises to over 95% (96.8%) of companies surveyed of between 50 and 250 employees.

Some changes in the collection period could be the result of economic conditions. However, we should also consider other possible reasons for (i) a reduction and (ii) an increase in the collection period.

A reduction in the collection period could arise from beneficial reasons such as improved credit control, prompt payment by customers to receive a cash discount, heavy discounting because the business has cash flow problems or to achieve sales targets and factoring of the debts. There might also be unwelcome reasons such as bad debts written-off and restriction of credit due to cash flow problems which could possibly lead to a reduction in sales.

An increase in the collection period could be due to poor credit control with credit extended to unreliable customers, late payment with the risk that these turn into bad debts, disputed debts with risk of non-payment, or fictitious sales with fictitious customer balances.

(c) Trade payables turnover – payment period

This indicates the rate at which creditors settle their accounts with suppliers. Ideally the ratio would be calculated as:

$$\text{Accounts payable turnover} = \frac{\text{Total supplier purchases}}{\text{Average accounts payable}}$$

However, working from published financial statements, the purchases figure is not available and the ratio can therefore, be calculated as:

$$\text{Payables turnover} = \frac{\text{Sales}}{\text{Accounts payable}} \text{ or more usually } \frac{\text{Cost of sales}}{\text{Accounts payable}}$$

Expressed in terms of the payment period (in days) the ratio is:

$$\frac{\text{Accounts payable}}{\text{Sales}} \times 365 \text{ or more usually } \frac{\text{Accounts payable}}{\text{Cost of sales}} \times 365$$

This ratio indicates the outstanding credit allowed to a company by its suppliers. Any changes in the payment period might be due to suppliers altering credit terms (either being more or less generous), the company taking advantage of early payment incentives or delaying payment beyond the agreed credit period.

27.6.6 Investment ratios

Investment ratios such as earnings per share (EPS), price/earnings ratio (PE ratio) and dividend cover are of great interest to investors.

Earnings per share

EPS indicates the amount of profit after tax, interest and dividends to preference shares has been earned for each ordinary share. Its importance is recognised by some managers who use the EPS as part of their strategic planning; e.g. the 2005 Annual Report of Gamma Holding NV states:

Financial targets
Gamma Holdings strives for an average annual growth of earnings per share of at least 10% over a number of years. This growth is related to the net result of the company, excluding restructuring, in 2004.

The company also targets profit to sales %, ROCE and statement of financial position ratios:

In addition, the company strives for an operating result of at least 8% of turnover for the Gamma Technologies sector and at least 9% of turnover for the Gamma Comfort & Style sector. For each of these sectors Gamma strives for a return on capital employed of at least 15%. With a view to a healthy statement of financial position, the company aims for a solvency percentage of at least 30% and gearing (ratio of total interest-bearing liabilities to total equity) of at most 1. It is the company's policy that net debt should not exceed 2.5 times EBITDA.

PE ratio

The ratio is calculated using the current share price and current earnings. It is a measure of market confidence in the shares of a company. However, the market price also takes into account anticipated changes in the earnings arising from their assessment of macro events such as political factors, e.g. imposition of trade embargoes and sanctions; economic factors, e.g. the downturn in manufacturing activity; and market conditions as in the following extract from the Sepracor 2003 Annual Report:

The price of our common stock historically has been volatile, which could cause you to lose part of your investment. The market price of our stock, like that of the common stock of many other pharmaceutical and biotechnology companies, may be highly volatile. In addition, the stock market has experienced extreme price and volume fluctuations. This volatility has significantly affected the market price . . . For reasons unrelated to or disproportionate to the operating performance of the specific companies. Prices . . . may be influenced by many factors, including variations in our financial results and investors' perceptions of us, changes in recommendations by securities analysts as well as their perceptions of general economic, industry and market conditions.

It is also, of course, influenced by company-related events, for example, the possibility of reconstruction, organic or acquired growth.

Dividend cover

Dividend cover is ascertained by comparing EPS to dividend per share. It indicates the cushion that exists to meet dividends in the future if earnings were to deteriorate. The cover is expressed as number of times or, in some annual reports, as a payout ratio. Dividend yield expresses dividend as a percentage of the share price.

27.6.7 Profitability ratios

Profitability ratios allow a more specific analysis of profit margin, e.g. expressing individual expenses as a proportion of sales or cost of sales. These ratios will identify any irregularities or changes in specific expenses from year to year. A list of these is set out in Figure 27.4.

27.6.8 Comparing current ratios with those of the previous year

It is normal practice for the financial director to make a comparison with the previous year's ratios to identify, investigate significant changes and make a report to the board. In approaching this there could be some preconceived ideas as to the reason based on local knowledge of the company. For students and those taking examinations, the task may be to consider what questions to ask in the absence of this local company knowledge. For example, consider the scenario where the inventory turnover rate has increased significantly. This should give rise to questions such as:

● Has the sales increased significantly? If so, is this from a one–off contract or is it likely to be a permanent increase? If a permanent increase, is there any risk of overtrading where there is insufficient capital to maintain inventory at a level which does not affect liquidity or a risk of stock–outs?

● Has the inventory level fallen? If so, is this because there is a restriction of credit and if so, why has that occurred? Have there been significant write–downs? If due to obsolescence, what is the possible affect on the reported inventory? Is the company experiencing liquidity problems and reducing inventory levels? Has there been a change in staff resulting in improved inventory control. Has the company divested itself of a segment late in the year whereby revenues have been achieved during the year and some inventory has been part of the disposal?

In addition to making comparisons with the previous year, many companies make comparisons with another competitor company, a selected peer group and industry sector averages.

27.7 Comparative ratios: inter-firm comparisons and industry averages

We have seen that financial ratios provide management with the means to question any significant changes arising during the financial year. They are also a convenient way of assessing the current financial health and performance of a company relative to similar companies in the same industrial sector. This enables a company to be judged directly against its competitors, rather than merely against its own previous performance. Provided that each company uses exactly the same bases in calculating ratios, inter-firm comparisons provide an objective means of evaluation. Every company is subject to identical economic and market conditions in the given review period, allowing a much truer comparison than a single company's fluctuating results over several years.

Inter-firm comparisons are ideal for identifying the strengths and weaknesses of a company relative to its immediate competitors and the industrial sector. These comparisons can be analysed by both internal users (management can take the necessary actions to maintain strengths and rectify weaknesses) and external users (lenders, creditors, investors, etc.). There are numerous sources of inter-firm information, but the organisations providing it can be divided into those which gather their data from external published accounts and those which collect the data directly from the surveyed companies on a strictly confidential basis.

27.7.1 Data collected from external published accounts

Organisations that prepare inter-firm comparisons from external published accounts face all the limitations associated with company accounts. These limitations include the following:

● The comparative ratios that can be included in an inter-firm comparison are limited to the information content of a set of published accounts. The inadequacies of compulsory disclosure restrict the amount of useful information and make it impossible to prepare every desirable ratio, for example, not all companies publish their gross profit percentage.

- There may be different accounting policies. For example, historical cost or revaluation of non-current assets, straight-line or reducing balance depreciation methods, and inventory valued at FIFO or average rate.
- The timeliness of any inter-firm comparison is dependent on the timeliness of published accounts. Companies may have different year ends and there will be a time lag in the publication of inter-firm comparison information.

Although these drawbacks affect the reliability and completeness of survey results, such agencies have several advantages:

- The scope of an inter-firm comparison is extremely wide as it can include an analysis of any firm that produces published accounts.
- The quality of ratio analysis is improved because survey organisations attempt to standardise the bases of every ratio in the survey. This increases the uniformity and comparability of the ratio information.
- The survey information is easy to access and available at a relatively low cost.

What organisations provide inter-firm comparisons prepared from external published accounts?

Useful sources for inter-firm ratio comparisons include *Company REFS*,[7] *Handbook of Market Leaders*,[8] Dun & Bradstreet's *Key Business Ratios: The Guide to British Business Performance*,[9] *The Company Guide*[10] and the online and CD-ROM computer services, including Datastream, OneSource,[11] Fame and Extel Financial Workstation. In addition, the World Wide Web provides an excellent source for corporate information.

27.7.2 Data collected direct from member companies of the private inter-firm comparison scheme

These inter-firm comparisons are prepared on a confidential basis and the analysed information is usually available only to the participating companies.

The advantages of private schemes are that inter-firm comparisons consist of a comprehensive analysis of every firm in the scheme, and a higher degree of reliability can be attached to their findings than if external published accounts alone were used.

The drawbacks of private schemes are as follows:

- There are onerous requirements concerning the quality of information that companies contribute to private schemes. All information must comply with strict uniformity requirements.
- The cost of these schemes may be relatively high.

The advantages of private schemes are that inter-firm comparisons consist of a comprehensive analysis of every firm in the scheme, and a higher degree of reliability can be attached to their findings than if external published accounts alone were used.

What organisations provide private schemes?

Numerous organisations co-ordinate private inter-firm comparison schemes for the majority of different trade groups and industrial sectors. One of the best known is the Centre for Interfirm Comparison, which was founded by the British Institute of Management.

27.7.3 Ensuring valid inter-firm comparisons

The necessity for comparing like with like has been stressed throughout this chapter. For valid comparisons, we must ensure not only that the bases of ratios are identical, but that a company is compared with companies in the same industrial sector and with similar principal activities. If it is compared with a company in a different industrial sector, the results might be interesting, but they might not be suitable for any decision-useful analysis. Of course, when using any published inter-company comparison data, it is essential to understand how the ratios are calculated. Most publications define key terms, how ratios are computed and the methodologies used.

As stressed before, ratio definitions are not 'set in stone'. Different publications and inter-company comparison schemes will use different definitions of seemingly identical ratios. For instance, when using FAME's profit margin, we would need to ascertain what measure of profit is used (e.g. has other income and/or interest received been included?).

There are a number of subscription databases available on CD-rom or online which provide annual reports and ratios with excellent search facilities e.g. FAME, Amadeus and OneSource.

FAME (Financial Analysis Made Easy) (www.bvdep.com)

FAME displays annual consolidated accounts, and performs company comparisons (Peer Analysis), as well as market sector reports (Statistical Analysis). The detailed information includes Company profile including subsidiaries and directors, Accounting and financial information including company turnover, Ratios and trends, Complete lists of holding companies and shareholder details, and the latest company news.

Search can be on a single criterion or over 100 criteria with results displayed or printed in various formats, e.g. text, charts or graphs, and exported to other applications, e.g. word processors, databases, Excel spreadsheets. The index supplies information on live and dissolved companies, which is particularly helpful for tracing old, new and very small companies. It also includes share prices from mid-2000 for quoted companies.

Amadeus (www.bvdep.com)

Amadeus is a comprehensive, pan-European database containing financial information on public and private companies. It provides standardised company accounts for up to ten years for European companies with twenty-five standard ratios. As with FAME, it is modular, with data for the top 200,000 companies, the top 1 million or all 5 million companies.

OneSource (www.onesource.com)

OneSource is a user-friendly database that can be accessed on line. It integrates business content from over 2,500 leading sources worldwide to provide world-class company and industry profiles, executive biographies, financial data, analyst reports, and business press coverage. OneSource gathers in-depth data on more than 100 major industries, including detailed SIC code-level information. Users can search to find companies that match their criteria – search by size, location or line of business or via a large selection of variables and get detailed financial information and analysts' reports. In addition to financial data it records key executive contacts and board members by name, location, line of business, job function or biographical details, news and articles.

27.8 Limitations of ratio analysis

Ratios are useful flags but there may be limitations that the reader needs to bear in mind relating to external factors, internal factors and problems specific to consolidated accounts.

27.8.1 External factors

There are a number of external factors that need to be understood. These include:

- Ratios need to be interpreted bearing in mind the political context within which a business has been operating as, for example, when governments adopt protectionist measures that can impact on a company's sales. For example, in 2009 the Argentine Production Ministry announced new anti-dumping measures to combat what it regarded as unfair competition and restricted foreign imports from a number of countries covering a range of imports such as metal cutlery, air conditioners and terminals.

- Ratios need to be interpreted bearing in mind the economic context within which a business has been operating by considering any changes that have occurred in the accounting period that could impact on:
  - non-current assets, e.g. tax incentives to invest;
  - inventories, e.g. a downturn in the economy leading to holding excessive amounts of inventory;
  - trade receivables, e.g. credit restrictions leading to a longer collection period;
  - costs affecting the gross profit, e.g. raw material shortages leading to inflated prices as with gas and oil supplies and wage increases due to a rise in minimum wage rates; and
  - costs affecting the profit before tax, e.g. increased bad debts and interest rate increases.

27.8.2 Internal factors

There are internal factors to consider:

- Ratios need to be interpreted in conjunction with reading the narrative and notes in the annual reports. The narrative could be helpful in explaining changes in the ratios, e.g. whether an inventory buildup is in anticipation of sales or a fall in demand. The notes could be helpful in corroborating the narrative, e.g. if the narrative explains that the increase in inventory is due to anticipated further production and sales, check whether the non-current assets have increased or whether there is a note about future capital expenditure.

- Whether confident that the financial statements give a true and fair view:
  - Whether there is a risk of fraudulent misrepresentation which can affect even major companies as, for example, in the case of Xerox.[12] The fraud was that Xerox overstated its true equipment revenues by at least $3 billion and its true earnings by approximately $1.5 billion during a four-year period. When Xerox finally restated its financial results for 1997–2000, it restated $6.1 billion in equipment revenues and $1.9 billion in pre-tax earnings – the largest restatement in US history up to that point.
  - Whether there is a risk of window dressing, e.g. dispatching goods at the end of the period knowing them to be defective so that they appear in the current year's sales and accepting that they will be returned later in the next period.

- Have the accounts been subject to fundamental uncertainty which could affect the going concern concept? There might be full disclosure in the notes but ratios might not be accurate predictors of earnings and solvency.

- Have liabilities been omitted, e.g. use of off balance sheet finance such as structuring the terms of a lease to ensure that it is treated as an operating lease and not a finance lease and special-purpose enterprises to keep debts off the statement of financial position?

● Ratios might be distorted because they are based on period-end figures:

- The end of year figures are static and might not be a fair reflection of normal relationships such as when a business is seasonal, e.g. an arable farm might have no inventory until the harvest and a toy manufacturer might have little inventory after supplying wholesalers in the lead up to Christmas. Any ratios based on the inventory figure such as inventory turnover could be misleading if calculated at, say, a 31 December year-end.

- Similarly, a decline in the rate of inventory turnover might have arisen from the management decision to stockpile scarce raw materials which will allow the company to meet customer demand when competitors are out of stock.

● Factors that could invalidate inter-company comparisons, such as:

- use of different measurement bases with non-current assets reported at historical cost or revaluation and revaluations carried out at different dates;

- use of different commercial practices, e.g. factoring trade receivables so that cash is increased – a perfectly normal transaction but one that could cause the comparative ratio of days' credit allowed to be significantly reduced;

- applying different accounting policies: e.g. adopting different depreciation methods such as straight-line and reducing balance; adopting different inventory valuation methods such as FIFO and weighted average; or assuming different degrees of optimism/ pessimism when making judgement-based adjustments to non-current and current assets, e.g.:

  ● on the impairment review of intangible and tangible non-current assets;

  ● on R&D spend (an interesting research study[13] looking at 243 initial public offerings from 1986 to 1990 found that there was a reduction by managers in R&D spending to increase current earnings and a manipulation of discretionary current accruals. One explanation might be that potential investors attach greater weight to current earnings and this could benefit insiders on the sale of their pre-offering shareholding);

- having different definitions for ratios, e.g.:

  ● the numerator for ROCE could be operating profit, profit before interest and tax, profit before interest, profit after tax, etc.;

  ● the denominator for ROCE could be total assets, total assets less intangibles, net assets, average total assets, etc.;

- the use of norms can be misleading, e.g.:

  ● a current ratio of 2:1 might be totally inappropriate for a company like Tesco which does not have long inventory turnover periods and as its sales are for cash it would not produce trade receivable collection period ratios;

- making the appropriate choice of comparator companies for benchmarking by finding companies with the same mix of products and markets and deciding on appropriate criteria, e.g. deciding if it should be the industry average ratios. However, these may be based on many companies of different size regarding the amounts of capital employed, turnover, number of employees, etc. The choice of benchmark is important as it affects the conclusions that are made but it is difficult to get an exact fit.

27.8.3 Problems when using consolidated accounts

Certain limitations need to be recognised when analysing a consolidated statement of financial position, making inter-company comparisons and forming a judgement on distributable profits based on the consolidated statement of comprehensive income. These are as follows:

- The consolidated statement of financial position aggregates the assets and liabilities of the parent company and its subsidiaries. The current and liquidity ratios that are extracted to indicate to creditors the security of their credit and the likelihood of the debt being settled will be valid only if all creditors have equal rights to claim against the aggregated assets. This may be the case if there are cross-guarantees from each company, but it is more likely that the creditors will need to seek payment from the individual group company to which it allowed the credit. One needs to be aware that the consolidated accounts are prepared for the shareholders of the parent company and that they may be irrelevant to the needs of creditors. This is not a criticism of consolidation, merely a recognition of the purpose for which the accounts are relevant.

- The consolidated statement of comprehensive income does not give a true picture of the profits immediately available for distribution by the holding company to its shareholders. It shows the group profit that could become available for distribution if the holding company were to exercise its influence and control, and require all its subsidiary companies and associated companies to declare a dividend of 100% of their profits for the year. Legally, it is possible for the company to exercise its voting power to achieve the passing up to it of the subsidiary companies' profits – although commercially this is highly unlikely. The position of the associated companies is less clear: the holding company only has influence and does not have the voting power to guarantee that the profit disclosed in the consolidated statement of comprehensive income is translated into dividends for the holding company shareholders.

27.9 Earnings before interest, tax, depreciation and amortisation (EBITDA) used for management control purposes

We have so far discussed the preparation of ratios based on the information reported in the published accounts. For example, we have used Operating profit before interest and tax in calculating the ROCE as a measure of the effective use of resources by management. Another measure is based on **EBITDA** – earnings before interest, tax, depreciation and amortisation.

EBITDA reflects the cash effect of earnings by adding back depreciation and amortisation charges to the operating profit. If this is not separately disclosed, the figure can be derived by adding back the depreciation disclosed in the statement of cash flows.

27.9.1 Why use EBITDA?

By taking earnings before depreciation we eliminate differences due to different ages of plant and equipment when making inter-period comparisons of performance and also differences arising from the use of different depreciation methods when making inter-firm comparisons.

This information is useful where a company has a number of segments. It allows performance to be compared by calculating the EBITDA for each segment which provides a figure that is independent of the age structure of the non-current assets. This is illustrated in the following extract from the 2008 Wienerberger Annual Report. The EBITDA for the Group showed a 20% reduction and the analysis of geographic segments (reported under IFRS 8) showed wide variations, as follows:

Operating EBITDA	2007 €m	2008 €m	Change %
Central-East Europe	282.8	262.0	−7
Central-West Europe	76.5	42.5	−44
North-West Europe	183.7	144.0	−22
North America	35.3	15.1	−57
Investment and Other	−27.1	−23.5	−13
Wienerberger Group	551.2	440.1	−20

The financial review dealt with each change. For example, noting that the housing market in North America, where there had been a 57% change, had not recovered with a resulting fall in the demand for bricks.

The EBITDA margin was also reported for the Group and segments, as follows:

Profitability ratios	2007 %	2008 %
Gross profit to revenues	39.0	34.8
Administrative expenses to revenue	6.0	6.1
Selling expenses to revenue	18.4	19.3
Operating EBITDA margin	22.3	18.1
Operating EBIT margin	14.5	9.9

This shows a decline in EBITDA from 22.3% to 18.1% which is explained as arising from the fall due to lower sales volumes, cost inflation and more flexible pricing policies in some countries as well as the costs related to plant standstills and idle capacity.

27.9.2 What other ratios may be produced based on EBITDA?

We have seen that EBITDA shows the cash impact of earnings. It differs from the Cash flow from operations reported in the Cash flow statement in that it is before adjusting for working capital changes. Other ratios commonly produced are:

● net debt/EBITDA to show the number of years that it would take to pay off the net debt;

● debt service coverage ratio defined as EBITDA/annual debt repayments and interest; and

● EBITDA/interest to show the times interest cover.

Summary

Financial ratio analysis is integral to the assessment and improvement of company performance. Financial ratios help to direct attention to the areas of the business that need additional analysis. In particular, they provide some measure of the profitability and cash position of a company.

Financial ratios can be compared against preceding period's ratios, budgeted ratios for the current period, ratios of other companies in the same industry and the industry sector averages. This comparison is meaningful and decision-useful only when like is compared with like. Users of financial ratios must ensure that the composition of ratios is clearly defined and agreed.

The problem of lack of uniformity in company reports is being progressively addressed by the IASB and FASB with a drive towards global standards.

Ratios are useful only if they are used properly. They are a starting point for further investigations and should be used in conjunction with other sources of information and other analytical techniques. Financial reports are only one of many sources of information available about an enter-prise; others include international, national and industrial statistics and projections, trade association reports, market and consumer surveys, and reports prepared by professional analysts.

Analysts and shareholders who have the full annual report are able to brief themselves by close reading of the narrative in the financial review and notes. In a student situation, the key is to raise relevant questions from the ratios that you have calculated.

In Chapter 28 we consider some additional techniques that complement the pyramid approach to ratio analysis.

REVIEW QUESTIONS

1 Explain how the reader of an annual report prepared for a group might become aware if any subsidiary or associated company was experiencing:

(a) solvency problems;

(b) profitability problems.[14]

2 (a) Explain the uses and limitations of ratio analysis when used to interpret the published financial accounts of a company.

(b) State and express two ratios that can be used to analyse each of the following:

   (i) profitability;

  (ii) liquidity;

  (iii) management control.

(c) Explain briefly points which are important when using ratios to interpret accounts under each of the headings in (b) above.

3 Discuss the importance of the disclosure of exceptional items to the users of the annual report in addition to the operating profit.

4 'Unregulated segmental reporting is commercially dangerous to companies making disclosures.'[15] Discuss.

5 Explain how a reader of the accounts might be able to assess whether the non-current asset base is being maintained.

6 Discuss why a company might decide to report EBITDA in addition to operating profit.

7 Explain in what circumstances an increase in the revenue to current assets might be an indication of a possible problem.

8 Explain in what circumstances a decrease in the rate of non-current asset turnover might be a positive indicator.

9 Discuss why an increasing current ratio might not be an indicator of better working capital management.

10 The management of Alpha plc calculate ROCE using profit before interest and tax as a percentage of net closing assets. Discuss how this definition might be improved.

11 Explain why shareholders might prefer to use Net profit after tax (rather than before tax) when calculating the ROCE.

12 The current ratio has doubled since the previous year. Explain the questions that you would have in mind when reviewing the accounts.

13 The asset turnover rate has increased by 50% over the previous year. Explain the questions you would have in mind and what other ratios would you review?

14 The finance director has proposed that the company buy back its debt, which is 20% below par value, in order to avoid the business showing a loss with this gain on the buyback exceeding the operating loss. Discuss how this would be reflected in the ratios.

EXERCISES

An outline solution is provided on the Companion Website (www.pearsoned.co.uk/elliott-elliott) for exercises marked with an asterisk (*).

Question 1

Belt plc and Braces plc were in the same industry. The following information appeared in their 20X9 accounts:

	Belt €m	Braces €m
Revenue	200	300
Total operating expenses	180	275
Average total assets during 20X9	150	125

Required:
(a) Calculate the following ratios for each company and show the numerical relationship between them:
  (i) Their rate of return on the average total assets.
  (ii) The net profit percentages.
  (iii) The ratio of revenue to average total assets.
(b) Comment on the relative performance of the two companies.
(c) State any additional information you would require as:
  (i) A potential shareholder.
  (ii) A potential loan creditor.

Question 2

Saddam Ltd is considering the possibility of diversifying its operations and has identified three firms in the same industrial sector as potential takeover targets. The following information in respect of the companies has been extracted from their most recent financial statements.

	Ali Ltd	Baba Ltd	Camel Ltd
ROCE before tax %	22.1	23.7	25.0
Net profit %	12.0	12.5	3.75
Asset turnover ratio	1.45	1.16	3.73
Gross profit %	20.0	25.0	10.0
Sales/non-current assets	4.8	2.2	11.6
Sales/current assets	2.1	5.2	5.5
Current ratio	3.75	1.4	1.5
Acid test ratio	2.25	0.4	0.9
Average number of weeks' receivables outstanding	5.6	6.0	4.8
Average number of weeks' inventory held	12.0	19.2	4.0
Ordinary dividend %	10.0	15.0	30.0
Dividend cover	4.3	5.0	1.0

Required:
(a) Prepare a report for the directors of Saddam Ltd, assessing the performance of the three companies from the information provided and identifying areas which you consider require further investigation before a final decision is made.
(b) Discuss briefly why a firm's statement of financial position is unlikely to show the true market value of the business.

Question 3

(a) The following ratios have been extracted from an analysis of the consolidated accounts of three companies – North, South and East:

	North	South	East
Profit/Sales × 100	5%	4%	3%
Asset turnover	5 times	3 times	4 times
Financial leverage	2	4	5

Required:
Comment on the respective performance of each of the three companies.

(b) 'The consolidation of financial statements hides rather than provides information.' Discuss.

* Question 4

The following are the accounts of Bouncy plc, a company that manufactures playground equipment, for the year ended 30 November 20X6.

Statements of comprehensive income for years ended 30 November

	20X6	20X5
	£000	£000
Profit before interest and tax	2,200	1,570
Interest expense	170	150
Profit before tax	2,030	1,420
Taxation	730	520
Profit after tax	1,300	900
Dividends paid	250	250
Retained profit	1,050	650

Statements of financial position as at 30 November 20X6

	20X6	20X5
	£000	£000
Non-current assets (written-down value)	6,350	5,600
Current assets		
Inventories	2,100	2,070
Receivables	1,710	1,540
	10,160	9,210
Creditors: amounts due within one year		
Trade payables	1,040	1,130
Taxation	550	450
Bank overdraft	370	480
Total assets less current liabilities	8,200	7,150
Creditors: amounts due after more than one year		
10% debentures 20X7/20X8	1,500	1,500
	6,700	5,650
Capital and reserves		
Share capital: ordinary shares of 50p fully paid up	3,000	3,000
Share premium	750	750
Retained earnings	2,950	1,900
	6,700	5,650

The directors are considering two schemes to raise £6,000,000 in order to repay the debentures and finance expansion estimated to increase profit before interest and tax by £900,000. It is proposed to make a dividend of 6p per share whether funds are raised by equity or loan. The two schemes are:

1 an issue of 13% debentures redeemable in 30 years;

2 a rights issue at £1.50 per share. The current market price is £1.80 per share (20X5: £1.50; 20X4: £1.20).

Required:

(a) Calculate the return on equity and any three investment ratios of interest to a potential investor.

(b) Calculate three ratios of interest to a potential long-term lender.

(c) Report briefly on the performance and state of the business from the viewpoint of a potential shareholder and lender using the ratios calculated above and explain any weaknesses in these ratios.

(d) Advise management which scheme they should adopt on the basis of your analysis above and explain what other information may need to be considered when making the decision.

Question 5

You are informed that the non-current assets totalled €350,000, current liabilities €156,000, the opening retained earnings totalled €103,000, the administration expenses totalled €92,680 and that the available ratios were the current ratio 1.5, the acid test ratio 0.75, the trade receivables collection period was six weeks, the gross profit was 20% and the net assets turned over 1.4 times.

Required:
Prepare the statement of financial position from the above information.

* Question 6

Liz Collier runs a small delicatessen. Her profits in recent years have remained steady at around £21,000 per annum. This type of business generally earns a uniform rate of net profit on sales of 20%.

Recently, Liz has found that this level of profitability is insufficient to enable her to maintain her desired lifestyle. She is considering three options to improve her profitability.

Option 1 Liz will borrow £10,000 from her bank at an interest rate of 10% per annum, payable at the end of each financial year. The whole capital sum will be repaid to the bank at the end of the second year. The money will be used to hire the services of a marketing agency for two years. It is anticipated that turnover will increase by 40% as a result of the additional advertising.

Option 2 Liz will form a partnership with Joan Mercer, who also runs a local delicatessen. Joan's net profits have remained at £12,000 per annum since she started in business five years ago. The sales of each shop in the combined business are expected to increase by 20% in the first year and then remain steady. The costs of the amalgamation will amount to £6,870, which will be written off in the first year. The partnership agreement will allow each partner a partnership salary of 2% of the revised turnover of their own shop. Remaining profits will be shared in the ratio of Liz 3/5, Joan 2/5.

Option 3 Liz will reduce her present sales by 80% and take up a franchise to sell Nickson's Munchy Sausage. The franchise will cost £80,000. This amount will be borrowed from her bank. The annual interest rate will be 10% flat rate based on the amount borrowed. Sales of Munchy Sausage yield a net profit to sales percentage of 30%. Sales are expected to be £50,000 in the first year, but should increase annually at a rate of 15% for the following three years then remain constant.

Required:
(a) Prepare a financial statement for Liz comparing the results of each option for each of the next two years.
(b) Advise Liz which option may be the best to choose.
(c) Discuss any other factors that Liz should consider under each of the options.

Question 7

Sally Gorden seeks your assistance to decide whether she should invest in Ruby plc or Sapphire plc. Both companies are quoted on the London Stock Exchange. Their shares were listed on 20 June 20X4 as Ruby 475p and Sapphire 480p.

The performance of these two companies during the year ended 30 June 20X4 is summarised as follows:

	Ruby plc £000	Sapphire plc £000
Operating profit	588	445
Interest and similar charges	(144)	(60)
	444	385
Taxation	(164)	(145)
Profit after taxation	280	240
Interim dividend paid	(30)	(40)
Preference dividend proposed	(90)	—
Ordinary dividend proposed	(60)	(120)
Retained earnings for the year	100	80

The companies have been financed on 30 June 20X4 as follows:

	Ruby plc £000	Sapphire plc £000
Ordinary shares of 50p each	1,000	1,500
15% preference shares of £1 each	600	—
Share premium account	60	—
Retained earnings	250	450
17% debentures	800	—
12% debentures	—	500
	2,710	2,450

On 1 October 20X3 Ruby plc issued 500,000 ordinary shares of 50p each at a premium of 20%. On 1 April 20X4 Sapphire plc made a 1 for 2 bonus issue. Apart from these, there has been no change in the issued capital of either company during the year.

Required:
(a) Calculate the earnings per share (EPS) of each company.
(b) Determine the price/earnings ratio (PE) of each company.
(c) Based on the PE ratio alone, which company's shares would you recommend to Sally?
(d) On the basis of appropriate accounting ratios (which should be calculated), identify three other matters Sally should take account of before she makes her choice.
(e) Describe the advantages and disadvantages of gearing.

Question 8

The statements of financial position, cash flows, income and movements of non-current assets of Dragon plc for the year ended 30 September 20X6 are set out below:

(i) Statement of financial position

	20X5 £000	20X5 £000	20X6 £000	20X6 £000
Tangible non-current assets				
Freehold land and buildings, at cost		1,200		1,160
Plant and equipment, at net book value		700		1,700
		1,900		2,860
Current assets				
Inventory	715		1,020	
Trade receivables	590		826	
Short-term investments	52		—	
Cash at bank and in hand	15		47	
	1,372		1,893	
Current liabilities				
Trade payables	520		940	
Taxation payable	130		45	
Dividends payable	90		105	
	740		1,090	
Net current assets		632		803
		2,532		3,663
Long-term liability and provisions				
8% debentures, 20X9		500		1,500
Provisions for deferred tax		100		180
		1,932		1,983
Capital and reserves				
Ordinary shares of £1 each		1,400		1,400
Share premium account		250		250
Retained earnings		282		333
		1,932		1,983

(ii) Statement of income (extract) for the years ended 30 September 20X6

		20X6
EBITDA		1,161
Depreciation		660
Operating profit		501
Interest payable: debentures		150
Profit before taxation		351
Income tax		125
Profit attributable to shareholders		226
Dividends : paid	70	
: proposed	105	175
Retained earnings for year		51
Retained earnings b/f		282
Retained earnings c/f		333

(iii) Statement of cash flows

Net cash flow from operating activities		1,033
Interest paid	(150)	
Income taxes paid	(130)	(280)
Net cash from operating activities		753
Cash flows from investing activities		
Purchase of property, plant and equipment	(1,620)	
Net cash used in investing activities		(1,620)
Cash flows from financing activities		
Proceeds from sale of short-term investments	59	
Proceeds from long-term borrowings	1,000	
Dividends paid	(160)	
Net cash from financing activities		899
Net increase in cash and cash equivalents		32
Cash and cash equivalents at the beginning of the period		15
Cash and cash equivalents at the end of the period		47

(iv) Tangible non-current assets (or PPE)

The movements in the year were as follows:

	Freehold land and buildings £000	Plant and machinery £000	Total £000
Cost			
At 1 October 20X5	2,000	1,600	3,600
Additions	—	1,620	1,620
At 30 September 20X6	**2,000**	**3,220**	**5,220**
Depreciation			
At 1 October 20X5	800	900	1,700
Charge during the year	40	620	660
At 30 September 20X6	**840**	**1,520**	**2,360**
Net book value			
Beginning of year	1,200	700	1,900
End of year	**1,160**	**1,700**	**2,860**

You are also provided with the following information:

(i) There was a debenture issue on 1 October 20X5 with interest payable on 30 September each year.

(ii) An interim dividend of £70,000 was paid on 1 July 20X6.

(iii) The short-term investment was sold for £59,000 on 1 October 20X5.

(iv) Business activity increased significantly to meet increased consumer demand.

Required:

(a) Prepare a Reconciliation of operating profit to net cash inflow from operating activities.

(b) Discuss the financial developments at Dragon plc during the financial year ended 30 September 20X6 with particular regard to its financial position at the year end and prospects for the following financial year – supported by appropriate financial ratios.

Question 9

Amalgamated Engineering plc makes specialised machinery for several industries. In recent years, the company has faced severe competition from overseas businesses, and its sales volume has hardly changed. The company has recently applied for an increase in its bank overdraft limit from £750,000 to £1,500,000. The bank manager has asked you, as the bank's credit analyst, to look at the company's application.

You have the following information:

(i) Statements of financial position as at 31 December 20X5 and 20X6:

	20X5		20X6	
	£000	£000	£000	£000
Tangible non-current assets				
Freehold land and buildings, at cost		1,800		1,800
Plant and equipment, at net book value		3,150		3,300
		4,950		5,100
Current assets				
Inventory	1,125		1,500	
Trade receivables	825		1,125	
Short-term investments	300		—	
	2,250		2,625	
Current liabilities				
Bank overdraft	225		675	
Trade payables	300		375	
Taxation payable	375		300	
Dividends payable	225		225	
	1,125		1,575	
Net current assets		1,125		1,050
		6,075		6,150
Long-term liability				
8% debentures, 20X9		1,500		1,500
		4,575		4,650
Capital and reserves				
Ordinary shares of £1 each		2,250		2,250
Share premium account		750		750
Retained earnings		1,575		1,650
		4,575		4,650

(ii) Statements of comprehensive income for the years ended 31 December 20X5 and 20X6:

	20X5		20X6	
	£000	£000	£000	£000
Turnover		6,300		6,600
Cost of sales: materials	1,500		1,575	
: labour	2,160		2,280	
: production: overheads	750		825	
		4,410		4,680
		1,890		1,920
Administrative expenses		1,020		1,125
Operating profit		870		795
Investment income		15		—
		885		795
Interest payable: debentures	120		120	
: bank overdraft	15		75	
		135		195
Profit before taxation		750		600
Taxation		375		300
Profit attributable to shareholders		375		300
Dividends		225		225
Retained earnings for year		150		75

You are also provided with the following information:

(iii) The general price level rose on average by 10% between 20X5 and 20X6. Average wages also rose by 10% during this period.

(iv) The debenture stock is secured by a fixed charge over the freehold land and buildings, which have recently been valued at £3,000,000. The bank overdraft is unsecured.

(v) Additions to plant and equipment in 20X6 amounted to £450,000: depreciation provided in that year was £300,000.

Required:
(a) Prepare a Statement of cash flows for the year ended 31 December 20X6.
(b) Calculate appropriate ratios to use as a basis for a report to the bank manager.
(c) Draft the outline of a report for the bank manager, highlighting key areas you feel should be the subject of further investigation. Mention any additional information you need, and where appropriate refer to the limitations of conventional historical cost accounts.
(d) On receiving the draft report the bank manager advised that he also required the following three cash-based ratios:
  (i) Debt service coverage ratio defined as EBITDA/annual debt repayments and interest.
  (ii) Cash flow from operations to current liabilities.
  (iii) Cash recovery rate defined as ((cash flow from operations proceeds from sale of noncurrent assets)/average gross assets) × 100.
  The director has asked you to explain why the bank manager has requested this additional information given that he has already been supplied with profit-based ratios.

Question 10

The Housing Department of Chaldon District Council has invited tenders for re-roofing 80 houses on an estate. Chaldon Direct Services (CDS) is one of the Council's direct services organisations and it has submitted a tender for this contract, as have several contractors from the private sector.

The Council has been able to narrow the choice of contractor to the four tenderers who have submitted the lowest bids, as follows:

	£
Nutfield & Sons	398,600
Chaldon Direct Services	401,850
Tandridge Tilers Ltd	402,300
Redhill Roofing Contractors plc	406,500

The tender evaluation process requires that the three private tenderers be appraised on the basis of financial soundness and quality of work. These tenderers were required to provide their latest final accounts (year ended 31 March 20X4) for this appraisal; details are as follows:

	Nutfield & Sons	Tandridge Tilers Ltd	Redhill Roofing Contractors plc
Profit and loss account for year ended 31 March 20X4			
	£	£	£
Turnover	611,600	1,741,200	3,080,400
Direct costs	(410,000)	(1,190,600)	(1,734,800)
Other operating costs	(165,000)	(211,800)	(811,200)
Interest	—	(85,000)	(96,000)
Net profit before taxation	36,600	253,800	438,400
Statement of financial position as at 31 March 20X4			
	£	£	£
Non-current assets (net book value)	55,400	1,542,400	2,906,800
Inventories and work-in-progress	26,700	149,000	449,200
Receivables	69,300	130,800	240,600
Bank	(11,000)	10,400	(6,200)
Payables	(92,600)	(140,600)	(279,600)
Proposed dividend	—	(91,800)	(70,000)
Loan	—	(800,000)	(1,200,000)
	47,800	800,200	2,040,800
Capital	47,800	—	—
Ordinary shares @ £1 each	—	250,000	1,000,000
Reserves	—	550,200	1,040,800
	47,800	800,200	2,040,800

Nutfield & Sons employ a workforce of six operatives and have been used by the Council for four small maintenance contracts worth between £60,000 and £75,000 which they have completed to an appropriate standard. Tandridge Tilers Ltd have been employed by the Council on a contract for the replacement of flat roofs on a block of flats, but there have been numerous complaints about the standard of the work. Redhill Roofing Contractors plc is a company which has not been employed by the Council in the past and, as much of its work has been carried out elsewhere, its quality of work is not known.

CDS has been suffering from the effects of increasing competition in recent years and achieved a return on capital employed of only 3.5% in the previous financial year. CDS's manager has successfully renegotiated more beneficial service level agreements with the Council's central support departments with effect from 1 April 20X4. CDS has also reviewed its non-current asset base which has resulted in the disposal of a depot which was surplus to requirements and in the rationalisation of vehicles and plant. The consequence of this is that CDS's average capital employed for 20X4/X5 is likely to be some 15% lower than in 20X3/X4.

A further analysis of the tender bids is provided below:

	Nutfield & Sons £	Chaldon Direct Services £	Tandridge Tilers Ltd £	Redhill Roofing Contractors plc £
Labour	234,000	251,400	303,600	230,400
Materials	140,000	100,000	80,000	140,000
Overheads (including profit)	24,600	50,450	18,700	36,100

The Council's Client Services Committee can reject tenders on financial and/or quality grounds. However, each tender has to be appraised on these criteria and reasons for acceptance or rejection must be justified in the appraisal process.

Required:

In your capacity as accountant responsible for reporting to the Client Services Committee, draft a report to the Committee evaluating the tender bids and recommending to whom the contract should be awarded.

(CIPFA)

Question 11

Chelsea plc has embarked on a programme of growth through acquisitions and has identified Kensington Ltd and Wimbledon Ltd as companies in the same industrial sector, as potential targets. Using recent financial statements of both Kensington and Wimbledon and further information obtained from a trade association, Chelsea plc has managed to build up the following comparability table:

	Kensington	Wimbledon	Industrial average
Profitability ratios			
ROCE before tax %	22	28	20
Return on equity %	18	22	15
Net profit margin %	11	5	7
Gross profit ratio %	25	12	20
Activity ratios			
Total assets turnover = times	1.5	4.0	2.5
Non-current asset turnover = times	2.3	12.0	5.1
Receivables collection period in weeks	8.0	5.1	6.5
Inventoryholding period in weeks	21.0	4.0	13.0
Liquidity ratios			
Current ratio	1.8	1.7	2.8
Acid test	0.5	0.9	1.3
Debt–equity ratio %	80.0	20.0	65.0

Required:

(a) Prepare a performance report for the two companies for consideration by the directors of Chelsea plc indicating which of the two companies you consider to be a better acquisition.

(b) Indicate what further information is needed before a final decision can be made.

References

1 I. Griffiths, *Creative Accounting*, Sidgwick & Jackson, 1986.

2 *Ibid.*

3 M. Stead, *How to Use Company Accounts for Successful Investment Decisions*, FT Pitman Publishing, 1995, pp. 134–136.

4 www.shareholderexecutive.gov.uk/publications/pdf/annualreport0708.pdf

5 N. Cope, 'Bitter battles in the beer business', *Accountancy*, May 1993, p. 32.

6 www.managementtoday.co.uk/search/article/410545/uk-gearing-down/

7 *Company REFS – Really Essential Financial Statistics*: Tables Volume devised by Jim Slater, Hemmington Scott.

8 *Handbook of Market Leaders*, Extel Financial Ltd.

9 *Key Business Ratios: The Guide to British Business Performance*, Dun & Bradstreet Ltd.

10 *The Company Guide*, HS Financial Publishing.

11 See www.onesource.com/.

12 www.sec.gov/litigation/complaints/comp17954.htm

13 M. Darrough and S. Rangan, 'Do Insiders Manipulate Earnings When They Sell Their Shares in an Initial Public Offering?', *Journal of Accounting Research*, March 2005, vol. 43, no.1, pp. 1–33.

14 P. Anderson, 'Are you ready for ratio analysis?', *Accountancy*, September 1996, p. 92.

15 G.J. Kelly, 'Unregulated segment reporting: Australian evidence', *British Accounting Review*, 26(3), 1994, p. 217.

CHAPTER 28

Analytical analysis – selective use of ratios

28.1 Introduction

The main purpose of this chapter is to explain the selective use of ratios required to satisfy specific user objectives.

Objectives

By the end of the chapter, you should be able to:

- prepare and interpret common size statements of income and financial position;
- explain the use of ratios in determining whether a company is shariah compliant;
- explain the use of ratios in debt covenants;
- critically discuss various scoring systems for predicting corporate failure;
- critically discuss remuneration performance criterion;
- calculate the value of unquoted investments;
- critically discuss the role of credit rating agencies.

28.2 Improvement of information for shareholders

There have been a number of discussion papers, reports and voluntary code provisions from professional firms and regulators making recommendations on how to provide additional information. These have some common themes which include: (a) making financial information more understandable and easier to analyse; (b) improving the reliability of the historical financial data; and (c) the opportunity for investors to form a view as to the business's future prospects.

28.2.1 Making financial information more understandable and easier to analyse

There has been a view that users should bring a reasonable level of understanding when reading an annual report. This view could be supported when transactions were relatively simple. It no longer applies when even professional accountants comment that the only people who understand some of the disclosures are the technical staff of the regulator and the professional accounting firms. Users need the financial information to be made more accessible and easier to interpret.

28.2.2 Making the information accessible

The ICAS (the Institute of Chartered Accountants in Scotland) produced a report in 1999, *Business Reporting: the Inevitable Change?* which proposed that financial and non-financial business information should be more timely, more forward looking and more accessible to non-expert users to assist them to understand the drivers of corporate performance. This would also help ensure the equal treatment of all investors and improve accountability for stewardship, investor protection and the usefulness of financial reporting. Such information would improve the level of transparency but there would be constraints arising from commercial confidentiality and potential litigation.

28.2.3 Making the information easier to interpret

Investors do not currently have the means to analyse the financial data easily. Traditionally attention has focused on financial data which have been paper-based. Investors have had to be dependent on analysts or access to the various commercial databases, e.g. Datastream, for data in electronic format for further analysis.

The Internet is about to change this by focusing on how to report rather than what to report. It has the capacity to give investors the means to readily analyse the financial data by providing it in a uniform format which can be easily transported into other systems, e.g. Excel. It achieves this through the Extensible Business Reporting Language (XBRL) which has been developed to allow information to be described uniformly and tagged. A demonstration website has been developed by Microsoft, NASDAQ and PricewaterhouseCoopers.[1] This is discussed in Chapter 29.

28.2.4 The reliability of current financial information

Investors rely on annual reports and the various mid-year reports and are entitled to assume that these give a fair view of a company's financial performance and position. However, following various accounting scandals such as Enron, there is a lack of confidence among investors that the information provided is a fair representation. There is a need for greater transparency, for example, reporting the commercial effect of any off balance sheet transactions that have a material impact on a company's viability and continuing existence.

28.2.5 Audit independence needs to be strengthened

Many of the schemes which have kept liabilities off the statement of financial position have been actively promoted by the auditors. This has meant that the auditors are not seen as protecting the interests of the shareholders. The profession is aware of this view held by the public and of the existence of an expectation gap that needs addressing. This is discussed further in Chapter 30.

28.2.6 Future business prospects

Shareholders rely on information provided by companies when they make their investment decisions. Traditionally this information has been historical and the narrative in the annual report has been to explain what has happened commercially during the financial year and provide sensitive information such as the make-up of directors' remuneration. The pressure now is for managers to share their assessment of future business prospects so that investors can make informed investment decisions.

28.2.7 Disclosure of strategies

In 1999 the ICAEW produced a report *No Surprises: The Case for Better Risk Reporting*. This report recognised the need for management to disclose their strategies and how they managed risk whilst stating that the intention was not to encourage profit smoothing but rather a better management of risk and a better understanding by investors of volatility.

28.3 Disclosure of risks and focus on relevant ratios

The ICAEW has proposed that listed companies should be at the forefront of improved risk reporting in financial statements. In a 1998 discussion paper, *Financial Reporting of Risk*,[2] it attempted to encourage the inclusion of better-quality information on business risks so that users of accounts had a better understanding of the risks underlying a business's activity. There is a benefit to the company in that the cost of capital is lower where there is more transparency and disclosure of risk management. With specific reference to ratio analysis, the discussion paper argued that 'the preparation of a statement of business risk should help preparers and users to focus on the ratios that are most relevant to the particular business risks that are most relevant to individual companies' (para. 6.16).

28.3.1 Focus on relevant ratios

In the previous chapter we applied a pyramid approach to the calculation of ratios covering profitability, liquidity and asset turnover rates.

In this chapter we are looking at targeting the ratios that are relevant to the particular interests of the user. We look at the use of techniques which raise flags indicating which of the ratios might be particularly relevant to the analysis of a specific individual company's financial statements.

We will start with the initial analytical overview that an auditor or potential investor might carry out. This will be followed by the use of ratios when identifying shariah compliant investments, companies at risk of failing and valuing shares in an unquoted company.

28.3.2 The initial overview

When beginning to analyse a company's financial statements it is a good starting point to prepare a common size statement of financial position which is simply a vertical analysis to assess the strength of the statement of financial position with assets and liabilities each shown as a percentage of a base figure.

A horizontal analysis is then carried out on areas that require further investigation.

28.3.3 Vertical analysis – common size statements

The vertical analysis approach highlights the structure of the statement of financial position by presenting non-current assets, working capital, debt and equity as a percentage of debt plus equity. It allows us to form a view on the financing of the business. In particular the extent to which a business is reliant on debt to finance its non-current assets. In times of recesssion this is of particular interest and is described as indicating the strength of the financial position.

Illustration – Vertigo plc

We will illustrate with using the statement of financial position of Vertigo plc as at 1 April 20X7. Let us assume that you are a trainee in an accounting firm that has been approached by a client to give an initial view on a possible investment in Vertigo. Vertigo is a family company. The major shareholder is nearing retirement and the younger family members are not interested in managing the business. The client is concerned that, with companies failing in the recession, the business might not be financed adequately and, with an older management team, might not be as efficient as she would hope. Apparently, Vertigo is seeking additional funds to replace some of its equipment which will soon need to be replaced.

There is a draft statement of financial position available and the auditors are soon due to start their audit.

Draft statement of financial position as at 1 April 20X7

	£000
Non-current assets:	
Equipment	2,240
Motor vehicles	441
Investments	340
	3,021
Current assets:	
Inventory	398
Trade receivables	912
Cash and bank	11
	4,342

	£000
Equity and reserves:	
Ordinary shares of 50p each	3,000
Retained earnings	262
5% Debentures	600
Current liabilities:	
Trade payables	398
Accrued expenses	12
Taxation	29
Bank overdraft	41
	4,342

Common size statement – making an initial assessment of the financial structure

as at 1 April 20X7

	£000	%
Non-current assets	3,021	78.2
Working capital	841	21.8
Total	3,862	100
Equity	3,262	84.5
Debt	600	15.5
Total	3,862	100

From this we can see that the company has a strong statement of financial position in that the long-term assets are fully financed by shareholders with a contribution also made towards funding the working capital. We can then express this in terms of the ratios from the previous chapter by calculating the debt/equity ratio – in this example it is reasonably low at 18.4%. First impression is that the financial structure is sound.

We can then extend this by restating assets, liabilities and equity as a percentage of total assets to see the relationships within the total assets, as follows:

	£000	%
Non-current assets	3,021	69.5
Current assets	1,321	30.5
Total	4,342	100
Equity	3,262	75.1
Debt	600	13.8
Current liabilities	480	11.1
Total	4,342	100

The long-term debt to total liabilities ratio is 13.8% and we can see the current position appears relatively high with a current ratio of 2.75:1.

Vertigo, to support its search for additional funds, has also produced a forecast statement for the following year as shown below.

Vertigo's statements for 20X7 and 20X8 are as follows:

	20X7 £000	20X8 £000
Non-current assets:		
Machinery	2,240	2,100
Motor vehicles	441	394
Investments	340	340
	3,021	2,834
Current assets:		
Inventory	398	563
Trade receivables	912	1,181
Cash and bank	11	9
	4,342	4,587
		£000
Equity and reserves:		
Ordinary shares of 50p each	3,000	3,000
Retained earnings	262	353
	3,262	3,353
5% Debentures (repayable in 8 years)	600	600
Current liabilities:		
Trade payables	398	498
Accrued expenses	12	15
Taxation	29	24
Bank overdraft	41	97
	4,342	4,587

Inter-period comparisons of financial structure
Both years are restated in common size format as follows:

	20X7 £,000	20X7 %	20X8 £,000	20X8 %
Non-current assets	3,021	69.5	2,834	61.8
Current assets	1,321	30.5	1,753	38.2
Total	4,342	100	4,587	100
Equity	3,262	75.1	3,353	73.1
Debt	600	13.8	600	13.1
Current liabilities	480	11.1	634	13.8
Total	4,342	100	4,587	100

This indicates that the financial strength is maintained in terms of the debt/equity relationship. The financing from current liabilities has increased and we need to review the current position. The current ratio has increased slightly to 2.78:1 and needs to be investigated and compared with an industry average.

There is no indication of a financing problem. However, it doesn't tell us whether the working capital is properly controlled. For that we would resort to the turnover ratios discussed in the previous chapter in relation to inventory, receivable and payable turnover rates.

28.3.4 Horizontal analysis

A horizontal analysis looks at the percentage change that has occurred. In this case it would be helpful to prepare this for the area that seems to require closer investigation i.e. current asset and liabilities. The anlysis is as follows:

	20X7 £,000	20X8 £,000	% change
Current assets:			
Inventory	398	563	+41.5
Trade receivables	912	1,181	+29.5
Cash and bank	11	9	−18.1
Trade payables	398	498	+25.1
Accrued expenses	12	15	+25.0
Taxation	29	24	−17.2
Bank overdraft	41	97	+136.5

This indicates that although there has been a 5% increase in sales, there has been a build up of inventory and the credit allowed and taken has increased significantly.

The next step would be to extract the turnover ratios for inventory, trade receivables and payables and ascertain the terms and limit of the overdraft.

These would be as follows showing that receivables credit period has been extended from 101 days to 126 days and payables period extended from 60 days to 69 days.

	20X7 Times	20X8 Times
Current assets:		
Inventory turnover:		
Cost of sales/Average inventory		
2,240/((253 + 398)/2)	6.9	
2,458/((398 + 563)/2)		5.1
Trade receivables turnover		
Sales/closing trade receivables		
3,296/912	3.6	
3,461/1,181		2.9
Trade payables:		
Purchases/Closing trade payables		
2,385/398	6.0	
2,623/498		5.3

The financial position is strong in relation to long-term debt to equity in both years. However, the increase in working capital has led to a greater reliance on bank overdraft facilities and is a cause for concern.

Further information is required to determine the risks arising from the inventory. Why has the increase occurred? Is there a greater risk of obsolescence or further pressure to reduce the gross profit margin to move the inventory?

Also with regard to the trade receivables build up. Has there been a change in the credit terms? Has that been a formal arrangement? Has the company changed its criteria for creating an allowance for bad debts? Bad debts have fallen but is this due to a reluctance to chase late payment?

28.3.5 Overview of the cost structures – vertical analysis

Preparing a common size statements of income gives an indication of the cost structure so that we an see the relative significance of costs.

The income statements of Vertigo plc for 20X7 and 20X8 are as follows:

	20X7 £000	20X8 £000
Sales revenue	3,296	3,461
Inventory – 1.4.20X7	253	398
Purchases	2,385	2,623
Inventory – 31.3.20X8	(398)	(563)
Cost of goods sold	(2,240)	(2,458)
Gross profit	1,056	1,003
Distribution costs:		
Depreciation	239	187
Bad debts	32	17
Advertising	94	24
Administrative expenses:		
Rent	60	60
Salaries & wages	316	362
Miscellaneous expenses	212	237
Operating profit	103	116
Dividend received	51	
Profit before taxation	154	116
Taxation	(39)	(25)
Profit after taxation	115	91

An overview is obtained by restating by function into a common size statement format as follows:

	20X7 £000	20X7 %	20X8 £000	20X8 %
Sales	3,296	100.0	3,461	100.0
Cost of sales	2,240	68.0	2,458	71.0
Total gross profit	1,056	32.0	1,003	29.0
Distribution costs	365	11.1	228	6.6
Administration expenses	588	17.8	659	19.0
Net profit before tax	103	3.1	116	3.4

We can see that there has been a change in the cost structure with a fall in the gross profit from 32% to 29% compensated for by a significant fall in the distribution costs.

28.3.6 Overview of the cost structures – horizontal analysis

An overview is obtained by calculating the percentage change as follows:

	20X7 £000	20X8 £000	% change
Sales	3,296	3,461	+5.0
Cost of sales	2,240	2,458	+9.7
Total gross profit	1,056	1,003	-5.0
Distribution costs	365	228	37.8
Administration expenses	588	659	+12.1
Net profit before tax	103	116	+12.6

Sales have increased by 5% and operating profit by 12.6%. The gross profit margin has fallen with the 9.7% increase in the cost of sales. This requires further enquiry. Has there been a change in the selling price? Has there been a change to maintain sales volume at the expense of the profit margin? Has there been discounting or longer running sales? Has there been a change in the sales mix? Have purchase prices risen? Have there been currency effects? Has there been a change in suppliers? If so, why?

Targeted for further enquiry

The change in both distribution costs and administrative expenses are significant and not in line with the increase in sales. This means that the detailed costs within both these headings require further analysis.

28.3.7 Analysis of the percentage changes in individual expenses

For our illustration we have assumed that it is an enquiry for a client considering investing. The detailed analysis that we are now preparing would also be a routine procedure when designing audit tests as it targets areas of significant change.

Horizontal analysis

	20X7 £000	20X8 £000	% change
Sales revenue	3,296	3,461	+5.0
Inventory – Opening	253	398	
Purchases	2,385	2,623	+10.0
Inventory – Closing	(398)	(563)	+41.5
Cost of goods sold	(2,240)	(2,458)	+9.7
Gross profit	1,056	1,003	−5.0
Distribution costs:			
Depreciation	239	187	−2.2
Bad debts	32	17	−46.9
Advertising	94	24	−74.5
Administrative expenses:			
Rent	60	60	
Salaries and wages	316	362	+14.6
Miscellaneous expenses	212	237	+11.8
Operating profit	103	116	+12.6

The changes are then reviewed for (a) distribution costs an (b) administrative expenses.

(a) Review of distribution costs

It is interesting to see that discretionary costs in the form of Advertising have been reduced by 74.5%. If the Advertising had been maintained at 20X7 levels the operating profit would be reduced by £70,000 to £46,000 which would have shown a fall from the previous year of 55% rather than an an increase of 12.6%.

There should be further enquiry to establish whether (a) the normal level over the previous three years – whether there was heavier advertising in 20X7 to achieve the 5% increase in sales in the light of the company's intention to attempt to obtain further investment in 20X8 and (b) whether this is likely to have an adverse effect on 20X9 sales and (c) what the company's reason was for reduced spending. This is more of a commercial relevance than audit relevance.

Bad debts have fallen although there has been an increase in sales and the credit period has increased to 126 days. This raises a query as to the company's credit control and possibility of more bad debts.

(b) Review of administration expenses

Salaries and administration expenses have increased significantly.

Administration costs have risen. Enquire whether this is due to salary increases or taking on extra staff – possibly connected with the increase in trade receivables and inventory holding.

From an audit point of view, attention would be directed towards the audit implications for salaries. For example, verification of existence of staff, approval of any rate increases and internal control over payments. Miscellaneous expenses were found to include loan interest.

28.3.8 Report following common size exercise

The long-term financing as evidenced by the debt/equity ratio is sound. There is not an excessive level of debt.

The current position needs further enquiry. There is a growing overdraft. However, the current ratio is high at 2.75:1 and if the trade receivables are recoverable and if the credit period were reduced to 90 days the overdaft would be eliminated.

The control over working capital requires further enquiry. The days credit allowed and taken and inventory turnover rates have been calculated. This appears to indicate a lack of control with the build up of receivables – it is uncertain if this is deliberate or a sign of difficulty in obtaining payment. There is also a decrease in the inventory turnover rate – this might be due to inefficiency or, of more concern, indicate that the market for the product is slipping.

The costs need exploring further. In particular the commercial impact of the fall in advertising needs to be assessed.

Stress testing

There needs to be a sensitivity check to see the effect of a fall in sales. For example, if there were to be a fall of 10% in 20X9 resulting from the cut in advertising, what would be the impact on operating profit and interest cover? Assuming that cost of sales remains at 71% and distribution costs and administrative expenses (excluding loan interest) are relatively fixed, then the operating profit would fall to £45,700 (20X8 £146,000 being £116,000 + interest £30,000) and interest cover would fall to 1.5 (45,700/30,000) from 4.9 (146,000/30,000).

28.4 Shariah compliant companies – why ratios are important

This use of ratios is included because of the growing importance of investment in shariah compliant companies. Islamic banking is gaining popularity all over the world with a forecast that investments worth $100 billion will be made globally in this system by 2010. There are many major multinationals included in shariah indices including companies such as Google Inc., TOTAL SA, BP plc, Exxon Mobil Corp., Petroleo Brasileiro, Novartis AG, Roche Holding, GlaxoSmithKline plc, BHP Billiton Ltd, Siemens AG, Samsung Eectronics, International Business Machines Corp, Nestle SA, and Coca-Cola. There are also major private equity investors. For example, the following is an extract titled *Shari'ah Compliant Private Equity Finance*:[3]

> Major private equity investors in the Gulf include the Gulf Finance House and Investment Dar of Kuwait . . . Investment Dar and Dubai based investment companies have Shari'ah boards . . . Investment Dar is perhaps the best known internationally as a result of its purchase of Aston Martin, the British based luxury sports car manufacturer. It has extensive interests in real estate . . . With its working capital exceeding KD 500 million, ($1.85 billion) Investment Dar is well positioned to undertake strategic private equity investments.

28.4.1 The criteria for determining that a company is shariah compliant

Islam, like some other religions, commands followers to avoid consumption of alcohol and pork and so Muslims do not condone investments in those industries. There is screening to check that (a) business activities are not prohibited and (b) certain of the financial ratios do not exceed specified limits.

Investors interested in establishing whether a company is shariah compliant are assisted by the service provided by various Islamic Indices where the constituent companies have been screened to confirm that they are shariah compliant with reference to the nature of the business and debt ratios.

A number of indices have been created which only include companies that are shariah compliant such as the MSCI[4] Global Islamic Indices and the Dow Jones[5] Islamic index. It is interesting to look at the methodology in preparing these two indices.

28.4.2 The MSCI Islamic Indices – methodology

The indices are compiled after:

- screening companies to confirm that their business activities are not prohibited (or fall within the 5% permitted threshold);
- calculating three financial ratios based on total assets; and
- calculating a dividend adjustment factor which results in more relevant benchmarks, as they reflect the total return to an Islamic portfolio net of dividend purification.

MCSI explains its methodology as follows.

Business activity screening

Shariah investment principles do not allow investment in companies which are directly active in, or derive more than 5% of their revenue (cumulatively) from, the following activities ('prohibited activities'):

- Alcohol: distillers, vintners and producers of alcoholic beverages, including producers of beer and malt liquors, owners and operators of bars and pubs.
- Tobacco: cigarettes and other tobacco products manufacturers and retailers.
- Pork-related products: companies involved in the manufacture and retail of pork products.
- Conventional financial services – an extensive range including commercial banks, investment banks, insurance companies, consumer finance such as credit cards and leasing.
- Defence/weapons: manufacturers of military aerospace and defence equipment, parts or products, including defence electronics and space equipment.
- Gambling/casino: owners and operators of casinos and gaming facilities, including companies providing lottery and betting services.
- Music: producers and distributors of music, owners and operators of radio broadcasting systems.
- Hotels: owners and operators of hotels.

Financial screening

Shariah investment principles do not allow investment in companies deriving significant income from interest or companies that have excessive leverage. MSCI Barra uses the following three financial ratios to screen for these companies:

- total debt over total assets;
- sum of a company's cash and interest-bearing securities over total assets;
- sum of a company's accounts receivables and cash over total assets.

None of the financial ratios may exceed 33.33%.

Dividend purification

If a company does derive part of its total income from interest income and/or from prohibited activities, shariah investment principles state that this proportion must be deducted from the dividend paid out to shareholders and given to charity. MSCI Barra will apply a 'dividend adjustment factor' to all reinvested dividends.

The 'dividend adjustment factor' is defined as: (total earnings − (income from prohibited activities + interest income)) / total earnings. In this formula, total earnings are defined as gross income, and interest income is defined as operating and non-operating interest.

MSCI Barra will review the 'dividend adjustment factor' on an annual basis at the May Semi-Annual Index Review.

28.4.3 Dow Jones Islamic Indexes

The Dow Jones Islamic Market Indexes were introduced in 1999 as the first benchmarks to represent Islamic-compliant portfolios. Today the series encompasses more than 70 indexes. The indexes are maintained based on a stringent and published methodology. An independent Shariah Supervisory Board counsels Dow Jones Indexes on matters related to the compliance of index-eligible companies.

The business activities screening carried out to confirm that shariah principles have been followed is the same as that which is carried out by MCSI. The financial ratios are calculated differently as follows:

All of the following should be less than 33%:

- total debt divided by trailing 12-month average market capitalisation;
- the sum of a company's cash and interest-bearing securities divided by trailing 12-month average market capitalisation;
- accounts receivables divided by trailing 12-month average market capitalisation.

MCSI explains that it uses total assets as the base rather than market capitalisation as this results in lower index volatility and lower index turnover, as market capitalisation can be more volatile than total assets.

It follows that the ratios of certain sectors, such as property developing companies that are frequently highly geared, would exceed the 33% criteria.

Subsequent screening

After the initial investment, subsequent screening would be similar to the checks that banks make to confirm that debt covenants have not been breached.

Other indices

There are a number of other indices including the FTSE Global Islamic Index Series; the FTSE SGX Shariah Index Series; the FTSE DIFX Shariah Index Series and the FTSE Bursa Malaysia Index Series.

28.5 Ratios set by lenders in debt covenants

Lenders may require borrowers to do certain things by affirmative covenants or refrain from doing certain things by negative covenants.

Affirmative covenants may, e.g. include requiring the borrower to:

- provide quarterly and annual financial statements;
- remain within certain ratios whilst ensuring that each agreed ratio is not so restrictive that it impairs normal operations:
  - maintain a current ratio of not less than an agreed ratio – say 1.6 to 1;
  - maintain a ratio of total liabilities to tangible net worth at an agreed rate – say no greater than 2.5 to 1;
  - maintain tangible net worth in excess of an agreed amount – say £1 million;
- maintain adequate insurance.

Negative covenants may, for example, include requiring the borrower **not** to:

- grant any other charges over the company's assets;
- repay loans from related parties without prior approval;
- change the group structure by acquisitions, mergers or divestment without prior agreement.

28.5.1 What happens if a company is in breach of its debt covenants?

Borrowers will normally have prepared forecasts to assure themselves and the lenders that compliance is reasonably feasible – such forecasts will also normally include the worst case scenario, e.g. taking account of seasonal fluctuations that may trigger temporary violations with higher borrowing required to cover higher levels of stock and debtors.

If any violation has occurred, the lender has a range of options, such as:

- amending the covenant, e.g. accepting a lower current ratio; or
- granting a waiver period when the terms of the covenant are not applied; or
- granting a waiver but requiring the loans to be restructured; or
- requiring the terms to be met within a stipulated period of grace, or, as a last resort;
- declaring that the borrower is in default and demanding repayment of the loan.

However, since the credit crisis it is unlikely that banks will be as relaxed about any breach as they might have been pre-2008 and serious thought has to be given to the risk to an entity's going concern if a breach has occurred.

In times of recession a typical reaction is for companies to take steps to reduce their operating costs, align production with reduced demand, tightly control their working capital and reduce discretionary capital expenditure.

In addition, steps may be taken to reduce interest by paying down overdrafts and loans. For example, the following is an extact from the Xstrata 2008 Annual Report:

> Our announcement of a 2 for 1 rights issue to raise £4.1 billion (approximately $5.9 billion) excluding costs, will provide a significant injection of capital, mitigate the risks presented by the current uncertainty and remove this potential constraint. The proceeds of the rights issue will be used to repay bank debt.

28.5.2 Risk of aggressive earnings management

In 2001, before the collapse of Enron, there was a consensus amongst respondents to the UK Auditing Practices Board Consultation Paper *Aggressive Earnings Management* that aggressive earnings management was a significant threat and actions should be taken to diminish it. It was considered that aggressive earnings management could occur when there was a need to meet or exceed market expectations and when directors' and managements' remuneration were linked to earnings – also, but to a lesser extent, to understate profits to reduce tax liabilities or to increase profits to ensure compliance with loan covenants.

In 2004, as a part of the *Information for Better Markets* initiative, the Audit and Assurance Faculty commissioned a survey[6] to check whether views had changed since 2001. This showed that the vulnerability of corporate reporting to manipulation is perceived as being always with us but at a lower level following the greater awareness and scrutiny by non-executive directors and audit committees.

The *analysts* interviewed in the survey believed the potential for aggressive earnings management varied from sector to sector, e.g. in the older, more established sectors followed by the same analysts for a number of years, they believed that company management would find it hard to disguise anything aggressive even if they wanted to – however, this was not true of newer sectors (e.g. IT) where the business models may be imperfectly understood.

Whilst analysts and journalists tend to have low confidence in the reported earnings where there are pressures to manipulate, there is a research report[7] which paints a rather more optimistic picture. This report aimed to assess the level of confidence investors had in different sources of company information, including audited financial information, when making investment decisions. As far as audited financial information was concerned, the levels of confidence in UK audited financial information amongst UK and US investors remained very high, with 87% of UK respondents having either a 'great deal' or a 'fair amount' of confidence in UK audited financial information.

The auditing profession continues to respond to the need to contain aggressive earnings management. This is not easy because it requires a detailed understanding not only of the business but also of the process management follow when making their estimates. The proposed ISA 540 Revised, *Auditing Accounting Estimates, including Fair Value Accounting Estimates, and Related Disclosures*, requires auditors to exercise greater rigour and scepticism and to be particularly aware of the cumulative effect of estimates which in themselves fall within a normal range but which, taken together, are misleading.

28.5.3 Audit implications when there is a breach of a debt covenant

Auditors are required to bring a healthy scepticism to their work. This applies particularly at times such as when there is a potential debt covenant breach. There may then well be a temptation to manipulate to avoid reporting a breach. This will depend on the specific covenant, e.g. if the current ratio is below the agreed figure, management might be more optimistic in setting inventory obsolescence and accounts receivable provisions and have a lower expectation of the likelihood of contingent liabilities crystallising.

28.5.4 Impact on share price

If there is a risk of bank covenants being breached, there can be a significant adverse effect on the share price, e.g. the Jarvis share price tumbled 24%, wiping £64 million off the engineering services group's stock market value as a result of fears that bank covenants would be breached.[8]

28.6 Predicting corporate failure

In the preceding chapter we extolled the virtues of ratio analysis for the interpretation of financial statements. However, ratio analysis is an excellent indicator only when applied properly. Unfortunately, a number of limitations impede its proper application. How do we know which ratios to select for the analysis of company accounts? Which ratios can be combined to produce an informative end-result? How should individual ratios be ranked to give the user an overall picture of company performance? How reliable are all the ratios – can users place more reliance on some ratios than others?

We will now discuss how Z-scores, H-scores and A-scores address this.

Z-score analysis can be employed to overcome some of the limitations of traditional ratio analysis. It evaluates corporate stability and, more importantly, predicts potential instances of corporate failure. All the forecasts and predictions are based on publicly available financial statements.[9] The aim is to identify potential failures so that 'the appropriate action to reverse the process [of failure] can be taken before it is too late'.[10]

28.6.1 What are Z-scores?

Inman describes what Z-scores are designed for:

> Z-scores attempt to replace various independent and often unreliable and misleading historical ratios and subjective rule-of-thumb tests with scientifically analysed ratios which can reliably predict future events by identifying bench marks above which 'all's well' and below which there is imminent danger.[11]

Z-scores provide a single-value score to describe the combination of a number of key characteristics of a company. Some of the most important predictive ratios are weighted according to perceived importance and then summed to give the single Z-score. This is then evaluated against the identified benchmark.

The two best known Z-scores are Altman's Z-score and Taffler's Z-score.

Altman's Z-score

The original Z-score equation was devised by Professor Altman in 1968 and developed further in 1977.[12] The original equation is:

$$Z = 0.012X_1 + 0.014X_2 + 0.033X_3 + 0.006X_4 + 0.999X_5$$

where

X_1 = Working capital/Total assets
(Liquid assets are being measured in relation to the business's size and this may be seen as a better predictor than the current and acid test ratios which measure the interrelationships within working capital. For X_1 the more relative Working Capital, the more liquidity.)

X_2 = Retained earnings/Total assets
(In early years the proportion of retained earnings used to finance the total asset base may be quite low and the length of time the business has been in existence has been seen as a factor in insolvency. In later years the more earnings that are retained the more funds that could be available to pay creditors. Also acts an indication of a company's dividend policy – a high dividend payout reduces the retained earnings with impact on solvency and creditors' position.)

X_3 = Earnings before interest and tax/Total assets
(Adequate operating profit is fundamental to the survival of a business.)

X_4 = Market capitalisation/Book value of debt
(This is an attempt to include market expectations which may be an early warning as to possible future problems. Solvency is less likely to be threatened if shareholders' interest is relatively high in relation to the total debt.)

X_5 = Sales/Total assets

(This indicates how assets are being used. If efficient, then profits available to meet interest payments are more likely. It is a measure that might have been more appropriate when Altman was researching companies within the manufacturing sector. It is a relationship that varies widely between manufacturing sectors and even more so within knowledge-based companies.)

Altman identified two benchmarks. Companies scoring over 3.0 are unlikely to fail and should be considered safe, while companies scoring under 1.8 are very likely to fail. The value of 3.0 has since been revised down to 2.7.[13] Z-scores between 2.7 and 1.8 fall into the grey area. The 1968 work is claimed to be able to distinguish between successes and failures up to two or three years before the event. The 1977 work claims an improved prediction period of up to five years before the event.

The Zeta model

This was a model developed by Altman and Zeta Services Inc in 1977. It is the same as the Z-score for identifying corporate failure one year ahead but it is more accurate in identifying potential failure in the period two to five years ahead. The model is based on the following variables:

X_1 return on assets:earnings before interest and tax/total assets;

X_2 stability of earnings:normalized return on assets around a five- to ten-year trend;

X_3 debt service:earnings before interest and tax/total interest;

X_4 cumulative profitability:retained earnings/total assets;

X_5 liquidity:the current ratio;

X_6 capitalisation:equity/total market value;

X_7 size:total tangible assets.

Zeta is available as a subscription service and the coefficients have not been published.

Taffler's Z-score

The exact definition of Taffler's Z-score[14] is unpublished, but the following components form the equation:

$$Z = c_0 + c_1 X_1 + c_2 X_2 + c_3 X_3 + c_4 X_4$$

where

X_1 = Profit before tax/Current assets (53%)

X_2 = Current assets/Current liabilities (13%)

X_3 = Current liabilities/Total assets (18%)

X_4 = No credit interval = Length of time which the company can continue to finance its operations using its own assets with no revenue inflow (16%)

c_0 to c_4 are the coefficients, and the percentages in brackets represent the ratios' contributions to the power of the model.

The benchmark used to detect success or failure is 0.2.[15] Companies scoring above 0.2 are unlikely to fail, while companies scoring less than 0.2 demonstrate the same symptoms as companies that have failed in the past.

PAS-score: performance analysis score

Taffler adapted the Z-score technique to develop the PAS-score. The PAS-score evaluates company performance relative to other companies in the industry and incorporates changes in the economy.

The PAS-score ranks all company Z-scores in percentile terms, measuring relative performance on a scale of 0 to 100. A PAS-score of X means that $100 - X\%$ of the companies have scored higher Z-scores. So, a PAS-score of 80 means that only 20% of the companies in the comparison have achieved higher Z-scores.

The PAS-score details the relative performance trend of a company over time. Any downward trends should be investigated immediately and the management should take appropriate action. For other danger signals see Holmes and Dunham.[16]

SMEs and failure prediction

The effectiveness of applying a failure prediction model is not restricted to large companies. This is illustrated by research[17] conducted in New Zealand where such a model was applied to 185 SMEs and found to be useful. As with all models, it is also helpful to refer to other supplementary information that may be available, e.g. other credit reports, credit managers' assessments and trade magazines.

28.6.2 H-scores

An H-score is produced by Company Watch to determine overall financial health. The H-score is an enhancement of the Z-score technique in giving more emphasis to the strength of the statement of financial position. The Company Watch system calculates a score ranging from 0 to 100 with below 25 being in the danger zone. It takes into account profit management, asset management and funding management using seven factors – these are profit from the profit and loss account, three factors from the asset side of the statement of financial position, namely, current asset cover, inventory and trade receivables management and liquidity; and three factors from the liability side of the statement of financial position, namely, equity base, debt dependence and current funding.

The factors are taken from published financial statements which makes the approach taken by the ASB to bring off balance sheet transactions onto the statement of financial position particularly important.

A strength of the H-score is that it can be applied to all sectors (other than the financial sector) and there is clear evidence that it can predict possible failures, e.g. the model indicated that European Home Retail (the parent company of Farepack, the Christmas hamper company) was at risk as far back as 2001 when its H-score was nine.

The ability to chart each factor against the sector average and to twenty-five level criteria over a five-year period means that it is valuable for a range of user needs from trade creditors considering extending or continuing to allow credit to potential lenders and equity investors and the big four accounting firms in reviewing audit risk. The model also has the ability to process 'what-ifs'. This is referred to in an article that gives as an example the fact that the impact on the H-score can be measured for a potential rights issue which is used to repay debt:

> That is a feature which Paul Woodley, a director of Postern, the group that provides company doctors for distressed companies, also finds useful. If a company is in trouble, the H score can be used to show exactly what needs to be done to sort it out.[18]

It appears to be a robust, useful and exciting new tool for all user groups. It is not simply a tool for measuring risk. It can also be used by investors to identify companies whose share price might have fallen but which might be financially strong with the possibility of the share price recovering – it can indicate buy situations. It is also used by leading firms of accountants for purpose of targeting companies in need of turnaround. Further information appears on the company's website at www.companywatch.net which includes additional examples.

28.6.3 A-scores

A-scores concentrate on non-financial signs of failure.[19] This method sets out to quantify different judgmental factors. The whole basis of the analysis is that financial difficulties are the direct result of management defects and errors which have existed in the company for many years.

A-scores assume that many company failures can be explained by similar factors. Company failure can be broken down into a three-stage sequence of events:

1 **Defects**. Specific defects exist in company top management. Typically, these defects centre on management structure; decision making and ability; accounting systems; and failure to respond to change.

2 **Mistakes**. Management will make mistakes that can be attributed to the company defects. The three mistakes that lead to company failure are very high leverage; over-trading; and the failure of the company's main project.

3 **Symptoms**. Finally, symptoms of failure will start to arise. These are directly attributable to preceding management mistakes. Typical symptoms are financial signs (e.g. poor ratios, poor Z-scores); creative accounting (management might attempt to 'disguise' signs of failure in the accounts); non-financial signs (e.g. investment decisions delayed; market share drops); and terminal signs (when the financial collapse of the company is imminent).

To calculate a company A-score, different scores are allocated to each defect, mistake and symptom according to their importance. Then this score is compared with the benchmark values. If companies achieve an overall score of over 25, or a defect score of over 10, or a mistakes score of over 15, then the company is demonstrating typical signs leading up to failure. Generally, companies not at risk will score below 18, and companies which are at risk will score well over 25.

The scoring system attaches a weight to individual items within defects, mistakes and symptoms. By way of illustration we set out the weights applied within defects which are as follows:

Defects in management:	*Weight*
The chief executive is an autocrat	8
The chief executive is also the chairman	4
There is a passive board	2
The board is unbalanced, e.g. too few with finance experience	2
There is poor management depth	1
Defects in accountancy:	
There are no budgets for budgetary control	3
There are no current cash flow plans	3
There is no costing system or product costs	3
There is a poor response to change, e.g. out-of-date plant, old-fashioned products, poor marketing	15

Consider our A-score assessment of DNB Computer Systems plc:

Defects:	Weak finance director	2	
	Poor management depth	1	
	No budgeting control	3	
	No current updated cash flows	3	
	No costing system	3	
			12
Mistakes:	Main project failure	15	
			15
Symptoms:	Financial signs – adverse Z-scores	4	
	Creative accounting – unduly low debtor provisions	4	
	High staff turnover	3	
			11
Total A-score:			38

According to our benchmarks, DNB Computer Systems plc is at risk of failure because the mistakes score is 15 and the overall A-score is 38. Therefore, there is some cause for concern, e.g. Why did the main project fail? To which of the symptoms was it due?

Whilst it is difficult to see the rationale for either the weightings or the additive nature of the A-score, and whilst the process can be criticised for being subjective, the identification of a defect or mistake can in itself be a warning light and give direction to further enquiry.

It is interesting to see the weighting given to the chief executive being an autocrat which is supported by the experience in failures such as WorldCom in 2002 with the following comment:[20]

'Autocratic style'
WorldCom pursued an aggressive strategy under Ebbers . . . In 1998, Ebbers cemented his reputation when Worldcom purchased MCI for $40bn – the largest acquisition in corporate history at that time . . . But according to one journalist in Mississippi who followed Worldcom from its inception, the seeds of the disaster were sown from the start by Ebbers' aggressive autocratic management style.

28.6.4 Failure prediction combining cash flow and accrual data

There is a continuing interest in identifying variables which have the ability to predict the likelihood of corporate failure – particularly if this only requires a small number of variables. A recent study[21] indicated that a parsimonious model that included only three financial variables, namely, a cash flow, a profitability and a financial leverage variable, was accurate in 83% of the cases in predicting corporate failure one year ahead.

28.6.5 Use of prediction models by auditor reporting on going concern status

Auditors are required to assess whether a company has any going concern problems which would indicate that it might not be able to continue trading for a further financial year. They are assisted in forming an opinion by the use of failure prediction models such as the scoring systems and analytical techniques discussed in this and the previous chapter when assessing solvency and future cash flows.

The following is an extract from the Notes to the 2008 Financial Statements of Independent International Investment Research plc:

The accounts have been prepared under the assumption that the Company is a going concern. The Company is engaged in an industry where losses represent the Company's investment in its development and it has remained the directors' policy to ensure that adequate finance is available to support this development. At the date of approving these accounts there exists a fundamental uncertainty concerning the Company's ability to continue as a going concern.

This fundamental uncertainty relates to the Company's ability to meet its future working capital requirements and therefore continue as a going concern.

The application of the going concern concept in preparing the accounts assumes the Company's ability to continue activities in the foreseeable future which in turn depends on the ability to generate free cash flow. The directors believe that sufficient revenue and free cash flow will be generated to meet the Company's working capital requirements for at least the next twelve months.

On this basis, in the opinion of the directors, the accounts have been properly prepared on the assumption that the Company is a going concern.

The accounts do not include any adjustments that would result from the Company's ability to generate sufficient free cash flow. It is not practical to quantify the adjustment that might be required but should any adjustment be required it would be significant.

The auditors accept that there has been adequate disclosure by the directors in modifying their report as follows:

Fundamental uncertainty – Going concern

In forming our opinion, we have considered the adequacy of the disclosure made in note 1 of the accounts concerning the fundamental uncertainty as to whether or not the Company can be considered a going concern. The validity of the going concern basis is dependant on the Company's ability to meet its future working capital requirements and generate free cashflow.

The accounts do not include any adjustments that would result from a failure to generate a free cash flow. It is not practical to quantify the adjustments that might be required, but should any adjustments be required they would be significant. In view of the significance of this fundamental uncertainty we consider that it should be drawn to your attention but our opinion is not qualified in this respect.

Following the uncertainties that have resulted from the credit crisis there were two concerns that needed to be addressed.

The first was the fear that the market would react badly if there were more reports of fundamental uncertainty in the audit report and assume that this meant that the company was insolvent. This risk could be reduced by making investors aware of the significance of the modified audit report, i.e. it did not mean that liquidation was imminent. Without such awareness general business confidence might be damaged and individual companies could suffer in a number of ways. For example, suppliers might stop allowing credit and lenders might call in their loans thinking that covenants had been breached.

The second concern was that auditors should exercise even greater attention when testing that the company is in fact a going concern. For example, at a macro level reviewing the industry to assess if it is likely to be adversely affected and at a company level reviewing the customers and suppliers to see if there is any indication that they are in difficulties that could materially affect the company.

28.7 Performance related remuneration – shareholder returns

The Greenbury Report recommended that,

> In considering what the performance criteria should be, remuneration committees should consider criteria which measure company performance relative to a group of comparator companies . . . reflecting the company's objectives such as shareholder return . . . Directors should not be rewarded for increases in share prices or other indicators which reflect general price inflation, general movements in the stock market, movements in a particular sector of the market or the development of regulatory regimes.

28.7.1 Shareholder value (SV)

It has been a longstanding practice for analysts to arrive at shareholder value of a share by calculating the internal rate of return (IRR %) on an investment from the dividend stream and realisable value of the investment at date of disposal, i.e. taking account of dividends received and capital gains. However, it is not a generic measure in that the calculation is specific to each shareholder. The reason for this is that the dividends received will depend on the length of period the shares are held and the capital gain achieved will depend on the share price at the date of disposal – and, as we know, the share price can move significantly even over a week.

For example, consider the SV for each of the following three shareholders, Miss Rapid, Mr Medium and Miss Undecided, who each invested £10,000 on 1 January 20X6 in Spacemobile Ltd which pays a dividend of £500 on these shares on 31 December each year. Miss Rapid sold her shares on 31 December 20X7. Mr Medium sold his on 31 December 20X9, whereas Miss Undecided could not decide what to do with her shares. The SV for each shareholder is as follows:

Shareholder	Date acquired	Investment at cost	Dividends amount (total)	Date of disposal	Sale proceeds	IRR%
Miss Rapid	1.1.20X6	10,000	1,000	31.12.20X7	11,000	10%*
Mr Medium	1.1.20X6	10,000	2,000	31.12.20X9	15,000	15%
Miss Undecided	1.1.20X6	10,000	2,000	Undecided		

* $((500 \times 9091) + (11,500 \times 8265)) - 10,000 = 0$

We can see that Miss Rapid achieved a shareholder value of 10% on her shares and Mr Medium, by holding until 31.12.20X9, achieved an increased capital gain raising the SV to 15%. We do not have the information as to how Miss Rapid invested from 1.1.20X8 and so we cannot evaluate her decision – it depends on the subsequent investment and the economic value added by that new company.

28.7.2 Total shareholder return

Miss Undecided has a notional SV at 31.12.20X9 of 15% as calculated for Mr Medium. However, this has not been realised and, if the share price changed the following day, the SV would be different. The notional 15% calculated for Miss Undecided is referred to as the total shareholder return (TSR) – it takes into account market expectation on the assumption that share prices reflect all available information but it is dependent on the assumption made about the length of the period the shares are held.

TSR has been used for performance monitoring, as a criterion for performance-based remuneration and, recently, to satisfy statutory requirements.

Performance monitoring

It has been used by companies to monitor their performance by comparing their own TSR with that of comparator companies. It is also used to set strategic targets. For example, Unilever set itself a TSR target in the top third of a reference group of twenty-one international consumer goods companies. Unilever calculates the TSR over a three-year rolling period which it considers 'sensitive enough to reflect changes but long enough to smooth out short-term volatility'.

Remuneration performance criterion

It is also used by companies as part of their remuneration package. For example, Vodafone in its 2009 Annual Report states:

> The long term incentive measures performance against free cash flow, which is believed to be the single most important operational measure; and total shareholder return ('TSR') relative to Vodafone's key competitors.

The choice of comparator companies rests with the directors.

Appropriate comparator companies are chosen by the Remuneration Committee taking into account their relative size and the markets in which they operate with a review before each performance cycle to maintain its relevance.

Statutory requirement

The Directors' Report Regulations 2002 now require a line graph to be prepared showing such a comparison. Marks & Spencer Group's 2009 Annual Report contained the following:

Performance graph

The graph illustrates the performance of the Company against the FTSE 100 over the past five years. The FTSE 100 has been chosen as it is a recognised broad equity market index of which the Company has been a member throughout the period. It looks at the value, at 28 March 2009, of £100 invested in Marks & Spencer Group plc on 3 April 2004 compared with the value of £100 invested in the FTSE 100 Index over the same period. The other points plotted are the values at the intervening financial period-ends.

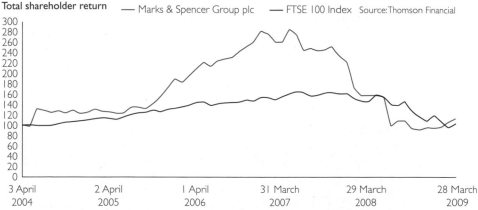

The above graph looks at the value, at 28 March 2009, of £100 invested in Marks & Spencer Group plc on 3 April 2004 compared with the value of £100 invested in the FTSE 100 Index over the same period. The other points plotted are the values at the intervening financial period-ends.

28.7.3 Performance related remuneration – Economic Value Added (EVA)

Need to generate above average returns

Companies are increasingly becoming aware that investors need to be confident that the company can deliver above average rates of return, i.e. achieve growth, and that communication is the key. This is why companies are using the annual report to provide shareholders and potential shareholders with a measure of the company's performance that will give them confidence to maintain or make an investment in the company.

EVA and managers' performance

In some organisations EVA has been used as a basis for determining bonus payments made to managers. There is some evidence that managers rewarded under such a scheme do perform better than those operating under more traditional schemes. However, research[22] indicated that this occurs when managers understand the concept of EVA and that it is not universally appropriate as other factors need to be taken into account such as the area of the firm in which a manager is employed. The following is an extract from the ThyssenKrupp 2009 Annual Report:

> This management and controlling system is linked to the bonus system in such a way that the amount of the performance-related remuneration is determined by the achieved EVA.

28.7.4 Formula for calculating economic value added

The formula applied is explained by Geveke nv Amsterdam in its 1999 Annual Report:

> EVA measures economic value achieved over a specific period. It is equal to net operating profit after tax (NOPAT), corrected for the cost of capital employed (the sum of interest bearing liabilities and shareholders' equity). The cost of capital employed is the required yield R times capital employed (CE).
>
> In the form of a formula: $NOPAT - (R \times CE) = EVA$
>
> A positive EVA indicates that over a specific period economic value has been created. Net operating profit after tax is then greater than the cost of finance (i.e. the company's weighted average cost of capital). Research has shown that a substantial part of the long-term movement in share price is explained by the development of EVA. The concept of EVA can be a very good method of performance measurement and monitoring of decisions.

We will illustrate the formula for Alpha nv, which has the following data (in euros):

	31 March 20X1	31 March 20X2	31 March 20X3
NOPAT	10m	11m	13m
Weighted average cost of capital (WACC)	12%	11.5%	11%
Capital employed	70m	77m	96m

The EVA is:

	% change
31 March 20X1 EVA = 10m – (12% of 70m) = 1.6m	—
31 March 20X2 EVA = 11m – (11.5% of 77m) = 2.145m	34%
31 March 20X3 EVA = 12.5m – (11% of 96m) = 1.94m	(10%)

The formula allows weight to be given to the capital employed to generate operating profit. The percentage change is an important management tool in that the annual increase is seen as the created value rather than the absolute level, i.e. the 34% is the key figure rather than the 2.145 million. Further enquiry is necessary to assess how well Alpha nv will employ the increase in capital employed in future periods.

It is useful to calculate rate of change over time. However, as for all inter-company comparisons of ratios, it is necessary to identify how the WACC and capital employed have been defined. This may vary from company to company.

WACC calculation

This figure depends on the capital structure and risk in each country in which a company has a significant business interest. For example, the following is an extract from the 2003 Annual Report of the Orkla Group:

Capital structure and cost of capital

The Group's average cost of capital is calculated as a weighted average of the costs of borrowed capital and equity. The calculations are based on an equity-to-total-assets ratio of 60%. The cost of equity is calculated with the help of the Capital Asset Pricing Model. The cost of borrowed capital is based on a long-term, weighted interest rate for relevant countries in which Orkla operates . . .

The table shows how Orkla's average cost of capital is calculated:

Description	Rates	Relative %	Weighted cost
Weighted average beta	1.0		
× Market risk premium	4.0%		
= Risk premium for equity	4.0%		
+ Risk free long-term interest rate	4.9%		
= Cost of equity	8.9%	60%	5.3%
Imputed borrowing rate before tax	5.9%		
Imputed tax charge	28%		
= Imputed borrowing rate after tax	4.2%	40%	1.7%
WACC after tax			7.0%

Capital employed definition

The norm is to exclude non-interest-bearing liabilities including current liabilities when determining net total assets. However, there are variations in the treatment of intangible assets, e.g. goodwill may be excluded from the net assets or included at book value or included, as by Koninklejke Wessanen, at market value rather than the historically paid goodwill.

Achieving increases in EVA

EVA can be improved in three ways: by increasing NOPAT, reducing WACC and/or improving the utilisation of capital employed.

- Increasing NOPAT: this is achieved by optimising strategic choices by comparing the cash flows arising from different strategic opportunities, e.g. appraising geographic and product segmental information, cost reduction programmes, appraising acquisitions and divestments.

- Reducing WACC: this is achieved by reviewing the manner in which a company is financed, e.g. determining a favourable gearing ratio and reducing the perceived risk factor by a favourable spread of products and markets.

- Improving the utilisation of capital employed: this is achieved by consideration of activity ratios, e.g. non-curent asset turnover, working capital ratio.

28.8 Valuing shares of an unquoted company – quantitative process

The valuation of shares brings together a number of different financial accounting procedures that we have covered in previous chapters. The assumptions may be highly subjective, but there is a standard approach. This involves the following:

- Estimate the maintainable income flow based on earnings defined in accordance with the IIMR guidelines, as described in Chapter 25. Normally the profits of the past five years are used, adjusted for any known or expected future changes.

- Estimate an appropriate dividend yield, as described in Chapter 27, if valuing a non-controlling holding; or an appropriate earnings yield if valuing a majority holding. In the UK there is now a Valuation Index focused on SMEs which is the result of UK200s Corporate Finance members providing key data on actual transactions involving the purchase or sale of real businesses (in the form of asset or share deals) over the past five years. The median P/E ratio at November 2009 stood at 5.2

- Make a decision on any adjustment to the required yields. For example, the shares in the unquoted company might not be as marketable as those in the comparative quoted companies and the required yield would therefore be increased to reflect this lack of marketability; or the statement of financial position might not be as strong with lower current/acid test ratios or higher gearing, which would also lead to an increase in the required yield.

- Calculate the economic capital value, as described in Chapter 3, by applying the required yield to the income flow.

- Compare the resulting value with the net realisable value (NRV), as described in Chapter 4, when deciding what action to take based on the economic value.

EXAMPLE ● The Doughnut Ltd is an unlisted company engaged in the baking of doughnuts. The statement of financial position of the Doughnut Ltd as at 31 December 20X9 showed:

	£000	£000
Freehold land		100
Non-current assets at cost	240	
Accumulated depreciation	40	
		200
Current assets	80	
Current liabilities	(60)	
		20
		320
Share capital in £1 shares		300
Retained earnings		20
		320
Estimated net realisable values:		
Freehold land		310
Plant and equipment		160
Current assets		70

It achieved the following profit after tax (adjusted to reflect maintainable earnings) for the past five years ended 31 December:

	20X5	20X6	20X7	20X8	20X9
Maintainable earnings (£000)	36	40	44	38	42
Dividend payout history: Dividends	10%	10%	12%	12%	12%

Current yields for comparative quoted companies as at 31 December 20X9:

	Earnings yield %	Dividend yield %
Ace Bakers plc	14	8
Busi-Bake plc	10	8
Hard-to-beat plc	13	8

You are required to value a holding of 250,000 shares for a shareholder, Mr Quick, who makes a practice of buying shares for sale within three years.

Now, the 250,000 shares represent an 83% holding. This is a majority holding and the steps to value it are as follows:

1 Calculate average maintainable earnings (in £000):

$$\frac{36,000 + 40,000 + 44,000 + 38,000 + 42,000}{5} = £40,000$$

2 Estimate an appropriate earnings yield:

$$\frac{14\% + 10\% + 13\%}{3} = 12.3\%$$

3 Adjust the rate for lack of marketability by, say, 3% and for the lower current ratio by, say, 2%. Both these adjustments are subjective and would be a matter of negotiation between the parties.

Require yield	=	12.3
Lack of marketability weighting	=	3
Statement of financial position weakness	=	2
Required earnings yield		17.3

The adjustments depend on the actual circumstances. For instance, if Mr Quick were intending to hold the shares as a long-term investment, there might be no need to increase the required return for lack of marketability.

4 Calculate share value:

$$(£40,000 \times 100/17.3)/300,000 = 77p$$

5 Compare with the net realisable values on the basis that the company was to be liquidated:

		£
Net realisable values = 70,000 + 160,000 + 310,000	=	540,000
Less: Current liabilities		60,000
		480,000
Net asset value per share = £480,000/300,000	=	£1.60

The comparison indicates that, on the information we have been given, Mr Quick should acquire the shares and dispose of the assets and liquidate the company to make an immediate capital gain of 83p per share.

Let us extend our illustration by assuming that it is intended to replace the non-current assets at a cost of £20,000 per year out of retained earnings, if Mr Quick acquires the shares. Advise Mr Small, who has £10,000 to invest, how many shares he would be able to acquire in the Doughnut Ltd.

There are two significant changes: the cash available for distribution as dividends will be reduced by £20,000 per year, which is used to replace non-current assets; and Mr Small is acquiring only a minority holding, which means that the appropriate valuation method is the **dividend yield** rather than the **earnings yield**.

The share value will be calculated as follows:

1 Estimate income flow:

	£
Maintainable earnings	40,000
Less: CAPEX	20,000
Cash available for distribution	20,000

Note that we are here calculating not distributable profits, but the available cash flow.

2 Required dividend yield:

	%
Average dividend yield	8
Lack of negotiability, say	2
Financial risk, say	1.5
	11.5

3 Share value:

$$\frac{£20,000}{300,000} \times \frac{100}{11.5} = 58\text{p}$$

At this price it would be possible for Mr Small to acquire (£10,000/58p) 17,241 shares.

28.8.1 Valuing shares of an unquoted company – qualitative process

In the section above we illustrated how to value shares using the capitalisation of earnings and capitalisation of dividends methods. However, share valuation is an extremely subjective exercise. For example, even the prospect of a takeover for Morgan Crucible in 2006 was enough to cause shares to increase by 48.5p to a five-year high of 282p. The values we have calculated for the Doughnut Ltd shares could therefore be subject to material revision in the light of other relevant factors.

A company's future cash flows may be affected by a number of factors. These may occur as a result of action within the company (e.g. management change, revenue investment) or as a result of external events (e.g. change in the rate of inflation, change in competitive pressures).

● **Management change** often heralds a significant change in a company's share price. For example, the new chief executive of Fisons made significant changes to Fisons in 1994/5 by reducing the business to its valuable core, which then saw the share price move from 103p to 193p.

● **Revenue investment** refers to discretionary revenue expenditure, such as charges to the Income Statement for research and development, training, advertising and major maintenance and refurbishment. The ASB in its exposure draft for FRS 3 *Reporting*

Financial Performance had proposed that this information should be disclosed in the income statement. The proposal did not find support at the exposure stage and it is suggested that such information should instead be disclosed in the operating and financial review.

- **Changes in the rate of inflation** can affect the required yield. If, for example, it is expected that inflation will fall, this might mean that past percentage yields will be higher than the percentage yield that is likely to be available in the future.

- **Change in competitive pressures** can affect future sales. For example, increased foreign competition could mean that past maintainable earnings are not achievable in the future and the historic average level might need to be reduced.

These are a few of the internal and external factors that can affect the valuation of a share. The factors that are relevant to a particular company may be industry-wide (e.g. change in rate of inflation), sector-wide (e.g. change in competitive pressure) or company-specific (e.g. loss of key managers or employees). They may not be immediately apparent from an appraisal of financial statements alone: e.g. the application and success of the balanced scorecard approach might not be immediately apparent without discussions with all the stakeholders. The valuer will need to carry out detailed enquiries in order both to identify which factors are relevant and to evaluate their impact on the share price.

If the company supports the acquisition of the shares, the valuer will be able to gain access to relevant internal information. For example, details of research and development expenditure may be available analysed by type of technology involved, by product line, by project and by location, and distinguishing internal from externally acquired R&D.

If the acquisition is being considered without the company's knowledge or support, the valuer will rely more heavily on information gained from public sources: e.g. statutory and voluntary disclosures in the annual accounts and industry information such as trade journals. Information on areas such as R&D may be provided in the OFR, but probably in an aggregated form, constrained by management concerns about use by potential competitors.[23]

There is an increasing wealth of financial and narrative disclosures to assist investors in making their investment decisions. There are external data such as the various multi-variate Z-scores and H-scores and professional credit agency ratings; there is greater internal disclosure of financial data such as TSR and EVA data indicating how well companies have managed value in comparison with a peer group and of narrative information such as the OFR, statements of business risk and key performance indicators. There will also increasingly be easier access to companies' financial data through the Web.

Literature search of qualitative factors which can lead to improved or reduced valuations

There is an interesting research report[24] investigating the nature of SME intangible assets in which the researchers have reported the following:

- Factors identified in the literature as enhancing achieved price: transportable business with a transferable customer base; provides attractive lifestyle for new owner; non-cancellable service agreements and beneficial contractual arrangements; unexploited property situations; synergistic and cost-saving benefits; under-exploited brands and products; customer base providing cross-selling opportunities; competitor elimination, increased market share; complementary product or service range; market entry – quick way of overcoming entry barriers; buy into new technology; access to distribution channels; and non-competition agreements.

- Factors identified in the literature as diminishing achieved price: confused accounts; poor housekeeping, doubtful debts, underutilized equipment, outstanding litigation, etc.; over-dependence upon owner and key individuals; over-dependence on small number of customers; unrelated side activities; poor or out-of-date company image; long-term contracts about to finish; poor liquidity; poor performance; minority and 'messy' ownership structures; inability to substantiate ownership of assets and uncertainties surrounding liabilities.

Not all of these satisfy the criteria for recognition in annual financial statements.

28.9 Professional risk assessors

Credit agencies such as Standard & Poor and Moody's Investor Services assist investors, lenders and trade creditors by providing a credit rating service. Companies are given a rating that can range from AAA for companies with a strong capacity to meet their financial commitments down to D for companies that have been unable to make contractual payments or have filed for bankruptcy with more than ten ratings in between, e.g. BBB for companies that have adequate capacity but which are vulnerable to internal or external economic changes.

28.9.1 How are ratings set?

The credit agencies take a broad range of internal company and external factors into account.

Internal company factors may include:

- an appraisal of the financial reports to determine:
  - trading performance, e.g. specific financial targets such as return on equity and return on assets; earnings volatility; past and projected performance; how well a company has coped with business cycles and severe competition;
  - cash flow adequacy, e.g. EBITDA interest cover; EBIT interest cover; free operating cash flow;
  - capital structure, e.g. gearing ratio; debt structure; implications of off statement of financial position financing;
  - a consideration of the notes to the accounts to determine possible adverse implications, e.g. contingent liabilities, heavy capital investment commitments which may impact on future profitability, liquidity and funding requirements;
- meetings and discussions with management;
- monitoring expectation, e.g. against quarterly reports, company press releases, profit warnings;
- monitoring changes in company strategy, e.g. changes to funding structure with company buyback of shares, new divestment or acquisition plans and implications for any debt covenants.

However, experience with companies such as Enron makes it clear that off balance sheet transactions can make appraisal difficult even for professional agencies if companies continue to avoid transparency in their reporting.

External factors may include:

- growth prospects, e.g. trends in industry sector; technology possible changes; peer comparison;
- capital requirements, e.g. whether company is fixed capital or working capital intensive; future tangible non-current asset requirements; R&D spending requirements;

- competitors, e.g. the major domestic and foreign competitors; product differentiation; what barriers there are to entry;
- keeping a watching brief on macroeconomic factors, e.g. environmental statutory levies, tax changes, political changes such as restrictions on the supply of oil, foreign currency risks;
- monitoring changes in company strategy, e.g. implication of a company embarking on a heavy overseas acquisition programme which changes the risk profile, e.g. difficulty in management control and in achieving synergies, increased foreign exchange exposure.

28.9.2 What impact does a rating have on a company?

The rating is a risk measure and influences decisions as to whether to grant credit and also as to the terms of such credit, e.g. if a company's rating is downgraded then lenders may refuse credit or impose a higher interest rate or set additional debt covenants.

The ratings are taken seriously by even the largest multinational because they are perceived by investors as possibly adversely affecting access to capital markets. Sony, for example, addressed this concern when it commented in its 2004 Annual Report:

> On June 25, 2003 Moody's downgraded Sony's long-term debt rating from Aa3 to A1 (outlook: negative). R&I downgraded Sony's long-term debt rating from AA+ to AA on June 16, 2003. These actions reflected the concerns of the two agencies that Sony may take longer than initially expected to regain its previous level of profit and cash flow under the severe competition, particularly in the electronics business . . . Despite the downgrading . . . Sony believes that its access to the global capital markets will remain sufficient for its financing needs going forward . . .

28.9.3 Regulation of credit rating agencies

Since the credit crisis there has been severe criticism that credit rating agencies had not been independent when rating financial products. The agencies have been self-regulated but this has been totally inadequate in curtailing conflicts of interest. The conflicts have arisen because they were actively involved in the design of products (collateralised debt obligations) to which they then gave an 'objective' credit rating which did not clearly reflect the true risks associated with investing in them. This conflict of interest was compounded by the fact that (a) agency staff were free to join a company after rating its products and (b) the companies issuing the products paid their fees.

The following swingeing comments were made by the ACCA:[25]

Regulation of credit agencies
It's a joke that an industry with such influence, particularly during the current volatile economic climate, is self-regulated and only subject to a toothless voluntary code of conduct.

The mere fact that credit rating agencies are paid by the companies they rate puts their independence in jeopardy . . . greater transparency is required . . . We have to strike the right balance when regulating the market between protecting and over-burdening. A range of measures is necessary to bring about transparency in the ratings process . . . Regulation would be part of the solution, but it can't be used in isolation . . . This is a perfect example for when an international set of regulations and other measures are imperative to regain trust in financial markets and avoid further credit crunched victims.

This has led to a call for both Europe and the US to regulate the agencies.

European Commission Agency Regulation[26]

In November 2008, the European Commission adopted a proposal for a Regulation on Credit Rating Agencies, which would require agencies to have procedures in place to ensure that:

● ratings are not affected by conflicts of interest;

● credit rating agencies have a high standard for the quality of the rating methodology and the ratings; and

● credit rating agencies act in a transparent manner.

The intention is that the agencies would remain responsible for the content of the ratings.

SEC agency regulation[27]

In December 2008 the US Securities and Exchange Commission (SEC) voted to adopt new regulations relating to credit agencies, referred to as 'nationally recognised statistical rating organisations' (NRSROs). Its approach is to require any issuer to make information used to obtain a rating available to all NRSROs. The new rules contain prohibitions and requirements including the following:

● recommendations on the structure of a structured finance product by an NRSRO that rates the product are prohibited;

● agency analysts receiving gifts and negotiating fees are prohibited;

● a record of any complaints against an analyst is required; and

● a record of the rationale for any difference between a rating implied by a model and a rating issued.

In the US there have been various applications to the court for permission to hold credit agencies responsible for losses incurred as a result of relying on ratings that were not set objectively. Whatever regulation is in place, however, investors should carry out their own due diligence enquiries – credit ratings are only one of the tools in arriving at a decision.

Summary

This chapter has introduced a number of additional analytical techniques to complement the pyramid approach to ratio analysis discussed in the previous chapter.

These techniques include common size vertical analysis and horizontal analysis. The use of ratios was discussed in determining shariah compliance and in setting debt covenants. Corporate failure multivariate models were introduced including the use of Z-scores, H-scores and A-scores.

The use of TSR and EVA were discussed in the context of performance related remuneration and the statutory disclosures that appear in annual reports. In addition, this chapter has described the use of ratios in the valuation of unquoted shares.

The prime purpose of each analytical method in the first half of the chapter was to identify potential financial problem areas. Once these have been identified, thorough investigations should be carried out to determine the cause of each irregularity which includes selecting additional ratios. Management should then take the necessary actions to correct any irregularities and deficiencies.

All users of financial statements (both internal and external users) should be prepared to utilise any or all of the interpretative techniques suggested in this chapter and the preceding one. These techniques help to evaluate the financial health and performance of a company. Users should approach these financial indicators with real curiosity – any unexplained or unanswered questions arising from this analysis should form the basis of a more detailed examination of the company accounts.

REVIEW QUESTIONS

1 Explain what you would look for when examining a company's common-sized statement of financial position.

2 Discuss the difficulties when attempting to identify comparator companies for benchmarking as, for example, when selecting a TSR peer group.

3 The Unilever annual review stated:

> Total Shareholder Return (TSR) is a concept used to compare the performance of different companies' stocks and shares over time. It combines share price appreciation and dividends paid to show the total return to the shareholder. The absolute size of the TSR will vary with stock markets, but the relative position is a reflection of the market perception of overall performance relative to a reference group. The Company calculates the TSR over a three-year rolling period... Unilever has set itself a TSR target in the top third of a reference group of 21 ... companies.

Discuss (a) why a three-year rolling period has been chosen, and (b) the criteria you consider appropriate for selecting the reference group of companies.

4 Discuss Z-score analysis with particular reference to Altman's Z-score and Taffler's Z-score. In particular:

(i) What are the benefits of Z-score analysis?

(ii) What criticisms can be levelled at Z-score analysis?

5 Robertson identifies four main elements which cause changes in the financial health of a company: trading stability; declining profits; declining working capital; increase in borrowings.[28]

Robertson's Z-score is as follows:

where

X_1 = (Sales − Total assets)/Sales
X_2 = Profit before tax/Total assets
X_3 = (Current assets − Total debt)/Current liabilities
X_4 = (Equity − Total borrowing)/Total debt
X_5 = (Liquid assets − Bank overdraft)/Creditors

Interpretation of the Z-score concentrates on rate of change from one period to the next. If the score falls by 40% or more in any one year, immediate investigations must be made to identify and rectify the cause of the decrease in Z-score. If the score falls by 40% or more for two years running, the company is unlikely to survive.

Compare and contrast Robertson's Z-score with:

(i) Altman's Z-score;

(ii) Taffler's Z-score and PAS-score.

6 Explain how and why EVA is calculated.

7 The details given below are a summary of the statements of financial position of six public companies engaged in different industries:

	A	B	C	D	E	F
	%	%	%	%	%	%
Land and buildings	10	2	26	24	57	5
Other non-current assets	17	1	34		13	73
Inventories and work-in-progress	44		22	55	16	1
Trade receivables	6	77	15	4	1	13
Other receivables	11			8	2	5
Cash and investments	12	20	3	9	11	3
	100	100	100	100	100	100

	A	B	C	D	E	F
Capital and reserves	37	5	62	58	55	50
Creditors: over one year	12	5	4	13	6	25
Creditors: under one year						
Trade	32	85	34	14	24	6
Other	16	5		14	15	11
Bank overdraft	3			1		8
Total capital employed	100	100	100	100	100	100

The activities of each company are as follows:

1 Operator of a chain of retail supermarkets.

2 Sea ferry operator.

3 Property investor and house builder. Apart from supplying managers, including site management, for the house building side of its operations, this company completely subcontracts all building work.

4 A vertically integrated company in the food industry which owns farms, flour mills, bakeries and retail outlets.

5 Commercial bank with a network of branches.

6 Contractor in the civil engineering industry.

Note: No company employs off statement of financial position financing such as leasing.

(a) State which of the above activities relate to which set of statement of financial position details, giving a brief summary of your reasoning in each case.

(b) What do you consider to be the major limitations of ratio analysis as a means of interpreting accounting information?

8 It has been suggested that 'growth in profits which occurred in the 1960s was the result of accounting sleight of hand rather than genuine economic growth'. Consider how 'accounting sleight of hand' can be used to report increased profits and discuss what measures can be taken to mitigate against the possibility of this happening.

9 Discuss whether all companies should adopt the ratio criteria required to be shariah compliant.

10 Describe the measures taken to reduce the risk that credit rating agencies can mislead investors.

EXERCISES

An extract from the solution is provided on the Companion Website (www.pearsoned.co.uk/elliott-elliott) for exercises marked with an asterisk (*).

Question 1

The following five-year summary relates to Wandafood Products plc and is based on financial statements prepared under the historical cost convention:

Financial ratios Profitability		20X9	20X8	20X7	20X6	20X5
Margin	$\dfrac{\text{Trading profit}}{\text{Sales}}\%$	7.8	7.5	7.0	7.2	7.3
Return on assets	$\dfrac{\text{Trading profit}}{\text{Net finance charge}}\%$	16.3	17.6	16.2	18.2	18.3
Interest and dividend cover						
Interest cover	$\dfrac{\text{Trading profit}}{\text{Net finance charge}}$ times	2.9	4.8	5.1	6.5	3.6
Dividend cover	$\dfrac{\text{Earnings per ordinary share}}{\text{Dividend per ordinary share}}$ times	2.7	2.6	2.1	2.5	3.1
Debt–equity ratios						
	$\dfrac{\text{Net borrowings}}{\text{Shareholders'}}\%$	65.9	61.3	48.3	10.8	36.5
	$\dfrac{\text{Net borrowings}}{\text{Shareholders' funds plus minority interests}}\%$	59.3	55.5	44.0	10.1	33.9
		20X9	20X8	20X7	20X6	20X5
Liquidity ratios						
Quick ratio	$\dfrac{\text{Current assets less stock}}{\text{Current liabilities}}\%$	74.3	73.3	78.8	113.8	93.4
Current ratio	$\dfrac{\text{Current assets}}{\text{Current liabilities}}\%$	133.6	130.3	142.2	178.9	174.7
Asset ratios						
Operating asset turnover	$\dfrac{\text{Sales}}{\text{Net operating assets}}$ times	2.1	2.4	2.3	2.5	2.5
Working capital turnover	$\dfrac{\text{Sales}}{\text{Working capital}}$ times	8.6	8.0	7.0	7.4	6.2

Per share

Earnings per	– pre-tax basis ....p	23.62	21.25	17.96	17.72	15.06
Share	– net basis....................................p	15.65	13.60	10.98	11.32	12.18
Dividends per share ....p		5.90	5.40	4.90	4.60	4.10
Net assets per share ....p		102.1	89.22	85.95	85.79	78.11

Net operating assets include tangible fixed assets, stock, debtors and creditors. They exclude borrowings, taxation and dividends.

Required:
Prepare a report on the company, clearly interpreting and evaluating the information given.

Question 2

You work for Euroc, a limited liability company, which seeks growth through acquisitions. You are a member of a team that is investigating the possible purchase of Choggerell, a limited liability company that manufactures a product complementary to the products currently being sold by Euroc.

Your team leader wants you to prepare a report for the team evaluating the recent performance of Choggerell and the quality of its management, and has given you the following financial information which has been derived from the financial statements of Choggerell for the three years ended 31 March 2006, 2007 and 2008.

Financial year ended 31 March	*2006*	*2007*	*2008*
Turnover (€ million)	2,243	2,355	2,237
Cash and cash equivalents (€ million)	−50	81	−97
Return on equity	13%	22%	19%
Sales revenue to total assets	2.66	2.66	2.01
Cost of sales to sales revenue	85%	82%	79%
Operating expenses to sales revenue	11%	12%	15%
Net income to sales revenue	2.6%	4.3%	4.2%
Current/Working Capital ratio (to 1)	1.12	1.44	1.06
Acid test ratio (to 1)	0.80	1.03	0.74
Inventory turnover (months)	0.6	0.7	1.0
Credit to customers (months)	1.3	1.5	1.7
Credit from suppliers (months)	1.5	1.5	2.0
Net assets per share (cents per share)	0.86	0.2	0.97
Dividend per share (cents per share)	10.0	14.0	14.0
Earnings per share (cents per share)	11.5	20.1	18.7

Required:
Use the above information to prepare a report for your team leader which:
(a) reviews the performance of Choggerell as evidenced by the above ratios;
(b) makes recommendations as to how the overall performance of Choggerel could be improved; and
(c) indicates any limitations in your analysis.

(The Association of International Accountants)

* Question 3

Growth plc made a cash offer for all of the ordinary shares of Beta Ltd on 30 October 20X9 at £2.75 per share. Beta's accounts for the year ended 31 March 20X9 showed:

	£000
Profit for the year after tax	750
Dividends paid and proposed	250
Retained profit for the year	500

Statement of financial position as at 31 March 20X9

		£000
Buildings		1,600
Other tangible non-current assets		1,400
		3,000
Current assets	2,000	
Current liabilities	1,400	
		600
		3,600
£1 Ordinary shares		2,500
Retained earnings		1,100
		3,600

Additional information:

(i) The half yearly profits to 30 September 20X9 show an increase of 25% over those of the corresponding period in 20X8. The directors are confident that this pattern will continue, or increase even further.

(ii) The Beta directors hold 90% of the ordinary shares.

(iii) Following valuations are available:

Realisable values

	£000
Buildings	2,500
Other non-current assets	700
Current assets	2,500

Net Replacement values

	£000
Buildings	2,600
Other non-current assets	1.800
Current assets	2,200

(iv) Shares in quoted companies in the same sector have a P/E ratio of 10. Beta Ltd is an unquoted company.

(v) One of the shareholders is a bank manager who advises the directors to press for a better price.

(vi) The extra risk for unquoted companies is 25% in this sector.

Required:
(a) Calculate valuations for the Beta ordinary shares using four different bases of valuation.
(b) Draft a report highlighting the limitaions of each basis and advise the directors whether the offer is reasonable.

Question 4

Quickserve plc is a food wholesale company. Its financial statements for the years ended 31 December 20X8 and 20X9 are as follows:

Statements of income

	20X9 £000	20X8 £000
Sales revenue	12,000	15,000
Gross profit	3,000	3,900
Distribution costs	500	600
Administrative expenses	1,500	1,000
Operating profit	1,000	2,300
Interest receivable	80	100
Interest payable	(400)	(350)
Profit before taxation	680	2,050
Income taxation	240	720
Profit after taxation	440	1,330
Dividends	800	600
(Loss)/profit retained	(360)	730

Statements of financial position

	20X9 £000	20X8 £000
Non-current assets:		
Intangible assets	200	—
Tangible assets	4,000	7,000
Investments	600	800
	4,800	7,800
Current assets:		
Inventory	250	300
Trade receivables	1,750	2,500
Cash & bank	1,500	200
	3,500	3,000
Total assets	8,300	10,800

	£000	£000
Equity and reserves:		
Ordinary shares of 10p each	1,000	1,000
Share premium account	1,000	1,000
Revaluation reserve	1,110	1,750
Retained earnings	3,190	3,550
	6,300	7,300
Debentures	1,000	2,000
Current liabilities	1,000	1,500
	8,300	10,800

Required:
(a) Describe the concerns of the following users and how reading an annual report might help satisfy these concerns:
   (i) Employees
   (ii) Bankers
   (iii) Shareholders.
(b) Calculate relevant ratios for Quickserve and suggest how each of the above user groups might react to these.

Question 5

R. Johnson inherited 810,000 £1 ordinary shares in Johnson Products Ltd on the death of his uncle in 20X5. His uncle had been the founder of the company and managing director until his death. The remainder of the issued shares were held in small lots by employees and friends, with no one holding more than 4%.

R. Johnson is planning to emigrate and is considering disposing of his shareholding. He has had approaches from three parties, who are:

1 A competitor – Sonar Products Ltd. Sonar Products Ltd considers that Johnson Products Ltd would complement its own business and is interested in acquiring all of the 810,000 shares. Sonar Products Ltd currently achieves a post-tax return of 12.5% on capital employed.

2 Senior employees. Twenty employees are interested in making a management buyout with each acquiring 40,500 shares from R. Johnson. They have obtained financial backing, in principle, from the company's bankers.

3 A financial conglomerate – Divest plc. Divest plc is a company that has extensive experience of acquiring control of a company and breaking it up to show a profit on the transaction. It is its policy to seek a pre-tax return of 20% from such an exercise.

The company has prepared draft accounts for the year ended 30 April 20X9. The following information is available.

(a) Past earnings and distributions:

Year ended 30 April £	Profit/(Loss) after tax %	Gross dividends declared
20X5	79,400	6
20X6	(27,600)	—
20X7	56,500	4
20X8	88,300	5
20X9	97,200	6

(b) Statement of financial position of Johnson Products Ltd as at 30 April 20X9:

	£000	£000
Non-current assets		
Land at cost		376
Premises at cost	724	
Aggregate depreciation	216	
		508
Equipment at cost	649	
Aggregate depreciation	353	
		296
Current assets		
Inventories	141	
Receivables	278	
Cash at bank	70	
	489	
Creditors due within one year	(335)	
Net current assets		154
Non-current liabilities		(158)
		1,176
Represented by:		
£1 ordinary shares		1,080
Retained earnings		96
		1,176

(c) Information on the nearest comparable listed companies in the same industry:

Company	Profit after tax for 20X9 £000	Retention %	Gross dividend yield %
Eastron plc	280	25	15
Westron plc	168	16	10.5
Northron plc	243	20	13.4

Profit after tax in each of the companies has been growing by approximately 8% per annum for the past five years.

(d) The following is an estimate of the net realisable values of Johnson Products Ltd's assets as at 30 April 20X9:

	£000
Land	480
Premises	630
Equipment	150
Receivables	168
Inventories	98

Required:
(a) As accountant for R. Johnson, advise him of the amount that could be offered for his share-holding with a reasonable chance of being acceptable to the seller, based on the information given in the question, by each of the following:

(i) Sonar Products Ltd;

(ii) the 20 employees;

(iii) Divest plc.

(b) As accountant for Sonar Products Ltd, estimate the maximum amount that could be offered by Sonar Products Ltd for the shares held by R. Johnson.

(c) As accountant for Sonar Products Ltd, state the principal matters you would consider in determining the future maintainable earnings of Johnson Products Ltd and explain their relevance.

(ACCA)

Question 6

Harry is about to start negotiations to purchase a controlling interest in NX, an unquoted limited liability company. The following is the statement of financial position of NX as at 30 June 2006, the end of the company's most recent financial year.

NX

Statement of financial position as at 30 June 2006

	$
ASSETS	
Non-current assets	3,369,520
Current assets	
Inventories, at cost	476,000
Trade and other receivables	642,970
Cash and cash equivalents	132,800
	1,251,770
Total assets	4,621,290
LIABILITIES AND EQUITY	
Non-current liabilities	
8% Loan note	260,000
	260,000
Current liabilities	
Trade and other payables	467,700
Current tax payable	414,700
	882,400
Equity	
Ordinary shares, 40 cent shares	2,000,000
5% Preferred shares of $1	200,000
Retained profits	1,278,890
	3,478,890
Total liabilities	1,142,400
Total liabilities and equity	4,621,290

The non-current assets of NX comprise:

	Cost	Depreciation	Net
	$	$	$
Property	2,137,500	262,500	1,875,000
Equipment	1,611,855	515,355	1,096,500
Motor vehicles	696,535	298,515	398,020
	4,445,890	1,076,370	3,369,520

NX has grown rapidly since its formation in 2000 by Albert Bell and Candy Dale who are currently directors of the company and who each own half of the company's issued share capital. The company was formed to exploit knowledge developed by Albert Bell. This knowledge is protected by a number of patents and trademarks owned by the company. Candy Dale's expertise was in marketing and she was largely responsible for developing the company's customer base. Figures for turnover and profit after tax taken from the statements of comprehensive income of the company for the past three years are:

	Turnover $	Profit after tax $
Profit for 2004	8,218,500	1,031,000
Profit for 2005	10,273,100	1,288,720
Profit for 2006	11,414,600	991,320

NX's property has recently been valued at $3,000,000 and it is estimated that the equipment and motor vehicles could be sold for a total of $1,568,426. The net realisable values of inventory and receivables are estimated at $400,000 and $580,000 respectively. It is estimated that the costs of selling off the company's assets would be $101,000.

The 8% loan note is repayable at a premium of 30% on 31 December 2006 and is secured on the company's property. It is anticipated that it will be possible to repay the loan note by issuing a new loan note bearing interest at 11% repayable in 2012.

As directors of the company, Albert Bell and Candy Dale receive annual remuneration of $99,000 and £74,000 respectively. Both would cease their relationship with NX because they wish to set up another company together. Harry would appoint a general manager at an annual salary of $120,000 to replace Albert Bell and Candy Dale.

Investors in quoted companies similar to NX are currently earning a dividend yield of 6% and the average PE ratio for the sector is currently 11. NX has been paying a dividend of 7% on its common stock for the past two years.

Ownership of the issued common stock and preferred shares is shared equally between Albert Bell and Candy Dale.

Harry wishes to purchase a controlling interest in NX.

Required
(a) On the basis of the information given, prepare calculations of the values of a preferred share and an ordinary share in NX on each of the following bases:
  (i) net realisable values;
  (ii) future maintainable earnings.
(b) Advise Harry on other factors which he should be considering in calculating the total amount he may have to pay to acquire a controlling interest in NX.

(The Association of International Accountants)

* Question 7

The major shareholder/director of Esrever Ltd has obtained average data for the industry as a whole. He wishes to see what the forecast results and position of Esrever Ltd would be if in the ensuing year its performance were to match the industry averages.

At 1 July 20X0, actual figures for Esrever Ltd included:

	£
Land and buildings (at written-down value)	132,000
Fixtures, fittings and equipment (at written-down value)	96,750
Inventory	22,040
12% loan (repayable in 20X5)	50,000
Ordinary share capital (50p shares)	100,000

For the year ended 30 June 20X1 the following forecast information is available:

1 Depreciation of non-current assets (on reducing balance)

Land and buildings	2%
Fixtures, fittings and equipment	20%

2 Net current assets will be financed by a bank overdraft to the extent necessary.

3 At 30 June 20X0 total assets minus current liabilities will be £231,808.

4 Profit after tax for the year will be 23.32% of gross profit and 11.16% of total assets minus all external liabilities, both long-term and short-term.

5 Tax will be at an effective rate of 20% of profit before tax.

6 Cost of sales will be 68% of turnover (excluding VAT).

7 Closing inventory will represent 61.9 days' average cost of sales (excluding VAT).

8 Any difference between total expenses and the aggregate of expenses ascertained from this given information will represent credit purchases and other credit expenses, in each case excluding VAT input tax.

9 A dividend of 2.5p per share will be proposed.

10 The collection period for the VAT-exclusive amount of trade receivables will be an average of 42.6 days of the annual turnover. All the company's supplies are subject to VAT output tax at 15%.

11 The payment period for the VAT-exclusive amount of trade payables (purchases and other credit expenses) will be an average of 29.7 days. All these items are subject to (reclaimable) VAT input tax at 15%. This VAT rate has been increased to 17.5% and may be subject to future changes, but for the purpose of this question the theory and workings remain the same irrespective of the rate.

12 Payables, other than trade payables, will comprise tax due, proposed dividends and VAT payable equal to one-quarter of the net amount due for the year.

13 Calculations are based on a year of 365 days.

Required:
Construct a forecast statement of comprehensive income for Esrever Ltd for the year ended 30 June 20X1 and a forecast statement of financial position at that date in as much detail as possible. (All calculations should be made to the nearest £1.)

Question 8

The directors of Chekani plc, a large listed company, are engaged in a policy of expansion. Accordingly, they have approached the directors of Meela Ltd, an unlisted company of substantial size, in connection with a proposed purchase of Meela Ltd.

The directors of Meela Ltd have indicated that the shareholders of Meela Ltd would prefer the form of consideration for the purchase of their shares to be in cash and you are informed that this is acceptable to the prospective purchasing company, Chekani plc.

The directors of Meela Ltd have now been asked to state the price at which the shareholders of Meela Ltd would be prepared to sell their shares to Chekani plc. As a member of a firm of independent accountants, you have been engaged as a consultant to advise the directors of Meela Ltd in this regard.

In order that you may be able to do so, the following details, extracted from the most recent financial statements of Meela, have been made available to you.

Meela Ltd accounts for year ended 30 June 20X4

Statement of financial position extracts as at 30 June 20X4:

	£000
Purchased goodwill unamortised	15,000
Freehold property	30,000
Plant and machinery	60,000
Investments	15,000
Net current assets	12,000
10% debentures 20X9	(30,000)
Ordinary shares of £1 each (cumulative)	(40,000)
7% preference shares of £1 each (cumulative)	(12,000)
Share premium account	(20,000)
Retained earnings	(30,000)

Meela Ltd disclosed a contingent liability of £3.0m in the notes to the statement of financial position.

(Amounts in brackets indicate credit balances.)

Statement of comprehensive income extracts for the year ended 30 June 20X4:

	£000
Profit before interest payments and taxation and exceptional items	21,000
Exceptional items	1,500
Interest	(3,000)
Taxation	(6,000)
Dividends paid – Preference	(840)
– Ordinary	(3,000)
Retained profit for the year	9,660

(Amounts in brackets indicate a charge or appropriation to profits.)

The following information is also supplied:

(i) Profit before interest and tax for the year ended 30 June 20X3 was £24.2 million and for the year ended 30 June 20X2 it was £30.3 million.

(ii) Assume tax at 30%.

(iii) Exceptional items in 20X4 relate to the profit on disposal of an investment in a related company. The related company contributed to profit before interest as follows:

To 30 June 20X4	£0
To 30 June 20X3	£200,000
To 30 June 20X2	£300,000

(iv) The preference share capital can be sold independently, and a buyer has already been found. The agreed purchase price is 90p per share.

(v) Chekani plc has agreed to purchase the debentures of Meela Ltd at a price of £110 for each £100 debenture.

(vi) The current rental value of the freehold property is £4.5 million per annum and a buyer is available on the basis of achieving an 8% return on their investment.

(vii) The investments of Meela Ltd have a current market value of £22.5 million.

(viii) Meela Ltd is engaged in operations substantially different from those of Chekani plc. The most recent financial data relating to two listed companies that are engaged in operations similar to those of Meela Ltd are:

	NV per share	Market price per share	P/E	Net dividend per share	Cover	Yield
Ranpar plc	£1	£3.06	11.3	12 pence	2.6	4.9
Menner plc	50p	£1.22	8.2	4 pence	3.8	4.1

Required:

Write a report, of approximately 2,000 words, to the directors of Meela Ltd, covering the following:

(a) Advise them of the alternative methods used for valuing unquoted shares and explain some of the issues involved in the choice of method.

(b) Explain the alternative valuations that could be placed on the ordinary shares of Meela Ltd.

(c) Recommend an appropriate strategy for the board of Meela Ltd to adopt in its negotiations with Chekani plc.

Include, as appendices to your report, supporting schedules showing how the valuations were calculated.

Question 9

Discuss the following issues with regard to financial reporting for risk:

(a) How can a company identify and prioritise its key risks?

(b) What actions can a company take to manage the risks identified in (a)?

(c) How can a company measure risk?

Question 10

Flash Fashions plc has had a difficult nine months and the management team is discussing strategy for the final quarter.

In the last nine months the company has survived by cutting production, reducing staff and reducing overheads wherever possible. However, the share market, whilst recognising that sales across the industry have been poor, has worried about the financial strength of the business and as a result the share price has fallen 40%.

The company is desperate to increase sales. It has been recognised that the high fixed costs of the factory are not being fully absorbed by the lower volumes which are costed at standard cost. If sales and production can be increased then more factory costs will be absorbed and increased sales volume will raise staff morale and make analysts think the firm is entering a turnaround phase.

The company decides to drop prices by 15% for the next two months and to change the terms of sale so that property does not pass until the clothes are paid for. This is purely a reflection of the tough economic conditions and the need to protect the firm against customer insolvency. Further, it is decided that if sales have not increased enough by the end of the two months, the company representatives will be advised to ship goods to customers on the understanding that they will be invoiced but if they don't sell the goods in two months they can return them. Volume discounts will be stressed to keep the stock moving.

These actions are intended to increase sales, increase profitability, justify higher stocks, and to ensure that more overheads are transferred out of the profit statement into stocks.

For the purposes of annual reporting it was decided not to spell out sales growth in financial figure terms in the managing director's report but rather to focus on units shipped in graphs using scales (possibly log scales) designed to make the fall look less dramatic. Also comparisons will be made against industry volumes as the fashion industry has been more affected by economic conditions than the economy as a whole.

To make the ratios look better, the company will enter into an agreement on the last week of the year with a two-dollar company called Upstart Ltd owned by Colleen Livingston, friend of the managing director of Flash Fashions, Sue Cotton. Upstart Ltd will sign a contract to buy a property for £30 million from Flash Fashions and will also sign promissory notes payable over the next three quarters for £10 million each. The auditors will not be told, but Flash Fashions will enter into an agreement to buy back the property for £31 million any time after the start of the third month in the new financial year.

Required:
Critically discuss each of the proposed strategies.

Question 11

Briefly state:

(i) the case for segmental reporting;
(ii) the case against segmental reporting.

References

1 www.nasdaq.com/xbrl
2 ICAEW, *Financial Reporting of Risk*, Discussion Paper, 1998.
3 www.djindexes.com/mdsidx/downloads/Islamic/articles/private-equity-finance.pdf
4 www.mscibarra.com/products/indices/islamic/
5 www.djindexes.com/mdsidx/downloads/brochure_info/DJIM_brochure.pdf
6 J. Collier, *Aggressive Earnings Management: Is it still a significant threat?*, ICAEW October 2004.
7 Alpa A. Virdi, *Investors' Confidence in Audited Financial Information Research Report*, ICAEW December 2004.
8 *The Times*, 28 January 2004.
9 C. Pratten, *Company Failure*, Financial Reporting and Auditing Group, ICAEW, 1991, pp. 43–45.
10 R.J. Taffler, 'Forecasting company failure in the UK using discriminant analysis and financial ratio data', *Journal of the Royal Statistical Society*, Series A, vol. 145, part 3, 1982, pp. 342–358.
11 M.L. Inman, 'Altman's Z-formula prediction', *Management Accounting*, November 1982, pp. 37–39.

12 E.I. Altman, 'Financial ratios, discriminant analysis and the prediction of corporate bankruptcy', *Journal of Finance*, vol. 23(4), 1968, pp. 589–609.

13 M.L. Inman, 'Z-scores and the going concern review', *ACCA Students' Newsletter*, August 1991, pp. 8–13.

14 R.J. Taffler, *op. cit.*; R.J. Taffler, 'Z-scores: an approach to the recession', *Accountancy*, July 1991, pp. 95–97.

15 M.L. Inman, *op. cit.*, 1991.

16 G. Holmes and R. Dunham, *Beyond the Statement of Financial Position*, Woodhead Faulkner, 1994.

17 K. Van Peursem and M. Pratt, 'Failure prediction in New Zealand SMEs: measuring signs of trouble', *International Journal of Business Performance Management (IJBPM)*, vol. 8, no. 2/3, 2006.

18 M. Urry, 'Early warning signals', *Financial Times*, 5 October 1999.

19 J. Argenti, 'Predicting corporate failure', *Accountants Digest*, no. 138, Summer 1983, pp. 18–21.

20 http://news.bbc.co.uk/l/hi/business/4352553.stm

21 A. Charitou, E. Neophytou and C. Charalambous, 'Predicting corporate failure: empirical evidence for the UK', *European Accounting Review*, 2004, vol. 13, pp. 465–497.

22 J. Stern, 'Management: its mission and its measure', *Director*, October 1994, pp. 42–44.

23 W.A. Nixon and C.J. McNair, 'A measure of R&D', *Accountancy*, October 1994, p. 138.

24 C. Martin and J. Hartley, *SME intangible assets*, Certified Accountants Research Report 93, London, 2006.

25 www.accaglobal.com/databases/pressandpolicy/unitedkingdom/3107831

26 http://ec.europa.eu/internal_market/consultations/docs/securities_agencies/consultation-cra-framework_en.pdf

27 www.sec.gov/news/press/2008/nrsrofactsheet-120308.htm

28 J. Robertson, 'Company failure – measuring changes in financial health through ratio analysis', *Management Accounting*, November 1983.

CHAPTER 29

An introduction to financial reporting on the Internet

29.1 Introduction

The main objective of this chapter is to explain what XBRL is and how reports in XBRL assist investors and analysts to access and analyse data in published financial statements.

Objectives

By the end of the chapter, you should be able to:

- understand the reason for the development of a business reporting language;
- explain the benefits of tagging in XML and XBRL code data for financial reporting;
- understand why companies should adopt XBRL;
- list the processes a company needs to take to adopt XBRL.

29.2 The reason for the development of a business reporting language

We saw in the previous chapter that various online subscription databases such as Datastream, FAME and OneSource are available, where selected financial reports have been formatted by each of the databases into a standardised format. This allows subscribers to select peer groups and search across a variety of variables. Students having access to such databases at their own institution may carry out a range of assignments and projects such as selecting companies suitable for takeover based on stated criteria such as ROCE, % sales and % earnings growth.

29.2.1 Financial reporting on the Internet in PDF files

At an individual company level we find that most companies have a website to communicate all types of information to interested parties including financial information. Stakeholders or other interested parties can then download this information for their own particular use. Most of the financial information is in the format of PDF files created by a software program called Adobe® Acrobat®. This program is used for the conversion of all their documents, which make up the financial information contained within the annual general reports, into one document, a PDF file, for publication on the Internet. This PDF file can be formatted to include encryption and digital signatures to ensure that the document cannot be changed.

In order for the user to be able to read the PDF files, a special software program called Adobe Reader® needs to be downloaded from the Adobe website www.adobe.com.

29.2.2 Data re-keyed for analysis

Other formats used to display company information are often in Hyper Text Mark-up Language (HTML). HTML mainly defines the appearance of the information on the computer screen such as placement, colour, font, etc. But even though it is helpful to be able to download the file and read or print the financial information on screen or on paper, when calculations need to be performed the information needs to be retyped unless, as with a few companies, the data is also in Excel format. When we need to consider and evaluate multiple years of a company's financial results or evaluate companies in a sector then this rekeying is an even more time-consuming task and subject to errors.

Other interested parties or stakeholders such as investment analysts, merchant bankers, banks, regulatory bodies and government taxation departments may be able to request information in specific electronic formats otherwise they also will need to rekey the data.

29.3 Reports and the flow of information pre-XBRL

The information flow from an organisation reporting to stakeholders and regulatory bodies and banks is considerable. The information required is not the same for each of the external parties and so one report is not appropriate.

A typical flow is set out in Figure 29.1 demonstrating how information is collated from Operational Data Stores and coded to the General Ledger (GL) using the chart of accounts

Figure 29.1 Today: a convoluted information supply chain

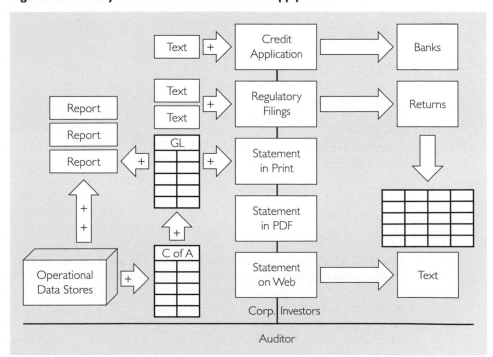

Source: www.xbrl.org.au/training/NSWWorkshop.pdf

(C of A). Once the data has been captured in the GL, statements of comprehensive income, financial position and cash flows can be produced for shareholders and for statutory filing. In addition, separate reports are produced for a variety of other stakeholders such as the tax authorities, stock exchanges, banks and creditors. The reports can be in different formats such as printed statements for internal management and audit use, hard copy annual reports for investors, and summary or full reports on a company's home webpage in PDF or HTML format now that this is becoming mandatory or encouraged. This is a very costly process which has led to the development of a special business reporting language called eXtensible **B**usiness **R**eporting **L**anguage or **XBRL** which is based on XML.

Accountants will become increasingly involved with its development and this chapter provides a brief oversight of a development that is going to make a major impact internationally on the availability of financial data for comparative analysis. Just as the IASB is gradually achieving uniformity of accounting policies, XBRL will gradually achieve uniformity in the presentation of data on the Internet. Note that XBRL is not an accounting standard. It is a language specifically constructed for the exchange of financial information. As with other financial statements, the reader needs to be aware of the accounting standards applicable to the statements under review. XBRL does not in any way attempt to specify accounting rules.

29.4 What are HTML, XML and XBRL?

XBRL is based upon the eXtensible Mark-up Language or XML. XML itself is an extension of the Hyper Text Mark-up Language (HTML) which controls the format and display of web pages. We will briefly comment on each:

HTML

HTML is extensively used in website creation for the purposes of display. For example, the following text using HTML would have tags that describe the format and placement of the text.

> **Assets $50,000**
> **Liabilities $25,000**

> \<p>\<b>Assets $50,000\</b>\</p>
> \<p>\<b>Liabilities $25,000\</b>\</p>

where \<p> instructs the item to be printed on the screen (and also where on the screen or in what format) and \<b> instructs the item to be displayed in bold print. The \</p> denotes the end of the commands and instructs the data to be 'printed' on the computer screen.

XML

XML is a language developed by the World Wide Web Consortium.[1] It goes one step further by allowing for 'tags' to be created which convey identification and meaning of the data within the tags. Thus instead of looking simply at format and presentation, the XML code looks for the text displayed within the code. For example, the user can design the tags used in XML as follows:

> **Assets $50,000** in this example of XML would be written as
> \<Assets>$50,000\</Assets> and similarly for **Liabilities $25,000** the XML code
> would be \<Liabilities>$25,000\</Liabilities>

The computer program reading the XML code would thus know that the value found of $50,000 within the tags relates to Assets.

XBRL

XBRL has taken XML one step further and designed 'tags' based upon the common financial language used. For example, the term ASSETS or LIABILITIES is a common term used in financial reports even though the calculations or valuations and the definitions used in different accounting standards may be dependent on those accounting standards applicable to the company.

29.4.1 Advantages of XBRL

Using XBRL means that it is easier for direct system-to-system information sharing between a company and its stakeholders and allows for improved analytical capacity. The numeric data in the financial statements of all companies filing their annual reports will be uniformly defined and presented and available for analysis, e.g. downloaded into Excel and other analytical software. The advantage of using XBRL according to XBRL International[2] is that:

> Computers can treat XBRL data 'intelligently': they can recognise the information in a XBRL document, select it, analyse it, store it, exchange it with other computers and present it automatically in a variety of ways for users. XBRL greatly increases the speed of handling of financial data, reduces the chance of error and permits automatic checking of information.

29.5 Reports and the flow of information post-XBRL

When XBRL is used (a) information flows from an organisation to stakeholders are much simpler as seen in Figure 29.2, and (b) it possible for stakeholders to receive information that can be understood by computer software and allow them to analyse the data obtained, as seen in Figure 29.3.

Figure 29.2 With XRBL: multiple outlets from a single specification

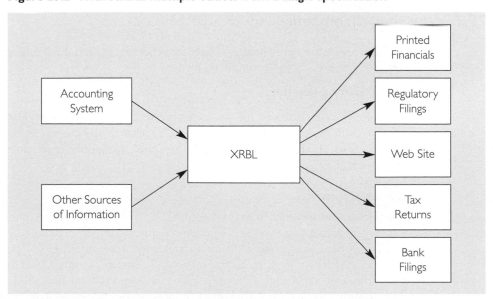

Source: http://xbrl.org.au/training/NSWWorkshop.pdf

Figure 29.3 XRBL: information flow to stakeholders

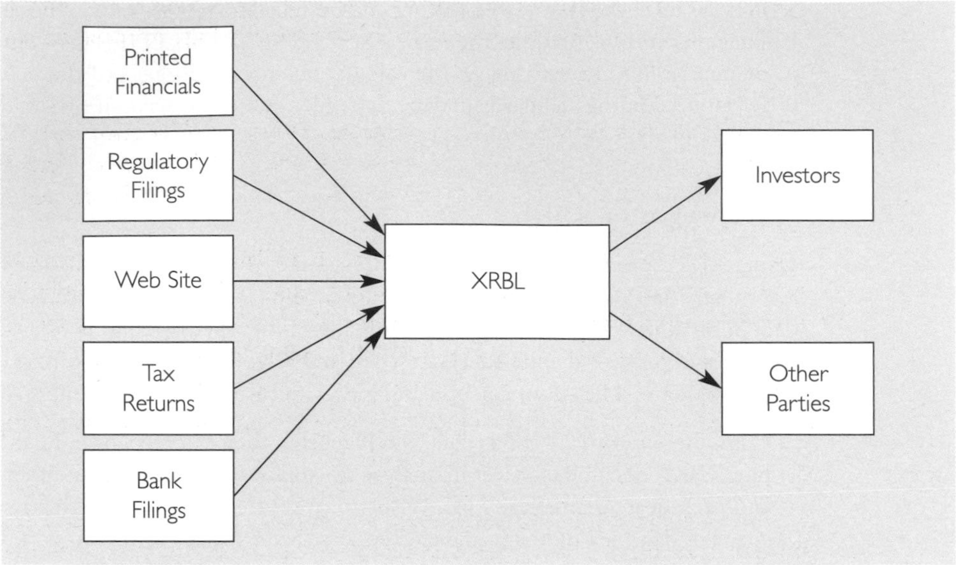

Source: http://xbrl.org.au/training/NSWWorkshop.pdf

29.6 XBRL and the IASB

Tags have been developed as a business reporting language and individual countries are setting their own priorities as to the reports that are being initially developed. As regards financial reporting, the IASB has developed XBRL applicable to IFRSs. We are on course for the content of financial statements to be standardised through IFRSs and that content to be presented in a standardised uniform digital format.

29.7 Why should companies adopt XBRL?

There are regulatory pressures and commercial benefits concerning the adoption of XBRL.

29.7.1 Regulatory pressures

One of the driving forces has been the pressure from national regulatory bodies for companies to file corporate tax returns, stock exchange and corporate statutory financial statements in XBRL format. In some countries there are specific requirements for financial statements filing.

US developments

The US Securities and Exchange Commission (SEC) requires[3] that public and foreign Companies with a float over $5 billion, representing approximately the top 500 companies listed with SEC, who prepare financial statements based on US GAAP must lodge their reports in XBRL from April 2009. Smaller US companies using US GAAP and foreign companies using IFRS must lodge their financial reports from June 2011. All companies lodging their statements in XBRL must also publish this information, on the same day they submit to the SEC, on their corporate websites and this information must be available for 12 months after lodging with SEC. The XBRL based statements still have the limited liability status as under the voluntary filing programme until 31 October 2014. After this date the XBRL based statements will have the same legal status as any other financial report. This will have implications for auditors and preparers of the financial reports.

UK developments

UK companies filing accounts at Companies House were notified that from April 2011 online submissions must be prepared using Inline XBRL (iXBRL). iXBRL is a specific form of XBRL that focuses on the human readable format. It is planned for commercial software to be available[4] from spring 2010.

HM Revenue and Customs (HMRC) require similar filing and have stated that companies with a turnover of more than £100,000 must lodge online for companies with accounting periods starting from 1 April 2010. For any new business registering for VAT there is no choice, all returns must comply[5] with iXBRL online filing.

Companies House and HMRC requirements mean that all companies submitting online must be familiar with iXBRL and understand the implications for their company.

EU developments and the accounting profession

A policy statement from the Federation of European Accountants (FEE) details the impact upon accountants.[6] The impacts considered are the ability to assist with the application of XBRL and the assurance/auditing process of accounting information prepared with XBRL. The accounting profession itself will have to educate their members about all aspects of XBRL.

29.7.2 Commercial benefits

The above is a brief introduction to just some of the XBRL developments that are occurring around the world whereby companies can easily generate tailored reports from a single data set and the data can be readily accessed at a lower cost by regulators, auditors, credit rating agencies, investors and research institutions.

29.8 What is needed to use XBRL for outputting information?

There are four processes, supported by the appropriate software, to be completed to adopt XBRL. The processes are (a) taxonomy design, (b) mapping, (c) creating an instance document and (d) selecting and applying a stylesheet.

(a) The taxonomy needs to be designed

Taxonomy has two functions. It establishes relationships and defines elements acting like a dictionary. For example, the taxonomy for assets in the statement of financial position would be to show how total assets are derived by aggregating each asset and defining each asset as follows:

	Relationship	Definitions
Non-current assets	a	Not expected to be converted into cash within one year
Current assets		Expected to be turned into cash in less than one year
Inventory	v	Finished goods ready for sale, goods in course of production and raw materials
Trade receivables	w	Amounts owed by customers
Cash	x	Cash and cash equivalents
Subtotal	v + w + x	
Total assets	a + v + w + x	

The taxonomy also contains linkbases which provide additional information. For example:

- a means to cross-reference with the para in the relevant IFRS;
- an indication of the language used in the financial report e.g. English, French;
- prompts when a note to the accounts is required for a particular element.

Calculation: contains the validation rules and weights given to monetary items. For example, gross profit is calculated by taking away the cost of sales from revenue (GP = Revenue − COS). Revenue would be assigned 1 and COS would be minus 1 (noted as −1) to achieve gross profit, also assigned a weight of 1.

Presentation: is used when reports need to be constructed. Business reports use parent–child type or tree type structures as in the term 'Assets'. Assets is the *parent* of Current and Non-Current Assets. Mimicking the business report structures helps users to find the terms they are interested in.

Each country has been developing its own taxonomies. Since the issue by the IASB of the *IFRS Taxonomy Guide* in 2008, future taxonomies could be designed based upon the IFRS guide.

(b) Mapping

The term 'mapping' relates to equating the terminology used in the financial statements to 'names' used in the taxonomy. For example, if the taxonomy refers to 'Inventory' as being products held for sale, but the organisation refers to this as 'Stock In Trade' in the financial statements then this needs to be 'mapped' to the taxonomy. All the names used in the financial statements, or any other reports, need thus be compared and mapped to (identified with) the taxonomy. This 'mapping' is done for the first time the taxonomy is used.

(c) Instance documents

The instance document holds the data which are to be reported. For example, if preparing the statement of financial position at 30 September 2010 then entries of individual asset values would be made in this document. This data would then be input to a stylesheet to produce the required report.

	Values	*Date*
Non-current assets	1,250	30.9.2010
Inventory	650	30.9.2010
Trade receivables	310	30.9.2010
Cash	129	30.9.2010

(d) Stylesheets

The format of a required report is specified in a template referred to as a stylesheet where the display is pre-designed. A stylesheet can be used repeatedly as, for example, for an annual report or new stylesheets can be designed if reports are more variable as in interim reports. The annual report would be displayed in correct format with appropriate headings, currency and scale. For example:

Statement of financial position as at 30 September 2010

	$000	$000
Non-current assets		1,250
Current assets		
Inventory	650	
Trade receivables	310	
Cash	129	
		1,089
Total assets		2,339

The taxonomy and stylesheets do not need to be changed every time a report is produced. The only changes that are made are those in the instance documents regarding data entries.

Summary of the four processes

A summary is set out in Figure 29.4.

Figure 29.4 Summary of the four processes

29.9 What is needed when receiving XBRL output information?

Institutional users

Institutions which receive XBRL formatted financial information from companies, such as Revenue Authorities, Stock Exchanges, Banks and Insurance companies, normally require the information to be lodged according to a pre-determined format and their software is specifically designed to be able extract and display the XBRL data.

Non-institutional users

For other interested parties, specific software is needed to make the XBRL format data readable. In order for the text to be understood by a human in a way that indicates that we are looking at a financial report, it needs to be 'translated', a process known as **rendering** by computer. 'Rendering' the items contained within XBRL is the current challenge.

Example of rendering

The text below represents the code for XBRL formatted data in an instance document:

Instance document in XBRL

```
<ifrs-gp:AssetsHeldSale contextRef=vCurrent_AsOf" unitRef="U-Euros"
   decimals="0">100000</ifrs-gp:AssetsHeldSale>

<ifrs-gp:ConstructionProgressCurrent contextRef="Current_AsOf"
   unitRBf="U-Euros" decimals="0">100000</ifrs-
   gp:ConstructionProgressCurrent>

<ifrs-gp:Inventories contextRef="Current_AsOf" unitRef="U-Euros"
   decimals="0">100000</ifrs-gp:Inventories>

<ifrs-gp:OtherFinancialAssetsCurrent contextRef="Current_AsOf"
   unitRef="U-Euros" decimals="0">100000</ifrs-
   gp:OtherFinancialAssetsCurrent>

<ifrs-gp:HedgingInstrumentsCurrentAsset contextRef="Current_AsOf"
   unitRef="U-Euros" decimals="0">100000</ifrs-
   gp:HedgingInstrumentsCurrentAsset>

<ifrs-gp:CurrentTaxReceivables contextRef="Current_AsOf" unitRef="U-Euros"
   decimals="0">100000</ifrs-gp:CurrentTaxReceivables>

<ifrs-gp:TradeOtherReceivablesNetCurrent contextRef="Current_AsOf"
   unitRef="U-Euros" decimals="0">100000</ifrs-
   gp:TradeOtherReceivablesNetCurrent>

<ifrs-gp:PrepaymentsCurrent contextRef="Current_AsOf" unitRef="U-Euros"
   decimals="0">100000</ifrs-gp:PrepaymentsCurrent>

<ifrs-gp:CashCashEquivalents contextRef="Current_AsOf" unitRef="U-Euros"
   decimals="0">100000</ifrs-gp:CashCashEquivalents>

<ifrs-gp:OtherAssetsCurrent contextRef="Current_AsOf" unitRef="U-Euros"
   decimals="0">100000</ifrs-gp:OtherAssetsCurrent>

<ifrs-gp:AssetsCurrentTotal contextRef="Current_AsOf" unitRef="U-Euros"
   decimals="0">1000000</ifrs-gp:AssetsCurrentTotal>
```

Looking at the first two lines of code, it is possible to see that the data contain financial information about assets held for sale, that these are 'Current' and that the unit of measurement is in euros and has zero decimals with a value of 100,000. This is possible for a few lines but it would not be feasible to do this for a complex financial statement. Rendering translates the code into readable format as follows:

Rendered XBRL data

CURRENT ASSETS

Assets Held for Sale	100,000
Construction in Progress, Current	100,000
Inventories	100,000
Hedging Instruments, Current [Asset]	100,000
Current Tax Receivables	100,000
Trade and Other Receivables, Net, Current	100,000
Prepayments, Current	100,000
Cash and Cash Equivalents	100,000
Other Assets, Current	100,000
Current assets, Total	**1,000,000**

The data can now be recognised as belonging to that part of the financial statement where the current assets are listed. This example can be found at http://www.xbrl.org/Example1/.

The rendering process is of particular interest to investors and other third parties who may want to access financial data in XBRL format for evaluation purposes and who may not have software capable of rendering the instance document into human readable format. The ability to render an XBRL document becomes even more important for an investor or analyst seeking to carryout trend or inter-firm comparison analysis. For a more in-depth discussion of the processes involved in rendering visit www.xbrl.org/uk/Rendering/.

29.9.1 How has XBRL assisted the user?

If we take the revenue authorities as an example, they have had their own in-house developed software for carrying out a risk analysis in an attempt to identify those that look as though they should be investigated. Such risk analysis was routine before XBRL but XBRL has allowed the existing analysis software to be refined – this allows obviously compliant companies to be identified and investigation to be targeted where there is possible or probable non-compliance. However, it was still not possible to read the data in human form.

29.9.2 Development of iXBRL

Inline XBRL (known as iXBRL) has been developed so that the XBRL data is capable of being read by the user. It achieves this by embedding the XBRL coding in an HTML document so that it is similar to reading a web page. iXBRL takes a report, say a company's published accounts, in Excel, MS Word or PDF and then 'translates' this to iXBRL. It is then still able to be viewed in human readable format. This would be an advantage for smaller businesses where there may not be accountants with XBRL skills or where the cost would be prohibitive and they also do not need more advanced software. Corefiling's software[7] would be a good example of iXBRL.

This is newly developed software and, if you want to explore this a little further, there are helpful websites – one that offers a software company's view[8] and one that offers another perspective.[9]

How has iXBRL assisted the user?

If we consider the position of the regulators we can see that there is an impact on narrative in reports. For example, there is the requirement of the SEC to include the notes to the business reports in a certain format in the near future. For the larger companies[10] this means that tags have to be developed for many more items than before. The inclusion of the notes to the accounts is not new but the new requirements from the SEC involve different levels of disclosure within the notes and this will require further development of either a linkbase or a standard approach to the application of stylesheets.

If we continue with the revenue authorities example, the availability of the data in readable format has meant that, once a high risk case has been identified, it is possible to drill down into the data and highlight relationships that would not have been possible before iXBRL.

XBRL data may be exported to Excel

Facilities are being developed all the time and access to financial data is being constantly improved.

29.9.3 International experience

US experience

In the US, SEC data are being exported to an Excel spreadsheet for analysis.[11] This facility also allows for downloading to Excel spreadsheets and charting operations on screen. However, because companies have different items in their financial reports, it is not possible to make a line by line comparison. The user needs to synchronise items and to do this needs to be conversant with the accounting definition of each individual item.

UK experience

In the UK, data that has been submitted to Companies House can be obtained but at a cost.[12] Investors who go to the company's individual website to download the financial information will find that most will be in Adobe Acrobat (PDF) format and not easily copied to Excel for comparative analysis.

XBRL UK reports[13] that both HMRC and Companies House are implementing the recommendations as set out in the Carter report of March 2006. Since the announcement[14] in 2009 this project is now progressing and iXBRL will be used to submit returns to both agencies by the summer of 2010. The advantage of using iXBRL is that the document produced using this method can be read by humans as the code is 'rendered' in HTML-looking documents. Businesses can continue to use their current software and then as an iXBRL software to render the document in that code.

Singaporean experience

Singapore's Accounting Corporate Regulatory Authority (ACCRA),[15] the regulating authority for businesses incorporated in Singapore, has been receiving company reports for most incorporated commercial companies in XBRL format since 2007. Company information can also be purchased from the ACCRA website. The information has been extracted from the data lodged with ACCRA[16] for a demo of the type of analysis available. The demo on this website also included evaluation of the company's position in relation to their peers within the industry or the whole industry. This extends the use of business reports from merely financial to the position of the company in the economic environment of their industry sector.

Most investment analysis providers have their analysis and rendering software written in-house to service their investment clients and investment brokers. For investors wanting to do their own investment analysis there is still a wait for suitable software to obtain XBRL data and then view it on a PC. iXBRL may be able to fill this gap.

Australian experience

In Australia, the Australian Prudential Regulatory Authority (APRA), is the government body that controls and regulates banking and superannuation funds in Australia. It collects regular data using its own Taxonomy D2A (Direct to APRA) based on XBRL. There may be changes to this as the Australian federal government is well on the way to implementing standard business reporting (SBR). The government estimated that the use of SBR, based on XBRL taxonomies, will provide savings per year of $800 million to Australian businesses. The process is facilitated by the Australian Treasury. Agencies currently participating in SBR include the Australian Taxation Office (ATO), the Australian Securities and Investments Commission (ASIC), the Australian Prudential Regulation Authority (APRA), all State and Territory government revenue offices (ROs) and the Australian Bureau of Statistics.

Participation is voluntary and the required files are distributed by the Treasury.[17] Taxation returns and Business Activity Statements (BAS), required to be lodged by businesses for Goods and Services Tax (GST, equivalent to the UK VAT) to the ATO. The ATO requires precise formatting for the collection of the business activities.

Estimates by the Australian government are that the application of SBR to the government data has resulted in the elimination of approximately 7,000 data elements.[18]

New Zealand experience

New Zealand has also joined Australia in the SBR project. The New Zealand government is developing a similar approach to SBR with the streamlining of business forms and business information collected by the NZ government agencies. To this effect the NZ budget provides for $3 million over the 2009/10 operational budget.[19]

European experience

In Europe there have been a number of projects,[20] in the last few years, some of which have been very extensive. For example, the Dutch project 'Renewal Government Services' is a €250 million project initiated by the Dutch Ministry of Justice and Finance to improve information to be lodged by businesses to government departments and access to published information by third parties. It also provides for €22.4 million for the next four years from 2008 to expand the Dutch taxonomy. It is envisaged that other government areas[21] such as health and education will be the focus of attention for further development of the project. An example[22] of the extended use of XBRL is demonstrated by the government of the Netherlands' use for the yearly budget. The Netherlands also has a taxonomy for use in the banking sector.[23]

In Germany[24] the electronic federal gazette so far has received almost half of the annual reports in XBRL since 2007.

29.9.4 Development of XBRL and iXBRL beyond statutory financial reporting

Sharing data

The development of the SBR projects in Australia, New Zealand, the Netherlands and the US are good examples of the extension and application of XBRL beyond financial reporting and accounting. Development of these projects is an enormous task and requires a lot of planning, design and testing by all parties involved.

The next logical step is for government agencies to share the data submitted rather than business having to lodge different reports for different purposes. This will mean though that governments need to rationalise the formats and volume in which they require businesses to lodge information.

We have discussed the use of XBRL and iXBRL for submitting reports to statutory authorities. There have also been interesting developments in their use for internal accounting.

29.10 Progress of **XBRL** development for internal accounting

Development in the general ledger area is continuing and will probably be one of the most important developments for companies with consolidation requirements when multiple general ledgers are involved. The general ledger specification has the advantage that organisational data is classified at source and the classification decision with respect to XBRL names will have been made at the Chart of Accounts level.

This is quite a task as the financial statements usually report aggregated data. For example, the total for administration expenses in the Income Statement is usually made up by aggregating a number of different account classifications in the General Ledger. A further consideration is the effect of IFRSs when aggregating expense accounts. For example, the Chart of Account structure for the disclosure of segmentation by product class or geographical areas, is distinctly different. The XBRL code also needs to reflect this.

The XBRL for the General Ledger may also bring great cost savings as data collection at source is automated and the extraction and processing of data into reports can be achieved in a much shorter time. A company such as General Electric has more than 150 general ledgers which are not compatible in use. XBRL has the potential to considerably streamline consolidation processes considerably.

The XBRL Global General Ledger Working Group (XBRL GL WG) within XBRL has released an updated GL module[25] to include the SRCD (Summary Reporting Contextual Data):

> SRCD is a module of the XBRL Global Ledger Framework (XBRL GL) designed to facilitate the link between detailed data represented with XBRL GL and end reporting represented with XBRL for financial reporting (XBRL FR) or other XML schemas.

This module should enable a streamlined preparation of business reports from the general ledger. In February 2010 the GL framework also released the GL module with Japanese labels and this is now awaiting feedback and then a final recommendation.

29.11 Further study

The XBRL International website (www.xbrl.org) has an extensive listing of companies and authorities currently using XBRL. This website also released a discussion paper[26] in February 2010 to obtain feedback from stakeholders and interested parties on the future directions for XBRL. The reader is encouraged to investigate further any of the resources available on the XBRL and other websites. A number of the links provided will lead to good discussions of the projects and demonstrate how XBRL is applied. Some of the links will also bring the reader to websites in languages other than English (Google translation toolbar may be helpful) and may be of particular interest to readers of this text living in these countries.

Summary

XBRL is still a developing area relating to organisational reporting. In the coming years this will continue and extend beyond the current focus on published financial statements. The general ledger area is developing and this will benefit the organisational information supply chain. Accounting software suppliers are also adopting XBRL in their developments and this will increase accessibility to XBRL. Accounting software companies such as MYOB, aimed at smaller organisations, are also using XBRL in their new developments. Future software development may also make it easier for accountants to use XBRL, especially when a country's taxonomies are in 'final' approved stage.

Financial statements presented in XBRL format are capable of being downloaded into an analyst/investor's own spreadsheet (such as Microsoft Excel). The advantage of this is that the analyst/investor does not need to retype the information. The commercial databases which compile specific information for analysts/investors are usually only concerned with public companies listed on the Stock Exchange. XBRL allows any type of financial information to be transferred to a statistical package without having to retype the information. XBRL could thus also benefit not-for-profit organisations and trusts, etc. Professional accounting consultants would also be able to use XBRL in transferring information from a client's accounting package into an analytical tool to prepare information to evaluate business efficiency. This information is often more extensive than the end of year financial information.

Large software developers such as SAP announced in February 2009 that 'SAP® BusinessObjects™' is now available for financial publications in XBRL. This conforms to Security and Exchange Commission (SEC) requirements to lodge specific financial information from June 2009. SAP also stated that its software also can be used to lodge financial information using XBRL with HM Revenue & Customs in the UK. The software allows for automatic and easy tagging of the information (see www.xbrlspy.org/ sap_announces_xbrl_publishing_support).

Accountants and students wishing to keep up-to-date with these developments are gaining a competitive advantage by creating and developing a 'niche' skill which can only add value to an organisation employing these professionals.

REVIEW QUESTIONS

1 Discuss how an investor might benefit from annual reports being made available in XBRL.

2 Explain how a body such as a tax authority might benefit from XBRL.

3 Explain what you understand by taxonomy and mapping.

4 Explain the use of instance documents.

5 Explain the use of stylesheets.

6 Explain iXBRL and where it is used.

EXERCISES

Question 1

Visit www.us.kpmg.com/microsite/xbrl/kkb.asp to attempt the XBRL tutorial and write a brief note on how you think it will affect the work of a financial accountant.

Question 2

Find the financial reports for a company of your own choice. List the company and in what format the Annual report is. See if you can also find information on the **company's own** website about its use of XBRL.

Question 3

Visit www.microsoft.com/msft/faq/xbrl.mspx and write a summary of Microsoft's involvement in XBRL.

Question 4 – for the adventurous!

(a) Go to the SAP website: https://www.sap.com/solutions/sapbusinessobjects/large/enterprise-performance-management/xbrl-publishing/index.epx?kNtBzmUK9zU

(b) Watch the demo: "SAP BUSINESSOBJECTS XBRL PUBLISHING DEMO" (on the right side of the screen). Take note of how the software facilitates the creation and validation of the XBRL taxonomies.

(c) Now compare this with the application of iXBRL. A good starting point would be http://blogs.corefiling.com/category/inline-xbrl/

(d) Write a review on both approaches to XBRL and discuss the differences. What type of company would be most suited to these two solutions?

Question 5

Find out more about any of the following topics and write a one page summary on:

(a) the XBRL general ledger work;

(b) use of XBRL by stock exchanges;

(c) the commitment by the IFRS to the XBRL project;

(d) accounting software companies involved in providing XBRL capabilities;

(e) public utilities who are using XBRL;

(f) government involvement in XBRL.

References

1   www/w3/org/Consortium/
2   www.xbrl/org/WhatIsXBRL
3   www.sec.gov/rules/final/2009/33-9002.pdf (accessed 27/2/2010); http://xbrl.us/Learn/Pages/USGAAPandSEC.aspx

4 www.companieshouse.gov.uk/about/pdf/hmrcCommonFiling1.pdf (accessed 1/3/2010).
5 www.hmrc.gov.uk/carter/compulsory-deadlines.htm (accessed 1/3/2010).
6 www.xbrl.org/eu/ and select 'FEE Policy Statement on XBRL' (accessed 1/3/2010).
7 www.corefiling.com/products/seahorse.html
8 www.tcsl.co.uk/ (accessed 28/2/2010).
9 www.xbrlspy.org/to_render_or_not_to_render_xbrl (accessed 28/2/2010).
10 www.claritysystems.com/ap/events/webcasts/Pages/XBRL4Tagging.aspx (accessed 3/3/2010).
11 http://viewerprototype1.com/viewer
12 www.companieshouse.gov.uk/
13 www.xbrl.org/uk/Projects/ (accessed 6/3/2010).
14 www.companieshouse.gov.uk/about/pdf/hmrcCommonFiling1.pdf
15 www.acra.gov.sg/
16 http://www.openanalyticsintl.com/
17 www.sbr.gov.au/About_SBR.aspx (accessed 6/3/2010).
18 www.sbr.gov.au/Learning.aspx (accessed 6/3/2010).
19 www.med.govt.nz/templates/MultipageDocumentTOC____41220.aspx#B0
20 www.xbrl.org.eu
21 www.xbrl-ntp.nl/english
22 see www.xbrl.org/eu/ and select 'XBRL in Action in Europe' and follow the links to 'Some Projects'.
23 www.xbrl-ntp.nl/banken/ (accessed 7/3/2010). Tip: use Google translate this page.
24 www.xbrlplanet.org/
25 www.xbrl.org/GLFiles/ (accessed 6/3/2010).
26 www.xbrl.org/Announcements/2010TechDiscussion.htm (accessed 6/3/2010).

Bibliography

H. Ashbaugh, K.M. Johnstone, and T.D. Warfield, 'Corporate Reporting on the Internet', *Accounting Horizons*, vol. 13, no. 3, 1999, pp. 241–257.

R. Debreceny and G. Gray, 'Financial Reporting on the Internet and the External Audit', *European Accounting Review*, vol. 8, no. 2, 1999, pp. 335–350.

R. Debreceny and G. Gray, 'The Production and Use of Semantically Rich Accounting Reports on the Internet: XML And XBRL', *International Journal of Accounting Information Systems*, vol. 1, no. 3, 2000.

D. Deller, M. Stubenrath and C. Weber, 'A Survey of the Use of the Internet for Investor Relations in the USA, UK and Germany', *European Accounting Review*, vol. 8, no. 2, pp. 351–364.

Ernst & Young, *Web Enabled Business Reporting. De invloed van XBRL op het verslaggevingsprocess*, Kluwer, 2004.

M. Ettredge, V.J. Richardson and S. Scholz, 'Going Concern Auditor Reports At Corporate Web Sites', *Research in Accounting Regulation*, vol. 14, 2000, pp. 3–21.

M. Ettredge, V.J. Richardson and S. Scholz, *Accounting Information at Corporate Web Sites: Does the Auditor's Opinion Matter?*, University of Kansas, February 1999.

Neil Hannon, 'XBRL Grows Fast in Europe', *Strategic Finance*, October 2004, pp. 55–56.

Mark Huckelsby and Josef Macdonald, 'The three tenets of XBRL – adoption, adoption, adoption!', *Chartered Accountants Journal of New Zealand*, March 2004, pp. 46–47.

V. Richardson and S. Scholz, 'Corporate Reporting and the Internet: Vision Reality and Intervening Obstacles', *Pacific Accounting Review*, vol. 11, no. 2, 2000, pp. 153–160.

Mike Rondel, 'XBRL – Do I need to know more?', *Chartered Accountants Journal of New Zealand*, vol. 83, no. 5, June 2004, pp. 37–40.

G. Trites, *The Impact of Technology on Financial and Business Reporting*, Toronto: Canadian Institute of Chartered Accountants, 1999.

The following websites were accessed:

www.adobe.com

www.xbrl.org/Example1/

www.xbrl.org/FRTaxonomies/

www.us.jkpmg.com/microsite/xbrl/train/86/start.htm

www.xbrl.org

www.oracle.com/applications/financials/OracleGeneralLedgerDS-1.pdf

www.xbrl.org.au/training.NSWWorkshop.pdf

www.microsoft.com/office/solutions.xbrl/default.mspx

www.ubmatrix.com/home/

www.semansys.com

www.j3technology.com/

www.sec.gov/spotlight/xbrl/xbrl-vfp.shtml

PART **6**

Accountability

CHAPTER 30

Corporate governance

30.1 Introduction

The main aim of this chapter is to create an awareness of what constitutes good corporate governance – how to achieve it, the threats to achieving it and the role of accountants and auditors.

> ### Objectives
>
> By the end of this chapter, you should be able to:
>
> - understand the concept of corporate governance;
> - have an awareness of how and why governance mechanisms may differ from jurisdiction to jurisdiction;
> - have an appreciation of the role which accounting and auditing play in the governance process;
> - have a greater sensitivity to areas of potential conflicts of interest.

30.2 The concept

When we pause to contemplate the contribution of corporations to our standard of living, we are reminded how important their contribution is to most aspects of our existence. It is therefore vital that they operate as good citizens. However, the complexity of their operations makes it difficult for stakeholders to be able to assess the culture of a corporation. Just as corporations are complex, stakeholders also have different perspectives.

30.2.1 Stakeholder perspectives

A stakeholder perspective addresses all the parties whose continued support is necessary to ensure the satisfactory performance of the business. The parties are normally seen as one of the following categories: financiers, employees, trade unions representing employees, shareholders, customers, governments and suppliers. However, a category cannot be viewed as being homogeneous and there may be conflicting interests within it. For example, shareholders could include dominant and minority shareholders, individual and institutional shareholders, short-term and long-term investors, domestic and foreign investors – the list is unending – further there are employee shareholders, government shareholders, environmentalist shareholders. Trade unions may be representing different groups of employees within the same company and have different objectives, power and understanding of the economic position of the company.

As well as there being conflicting interest, there are also differences in the influence that a stakeholder can exert. For example, dominant shareholders and institutional investors have a greater ability to hold management to account and achieve good corporate governance outcomes.

We have described the complexity of a stakeholder perspective which assumes that each stakeholder will pursue their individual view of what constitutes good governance. There is also a systems perspective.

30.2.2 A systems perspective

Corporations do not act in a vacuum. They form part of society and their corporate operations are influenced by the history, institutions and cultural expectations of society. A systems perspective recognises that an entity is not independent but is interdependent with its environment. Good corporate governance attempts to set up institutions and procedures to ensure that it achieves equilibrium with its environment. The objective is to minimise conflicts of interest and have a system that is fair to all parties so that all are able to achieve personal, corporate and societal objectives. There is no unique or universal system but rather governance systems with varying degrees of being able to match corporate and societal objectives.

30.3 Corporate governance effect on corporate behaviour

Corporate governance is defined by Oman[1] as:

> private and public institutions, including laws, regulations and accepted business practices, which together govern the relationship, in a market economy, between corporate managers and entrepreneurs ('corporate insiders') on the one hand, and those who invest resources in corporations on the other. Investors can include suppliers of equity finance (shareholders), suppliers of debt finance (creditors), suppliers of relatively firm-specific human capital (employees) and suppliers of other tangible and intangible assets that corporations may use to operate and grow.

What actions and information would flow from such a relationship under good governance?

Actions by management

- Compliance with the laws and norms of society.
- Act as a good citizen.
- Fair treatment of employees – avoiding discrimination.
- Striving to achieve the company objectives in a manner which does not involve excessive risks.
- Balancing short- and long-term performance.
- Establishing mechanisms to ensure that managers are acting in the interests of shareholders and are not directly or indirectly using their knowledge or positions to gain inappropriate benefits at the expense of shareholders.
- Establishing mechanisms for resolving conflicts of interests.

- Establishing mechanisms for whistle-blowing so that if inappropriate behaviour is taking place it is highlighted as quickly as possible so as to minimise the cost to the organisation and society.

Information flows:

- Providing lenders and suppliers with relevant, reliable and timely information that allows them to assess the performance, solvency and financial stability of the business.
- Providing confirmation that excessive risks are not being taken.
- Providing investors with an independent opinion that the financial statements are a fair representation.

This list does not cover all eventualities but is intended to indicate what could be expected from corporate governance – good being determined by the degree that the actions and information flows achieve fair outcomes.

The objective is to influence behaviour so that all parties act within the spirit of good governance. The actions and information flows above have been oriented towards business entities but we should expect all organisations to behave in the same way. For example, in the case of a not-for-profit enterprise such as a charity it is important that the money raised be used in a manner consistent with the uses envisaged by the donors and that an appropriate balance be achieved between administrative costs and the money devoted to assisting the beneficiaries of the charity.

30.4 Pressures on good governance behaviour vary over time

History shows that business behaviour is influenced by where we are in the economic cycle, whether it's a time of boom or bust.

30.4.1 Behaviour in boom times

During the booms there has always been a tendency to be over-optimistic and to expect the good times to continue indefinitely. In such periods there is a tendency for everyone to focus on making profits. The safeguards that are in the system to prevent conflicts of interest and to limit undesirable behaviour are seen as slowing down the business and causing genuine opportunities to be missed. Over-optimism leads to a business taking risks that the shareholders had not sanctioned and is, to that extent, excessive.

This is accompanied by a tendency to water down the controls or to simply ignore them. When that happens there will always be some unethical individuals who will exploit some of the opportunities for themselves rather than for the business.

30.4.2 Behaviour in bust times

We see a repetitive reaction from bust to bust. When it occurs some of the malpractices will come to light, there will be a public outcry and governance procedures will be tightened up. Although controls are weakly enforced during boom times, it is a fact of life that vigilance is required at all times. Fraud, misrepresentation, misappropriation and anti-social behaviour will be constantly with us and robust corporate governance systems need to be in place and monitored.

The ideal would be that the controls in place develop a culture that make individuals constrain their own behaviour to that which is ethical, having previously sensitised themselves to recognise the potential conflicts of interest. It is interesting to see the approach taken by the professional accounting bodies which are concentrating on sensitising students and members to ethical issues.

30.5 Types of past unethical behaviour

Some of the unethical behaviour which has been identified in earlier periods and which our governance systems should attempt to prevent are listed below:

- Looting – this is a term applied to executives who strip corporations of money for their own use i.e. misappropriation of funds. The misappropriation is often concealed by normal corporate activities such as entering into transactions with associates of the management or dominant shareholders at inflated prices or by falsifying the accounting records and financial statements.

  For example, in the US the SEC filed a complaint[2] against Richard E. McDonald, former CEO and chairman of World Health Alternatives, Inc. ('World Health'):

  > The Commission's complaint alleges that McDonald was the principal architect of a wide-ranging financial fraud at World Health by which McDonald misappropriated approximately $6.4 million for his personal benefit. Also named as defendants are Deanna Seruga of Pittsburgh, the company's former controller and a CPA, . . .
  >
  > A key aspect of the fraud involved the manipulation of World Health's accounting entries . . . repeatedly falsified accounting entries in World Health's financial books and records, understating expenses and liabilities. This made the Company appear more financially sound, and masked McDonald's misappropriation of funds.

- Insider trading particularly around major events. The regulators are refining their techniques for identifying insider trading if it relates to the use of sensitive information such as a forthcoming takeover because there is a specific date when the takeover is announced. Transactions occurring just before that date can be investigated if there has been an unexpected level of activity in the shares. Even then it is incredibly difficult to prove and there have been few convictions. It is even more difficult to identify that it has occurred if the information relates to internal business activity such as the successful development of a new drug or product.

- Excessive remuneration so that the rewards flow disproportionately to management compared to other stakeholders and often with the major risks being borne by the other stakeholders.

- Excessive risk taking which is hidden from shareholders and stakeholders until after the catastrophe has struck.

- Unsuccessful managers being given golden handshakes to leave and thus being rewarded for poor performance.

- Auditors, bankers, lawyers, credit rating agencies, and stock analysts, who might put their fees before the interests of the public for honest reporting.

- Directors who did not stand up to authoritarian managing directors or seriously question their ill advised plans.

- Management setting incentives for employees which encourage action which is not in the firm's interests leading to rogue trading (several banks) or emphasise project formulation over successful implementation (market to market accounting at Enron).

30.6 Different jurisdictions have different governance priorities

The predominant conflicts of interest will vary from country to country depending on each country's history, economic and legal developments, norms and religion.

England and United States, with their similar legal histories with considerable reliance on stock exchanges for the financing of public companies need an active, efficient capital market. This leads to their focus being on potential conflicts between management and shareholders.

Australia has been encouraging higher levels of investment through compulsory super-annuation providing institutions with access to large amounts of cash during the recent economic downturn. The overlevered companies almost guaranteed the institutional investors major capital gains through the issue of new shares at substantial discounts. This followed a period when some companies made issues to institutions on terms which handed tax advantages to them whilst not giving the same advantages to retail/individual shareholders. Individual shareholders perceived that there were conflicts of interests in that management in raising capital quickly and with little administration from institutions were generating conflicts between individual and institutional investors. As a result, several major companies then made offers to individual shareholders at discounts to the market.

In south-east Asia, because many of the large corporations have substantial shareholdings owned by members of a single family, the emphasis has been on avoiding conflicts between family and minority shareholders.

In some countries the presence of significant state investments in listed companies has created a different set of conflicts to be managed. China is an example of this but it is also true in some Middle Eastern countries. The country's economic and social objectives may not coincide with investor interests.

In countries in which the banks are the major suppliers of finance, as opposed to the lesser role of the stock market in such jurisdictions, there may be greater control over management because the banks can demand detailed information, but there is the potential for conflicts between the interests of bankers and other investors. Germany provides an example of a different legal history with companies having both a board of directors made up of investors as well as an advisory board representing both management and employees. This reflects the recognition that there is a need to reconcile both management and employee long-term interests and to ensure that both groups are motivated to achieve the organisation's long-term goals.

In Muslim countries companies should not be involved in activities related to alcohol and gambling; they cannot pay or charge interest and they have religious obligations to make a minimum level of donations. In the event that they have no alternative but to receive interest, such money has to be given to charity. Thus Muslim companies need a corporate governance mechanism to ensure that they comply with their religious obligations.

From the above we can see how the governance priorities differ from country to country. They result from the role of the political institutions, the stage of economic development, the diversity of stakeholder perspectives and a country's heritage in so far as it shapes the law, the religion and the social norms.

Just as governance priorities differ, so do the institutions and methods for controlling corporate governance. The institutions include statutory bodies enforcing detailed prescriptive requirements, statutory bodies that encourage voluntary adoption of good practices with disclosure through to private sector bodies trying to influence their membership to give due attention to corporate governance philosophies.

30.6.1 Future developments

Corporate governance requirements are less developed in the European Union (EU) countries (except the UK) and Japan. What about the future? Developments in the EU, Japan, China, Russia and other Eastern Bloc (former communist) countries are leading to a model of much wider ownership of shares (i.e. like the US and the UK). For example, in 2006 the market capitalisation as a percentage of GDP in China was 50%, Italy 52% and Spain 95%.

In the EU, restrictions on who may hold shares in major companies are inconsistent with the Union's desire for the free movement of goods and capital, so there will be a trend for a greater proportion of companies' shares being listed on a stock exchange.

In China, Russia and the former communist countries in Eastern Europe, the economies are being changed from state-controlled businesses to privately owned companies. The 'model' of these companies is similar to those in the US and UK. So, the trend is towards the US and UK model of companies' shares being listed on their national stock exchange. This trend to wider share ownership will slowly encourage the development of corporate governance criteria similar to those in the US and the UK. It is for some countries a real cultural shift and it will take time for the concept of good corporate governance to be applied. The following is an extract from an OECD Note of a meeting on Corporate Governance Development in State-owned Enterprises in Russia:[3]

> Finally, as stressed by investors, the OECD, and government officials at this expert's meeting, the emergence of a true corporate governance culture is vital. Such a culture-based approach should involve the understanding of the principles and values behind corporate governance, and replace the 'box-ticking' mechanistic approach in which superficial institutions fulfill certain criteria but do not bring real benefits in terms of effective achievement of corporate goals. This would complement the creation of specific incentives intended to guide the behaviour of economic actors.

30.7 The effect on capital markets of good corporate governance

Good governance is important to facilitate large-scale commerce. The mechanism of legal structures such as limited liability of companies exist because they allow the capital of many investors to be combined in the pursuit of economic activities which need large quantities of capital to be economically viable. There are also statutory provisions relating to directors' duties and shareholder rights. This is a good backcloth which is necessary but not sufficient to ensure the effective working of the capital market.

In addition there has to be a high level of trust by shareholders in their relationship with the management. Firstly, they need to believe the company will deal with them in an honest and prudent manner and act diligently. This means that shareholders need to be confident that:

● their money will be invested in ventures of an appropriate degree of risk;

● efforts will be made to achieve a competitive return on equity;

● management will not take personal advantage of their greater knowledge of events in the business;

● the company will provide a flow of information that will contribute to the market fairly valuing shares at the times of purchase and sale.

Failure to achieve appropriate levels of trust will lead to the risk of the loss of potential investors or the provision of lesser amounts of funds at higher costs. Similarly if other stakeholders, such as the bank, do not trust the management, there will be fewer participants and the terms will be less favourable. Another way of addressing this is to say that people have a strong sense of what is or is not fair. Whilst economic necessity may lead to participation, the level of commitment is influenced by the perceived fairness of the transaction.

Also from a macro perspective, the more efficient and effective the individual firms, the better allocation of resources and the higher the average standard of living. If management as a group is not diligent in its activities and fair in its treatment of stakeholders, there will be lower standards of living both economically and socially.

In addition the current focus on corporate social responsibility could be seen as a response to governance failures by some companies. For example, some managers ignored externalities such as the costs to society of rectifying pollution because management was only judged on the financial results of the firm, and not the net benefit to society.

30.8 The role of accounting in corporate governance

Accounting can contribute to the corporate governance process by acting as a control process and by providing economic information relevant to evaluating the effectiveness of corporate controls.

30.8.1 Control processes

In some jurisdictions the company and the external auditors have to explicitly state that the company has adequate internal controls and the accounts have integrity. In other jurisdictions it is implied that if the company receives a clean audit report that the internal controls are good and that the accounts have integrity.

In the US when the explicit requirement was introduced many companies spent considerable sums after the introduction of the Sarbanes–Oxley Act 2002 in upgrading their systems, particularly as the CEO and CFO were made personally liable for the effectiveness of the internal controls.

There is an opportunity cost in CEOs focusing on compliance issues rather than on strategic issues and an actual cost in upgrading systems. This led to some arguing that the costs were unjustified.

Whilst the need to consider cost benefit considerations in relation to all corporate governance measures is a valid concern, it is also important to remember the costs of bad corporate governance. These take the form of direct losses by shareholders, employees, customers and suppliers. There are also the indirect losses in the form of reluctance to invest in the stock market, credit squeezes and the loss of confidence in the economy leading to depressions, unemployment and under employment. However it is common for the costs of poor governance to be forgotten by each new generation, hence boom and bust. Obviously good governance will not stop all fraud but it will stop it from being so widespread.

The internal control systems should limit the ability of management to misdirect resources to their personal use. Thus internal controls combined with an internal audit unit should make it more difficult for senior managers to misappropriate resources. Naturally we know that the more senior the manager the more likely it is that they can override the internal controls or pressure others to do so. It can be argued that such a situation justifies the requirement that the internal audit unit (if one exists) should report to members of the board who are independent directors (presumably the audit committee of the board), however, that is not often the case.

30.8.2 Comprehensive financial statements

There are two aspects, namely, the financial data and the narrative.

Comprehensive financial data

There has been a serious problem with the use by companies of off balance sheet finance and special purpose entities which conceal certain of the company's activities.

For example, in the case of Enron, assets whose value were expected to have to be written down or were vulnerable to substantial market fluctuations were sold to special purpose entities which were intended to have 3% or more outside ownership. Under US rules at that time if the 3% condition was met then the special purpose entity's financial affairs did not have to be consolidated. The exclusion of such items led to the accounts being misleading. It could be argued that the legislators who created such loopholes were also responsible for encouraging poor corporate governance as were accounting bodies which did not speak against such legislation. Further, it could be argued that all instances of off balance sheet financing should be brought back onto the statement of financial position or being fully disclosed in some other way. In effect it should be an ongoing matter to identify all instances where full and frank disclosures are not occurring and to amend the rules to prevent poor corporate governance.

The use of such off balance sheet devices, or sales with the obligation to repurchase at a later date at a specified price, is a clear sign that management is breaching the intent of good corporate governance. The use of off balance sheet items of the investment bank Lehman Brothers is a good example of this.

Comprehensive narrative information

The financial data are backward looking. Comprehensive information would also include items which are likely to be very important in the future even though they are not currently required to be reported. This could in many jurisdictions include matters relating to future sustainability and comprehensive assessments of environmental impacts. Other future oriented information would have to relate to the company's strategic drivers and opportunities.

Annual reports can also be used as devices to disclose information which is solely oriented to corporate governance. For example, the disclosure of related party transactions is intended to make it more difficult for a major shareholder to exploit the company for their own benefit. Whilst the disclosure does not prevent that, it allows shareholders to view the level of activity and if they find the level of activity a matter of concern they can raise the issue at an annual general meeting.

There is a more general issue of the need for the board of directors to identify and report the potential risks which could have a significant impact on the organisation. These could include major reliance on individual suppliers, insurers, products, financiers or customers; exposure to environmental or product liabilities; or regulatory approvals of medical products.

In more recent times banks and other financial institutions misled investors when they did not disclose in a clear and unambiguous way the level of risks they were taking in relation to subprime mortgages. This size of exposure even if insured with other institutions was a breach of good corporate governance as it exposed the company to potentially fatal levels of risk. Accounting regulations were inadequate to ensure such information was adequately quantified and disclosed to the board and shareholders and bank regulators.

30.9 External audits in corporate governance

External audits are intended to increase participation in financial investing and to lower the cost of funds. They may be *ad hoc* reports or audit reports giving an opinion on the fair view of annual financial statements.

Ad hoc reports

In the case of lending to companies it is not uncommon for lenders to impose restrictions to protect the interests of the lenders. Such restrictions or covenants include compliance with certain ratios such as liquidity and leverage or gearing ratios. Auditors then report to lenders or trustees for groups of lenders on the level of compliance. In this way auditors facilitate the flows of funds at good rates.

Statutory audit reports

Similarly for shareholders the audit report is intended to create confidence that the financial statements are presenting a fair view of financial performance and position. If that confidence is undermined by examples of auditors failing to detect misrepresentation or being party to it, the public becomes wary of holding shares, share prices in the market tend to fall and the availability of new funds shrinks.

For the audit report to perform its role adequately, a number of things need to occur:

● Managers have to be perceived to be reporting in a forthright manner.

● That perception has to be reinforced by a review by independent people who should be in a good position to judge whether those accounts provide a fair representation of the company's achievements and current position – it is often recommended that the accounts be reviewed by directors who are independent of management and that those directors be assisted by internal and external auditors.

● The external auditors reviewing the accounts have industry knowledge and professional competence and identify with the needs of investors as the primary users of the accounts.

● The results of the audit are communicated in a clear manner.

To achieve the above, a number of corporate governance procedures are in place or have been recommended to ensure that auditor independence is not called into question.

30.9.1 Auditor independence

The external auditors should keep in mind that their main responsibility is to shareholders. However, there is a potential governance conflict in that for all practical purposes they are appointed by the board, their remuneration is agreed with the board and their day-to-day dealings are with the management. Appointments and remuneration have to be approved by the shareholders but this is normally a rubber stamping exercise.

It is not uncommon for auditors to talk of the management as the customer which is of course the wrong mindset. To reduce the identification with management and loss of independence arising from a personal interest in the financial performance of the client, a number of controls are often put in place, for example:

Financial threats to independence:

● Auditors and close relatives should not have shares or options in the company, particularly if the value of their financial interest could be directly affected by their decisions.

- Auditors must not accept contingency fees or gifts nor should relatives or close associates receive benefits.
- The audit firm is precluded from undertaking non-audit work for the company so it does not have to consider the loss of lucrative consulting contracts when making audit decisions. This is a contentious issue with some advocating that auditors should not undertake non-audit work, whereas the client might consider that to be cost effective. All the indications are that current practice will continue with disclosure of the amounts involved.

Familiarity threats:

- Appointments, terminations and the remuneration of auditors should be handled by the audit committee.
- Auditors should not have worked for the company or its associates.
- Audit partners should be rotated periodically so the audit is looked at with fresh eyes.
- Audit tests should vary so that employees cannot anticipate what will be audited.
- It is not desirable that audit staff be transferred to senior positions in a client company. This happens but it does mean that they will continue to have close relations with the auditors and knowledge of their audit procedures. Clients might regard this as a cost benefit.

However, the above are indications and not to be seen as taking a rule-based approach. Good governance is not just a matter of compliance with rules as ways can always be found to comply with rules whilst not complying with their spirit. It is really a question of behaviour – good governance depends on the auditors behaving independently, with professional competence and identifying with shareholders and other stakeholders whose interests they are supposed to be protecting. Failing to do this leads to what is described as the expectation gap.

30.9.2 The expectation gap

Another area of corporate governance and auditing relates to the expectation gap. The gap is between the stakeholders' expectation of the outcomes that can be expected from the auditors' performance and the outcomes that could reasonably be expected given the audit work that should have been performed.

The stakeholders' expectation is that the auditor guarantees that the financial statements are accurate, that every transaction has been 100% checked and any fraud would have been detected. The auditors' expectation is that the audit work carried out should identify material errors and misstatements based on a judgmental or statistical sampling approach.

There have been a number of high profile corporate failures and irregularities, for example, in the US, Enron failed having inflated its earnings and hidden liabilities in SPEs (special purpose entities). In 2008 the same problem of hiding liabilities appears to have occurred with Lehman Brothers where according to the Examiner's report[4] Lehman used what amounted to financial engineering to temporarily shuffle $50 billion of troubled assets off its books in the months before its collapse in September 2008 to conceal its dependence on borrowed money, and Senior Lehman executives as well as the bank's accountants at Ernst & Young were aware of the moves. In Italy, Parmalat, created a false paper trail and created assets where none existed; and in the US, the senior management of Tyco looted the company.

This raises the questions such as (a) Were the auditors independent? (b) Did they carry out the work with due professional competence? and (c) Did they rely unduly on management representations?

30.9.3 Lack of independence – Enron

The following is an extract from the United Nations Conference on Trade and Development G-24 Discussion Paper Series:[5]

Regarding auditing good corporate governance requires high-quality standards for preparation and disclosure, and independence for the external auditor. Enron's external auditor was Arthur Andersen, which also provided the firm with extensive internal auditing and consulting services. Some idea of its relative importance in these different roles during the period leading up to Enron's insolvency is indicated by the fact that in 2000 consultancy fees (at $27 million) accounted for more than 50 per cent of the approximately $52 million earned by Andersen for work on Enron . . . the following assessment by the Powers Committee: The evidence available to us suggests that Andersen did not fulfill its professional responsibilities in connection with its audits of Enron's financial statements, . . . Both the Powers Committee and bodies of the United States Senate which have investigated Enron's collapse have taken the view that lack of independence linked to its multiple consultancy roles was a crucial factor in Andersen's failure to fulfill its obligations as Enron's external auditor.

30.9.4 Failure to carry out audit in accordance with audit standards – TYCO

The following is an extract[6] from an SEC finding 2003–95:

SEC Finds PricewaterhouseCoopers's Engagement Partner Recklessly Issued Fraudulent Audit Report and Engaged in Improper Professional Conduct
The Commission's Order finds that multiple and repeated facts provided notice to Scalzo regarding the integrity of Tyco's senior management and that Scalzo was reckless in not taking appropriate audit steps in the face of this information. By the end of the Tyco annual audit for its fiscal year ended Sept. 30, 1998, if not before, those facts were sufficient to obligate Scalzo, pursuant to generally accepted auditing standards (GAAS), to re-evaluate the risk assessment of the Tyco audits and to perform additional audit procedures, including further audit testing of certain items (most notably, certain executive benefits, executive compensation, and related party transactions). Scalzo did not take sufficient steps in these regards. Accordingly, Scalzo recklessly failed to conduct the audits in accordance with GAAS. The Order, therefore, finds that Scalzo engaged in improper professional conduct. The Commission denies him the privilege of practicing before the Commission as an accountant.

Investors rely on auditors and are betrayed when auditors fail to conduct diligent audits, [according to Thomas C. Newkirk, Associate Director of Enforcement at the Securities and Exchange Commission]. In this case, senior management was looting the company, and Scalzo was confronted with numerous warning signs about management's integrity. Scalzo is not being sanctioned because he did not discover the looting; he is being charged because he did not look despite these warnings.

30.9.5 Undue reliance on management representations – Structural Dynamics Research Corporation

In the normal course of an audit it is usual to obtain a letter of representation from management, for example, providing information regarding a subsequent event occurring after year end and the existence of off balance sheet contingencies. It is confirmation to the auditor that management has made full disclosure of all material activities and transactions in its financial records and statements.

However, the representations do not absolve the auditor from obtaining sufficient and appropriate audit evidence. The following is an extract[7] from an SEC finding relating to two CPAs who were auditing a company which had improperly recorded sales and then written them off in the following accounting period:

> Despite the fact that the language in FEC purchase orders clearly stated the orders were conditional and subject to cancellation, the auditors accepted the controller's explanation and did not take exception to the recognition of revenue on these orders. This undue reliance on management's representations constitutes insufficient professional skepticism by Present (the engagement partner).
>
> Moreover, Present failed to corroborate management's representations regarding conditional purchase orders with sufficient additional evidence that these sales were properly recorded . . . Overall, Present failed to exercise due professional care in the performance of the audit.

In each of the above there is good reason for the expectation gap in that the audit had not been conducted in accordance with generally accepted audit standards and there was a lack of due professional care. If the auditors have been negligent then they are liable to be sued in a civil action. In the UK the profession has sought to obtain a statutory limit on their liability and, failing that, some have registered as limited liability partnerships – the path taken by Ernst & Young in 1996 and KPMG in 2002. In Australia some accountants operate under a statutory limit on their liability and in return ensure they have a minimum level of professional indemnity insurance.

30.9.6 Detection of fraud

An audit is designed to obtain evidence that the financial statements present a fair view and do not contain material misstatements. It is not a forensic investigation commissioned to detect fraud. Such an investigation would be expensive and in the majority of cases not be cost effective. It has been argued that auditors should be required to carry out a fraud and detection role to avoid public concerns that arise when hearing about the high-profile corporate failures. However, it would appear that it is not so much a question of making every audit a forensic investigation to detect fraud but rather enforcing the exercise of due professional care in the conduct of all audits. The audit standards reinforce this when they emphasise the importance of scepticism.

30.9.7 Enforcing audit standards

There are international audit standards. These are set by the International Auditing and Assurance Standards Board (IAASB) which sets high quality standards dealing with auditing and quality control and which facilitates the convergence of national and international standards.

Whilst the standards are international, the enforcement of the standards is carried out nationally. National practice varies. In the UK, the Financial Reporting Council (FRC) is the independent regulator for corporate reporting and corporate governance. Through several of its operating bodies (the Auditing Practices Board, the Professional Oversight Board for Accountancy and the Accountancy Investigation and Discipline Board) the FRC has primary responsibility for setting, monitoring and enforcement of auditing standards in the UK.

30.9.8 Educating users

Many surveys have shown that there has been a considerable difference between auditors and audit report users regarding auditors' responsibilities for discovering fraud and predicting failure. Users of published financial statements need to be made aware that auditors rely on systems reviews and *sample testing* to evaluate the company annual report. Based on those evaluations they form an opinion on the *likelihood* that the accounts provide a true and fair view or fairly present the accounts. However they cannot guarantee the accounts are 100% accurate.

A number of major companies collapsed without warning signs and the public criticised the auditors. In response to these pressures auditors have modified their audit standards to place more emphasis on scepticism. It is difficult, however, when there are such high-profile corporate failures to persuade the public that lack of due professional care is not endemic. Audit firms have their own governance procedures within the firms.

30.9.9 Governance within audit firms

Within the audit practices there is also the need to apply systems to ensure that audits are conducted in accordance with the spirit of the intent of the process, that there are adequate reviews of the performance of individual auditors and that the individual partners do not take advantage of their positions of trust.

The greatest control mechanism within an audit firm is the culture of the firm. Arthur Wyatt made the following observation:[8]

> The leadership of the various firms needs to understand that the internal culture of firms needs a substantial amount of attention if the reputation of the firms is to be restored. No piece of legislation is likely to solve the behavioural changes that have evolved within the past thirty years.

In particular Wyatt was drawing on his experience in Arthur Andersen and his observation of competitors. He indicated that in earlier times there was a culture of placing the maintenance of standards ahead of retention of clients, the smaller size of firms meant there was more informal monitoring of compliance with firm rules and ethical standards. Promotion was more likely to flow to those with the greatest technical expertise and compliance with ethical standards, rather than an ability to bring in more fees. The values of conservative accountants predominated over the risk taking orientation of consultants.

The large accounting firms separated from their consulting arms following public pressure only to evolve new consulting activities. Wyatt was saying that the growth and risk orientations of consulting are incompatible with the values needed to perform auditing in a manner which is independent in attitude. Also they need to have a sense of the importance of lobbying for quality forthright accounting standards and of taking a strong stand in audits.

Having established the appropriate attitudes, the systems of review must be able to identify and correct deviations, and to reinforce a conservative culture.

Also the firm needs controls in place to ensure its partners and its staff do not undertake activities incompatible with the firm's function as an auditor, for example, do not engage in insider trading based on information gained whilst conducting an audit, or are not feeling pressured to give favourable audit reports because of the possible impact on their personal investments.

It has been suggested that auditors are very conscious of the possibility of being sued over substandard audits. The ability of this device to influence behaviour depends on the awareness of the individual auditors of the likelihood of being sued, what the costs will be to them personally and how that compares to rewards of being a good revenue generator.

30.10 Corporate governance in relation to the board of directors

A properly functioning board makes for good corporate governance. What do we mean by properly functioning? It means that (a) there is no one person dominating the Board and (b) there are independent board members and (c) the board committees have independent members who are not unduly influenced by the executive directors. We will now discuss each of these points.

30.10.1 Separation of chairperson of the board and the senior executive

One of the roles of a board is to evaluate the executive management team and where necessary to remove non-performing executives. This is important in the sense that the senior executive (variously titled CEO, Chief Executive Officer, MD, Managing Director, Executive Director, Director General) and their team are being supervised. Where the senior executive has a forceful personality there is a real need for someone who can constructively challenge and make sure that major decisions are seriously reviewed. It is hard for subordinates to tell their boss that a strategy is wrong or too risky – an independent chairperson can.

30.10.2 Independent board members

To ensure that the company can appoint independent directors, the company should have a nominating committee for board and audit committee appointments so that board members are not beholden to the CEO for their positions. Those committees should not include management.

30.10.3 Audit committees

To ensure that the audit committee of the board of directors is independent, it is normally recommended that the chair of the audit committee be a person of high prestige who is knowledgeable in accounting and independent of management. Some believe that all members of the audit committee should be independent of management and of any substantial shareholders. Independence also requires the ability to look at events and scrutinise them from the perspectives of the relevant stakeholders. Independence is a state of mind which is much more difficult to achieve when there are personal connections with the CEO.

30.11 Executive remuneration

It is worth reinforcing the fact that the objective of corporate governance is to focus management on achieving the objectives of the company whilst keeping risks to appropriate levels and positioning the firm for a prosperous future. At the same time, sufficient safeguards must be in place to reduce the risks of resources being inappropriately diverted to any group at the expense of other groups involved.

Since management is the group with the most discretion and power, it is important to ensure they do not obtain excessive remuneration or perks, or be allowed to shirk, or to gamble with company resources by taking excessive risks.

30.11.1 What is fair?

Companies should pay enough, and no more than enough, to attract suitable directors and part of the remuneration should be linked to individual and corporate performance. In deciding whether something is fair or not, we tend to base it on a comparison. The problem is how to choose the comparator. This is true when looking at remuneration. For instance, a matter which has attracted considerable attention is executive remuneration. It is suggested that the heat which such matters generate is not just a matter of envy, although there may be elements of that, but relates to concepts of fairness. So what is fair? Management probably looks at fairness by comparing their remuneration with that of other executives; employees probably compare it with what other employees get, and institutional shareholders probably compare it with what they earn, and individual shareholders probably assess it in light of the company's performance.

The statistics show[9] that in recent years the remuneration of executives relative to the average employee has been considerably higher than it was twenty years ago and the remuneration of the top executive compared to the average of the next four executives is also better than in the past. That seems intuitively unfair – but is it a valid comparison to be referring back to a relationship that existed twenty years ago? Perhaps the question should be whether this higher relative remuneration reflects a greater contribution to performance, or does it reflect that as businesses increase in size the remuneration of the chief executive tends to increase to reflect the higher responsibilities, or has it been achieved because directors have been effectively able to set their own remuneration?

30.11.2 How to set criteria – in principle

There are a number of issues that will require a judgement to be made:

● What is the right balance between short-term performance and long-term performance?

● What if there are revenues and costs that are beyond the control or influence of management? Should these be excluded from the measure?

● Also to the extent that performance may be influenced by general economic conditions should the managers be assessed on absolute performance or relative performance?

– What if management has achieved an increase in profit but not at the same rate as a peer group? For example, assume that a firm had increased return on investment by 2% to 12% but the peer group showed medium increases from 14% to 17%. Should there be a bonus? Should it be on a proportional basis?

– Similarly, if the performance fell from 10% to minus 3% during an economic down turn, and competitors earned minus 5%, should the managers get a bonus even though shareholders saw their share price fall considerably?

Often companies resort to outside consultants but the observation has been made that one doesn't hear of outside consultants recommending a pay cut and are in part responsible for the ratcheting up levels of remuneration.

30.11.3 Where do accountants feature in setting directors' remuneration?

The equity of the remuneration is not normally seen as an accounting matter, but accountants should ensure transparent disclosure of the performance criteria and of the payments. In some jurisdictions there is legislation setting out in some detail what has to be disclosed.

30.11.4 Performance criteria

Directors are expected to produce increases in the share price and dividends. Traditional measures have been largely based on growth in earnings per share (EPS), which has encouraged companies to seek to increase short-term earnings at the expense of long-term earnings, e.g. by cutting back capital programmes. Even worse, concentrating on growth in earnings per share can result in a reduction in shareholder value, e.g. by companies borrowing and investing in projects that produce a return in excess of the interest charge, but less than the return expected by equity investors.

30.11.5 What alternatives are there?

It is interesting to identify the suggested criteria because they could have an impact on the financial information that has to be disclosed in the annual accounts. Suggested criteria include the following:

● **Relative share price increase**, i.e. using market comparisons. Grand Met has revised its scheme so that, before executives gain any benefit from their share options, Grand Met's share price must outperform the FT All-Share Index over a three-year period, i.e. the scheme focuses management on value creation.[10] If this policy is adopted, it would be helpful for the annual accounts to contain details of share price and index movements. Comparative share price schemes should also, in the opinion of the Association of British Insurers, be conditional on a secondary performance criterion, validating sustained and significant improvement in underlying financial performance over the same period.

● **Indicators related to business drivers**, i.e. using internal data. Schemes would need to identify business drivers appropriate to each company, such as customer satisfaction or process times, growth in sales, gross profit, profit before interest and tax, cash flow and return on shareholders' funds.

● **Indicators based on factors such as size and complexity**. Schemes would need to take account of factors such as market capitalisation, turnover, number of employees, breadth of product and markets, risk, regulatory and competitive environment, and rates of change experienced by the organisation. This information could again be disclosed in the business review section of the annual report.

The indications are that there will be a growth in the number of firms offering schemes. However, regulators will need to keep a close eye on the position to avoid schemes creeping in that avoid the existing disclosure requirements. For example, there has been a growth in long-term incentive plans, under which free shares are offered in the future if the executive remains with the company and achieves a certain performance level. This is a perfectly healthy development that retains staff, but such schemes fall outside the definition of a share option plan and allow companies to avoid disclosure.

One of the problems is the innovative nature of the remuneration packages that companies might adopt and the fact that there is no uniquely correct scheme. The Association of British Insurers, in its publication *Share Option and Profit Sharing Incentive Schemes* (February 1995), commented on this very point:

> There is growing acceptance that the benefit arising from the exercise of options should be linked to the underlying financial performance of the company.
>
> Initially, attention focused on performance criteria showing real growth in normalised earnings, however, a number of other criteria have subsequently emerged.

The circumstances of each individual company will vary and there is a reluctance, therefore, on the part of institutional investors to indicate a general preference for any particular measurement. On the other hand, a considerable number of companies have stated that they welcome indications of the sort of formulae that are considered to be acceptable. It is felt that remuneration committees should have discretion to select the formula which is felt to be most appropriate to the circumstances of the company in question. Nevertheless . . . it is important that whatever criterion is chosen . . . the formula should be supported by, or give clear evidence of, sustained improvement in the underlying financial performance of the group in question.

30.11.6 The role of share options

Share options have been offered to managers to encourage them to align their interest with those of the shareholders so that management incentives reflect the capital and income benefits they achieve for the shareholders. However, the match is not perfect because, if the managers and the company perform poorly, the worst outcome for managers is they receive no bonus but shareholders have their total investment at risk.

30.11.7 How to measure the benefit of an option?

The issue of share options raises some difficult measurement issues. What amount should the shareholders be told when voting on directors' remuneration? Should it be the value at the time of issue (grant date) and no subsequent accounting be required irrespective of the future fluctuations in the value of the option? Should it be performance related and the value reported at the date they are entitled to exercise the option?

30.12 Market forces and corporate governance

Another corporate governance mechanism is said to be the markets. These are (a) the market for gaining control, (b) the market for executives and (c) the market to replace executives.

30.12.1 The market for gaining control

If managers are inefficient, too greedy or reckless then the value of the company will fall. When that happens, an entrepreneurial manager or venture capitalist will recognise the potential for making the company more profitable and will make a takeover offer. If successful, the new owners will remove the old management and install a new experienced team. The threat of a takeover will place a limit on the extent to which management can coast or divert resources to excessive rewards. However, there is also the possibility that otherwise good managers will focus on short-term results to make it more difficult to take over their company.

30.12.2 The market for executives

If managers have ambitions to become managing directors at larger or more prestigious organisations, they will supposedly seek to achieve good economic returns to make them more marketable which results in good governance. However, good governance might be less of a concern if the focus is more on self-promotion and good public relations.

30.12.3 The market for removing directors

In general, individual shareholders have little prospect of removing a director or controlling their remuneration. It is the large investment and insurance firms that have the power to block resolutions which they believe are not in the interests of shareholders. The extent to which they exercise such powers varies from country to country depending on the requirements of the law and the traditions in the particular country. There is a major question over who imposes good governance on the superannuation and investment funds. There is generally little if any involvement of fund members in the supervision of fund managers.

30.12.4 Insider trading

Insider trading involves a person taking advantage of information which isn't available to the public to make an unfair gain or to transfer a loss to another party. Proven examples include directors selling shares before the announcement of unexpected poor results, an executive in a ratings firm using knowledge of an about-to-be announced takeover offer to tip off a friend to trade in shares and options, a senior executive in an investment bank gaining entry to the building at night to find out what his colleagues were working on and then traded on that information.

To discourage such activities most companies and audit firms expressly forbid it. It is also common practice for boards of directors to preclude directors from trading in shares in the periods leading up to major announcements such as quarterly/half yearly earnings, dividend changes, announcements of major changes in mineral reserves, or preceding disclosure of major takeovers.

Also most countries forbid separate briefings to analysts without the same information being released to the public at the same time.

There is no doubt that insider trading takes place as academic research looking at specific events shows abnormal returns being made immediately before the announcement of major events. This signifies that some people who know what is going to happen trade on that knowledge. In that sense the markets are not fair. However, proving it has traditionally been very difficult. To overcome that the laws have been made clearer, police investigative powers have been strengthened, and more resources have been put into investigating such cases.

30.13 Risk management

There is a growing pressure internationally for a company to disclose its risk management policy. In any company there is a range of risks that have to be managed. It is not a matter of just avoiding risks but rather of systematically analysing the risks and then deciding how to decide what risks should be borne, which to avoid, and how to minimise the possible adverse consequences of those which it is not economical to shift. A good governance system will ensure that comprehensive risk management occurs as a normal course of events.

There is a variety of approaches which could be adopted to the process of identifying the types of risks associated with a company. In this chapter we will discuss briefly strategic, operational, legal/regulatory and financial risks.

30.13.1 Strategic risks

Strategic risk is associated with maintaining the attractiveness and economic viability of the product and service offerings. In other words, current product decisions have to be made with a strong sense of their probable future consequences. To do that the business has to be constantly monitoring trends in the current markets, potential merging of markets,[11] shifting demographics and consumer tastes, technological developments, political developments and regulations so as to capitalise on opportunities and to counter threats. It must be remembered that to do nothing may involve as much or more risk as entering into new ventures. When entering into new projects there needs to be a thorough risk analysis to ensure there are no false assumptions in the projections, that there has been pilot testing, and the question of what is the exit strategy if the project fails has been seriously considered and costed.

30.13.2 Operational risks

Operational risks include those that are very familiar such as possible interruption to operations, fire, floods, accidental or malicious product contamination, quality issues, systems security, impacts on ability of staff to run the business in the event of an influenza pandemic, occupational health and safety, security, and public liability. This list is not exhaustive but rather illustrative. Each business will be different and must be looked at as a separate exercise. Once the list has been identified then questions could be asked such as – can we insure this risk? If so, is it desirable to do so? The question is, should this event happen could we comfortably bear the cost? If the answer is no then we should insure at least for the amount we couldn't afford to bear.

Another possible question is whether there are ways we could transfer the risk. This could involve outsourcing some of the work. However, that in itself creates risks such as dependence, quality control, reliability of delivery, lack of involvement in technological developments, and financial risks associated with the subcontractor.

In relation to risks like occupational health and safety, the steps involve identification of potential hazards, identifying the best physical process for handling them, and developing standard ways of operating. Then training personnel in those standard operating procedures, and then regularly checking to ensure those procedures are being followed.

Also there is a need to ensure that remuneration and other policies do not work counter to the standard operating procedures. A factory that rewards staff on the basis of volume of output may encourage short cuts which jeopardise safety.

The likelihood of one policy undermining another policy needs to be investigated. Consider a bank which has a policy of reducing risks by purchasing forward currency only to match expected customer demands. However, if it rewards traders on profits made then it is encouraging traders to ignore policy to get more remuneration. This is made worse if supervisors stress profitability all the time.

What areas of supply are critical? Do you have multiple suppliers to protect against normal hazards such as strikes at the supplier, adverse weather conditions blocking supply, or threats to supply caused by political factors?

In some companies a small number of key staff members are critical to their operations. Are there processes to monitor the level of staff morale and to act on the results?

30.13.3 Legal and regulatory risks

This refers to the possibility that the firm will breach its legal or regulatory requirements and thus expose the company to fines and injury to its reputation. This involves being aware of the requirements of each country in which it operates or in which its products and services are used. Further, the staff of the company need to know of the relevant requirements which apply to their activities. They should also have access to advice in order to avoid problems or to address issues that do arise. Once again, standard operating procedures and standard documentation can help reduce the risks. In some companies the protection of intellectual property should be of considerable relevance.

30.13.4 Financial risks

Financial risk management refers to the protection of assets from misappropriation and the avoidance of the incurrence of inappropriate liabilities, together with the financial management of cash flows so that the business can pay its obligations as they fall due. Accountants are very familiar with the protections provided by internal control systems supported by internal audits.

However, the recent global financial crisis has highlighted weaknesses in risk management. For example, the assumptions regarding the likelihood of sources of debt finance being rolled over were too optimistic and often items were looked at in isolation. By looking at it in isolation, the risk associated with an item was assessed on the assumption that an adverse event affected only that item whilst everything else was normal. However, when all parts of the economy deteriorated at the same time the impact of an adverse event was greater than expected.

Consider a property development company which is largely financed by debt. To reduce risk the company spread its investments across all types of properties (residential units, houses, industrial, office blocks, and shopping centres) and across several major cities. It did its stress analysis assuming one segment at a time (say, shopping centres) fell 15% in value. Under that analysis whichever segment fell, with the other segments remaining static, the company had more than sufficient asset backing to roll over its debt. However, during the great financial crisis all segments fell 12% to 20% with an overall fall of 17%, causing the debt financiers to question whether the asset backing was sufficient given the economists forecasting a further 5% fall in real estate prices.

Whilst it is not feasible to address all risk elements, the essential point is that each company needs to identify the risks that could pose serious threats to the prosperity of the business and put in place procedures to manage those risks. It should also be kept in mind that it is not a one off process but needs to be continually monitored. Every time the business changes its strategy or operations, and/or is involved in a takeover, or there is a change in laws the risk management programme has to be reviewed. With any programme there is a tendency for processes to slip either because of complacency or as a result of staff changes. This needs to be guarded against.

30.14 Corporate governance, legislation and codes

Investors looking to the safety and adequacy of the return on their investment are influenced by their level of confidence in the ability of the directors to achieve this. Good governance has not been fully defined and various reports have attempted to set out principles and practices which they perceive to be helpful in making directors accountable. These principles and practices are set out in a variety of Acts, e.g. Sarbanes–Oxley in the US and the Companies Act and regulations in the UK, and codes such as the Singapore Code of Corporate Governance 2005 and the UK Corporate Governance Code (formerly the Combined Code).

The various laws and codes that have been published set out principles and recommended best practice relating to the board of directors, directors' remuneration, relations with shareholders, accountability and audit. We now comment briefly on the position in Hong Kong, Malaysia and Singapore where there are common themes coming through from reviews – namely, how to make directors more accountable.

30.14.1 HK Code of Corporate Governance

There is a Hong Kong Code of Corporate Governance which was revised in 2005. Grant Thornton reviewed[12] the operation of the code in 2008 and commented:

Improved compliance
Our analysis makes it clear that overall compliance is improving. The year 2008 witnessed an increase in the compliance rate of HSCI companies to 62%. This shows that Hong Kong companies are making efforts to comply with the Code and improve their level of transparency . . . Our review notes that they still lag far behind expectations in many areas, and they should adhere to the Code's principles and best practices with greater determination.

The review then commented[13] on areas where performance needed to be improved. One of these was the problem of the lack of independence on the board:

A low level of independence on a company's board or committees greatly affects its ability to make objective decisions and critically monitor its performance . . . The Code requires that at least three INEDs should sit on the board . . . Even so, very few companies provide detailed and thorough information about their annual review of INED independence. The perception of independence will continue to be a strong element expected of top Hong Kong companies, as it is globally. Companies should therefore strive to improve their disclosures on this issue . . . the number of companies reporting that only INEDs serve on their audit committee remained unchanged at 60% . . . still far short of full compliance . . . The compliance rate is far lower where the composition of remuneration committees was concerned. Only 19% of companies had only INEDs serving on this committee.
   Another key area that is far more relevant to Hong Kong is the direct involvement and controlling influence of family members. Our business environment has a high concentration of familial involvement. While this is not an issue in itself, it should be properly handled in order to avoid perceptions of impaired objectivity or conflicts of interest . . . Even a higher percentage, 30%, noted that familial relationships existed within the board. The low involvement of INEDs further compounds the issue of independence, and companies should address these points.

30.14.2 Malaysian Code on Corporate Governance

The Malaysian Code on Corporate Governance was revised in 2007. The key amendments[14] to the code were designed to strengthen (a) the board of directors by spelling out the eligibility criteria for appointment of directors and the role of the nominating committee, and (b) the audit committees by spelling out that the committees should comprise only non-executive directors, all of whom should be able to read, analyse and interpret financial statements so that they will be able to effectively discharge their functions.

30.14.3 Singapore Code of Corporate Governance

A report[15] on the operation of the Singapore Code of Corporate Governance 2005 was carried out in 2007 for the Monetary Authority of Singapore and Singapore Exchange. The objective was to improve corporate governance standards to enhance Singapore's reputation as an international financial centre, help attract international investment, improve the liquidity of its stock markets, and reduce the cost of capital for its companies. There were a number of suggestions relating to directors' independence such as:

The proportion of directors who are labeled as independent generally meets the Code's recommendations. Nevertheless, there are concerns about the amount of influence which controlling shareholders have over the appointment of independent directors, the process by which independent directors are typically appointed, the relatively small pool from which independent directors are drawn, and how nominating committees are assessing the independence of directors. These could affect the ability or willingness of independent directors to act independently . . .

Regulators should consider supporting the creation of an online directors' register to increase the pool of independent directors and to assist companies in finding independent director candidates.

There is a Corporate Governance & Financial Reporting Centre (CGFRC) at the National University of Singapore[16] which aims to promote best practices in corporate governance and financial reporting.

30.14.4 Codes as a partial solution

As the nature of business and expectations of society change, the governance requirements evolve to reflect the new laws and regulations. By anticipating changing requirements, companies can prepare for the future. At the same time they should identify the special areas of potential conflict in their own operations and develop policies to manage those relationships.

Good governance is a question of having the right attitudes. All the corporate governance codes will not achieve much if they focus on form rather than substance. Codes work because people want to achieve good governance. People can always find ways around rules. Further, rules cannot cover all cases so good governance needs a commitment to the fundamental idea of fairness.

The research on whether good governance leads to lower cost of capital is very mixed reflecting both the difficulty of identifying the impact of good governance and the fact that some engage with the spirit of the concept and some don't. There are those who question the impact of good corporate governance and supporting the case of those who doubt that there is a positive impact on performance is an Australian research project[17] looking at companies in the S&P/ASX 200 index which found that companies which the researcher classified as having poor corporate governance outperformed companies classified as having good corporate governance over a range of measures including EBITDA growth and return on assets. There is an ongoing need for further research, particularly as to the effect on smaller listed companies, and it will be interesting to await the outcome.

30.15 Corporate governance – the UK experience

In the UK there have been a number of initiatives in attempts to achieve good corporate governance through (a) legislation, (b) the UK Corporate Governance Code, (c) supplementary reports, (d) non-executive directors (NEDs), (e) shareholder activism and (f) audit. We discuss each of these briefly below.

30.15.1 Legislation

Legislation is in place that attempts to ensure that investors receive sufficient information to make informed judgements. For example, there are requirements for the audit of financial statements and disclosure of directors' remuneration. There could be a case for increased statutory involvement in the affairs of a company by, for example, putting a limit on benefits and specifying how share options should be structured. However, the government has gone down the road of disclosure and transparency in reporting. There is still a need for further statutory requirements, such as fuller disclosure in the summary financial statements and improved voting mechanisms to avoid the high rate of proxy voting.

30.15.2 The UK Corporate Governance Code

The code is issued by the Financial Reporting Council (FRC). It is not a rule book but is principles-based and sets out best practice. It relies for its effectiveness on disclosure by requiring companies listed on a stock exchange to explain if they do not comply with its provisions.

The original code made an interesting development by separating its proposals into two parts:

- Part 1 containing Principles of Good Governance (Main and Supplementary) relating to

  A: directors

  B: directors' remuneration

  C: relations with shareholders

  D: accountability and audit.

- Part 2 containing Codes of Best Practice with procedures to make the Principles operational.

The code is regularly reviewed and updated but continues to distinguish between broad principles which companies are largely free to choose their own method of implementing. The detailed code provisions are those which companies are required to say whether they have complied with and, where they have not complied, to explain why not. The intention is to combine flexibility over detailed implementation with clarity where there was non-compliance.

The principles and code provisions relating to the board of directors are set out below to illustrate the code's approach. The six principles that relate to directors cover:

A1   the board

A2   chairman and chief executive

A3   board balance and independence

A4   appointments to the board

A5   information and professional development

A6   performance evaluation

As an illustration of the level of detail, the Principles (A1) and Provisions (A1.1 to A1.5) relating to **the board** are set out below.

A1 The Board

Main Principle
Every company should be headed by an effective board, which is collectively responsible for the success of the company.

Supporting Principles
- The board's role is to provide entrepreneurial leadership of the company within a framework of prudent and effective controls which enables risk to be assessed and managed.

- The board should
  - set the company's strategic aims;
  - ensure that the necessary financial and human resources are in place for the company to meet its objectives; and
- review management performance.
- The board should
  - set the company's values and standards; and
  - ensure that its obligations to its shareholders and others are understood and met.
- All directors must take decisions objectively in the interests of the company.
- As part of their role as members of a unitary board, non-executive directors should
  - constructively challenge and help develop proposals on strategy;
  - scrutinise the performance of management in meeting agreed goals and objectives and monitor the reporting of performance;
  - satisfy themselves on the integrity of financial information and that financial controls and systems of risk management are robust and defensible.
- As non-executive directors they
  - are responsible for determining appropriate levels of remuneration of executive directors; and
  - have a prime role in appointing, and where necessary removing, executive directors, and in succession planning.

Code Provisions

A.1.1   The board should meet sufficiently regularly to discharge its duties effectively. There should be a formal schedule of matters specifically reserved for its decision. The annual report should include a statement of how the board operates, including a high level statement of which types of decisions are to be taken by the board and which are to be delegated to management.

A.1.2   The annual report should identify the chairman, the deputy chairman (where there is one), the chief executive, the senior independent director and the chairmen and members of the nomination, audit and remuneration committees. It should also set out the number of meetings of the board and those committees, and individual attendance by directors.

A.1.3   The chairman should hold meetings with the non-executive directors without the executives present. Led by the senior independent director, the non-executive directors should meet without the chairman present at least annually to appraise the chairman's performance (as described in A.6.1) and on such other occasions as are deemed appropriate.

A.1.4   Where directors have concerns which cannot be resolved about the running of the company or a proposed action, they should ensure that their concerns are recorded in the board minutes. On resignation, a non-executive director should provide a written statement to the chairman, for circulation to the board, if they have any such concerns.

A.1.5   The company should arrange appropriate insurance cover in respect of legal action against its directors.

Revisions to the code

The code is regularly updated to reflect changes in perception of best practice. For example, a change was made which allowed the company chairman to sit on the remuneration committee provided he is considered independent on appointment and makes the use of proxies more transparent. Transparency was improved by allowing shareholders who vote by proxy the option of withholding their vote on a resolution and encouraging companies to publish details of proxies where votes are taken on a show of hands. It also removed the restriction on an individual chairing more than one FTSE 100 company because this was felt to be over-prescriptive and for listed companies outside the FTSE 350, allowed the company chairman to be a member of, but not chair, the audit committee provided that he or she was independent on appointment as chairman although there would still need to be two independent non-executive directors.

30.15.3 Supplementary reports

The code has been supplemented by a number of reports dealing with specific aspects of corporate governance. We discuss briefly three of these reports, namely, the Myners Report, the Smith Report and the Higgs Report.

Myners Report[18]

This was a Treasury Report issued in 2001 titled *Developing a Winning Partnership* which considered how companies and institutional investors were working together. It dealt with the role of the chair of the board when trustees were making an investment decision, for example, recommending that the chair of the board should be responsible for ensuring that trustees taking investment decisions are familiar with investment issues and that the board has sufficient trustees for that purpose and for funds with more than 5,000 members, the chair of the board and at least one-third of trustees should be familiar with investment issues (even where investment decisions have been delegated to an investment subcommittee).

Smith Report (2003)

This produced recommendations on the membership and functions of audit committees. Its recommendations on audit committees were that there should be at least three members, all independent NEDs with at least one member having significant, recent and relevant financial experience. It also recommended that the committee should monitor the integrity of the financial statements and the external auditor's independence, objectivity and effectiveness; review the company's internal financial control system and effectiveness of internal audit; recommend the appointment of the external auditor, and approve their remuneration.

The Higgs Report[19]

This report issued in 2003 made recommendations relating to the membership of NEDs on the board, their appointment, independence, effectiveness, and the appointment of a senior NED. It recommended that the main roles for NEDs was to constructively challenge and contribute to the development of strategy, scrutinise the performance of management in meeting agreed goals and objectives and monitor the reporting of performance, satisfy themselves that financial information is accurate and that financial controls and systems of risk management are robust and defensible and be responsible for determining the appropriate level of remuneration of executive directors and have a prime role in appointing, and where necessary removing, senior management in succession planning.

The code is periodically revised to adopt recommendations based on reports such as those above. This is one of the strengths of the code that it continually attempts to review current practice and improve the corporate governance regime.

30.15.4 NEDs

The main function of non-executive directors is to ensure that the executive directors are pursuing policies consistent with shareholders' interests.[20]

Review of their contribution

Considering the qualities that are required, the Cadbury Report recommended that the board should include non-executive directors of sufficient calibre and number for their views to carry significant weight in the board's decisions. Research[21] indicated that they are concerned to maintain their reputation in the external market in order to maintain their marketability.

NEDs on many boards bring added or essential commercial and financial expertise. For example, on a routine basis as members of the audit committee or, on an *ad hoc* basis, providing experience when a company is preparing to float or having specific industry knowledge, as explained in the following extract from the 2007 Beazley Group plc Annual Report:

The Board

The board consists of a non-executive chairman, Jonathan Agnew, together with five independent non-executive directors, of which Andy Pomfret is the senior non-executive director, and seven executive directors, of which Andrew Beazley is chief executive.

All five of the non-executive directors, who have been appointed for specified terms, are considered by the board to be independent of management and free of any relationship which could materially interfere with the exercise of their independent judgement. Given that the business of the group is insurance underwriting organised by line of business in divisions, the board continues to consider it appropriate that some of the underwriting heads of the major divisions should be executive directors.

Notwithstanding that the company is included in the FTSE 250 index, it does not consider it desirable to increase the number of non-executive directors to outnumber the executive directors since the range of skills and experience of the existing non-executive director is sufficient and the increased size of the board would make it unwieldy. Indeed the board intends over the medium term to reduce its size to some extent, provided that this can be achieved without significantly impairing the underwriting experience represented on it.

The fees of non-executive directors, other than the chairman, are determined by the board. When setting fee levels consideration is given to levels in comparable companies for comparable services. No non-executive director participates in the company's incentive arrangements or pension plan.

Non-executive directors are appointed for fixed terms, normally for three years, and may be reappointed for future terms. Non-executive directors are typically appointed through a selection process that includes the candidate bringing the desired competence and skills to the group. The board has identified several key competencies for non-executive directors to complement the existing skill-set of the executive directors. These competencies are as follows: Insurance sector expertise; Asset management skills; Public company and corporate governance experience; Risk management skills; and Finance skills.

However, NEDs are not and never can be a universal panacea. It has to be recognised that there may be constraints:

- They might have divided loyalties having been nominated by the chairman, the CEO or other board member.
- They might have other NED appointments and/or executive appointments which limit the time they can give to the company's affairs.
- They are not full-time directors.
- They cannot have the same detailed knowledge of the company as executive directors, particularly in relation to strategic planning.
- They might not have access to all relevant information if the company has a complex geographic or group organisation.
- They might not have the technical knowledge to be effective in a committee of which they are a member.
- They do not have a voting majority on the board.
- They might not be able to restrain an overbearing CEO, particularly if the CEO is also the chairman.

With so many caveats, it would not be unreasonable to assume that NEDs could not easily divert a dominant CEO or executive directors from a planned course of action. In such cases, their influence on good corporate governance is reduced unless the interest of directors and shareholders already happen to coincide. However if the issue is serious enough for one or more independent director to resign it is likely that the market will certainly take note.

There is great reliance placed on the use of NEDs as one mechanisms for achieving good corporate governance. Attention has been directed towards their role in setting directors' remuneration but their remit is much wider. It is also to consider a company's strategic planning and, in this, there is mixed evidence as to whether there is a positive or negative correlation between the proportion of independent directors and performance.

Investors, auditors and regulators need to be aware of conditions that can neuter NEDs, e.g. where there is a national culture of disregard for corporate guidelines and a strong CEO who is also chairman, as in the case of Parmalat.[22] Regulators, such as the FSA in the UK, have the responsibility for regulating financial services – if the regulators are unable to ensure good corporate governance, it is unreal to expect NEDs to do so in such a situation.

The public does not have the information to assess these situations and has to rely on auditors and institutional investors who have analytical expertise. Problems only tend to become known to the public when there is force on a company. This can come about for a number of reasons: e.g. if a company has to make a significant restatement of its financial statements or a company is acquired and the new management want to clean up the statement of financial position.

However, on a positive note, the presence of NEDs is perceived to be indicative of good corporate governance and a research report[23] indicated that good governance has a positive impact on investor confidence. The research examined 654 UK FTSE All-Share companies from 2003 to 2007 using unique governance data from the ABI's Institutional Voting and Information Service (IVIS). The service issues colour coded guidance to highlight breaches of governance best practice, with red being the most serious. An extract from the ABI research is as follows:

New research from the ABI (Association of British Insurers) shows that companies with the best corporate governance records have produced returns 18% higher than those with poor governance. It was also revealed that a breach of governance best practice (known as a red top in the ABI's guidance) reduces a company's industry-adjusted return on assets (ROA) by an average of 1 percentage point a year. For even the best performing companies, (those within the top quartile of ROA performance), that equates to an actual fall of 8.6% in returns per year.

The research also shows that shareholders investing in a poorly governed company suffer from low returns. £100 invested in a company with no corporate governance problems leads to an average return of £120 but if invested in the worst governed companies the return would have been just £102.

There are many highly talented, well-experienced NEDs but their ability to influence good governance should not be overestimated. They are always described as the *independent* directors. However, it is difficult to be confident when nominations are made by the board, future appointments might be affected if they prove difficult, i.e. challenging. Their effectiveness might be reduced if they have limited time, limited access to documents, limited respect from full-time executive directors and limited expertise within the remuneration and/or audit committees. When a company is prospering their influence could be extremely beneficial; when there are problems they may not have the authority to ensure good governance.

30.15.5 Shareholders

In the UK the need for good corporate governance is affected by how widely shares are held.

In the US and the UK, a large number of financial institutions and individuals hold shares in listed companies, so there is a greater need for corporate governance requirements. In Japan and most European countries (except the UK) shares in listed companies tend to be held by a small number of banks, financial institutions and individuals. Where there are few shareholders in a company, they can question the directors directly, so there is less need for corporate governance requirements.

The following table is an extract from the UK Office of National Statistics[24] showing the holdings in UK shares:

Beneficial ownership of UK shares 2006 and 2008

	Pounds (bn)		*Percentages*	
	2006	*2008*	*2006*	*2008*
Rest of the world	742.4	481.1	40.0	41.5
Insurance companies	272.8	154.9	14.7	13.4
Pensions funds	235.8	148.8	12.7	12.8
Individuals	238.5	117.8	12.8	10.2
Unit trusts	30.0	21.3	1.6	1.8
Investment trusts	45.1	22.1	2.4	1.9
Other financial institutions	179.1	115.3	9.6	10.0
Charities	16.1	8.7	0.9	0.8
Private non-financial companies	33.5	34.7	1.8	3.0
Public sector	2.0	13.0	0.1	1.1
Banks	63.0	40.6	3.4	3.5
Total	1858.3	1158.3	100.0	100.0

At the end of 2008 the UK Stock Market was valued at £1,158.4 billion, a decrease of £699.8 billion (37.7 per cent) since the end of 2006.

Figures for end-2008 show that: Investors from outside the UK owned 41.5 per cent of UK shares listed on the UK Stock Exchange, up from 40.0 per cent at end-2006. Rest of the world investors held £481.1 billion of shares – down from £742.4 billion at end-2006.

Individual shareholder influence on corporate governance

With the Rest of the world holding 41.5% and individual shareholders having fallen to just over 10% it is difficult for this group to exercise any significant group influence on management behaviour. In passing legislation, there is an implicit view that individual shareholders have a responsibility to achieve good corporate governance. Statutes can provide for disclosure and be fine-tuned in response to changing needs but they are not intended to replace share-holder activism. When the economy is booming there is a temptation to sit back, collect the dividends and capital gains, bin the annual report and post in-proxy forms.

Shareholder influence has to rely on that exercised by the institutional investors.

Large-block investors' influence on corporate governance

There is mixed evidence about the influence of large-block shareholders. The following is an extract from a Department of Trade and Industry Report:[25]

> The report observed from a review of economics, corporate finance and 'law and economics' research literature that there was no unambiguous evidence that presence of large-block and institutional investors among the firm's shareholders performed monitoring and resource functions of 'good' corporate governance. However, management and business strategy research suggests that it does have a significant effect on *critical* organisational decisions, such as executive turnover, value-enhancing business strategy, and limitations on anti-takeover defences.

Feedback from the experts' evaluation of the governance roles of various types of share-holders provided the following pattern:[26]

	Mean	*Standard deviation*
Pension funds, mutual funds, foundations	4.58	1.50
Private equity funds	4.52	1.76
Individual (non-family) blockholders	4.36	1.70
Family blockholders	4.20	1.63
Corporate pension funds	3.85	1.55
Insurance companies	3.69	1.69
Banks	3.31	1.49
Dispersed individual shareholders	2.18	1.41

The highest scores were assigned to the governance roles of pension funds, mutual funds, foundations and private equity investors:

> Some respondents also suggested that various associations of institutional investors such as NAPF, ABI, etc., play strong governance roles, as do individual blockholders and family owners. At the other end of the spectrum are dispersed individual shareholders whose governance roles received the lowest score. However, it must be kept in mind that none of the individual scores is above 5 indicating that, on average, our experts were rather sceptical about the effectiveness of large blockholders from the 'good' governance perspective.[27]

A further related factor is that US and UK companies have tended to have a low gearing with most of the finance provided by shareholders. However, in other countries the gearing of companies is much higher, which indicates that most finance for companies comes from banks. If the majority of the finance is provided by shareholders, then there is a greater need for corporate governance requirements than if finance is in the form of loans where the lenders are able to stipulate conditions and loan covenants, e.g. the maximum level of gearing and action available to them if interest payments or capital repayments are missed.

However, institutional investors do not represent a majority in any company. Their role is to achieve the best return on the funds under their management consistent with their attitude to environmental and social issues. Their expertise has been largely directed towards the strategic management and performance of the company with, perhaps an excessive concern with short-term gains. Issues such as directors' remuneration issues might well be of far less significance than the return on their investment.

The Walker Review of Corporate Governance of UK Banking Industry[28]

This reviewed corporate governance in the UK banking industry and financial institutions and made recommendations on the effectiveness of risk management at board level, including the incentives in remuneration policy to manage risk effectively; the balance of skills, experience and independence required on the boards; the effectiveness of board practices and the performance of audit, risk, remuneration and nomination committees and the role of institutional shareholders in engaging effectively with companies and monitoring of boards. The role of the institutional investors is important and a stewardship code has been proposed.

The Stewardship Code

The code consists of seven principles which, if followed, should benefit corporate governance. The principles are:

1 **Institutional investors should publicly disclose their policy on how they will discharge their stewardship responsibilities.** Such a policy should include how investee companies will be monitored with an active dialogue on the board and its policy on voting and the use made of proxy voting.

2 **Institutional investors should have a robust policy on managing conflicts of interest in relation to stewardship and this policy should be publicly disclosed.** Such a policy should include how to manage conflicts of interest when, for example, voting on matters affecting a parent company or client.

3 **Institutional investors should monitor when it is necessary to enter into an active dialogue with their boards.** Such monitoring should include satisfying themselves that the board and sub-committee structures are effective, and that independent directors provide adequate oversight and maintain a clear audit trail of the institution's decisions. The objective is to identify problems at an early stage to minimise any loss of shareholder value.

4 **Institutional investors should establish clear guidelines on when and how they will escalate their activities as a method of protecting and enhancing shareholder value.** Such guidelines should say the circumstances when they will actively intervene. Instances when institutional investors may want to intervene include when they have concerns about the company's strategy and performance, its governance or its approach to the risks arising from social and environmental matters. If there are concerns, then any action could escalate from meetings with management specifically to discuss the concerns through to requisitioning an EGM, possibly to change the board.

5 **Institutional investors should be willing to act collectively with other investors where appropriate.** Such action is proposed in extreme cases when the risks posed threaten the ability of the company to continue.

6 **Institutional investors should have a clear policy on voting and disclosure of voting activity.** Institutional investors should seek to vote all shares held. They should not automatically support the board and if they have been unable to reach a satisfactory outcome through active dialogue then they should register an abstention or vote against the resolution.

7 **Institutional investors should report periodically on their stewardship and voting activities.** Such reports should be made regularly and explain how they have discharged their responsibilities. However, it is recognised that confidentiality in specific situations may well be crucial to achieving a positive outcome.

The FRC proposes to extend these principles to all listed companies.

Legal safeguards

Corporate governance has to react to changing circumstances and threats. It evolves and will continue to need to be revised and updated. The law provides minimum safeguards but in the ever changing complexities of global trade and finance good governance is dependent on the behaviour of directors and their commitment to principles and values. The UK system is heavily dependent on codes which set out principles and the requirement for directors to explain if they fail to comply. The Governance Code and Stewardship Code will rely for their effectiveness on investor engagement. This recognises that investors cannot delegate all responsibility to their agents, the directors, accept their dividends and be dormant principals.

UK experience and international initiatives

It is interesting to note that what constitutes good corporate governance is evolving with new initiatives being taken globally.

For example, The OECD is responding to weaknesses in corporate governance that became apparent in the financial crisis by developing recommendations for improvements in board practices, the remuneration process and how shareholders should actively exercise their rights. It is also reviewing governance in relation to risk management which featured as such a threat in the way financial institutions conducted their business. However, there is some concern that measures that might be essential for the control of the financial sector should not be imposed arbitrarily on non-financial sector organisations.

30.15.6 Audit

Auditors are subject to professional oversight to ensure that they are independent, up-to-date and competent. However, where there is a determined effort to mislead the auditors, for example, creating false paper trails and misstatement at the highest level, then there is the risk that fraud will be missed.

There have been allegations of audit negligence in some high-profile corporate failures, in some of which auditors have been found liable. In part, the financial crisis arising from issues such as the use of special purpose entities and complex financial instruments has been made more difficult for auditors as it is quite clear that pressure groups, such as the investment banks, have influenced the regulators to allow, or not question, practices that have since been found to be highly risky and unreported.

In general, the audit appears to be a reliable mechanism for ensuring that the financial statements give a true and fair view.

Summary

Good governance is achieved when all parties feel that they have been fairly treated. It is achieved when behaviour is prompted by the idea of fairness to all parties. Independent behaviour is expected of the NEDs and auditors and they are expected to have the strength of character to act professionally with proper regard for the interest of the shareholders. The shareholders in turn should be exercising their rights and not be inert. They have a role to play and it is not fair to sit on their hands and complain.

Good corporate governance cannot be achieved by rules alone. The principle-based approach such as that of the FRC with the UK Corporate Governance Code recognises that it is behaviour that is the key – it sets out broad principles and a recommended set of provisions/rules which are indicative of good practice and disclosure is required if there is reason why they are not appropriate in a specific situation.

Good corporate governance depends on directors behaving in the best interest of shareholders. Corporate governance mechanisms to achieve this include legislation, corporate governance codes, appointment of NEDs, shareholder activism and audit. Such mechanisms are necessary when companies are financed largely by equity capital. It is noticeable that they are being developed in many countries in response to wider share ownership.

Corporate governance best practice is being regularly reviewed and improved as, for example, steps being taken to improve the ability of NEDs to exercise an effective corporate governance role.

REVIEW QUESTIONS

1 Explain in your own words what you understand corporate governance to mean.

2 Explain why governance procedures may vary from country to country.

3 What are the implications of governance for audit practices.

4 The Association of British Insurers held the view that options should be exercised only if the company's earnings per share growth exceeded that of the retail price index. The National Association of Pension Funds preferred the criterion to be a company's outperformance of the FTA All-Share Index.

(a) Discuss the reasons for the differences in approach.

(b) Discuss the implication of each approach to the financial reporting regulators and the auditors.

5 Research[29] suggests that companies whose managers own a significant proportion of the voting share capital tend to violate the UK Corporate Governance Code recommendations on board composition far more frequently than other companies. Discuss the advantages and disadvantages of enforcing greater compliance.

6 Good corporate governance is a myth – Just look at these frauds and irregularities:

- Enron   www.sec.gov/litigation/litreleases/lr18582.htm
- WorldCom   www.sec.gov/litigation/litreleases/lr17588.htm
- Xerox Corporation   www.sec.gov/litigation/complaints/complr17465.htm
- Dell   www.sec.gov/news/press/2010/2010-131.htm
- Lehman   http://lehmanreport.jenner.com/VOLUME%201.pdf

How realistic is it to expect good governance to combat similar future behaviour?

7 'Stronger corporate governance legislation is emerging globally but true success will only come from self-regulation, increased internal controls and the strong ethical corporate culture that organisations create.' Discuss.

8 In the modern commercial world, auditors provide numerous other services to complement their audit work. These services include the following:

(a) Accountancy and book-keeping assistance, e.g. in the maintenance of ledgers and in the preparation of monthly and annual accounts.

(b) Secretarial help, e.g. ensuring that the company has complied with the Companies Act in the maintenance of shareholder registers and in the completion of annual returns to Companies House.

(c) Consultancy services, e.g. advice on the design of information systems and organisational structures, advice on the choice of computer equipment and software packages, and advice on the recruitment of new executives.

(d) Investigation work, e.g. appraisals of companies that might be taken over.

(e) Receivership work, e.g. when the firm assumes the role of receiver or liquidator on behalf of an audit client.

(f) Taxation work, e.g. tax planning advice and preparation of tax returns to the Inland Revenue for both the company and the company's senior management.

Discuss:

(i) Whether any of these activities is unacceptable as a separate activity because it might weaken an auditor's independence.

(ii) The advantages and disadvantages to the shareholders of the audit firm providing this range of service.

9 The following is an extract from the *Sunday Times* of 8 March 2009:

Marc Jobling, the ABI's assistant director of investment affairs said: 'Pay consultants are a big contributor to the problems around executive pay. We have heard of some who admit that they work for both management and independent directors – which is a clear conflict of interest and not acceptable. We believe that remuneration consultants, whose livelihood appears to depend on pushing an ever-upward spiral in executive pay, should be obliged to develop a code of ethics.'

Discuss the types of issues which should be included in such a code of ethics and how effective they would be in achieving good corporate governance.

10 There has been much criticism of the effectiveness of non-executive directors following failures such as Enron. Some consider that their interests are too close to those of the executive directors and they have neither the time nor the professional support to allow them to be effective monitors of the executive directors. Draft a job specification and personal criteria that you think would allay these criticisms.

11 In 2000, the chairman of the US Securities and Exchange Commission (SEC), Arthur Levitt, proposed that other services provided by audit firms to their audit clients should be severely restricted, probably solely to audit and tax work.[31] Discuss why this still has not happened.

12 Discuss how remuneration policies may affect good corporate governance.

13 Discuss the major risks which will need to be managed by a pharmaceutical company and the extreme to which these should be disclosed.

14 Egypt is a country in which many of the public companies have substantial shareholders in the form of founding families or government shareholders. How do you think that would affect corporate governance?

15 Discuss whether corporate governance has any particular relevance to banks.

16 'Management will become accountable only when shareholders receive information on corporate strategy, future-based plans and budgets, and actual results with explanations of variances.' Discuss whether this is necessary, feasible and in the company's interest.

17 The Chartered Institute of Management Accountants (CIMA) has warned that linking directors' pay to EPS or return on assets is open to abuse, since these are not the objective measures they might appear.

   (a) Identify five ways in which the directors might manipulate the EPS and return on assets without breaching existing standards.

   (b) Suggest two alternative bases for setting criteria for bonuses.

18 Review reporting requirements in relation to disclosure of related party transactions and discuss their adequacy in relation to the avoidance of conflicts of interest.

19 Summarise the approach of the UK Financial Reporting Council to governance in audit practices and discuss in what situations audit independence could be compromised.

20 Discuss the extent to which a trade union is able to contribute to good corporate governance.

EXERCISES

Question 1: Scenario – Fred Paris

Manufacturing Co has been negotiating with Fred Paris regarding the sale of some property that represented an old manufacturing site which is now surplus to requirements. Because part of the site was used for manufacturing, it has to be decontaminated before it can be subdivided as a new housing development. This has complicated negotiations. Fred is a property developer and he has a private company (Paris Property Development Pty Ltd) and is also a major (15%) shareholder of FP Development of which he is chairman. The negotiators for Manufacturing Co note that the documents keep switching between Paris Property Development and FP Development and they use that as feedback as to how well they are negotiating. Is there a corporate governance failure? Discuss.

Question 2: Scenario – Harvey Storm

Harvey Storm is chief executive of West Wing Savings and Loans. Harvey authorises a loan to Middleman Properties secured on the land it is about to purchase. Middleman Properties has little money of its own. Middleman Properties subdivides the land and builds houses on them. It offers buyers a house and finance package under which West Wing provides the house loans up to 97% of the house price even to couples with poor credit ratings. This allows Middleman Properties to ask for higher prices for the houses.

Middleman Properties appoints Frontman Homes as the selling agent who kindly provides buyers with the free services of a solicitor to handle all the legal aspects including the conveyancing. Most of the profits from the developments are paid to Frontman Homes as commissions. Harvey Storm's wife has a 20% interest in Frontman Homes. Are these corporate governance failures? Discuss.

Question 3: Scenario – Conglomerate plc

Conglomerate plc was a family company which was so successful that the founding Alexander family could not fully finance its expansion. So the company was floated on the stock exchange with the Alexander family holding 'A' class shares and the public holding 'B' class shares. 'A' class shares held the right to appoint six of the eleven directors. 'B' class shares could appoint five directors and had the same dividend rights as the 'A' class shares. The company could not be wound up unless a resolution was passed by 75% or more of 'A' class shareholders. Is there any risk of a governance failure? Discuss.

Question 4: Scenario – White plc

The board of White plc is discussing the filling of a vacant position arising from the death of Lord White. A list of possible candidates is as follows:

(a) Lord Sperring who is a well known company director and who was the managing director of Sperring Manufacturers before he switched to being a professional director.

(b) John Spate, B.Eng., PhD who is managing director of a successful, innovative high technology company and will be taking retirement in four months time.

(c) Gerald Stewart B.Com who is the retired managing director of Spry and Montgomery advertising agency which operates in six countries being England and five other commonwealth countries.

The managing director leads the discussion and focuses on the likelihood of the three candidates being able to work in harmony with other members of the board and suggests that John Spate is too radical to be a member of the board of White plc. The other members of the board agree that he has a history of looking at things differently and would tend to distract the board.

The chairman of the board suggests that Lord Sperring is very well connected in the business community and would be able to open many doors for the managing director. It was unanimously agreed that the chairman should approach Lord Sperring to see if he would be willing to join the board.

Critically discuss the appointment process.

Question 5

(a) Describe the value to the audit client of the audit firm providing consultancy services.

(b) Why is it undesirable for audit firms to provide consultancy services to audit clients?

(c) Why do audit firms want to continue to provide consultancy services to audit clients?

Question 6

How is the relationship between the audit firm and the audit client different for:

(a) the provision of statutory audit when the auditor reports to the shareholders;

(b) the provision of consultancy services by audit firms?

Question 7

Why is there a prohibition of auditors owning shares in client companies? Is this prohibition reasonable? Discuss.

Question 8

The financial statements of Rolls-Royce plc (aero engine manufacturer) for the year ended 31 December 1999 disclose the following matters in relation to the directors:

(a) Remuneration committee

The remuneration committee, which operates within agreed terms of reference, has responsibility for making recommendations to the board on the Group's general policy towards executive remuneration. The committee also determines, on the board's behalf, the specific remuneration packages of the executive directors and a number of senior executives.

The membership of the committee consists exclusively of independent non-executive directors (*the financial statements disclose the names of these directors*). The committee meets regularly and has access to professional advice from inside and outside the Company.

The Chairman of the Company (*a part-time executive director*) and the Chief Executive (*an executive director*) generally attend meetings but are not present during any discussion of their own emoluments.

(b) Base salary

The committee believes that in order to attract and retain executive directors of the right calibre and to provide them with adequate incentives to deliver the Group's objectives, the Group should pursue a policy of offering median-level base salaries for its executive directors, and through the performance-related schemes, the opportunity of upper quartile earnings for upper quartile performance.

(c) Annual performance award scheme

The scheme enables a maximum performance award of up to 60% of salary to be paid to executive directors for exceptional performance against pre-determined targets based upon return on capital employed with a tapered and reducing scale of maximum percentages for senior employees. The targets are set by the committee based upon the Group's annual operating plans. Such payments do not form part of pensionable earnings. One-third of total awards made are paid in Rolls-Royce shares which are held in trust for two years, with release normally being conditional on the individual remaining in the Group's employment until the end of the period. The required shares are purchased on the open market. This arrangement provides a strong link between performance and remuneration and provides a culture of share ownership amongst the Group's senior management.

Required:
Comment on the notes to the financial statements included above.

References

1 C. Oman (ed.) *Corporate Governance in Development: The Experiences of Brazil, Chile, India and South Africa*, Paris and Washington, DC. OECD Development Centre and Center for International Private Enterprise, 2003, cited in N. Meisel, *Governance Culture and Development*, Paris: Development Centre, OECD, 2004, p. 16.
2 www.sec.gov/litigation/litreleases/2009/lr21350.htm
3 www.oecd.org/dataoecd/28/62/38699164.pdf
4 http://lehmanreport.jenner.com/
5 A. Cornford, *Enron and Internationally Agreed Principles for Corporate Governance and the Financial Sector*, G-24 Discussion Paper Series, United Nations.
6 www.sec.gov/news/press/2003-95.htm

7 www.sec.gov/litigation/admin/3438494.txt

8 A.R. Wyatt (2003) *Accounting Professionalism – They just don't get it!* (http: aaahq.org/AM2003/WyattSpeech.pdf

9 L. Bebchuk, M. Cremers and U. Peyer, 'Higher CEO salaries don't always pay off', *The Australian Financial Review*, 12 February 2010, p. 59.

10 *Accountancy*, September 1995.

11 An example of this is the convergence of computing, telephone, television and entertainment markets as new devices impinge on all fields compared to ten years ago when they were quite distinct fields.

12 *Corporate Governance Review*, Grant Thornton p. 7 (www.gthk.com.hk/web/en/publications/Research/review).

13 *Ibid.* p. 8.

14 sc.com.my/ENG/HTML/CG/cg**2007**.pdf

15 Professor Mak Yuen Teen, *Improving the Implementation of Corporate Governance Practices in Singapore*, Monetary Authority of Singapore and Singapore Exchange, 2007 (www.mas.gov.sg/resource/news_room/press_releases/2007/CG_Study_Complete_Report_260607.pdf).

16 www.cgfrc.nus.edu.sg

17 M. Gold, 'Corporate Governance Reform in Australia: The Intersection of Investment Fiduciaries and Issuers' in *International Corporate Governance after Sarbanes–Oxley*, P. Ali and G. Gregoriou (eds), John Wiley and Sons, New York, 2006.

18 http://archive.treasury.gov.uk/docs/2001/myners_report0602.html

19 www.berr.gov.uk/whatwedo/businesslaw/corp-governance/higgs-tyson/page23342.html

20 E. Fama, 'Agency problems and the theory of the firms', *Journal of Political Economy*, 1980, vol. 88, pp. 288–307.

21 E. Fama and M. Jensen, 'Separation of ownership and control', *Journal of Law and Economics*, 1983, vol. 26, pp. 301–325.

22 www.ethicalcorp.com/content.asp?ContentID=1673

23 *ABI Research: Corporate governance 'pays' for shareholders and company performance*, ABI, 27 February 2008, Ref: 12/08.

24 www.statistics.gov.uk/pdfdir/share0110.pdf

25 G. Igor Filatochev, H.G. Jackson and D. Allcock, *Key Drivers to Good Corporate Governance and Appropriateness of UK Policy Responses*, DTI, 2007 (www.berr.gov.uk/files/file36671.pdf).

26 *Ibid.*

27 *Ibid.*

28 www.hm-treasury.gov.uk/walker_review_information.htm

29 K. Peasnell, P. Pope and S. Young, *Accountancy*, July 1998, p. 115.

30 I. Fraser and W. Henry, *The Future of Corporate Governance: Insights from the UK*, ICAS 2003.

31 'PwC and E&Y in favour of rules to restrict services', *Accountancy*, October 2000, p. 7.

CHAPTER 31

Sustainability – environmental and social reporting

31.1 Introduction

The main purpose of this chapter is to provide an overview of the impact of sustainability on financial reporting.

Objectives

By the end of the chapter, you should be able to:

- discuss the evolution of sustainability reporting including:
  - triple bottom line reporting;
  - the connected framework;
  - IFAC Sustainability Framework;
  - the accountant's role in a capitalist society;
- discuss the evolution of environmental reporting in the annual report:
  - European Commission initiatives;
  - United Nations initiatives;
  - US initiatives;
  - Self-regulation schemes;
  - economic consequences;
  - environmental audit;
- discuss the evolution of social accounting in the annual report:
  - the corporate report;
  - corporate social reporting;
- need for comparative data:
  - Global Reporting Initiative;
  - benchmarking.

31.2 How financial reporting has evolved to embrace sustainability reporting

Primary stakeholders

When corporate bodies were first created the primary stakeholders were the shareholders who had invested the capital and it was seen as the directors' responsibility to maximise their return by way of dividends and capital growth. This view was promoted by Milton Friedman[1] writing that:

few trends would so thoroughly undermine the very foundations of our free society as the acceptance by corporate officials of a social responsibility other than to make as much money for their shareholders as they possibly can.

It follows from this that directors were accountable to the shareholders who in turn should hold them to account. The Friedman approach offers protection for shareholders provided they actually do exercise their ability to hold directors accountable. However, it does not have regard to the interests of any other group affected by a company's decisions, such as consumers, employees or communities impacted upon by a company's operations unless there is a financial benefit to the company.

Other stakeholders

Since Friedman's writing in the 1960s companies have been under pressure to be accountable to a growing number of stakeholders. The pressure can be seen to come from

- Europe, e.g. the limiting and charging for landfill waste;
- national legislation, e.g. the Companies Act 2006 requirement that the business review in the Directors' Report must include information about:
  - environmental matters (including the impact of the company's business on the environment);
  - the company's employees; and
  - social and community issues.

Companies are now expected to act responsibly in their relationships with other stakeholders who have a legitimate interest in the business. Although there was a fear within companies that their financial performance would be damaged if public costs and other stakeholder interests were taken into account, societal pressure has grown since the 1990s. The following is a quote from the World Business Council for Sustainable Development:[2]

> CSR is the continuing commitment by business to behave ethically and contribute to economic development while improving the quality of life of the workforce and their families as well as of the local community and society at large.

There are three interesting points to highlight in this quotation. The first is the reference to behave ethically, the second is the acknowledgement that a company has an economic objective and the third is the extension to improve the quality of life of other stakeholders which includes environmental and social impacts.

As far back as 1975 there have been various initiatives such as the corporate report proposing the disclosure of additional information, such as employment and value added reports. External corporate reporting has been evolving from the simple financial reporting of profits and losses, assets and liabilities to, for example, the inclusion of information on governance (e.g. disclosure of directors remuneration), as well as non-financial information such as environmental and social policies.

The concept of the triple bottom line was to integrate the reporting of economic, environmental and social impacts to recognise wider stakeholder interests.

31.3 The Triple Bottom Line (TBL)

TBL was a concept developed in the 1990s[3] under which financial, social and environmental performance were to be reported within the annual report. Economic performance was already highly developed, e.g. return on investment, gearing and liquidity ratios. The fact of reporting social and environmental impacts provided an incentive for a company to identify and establish performance indicators.

Environmental impacts were identified in relation, amongst other things, to waste, emissions and energy. Social impacts were identified in relation, amongst other things, to employment and human rights issues.

However, sustainability reporting is evolving and the author of TPL writes[4] that:

> In sum, the TBL agenda as most people would currently understand it is only the beginning. A much more comprehensive approach will be needed that involves a wide range of stakeholders and coordinates across many areas of government policy, including tax policy, technology policy, economic development policy, labour policy, security policy, corporate reporting policy and so on. Developing this comprehensive approach to sustainable development and environmental protection will be a central governance challenge – and, even more critically, a market challenge – in the 21st century.

31.4 The Connected Reporting Framework

The Accounting for Sustainability project[5] has developed a Connected Reporting Framework which will:

> help provide clearer, more consistent and comparable information for use both within an organisation and externally. The new Connected Reporting Framework developed by the Project explains how all areas of organisational performance can be presented in a connected way, reflecting the organisation's strategy and the way it is managed.

The principles which underlie the new Framework are:

- sustainability issues should be clearly linked to the organisation's overall strategy;
- sustainability and more conventional financial information should be presented together so that a more complete and balanced picture of the organisation's performance is given; and
- there should be consistency in presentation to aid comparability between years and organisations.

The Connected Reporting Framework has the following five key elements

1 An explanation of how sustainability is connected to the overall operational strategy of the organisation and the provision of sustainability targets.

2 Five key environmental indicators, which all organizations should consider reporting, being: polluting emissions, energy use, water use, waste and significant use of other finite resources

3 Other key sustainability information should be given where the business or operation has material impacts.

4 The inclusion of industry benchmarks, when available, for key performance indicators, to aid performance appraisal.

5 The up-stream and down-stream impact of the organisation's products and services: the sustainability impacts of its suppliers and of the use of its products or services by customers and consumers.

31.4.1 The Connected Reporting Framework illustrated

The following is an extract from the 2007 Aviva plc Annual Report:

Working with the Accounting for Sustainability project, Aviva is helping define a new reporting standard for sustainable business and a tool-kit to embed sustainable decision making. The table . . . (*see below for extract*) demonstrates some of the measures in the sustainability model. We continue to work towards internalising the cost of carbon and demonstrating how environmental impacts of the business can be brought into our reporting and accounting process:

	Key indicators	
Greenhouse gas Emissions	Waste	Resource usage
CO₂ emissions *Other significant emissions*	*Hazardous and non-hazardous waste* *Conservation investment*	*Water* *Energy intensity* *Paper usage*
	Direct company impacts **Cash flow performance**	
CO$_2$ emissions Total cost of offsetting 100% of our global CO$_2$ emissions in 2007 is approximately £909,000. We incur up to a 2% premium for zero emission / renewable electricity compared to fossil fuels.	Total disposal cost for hazardous and non hazardous waste in the UK was £464,000 in 2007 (**2006: £585,000**) which includes UK landfill tax at circa £80 per tonne.	The operating cost of water usage was £938,000 in 2007 (2006: £670,000)

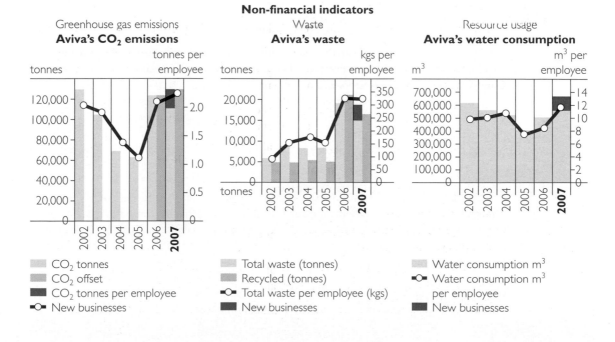

Non-financial indicators

Greenhouse gas emissions
Aviva's CO$_2$ emissions

Waste
Aviva's waste

Resource usage
Aviva's water consumption

Commentary on our performance, strategy and targets

Greenhouse gas emissions	Waste	Resource usage
In 2007, our total CO_2 emissions increased, mainly due to the inclusion of emissions data from our new business in Aviva USA, Aviva Global Services, Sri Lanka and Russia. From our existing businesses, emissions have shown an 11% decrease, by 13,555 tonnes reflecting significant focus on energy efficiency and resourcing renewable energy.	In 2007, the total volume of waste decreased and the total amount recycled increased. Plastic wrap from the Auto Windscreens operation is now being recycled – 70 tonnes per year with a value of £135 per tonne.	There is limited scope for the retro-fitting of latest technologies in water usage reduction in washrooms. However, where possible we take advantage of such technologies.

	Industry Benchmark Information	
Greenhouse gas emissions	Waste	Resource usage
• Carbon Disclosure Project CDP 5. 'Best in class' • Innovest ranking 'AAA'. • BREEAM minimum ranking 'Good' for new build and refurbishment.	200 kg of waste per employee per year. Recycling rate of 60–70% (BRE Office toolkit).	7.7 m³ per employee per year. (National Water Demand Management Centre).

31.5 IFAC Sustainability Framework[6]

The Framework indicates that the successful management of a sustainable organisation requires attention to four perspectives. These perspectives are: business strategy, internal management, financial investors and other stakeholders.

As far as accountants are concerned, in an organisation a business strategy perspective would typically be taken by finance directors, an internal management perspective by management accountants and financial controllers, and a financial investors'/other stakeholders' perspective by accountants preparing and auditing the published financial statements.

31.5.1 The Framework's four perspectives

Taking a perspective means being aware of needs and concerns in relation to sustainability. For example, the importance attached to the control of carbon emissions by other stakeholders influences the priority given to it by management. This might also have to be reconciled with the business strategy perspective which could be that funds are being diverted away from productive capital investment. Taking a perspective means being aware, communicating effectively and influencing behaviour within an organisation.

Figure 31.1 is an extract from the Framework summarising the four perspectives.

Figure 31.1 The four perspectives

Part A: Business strategy perspective – taking a strategic approach

The Framework emphasises the importance of adopting a strategic approach, so that sustainable development is a part of strategic discussions, objectives, goals and targets, and is integrated with governance and accountability arrangements and risk management. Only by taking a business strategy approach can organisations make sustainable development a part of doing business.

Part B: Internal management perspective – making it happen

In many organisations, (a) enhancing performance evaluation and measurement, (b) changing behaviours, and (c) introducing sustainability and environmental accounting as an extension of existing accounting/information systems to accommodate organisational plans for sustainable development, can be a challenge for organisations, and can take time to achieve. Therefore, this perspective also includes advice on how organisations can achieve relatively simple quick wins to improve energy efficiency and reduce waste, that can help them improve environmental performance while reducing their costs, all in a relatively short time frame.

Part C: Financial investors' perspective – telling the story to investors

The Framework offers advice on both incorporating environmental and other sustainability issues into financial statements in a way that supports an organisation's stewardship role and enhanced reporting to investors in financial reporting, including narrative reporting using management commentary.

Part D: Other stakeholders' perspective – wider transparency

The final perspective considers an evolving part of sustainable development that builds on the development of stakeholder relationships (covered in the business strategy perspective) to improve transparency and non-financial reporting against a broader set of expectations. Such reporting commonly takes the form of separate sustainability or corporate social responsibility (CSR) reports that may be based on *de facto* standards, such as those from the Global Reporting Initiative (GRI). This perspective also includes sustainability assurance, to help to improve credibility and trust.

The proposals in the triple bottom line, the Connected Reporting Framework and the Sustainability Framework are voluntary proposals for best practice.

31.5.2 Why is the qualitative information voluntary?

It is voluntary in recognition of the fact that market and political pressures exist; that each company balances the perceived costs (e.g. competitive disadvantage) and the perceived benefits of voluntary disclosure (e.g. improved investor appeal) in determining the extent of its voluntary disclosures.[7]

Companies have traditionally been ranked according to various criteria, e.g. their ability to maximise their shareholders' wealth or return on capital employed or EPS growth rates. However, there is a philosophical view that holds that a company:

> possesses a role in society because society finds it useful that it should do so . . . [It] cannot expect to find itself fully acceptable to society if it single-mindedly pursues its major objective without regard for the range of consequences of its actions.[8]

This means that a company is permitted to seek its private objectives subject to legal, social and ethical boundaries. This takes accounting beyond the traditional framework of reporting monetary transactions that are of interest primarily to the shareholders.

31.6 The accountant's role in a capitalist industrial society

In a capitalist, industrial society, production requires the raising and efficient use of capital largely through joint stock companies. These operate within a legal framework which grants them limited liability subject to certain obligations. The obligations include **capital maintenance provisions** to protect creditors (e.g. restriction on distributable profits) and **disclosure provisions** to protect shareholders (e.g. the publication of annual reports).

The state issues statutes to ensure there is effective control of the capital market; the degree of intervention depends on the party in power. Accountants issue standards to ensure there is reliable information to the owners to support an orderly capital market. Both the state and the accountancy profession have directed their major efforts towards servicing the needs of capital. This has influenced the nature of the legislation, e.g. removing obligations that are perceived to make a company uncompetitive, and the nature of the accounting standards, e.g. concentrating on earnings and monetary values.

However, production and distribution involve complex social relationships between private ownership of property and wage labour[9] and other stakeholders. This raises the question of the role of accountants. Should their primary concern be to serve the interests of the shareholders, or the interests of management, or to focus on equity issues and social welfare?[10]

Prior to the formation in the UK of the ASB, the profession identified with management and it was not unusual to allow information to be reported to suit management. If managers were unhappy with a standard, they were able to frustrate or delay its implementation, as with deferred tax. Often, reported results bore little resemblance to the commercial substance of the underlying transactions.

The ASB has concentrated on making reports reflect the substance of a transaction. It has developed a conceptual framework for financial reporting to underpin its reporting standards and criteria has been defined for the recognition of assets, liabilities, income and expense.

The ASB did not produce mandatory requirements for narrative or qualitative disclosures – the operating and financial review (OFR) was voluntary (now the business review in the directors' report). However, the fact that it proposed the publication of an OFR was an important in itself because it recognised that there was a need for narrative disclosure, even where this was not capable of audit verification.

31.7 The accountant's changing role

Accountants now make positive contributions to sustainability management by their responsible roles in systems and external reporting. They are responsible for the financial systems which provide the raw data for strategic planning, the management of risk, the measurement and reporting of performance and the allocation. For example, they identify environmental costs to measure and report on the efficiency of energy costs and social costs such as the cost of staff turnover and absenteeism.

Sustainability information reported to investors and other stakeholders needs to be based on sound systems of accounting, internal control and be externally assured. Professional accountants provide the expertise for the design and operation of systems and external auditors are increasingly providing an assurance capability.

Accountants have a central role in finance from which they are able to encourage a sustainability culture within an organisation by raising sustainability as a consideration when making decisions. This can be at an operating level as when they identify environmental or social costs or at a strategic level when capital investment decisions are being made.

31.8 Sustainability – environmental reporting

There has been a growing concern since the early 1990s that insufficient attention has been given to the impact of current commercial activities on future generations. This has led to the need for sustainable development which meets the needs of the present without compromising the ability of future generations to meet their own needs.

Why have companies become sensitive to the environmental concerns of stakeholders other than their shareholders? This has been a reaction to pressure from a variety of stakeholders ranging from the government to local communities and from environmental groups to individual consumers and individual investors.

We will now look at the development of environmental reporting.

31.9 Environmental information in the annual accounts

Much of the environmental information falls outside the expertise of the accountant, so why was it included in the annual report? The annual report had already become the accepted vehicle for providing shareholders with information on matters of social interest such as charitable donations and this extended to present qualitative information such as a statement of company policy.

However, in addition to recognising the concerns of other stakeholder, companies also began to realise that there could be adverse financial implications for their capacity to raise funds.

Potential individual investors

The government in *This Common Inheritance*[11] indicated that shareholders could seek information about environmental practices from companies that they invest in and make their views known.

Potential corporate investors

Acquisitive companies needed to be aware of contingent liabilities,[12] which can be enormous. In the USA the potential cost of clearing up past industrially hazardous sites has been estimated at $675 billion. Even in relation to individual companies the scale of the contingency can be large, as in the Love Canal case. In this case a housing project was built at Love Canal in upper New York State on a site that until the 1950s had been used by the Hooker Chemicals Corporation for dumping a chemical waste containing dioxin. Occidental, which had acquired Hooker Chemicals, was judged liable for the costs of clean-up of more than $260 million.[13] Existing shareholders and the share price would also be affected by these increased costs.

There is recognition that there is a wider interest than short-term profits.

31.10 Background to companies' reporting practices

Some companies have independently instituted comprehensive environmental management systems but many have not. There has been a tendency initially for companies to target the area that they considered to be the most sensitive and to treat it rather as a PR exercise or damage limitation. There was a concern that resources devoted to achieving environmental benefits would merely increase costs and companies made a point of referring to cost benefits to justify their outlay as in the following extract from the Scottish Power 1994 Annual Report:

> The company is committed to meeting or bettering increasingly stringent environmental controls for electricity generation and is developing new technologies and plant which can achieve significant benefits at realistic cost. At Longannet Power Station, more than £24 million is being invested in low Nox burners, which produce fewer nitrous oxides, and in renewing equipment to reduce dust from flue gases . . . This process is expected to be environmentally superior and lower in costs than alternative technologies.

This was quite understandable as it had been estimated that the enforcement of stringent environmental controls to reduce pollution could have substantial cost implications estimated at £15 billion for Britain in 1991.[14]

Companies were reactive and concentrated on satisfying statutory obligations or explaining their treatment of what they perceived to be the major environmental concern affecting their company. For example, in the case of Pearson, a major publishing company, a major concern was the use for printing of renewable resources and its 1993 Annual Report it included the following:

> One aspect of our company's environmental responsibilities is to keep purchasing policies under review. Pearson's most significant purchase is paper. Our publishing companies between them buy some 180,000 tonnes of paper a year . . . Pearson makes certain that it buys paper only from responsibly managed forests and avoids paper bleached with chlorinated organic compounds where possible . . .

By 2007 Pearson published a CSR report, *Our Business and Society*, which included the following extract on the environment:

> The environmental considerations relating to the purchase of paper continue to be a priority for us . . . Pearson has further developed its responsible paper sourcing practice. As part of an action plan on responsible paper sourcing agreed with the WWF UK Forest & Trade Network, we established a database on the environmental characteristics of the paper we purchase. We have also met a number of our key suppliers and manufacturers of paper and some NGOs to discuss and review environmental issues including certification and increasing the recycled content in the paper we use in our books.

Although this was an *ad hoc* approach to environmental reporting, it did not mean that significant benefits were not achieved. The following extract from the 2001 Annual Report of the Body Shop indicates the level of benefit:

At the Body Shop, we have made a significant commitment to reducing our CO_2 impact by switching electricity supply at both our Littlehampton sites and all UK company-owned shops to a renewable source. This initiative, together with our 15% investment in Bryn Titli wind farm, means that we offset an estimated 48% of electricity, gas and road freight used for all our UK operations including company-owned shops in the last financial year.

In some jurisdictions there have been mandatory requirements. In the USA, e.g. the Securities and Exchange Commission requires companies to disclose:

(a) the material effects of complying or failing to comply with environmental requirements on the capital expenditures, earnings and competitive position of the registrant and its subsidiaries;

(b) pending environmental legal proceedings or proceedings known to be contemplated, which meet any of three qualifying conditions: (1) materiality, (2) 10% of current assets, or (3) monetary sanctions; and

(c) environmental contingencies that may reasonably have material impact on net sales, revenue, or income from continuing operations.

A typical disclosure of amounts appears in the following extract from the Bayer Schering Pharma AG 2006 Annual Report:

We have spent substantial amounts on environmental protection and safety measures up to now, and anticipate having to spend similar sums in 2007 and subsequent years. In 2006, our operating and maintenance costs in the field of environmental protection and safety totaled €59m (2005: €65m). Our capital expenditure on environmental protection projects and other ecologically beneficial projects totaled €4m (2005: €5m).

31.11 European Commission's recommendations for disclosures in annual accounts

In May 2001 the European Commission issued a *Recommendation on the Recognition, Measurement and Disclosure of Environmental Issues in the Annual Accounts and Annual Reports of Companies.*[15]

The Commission's view was that there were two problems. The first was that there was a lack of explicit rules, which meant that any one or all of the different stakeholder groups, e.g. investors, regulatory authorities, financial analysts and the public in general, could feel that the disclosures were insufficient or unreliable; the second was that there was a low level of voluntary disclosure, even in sectors where there was significant impact on the environment.

31.11.1 Lack of explicit rules

The lack of harmonised guidelines has meant that investors have been unable to compare companies or to adequately assess environmental risks affecting the financial position of the company. Whilst recognising that there are existing financial reporting standards on the disclosure of provisions and contingent liabilities and that companies in environmentally sensitive sectors are producing stand-alone environmental reports, the Commission was of the opinion that there is a justified need to facilitate further harmonisation on what to disclose in the annual accounts.

As mentioned above, the cost of collecting and reporting is frequently perceived to be a deterrent and the Recommendation intends to avoid unjustified burdensome obligations. It also proposes that Recommendations should be within existing European directives, e.g. the Fourth and Seventh Directives.

31.11.2 Stakeholder groups' information needs

All groups require relevant disclosures that are consistent and comparable – particularly disclosure in the notes to the accounts relating to environmental expenditures either charged to the profit and loss account or capitalised including fines and penalties for non-compliance and compensation payments.

31.11.3 Key points relating to recognition, measurement and disclosure

The approach to recognition and measurement is a restatement of current financial reporting requirements with some additional illustrations and explanations. The disclosures are fuller than currently met within annual accounts.

Recognition and measurement

For the recognition of environmental liabilities the criteria are the same as for IAS 37 *Provisions, Contingent Liabilities and Contingent Assets* e.g. requirement for probable outflow of resources, reliable estimate of costs and recognition of liability at the date operations commence if relating to site restoration.

For the capitalisation of environmental expenditure the criteria to recognise as an asset apply, e.g. it produces future economic benefits. There are also detailed proposals relating to environmental expenditure which improves the future benefits from another asset and to asset impairment.

Disclosures

Disclosure is recommended if the issues are material to either the financial performance or financial position. Detailed proposals in relation to environmental protection are for the disclosure of:

- the policies that have been adopted and reference to any certification such as EMAS (see section 31.12.2 below);
- the improvements made in key areas with physical data if possible, e.g. on emissions;
- progress implementing mandatory requirements;
- environmental performance measures, e.g. trends for percentage of recycled packaging;
- reference to any separate environmental report produced.

There are, in addition, detailed cross-references to the requirements of the Fourth and Seventh Directives, e.g. description of valuation methods applied and additional disclosures, e.g. if there are long-term dismantling costs, the accounting policy and, if the company gradually builds up a provision, the amount of the full provision required.

31.12 Evolution of stand-alone environmental reports

There is a steady growth in the rate at which environmental reports are being produced. The rate is faster where there are clear risks such as paper, chemicals, oil and gas, and pharmaceuticals.

In some jurisdictions such as Denmark, the Netherlands, Norway and Sweden, there is legislation requiring environmental statements from environmentally sensitive industries either in their financial statements or in a stand-alone report; in other countries, voluntary disclosures are proposed.

The following is an extract relating to a Danish experience where most companies now produce separate CSR reports (www.sustainabilityreporting.eu/denmark/index.htm):

> Most Danish companies now publish separate CSR reports, independent of their statutory annual reporting. In recent years, more companies have started integrating their financial and non-financial data into the same report, for instance by adding a section on non-financial data at the end of the report. The companies preparing the best reports, however, are those which grasp the connection between the non-financial data and their business. As a result, these companies have fully integrated non-financial data with financial data in the report. In doing this, the companies clearly demonstrate their full understanding of the value of reporting on non-financial data. *They demonstrate that the data are being used as a serious management and communication tool and that they are able to link CSR to business strategy*. However, as statutory reports do not necessarily reach all stakeholders. These companies also make use of a number of other communication channels to report on their CSR work. When we consider the future focus on climate change, the companies' desire to adapt their reporting to their future stakeholders, the Danish Government's pressure on Danish companies to integrate CSR in their business strategy, and the need for cost cuts owing to the current crisis, we are convinced that the trend will be that more Danish companies begin to employ completely integrated reporting.

When considering inclusion of CSR reporting in the annual report, one of the problems has been the volume of data. Companies are overcoming this by issuing summary CSR reports in hard copy and uploading the full CSR report onto their websites. The following is an extract relating to experience in the Netherlands (www.sustainabilityreporting.eu/netherlands/index.htm):

> In the Netherlands, various companies are aiming for further integration of the CSR information into their annual reports. Companies are increasingly using the Internet in order to reduce the size of their CSR reports. They publish hard copy summary reports, with the full versions available on the Internet.

Attention is also being given to the increasing use of non-financial information:

> In the Netherlands, from 2006, health insurance became an entirely private activity. As a result, health insurance companies have certain responsibilities towards their clients. To monitor this process, these companies have to publish mandatory CSR reports to the health insurance authority. CSR reporting by health insurance companies to their stakeholders has consequently increased. Government departments (ministry, province, municipality) also have to provide information on their performance in relation to their policy plans.
>
> This includes both financial and non-financial performance indicators and will also lead to an increase in reporting. Amsterdam has already published its first CSR report.

CSR is also being progressively introduced into academic programmes. For example, the Erasmus University Rotterdam has started a one-year postgraduate course on CSR Management and CSR Auditing, which includes one module on CSR Reporting.

In Chapter 30 we discussed the development of corporate governance and the concentration was on the accountability of the board to the shareholders for its strategic control of the assets and its responsibility to act in the best interest of the shareholders. The effectiveness of its control would be assessed in financial terms by reference to ratios such as ROCE, ROI, growth rate of EPS, earnings and dividend yield.

In the early stages of environmental, social and now sustainability reporting the emphasis was on reporting to other stakeholders. This was extended by the concept of the triple bottom line and it is interesting to see that sustainability and corporate governance are potentially merging as companies see that the two do not have separate audiences. Shareholders and stakeholders are both beginning to look at both aspects. The following is an extract relating to Swedish experience (www.sustainabilityreporting.eu/sweden/index.htm):

> During the last year newspapers, television and other media have reported more than ever before on climate change and supply chain related issues. The media interest in corporate responsibility and the need for change and transparency has an even longer tradition. The manner in which these trends will have an impact on the further development of sustainability reporting is, of course, an interesting question. We are at a turning point in reporting on sustainability. The Accounting Modernisation Directive implemented in the Swedish Annual Accounts Act may help companies to focus their reporting on non-financial risks. Some companies are already integrating their efforts on sustainability and corporate social responsibility with their work on corporate governance. Interesting to note is the fact that some companies' governance reports include information on sustainability. There is a call for transparent non-financial reporting from the financial community. Last but not least, the Swedish Government's requirements on reporting sustainability will pave the way for GRI reporting also in the public sector.

There has been a growing pressure for CSR information to be subject to assurance reports to give stakeholders the same confidence as they have obtained from the audit reports on financial statements. The following is an extract relating to a UK experience (www.sustainabilityreporting.eu/uk/index.htm):

> The challenges facing companies are:
>
> ● starting assurance engagements using the updated, 2008 version of the AA1000AS;
> ● improving the standards of assurance statements (as in previous years), including: more detailed commentary on methodology and recommendations in the statement; and focusing more on the materiality, completeness and responsiveness principles rather than just simply checking accuracy of information;
> ● providing an organisational response to the assurance engagement in the report, including how any recommendations will be put into place; and
> ● dealing with the mandatory reporting on carbon emissions according to the requirements of the Climate Change Bill.

There is progress being made at varying rates around the world. One of the stimuli has been the environmental, social and sustainability award schemes. One of the earliest of the award schemes was that of the ACCA.

31.12.1 The ACCA award schemes

In 2000 the ACCA commemorated ten years of progress in environmental reporting. After these ten years the ACCA established in 2002 a new structure for the UK awards to reflect the ever-increasing public awareness of the environmental, social and economic impacts of business. The ACCA Award scheme was restructured in 2001 under the title 'The ACCA

Awards for Sustainability Reporting'. There are three different award categories: the ACCA UK Environmental Reporting Awards, the ACCA Social Reporting Awards and a new category, the ACCA Sustainability Reporting Awards. Details of Award winners can be found on the ACCA website.

These schemes have given environmental reporting a high profile and contributed greatly to the present quality of reports. The schemes now take place in a number of countries and regions. These include Hong Kong, Malaysia, Singapore, South Africa, Sri Lanka, Europe and North America.

The following is an extract relating to the Singapore awards (www.accaglobal.com/singapore/publicinterest/sustainability/sustainability).

Singapore Awards for Sustainability Reporting

ACCA is pleased to announce the launch of the ACCA Singapore Awards for Sustainability Reporting 2008. Formerly known as the Singapore Environmental and Social Reporting Awards (SESRA), the awards which are now into its seventh year are endorsed by the National Environment Agency and supported by the Singapore Environment Council and TüV SüD PSB. Joining the list of supporting organisations this year is Singapore Compact for CSR.

ACCA Singapore invites organisations of all sizes and sectors to submit their application into the awards. The closing date for entries is 31 March 2009. The Awards ceremony will be held in June 2009.

The aim of the awards is to promote transparency and give recognition to those organisations which report and disclose environmental, social and full sustainability information. The awards also provide a platform to raise awareness of corporate transparency issues.

ACCA has promoted sustainability reporting for more than a decade since the introduction of the environmental reporting awards in 1991 in the United Kingdom. ACCA is involved in reporting awards around the world in Europe, Africa, North America and the Asia Pacific region.

Any organisation of any size or industry sector; be it private or public with operations in Singapore can enter into the awards.

The entries are reviewed by a judging panel comprising of experts within the field of environmental and sustainability reporting. At the core of the judging criteria are completeness, credibility and communication.

This year ACCA will be giving out awards in the following categories; Environmental Reporting, Social Reporting and the newly added category of Sustainability reporting. In addition to the main awards and commendations, ACCA Singapore will also be introducing new awards for 'First Time Reporter'. The introduction of the new awards is to encourage greater participation and to acknowledge a wider range of efforts that organisations have taken towards enhancing sustainability and transparency.

The criteria that each scheme sets can vary and reflect local interests. For example, the Hong Kong awards for 2008 were in the following categories:

Best Sustainability Report	CLP Holdings Limited
Runner Up – Best Sustainability Report	Swire Pacific Limited
Commendation For Excellent Communication Using The Internet	MTR Corporation
Commendation For Demonstration Of Integrity In Reporting	Gammon Construction Limited
Commendation For Addressing Sectoral Issues	The China Navigation Company Limited

Encouragement has been actively given to SME reporting. For example, in 2000, at the Europe-wide level, the European Environmental Reporting Awards (EERA), in which entries are selected from the winners of national schemes organised by EU member states, selected four winners:

- Overall winner: Shell International (UK),
- Best first-time reporter: Acquedotto Pugliese (Italy),
- Best SME reporter: Obermurtaler Brauereigenossenschaft (Austria),
- Best sustainability report: Novo Nordisk (Denmark).

The judges commented on strengths, and in respect of the best SME reporter listed:

- its comprehensive reporting on corporate performance including five-year trend data for various indicators and quantified targets;
- an analysis of the environmental impact arising from the product development activity;
- detailed description of supplier audits;
- disclosure of internal audit procedures and results; and
- evidence of environmental interest including obtaining EMAS registration (the first site to do this in Austria).

SMEs continue to be encouraged to develop CSR reporting.

In the UK the ACCA awards again looked carefully at assurance and reported (www.accaglobal.com/uk/publicinterest/sustainability/):

- All the shortlisted companies for the 2008 ACCA UK Sustainability Reporting Awards have some form of external assurance of their reports, including the small and medium-sized enterprises (SMEs), but the scope and approach varies widely between reports.
- Many assurance statements continue to lack concrete recommendations from the assurance provider, meaning that they do not provide the reader with a clear account of the outcomes of the engagement. Assurance was picked up by the 2008 judges as being a general weakness, both in terms of the assurance statement itself and the organisational response to the assurance engagement's outcomes.
- As in previous years, non-accounting assurance providers tend to use the AccountAbility AA1000 Assurance Standard (sometimes in combination with the ISAE300) and Big 4 accounting firms are encouraged to use the ISAE3000.
- UK organisations (as well as those elsewhere in Europe) will have to start using the new version of AA1000AS, launched in October 2008, from 2009 onwards.
- There continues to be a wider scope of assurance processes than the traditional assurance statement approach. For example, the inclusion of an external stakeholder assurance panel (as demonstrated by Shell's report) and different 'niche' assurance providers for different areas of the business/reporting (as demonstrated by De Beers' sustainability report).

31.13 International charters and guidelines

There have been a number of international and national summits, charters and recommendations issued. In some jurisdictions such as Denmark, the Netherlands, Norway and

Sweden, there is now legislation requiring environmental statements from environmentally sensitive industries either in their financial statements or in a stand-alone report; in other countries, voluntary disclosures are proposed. Below are brief descriptions of just some of the voluntary disclosures proposed by the United Nations, Europe and the USA, and of some self-regulation schemes in which companies can elect to participate.

31.13.1 United Nations

At the United Nations we can see that the United Nations Environment Programme (UNEP)[16] has made major impacts, e.g. it was the driving force behind the 1987 Montreal Protocol on Substances that Deplete the Ozone Layer whereby industrialised countries ceased production and consumption of a significant proportion of all ozone-depleting substances in 1996. It is estimated that 1.5 million cases of melanoma skin cancer due to the sun's UV-B radiation will be averted by the year 2060 as a result of the Protocol. It has had similar success as the leading force for the sound global management of hazardous chemicals and the protection of the world's biological diversity by forging the Convention on Biological Diversity. It is innovative in its approach, e.g. entering into a partnership agreement with the International Olympic Committee (IOC) in 1995 as a result of which the environment now figures as the third pillar of Olympism, along with sport and culture, in the IOC's Charter. UNEP has initiated the development of environmental guidelines for sports federations and countries bidding for the Olympic Games.

UNEP is actively concerned with climate change. As a science-based organisation it is able to make available better and more relevant scientific information on climate change impacts to developing country decision-makers. UNEP states that 'it will help improve capacity to use this information for policy purposes, as well as providing scientific, legal and institutional support to developing country negotiators and their institutions so that they can meaningfully contribute to a strengthened international regime on climate change'.

31.13.2 Europe

In Europe the Eco-Management and Audit Scheme (EMAS)[17] was adopted by the European Council on 29 June 1993, allowing voluntary participation in an environmental management scheme. Its aim is to promote continuous environmental performance improvements of activities by committing organisations to evaluating and improving their own environmental performance.

The main elements of the current EMAS regulations include:

● making environmental statements more transparent;

● the involvement of employees in the implementation of EMAS; and

● a more thorough consideration of indirect effects including capital investments, administrative and planning decisions and procurement procedures.

Companies that participate in the scheme are required to adopt an environmental policy containing the following key commitments:

● compliance with all relevant environmental legislation;

● prevention of pollution; and

● achieving continuous improvements in environmental performance.

The procedure is for an initial environmental review to be undertaken and an environmental programme and environmental management system established for the organisation.

Verification is seen as an important element and environmental audits, covering all activities at the organisation concerned, must be conducted within an audit cycle of no longer than three years. On completion of the initial environmental review and subsequent audits or audit cycles a public environmental statement is produced.

An organisation's environmental statement will include the following key elements:

- a clear description of the organisation, and its activities, products and services;
- the organisation's environmental policy and a brief description of the environmental management system;
- a description of all the significant direct and indirect environmental aspects of the organisation and an explanation of the nature of the impacts as related to these aspects;
- a description of the environmental objectives and targets in relation to the significant environmental aspects and impacts;
- a summary of the organisation's year-by-year environmental performance data which may include pollution emissions, waste generation, consumption of raw materials, energy use, water management and noise;
- other factors regarding environmental performance including performance against legal provisions; and
- the name and accreditation number of the environmental verifier, the date of validation and deadline for submission of the next statement.

The following extract from the Schering 2000 Annual Report indicates the persuasive influence of schemes such as EMAS:

We aim at achieving the ISO 14001 certification or the Eco Management and Audit Scheme (EMAS) validation for all production sites. We have begun to integrate the existing management systems for quality, safety and environmental protection, and to organise throughout the Group. This Integrated Management System (IMS) is based on International Standard ISO 9000 (for quality) as well as ISO 14001 and EMAS (for environmental protection).

31.13.3 The USA

In the USA the Environmental Accounting Project began in 1992 to encourage companies to adopt environmental accounting techniques which would make environmental costs more apparent to managers and, therefore, make them more controllable. It was thought that this could result in three positive outcomes namely, the significant reduction of environmental costs, the gaining of competitive advantage and the improvement of environmental performance with the initial concern being to reduce pollution.

31.14 Self-regulation schemes

There are a number of examples of self-regulatory codes of conduct from institutions, e.g. the International Chamber of Commerce (ICC),[18] the International Organization for Standardization (ISO), and bodies representing particular industries, e.g. the European Chemical Industry Council (CEFIC).[19] We will describe briefly the ICC Charter and ISO standards.

31.14.1 The International Chamber of Commerce (ICC)

The ICC launched **the Business Charter for Sustainable Development** in 1991 to help business around the world improve its environmental performance relating to health, safety and product stewardship. The charter set out sixteen principles which include:

- *Policy statements* – such as giving environmental management high corporate priority; aiming to integrate environmental policies and practices as an essential element of management; continuing to improve corporate policies performance; advising customers, distributors and the public in the safe use, transportation, storage and disposal of products provided; promoting the adoption of these principles by contractors acting on behalf of the enterprise; developing products that have no undue environmental impact and are efficient in their consumption of energy and natural resources, and that can be recycled, reused, or disposed of safely; fostering openness and dialogue with employees and the public, anticipating and responding to their concerns about the potential hazards and impacts of operations, products, wastes or services; and measuring environmental performance.

- *Financially quantifiable practices* – such as employee education; assessment of environmental impacts before starting a new activity or decommissioning; conduct or support of research on the environmental impacts of raw materials, products, processes, emissions and wastes associated with the enterprise and on the means of minimising such adverse impacts; modification of the manufacture, marketing or use of products or services to prevent serious or irreversible environmental degradation.

The following extract from the Nestlé 2000 Environment Progress Report is a good example of a company that has applied the ICC approach and is proactive in seeking improvements:

Message from CEO

I am pleased about the clear progress in a number of key areas, including a significant decline in the amounts of water and energy used to bring each kilo of Nestlé product into your home, and a similar reduction in factors which potentially affect global warming. However, we are never completely satisfied with our current performance, and are committed to further environmental improvements.

We try to remain sensitive to the environmental concerns of our consumers and the public as a whole. . . . we have pledged our allegiance to *The Business Charter for Sustainable Development* of the International Chamber of Commerce, and we are committed to being a leader in environmental performance.

In 2007 Nestlé published its *Creating Shared Value Report* (see http://www.nestle.com/csv). This profiles Nestlé's global efforts to increase the delivery of high-quality, nutritious food products that add to consumers' health and well-being. The report also profiles Nestlé's ongoing commitment to develop nutritious, popularly positioned products that are affordable and accessible to consumers at the base of the global economic pyramid.

The following is an extract from the Nestlé CSV Report:

Nestlé is committed to reporting its performance openly. In 2008, we published our first global report on Creating Shared Value. It is a first step towards providing evidence that the successful creation of long-term shareholder value is dependent also on the creation of value for society.

We first explored the concept of Creating Shared Value in our 2005 report, 'The Nestlé concept of corporate social responsibility', which focused on our Latin American operations . . . Since then, in conjunction with our business areas and advisers including SustainAbility and AccountAbility, we have identified and assessed critical issues, developed global performance indicators and engaged stakeholders in debate.

In order to provide assurance to stakeholders over Nestlé Creating Shared Value reporting, an external auditor Bureau Veritas has been engaged. For more information, read the full Bureau Veritas Assurance Statement.

Nestlé is also among the first food companies to join the Global Reporting Initiative multi-stakeholder programme to develop global reporting standards and indicators on sustainability in the food industry.

31.14.2 The International Organization for Standardization (ISO)

The ISO is a non-governmental organisation established in 1947, and comprises a world-wide federation of national standards with the aim of establishing international standards to reduce barriers to international trade. Its standards, including environmental standards, are voluntary and companies may elect to join in order to obtain ISO certification.

One group of standards, the ISO 14000 series, is intended to encourage organisations to systematically assess the environmental impacts of their activities through a common approach to environmental management systems. Within the group, the ISO 14001 standard states the requirements for establishing an EMS and companies must satisfy its requirements in order to qualify for ISO certification.

What benefits arise from implementation of ISO 14001?

Those who support the ISO approach consider that there are a number of positive advantages, such as:

- **Top-level management become involved** – they are required to define an overall policy and, in addition, they recognise significant financial considerations from certification, e.g. customers might in the future prefer to deal with ISO compliant companies, insurance premiums might be lower and there is the potential to reduce costs by greater production efficiency.

- **Environmental management** – ISO 14001 establishes a framework for a systematic approach to environmental management which can identify inefficiencies that were not apparent beforehand resulting in operational cost savings and reduced environmental liabilities. We have seen above, for example, that Nestlé reduced its energy consumption by 20%.

- **A framework for continual improvements is established** – there is a requirement for continual improvement of the management system.

What criticisms are there of a compliance approach?

Compliance approaches which set out criteria such as a commitment to minimise environmental impact can allow companies to set low objectives for improvement and report these as achievements with little confidence that there has been significant environmental benefit.

31.15 Economic consequences of environmental reporting

There can be internal and external favourable economic consequences for companies. They can achieve cost reductions and become more attractive to potential investors.

31.15.1 Cost reductions

It has been reported that the discipline of measuring these risks can yield valuable management information with DuPont, for example, reporting that since it began measuring and reporting on the environmental impact of its activities, its annual environmental costs dropped from a high of US$1 billion in 1993 to $560 million in 1999.

31.15.2 Investors

Investors are gradually beginning to require information on a company's policy and programmes for environmental compliance and performance in order to assess the risk to earnings and statement of financial position. One would expect that the more transparent these are the less volatile the share prices will be which could be beneficial for both the investor and the company. This will be a fruitful field for research as environmental reporting evolves with more consistent, comparable, relevant and reliable numbers and narrative disclosures.

This has also given rise to Socially Responsible Investing (SRI) which considers both the investor's financial needs and the investee company's impact on society to an extent that in 1999 over US$2,000 billion in assets were invested in 'ethical' investment funds. In the UK there is pressure from bodies such as the Association of British Insurers for institutional investors to take SRI principles into account. Investors are also able to refer to indices such as the Dow Jones Sustainability Indices and the FTSE4Good Index.

Dow Jones Sustainability Indices

The Dow Jones Sustainability Indices were begun in 1999 and were the first global indices tracking the financial performance of the leading sustainability-driven companies worldwide.

FTSE4Good Index Series

The FTSE4Good Index Series provides potential investors with a measure of the performance of companies that meet globally recognised corporate responsibility standards. FTSE4Good is helpful as a basis for socially responsible investment and as a benchmark for tracking the performance of socially responsible investment portfolios.

However, research carried out by Trucost and commissioned by the Environment Agency (www.environment-agency.gov.uk/business) into quantitative disclosures found that direct links between management of environmental risks and shareholder value are almost non-existent, with only 11% of FTSE 350 making a link between the environment and some aspect of their financial performance and only 5% explicitly linking it to shareholder value.

31.16 Summary on environmental reporting

Environmental reporting is in a state of evolution ranging from *ad hoc* comments in the annual report to a more systematic approach in the annual report to stand-alone environmental reports.

Environmental investment is no longer seen as an additional cost but as an essential part of being a good corporate citizen and environmental reports are seen as necessary in communicating with stakeholders to address their environmental concerns.

Companies are realising that it is their corporate responsibility to achieve sustainable development whereby they meet the needs of the present without compromising the ability of future generations to meet their own needs. Economic growth is important for shareholders and other stakeholders alike in that it provides the conditions in which protection of the environment can best be achieved, and environmental protection, in balance with other human goals, is necessary to achieve growth that is sustainable.

However, there is still a long way to go and the EU's Sixth Action Programme 'Environment 2010: Our Future, Our Choice'[20] recognises that effective steps have not been taken by all member states to implement EC environmental directives and there is weak ownership of environmental objectives by stakeholders. The programme focuses on four major areas for action – climate change, health and the environment, nature and biodiversity, and natural resource management – and emphasises how important it is that all stakeholders should be involved to achieve more environmentally friendly forms of production and consumption as well as integration into all aspects of our life such as transport, energy and agriculture.

As with the other environmental reporting initiatives discussed above and the corporate governance approach we have seen with the Hampel Report and the OFR, the programme concentrates on setting general objectives rather than quantified targets apart from the targets relating to climate change where there is the EU's 8% emission reduction target for 2008–12 under the Kyoto Protocol. This is a sensible way to progress with an opportunity for best practice to evolve.

However, significant improvements are still required, with research indicating that although the majority of FTSE All Share companies discuss their interaction with the environment in their annual report and accounts, the vast majority lack depth, rigour or quantification.

31.17 Environmental auditing: international initiatives

The need for environmental auditors has grown side by side with the growth of environmental reporting. This is prompted by the need for investors to be confident that the information is reliable and relevant. There have been various initiatives around the world and we will briefly refer to examples from Canada, the USA and Europe.

Canada

The Canadian Environmental Auditing Association (CEAA) was founded in 1991 to encourage the development of environmental auditing and the improvement of environmental management through environmental auditor certification and the application of environmental auditing ethics, principles and standards. It is a multidisciplinary organisation whose international membership base now includes environmental managers, ISO 14001 registration auditors, EMS consultants, corporate environmental auditors, engineers, chemists, government employees, accountants and lawyers. The CEAA is now accredited by the Standards Council of Canada as a certifying body for EMS Auditors.[21]

USA

The Registrar Accreditation Board (RAB)[22] was established in 1989 by the American Society for Quality to provide accreditation services for ISO 9000 Quality Management Systems (QMS) registrars.

In 1991, the American National Standards Institute (ANSI) and RAB joined forces to establish the American National Accreditation Program for Registrars of Quality Systems.

In 1996, with the release of new ISO 14000 Environmental Management Systems (EMS) standards, the ANSI-RAB National Accreditation Program (NAP) was formed covering the accreditation of QMS and EMS registrars as well as accreditation of course providers offering QMS and EMS auditor training courses. Certification programmes for both EMS and QMS auditors are now operated solely by RAB.

RAB exists to serve the conformity assessment needs of business and industry, registrars, course providers and individual auditors.

Europe

Since 1999 the European Federation of Accountants (FEE) Sustainability Working Party (formerly Environmental) has been active in the project Providing Assurance on Environmental Reports[23] and is actively participating with other organisations and collaborating on projects such as GRI Sustainability Guidelines which are discussed further in section 31.23 below.

31.18 The activities involved in an environmental audit

There are many activities commonly seen in practice. These can be grouped into those assessing the *current position* and those evaluating decisions affecting the *future*.

31.18.1 Assessing the current position

The assessment embraces physical, systems and staff appraisal.

- Physical appraisal is carried out by means of:
  - **site inspections**;
  - **scientific testing** to sample and test substances including air samples;
  - **off-site testing and inspections** to examine the organisation's impact on its immediate surroundings; after all, the company's responsibility does not stop at the boundary fence.
- Systems appraisal is carried out by means of:
  - **systems inspections** to review the stated systems of management and control in respect of environmental issues;
  - **operational reviews** to review actual practices when compared to the stated systems;
  - **compliance audits for certification schemes.**
- Staff appraisal is carried out by means of:
  - **awareness tests for staff** to test, by questionnaire, the basic knowledge of all levels of staff of the systems and practices currently used by the organisation. This will highlight any areas of weakness.

31.18.2 Assessing the future

The assessment embraces planning and design processes and preparedness for emergencies.

- Planning and design appraisal is carried out by means of:
  - **review of planning procedures** to ensure that environmental factors are considered in the planning processes adopted by the organisation;
  - **design reviews** to examine the basic design processes of the organisation (if applicable) to ensure that environmental issues are addressed at the design stage so the organisation can avoid problems rather than have to solve them when they happen.
- Preparedness for emergencies is appraised by means of:
  - **review of emergency procedures** to assess the organisation's preparedness for specific, predictable emergencies;
  - **review of crisis plans** to review the organisation's general approach to crisis management with the audit covering such topics as the formation of **crisis management teams** and resource availability.

31.18.3 The environmental audit report

We can see from the above that an environmental audit may be wide-ranging in its scope and time-consuming, particularly when auditing a major organisation. A typical report could include:

- Current practice
  - a comprehensive review and comment on current operational practices.
- List of action required
  - areas of **immediate concern** which the organisation needs to address as a matter of urgency;
  - areas for improvement over a set period of time.
- Qualitative assessment
  - a **statement of risk** as seen by the audit team based on an overview of the whole situation with a qualitative assessment of the level of environmental risk being faced by the organisation.
- An action plan
  - a **schedule of improvement** may also be produced which gives a timetable and series of stages for the organisation to follow in improving its environmental performance.
- Encouraging good practice
  - a positive statement of 'good practice' may be included. This has a dual value in that it is a motivational tool for management and an educational tool to foster staff awareness of what constitutes 'good practice'.

31.18.4 What is the status of an environmental audit report?

Legal position

There is no legal obligation to carry out an environmental audit or to inform outside parties of any critical findings when such an audit is carried out. The reports are usually regarded as 'confidential' even when carried out by external auditors who provide the service as an 'optional extra' which is offered to the organisation for an additional fee.

Public interest

There is a strong case for requiring both environmental audits and the publication of the resultant reports. Requiring reports to be put into the public domain would encourage transparency in the process and avoid accusations of secrecy. However, this 'public interest' argument has been heard before in accounting and has met with some resistance in the guise of commercial sensitivity.

Mandatory position

The lack of legal obligation could be regarded as a crucial weakness of the environmental audit process as there could be a major danger to the environment which remains 'secret' until after the crisis when it is then too late. The responsible organisation will of course inform all appropriate parties of any revealed risk but it would be foolhardy to assume that all organisations are responsible. The ASB has become involved with potential liability for the company in its consideration of provisions. Whilst this is only viewing it from the viewpoint of the shareholder, it may well be the only pragmatic way forward at present.

31.18.5 Experience in the USA

The increasing importance of environmental accounting can be seen in the USA in the work of the United States Environmental Protection Agency (EPA) and its Environmental Accounting Project (EAP) which has been operating since 1992.

In this large project the EPA attempts to identify the currently 'hidden' societal costs faced by organisations. These costs are those which an organisation incurs in its interaction with the environment and which in theory are totally avoidable. By identifying these costs, the organisation is motivated to address them and by implication make every attempt to reduce them, thus improving the environment.

The EPA has a very impressive website, which can be found at the following address: www.epa.gov/epahome/aboutepa/htm. Here the basic ideas and concepts governing the EPA's study of environmental accounting are set out.

The work of the EPA has also been of a more practical nature in helping organisations address environmental issues from an environmental viewpoint. A brief review of three such cases may help explain the proactive approach to environmental accounting, which goes beyond traditional reporting.

A. The Chrysler Corporation (a major vehicle manufacturer) was faced with a problem with the use of mercury switches in its electrical systems on vehicles. Mercury is dangerous to use and is very dangerous as a waste product when the vehicle is scrapped. The company had always resisted the use of non-mercury switches on pure cost terms.

However, during the EPA project, by looking at the environmental cost it was seen that non-mercury switches actually made a saving of $0.11 per unit. The company on an annual basis would make an $18,000 annual saving on one plant alone by this component change.

B. Amoco Corporation (a major oil company) needed to identify the cost of complying with environmental protection regulations and used one of its refineries in Yorktown, Virginia, as an experimental site. From an analysis of the financial accounts it was found that environmental costs represented 21.9% of the non-crude cost of the product (crude oil being the major cost).

This figure was six times the level previously assumed to be the environmental cost of production. The realisation of the scale of the cost led to changes in managerial policies and practices.

C. Majestic Metals Inc. of Denver, Colorado, had a problem with pollution caused by its paint-spraying machinery and practices. Through an environmental accounting exercise, the company decided to use high-volume, low-pressure (HVLP) sprayers and this reduced the cost of environmental damage (as shown by fines and rectification costs) by $40,000 per year. From a capital investment appraisal viewpoint the project gave a positive NPV over eight years of $140,000, an internal rate of return (IRR) of 906% and a discounted payback of 0.12 years – an impressive range of results in any terms.

The EPA's website has many more cases showing the impact of an environmental accounting approach.

31.19 Concept of social accounting

This is a difficult place to start because there are so many definitions of social accounting[24] – the main points are that it includes non-financial as well as financial information and addresses the needs of stakeholders other than the shareholders. Stakeholders can be broken down into three categories:

- **internal stakeholders** – managers and workers;
- **external stakeholders** – shareholders, creditors, banks and debtors;
- **related stakeholders** – society as represented by national and local government and the increasing role of pressure groups such as Amnesty International and Greenpeace.

31.19.1 Reporting at corporate level

Prior to 1975, social accounting was viewed as being in the domain of the **economist** and concerned with national income and related issues. In 1975, *The Corporate Report* gave a different definition:

> the reporting of those costs and benefits, which may or may not be quantifiable in money terms, arising from economic activities and subsequently borne or received by the community at large or particular groups not holding a direct relationship with the reporting entity.[25]

This is probably the best working definition of the topic and it establishes the first element of the social accounting concept, namely **reporting at a corporate level** and interpreting corporate in its widest sense as including all organisations of economic significance regardless of the type of organisation or the nature of ownership.

31.19.2 Accountability

The effect of the redefinition by *The Corporate Report* was to introduce the second element of our social accounting concept: accountability. The national income view was only of interest to economists and could not be related to individual company performance – *The Corporate Report* changed that. Social accounting moved into the accountants' domain and it should be the aim of accountants to learn how accountability might be achieved and to define a model against which to judge their own efforts and the efforts of others.[26]

31.19.3 Comprehensive coverage

The annual report is concerned mainly with monetary amounts or clarifying monetary issues. Despite the ASB identifying employees and the public within the user groups,[27] no standards have been issued that deal specifically with reporting to employees or the public.

Instead, the ASB prefers to assume that financial statements that meet the needs of investors will meet most of the needs of other users.[28] For all practical purposes, it disassociates itself from the needs of non-investor users by assuming that there will be more specific information that they may obtain in their dealings with the enterprise.[29]

The information needs of different categories, e.g. employees and the public, need not be identical. The provision of information of particular interest to the public has been referred to as **public interest accounting**,[30] but there is a danger that, whilst valid as an approach, it could act as a constraint on matters that might be of legitimate interest to the employee user group. For example, safety issues at a particular location might be of little interest to the public at large but of immense concern to an employee exposed to work-related radiation or asbestos. The term 'social accounting' as defined by *The Corporate Report* is seen as embracing all interests, even those of a small group.

Equally, the information needs within a category – say, employees – can differ according to the level of the employees. One study identified that different levels of employee ranked the information provided about the employer differently, e.g. lower-level employees rated safety information highest, whereas higher-level employees rated organisation information highest.[31] There were also differences in opinion about the need for additional information, with the majority of lower-level but minority of higher-level employees agreeing that the social report should also contain information on corporate environmental effects.[32]

The need for social accounting to cope with both inter-group and intra-group differences was also identified in a Swedish study.[33]

31.19.4 Independent review

The degree of credibility accorded a particular piece of information is influenced by factors such as whether it is historical or deals with the future; whether appropriate techniques exist for obtaining it; whether its source causes particular concern about deliberate or unintentional bias towards a company view; whether past experience has been that the information was reasonably complete and balanced; and, finally, the extent of independent verification.[34]

Given that social accounting is complex and technically underdeveloped, that it deals with subjective areas or future events, and that it is reported on a selective basis within a report prepared by the management, it is understandable that its credibility will be called into question. Questions will be raised as to why particular items were included or omitted – after all, it is not that unusual for companies to want to hide unfavourable developments.

31.20 Background to social accounting

A brief consideration of the history of social accounting in the UK could be helpful in putting the subject into context. *The Corporate Report* (1975) was the starting point for the whole issue. This was at a time when there was the general dissatisfaction with the quality of financial reporting which had resulted in the creation of a standard-setting regulatory body (the Accounting Standards Steering Committee) and additional statutory provisions, e.g. Companies Act provisions relating to directors.

The Corporate Report was a discussion paper issued by the ASSC which represented the first UK conceptual framework. Its approach was to identify users and their information needs. It identified seven groups of user, which included employees and the public, and their information needs. However, although it identified that there were common areas of interest among the seven groups, such as assessing liquidity and evaluating management performance, it concluded that a single set of general-purpose accounts would not satisfy each group – a different conclusion from that stated by the ASB in 1991, as discussed above.[35] The conclusions reached in *The Corporate Report* were influenced by the findings of a survey of the chairmen of the 300 largest UK listed companies. They indicated a trend towards acceptance of multiple responsibilities towards groups affected by corporate decision-making and their interest as stakeholders.[36]

It was proposed in *The Corporate Report* that there should be additional reports to satisfy the needs of the other stakeholders. These included a statement of corporate objectives, a statement of future prospects, an employment report and a value added statement.

Statement of corporate objectives

Would this be the place for social accounting to start? Would this be the place for vested interests to be represented so that agreed objectives take account of the views of all stakeholders and not merely the management and, indirectly, the shareholders? At present, social accounting appears as a series of add-ons, e.g. a little on charity donations, a little on disabled recruitment policy. Corporate objectives or the mission statement are often seen as something to be handed down; could they assume a different role?

The employment report

The need for an employment report was founded on the belief that there is a trust relationship between employers and employees and an economic relationship between employment prospects and the welfare of the community. The intention was that such a report should contain statistical information relating to such matters as numbers, reasons for change, training time and costs, age and sex distribution, and health and safety.

Statement of future prospects

There has always been resistance to publishing information focusing on the future. The arguments raised against it have included competitive disadvantage and the possibility of misinterpretation because the data relate to the future and are therefore uncertain.

The writers of *The Corporate Report* nevertheless considered it appropriate to publish information on future employment and capital investment levels that could have a direct impact on employees and the local community.

Value added reports

A value added report was intended to give a different focus from the profit and loss account with its emphasis on the bottom line earnings figure. It was intended to demonstrate the interdependence of profits and payments to employees, shareholders, the government and the company via inward investment. It reflected the mood picked up from the survey of chairmen that distributable profit could no longer be regarded as the sole or prime indicator of company performance.[37]

The value added statement became a well-known reporting mechanism to measure how effectively an organisation utilised its resources and added value to its raw materials to turn them into saleable goods. Figure 31.2 is an example of a value added statement.

Several advantages have been claimed for these reports, including improving employee attitudes by reflecting a broader view of companies' objectives and responsibilities.[38]

There have also been criticisms, e.g. they are merely a restatement of information that appears in the annual report; they only report data capable of being reported in monetary terms; and the individual elements of societal benefit are limited to the traditional ones of shareholders, employees and the government, with others such as society and the consumers ignored.

There was also criticism that there was no standard so that expenditures could be aggregated or calculated to disclose a misleading picture, e.g. the inclusion of PAYE tax and welfare payments made to the government in the employee classification so that wages were shown gross, whereas distributions to shareholders were shown net of tax. The effect of both was to overstate the apparent employee share and understate the government and shareholders' share.[39]

In the years immediately following the publication of *The Corporate Report*, companies published value added statements on a voluntary basis but their importance has declined. There was a move away from industrial democracy and the standard-setting regulators did not make the publication of value added statements mandatory.

Figure 31.2 Barloworld Limited value added statement for year ended 30 September 2004

R million	2004	%	2003	%
Revenue	36,673		34,603	
Paid to suppliers for materials and services	26,184		25,486	
Value added	10,489		9,117	
Income from investments*	287		274	
Total wealth created	10,776		9,391	
Wealth distribution				
Salaries, wages and other benefits (note 1)	5,993	56	5,450	58
Providers of capital	1,298	12	1,512	16
Finance cost	468		531	
Dividends paid to Barloworld Ltd shareholders	626		736	
Dividends paid to outside shareholders in subsidiaries	204		245	
Government (note 2)	1,059	10	809	9
Reinvested in group to maintain and develop operations	2,426	22	1,620	17
Depreciation	1,535		1,226	
Retained profit	814		415	
Deferred taxation	77		(21)	
	10,776	100	9,391	100
Value added ratios				
Number of employees (30 September)	25,233		22,749	
Turnover per employee (Rand)#	1,528,615		1,506,410	
Wealth created per employee (Rand)#	449,168		406,086	

Notes:
1. Salaries, wages and other benefits

Salaries, wages, overtime payments, commissions, bonuses and allowances	4,483		4,385	
Employer contributions+	1,150		1,065	
	5,593		5,450	

2. Central and local government

Current taxation	828		637	
Regional Services Council levels	39		33	
Rates and taxes paid to local authorities	62		54	
Customs duties, import surcharges and excise taxes	122		76	
Skills development levy	13		11	
South African withholding taxation			2	
Cash grants and cash subsidies granted by the government	(5)		(4)	
Gross contribution to central and local government	1,059		809	

* Includes interest received, dividend income and share of associate companies and joint ventures retained profit.
\# Based on average number of employees.
\+ In respect of pension funds, retirement annuities, provident funds, medical aid and insurance.

31.20.1 Why *The Corporate Report* was not implemented

The Corporate Report's proposals for additional reports have not been implemented. There are a number of views as to why this was so. There is a view that the business community, despite the results of the chairmen survey, were concerned about the possibility of their reporting responsibility being extended through the report's concept of public accountability and welcomed the release of the Sandilands Report on inflation accounting which overshadowed *The Corporate Report*. There is a view that *The Corporate Report* fell short of making a significant contribution 'by virtue of its failure to select the accounting models appropriate to the informational needs of the individual user groups which it had identified'.[40]

However, the most likely reason for it not being fully implemented was the change of government. The Labour government produced a Green Paper in 1976, *Aims and Scope of Company Reports*, which endorsed much of *The Corporate Report* concept. The reaction from the business community and the Stock Exchange was hostile to any move away from the traditional stewardship concept with its obligations only to shareholders. The CBI view was that other users could ask for information, but that was no reason for companies to be required to provide it.[41] In the event, there was a change of government and the Green Paper sank without trace.

The new government supported the view of Milton Friedman, who wrote in 1962 that 'few trends could so . . . undermine the very foundations of our free society as the acceptance by corporate officials of a social responsibility other than to make as much money . . . as possible'.

Many responsible members of the business community pressed for change,[42] but the mid 1980s saw a decline in the commercial support for social accounting, as profit, dividends and growth superseded all other social goals in business. The movement continued but advocates were regarded at best as well-meaning radicals and at worst as dangerous politicised activists devoted to the destruction of the capitalist system.

By the early 1990s, interest was appearing in the commercial sector but from a free market rather than regulatory viewpoint. The thought was that socially responsible policies need not mean lower profits – in fact, quite the opposite. Given this change in perception, companies began to embrace social accounting concepts – suddenly accountants were able to make a contribution, e.g. evaluating the profit implication of crêche facilities for working mothers being provided by the employer rather than the state. There was also a growth within society in general of a socially responsible point of view which even extended to share investment decisions with the marketing of ethically sound investments.

31.21 Corporate social responsibility

Companies are increasingly recognising the importance of adopting a social, ethical and environmentally responsible approach to business activity and entering into dialogue with all groups of stakeholders. We have discussed the environmentally responsible approach above – the socially responsible approach includes a wide range of activities including the companies' dealings in the marketplace, the workplace, and the community, and in the field of human rights.

Reporting is slowly evolving from simply reporting the amount of charitable donations in the annual report to including additional activities which the company considers to be of key interest. The reporting might be brief but it gives an attractive picture of a company's social responsibility. For example, the 2001 Kingfisher Annual Report has a brief two-page section for social responsibility in which it gives information on:

- environmental issues, e.g. a commitment to sustainable forestry, winning the Business in the Environment award for energy saving; and

- social issues, e.g. from training young unemployed people to recycling electrical goods; making charitable donations that supported the Woolworth Kids First, You Can Do It and Green Grants schemes; and winning a Business in the Community award for Innovation relating to its work forming partnerships with local disability organisations.

We can see from this that community involvement can take many forms, e.g. charitable donations, gifts in kind, employee volunteering initiatives, staff secondments, and sustainable and mutually beneficial partnerships with community and voluntary organisations active in a variety of fields including education, training, regeneration, employment and homelessness.

The approach to CSR is becoming increasingly formalised with the setting up of committees reporting to the Board and more comprehensive CSR Reports.

Committees reporting to the board

The 2004 Kingfisher Annual Report described the role of the Social Responsibility Committee whose purpose is to review progress in fulfilling the Social Responsibility Plan, including monitoring the resources required to support the plan and ensuring that actions taken maximise the opportunity to meet the expectations of key group stakeholders and emerging corporate governance standards (e.g. investor surveys, Turnbull, Business in the Community Survey). The seniority of the committee members is an indication that it has significant influence in advising the board and ensuring the plan is delivered.

CSR Reports

The following is an extract from the CSR Report accompanying the Marks & Spencer 2004 Annual Report:

> **What Corporate Social Responsibility means to us**
> Marks & Spencer has a strong tradition of CSR . . . Our founders believed that building good relationships with employees, suppliers and wider society was the best guarantee of long-term success . . . Managing CSR well will allow us to identify potential risks to the Company and respond to areas of performance where we fall behind . . . it also means we can identify opportunities to differentiate ourselves from our competitors. CSR can help us to draw shoppers to our stores, attract and retain the best staff, make us a partner of choice with suppliers and create value for our shareholders.

Their approach is built around three principles, namely **products, people and places**, and a framework developed by their board-level CSR Committee during 2002 with a detailed statement for each principle. For example, the **principle for places** reads as follows:

> **Help make our communities good places in which to live and work**
> We recognise our obligations to the communities in which we trade. We were founding members of Business in the Community . . . Our relationship with communities is interdependent. Successful retailing requires economically healthy and sustainable communities . . . we provide employment and products and services and often become an important part of the fabric of the high street. We place much emphasis on our stores, their location, design, construction and activities. A 'Store of the Future' project has helped to improve the environmental standards we use to locate, build and refurbish them. Day-to-day operations are managed

within an overall compliance system that includes emergency planning, energy and water usage, health and safety, waste disposal, recycling, recovery of shopping trolleys and donations of unsold food to charities . . . We are also active in a wider sense . . .

A recent development is our growing co-operation with suppliers and business partners in community programmes.

31.22 Need for comparative data

There is evidence[43] that environmental performance could be given a higher priority when analysts assess a company if there were comparable data by sector on a company's level of corporate responsibility.

We will consider two approaches that have taken place to satisfy this need for comparable data: benchmarking and comprehensive guidelines.

31.22.1 Benchmarking

There are a number of benchmarking schemes and we will consider two by way of illustration – these are the London Benchmarking Group, established in 1994, and the Impact on Society, established in December 2001.

The London Benchmarking Group[44]

The Group started in 1994 and consists of companies which join in order to measure and report their involvement in the community, which is a key part of any corporate social responsibility programme, and which have a tool to assist them effectively to assess and target their community programmes. Organisations such as Deloitte & Touche, British Airways and Lloyds TSB are members.

The scheme is concerned with corporate community involvement. It identifies three categories into which different forms of community involvement can be classified, namely, charity donations, social or community investment and commercial initiatives, and includes only contributions made over and above those that result from the basic business operations.

It uses an input/output model, putting a monetary value on the 'input' costs which include contributions made in cash, in time or in kind, together with full cost of staff involved; and collecting 'output' data on the community benefit, e.g. number who benefited, leveraged resources and benefit accruing to the business.

Impact on Society[45]

This is a website created in 2001 which provides free access to corporate social responsibility information from leading companies. It is the first time a common set of indicators against which companies can be measured has been provided, offering insight into areas such as the environment, the workplace, the community in which the company operates, the market-place and human rights. The information ranges from relatively easy-to-measure numeric data, such as water usage, through to more complex, often perception-based information, e.g. from employee surveys. The information is then summarised into clear company profiles and can be compared and contrasted according to a range of parameters, such as specific indicators or industry sectors.

The site provides **qualitative** information for each company with key indicators as shown in Figure 31.3. It also provides quantitative information as a percentage, absolute cash value or physical volume.

Figure 31.3 Impact on Society key indicators

Indicator area	Indicators reported against
Marketplace	Advertising complaints upheld; upheld cases of anti-competitive behaviour; customer satisfaction levels; average time to pay bills to suppliers; customer retention; customer complaints about products and services; provision for customers with special needs.
Environment	Overall energy consumption; water usage; quantity of waste produced by weight; upheld cases of prosecution for environmental offences; CO_2/greenhouse gas emissions; percentage of waste recycled; environmental impact; benefits or costs of company's core products and services; environmental impact over the supply chain.
Workplace	Workforce profile by race, gender, disability and age; number of legal non-compliances with health and safety and equal opportunities legislation; upheld cases of corrupt or unprofessional behaviour; staff turnover; value of staff training, perception measures of the company by its employees; absenteeism rates; pay and conditions compared to local equivalent average; work profile compared to local community profile.
Community	Cash value of support as percentage of pre-tax profits; estimated combined value of staff company time; gifts in kind and management time; leverage of other resources; perception measure of company as a good neighbour.
Human rights	Existence of confidential grievance procedures for staff; proportion of suppliers or partners screened for human rights compliance; proportion of suppliers or partners meeting company's own standards on human rights; perception by staff and local community of company's performance on human rights; wage rates.

An illustration of the scheme applied to Marks & Spencer for human rights and the environment is as follows:

Human rights

Particularly applicable to countries with operations or suppliers in developing countries.

The issues measured under human rights largely apply to companies who operate in, or buy from suppliers in, developing countries. What does or does not constitute a human right is always under some debate. However, the Universal Declaration of Human Rights is a main reference point. Before they can report that they definitely fall outside the scope of this section, companies need to answer a 'gatekeeper' question. Unless they can answer that they are definitely not exposed to human rights issues, they need to do more research and report against this indicator area.

The human rights indicators are being developed further: in consultation with non-governmental organisations and businesses engaged in human rights issues. While some companies have chosen to report, others await more fully developed indicators in this area.

Environment

Use of recycled material
Percentage of material used from recycled sources
Non-weight bearing food product cardboard packaging

Recycled cardboard
2000   60%
1999   50%
1998   25%

Many types of packaging use recycled materials as a matter of course, e.g. glass bottles, tin cans and transport boxes. Where we believe that the use of recycled materials is the best environmental option and that we are able to achieve improvements we set targets. We have been working to increase our use of recycled cardboard (made from at least 50% post-consumer waste) for all our non-weight bearing food product packaging.

31.23 International initiatives towards triple bottom line reporting

There are no mandatory standards for sustainability reporting but there are Sustainability Reporting Guidelines which were issued in 2000 by the Global Reporting Initiative Steering Committee on which a number of international organisations are represented including ACCA, the Institute of Social and Ethical Accountability, the New Economics Foundation and SustainAbility Ltd from the UK.

31.23.1 The Global Reporting Initiative (GRI)

The GRI has a mission to develop global sustainability reporting guidelines for voluntary use by organisations reporting on the three linked elements of sustainability, namely, the economic, environmental and social dimensions of their activities, products and services.

Economic dimension

This includes financial and non-financial information on R&D expenditure, investment in the workforce, current staff expenditure and outputs in terms of labour productivity.

Environmental dimension

This includes any adverse impact on air, water, land, biodiversity and human health by an organisation's production processes, products and services.

Social dimension

This includes information on health and safety and recognition of rights, e.g. human rights for both employees and outsourced employees.

31.23.2 How will the guidelines assist organisations?

The aim is to assist organisations to report information that complements existing reporting standards and is consistent, comparable and easy to understand so that:

● Parties contemplating a relationship such as assessing investment risk, obtaining goods or services or entering into any other commercial partnership arrangement will have available to them a clear picture of the human and ecological impact of the business so that they can make an informed decision.

● Management has the means to develop information systems to provide the basis for monitoring performance, making inter-company comparisons and reporting to stakeholders.

31.23.3 What information should appear in an ideal GRI report?

There are six parts to the ideal GRI report:

1 CEO statement – describing key elements of the report.

2 A profile – providing an overview of the organisation and the scope of the report (it could, for example, be dealing only with environmental information) which sets the context for the next four parts.

3 Executive summary and key indicators – to assist stakeholders to assess trends and make inter-company comparisons.

4 Vision and strategy – a statement of the vision for the future and how that integrates economic, environmental and social performance.

5 Policies, organisation and systems – an overview of the governance and management systems to implement this vision with a discussion of how stakeholders have been engaged. This reflects the GRI view that the report should not be made in isolation but there should have been appropriate inputs from stakeholders.

6 Performance review.
The GRI issued Draft Sustainability Reporting Guidelines in 2006 (www.grig3.org/guide-lines/overviewg.html). The guidelines consist of principles for defining report content and ensuring the quality of reported information as well as standard disclosures comprising performance indicators and other disclosure items. There is also detailed guidance to assist users in applying the guidelines in the form of technical protocols that are being developed on indicator measurement, e.g. specific indicators for energy use, child labour and health and safety.

31.23.4 How are GRI reports to be verified?

CSR Reports are now able to be verified by independent, competent and impartial external assurance providers. The assurance providers now have a standard – the AA1000 Assurance Standard (www.accountability.org.uk) to provide a framework for their work. This standard was launched in 2003 to address the need for a single approach to deal effectively with the qualitative as well as quantitative data that makes up sustainability performance plus the systems that underpin the data and performance. It is designed to complement the GRI Reporting Guidelines and other standardised or company-specific approaches to disclosure. It requires reports against three Assurance Principles which are Materiality, Completeness and Responsiveness, as well as statements as to how conclusions were reached and on the independence of the assurance providers.

As an example, in the 2004 Annual Report of O_2 Ernst & Young, who were the assurance providers, stated that they were forming a conclusion on matters such as (a) *materiality* – whether O_2 had provided a balanced representation of material issues concerning O_2's corporate responsibility performance, (b) *completeness* – whether O_2 had complete information on which to base a judgement of what was material for inclusion in the Report, and (c) *responsiveness* – whether O_2 had responded to stakeholder concerns. They also explained what they did to form their conclusions:

What we did to form our conclusions
There are currently no statutory requirements in the UK in relation to the independent review of corporate responsibility reports. The AA1000 Assurance Standard sets out principles for social and environmental report assurance. We have been asked by O_2 to set out our conclusions by reference to the assurance principles described in the AA1000 Assurance Standard.

31.23.5 Will there be any impact on matters that are currently disclosed?

There may be an overlap with existing disclosures in the OFR and there is also a pressure for additional information to permit a greater understanding of future risks, e.g. the GRI acknowledges that in financial reporting terms a going concern is one that is considered to be financially viable for at least the next financial year but seeks additional information such as:

● The extent to which significant internal and external operational, financial, compliance, and other risks are identified and assessed on an ongoing basis. Significant risks may, for example, include those related to market, credit, liquidity, technological, legal, health, safety, environmental and reputation issues.

● The likely impact of prospective legislation, e.g. product, environmental, fiscal or employee-related.

31.23.6 The nature of the accountant's involvement

There will be inputs from accountants in each of the three elements with a greater degree of quantification at present for the economic and environmental dimensions. For example:
The economic dimension may require economic indicators such as:

● profit: segmental gross margin, net profit, EBIT, return on average capital employed;
● intangible assets: ratio of market valuation to book value;
● investments: human capital, R&D, debt/equity ratio;
● wages and benefits: totals by country;
● labour productivity: levels and changes by job category;
● community development: jobs by type and country showing absolute figures and net change;
● suppliers: value of goods and services outsourced, performance in meeting credit terms.

The environmental dimension may require environmental indicators such as:

● products and services: major issues, e.g. disposal of waste, packaging practices, percentage of product reclaimed after use;
● suppliers: supplier issues identified through stakeholder consultation, e.g. forest stewardship;
● travel: objectives and targets, e.g. product distribution, fleet operation, quantitative estimates of miles travelled by transport type.

Social dimensions may require social indicators such as:

● quality of management: employee retention rates, ratio of jobs offered to jobs accepted, ranking as an employer in surveys;
● health and safety: reportable cases, lost days, absentee rate, investment per worker in injury prevention;
● wages and benefits: ratio of lowest wage to local cost of living, health and pension benefits provided;
● training and education: ratio of training budget to annual operating cost, programmes to encourage worker participation in decision making;
● freedom of association: grievance procedures in place, number and types of legal action concerning anti-union practices.

Summary

Sustainability is now recognised as having three elements. These are the economic, environmental and social. It is recognised that advances in environmental and social improvement are dependent on the existence of an economically viable organisation.

As environmental and social reporting evolves, there are proposals being made to harmonise the content and disclosure. This can be seen with the publication of the triple bottom line, the Connected Framework and the IFAC Sustainability Framework.

In addition there are benchmark schemes which allow stakeholders to compare corporate social reports and evaluate an individual company's performance. The management systems that are being developed within companies should result in data that are consistent and reliable and capable of external verification. The benchmarking systems should assist in both identifying best practice and establishing relevant performance indicators.

Corporate social reporting is coming of age. Initially there were fears that it would add to costs and there are present concerns that it is diverting too much of a finance director's attention away from commercial and stragetic planning. However, it is becoming generally recognised that a company's reputation and its attractiveness to potential investors are influenced by a company's behaviour and attitude to corporate governance and sustainability.

Companies are reacting positively to the need to be good corporate citizens and it is interesting to see the developments around the world where sustainability, good corporate governance and strategic planning are merging into an integrated system. This will take time but companies are taking up the challenge to be transparent and innovative in their financial reporting. Award schemes are encouraging the spread of best practice. Companies are integrating their non-financial narrative and using the Internet to get their message out to a wider public.

The time has passed since corporate governance, sustainabilty, environmental and social reporting were seen purely as a PR exercise.

REVIEW QUESTIONS

1 Discuss the relevance of corporate social reports to an existing and potential investor.

2 Obtain a copy of the environmental report of a company that has taken part in the ACCA Awards for Sustainability Reporting and critically discuss from an investor's and public interest viewpoint.

3 'Charters and guidelines help make reports reliable but inhibit innovation and reduce their relevance.' Discuss.

4 Discuss the implications of the Global Reporting Initiative for the accountancy profession.

5 Discuss *The Corporate Report*'s relevance to modern business; identify changes that would improve current reporting practice and the conditions necessary for such changes to become mandatory.

6 (a) Explain the term 'stakeholders' in a corporate context.

   (b) 'Social accounting recognises all *Corporate Report* users as stakeholders.' Discuss.

7 Discuss the value added concept, giving examples, and ways to improve the statement.

8 Outline the arguments for and against a greater role for the audit function in corporate social reporting.

9 (a) 'Human assets are incapable of being valued.' Discuss.

(b) Football clubs have followed various policies in the way in which they include players within their accounts. For example, some clubs capitalise players, as shown by a 1992 Touche Ross survey:[46]

Club	Value £m	Basis	Which players
Tottenham Hotspur	9.8	Cost	Those purchased
Sheffield United	8.7	Manager's valuation	Whole squad
Portsmouth	7.0	Directors' valuation	Whole squad
Derby County	6.5	Cost	Those purchased

Other clubs disclose squad value in notes to the accounts or in the directors' report:

Manchester United	24.0	Independent valuation
Charlton Athletic	4.1	Directors' valuation
Millwall	11.0	Manager's valuation

Discuss arguments for and against capitalising players as assets. Explain the effect on the profit and loss account if players are not capitalised.

10 (a) Examine the recent financial press to identify examples of a failure to meet information needs in respect of an area of public interest.

(b) Obtain a set of accounts from a public listed company and assess the success in meeting the needs of the traditional users. Repeat the process for non-traditional users and discuss how you could improve the situation (i) marginally, (ii) significantly.

11 Discuss the impact of the following groups on the accounting profession:

(a) Environmental groups;

(b) Customers;

(c) Workforce;

(d) Ethical investors.

12 Nissan, the Japanese car company, decided that 'any environmentalism should pay for itself and for every penny you spend you must save a penny. You can spend as many pennies as you like as long as other environmental actions save an equal number.'[47] Discuss the significance of this for each of the stakeholders.

13 (a) 'Accounting should contribute to the protection of the environment.' Discuss whether this is a proper role for accounting and outline ways in which it could.

(b) Outline, with reasons, your ideas for an environmental report for a company of your choice.

(c) Discuss the arguments against the adoption of environmental accounting.

14 (a) Obtain the annual reports of companies that claim to be environmentally aware and assess whether these reports and accounts reflect the claim. The various oil, chemical and pharmaceutical companies are useful for this.

(b) Look at your own organisation/institution, outline the possible environmental issues and discuss how these could or should be disclosed in the annual report.

EXERCISES

An extract from the solution is provided on the Companion Website (www.pearsoned.co.uk/elliott-elliott) for exercises marked with an asterisk (*).

* Question 1

The following information relates to the Plus Factors Group plc for the years to 30 September 20X8 and 20X9:

	Notes	20X9 £000	20X8 £000
Associated company share of profit		10.9	10.7
Auditors' remuneration		12.2	11.9
Payables for materials			
At beginning of year		1,109.1	987.2
At end of year		1,244.2	1,109.1
Receivables			
At beginning of year		1,422.0	1,305.0
At end of year		1,601.0	1,422.0
11% debentures	1	500.0	600.0
Depreciation		113.7	98.4
Employee benefits paid		109.9	68.4
Hire of plant, machinery and vehicles	2	66.5	367.3
Materials paid for in year		3,622.9	2,971.4
Minority interest in profit of the year		167.2	144.1
Other overheads incurred		1,012.4	738.3
Pensions and pension contributions paid		319.8	222.2
Profit before taxation		1,437.4	1,156.4
Provision for corporation tax		464.7	527.9
Salaries and wages		1,763.8	1,863.0
Sales	3	9,905.6	8,694.1
Shares at nominal value			
Ordinary at 25p each fully paid	4	2,500.0	2,000.0
7% preference at £1 each fully paid	4	500.0	200.0
Inventories of materials			
Beginning of year		804.1	689.7
End of year		837.8	804.1

Ordinary dividends were declared as follows:

Interim   1.12 pence per share (20X8, 1.67p)
Final   3.57 pence per share (20X8, 2.61p)
Average number of employees was 196 (20X8, 201)

Notes:

1 £300,000 of debentures were redeemed at par on 31 March 20X9 and £200,000 new debentures at the same rate of interest were issued at £98 for each £100 nominal value on the same date. The new debentures are due to be redeemed in five years' time.

2 This is the amount for inclusion in the statement of comprehensive income.

3 All the groups' sales are subject to value added tax at 15% and the figures given include such tax. All other figures are exclusive of value added tax. This VAT rate has been increased to 17.5% and may be subject to future changes, but for the purposes of this question the theory and workings remain the same irrespective of the rate.

4 All shares have been in issue throughout the year.

The statement of value added is available for 20X8 and the 20X9 statement needs to be completed.

	Workings	£000	
Turnover	1	7,560.1	
Less: Bought-in materials and services	2	4,096.4	
Value added by group		3,463.7	
Share of profits of associated company		10.7	
		3,474.4	
Applied in the following ways			
To pay employees	3	2,153.6	62.0%
To pay providers of capital	4	566.5	16.3%
To pay government		527.9	15.2%
To provide for maintenance and expansion of assets	5	226.4	6.50%
		3,474.4	100.0%

Workings

1 *Turnover*

Sales inclusive of VAT		8,694.1
VAT at 15%		1,134.0
		7,560.1

2 *Bought-in materials and services*

Cost of materials

Creditors at end of year	1,109.1
Add: Payments in year	2,971.4
	4,080.5
Less: Payables at beginning of year	987.2
Materials purchased in year	3,093.3
Add: Opening inventory	689.7
Less: Closing inventory	(804.1)
Materials used	2,978.9
Add: Cost of bought-in services	
Auditors' remuneration	11.9
Hire of plant, machinery and vehicles	367.3
Other overheads	738.3
	4,096.4

	£000
3 *To pay employees*	
Benefits paid	68.4
Pensions and pension contributions	222.2
Salaries and wages	1,863.0
	2,153.6
4 *To pay providers of capital*	
Debenture interest	
11% of £600,000	66.0
Dividends	
Preference 20X8 7% of £200,000	14.0
Ordinary 20X8 8 million shares at 4.28p	342.4
Minority interest	144.1
	566.5
5 *To provide for maintenance and expansion of assets*	
Profit before tax	1,156.4
Less:	
tax	(527.9)
minority interest	(144.1)
dividends	(356.4)
Retained profits	128.0
Depreciation	98.4
	226.4

Required:

(a) **Prepare a statement of value added for the year to 30 September 20X9. Include a percentage breakdown of the distribution of value added.**

(b) **Produce ratios related to employees' interests based on the statement in (a) and explain how they might be of use.**

(c) **Explain briefly what the difficulties are of measuring and reporting financial information in the form of a statement of value added.**

Question 2

David Mark is a sole trader who owns and operates supermarkets in each of three villages near Ousby. He has drafted his own accounts for the year ended 31 May 20X4 for each of the branches. They are as follows:

	Arton		Blendale		Clifearn	
	£	£	£	£	£	£
Sales		910,800		673,200		382,800
Cost of sales		633,100		504,900		287,100
Gross profit		277,700		168,300		95,700
Less: Expenses:						
David Mark's salary	10,560		10,560		10,560	
Other salaries and wages	143,220		97,020		78,540	
Rent			19,800			
Rates	8,920		5,780		2,865	
Advertising	2,640		2,640		2,640	
Delivery van expenses	5,280		5,280		5,280	
General expenses	11,220		3,300		1,188	
Telephone	2,640		1,980		1,584	
Wrapping materials	7,920		3,960		2,640	
Depreciation:						
Fixtures	8,220		4,260		2,940	
Vehicle	3,000	203,620	3,000	157,580	3,000	111,237
Net profit/(loss)		74,080		10,720		(15,537)

The figures for the year ended 31 May 20X4 follow the pattern of recent years. Because of this, David Mark is proposing to close the Clifearn supermarket immediately.

David Mark employs 12 full-time and 20 part-time staff. His recruitment policy is based on employing one extra part-time assistant for every £30,000 increase in branch sales. His staff deployment at the moment is as follows:

	Arton	Blendale	Clifearn
Full-time staff (including managers)	6	4	2
Part-time staff	8	6	6

Peter Gaskin, the manager of the Clifearn supermarket, asks David to give him another year to make the supermarket profitable. Peter has calculated that he must cover £125,500 expenses out of his gross profit in the year ended 31 May 20X5 in order to move into profitability. His calculations include extra staff costs and all other extra costs.

Additional information:

1 General advertising for the business as a whole is controlled by David Mark. This costs £3,960 per annum. Each manager spends a further £1,320 advertising his own supermarket locally.

2 The delivery vehicle is used for deliveries from the Arton supermarket only.

3 David Mark has a central telephone switchboard which costs £1,584 rental per annum. Each supermarket is charged for all calls actually made. For the year ended 31 May 20X4 these amounted to:

Arton	£2,112
Blendale	£1,452
Clifearn	£1,056

Required:
(a) A report addressed to David Mark advising him whether to close Clifearn supermarket. Your report should include a detailed financial statement based on the results for the year ended 31 May 20X4 relating to the Clifearn branch.
(b) Calculate the increased turnover and extra staff needed if Peter's suggestion is implemented.
(c) Comment on the social implications for the residents of Clifearn if (i) David Mark closes the supermarket, (ii) Peter Gaskin's recommendation is undertaken.

Question 3

(a) You are required to prepare a value added statement to be included in the corporate report of Hythe plc for the year ended 31 December 20X6, including the comparatives for 20X5, using the information given below:

	20X6	20X5
	£000	£000
Non-current assets (net book value)	3,725	3,594
Trade receivables	870	769
Trade payables	530	448
14% debentures	1,200	1,080
6% preference shares	400	400
Ordinary shares (£1 each)	3,200	3,200
Sales	5,124	4,604
Materials consumed	2,934	2,482
Wages	607	598
Depreciation	155	144
Fuel consumed	290	242
Hire of plant and machinery	41	38
Salaries	203	198
Auditors' remuneration	10	8
Corporation tax provision	402	393
Ordinary share dividend	9p	8p
Number of employees	40	42

(b) Although value added statements were recommended by *The Corporate Report*, as yet there is no accounting standard related to them. Explain what a value added statement is and provide reasons as to why you think it has not yet become mandatory to produce such a statement as a component of current financial statements either through a Financial Reporting Standard or company law.

Question 4

Gettry Doffit plc is an international company with worldwide turnover of £26 million. The activities of the company include the breaking down and disposal of noxious chemicals at a specialised plant in the remote Scottish countryside. During the preparation of the financial statements for the year ended 31 March 20X5, it was discovered that:

1 Quantities of chemicals for disposals on site at the year-end included:

(A) Axylotl peroxide   40,000 gallons

(B) Pterodactyl chlorate   35 tons

Chemical A is disposed of for a South Korean company, which was invoiced for 170 million won on 30 January 20X5, for payment in 120 days. It is estimated that the costs of disposal will not exceed £75,000. £60,000 of costs have been incurred at the year-end.

Chemical B is disposed of for a British company on a standard contract for 'cost of disposal plus 35%', one month after processing. At the year-end the chemical has been broken down into harmless by-products at a cost of £77,000. The by-products, which belong to Gettry Doffit plc, are worth £2,500.

2 To cover against exchange risks, the company entered into two forward contracts on 30 January 20X5:

No. 03067   Sell 170 million won at 1,950 won = £1: 31 May 20X5
No. 03068   Buy $70,000 at $1.60   = £1: 31 May 20X5

Actual sterling exchange rates were:

	won	$
30 January 20X5	1,900	1.70
31 March 20X5	2,000	1.38
30 April 20X5 (today)	2,100	1.80

The company often purchases a standard chemical used in processing from a North American company, and the dollars will be applied towards this purpose.

3 The company entered into a contract to import a specialised chemical used in the breaking down of magnesium perambulate from a Nigerian company which demanded the raising of an irrevocable letter of credit for £65,000 to cover 130 tons of the chemical. By 31 March 20X5 bills of lading for 60 tons had been received and paid for under the letter of credit. It now appears that the total needed for the requirements of Gettry Doffit plc for the foreseeable future is only 90 tons.

4 On 16 October 20X4 Gettry Doffit plc entered into a joint venture as partners with Dumpet Andrunn plc to process perfidious recalcitrant (PR) at the Gettry Doffit plc site using Dumpet Andrunn plc's technology. Unfortunately, a spillage at the site on 15 April 20X5 has led to claims being filed against the two companies for £12 million. A public inquiry has been set up, to assess the cause of the accident and to determine liability, which the finance director of Gettry Doffit plc fears will be, at the very least, £3 million.

Required:
Discuss how these matters should be reflected in the financial statements of Gettry Doffit plc as on and for the year ended 31 March 20X5.

Question 5

Examine the EPA's website (www.epa.gov/epahome/aboutepa.htm) and prepare one of the cases as a presentation to the group showing clearly how environmental accounting was used and the results of the exercise.

Question 6

The following items have been extracted from the accounts:

	2005 (€m)	2004 (€m)
Other income	844	980
Cost of materials	25,694	24,467
Financial income	−188	54
Depreciation/amortisation	4,207	3,589
Providers of finance	1,351	1,059
Retained	1,815	1,823
Revenues	46,656	44,335
Government	1,590	1,794
Other expenses	4,925	5,093
Shareholders	424	419
Employees	7,306	7,125

Required:
(a) Prepare a Value Added Statement showing % for each year and % change
(b) Draft a note for inclusion in the Annual Report commenting on the Statement you have prepared.

References

1 M. Friedman, *Capitalism and Freedom*, University of Chicago Press, 1962, p. 133.
2 www.wbcsd.org/templates/TemplateWBCSD5/layout.asp?type=p&MenuId=MTE0OQ
3 J. Elkington, *Cannibals With Forks: The Triple Bottom Line of 21st Century Business*, Capstone, 1997.
4 www.johnelkington.com/TBL-elkington-chapter.pdf.
5 www.sustainabilityatwork.org.uk/strategy/report/0.
6 web.ifac.org/sustainability-framework/ip-introduction.
7 S.J. Gray and C.B. Roberts, *Voluntary Information Disclosure and the British Multinationals: Corporate Perceptions of Costs and Benefits, International Pressures for Accounting Change*, Prentice Hall, 1989, p. 117.
8 AICPA, *The Measurement of Corporate Social Performance*, 1977, p. 4.
9 C. Lehman, *Accounting's Changing Roles in Social Conflict*, Markus Weiner Publishing, 1992, p. 64.
10 *Ibid.*, p. 17.
11 *This Common Inheritance*, Government White Paper, 1990.
12 KPMG Peat Marwick McLintock, *Environmental Considerations in Acquiring*, Corporate Finance Briefing, 17 May 1991.
13 M. Jones, 'The cost of cleaning up', *Certified Accountant*, May 1995, p. 47.
14 M. Campanale, 'Cost or opportunity', *Certified Accountant*, November 1991, p. 32.
15 See http://www.iasplus.com/resource/0105euroenv.pdf
16 See www.unep.org
17 See http://ec.europa.eu/environment/emas/index_en.htm
18 See www.iccwbo.org
19 See www.cefic.be/
20 See http://ec.europa.eu/environment/newprg/
21 See www.ceaa-acve.ca/aboutus.htm
22 See www.rabnet.com/
23 See www.fee.be/issues/other.htm#Sustainability

24 M.R. Matthews and M.H.B. Perera, *Accounting Theory and Development*, Chapman and Hall, 1991, p. 350.

25 Accounting Standards Steering Committee, *The Corporate Report*, 1975.

26 R. Gray, D. Owen and K. Maunders, *Corporate Social Reporting*, Prentice Hall, 1987, p. 75.

27 ASB, *Statement of Principles: The Objective of Financial Statements*, 1991, para. 9.

28 *Ibid.*, para. 10.

29 *Ibid.*, para. 11.

30 F. Okcabol and A. Tinker, 'The market for positive theory: deconstructing the theory for excuses', *Advances in Public Interest Accounting*, vol. 3, 1990.

31 H. Sebreuder, 'Employees and the corporate social report: the Dutch case', in S.J. Gray (ed.), *International Accounting and Transnational Decisions*, Butterworth, 1983, p. 287.

32 *Ibid.*, p. 289.

33 *Ibid.*, p. 287.

34 AICPA, *op. cit.*, p. 243.

35 *Statement of Principles, op. cit.*

36 R. Gray, D. Owen and K. Maunders, *op. cit.*, p. 44.

37 *Ibid.*

38 S.J. Gray and K.T. Maunders, *Value Added Reporting: Uses and Measurement*, ACCA, 1980; B. Underwood and P.J. Taylor, *Accounting Theory and Policy Making*, Heinemann, 1985, p. 298.

39 *Ibid.*, p. 174.

40 M. Davies, R. Patterson and A. Wilson, *UK GAAP* (4th edition), Ernst & Young, 1994, p. 71.

41 R. Gray, D. Owen and K. Maunders, *op. cit.*, p. 48.

42 R.W. Perks and R.H. Gray, 'Corporate social reporting – an analysis of objectives', *British Accounting Review*, 1978, vol. 10(2), pp. 43–59.

43 Business in the Environment, *Investing in the Future*, May 2001.

44 See www.lbg-online.net/

45 See www.iosreporting.org

46 R. Bruce, *The Independent*, 25 October 1993, p. 29.

47 M. Brown, 'Greening the bottom line', *Management Today*, July 1995, p. 73.

Bibliography

The following references have been helpful for students carrying out assignments in the developing areas of environmental and social reporting:

Association of British Insurers, *Investing in Social Responsibility – Risks and Opportunities*, London: Association of British Insurers, 2001.

C.A. Adams, W.-Y. Hill and C.B. Roberts, 'Corporate social reporting practices in Western Europe: legitimating corporate behaviour?', *British Accounting Review*, vol. 30, no. 1, 1998, pp. 1–22.

C.C. Adams, A. Coutts and G. Harte, 'Corporate equal opportunities (non-) disclosure', *British Accounting Review*, vol. 27, no. 2, 1995, pp. 87–108.

P. Bartram, 'Go green, not into the red', *Accountancy Age*, 31 October 2002, p. 15.

J. Bebbington, 'Sustainable development: a review of the international development business and accounting literature', *Accounting Forum*, vol. 25, no. 2, 2001, pp. 128–157.

J. Bebbington and I. Thomson, 'Commentary on: Some thoughts on social and environmental accounting education', *Accounting Education: An international journal*, vol. 10, no. 4, 2001, pp. 353-355.

F. Birkin, P. Edwards and D. Woodward, 'Some Evidence on Executives' Views of Corporate Social Responsibility', *British Accounting Review*, vol. 33, 2001, pp. 357–397.

J.H. Blokdijk and F. Drieenhuizen, 'The environment and the audit profession – a Dutch research study', *The European Accounting Review*, December 1992, pp. 437–443.

K. Bondy, D. Matten and J. Moon, 'The adoption of voluntary codes of conduct in MNCs – a three countries comparative study', *Business and Society Review*, vol. 109, no. 4, 2004, pp. 449–478.

K. Bondy, D. Matten and J. Moon, 'Codes of conduct as a tool for sustainable governance in MNCs', in S. Benn and D. Dunphy (eds.) *Corporate Governance and Sustainability: Challenges for Theory and Practice*, Routledge, 2006.

W. Chapple and J. Moon, 'Corporate social responsibility (CSR) in Asia: a seven country study of CSR website reporting', *Business and Society*, vol. 44, no. 4, 2005, pp. 115–136.

Commission of the European Communities, *Commission Recommendation of 30 May 2001 on the Recognition, Measurement and Disclosure of Environmental Issues in the Annual Accounts and Annual Reports of Companies*, Luxembourg: OOPEC, 2001.

'Corporate social responsibility', Guidance for the Financial Services Sector, www.abi.org.uk

A. Crane, D. Matten and J. Moon, *Corporations and Citizenship*, UK, Cambridge University Press, 2006.

D. Crowther, *Social and Environmental Accounting*, Harlow: Financial Times Prentice Hall, 2000, p. 109 (Financial Times Executive Briefings), ISBN: 0273650920.

Deloitte & Touche, *Accounting for Carbon under the UK Emissions Trading Scheme – Discussion Paper*, London: Deloitte & Touche, 2002.

C. Evans, 'Sustainability: the bottom line', *Accountancy*, vol. 131, no. 1313, January 2003, p. 16.

R. Gray, J. Bebbington, D. Walters and M. Houldin (eds.), *Accounting for the Environment*, Paul Chapman Publishing, 1993.

R. Gray, D. Owen and C. Adams, *Accounting and Accountability: Changes and Challenges in Corporate Social and Environmental Reporting*, Prentice Hall, 1996.

R. Gray, J. Bebbington and M. Houldin, *Accounting for the Environment* (2nd edition), London: Sage Publications, 2001.

D. Hawkins, *Corporate Social Responsibility: Balancing Tomorrow's Sustainability and Today's Profitability*, Palgrave MacMillan, 2006.

A. Henriques and J. Richardson, *The Triple Bottom Line: does it all add up?*, Earthscan, 2004.

R. Howes, *Environmental Cost Accounting: An introduction and practical guide*, London: CIMA, 2002.

M.J. Jones, 'Accounting for biodiversity', *British Accounting Review*, vol. 28, no. 4, 1996, pp. 281–304.

B. O'Dwyer, *The State of Corporate Environmental Reporting in Ireland*, London: Certified. Accountants Educational Trust for the Association of Chartered Certified Accountants, 2001, p. 47 (Research Report 69).

D. Owen (ed.), *Green Reporting: Accountancy and the Challenge of the Nineties*, Thompson Business Press, 1992.

L.S. Paine, *Value Shift – why companies must merge social and financial imperatives to achieve superior performance*, New York: McGraw-Hill, 2002.

PricewaterhouseCoopers, *The Politics of Responsible Business – a survey of political and business opinion on corporate social responsibility*, London: PricewaterhouseCoopers in association with the Industry and Parliament Trust, 2001.

J. Rayner and W. Raven (eds.), *Corporate Social Responsibility Monitor*, London: Gee, 2002, 1 vol., looseleaf, updated.

R. Roslender and J.R. Dyson, 'Accounting for the worth of employees: a new look at an old problem', *British Accounting Review*, vol. 24, no. 4, 1992, pp. 311–330.

C.A. Tilt, 'Environmental policies of major companies: Australian evidence', *British Accounting Review*, vol. 29, no. 4, 1997, pp. 367–394.

T. Tinker and T. Puxy, *Policing Accounting Knowledge: The Market for Excuses Affair*, Paul Chapman Publishing, 1995.

J.S. Toms, *Environmental Management, Environmental Accounting and Financial Performance*, London: Chartered Institute of Management Accountants, 2000.

Index

A & J Muklow plc 426
A-scores 753–4
abandonment 232, 233
abbreviated accounts 120
ACCA *see* Association of Chartered
    Certified Accountants
Accor 117
accountability 143, 152, 179
    SME test: public 122
    stewardship *see separate entry*
accountants 443, 815
    environmental and social reporting
        844–5, 862, 872
    ethical behaviour *see separate entry*
    external reporting 3–4
    IFAC *Code of Ethics for Professional*
        Accountants 165–8
    income and asset value measurement
        43–7, 132
    influence and status 112
    internal reporting 3, 4–8
    loss of confidence in 102–3
    reporting role 5
    XBRL 787
Accounting and Actuarial Disciplinary
    Board 176
accounting bases 201–2
accounting policies 44, 201, 202
    changes in 202, 391
    consolidated accounts 577
    disclosure 111, 131, 201, 202, 203
    earnings per share 644
    ratio analysis 698, 719
    revenue 25–6
accounting principles 201
    see also individual principles
accounting standards
    arguments for and against 104–5
    cash flow concept 12
    company law 205
    effectiveness 123–5
    ethics and process of setting 164–5
    financial crisis and 314–15
    national differences 109–13,
        129–30
    need for mandatory 101–3, 104,
        123–5, 129
    non-publicly accountable entities
        119–23
    principles and 163

regulatory framework 105–8
standardise financial reports, efforts to
    113–19
see also Financial Reporting Standards;
    International Accounting
    Standards; International
    Financial Reporting Standards;
    Statements of Financial
    Accounting Standards;
    Statements of Standard
    Accounting Practice
Accounting Standards Board (ASB) 106,
    129, 133, 151
    accrual accounting 32
    conceptual framework developments
        150
    deferred tax 392–3
    IFRS and UK GAAP 381–2
    inflation accounting 81–3, 145–7
    operating and financial review: RS 1
        208–9
    review of narrative reporting 210
    SME reporting 123
    social and environmental reporting
        862, 863
    Statement of Accounting Principles 83,
        125, 134, 138–49, 844
    true and fair 204
Accounting Standards Committee (ASC)
    125, 203–4
accounting theory 112, 130–3
accrual accounting 16, 17, 22–3, 44, 110,
    125, 131, 189–90, 201
    concept 24
    cost of sales 198
    development costs 463
    dividends 16, 42
    goodwill 468
    historical cost convention 23–4, 32
    matching principle 27, 29, 404, 425,
        468
    mechanics of 24–5, 28
    non-current assets 29–32, 404, 425
    reconciliation of cash flow and data
        from 32–4
    statement of comprehensive income
        27, 28, 30, 31
    statement of financial position 28–9,
        30, 31
    subjective judgements 25–7, 164

summary 34
taxation 376
views on 32
acid test ratio 709
acquisitions 818
    after reporting date 236
    deferred tax 390–1, 393
    intangible assets 472, 477, 482–4
    share exchange 261, 555
    threat of takeover 817
    see also consolidated accounts; goodwill
actuarial method
    finance leases 446, 449
adaptability, financial 140, 145
administrative expenses 188
advance corporation tax (ACT) 381
advertising agencies 467
AEI/GEC merger 498
agency costs/principal–agent 8, 159
aggregation 201
Agrana Group 505–6
agriculture 427, 514–17
Ahold 124–5, 510
Amadeus 717
Amoco Corporation 861
amortisation 471, 472, 483
    development costs 464
    emissions trading certificates 478
    financial instruments 313–14, 322,
        323, 324–5, 326, 327–8, 334–5
    goodwill 466, 467, 468–9, 470, 483,
        554
    public–private partnerships 537, 538
analysts 117, 304, 463, 467, 482,
    641, 696, 737, 749, 756, 804,
    818, 847
analytical analysis
    A-scores 753–4
    aggressive earnings management
        748–9
    credit rating agencies 262, 317, 453,
        764–6, 787, 804
    debt covenants 747–9, 765
    failure prediction models 749–55
    H-scores 752–3, 763
    overview 738–45
    performance related remuneration
        756–9
    risk reporting 738
    sensitivity analysis 745

analytical analysis (*continued*)
  shareholders, improved information
      for 736–8
  shariah compliant companies 745–7
  unquoted company shares 760–4
  Z-scores 750–2, 763
  see also ratios
annual report and accounts 186, 206,
    696–7, 758
  chairman's report 207, 644
  directors' report 186, 207, 209–10,
      757, 844
  discontinued operations 233–5
  environmental reporting 845–6, 858
  events after reporting period 235–7
  financial data *see* cash flow statement;
      statement of changes in equity;
      statement of comprehensive
      income; statement of financial
      position
  intellectual property 482
  iXBRL filing 787
  mandatory separate disclosures 206
  non-current assets held for sale 232–3
  operating and financial review 208–9
  related party disclosures 237–41
  review of narrative reporting 210
  segment reporting 122, 223–32
annuity method of depreciation 413–15
Argentina 718
Arinso International 305
asset utilisation ratios 706, 709–13,
    741–2
  asset turnover 698, 700, 702, 705
  inventory 711–12, 715, 719, 742
  trade receivables 712–13, 718, 719,
      742
assets 510
  biological 514–17
  contingent 296, 297, 300–1, 303
  definitions 28, 137, 285–6, 471
  events after reporting period 236
  financial *see* financial instruments
  net 44–6
  prescribed format 194–5
  revaluations of non-current 44, 46, 85,
      130, 137, 146, 152, 191, 268–9,
      388, 390, 391, 393, 395, 408,
      417–18, 428–9, 569, 587
  segment 227, 228, 229
  unrealised capital profits 46
associates 720
  acquisition during year 606–8
  definitions 603–4
  equity method 604–6
  held for sale 604
  provisions for unrealised profits 606
  public–private partnerships 535–6
  segment reporting 228
  SMEs: cost method 122
Association of Chartered Certified
      Accountants (ACCA) 765
  award schemes 850–2
  ethical behaviour 173–4, 176, 178–9
AstraZeneca 199, 202, 203, 274, 560
audit committees 749, 814

auditors 4, 103, 106, 114, 119, 132, 133,
    151, 696
  breach of confidentiality 177
  corporate governance 804, 809–14,
      818, 831
  debt covenants 749
  environment 853–4, 858–60
  ethical behaviour 164, 166, 175, 177,
      178
  expectation gap 810–12
  fees 166, 193, 737, 804
  going concern 754–5
  internal 178
  internal controls 807
  inventories 506, 509–10, 511, 512–13,
      514
  public interest 166, 177
  qualified audit report 267
  rules-based approach 149
  scepticism 170, 172, 749, 813
  special purpose entities 304–5, 810
  true and fair 204
  XBRL based statements 787
Australia 152
  accounting profession 112, 114
  cash flow statement 671
  corporate governance 805, 812, 822
  historical cost accounting 84–5
  IFRSs 115, 117
  legal system 109
  XBRL 793
available-for-sale financial assets 191,
    323–5, 327, 537
average basis (inventory valuation)
    198–9
average cost (AVCO) 500
Aviva plc 484, 841–2

BAE Systems 173
Balfour Beatty 317–18, 352, 536–7
bank deposits 323
banks 110–11, 304, 748
  corporate governance 804, 805, 808,
      818, 830–1
  dormant accounts 326
  financial instruments 313–14
  security for loans 264
Barclays 305
Barloworld 702, 709, 865
Bayer Group 396, 398
Bayer Schering Pharma AG 847
Beazley Group plc 826
behavioural entity, economy as 49
benchmarks 197, 868–70
binomial model 361
biological assets 514–17
Black–Scholes model 361
Body Shop 846–7
bonds
  inter-company balances 571
bonus issues 644, 645
bonuses, employee 200, 356, 357,
    358, 697
  impact of changing to IFRSs 117
  taxation 376
BorsodChemNyct 416

BP 172, 275, 394, 745
brand accounting 474–7, 482–4, 560
Brewin Dolphin Holdings plc 477
bribes 173
Brighton plc 324
Brio 262
British Airways 174, 394
British Energy 479
British Gas 394
British Sky Broadcasting plc 425
British Telecommunications plc 41, 42,
    169, 261
Brixton plc 395

Cadbury report 826
Cal Micro 512
Canada 152, 858
  accounting profession 112, 114, 147
  IFRSs 115
  legal system 109
  SME reporting 123
capital
  gearing 283, 289, 707
  maintenance 30–2, 53–4, 62–4, 66,
      68–79, 80, 133, 138, 145, 146,
      258, 263–5, 844
  markets 806–7
  nature of accounting 44–5
  restructuring 258
  share 65
  sources of finance 110
  see also gearing
capital allowances 43, 111, 376
capital commitments 196–7, 644
capital investment appraisal 6–8, 9
cartels, price-fixing 174
cash at hand 323
cash debt coverage 680
cash dividend coverage 681
cash flow accounting 3–17, 32
  characteristics of data 11–12, 15–16
  dividends 16, 42
cash flow statement 186, 454, 668–70
  accrual accounting 32–4
  analysis of 679–84
  consolidated 591–2, 677–9
  critique 684
  direct method 669, 670–1, 676, 684
  disclosures 676–7, 683
  indirect method 670, 671–2, 673–6,
      679, 684
  notes to 676–7
  reconciliation of net cash flows to net
      debt 684
  segment information 677, 683
cash flows
  discontinued operations 234
  free cash flow (FCF) 682–3, 757
  information to predict future 206, 210,
      241, 681–2, 754
  public–private partnerships 535
  see also present values
chairman 814
  report 207, 644
Chartered Institute of Management
      Accountants (CIMA) 176, 392

Chartered Institute of Public Finance and Accountancy (CIPFA) 176
chief executive officer (CEO) 160, 170–1, 807, 814, 827
chief financial officer (CFO) 160, 807
China 805, 806
  Hong Kong 821, 851
  IFRSs 115
Chrysler Corporation 861
CIMA *see* Chartered Institute of Management Accountants
CIPFA *see* Chartered Institute of Public Finance and Accountancy
Citi 474
Citigroup Global Markets 175
civil liability
  safe harbour provisions 210
Coats Viyella plc 498
Coca-Cola 474, 745
coffee 502
Coil SA 417–18
commercial awareness 4
Commerzbank 111
Committee of European Securities Regulators (CESR) 107
commodity contracts 316
companies
  formation expenses 376
  restructuring 258, 261, 294–5, 302, 305
  tax *see* corporation tax
Companies Act 1929 40
Companies Act 1981 109
Companies Act 2006
  creditor protection 264–5
  disclosures 42
  distributable profits 266–7
  environmental and social reporting 839
  investment companies 266–7
  safe harbour 210
  share issue 258
  small companies 122
  treasury shares 275–6
comparability 104, 123, 137, 142, 143, 150, 848
  cash flow statement 684
  fair presentation 203
  government grants 427
  leases 453
  operating and financial review 208
  PPE, effect of accounting policy for 428–30
  principles-based approach 163
  segment reporting 224
  share-based payments and 359
completeness 15, 142
compound instruments 258, 317–18, 364, 391
conceptual framework 125, 131, 133
  ASB *Statement of Principles* 83, 125, 134, 138–49, 844
  comparison: share exchange and cash acquisition 555
  developments 85–6, 149–50
  FASB Concept Statements 133, 134–6, 149
  historical overview 130–3

IASC/IASB *Framework* 28, 32, 86, 115, 125, 133, 137–8, 141, 150, 201, 203, 284–5, 297, 298, 300, 303, 376, 387, 395–6, 410, 427, 443, 453, 462–3, 464–5, 469, 470, 471, 503, 517
  national differences 129–30
  off balance sheet finance 283
  summary 150–2
confidentiality 165, 177
conflicts of interest 802, 804, 805
  see also corporate governance
Connected Reporting Framework 840–2, 843–4
consignment stocks 286–8
consistency 12, 125, 130, 150, 191, 201, 498, 507, 513, 642, 848
consolidated accounts 381, 808
  accounting policies 577
  acquisition during year 588–92
  ASB *Statement of Principles* 148–9
  cash flow statement 591–2, 677–9
  consolidation adjustments 569, 571–2, 573, 586–7, 591, 678
  control 551–2, 555
  definitions 549, 551–2
  dividends/interest out of pre-acquisition reserves 587–8
  exclusion of subsidiary from 550–1
  fair override 205
  fair value 552, 556, 558–60, 632
  foreign operations 624, 627–8, 632
  inter-company balances 571–2
  materiality 551
  negative goodwill 554–5
  no need for 550
  non-controlling interests 555–8, 571, 577, 591
  parent company accounts 578, 587–8
  pension schemes, defined benefit 356
  pooling of interests method 552
  positive goodwill 554
  pre- and post-acquisition profit/loss 568–70
  public–private partnerships 535
  purchase method 552–4
  ratio analysis 720
  reasons to prepare 549–51
  reporting dates 577
  special purpose entities 305
  statement of changes in equity 586
  statement of comprehensive income 555, 556, 560, 583–5, 586–7, 588–90, 625, 628, 631–2, 720
  statement of financial position 554, 556–8, 560, 568–70, 571, 573–7, 625, 627, 628
  unrealised profit on inter-company sales 572–4, 575, 577
construction contracts 523–5
  costs identified 525–6
  definition 524
  public–private partnerships 532–8
  recognition of revenue and costs 523–5, 526–32
  revenue identified 525

contingent assets 296, 297, 300–1, 303
contingent liabilities 144, 197, 296, 297, 298–300, 303, 470
  constructive and/or legal obligation 301
  debt covenants 749
  environmental 845–6
contributions 205
control 141
  definition of 551–2
  internal control systems 509–10, 807
convertible loans 317, 653, 654
convertible preference shares 262, 317–18, 653–4
Cookson Group plc 261–2
copyright 479, 480
corporate failure prediction models 749–55
corporate governance 849–50
  accounting, role of 807–8
  auditors 804, 809–14, 818, 831
  behaviour, effect on corporate 802–3
  Board of Directors 814, 823–4
  capital markets 806–7
  concept of 801–2
  conflicts of interest 802, 804, 805
  definition 802
  economic cycle 803–4
  ethics and 158–9, 803–4
  executive remuneration 814–17
  insider information/trading 512, 719, 802, 804, 813, 818
  jurisdictional differences 805–6
  legislation and codes 820–31
  market forces and 817–18
  non-voting shares 260–1
  risk management 818–20, 830, 831
  UK experience 820, 822–31
corporate social responsibility (CSR) 807, 839, 843, 849–50, 866–8, 871
  ethics and 159, 165
corporation tax 42–3, 111–12, 123, 375–7
  avoidance and evasion 377–9
  from 6 April 1999 380–1
  IFRS and 381–2
  iXBRL filing 787
  until 5 April 1999: advance 381
corruption 173
cost of capital 169, 738
  weighted average 759
cost of sales 187, 198–200, 478, 586–7
cost–benefit analysis 131, 136, 137, 150
  accounting standards and SMEs 122–3
costs 718
  biological assets 515
  emissions trading certificates 478
  inventories 44, 503–6, 507–9
courts 163, 203
Cray Inc 526
credit crunch 119, 748, 755
credit rating agencies 262, 317, 453, 764–6, 787, 804
Credit Suisse First Boston 176
creditors
  protection of 258, 263–5, 269–71, 273, 276

cultures
  norms in different 164
  organisational 171
cumulative preference shares 262
current assets 85, 194–5, 205
  emissions trading certificates 478–9
  non-current assets held for sale 232
  ratio analysis 711–13, 719
  see also inventories; trade receivables
current entry cost or replacement cost
    42, 53–4, 60, 61–3, 64, 65,
    132–3
  ASB approach 146
  critique of 66–7
  IASB Framework 138
current exit cost or net realisable value
    60, 61–3, 64, 65, 66, 132–3
  ASB approach 146
  critique of 67–8
  IASB Framework 138
current liabilities
  prescribed format 194–5
current purchasing power (CPP) 60–5,
    112, 132–3
  critique of 65–6
current ratio 698, 700, 702–3, 705, 706,
    719, 720, 740, 741, 745
  debt covenants 748, 749
current value accounting see inflation
    accounting
customers 139, 165, 170
  segment reporting 226, 228–9

Daimler Benz 111
databases 716, 717, 737, 782
Datastream 716, 737
De La Rue 658
debentures see loan creditors
debt covenants 304, 305, 316, 467,
    747–9, 765
debts see receivables
decommissioning costs 293, 295, 305,
    406
deductive approach 131, 132–3
deferred income 205
deferred tax 384–93, 844
  critique of 393–6
Denmark 849
depreciation 429, 430
  accounting policy 202
  accrual accounting 29–30
  annuity method 413–15
  consolidation adjustments 586–7
  definition 408
  differences: method and estimates 200,
    429
  diminishing balance method 412–13,
    414, 415
  disclosure 111, 131, 193
  fair override 205
  finance leases 446
  government grants 426
  held for sale 233
  impairment 416
  investment properties 205
  leases 415, 446, 448, 455

machine-hour method 413, 415
nil 409, 410
NRV accounting 67
residual value 412
revaluations 408, 411
straight-line method 30, 202, 411,
    412–13, 414, 415–16
sum of the units method 413, 414
taxation 43, 111, 376, 385, 389–90
useful life 408–9, 411–12, 429
deprival value 82, 146, 147
derivatives 305, 321, 322, 325
  embedded 326
Deutsche Bank 111
Diageo 474
diminishing balance method 412–13,
    414, 415
directors 132
  agency costs/principal–agent 8, 169
  business objectives 6
  corporate governance 804, 808,
    814–18, 823–4
  fiduciary duties 267
  going concern issue 47
  mandatory accounting standards 104
  non-executive 749, 824, 825, 826–8
  remuneration 41, 101–2, 261, 304,
    359, 748–9, 756–9, 804, 814–17
  report 186, 207, 209–10, 757, 844
  safe harbour provisions 210
  SMEs: personal guarantees 122
  supervisory board 805
  true and fair 204
disclosures 644, 762–3, 808, 815, 844,
    848
  accounting policies 111, 131, 201, 202,
    203
  additional 203
  brands 475
  cash flow statement 676–7, 683
  consolidated accounts 577
  construction contracts 527, 528–30,
    531–2
  contingent assets 296
  contingent liabilities 296, 300
  controlling relationships 238
  cost/benefit 150
  depreciation 111, 131, 193
  discontinued operations 234–5
  earnings per share 642, 652, 656–8
  employees benefits 238, 347, 356, 361,
    363, 364–7
  events after reporting period 236
  financial instruments 315–20, 330–3,
    335
  Germany 111
  intangible assets 472–4, 475, 482, 484
  inventories 499, 513–14
  investment properties 428
  key managers: compensation 238
  leases 445–6, 449–51, 455
  mandatory separate 206
  materiality 150
  non-current assets held for sale 233, 424
  non-financial liabilities 302–3
  pensions 347, 356, 364–7

personal guarantees 122
principles–based approach 149
property, plant and equipment 424–5
provisions 294–5, 302–3
related party 238–41, 808
research and development 463,
    465–6
segment reporting 224, 227–9, 231–2,
    677
share-based payments 361, 363
small and medium-sized enterprises
    (SMEs) 120, 122
taxation 234, 383
  see also individual statements
discontinued operations 233–5
discounted cash flow (DCF) 50–2, 53,
    420–1, 423
Disney 474
distributable profits/reserves 258, 259,
    265–7
distribution costs 187–8, 587
dividend cover 706, 714
dividend yield 706, 762
dividends 236, 259
  cash flow 16, 42
  consolidated cash flow statement 591
  disclosure 197
  fair value accounting 267
  from pre-acquisition reserves 587–8
  impact of changing to IFRSs 117
  inflation accounting 65, 66, 81
  inter-company 572
  interim 267
  policies 42
  preference 316
  reinvestment plans 261
  scrip 261
  shariah compliant companies 746
  taxation 375, 376–7, 380–1
dot com boom 162
double entry principle 143
Dow Jones Islamic indexes 747
Dresdner Bank 111
DuPont 856–7

earnings per share (EPS) 41, 104, 118,
    152, 713–14
  alternative EPS figures 657, 658–9
  basic 642–3, 644–52
  consolidated accounts 550, 560
  deferred tax 394
  diluted 643, 652–6
  disclosures 642, 652, 656–8
  importance of 641–2
  inventory valuation 498, 514
  limitations as performance measure
    644
  property, plant and equipment 430
  purchase of own shares 274
  remuneration and 816
  rights issues 645, 647–52
  share price 259, 644
  shareholders use of 643–4
  SMEs 121, 122
earnings yield 642, 761
Eastern Europe 112, 806

EBITDA (earnings before interest, tax, depreciation and amortisation) 453, 454, 467, 707, 720–1, 764, 822
Eco-Management and Audit Scheme (EMAS) 853–4
economic income 49–53
economic value added (EVA) 758–9, 763
economists
  income and asset value measurement 47–53, 132
emissions trading 477–9
empirical inductive approach 131–2
employees 170, 804, 805
  bonuses 117, 200, 356, 357, 358, 376, 697
  disclosure of benefits 238, 347, 356, 361, 363, 364–7
  goodwill 484
  information needs/provided to 5, 139, 197
  pensions and other long-service benefits 343–57, 364–7
  principles–based approach 162, 164
  share-based payments 261, 275, 346, 359–64, 382
  short-term benefits 357–8
  social reporting 862–3, 864
  stakeholders 6, 165
  termination benefits 358
EnBW Energie Baden-Württemberg AG 554, 555
Eni 527
Enron 105, 107, 114, 124, 149, 160, 162, 170, 175, 304, 737, 804, 808, 810, 811
entity
  approach 150
  reporting 140–1
environmental auditing 853–4, 858–60
environmental liabilities
  provision for 295, 305, 848
environmental reporting 164–5, 838–9, 857–8, 861, 869–70
  ACCA award schemes 850–2
  accountant's role 844–5
  background 846–7
  Connected Reporting Framework 840–2, 843–4
  corporate social responsibility (CSR) 159, 165, 807, 839, 843, 849–50, 866–8, 871
  economic consequences 856–7
  European Commission 847–8
  evolution of stand-alone reports 848–50
  Global Reporting Initiative (GRI) 843, 870–2
  IFAC Framework 842–4
  international charters and guidelines 852–4
  self-regulation schemes 854–6
  triple bottom line (TBL) 839–40, 843–4, 850, 870–2

equity
  capital 45
  investors see shareholders
equity compensation plans see share-based payments
equity method
  associates 604–6
  joint ventures 609, 610
errors 391, 510, 512, 513–14, 526, 555
estimates 44, 49, 67, 108, 145, 201
  depreciation 200
ethical behaviour 804
  accounting profession: meaning of 159–61
  accounting standard setting process 164–5
  company code of ethics 172–4
  corporate governance 158–9, 803–4
  corporate social responsibility 159, 165
  ICAS research report 168–9, 171
  IFAC Code of Ethics for Professional Accountants 165–8
  impact on financial reports 169–72
  law 158
  maximisation of profits 161
  meaning of 156–61
  norms of society 161
  principles-based approach 162–4
  rules-based approach 162
  Sarbanes–Oxley Act (SOX) 160
  superfairness 158, 163, 179
  training in 178–9
  whistle-blowing 174–8
Europe 172, 806, 851, 853–4, 859
  stewardship reporting 85
European Home Retail 752
European Union 113, 313, 477, 839
  corporate governance 806
  credit rating agencies 766
  Eighth Directive 114
  environmental reporting 847–8, 858
  financial instruments 314
  Fourth Directive 109, 112, 113–14, 848
  historical cost accounting 82
  IFRSs 115, 381
  Parliament 229–30
  segment reporting 225
  Seventh Directive 114, 848
  sources of finance 110
  taxation 379, 385
  XBRL 787
Eurovestech 205
events after reporting period 235–7, 572
Excel 783, 791, 792
exceptional items 42, 194
  size, nature or incidence: require disclosure (IAS 1) 206
eXtensible Business Reporting Language see XBRL
eXtensible Mark-up Language (XML) 784
externalities 807
extraordinary items 42
Eybl International 550

failure prediction models, corporate 749–55
fair value
  accounting 85, 86, 119, 147, 267
  biological assets 515, 516, 517
  deferred tax 390
  emissions trading certificates 478
  finance leases 446, 447
  financial instruments 195, 313–14, 321–2, 323–5, 326–7, 328, 330, 334–5
  foreign operations, consolidation of 628, 632
  goodwill 466, 552–5
  held for sale assets 233, 604
  intangible assets 466, 477, 537–8
  investment properties 428, 444
  leases of land 444
  non-controlling interests 556, 558
  non-current assets held for sale 424
  parent company accounts 578
  pension schemes 349, 352, 366
  property, plant and equipment 406, 417
  public–private partnerships 537–8
  purchase method of consolidating 552, 558–60
  share-based payments 360, 361–3, 364
  see also market value
fairness 164–5, 179, 803, 807
  fair override 204–5
  fair view 202, 203, 206
  superfairness 158, 163, 179
  true and fair 16, 150, 162, 203–4, 205
faithful representation 15, 141, 143, 150, 285
FAME (Financial Analysis Made Easy) 717
fees
  accountants 166–7
  audit 166, 193
fiduciary duties
  directors 267
FIFO (first-in-first-out) 198–9, 202
filing of accounts 787, 792
finance costs 188, 318–20, 323
  finance leases 446–7
finance leases see under leases
Financial Accounting Standards Board (FASB) 108, 129
  accrual accounting 24, 26–7, 32
  Concepts Statements 133, 134–6, 149
  conceptual framework developments 85–6, 149–50, 152
  convergence project 391–2, 469–70, 659
  fair value 86, 147
  IFRSs 118–19
  negative pressures on standard setters 160–1
  objective of financial reporting 85–6, 149
  operating leases 454
  revenue recognition 523
  segment reporting 224, 230
  taxation 391, 392

financial accounting theory 112
  historical overview 130–3
Financial Action Task Force (FATF)
  177–8
financial adaptability 140, 145
financial assets *see* financial instruments
financial capital maintenance 30–2,
  53–4, 62–4, 79, 80, 145
financial crisis 313–15, 322, 327, 820,
  831
  credit crunch 119, 748, 755
financial decision model 5–6
financial instruments 85, 132, 267,
  312–13, 831
  2008 financial crisis 313–15, 322, 327
  amortised cost 313–14, 322, 323,
    324–5, 326, 327–8, 334–5
  available-for-sale financial assets 191,
    323–5, 327, 537
  compound instruments 258, 317–18,
    364, 391
  definitions 315–16, 321–4, 32708
  derecognition of financial assets
    325–6, 336
  developments 333–6
  disclosure and presentation 315–20,
    330–3, 335
  emissions trading certificates 478
  fair value 195, 313–14, 321–2, 323–5,
    326–7, 328, 330, 334–5
  finance costs on liabilities 188, 318–20
  four categories of 321–4, 334
  hedge accounting 313, 329–30, 382,
    625
  impairment of financial assets 335–6
  inter-company balances 571
  investment in subsidiaries 578
  measurement 326–9, 334–6
  offsetting 320
  perpetual debt 318
  public–private partnerships 536–7
  recognition of 325–6, 336
  rules versus principles 313
  scope of standards 315, 321
financial leverage multiplier 698, 700,
  701, 703, 705
financial reporting
  financial statements 134, 150
  fraudulent 510
  history of 40–1
  Internet *see separate entry*
  national differences 109–13, 129–30
  need for mandatory standards 101–3,
    104, 123–5, 129
  non-publicly accountable entities
    119–23
  objectives 22–3, 85–6, 134, 149
  regulatory framework 105–8
  standardise, efforts to 113–19
  tax and 111–12
Financial Reporting Council (FRC)
  16, 104, 105, 151, 204, 812,
  823, 831
Financial Reporting Review Panel
  (FRRP) 106–8, 129, 151
  fair override 205

segment reporting 230
  tangible assets 477
Financial Reporting Standard for
    Smaller Entities (FRSSE) 121–2,
    123
Financial Reporting Standards (FRS)
  106
  1 *Cash Flow Statements* 684
  2 *Accounting for Subsidiary
    Undertakings* 121
  3 *Reporting Financial Performance* 83,
    762–3
  5 *Reporting the Substance of
    Transactions* 122, 304, 536
  6 *Acquisitions and Mergers* 142
  8 *Related Party Disclosures* 122
  10 *Goodwill and Intangible Assets* 122
  15 *Tangible Fixed Assets* 30, 407
  16 *Current Tax* 122, 375, 384
  18 *Accounting Policies* 122
  19 *Deferred Tax* 122, 375, 392–3
  20 *Share-based Payment* 382
  22 *Earnings per Share* 121
financial risks 820
Financial Services Authority 150
financial statements 150
  contents for external users 23
  elements of 134–6, 143
  FASB Concept Statements 134–6
  IAS 1 *Presentation of Financial
    Statements* 131, 186, 187, 191,
    194, 201, 202, 203, 204, 206, 210,
    376
  IASC/IASB *Framework see under*
    International Accounting
    Standards Board
  measurement in 136, 145–7
  objectives 22–3, 86, 137, 138–40
  recognition in 136, 143–5
  see also individual statements
Findel plc 207, 331–3
FINRA (Financial Industry Regulatory
    Authority) 175–6
first-in-first-out (FIFO) 44, 499, 500
Fisher, Irving 49–50, 132
Fisons 762
fixed assets
  PPE *see* property, plant and equipment
  public–private partnerships 536–7
FLS Industries A/S 550
football sector 178, 236, 261
Ford 474
foreign exchange 391, 623–33
  conversion distinguished from
    translation 623
  definition of foreign currency
    transaction 623
  functional currency 624, 625, 627, 632
  monetary and non-monetary items
    624, 625
  presentation currency 624, 627–8, 632
France 114, 117, 314, 462
  bearer shares 110–11
  equity investment 110
  legal system 109
  tax and accounting rules 111

fraud 170–1, 175, 506, 510, 511, 718,
  803, 804, 810, 811
  audit and detection of 812, 813, 831
free cash flow (FCF) 682–3, 757
freehold land 409–10
Friedman, Milton 161
FRSSE (Financial Reporting Standard
    for Smaller Entities) 121–2, 123

G20 313, 314
Gamma Holdings NV 714
gearing 706–9, 707, 740, 754
  brands 475, 476
  corporate governance 829–30
  goodwill 467
  leases 442, 452–3, 454
  off balance sheet finance 283–4, 289,
    304, 305, 442, 452, 719
  preference shares 316–17
  property, plant and equipment 417,
    428–9
  shariah compliant companies 746
GEC/AEI 102–3
general or current purchasing power
  60–6, 112, 132–3
General Electric 394
Germany 40, 113, 114, 462
  banks 110–11
  bearer shares 110–11
  corporate governance 805
  fair override 204
  legal system 109
  sources of finance 110
  tax and accounting rules 111
  XBRL 793
Getronics 262
Geveke NV 758
Gibraltar 379
GKN 261, 550–1
Global Reporting Initiative (GRI) 843,
  870–2
Go-Ahead 426
going concern 16, 30, 46–7, 67, 119, 125,
  131, 164, 201, 510, 696
  events after reporting period 237
  failure prediction 754–5
Goldfields 409–10
goodwill 170, 205, 466–70, 471, 477,
  483–4
  definition 466
  equity depletion and brands 475
  foreign operations 628, 632
  impairment 421–2, 466, 467, 469, 470,
    483, 554
  negative 470, 554–5
  purchase method of consolidating
    552–5, 560
  SMEs 122
governments
  grants 425–6, 517
  income measurement 41–2
  information needs 139
  investments in companies 805
  protectionism 718
  public–private partnerships (PPPs)
    532–8

governments (*continued*)
related party disclosures 240–1
social reporting 866
grants 205
Great Portland Estates plc 395
Greenbury Report 756
gross profit 200–1
groups
accounts *see* consolidated accounts
definition 549
GUS 394

H-scores 752–3, 763
Harris Queensway 510
Hart plc 348
hedge accounting 313, 329–30, 382, 625
held-for-trading investments 321
held-to-maturity investments 322, 323,
324–5, 327
Hicks, John 50, 132
Higgs report (2003) 825
historical cost accounting (HCA) 23–4,
32, 43–4, 54, 84–5, 131, 195
accounting base 201
ASB approach 81, 82, 83, 145–6
CCA statements and 79–80
example 61–5
IASB *Framework* 137, 138, 503
intellectual property 482
modified 44, 46, 84–5, 130, 137, 145,
146, 152
problems of 59–60, 429
historical overview
accounting scandals 102–3, 112–13
financial accounting theory 130–3
Holman AB 515
Hong Kong 821, 851
Hooker Chemical Corporation 845–6
horizontal analysis 741–2, 743–4
hotels 410
HSBC 708
HTML (Hyper Text Mark-up
Language) 783, 784, 791
Hugo Boss 147, 476
human rights 840, 869
hyperinflation 83–4

IBM 474
ICAEW (Institute of Chartered
Accountants in England and
Wales) 103, 142, 267, 392, 395,
482, 669, 738
ethical behaviour 171–2, 176, 177
ICAS (Institute of Chartered Accountants
of Scotland) 149, 168, 171, 737
ICI 408–9, 420
impairment 416, 472, 483, 719
brands 477
emissions trading certificates 478
events after reporting period 236
financial assets 335–6
goodwill 421–2, 466, 467, 469, 470,
483, 554
held for sale assets 233
property, plant and equipment 416,
418–23
public–private partnerships 538

income
gearing 283, 289, 707
as means of control 41–2
as means of prediction 42
see also gearing
income and asset value measurement
accountant's view 43–7, 132
changing price levels 53–4
conceptual framework 136, 137
economist's view 47–53, 132
role and objective 40–3
summary 55
India 115
indirect control 141
inflation 24, 54, 65, 83, 84, 644, 763
inflation accounting 24, 112, 130, 866
ASB approach 81–3, 145–7
borrowings 75–6
critique of CCA statements 79–81
current entry cost or replacement cost
42, 53–4, 60, 61–3, 64, 65, 66–7,
132–3, 138, 146
current exit cost or net realisable value
60, 61–3, 64, 65, 66, 67–8, 85,
132–3, 138, 146
current or general purchasing power
60–6, 112, 132–3
depreciation 412, 428
examples 61–5, 68–79
future developments 84–6
IASC/IASB approach 83–4, 138
non-monetary assets 72–3
profit adjustments 70–2
restating opening position 69–70
value to the business model 82, 83,
146–7
Informa plc 552
information needs 22, 110
conceptual framework 85–6, 132–3,
134, 138–40, 149–50, 151–2
employees 5, 139, 197
environmental reporting 848
internal users 4–8
managers 3, 4–5
shareholders 3–4, 42, 110, 111, 124,
133, 134, 138, 139, 149, 151–2,
164, 206–10, 736–8, 817, 848
users of SME accounts 121, 123
initial public offerings (IPOs) 719
insider information/trading 512, 719,
802, 804, 813, 818
Institute of Chartered Accountants in
England and Wales (ICAEW)
103, 142
ethical behaviour 171–2, 176, 177
Institute of Chartered Accountants of
Scotland (ICAS) 149, 168, 171,
737
Institute of Investment Management and
Research (IIMR) 657
institutional investors 111, 260
insurance
brands 476
claims 300–1, 303
firms 818
intangible assets 170, 471–4, 482–4

brand accounting 474–7, 482–4, 560
emissions trading certificates 478, 479
goodwill *see separate entry*
intellectual property 479–82
public–private partnerships 536–8
R&D *see* research and development
small and medium-sized enterprises
(SMEs) 763
Intel 474
intellectual property 479–82
inter-company balances 571–2
interest
capitalisation 406–7
cover 680, 744
financial instruments: implicit rate of
319–20
present value calculations 49, 53
internal control systems 509–10, 807
internal rate of return (IRR) 7, 756
International Accounting Standards
Board (IASB) 114–15
conceptual framework developments
85–6, 149–50, 152
construction contracts 523–4
convergence project 391–2, 469–70, 659
discontinued operations 233
fair value 86, 147, 327
financial instruments 313, 314, 322,
327, 333, 334, 335, 336
financial statements 23, 85–6
*Framework for the Presentation and
Preparation of Financial
Statements* 28, 32, 86, 115, 125,
133, 137–8, 141, 150, 201, 203,
284–5, 297, 298, 300, 303, 376,
387, 395–6, 410, 427, 443, 453,
462–3, 464–5, 469, 470, 471,
503, 517
government grants 427
inflation accounting 83–4, 138
joint ventures 609
objectives of financial reporting 85–6,
149
operating leases 454
performance statement 382
principles–based approach 162
revenue recognition 523–4
segment reporting 224, 230
SME reporting 123
taxation 391–2, 395–6
United States: adoption of IFRSs
118–19
XBRL and 786
International Accounting Standards
Committee (IASC) 112, 114, 151,
152, 312, 463, 669
accrual accounting 24, 32
objective of financial statements 22–3
International Accounting Standards
(IAS) 115, 116
1 *Presentation of Financial Statements*
131, 186, 187, 191, 194, 201, 202,
203, 204, 206, 210, 376
2 *Inventories* 131, 195, 406, 427, 464,
497–8, 499–509, 511, 513–14,
517

International Accounting Standards (IAS) *(continued)*
7 *Cash Flow Statements* 32–4, 669–79, 680, 683–5
8 *Accounting Policies, Changes in Accounting Estimates and Errors* 202, 203, 382, 383, 391
10 *Events after the Reporting Period* 235–7, 283, 375, 572
11 *Construction Contracts* 118, 523, 524–32, 538
12 *Income Taxes* 118, 234, 375, 382–92, 393, 395, 426
14 *Segment Reporting* 118, 224, 225, 227, 229, 230
15 *Information Reflecting the Effects of Changing Prices* 83
16 *Property, Plant and Equipment* 29–30, 146, 195, 385, 391, 405, 406, 407, 408, 410, 411, 412, 415, 416, 417, 427, 430, 517, 569
17 *Leases* 133, 284, 427, 441, 442–56
18 *Revenue* 25, 26, 328, 523, 538
19 *Employee Benefits* 238, 343, 344, 346, 347–58, 359
20 *Accounting for Government Grants and Disclosure of Government Assistance* 405, 425–7, 517
21 *The Effects of Changes in Foreign Exchange Rates* 391, 623–33
22 *Business Combinations* 467
23 *Borrowing Costs* 118, 405, 406–7
24 *Related Party Disclosures* 237–41
26 *Accounting and Reporting by Retirement Benefit Plans* 364–7
27 *Consolidated and Separate Financial Statements* 315, 549–51, 572, 577, 578
28 *Investments in Associates* 118, 315, 536, 603–4, 610
29 *Financial Reporting in Hyperinflationary Economies* 83–4
30 *Disclosures in the Financial Statements of Banks* 330
31 *Interests in Joint Ventures* 315, 608–10
32 *Financial Instruments: Presentation* 297, 298, 312, 313, 315–20, 330, 333, 571
33 *Earnings per Share* 641, 642–3, 644–58, 659
35 *Discontinuing Operations* 424
36 *Impairment of Assets* 233, 405, 416, 418–23, 472, 554
37 *Provisions, Contingent Liabilities and Contingent Assets* 195, 283, 289–304, 344, 358, 406, 560
38 *Intangible Assets* 300, 461–2, 463–6, 469, 471–4, 476, 477, 538
39 *Financial Instruments: Recognition and Measurement* 195, 267, 297, 312, 313–14, 315, 316, 320–30, 331, 333, 334, 335–6, 382, 478, 537, 578, 625
40 *Investment Property* 405, 427–30, 444

41 *Agriculture* 427, 515–17
true and fair 204
International Auditing and Assurance Standards Board (IAASB) 812
International Chamber of Commerce (ICC) 855–6
International Federation of Accountants (IFAC)
Code of Ethics for Professional Accountants 165–8
Sustainability Framework 842–4
International Financial Reporting Interpretations Committee (IFRIC)
12 *Service Concession Arrangements* 537–8
14 *Limit on a Defined Benefit Asset* 349
International Financial Reporting Standards (IFRS) 115–17, 267
2 *Share-based Payments* 315, 343, 346, 359–64, 382
3 *Business Combinations* 85, 390–1, 466, 467, 469–70, 477, 482–4, 551, 555–60
5 *Non-current Assets held for Sale and Discontinued Operations* 232–5, 405, 424–5, 550, 604
6 *Exploration for and Evaluation of Mineral Resources* 410
7 *Financial Instruments Disclosures* 330–3
8 *Operating Segments* 118, 224–32, 551, 677
9 *Financial Instruments* 333, 334–5
additional disclosures 203
advantages and disadvantages 119
corporate social responsibility 165
Framework and 137
impact of changing to 117, 305–6, 316–17, 352, 359, 381–2, 394–5
principles–based approach 162
small and medium-sized enterprises (SMEs) 121, 122–3
International Forum on Accountancy Development (IFAD) 130
International Organization for Standardization (ISO) 856
International Valuation Standards Council 476
Internet 763, 782–4
Excel 783, 791, 792
eXtensible Business Reporting Language *see* XBRL
HTML (Hyper Text Mark-up Language) 783, 784, 791
inventories 118, 718
agricultural activity 514–17
audit of year-end count 510, 512–13
consignment 286–8
control 509–10
cost 44, 503–6, 507–9
cut-off procedures 509, 510
definition 497
disclosure 499, 513–14

errors, impact on profits of 513–14
net realisable value 44, 137, 195, 200, 236, 506–7, 511, 513
obsolete 511–12, 749
SMEs 122
subjectivity and creative accounting 499, 510–12
turnover ratio 711–12, 715, 719, 742
unrealised profit on inter-company sales 572–4, 575, 577
valuation 44, 131, 195, 198–200, 236, 497–509, 511–12
work-in-progress 507–9
investment companies
distributable profits 266–7
investment firms 164, 818
investment properties 205, 427–8
investment ratios 706, 713–14
dividend cover 706, 714
dividend yield 706
EPS *see* earnings per share
operating return on equity 698, 700, 701, 703, 705
price/earnings (PE) ratio 41, 259, 641–2, 714, 760
investments
available-for-sale 191
short-term 145
Ireland 109, 114, 379
Islam *see* Muslim countries
Islamic societies 157
Italy 806
ITOCHU Corporation 200–1
iXBRL (inline XBRL) 787, 791–2

James Hardie Group 170
Japan 114, 462
corporate governance 806
IFRSs 115
legal system 109
non-voting shares 261
sources of finance 110
Jarvis 749
JD Wetherspoon 703–6
Jenoptik AG 147
Johnson Matthey 101–2, 526–7
joint ventures 608–10
segment reporting 228
journal adjustments 511

key performance indicators (KPIs) 208–9, 210
Kier Group 710
Kingfisher 484, 866–7
knowledge management 480–1
KPMG 379
Kuoni Travel Holding AG 294

land and buildings 44, 46, 429
agricultural land 517
freehold land 409–10
leases 444, 451–2
see also property, plant and equipment
language 113
last-in-first-out (LIFO) 44, 499, 501–2, 503

leases 130, 427, 441–4
  definitions 441, 442–3
  depreciation 415, 446, 448, 455
  ethical behaviour 161
  finance 130, 284, 442–3, 444, 445,
    446–52, 455
  of land and buildings 444, 451–2
  lessors 442, 455
  new approach 453–4
  off balance sheet finance 441, 442,
    452–3
  operating 284, 442–3, 444, 445–6,
    451–2, 455
  substance over form 130, 133, 284,
    443, 444
legal claims 292, 297, 300
legal profession 159, 444, 804
legal and regulatory risks 819–20
legal systems, national 109
Lehman Brothers 808, 810
Lexmark 512
liabilities 40
  contingent 144, 197, 296, 297,
    298–300, 301, 470, 749, 845–6
  definitions 28, 285–6, 298, 300, 470
  events after reporting period 236
  financial see financial instruments
  hidden 170
  non-financial 297–304
  prescribed format 194–5
  segment 227, 228, 229
  trade creditors see separate entry
limited liability companies 264
Linde AG 551
liquidity 305, 683
  problems 262
liquidity ratios 698, 706, 709, 720
  current ratio 698, 700, 702–3, 705,
    706, 719, 720, 740, 741, 745, 748,
    749
loan creditors 257
  convertible loans 317, 326
  debt exchanged for shares 262
  information needs 138, 151–2
  leases 444
  principles–based approach 162
  protection of 258, 263–5, 269–71, 273,
    276
  reconstruction: debenture holders
    271–3
  see also credit rating agencies
long-term contracts 44, 46
  see also construction contracts
  SMEs 122
losses
  unrealised 46

machine-hour method of depreciation
    413, 415
macroeconomics 41–2, 49
maintainable earnings/profits 42, 162,
    206, 467, 643–4, 760–1
maintenance costs 293
Majestic Metals Inc 861
Malaysia 821, 851
  IFRSs 115

MAN 405
management 697, 762, 817–18
  accounting system 117
  buy-outs 200
  by objectives 172–3
  choice of accounting policies and EPS
    644
  decisions and brands 476
  inflation accounting 65, 80
  performance 81
  remuneration 101–2, 200, 210, 238,
    748–9, 756–9, 804, 814–17
  reporting to 3, 4–5
Manchester United plc 236, 296
market forces and corporate governance
    817–18
market position and share 208
market value 147, 195, 205
  financial assets 85
  IASB Framework 137
  see also fair value
Marks & Spencer 394, 757, 867–8,
    869–70
matching principle 16, 27, 29, 44, 131,
    143–4, 404, 408, 425, 468, 499,
    509
materiality 136, 137, 142, 150, 201, 405,
    551
  inter-company balances 572
measurability 136
measurement 55, 136, 145–7, 195, 503,
    848
  accountant's view 43–7, 132
  biological assets 515–17
  changing price levels 53–4
  conceptual framework 136, 137
  contingent assets 300
  contingent liabilities 299, 300, 301
  economist's view 47–53, 132
  employee benefits 349–52, 357, 358,
    360, 361–3, 364
  financial instruments 326–9, 334–6
  non-current assets held for sale 424
  non-financial liabilities 299, 300, 301,
    303–4
  provisions 291–3
  role and objective 40–3
  share-based payments 360, 361–3,
    364
  see also historical cost accounting;
    inflation accounting; net
    realisable value; present values;
    replacement cost
mergers
  suppliers 170
Merrill Lynch 175
Mexico 114
Microsoft 261, 474
Middle East 805
mineral resources 409–10, 415, 427
Miniscribe Corporation 510
Molins plc 467, 470
money laundering 177–8
Moody's Investor Services 764, 765
Morgan Crucible 762
MSCI Islamic indices 746–7

multinational companies
  ethical behaviour 164, 173
Muslim countries
  corporate governance 805
  shariah compliant companies 745–7
Myners report 825

national differences
  ethics and principles–based approach
    164
  financial reporting 109–13, 129–30
National Grid plc 577
Nemetschek AC 625
Nestlé Group 202, 345–6, 450–1,
    855–6
net assets and borrowing powers 475
net present value (NPV) 7, 9, 319–20
net realisable value (NRV)
  current value accounting 60, 61–3, 64,
    65, 66, 67–8, 85, 132–3, 138, 146
  emissions trading certificates 478
  IASB Framework 137, 138
  inventories 44, 137, 195, 200, 236,
    506–7, 511, 513
Netherlands 117, 849
  accounting profession 112, 114
  inflation accounting 112, 130
  tax and accounting rules 111
  true and fair 204
  XBRL 793
neutrality 15, 142, 164–5
  operating and financial review 208
New Zealand 752
  IFRSs 115
  legal system 109
  XBRL 793
Nike 172
Nissan 551
Nokia 345, 474
non-cumulative preference shares 262
non-current assets 404–5, 718
  capitalisation of own work 187
  cash flow concept 14–15
  consolidation adjustments 586–7
  cost of PPE 406–7, 416
  definition of PPE 405
  depreciation of PPE 408–16
  disclosure of PPE 424–5
  fair override 205
  government grants 425–7
  held for sale 232–3, 405, 424, 550, 604
  impairment 416, 418–23
  interpretation of accounts 428–30
  investment properties 205, 427–8
  prescribed format 194–5
  ratio analysis 709–10, 719
  revaluation of 44, 46, 85, 130, 137,
    146, 152, 191, 268–9, 388, 390,
    391, 393, 395, 408, 417–18, 569,
    587
non-distributable reserves 258, 259, 263,
    274
non-executive directors (NEDs) 749,
    824, 825, 826–8
non-financial liabilities 297–304

normalised earnings 162, 206
see also maintainable earnings
North America 851
see also individual countries
Norwalk Agreement 118
Norway 113, 849

objectives
  financial reporting 22–3, 85–6, 134, 149
  financial statements 22–3, 86, 137, 138–40
  income measurement 40–3
objectivity 11, 23–4, 43, 44, 46
  CPP model 65
  IFAC *Code of Ethics for Professional Accountants* 165, 167, 168
Occidental 845–6
OECD (Organisation for Economic Cooperation and Development) 481, 806, 831
off balance sheet finance 210, 283, 737, 808
  contingent assets 296, 297, 300–1, 303
  contingent liabilities 144, 197, 296, 297, 298–300, 301, 303, 470, 749, 845–6
  gearing 283–4, 289, 304, 305, 442, 452, 719
  IFRS, impact of converting to 305–6
  leases 441, 442, 452–3
  non-financial liabilities 297–303
  provisions *see separate entry*
  ratio analysis 283–4, 304, 305, 719
  special purpose entities (SPEs) 304–5, 808, 810, 831
  substance over form 130, 133, 284–9, 443, 444
oil 502–3
  pipeline 609
onerous contracts 294, 301
OneSource 716, 717
operating capital maintenance 53, 54, 64, 66, 68–79, 80, 133
operating and financial review 208–9
operating leases *see under* leases
operating margin ratio 698, 700, 702, 705
operating return on equity 698, 700, 701, 703, 705
operational risks 819
opportunity costs 8, 53, 61, 67
options
  pricing models 361, 363
  put 326, 659
  share 197, 261, 275, 346, 359, 361–3, 364, 653, 659, 816, 817
ordinary shares 258, 259–61, 272–3, 274
organic growth 710
Orkla Group 759

Palfinger AG 508
parent company
  consolidated accounts *see separate entry*
  statement of comprehensive income 587
  statement of financial position 578, 587–8

Parmalat 114, 810, 827
participating preference shares 258, 262
partnerships 375
PDF files 782–3, 791, 792
Pearson 682–3, 846
pension schemes 343–4
  deferred tax 390
  defined benefit 191, 345–6, 347–56, 365–7
  defined contribution 344–5, 346–7, 365, 366–7
  disclosure 347, 356, 364–7
  ex gratia 344
  example: defined benefit 353–5
  impact of IFRS 352
  multi-employer plans: defined benefit 355–6
Pergamon Press 103
perpetual debt 318
plant *see* property, plant and equipment
power base, world 164
preference/preferred shares 258, 259, 262, 271, 274, 316–18
  inter-company balances 571
prepayments 189–90
present values (PV) 45, 47–9, 50, 53, 138, 195
  finance leases 446, 447, 449
  impairment of assets 416
  intangible assets 473
  provisions 195, 292–3, 301
presentation of financial information 147–8
price level changes 53–4, 59
  inflation accounting *see separate entry*
  problems of historical cost accounting 59–60
price-fixing cartels 174
price/earnings (PE) ratio 41, 259, 641–2, 714, 760
principal–agent issue 8, 159
principles-based approach 149, 162–4, 313
private companies 259, 265, 266
  reduction in capital 267–8, 276
Private Finance Initiative (PFI) 532, 533–5
profit-sharing plans
  employees 356, 357, 358
profitability ratios 706, 714, 754
  operating margin ratio 698, 700, 702, 705
profits 44, 698
  capital 46, 259
  distributable 258, 259, 265–7
  ethical behaviour 161, 164–5
  maintainable 42
  maximisation of 161
  public–private partnerships 535
  realised 266, 267
  recognition in financial statements 145
  segment 227, 230
  unrealised 46, 267
  unrealised on inter-company sales 572–4, 575, 577
  unrealised on inter-company sales: associates 606

property, plant and equipment (PPE) 404–5
  agricultural land 517
  cost 406–7, 416
  definition 405
  depreciation 408–16
  disclosure 424–5
  government grants 425–7
  impairment 416, 418–23
  interpretation of accounts 428–30
  investment properties 205, 427–8
  leases of land and buildings 444, 451–2
  non-current assets held for sale 232–3, 405, 424
  revaluations 44, 46, 85, 130, 137, 146, 152, 191, 268–9, 388, 390, 391, 393, 395, 408, 417–18, 428–9, 569, 587
protectionism 718
provisions 406
  constructive and legal obligations 301, 303, 344
  definition 289, 303
  disclosures 294–5, 302–3
  IAS 37 195, 283, 289–95
  ED IAS 37 *Non-financial liabilities* 297, 298, 300–3
  measurement of 195, 291–3, 301, 303–4
  onerous contracts 294, 301
  present value 195, 292–3, 301
  prudence 201
  recognition of 290–1
  restructurings 294–5, 302, 305, 560
  scenarios 293
  use of 295
prudence 15, 29, 46, 110, 125, 142, 143, 144–5, 201
  contingent assets 300
  development costs 463
  government grants 426
  provisions 289, 292
  taxation 376
  termination payments 358
Prudential plc 261
Psion 261
public: information needs 139
public companies 259, 265, 266
  borrowing powers and brands 475
  fraudulent reporting 510
  reduction in capital 267, 276
public goods 132, 133
public interest 165, 166, 176, 177
public–private partnerships (PPPs) 532–8
Punch Taverns plc 410
purchase of own shares 267, 274–6
  earnings per share 646–7
purchasing power of money 54

quick ratio 709

ratios 696–8, 707
  asset turnover 698, 700, 702, 705
  cash debt coverage 680
  cash dividend coverage 681

ratios (*continued*)
  comparison with previous year 715
  consolidated accounts 720
  cost classification and 200–1
  current 305, 498, 514, 698, 700, 702–3, 705, 706, 719, 720, 740, 741, 745, 748, 749
  EBITDA 720–1
  financial instruments 316–17
  financial leverage multiplier 698, 700, 701, 703, 705
  free cash flow 683
  gearing *see separate entry*
  inter-firm comparisons and industry averages 715–17, 719–20
  inventory valuation 498, 514
  investment *see separate entry*
  key 698–706
  limitations of 718–20
  liquidity *see separate entry*
  non-financial liabilities 304
  off balance sheet finance 283–4, 289, 304, 305, 442, 452–3, 719
  operating margin ratio 698, 700, 702, 705
  operating return on equity 698, 700, 701, 703, 705
  PPE, effect of accounting policy for 428–30
  production efficiency 200–1
  profitability 698, 700, 702, 705, 706, 714, 754
  pyramid of 699, 705
  return on capital employed (ROCE) 53, 145, 208, 429–30, 453, 514, 550, 698, 700–2, 703, 705, 707, 719
  revaluations and 428–9
  subsidiary 706–7
  turnover *see separate entry*
  use of *see* analytical analysis
receivables 323, 327, 479, 510
  trade 43, 288–9, 323, 712–13, 718, 719, 742, 749
recognition 848
  ASB *Statement of Principles* 143–5
  biological assets 515
  construction contracts 523–5, 526–32
  criteria 136
  financial instruments 325–6, 336
  IASB *Framework* 137
  intangible assets 466, 471
  provisions 290–1
  revenue 25–6, 523–4
  share-based payments 359, 360
reconstructions
  write off of lost capital 267, 268–73
redeemable preference shares 262, 274, 322
redundancy payments 358, 470
reimbursements
  insurance claims 300–1, 303
related party disclosures 237–41, 808
relevance 15, 121, 123, 136, 137
  ASB *Statement of Principles* 141, 142, 143, 146, 147, 150

fair presentation 203
  principles-based approach 163
reliability 15–16, 119, 123, 136, 152
  ASB *Statement of Principles* 141–2, 143, 144–5, 146, 147, 150
  fair presentation 203
  IASB *Framework* 137, 284–5
  principles-based approach 163
  prudence 201
religious ethics 157, 164
remuneration
  directors 41, 101–2, 261, 304, 359, 748–9, 756–9, 804, 814–17
  disclosures 238
  inventory valuation 200
  performance related 756–9, 816–17
replacement cost (RC) 42, 53–4, 60, 61–3, 64, 65, 66–7, 82, 132–3
  inventories 502–3
reporting entity 140–1
research and development (R&D) 118, 719, 763
  deferred tax 390
  definitions 461–2
  development costs 461, 462, 463–6
  research 305, 461, 462–3
reserves
  distributable 258, 259, 265–7, 844
  non-distributable 258, 259, 263, 274
  retained earnings 362, 418
  revaluation 258, 428–9
  share-based payments 362
restructuring 258, 261
  provision for 294–5, 302, 305, 560
retail method 501
return of capital 145
return on capital employed (ROCE) 53, 145, 208, 698, 700–2, 703, 705, 707, 719
Reuters 394
revaluations
  assets 44, 46, 85, 130, 137, 146, 152, 191, 268–9, 388, 390, 391, 393, 395, 408, 417–18, 428–9, 569, 587
  depreciation 408, 411
  events after reporting period 236
  impairment loss 421
  intangible assets 472
  ratio analysis 710
  ratios and 428–9
  reserves 258
  statement of total recognised gains and losses 83
  taxation 388, 390, 393, 395
revenue 510
  accrued 323
  inflating total 26–7
  overstatement of 510
  recognition 25–6, 523–4
rights issue 261–2, 645
Rio Tinto 609
risk 683
  analysis: Revenue Authorities 791
  corporate failure prediction models 749–55

corporate governance 803, 808, 818–20, 830, 831
credit rating agencies 262, 317, 453, 764–6, 787
reporting 738
Rite Aid Corporation 511
Roche Group 396–7
Roche Holdings 420–1, 745
Rohan plc 317
Rolls Royce 274, 313, 465
Royal Mint 701
rules-based approach 149, 162, 313
Russia 806

SABMiller 473–4
safe harbour provisions 210
Sainsbury 501
sale and repurchase agreements 288
sales
  incentives 26–7
  inter-company balances 572
  unrealised profit on inter-company 572–4, 575, 577
Sanitec International SA 572
Sarbanes–Oxley Act (SOX) 160, 807, 820
scandals, accounting 102–3, 112–13, 123–4
  deficient corporate climate 173
  Enron 105, 107, 114, 124, 149, 160, 162, 170, 175, 304, 737, 804, 808, 810, 811
  Parmalat 114, 810, 827
Scandinavia 112
Scottish Power 295, 846
Sea Containers Ltd 147
Securities and Exchange Commission (SEC) 108, 113, 118, 119, 129, 142, 510
  credit rating agencies 766
  environmental reporting 847
  negative pressures on standard setters 160–1
  XBRL based statements 786–7, 791–2, 795
segment reporting 122, 223–7
  cash flow statement 677, 683
  consolidated accounts 551
  disclosures 224, 227–9, 231–2, 677, 683
  impact of IFRS 8 229–30
self-constructed assets 406
sensitivity analysis 745
Sepracor 714
Severn Trent 394
share capital 65
  minimum 265
  reduction in 258, 267–76
  writing off lost capital 267, 268–73
share-based payments 197, 261, 275, 346, 359–64
  corporation tax 382
shareholders 162, 838–9, 850
  agency costs 8, 159
  audit client 166
  corporate governance 801–2, 804, 805, 817, 818, 825, 828–31, 850
  CPP model 65, 66

shareholders (*continued*)
earnings per share, use of 643–4
ethics and principles–based approach
163, 164
expectation gap 124
Fisher/Hirshleifer separation theory 6
going concern issue 47
inflation accounting 65, 66, 80
information needs 3–4, 42, 110, 111, 124,
133, 134, 138, 139, 149, 151–2,
164, 206–10, 736–8, 817, 848
leases 444
limited liability 264
public–private partnerships 535
shareholder value (SV) 756, 816
shareholders' funds 45, 65, 475
stewardship *see separate entry*
taxation 375, 376–7, 380–1
total shareholder return (TSR) 756–7,
763
voting 260–1
shares 257–8
bearer 110–11
bonus issues 644, 645
compound instruments 258, 317–18
convertible preference 262, 317–18
France 110–11
Germany 110–11
issue of 236, 258–9, 261–3
issued after reporting date 236
options 197, 261, 275, 346, 359, 361–3,
364, 653, 659, 816, 817
ordinary 258, 259–61, 272–3, 274
participating preference 258, 262
preference/preferred 258, 259, 262,
271, 274, 316–18, 571
premium 259, 263
price 26, 41, 104, 119, 169, 175, 259,
304, 512, 644, 749, 762
purchase of own 267, 274–6, 646–7
redeemable preference 262, 274, 322
rights issues 261–2, 645, 647–50
share split 645, 646–7
treasury 257, 274, 275
United Kingdom 110, 258–9
unquoted companies: valuation of
760–4
warrants 653
shariah compliant companies 745–7
Shell 632
silver 503
Singapore 463, 851
corporate governance 820, 821–3
IFRSs 115
purchase of own shares 276
XBRL 792
Sirius XM 262
Sketchley plc 123–4
Slough Estates plc 395
small and medium–sized enterprises
(SMEs) 15, 763–4
definition 120, 122
disclosures 120, 122
environmental reporting 852
failure prediction models 752
FRSSE 121–2

IFRS for 122–3
national standards 120–2
objectives of small firms 14
reconstruction 271
role in UK economy 119–20
segment reporting 122, 230
unquoted companies: share valuation
760–4
Smith, Adam 161
Smith report (2003) 825
social reporting 164–5, 838–9, 861–2
accountability 862
background 863–6
comparative data 868–70
comprehensive coverage 862–3
corporate social responsibility (CSR)
159, 165, 807, 839, 843, 849–50,
866–8, 871
definition of social accounting 862
Global Reporting Initiative (GRI) 843,
870–2
triple bottom line (TBL) 839–40,
843–4, 850, 870–2
Sony 765
SORP (Statements of Recommended
Practice) 106
South Africa 851
South East Asia 805
Spain 113, 177, 379, 806
special purpose entities (SPEs) 304–5,
808, 810, 831
Sri Lanka 851
SSL International plc 262, 427
Stagecoach plc 148
stakeholders 6, 133, 147, 257
audit client 166
corporate governance 801–2, 804, 850
environmental and social reporting
838–9, 843, 844, 847, 848, 850,
861–2
fairness to all 165
operating and financial review 208
principles based approach 162
reconstruction 272
Standard & Poor 453, 764
Standard Chartered 483
standard cost 44, 501
start-ups 359
costs 305
statement of cash flows *see* cash flow
statements
statement of changes in equity (SOCE)
186, 191, 197–8
consolidated 586
corporation tax 382
statement of comprehensive income 40,
41, 108, 186, 669, 698
accrual accounting 27, 28, 30, 31
administrative expenses 188
associates 604, 606, 607–8, 720
available-for-sale financial assets 191,
323–5
biological assets 515
consolidated 555, 556, 560, 583–5,
586–7, 588–90, 625, 628, 631–2,
720

construction contracts 526, 528,
529–30, 531
cost of sales 187, 198–200
decision-useful 210
discontinued operations 234–5
distribution costs 187–8
finance costs 188, 318–20, 323, 325,
447, 448–9
financial instruments 318–20, 323–5,
325, 329, 330–1, 334, 335
foreign operations 625, 628, 631–2
Format 2 187, 192–3
fundamental accounting principles 201
goodwill 467, 468, 470
government grants 425–6
historical cost convention 24
identical transactions and formats
198–201
impairment 421, 422
inflation accounting 62–4, 70–2, 77, 80
inventories 512
IRFS, impact of converting to 117
joint ventures 608, 609
leases 443, 445, 446, 447, 448–9, 452,
454
note to 193–4
other comprehensive income 191–2,
325, 329, 334, 335, 418, 587
other operating income or expense 188
parent company 587
past–defined period of time 44
pensions 191, 347–8, 349, 352, 355
preference dividends 316
preparation of income statements
188–92
prescribed formats 187–94
property, plant and equipment 405
public–private partnerships 535–8
revaluations 191, 418
share-based payments 359, 361–3
taxation 234, 382, 383, 384, 391
year end adjustments 189–90
statement of financial position 40–1, 108,
186, 698, 808
accrual accounting 28–9, 30, 31
asset valuation 195
assets, recognition of 286
associates 604–5
biological assets 516
cash flow concept 12–15
conceptual framework 140, 145
consolidated 554, 556–8, 560, 568–70,
571, 573–7, 625, 627, 628
construction contracts 527, 529, 530,
532
emissions trading certificates 477–9
equity capital 258
explanatory notes 196–7
financial instruments 319, 320, 324–5,
330–1
foreign operations consolidated 625,
627, 628
fundamental accounting principles
201
goodwill 467, 469, 470
impairment 423

statement of financial position (*continued*)
  inflation accounting 61, 62–3, 66, 68–70, 72–6, 77–9
  intangible assets 467, 469, 470, 475, 477
  inventories 499, 512, 513
  IRFS, impact of converting to 117, 305–6
  joint ventures 608, 609
  leases 448, 449–50, 452, 454
  liabilities, recognition of 286
  non-current assets held for sale 232–3
  parent company 578, 587–8
  pensions 347–52, 355
  prescribed formats 194–7
  present values 53
  presentation 148
  property, plant and equipment 232–3, 405, 429
  public–private partnerships 535–8
  recognition of assets and liabilities 286
  share-based payments 362
  taxation 383, 387, 395
  unconsumed cost of assets 44–6
statement of total recognised gains and losses 83
Statements of Financial Accounting Standards (SFAS)(US)
  95 *Statement of Cash Flows* 669
  109 *Accounting for Income Taxes* 388
  128 *Earnings per Share* 659
  131 *Disclosures about Segments of an Enterprise and Related Information* 224, 229–30
  141R *Business Combinations* 118
Statements of Recommended Practice (SORP) 106
Statements of Standard Accounting Practice (SSAP) 103, 106
  5 *Accounting for Value Added Tax* 396–9
  9 *Stocks and Long-Term Contracts* 122
  22 *Accounting for Goodwill* 467
  25 *Segmental Reporting* 224
stewardship 12–13, 16, 22, 24, 41, 85–6, 123, 134, 149, 150, 186, 210
  ASB *Statement of Principles* 138, 143
  intangible assets 477
  maintainable profit 42
stock *see* inventories
straight-line method
  depreciation 30, 202, 411, 412–13, 414, 415–16
  goodwill amortisation 468
  leases 415, 447, 455
strategic risks 818–19
Structural Dynamics Research Corporation 811–12
subjectivity 25–7, 44, 49, 53, 54
  discontinued operation 233
  fair value accounting 119
  inflation accounting 67
  inventories 499, 510–12
  principles–based approach 163
  progress, concept of 164
  segment reporting 224, 229

subprime mortgages 808
substance over form 16, 110, 125, 133, 152, 844
  accounting for 285–6
  deferred tax 396
  examples 286–9
  financial instruments 316, 318
  IASB *Framework* 284–5, 396
  leases 130, 133, 284, 443, 444
sum of the digits method
  depreciation 413, 414
  finance leases 447, 448
superfairness 158, 163, 179
sustainability 838–9
  accountant's role 844–5
  Connected Reporting Framework 840–2, 843–4
  environmental reporting *see separate entry*
  Global Reporting Initiative (GRI) 843, 870–2
  IFAC Framework 842–4
  social reporting *see separate entry*
  triple bottom line (TBL) 839–40, 843–4, 850, 870–2
sustainable earnings 162, 206
Sweden 849, 850
synergies 484
Syskoplan 710

Taffler's Z-score 751–2
tangible assets 480, 510, 710
  PPE *see* property, plant and equipment
  public–private partnerships 536–7
taxation 426
  accounting for current 382–4
  avoidance and evasion 377–80
  corporation tax 42–3, 111–12, 123, 375–82
  deferred 384–96, 844
  discontinued operations 234
  IFRS and 381–2
  income measurement 42–3
  iXBRL filing 787, 792
  leases 441
  purchase of own shares 274
  reporting systems and 111–12, 123, 375–6
  share-based payments 359
  stamp duty 261
  value added tax (VAT) 396–9, 787
  XBRL based filing 787, 792, 793, 795
technical expertise 4
Technotrans 294
termination benefits 358
terrorist financing 177–8
Tesco 702, 719
ThyssenKrupp 758
TI Group 394
timeliness 150
T.J. Hughes 510
total shareholder return (TSR) 756–7, 763
total shareholders' funds 258–62
trade creditors/suppliers 257
  ethics 165, 170

information needs 139
  protection of 258, 263–5, 269–71, 273, 276
  turnover ratio 713, 742
trade receivables 323, 749
  doubtful debts 43
  factoring 288–9, 719
  turnover ratio 712–13, 718, 719, 742
trademarks 473, 479
transparency 314, 482, 737, 738, 765, 815, 825
  non-financial liabilities 304
  principles–based approach 149
  special purpose entities (SPEs) 304–5
Treadway Commission: COSO 510
treasury shares 257, 274, 275
trial balance 188–90
triple bottom line (TBL) 839–40, 843–4
true and fair 16, 150, 162, 203–4, 205, 498, 510, 813, 831
  off balance sheet finance 284, 442
Turkiye Petrol Rafinerileri 84
turnover 42
turnover ratios 706, 709–13, 741–2
  asset turnover 698, 700, 702, 705
  inventory 711–12, 715, 719
  trade receivables 712–13, 718, 719
Tyco 810, 811

UITF (Urgent Issues Task Force) 121, 122
uncertainty 144, 755
  contingent assets 296, 300
  contingent liabilities 296
  proposed revenue recognition approach 523
  provisions 289, 292, 298
understandability 142, 150, 163
  fair presentation 203
  operating and financial review 208
Unilever 233, 239–40, 757
unincorporated businesses 264
Uniq Group 627–8
United Kingdom 40, 104, 114, 117, 119, 462, 480
  Accounting and Actuarial Disciplinary Board 176
  banks: dormant accounts 326
  cash flow statement 671, 672, 680, 684
  corporate governance 805, 806, 812, 820, 822–31
  corrupt practices 173
  environmental and social reporting 857, 858, 863–6, 868–70
  equity market 110
  ethical behaviour 164, 173, 176, 178
  fair value accounting 119
  financial instruments 312
  goodwill 467, 470, 475, 482–3
  historical cost accounting 82, 84–5, 130, 145, 151–2
  institutional investors 111
  interest costs capitalised 407
  inventories 503
  iXBRL filing 787, 792
  joint ventures 610

United Kingdom (*continued*)
  legal system 109
  mandatory standards 101–3, 113
  minimum share capital 265
  money laundering 177
  off balance sheet finance 304
  pensions 349
  Private Finance Initiative (PFI) 532,
    533–5
  reduction in capital 267–76
  regulatory framework 105–8, 129
  share-based payments 359
  small and medium-sized enterprises
    (SMEs) 119–22
  taxation 111, 375, 378, 379, 381–2,
    384, 391, 392–3, 394–5
  total shareholders' funds 258–62
  Wider Markets Initiative (WMI)
    532–3
  XBRL 787, 792, 795
  see also Company Acts
United Nations 853
United States 152, 462
  accounting profession 112, 114
  corporate governance 805, 808, 820,
    829
  environmental reporting 854, 858, 861
  equity market 110
  ethical behaviour 164, 172, 173, 174,
    175–6, 178
  fair value accounting 86
  FASB *see* Financial Accounting
    Standards Board
  financial instruments 313, 314
  FINRA (Financial Industry
    Regulatory Authority) 175–6
  fraudulent reporting 510
  GAAP 118, 313, 314, 322, 349, 424,
    469–70
  historical cost accounting 82
  IFRSs 118–19
  institutional investors 111
  inventories 118, 502, 503
  legal system 109

materiality 142
negative pressures on standard setters
  160–1
pensions 349
regulatory framework 108, 112–13,
  129
rules-based approach 149, 162
Sarbanes–Oxley Act (SOX) 160, 807,
  820
SEC *see* Securities and Exchange
  Commission
segment reporting 224, 229
SME reporting 123
stewardship reporting 85, 134, 150
taxation 111, 379, 388
treasury shares, buyback of 275
XBRL 786–7, 791–2, 793, 795
unquoted companies 760–4

valuation
  accounting rules 195
  emissions trading certificates 477–9
  intangible assets 473, 476, 480, 483,
    484
  inventories 44, 131, 195, 198–200,
    236, 497–509, 511–12
  true and fair override 205
  unquoted company shares 760–4
  see also fair value; market value; net
    realisable value; present values;
    revaluations
value added reports 864–5
value added tax (VAT) 396–9
  iXBRL filing 787
Varia plc 226–7
verifiability 143, 150
vertical analysis 738–41, 742–3
Virgin Atlantic 174
Visa 474
Vodafone 176–7, 234–5, 757

WACC (weighted average cost of capital)
  759
Waddell & Reed, Inc 176

Wal-Mart Stores Inc 502
warrants, share 653
warranty provisions 291, 297, 301
Wartsila Corporation 551–2
Watford Leisure plc 261
weighted average
  inventories 499, 500
weighted average cost of capital (WACC)
  759
Wessanen 117
whistle-blowing 174–8, 803
Wider Markets Initiative (WMI) 532–3
Wienerberger 702
window dressing 718
Wolseley 201, 394
working capital 12, 13–14
World Health Alternatives Inc 804
World Intellectual Property Organisation
  (WIPO) 479–80
WorldCom 160, 754
WPP 476–7, 483

XBRL (eXtensible Business Reporting
  Language) 119, 737, 782–4, 785,
  794–5
  advantages of 785
  IASB and 786
  internal accounting 794
  international use of 786–7, 791–3
  iXBRL 787, 791–2
  processes to adopt 787–9
  reasons to adopt 786–9
  receiving XBRL output information
    789–91
  Revenue Authorities 787, 791, 793,
    795
  sharing data 793–4
Xerox 718
XML (eXtensible Mark-up Language)
  784
Xstrata 748

Z-scores 750–2, 763
Zeta model 751